GALE
ENCYCLOPEDIA OF
MULTICULTURAL
AMERICA

GALE
ENCYCLOPEDIA OF
MULTICULTURAL
AMERICA
SECOND EDITION

volume 2

Georgian Americans – Ojibwa

Contributing Editor

ROBERT VON DASSANOWSKY

Author of Introduction

RUDOLPH J. VECOLI

Edited by

JEFFREY LEHMAN

Endorsed by the Ethnic and Multicultural
Information Exchange Round Table,
American Library Association.

GALE GROUP

Detroit
New York
San Francisco
London
Boston
Woodbridge, CT

Jeffrey Lehman, *Editor*
Elizabeth Shaw, *Associate Editor*
Gloria Lam, *Assistant Editor*
Linda S. Hubbard, *Managing Editor*
Contributing editors: Ashyia N. Henderson, Brian Koski, Allison McClintic Marion,
Mark F. Mikula, David G. Oblender, Patrick Politano

Maria Franklin, *Permissions Manager*
Margaret A. Chamberlain, *Permissions Specialist*

Mary Beth Trimper, *Production Director*
Evi Seoud, *Assistant Production Manager*

Cynthia Baldwin, *Product Design Manager*
Barbara J. Yarrow, *Imaging and Multimedia Content Manager*
Randy Bassett, *Image Database Supervisor*
Pamela A. Reed, *Imaging Coordinator*
Robert Duncan, *Senior Imaging Specialist*

Copyright © 2000
Gale Group
27500 Drake Rd.
Farmington Hills, MI 48331-3535
http://www.galegroup.com
800-877-4253
248-699-4253

ISBN 0-7876-3986-9
Vol. 1 ISBN 0-7876-3987-7
Vol. 2 ISBN 0-7876-3988-5
Vol. 3 ISBN 0-7876-3989-3

Printed in the United States of America

Library of Congress Cataloging-in-Publication Data

Gale encyclopedia of multicultural America / contributing editor, Robert von
Dassanowsky ; edited by Jeffrey Lehman.— 2nd ed.
      p. cm.
      Includes bibliographical references and index.
      Summary: Essays on approximately 150 culture groups of the U.S., from Acadians to
Yupiats, covering their history, acculturation and assimilation, family and community
dynamics, language and religion.
      ISBN 0-7876-3986-9 (set : alk. paper) — ISBN 0-7876-3987-7 (vol. 1 : alk. paper) —
      ISBN 0-7876-3988-5 (vol. 2 : alk. paper) — ISBN 0-7876-3989-3 (vol. 3 : alk. paper)
      1. Pluralism (Social sciences)—United States—Encyclopedias, Juvenile. 2.
Ethnology—United States—Encyclopedias, Juvenile. 3. Minorities—United
States—Encyclopedias, Juvenile. 4. United States—Ethnic relations—Encyclopedias. 5.
United States—Race relations—Encyclopedias, Juvenile. [1. Ethnology—Encyclopedias.
2. Minorities—Encyclopedias.] I. Dassanowsky, Robert. II. Lehman, Jeffrey, 1969-

E184.A1 G14 1999
305.8'00973'03—dc21   99-044226

CONTENTS

Volume I

Volume II

Volume III

The second edition of the *Gale Encyclopedia of Multicultural America* has been endorsed by the Ethnic and Multicultural Information Exchange Round Table of the American Library Association

The first edition of the *Gale Encyclopedia of Multicultural America*, with 101 essays on different culture groups in the United States, filled a need in the reference collection for a single, comprehensive source of extensive information about ethnicities in the United States. Its contents satisfied high school and college students, librarians, and general reference seekers alike. The American Library Association's Ethnic Materials and Information Exchange Round Table *Bulletin* endorsed it as an exceptionally useful reference product and the Reference Users and Services Association honored it with a RUSA award.

This second edition adds to and improves upon the original. The demand for more current and comprehensive multicultural reference products in public, high school, and academic libraries remains strong. Topics related to ethnic issues, immigration, and acculturation continue to make headlines. People from Latin America, Africa, and Asia represent higher percentages of the new arrivals and increase the diversity of our population. The new *Gale Encyclopedia of Multicultural America*, with 152 essays, more than 250 images, a general bibliography updated by Vladimir Wertsman, and an improved general subject index, covers 50 percent more groups. Both new and revised essays received the scrutiny of scholars. Approximately 50 essays received significant textual updating to reflect changing conditions at the end of the century in America. In all essays, we updated the directory information for media, organizations, and museums by adding e-mail addresses and URLs, by deleting defunct groups, and by adding new groups or more accurate contact information. We have also created fresher suggested readings lists.

SCOPE

The three volumes of this edition address 152 ethnic, ethnoreligious, and Native American cultures currently residing in the United States. The average essay length is 8,000 words, but ranges from slightly less than 3,000 to more than 20,000 words, depending on the amount of information available. Essays are arranged alphabetically by the most-commonly cited name for the group—although such terms as

Sioux and Gypsy may be offensive to some members of the groups themselves, as noted in the essays.

Every essay in the first edition appears in the second edition of *Gale Encyclopedia of Multicultural America*, though some are in a different form. For example, the Lebanese Americans and Syrian Americans originally were covered in a single essay on Syrian/Lebanese Americans; in this book, they are separate entries. Additionally, the editors selected 50 more cultures based on the original volume's two main criteria: size of the group according to 1990 U.S. Census data and the recommendations of the advisory board. The advisors chose groups likely to be studied in high school and college classrooms. Because of the greater number of groups covered, some essays new to this edition are about groups that still have not established large enough populations to be much recognized outside of their immediate locations of settlement. This lower "visibility" means that few radio, television, or newspaper media report on events specific to very small minority groups. As a result, many of the essays are shorter in length.

The *Gale Encyclopedia of Multicultural America*'s essays cover a wide range of national and other culture groups, including those from Europe, Africa, Central America, South America, the Caribbean, the Middle East, Asia, Oceania, and North America, as well as several ethnoreligious groups. This book centers on communities as they exist in the United States, however. Thus, the encyclopedia recognizes the history, culture, and contributions of the first settlers—such as English Americans and French Americans—as well as newer Americans who have been overlooked in previous studies—such as Garifuna Americans, Georgian Americans, and Mongolian Americans. Moreover, such ethnoreligious groups as the Amish and the Druze are presented.

The various cultures that make up the American mosaic are not limited to immigrant groups, though. The Native Americans can more accurately be referred to as First Americans because of their primacy throughout the entire Western hemisphere. This rich heritage should not be undervalued and their contributions to the tapestry of U.S. history is equally noteworthy. Therefore, we felt it imperative to include essays on Native American peoples. Many attempts at a full-scale treatment of Native America have been made, including the *Gale Encyclopedia of Native American Tribes*, but such thorough coverage could not be included here for reasons of space. With the help of experts and advisors, the second edition added six new essays on Indian groups, again selected for their cultural diversity and geographical representation, bringing the total to 18.

The first edition contained two chapters devoted to peoples from Subsaharan Africa. Because the vast majority of people in the United States from this region identified themselves as African American in the 1990 U.S. Census, there is a lengthy essay entitled "African Americans" that represents persons of multiple ancestry. The census also indicated that Nigerian Americans—at 91,688 people—outnumbered all other individual national groups from Africa. This second edition adds nine more essays on peoples of African origin, most of whom are significantly less populous than Nigerian Americans. Nevertheless, the variety of customs evident in these cultures and the growing proportion of immigrants from Africa to America make it necessary and beneficial to increase coverage.

We also attempted to improve the overall demographic coverage. *Gale Encyclopedia of Multicultural America* now has 12 more essays on Asians/Pacific Islanders; five more on Hispanics, Central Americans, or South Americans; nine more on Middle Eastern/North Africans; and eight more on European peoples. The 49 essays on European immigrants treat them as separate groups with separate experiences to dispel the popular notions of a generic European American culture.

FORMAT

While each essay in the *Gale Encyclopedia of Multicultural America* includes information on the country of origin and circumstances surrounding major immigration waves (if applicable), they focus primarily on the group's experiences in the United States, specifically in the areas of acculturation and assimilation, family and community dynamics, language, religion, employment and economic traditions, politics and government, and significant contributions to American society. Wherever possible, each entry also features directory listings of periodicals, broadcast and Internet media, organizations and associations, and museums and research centers to aid the user in conducting additional research. Each entry also cites sources for further study that are current, useful, and accessible. Every essay contains clearly-marked, standardized headings and subheadings designed to locate specific types of information within each essay while also facilitating cross-cultural comparisons.

ADDITIONAL FEATURES

The improved general subject index in *Gale Encyclopedia of Multicultural America* still provides reference to significant terms, people, places, movements, and events, but also contains concepts pertinent to multicultural studies. Vladimir Wertsman, former librarian at the New York Public Library and member of the Ethnic and Multicultural Information Exchange Round Table of the American Library Association, has updated the valuable general bibliography. Its sources augment the further readings suggested in the text without duplicating them by listing general multicultural studies works. Finally, more than 250 images highlight the essays.

A companion volume, the *Gale Encyclopedia of Multicultural America: Primary Documents*, brings history to life through a wide variety of representative documents. More than 200 documents—ranging in type from periodical articles and autobiographies to political cartoons and recipes—give readers a more personal perspective on key events in history as well as the everyday lives of 90 different cultures.

ACKNOWLEDGMENTS

The editor must thank all the people whose efforts, talents, and time improved this project beyond measure. Contributing editor Professor Robert von Dassanowsky made the marathon run from beginning to end, all the while offering his insights, feedback, and unsolicited attention to details that could have been overlooked by a less observant eye; he made clear distinctions about how to treat many of the newer, lesser-known groups being added; he provided his expertise on 13 original essays and 12 new essays in the form of review and update recommendations; and he constantly served as an extra editorial opinion. The entire advisory board deserves a round of applause for their quick and invaluable feedback, but especially Vladimir Wertsman, who once again served as GEMA's exemplary advisor, tirelessly providing me with needed guidance and words of encouragement, review and update of key essays, and an updated general bibliography. The Multicultural team also aided this process considerably: especially Liz Shaw for just about everything, including accepting most of the responsibilities for other projects so that I could focus on *Gale Encyclopedia of Multicultural America*; handling the ever-changing photo permissions and selection; and coordinating the assignment, review, and clean-up inherent in having 152 essays written or updated. Also noteworthy is Gloria Lam, who took on some of Liz's tasks when necessary. I thank Mark Mikula and Bernard Grunow for helping out in a pinch with their technological prowess; the expert reviewers, including Dean T. Alegado, Timothy Dunnigan, Truong Buu Lam, Vasudha Narayanan, Albert Valdman, Vladimir Wertsman, and Kevin Scott Wong; and Rebecca Forgette, who deserves accolades for the improvement of the index.

Even though I laud the highly professional contributions of these individuals, I understand that as the editor, this publication is my responsibility.

SUGGESTIONS ARE WELCOME

The editor welcomes your suggestions on any aspect of this work. Please mail comments, suggestions, or criticisms to: The Editor, *Gale Encyclopedia of Multicultural America*, The Gale Group, 27500 Drake Road, Farmington Hills, MI 48331-3535; call 1-800-877-GALE [877-4253]; fax to (248) 699-8062; or e-mail galegroup.com.

CREDITS

The editors wish to thank the permissions managers of the companies that assisted us in securing reprint rights. The following list acknowledges the copyright holders who have granted us permission to reprint material in this second edition of the *Gale Encyclopedia of Multicultural America*. Every effort has been made to trace the copyright holders, but if omissions have occured, please contact the editor.

COPYRIGHTED IMAGES

The photographs and illustrations appearing in the *Gale Encyclopedia of Multicultural America*, were received from the following sources:

Cover photographs: **The Joy of Citizenship,** UPI/Bettmann; **Against the Sky,** UPI/Bettmann; **Leaving Ellis Island,** The Bettmann Archive.

Acadian man dumping bucket of crayfish into red sack, 1980s-1990s, Acadian Village, near Lafayette, Louisiana, photograph by Philip Gould. Corbis. **Acadian people dancing outdoors at the Acadian Festival,** c.1997, Lafayette, Louisiana, photograph by Philip Gould. Corbis. **Acadians** (re-enactment of early Acadian family), photograph. Village Historique Acadien. **African American family,** photograph by Ken Estell. **African American; Lunch counter segregation protest,** Raleigh, North Carolina, 1960, photograph. AP/Wide World Photos. **African American Rabbi,** photograph by John Duprey. ©New York Daily News, L.P. **African American school room in Missouri, c.1930,** photograph. Corbis-Bettmann Archive. **Albanian Harry Bajraktari** (Albanian American publisher, holding newspaper), photograph. AP/Wide World Photos. **Albanian woman** (shawl draped over her head), photograph. Corbis-Bettmann. **Amish boys** (five boys and a horse), photograph. AP/Wide World Photos. **Amish families** gathering to eat a traditional Amish meal in New Holland, Pennsylvania, photograph by David Johnson. **Amish farmers** (two men, woman, and horses), photograph. AP/Wide World Photos. **Apache boys and girls** (conducting physics experiments), Carlisle Indian School, Pennsylvania, c.1915, photograph. National Archives and Records Administration. **Apache Devil Dancers** (group of dancers), photograph. AP/Wide World Photos. **Apaches holding their last tribal meeting at Mescalera, NM,** 1919, photograph. Corbis-Bettmann. **Arab American woman in traditional Arab clothing** (blues and gold) riding a purebred Arabian horse, 1984, Los Angeles, California, photograph. Corbis/Kit Houghton Photography. **Arab Americans** (two women and five children, crossing the street), photograph. AP/Wide World Photos. **Arab; Alixa Naff,** sitting with Arab-American artifacts, photograph by Doug Mills. AP/Wide World Photo. **Young Arab girl/woman** (wearing yellow hairbow), 1998, Los Angeles, California, photograph by Catherine Karnow. Corbis. **Argentinean dancers,** Hispanic Parade, New York, photograph by Frances M. Roberts. Levine & Roberts Stock Photography. **Argentinean; Geraldo Hernandez,** (on float at Hispanic American Parade), photograph by Joe Comunale. AP/Wide World Photos. **Armenian rug making,** Jarjorian, Victoria, and Mrs. Paul Sherkerjian, with two women and children demonstrating Armenian rug making (in traditional garb), 1919, Chicago, Illinois, photograph. Corbis-Bettmann. **Armenian; Maro Partamian,** (back turned to choir), New York City, 1999, photograph by Bebeto Matthews. AP/Wide World Photos. **Armenian; Norik Shahbazian,** (showing tray of baklava), Los Angeles, California, 1998, photograph by Reed Saxon. AP/Wide World Photos. **Asian Indian woman, holding plate of food,** Rockville, Maryland, 1993, photograph by Catherine Karnow. Corbis. **Asian Indian; Three generations of an East Indian family** (sitting under trees), c.1991, Pomo, California, photograph by Joseph Sohm. Corbis/ChromoSohm Inc. **Australian; Marko Johnson,** (seated holding Australian instrument, didjeridoo, which he crafted, collection behind), 1998, Salt Lake City, Utah, photograph. AP/Wide World Photos. **Austrian; Arnold Schwarzenegger,** sitting and talking to President Gerorge Bush, photograph. AP/Wide World Photos. **Basque children wearing traditional costumes,** c.1996, Boise, Idaho, photograph by Jan Butchofsky-Houser. Corbis. **Basque couple wearing traditional costumes,** Boise, Idaho, photograph by Buddy Mays. Corbis. **Belgian; Waiter serving food in Belgian restaurant** (wearing black uniform), photograph by Jeff Christensen. Archive Photos. **Blackfoot Indians burial platform** (father mourning his son), 1912, photograph by Roland Reed. The Library of Congress. **Blackfoot Indians chasing buffalo,** photograph by John M. Stanley. National Archives and Records Administration. **Bolivian; Gladys Gomez,** (holding U.S. and Bolivian flags), New York City, 1962, photograph by Marty Hanley. Corbis/Bettmann. **Bosnian refugees,** Slavica Cvijetinovic, her son Ivan, and Svemir Ilic (in apartment), 1998, Clarkston, Georgia, photograph. AP/Wide World Photos. **Brazilian Street Festival,** Jesus, Michelle, and Adenilson Daros (on vacation from Brazil) dancing together, 15th Brazil Street Festival, 1998, New York, photograph. AP/Wide World Photos. **Brazilian; Tatiana Lima,** (wearing Carnival costume), photograph by Jeff Christensen. Archive Photos. **Bulgarian American artist, Christo** (kneeling, left hand in front of painting), New York City, c.1983, photograph by Jacques M.Chenet. Corbis. **Bulgarian; Bishop Andrey Velichky,** (receiving cross from swimmer), Santa Monica, California, 1939, photograph. Corbis/Bettmann. **Burmese Chart** (chart depicting the pronunciation and script for numbers and expressions), illustration. Eastword Publications Development. The Gale Group. **Cambodian girls standing on porch steps,** 1994, Seattle, Washington, photograph by Dan Lamont. Corbis. **Cambodian child, Angelina Melendez,** (standing in front of chart), photograph. AP/Wide World Photos. **Cambodian; Virak Ui,** (sitting on bed), photograph. AP/Wide World Photos. **Canadian American farmers in a field with a truck,** Sweetgrass, Montana, 1983, photograph by Michael S. Yamashita. Corbis. **Canadian; Donald and Kiefer Sutherland,** (standing together), Los Angeles, California, 1995, photograph by Kurt Kireger. Corbis. **Cape Verdean Henry Andrade** (preparing to represent Cape Verde in Atlanta Olympics), 1996, Cerritos, California, photograph. AP/Wide World Photos. **Cherokee boy and girl** (in traditional dress), c.1939, photograph. National Archives and Records Administration. **Cherokee woman with child on her back fishing,** photograph. Corbis-Bettmann. **Chilean; Hispanic Columbus Day parade** (children dancing in the street), photograph by Richard I. Harbus. AP/Wide World Photos. **Chinese Chart** (depicting examples of pictographs, ideographs, ideographic combinations, ideograph/sound characters, transferable characters, and loan characters), illustration. Eastword Publications Development. The Gale Group. **Chinese Dragon Parade** (two people dressed in dragon costumes), photograph by Frank Polich. AP/Wide World Photos. **Choctaw family standing at Chucalissa,** photograph. The Library of Congress. **Choctaw school children and their teacher** (standing outside of Bascome School), Pittsburg County, photograph. National Archives and Records Administration. **Colombian Americans perform during the Orange Bowl Parade** (women wearing long skirts and blouses), photograph by Alan Diaz. AP/Wide World Photos. **Creek Council House** (delegates from 34 tribes in front of large house), Indian Territory, 1880, photograph. National Archives and Records Administration. **Creek; Marion McGhee (Wild Horse),** doing Fluff Dance, photograph. AP/Wide World Photos. **Creole; elderly white woman holding Creole baby on her lap,** 1953, Saba Island, Netherlands Antilles, photograph by Bradley Smith. Corbis. **Creole; Mardi Gras** (Krewe of Rex floats travelling through street), photograph by Drew Story. Archive Photos. **Creole; Two men presenting the Creole flag,**

Zydeco Festival, c.1990, Plaisance, Louisiana, photograph by Philip Gould. Corbis. **Creole woman quilting** (red and white quilt, in 19th century garb), Amand Broussard House, Vermillionville Cajun/Creole Folk Village, Lafayette, Louisiana, c.1997, photograph by Dave G. Houser. Corbis. **Croatian Americans** (man with child), photograph. Aneal Vohra/Unicorn Stock Photos. **Croatian boy holding ends of scissors-like oyster rake,** 1938, Olga, Louisiana, photograph by Russell Lee. Corbis. **Cuban Americans** (holding crosses representing loved ones who died in Cuba), photograph by Alan Diaz. AP/Wide World Photos. **Cuban family reunited in Miami, Florida,** 1980, photograph. AP/Wide World Photos. **Cuban refugees** (older man and woman and three younger women), photograph. Reuters/Corbis-Bettmann. **Cuban children marching in Calle Ocho Parade,** photograph © by Steven Ferry. **Czech Americans** (at Czech festival), photograph. Aneal Vohra/Unicorn Stock Photos. **Czech immigrants** (six women and one child), photograph. UPI/Corbis-Bettmann. **Czech women,** standing in front of brick wall, Ellis Island, New York City, 1920, photograph. Corbis/Bettmann. **Danish American women** (at ethnic festival), photograph. © Aneal Vohra/Unicorn Stock Photos. **Danish Americans** (women and their daughters at Dana College), photograph. Dana College, Blair Nebraska. **Dominican; Ysaes Amaro** (dancing, wearing mask with long horns), New York City, 1999, photograph by Mitch Jacobson. AP/Wide World Photos. **Dominican; Hispanic Parade,** Dominican women dancing in front of building (holding flower baskets), photograph © Charlotte Kahler. **Dutch Americans** (Klompen dancers perform circle dance), Tulip Festival, Holland, Michigan, photograph. © Dennis MacDonald/Photo Edit. **Dutch immigrants** (mother and children), photograph. UPI/Corbis-Bettmann. **Dutch; Micah Zantingh,** (looking at tulips, in traditional Dutch garb), Tulip Festival, 1996, Pella, Iowa, photograph. AP/Wide World Photos. **English; Morris Dancers** (performing), photograph. Rich Baker/Unicorn Stock Photos. **English; British pub patrons,** Marty Flicker, Steve Jones, Phil Elwell, and Alan Shadrake (at British pub "The King's Head"), photograph by Bob Galbraith. AP/Wide World Photos. **Eritreans demonstrating against Ethiopian aggression,** in front of White House, 1997-1998, Washington, D.C., photograph by Lee Snider. Corbis. **Estonian Americans** (family sitting at table peeling apples), photograph. Library of Congress/Corbis. **Estonian Americans** (group of people, eight men, three woman and one little girl), photograph. UPI/Corbis-Bettmann. **Ethiopian; Berhanu Adanne** (front left), surrounded by Ethiopian immigrants Yeneneh Adugna (back left) and Halile Bekele (right front), celebrating his win of the Bolder Boulder 10-Kilometer Race, 1999, Boulder, Colorado, photograph. AP/Wide World Photos. **Filipino Immigrants,** photograph. Photo by Gene Viernes Collection **Filipino; Lotus Festival** (Fil-Am family, holding large feather and flower fans), photograph by Tara Farrell. AP/Wide World Photos. **Finnish Americans** (proponents of socialism with their families), photograph. The Tuomi Family Photographs/Balch Institute for Ethnic Studies. **Finnish Americans** (standing in line at festival), photograph.© Gary Conner /Photo Edit. **Finnish; Three generations of Finnish Americans,** Rebecca Hoekstra (l to r), Margaret Mattila, Joanna Hoekstra, with newspaper at kitchen table), 1999, Painesville, Michigan, photograph. AP/Wide World Photos. **French Americans** (woman playing an accordian) , photograph. © Joe Sohm/Unicorn Stock Photos. **French children in parade at Cape Vincent's French Festival,** photograph. Cape Vincent Chamber of Commerce. **French; Sally Eustice** (wearing French bride costume, white lace bonnet, royal blue dress), Michilimackinac, Michigan, c.1985, photograph by Macduff Everton. Corbis. **French-Canadian farmers,** waiting for their potatoes to be weighed (by woodpile), 1940, Arostook County, Maine, photograph. Corbis. **French-Canadian farmer sitting on digger,** Caribou, Maine, 1940, photograph by Jack Delano. Corbis. **French-Canadian; Grandmother of Patrick Dumond Family** (wearing white blouse, print apron), photograph. The Library of Congress. **French-Canadian; Two young boys** (standing on road), photograph. The Library of Congress. **German immigrants** (little girl holding doll), photograph. UPI/Corbis-Bettmann. **German people dancing at Heritagefest,** photograph. Minnesota Office of Tourism. © Minnesota Office of Tourism. **German; Steuben Day Parade** (German Tricentennial Multicycle), photograph. AP/Wide World Photos. **Greek American** (girl at Greek parade), photograph. Kelly-Mooney Photography/Corbis. **Greek American altar boys** (at church, lighting candles), photograph © Audrey Gottlieb 1992. **Greek; Theo Koulianos,** (holding cross thrown in water by Greek Orthodox Archbishop), photograph by Chris O'Meara. AP/Wide World Photos. **Guamanian boy in striped shirt leaning against doorjamb,** c.1950, photograph. Corbis/Hulton-Deutsch Collection. **Guatemalan boy and girl riding on top of van** (ethnic pride parade), 1995, Chicago, Illinois, photograph by Sandy Felsenthal. Corbis. **Guatemalan girls in traditional dress,** at ethnic pride parade, 1995, Chicago, Illinois, photograph by Sandy Felsenthal. Corbis. **Guatemalan; Julio Recinos,**

(covering banana boxes), Los Angeles, California, 1998, photograph by Damian Dovargnes. AP/Wide World Photos. **Gypsies; Flamenco** (wedding party group), photograph. UPI/Corbis-Bettmann. **Gypsy woman** (performing traditional dance), photograph. © Russell Grundke/Unicorn Stock Photos. **Haitian; Edwidge Danticat,** Ixel Cervera (Danticat signing her book for Cervera), New York City, 1998, photograph by Bebeto Matthews. AP/Wide World Photos. **Haitian; Fernande Maxton with Joseph Nelian Strong** (holding photo of Aristide), photograph by Bebeto Matthews. AP/Wide World Photos. **Haitian; Sauveur St. Cyr,** (standing to the right of alter), New York City, 1998, photograph by Lynsey Addario. AP/Wide World Photos. **Hawaiian children wearing leis in Lei Day celebration, Hawaii,** 1985, photograph by Morton Beebe. Corbis. **Hawaiian group singing at luau, Milolii, Hawaii,** 1969, photograph by James L. Amos. Corbis. **Hawaiian man checking fish trap,** photograph. The Library of Congress. **Hawaiian women dancing,** Washington D.C., 1998, photograph by Khue Bui. AP/Wide World Photos. **Hmong; Vang Alben** (pointing to portion of Hmong story quilt), Fresno, California, 1998, photograph by Gary Kazanjian. AP/Wide World Photos. **Hmong; Moua Vang** (holding fringed parasol), Fresno, California, 1996, photograph by Thor Swift. AP/Wide World Photos. **Hopi dancer at El Tovar, Grand Canyon,** photograph. Corbis-Bettmann. **Hopi women's dance,** 1879, photograph by John K. Hillers. National Archives and Records Administration. **Hungarian American debutante ball,** photograph by Contessa Photography **Hungarian Americans** (man reunited with his family), photograph. Special Collections and University Archives, Rutgers University. **Hungarian refugees** (large group on ship deck), photograph. UPI/Corbis-Bettmann. **Icelanders** (five women sitting outside of Cabin), photograph. North Dakota Institute for Regional Studies and Archives/North Dakota State University. **Icelandic girl kneeling, picking cranberries,** c.1990, Half Moon Lake, Wisconsin, photograph by Tom Bean. Corbis. **Indonesian; Balinese dancer wearing white mask, gold headdress and embroidered collar,** 1980-1995, Bali, Indonesia, photograph. CORBIS/David Cumming; Ubiquitous. **Indonesian; two Balinese dancers** (in gold silk, tall headdresses, with fans), Bali, Indonesia, photograph by Dennis Degnan. Corbis. **Indonesian; Wayang Golek puppets** (with helmets, gold trimmed coats), 1970-1995, Indonesia, photograph by Sean Kielty. Corbis. **Inuit dance orchestra,** 1935, photograph by Stanley Morgan. National Archives and Records Administration. **Inuit dancer and drummers,** Nome, Alaska, c.1910, photograph. Corbis/Michael Maslan Historic Photographs. **Inuit wedding people,** posing outside of Saint Michael's Church, Saint Michael, Alaska, 1906, photograph by Huey & Laws. Corbis. **Iranian; Persian New Year celebrations,** among expatriate community (boy running through bonfire), c.1995, Sydney, Australia, photograph by Paul A. Souders. Corbis. **Irish girls performing step dancing in Boston St. Patrick's Day Parade,** 1996, photograph. AP/Wide World Photos. **Irish immigrants** (woman and nine children), photograph. UPI/Corbis-Bettmann. **Irish; Bernie Hurley,** (dressed like leprechaun, rollerblading), Denver, St. Patrick's Day Parade, 1998, photograph. AP/Wide World Photos. **Irish; Bill Pesature,** (shamrock on his forehead), photograph. AP/Wide World Photos. **Iroquois steel workers at construction site,** 1925, photograph. Corbis-Bettmann. **Iroquois tribe members,** unearthing bones of their ancestors, photograph. Corbis-Bettmann. **Israeli; "Salute to Israel" parade,** children holding up Israeli Flag, photograph by David Karp. AP/Wide World Photos. **Israeli; "Salute to Israel" parade,** Yemenite banner, New York, photograph by Richard B. Levine. Levine & Roberts Stock Photography **Italian Americans** (men walking in Italian parade), photograph. Robert Brenner/Photo Edit. **Italian immigrants** (mother and three children), photograph. Corbis-Bettmann. **Italian railway workers,** Lebanon Springs, New York, c.1900, photograph by H. M. Gillet. Corbis/Michael Maslan Histrorical Photographs. **Jamaican women playing steel drums in Labor Day parade** (wearing red, yellow drums), 1978, Brooklyn, New York, photograph by Ted Spiegel. Corbis **Jamaican; Three female Caribbean dancers at Liberty Weekend Festival** (in ruffled dresses and beaded hats), 1986, New York, photograph by Joseph Sohm. Corbis/ChromoSohm Inc. **Japanese American children,** eating special obento lunches from their lunchboxes on Children's Day, 1985, at the Japanese American Community and Cultural Center, Little Tokyo, Los Angeles, California, photograph by Michael Yamashita. Corbis. **Japanese American girl with baggage** (awaiting internment), April, 1942, photograph. National Archives and Records Administration. **Japanese American girls,** wearing traditional kimonos at a cherry blossom festival, San Francisco, California, photograph by Nik Wheeler. Corbis. **Japanese immigrants** (dressed as samurai), photograph. National Archives and Records Administration. **Jewish; Bar Mitzvah** (boy reading from the Torah), photograph. © Nathan Nourok/Photo Edit. **Jewish; Orthodox Jews** (burning hametz in preparation of Passover), photograph by Ed Bailey. AP/Wide World Photos. **Jewish; Senator Alfonse D'Amato with Jackie Mason** (at

Salute to Israel Parade), photograph. AP/Wide World Photos. **Kenyan; David Lichoro,** (wearing "God has been good to me!" T-shirt), 1998, Iowa State University, Ames, Iowa, photograph. AP/Wide World Photos. **Kenyan; Samb Aminata** (with Kenyan sculptures for sale), 24th Annual Afro American Festival, 1997, Detroit Michigan, photograph. AP/Wide World Photos. **Korean American boy,** holding Korean flag, photograph by Richard B. Levine. Levine & Roberts Stock Photography. **Korean basic alphabet,** illustration. Eastword Publications Development. The Gale Group. **Korean; signs in Koreatown, NY** (Korean signs, people in lower left corner of photo), photograph. AP/Wide World Photos. **Laotian women** (standing around Vietnam Veterans Memorial, wearing traditional Laos costumes), photograph by Mark Wilson. Archive Photos. **Laotian; Chia Hang, Pahoua Yang** (daughter holding mother's shoulders), Brooklyn Center, Minnesota, 1999, photograph by Dawn Villella. AP/Wide World Photos. **Latvian Americans** (mother, father, 11 children), photograph. UPI/Corbis-Bettmann. **Latvian; Karl Zarins,** (Latvian immigrant holding his daughter), photograph. UPI/Corbis-Bettmann. **Lebanese Americans,** demonstrating, Washington D. C., 1996, photograph by Jeff Elsayed. AP/Wide World Photos. **Liberian; Michael Rhodes,** (examining Liberian Passport Masks), at the 1999 New York International Tribal Antiques Show, Park Avenue Armory, New York, photograph. AP/Wide World Photos. **Lithuanian Americans** (family of 12, men, women and children), photograph. UPI/Corbis-Bettmann. **Lithuanian Americans** (protesting on Capitol steps), photograph. UPI/Corbis-Bettmann. **Malaysian float at Pasadena Rose Parade, Pasadena, California,** c.1990, photograph Dave G. Houser. Corbis. **Maltese Americans** (girls in Maltese parade), photograph. © Robert Brenner/Photo Edit. **Maltese immigrant woman at parade,** New York City, photograph by Richard B. Levine. Levine & Roberts Stock Photography. **Mexican Celebration of the Day of the Dead festival** (seated women, flowers, food), c.1970-1995, photograph by Charles & Josette Lenars. Corbis. **Mexican soccer fans dancing outside Washington's RFK Stadium,** photograph by Damian Dovarganes. AP/Wide World Photos. **Mongolian "throat singer," Ondar,** performing at the Telluride Bluegrass Festival, 1999, Telluride, Colorado, photograph. AP/Wide World Photos. **Mongolian wedding gown being modeled,** at the end of the showing of Mary McFadden's 1999 Fall and Winter Collection, New York, photograph. AP/Wide World Photos. **"Mormon emigrants," covered wagon caravan,** photograph by C. W. Carver. National Archives and Records Adminis-

tration. **Mormon family in front of log cabin,** 1875, photograph. Corbis-Bettmann. **Mormon Women** (tacking a quilt), photograph. The Library of Congress. **Moroccan; Lofti's Restaurant,** New York City, 1995, photograph by Ed Malitsky. Corbis. **Navajo family courtyard** (one man, one child, two women in foreground), photograph. Corbis-Bettmann. **Navajo protesters,** marched two miles to present grievances to tribal officals, photograph. AP/Wide World Photos. **Navajo protesters** (walking, three holding large banner), 1976, Arizona, photograph. AP/Wide World Photos. **Nepalese; Gelmu Sherpa rubbing "singing bowl,"** May 20, 1998, photograph by Suzanne Plunkett. AP/Wide World Photos. **Nez Perce family in a three-seated car,** 1916, photograph by Frank Palmer. The Library of Congress. **Nez Perce man in ceremonial dress** (right profile), c.1996, Idaho, photograph by Dave G. Houser. Corbis. **Nicaraguan girls in a Cinco de Mayo parade** (flower in hair, wearing peasant blouses), c.1997, New York, photograph by Catherine Karnow. Corbis. **Nicaraguan; Dennis Martinez,** (playing baseball), photograph by Tami L. Chappell. Archive Photos. **Norwegian Americans** (gathered around table, some seated and some standing), photograph. UPI/Corbis-Bettmann. **Norwegian Americans** (Leikarring Norwegian dancers), photograph. © Jeff Greenberg/Photo Edit. **Ojibwa woman and child,** lithograph. The Library of Congress. **Ojibwa woman and papoose,** color lithograph by Bowen's, 1837. The Library of Congress **Paiute drawing his bow and arrow** (two others in festive costume), 1872, photograph by John K. Hillers. National Archives and Records Administration. **Paiute woman** (grinding seeds in hut doorway), 1872, photograph by John K. Hillers. National Archives and Records Administration. **Paiute; Revival of the Ghost Dance,** being performed by women, photograph. Richard Erdoes. Reproduced by permission. **Pakistani American family in traditional dress,** photograph by Shazia Rafi. **Palestinean; Jacob Ratisi,** with brother John Ratisi (standing inside their restaurant), photograph by Mark Elias. AP/Wide World Photos. **Palestinian; Faras Warde,** (holding up leaflets and poster), Boston, Massachusetts, 1998, photograph by Kuni. AP/Wide World Photos. **Peruvian shepherd immobilizes sheep while preparing an inoculation,** 1995, Bridgeport, California, photograph by Phil Schermeister. Corbis. **Polish Americans** (woman and her three sons), photograph. UPI/Corbis-Bettmann. **Polish; Kanosky Family,** (posing for a picture), August, 1941. Reproduced by permission of Stella McDermott. **Polish; Leonard Sikorasky and Julia Wesoly,** (at Polish parade), photograph. UPI/Corbis-Bettmann. **Portuguese American** (man fishing), photograph. © 1994 Gale Zucker. **Portuguese Americans** (children in traditional Portuguese dress), photograph. © Robert Brenner/Photo Edit. **Pueblo mother with her children** (on ladder by house), Taos, New Mexico, photograph. Corbis-Bettmann. **Pueblo; Row of drummers and row of dancers,** under cloudy sky, photograph by Craig Aurness. Corbis. **Pueblo; Taos Indians performing at dance festival,** c.1969, New Mexico, photograph by Adam Woolfit. Corbis. **Puerto Rican Day Parade** (crowd of people waving flags), photograph by David A.Cantor. AP/Wide World Photos. **Puerto Rican; 20th Annual Three Kings Day Parade** (over-life-size magi figures, Puerto Rican celebration of Epiphany), 1997, El Museo del Barrio, East Harlem, New York, photograph. AP/Wide World Photos. **Puerto Rican; Puerto Rican New Progressive Party,** photograph. AP/Wide World Photos. **Romanian Priests** (leading congregation in prayer), photograph. AP/Wide World Photos. **Romanian; Regina Kohn,** (holding violin), photograph. UPI/Corbis-Bettmann. **Russian Americans** (five women sitting in wagon), photograph. UPI/Corbis-Bettmann. **Russian; Lev Vinjica,** (standing in his handicraft booth), photograph. AP/Wide World Photos. **Russian; Olesa Zaharova,** (standing in front of chalkboard, playing hangman), Gambell, Alaska, 1992, photograph by Natalie Fobes. Corbis. **Salvadoran; Ricardo Zelada,** (standing, right arm around woman, left around girl), Los Angeles, California, 1983, photograph by Nik Wheeler. Corbis. **Samoan woman playing ukulele,** sitting at base of tree, Honolulu, Oahu, Hawaii, 1960's-1990's, photograph by Ted Streshinsky. Corbis. **Samoan men, standing in front of sign reading "Talofa . . . Samoa,"** Laie, Oahu, Hawaii, 1996, photograph by Catherine Karnow. Corbis. **Scottish Americans** (bagpipers), photograph. © Tony Freeman/Photo Edit. **Scottish Americans** (girl performing Scottish sword dance), photograph. © Jim Shiopee/Unicorn Stock Photos. **Scottish; David Barron** (swinging a weight, in kilt), 25th Annual Quechee Scottish Festival, 1997, Quechee, Vermont, photograph. AP/Wide World Photos. **Serbian; Jelena Mladenovic,** (lighting candle), New York City, 1999, photograph by Lynsey Addario. AP/Wide World Photos. **Serbian; Jim Pigford,** (proof-reading newspaper pages), Pittsburgh, Pennsylvania, 1999, photograph by Gene J. Puskar. AP/Wide World Photos. **Sicilian Archbishop Iakovos** (standing in front of stage, spreading incense), photograph by Mark Cardwell. Archive Photos. **Sioux girl** (sitting, wearing long light colored fringed clothing), photograph. The Library of Congress. **Sioux Police,** (on horseback, in front of buildings), photograph. National Archives and Records Administration. **Slovak immigrant** (woman at Ellis Island), photograph. Corbis-Bettmann. **Slovenian; Bob Dole** (listening to singing group), Cleveland, Ohio, 1996, photograph by Mark Duncan. AP/Wide World Photos. **Spanish American; Isabel Arevalo** (Spanish American), photograph. Corbis-Bettmann. **Spanish; United Hispanic American Parade** (group performing in the street, playing musical instruments), photograph by Joe Comunale. AP/Wide World Photos. **Swedish; Ingrid and Astrid Sjdbeck,** (sitting on a bench), photograph. UPI/Corbis-Bettmann. **Swedish; young girl and boy in traditional Swedish clothing,** 1979, Minneapolis, Minnesota, photograph by Raymond Gehman. Corbis. **Swiss; Dr. Hans Kung,** (signing book for Scott Forsyth), 1993, Chicago, photograph. AP/Wide World Photos. **Swiss; Ida Zahler,** (arriving from Switzerland with her eleven children), photograph. UPI/Corbis-Bettmann. **Syrian children in New York City** (in rows on steps), 1908-1915, photograph. Corbis. **Syrian man with a food cart,** peddles his food to two men on the streets of New York, early 20th century, photograph. Corbis. **Syrian man selling cold drinks in the Syrian quarter,** c.1900, New York, photograph. Corbis. **"Taiwan Independence, No Chinese Empire"** Demonstration, protesters sitting on street, New York City, 1997, photograph by Adam Nadel. AP/Wide World Photos. **Thai; Christie Wong, Julie Trung, and Susan Lond** (working on float that will be in the Tournament of the Roses Parade), photograph by Fred Prouser. Archive Photos. **Tibetan Black Hat Dancers,** two men wearing identical costumes, Newark, New Jersey, 1981, photograph by Sheldan Collins. Corbis-Bettmann. **Tibetan Buddhist monk at Lollapalooza,** 1994, near Los Angeles, California, photograph by Henry Diltz. Corbis. **Tibetan; Kalachakra Initiation Dancers,** dancing, holding up right hands, Madison, Wisconsin, 1981, photograph by Sheldan Collins. Corbis. **Tibetan; Tenzin Choezam** (demonstrating outside the Chinese Consulate, "Free Tibet...,"), 1999, Houston, Texas, photograph. AP/Wide World Photos. **Tlingit girls wearing nose rings,** photograph by Miles Brothers. National Archives and Records Administration. **Tlingit mother and child,** wearing tribal regalia, Alaska/Petersburg, photograph by Jeff Greenberg. Archive Photos. **Tlingit;** attending potlach ceremony in dugout canoes, 1895, photograph by Winter & Pont. Corbis. **Tongan man at luau, adorned with leaves,** Lahaina, Hawaii, 1994, photograph by Robert Holmes. Corbis. **Trinidadian; West Indian American Day parade** (woman wearing colorful costume, dancing in the street), photograph by Carol Cleere. Archive Photos. **Turkish Parade**

(Turkish band members), photograph. AP/Wide World Photos. **Turkish; Heripsima Hovnanian,** (Turkish immigrant, with family members), photograph. UPI/Corbis-Bettmann. **Ukrainian Americans** (dance the Zaporozhian Knight's Battle), photograph. UPI/Corbis-Bettmann. **Ukrainian; Oksana Roshetsky,** (displaying Ukrainian Easter eggs), photograph. UPI/Corbis-Bettmann. **Vietnamese dance troupe** (dancing in the street), photograph by Nick Ut. AP/Wide World Photos. **Vietnamese refugee to Lo Huyhn** (with daughter, Hanh), photograph. AP/Wide World Photos. **Vietnamese; Christina Pham,** (holding large fan), photograph. AP/Wide World Photos. **Virgin Islander schoolchildren standing on school steps,** Charlotte Amalie, Virgin Island, photograph. Corbis/Hulton-Deutsch Collection. **Welsh; Tom Jones,** photograph. AP/Wide World Photos.

ADVISORY BOARD

CONTRIBUTORS

Nabeel Abraham
Professor of Anthropology
Henry Ford Community College
Dearborn, Michigan

June Granatir Alexander
Assistant Professor
Russian and East European Studies
University of Cincinnati
Cincinnati, Ohio

Donald Altschiller
Freelance writer, Cambridge, Massachusetts

Diane Andreassi
Freelance writer, Livonia, Michigan

Carl L. Bankston III
Professor, Department of Sociology
Louisiana State University
Baton Rouge, Louisiana

Diane E. Benson ('Lxeis')
Tlingit actress and writer, Eagle River, Alaska

Barbara C. Bigelow
Freelance writer, White Lake, Michigan

D. L. Birchfield
Editor and writer, Oklahoma City, Oklahoma

Herbert J. Brinks
Professor, Department of History
Calvin College
Grand Rapids, Michigan

Sean T. Buffington
Professor, Department of Ethnic Studies
University of Michigan
Ann Arbor, Michigan

Phyllis J. Burson
Independent consultant, Silver Spring, Maryland

Kimberly Burton
Freelance copyeditor, Ann Arbor, Michigan

Helen Bush Caver
Associate Professor and Librarian
Jacksonville State University
Jacksonville, Alabama

Cida S. Chase
Professor of Spanish, Oklahoma State University
Stillwater, Oklahoma

Clark Colahan
Professor of Spanish, Whitman College
Walla Walla, Washington

Robert J. Conley
Freelance writer, Tahlequah, Oklahoma

Jane Stewart Cook
Freelance writer, Green Bay, Wisconsin

Amy Cooper
Freelance writer, Ann Arbor, Michigan

Paul Cox
Dean, General Education and Honors
Brigham Young University
Provo, Utah

Ken Cuthbertson
Queen's Alumni Review
Queen's University
Kingston, Ontario, Canada

Rosetta Sharp Dean
Counselor and writer, Anniston, Alabama

Stanley E. Easton
Professor of Japanese
University of Tennessee
Chattanooga, Tennessee

Tim Eigo
Freelance writer, Phoenix, Arizona

Lucien Ellington
Freelance writer

Jessie L. Embry
Oral History Program Director
Charles Redd Center for Western Studies
Brigham Young University
Provo, Utah

Allen Englekirk
Chairperson, Modern Languages and Literature
Gonzaga University
Spokane, Washington

Marianne P. Fedunkiw
Freelance writer, Toronto, Ontario, Canada

Ellen French
Freelance writer, Murrieta, California

Mary Gillis
Freelance writer, Huntington Woods, Michigan

Edward Gobetz
Executive Director
Slovenian Research Center of America, Inc.
Willoughby Hills, Ohio

Mark A. Granquist
Assistant Professor of Religion
Saint Olaf College
Northfield, Minnesota

Derek Green
Freelance writer, Ann Arbor, Michigan

Paula Hajar
Freelance writer, New York, New York

Loretta Hall
Freelance writer, Albuquerque, New Mexico

Francesca Hampton
Freelance writer, Santa Cruz, California

Richard C. Hanes
Freelance writer, Eugene, Oregon

Sheldon Hanft
Professor, Department of History
Appalachian State University
Boone, North Carolina

James Heiberg
Freelance writer, Minneapolis, Minnesota

Karl Heil
Freelance writer, Ann Arbor, Michigan

Evan Heimlich
Assistant Coordinator, Multicultural Resource
    Center
University of Kansas
Lawrence, Kansas

Angela Washburn Heisey
Freelance writer

Mary A. Hess
Teaching Assistant, Integrated Arts and
    Humanities
Michigan State University
Lansing, Michigan

Laurie Collier Hillstrom
Freelance writer, Pleasant Ridge, Michigan

Maria Hong
Freelance writer, Austin, Texas

Edward Ifkovič
Writer and lecturer, Hartford, Connecticut

Alphine W. Jefferson
Professor, Department of History
College of Wooster
Wooster, Ohio

Charlie Jones
Librarian, Plymouth-Canton High School
Canton, Michigan

J. Sydney Jones
Freelance writer, Soquel, California

Jane Jurgens
Assistant Professor, Learning Resources Center
St. Cloud State University
St. Cloud, Minnesota

Jim Kamp
Freelance writer and editor, Royal Oak, Michigan

John Kane
Freelance writer and copyeditor, Branford,
    Connecticut

Oscar Kawagley
Assistant Professor of Education
University of Alaska
Fairbanks, Alaska

Vituat Kipal
Librarian, Slavic and Baltic Division
New York Public Library

Judson Knight
Freelance writer, Atlanta, Georgia

Paul Kobel
Freelance writer, North Tonawanda, New York

Donald B. Kraybill
Professor, Department of Sociology
Elizabethtown College
Elizabethtown, Pennsylvania

Ken Kurson
Freelance writer, New York, New York

Odd S. Lovoll
Professor of Scandinavian American Studies
Saint Olaf College
Northfield, Minnesota

Lorna Mabunda
Freelance writer, Ann Arbor, Michigan

Paul Robert Magocsi
Director and Chief Executive Officer
Multicultural History Society of Ontario
Toronto, Ontario, Canada

Marguertie Marín
Freelance writer

William Maxwell
Contributing Editor
A Gathering of the Tribes Magazine
New York, New York

Jacqueline A. McLeod
Freelance writer, East Lansing, Michigan

H. Brett Melendy
University Archivist
San Jose State University
San Jose, California

Mona Mikhail
Professor, Department of Near Eastern Languages
    and Literatures
New York University
New York, New York

Olivia Miller
Freelance writer, Memphis, Tennessee

Christine Molinari
Manuscript editor, University of Chicago Press
Chicago, Illinois

Lloyd Mulraine
Professor of English
Jacksonville State University
Jacksonville, Alabama

Jeremy Mumford
Assistant News Editor
Courtroom Television Network
New York, New York

N. Samuel Murrell
Professor of Religion and Black Studies
College of Wooster
Wooster, Ohio

Sally A. Myers
Freelance copyeditor, Defiance, Ohio

Amy Nash
Freelance writer, Minneapolis, Minnesota

Fiona Nesbitt
Freelance writer, Mountain View, California

John Mark Nielsen
Professor of English
Dana College
Blair, Nebraska

Ernest E. Norden
Professor, Division of Spanish and Portuguese
Baylor University
Waco, Texas

Lolly Ockerstrom
Freelance writer, Washington, DC

John Packel
Freelance writer, Brooklyn, New York

Tinaz Pavri
Freelance writer, Columbus, Ohio

Richard E. Perrin
Librarian, Reference and Instructional Services
Timme Library, Ferris State University
Big Rapids, Michigan

Peter L. Petersen
Professor of History
West Texas A&M
Canyon, Texas

Annette Petrusso
Freelance writer, Austin, Texas

Matthew T. Pifer
Freelance writer

George Pozzetta
Professor, Department of History
University of Florida
Gainesville, Florida

Norman Prady
Freelance writer, Southfield, Michigan

Brendan A. Rapple
Reference Librarian/Education Bibliographer
O'Neill Library, Boston College
Boston, Massachusetts

Megan Ratner
Freelance writer, New York, New York

Gertrude Ring
Freelance copyeditor, Los Angeles, California

La Vern J. Rippley
Professor of German
Saint Olaf College
Northfield, Minnesota

Julio Rodriguez
Freelance writer, Walla Walla, Washington

Pam Rohland
Freelance writer, Bernville, Pennsylvania

Lorene Roy
Associate Professor and Minority
    Liaison Officer
University of Texas
Austin, Texas

Laura C. Rudolph
Freelance writer, Raleigh, North Carolina

Kwasi Sarkodie-Mensah
Chief Reference Librarian, O'Neill Library
Boston College
Boston, Massachusetts

Leo Schelbert
Professor, Department of History
University of Illinois
Chicago, Illinois

Sonya Schryer
Freelance writer, Lansing, Michigan

Mary C. Sengstock
Professor, Department of Sociology
Wayne State University
Detroit, Michigan

Elizabeth Shostak
Freelance writer, Cambridge, Massachusetts

Stefan Smagula
Freelance writer, Austin, Texas

Keith Snyder
Freelance copyeditor, Washington, DC

Jane E. Spear
Freelance writer, Canton, Ohio

Janet Stamatel
Freelance copyeditor, Detroit, Michigan

Bosiljka Stevanovič
Principal Librarian, Donnell Library Center
World Languages Collection
New York Public Library

Andris Straumanis
Freelance writer, New Brighton, Minnesota

Pamela Sturner
Freelance writer, New Haven, Connecticut

Liz Swain
Freelance writer, San Diego, California

Mark Swartz
Manuscript editor
University of Chicago Press
Chicago, Illinois

Thomas Szendrey
Freelance writer

Harold Takooshian
Professor, Division of Social Studies
Fordham University
New York, New York

Baatar Tsend
Mongolian Scholar
Indiana University
Bloomington, Indiana

Felix Eme Unaeze
Head Librarian
Reference and Instructional
    Services Department
Timme Library, Ferris State University
Big Rapids, Michigan

Steven Béla Várdy
Professor and Director, Department of History
Duquesne University
Pittsburgh, Pennsylvania

Drew Walker
Freelance writer, New York, New York

Ling-chi Wang
Professor, Asian American Studies
Department of Ethnic Studies
University of California
Berkeley, California

K. Marianne Wargelin
Freelance writer, Minneapolis, Minnesota

Ken R. Wells
Freelance writer, Aliso Viejo, California

Vladimir F. Wertsman
Chair, Publishing and Multicultural
    Materials Committee
American Library Association

Mary T. Williams
Associate Professor
Jacksonville State University
Jacksonville, Alabama

Elaine Winters
Freelance writer, Berkeley, California

Eveline Yang
Manager, Information Delivery Program
Auraria Library
Denver, Colorado

Eleanor Yu
Deputy news Editor
Courtroom Television Network
New York, New York

INTRODUCTION

RUDOLPH J. VECOLI

The term multiculturalism has recently come into usage to describe a society characterized by a diversity of cultures. Religion, language, customs, traditions, and values are some of the components of culture, but more importantly culture is the lens through which one perceives and interprets the world. When a shared culture forms the basis for a "sense of peoplehood," based on consciousness of a common past, we can speak of a group possessing an ethnicity. As employed here, ethnicity is not transmitted genetically from generation to generation; nor is it unchanging over time. Rather, ethnicity is invented or constructed in response to particular historical circumstances and changes as circumstances change. "Race," a sub-category of ethnicity, is not a biological reality but a cultural construction. While in its most intimate form an ethnic group may be based on face-to-face relationships, a politicized ethnicity mobilizes its followers far beyond the circle of personal acquaintances. Joined with aspirations for political self-determination, ethnicity can become full-blown nationalism. In this essay, ethnicity will be used to identify groups or communities that are differentiated by religious, racial, or cultural characteristics and that possess a sense of peoplehood.

The "Multicultural America" to which this encyclopedia is dedicated is the product of the mingling of many different peoples over the course of several hundred years in what is now the United States. Cultural diversity was characteristic of this continent prior to the coming of European colonists and African slaves. The indigenous inhabitants of North America who numbered an estimated 4.5 million in 1500 were divided into hundreds of tribes with distinctive cultures, languages, and religions. Although the numbers of "Indians," as they were named by Europeans, declined precipitously through the nineteenth century, their population has rebounded in the twentieth century. Both as members of their particular tribes (a form of ethnicity), Navajo, Ojibwa, Choctaw, etc., and as American Indians (a form of panethnicity), they are very much a part of today's cultural and ethnic pluralism.

Most Americans, however, are descendants of immigrants. Since the sixteenth century, from the earliest Spanish settlement at St. Augustine, Florida, the process of repeopling this continent has gone on apace. Some 600,000 Europeans and Africans were recruited or enslaved and transported across the Atlantic Ocean in the colonial period to what was to become the United States. The first census of 1790 revealed the high degree of diversity that already marked the American population. Almost 19 percent were of African ancestry, another 12 percent Scottish and Scotch-Irish, ten percent German, with smaller numbers of French, Irish, Welsh, and Sephardic Jews. The census did not include American Indians. The English, sometimes described as the "founding people," only comprised 48 percent of the total. At the time of its birth in 1776, the United States was already a "complex ethnic mosaic," with a wide variety of communities differentiated by culture, language, race, and religion.

The present United States includes not only the original 13 colonies, but lands that were subsequently purchased or conquered. Through this territorial expansion, other peoples were brought within the boundaries of the republic; these included, in addition to many Native American tribes, French, Hawaiian, Inuit, Mexican, and Puerto Rican, among others. Since 1790, population growth, other than by natural increase, has come primarily through three massive waves of immigration. During the first wave (1841-1890), almost 15 million immigrants arrived: over four million Germans, three million each of Irish and British (English, Scottish, and Welsh), and one million Scandinavians. A second wave (1891-1920) brought an additional 18 million immigrants: almost four million from Italy, 3.6 million from Austria-Hungary, and three million from Russia. In addition, over two million Canadians, Anglo and French, immigrated prior to 1920. The intervening decades, from 1920 to 1945, marked a hiatus in immigration due to restrictive policies, economic depression, and war. A modest post-World War II influx of refugees was followed by a new surge subsequent to changes in immigration policy in 1965. Totalling approximately 16 million—and still in progress, this third wave encompassed some four million from Mexico, another four million from Central and South America and the Caribbean, and roughly six million from Asia. While almost 90 percent of the first two waves originated in Europe, only 12 percent of the third did.

Immigration has introduced an enormous diversity of cultures into American society. The 1990 U.S. Census report on ancestry provides a fascinating portrait of the complex ethnic origins of the American people. Responses to the question, "What is your ancestry or ethnic origin?," were tabulated for 215 ancestry groups. The largest ancestry groups reported were, in order of magnitude, German, Irish, English, and African American, all more than 20 million.

Other groups reporting over six million were Italian, Mexican, French, Polish, Native American, Dutch, and Scotch-Irish, while another 28 groups reported over one million each. Scanning the roster of ancestries one is struck by the plethora of smaller groups: Hmong, Maltese, Honduran, Carpatho-Rusyns, and Nigerian, among scores of others. Interestingly enough, only five percent identified themselves simply as "American"—and less than one percent as "white."

Immigration also contributed to the transformation of the religious character of the United States. Its original Protestantism (itself divided among many denominations and sects) was both reinforced by the arrival of millions of Lutherans, Methodists, Presbyterians, etc., and diluted by the heavy influx of Roman Catholics—first the Irish and Germans, then Eastern Europeans and Italians, and more recently Hispanics. These immigrants have made Roman Catholicism the largest single denomination in the country. Meanwhile, Slavic Christian and Jewish immigrants from Central and Eastern Europe established Judaism and Orthodoxy as major American religious bodies. As a consequence of Near Eastern immigration—and the conversion of many African Americans to Islam—there are currently some three million Muslims in the United States. Smaller numbers of Buddhists, Hindus, and followers of other religions have also arrived. In many American cities, houses of worship now include mosques and temples as well as churches and synagogues. Such religious pluralism is an important source of American multiculturalism.

The immigration and naturalization policies pursued by a country are a key to understanding its self-conception as a nation. By determining who to admit to residence and citizenship, the dominant element defines the future ethnic and racial composition of the population and the body politic. Each of the three great waves of immigration inspired much soul-searching and intense debate over the consequences for the republic. If the capacity of American society to absorb some 55 million immigrants over the course of a century and a half is impressive, it is also true that American history has been punctuated by ugly episodes of nativism and xenophobia. With the possible exception of the British, it is difficult to find an immigrant group that has not been subject to some degree of prejudice and discrimination. From their early encounters with Native Americans and Africans, Anglo-Americans established "whiteness" as an essential marker of difference and superiority. The Naturalization Act of 1790, for example, specified that citizenship was to be available to "any alien, being a free white person." By this provision not only were blacks ineligible for naturalization, but also future immigrants who were deemed not to be "white." The greater the likeness of immigrants to the Anglo-American type (e.g., British Protestants), the more readily they were welcomed.

Not all Anglo-Americans were racists or xenophobes. Citing Christian and democratic ideals of universal brotherhood, many advocated the abolition of slavery and the rights of freedmen—freedom of religion and cultural tolerance. Debates over immigration policy brought these contrasting views of the republic into collision. The ideal of America as an asylum for the oppressed of the world has exerted a powerful influence for a liberal reception of newcomers. Emma Lazarus's sonnet, which began "Give me your tired, your poor, your huddled masses yearning to breathe free, the wretched refuse of your teeming shore," struck a responsive chord among many Anglo-Americans. Moreover, American capitalism depended upon the rural workers of Europe, French Canada, Mexico, and Asia to man its factories and mines. Nonetheless, many Americans have regarded immigration as posing a threat to social stability, the jobs of native white workers, honest politics, and American cultural—even biological—integrity. The strength of anti-immigrant movements has waxed and waned with the volume of immigration, but even more with fluctuations in the state of the economy and society. Although the targets of nativist attacks have changed over time, a constant theme has been the danger posed by foreigners to American values and institutions.

Irish Catholics, for example, were viewed as minions of the Pope and enemies of the Protestant character of the country. A Protestant Crusade culminated with the formation of the American (or "Know-Nothing") Party in 1854, whose battle cry was "America for the Americans!" While the Know-Nothing movement was swallowed up by sectional conflict culminating in the Civil War, anti-Catholicism continued to be a powerful strain of nativism well into the twentieth century.

Despite such episodes of xenophobia, during its first century of existence, the United States welcomed all newcomers with minimal regulation. In 1882, however, two laws initiated a progressive tightening of restrictions upon immigration. The first established qualitative health and moral standards by excluding criminals, prostitutes, lunatics, idiots, and paupers. The second, the Chinese Exclusion Act, the culmination of an anti-Chinese movement centered on the West Coast, denied admission to Chinese laborers and barred Chinese immigrants from acquiring citizenship. Following the enactment of this law, agitation for exclusion of Asians continued as the Japanese and others arrived, culminating in the provision of the Immigration Law of 1924, which denied entry to aliens ineligible for citizenship (those who were not deemed "white"). It was not until 1952 that a combination of international politics and democratic idealism finally resulted in the elimination of all racial restrictions from American immigration and naturalization policies.

In the late nineteenth century, "scientific" racialism, which asserted the superiority of Anglo-Saxons, was embraced by many Americans as justification for imperialism and immigration restriction. At that time a second immigrant wave was beginning to bring peoples from eastern Europe, the Balkans, and the Mediterranean into the country. Nativists campaigned for a literacy test and other measures to restrict the entry of these "inferior races." Proponents of a liberal immigration policy defeated such efforts until World War I created a xenophobic climate which not only insured the passage of the literacy test, but prepared the way for the Immigration Acts of 1921 and 1924. Inspired by racialist ideas, these laws established national quota systems designed to drastically reduce the number of southern and eastern Europeans entering the United States and to bar Asians entirely. In essence, the statutes sought to freeze the biological and ethnic identity of the American people by protecting them from contamination from abroad.

Until 1965 the United States pursued this restrictive and racist immigration policy. The Immigration Act of 1965 did away with the national origins quota system and opened the country to immigration from throughout the world, establishing preferences for family members of American citizens and resident aliens, skilled workers, and refugees. The unforeseen consequence of the law of 1965 was the third wave of immigration. Not only did the annual volume of immigration increase steadily to the current level of one million or more arrivals each year, but the majority of the immigrants now came from Asia and Latin America. During the 1980s, they accounted for 85 percent of the total number of immigrants, with Mexicans, Chinese, Filipinos, and Koreans being the largest contingents.

The cumulative impact of an immigration of 16 plus millions since 1965 has aroused intense concerns regarding the demographic, cultural, and racial future of the American people. The skin color, languages, and lifestyles of the newcomers triggered a latent xenophobia in the American psyche. While eschewing the overt racism of earlier years, advocates of tighter restriction have warned that if current rates of immigration continue, the "minorities" (persons of African, Asian, and "Hispanic" ancestry) will make up about half of the American population by the year 2050.

A particular cause of anxiety is the number of undocumented immigrants (estimated at 200,000-300,000 per year). Contrary to popular belief, the majority of these individuals do not cross the border from Mexico, but enter the country with either student or tourist visas and simply stay—many are Europeans and Asians. The Immigration Reform and Control Act (IRCA) of 1986 sought to solve the problem by extending amnesty for undocumented immigrants under certain conditions and imposing penalties on employers who hired undocumented immigrants, while making special provisions for temporary agricultural migrant workers. Although over three million persons qualified for consideration for amnesty, employer sanctions failed for lack of effective enforcement, and the number of undocumented immigrants has not decreased. Congress subsequently enacted the Immigration Act of 1990, which established a cap of 700,000 immigrants per year, maintained preferences based on family reunification, and expanded the number of skilled workers to be admitted. Immigration, however, has continued to be a hotly debated issue. Responding to the nativist mood of the country, politicians have advocated measures to limit access of legal as well as undocumented immigrants to Medicare and other welfare benefits. A constitutional amendment was even proposed that would deny citizenship to American-born children of undocumented residents.

Forebodings about an "unprecedented immigrant invasion," however, appear exaggerated. In the early 1900s, the rate of immigration (the number of immigrants measured against the total population) was ten per every thousand; in the 1980s the rate was only 3.5 per every thousand. While the number of foreign-born individuals in the United States reached an all-time high of almost 20 million in 1990, they accounted for only eight percent of the population as compared with 14.7 per cent in 1910. In other words, the statistical impact of contemporary immigration has been of a much smaller magnitude than that of the past. A persuasive argument has also been made that immigrants, legal and undocumented, contribute more than they take from the American economy and that they pay more in taxes than they receive in social services. As in the past, immigrants are being made scapegoats for the country's problems.

Among the most difficult questions facing students of American history are: how have these tens of millions of immigrants with such differing cultures incorporated into American society?; and what changes have they wrought in the character of that society? The concepts of acculturation and assimilation are helpful in understanding the processes whereby immigrants have adapted to the new society. Applying Milton Gordon's theory, acculturation is the process whereby newcomers assume American cultural attributes, such as the English language, manners, and values, while assimilation is the process of their incorporation into the social networks (work, residence, leisure, families) of the host society. These changes have not come quickly or easily. Many immigrants have experienced only limited acculturation and practically no assimilation during their lifetimes. Among the factors that have affected these processes are race, ethnicity, class, gender, and character of settlement.

The most important factor, however, has been the willingness of the dominant ethnic group (Anglo-Americans) to accept the foreigners. Since they have wielded political and social power, Anglo-Americans have been able to decide who to include and who to exclude. Race (essentially skin color) has been the major barrier to acceptance; thus Asians and Mexicans, as well as African Americans and Native Americans, have in the past been excluded from full integration into the mainstream. At various times, religion, language, and nationality have constituted impediments to incorporation. Social class has also strongly affected interactions among various ethnic groups. Historically, American society has been highly stratified with a close congruence between class and ethnicity, i.e., Anglo-Americans tend to belong to the upper class, northern and western Europeans to the middle class, and southern and eastern Europeans and African Americans to the working class. The metaphor of a "vertical mosaic" has utility in conceptualizing American society. A high degree of segregation (residential, occupational, leisure) within the vertical mosaic has severely limited acculturation and assimilation across class and ethnic lines. However, within a particular social class, various immigrant groups have often interacted at work, in neighborhoods, at churches and saloons, and in the process have engaged in what one historian has described as "Americanization from the bottom UP."

Gender has also been a factor since the status of women within the general American society, as well as within their particular ethnic groups, has affected their assimilative and acculturative experiences. Wide variations exist among groups as to the degree to which women are restricted to traditional roles or have freedom to pursue opportunities in the larger society. The density and location of immigrant settlements have also influenced the rate and character of incorporation into the mainstream culture. Concentrated urban settlements and isolated rural settlements, by limiting contacts between the immigrants and others, tend to inhibit the processes of acculturation and assimilation.

An independent variable in these processes, however, is the determination of immigrants themselves whether or not to shed their cultures and become simply Americans. By and large, they are not willing or able to do so. Rather, they cling, often tenaciously, to their old world traditions, languages, and beliefs. Through chain migrations, relatives and friends have regrouped in cities, towns, and the countryside for mutual assistance and to maintain their customary ways. Establishing churches, societies, newspapers, and other institutions, they have built communities and have developed an enlarged sense of peoplehood. Thus, ethnicity (although related to nationalist movements in countries of origin) in large part has emerged from the immigrants' attempt to cope with life in this pluralist society. While they cannot transplant their Old Country ways intact to the Dakota prairie or the Chicago slums, theirs is a selective adaptation, in which they have taken from American culture that which they needed and have kept from their traditional culture that which they valued. Rather than becoming Anglo-Americans, they became ethnic Americans of various kinds.

Assimilation and acculturation have progressed over the course of several generations. The children and grandchildren of immigrants have retained less of their ancestral cultures (languages are first to go; customs and traditions often follow) and have assumed more mainstream attributes. Yet many have retained, to a greater or lesser degree, a sense of identity and affiliation with a particular ethnic group. Conceived of not as a finite culture brought over in immigrant trunks, but as a mode of accommodation to the dominant culture, ethnicity persists even when the cultural content changes.

We might also ask to what have the descendants been assimilating and acculturating. Some have argued that there is an American core culture, essentially British in origin, in which immigrants and their offspring are absorbed. However, if one compares the "mainstream culture" of Americans today (music, food, literature, mass media) with that of one or two centuries ago, it is obvious that it is not Anglo-American (even the American English language has undergone enormous changes from British English). Rather, mainstream culture embodies and reflects the spectrum of immigrant and indigenous ethnic cultures that make up American society. It is the product of syncretism, the melding of different, sometimes contradictory and discordant elements. Multiculturalism is not a museum of immigrant cultures, but rather this complex of the living, vibrant ethnicities of contemporary America.

If Americans share an ideological heritage deriving from the ideals of the American Revolution, such ideals have not been merely abstract principles handed down unchanged from the eighteenth century to the present. Immigrant and indigenous ethnic groups, taking these ideals at face value, have employed them as weapons to combat ethnic and racial prejudice and economic exploitation. If America was the Promised Land, for many the promise was realized only after prolonged and collective struggles. Through labor and civil rights movements, they have contributed to keeping alive and enlarging the ideals of justice, freedom, and equality. If America transformed the immigrants and indigenous ethnic groups, they have also transformed America.

How have Americans conceived of this polyglot, kaleidoscopic society? Over the centuries, several models of a social order, comprised of a variety of ethnic and racial groups, have competed for dominance. An early form was a society based on caste—a society divided into those who were free and those who were not free. Such a social order existed in the South for two hundred years. While the Civil War destroyed slavery, the Jim Crow system of racial segregation maintained a caste system for another hundred years. But the caste model was not limited to black-white relations in the southern states. Industrial capitalism also created a caste-like structure in the North. For a century prior to the New Deal, power, wealth, and status were concentrated in the hands of an Anglo-American elite, while the workers, comprised largely of immigrants and their children, were the helots of the farms and the factories.

The caste model collapsed in both the North and the South in the twentieth century before the onslaught of economic expansion, technological change, and geographic and social mobility.

Anglo-conformity has been a favored model through much of our history. Convinced of their cultural and even biological superiority, Anglo-Americans have demanded that Native Americans, African Americans, and immigrants abandon their distinctive linguistic, cultural, and religious traits and conform (in so far as they are capable) to the Anglo model. But at the same time that they demanded conformity to their values and lifestyles, Anglo-Americans erected barriers that severely limited social intercourse with those they regarded as inferior. The ideology of Anglo-conformity has particularly influenced educational policies. A prime objective of the American public school system has been the assimilation of "alien" children to Anglo-American middle class values and behaviors. In recent years, Anglo-conformity has taken the form of opposition to bilingual education. A vigorous campaign has been waged for a constitutional amendment that would make English the official language of the United States.

A competing model, the Melting Pot, symbolized the process whereby the foreign elements were to be transmuted into a new American race. There have been many variants of this ideology of assimilation, including one in which the Anglo-American is the cook stirring and determining the ingredients, but the prevailing concept has been that a distinctive amalgam of all the varied cultures and peoples would emerge from the crucible. Expressing confidence in the capacity of America to assimilate all newcomers, the Melting Pot ideology provided the rationale for a liberal immigration policy. Although the Melting Pot ideology came under sharp attack in the 1960s as a coercive policy of assimilation, the increased immigration of recent years and the related anxiety over national unity has brought it back into favor in certain academic and political circles.

In response to pressures for 100 percent Americanization during World War I, the model of Cultural Pluralism has been offered as an alternative to the Melting Pot. In this model, while sharing a common American citizenship and loyalty, ethnic groups would maintain and foster their particular languages and cultures. The metaphors employed for the cultural pluralism model have included a symphony orchestra, a flower garden, a mosaic, and a stew or salad. All suggest a reconciliation of diversity with an encompassing harmony and coherence. The fortunes of the Pluralist model have fluctuated with the national mood. During the 1930s, when cultural democracy was in vogue, pluralist ideas were popular. Again during the period of the "new ethnicity" of the 1960s and the 1970s, cultural pluralism attracted a considerable following. In recent years, heightened fears that American society was fragmenting caused many to reject pluralism for a return to the Melting Pot.

As the United States enters the twenty-first century its future as an ethnically plural society is hotly contested. Is the United States more diverse today than in the past? Is the unity of society threatened by its diversity? Are the centrifugal forces in American society more powerful than the centripetal? The old models of Angloconformity, the Melting Pot, and Cultural Pluralism have lost their explanatory and symbolic value. We need a new model, a new definition of our identity as a people, which will encompass our expanding multiculturalism and which will define us as a multiethnic people in the context of a multiethnic world. We need a compelling paradigm that will command the faith of all Americans because it embraces them in their many splendored diversity within a just society.

SUGGESTED READINGS

On acculturation and assimilation, Milton Gordon's *Assimilation in American Life: The Role of Race, Religion, and National Origins* (1964) provides a useful theoretical framework. For a discussion of the concept of ethnicity, see Kathleen Neils Conzen, et al. "The Invention of Ethnicity: A Perspective from the USA," *Journal of American Ethnic History*, 12 (Fall 1992). *Harvard Encyclopedia of American Ethnic Groups*, edited by Stephan Thernstrom (Cambridge, MA, 1980) is a standard reference work with articles on themes as well as specific groups; see especially the essay by Philip Gleason, "American Identity and Americanization." Roger Daniels's *Coming to America: A History of Immigration and Ethnicity in American Life* (New York, 1991) is the most comprehensive and up-to-date history. For a comparative history of ethnic groups see Ronald Takaki's *A Different Mirror: A History of Multicultural America* (1993). On post-1965 immigration, David Reimers's *Still the Golden Door: The Third World Comes to America* (1985), is an excellent overview. A classic work on nativism is John Higham's, *Strangers in the Land: Patterns of American Nativism: 1860-1925* (1963), but see also David H. Bennett's *The Party of Fear: From Nativist Movements to the New Right in American History* (1988). On the Anglo-American elite see E. Digby Baltzell's *The Protestant Establishment: Aristocracy and Caste in America* (1964).

GEORGIAN AMERICANS

by
Vladimir F. Wertsman

OVERVIEW

Georgia, called Sakartvelo by Georgians, is a European country occupying about 27,000 square miles (69,700 square kilometers). It is almost half the size of Illinois and is located in the mountainous region of Transcaucasia. Georgia is bounded by Russia to the north and northeast, Azerbaijan to the east, the Black Sea to the west, and Armenia and Turkey to the south. The country's population, which was 5.5 million in 1995, is predominantly Georgian. The Georgians comprise 71 percent of the population. Ethnic minorities include Armenians (8 percent), Russians (6.5 percent), Azerbaijanis (4.6 percent), Greeks (3 percent), Ossets (3 percent), and Abkhazians (2 percent). There are also smaller groups of Ukrainians, Turks, Persians, and Jews. Georgians are Christians and belong to the Georgian Orthodox Church. Islam and Judaism, which are practiced by ethnic minorities, are tolerated.

Georgia has a rich cultural heritage that is expressed in the original architecture of its churches, castles, and fortresses. The country is also known for its exquisite gold and silver jewelry, polyphonic songs, and uniquely painted icons. The Georgian people are noted for their courage, passionate love of music, dancing, poetry, and longevity. Every 51 of 100,000 people in Georgia are 100 years of age or more.

Tbilisi is the capital of Georgia. The official language is Georgian, but Russian is used as a second language. The Georgian flag has a red background, with a white and blue horizontal square in the left corner.

HISTORY

According to traditional Georgian accounts, Georgians are descendants of Thargamos, the great-grandson of Japhet, son of the Biblical Noah. The ancient name of Georgia was Colchis, which was associated for centuries with the Greek myth of Jason and his 50 Argonauts, who sailed from Greece to Colchis to capture the Golden Fleece. The legend describes how Medea, the daughter of the King of Colchis, assisted Jason in his adventure, but at the end was deserted by him. Colchis is historically recorded by Herodotus (484-425 B.C.), Xenophon (c.430-354 B.C.), and Josephus Flavius (37-95 A.D.).

Georgia was formed as a kingdom in the fourth century B.C. and, over several centuries, was ruled by Romans, Persians, Byzantines, Arabs, and Turkish Seljuks. It regained full independence and unity under King David the Restorer (1089-1125), and reached the height of territorial expansion and cultural development under Queen Thamar (1183-1213). During the thirteenth and fourteenth centuries, Monoglian invasions by Genghis Khan and Tamerlane devastated the country and split its unity. In the fifteenth century, Georgia was divided into the three kingdoms of Iberia, Imertia, and Kakhetia. In 1555, Turkey took over the rule of West Georgia, while East Georgia fell under Persian rule. In 1783, Georgia became a protectorate of Russia. At the beginning of the nineteenth century, the country was annexed and incorporated into Russia's czarist empire. Georgia remained a part of Russia until 1917, when the Bolsheviks overthrew the czar and established a Communist state.

MODERN ERA

In 1918, Georgia became an independent state. However, three years later, the Soviet Red Army invaded Georgia and incorporated it into the Soviet Union. A rebellion that was designed to restore Georgian independence failed in 1924. In 1936, a new constitution was proclaimed and Georgia became a Soviet Socialist Republic under the dictatorship of Joseph Stalin (1879-1953), who was born a Georgian. Another Georgian, Lavrenti Beria (1899-1953), was a friend of Stalin and became the chief of NKVD, the Soviet secret police. Beria was notorious for extending Stalin's regime of terror through executions, mass arrests, and deportations to vast labor camps known as *gulags*.

Following the collapse of the Soviet Union, Georgia again became an independent nation in April of 1991. During the first half of the 1990s, the country had to cope with difficult political, economic, and ethnic problems. Two secessionist movements in the autonomous regions of Abkhazia and Inghushetia required military intervention. Both conflicts ended in 1996 with the signing of a peace agreement. A bitter political struggle between various parties and factions brought President Eduard Shevarnadze, a former Foreign Minister of the Soviet Union, to power. Shevarnadze quickly established a pro-Western government.

THE FIRST IN AMERICA

The Georgian presence in America began in 1890 with the arrival of 12 Georgian Cossack horsemen hired by Buffalo Bill Cody and his Wild Congress of Rough Riders. The Cossack horseman successfully competed with talented horsemen from Mexico, Argentina, France, England, Spain, and the United States. Under the leadership of Prince Ivan Rostromov Marcheradse, the Georgians charmed audiences with their energy, style, and riding skills. In 1910, a second group of 30 Georgian male and female riders successfully performed with the Ringling Brothers Circus. A third group of nearly 50 Georgians were hired as laborers to work on the West Coast railroads. Shortly before World War I, a few dozen Georgians returned to their native land, while those who decided to settle in America formed the nucleus around which the Georgian American community developed in later years.

SIGNIFICANT IMMIGRANT WAVES

Following the Soviet invasion of Georgia in 1921, hundreds of families, fearing repression by Communist authorities, became refugees abroad. About 200 Georgian refugees, including former political leaders, members of aristocracy, and military officers, came to the United States. Unable to speak English and lacking financial resources or help from charitable organizations, many Georgian refugees had a very hard time adjusting to their new life in America. Some gave up their professional occupations to take menial jobs, while others with aristocratic titles married wealthy American women. Those who could not cope with life in America returned to Europe, and joined other Georgian refugees who established themselves in Germany, France, Poland, Turkey, and Belgium.

A second wave of Georgian refugees was recorded after World War II. More than 250 men, women, and children came to the United States by virtue of the Displaced Persons Act of 1948 and the

Refugee Act of 1953. Several were former prisoners of war who feared reprisals if they returned to the Soviet Union. There were also some Georgians who lived in Europe as refugees from the Soviet Union before the start of World War II. These new immigrants, unlike the first wave, received assistance from various charitable and non-profit organizations, including the Georgian Association in the United States and The Tolstoy Foundation. Many immigrants from this second wave were skilled workers, professionals, military men, and clerical workers, and found it relatively easy to adjust to their new homeland.

During the final decade of Soviet rule in Georgia, a third wave of immigrants—consisting of a few hundred men and women—came to the United States for economic, religious, educational, business, or family reasons. This wave consisted of both professionals and non-professionals and included persons from various ethnic groups within Georgia. There are between 3,000 and 3,500 Georgian Americans, the majority of which have settled in or around New York, Boston, Washington, D.C., Chicago, Detroit, Seattle, Atlanta, and Los Angeles.

ACCULTURATION AND ASSIMILATION

Because Georgian Americans are small in number, less information is available about them than other ethnic groups. Despite this, Georgian Americans have preserved their heritage and culture through various organizations. As early as 1924, Georgian organizations were founded in San Francisco and in New York City. These organizations held cultural activities and social gatherings, and provided assistance to other immigrants. Between 1955 and 1975, the Georgian American press was very active. *Kartuli Azri* (Georgian Opinion) was the most popular newspaper and was it was heavily supported by donations from Georgian Americans. Over the years, Georgians have been fully assimilated into American culture. However, Georgian Americans continue to proudly preserve many aspects of their unique culture.

TRADITIONS, CUSTOMS, AND BELIEFS

In Georgia, some tribes forbid women to have children until after they have been married for three years. Georgian custom allows a maximum of three children per couple. The birth of a boy is cause for great celebration, while the birth of a girl is often met with disappointment. Many Georgian Ameri-

cans have long forsaken these customs. Other customs, however, are still observed. Formality and mutual respect guide the daily behavior of Georgian Americans. From an early age, children are trained in etiquette and the social graces. The display of any "sexual" behavior in public is considered a source of great shame. Privacy and modesty are greatly cherished and women are treated with respect.

PROVERBS

Georgians, like many other ethnic groups from Transcaucasia, are known for their many original proverbs. Examples include: Low places are considered high when high places are lacking; That which one loses by laughing one does not find again by crying; There is always a dirty spoon in every family; He who does not seek friends is his own enemy; If you put your nose into water you will also wet your cheeks; The cock cannot profit by the friendship of the fox; One blames one's friend to his face and one's enemy to his back; Don't spit into a well, one day it may serve to quench your thirst; It is better to drink water from a small spring than salt water from a great sea; The cart is heavy, but it makes the load light.

CUISINE

Georgian Americans have a very rich, healthy, and tasty cuisine. Other ethnic groups also enjoy Georgian cuisine, and it is typically featured on menus in Russian restaurants. Georgian women often cook according to the traditions of their homeland. A typical first course in a Georgian-style meal may include fresh herbs, radishes, scallions, tiny cucumbers, quartered tomatoes sprinkled with dill, home cured olives, pickled cabbage, red kidney beans dressed with walnut sauce, eggplant puree, cheese, and smoked sturgeon garnished with tarragon. *Khachapuri* (flat bread with cheese filling), *lobio* (kidney beans in plum sauce) and other types of appetizers are usually accompanied by *lavash* (thin white bread) and *raki* (a dry and strong liquor made from berries or grape) or *chacha* (a grape vodka). *Sulguni*, a type of cheese, is served with fresh coriander and scallions. *Khmeli-suneli*, a very popular dish, consists of mixtures of dill, coriander, pepper, and other strongly scented spices. Melons and oranges are often added to goat or chicken that has been strongly spiced with peppers and heavily seasoned with garlic. A chicken soup called *kharcho* is also served with walnuts.

Second courses may consist of skewers of fried or broiled fish such as *khramuli* or *kogak*, a white flesh fish that is delicately flavored. Lamb or chicken stews (*chakhokhbili*) are served with wine. *Shash-lik* is made of chicken, onions, and other vegetables on a skewer. *Kotmis satsivi* is a roast chicken or roast suckling pig served with walnut sauce. *Mtsvadi* is grilled lamb, pig or young goat, and *tabaka* is pressed fried chicken. Georgian cuisine also includes *pkhali* (vegetables and walnuts) *kinkali* (dumplings of beets), and pickled cabbage. All meals are served with excellent wines, especially *Kindzmarauli* and *Teliani*, both of which are prized for their aromatic flavors. Desserts include compotes, candied almonds or walnuts, various preserves, and *chuckella* (traditional candy made from grape juice and walnuts). Non-alcoholic beverages consist of yogurt, syrups, fruit juices, and Turkish coffee.

TRADITIONAL COSTUMES

Traditional clothing is still found in the homes of some older generation Georgian Americans, and is usually worn during Georgian folk festivals. Men wear black wool pants and a long-sleeved shirt that buttons half way down the front. This shirt is usually black and is often decorated around the edges with silver or gold thread. Soft, tight-fitting leather boots that extend above the knee are also worn. These boots have a thin sole and no heels. A wool coat, usually black, brown, white, or gray in color, is worn over the shirt and pants. It has no collar and is cut with a long, narrow, V shaped opening from the neck halfway to the waist. Rows of narrow pockets, six or eight on each side of the coat are sewn across the chest. A belt containing a dagger (*kinjal*) or sword is worn around the waist. The head is adorned with a *papakha*, a fur cap of sheep or goatskin with the fleece side out, which hangs down over the forehead. During winter months a *bashlik*, which is a hood of finely woven woolen material that can be tied around the neck, is worn. A cape made of goat or sheep wool, called a *bourka*, is worn around the shoulders. It is usually black and semicircular in shape, and fastened at the neck with thongs.

Georgian women wear long, floor-length gowns, with a tight bodice and long sleeves ending at the waist. The gowns are made of silk and come in white or a variety of pastel colors. A long, flowing scarf is often wrapped around the head and shoulders. The hair is worn in at least two braids, which frequently extend past the waist. An ornamental gold belt covers the waist. A headdress, in gold or another bright color, covers the head. Older women wear similar dresses, but in darker colors. They also wear a turban-like headdress. Georgian women, like their male counterparts, also wear boots. Unlike some of their neighbors, Georgian women do not wear a veil in front of their faces.

It should be noted that Georgian Americans, like their conationals in urban Georgia, dress in European or American-style clothes. Farmers also dress in European shirts and trousers that are conservative in color. Rural women typically wear blouses and long skirts.

DANCING, SONGS, AND MUSIC

Georgian men and women love to dance. Men dance on the tip of their toes at increasing speeds, incorporating breath taking leaps and swift head movements. Female dances employ scarves, handkerchiefs and pitches, intricate arm movements, and simple, gliding steps. The most popular Georgian dances are *Lezghinka*, in which men and women dance together; *partza*, a circular dance; *kartuli*, a dance of chivalry in which men are not permitted to touch the girls; and *Samaya*, which is performed by three young girls to celebrate a wedding feast. Young women often dance the *narnari*, which features beautiful arm and hand movements.

Dances are accompanied by highly rhythmic music in which drumming plays a leading role. The characteristic feature of Georgian folk music is polyphony. As a rule, multi-voice songs are performed by men. Women perform some solos and duets. Georgian folk music is also rich in lyrical songs honoring popular heroes. Georgian orchestras include flutes, lutes, drums, cymbals, bagpipes, and mandolins. Beginning in the 1950s Georgian singers and dancers, trained in their homeland, have performed in the United States and throughout the world. These groups are widely acclaimed for their exceptional artistic qualities. They have performed in New York, Chicago, Los Angeles, San Francisco, Oakland, Detroit, Cleveland, and many other cities.

HOLIDAYS

Dozens of religious holidays are celebrated in Georgia, depending on the region and locality. Several holidays are devoted to various saints, particularly St. George. Two religious holidays observed by Georgians and Georgian Americans are January 26 and May 19. Both of these days honor Saint Nino, the patron saint credited with bringing Christianity to the Georgians in the fourth century. Easter, Christmas, and New Year are also major holidays. Church services are followed by a meal and various festivities. Other important holidays include May 26, which celebrates the proclamation of Georgia's independence in 1918; and August 29, which marks Georgia's revolt against the Soviet Union in 1924. On April 9, 1991, Georgia declared its independence from the Soviet Union. This date has been added to the calendar of holidays.

HEALTH ISSUES

Georgian Americans are basically a vigorous people, with traditional longevity. As noted earlier, in Georgia, every 51 of 100,000 people are 100 years of age or more. There are no specific health problems affecting Georgian Americans.

LANGUAGE

Karthli, the Georgian language, is part of the Ibero-Caucasian family of languages and is distinct from Indo-European, Turkic, and Semitic languages. It does not have any connection to other Northern Caucasian language groups, even though it resembles them phonetically. Georgian is based on the Armenian alphabet and its roots are attributed to St. Mesrop. The Georgian language features a frequent recurrence of the sounds *ts, ds, thz, kh, khh, gh.* There are two systems of the Georgian alphabet. The first, Khutsuri, consists of 38 letters and dates back to the fifth century A.D. It was used in the Bible and liturgical works. The second Georgian alphabet, Mkherduli, consists of 40 letters and is used in ordinary writing.

The Georgian language is rich, flexible, and contains a complex grammar. High proportions of older Georgian Americans speak Georgian, while younger generations tend to speak English. Georgian is taught at Columbia University, Indiana University at Bloomington, University of North Carolina at Chapel Hill, and Emory University. Georgian books can be found at the Library of Congress, the New York Public Library, and universities that teach the language.

GREETINGS AND POPULAR EXPRESSIONS

Me kvia means my name is; *gamarjobat* is hello; *gmadlobt* is thank you; *inebet* is please; *nakhvamdis* is goodbye; *gauma . . . jobs* is cheers (when drinking wine). Other expressions: *deda* is mother; *mama* is father; *da* is sister; *zma* is brother; *mamuli* is fatherland; *ai* is this; *minda* is I want; *sadili* is dinner; "a" is pronounced like the a in the English word "car;" and "I" is pronounced in English like "ee."

FAMILY AND COMMUNITY DYNAMICS

Georgian American families are known for their strong ties. Women play an important role both in families and society, and divorce is frowned upon. Although the father is the head of the family, women may keep their own surnames when they marry, and there is no stigma when a husband lives with the wife's parents. Children are raised to value their family and respect older members. Young people are expected to be well-educated and encouraged to become professionals. Georgians enjoy gathering with family and close friends to gossip, praise traditions, and remember deceased family members. Georgians are also known for their hospitality.

WEDDINGS

Georgians usually marry at a young age, and married couples are expected to take care of their parents. In many cases, marriage is arranged by the parents of the bride and groom, relatives, or close friends. Wedding receptions traditionally include a series of toasts. The *tamada,* or toastmaster, is chosen by the audience, and leads toasts to the native land, to parents, to friends, to the memory of the dead, to women, to life, to children, and to the guests. After the toasts are made, all of the guests say "*gauma . . . jobs*" (cheers). No one except the tamada may make a toast without first asking permission. The couple then toasts the guests and thanks them for their good wishes. After each toast, the guests must drink an entire glass of wine.

Weddings in the Georgian Orthodox Church are performed according to old customs. In the wedding ceremony, the groom is called *mepe* (king) and the bride *dedopali* (queen). The couple sips wine from the same cup and puts crowns on their heads as a symbol of their union. The priest blesses the couple, and they officially become husband and wife. The wedding ceremony is followed by a reception with music and dancing.

BIRTH AND BAPTISMS

During a baby's christening (*natloba*), the godfather (*natlia*) plays a very important role. He first cuts the hair and nails of the newborn. By doing this, it is believed that the qualities and talents of the godfather are transmitted to the child. When the child is placed in water during the christening, small coins are thrown in to bring the child good luck and happiness.

FUNERALS

Following the death of a family member, church bells are rung three times a day until the funeral ceremony is completed. During the funeral ceremony the priest, assisted by a choir and deacon, sings prayers and hymns for the dead. In the name of the deceased, the priest asks for forgiveness of sins from family and friends. Prayers are recited at the cemetery and the Gospel is read. The coffin is then lowered into the grave, and soil sprinkled with holy water is tossed on top of the coffin. Another recitation from the Gospel concludes the funeral. After the funeral, the family of the deceased shares a light meal and beverages to honor their loved one.

INTERACTIONS WITH OTHER ETHNIC GROUPS

Georgian Americans maintain friendly ties with other ethnic groups who immigrated from Georgia. These groups include Circassians, Ossetians, and Cabardins. Many Georgian Americans have intermarried with Armenians, Russians, Jews, and Ukrainians. They have also developed good relations with Americans of other backgrounds and religious faiths.

RELIGION

Georgians became Christians in the fourth century A.D. under King Mirian (265-345) who erected the first Christian church, which was later renamed the Cathedral of Mtskhet. The Georgian Orthodox Church, a branch of the Eastern Orthodox Church, is headed by a Catholicos-Patriarch with its headquarters in Georgia. Georgian law grants the Catholicos the same power as that of a king, and the clergy actively participates in the life of state affairs. Bishops must be at least 35 years old, priests not less than 30 years, and deacons over 25 years.

Georgian liturgy uses characteristic liturgical texts called *Kondaki*, and various blessings for stated occasions called *Khurthkhevani*. Its system of chronology has a new *annus mundi*, its own order of ecclesiastical teachings and feasts. Mass is always accompanied by liturgical chants which employ specific Georgian styles and forms. The Georgian cross has a heraldic shape, which is different from the types of crosses used by other branches of the Eastern Orthodox Church. Georgian Americans do not have their own churches, and usually attend Russian Orthodox or Greek Orthodox churches.

EMPLOYMENT AND ECONOMIC TRADITIONS

Unlike the first wave of Georgian Americans who were employed as taxi drivers or in manual labor jobs, succeeding generations have enjoyed greater opportunities. Many are professionals (engineers, teachers, doctors, artists, military officers), some are businessmen, others are clerical workers. Most Georgian Americans belong to the middle class.

MILITARY

Some Georgian Americans became career military officers after World War II. A Georgian American officer, General John Shalikashvili (1936–), served as chairman of the Joint Chiefs of Staff between 1992 and 1996. Shalikashvili emigrated to the United States with his parents following World War II, completed a master's degree in international affairs at George Washington University, and joined the military in 1958. He was a decorated veteran of the Korean and Vietnam Wars, and eventually became commander of American troops in Germany. Shalikashvili was also the commander-in-chief of American armed forces in Europe before President Clinton named him chairman of the Joint Chiefs of Staff. It marked the first time that a Georgian American had been named to such a high position within the military.

RELATIONS WITH FORMER COUNTRY

Georgian Americans have always been extremely proud of their homeland and never accepted its forced incorporation into the Soviet Union. Georgian American organizations and newspapers lobbied constantly for the creation of an independent and democratic Georgia, a goal that was attained when the Soviet Union collapsed in 1991. New laws passed in Georgia have sought to facilitate increased economic, cultural, and educational ties with Georgian Americans.

INDIVIDUAL AND GROUP CONTRIBUTIONS

ACADEMIA AND EDUCATION

Dodona Kiziria was a professor of literature, cinema, and video at Indiana University at Bloomington; Timur Djordjaz was a professor in the Theater and Fine Arts Department, Pace University, New York City.

BALLET AND MUSIC

George Balanchine (1904-1983), was born Balanchivadze, and was a noted ballet master and choreographer. He was considered the most influential and finest choreographer of the twentieth century. Balanchine was the cofounder and artistic director of the New York City Ballet Company, worked for the New York Metropolitan Opera, created more than 200 ballets, and choreographed several Broadway musicals and movies. He also wrote a book about 101 ballet stories.

Alexander Toradze (1952-) was a pianist and winner of the 1977 Van Cliburn competition in Moscow. He joined the New York Philharmonic Orchestra in 1983, and was later conductor of the Minnesota Opera.

George Chavchavadze (1904-1962) was a noted pianist with international credits.

LITERATURE

George Papashvily (1898-1978) was an author who married American Helen White after immigrating to United States in the 1920s. Together they wrote *Anything Can Happen* (1944), which chronicled his immigrant experiences. The book was a bestseller, and was made into a 1952 movie by Paramount Pictures. Papashvily and his wife also published the novel *All the Happy Endings* (1956) and *Home and Home Again* (1973), which included their impressions of Georgia after a visit during the 1960s.

Svetlana Allilueva (1926–), was born Djugashvili, and was the daughter of Joseph Stalin. She defected from the Soviet Union to the United States in 1967, and subsequently wrote *Twenty Letters to a Friend* (1967), and *Only One Year* (1969), both in Russian and English, which detail her experiences before and after her defection, and her impressions about America.

Valerii Chalidze (1938–), was an author, editor, and publisher, who focused his writings on human rights violations in the former Soviet Union; published *To Defend These Rights: Human Rights and the Soviet Union* (1975), *Criminal Russia: Essays on Crime in the Soviet Union* (1977), *The Soviet Human Rights Movement: A Memoir* (1984).

David Chavchadze (1938–), was an author and linguist, former intelligence officer, and a descendant of a noble family. He specialized in tracing the nobility of Tsarist Russia, and published *Crowns and Trenchcoats: A Russian Prince in the CIA* (1990).

Paul Chavchavadze (1899-1971), was the author of fiction books, and the translator of writings from Georgian into English. He came from the same noble family as David Chavchadze.

JOURNALISM

Vladimir Babishvili (1923–), was an international broadcaster, and worked for the Voice of America for more than 20 years. He also translated the works of Georgian writers in exile into English.

CULINARY ARTS

George Papashvily and his wife (already described in the Literature section) published *Russian Cooking* (1970), which includes both Russian and Georgian recipes based on their own kitchen experiences and also collected from other Georgian American sources.

SCULPTURE

George Papashvily produced several pieces of sculpture, including *Georgian Folk Singer*, which was featured in the documentary film *Beauty in Stone*.

SCIENCE

Alexander Kartvelishvili was an aeronautical engineer, designing the P-47 (Thunderbolt fighter plane) and S-84 (Thunderjet) during World War II and the Korean War. He founded Republic Aviation.

BUSINESS

Prince Artchil Gourieli-Tchkonia (1895-1955), who emigrated to the United States in 1937, and his wife Madam Helena Rubinstein (1882-1965), known as the queen of cosmetic products, became a successful business couple. They launched Gourelli Apothecary with two new lines of expensive cosmetic products for women and men. The prince also established the "Prince Machiabelli" line, which included "Cachet" in 1970, and "Chimere" in 1980. These perfumes continued to remain popular after the prince's death.

SOCIAL WORK

Prince Teymuraz Bagration (1913-1992), a descendant of Georgian royalty, became president of the Tolstoy Foundation in New York City after World War II and remained in this position until his death. He was known for his efforts to resettle Georgian, Russian and other ethnic refugees from the Soviet Union and East European countries. He was also involved in the resettlement of refugees from Vietnam, Cuba, Uganda, and other countries. As a member of Care and Interaction, a coalition of more than 100 charitable organizations, Bagration was instrumental in assisting displaced persons who wanted to start a new life in the United States.

MEDIA

PRINT

The Georgian American League published *Voice of Free Georgia* (1953-1958) in English; the American Council for Independent Georgia published *Chveni Gza/Our Path* (1953-1960s), in Georgian with English summaries; and the Georgian National Alliance sponsored the publication of *Georgian Opinion* (1951-1975). All three publications focused on events in Georgia, the fight for a democratic and independent Georgia, and events in the Georgian American community. By the end of the 1990s, there were no Georgian American periodicals being published.

ORGANIZATIONS AND ASSOCIATIONS

Georgian Association in the United States (New York office).
Founded in 1931, this organization absorbed the Georgian National Alliance, and focused its activities on preserving Georgian heritage in America. It organizes cultural events, assists needy immigrants, maintains a library with books about Georgia, and publishes a newsletter.

Contact: Mrs. Elizabeth Zaldastani Napier, President.
Address: 164 Burns Street, Forest Hills, New York, New York 11375.
Telephone: (718) 268-5749 or (617) 227-0695.

Georgian Association in the United States (D.C. office).
Contact: Irakly Zurab Kakabadze.
Address: 3173 17th Street, NW, Washington, D.C. 20100.
Telephone: (202) 223-1770.
Fax: (202) 223-1779 or (617) 742-8353.

U.S.-Georgia Foundation.
Founded in 1992, its goal is to assist Georgia in becoming a more democratic society with a free market economy and a multi-party political system.

Contact: Eduard Gudava.
Address: 1110 Vermont Avenue, Suite 600, Washington, D.C. 20005.

Telephone: (202) 429-0108.
Fax: (202) 293-3419.

MUSEUMS AND RESEARCH CENTERS

Harvard University (Houghton Library).
Deposits-on-loan: (80 boxes with the archives of the Georgian government (1917-1921), and the correspondence of its legation abroad (Paris, Rome, Berlin, Constantinople, and Bern), expenses made by the government, domestic and foreign press about Georgia, and other valuable documents. The loan period is 1974-2004 and, since 1988, the microfilm of the archives has been available to scholars under the library's rules governing the use of manuscripts.

Contact: Librarian of Houghton Library.
Address: Cambridge, Massachusetts 02138.
Telephone: (617) 495-2401.
Fax: (617) 496-4750.

Indiana University Libraries.
Possesses a collection of rare materials about Georgia and the Caucasus region for the historical scholarly community. Access is restricted only to those researchers that have permission to use the collection.

Contact: Head Librarian.
Address: 10th and Jordan Street, Bloomington, Indiana 47405.
Telephone: (812) 455-3403 and 455-2452.
Fax: (812) 855-3143.

Projecto Sella.
Consists of more than 2,000 glass-plate negatives featuring people, landscape, and the architecture of Georgia and other regions of the Caucasus from the late 1890s. The pictures are well preserved and the negatives can be reproduced. They were taken by Vittorio Sella (1859-1945), a well-known Italian photographer with international credentials.

Contact: Paul Kallmes, Coordinator.
Address: P.O. Box 19928, Portland, Oregon 97280-0928.
Telephone: (503) 244-6319.
Fax: (503) 245-9879.

Russian Nobility Association.
Preserves biographical archives, and possesses more than 2,000 books on historical and genealogical subjects related to former members of nobility during Tsarist Russia. Among them are several Georgian princes who also belonged to the Russian nobility.

Contact: Alexis Shcherbatov.
Address: 971 First Avenue, New York, New York
10022.
Telephone: (212) 755-7528.

Tolstoy Foundation.
Founded in 1939 as a voluntary organization to help refugees who have escaped from oppressive regimes around the world. Its archives include documents and other materials regarding Georgian refugees who were helped by the organization from the end of World War II until the fall of communism in the Soviet Union.

Contact: Xenia Woyevodsky, Executive Director.
Address: 104 Lake Road, Valley Cottage, New
York 10989.
Telephone: (914) 268-6140; or (914) 268-6722.
Fax: (914) 268-6937.

SOURCES FOR ADDITIONAL STUDY

Curtis, Glenn. "Georgia." *Armenia, Azerbaijan and Georgia: Country Studies*. Washington, DC: Library of Congress/Federal Research Division, 1994, pp. 151-230.

Goldstein, Darra. *The Georgian Feast: The Vibrant Culture and Savory Food of the Republic of Georgia*. New York: Harper-Collins, 1992.

Papashvily, George and Helen. *Anything Can Happen*. New York: St. Martin's Press, 1985.

Wertsman, Vladimir. "Georgians in America." *Multicultural Review*, December 1995, pp. 28-31, 52-53.

Under the redemptioner system, a German peasant could travel on a sailing vessel without charge. On arrival at an Atlantic port he was sold to an American businessman to work from four to seven years to redeem his passage and win his freedom.

GERMAN AMERICANS

by
La Vern J. Rippley

OVERVIEW

Situated in the heart of Europe, Germany today adjoins nine neighbors: Denmark to the north; Poland and the Czech Republic to the east; Austria and Switzerland to the south; and the Netherlands, Belgium, Luxembourg, and France to the west. With a population of nearly 80 million, Germany follows Russia as the most populous nation in Europe. In size, however, Germany is smaller than either France or Spain and equates roughly with the combined area of Minnesota and Wisconsin. With an average of 222 people per square kilometer, Germany has one of the highest population densities in Europe.

HISTORY

Recorded German history begins with the battle between the Roman legions and Arminus, a prince of the Germanic Cherusci tribe, recounted in the chronicles of Tacitus. *Deutschland*, the Germans' name for their country, came into use in the eighth century when Charlemagne incorporated German and French speakers into a common nation. As cohesion among the population of the eastern realm increased, the term *Deutschland* applied to all German speakers. Once confined west of the Elbe River, Germans gradually penetrated father east into former Slavic territory, often peacefully, but sometimes by force.

Almost from the time of Charlemagne, Germany bore versions of the name Holy Roman Empire of the German Nation, beginning with the Salian dynasty and proceeding with the rule of the Hohenstaufens, the Habsburgs, and the Hohenzollerns. Germany suffered religious schism when Martin Luther proposed reforms in 1517, which led to the pillaging of the country by those who profited from the weakened central political, religious, and social ruling structures. The religiously motivated Thirty Years' War (1618-1648), which erupted a century after Luther's death, devastated Germany's territory and its moral fiber until the age of French absolutism. During this period, also known as the Enlightenment, Prussian king Frederick the Great (1740-1786) became a patron of the American Revolution. Frederick sent Baron von Steuben, Johannes DeKalb, and others to train American military novices at Valley Forge and elsewhere.

During the Napoleonic period, the Holy Roman Empire dissolved in favor of the *Deutscher Bund* (German Confederation), a loose confederation of individual sovereign states that functioned with a single participatory government unit, the *Bundestag*, a delegated parliament in Frankfurt. The *Bundestag* often behaved like a monarchical oligarchy, suppressing freedom, enforcing censorship, and controlling the universities and political activity.

Arguments arose among the liberals over whether to establish a "greater Germany," along the lines of Great Britain, or a "smaller Germany," which would include only the more traditionally German principalities without Austria. Because Austria wanted to bring into the union its more than a dozen ethnic groups, the National Assembly opted for a smaller Germany, for which they offered a constitution to King Friedrich Wilhelm IV of Prussia. The king's rejection of the constitution triggered popular uprisings in the German states, which were in turn met by military suppression. A large group of German intellectual liberals, known as the Forty-eighters, immigrated to the United States during this period to escape persecution. The contemporary flag of Germany with its black, red, and gold stripes derives from the flag of the Forty-eighter parliament.

Following three short wars in 1864, 1866, and 1870, the new Prussian chancellor Bismarck united the remaining German states into the smaller German Reich, which lasted until World War I. German industry grew during the late nineteenth century. Domestic unrest erupted when Kaiser Wilhelm I attempted to suppress the domestic socialist working class. In the early twentieth century, Germany struck up alliances with Austria and the age-old Ottoman Turkey, triggering fear abroad. Ultimately, the entente between France, England, and Russia led to Germany's defeat in World War I in November 1918.

MODERN ERA

With the framers of the Versailles Treaty, German Social Democrats and the Catholic Center Party succeeded in writing a constitution dubbed the Weimar Republic. The Republic was doomed from the outset by its struggles with burdensome war reparations, inflation, foreign military occupation west of the Rhine, a war guilt clause in the Versailles Treaty, and heavy losses of territory. In 1925 Field Marshal von Hindenburg, a hero on the Eastern Front in World War I, was elected president. Stricken by the political-economic disaster of 1929, Hindenburg in 1933 appointed to the chancellorship Adolf Hitler. Hitler promptly banned parties, expelled Communists from the government, and restructured the military. Hitler's goals were to purify Germany by removing people with all but the purest Teutonic blood and to expand German territory throughout Europe. In 1940 Germans occupied France, Czechoslovakia, Poland, Austria, and Hungary, and acted on the policy of extermination of unwanted peoples that nearly resulted in destroying the Jews and Gypsies of Europe.

Hitler's troops rounded up Jews in Germany and in other countries forcing them to give up their lands and property. Systematically, Jews and political prisoners in Western Europe were shipped from Belgium, France, Germany, Greece, Italy, and Holland to forced-labor camps and to prisons. Concentration camps, which held Jews captive without regard for the accepted norms of arrest, appeared in France, Germany, and Austria, as well as Poland and Czechoslovakia. There were camps built to exterminate the Jews; most were gassed, but some were shot, drowned, or starved to death. Nearly six million people were killed by Nazi command although there was some national resistance. When Germany was defeated in World War II, the country was divided into several parts governed by the various countries of the opposing armies. Eventually the Western countries that had opposed the Germans combined their sections into a European-influenced West Germany. This part of Germany was established as a democratic republic in 1949. The territory of Germans in the east was formed into a Russian satellite, and East Germany became a communist people's republic. For nearly 40 years distrust among Germans was encouraged by the Soviet Union on the one hand and by the West on the other. Both feared a united Germany. Finally in 1990 a revolution in

East Germany deposed the communist regime there and the leaders sought reunification with West Germany. The two German states agreed to reunite under a two-house parliament and the pattern of free elections that had been developed by West Germany. Germany has worked to balance the economies of an agriculturally entrenched east and a west with a long-standing industrial sector.

THE FIRST GERMANS IN AMERICA

Since their arrival at Jamestown in 1607 along with the English, Germans have been one of the three largest population components of American society. When Columbus arrived in America in 1492, he did so in the name of Ferdinand and Isabella of Spain, that is, with the entitlement of the Habsburgs who also ruled Germany as part of the Holy Roman Empire. It was a German cosmographer, Martin Waldseemüller, who suggested that the New World be designated "America."

German immigration began in the seventeenth century and continued throughout the postcolonial period at a rate that exceeded the immigration rate of any other country; however, German immigration was the first to diminish, dropping considerably during the 1890s. Contrary to myth, the first German immigrants did not originate solely in the state of Pfalz. Although emigrants from Pfalz were numerous from 1700 to 1770, equally high percentages came from Baden, Württemberg, Hesse, Nassau, and the bishoprics of Cologne, Osnabrück, Münster, and Mainz. During the American pre-Revolutionary War period, immigrants came primarily from the Rhine valley, an artery that gives access to the sea. German emigration during this period was almost exclusively via French or Dutch ports like LeHavre or Rotterdam.

SIGNIFICANT IMMIGRATION WAVES

Between 1671 and 1677 William Penn made trips to Germany on behalf of the Quaker faith, resulting in a German settlement that was symbolic in two ways: it was a specifically German-speaking ward, and it comprised religious dissenters. Pennsylvania has remained the heartland for various branches of Anabaptists: Old Order Mennonites, Ephrata Cloisters, Brethren, and Amish. Pennsylvania also became home for many Lutheran refugees from Catholic provinces (e.g., Salzburg), as well as for German Catholics who also had been discriminated against in their home country.

By 1790, when the first census of Americans was taken, more than 8.6 percent of the overall population of the United States was German, although in Pennsylvania more than 33 percent was German. During the Revolutionary War, these German Americans were numerically strengthened by the arrival of about 30,000 Hessian mercenaries who fought for England during the hostilities, of whom some 5,000 chose to remain in the New World after the war ceased.

In addition to those who had arrived for political and religious reasons until about 1815, Americans and some foreign shippers brought many Germans to America under the redemptioner system. The scheme was that a German peasant traveled on a sailing vessel without charge and on arrival at an Atlantic port was sold to an American businessman to work from four to seven years to redeem his passage and win his freedom. Some of the early sectarians—Baptist Dunkers, Schwenkfelders, Moravian Brethren, and others—were only able to reach America in this way.

Populous as German immigrants to America were by the end of the eighteenth century, the major waves of immigration came after the conclusion of the Napoleonic Wars in 1815. Germany's economy suffered in several ways. Too many goods were imported, especially cloth from industrialized England. Antiquated inheritance laws in southwestern Germany caused land holdings continuously to be divided, rendering farms too minuscule for assistance. A failing cottage industry collapsed when faced by a flood of foreign products. Finally, the population had grown artificially large because of growing dependence on the potato. Like Ireland, rural Germany in the 1840s was suddenly hit by famine precipitated by the potato blight.

Because the 1848 revolutions in Europe failed to bring democracy to Germany, several thousand fugitives left for America in addition to the nearly 750,000 other Germans who immigrated to America in the following years. While a mere 6,000 Germans had entered the United States in the 1820s, nearly one million did so in the 1850s, the first great influx from Germany. Despite annual fluctuations, especially during the Civil War period when the figure dropped to 723,000, the tide again swelled to 751,000 in the 1870s and peaked at 1,445,000 in the 1880s.

During the nineteenth century religious and political refugees were numerous. During the 1820s, for example, Prussia forced a union of the Reformed and Lutheran congregations, which by the late 1830s caused many Old Lutherans to emigrate. Saxon followers of Martin Stephan came in 1839 to escape the "wickedness" of the Old World. Other refugees were the Pietists, who founded communal

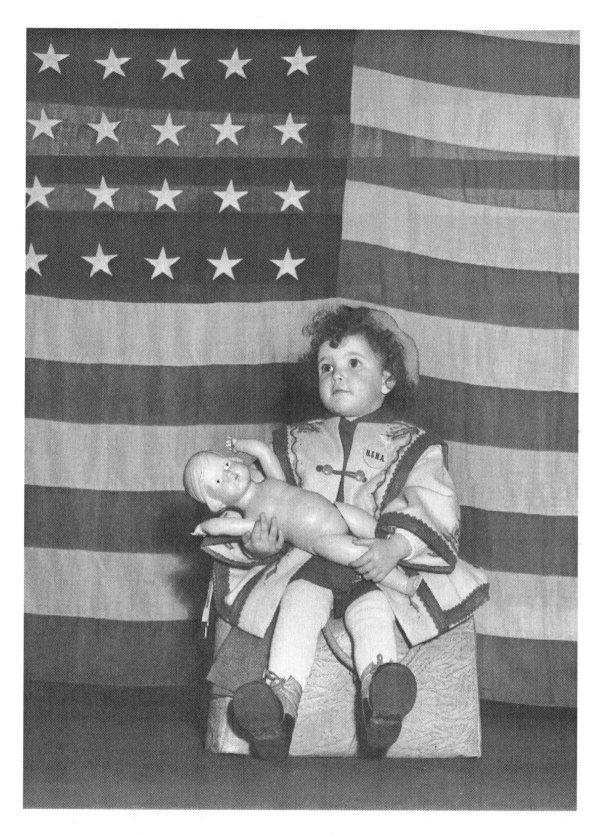

societies in America (including Harmony and Economy Pennsylvania—established by the Rappists—as well as Zoar in Ohio, St. Nazianz in Wisconsin, and Amana in Iowa).

Societies sponsored by German princes sought to use emigration as a solution to social problems at home. For example, the Central Society for German Emigrants at Berlin (1844), the National Emigration Society at Darmstadt (1847), the Giessener Emigration Society (1833), and the Texas Braunfels Adelsverein (1843) operated on the principle that a one-way ticket for the downtrodden was cheaper than a long-term subsidy. Also influential in unleashing a tidal wave of German emigration were writers like Gottfried Duden whose book (1829) about Missouri became a best-seller.

During the 1850s small farmers and their families dominated the first major wave of immigrants, who often came from southwest Germany. Soon after artisans and household manufacturers were the main arrivals from the more central states of Germany, while day laborers and agricultural workers from the rural northeast estates characterized subsequent waves of German immigrants. Not until German industrialization caught up with the English in the late nineteenth century did German emigrants no longer have to leave the country to improve their lives. Beginning in the late 1880s and for several decades thereafter, migrants from depressed German agricultural regions were destined less for America than for the manufacturing districts of Berlin, the Ruhr, and the Rhine in Germany itself.

"We were stationed in Hamburg in a tremendous big place. It was sort of an assembly building where you got processed. There was an exodus from Europe at that time, and they had all races in this place. You could see people from Russia, Poland, Lithuania, you name it. I can't describe the way I felt—it was part fear, it was exciting. It's something I'll never forget."

Ludwig Hofmeister in 1925, cited in *Ellis Island: An Illustrated History of the Immigrant Experience*, edited by Ivan Chermayeff et al. (New York: Macmillan, 1991).

Interspersed among these waves of economic emigrants were fugitives from oppression, including thousands of German Jews who left because of economic and social discrimination. Young men sometimes fled to avoid serving in the Prussian military. Organized industrial laborers also fled the antisocialist laws enacted when a would-be assassin threatened the life of Germany's Kaiser Wilhelm I, who blamed socialist labor leaders for the attempt. Catholics, too, were oppressed by Bismarck's infamous May Laws during the 1870s, which suppressed the influence of the Catholic Center Party and its drive for greater democracy during the first decade of the new emperor's reign.

Also during the latter half the nineteenth century, a host of agents fanned out across Germany to drum up emigration. Some were outright recruiters who were technically outlawed. More often these agencies took the form of aid societies working to better the lot of the emigres in Germany, such as the Catholic Raphael Society, the Bavarian *Ludwigsmissionsverein*, the Leopoldinen *Stiftung* in Vienna, the Pietist society of Herrnhut in Saxony, and the Lutheran support groups at Neuendettelsau of Franconia in northern Bavaria. Frankenmuth, Michigan, for example, traces its roots to the latter organization. Aiding the immigrants on this side of the Atlantic were such agencies as the Catholic Leo House in New York and the Central-Verein in St. Louis. Much better funded promoters were those established by the north-central states (most prominently, Michigan, Wisconsin, and Minnesota) as they joined the Union, many of which had ample support from their legislatures for their Immigration Commissioners. Even more influential were transcontinental railroads that sent agents to the ports of debarkation along the Atlantic and Germany to recruit immigrants to either take up their land grants or supply freight activity for their lines. Especially active was the Northern Pacific during the time when German immigrant Henry Villard headed the corporation and sought to populate his land grant with industrious German farmers.

In the latter phases of German immigration, newcomers joined established settlers in a phenomenon called "chain migration." Chain migration is defined as the movement of families or individuals to join friends and family members already established in a given place. Chain migration strengthened the already existing German regions of the United States. One such concentrated settlement pattern gave rise to the phrase "German triangle," that is, St. Paul, St. Louis, and Cincinnati, with lines stretching between them so that the triangle incorporates Chicago, Milwaukee, Indianapolis, Fort Wayne, Davenport, and other strongly German cities. Other descriptors include the more accurate "German parallelogram," which stretches from Albany westward along the Erie Canal to Buffalo and farther westward through Detroit to St. Paul and the Dakotas, then south to Nebraska and Kansas, back to Missouri, and eastward along the Ohio River to Baltimore. Except for large settlements in Texas, San Francisco, and Florida, German American settlement is still largely contained within the German belt.

The number of German Americans has remained constant. From 1850 to 1970 German was the most widely used language in the United States after English. In the 1990 U.S. census, 58 million Americans claimed sole German or part-German descent, demonstrating the persistence of the German heritage in the United States.

SETTLEMENT

Germans settled in different locations depending upon when they arrived and where the best locations for economic opportunity were situated. When France, which had attempted to colonize Louisiana in the early eighteenth century with the help of Germans, assumed an important role in the cotton trade, German immigrants arrived in New Orleans and made their way up the Mississippi, Ohio, and Missouri rivers. Others arrived in New York and travelled the Erie Canal and the Great Lakes to the Midwest. The primary port of arrival for early immigrants was Philadelphia and many Germans chose to settle in Pennsylvania. The German American population of 58 million breaks down demographically as follows: 39 percent live in the Midwest, 25 percent in the South, 19 percent in the West, and 17 percent in the Northeast. With regard to specific states, Americans reporting German ancestry are the most numerous in California, followed by Pennsylvania, Ohio, Illinois, and Texas. In terms of absolute numbers, the Germans have always been at their largest in New York City. The German Americans are nowhere more densely settled than in Wisconsin, Minnesota, North Dakota, South Dakota, Nebraska, and Iowa-in the traditional German belt.

ACCULTURATION AND ASSIMILATION

In many respects, the Germans were slower to assimilate than their fellow immigrants from other countries. This was due in part to their size and in part to their overall percentage of the population. When a cross-section of basic needs can be supplied within an ethnic community, the need to assimilate in order to survive is less urgent. Germans had their own professionals, businesses, clergy, churches, and especially schools. However, second generation German immigrants were drawn more quickly into the mainstream and the survival of German communities depended upon immigration.

TRADITIONS, CUSTOMS, AND BELIEFS

The true picture of German culture differs substantially from that presented in the popular media

This German
American
Tricentennial
Multicycle from
Philadelphia,
Pennsylvania, is
traveling along
Fifth Avenue in
New York City
during the 1988
Steuben Day
Parade.

where Germans are presented as either brutal or as jolly, overweight, and beer-guzzling. Equally enigmatic is post-World War II German Americans' perception of their heritage as inseparable from certain icons and costumes, notably, beer mugs, fast high-quality cars, sausage and sauerkraut—enlivened by the spirit of Bavarian folk music. In the United States Bavarian culture is regarded as synonymous with all German culture, even though Bavarian customs and language are confined to the regional state of Bavaria and its capital, Munich. German Day festivals almost always feature Bavarian dance and clothing such as the *lederhosen* (men's shorts with suspenders) and the *dirndl* (women's full skirt). Replicas of German cities—such as Leavenworth, Washington, or Frankenmuth, Michigan—invariably assume an air of Alpine Bavaria.

HOLIDAYS

In addition to traditional American holidays, Catholic communities celebrate the feast of Corpus Christi in which there are outdoor processions to altars decorated with flowers. At the Epiphany, neighbors visited from house-to-house and young men adorned with paper crowns would sing in exchange for treats. The German Christmas served as the basis for the American celebrations; it emphasizes the family and the exchange of gifts; often, the Christmas tree is not illuminated until Christmas eve. December 6 was the traditional time of St. Nicholas' visit. Another tradition that has survived from German American communities is the greeting of the New Year by gunfire—young men would ride horses through the neighborhood and fire their shotguns when midnight arrived.

LANGUAGE

The German language is related to Danish, Norwegian, Swedish, Dutch, and Icelandic, as well as to English. High German, the dialect spoken in the east-west central geographic elevation, differs linguistically from the language spoken in the lower-lying geographic regions of northern Germany, where once Low German was in everyday usage. It is also radically different from Bavarian and Swiss German which typically is voiced in the southern, more Alpine regions. Spoken natively by 100 million people, German is the mother tongue of thousands of people who live beyond all of Germany's current borders. Ten percent of all books published in the world are in German.

FAMILY AND COMMUNITY DYNAMICS

There was a low rate of tenancy among early German immigrants, who purchased homes as early as possible. German Americans have traditionally placed a high value upon home ownership and prefer those made of brick. The traditional German American family was essentially patriarchal with women assuming subservient roles. Because many German immigrants were from agricultural areas, they brought with them a traditional concept of the family. Farm families were, of necessity, large and family members worked together for the good of all. Wives and daughters worked together with husbands and sons to manage the harvests. In families whose work was not farm-centered, though, wives worked with their husbands in small family operated businesses. Children frequently left school early with the boys entering family businesses and the girls entering domestic service. According to 1880 census figures, though, a smaller proportion of German American women were part of the work force than other immigrant groups. Those who were employed outside the home did not work in factories or in jobs in which a knowledge of English was necessary; instead, they labored in janitorial work or the service industry.

EDUCATION

To emphasize the importance of their language in the transmission of cultural values, German Americans strove to maintain their own German-language schools, first by establishing private institutions and later, after 1849, by pressuring school districts to offer German or bilingual education where parents requested it. In addition to the German-language instruction offered in the public schools, there was the instruction in the parochial schools operated especially by Catholics and Lutherans, which enrolled thousands of the children of German immigrants.

Parochial schools started in colonial times and continued through the nineteenth century, sometimes sponsored by nonreligious organizations such as a local German school society which functioned as legal owner of the school. Some of these schools operated according to new pedagogical principles and had a lasting impact on the American school system. For example, they introduced kindergarten. At all school levels sports programs, which had their origin in the German socialist *Turner* societies, became an integral aspect of American training for physical fitness. A few German American leaders dreamed of having their own university with German as the language instruction, but in spite of *Kultur* enthusiasm, it never came to fruition.

At the lower levels Germans achieved success in the political arena. When the question of teaching subjects in German drew the attention of truancy alarmists in Wisconsin and Illinois around 1890, the Wisconsin legislature passed the infamous Bennett Law, which required that children attend school more faithfully and which added the stipulation that at least some of the subjects be taught in English. In Illinois a similar measure was called the Edwards Law. As a result, the Lutheran and Catholic constituents of these states campaigned to defeat Wisconsin's governor William Dempster Hoard and to free the German language schools of state intervention. Over time, however, German faded in favor of English.

To supply teachers for these many schools, German Americans maintained a teachers' college while the *Turner* gymnastic societies developed their own teacher preparation institute for the production of scholars who would educate pupils. After the turn of the twentieth century, a special three-million-strong organization, the German American Alliance, actively promoted the cause of Germans. It did so in part to preserve their culture and in part to maintain a clientele for German products like newspapers, books, and beer. In 1903 the Alliance urged in its *German-American Annals,* "Only through the preservation of the German language can our race in this land be preserved from entire disappearance. The principal aim should be the founding of independent parochial schools in which the language of instruction would be German, with English as a foreign language."

Elementary German language school enrollments reached their zenith between 1880 and 1900. In 1881 more than 160,000 pupils were attending German Catholic schools and about 50,000 were in Missouri Synod Lutheran schools. Of the roughly one-half million people attending school with a curriculum partly or all in German, as counted by the German American Teachers Association around 1900, 42 percent were attending public schools, more than a third were in Catholic schools, and 16 percent were in Lutheran private schools.

However, when World War I broke out, the German element was so discredited in the United States that when Congress declared war in April 1917, within six months legal action was brought not only to dampen considerably German cultural activities but also to eliminate the German language from American schools. The flagship case was the Mockett Law in Nebraska, which anti-German enthusiasts repealed. Eventually, 26 other states followed suit, banning instruction *in* German and *of* German. When the Missouri Synod Lutherans of Nebraska brought the test case, *Meyer v. Nebraska*, the ban on German was reconfirmed by all the courts until it reached the U.S. Supreme Court. On June 4, 1923, the Supreme Court held that a mere knowledge of German could not be regarded as harmful to the state, and the majority opinion added that the right of parents to have their children taught in a language other than English was within the liberties guaranteed by the Fourteenth Amendment. Nevertheless, as a language of instruction in schools, during church service, and at home, German gradually drifted into oblivion as assimilation accelerated.

RELIGION

Religious differences have characterized the German people. Most of the population is Protestant and practice a form of Lutheranism—the Protestant Reformation church created by the German religious leader Martin Luther. Religion was important to German immigrants and the lack of ministers attracted Moravian missionaries in the early eighteenth century. The success of these churches strengthened the established Reformed churches, which rejected the ecumenical stance of the Moravians. In the eighteenth century the language, doctrine, and rituals of some of the established synods of the Reformed church had become Americanized and they were unable to attract new immigrants. The conservative synods, such as the Missouri Synod, were more successful, however.

Many German immigrants were Catholic; but because the Catholic church was controlled essentially by the Irish there was much friction between the two groups. Many parishes were established by lay people, which resulted in frequent friction between the pastors and trustees in pioneer churches. The German American churches, which used the German language exclusively, featured a liturgy rich with ritual and music and offered its parishioners a variety of associations and societies. They also addressed numerous social needs by supporting and operating orphanages and hospitals. By the

twentieth century, however, many of the German American Catholic parishes underwent severe attrition when many of its members moved to suburban mixed parishes.

POLITICS AND GOVERNMENT

On the whole, Germans in America have been reluctant to participate in politics. They arrived without the necessary language skills, even if they had *not* lacked a tradition that conditioned them for political participation. Thus, at the national level, the first and most prominent German figure in American politics was Carl Schurz, who was influential in the election of Abraham Lincoln, served as ambassador to Spain, became a general in the Civil War, later was elected U.S. senator from Missouri, and finally was appointed Secretary of the Interior under Rutherford Hayes. At the state level, too, the Germans seem to have avoided public office. Except for John P. Altgeld, the German-born governor of Illinois from 1893 to 1897, no German was ever elected to head an American state. Even in the U.S. Senate, few German-born and a surprisingly small number of German Americans have ever entered that upper house.

Not until Dwight D. Eisenhower was there an American president with a German surname. Eisenhower's ancestors were colonial Pennsylvania Germans who had moved to Texas and then Kansas, but certainly this president was no friend of Germans. Political scientists have shown how strongly the Germans came to resent Franklin Roosevelt and General Eisenhower for their defeat of Germany during World War II. This resulted in a fading from Democratic Party support until the candidacy of President Harry Truman in 1948. During that campaign the German American electorate returned in droves to their traditional Democratic Party, handing Truman a surprise victory over Republican Thomas E. Dewey. Apparently, Truman's strong stand against Stalin at Potsdam, his subsequent anti-communist actions in Greece, and his May 1948 decision to save Berlin by airlift aided his November reelection chances with German Americans. There was no similar outpouring for Eisenhower in 1952, who won in spite of only mild German support.

LABOR UNIONS

Occupationally, the Germans were skilled in such trades as baking, carpentry, and brewing. They were also laborers, farmers, musicians, and merchants. According to the 1870 census figures, 27 percent of

German Americans were employed in agriculture, 23 percent in the professions, and 13 percent in trades and transportation. By 1890, however, some 45 percent reportedly were laborers or servants, perhaps as a result of industrial workers' migration rather than a farmers' migration. This may explain why the labor movement in the United States gained considerable impetus from its German component.

The mid-nineteenth century witnessed the introduction of the communist ideologies of Wilhelm Weitling (1808-1871) and Joseph Weydemeyer (1818-1866), which gave impetus to early struggles for social and economic reform. The International Workingmen's Association in America was founded in 1869 as the first of the communist and socialist groups in America; and its membership was predominantly German American. And in 1886, German American anarchists were also instrumental in the forming of the labor movement implicated in the infamous Chicago Haymarket bombing during the labor strikes of that period. Had it not been for the greater need for workers to unite against their employers and join the American Federation of Labor (AFL), German trade unions might have been consolidated in the late 1880s. In future years many leaders of American labor were German American, including Walter Reuther, who fought on the picket lines during the 1930s before becoming president of the AFL-CIO following World War II. For German immigrants, labor union membership enabled them to not only improve working conditions, it helped them to form a solidarity with workers from other ethnic backgrounds.

RELATIONS WITH GERMANY

During the period from 1945 to 1990, the United States, with allies Great Britain and France, officially occupied West Germany, each in a special zone. The Americans occupied Bavaria, the Rhine-Main Frankfurt, and Palatinate areas. Each country was also allocated a sector in the capital of Berlin. During the Cold War, dramatic confrontations focused on Berlin because it lay 110 miles behind the Iron Curtain. For 11 months in 1948 and 1949, the Soviets noosed a land blockade around the city, only to have the Allies supply the needs of two million inhabitants by air. For example, when the city's electrical power supply was severed, West Berliners lived in darkness until an entire generating plant could be flown in and assembled on site.

After Khrushchev met John F. Kennedy at a June summit in Vienna, East German border police erected the Berlin Wall on August 13, 1961. Throughout the Cold War, the wall was an important political symbol. It figured in the political phraseology of each U.S. president, most prominently in Kennedy's "Ich bein ein Berliner" speech at the city hall, which endeared him to Berliners for all time. After the collapse of Communism the wall was dismantled in 1990. Today a small portion of the wall stands as a museum. Before unification of the two Germanies on October 3, 1990, the four World War II Allied victors' flags were lowered from the *Komandatura* palace in Berlin. Thus ended four decades of control, returning Germany to full international autonomy, which further restored the confidence of Americans in their German descent. With its strong economy and continuous universal military conscription, Germany remains the linchpin of NATO and the core member in the European Community.

INDIVIDUAL AND GROUP CONTRIBUTIONS

German immigrants to the United States have distinguished themselves in virtually every field of endeavor. John Roebling (1806-1869) is still known from his prowess with bridges, although the once famous empire builder, John Jacob Astor (1763-1848), is little remembered for his American Fur Company. Baron Friedrich von Steuben (1730-1794) commands respect as a military hero, but cartoonist Thomas Nast (1840-1902) is all but forgotten, although his elephant and donkey mascots for the Republicans and Democrats and his Santa Claus are not. With the arrival of the computer screen, Ottmar Mergenthaler's (1854-1899) famous Linotype printing system has met oblivion. Even Wernher von Braun's (1912-1977) pioneer rocketry, which still carries Americans and their satellites into outer space, is fading from consciousness.

BUSINESS

In business John August Sutter (1803-1880) is remembered less for his Pacific trading prowess than for the fact that gold was found on his California land holdings in 1848. Claus Spreckels developed sugar refining in California and Hawaii, while Frederick Weyerhaeuser masterminded the Northwest timber industry. Henry Villard, born Heinrich Hilgard, completed the Northern Pacific Railroad. Prominent brewers include Philip Best, Valentin Blatz, Frederick Miller, Joseph Schlitz, and the Coors and the Anhaeuser-Busch families.

MUSIC

In music there were the father and son Walter Damrosch (1862-1950) and Leopold Damrosch, and Bruno Walter Schlesinger, all conductors in New York; opera singers Ernestine Schumann-Heink (1861-1936) and Lotte Lehmann (1888-1976); the composers Paul Hindemith (1895-1963) and Kurt Weill (1900-1950); film musicians such as Franz Waxman (1906-1967), Frederick Hollander (1896-1976), and Andre Previn (1929–), also renowned for his classical music.

SCIENCE AND TECHNOLOGY

In atomic energy Albert Einstein (1879-1955) is the most prominent scientist. In the laboratories it was his German-born colleagues, Nobel laureates James Franck (1882-1964), Otto Loewi (1873-1961), Victor Hess (1883-1964), Felix Bloch (1905-1983), Otto Stern (1888-1969), and Hans Bethe (1906–) who mattered. On the Manhattan Project they worked with two German-educated Hungarians, Edward Teller (1908–) and Leo Szilard (1898-1964), all under the command of Julius Robert Oppenheimer (1904-1967), the American-born son of Forty-eighter immigrants, who had taken his Ph.D. at the University of Goettingen before engineering the bomb. Szilard and the German-born scientists Erwin Schrödinger (1887-1961) and Max Delbrück (1906-1981) later worked closely with colleagues to develop the Crick-Watson model of DNA. George Westinghouse (1846-1914) invented, among many other things, the air brakes to stop trains. For his electric motors, Charles Steinmetz (1865-1923) became known as the wizard of Schenectady.

SPORTS

George Herman Erhardt Ruth (1895-1948), better known as Babe, and Lou Gehrig, both the sons of German immigrants, continue to enjoy sports fame.

STAGE AND SCREEN

Carl Laemmle (1867-1939) founded Universal Studios. Famous actors of German descent include: one of the best known actresses of her time, Marlene Dietrich (1902-1992); Conrad Veidt (1893-1943), who appeared in *The Thief of Baghdad* and *Casablanca*; Lilli Palmer (1914-1986); Werner Klemperer (1920-1996), known most for his role of Colonel Klink in the 1960s television series *Hogan's Heroes*; and leading lady in many films during the 1960s and 1970s, Elke Sommer (1940–).

Renowned directors include: Ernst Lubitsch (1892-1947), known for the "Lubitsch Touch" in his comedies and an inspiration to fellow directors Orson Welles and Billy Wilder; William Dieterle (1893-1972), director of *Elephant Walk* (1954); Anthony Mann (1906-1967) of *El Cid*; and Roland Emmerich (1955–), famed for modern-day blockbusters *Independence Day* and *Godzilla*.

VISUAL ARTS

In architecture the famous Bauhaus School was headed by Walter Gropius (1883-1969) at Harvard and Ludwig Mies van der Rohe (1886-1969) in Chicago. Marcel Breuer and Josef Albers (1888-1976) created the designation "modern design," overshadowed now by the so-called postmodern style.

MEDIA

PRINT

Amerika Woche.
Newspaper with text in English and German.

Contact: Werner Baroni, Editor.
Address: 4732 North Lincoln Avenue, Chicago, Illinois 60625.
Telephone: (312) 275-5054.

Der Deutsch-Amerikaner/German American Journal.
Newspaper published by the German American National Congress; promotes the organization's efforts to maintain German culture, art, and customs.

Contact: Ernst Ott, Editor.
Address: 4740 North Western Avenue, Second Floor, Chicago, Illinois 60625.
Telephone: (312) 275-1100.
Fax: (312) 274-4010.

German Life.
Bi-monthly magazine on German culture, history, and travel, which also focuses on the German-American experience.

Contact: Heidi L. Whitesell, Editor-in-Chief.
Address: Zeitgeist Publishing, 226 N. Adams St., Rockville, Maryland 20850-1829.
Telephone: (301) 294-9081.
Fax: (301) 294-7821.
E-mail: info@germanlife.com.
Online: http://www.GermanLife.com.

IGAR News.

Monthly publication of the Institute for German American Relations; promotes friendly German American relations through education.

Contact: Dr. Bruce D. Martin, Editor.
Address: 9380 McKnight Road, Suite 102, Pittsburgh, Pennsylvania 15237-5951.
Telephone: (412) 364-6554.

Nordamerikanische Wochen-Post.

Published in Troy, Michigan, this weekly carries a front page directly from Germany, reports on many German American organizations, and includes coverage of business activity in Germany. It is currently the best-edited and most widely distributed such publication in America.

Contact: Regina Bell, Editor.
Address: Detroit Abend-Post Publishing Co., 1120 East Long Lake Road, Troy, Michigan 48098.
Telephone: (313) 528-2810.
Fax: (313) 528-2741.

Society for German-American Studies— Newsletter.

Quarterly publication of the Society; focuses on German immigration and settlements in the United States and on German American history and culture.

Contact: LaVern J. Rippley, Editor.
Address: St. Olaf College, Northfie, Minnesota 55057.
Telephone: (507) 663-3233.

New Yorker Staats-Herold is the oldest and among the best North American German-language publications. *America Woche*, *Wächter und Anzeiger*, *California Staats-Zeitung*, and similar publications typify efforts of regional German-language newspapers to continue their noble traditions. The Deutsch-Amerikanische Nationalkongress, headquartered in Chicago, publishes its own monthly, as do a number of its chapters.

RADIO

German-language programs on radio stations abound. There are at minimum one-hour radio programs on perhaps a dozen radio stations in Chicago, and several radio programs in Milwaukee; Pittsburgh; Detroit; Saginaw; St. Paul; Cleveland; Toledo; Cincinnati; Denver; Seminola, Florida; New Braunfels, Texas; and on the West Coast.

ORGANIZATIONS AND ASSOCIATIONS

Throughout the German belt there continue to exist hundreds of German societies. In Michigan alone where the *Wochen-Post* carries a listing, there are 28 ranging from the Arion singers and the *Berlin Verein* to *Schwäbischer Männerchor* and the *Verein der Plattdeutschen* (Low German speakers). In other states there are dozens more, some representing Germans from beyond the borders of the nation, such as the German-Bohemian Society of New Ulm, the Germans from Russia Heritage Society in Bismarck, and the Transylvanian Saxons in Cleveland. New York City alone has perhaps 100 German clubs, listed periodically in the local German newspaper. So, too, hundreds of once German-language churches offer services routinely but not regularly, sometimes weekly, more often monthly for a persistent but waning German-language clientele.

German American Information and Education Association (GIEA).

Patriotic conservative organization seeking to improve the public image of "Germanity" and to publicize contributions to American culture made by German Americans.

Contact: Stanley Rittenhouse, President.
Address: P.O. Box 10888, Burke, Virginia 22015.
Telephone: (703) 425-0707.

German American National Political Action Committee (GANPAC).

Seeks to represent what the committee considers to be the interests of German Americans.

Contact: Hans Schmidt, Chair.
Address: P.O. Box 1137, Santa Monica, California 90406.

MUSEUMS AND RESEARCH CENTERS

The Society for German American Studies, headquartered at the University of Cincinnati, functions as a scholarly umbrella for many others that have a more social or genealogical orientation. The Pennsylvania German Society in Philadelphia has a major library, while research centers with the name Max Kade Institutes recently have sprung up on university campuses, notably, at Madison, Wisconsin; Lawrence, Kansas; Indianapolis; and Penn State. There is no semblance of a German American museum, although local historical societies in the "German" states have much material.

SOURCES FOR ADDITIONAL STUDY

America and the Germans: An Assessment of a Three-Hundred-Year History, two volumes, edited by Frank Trommler and Joseph McVeigh. Philadelphia: University of Pennsylvania Press, 1985.

Cook, Bernard A., and Rosemary Petralle Cook. *German Americans*. Vero Beach, Florida: Rourke Corp., 1991.

Emigration and Settlement Patterns of German Communities in North America, edited by Eberhard Reichmann, La Vern J. Rippley, and Jörg Nagler. Indianapolis: Max Kade German-American Center, Indiana University-Purdue University at Indianapolis; Nashville, Indiana: Produced and distributed by NCSA LITERATUR, 1995.

Kloss, Heinz. *Atlas of German-American Settlements*. Marburg: Elwert, 1974.

News from the Land of Freedom: German Immigrants Write Home, edited by Walter D. Kamphoefner, Wolfgang Helbich, and Ulrike Sommer, translated by Susan Carter Vogel. Ithaca, New York: Cornell University Press, 1991.

Piltz, Thomas. *The Americans and the Germans*. Munich: Heinz Moos, 1977.

Pond, Elizabeth. *Beyond the Wall: Germany's Road to Unification*. Washington, D.C.: Brookings Institution, 1993.

Rippley, La Vern J., and Eberhard Reichmann. *The German-Americans: An Ethnic Experience*, translated by Willi Paul Adams. Indianapolis: Max Kade German-American Center, 1993.

Totten, Christine M. *Roots in the Rhineland: America's German Heritage in Three Hundred Years of Immigration, 1683-1983*. New York: German Information Center, 1988.

Wust, Klaus. *Three Hundred Years of German Immigrants in North America, 1683-1983: A Pictorial History*. Baltimore and Munich: Heinz Moos, 1983.

GHANAIAN AMERICANS

by
Drew Walker

Ghana was the origin of a great many African-Americans who were brought to America as slaves and thus significant numbers of African Americans can also claim an original identity as Ghanaians.

OVERVIEW

The nation of Ghana is located in West Africa. With an area of 92,098 square miles (238,533 square kilometers), it borders Burkina Faso to its north and northwest, the Ivory Coast to its west, Togo to its east and the Atlantic Ocean's Gulf of Guinea to its south. With a population of 16,445,000, Ghana is by no means a large African nation, yet its economy and production statistics are among the highest in the continent. Most of the land in Ghana is low-lying, with the highest altitudes not exceeding 3,000 feet (900 meters). Bisecting the landmass of the country is the Volta River Basin and the artificially created Lake Volta. The greatest masses of population are found in the country's southern and southeastern areas.

Within Ghana, there are many distinct ethnic groups, all of which affect Ghanaian Americans as an ethnic group. Ghanaians cannot be easily encapsulated into one shared Ghanaian cultural identity, as they also have strong local identities. Within Ghana there are roughly 100 distinct ethnic groups, most of which also differ in language. The major ethnic groups of Ghana are the Akan, Ewe, Guan, Mole-Dagbane, and Ga-Adangbe. The different communities which make up these groups share a common history, language, and cultural practices. Although a great number of Ghanaians and Ghanaian immigrants to the United States belong to these main groups, there are some who have different cultural practices.

HISTORY

The early history of the land which is today known as Ghana consists of migrations of peoples who lived as fishers and hunters. These peoples shared traditions, technologies and trade among themselves and larger trade networks to the north. From the eleventh to mid-fourteenth centuries there arose distinct states which were involved in the ever-growing trade networks from the north. Within these networks, gold was the most valuable and powerful commodity traded. In central Ghana, gold mining grew to become one of the key indirect exports across the Sahara to Europe and Asia via the great Malian kingdom to the north. With the first direct trading contact with European traders in 1471, North African routes of trade began to diminish in importance and the gold route began moving south to the Atlantic coast. With the trade in gold and other commodities underway, other European countries began coming to the coast and establishing trading posts, forts, and even castles to solidify their positions and relations within the region. These other European trading groups included the British, Danes, French and the Germans. It was not long before slaves also became objects of sale. With the growth of the slave trade, different groups from the interior grew in wealth and power, now using firearms and gunpowder to affect their neighboring groups. It was by this trade, competition, and violence that the modern history of Ghana was inaugurated. By the middle of the 18th century, the coast of Ghana had nearly 40 separate active forts controlled by European slave and gold traders. From early on much of the area today known as Ghana was called the Gold Coast, only taking the name Ghana in 1957.

MODERN ERA

As the power of the forts grew, southern coastal peoples like the Asante built ever stronger relations with the European traders, establishing themselves as middlemen between the Europeans and the peoples of the north. Growing throughout the 17th and 18th century, the Asante came to control the supply and market of slaves and other goods from the north. In doing so, they also led a series of successful conquests of the coastal peoples to further secure their power. By the early nineteenth century, however, the slave trade was losing strength and by 1814, the British, Dutch, and Danes had outlawed it altogether. In the following decades the British asserted their power over the Asante by making various alliances with other groups like the Fante. They also began to gain control of the Gold Coast by buying out the interests of other nations such as Denmark. The British and Asante fought in a series of conflicts, until the British gained control after a decisive move in 1874 in which they sacked the Asante capital Kumasi. Later that year that the British declared the Gold Coast a colony of the British Empire.

Perhaps one of the most historically significant changes of this period in Ghanaian history was the introduction of cocoa farming, beginning in 1878. As the British government made various moves in the following decades to organize Northern and Asante territories into a colony under one government, the cocoa trade led to the creation of an entire infrastructure, including educational institutions, which was unique in West Africa at the time. Despite these developments, however, the political situation of the Ghanaian people left much to be desired. Divisions and long-standing resentment between the northern and southern peoples led to political unrest and riots in larger towns. Feeling that all-African control of the government would lead to a more just political and economic situation between laborers of different ethnicity and class, prominent Ghanaians and British colonial officials began to draw up plans for an all-Ghanaian legislative assembly which would be, for the most part, organized and run by the Ghanaians. While this plan was slowly developing, impatience and doubt began to grow. The leftist politician Kwame Nkrumah sought to exploit this situation and led his Convention People's Party (CCP) into power. Through popular support and loud demands for Ghanaian autonomy the CCP led their campaign for self-government with strikes and other forms of mass persuasion. In the elections of 1951, the CCP under Nkrumah had secured nearly every seat in the legislative assembly. The colonial Governor of the Gold Coast, Sir Charles Arden-Clarke, invited Nkrumah and his cabinet to lead the new administration and they soon came to hold power almost entirely independent of British rule. In 1957 Nkrumah renamed the new country Ghana and obtained recognition from the United Nations as an independent member of the British Commonwealth.

Leading Ghana for the next nine years, Nkrumah solidified his power by establishing a one-party system and making himself leader for life of both the government and the CCP. Facing a decline in living standards, corruption and massive debt, Nkrumah was ousted in a 1966 coup led by general Joseph A. Ankrah. Serving three years as the head of the governing National Liberation Council, Ankrah lost leadership to another coup leader and general named Akwasi Amankwaa Afrifa. In the following decades, Ghana has undergone a series of coups broken by elections which have failed to secure a democratic leadership. Under the leadership of such figures as Ignatius Kutu Acheampong and Jerry Rawlings, Ghana has been subjected to periods of governmental and economic change which have affected both emigration and foreign economic relations.

THE FIRST GHANAIANS IN AMERICA

Although there is no clear record of early Ghanaian immigrants in the United States, Ghana produced many sailors and it is likely that some of them found homes in the port cities of the United States. This lack of documentation is probably the result of Ghanaian immigrants being grouped into a larger category of African immigrants. It is also notable that Ghana was the country of origin of many African Americans who were brought to America as slaves.

SIGNIFICANT IMMIGRATION WAVES

The most significant influx of Ghanaians emigrating to the United States has been in the four decades since independence. While many long-time Ghanaian American immigrants in the United States came as students, many of the immigrants of 1980s and 1990s came seeking business opportunities as well as specialized experience and training. While times of economic hardship in Ghana have affected the number who emigrate, sometimes it was the temporary cessation of hardship which allowed emigrants to save money and to build resources for their emigration to the United States.

SETTLEMENT PATTERNS

The highest concentrations of Ghanaians are found in the large cities of the United States including New York, Chicago, Washington D.C., Boston, Atlanta, and Los Angeles. According to 1996 population estimates, 8,000 Ghanaian Americans lived in the New York City metropolitan area; 4,000 in Los Angeles; 13,000 in the Washington, D.C. and Baltimore metropolitan areas; 6,000 in Chicago; and 5,000 in Boston.

ACCULTURATION AND ASSIMILATION

Many Ghanaian American communities have support networks to aid recent immigrants. Often divided by ethnic group of origin, these networks are a crucial source for both the construction of new and the preservation of old cultural forms.

TRADITIONS, CUSTOMS, AND BELIEFS

The traditions, customs, and beliefs of Ghanaian Americans can be roughly divided in terms of the major Ghanaian ethnic groups which have settled in the United States. Below are descriptions of these major groups.

The Akan people occupy the greatest part of the areas south and west of the Black Volta River. The primary form of social organization among the Akan is the extended family, or the *abusua*. The Akan are a matrilineal society, which means that a child's family and group membership is determined by his or her mother's lineage. Every member of the Akan becomes a member of a corporate group which has its own symbols, property, and individual identity. Each corporate group has its own symbolic, carved stool or chair. This chair is often named after the female founder of the group who often lived in the past. Such stools or chairs are seen as the most important possessions of each group. Each group also shares a belief in certain spirits and gods around whom many traditions and beliefs are centered. The Akan are also exogamous, which means that each person is obligated to marry outside of his or her own corporate group.

The Ewe live in southeastern Ghana as well as the southern regions of neighboring countries Togo and Benin. The majority of the Ewe make their living as farmers, although fishing is also a common profession some areas. The Ewe are also known as traders and makers of textiles and pottery. They are a patrilineal society who regard children as descending their father's family. The head of the patrilineal family or group is often the oldest man; he is responsible for keeping the peace, representing his group in political affairs with other groups, and heading rituals regarding the ancestors of the group. In addition to honoring their ancestors, the Ewe participate in group and village rituals involving local spirits and gods. Along with these rituals, many Ewes also practice Christianity.

The Guan are thought to have originated north of Ghana, in what is today Burkina Faso. The settlement of the Guan moved down the Black Volta, eventually reaching the coastal plains. Today the Guan form enclaves in or near areas settled by other groups such as the Akan, Ewe, and Ga-Adangbe. Guan culture has often been eclectic, taking customs and practices from their neighbors and adapting them for their own purposes.

Although many groups inhabit the northern parts of Ghana, the three most prominent groups are the Mole-Dagbane (also referred to as the Mossi-Grunshi), the Gurma, and the Grusi. Of these three subfamilies of the Gur language group,

Mole-Dagbane make up 15 percent of Ghana's population and are by far the largest group in their region. Being quite varied culturally, the Mole-Dagbane group includes subgroups such as the Dagomba, Wala, Mamprusi, Frafra, Talensi, Nanumba, and the Kusase. Known for their diversity of political structure, Gur-speaking peoples traditionally lived in small, self-governed communities which maintained relations among themselves through intermarriage and trade. In many of these communities, a traditional religious leader would sometimes be summoned to settle disputes. This was not, however, the rule in all Mole-Dagbane communities. Some, like the Dagomba, Mamprusi, and Gonja, lived in societies of a larger scale and had kings.

The Ga-Adangbe live in the Accra Plains along Ghana's southern coastal area. They are two distinct yet culturally similar groups, the Ga and the Adangbe. Their languages stem from the same root, but are today unintelligible to each other. Today the Adangbe include a number of subgroups all speaking different dialects like the Shai, Ningi, Kpone, La, Gbugle, Krobo, and the Ada. Among the Ga are groups such as the Ga-Mashie, who are found in the neighborhoods of central Accra, as well as those who have immigrated to this area from Akwamu, Akwapim, Anecho (in neighboring Togo), and other areas surrounding Accra. Ga communities are prominent within the capital city of Accra, and much of Ga culture is still practiced in such urban settings.

PROVERBS

Proverbs have traditionally been very important to Africans, including the people of Ghana and Ghanaian Americans. Proverbs often play quite complex roles which vary greatly from group to group. In many cases, proverbs can be brought out through reference to short stories. Sometimes a series of proverbs is sung and accompanied by drums, a form of expression which reveals levels of emotion and meaning that bare proverbs cannot well relate. Among different groups, the recognized forms of proverbs differ. For example, the Ga and Adangbe make strict separations between proverbs and riddles, but not between epigrams and proverbs. The Ewe divide proverbs into two groups of metaphorical use according to social status and age of their performers. Many proverbs contain simple truths in the form of simple statements, such as the Akan proverb 'Anomuto ne nam nye fan' or 'The toothless man's meat is cabbage,' or in the Adangbe proverb 'Bubulo yo bu we ba' or 'Even a pauper manages to cover his nakedness with cloth instead of leaves.' Other proverbs take the form of simple statements of everyday fact, such as the Akan sayings 'Bosompo botoo abotam' or 'The rocks existed long before the sea,' and 'Dam wobo kyere aman' or 'An insane person's behavior does not escape the notice of the community.' Another popular form of proverb reports the words of animals. The following are examples of this form: Akan-Abowa apatabi se de 'Adze woye no nano nano' (The squirrel sings 'things must be done in the proper way'); Adangbe-Ateplee ke efi nge mi ne ake yahe na (The cockroach says it gave its excrement as its contribution toward the purchase of a cow) and Krakpahe ke enyuwumi nge enane mi ne kee su pa mi loko emaafo, se kpo no lohwehu tsuo ke eza we (The duck says its activity rests in its feet and that it can run only when it is in the water, but all other animals accuse it of sluggishness).

CUISINE

Of the many traditional foods prepared by Ghanaian Americans, most vary from group to group. Ghanaian Americans can often obtain the items they need to prepare specialty foods at African food stores in the large cities in which they live. Many Ghanaian Americans who have immigrated to the United States from the more forested zones of Ghana eat foods prepared from maize, coco yam, plantain, and cassava, while those from savanna prepare dishes from cereals such as millet, rice, guinea-corn, and maize. A common staple food is the yam and pounded yam (known as fufu). Wet and dry vegetables as well as beans are also prepared and eaten with yams and other foods. Meat of all sorts is also commonly consumed. Traditional alcoholic beverages include palm wine and a drink known as *pito*, which is brewed from guinea-corn, sorghum of maize.

MUSIC

Ghanaian music, which varies among ethnic groups, is often performed at festivals. Such musical performances often feature traditional instruments. A *Gangkogui*, a double iron bell, is one of the most important instruments in many ensembles; it is used to anchor tempo and timing. The drum is also a key instrument. The complex drumming techniques of many African cultures are said to speak an intricate language.

The *Atsimewu* is a lead drum. Standing four and a half feet tall, the bottom of the drum is open and smaller in diameter than the top head. Played by striking it on the head as well as the rim and sides, this lead drum is a 'talking drum' and a powerful speaker of song in rhythm, often reciting syllables of prose with drum strokes.

The Sogo/Kidi are a pair of barrel drums which are closed at the bottom. The Sogo is larger and lower in pitch than the Kidi. Each drum is played by a single person who uses a combination of open and closed stick strokes and hand muting while playing.

Other instruments include the Agboba, a large barrel bass drum, three feet high, with a closed bottom, and the Kloboto/Totodzi, which are short open bottom barrel drums. The Kaganu is a narrow barrel drum which is played with light sticks and is of similar proportions to the Atsimewu but built to the height of the Kidi. The Atoken is a small single boat-shaped bell laid in the open palm and played by striking it with piece of metal. The Axatse is a gourd rattle which is usually shaken and struck with the hand and thigh.

TRADITIONAL COSTUMES

Roughly speaking, traditional Ghanaian American modes of dress can be divided according to their geographic origin. These divisions, like many others in Ghanaian society, are drawn between north and south. For men, the cloth, a piece of fabric hanging over the shoulder and wrapped around the body, has traditionally been associated with the south. However, the smock, traditionally associated with the north, has become more popular overall. Among Muslims of the north, forms of Islamic clothing such as robes are also worn. Among the traditional outfits of Ghanaian American women, the slit and the Kaba, fashioned into long colorful dresses, are the most well known.

Of the cloths, Kente cloth is the most popular. Kente cloth has a long history, dating from 12th century Ghana. It was traditionally worn by kings, queens and other great figures of state during ceremonial events and functions. The name 'Kente' comes from the word kenten, which means 'basket,' due to its resemblance to the woven design of a basket. Traditionally each pattern of Kente was unique and had its own name and meaning, much the same way as great paintings or sculptures. Traditional smocks designs are often associated with a certain ethnic group. Among the noted areas in which smocks are manufactured are Yendi, Bimbilla, Tamale, Bawku, Bolgatanga, Lawra, Jirapa, Babile, and Nandom. Sites of Kente manufacture are Bonwire, Adansi, Accra, Keta, and Agbozume.

DANCES AND SONGS

At festivals, Ghanaian American ethnic groups often perform their varied dances and songs, which are often unique to the celebrated occasion. In addition to performing at festivals, a number of Ghanaian American groups also perform innovative and traditional dances within the United States. The following are examples of some of the dances performed by the California-based Ghanaian American performance group called Zadonu.

One prominent dance is called dowa. Dowa is a graceful dance that borrows from other dances like Kete and Denesewu. Originally a funeral dance, this graceful character is preserved in its own particular form of a dignified walking movement. Dowa is usually preceded by a chorus of voices which are accompanied at first by two boat-shaped bells and later joined by two drums. When the singing and drumming have set the mood in song, the Atumpan drums enter with parts of the drum rhythms being picked up by different parts of their bodies. This is accompanied by a spinning and bowing which the melody of the song suggest to the dancer. This dance is popular among the Twi, the Fante (who call it Adzewa), and the Ga.

Adzohu was originally a cult dance associated with a war god of Benin. In the first part of this dance, called Kadodo, only women dance. Gathering in a group as a chorus, the women sing and perform rituals while the young men are spiritually prepared for war. Then, in the second part called Atsia, the young men preparing for war begin to dance. Here, many of its movements imitate the various positions of battle, from moving in formation, to hand to hand combat, to reconnaissance.

Aside from these two examples, there are a number of other various dances and songs found in the Ghanaian American community. Dance and song are perhaps the most important cultural possessions of Ghanaian ethnic groups.

HOLIDAYS

In addition to celebrating most of the holidays of Anglo Americans, Ghanaian Americans try to preserve the traditional festivals and holidays of Ghana. Among them are: Adaekese, celebrated by the Asante; Odwira, celebrated by the Asante and Akuapim; Akwambo, celebrated by the Fantes of Agona and Gomoa; Homowo, celebrated by the Ga people of Accra; Hogebetsotso, celebrated by the Ewe people of Anlo; Damba, celebrated by the people of the northern and upper regions of Ghana; Bugum, celebrated by the Dagombas of the northern region; Kwafie, celebrated by the Dorma in the Brong Ahafo Region; Aboakyere, celebrated by the Effutu people of Winneba; and Oguaaa Fetu Afahye, celebrated by the people of the Cape Coast. The celebrations of these festivals are often sponsored by ethnic associations within the Ghanaian American community. They include traditional dancing, music and drumming, storytelling, and the display of traditional costumes. For example, the Homowo Festival celebrated in New York City annually is known as the most popular festival in the greater New York area. There is also a well-known Homowo Festival celebrated in Philadelphia. This celebration includes a pilgrimage to the Amugi Naa shrine at which participants pour libations and give thanks to ancestors and spirits. Most of these festivals are meant to give thanks to ancestors and gods, to provide purification of the group, and to offer times of reunion of families and groups. To many Ghanaians, these ceremonies are very important to maintaining links between the living and the dead by paying tribute to the departed and their memory. It is not uncommon for Ghanaian Americans, when possible, to return to the homeland, town, or village of their ancestors during one of the many such festivals to maintain links with their heritage and tradition.

Odwira is a traditional Akan festival which functions as a thanksgiving, dedication, purification, and reunion observed in Ghana and in the United States. Sponsored by the Okuapeman Association in America, it is one of the festivals observed by different groups of Ghanaian Americans. This festival is traditionally religious, reflecting and displaying many of the long-held cultural practices of the Akan people. It is considered key to maintaining a strong and respectful link between the living and the dead, and is therefore dedicated to the honor of ancestors and their spirits. This festival is usually celebrated on the ninth Sunday of the year according to the traditional Akan calender.

The main ritual activity in this festival is the purification of the sacred royal black stools, called the Nkonnwa tuntum, and the calling for blessings of the ancestors.

The Aboakyer festival is celebrated by a Guan-speaking people called the Effutu. It begins in some communities on the first Saturday of May. The term "Aboakyer" means "animal hunt" and requires capturing a live antelope from the bush with bare hands, then bringing it to be offered in sacrifice to one of many important gods or spirits. After the antelope is captured and brought to the community, various rites, including the pouring of libation and the recitation of incantations, are performed. Thereafter the antelope is slaughtered, cooked, and parts are offered to important gods before the members of the community eat the rest of the meat. The next day, after continuing to feast, dance, and celebrate through the night, consultation rites are performed and the future of the community is discussed. Festivals such as the Aboakyer are well known and often attract observers and visitors from other Ghanaian groups as well.

HEALTH ISSUES

For more recent immigrants from Ghana, diseases common in Ghana are an issue, including malaria and sickle cell anemia. Health insurance is also a concern to this group, as many immigrants, especially the more recent arrivals, are without it. However, because of the large number of Ghanaian American physicians, nurses, and health care workers, disease prevention and treatment are more manageable.

LANGUAGE

Among Ghanaian Americans, more than 100 languages and dialects are spoken. In addition, Ghanaians use English both in Ghana and in the United States to communicate with other Ghanaians outside of their own ethnic group. Today English is the official language of Ghana. The languages of Ghanaians are placed by linguists into two subfamilies of the greater family of Niger-Congo languages found throughout Africa. These two language groups are referred to as the Kwa group and the Gur group.

The Kwa group of languages, spoken by 75 percent of the population of Ghana, is generally spoken in the southern part of the country. This group includes such major languages as Akan, Ga-Adangbe, and Ewe. Further subdivisions are made within these groups as well, including: Asante, Bono, Akwapim, Akyem, Fante, Akwamu, Kwahu, Ahanta, Nzema, and Safwi (all belonging to the Akan subgroup); Ga, Adangbe, Ada, and Krobo or Kloli (belonging to the Ga-Adangbe subgroup); and the Nkonya, Tafi, Logba, Lolobi, Likpe and Sontrokofi (belonging to the Ewe subgroup). The Gur group of languages is primarily spoken in the northern parts of Ghana and includes subgroups called Gurma, Mole-Dagbane, and Grusi within which further subgroups can also be classified.

Since European colonialism, systems of writing based on the same Latin alphabet as English have been developed for many of these languages. While most publications in the Ghanaian and Ghanaian American communities are written in English, some are also written in the Twi dialects of Asante, Fante, and Akwapim and in other languages such as Ewe, Ga, Dagbane, and Nzema.

GREETINGS AND POPULAR EXPRESSIONS

Traditionally, greetings are very important in Ghana and usually entail extended conversation and inquiries about the other person's health, family, and other subjects. To neglect greeting someone is considered a great insult, as witnessed in the popular African sentiment that to forgo greeting someone invites bad fortune. Greetings and popular expressions differ within the native languages of Ghana. In greeting a group of people, it is the custom to start from those to your right.

FAMILY AND COMMUNITY DYNAMICS

Ghanaian American family and community dynamics vary greatly from group to group. However, extended family ties are strong and create ongoing commitments to many Ghanaian Americans. For example, wealthy Ghanaian Americans often support relatives in Ghana or in the United States. Like many recent immigrant groups, Ghanaian Americans push themselves and their children to succeed while seeking a balance of the traditions and customs of both Ghana and the United States.

One of the most important factors in the community dynamics of Ghanaian Americans is the numerous ethnic associations found in cities there the bulk of Ghanaian Americans have made their homes. These associations are not a phenomenon of the Ghanaian immigrant experience in the United States, but rather have their roots in the urban centers of Ghana. Even in 1956, nearly 17,000 people belonged to one of the 94 ethnic associations in the greater metropolitan area of Accra alone. Of these associations, 45 were dedicated to people of the same ethnic group, district or state, and 35 were dedicated to persons from the same town or village; in total, 22 ethnic divisions were represented. Many of the ethnic associations in Ghana could be classified as cultural, political, economic, or any combination of these roles.

Ghanaian Americans ethnic associations came later; most of them were founded in the 1980s. Like the ethnic associations in Ghana's urban centers, many of these associations were created as support organizations for Ghanaian immigrants of a particular ethnic origin. In 1995 there were 11 major Ghanaian ethnic associations in New York City alone, and such organizations can be found in most major cities in which Ghanaian Americans have congregated. While membership is usually not restricted to persons of a particular ethnicity, most of the members of these organizations can claim common roots in one of Ghana's ethnic groups. In addition, while an increasing number of Ghanaian Americans identify themselves as having two or more ethnicities, membership to most ethnic associations is granted on the understanding than a person does not belong to more than one such association. It is also not uncommon for Ghanaian Americans living in non-urban communities where there is no ethnic association to be members of an ethnic association in the nearest large city.

Ghanaian American ethnic associations are dedicated to cultural issues and charitable causes. Most associations operate as non-profit entities, channeling the excess from dues and fundraising into cultural education, group events, and aiding the families of members in the United States and Ghana. For the most part, these associations, unlike their earlier counterparts in Ghana, are not devoted to economic or political concerns. Of the many benevolent roles played by these associations, the provision of help for newly arrived immigrants and the families of members in times of distress are the most prominent. Most associations are run by volunteers and are headed and staffed by officials elected by the membership as a whole.

EDUCATION

The Ghanaian American community is devoted to both cultural and institutional education. Ethnic associations and related groups often educate the young in cultural traditions and art forms. In terms of more formal education, Ghanaian Americans are a very well-educated group, and many work in professions which require advanced degrees. Many earlier Ghanaian immigrants first came to the United States as foreign students and decided to stay. It is also not uncommon for Ghanaian Americans to continue their studies while in the workforce, with the hope of advancing their careers.

BIRTH AND BIRTHDAYS

Ghanaians both within and outside of the Akan group have a custom of deriving names from the seven days of the week. Children born on a given day of the week are given a name, called the kra din, that is derived from that day's name. According to this custom, a child born on Tuesday, whose parents speak the Twi language, would have a name derived from Benada, the Twi word for Tuesday. A boy would have the name Kwabena and a girl, Abena. If born on Friday (Fiada), a boy would be named Kofi and a girl Afua, and so on. In addition, it is common among the Fante that nicknames or pet names, like

Siisi and Fiifi, are derived from these names. People from the northern and upper regions of Ghana practice a variation of this tradition by using the Hausa names of the week as their base for naming. Among these people names such as Teni, Lariba, Alamisa, Azuma and Atlata are common. Although different groups have their own variations on these names, this practice is a special element of Ghanaian and Ghanaian American culture.

THE ROLE OF WOMEN

The traditional roles of Ghanaian and Ghanaian American women have included retailers, farmers, and mothers. Motherhood has been particularly emphasized due to various cultural pressures. In a 1983 survey of Ghanaian women, childbirth was named as an essential role for women due to the benefits and honor it bestows on women and their families, and 60 percent of the women surveyed found it important to have five or more children. However, in the United States, as in urban centers in Ghana, the lower rates of infant mortality, the costs of child rearing, and the constraints of time and career are impacting the traditional views of Ghanaian women regarding their roles. Many Ghanaian American women have found successful careers in education, nursing, and secretarial work, and many others have also begun to seek training and pursue careers as entrepreneurs and businesswomen.

BAPTISMS

Baptisms and other related forms of traditional cultural practice are found throughout the Ghanaian American community. However, the importance and forms of these practices vary among both Christian and traditional groups. Among Christians, for example, non-Pentecostal, Pentecostal, and Catholic rites and traditions vary greatly.

COURTSHIP

While Ghanaian Americans have the opportunity to meet other Ghanaian Americans in group meetings and festivals held in the United States, the possibilities to meet others of African and non-African descent have increased. Traditional courtship practices vary among the ethnic groups of Ghanaian Americans, and many younger Ghanaians find it difficult to carry on the courting traditions of their parents in the urban centers in which most of them live. Nevertheless, many Ghanaian Americans are aware of the traditional practices which many older members of the community followed before emigrating to the United States.

WEDDINGS

It is not uncommon for Ghanaian Americans, especially when marrying within the group, to be married in both a Christian ceremony as well as a traditional religious ceremony most often held in Ghana, though the ceremonies may be performed at times well removed from each other. Generally speaking, Christian ceremonies differ little from the way Americans have them performed. Ghanaian traditions involve many preliminary steps in which the man gains the grace of the family of his prospective wife. During the ceremony, the families come together and gifts are bartered and exchanged according to local customs. When an agreement is reached and all are satisfied, the couple is considered to be married. Afterwards a long-running feast is usually held in which songs are sung (most often by women), and music is played, often accompanied by dancing.

FUNERALS

Among Ghanaian Americans there is no more critical and profound time than the death of a loved one. After services are performed in the United States according to the family's religious orientation, it is not uncommon for the ethnic association of the family of the deceased to hold a memorial service and to aid the family in returning the deceased to Ghana for burial, as Ghanaians believe the deceased must be returned to their ancestral homeland. Such memorial services are one of the major functions of Ghanaian American associations.

INTERACTIONS WITH OTHER ETHNIC GROUPS

Outside of their ethnic groups, Ghanaian Americans often interact with other African immigrants with whom they often share common sentiments, traditions, and experiences as immigrants. To a lesser extent, Ghanaian Americans interact with the African Americans with whom they often live. Interaction with and assimilation into African American culture is more pronounced in younger Ghanaian Americans, who share many of the same experiences as other African Americans.

RELIGION

The spectrum of religious affiliation among Ghanaian Americans is quite varied. In the first census taken after Ghana's independence in 1960, 41 percent of Ghanaians identified themselves as Christian, 38 percent as following traditional religions, 12 percent as Muslims (mostly of the Sunni sect), and nine percent as having no affiliation. Among the Christian population, 25 percent identified themselves as non-Pentecostal Protestants, 13 percent as Roman Catholics, two percent as Pentecostal Protestants, and one percent as belonging to independent African churches.

Since this time, Protestant Christianity has grown considerably within Ghana. The diverse religious affiliations of Ghanaian Americans reflects the affiliations of Ghanaians on the whole. Among Ghanaian Americans, church attendance and devotion at mosques are regular features of life. Overall, Ghanaian Americans are tolerant not only of different Christian and Muslim religious practices, but they are also inclusive of traditional Ghanaian religious practices. In this community, one religious interest and commitment rarely rules out another.

EMPLOYMENT AND ECONOMIC TRADITIONS

Ghanaian Americans are employed across the spectrum of jobs found in the urban United States. There is a strong sense of entrepreneurship which stems from long traditions of trade within Ghana. A significant number of women work in healthcare professions and business. As a group, Ghanaian Americans are upwardly mobile, pursuing advanced degrees in practical areas of study and using networks to compete in the global economy. There is also a large number of Ghanaian Americans in the arts, art education, the social and natural sciences, and the humanities.

POLITICS AND GOVERNMENT

Being a relatively young ethnic group in the United States, Ghanaian Americans have gained few notable positions in United States government. However, many are politically active, keep themselves abreast of government, and, when necessary, are outspoken and eloquent critics. While many of their concerns relate to the politics of Ghana and other African nations, Ghanaian Americans are also active in issues of immigration, racism, and economic concerns.

RELATIONS WITH GHANA

Relations with Ghana are very much alive in Ghanaian American communities. Extended family, village, and other group ties continually influ-

ence events among groups in Ghana and their related groups in the United States. Ghanaian Americans often act as connections between the Ghanaian and the United States economies, whether through investment or the wealth of international connections found in the major urban centers of the United States.

It is common for Ghanaian Americans to visit their homelands frequently and to sponsor relatives and other Ghanaians for visits, immigration, or study stays in the United States. The relations between Ghanaian Americans and Ghanaians is generally strong and beneficial to both groups.

INDIVIDUAL AND GROUP CONTRIBUTIONS

With only a short time in the United States as a large group, Ghanaian Americans have made many notable contributions to its culture.

ACADEMIA

Among the many successful scholars in the Ghanaian American community is Kwame Anthony Appiah. Having earned his doctorate at Oxford University, Appiah is a professor in the departments of philosophy and Afro-American studies at Harvard. Born in Ghana, Appiah's work deals with diversity, cultural identity, and community building. Covering areas a diverse as metaphysics, anthropology, history, and sociology, his work weaves together African, European, and American thought.

Among his many published works is a popular book entitled In My Father's House: Africa in the Philosophy of Culture (1992), a collection of essays on race and culture which was named the New York Times Notable Book of the Year in 1992 and was the winner of the African Studies Association's Herskovits Award in 1993. With Henry Louis Gates, Jr., he has co-edited numerous volumes of critical perspectives on different African American writers, including Langston Hughes and Toni Morrison.

EDUCATION

Among the many great educators of Ghanaian descent, James Emman Aggrey is of special note. Born in 1875 in Ghana, Aggrey was educated at Methodist mission schools in which he also taught. His first major contribution was his work on translating the Bible into the Fante language. Working as an editor at the Gold Coast Methodist Times, Aggrey rallied a successful campaign against the Lands Bill of 1897, thus stopping the colonial government from seizing all land which was not in visible use. It was in 1898 that Aggrey first came to the United States to study at Livingstone College in Salisbury, North Carolina. Studying on a scholarship from an American church, the African Methodist Episcopal Zion Church, he stayed to work at the college as a registrar and teacher. During the next two decades, Aggrey engaged in ministerial work and studied theology at Columbia University and the Hood Theological School, where he received his doctorate in 1912. Serving in various posts, including a board member of the commission on education for the prestigious Phelps-Stokes Fund, Aggrey spent years working for the promotion of education and social transformation of African people. After founding the new university college of Achimota in Ghana in 1924, he was pressured to return to the United States in 1927. Shortly afterwards he died in New York. For further study of this remarkable figure see the 1929 biography of Aggrey by Edwin Smith, *Aggrey: A Study in Black and White*.

LITERATURE

Among the many great writers of Ghanaian descent is Kofi Nyidevu Awooner. Known mainly as a poet, Awooner (b.1935) has also written novels, short stories, essays, biographical pieces, plays, and scholarly works. After obtaining degrees in Ghana and the United Kingdom, Awoonor obtained a doctorate from the State University of New York-Stony Brook, where he became professor and chair of the department of comparative literature. At Stony Brook, Awooner developed one of the first black studies programs in the United States and completed most of the writing for which he is known. Living in Harlem while at Stony Brook, Awooner developed an ever-growing political consciousness. He returned to Ghana, where he held many important positions and his reputation as a writer, thinker, activist, and statesman continues to grow.

MUSIC

Among many successful Ghanaian American musicians and performance artists, Kobla and Dzidzorgbe Ladzekpo have had a wide range of successes. Kobla and Dzidzorgbe, a couple, are perhaps best known for founding the Zadonu Group in California. Both are long-time performers and instructors, having taught at the University of California-Los Angeles and the Naropa Institute. They have both been on the faculty of the California Institute of the Arts for 25 years, and Kobla is chair of the music department. The Zadonu Group is known throughout the world for its workshops, seminars, and performances which have been successful for bringing together African cultural groups in the United States. They have performed for the president of Ghana and at the NFL Super Bowl XXVIII. The name Zadonu is derived from a combination of the names of Kobla's late father and brother, who were highly respected composers of the Anlo clan in their native Ghana. Among the credits of Zadonu are the score for the Hollywood film *Mississippi Masala*, the Chasima Series for PBS, and the advertisement for the Los Angeles Arts Festival. The couple has also appeared and taught across in the United States and abroad.

SCIENCE AND TECHNOLOGY

Edward Ayensu (b.1935) has been a very prominent Ghanaian American scientist. Ayensu, a noted international plant physiologist, is also widely known as a policymaker on international environmental issues. Born in Ghana, Ayensu was first educated at Achimota College, then went on to receive bachelor's and master's degrees in the United States, and earned a doctorate from the University of London. After receiving his degree in London, Ayensu returned to the United States, where he served as an associate curator of botany at the Smithsonian Institution, then as chair and curator from 1970 to 1989. While at the Smithsonian, Ayensu also served a director of the institution's Endangered Species Project from 1976 to 1980. During this time Ayensu also served on many prominent international boards for the environment. Among his more than 20 books and 100 published professional papers are *Tropical Forest Ecosystems in Africa and South America* (1973) and *Medicinal Plants of West Africa* (1978).

ORGANIZATIONS AND ASSOCIATIONS

A good resource on Ghanaian American performance can be obtained from the Zadonu group at shoko.calarts.edu/~kozadonu/index.html.

A site for Ghanaian American children can be found at: heritage-international.com/cyberkid.htm.

Information on the Homowo harvest festival in Fairmont Park, Philadelphia is located at ghanaforum.com/news/phillynews080198.htm.

A good deal of other information can be found at Ghana Forum (http://www.ghanaforum.com) and at the Ghana Discussion Forum (http://www.ghanaforum.com/discuss.pl?read=5504), a bulletin board for issues affecting Ghanaians.

MUSEUMS AND RESEARCH CENTERS

Schomburg Center for Research in Black Culture.
Address: 515 Malcolm X Boulevard, New York, New York 10037-1801.
Telephone: (212) 491-2200.
Online: http://www.nypl.org/ns-search/research/sc.

Smithsonian Institution.
Address: Smithsonian Information, SI Building, Room 153, Washington, DC 20560-0010.
Telephone: (202) 357-2700; or (202) 357-1729 [TTY].
Online: http://www.si.edu.

SOURCES FOR ADDITIONAL STUDY

Attah-Poku, Agyemang. *The Socio-cultural Adjustment Question: The Role of Ghanaian Immigrant Ethnic Associations in America.* Brookfield, Vermont: Avebury, 1996.

Kondor, Daniel. *Ghanaian Culture in Perspective.* Accra: Presbyterian Press, 1993.

Ghana: A Country Study. Edited by LaVerle Berry. Washington, DC: Federal Research Division, Library of Congress, 1995.

If there is one self-defining concept among Greeks, it is the concept of *philotimo,* which may be translated as "love of honor."

GREEK AMERICANS

by
Jane Jurgens

Overview

Officially known as the Hellenic Republic, Greece is a mountainous peninsula located in southeastern Europe, between the Aegean and Mediterranean Seas. With a landmass of 51,000 square miles (132,100 square kilometers), Greece is bordered to the north by Bulgaria and Macedonia. Nearly 2,000 islands surround its eastern, southern, and western borders. The nine major land areas that constitute Greece include Central Pindus, Thessaly, the Salonika Plain, Macedonia/Thrace, Peloponnesus, the Southeastern Uplands, the Ionian Islands, the Aegean Islands, and Crete.

The capital city, Athens, and the cities of Thessaloniki (Salonika), Patras, Volos, and Larissa have the largest populations in Greece, which has a total population of approximately ten million. Ninety-seven percent of the ethnically and linguistically homogeneous nation speaks Greek, and one percent, Turkish. The Eastern Orthodox church is the dominant religion; only about 1.5 percent of the population is Muslim, and a small percentage is Roman Catholic, Greek Catholic, or Jewish.

Traditionally, Greeks referred to themselves as "Hellenes" and to the country of Greece as "Hellas." The word "Greek" comes from the Latin *Graeci,* a name given to the people of this region by the Romans.

The Greek flag features a small white cross in the upper left corner flanked to the right and bottom by alternating white and blue stripes. The white cross symbolizes the Greek Orthodox religion, while the blue stripes stand for the sea and sky, and the white stripes for the purity of the Greek struggle for independence. The national anthem is "The Hymn to Freedom" ("*Imnos pros teen elefteeriahn*"). The basic monetary unit is the drachma.

HISTORY

Greece is an ancient country that has been continuously occupied from 6000 B.C., the beginning of its Neolithic period, until the present. The Bronze Age, traditionally divided into early, middle, and late phases, dated from 2800 B.C. to 1000 B.C. It was during this period that Minoan civilization of Crete and the Mycenean civilization of mainland Greece flourished. These civilizations were destroyed around 1000 B.C. just as the individual city-state or "polis" was beginning to experience rapid growth. In 479 B.C. the city-states united to defeat Persia, a common enemy, but national unity proved to be short-lived. The power struggle between Athens and Sparta, the principal city-states, dominated the period.

Athens reached its zenith during the fifth century B.C., a period known as its Golden Age. At this time Athens experimented with a form of internal democracy unique in the ancient world, achieved a singular culture, and left enduring literary and architectural legacies. Socrates, Plato, Xenophon, Herodotus, Sophocles, Euripides, and Aeschylus came into prominence, and in 432 B.C. the Parthenon on the Acropolis was completed. The Peloponnesian War fought between Athens and Sparta from 431 to 404 B.C. and a plague that raged through Athens in 430 contributed to bring the Golden Age to an end. For a time Sparta dominated the Greek world, but war and severe economic decline hastened the decline of all of the city-states.

Greece came under Macedonian domination between 338 and 200 B.C. The Macedonian king, Alexander the Great, conquered Greece, Persia, and Egypt to create an empire, and he carried the idea of Hellenism to places as far away as India. The Hellenistic Age that followed Alexander's rule lasted until 146 B.C. As a Roman state from 127 B.C. to A.D. 330, Greece and its city-states had no political or military power. When the Roman Empire was divided in A.D. 395, Greece became part of the Eastern Empire, which continued as the Byzantine Empire until 1453. That year the Turks captured Constantinople, the capital of Byzantium, and Greece became part of the Ottoman Empire.

MODERN ERA

Greece's declaration of independence from the Ottoman Empire on March 25, 1821, resulted in the Greek War of Independence, which lasted until 1829, and began the history of independent modern Greece. Great Britain, France, and Russia assisted Greece in its struggle for independence, and Greece came under the protection of these powers by the London Protocol of 1830. In 1832 the Bavarian Otto I became the first king of Greece, and in 1844 a conservative revolutionary force established a constitutional monarchy. George I, who succeeded Otto I, created a more democratic form of government with a new constitution in 1864.

During the 1880s and 1890s, transportation, education, and social services rapidly improved. Then in 1897 a revolt against the Turks in Crete led to war between Greece and the Ottoman Empire and to eventual self-governance for Crete. A revolt by the Military League in 1909 prompted the appointment of Eleuthérios Venizélos as Prime Minister of Greece. Between 1910 and 1933 Venizélos enacted major financial reforms.

During World War I Greece joined the Allied forces in opposing Germany. After the war Greece regained much of the territory it had lost to the Ottoman Empire. But in 1921 Greece began a war against the Turks in Asia Minor and suffered a crushing defeat in 1922. In 1923, under the Treaty of Lausanne, more than 1.25 million Greeks moved from Turkey to Greece, and more than 400,000 Turks in Greece moved to Turkey.

Between the World Wars, the Greek population vacillated between the establishment of a republican form of government and the restoration of monarchy. In 1936 Greece became a military dictatorship under General Ioannis Metaxas, who remained in power until 1944. The Germans occupied Greece during World War II, and the country did not recover until the 1950s, when it began slowly to regain economic and political stability. In 1952 Greece joined the North Atlantic Treaty Organization and also granted women the right to vote and to hold political office. During 1952 to 1963 Alexander Papagos and Konstantinos Karamanlis each held the office of prime minister.

On April 27, 1967, Colonel George Papadopoulos led a military coup, resulting in the suspension of constitutionally guaranteed rights and the imposition of harsh social controls. Papadopoulos declared Greece a republic in 1973 and put an end to the monarchy before his government was overthrown. In November 1974 Greece held its first free elections in more than a decade. Parliament adopted a new constitution in 1975, and a civilian government was established.

The first Socialist government in Greece gained control in 1981, the year Andreas Papandreou—the son of George Papandreou and a member of the Panhellenic Socialist movement—succeeded conservative Georgios Rallis as prime minister. In 1989 a conservative-communist coalition formed a new government, and pledging that Greece would be an active participant in the greater European community, Papandreou was reelected.

THE FIRST GREEKS IN AMERICA

According to official records, the Greek sailor Don Teodoro or Theodoros, who sailed to America with the Spanish explorer Panfilio de Narvaez in 1528, was the first Greek to land in America. The names of other Greek sailors who may have come to America during this period are John Griego and Petros the Cretan. There is some speculation that Juan De Fuca, who discovered the straits south of Vancouver Island, may have been a Greek named Ionnis Phocas.

One of the first Greek colonies was at New Smyrna near Saint Augustine, Florida. Andrew Turnball and his wife Maria Rubini, daughter of a wealthy Greek merchant, persuaded approximately 450 colonists to journey to America and settle. With the promise of land, Greek colonists primarily from Mani in the south of Greece, as well as Italians, Minorcans, and Corsicans, began arriving in Florida on June 26, 1768. The colony was an overwhelming failure and was officially disbanded on July 17, 1777, but many of the colonists had already moved to neighboring Saint Augustine, where they were becoming successful as merchants and small businessmen. A small community of Greeks also built a chapel and school there.

SIGNIFICANT IMMIGRATION WAVES

The first wave of Greek immigrants included about 40 orphans who had survived the Greek Revolution of 1821 and who were brought to the United States by American missionaries; survivors of the 1822 massacre of Chios by the Turks; and merchant sailors who settled in the Americas. Most of these Greeks were from islands such as Chios, and others came from Asia Minor, Epirus, and Macedonia. By 1860 about 328 Greeks were living in the United States, with the majority residing in California, Arkansas, New York, and Massachusetts.

The U.S. Greek population remained small until the 1880s, when poor economic conditions in Greece prompted many Greeks to immigrate to the United States. During the 1880s most who came were from Laconia (notably, from the city of Sparta), a province of the Peloponnesus in southern Greece. Beginning in the 1890s, Greeks began arriving from other parts of Greece, principally from Arcadia, another province in the Peloponnesus. The largest numbers arrived during 1900-1910 (686) and 1911-1920 (385). Most were young single males who came to the United States to seek their fortunes and wished to return to Greece as soon as possible. About 30 percent of those who came before 1930 did return, some of whom went to fight in the Balkan Wars of 1912-1913.

The Immigration Acts of 1921 and 1924 reversed the open-door policy of immigration and established quotas. The Act of 1921 limited the number of Greek admittants to 3,063, while the Act of 1924 limited the number to 100. Legal petition increased the quota, and during 1925-1929 about 10,883 Greeks were admitted. Another 17,000 Greeks were admitted under the Refugee Relief Act of 1953, and 1,504 were accepted as a result of further legislation in 1957.

The Immigration Act of 1965 abandoned the quota system and gave preference to immigrants with families already established in the United States. The new Greek arrivals usually were better educated than their predecessors and included men and women in equal numbers, as well as family groups.

From 1820 to 1982 a total of 673,360 Greeks immigrated to the United States. After 1982, the number of Greeks entering the United States is as follows: 1983 (3,020); 1984 (2,865); 1985 (2,579); 1986 (2,512); 1987 (2,653); 1988 (2,458); 1989 (2,157); 1990 (2,742); 1991 (1,760); 1992 (1,790). The 1990 Census reported the number of people claiming at least one ancestry as Greek at 1,110,373.

SETTLEMENT

During the 1890s Greeks began settling in major urban areas, including the industrial cities of the Northeast and Midwest. The first immigrants settled in Massachusetts and southern New Hampshire. The city of Lowell, Massachusetts, attracted the majority of Greeks, and by 1920 it had the third largest Greek community in the United States. Greeks also settled in the New England towns of Haverhill, Lynn, Boston, Peabody, and Manchester. The largest Greek settlement in the twentieth century was in New York. Greeks also settled in western Pennsylvania, particularly Pittsburgh, and in the Midwestern cities of Detroit, Milwaukee, Cleveland, Youngstown, and Chicago.

Small Greek communities existed in Galveston, Texas, and Atlanta, Georgia, but the largest concentration of Greeks in the South was at Tarpon Springs, Florida. In the first half of the twentieth century, this unique settlement of Greeks made its living by sponge diving.

Attracted to mining and railroad work, large numbers of Greeks settled in Salt Lake City, with smaller numbers inhabiting Colorado, Wyoming, Idaho, and Nevada. The heaviest early concentration on the Pacific Coast was in San Francisco. Today, Greeks live primarily in urban areas and are increasingly moving to the South and West. The 1990 Census reveals that New York State still has the largest population of Greeks, with the highest concentration in the Astoria section of the borough of Queens. The next largest populations are in California, Illinois, Massachusetts, and Florida.

ACCULTURATION AND ASSIMILATION

Few negative Greek stereotypes persist. Greeks share the American work ethic and desire for success and are largely perceived as hardworking and family-oriented. They are also said to possess a "Zorba"-like spirit and love of life. However, many Greek Americans perceive the recent Greek immigrants as "foreign" and often as a source of embarrassment.

TRADITIONS, CUSTOMS, AND BELIEFS

Greeks have an assortment of traditional customs, beliefs, and superstitions to ensure success and ward off evil and misfortune. Old beliefs persist in some communities in the United States. For example, belief in the "evil eye" is still strong and is supported by the Greek Orthodox church as a generalized concept of evil. Precautions against the evil eye (*not* endorsed by the church) include wearing garlic; making the sign of the cross behind the ear of a child with dirt or soot; placing an image of an eye over the lintel; wearing the *mati*, a blue amulet with an eye in the center; and recitation of a ritual prayer, the *ksematiasma*. Greeks may also respond to a compliment with the expression *ptou, ptou*, to keep the evil eye from harming the person receiving the compliment. Greeks also "knock wood" to guard against misfortune, and reading one's fortunes in the patterns of coffee dregs remains popular.

PROVERBS

The Greeks "have a saying for it": In wine there is truth; You make my liver swell (You make me sick);

God ascends stairs and descends stairs (Everything is possible for God); An old hen makes the tastiest broth (Quality improves with age); He won't give her any chestnuts (He wouldn't cut her any slack); I tell it to my dog, and he tells it to his tail (To pass the buck); I went for wool, and I came out shorn (To lose the shirt off one's back); Faith is the power of life.

CUISINE

Greek food is extremely popular in the United States, where Greek American restaurants flourish. In Greek restaurants and in the home, many of the traditional recipes have been adapted (and sometimes improved on) to suit American tastes. In Greece meals are great social occasions where friends and family come together and the quantity of food is often impressive. Olive oil is a key ingredient in Greek cooking and is used in quantity. Traditional herbs include parsley, mint, dill, oregano (especially the wild oregano *rigani*), and garlic. You will find on most Greek tables olives, sliced cheese (such as feta, *kaseri*, and *kefalotiri*), tomato, and lemon wedges, along with bread. Fish, chicken, lamb, beef, and vegetables are all found on the Greek menu and are prepared in a variety of ways. Soup, salad, and yogurt are served as side dishes. Sheets of dough called *phillo* are layered and filled with spinach, cheese, eggs, and nuts. Greeks create such masterpieces as *moussaka*, a layered dish of eggplant, meat, cheese, and bread crumbs sometimes served with a white sauce. Other popular Greek dishes in the United States include *souvlakia*, a shish kabob of lamb, vegetables, and onions; *keft-*

edes, Greek meatballs; *saganaki*, a mixture of fried cheese, milk, egg, and flour; *dolmathes yalantzi*, grape leaves stuffed with rice, pine nuts, onions, and spices; and gyros, slices of beef, pork, and lamb prepared on a skewer, served with tomatoes, onions, and cucumber yogurt sauces on pita bread.

Soups include *psarosoupa me avgolemono*, a rich fish soup made with egg and lemon sauce; *spanaki soupa*, spinach soup; *mayeritsa*, an Easter soup made with tripe and/or lamb parts and rice; and *fasolatha*, a white bean Lenten soup made with tomatoes, garlic, and spices. Salads always accompany a meal. The traditional Greek salad (*salata a la greque*) is made with lettuce or spinach, feta cheese, tomatoes, onions, cucumbers, olives, oregano, and olive oil.

The national drink of Greece is *ouzo* ("oozoh"), an anise-flavored liquor that tastes like licorice and that remains popular with Greek Americans. Traditionally, it is served with appetizers (*mezethes*) such as olives, cheese, tomato, and lemon wedges. A popular Greek wine, *retsina*, is produced only in Greece and is imported to the United States.

TRADITIONAL COSTUMES

Greek traditional costumes come in a variety of styles, some dating back to ancient times. Women's clothing is heavy, with many layers and accessories, designed to cover the entire body. The undergarments include the floor-length *poukamiso* (shirt) made of linen or cotton and the *mesofori* (underskirt) and *vraka* (panties), usually of muslin. The outer garments consist of the *forema-palto*, a coat-dress of embroidered linen; the *fousta* (skirt) of wool or silk; the *sigouni*, a sleeveless jacket of embroidered wool worn outside the *forema-palto*; the *kontogourni* or *zipouni*, a short vest worn over the *fousta*; the *podia*, an apron of embroidered wool or linen; and finally the *zonari*, a long belt wrapped many times around the waist. Buckles on these belts can be very ornate.

Traditionally, men's costumes are less colorful than women's costumes. Men's urban and rural clothing styles vary by region. The *anteria* is a long dress coat with wide sleeves once worn in the city. In rural areas, men wore the *panovraki* (or its variation, the *vraka*), white or dark woolen pants, narrow at the bottom and wide at the waist, with the *poukamiso*, a short pleated dress. The *foustanela* is a variation on the old style and soon became the national costume of Greece. The *foustanela* is a short white skirt of cotton or muslin with many folds that is worn above the knee. It is worn with the *fermizi*, a jacket of velvet or serge with long sleeves that is thrown over the back; waist-high white stockings; and a shirt with wide sleeves made of cotton, muslin, or silk. The *foustanela* is a common sight on Greek Independence Day.

HOLIDAYS AND CELEBRATIONS

Greeks celebrate many Greek Orthodox holy days throughout the year, in addition to Christmas Day, Easter Day, and New Year's Day. Greeks in the United States also celebrate Greek Independence Day on March 25, commemorating their independence from the Ottoman Empire in 1821. In Chicago and New York, cities with a sizable Greek population, people dress in traditional costumes and sing the national anthem. The program of events also includes a parade, public address, folk dance, song, and poetry recitation.

DANCE AND SONGS

Greek music and dance are an expression of the national character and are appreciated by people of all ethnic backgrounds. As Marilyn Rouvelas stated in *A Guide to Greek Traditions and Customs in America*: "To the uninitiated, the music invites images of intriguing places, food and people. For the Greeks, the sounds and rhythms express their very essence: their dreams, sorrows and joys. Add dancing and nothing more need be said."

Varieties of Greek popular music include *dimotika* (*thimotika*), *laika*, and *evropaika*. *Dimotika* are traditional rural folk songs often accompanied by a clarinet, lute, violin dulcimer, and drum. *Laika* is an urban style of song, developed at the beginning of the twentieth century, which may feature the bouzouki, a long-necked stringed instrument. *Evropaika* is Eurostyle music set to Greek words that is popular with the older generation.

Traditional Greek dances may be danced in a circle, in a straight line, or between couples. The *kalamatianos* is an ancient dance with many variations in which both men and women participate. It has 12 basic steps and is danced in a semicircle to 7/8 time. All variations are performed by the leader who stands facing the semicircle. The *sirtos*, perhaps the most ancient dance, is similar to the *kalamatianos*, but it is more controlled, performed to 2/4 time. First danced in the mountainous region of Epirus in northwestern Greece, the *tsamiko*, traditionally danced by men, is today performed by both men and women. It was danced by the fighters and rebels in the Greek Revolution of 1821. The *hasapiko* is a popular folk dance for both men and women that is danced in a straight line, with one dancer holding the shoulder of the other. The *sirtaki*, a variation of the *hasapiko*, culminates with the "Zorba" dance popularized in the movie *Zorba the Greek*. Although the Zorba has no roots in Greek dance history, it does capture the mood and temperament of the Greek spirit. Originating in the Middle East, the *tsifteteli* is a seductive dance performed by one or two people. The *zeibekiko* is a personal dance traditionally danced only by men, either singly or as a couple. It is a serious, completely self-absorbed dance in which the dancer freely improvises the steps.

LANGUAGE

Greek is a conservative language that has retained much of its original integrity. Modern Greek is derived from the Attic Koine of the first century A.D. During Byzantine times, the language underwent modifications and has incorporated many French, Turkish, and Italian words. Modern Greek retained the ancient alphabet and orthography of the more ancient language, but many changes have taken place in the phonetic value of letters and in the spelling. Although about 75 percent of the old words remain from the ancient language, words often have taken on new meanings. Modern Greek also retains from the ancient language a system of three pitch accents (acute, circumflex, grave). In 1982, a monotonic accent (one-stress accent) was officially adopted by the Greek government.

Greeks are fiercely proud of the continuity and relative stability of their language and much confusion and debate persists about "correct Greek." Two separate languages were once widely written and spoken in Greece: demotic Greek (*Demotiki*), the more popular language of the people, and *Katharevousa*, the "pure" archaic language of administration, religion, education, and literature. In 1967 demotic Greek was recognized as the official spoken and written language of Greece and is the language adopted for liturgical services by the Greek Orthodox church in the United States.

Modern Greek contains 24 characters with seven vowels and five vowel sounds. It is traditionally written in Attic characters; the letters, their names, transliterations, and pronunciations are: "Αα"— alpha/a ("ah"); "Ββ"— veta/v ("v"); "Γγ"— gamma/g ("gh," "y"); "Δδ"— delta/d, dh ("th"); "Εε"— epsilon/e ("eh"); "Ζζ"— zeta/z ("z"); "Ηη"—eta/e ("ee"); "Θθ"— theta/th ("th"); "Ιι"— yiota/i ("ee"); "Κκ"—kappa/k, c ("k"); "Λλ"— lambda/l ("l"); "Μμ"—mu/m ("m"); "Νν"—nee/n ("n"); "Ξξ"— kse/x ("ks"); "Ωω"— omicron/o ("oh"); "Ππ"— pi/p ("p"); "Ρρ"— rho/r ("r"); "Σσ"—sigma/s ("s"); "Ττ"— taf/t ("t"); "Υυ"— ypsilon/y ("ee"); "Φφ"—fee/ph ("f'); "Χχ"— khee/h ("ch" [as in "ach"]); "Ψψ"—psee/ps ("ps" [as in "lapse"]); "Οο"— omega/o ("oh").

Today Greek language schools continue to encourage the study of Greek, and new generations are discovering its rich rewards.

GREETINGS AND OTHER COMMON EXPRESSIONS

Some of the more common expressions in the Greek language include: Ωχι ("ohchi")—No; Ναι ("neh")—Yes; Ευχαριστο (Efcharisto)—Thank you; Καλημερα ("kahleemera")—Good morning; Καλησπερα ("kahleespehrah")—Good afternoon/evening; Γεια σωυσασ ("yah soo"/"yah sahs")—Hello/Good-bye (informal); Χαιρετε ("chehrehteh")—Greetings/Hello (formal); Ωπα! ("ohpah")—Hooray! Toasts may include Για χαρα ("yah chahrah")—For joy; Καλη τυχη ("kahlee teechee")—Good luck. Other popular expressions are Χρωνια πωλλα ("chrohnyah pohllah")— Many years/Happy birthday; Χαλη χρωνια ("kahlee chrohnyah")—Good year; Καλη Σαρακωστη ("kahlee sahrahkohstee")—Good Lent; Καλα Χριστωυγεννα ("kahlah christooghehnna")—Merry Christmas. Expressions used at Easter are Καλω Πασχα ("kahloh pahschah")—Happy Easter (used before Easter); Καλη Ανασταση ("kahlee ahnahstahsee")—Good Resurrection (said after the Good Friday service); Χριστωσ ανεστη ("christohs ahnehstee")—Christ has risen (said after the Good Friday service) and its response, Αλη θωσ ανεστη ("ahleethohs ahnehstee")—Truly he has risen.

FAMILY AND COMMUNITY DYNAMICS

If there is one self-defining concept among Greeks, it is the concept of *philotimo*, which may be translated as "love of honor." *Philotimo* is a highly developed sense of right and wrong involving personal pride and honor and obligation to family and community. It shapes and regulates an individual's relationships as a member of both a family and the community. Because the acts of each individual affect the entire family and community, each person must work to maintain both personal and family honor. It is *philotimo* that "laid the foundation for Greek success in America," wrote G. Kunkelman in *The Religion of Ethnicity*.

The idea of family and attachment to the Greek Orthodox church remains strong among Greek Americans. In many communities, the ideal family is still a patriarchy where the man, as husband and father, is a central authority figure and the woman a wife and mother. Children are highly valued, and frequently parents will sacrifice a great deal to see that their children accomplish their goals. Elderly parents may still move in with their children, but "Americanization," with accompanying affluence, assimilation, and mobilization, has rendered this arrangement less practicable.

Another change from traditional Greek custom is the rising number of marriages between Orthodox and non-Orthodox Greeks. The 1994 *Yearbook* of the Greek Orthodox Archdiocese of North and South America reports that between 1976 and 1992, the number of marriages between Orthodox Greeks was 35,767, while the number between Orthodox and non-Orthodox Greeks was 53,790; the divorce rate is 6,629 and 5,552, respectively.

WEDDINGS

The wedding service conducted by a Greek Orthodox priest may be said in both Greek and in English, but the traditional elements of the Greek wedding remain unchanged. The hour-long ceremony is conducted around a small table on which two wedding crowns, the book of the Gospels, the wedding rings, a cup of wine, and two white candles are placed. The two-part Greek Orthodox wedding includes the betrothal and the wedding proper. During the betrothal the rings are blessed to signify that the couple is betrothed by the church. The priest first blesses the rings and then, with the rings, blesses the couple, touching their foreheads with the sign of the cross. The rings are placed on the bride's and groom's right hands, and the official wedding sponsors (*koumbari*) exchange the rings three times. During the wedding ceremony the bride and groom each hold a lighted white candle and join right hands while the priest prays over them. Crowns (*stephana*) joined with a ribbon are placed on their heads, and the *koumbaros* (male) or *koumbara* (female) is responsible for exchanging the wedding crowns three times above the heads of the couple during the service. Traditionally read are the Epistle of Saint Paul to the Ephesians and the second chapter of the Gospel of Saint John, which stress the mutual respect and love the couple now owe each other and the sanctity of the married state. After the couple shares a common cup of wine, they are led around the table by the priest in the Dance of Isaiah, which symbolizes the joy of the church in the new marriage. The *koumbaros* follows, holding the ribbon that joins the crowns. With the blessing of the priest, the couple is proclaimed married, and the crowns are removed.

The wedding reception reflects the influence of both Greek and American tradition and is notable for its abundance of food, dancing, and singing. The wedding cake is served along with an assortment of Greek sweets that may include baklava and *koufeta*—traditional wedding candy—is often distributed in candy dishes or in *bombonieries* (small favors given to guests after the wedding).

BAPTISMS AND CHRISMATIONS

The *koumbari* who act as wedding sponsors usually act as godparents for a couple's first child. The baptism begins at the narthex of the church, where the godparents speak for the child, renouncing Satan, blowing three times in the air, and spitting three times on the floor. They then recite the Nicene Creed. The priest uses the child's baptismal name for the first time and asks God to cleanse away sin. The priest, the godparents, and the child go to the baptismal font at the front of the church, where the priest consecrates the water, adding olive oil to it as a symbol of reconciliation. The child is undressed, and the priest makes the sign of the cross on various parts of the child's body. The godparents rub olive oil over the child's body, and the priest thrice immerses the child in the water of the baptismal font to symbolize the three days Christ spent in the tomb. The godparents then receive the child and wrap it in a new white sheet. During chrismation, immediately following baptism, the child is anointed with a special oil (*miron*), which has been blessed by the Ecumenical Patriarch of Constantinople. The child is dressed in new clothing, and a cross is placed around its neck. After the baptismal candle is lighted, the priest and godparents hold the child, and a few children walk around the font in a dance of joy. Finally, scriptures are read, and communion is given to the child.

FUNERALS

The funeral service in the Greek Orthodox church is called *kithia*. Traditionally, the *trisayion* (the three holies) is recited at the time of death or at any time during a 40-day mourning period. In the United States the *trisayion* is repeated at the funeral service. At the beginning of the service, the priest greets the mourners at the entrance of the church. An open casket is arranged so that the deceased faces the altar. During the service mourners recite scriptures, prayers, and hymns, and they are invited by the priest to pay their last respects to the deceased by filing past the casket and kissing the icon that has been placed within. The family gathers around the casket for a last farewell, and the priest sprinkles oil on the body in the form of the cross and says a concluding prayer. After the priest, friends, or family members deliver a brief eulogy, the body is taken immediately for burial (*endaphiasmos*). At the cemetery the priest recites the *trisayion* for the last time and sprinkles dirt on the casket while reciting a prayer. After the funeral guests and family share a funeral meal (*makaria*), which traditionally consists of brandy, coffee, and *paximathia* (hard, dry toast). A full meal may also be served, with fish as the main course.

THE ROLE OF WOMEN

As stated in the introduction to *American Aphrodite*, "Greek-American women have been without a voice since the first Greek immigrants arrived here as wives, mothers, sisters and daughters, usually, but not always, some months behind the menfolk, making no sound, proclaiming no existence." Traditionally, the lives of Greek women have centered on the home, the family, and the Greek Orthodox church. Since the earliest period of settlement in the United States, the burden of preserving Greek culture and tradition has been the responsibility of women. Women among the first and second generations of immigrants became the traditional keepers of songs, dances, and other folk customs and often cut themselves off from the *xeni*, the foreigners, who were essentially anyone outside the Greek community.

Today many Greek women are seriously challenged in their efforts to accommodate the values of two different worlds. The pressure to remain part of the community, obey parents' rules, and be "good Greek girls" who marry "well" and bear children is still strong. The conflict arises between family loyalty and self-realization, between duty to parents and community and the pursuit of the "American way of life." Many Greek American girls are given less freedom than their male counterparts and tend to remain close to their mothers even after marriage. The pursuit of education and a career is secondary and may even be perceived as "un-Greek" or unwomanly.

Although Greeks tend to be a highly educated ethnic group, the pursuit of higher education remains the province of men. The 1990 Census reports that twice as many Greek men as women received university degrees, with a significantly higher proportion of men going on to receive advanced degrees.

"**I** felt grateful the Statue of Liberty was a woman. I felt she would understand a woman's heart."

Stella Petrakis in 1916, cited in *Ellis Island: An Illustrated History of the Immigrant Experience*, edited by Ivan Chermayeff et al. (New York: Macmillan, 1991).

RELIGION

Theodore Salutos in *The Greeks in the United States* wrote: "Hellenism and Greek Orthodoxy—the one intertwined with the other—served as the cord that kept the immigrant attached to the mother country, nourished his patriotic appetites and helped him preserve the faith and language of his parents." The Greek Orthodox church helped to meet the emotional and spiritual needs of the immigrant. The early churches grew out of the *kinotitos* (community) where a *symvoulion* (board of directors) raised the money to build the church. The first Greek Orthodox church in the United States was founded in New Orleans in 1864. As Greek communities grew, other churches were established in New York (1892); Chicago (1893); Lowell, Massachusetts (1903); and Boston (1903). By 1923, there were 140 Greek churches in the United States.

Today, the liturgy and spirit of the Greek Orthodox church help to keep alive Greek ethnic cultural traditions in the United States. According to Kunkelman, to a Greek American, "ethnicity is synonymous with the church. One is a Greek not because he is a Hellene by birth; indeed many of Greek parentage have abandoned their identities and disappeared into the American mainstream. Rather one is Greek because he elects to remain part of the Greek community and an individual is a member of the Greek community by virtue of his

attachment to the Greek Orthodox church, the framework on which the community rests."

For many, the Greek Orthodox church is the center of community life. In the United States all dioceses, parishes, and churches are under the ecclesiastical jurisdiction of the Archdiocese of North and South America, an autonomous self-governing church within the sphere of influence of the Ecumenical Patriarch of Constantinople and New Rome. The Ecumenical Patriarch has the power to elect the archbishop and the bishops, directs all church matters outside the American church, and remains the guiding force in all matters of faith. Founded in 1922, the Archdiocese is located in New York City. It supports 62 parishes in the Archdiocesan District of New York, as well as the parishes in ten dioceses across the Americas.

"Orthodox" comes from the Greek *orthos* (correct) and *doxa* (teaching or worship). The Greek Orthodox share a common liturgy, worship, and tradition. In its fundamental beliefs, the church is conservative, resistant to change, and allows little flexibility. The Orthodox tradition is an Eastern tradition with the official center of Orthodoxy at Constantinople. After the tenth century Eastern and Western traditions grew apart on matters of faith, dogma, customs, and politics. East and West finally divided on the issue of papal authority.

The basic beliefs of the Orthodox are summarized in the Nicene Creed dating back to the fourth century. The Orthodox believe that one can achieve complete identification with God (*theosis*). All activities and services in the church are to assist the individual in achieving that end. The most important service is the Divine Liturgy in which there are four distinct liturgies: St. John Chrysostom (the one most frequently followed), St. Basil (followed ten times a year), St. James (October 23), and the Liturgy of the Presanctified Gifts (Wednesdays and Fridays of Lent and the first three days of Easter Holy Week). The church uses Greek Koine, the language of New Testament Greek, as its liturgical language. The seven sacraments in the church are Baptism, Chrismation, Confession, Communion, Marriage, Holy Unction (Anointing of the Sick), and Holy Orders. The Greek Orthodox calendar has many feast days, fast days, and name days. The most important feast day ("the feast of feasts") is Holy Pascha (Easter Sunday). In addition to Easter, the "twelve great feasts" are the Nativity of the Mother of God, the Exaltation of the Holy Cross, the Presentation of the Mother of God in the Temple, Christmas, Epiphany, the Presentation of Jesus Christ in the Temple, Palm Sunday, Ascension of Jesus Christ, Pentecost, the Transfiguration of Jesus Christ, and the Dormition (death) of the Mother of God.

The Greek Orthodox church also follows the Byzantine tradition in its architecture. The church is divided into the vestibule (the front of the church representing the world), the nave (the main area where people assemble), and the sanctuary. The sanctuary is separated from the nave by an iconostasis, a screenlike partition. Only the priests enter the sanctuary. Icons (images of saints) decorate the iconostasis in prescribed tiers. The service takes place in the sanctuary, which contains an altar table and an oblation (preparation) table. The Greek Orthodox church is filled with symbols, including crosses and icons, which create an aura of heaven on earth.

The church continues to face the process of Americanization. The American Orthodox church has many American elements: an American-trained clergy, the introduction of English into the service, modern music written for organ, modern architecture and architectural features (pews, choir lofts, separate social halls). The limited role of women in the church is being questioned. Until the second century, women fully participated in the church as teachers, preachers, and deacons. After that period, however, their roles were limited by official decree. Today women are taking more active leadership roles; however, the question of ordaining women to the priesthood has not been seriously considered.

Internal dissent has plagued the Greek Orthodox community in the United States in recent years. Dissenters have petitioned Ecumenical Patriarch Bartholomeos of Constantinople for the removal of Archbishop Spyridon, appointed leader of the Greek Orthodox archdiocese in the United States in 1996. They claim that Spyridon ignored input from the lay community in church affairs, including the firing of three priests from the faculty of Hellenic College in Brookline, Massachusetts. A spokesperson for the archdiocese commented that this group does not speak for the entire Greek Orthodox community in America, but a *New York Times* article suggested that the movement against Spyridon reveals that the church is in "serious turmoil."

EMPLOYMENT AND ECONOMIC TRADITIONS

The first immigrants were for the most part young single men who had no intention of remaining permanently in the United States. They came to work in the large industrial cities of the Northeast and Midwest as factory laborers, peddlers, busboys, and bootblacks. Those who went to the mill towns of New England worked in textile and shoe factories, while the Greeks who went West worked in mines and on the railroads. These Greeks often were subject to the *padrone* system, a form of exploitative indentured servitude employed in many of the larger industrial cities of the North and in the large mining corporations of the West.

Greeks in America have stressed individual efforts and talent and have had a long tradition of entrepreneurship in the United States, and many who were peddlers and street merchants in the United States became owners of small businesses. First-generation Greeks who were fruit and vegetable peddlers became owners of grocery stores; flower vendors opened florist shops. Greeks in Lowell, Massachusetts, became successful in numerous businesses. By 1912, according to a publication of the National Park Service, *Lowell: The Story of an Industrial City*, they owned "seven restaurants, twenty coffee houses, twelve barber shops, two drug stores, six fruit stores, eight shoeshine parlors, one dry-goods store, four ticket agencies, seven bakeries, four candy stores [and] twenty-two grocery stores."

In the 1920s Greeks owned thousands of confectionery stores across the country and usually owned the candy-manufacturing businesses that supplied the stores. When the candy businesses collapsed, Greeks became restaurant owners. By the late 1920s several thousand Greek restaurants were scattered across the country. Many immigrants of the 1950s and 1960s went into the fast-food restaurant business.

The Greek professional class remained small until the 1940s. During the first quarter of the twentieth century, most Greek professionals were doctors. The next largest group comprised lawyers, dentists, pharmacists, and chemists. A few became professors of literature, philosophy, and the classics. Although the Greeks were slow to develop an academic tradition in this country in part because of low economic incentive, a new professional class began to emerge after World War I. Today Greek Americans engage in many professional academic endeavors. Instead of remaining in family-held businesses, third- and fourth-generation Greek Americans increasingly are pursuing professional careers.

Currently, Greeks are found in almost every occupation and enterprise and constitute one of the wealthier economic groups in the United States. The average per capita income of all persons with Greek ancestry according to the 1990 Census was $18,361.

POLITICS AND GOVERNMENT

Numerous Greek American political and social organizations have existed since the 1880s. These organizations often were made up of Greeks who had come from the same region in Greece. They had a shared sense of Hellenism and a common religion and language and often aligned themselves with native Greek concerns. The *kinotitos* (community) was an organization similar to the village government in Greece. Although the *kinotitos* helped to preserve Greek traditions, it sometimes hindered assimilation.

In 1907 the Pan-Hellenic Union was founded to coordinate and incorporate local organizations; to provide a means of helping Greece obtain more territory from the Ottoman Empire; and to support the return of Constantinople to Greece and the consolidation of all Greek colonies in the Eastern Mediterranean under Greek authority. It also helped Greeks to adapt to their new home in the United States. Many Greek immigrants were slowly beginning to accept the fact that they would not be returning to Greece and that the United States was their permanent home. In 1922 the American Hellenic Educational Progressive Association (AHEPA) was founded. Although the AHEPA supported the assimilation of Greeks to the American way of life, it did not relinquish its strong attachments to Greece. During World War II, the AHEPA was a major contributor to the Greek War Relief Association.

The one issue that mobilized the Greek American community to political action was the Turkish invasion of Cyprus on July 15, 1974. The efforts of well-organized lobby groups to effect an arms embargo against Turkey were impressive. The AHEPA played a leading role in these activities, along with other lobby groups—the American Hellenic Institute and its public affairs committee, the influential United Hellenic American Congress, and the Hellenic Council of America. The Greek Orthodox church and local community organizations also assisted. Primarily because of the successful lobbying of these groups, the United States imposed an arms embargo on Turkey on February 5, 1975.

Greek American politicians were also instrumental in shaping U.S. policy toward the Republic of Macedonia, established after the breakup of the communist Yugoslav federation in the early 1990s. Greece strenuously objected to Macedonia's use of a name that also refers to a region in Greece, and announced a trade embargo against the new country. When, on February 9, 1994, President Clinton announced that the United States would officially recognize Macedonia, Greek American politicians launched an intensive campaign to reverse this policy, gathering 30,000 signatures on a protest petition. Clinton succumbed to this pressure and announced that the United States would withhold diplomatic relations until an envoy could resolve Greece's objections.

Greek political figures are almost overwhelmingly Democratic. They include Michael Dukakis, Paul Tsongas, John Brademas, Paul Spyro Sarbanes, Michael Bilirakis, Andrew Manatos, and George Stephanopoulos. Although Greek Americans traditionally have voted Democratic, their increasing wealth and status have led to an even division within the Greek American community between Republicans and Democrats.

MILITARY

Greek Americans have participated in large numbers in all major wars fought by the United States. Greek American men with veteran status number 90,530; women number 2,635.

INDIVIDUAL AND GROUP CONTRIBUTIONS

Greek Americans have made significant contributions in virtually all of the arts, sciences, and humanities, as well as in politics and business. Following is a sample of their achievements.

ACADEMIA

Aristides Phoutridis, a distinguished professor at Yale University, established Helikon, the first Greek student organization, in 1911 in Boston. George Mylonas (1898-1988) had a distinguished career in the fields of Classical and Bronze Age art and archaeology. His numerous books include *Mycenae, the Capital City of Agamemnon* (1956), *Aghios Kosmos* (1959), *Eleusis and the Eleusinian Mysteries* (1961), *Mycenae and the Mycenean Age* (1966), *Mycenae's Last Century of Greatness* (1968), *Grave Circle B of Mycenae* (1972), *The Cult Center of Mycenae* (1972), and *The West Cemetery of Eleusis* (1975). Theodore Salutos (1910-1980) was a professor of history at the University of California, Los Angeles, who is well known for his studies of the Greek immigration experience. His most important work, *Greeks in the United States* (1964), became a model for other works on this topic.

EDUCATION

John Celivergos Zachos (1820-1898), one of 40 orphans who came to the United States during the Greek Revolution of 1821, was associate principal of the Cooper Female Seminary in Dayton, Ohio (1851-1854), principal and teacher of literature in the grammar school of Antioch College in Yellow Springs, Ohio (1854-1857), a surgeon during the Civil War, a teacher at Meadville Theological School (1866-1867), and a teacher and curator at Cooper Union in New York until 1898. Michael Anagnos (1837-1906) became the director of the famous Perkins Institute for the Blind in Boston where he promoted vocational training and self-help.

FILM, TELEVISION, AND THEATER

Olympia Dukakis (1931-), a well-known film actress and the cousin of politician Michael Dukakis, has appeared in a number of roles since the 1960s. Selected films include *Lilith* (1964), *Twice a Man* (1964), *John and Mary* (1969), *Made for Each Other* (1971), and *The Idolmaker* (1980). Her most recent films are *Steel Magnolias* (1989) and *Moonstruck* (1987), for which she won an Academy Award for Best Supporting Actress. John Cassavetes (1929-1989) was a well-known stage, screen, and television actor, director, playwright, and screenwriter. His many film appearances include *Fourteen* (1951), *Affair in Havana* (1957), *The Killers* (1964), *The Dirty Dozen* (1967), and *Rosemary's Baby* (1968). He directed and produced many films including *Too Late Blues* (1962), *A Child Is Waiting* (1963), *A Woman under the Influence* (1974), and *Big Trouble* (1986). George Tsakiris (1933-), a singer, dancer, and actor, has been in films since the 1940s. He starred in roles in *Gentlemen Prefer Blondes* (1953); *White Christmas* (1954); *West Side Story* (1961), for which he won a Golden Globe Award and an Academy Award for Best Supporting Actor; *Diamond Head* (1962); and *Is Paris Burning?* (1963). Elia Kazan (1909-) was born Elia Kazanjoglou in Constantinople. He is well known as a director, producer, actor, and writer. His best-known productions include *A Streetcar Named Desire* (1951), *A Face in the Crowd* (1957), *Splendor in the Grass* (1961), *America, America* (1963), and *The Arrangement* (1969). He directed such films as *A Tree Grows in Brooklyn* (1945), *Gentlemen's Agreement* (1947), *On the Waterfront* (1953), and *East of Eden* (1954). His writings include *America, America* (1962), *The Arrangement* (1969), *The Assassins* (1972), *The Understudy* (1974), *Acts of Love* (1978), and *The Anatolian* (1982). Katina Paxinou (1900-1973), born Katina Constantopoulos, was a popular actress who starred in many films, including *For Whom the Bell Tolls* (1943), *Confidential Agent* (1945), *Mourning Becomes Electra* (1947), *The*

Inheritance (1947), and *Prince of Foxes* (1945). Telly Savalas (1923-1994), a popular film and television actor, is best known for his role as Theo Kojack in the National Broadcasting Corporation's television series "Kojack" (1973). Born in Garden City, New York, Savalas starred in several films including *The Young Savages* (1961), *Birdman of Alcatraz* (1962), *The Greatest Story Ever Told* (1965), and *The Dirty Dozen* (1967).

FINE ARTS

Christos G. Bastis, born in Trikala, Greece, established the Sea Fare restaurant in New York City, and became a notable collector of ancient sculpture. He donated several works from his collection to the Metropolitan Museum of Art, and was an honorary trustee of that institution and a member of the board of trustees of the Booklyn Museum.

JOURNALISM

Constantine Phasoularides published the first Greek American newspaper in New York in 1892, the *Neos Kosmos (New World)*. Nicholas Gage (1939-), born in Lia, is a journalist and writer, associated with the *Worcester Telegram and Evening Gazette*, *Boston Herald Traveler*, Associated Press, *Wall Street Journal*, and the *New York Times*. He left the *New York Times* in 1980 to write *Eleni*, a work detailing the events surrounding the execution of his mother by Communist guerrillas in Greece in the 1940s.

LITERATURE

In 1906 Mary Vardoulakis wrote *Gold in the Streets*, the first Greek American novel. Olga Broumas (1949-), born in Syros, is a feminist poet who writes a poetry of the "body" with distinct lesbian-erotic motifs. Many of her poems capture the spirit of the Greek homeland. Her works include *Beginning with O* (1977), *Sole Savage* (1980), *Pastoral Jazz* (1983), and *Perpetua* (1985). Kostantinos Lardas (1927-) writes both poetry and fiction. His major works are *The Devil Child* (1961) and *And In Him Too; In Us*, which was nominated for a Pulitzer Prize in 1964. Henry Mark Petrakis (1923-) is a major figure in Greek American fiction. His novels include *Lion of My Heart* (1959), *The Odyssey of Kostas Volakis* (1963), *The Dream of Kings* (1966), *In the Land of Morning* (1973), and *Hour of the Bell* (1976). Petrakis writes of the immigrant experience of the conflict between the old and new generations.

MILITARY

Captain George Partridge Colvocoresses (1816-1872) distinguished himself as commander of the *Saratoga* in the Civil War. His son Rear Admiral George P. Colvocoresses fought in the Spanish-American War was appointed the commandant of midshipmen at the U.S. Naval Academy.

MUSIC

Dimitri Mitropoulos (1896-1960), a well-known composer-conductor, conducted the Minneapolis Symphony (1937-1949) and the New York Philharmonic. Maria Callas (1923-1977), born Mary Kalogeropoulou, was a noted operatic soprano. Callas made her film debut in *Tosca* (1941). She is remembered as a true artist for her original interpretations of Bellini, Donizetti, and Cherubini and in her roles as Norma, Medea, Violetta, and Lucia, as well as Tosca.

POLITICS

The first Greek American to be elected to the U.S. Congress was Lucas Miltiades Miller (1824-1902). Miller, a Democrat from Wisconsin, served in Congress from March 4, 1891, to March 3, 1893. Spiro Agnew (1918-), a Republican who served as governor of Maryland in 1966, became vice president of the United States under Richard Nixon on November 5, 1968, and was reelected as vice president on November 7, 1972. John Brademas (1927-), a Democrat from Indiana, served in Congress from 1959 to 1981. He became president of New York State University in 1981 until his retirement in 1992. Michael Dukakis (1933-) was governor of Massachusetts in 1975-1979 and 1983-1991 and was Democratic candidate for president in 1988. Paul Efthemios Tsongas (1941-), congressman from Massachusetts, served in the House of Representatives during 1974-1979 and in the U.S. Senate during 1979-1985. Paul Spyro Sarbanes (1933-) was a Democratic congressman from Maryland who was reelected to the Senate in 1982. Gus Yatron (1927-), Democratic congressman from Pennsylvania, served in the U.S. House of Representatives during 1969-1989. George Stephanopoulos (1961-) was director of communications for President Bill Clinton's administration during 1992-1993 before becoming senior advisor to the president for policy and strategy.

SCIENCE AND TECHNOLOGY

George Papnicolaou (1883-1961) was professor emeritus of anatomy at Cornell Medical College. His research led him to develop the "pap smear," a test designed to detect cervical cancer. Polyvios Koryllos was a professor of medicine at the University of Athens and Yale University. He is well known for his work in diagnosing tuberculosis. John Kotzias was a neurologist who discovered the drug L-dopa for the treatment of Parkinson's disease.

SPORTS

Alex Karras (1935-) was a well-known football player (a two-time All-American) for the Detroit Lions from 1958 to 1971. He hosted the National Football League's Monday Night Football and has made numerous television appearances. Alex Grammas (1926-) was a professional baseball player between 1954 and 1963 who played with the St. Louis Cardinals, Cincinnati Reds, and the Chicago Cubs. He was a baseball manager in 1969 and 1976-1977. Harry Agganis (1930-1955) distinguished himself in baseball, football, and basketball. Although he was drafted by the Cleveland Browns football team on graduation from Boston University in 1953, he signed with the Boston Red Sox. Jimmy Londos (c. 1895-1975), born Christopher Theophilus, won the world heavyweight wrestling championship on June 25, 1934.

MEDIA

PRINT

Historically, the Greek ethnic press in the United States has kept pace with the needs of Greek Americans, and its presence has contributed to a strong ethnic cohesion in the Greek community. The first Greek American newspaper in the country was *Neos Kosmos* (*New World*), first published in New York by Constantine Phasoularides in September 1897. It was followed by the *Thermopylae*, published by John Booras in 1900. The *Ethnikos Keryx* (*National Herald*), which began publication in New York on April 2, 1915, was one of the few newspapers to have a significant influence on the Greek reading public. Its serious competitors in New York are *Proini* (*Morning News*), which publishes only in Greek, and the *Greek American*, which publishes only in English. In Chicago the *Greek Star* (*Hellenikos Aster*) and the *Greek Press* (*Hellenikos Typos*), both published in Greek and English, still hold a sizable readership.

There are 27 Greek American newspapers in the United States; seven are published in either Greek or English, respectively, and 14 are published in both languages. The majority focus on community events and church news, as well as on news from Greece and the lobbying activities of Greek American politicians.

Ethnikos Keryx (The National Herald).
Begun in 1915, the *Herald* is the oldest daily newspaper in the Greek language in the United States. Features international, national, and local news and items about Greece of interest to the community.

Contact: Anthony Diamataris, Editor.
Address: 41-17 Crescent Street, Long Island City, New York 11101.
Telephone: (718) 784-5255.

The Greek American.
Widely read English-language publication that focuses on the political events in Greece and in the United States. Publishes a national calendar of events that lists activities taking place in the larger Greek community.

Contact: Tina Maurikos, Editor.
Address: 25-50 Crescent Street, Astoria, New York 11102.
Telephone: (718) 626-7676.
Fax: (718) 956-8076.

Greek Press (Hellenikos Typos).
Founded in 1929 and published bi-weekly in English and Greek, *Greek Press* covers political, educational, and social events, as well as local and international news of interest to the Greek community.

Contact: Helen Angelopoulos, Editor.
Address: 808 West Jackson Boulevard, Chicago, Illinois 60607.
Telephone: (708) 766-2955.
Fax: (708) 766-3069.

Greek Star (Hellenikos-Aster).
Founded in 1904, *Greek Star* is the oldest continuously published Greek newspaper in the United States. A bi-weekly publication of the United Hellenic American Congregation, it appears in Greek and English and features local and international news of interest to the Greek community in Chicago. Covers news from Cyprus and Greece.

Contact: Nicholas Philippidis, Editor.
Address: 4715 North Lincoln, Chicago, Illinois 60625.
Telephone: (312) 878-7331.

The Hellenic Chronicle.
A weekly English-language publication dedicated to the promulgation of American, Hellenic, and Orthodox ideals. Features political, national, international, and local news of interest to the Greek community. Contains an Entertainment Arts and Social section.

Contact: Nancy Agris Savage, Editor.
Address: 5-6 Franklin Commons, Framingham, Massachusetts 01701-6637.
Telephone: (508) 820-9700.
Fax: (508) 820-0952.

Kampana—Campana.
Founded in 1917, *Campana* is published semimonthly in Greek and English and features the news from Greece, with information about Greeks abroad. Covers local and community events.

Contact: Costas Athansasiades, Editor.
Address: 30-96 42nd Street, Long Island City (Astoria), New York 11103-3031.
Telephone: (718) 278-3014.
Fax: (718) 278-3023.

Proini.
Competing with *The National Herald*, this daily publishes community news and news from Greece and Cyprus, sporting events, artistic and cultural events, and editorials.

Contact: Fanny Holliday Petallides, Publisher.
Address: 25-50 Crescent Street, Astoria, New York 11102.
Telephone: (718) 626-7676.

RADIO

WEDC-AM (1240).
"Hellenic American Radio Hour" airs every Saturday, 7:00p.m. to 8:00 p.m. One of the oldest Greek radio shows in the Chicago area (75 years). Features community events, discussion of family problems, religious issues, music, and news from Greece.

Contact: Carmen Castro.
Address: 5475 North Milwaukee Avenue, Chicago, Illinois 60630-1229.
Telephone: (312) 631-0700.

WEEF-AM (1430).
"Greek Orthodox Hours of the Chicago Diocese" airs every Tuesday and Wednesday, 11:00 p.m. to 12:00 a.m. Discusses topics related to the Greek Orthodox church.

Contact: Paula Rekoumis and Sotirios Rekoumis.
Address: 210 Skokie Valley Road, Highland Park,
    Illinois 60035.
Telephone: (708) 831-5440.

WNTN-AM (1550).

"Greek Cultural Radio Program of Boston," a non-commercial, one-hour program that broadcasts twice a week. Features topics relating to Greek heritage, customs, and history. In Greek and English.

Contact: Athanasios Vulgaropoulos.
Address: 143 Rumford Avenue, Newton,
    Massachusetts 02166.
Telephone: (617) 969-1550.

WUNR-AM (1600).

"The Other Program," a talk show where people can call in with questions; "The Athenian Hour," featuring cultural and news events; "Hellenic Voice of Massachusetts"; "Let Us Sing," playing selections of Greek music.

Contact: Jane A. Clarke.
Address: 160 North Washington Street, Boston,
    Massachusetts 02114-2142.
Telephone: (617) 367-9003.
Fax: (617) 367-2265.

ORGANIZATIONS AND ASSOCIATIONS

American Hellenic Educational Progressive Association (AHEPA).

Founded in 1922. The AHEPA is dedicated to the preservation of the Greek national identity in the United States. The oldest Greek fraternal organization in the United States has a membership of more than 500,000 members, with many chapters across the county. It engages in numerous charitable, publishing, and educational activities. It includes the Daughters of Penelope, a women's auxiliary; the Maids of Athens, a girls' organization; and the Sons of Pericles, a boys' organization. Publishes *AHEPAN*, a bimonthly.

Contact: Timothy Mauiatis, Executive Director.
Address: 1909 Q Street, N.W., Suite 500,
    Washington, D.C. 20009.
Telephone: (202) 232-6300.
Fax: (202) 232-2140.

Greek Orthodox Ladies Philoptochos Society.

Founded in 1931. The Society promotes the values of the family and the Greek Orthodox faith and engages in many charitable, educational, and religious activities on behalf of the church. Its membership of more than 400,000 includes women 18 years and older.

Contact: Eve C. Condakes, President.
Address: 345 East 74th Street, New York,
    New York 10021-3701.
Telephone: (212) 744-4390.
Fax: (212) 861-1956.

Greek Orthodox Youth Adult League.

Conducts workshops on religious education for Greek youth. Assists the church both nationally and locally, with 6,000 to 10,000 members.

Contact: Tom Kanelos.
Address: 8 East 79th Street, New York,
    New York 10021.
Telephone: (212) 570-3560.
Fax: (212) 861-2183.

United Hellenic American Congress (UHAC).

Founded in 1974. The UHAC was established to preserve the cultural traditions of Greece. It coordinates many of the cultural activities of the Greek community in the Chicago area. Every year the UHAC issues a Greek Heritage Calendar of Events and is active in promoting the Greek Independence Day parade. The UHAC was a prominent lobbyist in the Greek American protest against the Turkish invasion of Cyprus.

Contact: Andrew Athens, National Chair.
Address: 75 East Wacker Drive, Suite 500,
    Chicago, Illinois 60601.
Telephone: (312) 345-1000.
Fax: (312) 345-1025.

MUSEUMS AND RESEARCH CENTERS

Greek-American Folklore Society.

Founded 1983. Society members conduct classes and workshops on traditional dances and songs from every region of Greece. The Society presents hundreds of performances throughout the year and offers exhibits of and lectures on traditional Greek costumes. It coordinates the *Panegyri*, an annual conference of Greek folklore societies, as well as the Hellenic Folk Music Festival. The Society has 50 to 60 members.

Contact: Paul Ginis.
Address: 29-04 Ditmars Boulevard, Astoria, New
    York 11105.
Telephone: (718) 728-8048.

Hellenic Cultural Museum at Holy Trinity Cathedral.

Opened on May 3, 1992. The museum is considered to be the first Greek cultural museum in the United States. This "people's museum" contains important collections of scrapbooks, diaries, letters, artifacts, newspapers, and photographs documenting the lives of the Greeks who settled in Utah from 1905 to the present. The museum contains a unique display of mining operations.

Contact: Chris Metos.

Address: 279 South 300 West, Salt Lake City, Utah 84101.

Telephone: (801) 328-9681.

Hellenic Museum and Cultural Center.

Opened 1992. The center preserves original documents, artifacts, and other archival source materials relating to the Greek American immigrant experience. It also collects the artistic works (crafts, embroideries, furniture) of Greek Americans.

Contact: Elaine Kollintzas, Executive Director.

Address: 400 North Franklin Street, Chicago, Illinois 60610.

Telephone: (312) 467-4622.

Immigration History Research Center.

Located at the University of Minnesota, this center contains important primary source materials on many aspects of the life of Greek immigrants in the United States. The collection includes the papers of the immigrant historian Theodore Salutos.

Contact: Joel Whurl, Curator.

Address: 826 Berry Street, St. Paul, Minnesota 55114.

Telephone: (612) 627-4208.

Saint Photios Foundation.

Founded in 1981. A Greek fraternal organization dedicated to preserving a shrine in Saint Augustine, Florida, commemorating the Greeks of New Smyrna, the first Greeks immigrants to arrive in America in 1768. The museum has a small library and cultural exhibit.

Contact: Father Dimitrios Couchell.

Address: 41 Saint George Street, Post Office Box 1960, Saint Augustine, Florida 32085.

Telephone: (904) 829-8205.

SOURCES FOR ADDITIONAL STUDY

Callincos, Constance. *American Aphrodite: Becoming Female in Greek America.* New York: Pella, 1990.

Kunkelman, Gary. *The Religion of Ethnicity: Belief and Belonging in a Greek-American Community.* New York: Garland, 1990.

Moskos, Charles C. *Greek Americans: Struggle and Success,* second edition. New Brunswick, New Jersey: Transaction, 1989.

Mouzaki, Rozanna. *Greek Dances for Americans.* Garden City, New York: Doubleday, 1981.

Pappas, Susan. "The Greek-American Press Marks Its 100th Anniversary This Year," *Editor and Publisher,* September 1992, pp. 18-19.

Rouvelas, Marilyn. *A Guide to Greek Traditions and Customs in America.* Bethesda, Maryland: Attica, 1993.

Salutos, Theodore. *The Greeks in the United States.* Cambridge: Harvard University Press, 1964.

Scourby, Alice. *The Greek Americans.* Boston: Twayne, 1977.

Treasured Greek Proverbs, compiled, edited, and translated by Elaine G. Bucuvalas, Catherine G. Lavrakas, and Poppy G. Stamatos. (1980)

Grenadians are known traditionally as a friendly people. A willingness to "lend-a-hand" is not uncommon. Most Grenadian Americans try to maintain an "up-beat" approach to many day-to-day concerns.

GRENADIAN AMERICANS

by
Charlie Jones

OVERVIEW

The country of Grenada is located 1,500 miles (2415 kilometers) south of Miami, Florida, and 200 miles (3220 kilometers) north of the South American continent, in the southeast waters of the Caribbean Sea. Grenada shares its west shoreline with the Caribbean Sea and the Atlantic Ocean is located on its eastern shoreline. Existing as part of the southernmost Windward Islands of Great Britain, Grenada also comprises the islands of Carriacou and Petite Martinique. The total landmass of Grenada encompasses about 133 square miles (345 square kilometers) of territory, making it twice as large as Washington, D.C.

The island itself is home to beautiful picturesque white, sandy beaches, rain forests, and breathtaking lofty mountaintop views. Its long coastline and tropical climate make it an ideal retreat for surfing, fishing, and other relaxing aquatic activities. Grenada's natural wonders make the islands a much visited tourist destination. The tropical climate also lends itself well to the production of tropical crops such as bananas, cocoa, sugarcane, citrus and other fruits and vegetables. Spices such as cinnamon, nutmeg, and mace also grow well here, thus giving the island its internationally known nickname, "the isle of spice."

As of July 1998, a population of approximately 96,217 inhabits the islands of Grenada. Most Grenadians speak English. The majority, more than 82 percent, are of black African descent. The rest of the population is a mixture of European, East Indian, and Native Indian persons. Most Grenadians are of the Roman Catholic faith (53 percent), with Protestant sects comprising about 47 percent of the population. The Government is a parliamentary democracy consisting of three branches, executive, legislative and judicial. In 1999, the British monarch, Queen Elizabeth II of the United Kingdom, served as head of state, with Dr. Keith Mitchell, the prime minister, acting as the head of the government.

HISTORY

The Ciboney Indians from South America settled the islands around 4000 B.C. Several centuries later the Arawak Indians settled the island. During the period 1000 to 1300 A.D. the Carib Indians arrived on the island, which they called "Camerhogne," and killed or enslaved the Arawaks. Christopher Columbus sighted the island in 1498 but did not land there. He called the island "Concepcion." It is not clear how the island received its current name, "Grenada" (pronounced "Gruh-NAY-duh"). Some scholars believe Columbus's sailors called the island Granada. Others believe the Spanish renamed the island for the city of Granada, Spain. Nevertheless, in the eighteenth century the name "Grenada" was in common use.

Due in part to the defensive capabilities of the Carib Indians, Grenada remained uncolonized by European countries for most of the sixteenth century and half of the seventeenth century. However, by 1650 a French company purchased the island from the British and established a settlement in the islands. The Carib Indians resisted the French settlers. The French consequently brought in military reinforcements and slaughtered the Carib population. The French controlled the island until British forces captured it in 1762. The British regained control Grenada through the Treaty of Paris in 1763, under which the French ceded the island to Great Britain. Although the French regained control of Grenada in 1779, the Treaty of Versailles in 1783 restored the island to Britain.

Grenada's climate made it ideal for growing sugar, nutmeg, cocoa and other spices, and in the eighteenth century slave labor was considered key to the production of these and other commercially valuable crops. Black Africans were therefore imported to Grenada in large numbers to work on plantations as slaves. Both the British and French made use of African slaves to support agricultural production on the Island of Grenada. In 1833, the British government outlawed slavery, ending its institution.

MODERN ERA

Between 1855 and 1958 the British governing body of the Windward Islands was headquartered on Grenada. In 1877 Grenada became an official British colony. From 1900 to 1945 West Indians throughout the Caribbean developed even stronger ties to labor movements. Labor strikes occurred among sugar harvesters in Saint Kitts, coal miners in Saint Lucia, and oil field workers fields in Trinidad. All struck for higher wages and better working conditions.

From 1958 to 1962 Grenada was a member of the West Indian Federation. By 1967 Grenada had become self-governing in association with the United Kingdom. Grenada gained its independence on February 7, 1974 under the leadership of Eric Gairy, a labor unionist turned politician.

The first prime minister of Grenada, Eric Gairy, governed in a somewhat heavy-handed manner. In March of 1979 a coup d'etat occurred, bringing to power Maurice Bishop. Under his People's Revolutionary Government (PRG), Bishop served as a popular leader. Many still consider him a national hero. The PRG began forming ties with Cuba and the Soviet Union. Some members of the PRG were not satisfied with the leadership of the PRG and the direction it was taking, and under General Hudson Austin and Bernard Coard an internal coup took place, which resulted in the execution of Maurice Bishop and other key government officials.

Using the pretext of government instability and protection of U.S. citizens, the U.S. government under President Ronald Reagan along with other nations of the Caribbean invaded the island of Grenada in 1983. Military power was used to force a change from the government's communist bent to a more prodemocratic form of government. Elections were held in 1984, and the peacekeeping nations of Jamaica and Barbados departed by 1985, along with the U.S. Marines.

The Grenadian elections of 1990 did not result in a clear mandate for any one political party. The 1995 elections saw Dr. Keith Mitchell's New National Party receiving the most votes, and Dr. Mitchell became the prime minister. Mitchell's administration has sought ties with Cuba and the United States, and Mitchell has been working to end drug trafficking by the creation of a Grenadian Coast Guard based on Petite Martinique.

THE FIRST GRENADIANS IN AMERICA

In comparison to other ethnic groups entering the United States from Europe, little formal information regarding eighteenth- and early nineteenth-century Grenadian immigration to the United States exists. Indeed, it is very difficult to find any substantiated information regarding Grenadian citizens entering the United States willingly before the mid-nineteenth century. Some information that seems to suggest that a few black African slaves may have been imported from Grenada to the United States in the early nineteenth century. Most of these Grenadians would have been settled in the southeastern portion of the United States, where slavery existed and there was a great need for labor in support of tobacco, rice and other crops. As U.S. importation of slaves from Africa continued, a dependency on Grenadian slaves would have ceased. Therefore, after the British slave trade ended in 1834, there is no record of Grenadians arriving in the United States for many decades.

SIGNIFICANT IMMIGRATION WAVES

Grenadians began immigrating to the United States after the turn of the twentieth century. They settled in urban areas of the northeastern United States, according to Paula Aymer's article in *American Immigrant Cultures*, by "apprenticing on [U.S.] boats that transported bananas from Central America via Barbados and jumping ship once they docked in New York or Boston." The number of Grenadians coming to the United States in this manner amounted only to a few hundred, perhaps around three hundred.

Records of the U.S. immigration from 1900 through the 1930s indicate only a few Grenadians entering the United States as immigrants. By comparison to European immigration figures, their numbers were extremely low. Immigration from Grenada to the United States increased after the war years of the 1940s. Again, the number of Grenadians allowed to enter the United States legally was very low. This increase nevertheless occurred through the immigration of Grenadian women to the United States in the late 1950s. Grenadian women worked as nurses and/or domestics in the oil-rich areas of Venezuela, Aruba, and Curaçao. During the mid-1950s, when the Grenadian oil refineries were mechanized and downsized operationally, a group of Grenadian oil workers were allowed entrance into the United States as immigrants. According to Paula Aymer, "these restless men and women were determined to find their way into the United States, and they used various means. Some had made important job connections while working in the oil enclave or on the naval base (at Chaguaramas, Trinidad) and had been given references by American employers. Others

had sent their children to [U.S.] schools, and once these children found jobs and sponsors to help them with the immigration requirements, they applied for permanent residence for their parents. Still others first found work on oil refineries in the United States Virgin Islands, or traveled first to England, and from there found their way, often via Canada, into the United States."

Canadian-sponsored live-in maid programs for people of the Caribbean also enabled a few hundred Grenadian women to enter the United States as immigrants. These women settled in parts of Washington, D.C., New York, and Boston after serving the mandatory two-year requirement of the Canadian program. During the 1960s the United States developed its own program that sponsored domestic workers from the Caribbean. Hundreds of Grenadian woman entered the United States as live-in domestics in the northeastern section of the country, particularly in the New York area.

A much larger number of Grenadians immigrated to the United States after the U.S. Congress passed the Hart-Celler Immigration Reform Act of 1965. This law shifted favoritism in immigration from Europe to Caribbean nations, as the U.S. government found this foreign policy more advantageous due to a revived interest in the Caribbean region.

According to statistics of the U.S. Immigration and Naturalization Service, in the period between 1960 and 1980 a total of 10,391 Grenadians entered the United States legally. Between 1971 and 1984 just over 12,000 Grenadian immigrants entered New York. Since 1984, according to *American Immigrant Cultures*, approximately 850 Grenadians have legally entered the United States each year. Again, the number of Grenadians allowed to enter the United States was very low, by comparison to European immigrants entering the United States, but greater than the number allowed earlier in the century.

Grenadians moved to the United States for a number of reasons, ranging from better economic conditions in the United States to a desire to live with relatives who immigrated to America earlier. While living in the United States, many Grenadians maintain contact with family members still residing on the island. A large number of Grenadian Americans visit relatives on the island constantly and islanders fly to the United States to visit relatives living on the continent. Some of these visitors from the island use their visit as a means of illegal entry into the United States. These persons find jobs in the United States or attend schools in the United States and do not return to Grenada.

As Grenadians moved to the United States, older immigrants continued to maintain many traditional Grenadian customs and values, while younger Grenadian Americans began taking on more traditional American customs and values, in particular those of African Americans.

Even though this change in values was occurring, contact with and support for Grenadians on the island remained high. Many organizations have been set up by Grenadian Americans in the United States whose main objective is to send monies for support back to the Island.

By the 1970s and 1980s many Grenadians who emigrated from Grenada to the United States were not leaving the island primarily for economic reasons. Insead, another reason for entering the United States was political; many disapproved of Grenada's shift away from prodemocratic values to plitical ideas associated with communism.

ACCULTURATION AND ASSIMILATION

Grenadian Americans have many traditions, customs and beliefs, some dating as far back as their ancestral ties to Africa. Upon leaving Grenada for the United States, Grenadians did not quickly change their beliefs, traditions or customs too rapidly. Most Grenadian Americans are descendants of African slaves. Other Grenadians ethnic groups are mulattos (mixture of black and European), East Indians (who are descended from laborers who worked on plantations after the slaves were freed), and whites of European origin. Immigrating to the United States has in many cases meant moving into neighborhoods dominated by African American culture. Consequently, many Grenadian immigrants have shared and integrated their culture with that of African Americans.

TRADITIONS, CUSTOMS, AND BELIEFS

Grenadians are known traditionally as a friendly people. A willingness to lend a hand is not uncommon. Most Grenadian Americans try to maintain an upbeat approach to many day-to-day concerns. Difficult circumstances involving other persons rarely lead to prolonged bitter feelings. Grenadian Americans like to work as a group to strengthen their neighborhood and community. The philosophy of community support and shared work in a spirit of cooperation is called a "maroon" by those Grenadian Americans who remember this lifestyle from their days of living on the island. This lifestyle has been brought to America by some Grenadians and is practiced in some Grenadian neighborhoods.

Grenadian Americans believe that dressing well while in public is very important. Pride is exhibited in choice of clothing for social events such as going to church. Bright colors are customary. Sloppy dress in public, especially among adult Grenadian Americans, is looked upon as inappropriate. While in private, a more casual dress style is considered acceptable. For example, walking barefoot is common.

Most Grenadians like to chat and socialize with friends. Visiting is very common and reinforces the friendly approach Grenadians have toward people in general and other Grenadians in particular. When on a visit to a friend or family member's home, it is customary to be offered some sort of refreshment to eat or drink. One should not be too quick to refuse such offers; Grenadian Americans sometimes feel that to refuse an offer of refreshment is impolite.

Traditionally, women socialize by spending many volunteer hours doing church activities with friends. Men on the other hand, socialize more at work and at sporting events. Funerals are considered social gatherings by Grenadian Americans, which traditionally require men to dress in suits, usually black, while women dress in black or white dresses and hats. Socialization at such events usually continues long after the formal funeral procession and graveside activities have concluded.

CUISINE

Being from "the isle of spice" has influenced Grenadian American cuisine, especially its heavily spiced flavor. Grenadian Americans will use hot pepper sauces, curries and other spices while cooking. Corn, rice, and peas are eaten with meats such as chicken, fish, pork, and beef. Seafood is very popular among Grenadian Americans. Iguana and *manicou*, (a type of opossum) are also enjoyed. Fruits are a favorite among Grenadians as well. Bananas, grapefruit, coconuts, and papaya are purchased by Grenadians living throughout the United States. Barbecues and roasted foods are also enjoyed among Grenadians.

DANCES AND SONGS

When Grenadian Americans came to the United States, they brought their music with them. One style, called *calypso*, is influenced by African music and consists of singing and dancing. The lyrics deal with issues including love, humor, politics, and controversial current events. The musical beat is somewhat African in sound. The origins of calypso have been traced to West Indian slave singing. This form of music and its lyrics were apparently used as a form of slave communication. Primitive instruments such as the bamboo pipe, flute, and specially carved gourds are still used in performing calypso music today. Some of today's Grenadian American calypso bands also use electric guitars, maracas, and steel drums.

While listening to calypso music, many of those being entertained like to dance the limbo, a dance very popular among Grenadian Americans. This dance consists of bending backward in such a way as to allow for wiggling of the body while passing beneath an elongated pole. Success means clearing the pole without touching the floor or pole with any part of the body. The pole is continually lowered after each dancer successfully passes under it. A dancer is eliminated from the dance when he or she is unable to clear the lowered pole successfully. This dance, as with the music, seems to have originated from Africa.

The playing of steel drums is also popular among Grenadian American bands. Indeed, Grenadian steel drum bands exist in the United States and are often heard at U.S. Grenadian American festivals. This form of music seems to have originated in Trinidad, but it is quite popular on the Grenadian Island.

RECREATIONAL ACTIVITIES

Cricket and football (soccer) teams are abundant on the West Indian islands. Upon arriving in the United States, Grenadians brought their passion for football, which is called soccer in the United States, and the British game of cricket with them. Many Grenadian Americans who grew up in the islands learned to play cricket and/or football, and some played on professional teams. This explains why so many Grenadians enjoy these two forms of recreation in particular.

Other sports enjoyed by Grenadians include basketball and track and field. Grenadian Americans also practice aquatic activities such as fishing, diving, swimming, and sailing.

Many Grenadians learn to play guitar, violin, and drums, and private playing of these instruments for enjoyment is a wonderful and much enjoyed pastime for many Grenadian Americans.

HOLIDAYS

Grenadian Americans celebrate the traditional Christian religious holidays of Christmas, Good Friday, and Easter. The Eastern Orthodox holidays of Whitmonday and Corpus Christi are also celebrat-

ed. Many Grenadian Americans also celebrate the secular holidays of Grenada. These include Independence Day (celebrated February 7) and Emancipation Day (celebrated the first Monday in August). In addition, Grenadians enjoy carnivals, which may be held throughout the year. Carnivals are usually festive occasions commemorating special events in the history of Grenada. They usually involve street dancing, concerts, and parades.

Some Grenadians living in America also honor Grenadian thanksgiving. On the Grenadian islands, thanksgiving is observed in relationship to the 1983 United States invasion of the island, which was intended to restore order and democracy to Grenada. This observance is usually marked by official ceremonies.

LANGUAGE

Grenadian Americans speak English. However, some of their English expressions differ from American English expressions. For example, Grenadian Americans prefer "Happy Christmas" over the expression "Merry Christmas." A "bounce" in Grenadian English is a reference to a car accident, while "now for now" means "urgent" to the Grenadian American.

Informal Grenadian English is a combination of French, English, and African *patois*, which is sometimes referred to as "creole" or "broken English." Grenadian patois is different from that spoken on the other Windward Islands that make up Grenada, Carriacou and Petite Martinique. The dialect does not have a past or future tense. To indicate tense, body gestures are used. Among those Grenadians entering America, patois is sometimes spoken until the language is infused with the English spoken in America. This, in some instances, means an infusion with the English spoken in African American urban neighborhoods or other ethnic neighborhoods where Grenadian Americans live and socialize. Most Grenadians do not like to hear outsiders speak patois. Children are therefore asked to use standard English when speaking publicly.

GREETINGS AND POPULAR EXPRESSIONS

Grenadian Americans will speak to a friend when passing on the street. Not to do so is considered disrespectful. As is the American way, Grenadian Americans generally prefer to greet another person with a traditional handshake. It is also very common to end a conversation by saying "later." Gesturing with the hands is also a Grenadian American custom. The "thumbs up" usually means "good," "great," or "I agree." Waving the hand back and forth at waist level, palm down, means "no" or "I disagree."

The expressions of American teenagers are being incorporated into Grenadian American greetings. It is not uncommon to hear Grenadian Americans greet another by saying "W's happ nen," with the response being "cool," meaning "everything is all right." These expressions may derive from Grenadian immigrants associating with African Americans as neighbors. Many Grenadian American and African American traditions, customs, and values are merging in American cultural society.

FAMILY AND COMMUNITY DYNAMICS

Grenadian American families may consist of parents, children, grandparents, uncles, aunts, and cousins living within the same home. While all Grenadian families are not necessarily large, the norm of the extended family is real among many Grenadian families living in the United States. Children often are raised by the female head of the family. Male duties usually include working outside the home to provide income for the family. Grenadian American women also desire to work outside the home and provide for the household as well. Many Grenadian children live at home well past the age of adulthood. Each family member has a job to do to maintain the family within the home.

EDUCATION

Grenadians take education seriously, viewing it as a means to advancement in America. Children are expected to attend schools daily, as American law requires. Most attend public schools, but a few attend private schools, mostly parochial. Many adults also are returning to school to receive either technical training or to receive a high school diploma. The literacy rate of Grenada is around 98 percent. College attendance among Grenadian Americans is growing. Many Grenadians are in America for the purpose of attending school and/or college. After graduation, many choose to remain in America, taking a spouse and raising a family. Some however, return to the island of Grenada to help others on the island.

BIRTH AND BIRTHDAYS

Grenadian American families on average are generally somewhat smaller on average than the four to five children per family found on the island of Grenada. This may be due in part to a desire of Grenadian American women to enter the American workforce, thereby giving up larger families. Also, some Grenadian women are single mothers, as many Grenadian children are born out of wedlock and sometimes fathers leave the home.

COURTSHIP AND WEDDINGS

Grenadians usually meet in places of American social gatherings. These include restaurants, educational facilities, dance halls, entertainment venues and sporting venues. Grenadian Americans usually do not display affection publicly. Most couples generally like to live together before committing to marriage, and some couples prefer to live together instead of marrying.

When weddings do occur, they are very festive. After the church ceremony, the reception is enjoyed by all, with plenty of food, music and dancing. Gifts are also provided for the newlyweds. A honeymoon vacation sometimes follows the reception, when financially possible.

RELIGION

Most Grenadians, 53 percent, are Roman Catholic. Protestant sects are many and make up about 33 percent of the population. Islam is also practiced by some Grenadian Americans. A small number of Grenadians practice a faith known as Rastafarianism. Those who practice Rastas, generally believe that Haile Selassie, emperor of Ethiopia from 1930 to 1974, was a god. They also consider marijuana to be a sacred herb, and that all Afro-West Indians must move eventually to Ethiopia, which is viewed by Rastas believers as "the promised land."

POLITICS AND GOVERNMENT

Americans from Grenada maintain close ties with their former country. News concerning political and governmental activities comes to America from radio, newspapers, and television. Conversations by phone with friends and family also help Grenadian Americans know what the current state of affairs in Grenada. Most American Grenadians supported the 1983 invasion of Grenada by the United States, ostensibly to restore democracy.

Those living in the United States constantly express concern for helping islanders. According to a news release from the office of the Grenadian prime minister dated January 28, 1999, on January

27, 1999, nearly 300 Grenadian Americans met with Prime Minister Mitchell in Boston to ask how they could become involved in assisting with the development of Grenada. He responded by saying that they could help by "providing more training opportunities for young Grenadians in American learning institutions, as well as supplying computers and assisting with technology transfer to improve the working skills of Grenadians." To meet this challenge, Bostonian Grenadian Americans plan to adopt a school in Grenada and donate equipment and supplies on an annual basis. Americans from Grenada have always demonstrated a willingness to aid their countrymen on the island.

SOURCES FOR ADDITIONAL STUDY

Culturegram, 1998: Grenada. Provo, UT: Brigham Young University, 1998.

Eisenberg, Joyce. Places and Peoples of the World: Grenada. New York, Chelsea House, 1988.

Factbook: Grenada. http://www.odci.gov/cia/publications/factbook/gj.html. Cited May 1999.

Hague, Harlan. Grenada. http://www.softadventure.net/grenada.htm. Cited May 1999.

Herda, D. J. Ethnic America: The Northeastern States. Brookfield, CT, Millbrook, 1991.

Levinson, David. American Immigrant Cultures: Builders of a Nation. New York, Simon & Schuster, 1997.

Payne, Anthony. Grenada: Revolution and Invasion. New York, St. Martin's Press, 1984.

Thomas, Hugh. The Story of the Atlantic Slave Trade: 1440–1870. New York, Simon & Schuster, 1997.

U.S. Department of State Background Notes: Grenada. http://www.tradecompass.com/library/dos/bnotes/GRENADA.html. Cited May 1999. Originally published November of 1994 by the U.S. Bureau of Public Affairs.

GUAMANIAN AMERICANS

by
Jane E. Spear

OVERVIEW

Guam, or *Guahan*, (translated as "we have") as it was known in the ancient Chamorro language, is the southernmost and largest island of the Mariana Islands, in the west central Pacific. Located about 1,400 miles east of the Philippines, it is approximately 30 miles long, and varies in width from four miles to 12 miles. The island has a total landmass of 212 square miles, without calculating reef formations, and was formed when two volcanoes joined. In fact, Guam is the peak of a submerged mountain that rises 37,820 feet above the bottom of the Marianas Trench, the greatest ocean depth in the world. Guam has been a territory of the United States since 1898, and is the furthest west of all U.S. territories in the Pacific. Lying west of the International Dateline, it is one day ahead in time than the rest of the United States. (The International Dateline is the designated imaginary line drawn north and south through the Pacific Ocean, primarily along the 180th meridian, that by international agreement marks the calendar day for the world.) Guam's official slogan, "Where America's Day Begins," highlights its geographical position.

According to the 1990 census, Guam's population was 133,152, up from 105,979 in 1980. The population represents the Guamanians, who account for only half of Guam residents, Hawaiians, Filipinos, and North Americans. The majority of North Americans are either U.S. military personnel or support staff. As residents of a U.S. territory, Guamanians on the island are U.S. citizens with a U.S. passport. They elect a representative to the Congress of the United States, but citizens do not vote in the Presidential election. The representative who sits in the House votes only in committees, but does not vote on general issues.

The island's population is centered in Agana, the island's capital since ancient times. The city has a population of 1,139 and the surrounding Agana Heights' population is 3,646. The city was re-built after World War II, following two years of occupation by Japanese forces. In addition to the government buildings, the centerpiece of the city is the *Dulce Nombre de Maria* (Sweet Name of Mary) Cathedral Basilica. The cathedral is located on the site of the island's first Catholic church, which was constructed in 1669 by the Spanish settlers, directed by Padre San Vitores. The original church was destroyed by bombing during the Allied American forces' retaking Guam in 1944. Today the cathedral is the church of most of the islanders, the majority of whom are Roman Catholic.

The Seventh Day Adventists are the other major religious denomination on the island, active in Guam since the American reoccupation in 1944. They represent approximately one-fifth of Guamanians on the island. Spanish explorers brought Roman Catholicism to the island. Early Spanish and Portuguese missionaries to the Americas sought to convert the natives to Catholicism. These missionaries taught native Guamanians the Spanish language and customs, as well.

Other settlements are located in Sinajana, Tamnuning, and Barrigada, at the center of the island. The Anderson (U.S.) Air Force Base, a major presence on the island, temporarily housed refugees from Vietnam in 1975, after the fall of Saigon to the northern Vietnamese Communists.

The official Guam flag represents the history of the island. The flag's blue field serves as a background for the Great Seal of Guam, representing Guam's unity with the sea and the sky. A red strip surrounding the Guam seal is a reminder of the blood shed by the Guamanian people. The seal itself has very distinctive meanings in each of the visual symbols pictured: the pointed, egg-like shape of the seal represents a Chamorro sling stone quarried from the island; the coconut tree depicted represents self-sustenance and the ability to grow and survive under adverse circumstances; the flying *proa*, a seagoing canoe built by the Chamorro people, which required skill to build and sail; the river symbolizes the willingness to share the bounty of the land with others; the land mass is a reminder of the Chamorro's commitment to their environment—sea and land; and the name Guam, the home of the Chamorro people.

HISTORY

Guam was the earliest settlement of a Pacific island. Archaeological and historical evidence has indicated that the ancient Chamorros, the earliest known inhabitants of the Mariana Islands, lived there as early as 1755 B.C. These people were of Mayo-Indonesian descent and originated in southeast Asia. Spanish explorer Ferdinand Magellan reportedly landed at Umatac Bay on the southwestern coast of Guam on March 6, 1521, following a 98-day voyage from South America. One member of that expedition, by the last name of Pifigetta described the Chamorros at that time as being tall, big-boned, and robust with tawny brown skin and long black hair. The Chamorro population at the time of the first Spanish landing was estimated to be 65,000 to 85,000. Spain took formal control of Guam and the other Mariana Islands in 1565, but used the island only as a stopover point on the way from Mexico to the Philippines until the first missionaries arrived in 1688. By 1741, following periods of famine, Spanish conquest wars, and new diseases introduced by the explorers and settlers, the Chamorro population was reduced to 5,000.

Long before the Spanish arrived, the Chamorros maintained a simple and primitive civilization. They sustained themselves primarily through agriculture, hunting and fishing. In prehistoric times, the Chamorros dug up warriors' and leaders' (known as *maga lahis*) bones one year after their burial and used them to make spear points for hunting. They believed that ancestral spirits, or *taotaomonas*, assisted them in hunting, fishing and warfare against the Spaniards. The average age of adult death at that time was 43.5 years.

According to Gary Heathcote, of the University of Guam, Douglas Hanson, of the Forsyth Institute for Advance Research in Boston, and Bruce Anderson of the Army Central Identification Lab of Hickam Air Force Base in Hawaii, 14 to 21 percent of these ancient warriors "were unique with respect to all human populations, past and present by the presence of cranial outgrowths on the backs of Chamoru [Chamorro] skulls where the tendons of trapezius shoulder muscles attach." The information provided by Guam's official cultural page adds that the study indicated these characteristics were found only in indigenous (native) Mariana Islanders, and later on Tonga. The causes for such a body structure points to the following facts about the natives: 1) carrying heavy loads at the sides; 2) power lifting heavy loads with neck forwardly flexed; 3) mining/limestone quarrying; 4) transporting heavy loads by use of a tumpline (a broad band passed across the forehead and over the shoulders to support a pack on the back); 5) long-distance canoeing and navigation; and, 6) underwater swimming/spear fishing.

The Latte Stone of Guam gave further insight into Guam's ancient past. They are stone pillars of ancient houses, constructed in two pieces. One was the supporting column, or *halagi*, topped with a capstone, or *tasa*. These have been only on the Mariana Islands. Latte Park is located in the capital city of Agana, the stones having been moved from their original location at Me'pu, on Guam's southern interior. The ancient natives buried the bones of their ancestors under these, as well as jewelry or canoes they might have owned. The social structure of the Chamorros was divided into three groups. These were the Matua, the nobility, who lived along the coast; the Mana'chang, the lower caste, who lived in the interior; and, the third, a caste of medicine, or spirit Manmakahnas. The warring struggles existed between the Matua and Mana'chang before the Spanish landed. The two castes, according to missionary accounts, settled the island in two separate immigration waves, explaining their conflicting co-existence. These were the ancestors of present-day Guamanians, who eventually mixed blood with various settlers, including Asians, Europeans, and peoples from the Americas.

The Spanish administered Guam as a part of the Philippines. Trade developed with the Philippines and with Mexico, but for native Guamanians, whose numbers were brutalized by the conquering country, survival occurred at subsistence levels throughout the Spanish rule. They were considered a colony of Spain, yet did not enjoy the economic progress that Spain cultivated in other colonies. The Jesuit missionaries, however, taught the Chamorros to cultivate maize (corn), raise cattle, and tan hides.

MODERN ERA

The Treaty of Paris, which designated the end of the Spanish-American War in 1898, ceded Guam to the United States. After ruling Guam for more than 375 years, Spain relinquished their control. U.S. President William McKinley placed Guam under the administration of the Department of the Navy. The naval government brought improvements to the islanders through agriculture, public health and sanitation, education, management of land, taxes, and public works.

Immediately following the Japanese attack on Pearl Harbor on December 7, 1941, Japan occupied Guam. The island was renamed "Omiya Jima," or "Great Shrine Island." Throughout the occupation, Guamanians remained loyal to the United States. In a plea to include Guam's inclusion in the World War II Memorial planned as an addition to the other memorials in the nation's capital, Delegate Robert A. Underwood (D-Guam) noted that, "The years 1941 to 1944 were a time of great hardship and privation for the Chamorros of Guam. Despite the brutality of the Japanese occupying forces, the Chamorros, who were American nationals, remained steadfastly loyal to the United States. Consequently, their resistance and civil disobedience to conquest further contributed to the brutality of the occupation." Underwood went on to point out that hundreds of young Guamanian men have served in the U.S. armed forces. "Six of Guam's young men are entombed in the USS Arizona Memorial at Pearl Harbor," Underwood said. "During the defense of Wake Island, dozens of young men from Guam, who were working for Pan American and the U.S. Navy, gallantly participated alongside Marines in combat against the Japanese invaders." Liberation Day came on July 21, 1944; but the war continued for three more weeks and claimed thousands of lives before Guam was again quiet and restored to American rule. Until the end of the war on September 2, 1945, Guam was used as a command post for U.S. Western Pacific operations.

On May 30, 1946, the naval government was re-established and the United States began rebuilding Guam. The capital city of Agana was bombed heavily during the recapture of the island from the Japanese, and had to be completely rebuilt. U.S. military build-up also began. Mainland Americans, many of them connected to the military, surged into Guam. In 1949 President Harry S. Truman signed the Organic Act, which established Guam as an unincorporated territory, with limited self-rule. In 1950, Guamanians were given U.S. citizenship. In 1962 President John F. Kennedy lifted the Naval Clearing Act. Consequently, western and Asian cultural groups moved to Guam, and made it their permanent home. Filipinos, Americans, Europeans, Japanese, Korean, Chinese, Indian, and other Pacific Islanders were included in that group. When Pan American Airways began air service from Japan in 1967, the tourism industry for the island also began.

THE FIRST GUAMANIANS ON THE AMERICAN MAINLAND

Since 1898 Guamanians have arrived on the United States mainland in small numbers, primarily set-

This Guamanian
boy has enjoyed a
day of playing
outside.

tling in California. Guamanians who began migrating to the mainland United States following World War II, some of whom worked for the U.S. government or military, represented more significant numbers. By 1952 Guamanians living in the Washington, D.C. area established The Guam Territorial Society, later known as The Guam Society of America. The Chamorros had moved to Washington to work for the Department of Defense and military operations, and for the educational opportunities afforded them through citizenship. In 1999, family memberships in The Guam Society of America numbered 148. Guamanians in the United States have settled throughout Hawaii, California, and Washington State, in addition to Washington, D.C. Due to their citizenship status, once a Guamanian moves to one of the 50 states, and is considered a resident, full benefits of citizenship can be enjoyed, including the right to vote.

SIGNIFICANT IMMIGRATION WAVES

Guamanians do not represent a large number of people. Even with the 1997 estimate of 153,000 Guam residents, with 43 percent of them native Guamanians, immigration by any standards would be different from the vast numbers of immigrants from other cultural groups, past and present. Not until the 2000 census would Pacific Islanders as a whole be separated from Asians in the count. Until then, statistics of the number of Guamanians, especially those living in the United States itself, are difficult to determine.

ACCULTURATION AND ASSIMILATION

Under Spanish rule, the native Chamorros were expected to adopt Spanish customs, and religion. For some of them, that proved deadly, as they succumbed to the European diseases the Spanish brought with them. They managed to maintain their identity, even as the population diminished throughout the years of struggle with their Spanish conquerors. The ancient customs, legends, and language remained alive among their descendants throughout Guam and the United States. Because the Chamorro culture was matrilineal, with descent traced through the mother's line, a fact unrecognized by the Spanish when they removed young male warriors through battle, or displaced from their island homes, the traditions did not die. The matriarchs, or *I Maga Hagas*, represented the strength of the Chamorros throughout the years of Spanish conquest and through modern times, when assimilation threatened the culture. Furthermore, the village churches have remained the center of village life since the seventeenth century.

TRADITIONS, CUSTOMS, AND BELIEFS

Ancient Chamorro legends reveal the heart and soul of native Guamanian identity. The Guamanians believe they were born of the islands themselves. The name of the city of Agana, known as *Hagatna* in the Chamarro language, is from the tale of the formation of the islands. Agana was the capital and the seat of government of the island since recorded history there began. The ancient Chamorro legends tell the story of the island's beginnings. Fu'una used the parts of the body of her dying brother, Puntan, to create the world. His eyes were the sun and moon, his eyebrows were rainbows, his chest the sky and his back the earth. Then Fu'una turned herself into a rock, from which all humans originated. *Agana*, or *Hagatna*, means blood. It is the lifeblood of the larger body called Guahan, or Guam. *Hagatna* is the lifeblood of the government. In fact, most of the parts of the island refer to the human body; for example, *Urunao*, the head; *Tuyan*, the belly; and *Barrigada*, the flank.

According to the Guam Culture webpage, "The core culture, or *Kostumbren Chamoru*, was comprised of complex social protocol centered upon respect." These ancient customs included kissing the hands of elders; the passing of legends, chants, courtship rituals; canoe making; the making of the *Belembautuyan*, a stringed musical instrument; making slings and sling stones; burial rituals, preparation of herbal medicines by *suruhanas*, and a person requesting forgiveness from spiritual ancestors upon entering a jungle.

The chewing of betelnut, also known in Chamorro as *Pugua*, or *Mama'on*, is a tradition passed from grandparent to grandchild. The tree that produces the hard nuts is the *areca catechu*, and resembles a thin coconut palm tree. Guamanians and other Pacific Islanders chew betelnuts as Americans chew gum. Sometimes, betel leaves are also chewed along with the nuts. The leaves of the tree has a green pepper taste. Each island has its own species, and each species tastes different from each other. Guamanian islanders chew the hard red-colored nut variety called *ugam*, due to its fine, granular texture. When that is out of season, the coarse white *changnga* is chewed instead. This is an old tradition that Chamorros do not question, but include naturally as a part of any social event. Friends and strangers alike are invited to partake. Archaeological investigations of prehistoric skeletons show that ancient Chamorros also had betel-stained teeth. And as with their modern counterparts, the changes that occur in the enamel of the teeth, are what also prevents cavities. Chamorros usually chew Betelnut after a meal, often mixed with powdered lime and wrapped in the peppery leaves.

Another important tradition to Guamanians and other Pacific Islanders was canoe building, or carving. For the ancient Chamorros, navigation of rough waters was a spiritual undertaking as much as it initially served other purposes in hunting, fishing and travel. Modern day Pacific Islanders again embrace the tradition as another part of restoring their cultural history.

Inafa'maolek, or interdependence, was at the root of Chamorro culture, and was passed on even to modern generations who left the island. Guamanians working to help defend America from the Japanese during World War II demonstrated this spirit in their concern for not only their own welfare, but that of the United States. The following proverb sums up these various customs: "*I erensia, lina'la', espiriitu-ta,*"—"Our heritage gives life to our spirit."

CUISINE

Native island delicacies constituted the original simple diet of the Chamorros. The island provided fresh fish, *escabeche*, shrimp patties, red rice, coconut, *ahu*, bananas, *bonelos*, and other tropical fruits. A hot sauce native to Guam, *finadene*, remained a favorite spice alongside fish. The sauce is made with soy sauce, lemon juice or vinegar, hot peppers, and onions. As Asians settled on the island, Chinese and Japanese food combined with other ethnic cuisine provided a variety of foods. Guamanian celebrations throughout the island and the United States usually include fish, or the dish *kelaguen*, made from chopped broiled chicken, lemon juice, grated coconut, and hot peppers. The Filipino noodle dish, *pancit*, along with barbecued ribs and chicken, have become popular among Guamanians during celebrations.

TRADITIONAL COSTUMES

Native costumes were typical of many other Pacific islands. Natural fibers from the island were woven into short cloths for the men, and grass skirts and blouses for the women. In celebrations, Chamorro women also adorned their hair with flowers. The Spanish influence appears in the *mestiza*, a style of clothing village women still wear.

DANCES AND SONGS

The music of the Guamanian culture is simple, rhythmic, and tells the stories and legends of the island's history. The *Belembautuyan*, made from a hollow gourd and strung with taut wire, is a stringed musical instrument native to Guam. The nose flute, an instrument from ancient times, made a return at the end of the twentieth century. The Chamorros style of singing was born from their workday. The *Kantan* started with one person giving a four-line chant, often a teasing verse to another person in the group of workers. That person would pick up the song, and continue in the same fashion. The songs could continue this way for hours.

Other contemporary songs and dances also represented the many cultures that settled in Guam. The folk dances of the Chamorros portrayed the legends about the ancient spirits, doomed lovers leaping to their death off Two Lovers' Point (*Puntan Dos Amantes*) or about Sirena, the beautiful young girl who became a mermaid. The official Song of Guam, written by Dr. Ramon Sablan in English and translated into Chamoru, speaks of Guamanians' faith and perseverance:

> Stand ye Guamanians, for your country
> And sing her praise from shore to shore
> For her honor, for her glory
> Exalt our Island forever more
> May everlasting peace reign o'er us
> May heaven's blessing to us come
> Against all perils, do not forsake us
> God protect our Isle of Guam
> Against all perils, do not forsake us
> God protect our Isle of Guam.

HOLIDAYS

Guamanians are U.S. citizens, and therefore celebrate all of the major U.S. holidays, especially July 4th. Liberation Day, July 21, celebrates the day that American forces landed on Guam during World War II and marked an end to Japanese occupation. The first Monday in March is celebrated as Guam Discovery Day. On the island itself, due to the dominance of Roman Catholicism, the feast of saints and other Church holy days are observed. Each of the 19 villages has its own patron saint, and each holds a fiesta, or festival, in that saint's honor on the feast day. The entire village celebrates with Mass, a procession, dancing, and food.

HEALTH ISSUES

An issue of major concern to most native Guamanians and Guamanian Americans is Amyotrophic Lateral Sclerosis, or ALS, a disease also known as Lou Gehrig's disease, named after the famous New York Yankee ballplayer who lost his life to it. The incidence of ALS among Guamanians is disproportionately high when compared to other cultural groups— enough so to have one strain of the disease called "Guamanian." Records from the Guam from 1947 to 1952 indicate that all of the patients admitted for ALS were Chamorro. According to Oliver Sacks in *The Island of the Colorblind*, even the Chamorros who had migrated to California showed the incidence of *lytico-bodig*, the native term for the disease that affects muscle control and is ultimately fatal. Sacks noted that the researcher John Steele, a neurologist who had devoted his career to practicing throughout Micronesia during the 1950s also noted that these Chamorros often did not contract the disease until 10 or 20 years after their migration. The non-Chamorros immigrants seemed to develop the disease 10 or 20 years after they moved to Guam. Neither the discovery of the disease's origins or a cure for it had been occurred by the end of the twentieth century. Although many causes have been hypothesized regarding why the incidence is high among Chamorros, a conclusion has yet to be made.

An American Association of Retired Persons study indicated that U.S. Pacific Islanders over age 65 show a higher incidence of cancer, hypertension, and tuberculosis; the study did separate the various cultures represented to indicate the validity of those figures specific to Guamanians. An explanation for the higher incidence of these diseases is that older Pacific Islanders—due to financial reasons and ancient customs and superstitions—are less likely to consult a physician at a time when these diseases might be controlled.

LANGUAGE

Chamoru, the ancient language of the Chamorros on Guam, and English are both official languages in Guam. Chamoru remains intact as younger generations continue to learn and speak it. The Guam Society of America is responsible for heightening awareness of the language in the United States. Chamorus' origins can be traced back 5,000 years and belongs to the western group of the Austronesian language family. The languages of Indonesia, Malaysia, the Philippines, and Palau, are all included in this group. Since Spanish and American influences merged on the island, the Chamoru language has evolved to include many Spanish and English words. Besides Spanish and English, other immigrants to Guam brought their own languages, including Filipino, Japanese, and many other Asian and Pacific Islander tongues. An important Chamoru expression is *Hafa Adai*, which is translated as "Welcome." For the hospitable Guamanians, nothing is as important as welcoming friends and strangers to their country, and to their homes.

FAMILY AND COMMUNITY DYNAMICS

Guamanians in the United States and on the island view family as the center of cultural life, and extend that to the community surrounding them. As expressed, the notion of interdependence among everyone in a community is vital to the cooperation that runs a society. Chamorro culture is a matriarchy, meaning that the women are central to the culture's survival. In ancient times, men were traditionally warriors, leaving women to run the operation of daily life. In modern culture, especially in America, where education has offered the Guamanians greater opportunity to improve their economic status, women and men work together to support the family.

Due to the Catholicism practiced by most Guamanians, weddings, baptisms, and funerals are celebrated with solemn significance. The Chamorro customs have blended with the customs of other cultures settled there, and those of the mainland United States. The respect of elders remains a time-honored practice observed among Guamanians. Some ancient customs linger into modern day culture, including those related to courtship, burial, and honoring dead ancestors. Modern-day Guamanians are a blend of several different ethnic groups and cultures.

EDUCATION

Education is required among islanders between the ages of six and 16. Guamanians living in the 50 states, have fostered a strong appreciation for education among the younger generations as a means to improve their economic status. An increasing number of Guamanians have entered the professions of law and medicine. The University of Guam offers a four-year degree program. Many Guamanian Americans also enter colleges and universities from parochial Catholic schools with the intention of entering a profession, or the business sector.

INTERACTIONS WITH OTHER ETHNIC GROUPS

Guamanians have become a vital part of the Asian-American community. The younger generation has become involved in organizations such as the Atlantic Coast Asian American Student Union (ACAASU). In January of 1999, the group met at the University of Florida for their ninth annual conference. They include all Asians and Pacific Islanders. The ability of such a diverse group of cultures to find common bonds proved challenging, but rewarding, according to students who participated in the conference. The ACAASU provides a forum where all Asian Americans and Pacific Islanders of college age can share their stories and their concerns.

The Pork Filled Players of Seattle, an Asian comedy troupe, formed to reflect Asian issues and topics. The ethnicities represented in that group include Japanese, Chinese, Filipino, Vietnamese, Taiwanese, Guamanian, Hawaiian, and Caucasian Americans. The purpose of the group is to present images different from the often negative stereotypes of Asian Americans, in addition to making people laugh at those aspects of the culture that are not stereotypical.

RELIGION

The majority of Guamanians are Roman Catholic, a religion that represents approximately four-fifths of the population on the island, as well as that of Guamanians living in the 50 states. Since the first Spanish missionaries settled the island in the seventeenth century, when the Chamorros converted at the encouragement and sometimes mandate of the Spanish, Catholicism continued to dominate. As with other primitive cultures converted to Catholicism, the rituals of the Roman Catholics were often found suitable in the environment of their own ancient native superstitions and rituals. Some ancient customs were not abandoned, only

enhanced by the new faith. Pope John Paul II visited Guam in February of 1981. It marked the first papal visit in the history of the island. The Pope concluded remarks upon his arrival with, ""*Hu guiya todos hamyu,*" in Chamoru ("I love all of you," in English) and was warmly received by natives and other residents. From his outdoor Mass to his visit to the infirm at the Naval Regional Medical Center, Pope John Paul II affirmed the continued devotion thousands of Guamanians maintain for the Catholic Church.

Congregationalists arrived on Guam in 1902, and established their own mission, but were forced to abandon it in 1910, due to the lack of financial support. The following year, Americans who were with the General Baptist Foreign Missionary Society moved into the abandoned Congregationalist mission. In 1921, the Baptists built Guam's first modern Protestant church on a grander scale than the previous missions. A Baptist church built in 1925 in Inarajan was still in use in the mid-1960s. After World War II, the Seventh Day Adventists established missions in Guam, first by a Navy chief, Harry Metzker. The first congregation consisted entirely of military families, except for the family of a local woman of Dededo. The Seventh Day Adventists, who were well known for much of the twentieth century for their attention to health and well-being, also set up a clinic in Agana Heights. The Adventists operate hospitals throughout United States. They are considered at the front of treating various eating disorders, including anorexia nervosa and bulimia.

EMPLOYMENT AND ECONOMIC TRADITIONS

Half of the economy on the island of Guam emerged from American military establishment and related government services. A majority of Guamanians have been employed by the U.S. government and military, serving as cooks, office personnel, and other administrative positions, advancing to the upper-levels of the government salary tracks following years of service. The tourism industry is the second largest employer on the island. Other industries include agriculture (mostly for local consumption), commercial poultry farming, and small assembly plants for watches and machinery, brewery, and textiles.

According to Arthur Hu in *Order of Ethnic Diversity*, Guamanian income falls below the U.S. average. His figures indicated that the average household income of Guamanians was $30,786 in 1990. The American Association for Retired Persons offered that the income of Asian and Pacific Islander men over age 65 was $7,906—in contrast to $14,775 among white Americans men. Thirteen percent of Asian and Pacific Islander women over 65 live in poverty, in contrast to 10 percent of white American women over 65.

POLITICS AND GOVERNMENT

At the end of the twentieth century, the issues of politics and government were complicated, both for those Guamanians living on the island, and for those living in the mainland, who felt loyalty to their native land. The Guam Commonwealth Act was first introduced in to Congress in 1988, following two plebiscites by the people of Guam. (A plebiscite refers to an expression of the people's will by a direct ballot, usually, as in this case, a vote that calls for independent statehood, or affiliation with another nation). In an article for the Associated Press, Michael Tighe quoted Rep. Underwood: "The core, American democratic creed is that the only legitimate form of government is by consent of the governed. How do you deal with the fact the people on Guam are not participants in the legislative process?" As U.S. citizens, they can enter the military, but are not able to vote for the President. The representative they elect to Congress can vote only in committees.

Underwood published the document, along with an explanation, on his official website. As the terms are officially listed, the Guam Commonwealth Act held five major portions: 1) Creation of Commonwealth and the Right of Self-Determinism, under which a three-branch republican form of government would be established, and would allow the indigenous people of Guam (the Chamoros) to choose their preference for their final political status; 2) Immigration Control, which would allow the people of Guam to limit immigration to prevent further reduction of the indigenous population, and allow the people of Guam to enforce an immigration policy more appropriate for a developing economy in Asia; 3) Commercial, Economic, and Trade Matters, under which various specific negotiated authorities which allow consideration of Guam as an identifiably unique economy in Asia, and requiring certain approaches to managing such matters with full benefit both to Guam and to the United States, as well as maintaining status outside customs zone, with representation in regional economic organizations, recognition of local control of resources; 4) the Application of Federal Laws, which would provide a mechanism to allow for input from the people of Guam through its elected leadership as regards the appropriateness of a U.S. law or regulation and as applied to Guam—Guam would prefer a "joint commission" appointed by the President with final authority in Congress; and, 5) Mutual Consent, meaning that neither party could make arbitrary decision that would alter the provisions of the Guam Commonwealth Act. By early 1999, commonwealth status had not yet been determined. Opposition from President Clinton, and other non-Chamoro Guam residents to the particular point of Chamoro self-determination of the island remained an obstacle.

MILITARY

Guamanians are well represented in the military as enlisted men, officers, and support personnel. They served the United States in World War II without any legal military status. The military is the primary employer of residents on Guam. Among those Guamanian Americans living in the Washington, D.C. area are employees of the Defense Department.

INDIVIDUAL AND GROUP CONTRIBUTIONS

Cecilia, an indigenous poet from Guam, captures the Chamoru history, culture, and spirit in her compilation *Signs of Being—A Chamoru Spiritual Journey*. Her other works include, "Sky Cathedral," "Kafe Mulinu, "Steadfast Woman," "Strange Surroundings" and "Bare-Breasted Woman."

MEDIA

Guamanians can learn about their history and culture, and keep in touch with current topics through websites that focus on Guam and Chamoros. Some of the many sites include:

Guam's official website.

Online: http://www.guam.net.

The University of Guam.
Online: http://www.uog2.uog.edu.
A website devoted to Guam culture, history and tourism.

Online: http://www.visitguam.org.
Website featuring stories and news of Guamanians off and on the island, providing the source of news for the Guam Society of America, along with photos, armed forces news, poems, and short stories.

Online: http://www.Offisland.com.
The official Guam government site.

Online: http://www.gadao.gov.gu/.
Representative Robert A. Underwood's website featuring news from the U.S. Congress, current news stories, and other links to various Guam sites.

Online: http://www.house.gov/Underwood.

ORGANIZATIONS AND ASSOCIATIONS

Guam Society of America.
Chartered in 1976 as a non-profit, 501-C3 tax exempt, corporation in the District of Columbia. Founded in 1952 as the *Guam Territorial Society*. Changed name to Guam Society in 1985. Stated purposes are: 1) to foster and encourage educational, cultural, civic and social programs and activities among the members of the Society in the District of Columbia and its surrounding communities, and throughout the United States and its territories. 2) to foster and perpetuate the Chamorro language, culture and traditions. Any Chamorro (a native of Guam, Saipan, or any Marian Islands) or any person who has a bona fide interest in the purposes of the

Society is eligible for membership. The society sponsors events and activities throughout the year that include, Chamorro language classes in the D.C. metropolitan area, a Golf Classic, the Cherry Blossom Princess Ball and Chamorro Night.

Contact: Juan Salas or Juanit Naude.
E-mail: SALASVA@aol.com or
　　JMNaude@erols.com.

SOURCES FOR ADDITIONAL STUDY

Gailey, Harry. *The Liberation of Guam*. Novato, CA: Presidio Press, 1998.

Kerley, Barbara. *Songs of Papa's Island*. Houghton Mifflin, 1995.

Rogers, Robert F. *Destiny's Landfall: A History of Guam*. Honolulu: The University of Hawaii Press, 1995.

Torres, Laura Marie. *Daughters of the Island: Contemporary Chamorro Women Organizers on Guam*. University Press of America, 1992.

Although Guatemalan Americans constitute a very small percentage of the American population and are one of the most recently established American ethnic groups, they have contributed significantly to American life through political and cultural organizations and as individuals.

GUATEMALAN AMERICANS

by
Maria Hong

OVERVIEW

The most populous country in Central America, Guatemala is located in the northern part of the Central American region. Its land mass encompasses 42,042 square miles (108,889 square kilometers), bordered by Mexico to the north and west, El Salvador and Honduras to the south and east, the Pacific Ocean along its West Coast, and Belize and the Caribbean Sea to the north and east. The southern half of the Republic of Guatemala mainly consists of beautiful mountain highlands and plateaus, which are susceptible to devastating earthquakes. The northern region contains the department of the Petén, a sparsely populated lowland tropical jungle. There is also a narrow Pacific coastal plain and a small Caribbean lowland area. Most of Guatemala's population and its major cities, including the capital, Guatemala City, are located in the southern region.

Guatemala has a population of about ten million people and the largest indigenous population in Central America. Although estimates of the indigenous population vary greatly from as low as 40 percent of the total population to as high as 85 percent, most sources estimate it at over 50 percent. Most of the indigenous groups are Mayan, although small numbers of Pipil Aztecs live in the southern and eastern areas and Xincas in the east. More than a racial classification, the term *indigena* (indigenous) refers to cultural and linguistic groups.

The population of Spanish-speaking *ladinos* consists of the small Caucasian elite class; the substantial number of *mestizos* of mixed Spanish and indigenous race; minorities of African, Chinese, and Arab descent; and indigenous people who no longer consciously identify themselves as such. Guatemala's smallest ethnic group is the Garifuna, descendants of African and Carib people formerly from the island of St. Vincent who reside along the Caribbean coast.

Guatemala's official language is Spanish. However, the Maya speak over 20 distinct languages and numerous dialects, and many do not speak Spanish. The four main Mayan languages—Quiché, Mam, Cakchiquel, and Kekchi—are spoken by about 40 percent of the population. Other indigenous languages include Kanjobal, Chuj, Jacalteco, Ixil, Achi, Pocomchi, Central Pocomam, Eastern Pocomam, and Tzutuhil. These languages are spoken by distinct indigenous groups.

Although Roman Catholicism is the dominant religion, many Mayan Guatemalans have traditionally practiced a syncretist form of Catholicism, blending Catholic and Mayan rites and beliefs. Since the 1950s, Evangelical Pentecostal Protestantism has been on the rise in Guatemala, and it surged in popularity during the 1980s. Two modern presidents have been Evangelical Pentecostal Protestants and up to one-third of the population now practices this religion.

Guatemala's national symbol of independence and pride is the quetzal, a brilliantly colored tropical bird native to Central America. According to legend, the quetzal lost its voice after the Spanish Conquest in the sixteenth century.

HISTORY

Guatemala's roots lie in the great Mayan civilization, concentrated in separate city-states established throughout what is now southern Mexico and Central America. From 2000 B.C. through 900 A.D., Mayan civilization accomplished much in the areas of astronomy, written language, architecture, the arts, and religion. Some of these achievements remain for us to appreciate today, such as the immense stone temples and pyramids at Tikal in the Petén.

However, the Mayan city-states were also very militaristic, usually warring with each other and devoting much of their energies and resources to military efforts. This penchant for warfare may have contributed to the mysterious disappearance of Mayan civilization by 900 A.D. By the time the Spanish arrived, there were about one million indigenous people whose violent feuding facilitated their conquest. By 1650, most of the indigenous people had been wiped out by disease, war, and exploitation, and their numbers had dwindled to about 200,000.

From 1523 to 1524, the Spanish, led by Pedro de Alvarado, colonized many Mayan city-states. De Alvarado became the first captain general of Guatemala, which then encompassed most of Central America. In 1821, Guatemala gained independence from Spain, and in 1824 it joined the Central American Federation. In 1838, the Federation disbanded, due mostly to a revolt against it led by an indigenous general, Rafael Carrera, who then seized control of the newly independent nation of Guatemala.

In 1871, a liberal *caudillo* or military dictator, Justo Rufino Barrios, took power and ruled as president from 1873 to 1885. Barrios enacted anticlerical legislation, began to establish a national education system, and fostered the inception of Guatemala's coffee industry. Guatemala was ruled by a succession of military dictators until the last *caudillo*, Jorge Ubico, was overthrown in 1944. Shortly thereafter, Juan Jose Arevalo, a university professor exiled to Argentina, was called back and elected president. Arevalo instituted political democracy in Guatemala, encouraging organized labor, the formation of a social security system, and industrialization.

Arevalo's successor, Colonel Jacobo Arbenz Guzman, introduced a radical agrarian reform program that redistributed land from wealthy landowners and much of the holdings of the U.S.-based United Fruit Company. United Fruit had dominated the commercial banana industry and exploited peasant workers since the early twentieth century. Arbenz's challenge to United Fruit and his support of Guatemala's Communist party resulted in conflict with the company and U.S. President Dwight D. Eisenhower's administration. In mid-1954, Arbenz was overthrown by a U.S.-supported, largely CIA-directed revolt, led by Colonel Carlos Castillo Armas.

During the next 30 years, most of the agrarian and labor reforms achieved under Arevalo and Arbenz were undone by a succession of mostly military rulers. Since the 1960s, leftist guerrillas have attempted to undermine these regimes, while right-wing paramilitary death squads have fought back against the guerrillas by brutally repressing the civilian population. According to Amnesty International, at least 20,000 civilians were killed by the death squads from 1966 to 1976.

During the late 1970s, a popular resistance

movement to the military governments began to operate through a collaboration among *ladinos, indigenas*, peasants, labor leaders, students, journalists, politicians, and Catholic priests. In response, the army and paramilitary counterinsurgency units stepped up their repression efforts. From 1980 to 1981, guerrilla forces encouraged and sometimes coerced large numbers of highland *indigenas* to join them in their armed revolutionary efforts. The army retaliated by massacring whole indigenous villages; kidnapping, torturing, and murdering people suspected of supporting the guerrillas; and scorching peasant crops and homes.

Although the army's terrorism techniques affected all sectors of the resistance movements, indigenous communities suffered the brunt of the violence of the 1980s. Most authorities have called the military efforts an ethnic genocide campaign, stemming from pervasive discrimination against *indigenas* in Guatemalan society. In addition to destroying indigenous villages, the government army forced more than one million indigenas into military-controlled "model villages" and "reeducation camps," and conscripted men into the army's civil defense patrols.

Violence in the villages peaked under Efrain Rios Montt, a Pentecostal Protestant, who became president through a military coup in 1982. By the army's own count, the counterinsurgency movement destroyed 440 villages and damaged numerous others between 1980 and 1984. Widespread terrorism continued under Rios Montt's successor Brigadier General Oscar Humberto Mejia Victores, who became president in 1983. In 1984, the Guatemalan Supreme Court reported that around 100,000 children had lost at least one parent in the massacres.

In 1985, Marco Vinicio Cerezo Arevalo, a Christian Democratic Party leader, won the presidential election, initiating a transition from military to civilian government. Cerezo tried unsuccessfully to carry out reforms, and political killings by the right-wing death squads continued. He was succeeded in 1991 by Jorge Serrano Elias, an Evangelical Protestant and former member of the Rios Montt regime.

Although right-wing violence persisted, Serrano's government reached a tentative accord with the major guerrilla coalition, the Guatemalan National Revolutionary Unity (URNG) and police and military men were arrested for death-squad activity for the first time. In 1993, Serrano and military leaders attempted to dissolve Guatemala's Congress and suspend the constitution. After a short period of political turmoil, the Congress elect-ed Ramiro de Leon Carpio, a former human rights ombudsman, as president.

De Leon Carpio resumed the peace talks between the government and the URNG, which had been going on intermittently since 1991, and he has made significant breakthroughs in the peace process. On March 29, 1994, the government and the URNG signed three peace agreements brokered by the United Nations. Among other provisions, the agreements call for human rights investigations and monitoring, guerrilla demobilization, and prosecution of human rights violators.

Despite the achievements of the peace accords, however, widespread violence, including abductions, torture, and executions by army and paramilitary men, continues in Guatemala. In the political arena, the Guatemalan Republican Front, the right-wing party of Rios Montt, gained many seats in the Congress and Rios Montt himself was elected to the Congress in August of 1994. Members of the Party of National Advancement, another conservative party that opposes de Leon Carpio, also won many Congressional seats. In December of 1996 the long civil war finally ended when rebels and the government announced a peace treaty.

Sixty-three percent of the population lives in extreme poverty. In this mostly rural, agrarian country, two percent of the population owns over 64 percent of the arable land. Peasants survive by farming sub-subsistence land or by doing seasonal migratory work on coastal coffee, sugar, and cotton plantations. Among Central American nations, Guatemala has the highest infant and child mortality rates, the lowest life expectancy, and most malnourished population, with rampant severe hunger.

The efforts of activists such as Guatemalan Nobel Peace Laureate Rigoberta Menchú Tum have focused international attention on the oppression of indigenous people in Guatemala. However, an apartheid-type of oligarchic system remains entrenched with the government and other power centers controlled by a small European-descended minority. The long armed conflict has resulted in the disappearnce or murder of tens of thousands of people and the displacement of over a million more. Although several hundred thousand Guatemalans remain uprooted within Guatemala, hundreds of thousands have fled to the United States and Mexico to escape the violence since the late 1970s.

IMMIGRATION TO THE UNITED STATES

Until 1960, the United States did not keep separate statistics on the number of immigrants from Guatemala, and figures reflect migration from the entire Central American region. However, it is fair to conclude that few Guatemalans immigrated to the United States before 1960, since the numbers for all Central American immigrants were small.

During the 1830s, only 44 arrivals of Central Americans were recorded. Between 1890 and 1900, 500 Central Americans immigrated to the United States according to records of legal migration. The numbers increased during the next two decades, with 8,000 arriving from 1900 to 1910 and 17,000 migrating between 1910 and 1920. Emigrants from Guatemala may have been seeking a better life following a devastating earthquake in 1917.

During the 1930s, the number of immigrants fell to less than 6,000 in the decade, due in part to quotas on immigration from Western Hemisphere nations enacted in the 1920s. However, since the mid-1950s the annual number of legally admitted Central Americans has steadily risen, with 45,000 arriving from 1951 to 1960.

Due to political upheavals and related economic crises throughout the region, large numbers of undocumented Guatemalans and other Central Americans have been coming to the United States since the late 1970s. During the early 1970s, several factors, including inflation, political turmoil and violence, unemployment, low wages, land scarcity due to inequitable land allocation, and the population explosion, especially among indigenous people, precipitated the mass internal and external displacement of Guatemalan *campesino* peasants, *indigenas*, and professionals. In February of 1976, an earthquake destroyed much of Guatemala City, causing some to emigrate. From 1967 to 1976, 19,683 Guatemalans immigrated to the United States, and the 1970 U.S. Census recorded a Guatemalan American population of 26,865 persons. The 1980 U.S. Census recorded 62,098 Guatemalan Americans, with 46 percent arriving from 1975 to 1980.

However, the vast majority of the Guatemalan American population has arrived since 1980. Official immigration statistics do not reflect the true number of immigrants from Guatemala since most arrivals are undocumented refugees. In 1984, there were an estimated one million Guatemalan refugees, with many displaced within Guatemala and hundreds of thousands fleeing to Mexico and the United States. Thousands also escaped to neighboring Belize, Costa Rica, Nicaragua, and Honduras.

Since the 1920s or earlier, Mayan Guatemalans had traveled annually to southern Mexico to work on seasonal coffee harvests, attracted by the wages and low cost of living. Others possibly planned to sell contraband items upon their return home. By the late 1950s, ten to fifteen thousand men and women were crossing the border into Mexico and back every year. In the 1960s and 1970s, the number increased to around 60,000 annually; some of these settled in the state of Chiapas in southern Mexico, where Mayan communities also reside. After the massacres of Mayan villages in Guatemala, *indigenas* from the departments of Quiché, Alta Verapaz, Huehuetenango, Itzabal, and the Petén fled to this region, and many seasonal workers remained in Mexico. Refugee camps were established in Chiapas and in Campeche and Quintana Roo. Due to the desperate economic and health conditions in these camps many Guatemalan refugees moved on to the United States, often enduring great hardships on the way. Migration spurred by these circumstances continues today.

Since they must cross the border illegally, the emigrants usually hire guides called *coyotes*, who facilitate the crossings for high fees costing up to $1,500 per person. During the trips many experience graft, robbery, rape, or imprisonment by people who exploit their precarious status. Some are smuggled to the United States by religious workers who also give them sanctuary once they arrive. Due to the expense of the trip, those who migrate to the United States are not generally the poorest of the poor.

According to the 1970 U.S. Census, 90 percent of Guatemalans in the United States were white. During the 1950s and 1960s most Guatemalan immigrants were middle class. Before the 1980s, most Guatemalan political emigrants were *ladino* activists and politicians from urban centers. After 1980 large numbers of indigenous people and *campesinos* fled to the United States from counter-insurgency campaigns in the western highland areas. Significant numbers of schoolteachers, student activists, journalists, and other professionals accused of being guerrilla sympathizers also migrated for political reasons. More than 300,000 Guatemalans have entered the United States illegally since 1980.

The United States has not recognized Guatemalans as political refugees. Most recent immigrants from Guatemala are considered economic migrants, and only one to two percent of Guatemalan requests for political asylum are granted. Many sources state that immigration officials view Guatemalan asylum cases less favorably than those from applicants from other countries where human rights abuses are common, because U.S. refugee policy is politicized. They say that the United States has historically granted asylum to people fleeing Communist regimes rather than those from countries the United States is friendly with. Immigration officials deny bias in assessing asylum cases.

Illegal migrants who are caught by the Immigration and Naturalization Service are usually deported back to Guatemala, where they may face dangerous situations as repatriates. Some Guatemalan migrants travel to Canada, where they can receive refugee status. Despite the threat of deportation, the difficulty of the trip to the United States, and problems here as undocumented persons, Guatemalans have continued to arrive in the United States and are one of the fastest growing American immigrant groups.

SETTLEMENT PATTERNS

According to the 1990 U.S. Census, there are 268,779 persons of Guatemalan origin in the United States. The 1990 Census also listed 225,739 foreign-born persons from Guatemala, reflecting the large portion of recent immigrants among Guatemalan Americans. However, the actual number of Guatemalan Americans is higher than the census figures, since many are migratory and/or undocumented and thus reluctant to have contact with officials. In reality, there are probably over half a million Guatemalan Americans, and they are the second largest group among Central Americans after Salvadorans.

Guatemalan Americans have settled primarily in cities with large existing Latino communities. The greatest number—probably over 100,000—are in Los Angeles, where the biggest concentration of Central Americans in the United States resides. There are also significant numbers of Guatemalan Americans in Houston, Chicago, New York City, Washington D.C., southern Florida, and San Francisco. Smaller enclaves are found in Miami, New Orleans, Phoenix/Tucson, and other cities in Texas and North Carolina.

During the early 1980s, Phoenix/Tucson became an important center for the Sanctuary Movement, a group of mostly Christian religious organizations that provided sanctuary to illegal migrants from Guatemala and El Salvador. These groups supported migrants in their efforts to gain legal status and helped them obtain work and housing. However, most Guatemalans moved on to other areas cities or towns outside of Arizona.

The communities in Chicago and New York expanded considerably during the mid- to late-1980s. In these cities, Guatemalan Americans tend to be inconspicuous, blending in with the more established Mexican or Cuban American populations, for fear of being detected by the Immigration and Naturalization Service (INS). In the San Francisco Bay area and Washington D.C., Central

Americans predominate among Latinos. A number of wealthy Guatemalan Americans live in Miami, the commerce gateway to Latin America.

Many of the Guatemalan Americans in Los Angeles live in or near the Central American-dominated Pico-Union district. Once primarily a Mexican American area, Pico-Union is now characterized by businesses that cater to Central Americans, including bakeries, restaurants, grocery stores, and social service organizations. A substantial portion of the Guatemalan Americans in Los Angeles and in southern Florida are Kanjobal Mayans. In Houston, there are over a thousand Mayans from the provinces of Totonicapan and Quiché. These indigenous communities represent the best-documented Guatemalan American populations.

Guatemalan Americans have met with both hostility and empathy from the general American public. Many of the negative reactions by "established" Americans have focused on immigration issues. During recent recessions and concurrent waves of anti-immigrant sentiment, Guatemalans and other Central Americans have been depicted as economically threatening migrants who overwhelm government social services and undermine American labor by taking low-paying jobs. However, others have described newly arrived Central Americans as resourceful contributors to the economy.

The U.S. government's refusal to designate Guatemalan emigrants as political refugees and its persecution of Sanctuary Movement workers can also be interpreted as an unsympathetic stance toward Guatemalan Americans. On the other hand, grassroots supporters and many major city governments have defended recent Guatemalan immigrants. In the mid-1980s some members of Congress and at least a dozen cities, including Los Angeles, St. Paul, and Chicago criticized President Ronald Reagan and his administration's federal policy concerning illegal Central Americans and limited city cooperation with INS officials.

Relations with other Latino groups near whom Guatemalan Americans often live have been similarly mixed. The more established Chicano communities have expressed both resentment and support for the newer residents. Sometimes there is rivalry among Central American and Mexican groups for jobs, and cultural differences can preclude social interaction among people of different national origin. A number of Native American groups have been very supportive of indigenous Guatemalan immigrants to United States and empathize with their struggle against genocide and cultural obliteration.

Although there are many Guatemalan Americans whose ancestors came to America generations ago, the key issues facing the group in the near future are generally linked with immigration and their previous lives in Guatemala, since the majority of Guatemalan Americans have arrived since the mid-1980s. Most Guatemalan Americans face a host of challenges in the areas of work, health, and cultural preservation due to their undocumented status and the terrible economic and political conditions they left behind.

ACCULTURATION AND ASSIMILATION

Guatemalan Americans comprise a very culturally diverse group of people. Within Guatemala there are about 23 distinct ethnic groups that speak different languages and maintain unique cultural traditions. The majority of these groups are Mayan; and *ladinos*, or Hispanic Guatemalans, constitute a separate population as persons of Spanish language and culture. Guatemalan Americans represent a broad cross-section of this multicultural society, and assimilation processes, traditional beliefs, and customs vary from group to group. Given the diversity of the Guatemalan American population, it is impossible to generalize about the group as a whole.

Immigrant Mayan American communities have maintained their traditional practices the most visibly. Hispanic Guatemalans have tended to blend in more with other Latino cultures and very little information about them or third-, fourth-, and fifth-generation Guatemalan Americans exists. For instance, no studies have been conducted on how traditions are being passed on beyond the second generation. Further inquiry into these areas is needed and will probably occur as the recent wave of immigrants matures into second- and third-generation adults.

Certain practices like the celebration of *quinceñeros*, the formation of soccer leagues, and the organization of patronal fiestas have been maintained in most of the newer Guatemalan American neighborhoods. Specific Guatemalan American groups in Los Angeles, Houston, and southern Florida have received the most attention from sociologists and the media. The following sections on these three communities illustrate how some Guatemalan traditions are being preserved, transformed, and lost through the process of acculturation.

GUATEMALAN AMERICANS IN LOS ANGELES
Until the late 1970s, Los Angeles's Pico-Union district was populated by Mexican immigrants, Chicanos, African Americans, and European Ameri-

cans. Some Central and South Americans began arriving in the mid-1950s, and after 1980 an influx of Central Americans settled the neighborhood. These Central American immigrants, including university students, teachers, clergy, and *campesinos*, came from all classes and political persuasions. New residents could shop at Latino-owned businesses such as grocery stores, *botánicas* selling religious articles and herbs, dance halls, informal vendors, and record companies specializing in Latino music.

Among the Guatemalan immigrants were Mayan Chujes, Quichés, and Kanjobals. The Kanjobals from the highlands of Huehuetenango near Mexico constitute the largest Mayan group in Los Angeles, with a population of about 4,000 in 1984. Many call themselves *Migueleños* after their hometown of San Miguel Acatán. The first Kanjobal immigrants to Los Angeles came during the late 1970s in search of work, and large numbers followed during the early 1980s, when Kanjobals were targeted as guerrilla sympathizers, and both guerrillas and the army pressured men and boys to fight on their sides.

Coming from an agrarian society, the Kanjobals have made many adjustments to living in urban Los Angeles. Many had not used electricity or cars before. Women who had washed their clothes by hand in rivers became accustomed to coin laundromats. Both men and women encountered unfamiliar appliances such as refrigerators and strange products like hot dogs and commercial cleaning agents in the supermarkets.

To avoid deportation to Guatemala, many have become inconspicuous by passing for Mexican American. For example, women generally do not wear traditional clothing such as the bright embroidered blouses called *huipils* outside the home. Rather than using colorful cloth *rebozos* to carry infants on their backs, they now use baby carriages.

Deeper forms of integration into American society may be more elusive. Jacqueline Maria Hagan, who researched Houston's Mayan community, noted that assimilation can be intimately tied to legalization. Legal status affords the opportunity to develop bonds with the established society in areas like higher education, sports, stable jobs, and access to banks and other institutions. As undocumented immigrants, many Guatemalan Americans cannot interact with mainstream society in these areas.

A few organizations in Los Angeles have formed to promote and preserve Guatemalan and Mayan American culture. A group called Integración de Indígenas Mayas (IXIM), sponsors a range of political and cultural activities to foster community solidarity among Mayans in southern California.

FROM TOTONICAPAN TO HOUSTON

There are approximately 30,000 Guatemalan Americans living in Houston. As in Los Angeles, most Guatemalans emigrated after 1980 to escape political violence and economic repression. Both Hispanics and *indigenas* migrated to Houston, including Mayans from Quiche and Totonicapan in the southwestern highlands.

The thousand or so Mayans have maintained many of their traditional social and cultural customs, and *indigenas* from Totonicapan can depend on a well-developed community for support upon arrival. Life-cycle events such as birthdays, baptisms, weddings, and funerals are celebrated with the involvement of the whole group.

One such event is *quinceñeros*, which is like an elaborate coming-out party for girls celebrating their fifteenth birthdays. *Quinceñeros* is observed by most Guatemalan American groups, although only wealthier families may be able to afford it. Sometimes *padrinos*, or godparents, of the celebrant from the same locale but of higher social standing participate in the event. *Padrinos* have traveled from Totonicapan to Houston to honor *quinceñeros* celebrants and to give away brides.

The marimba, an ancient Mayan instrument made of hormiga wood native to Guatemalan forests, is played by bands at Guatemalan American holiday fiestas and special events throughout the United States. Marimba bands play both popular songs and sacred music and may play all night during certain occasions. The music is often accompanied by festive folk dancing. Another instrument native to the highlands is the flutelike *chirimías*.

Sports and church activities also spur much communal interaction in Guatemalan American communities. Soccer is the most popular national sport, and Guatemalan American men have formed soccer leagues in Los Angeles, Houston, San Francisco, and other cities. In Houston, the Community Soccer Club has played against other immigrant soccer teams on a weekly basis and the sports events have served to raise funds for fiesta in San Cristobal Totonicapan. In Los Angeles, Mayan Americans also play basketball, and both men's and women's tournaments are organized.

Some traditions have been lost upon settlement in the United States. Totonicapan is known as the capital of artisan production in Guatemala, and most of the male immigrants to Houston were previously craft tailors, weavers, or bakers. Since those skills were not transferable to the Houston workplace they have had to make the transition from cottage industry production to wage labor. Women, however, still buy traditional garments from Totonicapan for special events.

Close relations between Guatemalan home villages and Mayan American communities also sustain cultural practices on both ends. Many Guatemalan Americans have close family members remaining in Guatemala. Often they communicate regularly with them by sending letters and cassette tapes back and forth. In the 1980s, couriers traveled monthly between Houston and San Cristobal Totonicapan to deliver news, money, and goods. As they have achieved temporary or permanent residency status, some Guatemalans in Houston have been able to make the trips themselves. Items typically transported include traditional clothing, Guatemalan foods and spices, and occasionally things like wedding bands or other special celebratory objects.

Some families have moved out of the Houston Totonicapan community after gaining legal status and saving enough money. Researcher Hagan saw this as part of a shift toward adopting American Texan culture, which included buying new types of cars and women modernizing their hairstyles and clothes.

KANJOBALS IN SOUTHERN FLORIDA

A small farming town 25 miles inland from the East Coast of Florida called Indiantown is home to several thousand Guatemalan refugees. Along with other migrant workers, the Guatemalan Americans here harvest sugar, oranges, cucumbers, and other crops during the winter growing season. Indiantown derived its name from the Seminole Native Americans who used to inhabit the area, and is the center of the Guatemalan American population of southern Florida, which extends to other small towns like Immokalee.

Most of the Guatemalans in Indiantown are Kanjobals, although there is a small non-Kanjobal speaking group from the mostly *ladino* town of Cuilco. The Kanjobals first arrived in late 1982, when a Mexican American crew boss brought some refugees from Arizona to Indiantown to pick crops. These workers subsequently led family and friends from Kanjobal communities in Los Angeles and Guatemala to the area, and the town became a refuge from both the civil war and urban environments.

As in other Mayan American communities, the tradition of going to the weekly market to exchange news and gossip and buy fresh fruit, meat, and vegetables has been supplanted by going to supermarkets. However, other customs remain intact and the Kanjobals maintain a visible ethnic presence.

Kanjobal marimba players from Indiantown played at the U.S. Folk Festival in 1985 and they also received a grant to teach Kanjobal American teenagers traditional music. The local Catholic Church and Mayan American associations sponsor an annual fiesta in honor of the patron saint of San Miguel Acatán. Committees of men and women organize entertainment, sports, and the election of festival queens who give speeches in Kanjobal, Spanish, and English. Participants wear traditional clothing and teach children how to dance to marimba music. The dances traditionally involve costumed performances with masks made from paper maché, but in the first year of the masked dances, the masks were purchased from a local store. The patronal fiesta functions as an important gathering of Kanjobals who must work and live outside of Indiantown, and as an affirmation of identity.

Although many Mayan Americans have strived to preserve traditions such as these, others eschew former customs. Since acculturation is ultimately a personal choice, degrees of assimilation will vary from individual to individual. As in every other ethnic group, there are many like Mateo Andres, a first-generation Kanjobal American farmworker who told *New York Times* reporter Larry Rohter that he sees no need to pass on Mayan languages or practices and hopes that his newborn son grows up "100 percent American."

STEREOTYPES AND MISCONCEPTIONS

Guatemalan Americans face the stereotypes that have historically plagued almost all immigrant groups in the United States. Like the Irish, Eastern European, Asian, and other groups that have preceded them, Guatemalan Americans have been scapegoated as new immigrants by nativists who depict them as docile, ignorant workers who do not mind being exploited, overwhelm American economic and social resources, and are of little value except as workers in undesirable jobs. During economic recessions, politicians have exploited this anti-immigrant bias to curry favor with constituents who want to blame their financial woes on vulnerable targets rather than coming to terms with the real sources of the problem.

Guatemalan Americans are also generally lumped together with other Central American and Latino groups as indistinguishable from one another. Although there is great diversity within and among the different Central American and Latino groups, the American populace tends to perceive them as one entity, and subjects Guatemalan, Nicaraguan, Salvadoran, Honduran, Mexican, Cuban, and Puerto Rican Americans to the same stereotypes.

CUISINE

Savory sometimes spicy Guatemalan cuisine has its origins in pre-Hispanic foods. Mayan staples such as corn, beans, hot chile peppers, and tomatoes are still the staples of Guatemalan cooking. During the Spanish conquest rice and other European and Asian ingredients were introduced into the cuisine. Guatemalan cooking falls into three categories: the highland indigenous cuisine; the Spanish colonial style cultivated by *ladinos;* and the food of the Caribbean coast town Livingston. The last style of cooking developed with the culinary input of indentured laborers from India and Africa and it resembles the cuisine of Belize. Unlike the other two kinds of Guatemalan cooking, this type is tropical and uses a lot of seafood, coconut, and bananas in its recipes.

The indigenous and Spanish styles are much more prevalent and are somewhat intermixed. They make use of many of the vegetables and fruits native to the New World. Some of the most popular ingredients include *chayote* or *huisquil,* a pear-shaped vegetable with firm, deep to pale green skin, which can be boiled, fried, mashed, baked, or used in salads and deserts; *cilantro* or *culantro,* a green, leafy herb otherwise known as Chinese parsley or fresh coriander; and *cacao,* a chocolate made from local cacao beans sold in small cakes or tablets, which is used in cooking and to make hot chocolate.

Tortillas and black beans are among the most common foods in Guatemala. In indigenous villages, women often make the *tortillas* the traditional way by grinding corn with a rounded pestle on a flat lava stone called a *piedra* or *metate* and baking the flat corn disks on a dry, clay platter known as a *comal.* (This process is very time-consuming and generally cannot be sustained in the United States.) The black beans, which are difficult to find in the United States, are prepared whole, pureed, as soup, or paste and can be eaten at all meals. On the Caribbean coast and in cities the beans may be eaten with rice.

There are many varieties of *tamales,* which are essentially dough with meat and/or vegetables wrapped and steamed in a corn husk, leaf, or other wrapping. The dough can derive from cornmeal, flour, potatoes, or green bananas. In Guatemalan towns, women sell home-made *tamales* in markets. *Chuchitos* are a delicious type of cornmeal *tamale* made with chicken, pork, or turkey, tomatoes, and chiles.

Chilaquiles/as consist of *tortillas* stuffed with cheese or other ingredients dipped in a batter and then fried or baked. They can be served with a savory tomato sauce. In the chilly Guatemalan highlands, *caldos* or soups are frequently made and consumed.

Soup ingredients can include beef, chicken, lamb, potatoes, carrots, *chayotes*, onions, mint, eggs, tomatoes, beans, garlic, cilantro, and *epazote*, a mildly antiseptic herb, which also has medicinal purposes.

Turkey is native to the Americas and was raised, eaten, and sacrificed as a ceremonial bird in Mayan times. In Guatemala, turkey is still prepared and eaten during fiestas and national holidays. Another festive meat dish is *pepián*, which is eaten on Corpus Christi Day in June. *Pepián* consists of beef stewed with rice, spices, and vegetables such as tomatoes, green snap beans, chiles, and black peppercorns.

Plantains or *plátanos* are commonly eaten in the cities and in the more tropical areas. This very versatile fruit/vegetable, which looks like a banana, can be eaten ripe or green (but always cooked) and is alternately boiled, mashed, pan-fried, and deep-fried. Ripe plantains are sweet and can be prepared as a dessert with chocolate, cinnamon, or honey.

Sweets are quite popular in Guatemala and there is a wide variety of desserts and sweet breads like *pan dulce*, a sweet corn bread. *Hojuelas* are fried flour crisps drizzled with honey, which are sold in cities and in village markets. There are also prepared drinks like *boj*, a fermented sugar cane liquor drunk by Kekchi *indigenas* in Cobán. *Atol de maíz tierno* is a popular beverage made by boiling the paste of young corn, water, cinnamon, sugar, and salt.

TRADITIONAL COSTUMES

Since the 1930s, most men have worn European-style clothing, but women of the highlands still wear the brightly colored garments distinct to each Mayan village. The wearing of traditional clothing or *traje típico* has evolved into a way to preserve ethnic identity and pride in both Guatemala and in the United States. Mayan American women may wear *traje* at home and especially at cultural events like fiestas, church meetings, and weddings. The *huipil* is a multicolored, intricately embroidered blouse. The *corte* is an ankle-length brightly woven skirt that may also be embroidered. Traditionally, hair is kept long and worn in a braid or ponytail. On festive occasions women may also wear colorful beaded or silver necklaces and sparkly earrings. The cloth for *traje típico* is traditionally hand-woven on a loom, but today machine-produced cloth is widely available in Guatemala, although the hand-woven might be preferred for special occasions.

HOLIDAYS

Guatemalan Americans celebrate Thanksgiving, Christmas, and New Year's Day, as well as Guatemalan holidays like *Semana Santa* and patronal festivals. Totonicapan immigrants in Houston sometimes travel to San Cristobal to celebrate their town's patron saint fiesta *La Fiesta de Santiago*, Christmas, and *Semana Santa*. *Semana Santa* is based on the Catholic Holy Week. The week-long festivities reflect the blending of Mayan and Catholic rites and include costumed allegorical dramas that depict the Spanish conquest. During the week, participants cover the streets with *alfombras*, literally carpets, made of colored sawdust arranged in intricate patterns. The celebration reaches its climax on the last day when the parish priest leads a procession of the townspeople across the *alfombras*.

Although they are not national holidays, preparations for fiestas that honor a town's patron saint are elaborate, and Guatemalan Americans dynamically maintain these traditions. Kanjobals in both Los Angeles and southern Florida celebrate the fiesta of the patron saint of San Miguel Acatán on September 29th every year.

In 1990, more than 900 people attended the patronal festival in Los Angeles, which involved the coronation of festival queens, serving traditional Guatemalan food, the awarding of trophies to athletes, and a Deer Dance. The ancestral Deer Dance is performed by people dressed as animals and different types of people. In Guatemala, 60 to 80 dancers participate in the dance. The costumes have religious meaning and prayers are said before the dance commences. Celebrants set off firecrackers and rockets and play music on the marimba and on a drum made of wood and deer skin during the dance.

The theory of health and illness common in Mesoamerica is based on a humoral dichotomy of hot and cold, which should be in balance. The idea is derived from the Spanish importation of the Hippocratic quadratic that also considered the forces of wet and dry. In her study of the health practices of Mayan Americans in Florida, Maria Miralles observed that they sometimes attributed their illnesses to an imbalance in hot and cold or to the weather and heat.

Many of the indigenous and rural refugees are not accustomed to relying on modern American medicine to cure their health problems. In rural Guatemala and in some cities, *curanderos*, or traditional curers, use teas, herbs, and other natural remedies to heal the sick. *Curanderos* are also consulted as spiritual diviners and healers. Some *curanderos* are specialists trained in bone-setting or the treatment of tumors. In Los Angeles, the Kanjobals can go to local *curanderos* for problems like stress or depression. However, *curanderos* have been mostly supplanted by U.S. doctors, because they cannot get licenses to practice medicine here. *Promotores de salud* or health promoters trained by Catholic Action missionaries to know first-aid and preventative medicine also work in Guatemalan villages.

In many Mayan cultures, birth ceremonies are extremely important and the infant is received as a part of the community. Babies are traditionally delivered by midwives, and it is considered scandalous to go to a hospital to give birth. However, in the United States women may go to hospitals to deliver in order to obtain birth certificates for their newborns, despite their preferences.

Curative herbs can be consumed or used in medicinal steam baths. In Guatemala, the herbs can be bought from herb vendors; here they can found at *botánicas*, although not all of them are available. Some of the herbs used are *manzanilla* or chamomile and *hierba buena*, a mixture from Mexico. These can be taken for stomach disorders or headaches. Medicines can also be purchased without a prescription at pharmacies in Guatemala. Guatemalan immigrants who relied on traditional curative practices may prefer them to those of the American medical establishment. However, many also go to clinics and hospitals to cure their ailments.

HEALTH PROBLEMS AMONG REFUGEES

The journey from Guatemala to the United States is usually traumatic for emigrants escaping persecution or extreme poverty. Traveling by foot for up to thousands of miles with little money and few pos-

sessions, many become dehydrated, malnourished, and exhausted. Most refugees travel through Mexico, where they may stay in overcrowded refugee camps that provide little food and shelter and have poor sanitary conditions. Under these circumstances, refugees are susceptible to serious diseases like malaria and tuberculosis as well as parasites, gastrointestinal disorders, severe malnutrition, cracked and damaged feet, and skin infections.

Many refugees are also surviving the shock of experiencing extreme violence and subsequently suffer from mental health problems. Physical and mental health problems from conditions in Guatemala and the journey are compounded by the precariousness of the refugees positions once they settle here. Poor housing, underemployment, fear of deportation, and drastic changes can induce stress-related ailments such as ulcers and high blood pressure. Anxiety, depression, and alcohol abuse (among men) have also afflicted survivors.

Undocumented refugees usually do not receive insurance from employers, Medicaid, or other government health-care benefits, and often do not have access to affordable health care. However, in Los Angeles and Indiantown, health clinics have been established for Guatemalan and other immigrants without papers. In Indiantown, a county-sponsored health clinic known as *el corte* operates a Woman, Infant, and Child program for family planning and gives vaccinations to migrant workers' children. A privately run clinic known as *la clinica* provides screening, acute episode care, chronic disease management, and laboratory and x-ray services on a sliding fee basis. Kanjobal immigrants use both clinics, although they may also use traditional remedies at home.

In 1983, several social service and ecumenical religious groups created the Clinica Monsenor Oscar A. Romero as a free health care center for Central American refugees in Los Angeles. It was formed to address the special needs of refugees who cannot go to public medical facilities where they risk being deported and who contend with language and financial barriers that keep them from going to other clinics.

LANGUAGE

Spanish is the official language of Guatemala and is spoken by most first-generation Guatemalan Americans. However, some indigenous immigrants, especially women from the rural areas, speak exclusively Mayan languages and are unfamiliar with Spanish. Many first- and second-generation Mayan Americans are trilingual, and can communicate in Spanish, English, and a Mayan dialect. The Mayan languages spoken by Guatemalans in the United States include Kanjobal, Quiché, Mam, Cakchiquel, Chuj, Jacaltec, and Acatec. In Los Angeles, several dialects of Kanjobal are spoken, according to what village the person originates from.

The Mayan Americans in Houston speak both Quiché and Spanish. However, Hagan noted that the use of Quiché is diminishing both in Houston and in Guatemala, due to the predominance of Spanish in both areas. Children in Latino communities in Houston and Los Angeles learn Spanish in school and in their neighborhoods. Since Spanish is the language of access in Guatemala and in Latino areas, parents may encourage children to learn Spanish so they can interpret for them in various situations.

Language issues can be intimately linked with assimilation, as children sometimes reject both their Mayan language and customs. In Los Angeles, some second-generation Kanjobal Americans attend a Spanish-language church rather than one that holds services in Kanjobal, espousing the larger Latino community.

Guatemalan American refugees sometimes learn to speak Mexican Spanish to disguise their national origin. By passing for Mexican, they may be able to evade detection by the immigration authorities. For example, they may use Mexican terms such as "*lana*" instead of the Guatemalan term "*pisto*" for money. In some cities, Guatemalan immigrants learn to speak Puerto Rican Spanish for the same reasons. As one Guatemalan refugee aid worker put it: these more established Latino groups have "provided us with the tools to get along in an environment that doesn't accept us."

GREETINGS AND OTHER POPULAR EXPRESSIONS

Popular Guatemalan greetings and expressions include: *Buenos días* ("bwe'nos de'âs")—good morning, good day, hello; *buenas noches* ("bwe'nâs no'ches")—good night; *gracias* ("grâ'syâ"s)—thank you; *con mucho gusto* ("kon mü'cho gus'to")—with much pleasure, often used as "You're welcome," and as "It's a pleasure to meet you;" *sí pues* ("se pwes")—It's okay; or, Yeah, you're right; *con permiso* ("kon per me'so")—excuse me; *que rico, que riquíssimo* ("ke rre'ko, ke rreke'semo")—How rich, delicious, great!; ¡*Salud*! ("sâ luth'")—To your health! Cheers!; and ¡*Buen provecho*! ("bwen pro ve'cho")—literally "Good digestion!" said before a meal as in *bon apetit* or Enjoy!

In Cakchiquel, common sayings include: *Raxnek, seker, xseker*—good morning; *xocok'a', xok'a*—good night; *nuch' ocob'a'*—I'm sorry;

matiox—thank you; *ja'e*—with pleasure (like *con gusto*); and *rutzil, ruwech*—hello.

FAMILY AND COMMUNITY DYNAMICS

The family is very important among Guatemalan Americans. In many cases, large extended kinship groups maintain close bonds of loyalty, obligation, and social support. The family group traditionally includes grandparents and fictive kin such as *comadres* or godmothers.

However, among immigrants, many family members are now separated, since it is generally impossible for everyone to immigrate at the same time. Many men were forced to flee without their families because they were in immediate danger of being killed or conscripted into the fighting. Undocumented migrants usually have traveled to the United States alone, because they cannot afford to pay the *coyotes* for everyone at once and because their chances of making the crossing and surviving in the new environment are better.

After establishing their lives here, immigrants generally try to bring the rest of their families over. Spouses, children, and siblings frequently reunite with the original migrant. However, elderly parents and grandparents often cannot make the difficult trip north, which can require withstanding physical dangers and hardships. Children are sometimes left with grandparents in Guatemala, because both parents must work long hours and cannot afford day care or similar services.

Separation and reunification after long periods of living apart can strain family relations. Housing conditions may also change family dynamics. In refugee enclaves like Indiantown, families live in very crowded, tenement apartments due to low wages and the lack of adequate housing. In these situations, a family may share a one-room apartment with other families. Because of the lack of privacy and pressures these conditions create, many families move out of the community if they can save enough money to do so.

Despite the difficulty of finding work and making a living as undocumented persons, most Guatemalan Americans do not receive public assistance. Illegal aliens are not eligible for public assistance and are usually wary of government institutions. Citizen children may be eligible for welfare and food stamps, but undocumented parents are often afraid to apply for it. There are no official statistics on the percentage of Guatemalan American families who receive public assistance.

As in all immigrant communities, younger family members adjust much more quickly to American life, and may become alienated from older members. In urban Latino neighborhoods, adolescents may conflict with their parents if they assume *cholo* identities. *Cholo* refers to an originally Chicano teenage subculture that involves the use of slang, a street-wise pose and walk, activities like low-riding, using marijuana, and a specific style of dress—pressed Chinos, plaid shirts, and oversized brimmed hats for boys, and lots of make-up for girls.

Attitudes toward marriage have also changed in several Guatemalan American communities. Divorce and couples living together without being married are more common in the United States than they are in Guatemala. The absence of older generations in some communities may lead to a decline in the observance of traditional customs. In general, there is little intermarriage with other ethnic groups among the first-generation. Immigrant men are more likely to date or marry non-Guatemalans than women, and second-generation girls may be encouraged more than boys to date only Guatemalan Americans.

THE ROLE OF WOMEN

Guatemalan American women occupy complex and important positions within their families and communities. Guatemalan society is patriarchal and patrilineal, with men controlling most of the major institutions. However, within the last two decades women have garnered more leadership roles in all areas of society and they have led and played crucial parts in many of the popular resistance movements. During the 1980s, organizations like CONAVIGUA, composed mostly of indigenous widows of murdered or disappeared men, formed and fought for women's and human rights.

In many cases, women take on a larger economic role in the family when they immigrate to the United States. In migrant worker communities, women as well as men do wage field work. In addition, women are often expected to do all the domestic labor—child-rearing, cooking, and cleaning. Given the large size of households in some neighborhoods, this can involve an enormous amount of work, cooking and cleaning for ten to 20 people.

Immigrant women tend to transmit and sustain traditional culture more than the men, especially in

Mayan Guatemalan groups. By maintaining religious practices and language, preparing foods, and wearing traditional clothes and hairstyles, women preserve the cultural fabric of their group. Women also frequently organize church-related or community-oriented events like fiestas.

EDUCATION

Education is a high priority for many Guatemalan American parents. In urban areas, like Los Angeles and Houston, the available public schools often have poor reputations, and parents prefer to send their children to private Catholic schools. In Guatemala, schoolchildren generally attend private or boarding schools, if their parents can afford it. Guatemalan American parents whose children remain in Guatemala will often pay for their education there through wages earned here.

Children who were previously educated in Guatemalan schools in which the curricula are rigorous generally adjust easily to American schools once they learn English. However, a good number of refugee children have not had prior access to much education, since many Guatemalan schools were closed during recent decades due to poverty or violence. In southern Florida, two schools have been set up to address the needs of the migrant workers' children, who may not yet speak English and must deal with other challenges. The Migrant Head Start Program and the Hope Rural School are attended by Guatemalan American and many other children from Indiantown's diverse community. No statistics on the number of Guatemalan Americans who go to four-year universities and graduate schools are available. Undocumented refugee students cannot apply for financial aid for college and therefore it is almost impossible for them to attend institutions of higher learning.

RELIGION

Organized religion has greatly influenced the lives of Guatemalans and Guatemalan Americans in various ways. Since the time of the Spanish conquest, Guatemalans have practiced Roman Catholicism, while maintaining Mayan religious customs and beliefs. The Roman Catholic church is still dominant in Guatemala and has been involved with all aspects of life there, including politics, community development, social services, and internal refugee relief.

During the early 1980s when two Evangelical Pentecostal Protestant presidents ruled, the Catholic clergy were associated with rebel forces and became targets for violence. In some areas it was dangerous to identify with Catholicism. Protestant Evangelism grew dramatically during this time, as the U.S. churches sent missionaries to convert people. The rise in Pentecostal and other types of Protestant religions is evident in some Guatemalan American communities, where a large percentage are Protestants.

Norita Vlach, who interviewed Guatemalan refugee families in San Francisco, observed that many Catholic families switch to the Pentecostal church during their first years in that city. The churches offer women's groups, youth groups, and Spanish language classes. In Houston, La Iglesia de Dios, the Protestant Evangelical church, is similarly active among the Totonicapan community, holding Bible readings for women and multiple services during the week, and hosting cultural events like *quinceñeros* for church- and non-church-goers alike. The Evangelical Protestant church forbids dancing and drinking.

Other Protestant religions and Catholicism are practiced by the majority of Guatemalan Americans in Houston. In Indiantown and Los Angeles, the Kanjobal are Catholics, Seventh Day Adventists, Catholic Charismatics and Protestants, and many do not practice any religion although they may be nominally Catholic. A few practice traditional Mayan rituals of *costumbre*. Some *cofradias* or indigenous village elders who interpreted Catholicism in villages, mixing Mayan and Catholic customs, have immigrated to the United States, but they often have a diminished role in their new environments. It is difficult to maintain all Mayan religious practices here since some depend on being in sacred places in Guatemala. *Catequistas* or followers of the Catholic Action Movement seek to remove indigenous practices from Catholicism.

The Catholic church has provided asylum and many social services for Guatemalan American refugees. In Indiantown, the Holy Cross Church funded a social service center that helped process asylum and immigration papers, and supplied emergency relief, health referrals, and organizational help. Services are in Spanish and Kanjobal, and the annual patron saint's festival is held there. The Presbyterian Church's Office of World Service and World Hunger has also the supported the formation of local cultural groups.

EMPLOYMENT AND ECONOMIC TRADITIONS

Although Guatemalan Americans with legal resident or citizen status work in any number of professional fields such as law, teaching, and medicine, the large percentage of undocumented recent immigrants have little access to decently paying jobs. Since they have not been granted refugee status that would enable them to work here legally, these Guatemalan Americans have been forced to take low-paying jobs in the service sector, manufacturing, and agriculture. These are the same jobs that have historically been held by other new immigrant groups upon arrival in the United States. In rural areas throughout the United States Guatemalan immigrants work as migrant harvesters, picking fruit, flowers, vegetables, and commodities like tobacco in places like the San Joaquin Valley. The Kanjobal in Los Angeles and southern Florida frequently do migrant work when they first come to United States.

Field work of this type is often dangerous because of accidents and exposure to pesticides that can cause rashes and burns, and it demands long hours of physical exertion and a lifestyle of constant mobility. Exploitation of migrant workers is also common, as it is easy for agricultural contractors to pocket their Social Security payments or refuse to pay them altogether. If legal status is obtained, Guatemalan Americans usually move on to other types of work such as construction, or jobs where they can apply their professional skills in areas like education or social services. Many Guatemalan immigrants worked as trained professionals in Guatemala but cannot obtain the same type of work here because of their undocumented status.

The Mayan American men and women of southern Florida and Los Angeles sometimes work in garment factories during the off-season. In 1984, less than one percent of the undocumented garment workers in Los Angeles belonged to unions, although they legally have a right to unionize to demand better working conditions and wages. There have been a few successful efforts at unionizing illegal workers (including Guatemalan Americans) in agriculture and manufacturing, but most attempts have not gotten off the ground. The difficulty of organizing itinerant laborers, language differences, lack of experience with unions, and fear of being deported may all contribute to the lack of union activity.

Other Guatemalan Americans in Los Angeles and Florida work as gardeners in nurseries, landscapers on golf courses, and in restaurants and hotels. During the last few years, a textile cooperative was developed in Indiantown to create safe, year-round work in the Kanjobal neighborhood. The cooperative produces women's clothing that incorporates Mayan-style weaving.

Men may also do odd jobs as carpenters, roofers, or as informal vendors. Women often work as domestics throughout the United States, cooking, cleaning, or looking after children for individual families with whom they live. Women may also earn money by baby-sitting, doing laundry by hand, or cooking for people within their community.

In an unusual situation, many of the Totonicapan American men in Houston work as maintenance or stock workers in one retail chain. The employers who hired the original migrants from Totonicapan think of the Mayans as hard-working, responsible, and loyal. As more Totonicapan immigrants arrived, they obtained jobs with the company, creating a steady labor supply for the chain. This situation and the legalization of community members has made the acculturation process relatively smooth for this group.

Most of the work available to immigrants without legal papers is sporadic, and underemployment is a problem for many. However, the same people who have limited access to nonexploitative work are also ineligible for unemployment benefits. (There are no statistics on the number of Guatemalan Americans who receive unemployment, since figures are not categorized by national origin/individual ethnic groups.) The need for reliable, fairly paid employment is the most pressing issue in many Guatemalan American communities.

POLITICS AND GOVERNMENT

Since immigration in general and refugee status in particular are at the heart of the issues affecting many Guatemalan Americans, changes in federal immigration law have influenced the group. Since the 1980s, there have been several key pieces of federal legislation regarding immigration.

The 1980 Refugee Act mandates that immigration officials judge political asylum cases individually, rather than by national origin and that the rulings be independent of the government's relations with the country the applicant has come from. However, critics of asylum processes say that the INS still bases asylum decisions on national origin. This criticism is borne out by the fact that so few Guatemalan applicants receive asylum (fewer than two percent) when compared with applicants from countries the United States does not support like Nicaragua or the former Eastern Bloc countries. Although the act did not immediately change the way asylum decisions are made, it paved the path for later legislation and court decisions. The complex Immigration Reform and Control Act (IRCA) of 1986 enabled immigrants living in the United States continuously since January 1, 1982 and arriving before that date to apply for legalization status. This provision helped the small percentage of Guatemalan emigrants who arrived before 1982. Another provision of IRCA called for employer sanctions that penalize employers who hired unauthorized workers after November 6, 1986. Observers noted that this provision could reduce the demand for undocumented workers, force repatriation, and restrict immigration, but it is difficult to ascertain what the results of this part of IRCA have been. Some Guatemalan American migrant workers benefited from the farmworker amnesty portion of IRCA that provided resident alien status to farmworkers. Farmworkers who did agricultural labor for at least 90 days from 1985-1986 were eligible for this status under SAW or the Seasonal Agricultural Worker provision.

Several court cases have questioned the government's handling of political asylum proceedings for people from Central America and have prohibited discriminatory practices in these hearings. In February 1991, a Federal district judge in San Francisco approved a settlement that blocked deportation of up to 500,000 Salvadoran and Guatemalan immigrants and allowed them to reopen their asylum cases. Under the decision, the INS had to reconsider an estimated 150,000 cases of Guatemalan and Salvadoran refugees whose asylum cases had been denied since 1980 but who had not yet been deported.

Refugee advocacy groups lobbied for Temporary Protected Status (TPS) for Guatemalan refugees in the United States under the Immigration Act of 1990. The act authorizes TPS where there is an ongoing armed conflict that would seriously threaten the safety of an individual upon return, or where conditions prevent nationals from returning safely. The end of the civil war in Guatemala terminated these efforts. The governments of the two countries are working on a solution to the status of the nearly 200,000 Guatemalans living in the United States who are not U.S. citizens.

INVOLVEMENT IN U.S. POLITICS AND GOVERNMENT

Since Guatemalan Americans comprise a small and largely unestablished group, they have not yet been very involved with American politics. A number of grass-roots refugee advocacy groups, however, have lobbied for immigrant rights. There are no statistics on Guatemalan American voting patterns, the number of elected officials, or participation in the armed forces. The National Association of Latino Elected and Appointed Officials in Houston does not categorize their listing of Latino politicians by national origin. However, there are at least two Guatemalan American city officials in California.

Veronica Cardenas-Jaffe helped to incorporate Mission Viejo into the City of Mission Viejo in 1988. She was subsequently elected to the charter city council in 1988 and has served as Mayor pro tem since 1990. Jim Gonzalez was appointed to City and County Supervisor on the San Francisco Board of Supervisors in 1988. He has also worked as a special assistant to former San Francisco Mayor now Senator Dianne Feinstein from 1981 to 1986.

RELATIONS WITH GUATEMALA

Most Guatemalan Americans have family or close friends remaining in Guatemala, and the majority are very concerned about the state of affairs there. While many Guatemalan Americans do not have the resources or time to address the conditions they fled from, there are already several Guatemalan American organizations that actively strive for an end to violence and corruption in Guatemala. These groups include many refugee aid organizations, since political and economic turmoil in Guatemala continues to have a direct impact on the situation of refugees here.

INDIVIDUAL AND GROUP CONTRIBUTIONS

Although Guatemalan Americans constitute a very small percentage of the American population and are one of the most recently established American ethnic groups, they have contributed significantly to American life through political and cultural organizations and as individuals. Personal contributions have been especially numerous in the arts and sciences. The following subsections list some notable Guatemalan Americans and their accomplishments.

BUSINESS

Marta Ortiz-Buonafina (1933–) is an associate professor of marketing at Florida International University. She has published many articles and books, including the second edition of *Profitable Export Marketing* in 1992. Luis Alfredo Vasquez-Ajmac (1961–) is president of MAYA, a marketing communications firm targeting Latinos in Washington, D.C., that he established in 1990. He has also served as an advisory member to the Corporation for Public Broadcasting.

MEDICINE, SCIENCE, AND MATHEMATICS

In 1990, Hermann Mendez (1949–), associate professor of pediatrics at the State University of New York-Health Science Center at Brooklyn, received awards from the Department of Health and Human Services and the Assistant Secretary of Health for his outstanding contributions to the fight against AIDS. He was also named as one of the Best Doctors in New York by *New York Magazine* in 1991 and as one of the Best Doctors in America by Woodward/White Inc. in 1992.

John Joaquin Munoz (1918–) is a scientist emeritus at the National Institute of Health's Rocky Mountain Laboratories. He served as chairman of the immunology section of the American Society of Microbiology from (1980-1981), and received an NIH Director's Award in 1979. He has also published many papers and is the co-author of *Bordetella Pertussis: Immunological and Other Biological Activities* (1977).

Psychiatrist Julio Alfredo Molina (1948–) is the founder and director of the Anxiety Disorders Institute of Atlanta. Psychologist and government official Carmen Carrillo (1943–) is the director of Adult Acute Services at San Francisco's Department of Public Health. She has earned many awards for her work in education, psychology, mental health, and Latino issues, including the City and Council of San Francisco Distinction and Merit Award in 1988, the National Women's Political Caucus Public Service Award in 1989, and the California School Boards Association Service Award in 1991.

Sergio Ramiro Aragón (1949–), a professor of chemistry at San Francisco State University, established a supercomputer center at California State University in 1989. Sergio Roberto López-Permouth (1957–), assistant professor of math at Ohio University, has published several articles and co-edited a book called *Non-Commutative Ring Theory* with S. K. Jain in 1990. Victor Perez-Mendez (1923–) has edited two books, written over 300 articles, and is a professor of physics and faculty senior scientist at the University of California at Berkeley. Statistician Jorge Huascar del Pinal (1945–) is the chief of the U.S. Bureau of the Census's Ethnic and Spanish Statistics Branch. He published *Microcomputer Programs for Demographic Analysis* in 1985.

MUSIC AND LITERATURE

Aida Doninelli (1898–), Guatemalan-born and raised daughter of Italian immigrants to Guatemala, made her American debut as an opera singer in Chicago in 1927. A dramatic soprano, she performed in the major concert stages of the United States and Latin America and sang with New York's prestigious Metropolitan Opera from 1928 to 1933. During her tenure at the Met, Doninelli performed in many operatic roles, including Micaela in *Carmen*, Mimi in *La Bohème*, and Cio-Cio San in *Madame Butterfly*. She also appeared in some of the earliest musical films like *La Traviata* and *Tosca*, and introduced Latin American music to a wide U.S. audience by singing in radio shows broadcast from New York.

Several contemporary Guatemalan American authors and academics have augmented the field of American literature. Donald Kenneth Gutierrez (1932–), a professor of English at Western New Mexico University, has published numerous essays and scholarly books, including *The Dark and Light Gods: Essays on the Self in Modern Literature* in 1987. David Unger (1950–), a writer, translator, and co-director of the Latin American Writers' Institute, edited *Antipoems, new and selected* (1985) by Nicanor Parra and co-translated *World Alone: Mundo a Solas* (1982). He has received awards for his translation work from the New York State Council on the Arts.

Author Arturo Arias (1950–) co-wrote (with Gregory Nava and Anna Thomas) the screenplay for *El Norte*, which won the Montreal Prize and was nominated for an Academy Award for best screenplay in 1982. The film portrays the experiences of a Kanjobal brother and sister who flee from persecution in Guatemala and make the arduous journey to Los Angeles. The realistic depiction of their struggles on the way and in the United States was well-received by the Kanjobal American community in Los Angeles, on which it is based. Arias has also written several novels, including *Jaguar en llamas* in 1989, and he is a professor of humanities at Stanford University and San Francisco State University.

Journalist and author Francisco Goldman's first novel *The Long Night of White Chickens* was published in 1992 and received much critical acclaim. The book evokes contemporary Guatemala and is narrated by a Guatemalan American character who travels to Guatemala in search of Guatemalan American friend who was murdered under mysterious circumstances.

MEDIA

PRINT

El Vocero de IXIM: Boletín Informativo de Integración de Indígenas Mayas (IXIM).
Trilingual newsletter in Acatec Mayan, Spanish, and English published by IXIM. Reports on cultural activities, news of interest to the Guatemalan American community, and sometimes features traditional folk tales. Frequency is roughly quarterly.

Contact: Pascual Francisco, President.
Address: 1432 West Olympic Boulevard, No. 2, Los Angeles, California 90015.
Telephone: (213) 384-4134.

Guatemala Review.
Bilingual Spanish and English publication published by the Guatemalan Education Action Project. Features articles on the political situation in Guatemala and Chiapas.

Guatemala: The Bulletin of the Guatemala Human Rights Commission/USA.
Quarterly publication that provides information on the human rights situation in Guatemala.

Contact: Patricia Davis, Editor.

Guate-Noticias.
An English-language bi-monthly newsletter published by the Guatemala Support Network. In-depth articles on the peace process in Guatemala and announcements on conferences, events.

Contact: Benito Juarez, Director.
Address: Guatemala Support Network, 4223 Richmond Avenue, No. 112, Houston, Texas 77027.
Telephone: (713) 850-0441.

La Opinión.
A Spanish-language daily newspaper popular among Central Americans in Pico-Union.

Contact: Monica Lozano, Editor.
Address: Lozano Enterprises, 411 West Fifth Street, Los Angeles, California 90013.
Telephone: (213) 896-2020.
Fax: (213) 896-2144.

Report on Guatemala.
Published quarterly by the Guatemala News and Information Bureau. Focuses on news and analysis of events in Guatemala.

Contact: Todd Kolze, Coordinator.
Address: GNIB, P.O. Box 28594, Oakland,
California 94604.
Telephone: (510) 835-0810.

RADIO

WZOR-AM (1490).
Broadcasts programs for the Hispanic community in
Immokalee, Florida, specifically for the large
Guatemalan American population in the area.

Contact: Jose Quiatanilla, Station Manager.
Address: 2105 West Immokalee Drive,
Immokalee, Florida 33934.

ORGANIZATIONS AND ASSOCIATIONS

Casa Guatemala.
A member of Atanasio Tzul-Guatemala Support
Network, the umbrella organization for ten
Guatemalan refugee services groups in the United
States. Provides legal assistance for immigration
cases, English as a second language classes, and
organizes cultural activities.

Contact: Julio Revolorio, Executive Director.
Address: c/o Atanasio Tzul, 4554 North
Broadway, Suite 273, Chicago, Illinois 60640.
Telephone: (773) 465-2463.

La Comité Unidad Guatemalteca.
A mostly *ladino* cultural and political group organized by the Guatemalan American refugee community in San Francisco.

Contact: Mario Ordonez, Coordinator.
Address: 1200 Florida Street, San Francisco,
California 94110.
Telephone: (415) 550-9225.

Grupo Maya Qusamej Junan.
Promotes the culture of Guatemalan Mayans and
indigenous people in the United States through the
production of art exhibits, language classes, and traditional dances and ceremonies. It also supports
projects in Guatemala.

Contact: Adrian Cuyuzh, Coordinator.
Address: P.O. Box 40892, San Francisco,
California 94140.
Telephone: (415) 824-2534.

Guatemala Education Action Project.
Formed in 1986 by Guatemalan refugees in the
United States to build awareness, response, and
respect for the people of Guatemala.

Address: 8124 West Third, Suite 105, Los
Angeles, California 90048-4328.
Telephone: (213) 782-0953.
Fax: (213) 782-0954.

Guatemala Human Rights Commission/USA.
Monitors and provides current information about
human rights in Guatemala.

Contact: Alice Zachmann, Director.
Address: 3321 12th Street, N.E.,
Washington, D.C. 20017-4008.
Telephone: (202) 529-6599.
Fax: (202) 526-4611.
E-mail: ghrc@igc.apc.org.

International Mayan League.
Promotes Mayan thought in the areas of culture,
science, technology, and art. It produces
brochures and other media and participates in
speaking engagements. Headquarters are in Costa
Rica, with offices throughout the world, and it
serves as the parent organization of Guatemala
Watch of Vermont.

Contact: Felipe or Elena Ixzot, Coordinators.
Address: 11 Cider Mill Road, Weston, Vermont
05161.
Telephone: (802) 824-3529.
Fax: (802) 824-3529.
E-mail: ixcot@juno.com.
Online: http://www.alternativemedia.org/
imlconnect.html.

**Network in Solidarity with the People of
Guatemala (NISGUA).**
Founded in 1981. NISGUA acts as an umbrella
organization for groups that support human rights
in Guatemala. Collects and disseminates information about the political, military, and economic situation there.

Contact: Lael Parish, Executive Director.
Address: 1500 Massachusetts Avenue, N.W.,
No. 214, Washington, D.C. 20005.
Telephone: (202) 223-6474.
Fax: (202) 223-8221.
E-mail: nisgau@igc.apc.org.

MUSEUMS AND RESEARCH CENTERS

Dallas Museum of Art.
The museum displays an extensive collection of pre-Columbian and eighteenth- to twentieth-century textiles, censers, and other art objects from Guatemala.

Contact: Karen Zelanka, Associate Registrar, Permanent Collection.
Address: 1717 North Harwood, Dallas, Texas 75201.
Telephone: (214) 922-1200.

Human Rights Documentation Exchange.
Formerly known as the Central America Resource Center, the Documentation Exchange maintains a library of information on human rights and social conditions in many countries, including Guatemala, as well as some information on Guatemalan Americans.

Contact: Faye Kolly, RLSS Coordinator.
Address: P.O. Box 2327, Austin, Texas 78768.
Telephone: (512) 476-9841.
Fax: (512) 476-0130.

Middle American Research Institute (MARI).
Part of Tulane University. Features a collection of pre-Hispanic, Mayan textiles and archeological artifacts from Guatemala.

Address: Middle American Research Institute, Tulane University, New Orleans, Louisiana 70118.
Telephone: (504) 865-5110.
Fax: (504) 862-8778.
E-mail: mari@mailhost.tcs.tulane.edu.
Online: http://www.tulane.edu/~mari.

Nettie Lee Benson Latin American Collection at the University of Texas at Austin.
This internationally renowned library of books and periodicals on Latin America, maintains one of the best collections on Guatemalan Americans and Guatemala.

Contact: Laura Gutiérrez-Witt, Head Librarian.
Address: Sid Richardson Hall 1.109, General Libraries, University of Texas at Austin, Austin, Texas 78713-7330.
Telephone: (512) 471-3818.

San Antonio Museum of Art.
The museum features a variety of textiles and sculpture from Guatemala.

Contact: Dr. Marion Oettinger, Jr., Curator, Latin American Folk Art.

Address: 200 West Jones Avenue, San Antonio, Texas 78215.
Telephone: (210) 978-8100.
Fax: (210) 978-8118.

Textile Museum.
The museum displays a collection of handmade historic and ethnographic textiles from Guatemala and other Latin American countries.

Contact: William J. Conklin, Research Associate, Pre-Columbian textiles.
Address: 2320 South Street, N.W., Washington, D.C. 20008.
Telephone: (202) 667-0441.
Fax: (202) 483-0994.

The University of Texas Institute of Texan Cultures at San Antonio.
The multicultural museum and educational resource center maintains a library of books, files, and photographs of 90 ethnic groups in Texas, including Guatemalan Americans.

Contact: Diane Bruce, Librarian.
Address: 801 South Bowie, San Antonio, Texas 78205.
Telephone: (210) 558-2298.

SOURCES FOR ADDITIONAL STUDY

Ashabranner, Brent. *Children of the Maya: A Guatemalan Indian Odyssey.* New York: Dodd, Mead & Company, 1986.

Hagan, Jacqueline Maria. *Deciding to be Legal: A Maya Community in Houston.* Philadelphia: Temple University Press, 1994.

Hernandez, Marita. "Kanjobal Indians: Guatemala to L.A.—Bid for Survival," *Los Angeles Times,* September 24, 1984, Part I; pp. 1, 3, 12.

Miralles, Andrea Maria. *A Matter of Life and Death: Health-Seeking Behavior of Guatemalan Refugees in South Florida.* New York: AMS Press, Inc, 1989.

Rohter, Larry. "In a Florida Haven for Guatemalans, Seven Deaths Bring New Mourning," *New York Times,* October 24, 1991; p. A18.

Vlach, Norita. *The Quetzal in Flight: Guatemalan Refugee Families in the United States.* Westport, Connecticut: Praeger, 1989.

GUYANESE AMERICANS

by
Jacqueline A. McLeod

Guyanese Americans represent a minuscule percent of America's total population, but they have made significant contributions to American popular culture, the arts, academia, and politics.

OVERVIEW

The Cooperative Republic of Guyana—formerly the colony of British Guiana—is a country the size of its former colonial master, Great Britain, and slightly bigger than the state of Kansas. As one of many Caribbean nations, Guyana is often assumed to be an island rather than a continental country. Larger than the rest of the English-speaking Caribbean put together, it sprawls across 83,000 square miles of the northeastern coast of South America, bounded on the west by Venezuela, on the southwest by Brazil, and on the east by Suriname. Its northern boundary consists of 250 miles of coastline on the Atlantic Ocean. Of the country's total area, 86 percent is forest, 10.5 percent is savannah grassland, and 3.5 percent is the coastal belt on which nearly all its people live.

Guyana has a population of about three-quarters of a million people; 50 percent are of East Indian descent and about 30 percent are of African ancestry. Amerindian, Chinese, Portuguese, and British peoples all have contributed to the cultural heritage of the land. (The name Amerindian is used to distinguish Guyana's native groups from the immigrant East Indian population.) Primarily because of ambitious missionary activities during the nineteenth century, the Afro-Guyanese are mostly Christian. In fact, more than half of Guyana's people—regardless of race or ethnicity—are classified as Christian: 18 percent of the population is Roman Catholic, and 16 percent is Anglican. Of the non-Christian Guyanese, 35 percent Hindu, and 9 percent Muslim. The major religious holidays of each of the three faiths—Christianity, Hinduism, and Islam—are observed nationally.

Guyana's capital city is Georgetown. No other cities or towns rival it in importance. The official language of the country is English, but almost everyone speaks Creolese, a fusion of European and African dialects. Amerindian dialects and East Indian tongues are spoken as well, and three major Indian languages—Hindi, Tamil, and Telugu—are still in use among the Indo-Guyanese. Each of a dozen native groups speaks a different Carib, Arawak, or Warrau dialect. About 91 percent of the Guyanese population is literate—one of the highest rates among new nations of the world. Guyana's national flag consists of five colors: the green background symbolizes agriculture and forests, the golden arrowhead represents mineral wealth, the white border stands for water resources, and the red triangle edged in black signifies the energy and zeal of the Guyanese in building their nation.

HISTORY

Guyana is an Amerindian word that means "land of [many] waters." The Europeans first used the name to refer to the triangle formed by the Orinoco, Amazon, and Negro rivers. The British used "Guiana"—an English spelling of the same Amerindian name—to refer to their New World colony. Before the arrival of the Europeans, Guyana was inhabited by several native groups. The largest group was the Caribs, who lived in the upper reaches of the Essequibo River, as well as near the Mazaruni, Cuyuni, Pomeroon, and Barima rivers. The Caribs roamed the heavily forested regions of the interior. Between the Corentyne and Waini rivers lived the Arawaks, a friendly, peace-loving native group whose people were the first to greet Christopher Columbus in other areas of the Caribbean. Another native group, the Warrau, inhabited the swampland near the mouth of the Orinoco in present-day Venezuela but eventually moved east into Guyanese territory.

Christopher Columbus was the first European known to have sailed along the coast of Guyana. But during his voyage to the New World in 1498, Columbus only viewed the land's low-lying tropical shore. It was not until 1499 that Alonso de Ojeda became the first Spaniard to actually set foot on the land that would later be known as Guyana. No settlement, however, resulted from this early exploration. Between 1595 and 1616, English explorer

Sir Walter Raleigh—who dreamed of "El Dorado" (the mythical land of gold)—led three expeditions to the Guyanese territory. Although Raleigh failed to locate any gold, his efforts resulted in the earliest mapping of the Guyanese coastline.

The Dutch were the first Europeans to gain a real foothold in Guyana. In 1616 Dutch colonists selected a site on an island peak overlooking the junction of the Mazaruni and Cuyuni rivers, about 40 miles upstream from the mouth of the Essequibo River. The settlement was named Kijk-over-al ("Overlooking All"). Early attempts at farming included the growth of coffee, tobacco, and cotton crops. Meanwhile in Europe, the Dutch States-General (governing the provinces of present-day Holland) granted a charter over the Guyana territory to the Dutch West India Company in 1621. The charter gave the company complete political and economic authority, the privilege to undertake pirate raids against Spanish shipping, and the right to carry slaves from West Africa to the New World. By 1770 more than 15,000 Africans were enslaved in Guyana.

With a slave labor force, which consisted of men and women forcibly removed from their native Africa, the farms began to grow in size and in yield. The success of the Dutch venture encouraged the development of sugar plantations in other inland regions of Guyana. Similar settlements sprang up along the Berbice, Demerara, and Pomeroon rivers. The Berbice district became a separate territory in 1732, and a Demerara district was established in 1741.

In 1781 war broke out between the Dutch and the British over ownership of the colony, resulting in a year of British control over Guyana. In 1782 the French seized power and governed for two years, during which time they created the new town of Longchamps at the mouth of the Demerara River. When the Dutch regained power in 1784, they moved their colonial capital to Longchamps and renamed it Stabroek; the city was later renamed again—this time "Georgetown" after the British king, George III.

The Dutch maintained control over the Berbice, Essequibo, and Demerara settlements until 1796, when a British fleet from the Caribbean island of Barbados conquered the country. The British governed until 1802, at which time Guyana was restored to the Dutch under a truce established by the Treaty of Amiens. The next year the British once again conquered the colony, which was finally ceded to them in 1814 under agreements contained in the Treaty of Paris and the Congress of Vienna. In 1831, three years before slavery ended in the region, the British merged Berbice, Essequibo, and Demerara to form British Guiana. After slavery was abolished throughout the British colonies on August 1, 1834, former slaves were subjected to a four-year apprenticeship to facilitate their transition to a wage labor system. However, after emancipation, few former slaves chose to work—even for wages—for the plantation owners who had once enslaved them.

Faced with a critical shortage of workers, planters decided to import workers under a system of indentured servitude. Immigrants under this system included people from Portugal, China, the West Indies, and Africa, but by 1844 indentured servitude in Guyana was almost solely the domain of East Indian laborers. After a five-year indenture period, the East Indians were "free" to return to India at their own expense. This indenture system, which had satisfied the planter aristocracy's demand for workers, was abolished in British Guiana in 1917. But no matter how much headway was achieved by the former slaves or by former indentured laborers, the reins of political power remained in the firm grasp of a European elite.

MODERN ERA

Guyana's road to independence was a rocky one. In 1953, a new constitution granted universal adult voting rights and established a two-house legislature. But political turmoil followed the first general election. The British government feared the communist leanings of the winning People's Progressive Party (PPP), which was led by Cheddi Berret Jagan (1918–). Consequently, the British suspended the new constitution and the elected government. (Guyana's constitution did not go into effect until 1961.)

In addition to the PPP's communist stance, the party also advocated independence from Great Britain. From 1954 until the time that new elections were held in 1957, an interim government ruled British Guiana. Meanwhile, Jagan, an East Indian, and his fellow PPP cofounder, Linden Forbes Sampson Burnham (1923-1985), an African, had a major disagreement that ended their collaboration. Burnham left the PPP in 1957 and formed the People's National Congress (PNC), which eventually became an opposition party to the PPP. The split weakened the party's majority, but the PPP still won the most legislative seats in 1957 and again in 1961.

As head of the PPP, Jagan was elected prime minister of the colonial Guyanese government in 1957 and remained in office until the heavily contested election of 1964. That year, the colonial gov-

ernor declared Burnham the victor by virtue of his ability to lead a coalition of the PNC and the United Force (UF), a third party led by Portuguese businessman Peter Stanislaus d'Aguiar. Under Burnham's leadership, the nation's long struggle for independence ended on May 26, 1966, when he assumed the office of prime minister of an independent Guyana.

In an attempt to put an end to foreign meddling in Guyanese affairs, Burnham steadfastly positioned Guyana among the world's non-aligned nations in world affairs. With Burnham at the helm, Guyana declared itself a "Cooperative Republic" in 1970. The change meant that Guyana became a socialist nation—a country committed to achieving prosperity by pooling its material and human resources. The Guyanese government also nationalized its industries, including foreign-owned bauxite companies (bauxite is used in the production of aluminum), which produced much of the country's wealth. By 1985, the end of Burnham's 20-year tenure as chief executive and the year of his death, more than three-quarters of the country's economy had been brought under government control.

Immediately following Burnham's death, vice president Hugh Desmond Hoyt was sworn into office. Regularly scheduled elections, criticized as fraudulent, were held in December of 1985. Hoyt and the PNC won a solid but questionable victory. However, in national elections held in October of 1992—under the watchful eyes of the international community—the Jagan-led PPP won, bringing the tenure of the PNC as ruling party to a close after almost three decades.

THE FIRST GUYANESE IN AMERICA

The Guyanese people were part of the two major waves of British West Indian immigration to the United States. The earlier wave encompassed the first two decades of the twentieth century, showing a steady increase in immigration until the passage of the Immigration Act of 1924. This act placed race and ethnicity restrictions on entry to the United States and included the English-speaking Caribbean in the quota allotted to Great Britain, with a visa limit of 800 per year and a preference system for skilled workers and relatives of United States citizens. Throughout the 1940s and 1950s, Guyanese immigrants primarily chose Britain as their destination. However, following the passage of the Immigration and Nationality Act of 1952, also known as the McCarran-Walter Act, which removed race and ethnicity as conditions of entry, the second wave of immigration to the United States began; the

Guyanese American migration pattern continued to accelerate in the ensuing decades.

SIGNIFICANT IMMIGRATION WAVES

Guyanese immigration to the United States increased sharply with the passage of Britain's 1962 Commonwealth Immigration Act, which overturned the British Nationality Act of 1948. The earlier act allowed citizens of Guyana to claim citizenship in the United Kingdom and granted all Commonwealth citizens the same legal rights accorded to British citizens. Many Guyanese took advantage of this opportunity to further their education and improve their economic status. However, the concentration of nonwhite manual workers and their families in British cities stimulated an outcry against unregulated immigration, culminating in the 1962 act, which restricted their entry. With the doors of their "mother country" virtually closed to them, many Guyanese, mostly of the professional and technical classes, began to turn to the United States as their new land of opportunity.

In 1965 the McCarran-Walter Act was amended to protect American workers while restricting immigration from the Western Hemisphere. But with the introduction in 1968 of an annual ceiling of 120,000 immigrant visas for the Western Hemisphere, the intent of the act of 1965 was negated. Skilled laborers from Western Hemisphere countries journeyed to the United States in record numbers. The response from Guyana was immediate and dramatic. The majority of Guyanese applicants fell into the categories of "professional," "technical," and "kindred" (or skilled) workers.

The outward flow from Guyana intensified as the country experienced drastic economic and political changes during the 1970s and 1980s. After declaring itself a "Cooperative Republic" in 1970, Guyana began taking steps toward the nationalization of resources. During this time the country was under progressively heavier stresses and strains, resulting in declining productivity, massive unemployment, and skyrocketing inflation. It was also during this period that the Burnham regime came under increasing fire for its repression of political opposition.

Between 1960 and 1970, more Guyanese entered the United States than ever before. Around this time, the United States experienced labor shortages—especially in the health industry and in private households, traditional areas of employment for women. Guyanese women, like other Caribbean women, met demands in the United States for workers in the health and domestic fields. The first Guyanese to arrive in 1968, either as "private household workers" or as nurses' aides, were of African descent. East Indian Guyanese women were forbidden by custom to venture to the United States alone.

Guyanese immigrants no longer fit the traditional immigration pattern, in which the men settle in a new country first and send for their families later. Since the 1960s, female immigrants have assumed the status of "principal alien," the term given to an immigrant worker within a specific or delineated labor force capacity, whose status activates other provisions in the migration process of family members. According to Monica Gordon in *In Search of a Better Life: Perspectives on Migration from the Caribbean,* more Guyanese women than men settled in the United States in the 1960s and 1970s, making them primarily responsible for securing immigrant status for their families. These women, Gordon concluded, tended to see migration as a means to improve their economic and social status and the educational opportunities of their children. U.S. Census Bureau records indicate that of the 48,608 people of Guyanese ancestry living in the United States in 1980, 26,046 were female. By 1990 approximately 81,665 people of Guyanese ancestry had settled in the United States.

SETTLEMENT

Because the overwhelming majority of Guyanese were migrating from urban centers (90 percent of Guyana's population is clustered along the coastal plain), they tended to settle mostly in the northeastern cities of the United States. As of 1990, 80 percent of Guyanese Americans lived in the Northeast. The heaviest concentration of Guyanese Americans can be found in New York (56,462), New Jersey (6,697), and Maryland (3,106), although a significant portion of the population also settled in Florida, California, Texas, and Pennsylvania.

Guyanese American communities are not localized. There are no clearly demarcated spatial boundaries between them and other Caribbean groups. Rather, a multiplicity of Caribbean peoples tend to settle in the same regions. New York City's immigrant pool from 1982 to 1989 was drawn mostly from the Caribbean. Of the top five source countries, four were the Caribbean nations of the Dominican Republic, Jamaica, Haiti, and Guyana. Seventy percent of all Guyanese immigrants move to New York. In fact, about eight percent of the total population of Guyana moved to New York City—particularly the East Flatbush, Flatbush, and Crown Heights sections of Brooklyn—in the 1980s, according to a July 1, 1992, *New York Times* article entitled "A City of Immigrants Is Pictured in Report." Of the 46,706 Guyanese immigrants in the United States from 1983 to 1989, a total of 8,912, or approximately 19 percent, settled in these sections of the city.

ACCULTURATION AND ASSIMILATION

Many immigration studies on the Caribbean focus on the island nations of Jamaica, Haiti, Barbados, and Trinidad and Tobago because of their large populations abroad. Guyana's immigrant population in the United States noticeably increased in the 1980s. Guyana first grabbed the international spotlight in November of 1978, after the shocking People's Temple incident involving the mass suicide by poison of more than 900 Americans in the country's interior. The People's Temple, a cult that originated in California, consisted of U.S. citizens under the leadership of Reverend Jim Jones. Members of the Guyanese government found Jones's credentials sound and granted him permission to construct a religious center in Guyana's western region, near Port Kaituma. The enterprise, however, ended in tragedy when Jones—under scrutiny by the U.S. government for his questionable dealings—has his followers kill themselves. For years after, the country of Guyana was associated with the cult members' deaths.

TRADITIONS, CUSTOMS, AND BELIEFS

Guyanese folklore and traditions date back centuries. Many Guyanese superstitions or belief systems are maintained among Guyanese Americans, especially those who identify with some Caribbean enclave. The following are some examples of Guyanese beliefs: Good Friday is considered a very unlucky day to be involved in outdoor activities if they are not church-related. When entering a house late at night, a person should go in backwards in order to keep evil spirits out. To cure a fever, a sliced potato should be placed on the ill person's forehead. To cure the effects of a stroke (like a twisted mouth), a whole nutmeg should be placed inside of the mouth on the affected side. A woman whose feet have been swept will not get married. A black cat crossing in front of a pedestrian will bring bad luck. A dog howling at a particular house is a sign that death will soon come to someone in that household. A pondfly in the house is a sign of news or correspondence. Stepping over someone's leg will stunt their growth. All references to the dead must be prefaced with the words: "God rest the dead in the living and the looking."

PROVERBS

A wealth of proverbs from Guyanese culture have survived through the generations: "Hint at Quashiba mek Beneba tek notice" (Pay attention to the hints someone drops); "Wuh is fun fuh school boy is dead fuh crappo" (One man's meat is another man's poison); "Bush gat ears, goobie gat hole" (When you least expect it, people are eavesdropping); "Mouth open, story jump out" (Some people can't keep a secret); "Show me yuh company, I'll tell you who you be" (People judge you by the friends you keep); "Moon run til day ketch he" (Your deeds usually catch up with you); "Greedy man y'eye does yalla twice, fuh he own and he mattie own" (Some people are never satisfied); "Monkey mek he pickney til he spoil'um" (Similar to "Too many cooks spoil the broth"); "Wuh fall from head drop pun shoulder" (Sins of the parents fall on the children); "If yuh guh to crab dance, yuh mus get mud" (What you sow you reap); "Who lif yuh up doan put yuh dung" (Those who get you into trouble don't get you out); "It's a lazy horse that can't carry its own oats" (Your burden is yours to carry); "Hand wash hand mek hand come clean" (More is accomplished through cooperation); "Mocking is ketching" (Don't laugh at another's situation, it might be yours); "Monkey know wuh limb to jump pun" (Bullies know exactly on whom to pick); "Donkey ears long, but he doan hear he own story" (Some people mind other people's business); "Do suh nuh like suh" (Treat others as you would like to be treated); "If yuh nuh gat muhma suck granny" (Make do with what you have).

CUISINE

Guyanese cuisine is appetizing, spicy, and delicious. Spices and herbs are used in abundance, and one-dish meals occupy an important place in Guyanese cuisine. These dishes, sometimes called "poor man food," are nourishing, inexpensive, and very easy to prepare. Guyanese men and women both enjoy cooking, each trying to outdo the other in excellence. *Pepperpot*, considered a national dish, is a combination of different meats (beef, pork), spices, a dash of sugar, lots of onions, and *cassareep* (a sauce made from fermented juice from the bitter cassava plant); it is eaten with rice or bread. *Cookup rice*, another national dish, is a blend of rice, split peas or black-eyed peas, spices, onions, coconut milk, and meats. Also central to the repertoire of Guyanese recipes is the array of Indian curried dishes, made with curry powder, an East Indian spice with a distinctive flavor. *African Metemgee*, an inexpensive dish that is very filling, is made from coconut milk, meat or fish, onions, spices, plantains, and dumplings. *Souse* is a very spicy and tangy dish made from boiled pig ears and pig feet, flavored with cucumber, hot pepper, scallions, and lemon juice. Portuguese garlic pork is highly spiced pork pickled in garlic and vinegar. It is served fried, and eaten with bread. *Dahl* is a blend of boiled split peas, onions, garlic, curry powder, and cumin. This can be served over rice or eaten with *roti*, a pancake-like bread. Guyanese cuisine is not complete without Chinese noodles and chow mein, and black pudding, also called blood pudding, which is served with a tangy hot sauce.

Konkee is a sweet dish made from corn flour, sugar, spices, grated coconut, and raisins. The mixture is then wrapped in a banana leaf and boiled. *Foofoo*, one of several substitutes for rice, is simply boiled plantains pounded in a mortar with a pestle. This is usually served with some type of stew. *Coocoo*, another substitute for rice, is a corn meal mush blended with seasoned boiled okra. *Cutty Cutty soup*, a "poor man" dish, is made with okra, salt beef, pig tail, tripe (stomach tissue, usually of a cow), onions, green plantains, and dumplings. *Salt fish cakes*, also called codfish cakes, are made from shredded salted codfish mashed together with boiled potatoes, onions, and pepper, then placed in a batter and fried. Black cake is Guyanese fruit cake, usually made at Christmas or for weddings. It is a very dark and very rich fruit cake made with rum. Ginger beer is a non-alcoholic homemade drink made from grated ginger and sweetened water.

TRADITIONAL COSTUMES

Many Indo-Guyanese women wear their traditional *sari* for special occasions such as weddings or East Indian holidays. *Saris* are garments made from long pieces of light cloth: one end is wrapped around the waist to form a skirt and the other is draped over the shoulder or the head. Some Afro-Guyanese wear the African *booboo* and *head wrap*. During the 1970s, when Guyana became a socialist republic, Prime Minister Burnham formally declared the official business attire for men to be *shirtjacks* and pants, instead of the European suit and tie.

DANCES AND SONGS

Guyana's National Dance Company—a multiethnic troupe—performs East Indian and African dances during national holidays, including Independence Day; *Deepavali*, the Hindu celebration of lights; *Phagwah*, the Hindu festival to welcome spring; and the Republic celebrations.

HOLIDAYS

In addition to Christmas Day, New Year's Day, and Easter Sunday, Guyanese Americans celebrate Guyana's Independence on May 26, and to a lesser degree "August Monday," the first Monday in August, symbolizing Emancipation Day. At Independence Day celebrations, the national anthem, "Dear Land of Guyana," is sung.

HEALTH ISSUES

There are no documented health problems or medical conditions that are specific to Guyanese Americans. Many families have health insurance coverage through their employers. Like most Americans, Guyanese American business owners and professionals in private practice are insured at their own expense.

LANGUAGE

Guyanese generally speak and understand Creole or Creolese, which is a linguistic fusion of African dialects and English. Standard English is used for formal communication, although it is spoken in a definite Guyanese vernacular. For the first generation of immigrants who settled (as most did) among other Caribbean enclaves, there was no real attempt to alter their speech patten, since others in their community could understand them. For those immigrants who moved away from their Caribbean neighbors and integrated socially into the host society, their speech pattern gradually lost its distinctive Guyanese sound. Some immigrants, however, chose to hold onto their speech pattern as a way of maintaining their identity.

GREETINGS AND OTHER POPULAR EXPRESSIONS

Common Guyanese words and expressions include: Howdy—How are you?; God spare life—an expression used after promising to do something; God rest the dead—expression used before speaking the name of the dead; *Beannie*—referring to a young female; *Banna*—referring to a young male; *Jert*—to eat; *Tassay*—to get lost; *Ahgee*—grandmother; *Bambuy*—leftovers; *Eye wata*—tears; *Mamoo*—uncle (Indo-Guyanese); *Pagaly*—silly; "Don't mek yuh eyes pass me"—meaning don't disrespect me.

FAMILY AND COMMUNITY DYNAMICS

The first wave of Guyanese immigrants in the early decades of the twentieth century were typically single males who had left their families and possibly a fiancee behind temporarily in the hopes of sending for them later; in the interim, they supplemented the income of the family back home. Many married men did not immigrate ahead of their families, since their jobs at home provided the only income the family had. In the case of the Indo-Guyanese, some husbands and wives came together, leaving children with grandparents or other relatives. Recently there has been an increase in the numbers of Indo-Guyanese women who have immigrated without their families, but these numbers are still minuscule in comparison to the Afro-Guyanese women, who began moving to the United States alone in the 1960s. Typically these newcomers first stayed for a short time with friends or relatives. After finding work, however, they usually rented rooms in crowded boarding houses (often occupied by other Guyanese and Caribbean immigrants).

Like typical first generation immigrants, the Guyanese worked hard and saved most of their earnings, doing without the simplest of pleasures. Their primary goal was to facilitate the passage of their family members to the United States. Many of the males worked around the clock and went to night classes to better themselves educationally; women typically performed "sleep in" work—living six days per week at their place of employment and returning to the boarding house for one day, usually beginning Saturday night and ending Sunday night. That one day off was spent in church and at stores shopping for things to "pack a barrel" for their kin back home.

After acquiring permanent resident status and securing their family's passage to the United States, Guyanese immigrants then concentrated on improving their economic and educational status. Many women pursued nursing degrees part-time while holding multiple jobs.

The core of the social network of the Guyanese is the family. Other Guyanese are preferred as marriage partners, but many Guyanese marry persons from other Caribbean nations, or Americans of Caribbean parentage. The percentage of marriages between Guyanese and Americans—black or white—is low.

INTERACTIONS WITH OTHER ETHNIC GROUPS

From their first arrival, the Guyanese began to interact with other ethnic groups, particularly Jamaicans, Trinidadians, Barbadians, Grenadians, and people from other English-speaking Caribbean nations. This nurturing of a Caribbeanness contributes to the resistance to marry outside of the Caribbean group. Guyanese American cultural traditions have been preserved by the religious observances of weddings, baptisms, and funerals.

WEDDINGS

The bridal shower is a social custom practiced in Guyana among many Christians and non-Christians. Many Guyanese Hindus, for example, have simultaneous Christian celebrations to include their Christian friends. For Christian weddings, bans are usually announced in the church for three consecutive Sundays so that impediments to the marriage—if any—can be brought to the attention of the priest. During this period the priest counsels the couple on the duties of marriage. As in the United States, the couple selects a best man, maid (or matron) of honor, bridesmaids, and attendants. In most cases the best man and maid/matron of honor serve as godparents to the couple's first child. The godmother then becomes the couple's *mac mae* ("mac may"), and the godfather the *com pae* ("com pay").

On the night before the wedding, in a celebration of song and dance called a *kweh kweh*, the bride is feted by the older women of her family. The actual wedding ceremony mirrors the traditional American church wedding. Silver coins are also blessed by the priest and given to the bride and groom for good luck and prosperity. The priest wraps a robe around the bride and groom, symbolizing their union, and blesses them before concluding the ceremony.

Most Guyanese American weddings are held at a private home or at a Caribbean catering hall to ensure a Guyanese menu. Gifts are usually delivered before the day of the wedding. Toasting or paying respects to the newlyweds is the focal point of the reception. The best man gives his blessings and advice first, then directs the parents of the couple to speak, then any elders in the audience. The bridegroom then speaks, thanking everyone for attending. The reception is accompanied by Caribbean music and dancing. Two weeks after the wedding, the couple entertains family and friends at a gala called a "Second Sunday."

BAPTISMS

The Guyanese American community is a dispersed one, but family members often travel hundreds of miles for celebrations such as baptisms. According to Guyanese tradition, a female child will have two godmothers and one godfather, and a male child will have two godfathers and one godmother. The godparents are responsible for purchasing the baptismal gown for the child; however, if the mother still has her wedding dress, she may choose to make a baptismal dress from it for her first born. The godparents take the child to church; the priest then confers the grace of God on the baby by placing his hand on his or her head. The godparents promise to lead the child in the way of the Lord. Then, the priest blesses the child in the name of the Holy Trinity while rubbing incense on the forehead and chest; pours holy water over the child's forehead; and finally offers the child up to God.

After the baptism, it is customary to have a large gathering with lots of music, dancing, and food. Family members and friends shower the child with gifts, and money is pinned on the child for good luck and prosperity. Guyanese custom dictates that the child be given a piece of gold jewelry for good luck soon after birth. Girls usually are given a pair of gold bangles (bracelets) and a pair of gold earrings, and boys are given a gold ring and a gold bracelet.

FUNERALS

Among the Guyanese, a death in the family is announced by word of mouth. In Guyana, the body of the dead is usually washed and dressed by family members, but because of health regulations this tradition is not practiced in the United States. The deceased is remembered and mourned during a wake, which is followed by a gathering of loved ones and friends. Food and liquor abound, tall tales are told, and folksongs are sung.

After the funeral service at church, prayers are said by the priest at the cemetery, and family members are invited to place flowers on the coffin. Before the deceased is lowered into the grave, the priest sprinkles soil on top of the coffin and while saying: "Ashes to ashes, dust to dust." The congregation then returns to the home of the deceased where friends and relatives have gathered bearing food and beverages. Nine days after the death of a loved one, there is another wake—called "Nine Night"—held in memory of the deceased.

For many days before and after the burial, the family of the deceased is never left alone. Mirrors in the house are covered, for fear of seeing the deceased. Homes are not swept out for days after the burial, for fear of the dead taking more family members with him or her.

RELIGION

Guyanese Americans generally maintain an affiliation with the religious denomination of their homeland. The vast majority of Guyanese American churchgoers are Episcopalian. Priests from Guyana who immigrate to the United States often go on to lead Guyanese American churches. These churches also serve as network centers for newly arrived immigrants. Many Caribbean-led Episcopalian churches in the New York City area have established schools that cater to the educational demands of Caribbean parents and are staffed by former Caribbean schoolteachers. Guyanese parents view education as a combination of learning and discipline; many opt to pay for private schooling for their children, feeling assured that they will be taught in the "home way."

Beginning in the 1970s, a surge of nondenominational churches were established by the Guyanese in the New York and New Jersey areas. These "churches," which are more like teaching centers, have attracted many newly settled Guyanese Americans. So-called "Unity Centers" serve as community centers and teach positive thinking and ways to attain a closer relationship with God. The congregation reflects the many faces of the nations in the Caribbean, although Guyanese usually predominate in those Unity Centers run by Guyanese priests and priestesses.

EMPLOYMENT AND ECONOMIC TRADITIONS

Because the early Guyanese immigrants settled in the northeastern region of the United States, particularly New York, they found work in the health care, domestic labor, banking, clerical, and physical security fields. They were paid the lowest wages, and—like members of other immigrant groups—many worked several jobs at a time. After accumulating work experience and permanent resident status, many Guyanese advanced to better paying positions.

Some Guyanese established their own small, family-run businesses, such as bakeries and take-out restaurants catering to the tastes of a Caribbean community. Others who could not afford to rent business space in Caribbean neighborhoods sold Guyanese food out of their homes on weekends. As the Guyanese immigrants became more established, they opened real estate offices, guard services, small grocery stores (specializing in food products from home, like *cassareep*), neighborhood law offices (specializing in immigration and real estate law), beauty salons, and travel agencies.

POLITICS AND GOVERNMENT

Guyanese are active in the organizations of the larger Caribbean region. There are many Guyanese nurses' and police associations. Guyanese Americans have not yet made a collective impact on political activity nationally. Locally, however, they have organized through their churches with other ethnic groups to call attention to problems in their neighborhoods. They have also entered politics on a local level.

RELATIONS WITH GUYANA

Guyanese Americans maintain close ties to their homeland and its people and provide significant financial support to their native country. During the late 1970s and 1980s—when Guyana was experiencing a terrible economic crisis owing to the further devaluation of the Guyanese dollar, skyrocketing prices for consumer goods, and shortages of basic necessities—Guyanese organizations pooled their resources from fund-raising and made generous donations of money, food, clothing, and equipment to Guyanese hostels, orphans, almshouses, schools, and hospitals. High school alumni associations furnished their alma maters and other schools with chairs, desks, books, and office supplies. Nurses' organizations donated syringes, bed sheets, thermometers, penicillin, and other scarce supplies to hospitals.

There is a steady flow of scholarly exchanges between Guyana and the United States in the form of academic conferences. In almost every college or university with a sizable Caribbean student body, there are Caribbean associations that encourage the connections with home through guest lecturers, trips, and networking. In the United States, academic organizations such as the Association of Caribbean Historians, the Caribbean Studies Association, and the Caribbean Writers Association cater to scholars from the Caribbean.

INDIVIDUAL AND GROUP CONTRIBUTIONS

Guyanese Americans represent a minuscule percent of America's total population, but they have made significant contributions to American popular culture, the arts, academia, and politics:

LITERATURE AND THE ARTS

Guyana has long provided a theme for literary expression. Popular Guyanese authors include Jan Carew (1925–), Wilson Harris (1921–), Denis Williams (1923–), O. R. Dathorne (1934–), Christopher Nicole (1930–), Gordon Rohlehr, and E. R. Braithwaite (1920–). Braithwaite's memoir *To Sir With Love* details his experiences as a black high school teacher in a white London slum. The work was praised for its hopeful view of difficult race relations and was adapted for a 1967 film of the same name.

Edgar Mittelholzer (1909-1965) became well known outside of Guyana for such novels as *Corentyne Thunder*, *Shadows Move Among Them* (which won high critical acclaim in America and Britain), *Morning at the Office*, *The Life and Death of Sylvia*, *The Piling of Clouds*, and a three-part novel known as the *Kaywana Trilogy* (*Children of Kaywana*, *Kaywana Stock*, and *Kaywana Blood*). This trilogy follows the fortunes of a Dutch planter family, the Van Groenwegels, over three centuries of Guyanese history and attempts to capture the raw and violent spirit of those times.

Miramy, a full-length Guyanese comedy by Frank Pilgrim, is set on an imaginary island in the West Indies. It became the first locally written play to be performed outside of Guyana. The works of Jan Carew include *Black Midas*, a picaresque novel acclaimed for its vivid portrayal of raw and roguish types in the diamond fields of Guyana; *The Wild Coast*, a sensitive study of a young man's difficult passage from puberty to manhood; and *The Last Barbarian*, a study of West Indian and African life in Harlem. Works by Wilson Harris include a series of poems entitled *Eternity to Season* and the novel *The Palace of the Peacock*, about the journey of a river crew through the jungles of Guyana. Among his other works are *The Far Journey of Oudin*, *The Whole Armour*, and *The Secret Ladder*.

Gregory A. Henry, a Guyana-born artist, draws upon the endemic storytelling traditions of his culture for his paintings and sculpture. His work, which has been featured in several travelling exhibits and solo and group shows, has been praised by art critics who number him among a select group of artists projected to come to national prominence in the 1990s.

MUSIC

Alvin Chea is a member of Take 6, a Grammy Award-winning, all-male, *a cappella* gospel-pop group. Chea is first generation Guyanese American, born to a Guyanese mother.

POLITICS

Colin Moore is a Guyanese American who has made a name for himself in New York politics. An attorney in private practice in Brooklyn, Moore is known for representing many Guyanese Americans and other Caribbean immigrants throughout the New York area. He sought election to the office of governor of New York in 1994, ran unsuccessfully in the past for New York City councilman and district attorney, and—with a group of politically active African Americans—helped found the Freedom Party.

ORGANIZATIONS AND ASSOCIATIONS

Guyana Republican Party (GRP).
Address: P.O. Box 260185, Brooklyn, New York 11226-0185.
Telephone: (973) 484-3431; or (800) 577-7468.
Fax: (973) 484-1615.
E-Mail: 103203.652@compuserve.com.

SOURCES FOR ADDITIONAL STUDY

The Caribbean Exodus, edited by Barry B. Levine. New York: Praeger, 1987.

Caribbean Immigration to the United States, edited by Roy S. Bryce-Laporte and Delores M. Mortimer. Washington, D.C.: Research Institute on Immigration and Ethnic Studies, 1983.

In Search of a Better Life: Perspectives on Migration from the Caribbean, edited by Ransford W. Palmer. New York: Praeger, 1990.

Udeogalanya, Veronica. *Demographic and Socio-Economic Characteristics of Caribbean Immigrants and Non-Immigrant Population in the United States.* Brooklyn, New York: Caribbean Research Center, Medgar Evers College, 1989.

GYPSY

by
Evan Heimlich

AMERICANS

OVERVIEW

The term *Gypsy* derives from *Egyptian,* reflecting a
mistaken assumption of the origins of the people
who refer to themselves as the Roma. Ethnic Gypsies are the descendants of diverse groups of people
who were assembled in northern India as a military
force to resist the eastward movement of Islam.
Over the centuries, they moved westward into
Europe and northern Africa, adapting their language and culture in their migrations. Gypsy Americans represent family groups from England (Romnichals), Eastern Europe (the Rom, subdivided into
Kalderash, Lovari, and Machvaya), Romania
(Ludar), and Germany. They sometimes entered the
United States after residing in other parts of the
western hemisphere for a period of time. An accurate estimate of their numbers is difficult to achieve.
If counted in a census at all, it is typically by their
country of origin. Estimates of the total population
of ethnic Gypsies in the United States range from
fewer than 100,000 to one million.

HISTORY

The Rom linguist W. R. Rishi gives the etymology
of *Rom* from the Sanskrit *Rama,* with meanings that
include "one who roams about." The number of Persian, Armenian, and Greek terms in the various
Romani dialects reflect their migrations, just as
those related to Sanskrit and Hindi point to their

common origin. Although a Persian story has been cited as proof they came from a single caste of entertainers, more recent evidence, including blood-type research, points to a gathering of diverse peoples in the Punjab region of India to form an army and its support groups to counter Muslim invaders. In the eleventh century some of this group moved north through Kashmir and west into Persia. After some generations they pushed on to Armenia, then fled Turkish invaders by entering the Byzantine Empire. By the thirteenth century they reached the Balkan Peninsula; Serbian and Romanian terms came into their language. Thereafter they split into smaller groups that dispersed throughout Europe, absorbed cultural and linguistic influences of their host countries, and developed differences that persist among Gypsy subgroups today.

The Roma had reached Western Europe from regions dominated by the feared Ottoman Empire. Their language and appearance set them apart from the resident populations; they repeatedly suffered harassment or worse at the hands of the local majority. Such treatment likely encouraged their traditionally nomadic way of life. Eventually Europeans used "Gypsies" or related words to name not only a particular ethnic group of people, but also other groups of people, unrelated by blood, whose traveling lifestyles made them resemble ethnic Gypsies. For the most part, Gypsies kept to themselves as a people; however, as Matt Salo suggests in his introduction to *Urban Gypsies*, "The existence of a number of Gypsy-like peripatetic groups, some of which (such as British Travellers) have intermarried with Gypsies ... complicate our attempts at classification" of who should not count and who should count as Gypsies. Although purists tend to define the group narrowly, loose classifications of ethnic Gypsies include all nomads who live and identify themselves as Gypsies.

The two groups of Gypsy Americans about whom scholars know the most are the Rom and the Romnichals. Many of the Rom came to the New World from Russia or Eastern or Central Europe; the Romnichals came from Great Britain. Although these two groups have much in common, they also are divided by the cultural differences and prejudices between Great Britain and Eastern Europe. The Romnichals came to the United States earlier than the Rom, and ran successful horse-trading operations in New England. The Rom arrived in the United States during the late nineteenth century. It is uncertain how many Gypsies are in the United States because many Gypsies' entry was undocumented, and others were recorded by their country of origin and not as Gypsies. The Roma-sponsored Patrin website explains, "Many Roma themselves do not admit to their true ethnic origins for economic and social reasons." Most chillingly, the Nazis rounded up and killed one million Gypsies during World War II.

Almost all Gypsies in the United States originated from some part of Europe, although there are a few small groups from elsewhere, such as parts of Asia. Some "black Dutch," from Germany, the Netherlands, and Pennsylvania, intermarried with Romnichals and are counted as Anglo-Americans. Besides the Eastern Europeans who make up the large group of Rom, there are in the United States two other large groups of Gypsies: the Baschalde (from Slovakia, Hungary, and Carpagia), who may number close to 100,000; and the Romungre (from Hungary and Transylvania) who may number as many as 60,000. There are also some Horchanay, who are historically Muslims from the South Balkans, and a small population of Sinti Gypsies, who came from Northern Europe—Germany, Netherlands, France, Austria, Hungary—where they, like other Gypsies, were targets of the Nazis. There are also Bosnian and Polish Gypsies present in the United States. Within the category of Rom Gypsies, there are several subgroups in the United States, such as the Kalderash and Machwaya. One of the most recent immigrations of a Gypsy group is that of the Lovara, which arrived in the 1990s. There are also a few small groups of Rumanian Ludar, who may be Gypsies, in addition to the population of Gypsy Americans who emigrated from the Gypsy stronghold within the nation of Romania.

IMMIGRATION WAVES TO THE UNITED STATES

Gypsies have come to the United States for reasons similar to those of other immigrants; however, since European powers have tended to oppose Gypsies, this hostility has hastened Gypsy emigrations. According to Sway, "Gypsy deportations from England, France, Portugal, and Spain created the genesis of Gypsy life in the New World." Gypsies' social marginality left them little institutional power in Europe. Sway adds that England deported some Gypsies to Barbados and Australia, and by the end of the seventeenth century, every European country with New World holdings followed the practice of deporting Gypsies to the Americas.

Suspicion between Gypsies and established institutions also spurred Gypsy emigration. Christian churches of Europe attacked Gypsy fortunetellers, prompting deportations. Sending Gypsies home was not an option—no nation welcomed them since their origin in India was unknown to the Western world until the eighteenth century. Near the end of the nineteenth century, Eastern European emigrants spread throughout Europe and the Western Hemisphere; within this mass movement came the biggest immigrant waves of Gypsies to the United States.

Although Europeans have historically treated Gypsies poorly, Gypsies tended to fare better in Western Europe than in Eastern Europe, where they suffered the extremes of racial prejudice, including enslavement. Still, the Roma hoped to escape social oppression in the New World. Of Gypsies deported to South American colonies, some migrated North. Some Gypsies were annexed into America with territory itself: for example, Napoleon transported hundreds of Gypsy men to Louisiana during the two-year period before selling the Louisiana Territory to the United States in 1803. More recently, toward the end of the twentieth century, the collapse of Communism in Eastern Europe has enabled Gypsies to emigrate more freely, at times with renewed harassment as incentive, bringing new waves of Eastern European Gypsies to the United States.

SETTLEMENT PATTERNS

The traditional stereotype of the Gypsy is the wanderer, and some modern Gypsy Americans continue to travel in pursuit of their livelihoods. Rather than wander, they tend to move purposefully from one destination to another. Historically, some families have reportedly traveled in regular circuits, often returning to the same places; others have ranged more widely, following no set route. Awareness of the best cities, small towns, or rural areas as markets for their services has guided all travel. A group might camp for weeks, sometimes months, at especially productive urban areas, returning to these spots year after year.

Gypsy Americans might maintain a sequence of home bases; they often live in mobile homes, settling indefinitely in a trailer park. They may tear down walls or and enlarge the doorways of their homes to combine rooms or make them larger to create a wide open space suitable for the large social gatherings that occur in Rom homes. In *Urban Gypsies*, Carol Silverman noted that Gypsies frequently pass along the houses, apartments, or trailers that they modify to a succession of Gypsy families. While some Gypsy Americans travel to make their living, others pursue settled careers in a variety of occupations according to their education and opportunities.

The Gypsy population has been participating in American migrations from countryside into cities. Yet estimates tend to support that the Gypsy American population at any given time is evenly divided between urban and rural areas. Generally, as noted by Silverman, the urbanization of the Rom began as early as the end of the eighteenth century when various groups began to spend the winter months camping in vacant lots on the outskirts of cities, and intensified when "a large number of *Rom* flocked to the cities during the 1920s and 1930s to take advantage of various relief programs, and remained there because of gas rationing and because of increasing business opportunities within the city."

Because Gypsies tend to follow economic opportunities, the most populous cities, such as Los Angeles, San Francisco, New York, Chicago, Boston, Atlanta, Dallas, Houston, Seattle, and Portland, have the largest concentrations of Gypsies. Currently, there are Romnichal strongholds of very conservative Gypsies who reside in Texarkana, southern Arkansas, and other predominantly rural regions. Gypsies also have joined American movement westward. Many live in California.

CONTINUED HARASSMENT

Gypsy Americans who can do so often travel to other parts of the Western Hemisphere and to Europe. Many repeatedly visit certain places as part of a set route, including places where their kinfolk lived for generations. Gypsy Americans largely consider Eastern Europe their peoples' home. "In 1933 at the first International Conference on Gypsy Affairs held in Bucharest, Romania," stated Sway, "the United Gypsies of Europe asked for a piece of land in Bucharest where Gypsies in trouble could settle. Later in 1937, Janus Kwiek, the 'Gypsy King of Poland,' asked Mussolini to grant the Gypsies a strip of land in Abyssinia (present-day Ethiopia) so they might escape persecution in various host societies."

Many Americans have romanticized Gypsies as exotic foreigners. Some Americans draw on the supposedly romantic appeals of Gypsy traditions—especially traditions of dancing and music-making, lives on the road, and maintaining a traveling culture. Often, established Americans maintain or adopt European prejudices against Gypsies and treat Gypsy immigrants poorly. Just as Europeans have often attributed the fortune-telling skills of Gypsies to "black magic," Gypsy traders have been accused of fencing stolen goods, and of stealing their goods themselves. Laws attempting to deter, prevent, and punish fortune-tellers and thieves in America have singled out Gypsy Americans. According to Sway, until 1930, Virginia legally barred Gypsies from telling fortunes. And in New Jersey in the middle 1980s, special regulations and licensing requirements applied to Gypsies who told fortunes. Gypsy households have been labeled as "dens of thieves" so that charges brought against one resident may apply to any and all. In Mississippi in the middle 1980s, such application of liability "jointly-and-severally" is law. There have also been cases in the Pacific Northwest. As recently as the 1970s, New Hampshire expelled some Gypsies from that state on the grounds merely that they were Gypsies.

The fearsome shadow of attempted genocide of Gypsies in Europe still menaces Gypsies. Gypsy Americans are concerned about worsening oppression of fellow Gypsies, most severely in Eastern Europe. This concern is understandable in light of the first two genocidal massacres: during World War I Turks killed Gypsies and Armenians; and during the Holocaust, Nazis massacred Gypsies alongside Jews. Because too few people know about the Gypsy victims of the Nazis, Gypsies advocate public recognition of that loss. They attempt to draw attention, too, to the current plight of Eastern European Gypsies. Though the collapse of Communist regimes—especially that of Ceauşescu, which conducted sterilizations and other genocidal persecutions of Gypsies—has alleviated some of the worst oppression, "ethnic cleansing" in Eastern Europe is a cause for Gypsy concern.

ACCULTURATION AND ASSIMILATION

Gypsies have repeatedly shown the ability to adapt without surrendering the essence of their culture. Traditional Gypsy Americans continue to resist the inroads of acculturation, assimilation, and absorption in the United States. Even groups such as the Gitanos or Romnichals, despite having lost most of their original language, still maintain a strong sense of ethnic identity and exclusiveness. A major issue facing Gypsy Americans since the 1980s is a worldwide Christian Fundamentalist revival that has swept up Gypsies around the world. As masses of Gypsies practice versions of Pentecostal Christianity, currents of Gypsy culture may be undergoing a sea-change.

Gypsies maintain a powerful group identity, though. Their traveling itself sets them apart from other cultures, as does their common rejection of international borders. Another area of difference from mainstream America is attitude toward formal, public schools. Until recently, many Gypsies sent their children to schools only until the age of ten to keep them from being exposed to alien practices and teachings.

Prejudice against Gypsies has strengthened their isolation. One might suppose that economic interactions would dispel the insularity of Gypsies, if insular social techniques did not pull Gypsies together. These opposing tensions give Gypsies a flexible identity. Gypsy people may seem split between their business life, which focuses outwardly on non-Gypsies, and on the other hand, their social life, which focuses inwardly on only Gypsies. Nevertheless, as Silverman noted, some Gypsy Americans may present themselves as Puerto Ricans, Mexicans, Armenians, Greeks, Arabs, and as other local ethnics in order to obtain jobs, housing, and welfare.

Contemporary urban Rom usually live interspersed among the non-Gypsy population, establishing *ofisi* (fortune-telling parlors, one means of livelihood) in working areas or in their homes. Their businesses may make many Gypsies seem quite assimilated, and at other times the same Gypsies may seem very traditional. Gypsies have tended to maintain two distinct standards of public behavior, one among themselves, another among outsiders, and Sway pointed to a "form of body language and interactional style" that Gypsies often use when interacting with non-Gypsies. "A Gypsy's very survival among non-Gypsies often depends on his [or her] ability to conceal as well as exaggerate his Gypsiness at appropriate times," observed Silverman. For example, an appropriate time for a Gypsy to play to stereotype is while performing as a musician or fortune-teller for audiences who are known to value Gypsies' exoticism. On the other hand, Silverman added that "a large part of behaving appropriately as a Gypsy involves knowing when to conceal one's Gypsiness." By passing as someone from a less stigmatized group, one can circumvent anti-Gypsy prejudice. For many, noted Silverman, "the process of boundary crossing [is] a performance strategically enacted for survival."

Gypsies and non-Gypsy Americans have subjected each other to prejudices. To many Americans, Gypsy Americans seem to be sinister foreigners. To the Gypsies, Sway observed, "non-Gypsies seem cold, selfish, violent," as well as defiled or polluted. However, because Gypsies depend economically on non-Gypsies as customers for their services, they cannot afford to isolate themselves physically from non-Gypsies. Instead, social techniques enable Gypsies to maintain their cultural separateness from the people near whom they live, and with whom they do business. Basically, these techniques consist of taboos. A Gypsy court system enforces the taboos, to effectively limit social interactions with non-Gypsies. Gypsy Americans may bend their taboos by eating in a restaurant with non-Gypsies, and then attend to the taboos by remarking that some uncleanliness made them sick or unlucky.

IMAGES OF GYPSY AMERICANS

Stereotypes of Gypsies have focused on their nomadism, fortune-telling, and their trading. Non-Gypsies have stereotyped Gypsies, their cultures, and their skills as exotically different at best, but often much more offensively. As a result, English-speakers say that to defraud, swindle, or cheat some-one is to "gyp" them. This sensational image of Gypsies as criminals does not find support from sta-tistical analysis of court records, since conviction rates of Gypsy Americans seem to be lower than rates of other ethnic Americans for rape and mur-der; and the conviction rate of Gypsies for theft is no higher than the rate for other Americans. How-ever, Hancock pointed out in his *The Pariah Syn-drome* that the association of Gypsies with crime goes deep and is sometimes justified since Gypsies have resorted to theft as a means of survival; but "much of it is not justified, however, and is the result of exploitation of a stereotype by a popular press which is less interested in the honest Gypsies."

Western stereotypes of Gypsies as criminals arose when Gypsies first entered Europe. Confusion reigned over Europe's attempts to know who the Gypsies were. Matt Salo stated in his introductory essay to *Urban Gypsies* that "many early [European] accounts describe Gypsy bands as conglomerations of various segments of the underclass of society," adding that Gypsies were widely thought to be "a motley assemblage of rogues and vagabonds." Euro-pean Christians, especially, tended to believe that dark-skinned people were evil. Sway suggested that because the Gypsies were dark, strangely dressed, and spoke a language believed to be "a kind of gib-berish used to deceive others" lent credence to the fear that they were spies for the Turks and enemies of Christendom.

Many Europeans and Americans have romanti-cized Gypsies in literature, music, and folklore; part of the strength of the Gypsy-figure's appeal was that s/he seemed free from the constraints of life in con-temporary industrial society. This stereotypical fig-ure's popularity has captured audiences and helped to conceal ethnic Gypsies. In addition to their sup-posed criminality and freedom, the Gypsies have been portrayed as beautiful, loose, loose-bodied, flexible, and insolent—as in British novelist D. H. Lawrence's portrayal of a Gypsy man in *The Virgin and the Gipsy*, first published in 1931. Desire for the other tends to represent itself culturally as the other's desire; as Hancock notes, "Gypsy women

A gypsy wedding party poses for the camera in this 1941 photograph.

have long been represented as sexual temptresses, and Gypsy men as a sexual threat to non-Gypsy women, in both song and story."

Conversely, the roles of non-Gypsies as cus-tomers for some Gypsy businesses have contributed to Gypsies' negative stereotypes of non-Gypsies. To fortune-tellers non-Gypsies tend to seem depraved. "Many regular customers are lonely, mal-adjusted, or both," wrote Sway. "They reveal aspects of *gaje* (non-Gypsy) life to the fortune-teller which sound deviant to her; in turn, she tells her family every-thing she has heard."

Until relatively recently, when some Gypsy activists and scholars have begun to try to present their people in a better light, stereotypes faced little or no opposition. Gypsies had little basis of trust for attempts to reveal how they "really" are, and lacked the resources to publish denials of specific claims. However, many Gypsy Americans now are actively trying to debunk oppressive stereotypes of Gypsies and promote a new public image. The film, *King of the Gypsies*, which was "suggested by" the best-selling book by Peter Maas, focuses on the squalor of Gypsy life from the perspective of a Gypsy-born boy who reviles Gypsies. Gypsies have protested the inaccu-rate and garish portrayals in this film. At the other end of the film spectrum is *Latcho Drom*—a "musical journey from India to Iberia, a seamless anthology of Gypsy music as played by an assortment of profes-sionals on a variety of stringed instruments—sitars, zithers, violins, guitars—against means of percussion that range from small drums to brass vases to paired spoons to castanets," wrote J. Hoberman (*Village*

Voice, July 26, 1994, p. 47). "The vocals are as wailing and soulful as the rhythms are hypnotic and infectious." Community scenes feature children in Istanbul; an old man sings of the fall of Ceauşescu; a woman sings a lament of Auschwitz. The film ends in Western Europe, with singers, players, and dancers performing in France and Spain.

TRADITIONS, CUSTOMS, AND BELIEFS

Gypsies' patterns of kinship structures, traveling, and economics characterize them as an ancient people who have adapted well to modern society. Much scholarship on U.S. Gypsies treats only the Rom; and although other groups differ in some ways, Silverman states that the folk belief or folk religion of all ethnic Gypsies consists mainly of "the taboo system, together with the set of beliefs related to the dead and the supernatural."

Gypsy taboos separate Gypsies—each group of Gypsies—from non-Gypsies, and separate the contamination of the lower half of the adult Gypsy's body (especially the genitals and feet) from the purity of its upper half (especially the head and mouth). The waist divides an adult's body; in fact, the *Romani* word for waist, *maskar*, also means the spatial middle of anything. Since a Gypsy who becomes polluted can be expelled from the community, to avoid pollution, Gypsies try to avoid unpurified things that have touched a body's lower half. Accordingly, a Gypsy who touches his or her lower body should then wash his or her hands to purify them. Similarly, an object that feet have touched, such as shoes and floors, are impure and, by extension, things that touch the floor when someone drops them are impure as well. Gypsies mark the bottom end of bedcovers with a button or ribbon, to avoid accidentally putting the feet-end on their face.

To Gypsies, it seems non-Gypsies constantly contaminate themselves. Non-Gypsies might neglect to wash their hands after urinating in public restrooms, they may wash underwear together with face towels and even tablecloths, or dry their faces and feet with the same towel. According to Silverman, when non-Gypsies move into a home, "they often replace the entire kitchen area, especially countertops and sinks, to avoid ritual contamination from previous non-Gypsy occupants."

Taboos apply most fully to adult Gypsies who achieve that status when they marry. Childbearing potential fully activates taboos for men and especially for women. At birth, the infant is regarded as entirely contaminated or polluted, because s/he came from the lower center of the body. The mother, because of her intensive contact with the infant,

is also considered impure. As in other traditional cultures, mother and child are isolated for a period of time and other female members will assume the household duties of washing and cooking. Between infancy and marriage, taboos apply less strictly to children. For adults, taboos, especially those that separate males and females, relax as they become respected elders.

CUISINE

Hancock generalized that for mobile Gypsies, methods of preparing food have been "contingent on circumstance." Such items as stew, unleavened bread, and fried foods are common, whereas leavened breads and broiled foods, are not. Cleanliness is paramount, though; and, "like Hindus and Muslims, Roma, in Europe more than in America, avoid using the left hand during meals, either to eat with or to pass things" (Ian Hancock, "Romani Foodways," *The World and I*, June 1991, p. 671; cited hereafter as Foodways).

Traditionally, Gypsies eat two meals a day—one upon rising and the other late in the afternoon. Gypsies take time from their "making a living in the *gadji-kanó* or the non-Gypsy milieu," in order to have a meal with other Gypsies and enjoy *khethanipé*—being together (Foodways, p. 672). Gypsies tend to cook and eat foods of the cultures among which they historically lived: so for many Gypsy Americans traditional foods are Eastern European foods. Those who have adopted Eastern Orthodox Catholicism celebrate holidays closely related to the *slava* feast of southeastern Europe, and eat *sarmaa* (cabbage rolls), *gushvada* (cheese strudel), and a ritually sacrificed animal (often a lamb). Gypsies consider these and other strong-tasting foods *baxtaló xabé*, or lucky.

For all Gypsies, eating is important. Gypsies commonly greet an intimate by asking whether or not s/he ate that day, and what. Any weight loss is usually considered unhealthy. If food is lacking, it is associated with bad living, bad luck, poverty, or disease. Conversely, for men especially, weight gain traditionally means good health. The measure of a male's strength, power, or wealth is in his physical stature. Thus a *Rom baro* is a big man physically and politically. A growing awareness of the health risks of obesity tempers some Gypsies' eating.

Eating makes Gypsy social occasions festive, and indicates that those who eat together trust one another. Taboos attempt to bar anybody sickly, unlucky, or otherwise disgraced from joining a meal. Because of these taboos, it is more than impolite for one Gypsy to refuse an offer of food from another.

Such refusal would suggest that the offerer is *marimé*, or polluted. Since Gypsies consider non-Gypsies unclean, in Gypsy homes they serve non-Gypsies from special dishes, utensils, and cups that are kept separate, or disposed of and replaced. Though some Gypsies will eat in certain restaurants, traditionally Gypsies cook for themselves.

CLOTHING

Gypsies have brightly colored traditional costumes, often in brilliant reds and yellows. Women then wear dresses with full skirts and men wear baggy pants and loose-fitting shirts. A scarf often adorns a woman's hair or is used as a cumberbund. Women wear much jewelry and the men wear boots and large belts. A married Gypsy woman customarily must cover her hair with a *diklo*, a scarf that is knotted at the nape of the neck. However, many Gypsy women may go bareheaded except when attending traditional communal gatherings.

HOLIDAYS AND FESTIVALS

In addition to religious holidays, Gypsy funerals are the biggest community holidays. Groups of Gypsies travel and gather to mark the passing of one of their own. Marriages are also important gatherings.

HEALTH ISSUES

Ideas about health and illness among the Rom are closely related to a world view (*romania*), which includes notions of good and bad luck, purity and impurity, inclusion and exclusion. Sutherland, in an essay entitled "Health and Illness Among the Rom of California," observes that "these basic concepts affect everyday life in many ways including cultural rules about washing, food, clothes, the house, fasting, conducting rituals such as baptism and the slava, and diagnosing illness and prescribing home remedies." In Gypsy custom, ritual purification is the road to health. Much attention goes to avoiding diseases and curing them.

The most powerful Gypsy cure is a substance called *coxai*, or ghost vomit. According to Gypsy legends, *Mamorio* or "little grandmother" is a dirty, sickness-bringing ghost who eats people, then vomits on garbage piles. There, Gypsies find and gather what scientists call slime mold, and bake it with flour into rocks. Gypsies also use *asafoetida*, also referred to as devil's dung, which has a long association with healing and spiritualism in India; according to Sutherland, it has also been used in Western medicine as an antispasmodic, expectorant, and laxative.

Sutherland also recounts several Gypsy cures for common ailments. A salve of pork fat may be used to relieve itching. The juice of chopped onions sprinkled with sugar for a cold or the flu; brown sugar heated in a pan is also good for a child's cold; boiling the combined juice of oranges, lemons, water, and sugar, or mashing a clove of garlic in whiskey and drinking will also relieve a cold. For a mild headache, one might wrap slices of cold cooked potato or tea leaves around the head with a scarf; or for a migraine, put vinegar, or vinegar, garlic, and the juice of an unblemished new potato onto the scarf. For stomach trouble, drink a tea of the common nettle or of spearmint. For arthritis pain, wear copper necklaces or bracelets. For anxiety, sew a piece of fern into your clothes. Sutherland notes that elder Gypsies tend to "fear, understandably, that their grandchildren, who are turning more and more to American medicine, will lose the knowledge they have of herbs and plants, illnesses, and cures."

When a Gypsy falls sick, though, some Gypsy families turn to doctors, either in private practices or at clinics. As Sutherland notes in her essay in *Gypsies, Tinkers and Other Travellers*, "The Rom will often prefer to pay for private medical care with a collection rather than be cared for by a welfare doctor if they feel this care may be better." The Romnichals seem to have been historically prone to respiratory illnesses. In general, Gypsy culture seems to facilitate obesity, and thus heart trouble.

LANGUAGE

Most Gypsies are at least bilingual, speaking the language of the country in which they live as well as some branch of the Gypsy language, *Romani*. Sway observes that "since the Gypsy language has [almost] never been written, it has been easily influenced by the sounds of local languages." The Armenian language strongly influenced that of the Gypsies in their sojourns. Next, modern Greek contributed words to the vocabulary.

The language of the Gypsies was the key that unlocked the mystery of their supposed origin. Sway reports that the discovery that Gypsies originated in India was made by a scholar who noticed a close similarity between the language of the Hungarian Gypsies and the Sanskritized Malayalam of subcontinent Indians. This discovery, by a Hungarian theology student, Istvan Valyi, did not come until the middle of the eighteenth century. Matt Salo suggests that "from the realization that Gypsies indeed had their own language, the step to the recognition of their separate ethnicity followed automatically."

Matt Salo points to linguistic histories that help account for Gypsies who do not speak *Romani:* groups of Gypsies split when they left the Balkans, leaving behind others, including those who were enslaved. Fraser indicates that currently, some dialects of *Romani* are classified as Armenian, others as Asiatic (other than Armenian), and the rest as European. Groups from each of the language branches are now widespread. And, according to Fraser, the English word, "pal," (first recorded in 1681) is one of the few *Romani* words to have entered the English lexicon.

When non-Gypsies ask Gypsies speaking *Romani* to identify the foreign language, explains Silverman, "Gypsies usually answer Romanian, Greek, or Yugoslavian," to minimize curiosity and prejudice toward them. Among themselves, Gypsies are also said to use a sort of sign language, *patrin*—marks meaningful to themselves but unintelligible to others. They seemingly used these symbols to describe conditions of camps for future campers, as well as to provide information about people in the area that might be useful for those practicing fortune-telling. Furthermore, Gypsies usually use their Gypsy name only among other Gypsies, and adopt an Americanized name for general and official uses. Particularly because many Gypsies pick common names, they are hard to trace.

GREETINGS

P'aves Baxtalo/Baxtali! ("pah-vis bach-tah-low/bach-tah-lee")—May you be lucky (to a male/female).

FAMILY AND COMMUNITY DYNAMICS

Traditionally Gypsies maintain large extended families. Clans of people numbering in the scores, hundreds, or even thousands gather for weddings, funerals, other feasts, or when an elder falls sick. Although Gypsy communities do not have kings as such, traditionally a group will represent a man as king to outsiders when it needs one to serve as a figurehead or representative. Often, too, a man and his family will tell hospital staffers that he is "King of the Gypsies" so that he will receive better treatment—the title can help provide an excuse for the hospital to allow the large family to make prolonged visits.

In units bigger than a family and smaller than a tribe, Gypsy families often cluster to travel and make money, forming *kumpanias*—multi-family businesses. During recent decades in the United States, on the other hand, Gypsies have been acculturating more closely to the American model by consolidating nuclear families. Currently, after the birth of their first child, some Gypsy couples may be able to move from the husband's parents' home into their own. This change has given more independence to newly wedded women as daughters-in-law.

Gypsy families and communities divide along gender lines. Men wield public authority over members of their community through the *kris*—the Gypsy form of court. In its most extreme punishment, a *kris* expels and bars a Gypsy from the community. For most official, public duties with non-Gypsies, too, the men take control. Publicly, traditional Gypsy men treat women as subordinates.

The role of Gypsy women in this tradition is not limited to childbearing: she can influence and communicate with the supernatural world; she can pollute a Gypsy man so that a *kris* will expel him from the community; and in some cases she makes and manages most of a family's money. Successful fortune-tellers, all of whom are female, may provide the main income for their families. Men of their families will usually aid the fortune-telling business by helping in some support capacities, as long as they are not part of the "women's work" of talking to customers.

MARRIAGE AND CHILDREN

Gypsies of marriageable age may travel with their parents to meet prospective spouses and arrange a marriage. In making a good match, money, and the ability to earn more of it, tend to be factors more important than romance. A Gypsy woman who marries a non-Gypsy can expect her community to expel her permanently. A Gypsy man, however, may eventually get permission to return to his people with his non-Gypsy wife. Once married, a new daughter-in-law must subject herself to the commands of her husband's family, until her first pregnancy. With the birth of her first child, she fully enters womanhood.

Gypsy cultural practices attempt to prevent Gypsy children from learning non-Gypsy ways, and to facilitate raising them as Gypsies. Gypsy children, or at least post-adolescents, generally do not go to school, day-care centers, or babysitters who are not friends or relatives. Furthermore, Gypsy culture forbids them to play with non-Gypsies. Instead, they socialize with Gypsies of all ages. Formal schooling, as such, is minimal. Traditionally, Gypsies devalue education from outside their own culture. They educate their own children within extended families. An important reason Gypsies do not like to send their children to school is that they will have to violate Gypsy taboos: they will have to use public restrooms, and the boys and girls will come into contact too closely in classrooms and on playgrounds. Many Gypsy Americans send their children to schools until the age of ten or 11, at which time the parents permanently remove them from school.

Children are expected to watch and act like their elders. Rather than bar children from adult life, Gypsies often include them in conversations and business. Children learn the family business, often at home. Many Gypsies marry and become partners in family businesses by their late teens. For example, daughters, but not sons, of a fortune-teller train early to become fortune-tellers. Boys may train to sell cars.

RELIGION

Gypsy spirituality, part of the core culture of Gypsies, derives from Hindu and Zoroastrian concepts of *kintala*—balance and harmony, as between good and evil. When that balance is upset, ancestors send signals to keep people on track. The mysticism of fortune-tellers and tarot readers—though such services to non-Gypsies are not the same as Gypsies' own spirituality—has bases in Gypsy spirituality. Many Gypsies are Christians, with denominational allegiances that reflect their countries of origin.

Historically, toward the beginning of the second millennium B.C., Gypsies invented a story of their origins in Egypt—hence the name, "Gypsies"—which gave many of them safe passage in a hostile Europe. The story claimed that they had been oppressed and forced into idol-worship in Egypt, and that the Pope had ordered them to roam, as penitence for their former lack of faith. This story also played on legends of a common heritage of Gypsies and Jews, which were partly based on actual overlap of these two ethnic cultures in marginal trades and ghettos. Sway indicated that the story of an Egyptian origin convinced Europeans until the early sixteenth century when the church became convinced these "penitents" were frauds. The church moved to isolate its followers from Gypsies: "As early as 1456 excommunication became the punishment for having one's fortune told by a Gypsy.... More effective than the policy of excommunication was the assertion by the Catholic Church that the Gypsies were a cursed people partly responsible for the execution of Christ."

Although European churches have a long history of condemning Gypsies, their magic, and their

This gypsy woman is participating in a traditional dance.

arranged marriages, most Rom Gypsy Americans are Eastern Orthodox. They celebrate the *pomona* feast for the dead, at which the feasters invite the dead to eat in heaven. Also, preparation for their *slava* feast requires thorough cleaning of the interior of the host's house, its furniture, and its inhabitants, as the host transforms a section of the house into a church. The feast ceremony begins with coffee for the guests, prayer and a candle for the saints.

Today, around the world, Christian fundamentalist revival movements have been sweeping through Rom, Romnichal, and other groups of Gypsies. Since the mid-1980s, through Assemblies of God, various American groups have formed Gypsy churches. In Fort Worth, Texas, for example, a church integrates traditional Gypsy faith with Christian Pentecostal ritual.

Gypsies have tended to syncretize or blend their ethnic Gypsy folk religion with more established religions, such as Christianity. Gypsy religious beliefs are mostly unrelated to the business of fortune-telling. Silverman pointed out that while Gypsies may disbelieve Gypsy "magic," and "often joke about how gullible non-Gypsies are," in some ways, others act as believers; fortune-tellers generally treat their reading room as sacred and may "consult elder Gypsy women who are known to be experts in dream interpretation, card reading, and folk healing". Gypsies use code-names to mention certain evil-spirits to other Gypsies; and Gypsies sometimes cast curses on other Gypsies (or ward them off). Also, stated Silverman, Gypsy fortune-tellers use diverse religious iconography to create impressions out of a belief "that good luck and power can come from the symbols of any religion."

EMPLOYMENT AND ECONOMIC TRADITIONS

Gypsy Americans have found customers for their enterprises among other poorer members of U.S. society, usually other ethnic minorities, such as Hispanic Americans, African Americans, and immigrants to America from Eastern and Central Europe.

Mobility and adaptation characterize Gypsy trades. From their beginnings, their traditional occupations have catered to other groups, and at the same time maintained Gypsies' separation. In their essay in *Urban Gypsies,* Matt and Sheila Salo explain that "the main features of all occupations were that they were independent pursuits, required little overhead, had a ubiquitous clientele, and could be pursued while traveling" in urban and rural areas. Moreover, Gypsies have adapted to different locales and periods. Silverman discusses a change in occupations in twentieth century America that parallels the urbanization of the Rom. After their arrival in the 1880s, the Rom followed nomadic European trades such as coppersmithing, refining, and dealing in horses for the men, and begging or fortune-telling for the women. They would camp in the country and interact mostly with the rural population, venturing into the cities only to sell their services and purchase necessities. As the automobile supplanted horse travel, the Rom became used-car dealers and repairmen, occupations that they still pursue. When metalworking skills became less important, Gypsies learned new trades, including the selling of items such as watches and jewelry.

As Sutherland points out in *Gypsies, Tinkers and Other Travellers,* "In the *kumpania* men and women cooperate with each other in exploiting the economic resources of their area." Although jobs may be exploited by an individual, the Rom prefer to work in groups called *wortacha,* or partners. These groups always comprise members of the same sex, however, women often take along children of either sex. *Wortacha* may also include young unmarried Gypsies who learn the skills of the adults. Adults work as equals, dividing expenses and profits equally. As a token of respect for an elder, an extra amount may be given, but unmarried trainees receive only what others will give them. The Rom do not earn wages from another Rom. As a rule, Gypsies profit from non-Gypsies only. In the United States and other countries (including England and Wales), Gypsy Americans divide geographic territories to minimize competition between Gypsy businesses.

Gypsies, supremely mobile and profit-making traders, became dealers of vehicles. Romnichals took an early American role as horse traders, and achieved particular success in Boston. According to Matt and Sheila Salo, "During World War I, Gypsies brought teams of their horses to the Great Plains to help harvest crops. For a while at least, the label 'horse trader' or 'horse dealer' seemed almost synonymous with 'Gypsy.' The colorful wagons used by Romnichals to advertise their presence to any community they entered further reinforced this identification by the professionally painted side panels depicting idealized horses and the horse trading life." The pride of Romnichals in their ability to trade horses is reflected in the carved figures of horses on the tombstones of horse dealers, say Matt and Sheila Salo. Many of the Rom, who arrived in America after the horse trade's heyday, sell cars. Other mobile service contributions of the Gypsies have included driveway blacktopping, house painting, and tinsmithing. Gypsy tinkers, who were mostly Romanian-speaking Gypsies, were essential to various industries such as confectioneries, because they re-tinned large mixing bowls and other machinery on-site. They also worked in bakeries, laundries, and anywhere steam jackets operated.

By the 1930s the Rom group of Gypsy Americans virtually controlled the business of fortune-telling. Their advertisements and shop windows have their undeniable place on American boardwalks, roads, and streets. Gypsy mysticism, as represented in fortune-teller costumes and props such as the crystal ball and tarot deck, have impacted on American culture directly, and through their media representations and imitations, such as the likes of commercially produced Ouija boards. Gypsies have maintained a presence and influence in America's quasi-religious, commercially mystical functions.

MUSIC AND MINSTRELSY

Worldwide, Gypsies are most famous for their contributions as musicians. In the United States, Hungarian Slovak Gypsies, mostly violists, have played popular Hungarian music at immigrant weddings. Historically, Gypsies have contributed to music Americans play. Flamenco, which Gypsies are credited with creating in Spain, has its place in America, particularly in the Southwest. Django Rheinhardt, a well-known European Gypsy who contributed to American culture, is perhaps the all-time greatest jazz guitarist. Furthermore, Klezmer music of Jewish immigrants overlaps with music of

Eastern European Gypsies, especially in oriental, flatted-seventh chords played on a violin or clarinet.

There are intriguing parallels between Gypsies and African Americans in European and American cultural history. The rhythmic innovations that Gypsies brought to Europe were not only Asiatic and Middle Eastern, but also African, at least North African; similarly, African Americans brought innovations of African music to America. Some Gypsies owned slaves or employed African American laborers and stevedores (loaders/unloaders). According to legend, some of these men had eloped with Gypsy daughters. When African American ex-slave minstrels first attempted to taste the freedom of the road in post-Reconstruction America, some claimed to adopt the ethnicity, or at least the title, of Gypsies (Konrad Bercovici, "The American Gypsy," *Century Magazine*, 103, 1922, pp. 507-519). In popular American musical traditions of jazz, blues, and rock, the Gypsy has remained a powerful referent.

FORTUNE-TELLERS

In the United States, Rom Gypsies have dominated a niche for fortune-tellers, who are also known as palmists, readers, or advisers. "Fortune-telling actually includes elements of folk psychotherapy and folk healing," made into a business to serve non-Gypsies, wrote Silverman, who adds that one fortune-teller describes her relationship with her customers in this way: "All they need is confidence and strength and a friend and that's what I am." Some customers come only once, and others make themselves more valuable by returning. A reader will try to establish a steady relationship with the customer, whether in person, by telephone, or by mail. Readers will also try to use the customer's language, usually English or Spanish. Moreover, readers often adopt and advertise names for themselves that help them claim the ethnicity of their clientele; and/or, they choose an ethnicity renowned for mystical perception, such as an Asian, African, or Native American one. Fortune-tellers set up shop where they can make money. Often, they serve a working-class clientele composed of other ethnic minorities. They tend to choose visible locales where they can operate freely: New York supports a great many fortune-tellers, while Los Angeles (where more Gypsies sell real estate and cars) has relatively few because of strict laws governing fortune-telling. Daughters of successful fortune-tellers traditionally become fortune-tellers whether or not they are interested. Their family business is part of their household.

POLITICS AND GOVERNMENT

Special attention from American government authorities has seldom benefitted Gypsies. Some states and districts maintain policies and statutes that prohibit fortune-tellers, require them to pay hundreds of dollars for annual licenses, or otherwise control activities in which Gypsies engage. Despite the unconstitutionality of such measures, some rules apply specifically to Gypsies by name. One excuse for this discrimination is the confusion between ethnic Gypsies and vagrants. Gypsy parents skeptical of non-Gypsy schooling have run afoul of truant officers. After a long history of avoidance of local authorities, Gypsies in the United States and elsewhere are becoming more politically active in defense of their civil and human rights; an international organization of Roma people has been recognized by the United Nations.

INDIVIDUAL AND GROUP CONTRIBUTIONS

CULTURE

Brian Vessey-Fitzgerald, who authored *The Gypsies of England*; Jane Carlisle, Thomas's wife; Vita Sackville West; David Birkenhead Smith; and scholar Ian Hancock.

PERFORMING ARTS

Many Gypsy contributors to American culture have been performers. Among Romnichal (English Gypsies) who lived some in America, we can count Charlie Chaplin and Rita Hayworth. Ava Gardner, Michael Cain, and Sean Connery are reported to have Gypsy ancestry. Freddy Prinze (born Freddie Preutzel; 1954-1977), the late comedian and television star on *Chico and the Man*, was Hungarian Gypsy.

ORGANIZATIONS AND ASSOCIATIONS

Baschalde.
Contact: Bill Duna.
Telephone: (612) 926-8281.

Gypsy Folk Ensemble.
Also performs for school assemblies.
Contact: Juli Nelson, Director.

Address: 3265 Motor Avenue, Los Angeles, California 90034.
Telephone: (818) 966-4751.

Gypsy Lore Society.
Scholars, educators, and others interested in the study of the Roma and analogous itinerant or nomadic groups. Works to disseminate information aimed at increasing understanding of Romani culture in its diverse forms. Publishes the *Journal of the Gypsy Lore Society.*

Contact: Sheila Salo, Treasurer.
Address: 5607 Greenleaf Road, Cheverly, Maryland 20785.
Telephone: (301) 341-1261.
Fax: (301) 341-1261.
E-mail: isalo@capaccess.org.
Online: http://www.gypsy.net/gls.

International Romani Union (IRU).
Works to foster unity among members; promotes human rights and obligations; advocates protection and preservation of Romani culture and language. Publishes the quarterly *Buhazi,* the bi-monthly *Lacio Drom,* the bi-weekly *Nevipens Romani,* the monthly *Romano Nevipen,* the monthly *Rrom po Drom,* and the quarterly newspaper *Scharotl.*

Contact: Dr. Ian F. Hancock, Executive Officer.
Address: P.O. Box 822, Manchaca, Texas 78652-0822.
Telephone: (512) 295-4858.
Fax: (512) 295-4772.
E-mail: xulaj@mail.utexas.edu.

MUSEUMS AND RESEARCH CENTERS

Texas Romani Archives, University of Texas at Austin.
Address: Calhoun Hall 501, University of Texas 8-5100, Austin, Texas 78712.

Victor Weybright Archives of Gypsy Studies.
Part of the Gypsy Lore Society (see above).

SOURCES FOR ADDITIONAL STUDY

Fraser, Angus. *The Gypsies.* Cambridge, Massachusetts: Blackwell, 1992.

Gypsies and Travelers in North America: An Annotated Bibliography, compiled by William G. Lockwood and Sheila Salo. Cheverly, Maryland: The Gypsy Lore Society, 1994.

Hancock, Ian. *The Pariah Syndrome: An Account of Gypsy Slavery and Persecution.* Ann Arbor, Michigan: Karoma Publishers, 1987.

Miller, Carol. "The American Rom and the Ideology of Defilement," in *Gypsies, Tinkers and Other Travellers,* edited by Farnham Rehfisch. New York: Harcourt, Brace Jovanovich, 1975; pp. 41-54.

The Patrin Web Journal: Romani Culture and History, website (accessed September 7, 1999) at http://www.geocities.com/Paris/5121/patrin.htm (last modified September 3, 1999).

Rishi, W. R. *Roma: The Panjabi Emigrants in Europe, Central and Middle Asia, the USSR, and the Americas.* Chandigarh, India. Roma Publishers, 1976 and 1996.

Romani.org Home Page, website (accessed September 7, 1999) at http://www.romani.org/ (last modified August 1998).

Salo, Matt and Sheila. "Romnichal Economic and Social Organization in Urban New England 1850-1930," *Urban Gypsies* (special issue of *Urban Anthropology*), Volume 11, No. 3-4 (fall-winter) 1982.

Silverman, Carol. "Everyday Drama: Impression Management of Urban Gypsies," *Urban Gypsies* (special issue of *Urban Anthropology*), Volume 11, No. 3-4 (fall-winter) 1982.

Sutherland, Anne. "The American Rom: A Case of Economic Adaptation," in *Gypsies, Tinkers and Other Travellers,* edited by Farnham Rehfisch. New York: Harcourt, Brace Jovanovich, 1975; pp. 1-40.

————. *Gypsies: The Hidden Americans.* London: Tavistock Publications, 1975.

————. "Health and Illness Among the Rom of California," *The Journal of the Gypsy Lore Society,* February 1992.

Sway, Marlene. *Familiar Strangers: Gypsy Life in America.* Chicago: University of Illinois Press, 1988.

Urban Gypsies (special issue of *Urban Anthropology*), introduction by Matt Salo, Volume 11, No. 3-4 (fall-winter), 1982.

HAITIAN AMERICANS

by

Felix Eme Unaeze and
Richard E. Perrin

Haitian Americans,
by nature, have a
strong belief in the
culture, traditions,
and mores of
their homeland.

OVERVIEW

Haiti, an independent republic since 1804, is the oldest black republic in the world. It is located in the West Indies on the western third of the Island of Hispaniola, which lies between Cuba and Puerto Rico in the Caribbean Sea. The eastern two-thirds of the island is the Dominican Republic. Haiti, which occupies a total area of 10,714 square miles (27,750 sq. km.), is slightly larger than the State of Maryland. Mostly rough and mountainous in terrain with Massif de la Selle and La Hotte among the main ranges, Haiti also contains a few plateaus and plains such as the Northern Plain, Artibonite, and Cul-de-Sac. Haiti has a tropical climate with temperatures that vary between 70 and 90 degrees all year, although December and January can be quite cool. There are two rainy seasons, one beginning in April and ending in May, and the other beginning in October and ending in November. Tropical thunderstorms are frequent during the summer.

In 1992, Haiti's population was estimated to be about 6.5 million inhabitants, with approximately 71 percent living in rural areas and about 29 percent in urban centers. Haiti records one of the highest population densities in the world, with about 600 persons per square mile. The birth rate is about 44.6 per 1000 people and the fertility rate is about six children per woman. The death rate is about 15.6 deaths per 1000 persons. Life expectancy at birth is 53 years for males and 55 years for females.

The people of Haiti are primarily of African descent, although a smaller percentage is mulatto, and therefore of European and African descent. Creole is the main language spoken with about ten percent of the population fluent in French. The literacy rate is 23 percent. About 80 percent of the population is Roman Catholic and ten percent is Protestant; Voodoo is practiced by a majority of the people. The capital city is Port-au-Prince, the country's largest city, which boasts a population of about 1,148,000 people. Other major cities are Cap-Haitien, Gonaives, Les Cayes, Jeremie, and Jacmel. The national flag is horizontally blue over red with the national arms on a centered white panel. The national anthem is *La Dessalinienne: Pour le pays, pour les ancêtres*, which translates as "for the country, for the ancestors," with lyrics by J. Lherisson and music by N. Geffrand (1903).

HISTORY

The island, which was first inhabited by Indian tribes—the Arawaks, the Tainos, and lastly the Caraibes—called their country "Quisqueya" and later "Haiti," which means "the body of land." The island has had a turbulent and bitter history. When Christopher Columbus landed at the Mole St. Nicholas Bay on December 5, 1492, he claimed the island in the interest of the Spanish rulers who had financed the expedition—Ferdinand and Isabella—and called it "Hispaniola," which means "Little Spain."

Although the Indians welcomed the new settlers, the discovery of gold in the riverbeds sent the Spaniards into a frenzied search for the coveted nuggets. The Indians died by the thousands from diseases introduced by the Spaniards, who also enslaved the natives, treated them with extreme cruelty, and massacred them. The Indian population was reduced from about 300,000 to less than 500. In 1510, the Spaniards began to import their first African slaves from the West Coast of Africa to work in the gold mines. The French, who came in 1625 and changed the name of the island to Saint Domingue, fought the Spaniards to keep a hold on part of the territory. After Spain signed a treaty in 1697 in which it conceded the western part of the island to France, the colony developed rapidly under French rule. The 700,000 slaves who worked cotton, sugar cane, and coffee plantations generated great wealth for the plantation owners; Saint Domingue became a prosperous colony in the New World and was called "the Pearl of the Caribbean."

After the French Revolution in 1789, the slaves revolted against the colonists and the movement spread to the north and then to the west and the south. Under the leadership of such famous generals as Toussaint L'Ouverture, the slaves made significant progress in their struggle. Self-educated, Toussaint served first in the Spanish army and then in the French army. He was one of the main instruments of Haiti's independence, defeating the English who had invaded Saint Domingue. He also administered and divided the country into districts without the approval of the mainland "Metropole." The French later grew angry with General Toussaint and placed him in a French prison where he died on April 7, 1803 from hunger and lack of medical care. Although disheartened, the indigenous army fought under Generals Dessalines and Petion, and beat the French army at every turn. French General Leclerc died of yellow fever on November 2, 1803; his successor, General Rochambeau, took refuge. Dessalines surrounded his officers and proclaimed the independence of Saint Domingue in Gonaives on January 1, 1804, and restored the former name of Haiti. Independence was won and the country became the second, after the United States, in the Western Hemisphere to become an independent republic.

MODERN ERA

Dessalines became Haiti's first head of state. Following the elaboration and ratification of a constitution, full powers were given to Dessalines on September 2, 1804. He proclaimed himself Emperor and took the name Jacques the First. He redistributed the country's wealth and converted most of the colonist plantations to state property. He made many political enemies who later resented his manner of governing. Ambushed on his way to Port-au-Prince, he was killed on October 17, 1806. After his death, a constituent assembly amended the Constitution and limited the powers of the president. General Henri Christophe, who had started a power struggle with General Alexandre Petion, withdrew to the northern part of the country and formed a new government; Petion was elected president in March of 1807, thus dividing the new nation. Petion governed the West and South while Christophe ruled the North. In March of 1811, Christophe proclaimed himself king and took the name of Henri the First. Because of his strict regulations, the Kingdom of the North became prosperous, and he erected monuments, which became symbols of power and authority. For example, the Citadel Laferriere, a monument to human endurance, was constructed by the labor of 20,000 men between 1805 and 1814 as a center of resistance against any attempt by foreigners to conquer the island. His ornate palace at Sans Souci near Cap

Haitien and his vast citadel, though in ruins, are likewise marvels of massive masonry. When Christophe died in an apparent suicide in 1820, the North and South were reunited with Jean-Pierre Boyer succeeding Petion.

Twenty different presidents headed the Haitian government from 1867 to 1915, and Haiti's unstable political and economic conditions made it vulnerable to outside intervention. Haiti's rising external debt caused European countries to threaten force to collect. At this time, World War I was at its peak in Europe and in July of 1915, the United States Marines landed on Haiti's coast and occupied the country. Under the Monroe Doctrine—a document stating U.S. opposition to European involvment in the Western Hemisphere—the U.S. Marines remained in Haiti for 19 years from 1915 until 1934. The Haitian people resented American occupation and wanted to restore their national sovereignty. Guerrilla resistance movements were in place but were crushed. In 1946, a popular movement brought forth a rising middle class whose members asked for the sharing of power and liberalization of governmental institutions. The movement was aborted, which contributed to the fall of then-President Elie Lescot (1941-1946), and Dumarsais Estime was elected president. From that period on, all Haitian presidents, with the exception of François "Papa Doc" Duvalier, have been deposed by military coup d'état.

In 1957, François Duvalier was elected president. He became a dictator, enforcing a reign of terror with his secret police, sometimes referred to as *tonton macoute*. Duvalier proclaimed himself President-for-Life in 1964 and his reign of terror continued. The Haitian economy began to deteriorate and the people were suffering seriously in the 1960s. He died in 1971 and his son, Jean-Claude "Baby Doc" Duvalier, who was only 19 years old, succeeded his father. Both Duvaliers ruled for nearly 30 years. It was during this period that many Haitians fled Haiti. Jean-Claude followed in his father's footsteps, maintaining the same policies of hate and oppression. He was ousted by the Haitian people on February 7, 1986. From 1986 until 1990, four different provisional governments were put into power with the sole purpose of holding general elections, but popular discontent forced them out. Free elections were held on December 16, 1990; and, although the Reverend Jean-Bertrand Aristide was elected by a majority of 67 percent, he was overthrown by the army on September 30, 1991, and took refuge in the United States. He was restored to his position through peaceful negotiation; he returned to Haiti under a United States military escort and was reinstated on October 15, 1994.

THE FIRST HAITIANS IN AMERICA

During the 1790s, Haiti was the most affluent of the French colonies. It was then that the black populace of the island revolted against slavery and there was a panicked exodus. Thousands of whites, free blacks, and slaves fled to American seaports, culminating in large French-speaking communities in New Orleans, Norfolk, Baltimore, New York City, and Boston. Immigrants from Haiti who arrived in the United States during the eighteenth and nineteenth centuries were determined to survive in their new land. Jean-Baptiste Point du Sable, a trapper who settled on the shore of Lake Michigan was an early Haitian arrival; he settled and established a trading post on the river at a point that would later become the City of Chicago. Pierre Toussaint, a devout Catholic who came to New York as a slave of a French family in 1787, became a prominent hair dresser to wealthy New York patrons and also became a fund-raiser who helped the poor and destitute. France was a safe haven for many educated Haitians, and only a few middle-class Haitians chose to go to the United States. Many of them stayed to receive a university education. A renowned poet and playwright, Felix Morisseau-Leroy was one of the post-World War II immigrants.

SIGNIFICANT IMMIGRATION WAVES

According to the United States Census of 1990, there were about 290,000 people who claimed Haitian ancestry; however, this figure does not include the tens of thousands who were in the United States illegally. Moreover, there are second- and third-generation Haitian Americans who simply identify themselves as black; also, some legal immigrants may find it difficult to admit to roots that go back to a Caribbean nation so often associated with superstition and poverty. However, anthropologists estimate that about 1.2 million people in the United States are of Haitian ancestry.

There are five major documented periods of Haitian immigration to the United States: the period of French colonization; the Haitian revolution (1791-1803); the United States occupation of Haiti (1915-1934); the period of the Duvaliers (1957-1986); and the overthrow of President Aristide (1991). For almost three decades, from 1957 to 1986, when François "Papa Doc" and Jean-Claude "Baby Doc" Duvalier were in power, political persecution caused Haitian professionals, the middle class, and students to leave the island in large numbers. Haitians emigrated in search of political asylum or permanent residence status in various countries such as the United States, Mexico, Puerto

Rico, Jamaica, France, Dominican Republic, French Guyana, and Africa.

In the 1980s, many Haitian immigrants arrived in the United States by boat on the shores of Florida and were known as the "boat people." While President Carter gave such refugees a legal status similar to Cubans in 1980 with his Cuban-Haitian entrant program, 18 months later, President Reagan subscribed to a policy of interdiction and indefinite detention for Haitian boat people refugees. Six months later, in June 1982, a federal court ruled against such detention and several thousand refugees were released. In 1986, 40,000 Haitians who came to the United States seeking political asylum were given permanent resident status.

A similar pattern of events occurred in the 1990s. When Aristide was removed by military coup in 1991, there was another wave of Haitian boat people. Under Presidents Bush and Clinton, many were not allowed to reach the shores of the United States. Instead they were stopped at sea, and returned to Haiti. Others were put in detention camps; indefinite detention still occurred. Between 1995 and 1998, 50,000 Haitians were given asylum and temporary legal status, but not permanent like many of their Nicaraguan and Cuban counterparts. The National Coalition for Haitian Rights pushed for legislation to address this issue. In 1998, the Haitian Refugee Immigration Fairness Act was adopted, and those immigrants were given the opportunity to apply for such status.

As with the National Coalition for Haitian Rights, Michel S. Laguerre has documented that volunteer lawyers and local activists have helped many refugees remain in their adopted country, through the generosity of various humanitarian organizations. However, Laguerre—in his book *American Odyssey: The Haitians in New York City*—has also recorded that some refugees attempted suicide while in detention. Despite the odds, the Haitian refugees had the energy and determination to survive in the United States. In her book, *Demele: "Making It"*, social anthropologist Rose-Marie Chierici, herself a Haitian American, has recounted how Haitian immigrants used the Creole word "demele" to manage life in the face of hardship.

Every wave of migration from Haiti has come during political turmoil there; however, economic malaise has always accompanied such turmoil so it has been difficult to distinguish political from economic migrants. Some of the Haitian refugees were thought to have left their homeland because of economic rather than political reasons. Early Haitian immigrants stayed in cities in the United States where they could work and maintain contact with their homeland. The greatest concentration of immigrants are found in New York City, Miami, Chicago, New Orleans, Los Angeles and Boston. Until 1977, Brooklyn was the heart of Haitian America; however, between 1977 and 1981, 60,000 Haitian boat people landed in South Florida, and the center of the Haitian Diaspora moved south to a community of stucco cottages and mom-and-pop businesses anointed "Little Haiti."

In the early 1980s, thousands of Haitian doctors, teachers, social workers and entrepreneurs moved from New York to Miami. Restaurants serving conch and goat meat and record shops blaring Haitian meringue music sprang up on 54th Street and Northeast Second Avenue. The Tap Tap Haitian Restaurant in Miami Beach also serves as a Haitian hangout.

Haitian immigrants are employed in all types of fields. Deborah Sontag reported in the *New York Times* on June 3, 1994, that among the early immigrants, Haitian workers include not only migrant workers in Homestead, Florida, but also wealthy doctors on Long Island, taxi drivers in Manhattan as well as college professors in Washington, D.C.

ACCULTURATION AND ASSIMILATION

Like most immigrants in the United States, Haitians are busy in the pursuit of the American dream. Almost every Haitian American wishes to buy a home as a matter of status and security. This is implied in the saying, "Se vagabon ki loue kay," which means, "Respectable people don't rent." However, behind the facade of pride and achievement, there is a litany of social problems—battered women, homeless families, and economic exploitation. The problems that face Haitian immigrants are enormous and complex. Moreover, the problem of undocumented immigrants who live in constant fear of being deported and thrown into Haitian jails has also led to stress-related emotional disorders, which frequently keep the immigrants from using such facilities as public hospitals. Instead, they rely on folk medicine to cure ordinary aliments or they seek a private clinic with Haitian medical personnel. Marc Abraham, a Haitian who has lived on Long Island for 37 years, "I think Americans see Haitians as desperate people instead of decent people who struggle." Abraham continues: "I have to understand that hostility, I guess, to take it off my heart. I mean, this country has enough problems without ours too."

According to Father Thomas Wenski, director of Pierre Toussaint Haitian Catholic Center in

Miami, Haitians have been specifically and harshly excluded because of "America's endemic 'negrophobia' and inherent racism." Haitians have been excluded because of their race and economic condition. "Thus," says Wenski, "one must ask: will the Haitians be able to assimilate into American society as other immigrant groups of the past? Again, Haitians are black and can Haitians hope for a 'piece of the American pie' while native-born American blacks still fight for crumbs? Many would see an eventual amalgamation into the African American community but does such a view give too much importance to race as a determinant and underrate such values as religion and culture?" (Fr. Thomas Wenski, "Haitians in South Florida," unpublished research done in Miami, Florida, July 1991.)

The tide seemed to be changing by 1998. In a box office, black-oriented hit movie that summer, *Stella Got Her Groove Back,* a remark is made about Haiti being full of carriers of the disease AIDS. The Haitian-American community, led by the National Coalition for Haitian Rights, organized a protest. The film's distributor, Universal, apologized, and the line was removed from the video version of the film. This was seen by the Haitian American community as a victory in respect for Haitian Americans.

TRADITIONS, CUSTOMS, AND BELIEFS

Haitian Americans, by nature, have a strong belief in the culture, traditions and mores of their homeland. Haitian Americans believe, for example, that several types of illness are of supernatural origin and caused by angry spirits. Most believe that a Voodoo family has a spirit protector whose role is to protect its members from the malevolent powers of other spirits.

The institution of the family has made possible their enclaves in the United States. It is here that a bond with the old country is maintained, consciously or unconsciously. Laguerre has noted: "The family provides a niche within which a cultural continuity can be adapted to the exigencies of the new environment. Through the medium of the family, which influences the behaviors of its members through the mechanism of socialization, immigrants were able to retain some of their cultural heritage and develop an awareness of their ethnic legacy."

Haitian families spend their leisure time within their own family and friendship groups. Visits are made to friends and relatives especially on the weekends. It is important to be warm and hospitable to visitors by offering them food and drink. Visitors are usually parents, other relatives, in-laws, and friends. Haitian social circles commonly celebrate

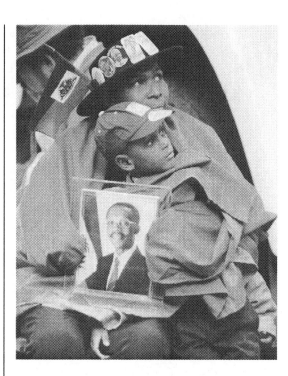

Two Haitian Americans hold a photo of deposed Haitian president Jean-Bertrand Aristide while listening to Aristide speak in New York City in 1992. Arisitide returned to Haiti as president in 1994.

birthdays, first communions, and baptisms among other special occasions and holidays. Larger numbers of people attend weddings and funerals.

PROVERBS

Haitians have a keen sense of humor which is reflected in many of their proverbs: Beyond the mountains there are more mountains; A dog has four paws, but it can go only one way; Little by little the bird makes its nest; Only the knife knows what is in the heart of the yam; The goat looks at the home owner's eyes before entering his house; Every vein affects the heart; An empty sack cannot stand up; With patience you will see the belly button of an ant; All that you do not know is greater than you; The big water pot is not a spring; You can hurry as much as you like, but being in too big a hurry will not make the day dawn.

CUISINE

Haitian cooking is a unique blend of many cultural influences. It is a mixture of the traditions of Europeans, West African slaves, and indigenous people of the island. The most common ingredients used in Haitian cuisine are black-eyed peas, squash, pumpkins, cassava, rice, cornmeal, and plantain. The meat served tends to be spicy and high in salt and fat. In the United States, Sunday dinners often consist of spicy chicken and goat, rice and djondjon, a dried mushroom.

Pois et ris is a combination of kidney beans and rice and is considered the national dish of Haiti.

Vodoo priest
Saveur St. Cyr
poses at the alter
to Azaka, the god
of agriculture.

Kabrit boukannen ak bon piman is a traditional favorite both in Haiti and the United States. It is barbecued goat with hot pepper. *Soup joumou* is a pumpkin soup. *Kasav ak manba* is homemade peanut butter, made with or without spices and hot peppers; it is often eaten with cassava bread. *Griyo ak bannan* is deep-fried pork and fried plantain. *Pwason fri* is a fried fish often sold with fried plantain and fried sweet potatoes. *Accra* or *calas* are black-eyed pea patties and the tradition of eating them on New Year's Eve means luck for the coming year.

HOLIDAYS

Haitians celebrate Christmas Day, New Year's Day, Carnival or Mardi Gras, All Saints' Day, and All Souls' Day on the days that are traditionally celebrated in other parts of the world. Flag and University Day is the most celebrated national holiday and is held on May 18. Other important holidays are Independence Day (January 1), Ancestors Day (January 2), the Anniversary of Dessalines' Death (October 17), and Discovery of Haiti Day (December 5).

HEALTH ISSUES

Health care beliefs vary widely among Haitian Americans. Immigrants from rural areas usually do not seek help from a physician but rely instead on folk healers. Immigrants from the cities are more likely to go to a physician or other professional health care provider. Social class and education also influence the type of medical help sought. Those from a lower social class or those who have not attained legal status in the United States rely on health care that is readily available to them such as home remedies, family recommendations, folk healers, and Voodoo medicine. The mother or grandmother is usually responsible for diagnosing symptoms and keeping alive the traditions of the family in treating sickness. First-generation Haitian Americans initially try home remedies prepared by members of the older generation; if these are unsuccessful, the person is advised to seek help from a physician, folk healer, or Voodoo priest. The use of folk healers is often limited because the medicinal preparations and elements of traditional health care are not available locally. The size of the local Haitian group affects the number of traditional healers.

The Voodooist folk healer is a Voodoo priest who has studied the mythology of spirits and which plants have the properties necessary for home remedies. Treatment involves prayers and herbal remedies. Neighborhood licensed pharmacies specialize in herbal remedies and French medications. They have Haitian personnel and sell the type of products from home which are familiar to Haitian Americans. Haitians consider eating well, good personal hygiene, and keeping regular hours as important qualities for maintaining good health. Fat people are considered healthy and happy, whereas thin people are believed to be in poor health caused by psychological and emotional problems.

The following statements may be used by a Haitian American when he is ill: *Kom pa bon* (I do not feel well)—indicates a temporary situation and that the person will soon be well; *Dan tan zan tan moin malad* (I feel sick from time to time)—indicates how the person feels about his/her general health; *Moin an konvalesans* (I am convalescing)—indicates that the person was sick and is now getting better; *Moin malad* (I am sick)—indicates the person is ill but the illness will not lead to death; *Moin malad anpil* (I am very sick)—indicates that the person is in a critical condition; *Moin pap refe* (I will never get well again)—indicates that the person is going to die from the illness.

Haitians from rural areas believe that illness can be of supernatural origin or natural origins. Natural illnesses are called *maladi pei* (country diseases) or *maladi bon die* (diseases of the Lord). Natural illnesses last for only a short time. Supernatural illnesses appear suddenly and the person does not feel any previous signs of illness. Angry Voodoo spirits are believed to cause several types of illness. This occurs when a person offends the family's Voodoo spirit protector in some manner. A Voodoo priest is consulted to help in diagnosing the illness. The priest attempts to contact the spirit to find out the reason for the spirit's unhappiness, what the person must do to make the spirit happy, and what medications the ill person must take.

Another belief commonly held by Haitians of all classes is that of the effect of blood irregularities on causing dangerous illnesses. Terms such as *san cho* (hot blood) and *san fret* (cold blood) are used to describe various conditions. Blood is believed to control the hot or cold state of the body. Various "blood" terms are used to describe what condition or state of health a person is in during certain types of activity.

Gaz (gas), a common complaint, can cause pain and anemia. It can occur in the head, shoulder, back, legs, or appendix. It is believed to cause *kolik*

(stomach pain) and *van nan tet* (gas in the head), which causes headaches. A tea made of garlic, cloves, and mint or solid foods, such as corn, is used to treat these conditions. The milk of a nursing mother is believed to cause certain illnesses if it becomes "too thick" or "too thin." If a mother becomes frightened, the belief is that the milk moves to her head and causes a bad headache. It may also cause depression in the nursing mother and diarrhea in the baby.

Foods may be divided into hot, cold, or neutral categories and are believed to affect the health of an individual. Anything that creates an imbalance between "hot" and "cold" factors may cause illness or discomfort. Treatments which must be used to treat these illnesses are the opposite of the class of the disease. "Hot" medicines are used to treat "cold" conditions. Patent or herbal medicines are also used to treat these diseases. Cough medicines ("hot") are used to treat coughs and colds ("cold").

The following home remedies are used: *Asorousi* is a tea boiled from leaves that will restore a person's appetite; *Fey korosol* is used to bathe a child's head to cure insomnia; a variety of leaves are used for gas or if a child's stomach is swollen; and warm oils are used in combination with massage to solve a number of problems from aching or sprained bones to displaced organs.

Haitian Americans often believe that only traditional healers have the knowledge and skills to treat particular illnesses so that it does not make sense to take these complaints to an American doctor. Haitian Americans often have problems with the behavior of American physicians during an office visit. The patient expects the physician to receive him or her with a few moments of conversation about the patient's life in general and then a straightforward, hands-on examination of the patient. The examination should not include a long list of questions by the doctor; it is the doctor, not the patient, who is supposed to determine what is wrong. Patients respect doctors who try to learn about their cultural beliefs and practices.

LANGUAGE

Two languages are spoken in Haiti: Creole and French. French is the official language and is spoken by the educated elite. The great majority of Haitians, however, speak only Creole.

The term Creole derives from the Portuguese word "*crioulo*" meaning an individual of European ancestry who was born and reared abroad. Haitian Creole developed when slaves who were taken to the Caribbean island of Saint Domingue from various areas of the west coast of Africa interacted with each other and with Europeans. Although predominantly French, some Spanish and Amerindian (Carib and Arawak) words have entered the language. While Haitian Creole has a French word base, the two languages are distinct. The sentence structure of Creole is basically African, but it has its own grammar, morphology, and syntax.

Haitian immigrants to the United States, especially the more recent ones, communicate best in Creole. This causes problems in interaction with Americans who have little knowledge of Creole and believe that all Haitians speak French.

GREETINGS AND OTHER COMMON EXPRESSIONS
Common Haitian greetings and other expressions include: *Allo* ("ah-low")—Hi!; *Bonjou* ("boon-ZHEW")—Good morning/day; *Bonswa* ("bon-SWA")—Good afternoon/evening; *Ki jan ou rele?* ("kee jan oo ray lay")—What is your name?; *M rele ...* ("m ray lay ...")—My name is ...; *Kote ou rete?* ("ko TAY oo ray TAY")—Where do you live?; *Ki numewo telefon ou?* ("kee new meh-wo tele FON OO")—What is your telephone number?; *Suple* ("soo-PLAY")—Please; *Chita!* ("SHEE-tah")—Sit down!; *Kanpe!* ("kan PAY")—Stand up!; *Mesi* ("MAY-see")—Thank you; *Orevwa* ("oh-ray-VWAH")—Goodbye.

FAMILY AND COMMUNITY DYNAMICS

The family is the nucleus of Haitian society; within it, individuals are dependent upon each other. The traditional Haitian family is a composed of father, mother, children, and grandparents. The family is involved in all decision-making for its members. The patriarchal system is prevalent, but many women rear children without the consistent presence of the father. By tradition, the father is the breadwinner and authority figure. The mother is the household manager and disciplinarian.

Family honor is of utmost importance. Family reputation is so important that the actions of a member of the family are considered to bring either honor or shame to the entire family. A family's reputation in society is based on honesty and former family history. Offspring of the *grandes familles* are considered excellent prospects for marriage.

From birth, males are granted more freedom and educational opportunities than females. Transgressions in behavior are more readily overlooked in males, and the male "macho" image is admired since men play the dominant role in society. Females in urban areas of Haiti lead a sheltered and protected life. The family and educational system prepares them for marriage and respectability. Social mobility outside the home is usually limited. Adolescent girls do not go out alone and their activities are closely controlled. They are expected to help with chores and care for siblings at home. Women in rural areas have always worked. They farm as well as perform household tasks. They are the backbone of the economic stability of the family. Traditionally, clear distinctions have existed between male and female roles. These are changing due to economic conditions. More urban women are working outside the home, enjoying some degree of freedom, and are less willing to play a subservient role to the male. This is especially true in the United States. Many women want a greater voice in the decision-making processes of their homes.

Haitian American parents are generally strict with their children, as is customary in Haiti. The children are monitored by the adults of the family. Adult rules are to be respected and obeyed without question. Children are expected to live at home until they are married. Haitian American children seem to accept these customs and values despite the freer attitudes and lifestyles they see in their American counterparts. Haitian parents have immigrated to seek a better standard of life for their children and they want to obtain a good formal education for them. They want their children to grow up to be obedient, responsible, and close to the family.

Treatment of the elderly in Haiti differs from that in the United States. Senior citizens are highly respected because they have wisdom that can only come from living a long life. Sending an aged parent to a nursing home is unthinkable for Haitians. Children vie with each other as to whom will be granted the privilege of caring for the parents.

Haitian families maintain regular contact with relatives in Haiti by visiting them during winter or summer vacations. Some also return during the carnival period and for relatives' funerals. Still others return for familial Voodoo gatherings. The Voodoo believers, who cannot return to the island because they do not have resident status, often help pay for such ceremonies. Haitian Americans keep in regular contact with family members in Haiti and even send money home for child care and other family matters. There is a common belief that once you take in a Haitian there will come other Haitians.

Haitian Americans also maintain contact with a network of friends and neighbors. This network enables them to know what is happening around their communities and to help each other. Old friends in Haiti have a common background and maintain their relationships in the United States. The immigrants try to maintain survival contacts with neighbors in the same apartment buildings. The more interaction the family has with other Haitian immigrants, the more the community is able to maintain its cultural tradition, its folklore, the Creole language, and other aspects of social life.

WEDDINGS

The most common marital relationship among the rural and urban lower class was *plasaj*, an arrangement not recognized by the state. The man and woman often make an explicit agreement about their economic relationship at the beginning of the marriage. The husband is required to cultivate at least one plot of land for the wife and to provide her with a house. The wife is expected to perform most household tasks. The *plasaj* previously would take place with beautiful traditional ceremonies and secret ritualistic sacrifices to the ancestors. Because weddings were expensive, many couples waited several years before having them. Due to the expense, however, few of these ceremonies remain today. The upper class traditionally had civil and religious marriage ceremonies, which were arranged mainly for prestige rather than legality. The "best" families could trace legally married family members back to the nineteenth century.

FUNERALS

To Haitians, death goes far beyond the immediate family. It includes the various *loa* (lesser deities) and the many dead relatives and ancestors. Some Haitians believe that the dead live in close proximity to the loa, in a place called "Under the Water." Others hold that the dead have no special place after death. Many believe that a dead person will become a loa. Sometimes the spirits of the dead do not go quietly but remain behind to annoy the living.

Burial ceremonies vary according to local tradition and the status of the person. Relatives and friends expend considerable effort to be present when death is near. The family does not express grief aloud until most of the deceased's possessions have been removed from the home. Persons who are knowledgeable in the funeral customs wash, dress, and place the body in a coffin. Mourners wear white clothing which represents death. A priest may be summoned to conduct the burial service. The burial usually takes place within 24 hours.

Haitian American author Edwidge Danticat, 29, signs a copy of her third novel "The Farming of Bones" for a fan after a benefit reading in New York City.

INTERACTIONS WITH OTHER ETHNIC MINORITIES

Haitians face a identity dilemma in the United States. Although they are different in national origin, they are almost physically indistinguishable from other black Americans. They cannot easily merge with the rest of the black population because of their language and culture. Haitian Americans perceive differences between themselves and other blacks. Most seek a middle ground between being merged with the rest of the black population and complete isolation. Haitian language and culture are preserved at home, which makes it possible for Haitian immigrants to separate themselves from the Afro-American culture around them. Traditional Haitian values are carefully guarded. They adapt to the dominant American culture while retaining their distinctive lifestyle at home. By the late 1990s, a distinct Haitian American identity was slowly forming in the public eye.

RELIGION

Religion is a basic force in the lives of Haitians who have migrated to the United States and they continue the beliefs that they brought with them from Haiti. Religious groups and churches serve as a powerful unifying element in the lives of the immigrants.

The national religion of Haiti is Roman Catholicism. The first missionaries were Catholic, and the schools that they established are still highly regarded for their educational standards; it is common for even the non-Catholic children to attend Catholic schools. Protestant churches are strong and vigorous in Haiti. Protestant missionaries have increased substantially and represent Baptist, Methodist, and Pentecostal as well as other evangelical denominations.

VOODOO

An important focus of Haitian religious life centers around Voodoo, which blends elements of Catholicism with those of diverse African beliefs resulting in Haitian Voodoo. It appears throughout the art, music and social customs of Haiti. Voodoo is a set of beliefs and practices that deals with the spiritual forces of the universe and attempts to keep the individual in harmonious relation with them as they affect his life.

A key to understanding the relationship and interplay between Catholicism and Voodooism is the fusion of the two belief systems. Children born into rural families are generally baptized twice, once into the Voodoo religion and once in the Catholic church. Voodoo means many things. It means an attitude toward life and death, a concept of ancestors and the afterworld, and a recognition of the forces which control individuals and their activities.

Those who practice Voodooism believe in a pantheon of gods who control and represent the laws and forces of the universe. In this pantheon, there is the Supreme Deity, the master of all gods, the loa who are a large group of lesser deities, and the twins known as marassas. Twins are believed to have special powers and once a year special services are held for them.

In Voodoo the major gods are classified into the four natural elements: water, air, fire and earth. There is also a god of love, of death, etc. These lesser gods (loas) are analogous to the saints of the Catholic Church and those of African gods. These gods are not only expected to protect people, but they are also expected to accord special favors through their representatives on earth which are the *hougans* (priests) and *mambos* (priestesses). In Voodoo, the soul continues to live on earth and may be used in magic or it may be incarnated in a member of the dead person's family. This belief is similar to Catholicism in that the soul is believed to be immortal. Elaborate burial customs have been established to keep the dead buried in the ground. It is believed that corpses that have been removed from their tombs may be turned into zombies, who then serve the will of their masters.

Voodoo worship centers in family groups and cult groups headed by a *hougan* or *mambo*. Ceremonies are performed annually for such events as Christmas and the harvest and also for specials occasions such as initiations and memorial services. Believers have obligations for the worship of their loa and their ancestors. Expert help is called in to help with the ceremonies which consist of Roman Catholic prayers, drumming and dancing, and the preparation of feasts. Each group of worshipers is independent and there is no central organization, religious leader, or set of beliefs. Beliefs and ceremonies often vary, depending upon family traditions.

EMPLOYMENT AND ECONOMIC TRADITIONS

When François Duvalier came to power in 1957, many dissident politicians, middle-class professionals, and tradespeople left Haiti and headed for New York City. The most recent wave of immigrants has included the poorer people of Haiti, who have entered the migrant workforce or the menial jobs in the New York City area. Haitian Americans are hard-working and use the lower-status jobs as springboards to better, more permanent positions. Many businesses dependent on trade with Haiti have been hurt by the international embargo against the country. This is especially true in Little Haiti in Miami where unemployment is running about 30 percent. From an analysis of the 1990 U.S. Census data, about six percent of the nation's Haitian households or about 5,300 individuals collect welfare benefits, compared to about five percent of households generally. Groups like the National Coalition for Haitian Rights was trying to change that in 1998. The Coalition was developing leadership training and education programs to empower the Haitian community.

Haitian Americans are accustomed to using rotating credit associations as an avenue of saving. Such associations are called in Creole "sangue," "min," or "assosie." They rotate money to members of the association from a lump-sum fund into which each member has contributed an amount of money. It is assumed that the Haitians adapted this system of contribution from their West African friends who call it "esusu." Haitian immigrants, especially undocumented ones who have no banking accounts, use the sangue to buy homes and finance various business ventures.

POLITICS AND GOVERNMENT

New York City has traditionally been the center for Haitian opposition politics. More than 30 political groups opposed to the dictatorship of François Duvalier have been in existence there since 1957. Some have had to operate secretly because of fear of reprisals against family members back home in Haiti. Political activities in New York have occurred during three periods. The first period was from 1956 to 1964 when former Haitian officials dominated and hoped to install a new president and to introduce reforms in the Haitian government system. Several attempted invasions of Haiti occurred during this period. The next period of activity occurred during the years from 1965 through 1970. The Haitian American Coalition (La Coalition Hatienne) was formed in 1964, composed of the groups Jeune Haiti, Les Forces Revolutionnaires Haitiennes, Le Mouvement Revolutionnaires du 12 Novembre, and followers of ex-President Paul-Eugene Magloire. The Coalition published a newspaper *Le Combattant Haitien* and broadcast messages to Haiti on Radio Vonvon. In 1970 the coalition was dissolved and La Resistance Haitienne was organized, which had more popular support. In 1971, the Comité de Mobilisation was formed to attempt to overthrow Jean-Claude Duvalier. This group was dissolved and in 1977, Le Regroupement de Forces Democratiques was formed to force Duvalier from power after he had completed his six-year term. Involvement in the American political process began in earnest in 1968 when Haitian Americans formed the Haitian American Political Organization. This organization was formed to lobby on behalf of the Haitian American community. Haitian Americans have worked in various elections to increase their presence as political force to obtain public services to be provided to the community.

On April 20, 1990, more than 50,000 Haitian Americans marched across the Brooklyn Bridge to City Hall to protest the action of the Centers for Disease Control and the American Red Cross. These organizations had ruled that no Haitian could donate blood because all Haitians were AIDS risks. This was one of the largest demonstrations of its type and encouraged local leaders to find a Haitian candidate for the city council from Brooklyn.

Currently, an increasing amount of political activity has involved attempts to help the "boat people" who have tried to escape oppressive conditions in Haiti. The Haitian Refugee Center in Miami and the National Coalition for Haitian Rights work to help those refugees trapped in the American legal system and facing possible deportation. The Coalition also worked to help Haitians in Haiti. The group reported in 1997 that the police force in Haiti, trained by the United States, engaged in abusive tactics. It also showed that the United States and the European Union were engaging in useless judicial reform efforts, prompting a policy change.

MILITARY

The American Revolution saw the participation of freedmen from Saint Domingue who fought under General Lafayette at Savannah in 1779. From 1814 to 1815, Joseph Savary headed the Second Battalion of Freemen of Color which fought under General Andrew Jackson. Savary was the first black to hold the rank of major in the U.S. Army.

Since the largest number of immigrants arrived in the United States after World War II, there was not a great involvement on their part in earlier wars. Many Haitian Americans, however, served in Vietnam. Haitian Americans currently serve in the U.S. armed forces; indeed, many of them were sent to Haiti to serve as Creole interpreters during the efforts to reinstate President Jean-Bertrand Aristide.

INDIVIDUAL AND GROUP CONTRIBUTIONS

ACADEMIA

Michel S. Laguerre, an anthropologist in the Department of Afro-American Studies, University of California at Berkeley, has researched many aspects of Haitian American life and has published numerous books and articles. Tekle Mariam Woldemikael, a sociologist in the Department of Sociology and Anthropology at Whittier College in Whittier, California, has written several studies concerning Haitian Americans. Carole M. Berotte Joseph, who was born in Port-au-Prince and came to the U.S. in 1957, is the Assistant Dean and Director of the Office of Student Services at the City College School of Education in New York City where she is an authority on bilingual and foreign language teaching; she is a founder of the International Alliance for Haiti, Inc. Michaelle Vincent, the District Supervisor Binlingual and Foreign Language Skills of the Dade County (Florida) Public Schools, is a consultant on Haitian culture and the Creole language, developing and implementing seminars on Haitian culture; she also hosted a daily radio show in Haitian Creole on WLRN in Miami.

JOURNALISM AND BROADCASTING

Joel Dreyfuss, editor of *PC Magazine*, emigrated from Haiti in the 1950s; he has published extensively in computer magazines as well as the *New York Times*. Marcus Garcia is the editor and publisher of *Haiti En Marche*, a weekly newspaper published in Miami; most articles are published in French but there is a section in Creole for Creole language speakers. Raymond Cajuste is a filmmaker and host of a program on Radio Tropicale. Ricot Dupuy is the station manager of Radio Soleil which was created after the 1991 coup in Haiti; he also helps new refugees with their needs upon arriving in New York.

MUSIC

The migration of Haitians to the United States has caused a boom in its music. Haitian music serves as an anchor connecting individuals with their country, one another, and themselves. Music functions as a sanctioned means of social protest. Wyclef Jean, one-third of the rap group, The Fugees, is a source of pride for Haitians and Haitian Americans. Not only does he incorporate his country's music in his rap songs but he also gives back to his fellow countrymen through benefit concerts. Theodore Beaubrun is the lead singer and composer of the Boukman Eksperyans whose songs assault Haiti's evildoers; the music is steeped in the symbolism of Voodoo and Haitian history. Dieudonne Larose, a composer who lives in Montreal, is transforming Haitian music and writes in the style of the old favorites of compas, Haiti's well-known dance music; he criticizes whites for racist attitudes toward black governments and warns Haitians to work hard and to respect the law.

SCIENCE AND TECHNOLOGY

John James Audubon (1785-1851) was born in Cayes. His drawings of birds in America are an invaluable source of information for naturalists and anthropologists.

VISUAL ARTS

Marc Jean-Louis emigrated to the United States at a very young age. He lives in South Florida and has made many contributions to Haitian art.

MEDIA

PRINT

Haiti en Marche.
Published weekly in French. There is a section in Creole for Creole speakers.

Address: Miami, Florida.

Haiti Observateur.
Published weekly in French, Creole, and English.

Address: 50 Court Street, Brooklyn, New York 11201.

Haiti Progress.
Published weekly in French.

Address: 1398 Flatbush Avenue, Brooklyn, New York 11210.

RADIO

WKCR-FM (89.9).
"L'Heure Haitienne" is broadcast on Sunday mornings.

Address: Columbia University, 208 Ferris Booth Hall, New York, New York 10027.

WLIB-AM (1190).
"Moment Creole" is broadcast every Sunday from 10:00 a.m. to 4:00 p.m.

Contact: Claude Tait.
Address: 801 Second Avenue, New York, New York 10017.

WNWK-FM (105.9).
"Eddy Publicité" is broadcast every Saturday from 8:00 p.m. to 10:00 p.m. It features a mix of Haitian music, news and discussion of community issues.

Contact: Otto Miller.
Address: 449 Broadway, Second Floor, New York, New York 10013.

WNYE-FM (91.5).
This station broadcasts various programs daily aimed at the Haitian American audience.

Address: 112 Tillary Street, Brooklyn, New York 11201.

Radio Tropical and Radio Soleil d'Haiti are subcarrier stations that broadcast 24 hours a day over special radios sold to listeners. They broadcast talk, call-in shows, news, gossip, and social announcements.

TELEVISION

Several cable companies offer programs aimed at their local Haitian American communities. Programs air political debates and instructions on coping with life in the United States.

ORGANIZATIONS AND ASSOCIATIONS

Caribbean Haitian Council (CAHACO).
Provides cultural normalization of and advocacy for Haitians and other Caribbean groups.

Address: 26 Ashland Avenue, East Orange, New Jersey 07017.
Telephone: (201) 678-5059.

Friends of Haiti (FOH).

Founded in 1971, FOH attempts to generate support for the Haitian national liberation struggle. It distributes information on the Haitian social structure and the liberation process, with an emphasis on U.S. economic, political and military involvement. Friends of Haiti maintains a data center on Haiti and has a library of 3,000 volumes.

Contact: Mauge Leblanc, Coordinator.
Address: 1398 Flatbush Avenue, Brooklyn, New York 11210.
Telephone: (718) 434-8100.
Fax: (718) 434-5551.

Haitian American Foundation, Inc. (HAFI).

Founded in 1990, HAFI works to help, educate and assist Haitian immigrants and other ethnic groups become self-sufficient. It sponsors programs that provide acculturation, vocational skills training, English classes, counseling, food distribution, and technical assistance to small business.

Contact: Ringo Cayard, President.
Address: 8340 Northeast Second Avenue, Suite 103, Miami, Florida 33138.
Telephone: (305) 758-3338.
E-mail: meera@mcione.com.

Haitian Refugee Center (HRC).

Founded in 1974, the Center provides free legal support and educational services to indigent Haitian aliens in their political asylum proceedings. It works to impede deportations and to publicize the plight of refugees.

Contact: Philies Auguh, Executive Director.
Address: 119 Northeast 54th Street, Miami, Florida 33137.
Telephone: (305) 757-8538.
Fax: (305) 758-2444.

Haitian Studies Association.

Encourages research and interest in Haiti, the Haitian people, and their culture.

Contact: Dr. Leslie G. Desmangles, President.
Address: Trinity College, McCook Hall, 300 Summit Street, Hartford, Connecticut 06106.
Telephone: (617) 287-7138.
E-mail: hsa@umbsky.cc.umb.edu.

National Coalition for Haitian Rights (NCHR).

Founded in 1982, NCHR attempts to obtain humane treatment, due process of law, and legal status for Haitians seeking asylum in the United States. Its goals are to obtain fair treatment for Haitians in their quest for asylum; convince the public of the need for legal status for refugees; stop the U. S. Coast Guard interdiction of Haitian boats; and increase the awareness of the social, economic, and political causes of the Haitian flight from Haiti.

Contact: Jocelyn McCalla, Executive Director.
Address: 275 Seventh Avenue, 25th Floor, New York, New York 10007.
Telephone: (212) 337-0005.
Fax: (212) 337-0028.
E-mail: jmccalla@nchr.org.
Online: http://www.nchr.org.

MUSEUMS AND RESEARCH CENTERS

Many museums of African American history contain Haitian collections or substantial exhibits of Haitian culture items, including: Afro-American Historical and Cultural Museum in Philadelphia; Black Heritage Museum in Miami; Museum for African Art in New York City; Museum of African American Art in Los Angeles; and National Museum of African Art at the Smithsonian Institute in Washington, D.C.

Amistad Research Center.

The Center contains material relating to ethnic history and race relations in the United States, with concentration on blacks, Native Americans, Chicanos, Asian Americans, Puerto Ricans, and Haitians.

Contact: Dr. Donald E. DeVore, Director..
Address: Tulane University, 6823 St. Charles Avenue, Tilton Hall, New Orleans, Louisiana 70118.
Telephone: (504) 865-5535.
Fax: (504) 865-5580.
E-mail: amistad@mailhost.tcs.tulane.edu.
Online: http://www.arc.tulane.edu.

Schomburg Center for Research in Black Culture (Harlem).

This is a reference library devoted to material by and about Black people throughout the world, with major emphasis on Afro-America, Africa, and the Caribbean, especially Haiti. Among its Haitian holdings is the Kurt Fisher and Eugene Maximilien Collection of Haitian manuscripts.

Contact: Howard Dodson, Chief Librarian.
Address: 135 Malcolm X Boulevard, New York, New York 10037-1801.
Telephone: (212) 491-2255.
Fax: (212) 491-6760.
Online: http://www.nypl.org.

SOURCES FOR ADDITIONAL STUDY

Chierici, Rose-Marie Cassagnol. *Demele: "Making It": Migration and Adaptation Among Haitian Boat People in the United States.* New York: AMS Press, 1980; pp. 1-12.

Dreyfuss, Joel. "The Invisible Immigrants: Haitians in America Are Industrious, Upwardly Mobile and Vastly Misunderstood," *New York Times Magazine,* May 23, 1993; pp. 20-21, 80-82.

Gollab, Caroline. *The Impact of Industrial Experience on the Immigrant Family: The Huddled Masses Reconsidered.* Charlottesville: University Press of Virginia, 1977.

Laguerre, Michel S. *American Odyssey: Haitians in New York City.* New York: Cornell University Press, 1984.

————. *The Complete Haitiana: A Bibliographic Guide to the Scholarly Literature, 1900-1980.* Millwood, New York: Kraus International Publications, 1982.

Sontag, Deborah. "Haitian Migrants Settle In, Looking Back," *New York Times,* June 3, 1994; p. A1.

Valburn, Marjorie. "Former Ragtag Immigrant Organization Evolves Into Coalition Pushing Haitian-American Rights," *The Wall Street Journal,* February 4, 1999; p. A24.

HAWAIIANS

by
**Elaine Winters and
Mark Swartz**

While native
Hawaiians almost
invariably suffered
as their homeland
underwent its
transformations, it is
also true that the
Hawaiian culture
greatly affected the
attitudes and
perspectives of many
immigrant groups.

OVERVIEW

The Pacific Ocean surrounds the Hawaiian archipelago. There are eight major and 124 minor islands, volcanic in origin, with a total land mass of 6,425 square miles (16,641 square kilometers). The eight major islands are Niihau, Kauai, Oahu, Molokai, Maui, Kahoolawe, Lanai, and Hawaii. Honolulu, the capital, is located on Oahu, and is 6,200 kilometers southwest of San Francisco. The islands' topography includes such diverse features as active volcanos, grassy pastures, and endless stretches of beach.

According to U.S. Census Bureau figures (1990), the population of the entire state is 1,108,229, with 836,231 persons living within the incorporated city of Honolulu and its immediate environs. Seventy-three percent of the entire population of the state lives on Oahu. Statewide, 135,263 persons identify themselves as native Hawaiians, though it is not known how many of these people are of mixed race. There has been a widespread diaspora of native Hawaiians, largely to the west coast of the United States and also to other Pacific Island nations.

HISTORY

The islands in the triangle formed (roughly) by Tahiti, New Zealand, and Hawaii are inhabited by people who possess prominent genealogical traits in common, speak related languages, and live similar lifestyles. They are descendants of Polynesians (Polynesia is Greek for "many islands"), who began settling in the South Pacific islands around 1100 B.C. They are believed to have reached the Hawaiian islands sometime between A.D. 300 and 500. They called the largest island *Havaiki* after one of the major islands of their former home. Dogs, pigs, chickens, tuber (taro), coconuts, bananas, breadfruit, yams, and sugar cane comprised much of the traditional Polynesian diet. The mulberry plant called *wauke* was pounded and bleached to make *kapa* or bark-cloth. Ti, a lily, provided leaves for *hula* skirts and roots to weave into matting or brew into a liquor called *okolehao*.

The population of native Hawaiians has diminished considerably since Western contact, usually dated from the arrival of the English seaman Captain Cook in 1778. From an estimated 300,000 that year, the population fell to 71,019 in 1853. This dramatic decrease was largely due to the introduction of various diseases (including cholera, chicken pox, influenza, measles, mumps, and syphilis), for which the immune systems and medical expertise of the natives were completely unprepared. Furthermore, Cook and those who came after him introduced firearms to the archipelago, making tribal conflicts much deadlier.

EUROPEAN SETTLEMENT IN THE HAWAIIAN ISLANDS

January 18, 1778 marked the arrival of Captain James Cook and the crews of his two ships, H.M.S. *Resolution* and H.M.S. *Discovery*, off the coast of the island Kauai. The British visitors recorded trading iron nails for fresh water, pigs, and sweet potatoes. Captain Cook named the archipelago the "Sandwich Islands," after his patron, the Earl of Sandwich. Cook was killed by natives on the island of Hawaii one year after his arrival in a skirmish over a small boat that had been stolen from him.

Prior to European settlement, native Hawaiians viewed land as the common property of everyone. The economic interests of the common people, the king, and the chiefs were collaborative, mutually beneficial, and intertwined. The arrival of settlers and their Western ideas of title and ownership, however, terminated that approach to government.

In 1780, Kamehameha, the first and mightiest of four leaders with the name, began a campaign to unite the islands under a single chiefdom. Hawaiian chiefs had traditionally clashed over land and the resources of the sea, but many of their disputes were settled in ritualized combat, which resulted in relatively few casualties. Kamehameha, however, adapt-

ed the modern weapons and armaments of the British visitors to suit his own purposes and hired two of Cook's seamen as war advisors. By 1795 he had obtained complete power over the eight main islands.

With the technological know-how introduced by foreigners, called *haoles*, (a term that later came to apply exclusively to white people), Kamehameha was able to take advantage of political and economic opportunities. He established a trade advantage and created a personal monopoly over foreign commerce. He used *Kapu*, the existing system of religious and social customs, to exclude both commoners and lesser chiefs from engaging in commerce with ships that passed by, and brought fresh provisions to these ships personally. As soon as he realized the value that foreigners placed on pearls, he reserved pearling in Pearl Harbor for himself and employed commoners to dive. Furthermore, he exacted tolls for the privilege of using Honolulu's harbor. In these ways, Kamehameha accumulated enormous wealth and power over the Hawaiian people and lesser royalty.

Westerners ventured to the Sandwich Islands in large numbers. Missionaries from various Protestant sects, particularly Calvinism, were the first major group of *haoles*, followed by Norwegian whalers, Mormons, diplomatic representatives from various countries, plantation owners, and Filipino, Japanese, and Chinese workers.

Sandalwood became a trading commodity as soon as it became known that the Chinese held it in high regard and were willing to pay virtually any price. Kamehameha incorporated sandalwood into his tribute demands from commoners and left the collection process to lesser chiefs. The sandalwood trade, however, required substantial labor, thus drawing workers from food production. Moreover, demand for provisions by ships stopping in Hawaii drew on local food supplies, causing a famine in 1810 that significantly weakened the small nation. Hawaii's position further degenerated when all the sandalwood was sold and trade ceased altogether.

In 1794 George Vancouver, a British navigator, drafted an agreement with island chiefs to transfer ownership of the islands to Great Britain. He believed the chiefs had formally granted the islands to Great Britain, while the chiefs thought they had a defense agreement. Although Britain did not ratify the agreement, the English Empire, which held sway over lands in Asia, the Middle East, and Africa, established a dominant presence in Hawaii.

In 1819 *Kapu* was overthrown and abandoned when Kamehameha II violated one of its cardinal rules by accepting an invitation to dine alongside women. In the ensuing chaos, many temples and works of sacred art were destroyed. As Christianity, fueled by the influx of missionaries, supplanted *Kapu*, such cultural hallmarks as *hula* dancing, surfing, and kite flying were forbidden along with other so-called pagan practices.

U.S. INVOLVEMENT IN THE HAWAIIAN ISLANDS

U.S. President William McKinley, acting according to the national spirit of Manifest Destiny, supported a policy of amplified political, military, and economic activity in the Pacific. Citing such reasons as resolving racial unrest on the islands, arresting the influence of Japan, and boosting American shipping and commerce, the United States officially annexed Hawaii in 1893, a few months after an unofficial coup d'état (supported by white plantation owners and enforced by U.S. Marines) and the imprisonment of Queen Liliuokalani. For her refusal to go along with annexation and her support of an attempted uprising against American domination, Liliuokalani is remembered by politically liberal native Hawaiians as a freedom fighter, whereas Kamehameha is regarded as an opportunist and an accomplice in the decline of native Hawaiian culture.

U.S. involvement with Hawaii reached a new plateau after Japan bombed Pearl Harbor on December 7, 1941. The islands were placed under martial law for the duration of the war and were used extensively as bases, bombing practice sites, and rest and recreation spots for soldiers and sailors. The memorial at the site of the sunken battleship *Arizona* attracts many visitors each year, as does the national cemetery at Punchbowl (an extinct volcanic crater), with its spectacular view of Honolulu and the harbor. Hawaii joined the union in 1959, thus becoming the fiftieth state. The current flag of the State of Hawaii has eight horizontal stripes (red, white, and blue), to symbolize the eight major islands, and a Union Jack in the upper left corner, to symbolize the occupation of the islands by the British.

ACCULTURATION AND ASSIMILATION

Writing in 1916, W. Somerset Maugham described Honolulu, in a story of the same name: "It is the meeting of East and West. The very new rubs shoulders with the immeasurably old." The ethnic variety of immigrants since the arrival of Captain Cook has created many opportunities for cultural exchange and hybridization. Of the 1,108,229 people living in Hawaii, 23 percent describe themselves as white, 22 percent as Japanese, 20 percent as part Hawaiian, 11 percent as Filipino, four percent as Chinese, two percent as black, and about one percent each as Korean and pure Hawaiian. Such clear-cut terms blur when faced by another statistic, however; about half of all Hawaiian marriages now occur between men and women of different races.

While native Hawaiians almost invariably suffered as their homeland underwent its transformations, it is also true that the Hawaiian culture greatly affected the attitudes and perspectives of many immigrant groups. The most striking example of this is the spirit of *aloha*, which is found on all the islands and among all ethnic groups. Although many consider the term to have been corrupted by colonialist opportunism and the tourist industry, it remains an important aspect of the culture of the State of Hawaii. The word *aloha* means many things: hello, good-bye, peace, and, perhaps most importantly, a sense of welcome and identity within the larger community.

TRADITIONS, CUSTOMS, AND BELIEFS

Storytelling is a great Hawaiian tradition. Before the Hawaiian language was written, the literature was spoken. The Hawaiian legend of the King of *Ku-ai-he-lani* is similar to the western tale of *Cinderella*; and *Au-ke-le* recalls Rip Van Winkle, or perhaps Odysseus. *Menehunes* are small people, rather like Irish leprechauns. Legends of their mischievous ways abound. For example, *menehunes* are held to be responsible when something is misplaced. In various locations, on all the islands, there are elaborate fish ponds that do not appear to have been formed naturally. Native Hawaiians believe *menehunes* built them, and there are strict rules about these ponds. Nothing must be removed or the *menehunes* will come at night and take it back. The implication is that the retrieval will be unpleasant.

Many of the old superstitions and traditions in Hawaii are still observed in modern form; ti leaves, for example, are still reputed to ward off evil spirits. Today, students in dormitories decorate entries and windows with ti leaves when they think there is an evil spirit afoot. Hawaiians bring ti leaves to football games and wave them like pom-poms to keep bad spirits away from a favorite team. Feasts, or *luaus*, are a native Hawaiian tradition still held on every important occasion. The traditional practice involves roasting a pig in a large oven (*imo*) dug into the ground. Weddings, childbirth, the completion of a canoe or a house, and a good catch or an abundant harvest are typical occasions for a native

Canoes have
figured
prominently in the
marine culture of
the native
Hawaiians.

Hawaiian *luau*. Today, *luaus* are held everywhere in Hawaii. Churches frequently hold *luaus* as fundraising events, and the entire community joins in the festivities and the eating. Tourists expect to enjoy a *luau* before leaving the islands.

AGRICULTURE

The Hawaiian farmer of ancient times was a superior cultivator who systematically identified and named plants—both those cultivated as well as the wild species gathered for use when crops failed. Procedures for cultivation at every arable location on an island (approximately 15 percent of the land), for the variety of altitudes, exposures, and weather conditions were likewise developed by farmers. They practiced organic farming, meaning that the unused leaves of plants were combined with plants that grew during fallow periods in a "green" manure; that is, no animal excrement was used.

Elaborate systems of aqueducts and ditches brought water from dammed springs to planted terraces, demonstrating engineering and building skills as well as planning and organizing abilities. The rem-

nants of these systems can still be seen from the air. Plants cultivated for food included such staples as taro, breadfruit, and yam, as well as foods that offered variety and additional nutrients, including banana, sugarcane, coconut, candelnut, arrowroot, and ti.

About three hundred varieties of taro are known to have existed in Hawaii. Early natives used the entire taro plant. The leaves were steamed alone or used to wrap potatoes or fish for steaming. The root was steamed in an *imo* and then peeled and pounded into a stiff paste handy for traveling when wrapped in pandanus leaves. Adding water to this paste produces *poi*, a starchy thick paste sometimes allowed to ferment. The entire coconut was used as well. Unripe coconuts provided nourishing liquid for journeys when no fresh water was available. The flesh of the mature nut was grated and pressed to produce a cream. Pudding was made by mixing this cream with arrowroot. The husks were halved when the mature coconut was harvested and, when empty, were used as drinking or baking cups. The fibers on the outside of the husks were pounded and then woven into rope. The leaves of the plant were sometimes used for thatching houses.

In addition to attracting laborers from China, Japan, and elsewhere, sugar production has been a major source of employment for native Hawaiians. In 1873, for instance, more than half the native male population was engaged in cultivating sugar. Women were employed stripping, grinding, and boiling cane and were paid half the wages of male natives.

MARINE CULTURE

Fish has traditionally supplied most of the protein in the Hawaiian diet. It is also a crucial and highly developed trade. Early Hawaiian fishermen were often accompanied by an individual responsible for actually finding the fish—the fish watchman. This skill involved understanding the sea floor, both inside and outside of the reef; the shape of the reef, including where the fish liked to hide; and what kind of net, hook, and bait were appropriate for each fish. Various traps were also devised for catching fish and other marine animals that lived in streams. Not everyone was allowed to eat every species of fish; certain fishes were for special events and then only for royalty. Priests were consulted every step of the way when it came to consumption of various foods. Rarely did women consume fish; rather, they were permitted shrimp and other shellfish.

Nautical culture was an important aspect of early Hawaiian life. There were freshwater ponds and shore ponds. The shore ponds were enclosures built of stone that encompassed both shallow and deep water; some ponds were as large as 60 acres. The walls had sluice gates made of wood. Native Hawaiians have long believed in the conservation of fresh water. In early times, after growing fish, the water was used to irrigate crops. Waste from ponds, a rich source of calcium, provided for an excellent fertilizer. (Hawaiian soil is low in calcium.) Some of these early conservation traditions have been revived and are practiced by native Hawaiians today.

Canoes were built for either transportation or racing. Racing is believed to have been reserved for royalty, and the large double canoes are thought to have been used for major inter-island travel and trading. The elaborate process of building a canoe began with a priest selecting the appropriate lumber. Suitable animal sacrifices (pigs or chickens) were offered and incantations and ceremonies accompanied each step of the process. For example, ti leaves were wrapped around the tree at various stages of the carving and building to ward off evil spirits. Canoe racing remains an active sport in modern Hawaii. One organization devoted to perpetuating the tradition of building and racing canoes is the Hawaiian Canoe Racing Association in Honolulu.

CUISINE

Hawaii's patchwork past is most apparent in its varied cuisine. Japanese *manju* (sweet black bean pastry), Portuguese sweet bread, Chinese noodles or crispy duck, and spicy Korean *kim chee* are as easy to find as Hawaiian *poi*, which is served as the traditional island staple. Hawaiians eat about twice as much fish as residents of any other state, as well as more fresh fruit. Mangoes, papayas, bananas, pineapples, oranges, and avocados are grown locally. Different areas are famed for specialty crops: open-air markets on Oahu overflow with Kahuku watermelons, Maui onions, Waimanalo corn, Manoa lettuce, and Puna papayas. During a *luau*, a pig is roasted in a pit lined with wood, lava rocks, and banana stumps. The pig is stuffed with hot rocks, wrapped in leaves, and buried along with pieces of fish, taro, yams, and breadfruit. A festive banquet for friends and extended family, the *luau* has absorbed many non-Hawaiian elements. In the 1800s, missionaries brought cakes, Chinese brought chicken, and Norwegian whalers brought salmon marinated with onion and tomato (lomi salmon). All are now standard *luau* dishes.

TRADITIONAL COSTUMES

Because of Hawaii's tropical climate, early natives usually wore no more than a strip or two of barkcloth (*kapa*). Many Hawaiians also covered much of their bodies with tattoos. Warriors ornamented themselves with spectacular yellow and gold capes and helmets of woven feathers. Today, Hawaiians continue to dress casually. Some Hawaiian women wear the *muumuu*, a voluminous dress originally designed by modest missionaries for Hawaiian women. Today these dresses are printed in bright and colorful cotton or silk. More firmly grounded in Hawaiian culture is the *lei*, a colorful wreath of fresh flowers or other decorative objects worn around the neck. Originally an artful offering to the gods, *leis* have become an emblem of Hawaiian hospitality and warmth.

DANCES AND SONGS

Although it has long been associated with Hawaii, the ukulele originated in Portugal. "Aloha Oe," a song written by Queen Liliouokalani, is a perennial favorite on this small, four-stringed, guitar-like instrument. Hawaiian musicians have also developed the distinctive slack-key style (a type of open tuning) for guitar, an instrument introduced to the islands from Spain. Instruments native to Hawaii include beating sticks, bamboo pipes, and rattles

These Hawaiian
dancers are
performing in
Washington D.C. to
commemorate the
loss of the
Hawaiian Islands as
an independent
kingdom.

and drums of various kinds. According to historians, native Hawaiians also played a bamboo nose flute, a whistle made from a gourd, and an instrument having one string that was played with a bow. A variety of Jew's harp was also used.

Singing, drumming, and the *hula* dance are sacred forms of worship and remain integral to the daily life of some native Hawaiians. Certain superstitions continue to be observed with regard to modern *hula*; for example, while black can be used to ornament a costume, one never dresses totally in black for *hula*, since black is the traditional color of mourning. It is believed that ancient Hawaiians blackened their faces and limbs when in mourning.

HOLIDAYS

Ancient religious holidays are not known, owing to the determination on the part of missionaries to enforce the celebration of only the Christian holidays. In addition to federal holidays observed by the entire United States, Hawaii also celebrates Kuhio Day (Kuhio was a prince) on March 26, and Kamehameha Day on June 11. Hawaiians also observe

"Aloha Friday" each week. On Fridays Hawaiians wear especially bright clothing and women wear a flower tucked behind one ear and perhaps a *lei* around their neck. The occasion is marked by a celebratory attitude and a sense of good fun.

HEALTH ISSUES

Religion and medicine were closely related in traditional native Hawaiian life. People expected prayer to heal most things. There were several classes of *Kahuna lapa'au* (medical priest/healer) who treated physical and mental ailments according to a variety of traditions now mostly lost to history.

Drinking seawater followed by fresh water was considered a universal remedy. Various native plants were used as compresses for relieving pain or injury, and the leaves of plants were brewed in teas and used for healing purposes. *Piper methysticum* (the source of the intoxicating *awa* or *kava*) was used in many ways. Today, this species is a sedative given in mild form to infants during teething and is used in commercial diuretics. Seasonal changes and extremes of humidity and dryness produced many respiratory problems among native Hawaiians. There were as many as 58 herbal remedies for asthma, many of which have been studied or adapted by modern medical science.

In addition to the diseases brought over by the first wave of immigrants to Hawaii, leprosy, whose origin is not known and for which there has never been a cure, had a profound effect on the public health of native Hawaiians. Because of the social stigma attached to the diseases (it was mistakenly thought to be a venereal disease) as well as its extreme contagiousness, lepers were isolated on the island of Molokai beginning in 1886. For 16 years, a Belgian priest named Demian Joseph de Veuster provided medical care for these patients, whom the medical community refused to treat, before succumbing to the illness himself in 1889.

Compared to Hawaiians of European and Asian ancestry, native Hawaiians have continued to bear the brunt of the archipelago's health problems. Whereas Hawaii as a whole boasts the longest average life span of any state (males live an average 75.37 years, females, 80.92 years), the death rates of native Hawaiians at all ages are above average. The infant mortality rate for native Hawaiians is 6.5 per 1,000 live births. In addition, native Hawaiians experience high rates of diabetes and hypertension. Health workers consider poor diet a major factor, and economic problems undoubtedly contribute to this situation.

LANGUAGE

Polynesian-based Hawaiian is dying out as a spoken language. Today, it survives mostly on the island of Niihau, in some religious services, and in words and phrases used by English-speakers (the predominant group of Hawaiians), rather than as a language of everyday use. Traditionally unwritten, Hawaiian had no alphabet until the arrival of the *haole*. The Hawaiian alphabet was Romanized and first written by early missionaries. It contains twelve letters: "a," "e," "i," "o," "u," "h," "k," "l," "m," "n," "p," and "w." In general, vowels are pronounced separately, except for diphthongs such as "*ai*" ("eye"), "*au*" ("ow"), and "*ei*" ("ay"). Thus, Kamehameha is pronounced "kah may hah MAY hah." Fewer than 2,500 people speak Hawaiian as their mother tongue, most of whom are older people. It is estimated that within 30 years, Hawaiian will survive only in isolated phrases and in place names throughout the islands. All the languages of Oceania, and particularly those of Polynesia, are linguistically related. New Zealand, Tahiti, Fiji, Samoa, and Hawaii share many words, with slight variations. Some representative words in Hawaiian are *ali'i* (chief or royalty); *kahuna* (priest

and/or expert healer); *kapu* (taboo or sacred); *mahalo* (thank you); *mana* (energy or spiritual power); and *ohana* (extended family).

FAMILY AND COMMUNITY DYNAMICS

Although for centuries women had to endure cultural and domestic oppression, the segregation of men and women under the *Kapu* system provided women with a good deal of autonomy. They led their own lives, cooked food for themselves, had their own deities, and had their own function in matters of royal inheritance and social stature. Women's status depended on social position and birth order. Older sisters were respected and generally wielded greater authority than junior siblings, including males. Older women continue to command respect in the community, relative to younger men and women.

Traditionally, the differences in raising native Hawaiian boys and girls center around their eventual roles as adults. Boys learn to plant, cultivate, cook, and fish; girls learn to cook and are taught how to prepare *tapa* for decoration or clothing. In the past, children were raised by the entire extended family, a practice called *hanai*. Grandparents usually had more to say in the upbringing of children than did parents. When the first child was a boy, it was taken by the father's parents and raised by them and the father's siblings—the child's aunts and uncles. If the first child was a girl, it was raised by the mother's parents and her extended family. Childless couples were unheard of in the social sense; there were always children who needed attention and instruction.

Among native Hawaiians today, the old ways, while fragmented, are still observed. For example, in neighborhoods that are predominantly Hawaiian, children move in and out of houses freely, and adults are clearly watching out for all the children in view. The concept of children belonging to and being the responsibility of the larger extended family remains vital.

WEDDINGS

Hawaiian chiefs created political alliances by marrying both commoners and other royalty. Most chiefs had many wives and provided for adopted as well as biological children. Engagements were arranged by the parents of the prospective bride and groom during their late childhood or early adolescence. When arrangements were settled by the par-

ents, the young people were consulted, and once agreement to the match was obtained from all parties, the engagement became binding. The extended community that constituted the couple's family gave the bride and groom away. Hawaiian weddings were traditionally, and continue to be, associated with flowers. Both the bride and groom wear elaborate *leis*—necklaces of flowers, nuts, seeds, and other plant material woven together. Traditional Hawaiian weddings are still performed with the addition of whatever civil or religious sanction is necessary for legal purposes.

There are also superstitions linked with weddings: The bride and groom are not wished good luck on their wedding day, as this can result in bad luck. The only way this unfortunate situation can be reversed is for the individual who was offered the wish to cross his or her fingers immediately after it is offered, thus counteracting the curse. In addition, pearls should not be worn on the wedding day, as they resemble tears and will cause the marriage to be filled with sorrow.

FUNERALS

When someone died, the *kahuna aumakau* (priest of the appropriate ancestral deity) of the dead person came and ritually sacrificed a pig or a chicken to ensure that the soul would live with its ancestors. There were several ways of disposing of the dead. Burial in the ground was the most common method; there are ancient graveyards found on all the major islands. In another disposal ritual, the corpse was

eviscerated, filled with salt, and burned. Sometimes, the flesh was scraped off the bones, and the skull, femur, and humerus were saved. The rest of the body was taken by boat far out to sea and dumped. Those in the boats were not permitted to look back once the remains were deposited into the sea, or the soul would follow them back to the land and thus not rest properly. Remnants of special, woven caskets have been found, and it is believed they were used to hold the bones of kings. Such caskets are considered extraordinary works of art and are unique to Hawaii.

The bones of the dead are revered among native Hawaiians. Water is sprinkled in the house of the deceased so the soul will not return. After attending a funeral, it is important to sprinkle one's body with water so that the soul will not follow a mourner home.

PRIMARY EDUCATION

Many bilingual programs exist to accommodate children for whom English is not a first language. Many classes are given in Hawaiian, which is the second official language of the State of Hawaii. For native Hawaiian children there are the well-endowed Kamehameha Schools, which were established in perpetuity by the estate of Bernice Pauahi Bishop, the last descendant of Kamehameha. The schools were intended to provide native Hawaiian children with a place where they could learn together, away from the influences of the children of various immigrant groups.

HIGHER EDUCATION

The University of Hawaii has two major campuses (Manoa and Hilo), and several smaller ones, which provide both education and employment to various strata of the native Hawaiian population. There are also several community colleges. The 1990 Census revealed that 22 percent of those between 18 and 24 years old who identify themselves as native Hawaiians are enrolled in school. There were 318 people under the age of 24 identifying themselves as native Hawaiians who had a bachelor's degree or higher. Of those native Hawaiians aged 25 or older, 1,549 are reported as having graduate or professional degrees.

RELIGION

The ancient religion of Hawaii incorporates hundreds of deities as well as magical and animist beliefs. Hawaiians worshipped both in their homes and in open-air temples called *heiau*. Ruins of these temples are still visible on all the islands. The largest were *heiau waikaua*, or war temples, at which sacrifices occurred. Chief gods were *Ku* (god of war and male fertility), *Kane* (the creator and chief god), *Lono* (god of thunder and agriculture), and *Kanaloa* (god of the ocean and winds). With the arrival of other immigrant groups, particularly early explorers in the early 1800s, ancient Hawaiian religious practices disappeared completely. Today, many Hawaiians practice Buddhism, Shinto, and Christianity.

EMPLOYMENT AND ECONOMIC TRADITIONS

Before tourism and the establishment of the U.S. military on the islands, agriculture was the biggest industry in Hawaii. Sugar, coconut, and pineapple formed the core of the plantation system. When the large plantations were established in the 1820s and 1830s, native Hawaiian men were employed as farm workers while Hawaiian women worked in the houses of white immigrants as maids and washerwomen.

Wage labor first developed to meet foreign demand and was centered in Honolulu and Lahaina. Beginning around 1820, commoners were enticed to work for wages (although records show that such payment was usually practiced to avoid taxation). By the mid-1840s there existed a group of landless native Hawaiian laborers in Honolulu; these people were paid about a dollar a day in 1847, less than half of what *haoles* earned. Plantation owners, in fact, set wages at different levels for each of the different racial groups, in order to maintain distrust among them and thereby prevent workers from organizing.

A statement made by the plantation kingpin Sanford B. Dole (who also served for a time as president of the Hawaiian Republic) at a planter's convention in the 1880s captures the disregard in which the planters held their native Hawaiian employees: "I cannot help feeling that the chief end of this meeting is plantation profits, and the prosperity of the country, the demands of society ... the future of the Hawaiian race only comes secondarily if at all." Even to those commoners who were conscious of their exploitation, however, working for wages on plantations seemed a better way of life than working to pay tribute to chiefs. Plantation workers, for example, had taxes paid for them by plantation owners, and an early strike forced plantations to pay workers directly rather than through the chief.

Emigration of male native Hawaiians to the west coast of the United States occurred during the California Gold Rush. The growing absence of local labor resulting from this exodus, as well as from the dwin-dling native Hawaiian population, encouraged the importation of Chinese, Japanese, and Portuguese farm workers; a total of 400,000 came between 1850 and 1880. Smaller numbers of European workers came from Germany, Norway, and other countries.

From the time of the missionaries until the beginning of World War II, Hawaii was economically controlled by five powerful companies: Castle and Cooke, Alexander and Baldwin, Theodore Davies, C. Brewer, and American Factors (Amfac). About one-third of the Directors of these five companies were direct descendants of missionary families or immediately related to them by marriage. Collectively, these companies formed an alliance that, by 1930, controlled 96 percent of the islands' sugar industry and every business associated with that crop. They therefore manipulated virtually all the sizable businesses and institutions on the islands: banking, insurance, utilities, transportation, wholesale and retail sales, marketing, and inter-island and mainland shipping. In 1932, the Big Five gained control of the pineapple industry, Hawaii's second most important agricultural crop prior to World War II. After the war, in which many Japanese Americans served with great distinction, the Japanese vote broke the political power of the planter elite.

In the 1980s and the early 1990s, the economy of the State of Hawaii was based on tourism. Visitors to Hawaii spent almost $10 billion in 1990. The second largest employer was the U.S. Department of Defense, which spent more than $3 billion in 1990. Native Hawaiians often took jobs as domestic servants or serve in other, often menial, capacities to meet the needs of those who are staying on the islands for a short time. As agriculture diminished in magnitude and economic importance, opportunities became scarce for native Hawaiians who traditionally worked in the fields and canneries. At the same time, the economic boom through the 1980s and 1990s, when tourism peaked, began to decline. Unemployment in Hawaii was about 5.6 percent in 1998, above the national average of 4.5 percent, and the cost of living remains high, with average home prices around $300,000. These economic factors have caused many native Hawaiians to leave the islands for better opportunities on the mainland.

Statistics gathered for the 1990 census indicate that 57,185 persons over the age of 16 who identify themselves as native Hawaiians are employed. Median income for a native Hawaiian family living in Honolulu was $37,960. (No family size is given with this statistic.) That many native Hawaiian families may live on public assistance is surmised by the percentages who are reported as living below the poverty line; 14 percent of the native Hawaiian population is given as living below the standard U.S. poverty line. Some impoverished families are taken care of by those who honor the tradition of supporting extended family; many are not so fortunate. Unemployment for the entire state was calculated at 15 percent by the census taken in 1990. No figures are available for native Hawaiians as a separate category.

POLITICS AND GOVERNMENT

Native Hawaiians have expressed a mix of determination and apprehension as they face the beleaguered state of their centuries-old culture. The Hawaiian language, considered a crucial aspect of cultural identity, has been the object of renewed attention. In 1978, Hawaiian won recognition as an official state language. For many, cultural survival is inextricably linked to having a political voice. More than a century after the overthrow of the last Hawaiian monarch, the issue of sovereignty has resurfaced. The organization Ka Lahui Hawai'i (The Nation of Hawaii), founded in 1987, is dedicated to mobilizing support for this objective, thus galvanizing anti-*haole* sentiment that dates back to the age of Captain Cook. Chief among their complaints is that native Hawaiians are the only indigenous people living within the borders of the United States not recognized as a separate nation by the federal government. Rather, they are regarded as "wards" of the State of Hawaii. Informed by the Civil Rights movement of the 1960s and encouraged by sovereignty movements around the globe, Ka Lahui Hawai'i asks that native Hawaiians be treated as other Native Americans and be given their own lands (in addition to homestead lands), as well as rights of self-governance.

The sovereignty movement maintains that the independent and internationally recognized government of the Hawaiian islands was illegally overthrown by the government of the United States. It is further argued that acculturation—produced by intermarriage and lack of attention to native traditions, customs, and language—is a form of racial genocide. Because native Hawaiian religion, traditions, and values are closely associated with 'aina (the land) and respect for the environment, many native Hawaiians feel that American desecration of the environment, resulting from military and commercial exploitation, constitutes a grievous crime. The island of Kahoolawe, which was rendered uninhabitable after its use as target practice by the U.S. military, is cited as a prime example of these destructive policies—as are the crowds of tourists.

In 1993, sovereignty activists picketed President Clinton while he attended fund-raising activities on Waikiki Beach. Four months later, Clinton issued a formal apology for the United States' overthrow of the Hawaiian monarchy and for "the deprivation of the rights of native Hawaiians to self-determination." In 1994, activists delivered a Proclamation of Restoration of the Independence of the Sovereign Nation State of Hawaii, and began work on a new Constitution, which was signed and ratified on January 16, 1995. This document called for the restoration of the inherent sovereignty of the Native Hawaiian people and guaranteed equal rights to all citizens regardless of race. In 1999, a Native Hawaiian Convention convened in Honolulu to begin the process of forming a Native Hawaiian government.

The sovereignty movement, however, is far from unified. Ka Lahui Hawaii is but the largest of some 100 organizations working for native Hawaiian issues, and members disagree on what form sovereignty should take. For some, secession from the United States is the goal; others envision a status similar to that of American Indian reservations, or one that designates certain areas in Hawaii as zones for traditional lifestyles.

RACE RELATIONS

The circumstances surrounding the alleged rape of Thalia Massie in 1931 represent for many native Hawaiians the racial injustice of the present as well as the past. Massie testified that two Japanese, two Hawaiians, and a Chinese Hawaiian had attacked her near Waikiki, but the trial resulted in a hung jury. Massie's husband took matters into his own hands and killed one of the Hawaiians—a crime that brought him a sentence of only one hour. In a separate instance, a convicted murderer named Keanu was purposely infected with leprosy.

For a long time after annexation, Hawaii's politics were dominated by conservative men of European descent who served the interests of the plantations. In the wake of World War II and statehood, the labor unions, especially the International Longshoremen's and Warehousemen's Union, exerted a strong political influence, creating a tradition of support for the Democratic party and a politically liberal climate. The presence of Hawaiians of Japanese descent in the political arena has created the impression of progressive attitudes regarding race. Nevertheless, native Hawaiians have not always benefited from liberal politics. "On the issue of the original Hawaiians," wrote Francine Du Plessix Gray in her book, *Hawaii: The Sugar-Coated Fortress*, "the most far-sighted men would tend to maintain their paternalism."

INDIVIDUAL AND GROUP CONTRIBUTIONS

ACADEMIA

Haunani-Kay Trask, a political theorist, is professor of Political Science at the University of Hawaii and author of *From a Native Daughter: Colonialism and Sovereignty in Hawaii* (1993). Trask is also the author of a book of poetry, *Light in the Crevice Never Seen*, published in 1994.

ART AND ENTERTAINMENT

Keanu Reeves (1964–), whose film credits include *Bill and Ted's Excellent Adventure* (1989), *My Own Private Idaho* (1991), *Point Break* (1991), *Much Ado about Nothing* (1993), *Speed* (1994), *A Walk in the Clouds* (1996), *The Devil's Advocate* (1997), and *The Matrix* (1999), is part Hawaiian. The artist Polani Vaughan has produced a work of his photos and verse called *Na leo*. Don Ho (1930–), Hawaii's beloved singer, achieved fame for his recording "Tiny Bubbles" (1967). Keola (Keolamaikalani Breckenridge) Beamer, a descendant of Queen Ahiakumai Ki'eki'e and Kamahameha I, has played a central role in integrating traditional chants and instruments into contemporary music. He is also an expert in slack-key guitar. He tours widely, has recorded several slack-key albums, and has won numerous Hoku Awards.

LITERATURE

John Dominis Holt is a playwright and author of fiction and nonfiction. Dana Naone Hall is the author of *Malama: Hawaiian Land and Water* (1985).

POLITICS

In the political arena, Mililani Trask is *Kia'aina* (governor) of *Ka Lahui Hawai'i* (The Hawaiian Nation). Congressman Daniel Akaka (1924–) was elected to the U.S. Senate in 1990 and John Waihee (1926–) became Governor of the State of Hawaii in 1987.

MEDIA

RADIO

KCCN-AM (1420).
Plays ethnic-contemporary Hawaiian music on weekends.

Contact: Michael Kelly, Manager.
Address: Pioneer Plaza, Suite 400, Honolulu, Hawaii 96814.
Telephone: (808) 536-2728.

KPOA-FM (93.5).
Plays ethnic Hawaiian music.

Contact: Chuck Bergson, Manager.
Address: Lahaina Broadcasting Company, 505 Front Street, Suite 215, Lahaina, Hawaii 96761.
Telephone: (808) 667-9110.
Fax: (808) 661-8850.
Online: http://www.mauigateway.com/~kpoa/.

KUAI-AM (720).
Plays ethnic Hawaiian music.

Contact: William Dahle, Manager.
Address: P.O. Box 720, Eleele, Hawaii 96705.
Telephone: (808) 335-3171.
Fax: (808) 335-3834.

TELEVISION

Hawaiian Cable Vision Co.
Founded in 1969, this station serves Lahaina and West Maui with 31 channels, two community access channels, and 30 hours per week of community access programming.

Contact: Jim McBride, General Manager.
Address: Daniels Communications Partners, 910 Honoapiilani Highway, Suite 6, Lahaina, Hawaii 96761.
Telephone: (808) 661-4607.
Fax: (808) 661-8865.

ORGANIZATIONS AND ASSOCIATIONS

Daughters of Hawaii.
An organization of native Hawaiian women working to perpetuate the memory and spirit of old Hawaii; preserves the nomenclature and pronunciations of the Hawaiian language. Offers classes in Hawaiian.

Contact: Kim Ku'ulei Birnieor.
Address: 2913 Pali Highway, Honolulu, Hawaii 96817.
Telephone: (808) 595-6291.

Halau Mohala Ilima.
A group of professional dancers offering instruction in *hula* and traditional Hawaiian culture.

Contact: Mapauna deSilva.
Address: 1110 'A'alapapa Drive, Kailua,
    Hawaii 96734.
Telephone: (808) 261-0689.

Hana Cultural Center.
Community facility which mounts exhibits about
Hana history.

Address: P.O. Box 27, Hana, Hawaii 96713.
Telephone: (808) 248-8620.
E-mail: hccm@aloha.net.
Online: http://planet-hawaii.com/hana.

Nation of Hawaii.
Organization working toward renewed Hawaiian
sovereignty.

Telephone: (808) 259-3389; or (808) 259-3391.
Online: http://hawaii-nation.org/index.html.

State Council on Hawaiian Heritage.
State-funded agency which sponsors seminars in
dance and presents the annual King Kamehameha
hula Competition. Also sponsors conferences and
seminars on traditional storytelling and ancient legends of Native Hawaiians.

Address: 355 North King Street, Honolulu,
    Hawaii, 96817.
Telephone: (808) 536-6540.

MUSEUMS AND
RESEARCH CENTERS

Bernice P. Bishop Museum.
Founded by Charles Bishop in memory of his wife,
Bernice (the last known surviving member of the
Kamehameha family), it is one of the most significant scientific and cultural facilities in the Pacific
Region. The collection of ancient Hawaiian artifacts is world famous. The Museum owns extensive
collections and mounts frequent exhibits related to
the cultural and natural history of Hawaii. There is
also an Immigrant Preservation Center that houses
collections and permits scholarly research of immigrant artifacts from all the major ethnic groups.

Contact: Siegfried Kagawa, President.
Address: 1525 Bernice Street, Honolulu, Hawaii
    96817-0916.
Telephone: (808) 847-3511; or General
    Information Recording (888) 777-7443.
Fax: (808) 841-8968.
E-mail: museum@bishopmuseum.org.
Online: http://www.bishop.hawaii.org/.

Hawaiian Historical Society.
Founded in 1892. Maintains historical documents
from Hawaii and the Pacific Region. Publishes
scholarly works on Hawaiian history. Offers free
programs to the public.

Address: 560 Kawaiahao, Honolulu, Hawaii 96813.
Telephone: (808) 537-6271.

Lyman House Memorial Museum.
Historical residence containing both modern native
Hawaiian history and Pre-Cook history. There is
also information about native flora and fauna, geol-
ogy, and local family genealogies.

Contact: Gloria Kobayashi, Curator.
Address: 276 Haili Street, Hilo, Hawaii 96720.
Telephone: (808) 935-5021.

Polynesian Cultural Center.
Presents, preserves, and perpetuates the arts, crafts,
culture, and lore of Fijian, Hawaiian, Maori, Mar-
quesan, Tahitian, Tongan, Samoan, and other Polynesian peoples.

Contact: Lester W. B. Moore, President.
Address: 55-370 Kamehameha Highway, Laie,
    Hawaii 96762.
Telephone: (808) 293-3333.
Online: http://www.polynesia.com/.

Queen Emma Summer Palace.
Historical building which houses ancient Hawiiana,
including tapa, quilts, furniture, and other artifacts
belonging to Queen Emma and her family.

Contact: Mildred Nolan, Regent.
Address: 2913 Pali Highway, Honolulu,
    Hawaii 96817.
Telephone: (808) 595-3167.

University of Hawaii at Manoa: School of
Hawaiian, Asian and Pacific Studies.
Umbrella center for ten research programs and centers on the main Manoa campus, including Hawaiian Studies. Their publication is *Journal of Contemporary Pacific*.

Contact: Professor Lilikala Kame'eleihiwa,
    Director.
Address: Hawaiian Studies Building, Room 209A,
    2645 Dole Street, University of Hawaii,
    Honolulu, Hawaii 96822.
Telephone: (808) 973-0989.
Fax: (808) 973-0988.
E-mail: chsuhm@hawaii.edu.
Online: http://www2.hawaii.edu/shaps/enter/
    hawaiian.html.

SOURCES FOR ADDITIONAL STUDY

Buck, Elizabeth. *Paradise Remade: The Politics of Culture and History in Hawai'i*. Philadelphia : Temple University Press, 1993.

Clarke, Joan, with photography by Michael A. Uno. *Family Traditions in Hawai'i: Birthday, Marriage, Funeral, and Cultural Customs in Hawai'i*. Honolulu: Namkoong Pub., 1994.

Gray, Francine Du Plessix. *Hawaii: The Sugar-Coated Fortress*. New York: Random House, 1972.

Stannard, David E. *Before the Horror: The Population of Hawai'i on the Eve of Western Contact*. Honolulu: Social Science Research Institute, University of Hawaii, 1989.

HMONG
by
Carl L. Bankston III
AMERICANS

Hmong Americans generally have a very positive view of their new country and younger generations tend to understand both cultures quite well.

OVERVIEW

Social scientists estimate that there are between six and seven million Hmong in the world. Until recently, almost all Hmong lived in the mountains of southern China, Laos, Thailand, and northern Vietnam. Chinese oppression during the nineteenth century and the rise of communism in Vietnam following World War II pushed many Hmong into Laos, where about 300,000 Hmong lived peacefully during the 1960s. After the royal Laotian government was overthrown by Communist forces in 1975, about one-third of the Laotian Hmong were killed, another third fled to Thailand, and the remaining third stayed in Laos. Many of those who took refuge in Thailand found homes in France, Australia, or the United States. Overall, about 95,000 Hmong have settled in the United States. The Hmong are sometimes referred to as the *Meo* in Laos, Thailand, and Vietnam. In China, one of the official "nationalities" is *Miao*, a group that includes Hmong, ancient predecessors of the Hmong, and non-related peoples. Each of these terms means "savage," a name that the Hmong understandably find insulting.

The Hmong can be grouped in many ways, including by the typical color or design of their clothing. According to Hmong legend, these divisions developed as a result of ancient Chinese conquerors who forced the Hmong to divide into different groups and to identify themselves by wearing distinctive clothing. White, Black, Flowery, Red,

Striped, and Cowery Shell are some of these divisions. Another method of identifying subgroups is by their dialect. Most Hmong Americans are speakers of either Hmoob Dawb ("White Hmong") or Moob Leeg (no English translation). Though the Moob Leeg do not identify themselves as such, the White Hmong call them the Blue Hmong or the Green Hmong. This does not mean that most Hmong Americans are members of the White or Blue/Green color group, because the linguistic and color distinctions overlap and cut across groups. The kingroup is a more important identifier than language or color affiliation. In Laos, there are about 20 of these patriclans, all identified by family names.

Though Hmong agriculture has undergone many changes since the establishment of the People's Republic of Laos, the Hmong live in villages with economies based on raising livestock—mostly cattle and pigs—and growing crops. They grow rice, mostly of the dry land varieties, and vegetables in abundance. They practice *swidden* (slash and burn) agriculture, meaning that the Hmong clear fields by burning, thereby fertilizing the ground with ashes. Since this kind of agriculture exhausts soil rapidly, Hmong villages must constantly be on the move. Their principal crops are corn and opium poppies, which they use for medicines and spiritual ceremonies or sell to local traders.

HISTORY

Chinese historical sources indicate that the Hmong have lived in China since 2000 B.C. Many scholars believe that they may have lived in Siberia prior to this date because blond hair and blue eyes are occasionally found among the Hmong.

For centuries, the Hmong, who lived in the mountainous regions of southern China, struggled against the Chinese government to maintain their distinctive ethnic identity. In the 1700s Chinese generals convinced Sonom, the last Hmong king, to surrender, promising him that the Hmong would be treated well and that his surrender would bring an honorable peace to the mountains. Instead, Sonom was taken to Beijing where he, his officers, and his advisors were tortured to death in the presence of the Chinese Emperor.

After China was defeated by the British in the first Opium War (1842), the imperial Chinese government was forced to pay indemnities to the victors. To raise money, the government of China levied heavy taxes on its subjects, thus increasing tension between Chinese authorities and the Hmong minority. Between 1850 and 1880, the Hmong waged a series of wars against the Chinese. Unsuccessful in their rebellion, the Hmong fled southward; the majority of these emigrants settled in Laos, although many Hmong also migrated to Vietnam and Thailand.

THE HMONG IN LAOS

In Laos, the Hmong met new oppressors—the French—who had claimed Vietnam, Laos, and Cambodia as part of their vast Indochinese Empire. French taxation led to two major revolts against the French by the Hmong, one in 1896 and one in the 1920s. (The second revolt was initiated by Pa Chay, who called for the establishment of an independent Hmong kingdom and remains a hero to many Hmong today.)

In an effort to pacify the Hmong, the French established an autonomous Hmong district that was allowed to partake in self-government. This created competition, however, between the heads of two prominent families in the district, one headed by Fong and one by Bliayao. In 1922 a feud broke out between their over which group would rule the district. To defuse the perilous situation, the French organized a democratic election for chief of the district in 1938. Touby Lyfong, the son of Fong, won the election, defeating his cousin Faydag Lobliayao, the son of Bliayao. The subsequent rivalry between these two men and their followers led to the permanent political separation of the Hmong in Laos. Touby Lyfong made common cause with the French and later allied himself with the Americans in their fight against the North Vietnamese. Faydang Lobliayao, on the other hand, joined forces with the Lao nationalists, who favored total independence from France, and later became an important leader of the Lao Communist forces.

U.S. INVOLVEMENT IN SOUTHEAST ASIA

The United States became involved in Southeast Asia to preserve a non-Communist regime in South Vietnam. Because the *Pathet Lao*, the communist guerrillas of Laos, were allied with North Vietnam's *Viet Minh* (later known as the *Viet Cong*), the United States provided economic and tactical support to the royal Lao government to fight the guerrillas as well as North Vietnamese troops. Many of the individuals recruited by the U.S. government were Hmong led by Vang Pao, an anti-Communist Hmong military leader who had earlier assisted the French. According to many sources, the Central Intelligence Agency (CIA) officials who organized the Hmong army promised the soldiers, who numbered 40,000 by 1969, that the United States would resettle the Hmong if they were defeated.

After American troops were withdrawn from Indochina in 1973, the Lao government was forced to negotiate with its enemies and to bring the pro-North Vietnamese leftists into a coalition government. Following the fall of South Vietnam in April 1975, the leftists in Laos consolidated their political power, the royal government crumbled, the king abdicated his throne, and the Lao People's Democratic Republic was proclaimed. Despite General Vang Pao's insistence that the United States resettle all of the Hmong soldiers, the U.S. government evacuated only about 1,000 Hmong in the first year.

The new Laotian government sent many Hmong to harsh reeducation camps. Others continued to fight against the new government. Still other Hmong made their way across the border into Thailand, where they stayed in refugee camps for months or, in some cases, years. It has been estimated that some 55,000 Hmong remain in such camps.

"**B**eing an American is really espousing the founding principles of freedom, no matter whether you speak the language or not.... And I think the Hmong ... know in their hearts that these principles are what they have fought for, even in Laos—the basic principles of freedom."

Mouachou Mouanoutoua in 1988, cited in *Hmong Means Free: Life in Laos and America,* edited by Sucheng Chan (Philadelphia: Temple University Press, 1994).

SIGNIFICANT IMMIGRATION WAVES

In December 1975 the United States agreed to begin resettling the Hmong in America and Congress admitted 3,466 individuals. In 1976, 10,200 refugees from Laos (who had fled across the border into Thailand) were admitted to the United States; some of these immigrants were Hmong, although there is no official record of them. The number of Laotian immigrants then dipped to only 400 in 1977, but climbed to 8,000 in 1978. By the early 1980s, about 50,000 Hmong were living in the United States. By the time of the 1990 U.S. Census the number of Hmong in the United States had doubled to almost 100,000 people. Of the foreign-born Hmong in the United States in 1990, 75 percent had arrived during the 1980s, the majority of whom had arrived in the first half of the decade.

SETTLEMENT PATTERNS

In 1990 the majority of Hmong Americans lived in California (43,000), Minnesota (more than17,000), and Wisconsin (16,000). By the summer of 1999, the

number of Hmong in Minnesota had reached an estimated 70,000. When the Hmong began arriving in the United States in the mid- to late-1970s, American refugee resettlement agencies dispersed the 12 traditional groups all over the country, placing small groups in 53 different cities and 25 different states, where voluntary agencies such as churches could be found to sponsor the refugees. Between 1981 and 1985, however, the Hmong reassembled through massive secondary migration, making their way across the country in small family groups. Drawn by the lure of reforming their kingroup-based society and by the moderate climate of the Pacific Coast, the majority congregated in farming towns and small cities in California, primarily Fresno (18,000), Merced (7,500), Sacramento (5,000), Stockton (5,000), and Chico, Modesto, and Visalia (6,000).

ACCULTURATION AND ASSIMILATION

Hmong Americans generally have a very positive view of their new country and younger generations tend to understand both cultures quite well. However, there is a general ignorance of the Hmong on the part of most Americans. Many Americans find it difficult to distinguish them from the Vietnamese or other Asian groups. Insofar as stereotypes have arisen, the Hmong are often seen as hard-working, but also extremely foreign. Many Americans are also perplexed by the rituals of the Hmong and by the music that often accompanies them. Nonetheless, Hmong Americans tend to be friendly to members of other groups and welcome attempts on the part of outsiders to learn more about their culture. The Hmong themselves are rapidly becoming an American minority, rather than an alien group in American society. As of 1990, about one-third of the Hmong in the United States were born in this country. Since Hmong Americans tend to be very young, the proportion of Hmong who have personal memories of Laos is decreasing rapidly.

Many Hmong customs are not practiced in the United States, especially by those who have converted to Christianity. As might be expected in a group that has experienced such rapid social change, Hmong Americans are still trying to sort out which traditions may be retained in the new land, and which traditions must be left behind.

MYTHS, LEGENDS, AND FOLKTALES

In recent years, efforts have been made to record and preserve the Hmong's ancient stories as younger

The Hmong story cloth plays an important part in remembering one's ancestry and passing down stories from generation to generation.

members of the ethnic group are drawn into the mass media-based American culture. One of the most comprehensive collections is the large, bilingual volume *Myths, Legends, and Folktales from the Hmong of Laos* (1985), edited by Charles Johnson.

The stories told by the Hmong date back to before they became part of the Chinese Empire. Magic, supernatural events, and spirits occupy a prominent place in these stories and, as in the folktales of other nations, animals can often talk. People are occasionally transformed into animals, or animals into people. Reincarnation is common and characters may reappear after their deaths. Many Hmong stories convey moral lessons, relaying happy outcomes for honest, hard-working, and virtuous individuals, and unfortunate outcomes for the evil, lazy, or selfish.

Hmong literature in America is largely preserved by older Hmong. Young Hmong Americans, like young Americans of many ethnic groups, are frequently more familiar with the lore of pop culture than with the lore of their ancestors. The Hmong and those familiar with them, however, recognize the oral literature as a unique repository of spiritual values and hope that some of it may be saved.

HOLIDAYS

The New Year Festival (*noj peb caug*) is the most important Hmong American holiday. In Laos, this holiday begins with the crowing of the first rooster on the first day of the new moon in the twelfth month, or harvest time, and lasts four to seven days. The scheduling is somewhat more flexible in America and does not usually last as long, but it always takes place around the time of the new moon in December. The New Year festival is the only holiday shared by the entire Hmong community and is an important occasion for bringing different Hmong families together.

The purpose of the New Year ceremonies is to get rid of the evil influences of the old year and to invoke good fortune for the new. One of the central rituals of the New Year ceremonies is the "world renewal ritual." This involves a small tree traditionally brought in from the forest (although Hmong Americans may use a green stick, or other symbolic tree), which is placed in the ground at the celebration site. One end of a rope is tied to the top of the tree and the other end is held by one of the participants or tied to a rock. An elder stands near the tree

Hmong American
Moua Vang is
dressed up to
celebrate at the
New Years Festival
in Fresno,
California.

Hmong American Moua Vang is dressed up to celebrate at the New Years Festival in Fresno, California.

holding a live chicken. The elder chants while the people circle the tree three times clockwise and four times counter-clockwise. The chanting during the clockwise movement is intended to remove the accumulated bad fortune of the previous year and the chanting during the counter-clockwise movement is intended to call out good fortune. The evil fortune, in the traditional perspective, is believed to accumulate in the blood of the chicken. After the participants have finished circling the tree, the elder is supposed to take the chicken to a remote place in the forest and cut its throat to take away the evil influences, but this practice is frequently not carried out in the United States.

Other rituals associated with the New Year ceremonies involve calling home the ancestral spirits to enjoy the festivities with the living and offering sacrifices to the guardian spirits of each house. For American Hmong, the New Year serves as an opportunity to reaffirm their culture and to teach their children about their traditions. For this reason, New Year celebrations in the United States usually involve displays of traditional cultural practices, such as dances, intended to educate Hmong children born in the United States. Aspects of western culture, such as performances by rock bands, have been integrated into the ceremonies. Many New Year exhibitions and practices show a merging of custom with newly acquired cultural practices, as when young Hmong women participate in beauty pageants wearing their elaborate traditional dresses.

Because the New Year holiday brings together people from different clans, it is considered an important occasion for young couples to meet one another. Ball games, in which long lines of young unmarried men and women toss a ball back and forth with their favorites, are a colorful tradition brought to America that may be seen at each New Year celebration.

HEALTH ISSUES

Traditional Hmong methods for healing are based on shamanism, which includes the use of herbal medicines and massage. Shamanistic health practices stem from the belief that illness is essentially spiritual in nature. For this reason, some western students of Hmong shamanism have characterized it as a form of psychotherapy.

The shamanistic view of the world considers reality as being composed of two parts: the visible and the invisible. The visible part of the world is the material reality that we see around us. The invisible part of the world is the realm of spirits, including the souls of the living, the spirits of the dead, care-taker spirits, malevolent spirits, and others. The shaman is capable of making contact with the spirit world and dealing with it on the behalf of others.

The Hmong recognize that illness can result from many causes, so the method of treatment depends on the source of disease. One of these causes is the loss of one's spirit or soul. It may become disconnected from the body and wander away, so that the body becomes alienated from the spiritual essence. Fear, loneliness, separation from loved ones, and other emotional stresses can rip the soul away from the body. This leads to a variety of physical symptoms, such as loss of weight and appetite, which usually lead to more serious diseases.

The "soul-caller" is one of the most important roles of traditional Hmong health care experts. There are many methods of calling a wandering soul back to its body. In less serious illnesses, parents or other family members may be able to perform the rituals needed. If a baby cries during the night, for example, an adult family member may go to the door and swing a burning stick back and forth to light the way for the baby's soul to return. In more serious illnesses, a shaman will be needed to perform rituals that typically include animal sacrifices.

Lost souls may also be found by someone who has a *neng*, a healing spirit in his own body. The *neng* and the healing skills that accompany it must be inherited from a clan member. A healer who has a *neng* can not only find lost souls, but he can also cure illnesses caused by evil spirits, frequently by engaging in battle with the evil spirit that has brought the sickness.

The Hmong have a great knowledge of curative herbs and most Hmong households in the United States have small herbal gardens. Women are almost always experts in herbal medicines. Herbs and massages are often combined to treat ailments such as stomach aches.

While the Hmong are, generally speaking, a healthy people, during the late 1970s and 1980s, Hmong Americans attracted nationwide attention as victims of Sudden Unexpected Nocturnal Death Syndrome. Similar to Sudden Infant Death Syndrome, the illness strikes during sleep. The mysterious fatalities occurred almost exclusively among men, most of whom showed no prior signs of illness. Physicians have connected the disease to breathing difficulties, but many Hmong ascribe it to an evil spirit that sits on the chests of victims during slumber.

Western-style health care professionals often have difficulty winning the confidence of Hmong patients because their concepts of illness are so different. Those who have written on the subject feel that doctors, nurses, and other health-care providers who work with the Hmong must try to better understand the Hmong approach. Some have also pointed out that the Hmong, with their intimate knowledge of herbal medicines, have much to teach American doctors.

LANGUAGE

The primary dialect spoken by most Hmong in the United States is either *Hmoob Dawb* ("White Hmong") or *Moob Leeg* (no English translation). *Hmoob Dawb* speakers refer to *Moob Leeg* speakers as *Hmoob Ntsaub*, Blue/Green Hmong. Hmong is monosyllabic and tonal, meaning that it consists mainly of one-syllable words and that the tone of a word affects meaning. Hmong uses eight different tones, more than the average of other Asian tonal languages.

According to Hmong oral tradition, after joining the Chinese Empire, the Hmong lost their original writing system and any Hmong caught using the Hmong alphabet was punished with death. Women of the tribes tried to keep the alphabet alive by sewing the letters into the patterns of their traditional clothes. Portions of this alphabet can be found on Hmong clothing today, but few people are capable of reading these carefully preserved designs.

Prior to the mid-twentieth century, those Hmong who could write their language usually did so with Chinese characters. In the 1950s, American and French missionaries in Laos developed the Romanized Popular Alphabet (RPA), a means of writing Hmong with a version of the alphabet used by English and other western European languages. Because the Hmong language is substantially different from European languages, however, some characteristics of the RPA are not familiar to English speakers.

Each of the eight tones is indicated by a consonant written at the end of the word. When the letter "b," for example, is written at the end of a word, it is not pronounced. It serves merely to indicate that this word is spoken with a high tone. The letter "j" at the end of a word indicates a high-falling tone, a bit like the descending intonation or pitch of "day-o" in the popular Caribbean song. A word ending in "v" is to be spoken with a mid-rising tone, similar to the intonation at the end of a question in

English. Moreover, at the end of a word, "s" indicates a mid-low tone, "g" indicates a mid-low breathy tone, and "m" at the end of a word is spoken with a low, glottalized tone, a tensing of the throat. Words ending in "d" have a low-rising tone.

Most of the vowels and consonants that do not occur at the ends of words have pronunciations similar to those of western European languages, but there are some differences. The consonant "x" is pronounced like the English "s," while "s" is pronounced like the English "sh." Likewise, "z" in the RPA has the sound of the "s" in "leisure." The Hmong "r" has no equivalent in English, but is closer to the English "t" or "d" than to the English sound "r." The consonant "c" in this writing system has a sound similar to the sound that "t" and "y" would make if we pronounced the words "quit you" very rapidly. The consonant "q" is like the English "k" or "g" but is pronounced further back in the throat. Finally, "w" has a sound that linguists call the "schwa," the vowel sound in the word "but," and "aw" is a longer version of this sound, somewhat like the vowel sound in "mud."

GREETINGS AND OTHER POPULAR EXPRESSIONS

The White Hmong phrases given here are written in the Romanized Popular Alphabet described above. Therefore, in words that end in consonants, the final consonant is not pronounced. It indicates the tone with which the word should be spoken.

Common greetings include: *Koj tuaj los?*—"You've come?"; *Kuv tuaj*—"I've come"; and *Mus ho tuaj*—"Come again." It is not usually regarded as polite to ask a stranger's name but a Hmong may turn to someone else and ask *Tus no yog leej twg tub?*—"Whose son is this?"; *Tus no yog leej tus ntxhais?*—"Whose daughter is this?"; *Tus no yog leej tus pojniam?*—"Whose wife is this?"; or *Tus no yog leej tus txiv?*—"Whose husband is this?" It is both polite and common to ask where someone lives: *Koj nyob qhov twg?*—"Where do you live?" If a visitor starts to leave, a Hmong host may say *Nyob. Wb tham mentsis tso maj*—"Stay, and we'll chat a little first," since it is considered polite to try to keep visitors from leaving. Two useful phrases for anyone wanting to learn a little Hmong are: *Qhov no yog dabtsi?*—"What's this?" and *Lus Hmoob hais li cas (English concept)?*—"How is (English concept) said in Hmong?"

FAMILY AND COMMUNITY DYNAMICS

Adjusting to life in a highly industrialized society has not been easy for the Hmong. In 1990, almost two-thirds of Hmong Americans (63.6 percent) lived below the poverty level, compared to seven percent of white Americans, and just over 23 percent of black Americans. Their median household income of $14,276 was one of the lowest of any ethnic or national group in the United States. As a result, about three out of every four Hmong families (74.1 percent) were receiving public assistance in 1990.

Many of the difficulties faced by Hmong Americans result from inadequate educational preparation. Having lived in a society based on agriculture and hunting, formal education was simply not a part of the traditional Hmong upbringing. Most adults, therefore, have very few educational credentials. Nearly 55 percent of Hmong over the age of 25 in the United States have less than a fifth grade education, and nearly 70 percent are not high school graduates. Despite these handicaps, however, Hmong born or raised in the United States have shown surprisingly high rates of college attendance. Almost 32 percent of Hmong aged 18 to 24 were in college in 1990, a rate of college attendance that is slightly below that of white Americans (39.5 percent) and slightly above that of black Americans (28.1 percent).

According to the 1990 U.S. Census, the average Hmong family has 6.38 individuals, compared to 3.73 individuals for the average Asian American family, 3.06 for the average white American family, and 3.48 for the average African American family. Over 60 percent of Hmong Americans were below the age of 18 in 1990 and the median age of Hmong Americans was 12.7 years, compared to 30.4 years for other Asian Americans and 34.1 years for Americans in general. The size of Hmong families, therefore, contribute to the economic difficulties of the group, since adults must use their incomes to support more children than are found in most American households. However, while the extreme youth of Hmong Americans may complicate family economic situations at present, this youth, combined with the educational achievement of young Hmong people, is a source of great potential for future upward mobility.

Hmong families in America generally regard men as the head of the family and chief decision-maker. Nonetheless, women often wield a great deal of power in the family, since they usually have primary responsibility for the household. This is partially due to the fact that Hmong homes are viewed as "child-centered" places, where small children are regarded as treasures. As chief care-givers for children, Hmong-American women can be extremely influential in their communities.

The ways in which Hmong American parents try to keep track of their children reflects their situation as new immigratns. They do not want the enculturation of their children taken completely out of their hands. The language and ways of their ancestors remain important to the parents who wish to see such valuable social attributes live on. Though some might view this as exercising a high degree of control over their children's lives, it would be more accurate to say that they want to teach and guide their children just like other American parents. Young Hmong Americans, however, sometimes have difficulty in seeing the relevance of cultural values important to their parents. As a result of this generation gap, some social workers and people who work with agencies serving the Hmong say that teenaged runaways have become a major issue among Hmong Americans and other Southeast Asian refugee groups.

While the extended family is the basic unit of social organization for the Hmong in Asia, those in the United States often find difficulty in maintaining the tradition of the extended family. It is not possible for large numbers of people to live together under one roof in the new country due to landlord and government regulations on fire and housing codes. Hmong Americans, therefore, have had to break up into nuclear-style families. However, extended family members almost always live in close proximity to one another and assist newcomers with living expenses, child care, and adaptation to American society.

Although Hmong kinship groups are still recognized in the United States, they have become less important to Hmong Americans. Respected elders previously took their functions from the rituals they performed in traditional ceremonies. Since the conversion of some Hmong to Christianity, however, these traditional ceremonies have become less important and less common. Also, many of the ceremonies require the sacrifice of animals, which is often illegal and typically frowned upon by other Americans. Many elders are gradually being replaced by newer and younger leaders who are well-educated and fluent in English and are, therefore, better able to help their families and other Hmong with the nuances of American society. These elders, however, are still held in high regard and receive deference from the young. Newer leaders rely on the moral authority and blessings of the elders.

BIRTH

Mus Thawj thiab, "go become again" or more simply "reincarnation," is a traditional Hmong belief. Thus, every child born is seen as a reincarnated soul. Children officially join human society three days after they are born. If a child dies within three days, no funeral ceremonies are held since the child did not have a soul yet. After three days of life, a shaman evokes a soul to be reincarnated in the baby's body. The family's ancestors are called upon to join the living family members in blessing the incarnation and in protecting the baby. The baby is then given a silver necklace that is supposed to keep the newly reincarnated soul from wandering.

MARRIAGE

Hmong marriage customs, as well as popular attitudes toward marriage, have undergone rapid change as a result of the move to America. In Laos, it is incestuous, and, therefore, forbidden for members of the same patriclan who share the same family to marry. Men and women with different family names, however, may get married regardless of their blood relationship. Most often, young people in Laos met potential mates at the New Year's Festival, which brought together people from different villages. At the Festival, young women wore their most colorful skirts and showed off their sewing and embroidery skills, while young men displayed their horse-riding and other skills, and sometimes played musical instruments to serenade the young women. Men generally married at any age between 18 and 30, while women often married between 14 and 18.

Traditional Hmong marriages required the prospective groom to secure a go-between, most often a relative, who bargained with the young woman's family for a bridal price, usually paid in silver bars. Marriages were made public by a two-day feast, featuring a roasted pig. This feast symbolically joined the clans of the bride and groom as well as the bride and groom themselves.

When a suitor could not reach an agreement on bridal price with the woman's family, the couple sometimes eloped. This practice became especially common after World War II when the social disruptions of war loosened parental control. Following the elopement, outside arbitrators helped to find an acceptable bridal price to pay in settlement.

Though always regarded as a serious transgression by the Hmong, young men with poor marriage prospects might attempt to abduct a woman and force her into marriage. Families without a formidable kin group to back them could not always prevent this from happening to their daughters. Usually the abductor and his relatives would offer the unwilling bride's family some form of payment in hopes of mollifying them. The government in Laos did not intervene in such situations, but the U.S. government does. Naturally, the practice has become extremely rare here.

Although most Hmong men had one wife, polygyny, or marriage with several women, was an accepted practice. During the war, polygyny became common due to the custom that required Hmong men to marry the widows of their dead brothers in order to provide a means of support for the brothers' families. Wealthy men often had several wives as symbols of affluence. Moreover, leaders sometimes married several times to establish political alliances.

American culture and law has made it necessary for the Hmong to change many of their attitudes and practices with regard to family. On occasions, those who have failed to drop older practices have found themselves in conflict with the American legal system. There have been a few instances of young Hmong American men kidnapping and sexually assaulting young females. While they may have considered this a culturally acceptable way to enter into marriage, American law defines this kind of activity as illicit abduction and rape. Some of the young women who have been abducted have viewed the events from an American perspective and have pressed charges.

The use of negotiators to arrange a marriage remains fairly common among Hmong Americans. However, many young women wait until their late teens or early twenties to marry. Surveys of Hmong Americans indicate that the majority believe that it is best for women to delay marriage until they are at least 18 years of age. Polygyny is rarely found among Hmong Americans.

FUNERALS

Before the Hmong came to America, the death of a family member was announced by firing three shots into the air. This action was thought to frighten away evil spirits. Today, this tradition is rarely followed by Hmong in the United States because of laws regulating the use of guns in populated areas.

The deceased is washed, dressed in new clothes, and left to lie in state. Mourners bearing gifts visit the home of the deceased, where they are fed by the family of the departed. A shaman makes an offering of a cup of alcohol to the dead person and tells the soul that the body has died. Colorful bits of paper, representing money for use in the spirit world are burned and the shaman tells the soul the route it must follow to get to the ancestors and how to avoid dangers during the journey.

INTERACTIONS WITH OTHER ETHNIC GROUPS

Hmong Americans interact most closely with ethnic Laotian Americans, with whom they work in a number of Southeast Asian refugee assistance organizations. Most Hmong who grew up in Laos or had some schooling there speak Laotian, facilitating interaction. The Hmong also maintain friendly relations with members of most other groups, but intermarriage is still relatively rare because of the continued importance of kinship groups.

RELIGION

The cult of spirits, shamanism, and ancestor worship compose the three major parts of traditional Hmong religion. It is a pantheistic religion, teaching that there are spirits residing in all things. According to Hmong religious beliefs, the world consists of two worlds, the invisible world of *yeeb ceeb*, which holds the spirits, and the visible world of *yaj ceeb*, which holds human beings, material objects, and nature.

The shaman is important because he can make contact with the world of the spirits. Each shaman has a set of spirits that serve as his allies in intervening with the unseen world on behalf of others. Some spirits, particularly those of ancestors, also make themselves accessible to people who are not shamans. Some households, for example, feed the spirits of their ancestors at feasts by placing a spoonful of rice and a spoonful of pork in the center of the table and inviting the spirits to share in the feast. Because women are most often in charge of medicinal herbs, they are responsible for propitiating the spirits of medicine on special altars.

Some Hmong Americans adhere to the *Chao Fa* (in Lao, literally, "Lord of the Sky") religion. This religion is said to have begun in Laos in the 1960s when a Hmong prophet, Yang Chong Leu (sometimes written as Shang Lue Yang), announced that the Hmong would be sent a king who would lead them to salvation from their enemies provided the Hmong rejected lowland Laotian and western ways, and returned to the ways of their ancestors. Yang Chong Leu also taught an original system of writing known as *Pahawh Hmong*, which is still used by adherents to *Chao Fa*. The prophet was killed in 1971, but his followers continued to grow in numbers and were active in the fight against the new Laotian government after 1975.

Missionaries from a wide variety of Christian denominations converted many Hmong in Laos. Even more Hmong converted to Christianity after their arrival to the United States. Baptists, Catholics, Presbyterians, members of the Church of Christ, Mormons, and Jehovah's Witnesses have all been energetic in seeking converts among the

Hmong in America. Since religion is regarded as the foundation of life among the Hmong, conversion has been among the most drastic social changes. In many cases, conversion to Christianity has split families, with some members taking up the new faith and some members adhering to traditional beliefs. Marriage practices, in particular, have been affected by religious conversion since many traditional Hmong practices, such as the bridal price, arranged marriage, and the marriage of girls, are strongly discouraged by Christian churches.

EMPLOYMENT AND ECONOMIC TRADITIONS

Since most Hmong in Asia practice agriculture, early arrivals had few transferable skills, considering America's vast industrial economy. Hence, of the 40,649 Hmong Americans who were over the age of 16 in 1990, only 11,923 had participated in the American labor force; 18.3 percent of this group were unemployed. Almost 80 percent of the Hmong Americans who are employed have blue-collar, or manual, occupations.

Employers who hire Hmong Americans generally hold high opinions of them. Most employers and managers who have experience with members of this group praise them for their hard work and honesty. Some supervisors have remarked that the Hmong have a more flexible concept of time than the American majority, and that this can sometimes lead to minor difficulties in the workplace. Most of the problems faced by Hmong Americans, though, appear to result from an inadequate command of the English language.

One of the most interesting aspects of Hmong adaptation to the American economy has been their discovery of a demand for traditional handicrafts in the American market. For centuries, Hmong women have practiced an elaborate needlecraft known as *paj ntaub* (also frequently spelled *pa ndau*). This art combines the techniques of embroidery and applique to produce colorful, abstract, geometric designs. The needlecraft is done entirely by hand, without the use of instruments for measurement.

During the 1980s, the cottage industry of *paj ntaub*—which had begun in the Thailand refugee camps—emerged in large Hmong communities, especially in California. Responding to the American marketplace, Hmong artisans have begun to produce bedspreads, pillow cases, wall hangings, and other items that appeal to buyers. This emerging industry confirms Hmong cultural value, while demonstrating the economic importance of women to their families and communities.

POLITICS AND GOVERNMENT

Adaptation to American society is a matter of overriding concern to Hmong organizations, most of which are geared toward helping Hmong Americans with housing, employment, language issues, and other immediate problems. The Hmong National Development is one of the largest organizations of this kind and, as such, functions as an advocate in obtaining funding for local Hmong organizations.

Hmong Americans are also passionately concerned with political events in their native land, where the Communist party that overthrew the Laotian government remains in power today. Although the government of Laos appears to have moderated its position toward political opponents in recent years, most Hmong remain strongly opposed to the regime. In fact, some American Hmong communities provide economic aid for small groups of Hmong in Laos who are still fighting the government. It has been suggested that Hmong Americans have been coerced into making contributions to anti-Communist forces in their homelands by groups operating in the United States, but this has not been definitely established.

INDIVIDUAL AND GROUP CONTRIBUTIONS

Despite the fact that the Hmong have lived in the United States for only a short period of time, many members of the Hmong American community have made significant contributions to American society. The following list represents only a few such individuals.

MEDICINE

Dr. Bruce (Thow Pao) Bliatout is Director of the International Health Center in Portland, Oregon. Dr. Bliatout first came to the United States in 1966, as a young exchange student. He returned to Laos, where he worked for the Laotian government until 1975. He then returned to the United States and earned a Ph.D. in public health. Dr. Bliatout is an authority on Sudden Death Syndrome (SUDS), and has written widely on the subject.

Dr. Xoua Thao arrived in the United States in 1976 at the age of 14. Dr. Thao's mother is a traditional herbalist and his father is a shaman. As a result of this family background in healing, Dr. Thao developed an interest in medicine and attended medical school at Brown University, where he received his medical degree in 1989. He is currently president of Hmong National Development and is studying for a law degree.

SOCIOLOGY

Dr. Dao Yang lives in St. Paul, Minnesota. Dr. Yang became the first Hmong to receive a Ph.D. when he received a doctorate in social economics in France. He was one of the co-founders of Hmong National Development and remains active in social issues, such as the prevention of teenage pregnancy.

Community leader Vang Pao lives in Santa Ana, California. He was leader of the Hmong army in Laos and is still widely respected, especially among older Hmong Americans.

Community activist Dia Cha (1962?–) worked as the Asian Community Outreach Coordinator at the Mental Health Center of Boulder County in Colorado where she provided support service to Asian students and served as an intermediary between parents and faculty in the Boulder Valley Public Schools. For the Southeast Asian Tribal Collections Project at the Denver Museum of Natural History, Cha organized collection materials, conducted research, and interviewed people to gather information. As a project director with the United Nations Development Fund for Women she assessed the needs of Lao and Hmong refugee women repatriates in Laos and in the refugee camps in Thailand. She authored the book *Dia's Story Cloth: The Hmong People's Journey of Freedom* (1996) and compiled *Folk Stories of the Hmong* (1991) with Norma Livo.

MEDIA

PRINT

California Hmong Times.
The chief Hmong publication in the United States, it publishes news and general interest articles, with a focus on the American Hmong community.

Address: 1945 North Fine Avenue #100, Fresno, California 93727-1528.
Telephone: (209) 268-8567.

ORGANIZATIONS AND ASSOCIATIONS

Hmong American Partnership.
Provides support services to the Minneapolis-St. Paul metropolitan area.

Address: 1600 West University Avenue, Suite 12, St. Paul, Minnesota 55104 .
Telephone: (651) 642-9601.
Fax: (651) 603-8399.
E-mail: hapmail@hmong.org.
Online: http://www.hmong.org/.

Hmong Council.
A community organization serving America's largest Hmong population. Helps with housing problems, translations, health and social services, and conflict resolution.

Contact: Houa Yang, President.
Address: 4753 East Olive Avenue, Suite 102, Fresno, California 93702.
Telephone: (209) 456-1220.

Hmong National Development (HND).
A national, non-profit organization that promotes the interests of Hmong Americans throughout the United States. The HND helps to facilitate communication among local Hmong organizations and to advocate for increased resources to Hmong organizations and communities.

Contact: Lee Pao Xiong, President.
Address: 1326 18th Street NW, Suite 200A, Washington, D.C. 20036.
Telephone: (202) 463-2118.
Fax: (202) 463-2119.
Email: Hndlink@aol.com.
Online: http://members.aol.com/Hndlink.

Lao Family Community of Minnesota.
A nonprofit mutual assistance association founded in 1977 as the Hmong Association of Minnesota. Strives to help the Hmong community strike a balance between traditional Hmong culture and modern American life.

Address: 320 West University Avenue, St. Paul, Minnesota 55103.
Telephone: (651) 221-0069.
Fax: (651) 221-0276.
E-mail: admin@laofamily.org.
Online: http://www.laofamily.org/.

Lao Family Community, Inc.
Provides English training and vocational education, a variety of youth programs, and a gang prevention program to Hmong, Laotians, and other minorities from Southeast Asia.

Contact: Pheng Lo.
Address: 807 North Joaquin, #207, Stockton, California 95202.
Telephone: (209) 466-0721.

South-East Asia Center (SEAC).

Grassroots organization seeking to assist Lao, Hmong, Cambodian, Vietnamese, and Chinese refugees from Indochina.

Contact: Peter R. Porr, Executive Director.
Address: 1124-1128 West Ainslie, Chicago, Illinois 60640.
Telephone: (773) 989-6927.
Fax: (773) 989-4871.
Email: seac1@hotmail.com.

Sources for Additional Study

Dunnigan, Timothy, et al. "Hmong" in *Refugees in America in the 1990s: A Reference Handbook*, edited by David W. Haines. Westport, CT: Greenwood Press, 1996.

Hmong Means Free: Life in Laos and America, edited by Sucheng Chan. Philadelphia: Temple University Press, 1994.

The Hmong Homepage. http://www.hmongnet.org (accessed August 31, 1999), last updated July 26, 1999.

Quincey, Keith. *Hmong: History of a People*. Cheney: Eastern Washington University Press, 1988.

Sherman, Spencer. "The Hmong in America: Laotian Refugees in the 'Land of the Giants,'" *National Geographic Magazine*, October 1988, pp. 586-610.

Southeast Asian-American Communities, edited by Kali Tal. Woodbridge, Connecticut: Viet Nam Generation, 1992.

Vang, Pao. *Against All Odds: the Laotian Freedom Fighters*. Washington, D.C.: Heritage Foundation, 1987.

While new arrivals have traditionally entered fields involving basic labor, established Honduran American immigrants have shown impressive success in moving into more lucrative professions.

HONDURAN AMERICANS

by
William Maxwell

OVERVIEW

Honduras is a Central American country bordered on the northwest by Guatemala, on the southwest by El Salvador, and on the southeast by Nicaragua. It has a population of 5.8 million and an area of 43,277 square miles, about the size of Virginia. The population is composed of 89 percent mestizo (people of mixed ancestry, often Indian and Spanish), seven percent pure Indian, two percent black, and one percent Caucasian.

HISTORY

It is not known when the geographical area that is now Honduras was originally settled by humans. However, archaeologists have recently found evidence of complex society that is at least 3,000 years old. Over the millennia, city-states gradually developed in the vast geographical area that includes large parts of present-day southern Mexico, Guatemala, and western El Salvador and Honduras. These city states had many common cultural characteristics, including a common spoken and written language. People of this region called themselves Maya.

One of the centers of Mayan civilization during its Classic period, between 250 and 900 A.D., was Copán, a metropolis on the Copán river in what is now western Honduras. Copán boasts the largest collection of mural hieroglyphics in the

Americas. In recent decades, anthropologists and archaeologists have been able to decipher large parts of the hieroglyphic code. What they formerly assumed to be a collection of astronomical and religious treatises has turned out to be a comprehensive history of Copán.

The Great Hieroglyphic Stairway, on one side of a pyramid in central Copán, is a collection of about 6,000 glyphs, where one glyph is equivalent to a word, idea, or sentence. They tell the story of the 16 god-kings of Copán's Classic period, of their births, ascensions, conquests, defeats, and deaths; and of the significant political, social, and astronomical events during their reign.

The Maya, through these writings, portrayed themselves as a warlike people, with a rigid class system and a very high level of civilization, involving complex religion, science, art, and architecture. For reasons not well understood, the major centers of Maya civilization, Copán, Teotihuacan in Mexico, Utatlan in Guatemala, and many others, lost their populations and became ghost towns in the twelfth century. Christopher Columbus, in 1502, found Honduras to be a land of peoples who lived mostly in small villages and hunted and farmed for their food.

THE COLONIAL ERA

In 1524, *Conquistador* (conqueror) of the Mexican Aztecs Hernan Cortés sent Cristóbal de Olid to conquer and rule Honduras in the name of the Spanish Crown. When Olid arrived in the region, he decided to rule it for himself and declared independence from Spain. Cortés sent an army to take it back, but Olid was assassinated by rivals before the army arrived. In the meantime, Cortés decided to go to Honduras himself, with another army. When he arrived, he consolidated Spanish power over Honduras and returned to Mexico. Shortly thereafter, Spain appointed Diego López de Salcedo as the first royal governor of Honduras.

The sixteenth, seventeenth, and eighteenth centuries saw relatively little change in this land. In the eighteenth century, gold and other mineral deposits were found in the central mountains and near the Caribbean coast, and the Spanish colonists employed nearby Indians in the mines. As mining expanded, larger numbers of Indians had to be found to work in them, and forced labor, severe working conditions, and forced migration led to the deaths of large numbers of Indians. Indian revolts then led to massacres of many other Indians at the hands of the armies of the Spanish colonists. Mistreatment of and violence against the Indians remains to this day a problem in Honduras.

In the eighteenth century, most colonists settled in the highlands near the Pacific coast, in cities including Tegucigalpa and Comayagua. The Caribbean coast was and is inhabited by the Mosquito and black Carib Indians (and more recently by banana plantation workers, managers, and owners). An island chain off Honduras's Caribbean coast, the Bay Islands, was also settled by the black Caribs, who are part Indian and part descendants of African runaway or emancipated slaves.

THE INDEPENDENT REPUBLIC OF HONDURAS

In 1823, the Central American provinces of Mexico broke away to form the United Provinces of Central America. Then, after years of interstate tension, squabbling, rewriting of the constitution, and moving of the capital, the Central American states decided to form independent, sovereign nations. Honduras declared independence on October 26, 1838, and adopted a constitution as the Republic of Honduras in January of 1839. The constitution of 1839 provided a single legislative body, a president elected by a majority of the registered male population, and a supreme court whose justices are appointed by the president; thus, it was a constitution in part inspired by the U.S. model.

Wars, military skirmishes, coups, and political intrigues across regional borders have been common in Central America since initial settlement. The Conservative and Liberal parties had been active for some time even before the founding of the Republic. When the candidate of one party was winning a campaign in one country, the presidents of the Central American countries who were members of the other party frequently took political and sometimes military action to prevent his election.

Throughout its history as an independent republic, Honduras has had to cope with an understandably hostile Indian population, a colonist population that was frequently at odds with other cultures within Honduras, meddling neighbors, and a massive U.S. economic, political, and military influence over the country. These are some of the reasons Honduras has one of the world's smallest annual per capita gross domestic products ($1,090 U.S. dollars in 1995), which is the value of what the average Honduran worker produces in a year.

THE TWENTIETH CENTURY

In 1899, the Vaccaro brothers of New Orleans, Louisiana, founded the Standard Fruit and Steamship Company to ship bananas and other fruit on the Caribbean coast of Honduras to the United

States. After a few years, when the company wanted to begin to cultivate its own fruit in Honduras, the Honduran government leased land to the company at a very favorable rate, and the company employed Mosquito Indians to work on the plantations they created. Other fruit companies followed, and Honduras's Caribbean coast has become a vast network of giant plantations owned by U.S. companies. La Ceiba and Trujillo became huge ports where the fruit was and is still today loaded onto ships bound for the United States and countries around the world. To this day, Honduras charges American companies very low taxes for the export of fruit and charges no taxes at all on profits from sales.

Over the last 95 years, the fruit companies have built schools, hospitals, and housing for their workers and connected cities in the region to a railroad network. It has been the region with the country's best infrastructure and standard of living, even for the peasants.

In 1956, the problems with political instability that Honduras had had since its foundation came to a head. The 1954 presidential election was inconclusive; no candidate won a majority of votes. As had happened in 1923 in a similar situation, the Honduran Congress, the arbiter of such dilemmas, was not able to reach a decision on any of the candidates. Lozano Díaz, the vice president in power after the president had had a heart attack and had been flown to Miami, unconstitutionally proclaimed himself president and arrested the leaders of principal parties, labor unions, and farmers' unions. As the political situation became more and more repressive in Honduras under Díaz, the military seized power in a bloodless coup and replaced him with a *junta*, a governing council of military officers. The next 40 years would see a revolving door leadership between the military- and civilian-elected governments.

The situation in Honduras continues to be a product of its past. Political instability is still one of the country's major problems. Throughout the 1980s, for example, the war on Nicaragua's revolutionary Sandinista government by the United States, using Nicaraguan *Contra* rebels stationed and trained in Honduras near the Nicaraguan border, threatened to embroil Honduras itself in a war with Nicaragua.

Today, the democratically elected civilian President Carlos Roberto Reina is attempting reforms in business, education, and in labor policy. However, he is, as others in his place have been, under tight reins from the military.

In 1998, Hurricane Mitch devastated Honduras, in addition to other Central American countries. La Alizanza Pro Ninez Hondurena, Inc., a non-profit organization established in September 1993 by a group of Honduran American educators and Honduran Americans in New York city, provided aid to elementary schools in Honduras. Hurricane Mitch killed some 6,000 persons and left about 6,000 more missing. More than one million persons had their homes destroyed by the hurricane, which also destroyed the majority of the country's agricultural crops.

IMMIGRATION WAVES

The first Hondurans came to this country in the late eighteenth and early nineteenth centuries during the turmoil of independence from Spain and the founding of the republic of Honduras. Since then, every major period of conflict has seen a minor immigration wave, never exceeding a few thousand people. The turbulence surrounding the 1956 succession dilemma saw another spurt in immigration. The 1980s have seen a steady rise in immigration rates, as the 1986 Immigration Reform and Control Act raised the hopes of potential illegal immigrants that they would eventually gain legal status. Another factor impacting immigration rates has been the hardships created by Central American unrest, including civil wars raging in all of Honduras's neighboring countries throughout the decade, often partially fought or launched from Honduran soil. It is too early to tell what will be the impact of California's Proposition 187, passed in 1994 to bar all government services except emergency medical aid from undocumented immigrants.

Many Honduran Americans are migrant farm laborers, and their number is difficult to measure since many of them are undocumented residents. The 1990 Census records 1,272 working-age people in farming, forestry, and fishing operations, but by all accounts, the actual number is much higher. Of those who have settled into a particular area, the largest numbers are found in New York City (33,000), Los Angeles (24,000), and Miami (18,000). Hondurans have followed the immigration patterns of previous groups; they first settled in the largest cities, in which they found support networks in the large Honduran American communities already present. Cities provide the most accessible market for jobs requiring the kind of basic labor skills most Hondurans possess upon arrival.

IMMIGRATION ISSUES

The families of the vast majority of Honduran Americans have entered the United States in the last 40 years to seek better economic opportunities and to escape political turmoil or oppression in Honduras. Many have had to leave their families in Honduras and regularly send a large part of their income home to support them. As a new immigrant group, Hondurans are experiencing the same prejudices and suspicions that arrivals have always felt from the longer-established population. Some Americans are under the impression that Hondurans have come here to live off the welfare state and simply take advantage of social services. Proposition 187 can be seen as a legal result of this attitude. It declares that every immigrant without visa and working papers shall be barred from all government services except emergency medical care. Apparently, those who voted for it believe that illegal immigrants take more social services than they pay for through taxes and consumer spending. However, there is substantial evidence that illegal immigrants pay for more social services than they use. This is due to the fact that many immigrants first come alone and attempt to secure working papers before bringing their families over. They need very few government services. Those who do bring their children often do not send them to school because they need the revenue from their work.

If Proposition 187 represents the locking of the door to Honduran undocumented immigrants, the federal Immigration Reform and Control Act of 1986 represents the legal welcome mat. It stipulates that those illegal immigrants who can prove they were in the country before January 1, 1982, may apply for legalization and may legally work until their cases are decided by the Immigration and Naturalization Service. Furthermore, if they have been granted working papers and legal status, they may apply for citizenship after five years.

Honduran Americans are a very diverse group. They include those of Spanish, mixed, Mayan, black Carib, African, Palestinian and Chinese ancestry, among many others. They have made important improvements in their own standards of living, major educational and professional achievements, and important cultural contributions to American society. In the future, they must face the challenges of prejudice from some Americans and overcome a history of poverty.

ACCULTURATION AND ASSIMILATION

There is no particular stereotype of the Honduran American in this country. However, this lack of specific prejudice is part of the prejudice. More established non-Hispanic Americans, when they exhibit prejudice, like to lump all Hispanic Americans together, contributing to the racist notion that all Hispanics are alike. Some will refer to Latin American immigrants derogatorily as "wetbacks," as economic refugees who "all just swam the Rio Grande to fall into the arms of Sweet Mother United States." So, the fact that Honduran Americans are rarely if ever singled out as an undesirable group does not mean Hondurans are free from prejudice; instead, that fact may only suggest ignorance of Latin American people and differences between their countries.

One notable observation about established American prejudice toward Latin American immigrants is that it is not limited to white Americans. Ladera Heights, California, is a wealthy suburban community primarily comprised of African Americans. Its citizens have attempted to pass an ordinance making it illegal for day laborers to solicit work in public places. They describe the day laborers, who are almost exclusively Hispanic American immigrants, as dirty, loud, disruptive, dangerous, and potentially criminal. While the sheriff's office had no criminal complaints against the day laborers when this case was reported in the *Los Angeles Times* by Robert J. Lopez on March 6, 1994, residents assumed that the Latin American immigrant workers were up to no good. "I do not want welfare. I want work," commented one Latin American day laborer criticizing the proposed ordinance. The issues raised in Ladera Heights reflect broader concerns about illegal immigration, concerns that have led to the passage of California's Proposition 187. Responding to this bill in an August 29, 1994, in a *Los Angeles Times* article by Lorenza Muñoz, one undocumented immigrant named Amanda expressed the often-ignored immigrant perspective: "We do pay taxes—we consume goods and services. This issue of illegal immigration needs to be looked at in a more creative way such as understanding the factors of immigration, and how much immigrants contribute to this country, economically and culturally. It cannot be looked at only in a negative light."

CUISINE

The staple of the mestizo Honduran diet is rice and beans. Other mainstays include *atól*, corn soup; *mondongo*, tripe soup in a tomato base with corn; and *tamale*, a corn pie stuffed with chicken, olives, and capers, among other ingredients. The diet of the Garifuna is based largely on cassava, a starchy root that is similar in texture, consistency, and taste to the potato. The Garifuna create combinations of cassava, coconuts, plantains, avocado, pineapples, and pigs' feet and tails, sometimes all in the same stew. A favorite is *Machuca*, a stew of fried fish and mashed plantains in a coconut base.

MUSIC

As a group, Hondurans have made their mark in American music. One important contribution is Garifuna music. Geoffrey Himes described this music in the *Washington Post* (April 2, 1993): "Legend has it that the Garifuna culture sprang from the survivors of a shipwrecked slave vessel who swam ashore on St. Vincent Island in the sixteenth century. There they intermarried with the local Carib and Arawak Indians and created a music that blended West African drumming and Caribbean Indian group singing. The culture then spread to Belize and Honduras." Garifuna is described as an astonishingly melodic and intricate music. The beat is usually carried by two to four large tuba (or hollow log) drums. The tercera drum provides the booming bass notes that establish the foundation rhythm. The primera drum supplies the melodic lead pattern, and the segunda drum shadows the primera with a counter rhythm. These three main patterns are amplified by turtle shells, claves, timbales, bongos, congas, maracas and tambourines. Himes noted: "Because each drum has its own pitch and timbre and because the vocals are woven inextricably into the drumming, the music has a richness you'd never expect from just percussion and voice."

Musical styles popular among Honduran American mestizos include salsa and meringue, both big-band styles of music, with many brass instruments, a driving, steady beat, and a high melody sung over the instruments.

HEALTH ISSUES

There are problems related to medical care that affect Honduran Americans more than other groups. The mass of Honduran American migrant farm workers suffer from a lack of organized medical care. This class of Honduran American workers is severely damaged by a lack of financial resources to obtain crucial medical care. Officially, New Jersey grants medical care to immigrants, legal or illegal, who demonstrate need and the lack of money for medical care and medicine. However, many illegal aliens from Honduras are wary of going through a government process like applying for Medicaid. They see the danger of being turned over to the Immigration and Naturalization Service as too great. Compounding this problem is the lack of adequate education for migrant farm workers. The average farm worker, especially the male, has only a few years of formal schooling, if any. There is a general lack of health, nutrition, and medical knowledge, especially as it pertains to the safe-keeping of foodstuffs.

The attitude of Honduran Americans in general to the American medical establishment is suspicious. Most Honduran Americans came to the United States as undocumented immigrants or legally working laborers, and in both categories, the level of medical care has been low, marked by neglect and indifference, especially on the part of government officials.

Psychiatry presents another area in which Honduran Americans, particularly new arrivals, have felt alienated. This is due less to neglect than to different cultural attitudes to psychiatry in Latin American and in the United States: "I thought that if you went to a psychologist, you were crazy," said Maximina Machado of the Bronx, originally from Honduras, as reported by Elaine River in New York *Newsday*, August 24, 1994. Older, traditional therapy in Honduras for psychological problems has included *Santeria*, a Caribbean-based faith that combines elements of African ritual with Catholicism, and *espiritualismo* (spiritualism). Both therapies see the psychological problem as a spiritual problem, an imbalance of supernatural forces. Therapy can then take the form of an attempt to reach a transcendent consciousness by using meditation, concentrating on specific personal objects, or consulting a medium. It can also take the form of an exorcism, where the treatment is meant to drive out an evil spirit or devil from the victim.

Psychiatrists and clinical psychologists in some urban medical centers around the country are seeking to break down cultural barriers to clinical therapy and begin addressing the psychological traumas that particularly affect Latin American immigrants. Dr. Arnold Ruiz's Latin American Immigrant Services program, founded in June 1993 in the Fordham-Tremont Mental Health Center in the Bronx, New York, is one such clinic. Here, Dr. Ruiz and his colleagues treat immigrants for adjustment disorders that arise from culture shock—a sense of confusion due to coming into a culture in which the immigrant does not know the language or the cultural mores. They also treat anxiety disorders and depression due to immigrants' feelings of isolation. Especially acute is post-traumatic stress, caused by witnessing horrors in the immigrants' home countries. Hondurans have had to endure the Horcones Massacre, in which the army slaughtered ten unarmed peasants, two students, and two foreign priests; terrorist groups such as the *Mancha Brava*, a covert group that struck terror into the hearts of all opposition activists from 1963 to 1978; and the 1969 war with El Salvador and part of the Nicaraguan war with the Contra rebels. Fordham-Tremont employees have been successful in breaking down some of the suspicions Honduran American immigrants typically have had toward clinical psychologists and psychiatrists. Most clinic employees are bilingual, and they have a respectful attitude toward the patients, taking their religious beliefs into account during therapy.

The American Psychiatric Association's manual of mental disorders lists some disorders specifically afflicting Latin Americans. They include *Ataque de nervios* (attack of nerves), which is characterized by uncontrollable shouting, trembling, fainting, seizures, and verbal and physical aggression; and *mal de ojo* (evil eye), which afflicts children and some adults and causes fitful sleep, diarrhea, vomiting, and crying spells.

A further example illustrates the confusion that arises from cultural differences in psychological and sexual mores between Hondurans and Americans. Attorney General Janet Reno, a Nevada prosecutor in the early 1990s, prosecuted a Honduran immigrant, Ileana Fuster, for child sexual abuse. Ms. Fuster ran a small day-care center from her home, where she kissed the babies all over their bodies in a non-sexual way when caressing them. Anthropologists commented that this practice is common in rural Latin American communities like the one in which Ms. Fuster grew up. Ms. Reno, with the help of two psychologists, extracted a confession after Ms. Fuster had initially asserted no wrongdoing and after several days of hours-long interrogations. Ms. Fuster's Honduran child-rearing practices had come head-to-head with a different set of cultural practices in suburban Nevada.

Another difference between Hondurans and Americans involves a congenital condition among certain Hondurans that affords them a specific medical immunity. The Garifuna, whose ancestors include black Africans and Caribbean Indians, have an African-component sickle-cell genetic adaptation to malaria. This means that, due to their genes, they are immune to malaria.

LANGUAGE

The almost universally spoken language of Honduran Americans, besides English, is Spanish. Most Honduran Indians speak it also. In addition, most Maya speak their own language, and the black Caribs speak Garifuna. Far from being a dead or obscure language, Garifuna is a living, vibrant, and growing language in the United States. Some estimates put the number of Garifuna around 10,000 for New York City, the Garifuna nexus in this country. The following are some Garifuna expressions: *Jin!* ("hing")—Hey, you!; *Buiti binafi illawuritei* ("booitey binaffy illawoorittay")—"Good morning, Uncle." *Abau isilledu eiguini, fulesei* ("ab-bow eesee-laydoo aiguiny, foolasay")—A plate of food, please.

Spanish expressions include *Buenos días* ("buaynos deeass")—Good day; *Feliz navidad* ("feleece navidad")—Merry Christmas; and *¿Donde están mis zapatos?* ("DONday isTAHN meese saBATTose")—Where are my shoes?

FAMILY AND COMMUNITY DYNAMICS

Since many Hondurans initially come to the United States alone, without their spouse or families, life in the United States can represent a strain on the family. Nonetheless, a sizeable percentage of adult Honduran Americans are married. The 1990 Census shows 20,529 of 44,132, or 46.5 percent, of Honduran American men 15 years and older as being married or having been married and 25,722 of 55,933 Honduran American women, or 46 percent, as being married at least once. These figures paint a picture of the typical Honduran American family as similar to that of the typical American family. The percentage of Honduran Americans married is similar to the percentage of other Americans who are married. The average number of children in Honduran American families is also similar to the average number of children in American families in general. The average married Honduran American woman aged 25 to 34 years old has 1.8 children, while the married Honduran American women 35 to 44 years old will have an average of 2.6 children.

The family experience of black Caribs, or Garifuna, presents a different, unique picture. They first came to Honduras's Bay Islands and Caribbean Coast from St. Vincent in 1797, crossing in ocean-going giant canoes, rowing thousands of sea miles from all over the Western Hemisphere. In ensuing years, young men had to migrate to find work and support their families. This became an accepted and permanent part of the Garifuna family structure. Soon after a young Garifuna couple married, the husband began his travels to find work to support his wife and young children. She would rely on brothers or other male family members to help her with what she herself could not do around the house. And often, she would take another lover to fill the void left by her absent husband. So, the Garifuna immigrant wave to the United States, which peaked in 1975, did not represent a big change for Garifuna society. Nancie González has advanced the thesis that Garifuna immigration to the United States allows the black Caribs in Honduras to retain ancient customs and their traditional family and cultural structure. American dollars earned by Garifuna in the United States are, according to her, helping to preserve the Garifuna way of life in Honduras (Nancie González, "Garifuna Settlement in New York: A New Frontier," *International Migration Review*, 1976). Of the 33,426 Honduran American households, 3,794, or 11.3 percent, are on public assistance.

EDUCATION

It has been easier for Honduran American girls to stay in school than for Honduran American boys. Especially in working-class families, there is tremendous pressure for boys, once they turn 12 or 14, to start working full time. This pressure is not as strong on the girls. As a result, statistics show Honduran American women to have more years of school than Honduran American men, with 10.9 percent of Honduran American women 25 years and older having a bachelor's degree, while the number drops to 6.4 percent for both women and men are in the same age category. In terms of high school education, 22.4 percent of the women 25 and older have a diploma, while the figure is 20.9 percent for the general Honduran American population according to the 1990 Census. The numbers even out, however, when it comes to advanced degrees. Of the 43,482 women 25 years and older, 602 have a master's degree, 411 have a professional degree, and 60 have a doctoral degree. For the total Honduran American population in the age category, the figures are 1,091 for a master's degree, 862 for a professional degree, and 151 for a doctoral degree.

Due to economic circumstances, it is easier for girls to stay in school through college. The fact that young men are more encouraged than women to seek advanced degrees, however, means that men who go to college are more likely to stay in school. Women, however, when they reach 22 or 23, experience strong pressure to marry, settle down, have a family, and focus their ambitions on their children.

Honduran American women are more likely to pursue professional careers than to complete advanced degrees. As a matter of fact, 11.3 percent of employed females 16 years and over, according to the 1990 Census, work in managerial and professional specialty occupations, versus 10.4 percent for the population as a whole.

Honduran American women have also become active in the community, fighting for their rights and the rights of their families. Mugama: Garifuna Women on the March, for example, is an organization dedicated to working with young Garifuna in New York City, giving them counseling and support and guiding them on their educational and professional paths. The organization also fights for the rights of Garifuna women, organizing rallies and creating banners for Hispanic parades.

RELIGION

An overwhelming majority of Hondurans are Catholic. The church exerts less influence than in the past. Honduran Americans are active in their church communities, and women take major responsibility for church affairs, such as attending Sunday church suppers and helping to organize parish charity drives. Yet, the move to the United States has brought with it a new phenomenon for the Honduran community. More and more Honduran Americans are exploring Protestant religions, with a sizeable number converting. Particularly popular are the storefront churches opening across the country. These storefront churches allow virtually anybody to take an active role in religion, even to become a minister. In particular the evangelical and Pentecostal churches stress energetic recruitment and a very close, equal relationship between minister and flock.

Storefront churches are a common sight in Latin neighborhoods across the Northeast. In New York, they can be found in Jackson Heights, Queens, and in the Lower East Side of Manhattan. The service, especially in Pentecostal churches, is typically very high-energy, with the reverend building to a shouting rant and the congregation responding in turn with a unified "amen." Sometimes, a parishioner will collapse in a type of "seeing" trance and experience a religious epiphany or rebirth. Such worship links Pentacostals closely to southern evangelical Baptists.

EMPLOYMENT AND ECONOMIC TRADITIONS

While new arrivals have traditionally entered fields involving basic labor, established Honduran American immigrants have shown impressive success in moving into more lucrative professions. Of the 34,220 Honduran Americans who came to this country between 1980 and 1990, according to the U.S. Census, 33.7 percent described themselves as being in service occupations, which include waitering, other restaurant work, janitorial work, and work in laundries and retail stores. Only 24.2 percent of the immigrants who arrived before 1980 are in that industry. Of those who came during the 1980s, 27.3 percent were operators, fabricators, and laborers; for those who came before, only 18.7 percent fit in that category. Those who came before 1980 are more heavily represented in managerial and professional specialty occupations, 14.6 percent as opposed to 5.6 percent for the newer arrivals. The contrast in public administration is similar, with a ratio of three percent for established Honduran Americans to one percent for newer arrivals; the same is true of educational services, the ratio being 4.9 percent to 2.4 percent. These figures demonstrate the trend towards self-improvement as Honduran Americans establish themselves in the United States.

The largest trading partner of Honduras is the United States. In 1995, the two nations traded 1.27 billion dollars in goods and services. The amount of business exported from the United States to Honduras in 1995 totaled 680 million dollars. Approximately 100 American companies operate in Honduras, many of them based in agriculture, petroleum products, bond assembly plants (*maquilas*), electric power generation, banking, and insurance.

American aid to Honuras, military and otherwise, declined in the 1990s. To compensate for this lost income, Honduras redoubled its efforts to export its agricultural products, such as coffee, fruits and vegetables, seafood, and beef. The United States, for its part, is encouraging investment in Honduras. The Most successful markets are in fruit, petroleum refining and marketing, and mining.

POLITICS AND GOVERNMENT

Being a relatively new immigrant group from a country that has seen its share of political turmoil, Honduran Americans have not been very conspicuous in American politics or unions, nor has there been much overt action on the part of Honduran Americans to influence politics in the mother country. For the most part, the overriding political issue for Honduran Americans has been the right to participate in the political process. As reported by Jorge Zarazua and Marty Gra of *The Houston Post* on July 10, 1994, a recently naturalized citizen represents a case in point: "Mario Casildo no longer wants to be one of the thousands of voiceless immigrants in America ... as soon as he takes the oath of citizenship, the 60-year-old Honduran immigrant intends to register to vote."

To address problems of the undocumented alien community, a group of Honduran American and other Central American undocumented aliens formed the Aliens for Better Immigration Laws in February 1994. At that time the group filed a class-action law suit in federal court to allow undocumented aliens to work while they are on a decade-long waiting list for green cards. This grassroots lobbying organization has fought to bring the issues of undocumented immigrants to the forefront, not only in the courts, but also in the consciousness of the American public.

MILITARY SERVICE

Honduran Americans have taken an active role in defending the United States. Of all the native (U.S.) Honduran American males 16 years old and over, 13.7 percent are military veterans. Even 769 Honduran American male non-citizens are veterans. The percentage of naturalized Honduran American male civilians 16 years old and over who have served in the armed forces is 13.2 percent. For those who came to the United States before 1980, this number jumps to 18.4 percent, almost one-fifth.

INDIVIDUAL AND GROUP CONTRIBUTIONS

ART

Julian Albert Touceda is a New Orleans artist and supporter of Latin art who was born and lived the first years of his life in Honduras. Born in the early 1940s, Touceda has been instrumental in preserving Latin American culture and exposing the local community to Latin artists. Touceda's main influences are the Spanish painters Francisco Goya and Diego Balasca, Mexican muralist Diego Rivera, and painter Rufino Tamayo. Since 1976, Touceda has had 23 exhibits in Louisiana, Mississippi, Florida, and New York. Among more than 50 prominent artists, he was the only Hispanic artist selected to exhibit his works at the Louisiana World Exposition in 1984.

MUSIC

Chatuye is a ten-man Garifuna band of Belizean and Honduran immigrants in Los Angeles.

PUBLISHING

One Honduran American who has contributed significantly to the United States is Julio Melara, a second-generation Honduran American who grew up in Kenner, Louisiana, before establishing himself in New Orleans. As a freshman in college, Melara worked as a courier at a local business newspaper. A graduate of the University of New Orleans, Melara was only 28 years old when he became the top sales executive at WWL radio in New Orleans and the only million-dollar producer in the radio industry in Louisiana. Determined and committed to excellence, Melara became the publisher of *New Orleans Magazine*. He joined the New Orleans Publishing Group in 1993 as vice president for sales and training. He also owns Action Inc., a sports marketing firm, and is writing a book called *Do You Have Time for Success?* In addition, he publishes *Arriba,* a magazine in Spanish for tourists coming to New Orleans from Latin America and Spain.

MEDIA

PRINT

Honduras This Week.
International weekly newspaper in English. Covers news in Honduras as well as items of interest to Hondurans abroad.

Address: P.O. Box 1312, Tegucigalpa, Honduras, C.A.
E-mail: hontweek@hondutel.hn.
Online: http://www.marrder.com/htw/.

TELEVISION

"Abriendo brechas" (Opening Gaps).
This three-hour weekly program on Cable Channel 69 is also known as BronxNet, a New York City public access cable channel.

Contact: Murphy Valentine, Producer.
Address: 1465 Fulton Avenue, Apartment 5B, Bronx, New York 10456.
Telephone: (718) 538-2244.

"Conversando con Antonieta Máximo" (Conversing with Antonieta Máximo).
Airs on Manhattan Neighborhood Network Channel 16 for three hours each week. The program features prominent Honduran and other Latin American community and cultural leaders discussing current issues.

Contact: Antonieta Máximo.
Address: 484 West 43rd Street, Apartment 9-M, New York, New York 10036.
Telephone: (212) 947-5712.

ORGANIZATIONS AND ASSOCIATIONS

Federation of Honduran Organizations in New York (FEDHONY).
Founded by Myriam DeMéndez and others as a response to the 1990 Happy Land Social Club fire in the Bronx that killed 87 people, most of whom were Honduran American. The Federation is a valuable resource for contacts of every kind for Honduran American communities.

Contact: Antonia Máximo, President.
Address: 100 East 175th Street, First Floor (NYNEX Building), Bronx, New York 10453.
Telephone: (718) 716-4882.
Fax: (718) 716-4964.

Honduran American Cultural Association.
A nexus for news of the local Honduran American communities and sponsor of concerts and other cultural events.

Contact: Jorge Cotto, President.
Address: 41-42 42nd Street, Sunnyside, New York 11104.
Telephone: (718) 784-7517.

SOURCES FOR ADDITIONAL STUDY

Fash, William L. *Warriors and Kings: The City of Copán and the Ancient Maya,* London: Thames and Hudson, 1991.

González, Nancie. "Garifuna Settlement in New York: A New Frontier," *International Migration Review* 13, No. 2, 1975.

Himes, Geoffrey. "Chatuye: Upholding the Garifuna Beat," *Washington Post,* April 2, 1993.

Honduras: A Country Study, edited by Tim L. Merrill. Washington, DC: U.S. Government Printing Office, 1995.

Norsworthy, Kent, with Tom Barry. *Inside Honduras.* Albuquerque, New Mexico: Inter-Hemispheric Education Resource Center, 1993.

River, Elaine. "Erasing a Stigma—Mental Health Center Deals with Latinos' Special Needs," *Newsday,* August 24, 1994.

HOPIS

by

**Ellen French and
Richard C. Hanes**

Traditional ceremonies
are performed as
instructed in sacred
stories and relate to
most aspects of daily
Hopi life. Such
occasions include
important times in an
individual's life,
important times
of the year, healing,
spiritual renewal,
bringing rain,
initiation of people
into positions, and
for thanksgiving.

OVERVIEW

The westernmost of the Pueblo Indian tribes, the independent Hopi (HO-pee) Nation is the only Pueblo tribe that speaks a Shoshonean language of the Uto-Aztecan linguistic family. "Hopi" is a shortened form of the original term *Hopituh-Shi-nu-mu*, for which the most common meaning given is "peaceful people." The Hopis have also been referred to as the Moqui, based on what the Spanish called them. The Hopi reservation, almost 2.5 million acres in size and located in northeastern Arizona near the Four Corners area just east of the Grand Canyon, is surrounded completely by the Navajo reservation. The Hopis inhabit 14 villages, most of which are situated atop three rocky mesas (called First Mesa, Second Mesa, and Third Mesa) that rise 600 feet from the desert floor. Estimated at 2,800 in 1680, the Hopi Nation had 7,360 members in 1990, about 1,000 of whom lived off the reservation. The Hopies are ancient, having lived continuously in the same place for a thousand years. They are also a deeply religious people, whose customs and yearlong calendar of ritual ceremonialism guide virtually every aspect of their lives. Although some concessions to modern convenience have been made, the Hopis have zealously guarded their cultural traditions. This degree of cultural preservation is a remarkable achievement, facilitated by isolation, secrecy, and a community that remains essentially closed to outsiders.

HISTORY

According to Suzanne and Jake Page's book *Hopi*, the Hopis are called "the oldest of the people" by other Native Americans. Frank Waters wrote in *The Book of the Hopi* that the Hopis "regard themselves as the first inhabitants of America. Their village of Oraibi is indisputably the oldest continuously occupied settlement in the United States." While Hopi oral history traces their origin to a Creation and Emergence from previous worlds, scientists place them in their present location for the last thousand years, perhaps longer. In her book *The Wind Won't Know Me*, Emily Benedek wrote that "anthropologists have shown that the cultural remains present a clear, uninterrupted, logical development culminating in the life, general technology, architecture, and agriculture and ceremonial practices to be seen on the three Hopi mesas today." Archaeologists definitively place the Hopis on the Black Mesa of the Colorado Plateau by 1350.

The period from 1350 to 1540 is considered the Hopi ancestral period, marked primarily by the rise of village chieftains. A need for greater social organization arose from increased village size and the first ritual use of *kivas*, the underground ceremonial chambers found in every village. Additionally, coal was mined from mesa outcroppings, requiring unprecedented coordination. The Hopis were among the world's first people to use coal for firing pottery.

The complex Hopi culture, much as it exists today, was firmly in place by the 1500s, including the ceremonial cycle, the clan and chieftain social system, and agricultural methods that utilized every possible source of moisture in an extremely arid environment. The Hopis' "historical period" began in 1540, when first contact with Europeans occurred. In that year a group of Spanish soldiers led by the explorer Francisco Vásquez de Coronado arrived, looking for the legendary Seven Cities of Gold. After a brief, confrontational search produced no gold, the Spanish destroyed part of a village and left.

The Hopis were not molested further until 1629, when the first Spanish missionaries arrived, building missions in the villages of Awatovi, Oraibi, and Shungopavi. Historians speculate the Hopis pretended to adopt the new religion while practicing their own in secret. Hopi oral history confirms this interpretation. Rebelling finally against the Spanish yoke of religious oppression, the Hopis joined the rest of the Pueblo people in a unified revolt in 1680. During this uprising, known as the Pueblo Revolt, the Indians took the lives of Franciscan priests and Spanish soldiers and then besieged Santa Fe for several days. When the Hopis finally returned to their villages, they killed all the missionaries.

The Hopis then moved three of their villages to the mesa tops as a defensive measure against possible retaliation. The Spanish returned to reconquer the Rio Grande area in 1692. Many Rio Grande Pueblo Indians fled west to Hopi, where they were welcomed. Over the next few years, many living in Awatovi invited the Spanish priests back, a situation that caused a serious rift between those who wanted to preserve the old ways and those who embraced Christianity. Finally, in 1700 Hopi traditionalists killed all the Christian men in Awatovi and then destroyed the village. The destruction of Awatovi signaled the end of Spanish interference in Hopi life, although contact between the groups continued.

MODERN ERA

In response to the growing problem of Navajo encroachment on traditional Hopi land, President Chester A. Arthur established the Hopi reservation in 1882, setting aside 2,472,254 acres in northeastern Arizona for "Moqui and other such Indians as the Secretary of the Interior may see fit to settle thereon." The Hopi reservation was centered within a larger area (considered by the Hopis also to be their ancestral land) that was designated the Navajo reservation. As populations increased, the Navajo expanded their settlements well beyond their own borders, encroaching even more on the Hopi reservation. Despite the executive order, this situation continued for many decades. The Hopis complained, but the government failed to act, and the Navajo continued to overrun Hopi lands until they had taken over 1,800,000 acres of the original Hopi designation. The Hopis were left with only about 600,000 acres. Recognizing the problem, Congress finally passed the Navajo-Hopi Settlement Act in 1974, which returned 900,000 acres to the Hopis. The dispute over resettlement and the remaining 900,000 original acres continues, however, as a number of Navajo families have refused to leave due to ancestral ties to the land. A 1975 film titled *Dineh: The People*, produced by Jonathan Reinis and Stephen Hornick, examined the relocation of Navajo from the joint-use area around the Hopi reservation, looking at the many sociocultural issues it raised. A more recent film, *In the Heart of Big Mountain* (1988), produced by Sandra Sunrising Osawa, looks at the background and history of the land dispute and the sacredness of the Big Mountain area to affected Navajo. Thomas Banyacya Sr. (b.1910), born in New Oraibi, became an outspoken traditionalist Hopi elder in opposition to Navajo relocation.

Another ongoing issue facing the Hopi concerns the preservation of the Hopi Way. Two 1980s films examine the Hopi Way. A 1983 film directed by Pat Ferrero takes an in-depth look at the Hopi

Way, the ideal way of life from the point of view of many Hopi community members. Titled *Hopi: Songs of the Fourth World*, the film shows Hopi people in everyday life and contrasts Hopi society and world-view with other societies. The 1984 film *Itam Hakim, Hopit*, produced, directed, and filmed by noted Hopi filmmaker Victor Masayesva Jr., examines the life of a member of a Hopi storytelling clan and various periods of Hopi history.

These modern-day concerns have split the tribe into two factions, the Traditionalists and the Progressives. Traditionalists fear the erosion of Hopi culture by white cultural influences. Progressives feel that adoption of some aspects of modern American culture is necessary if the tribe is to survive and grow economically.

ACCULTURATION AND ASSIMILATION

TRADITIONS, CUSTOMS, AND BELIEFS

By the end of the twentieth century, the Hopi tribe was considered one of the more traditional Indian

societies in the continental United States. As far back as they can be reliably traced by archeologists (to the period called Pueblo II, between 900 and 1100), the Hopis have been sedentary, living in masonry buildings. Their villages consisted of houses built of native stone, arranged around a central plaza containing one or more kivas. Hopi villages are arranged in much the same way today. During the Pueblo III Period (1100 to 1300), populations in the villages grew as the climate became more arid, making farming more difficult. The village buildings grew in size as well, some containing hundreds of rooms. During the Pueblo IV Period, the Hopi ancestral period from 1350 to 1540, the houses, made "of stone cemented with adobe and then plastered inside were virtually indistinguishable from the older houses of present-day Hopi, except that they were often multistoried," according to Page and Page. They added that the houses of that period contained rooms with specific functions, such as storage or grinding corn, and that kiva design was "nearly identical" to that of today. The houses and kivas of this period were heated with coal, which was also used for firing pottery. Today the Hopis occupy the older masonry houses as well as modern ones. The kiva remains largely as it was in ancient times: a rectangular room built of native stone, mostly below ground. "Sometimes," wrote Waters, "the kiva is widened at one end, forming the same shape as the T-shaped doorways found in all ancient Hopi ruins." This design is intended to echo the hairstyle of Hopi men, which generally forms a "T" shape. The kiva contains an altar and central fire pit below the roof opening. A ladder extends above the edge of the roof. When not in use for ceremonies, kivas are also used as meeting rooms.

The number four has great significance in the Hopi religion, so many ritual customs often call for repetitions of four. In accordance with Hopi tradition, both boys and girls were initiated into the *kachina* cult between the ages of eight and ten. Leitch wrote that the rite included "fasting, praying, and being whipped with a yucca whip. Each child had a ceremonial mother (girls) or father (boys) who saw them through the ordeal." She also noted, "All boys were initiated into one of the four men's societies Kwan, Ahl, Tao, or Wuwutcimi, usually joining the society of their ceremonial father. These rites commonly occurred in conjunction with the Powama ceremony, a four-day tribal initiation rite for young men, usually held at planting time." A tradition no longer observed is the prepuberty ceremony for ten-year-old girls, which involved grinding corn for an entire day at the girl's paternal grandmother's house. "At the onset of menses," Parsons wrote in 1950, "girls of the more conservative families go through a puberty ceremony marked by a four-day grinding ordeal." The girl would also receive a new name and would then occasionally assume the squash blossom hairstyle, the sign of marriageability.

TRADITIONAL STORIES

A tradition of oral literature has been crucial to the survival of the Hopi Way because the language has remained unwritten until recent years. The oral tradition has made it possible to foster Hopi pride during modern times and to continue the custom, ritual, and ceremony that sustain the religious beliefs that are the essence of the Hopi Way. The body of Hopi oral literature is huge.

CUISINE

The Hopis have long been sedentary agriculturalists, with the men handling the work of cultivating and harvesting the crops. A great drought occurred from 1279 to 1299, requiring the Hopis to adopt inventive farming methods still in use today. Every possible source of moisture is utilized. The wind blows sand up against the sides of the mesas, forming dunes that trap moisture. Crops are then planted in these dunes. The Hopis also plant in the dry washes that occasionally flood, as well as in the mouths of arroyos. In other areas they irrigate crops by hand.

In the ancestral period, wild game was more plentiful, and Hopi men hunted deer, antelope, and elk. They also hunted rabbit with a boomerang. Page and Page listed corn, squash, beans, and some wild and semi-cultivated plants such as Indian millet, wild potato, piñon, and dropseed as staples of this period. They also noted that salt was obtained, although not without difficulty, by making long excursions to the Grand Canyon area. Barbara Leitch wrote in *A Concise Dictionary of Indian Tribes of North America* that the women gathered "pinenuts, prickly pear, yucca, berries, currants, nuts, and various seeds." Hopi women also made fine pottery, a craft that still flourishes today. The Hopis raised cotton in addition to the edible crops, and the men, Leitch wrote, "spun and wove cotton cloth into ceremonial costumes, clothing, and textiles for trade." In the sixteenth century the Spanish introduced wheat, onions, peaches and other fruits, chiles, and mutton to the Hopi diet.

The Hopis continue to depend on the land. Wild game had dwindled significantly in the region by 1950, leaving only rabbit as well as a few quail and deer. Modern Hopi farmers still use the old methods, raising mainly corn, melons, gourds, and many varieties of beans. Corn is the main crop, and the six traditional Hopi varieties are raised: yellow, blue, red, white, purple, and sweet. All have symbolic meaning stemming from the Creation story. A corn roast is an annual ritual, and corn is ground for use in ceremonies as well as to make *piki*, a traditional bread baked in layers on hot stones. A 1983 film *Corn Is Life*, documents the importance of corn to Hopi culture and its religious significance. The film shows traditional activities in planting, cultivating, harvesting, and preparing corn, including the baking of piki bread on hot, polished stone.

TRADITIONAL APPAREL

In earlier times Hopi men wore fur or buckskin loincloths. Some loincloths were painted and decorated with tassels, which symbolized falling rain. The men also raised cotton and wove it into cloth, robes, blankets, and textiles. These hand-woven cotton blankets were also worn regularly. The Hopis were reported in 1861 as being wrapped in blankets with broad white and dark stripes. At that time, women also commonly wore a loose black gown with a gold stripe around the waist and at the hem. Men wore shirts and loose cotton pants, covered with a blanket wrap. During the ritual ceremonies and dances, Hopi men wear elaborate costumes that include special headdresses, masks, and body paints. These costumes vary according to clan and ceremony.

Women had long hair, but marriageable girls wore their hair twisted up into large whorls on either side of their heads. These whorls represented the squash blossom, which was a symbol of fertility. This hairstyle is still worn by unmarried Hopi girls but due to the amount of time required to create it, the style is reserved for ceremonial occasions. The hairstyle for married women was either loose or in braids. The traditional hairstyle for Hopi men, after which kiva design was sometimes patterned, was worn with straight bangs over the forehead and a knot of hair in the back with the sides hanging straight and covering the ears. This style of bangs is still seen among traditional Hopi men.

Hopi women and girls today wear a traditional dress, which is black and embroidered with bright red and green trim. A bride, as in early days, wears a white robe woven of white cotton by her uncles. This bridal costume actually consists of two white robes. The bride wears a large robe with tassels that symbolize falling rain. A second, smaller robe, also with tassels, is carried rolled up in a reed scroll called a "suitcase" in English. When the woman dies, she will be wrapped in the suitcase robe.

DANCES AND SONGS

Benedek wrote that "in spirit and in ceremony, the Hopis maintain a connection with the center of the earth, for they believe that they are the earth's caretakers, and with the successful performance of their ceremonial cycle, the world will remain in balance, the gods will be appeased, and rain will come." Central to the ceremonies are the kiva, the *paho*, and the Corn Mother. The kiva is the underground ceremonial chamber. Rectangular in shape (the very ancient kivas were circular), the kiva is a symbol of the Emergence to this world, with a small hole in the floor leading to the underworld and a ladder extending above the roof opening, which represents the way to the upper world. Kivas are found in various numbers in Hopi villages, always on an east–west axis, sunk into the central plaza of a village. Following the secret ceremonies held inside the kiva, ceremonial dances are performed in the plaza. The *paho*, a prayer feather, usually that of an eagle, is used to send prayers to the Creator. *Pahos* are prepared for all kiva ceremonies. Corn has sus-

tained the Hopis for centuries, and it plays a large role in Hopi ceremonies, such as in the sprinkling of cornmeal to welcome the kachinas to the Corn Mother. Waters described the Corn Mother as "a perfect ear of corn whose tip ends in four full kernels." It is saved for rituals.

The kachinas are spirits with the power to pass on prayers for rain and are mostly benevolent. Humans dressed and masked as these spirits perform the kachina dances, which are tied to the growing season, beginning in March and lasting into July. Kachina dolls, representing these gods, are carved and sold as crafts today, although they were originally toys for Hopi children. One of the most important ceremonials is held at the winter solstice. This ceremony, Soyal, as the first ceremony of the year and the first kachina dance, represents the second phase of Creation. The Niman ceremony, or the Home Dance, is held at the Summer Solstice, in late July. At that point the last of the crops have been planted and the first corn has been harvested. The Home Dance is the last kachina dance of the year. Although other ceremonial dances are also religious, they are less so than the kachina rituals. These other dances include the Buffalo Dance, held in January to commemorate the days when the buffalo were plentiful and Hopi men went out to the eastern plains to hun them; the Bean Dance, held in February to petition the kachinas for the next planting; and the Navajo Dance, celebrating the Navajo tribe. While the well-known Snake Dance is preceded by eight days of secret preparation, the dance itself is relatively short, lasting only about an hour. During this rite the priests handle and even put in their mouths unresistant snakes gathered from the desert. Non-Hopi experts have tried to discover how the priests can handle snakes without being bitten, but the secret has not been revealed. At the conclusion of the dance the snakes are released back into the desert, bearing messages for rain. The Snake and Flute Dances are held alternately every other year. The Flute Dance glorifies the spirits of those who have passed away during the preceding two years. In addition, the Basket Dance and other women's dances are held near the end of the year. The Hopi ceremonial cycle continues all year. The ritual ceremonies are conducted within the kivas in secrecy. The plaza dances that follow are rhythmic, mystical, and full of pageantry. Outsiders are sometimes allowed to watch the dances.

HOLIDAYS

Traditional ceremonies are performed as instructed in sacred stories and relate to most aspects of daily Hopi life. Such occasions include important times in an individual's life, important times of the year, healing, spiritual renewal, bringing rain, initiation of people into positions, and for thanksgiving. Hopi ceremonies included the Flute ceremony, New Fire ceremony, Niman Kachina ceremony, Pachavu ceremony, Powamu ceremony, Snake-Antelope ceremony, Soyal, and Wuwuchim ceremony.

PHYSICAL AND MENTAL HEALTH ISSUES

Page and Page stated that much of Hopi healing is psychic but that the Hopis also utilize many herbal remedies. The Hopis are quite knowledgeable about the various medicinal properties of certain plants and herbs. Ritual curing, however, is done by several societies, including the kachina society. Parsons wrote, "The Kachina cult is generally conceived as a rain-making, crop-bringing cult; but it has also curing or health-bringing functions." She added that "On First Mesa kachina dances (including the Horned water serpent and the Buffalo Dance) may be planned for afflicted persons." In addition to holding dances expressly for sick people, for some illnesses the cure is administered by a specific society. For example, snakebite is treated by the Snake society on First Mesa, according to Parsons, and rheumatism is treated by the Powamu society, which then inducts the afflicted into the society. Other cures are less logical to an outsider. "On First Mesa," Parsons wrote, "lightning-shocked persons and persons whose fields have been lightning-struck join the Flute society. A lightning-shocked man is called in to cure earache in babies." Other rituals include the practice of "sucking out" the disease, usually when dealing with sick infants and children. Cornmeal is actually held in the mouth during this procedure, and then the curer "spits away" the disease. The Hopis also utilize modern medical science, doctors, and hospitals. A government hospital was established in 1913. Now, the Office of Native Healing Services is located in nearby Window Rock, Arizona. In the late 1990s a new health care center was planned for First Mesa.

LANGUAGE

The Hopis speak several dialects of a single language, Hopi, with the exception of the village of Hano, where the members speak Tewa, which is derived from the Azteco-Tanoan linguistic family. Waters noted in 1963 that "Hopi is not yet a commonly written language, perhaps because of the extreme difficulty in translation, as pointed out by Benjamin Lee Whorf, who has made a profound analysis of the language." Despite being unwritten

and untranslated, the strong Hopi oral tradition has preserved and passed down the language. Most Hopis today, including the younger generations, speak both Hopi and English. Both Arizona state universities began developing a Hopi writing system with a dictionary containing over 30,000 words.

COMMON WORDS AND EXPRESSIONS

Some Hopi words and phrases include: *tiva*—dance; *tuwaki*—shrine in the kiva; *kahopi*—not Hopi; *kachada*—white man; *Hotomkam*—Three Stars in Line (Orion's Belt); *kachinki*—kachina house; *Hakomi?*—Who are you?; and, *Haliksa'I*—Listen, this is how it is.

FAMILY AND COMMUNITY DYNAMICS

EDUCATION

Hopi children gain their education through available formal school systems and through traditional educational activities in such places as kivas. Education is provided through local public schools, federal government schools, local village schools, private schools, and kivas. Between 1894 and 1912, schools were established near Hopi villages. But until the late twentieth century, children had to leave home to attend government-sponsored or private off-reservation boarding high schools. In 1985, new Hopi middle and high schools were opened for all tribal students. The on-reservation schools have facilitated traditional education by having students live at home, attending year-round village rituals and ceremonies. The traditional education begins in earnest around age of eight, with a series of initiation rites. The young are taught the Hopi Way, composed of traditional principles and ethics and the value of kinship systems.

THE ROLE OF WOMEN

The social organization of traditional Hopi society is based on kinship clans determined through the woman's side of the family. The clans determine various kinds of social relations of individuals throughout their lives, including possible marriage partners and their place of residence. Women own the farming and garden plots, though men are responsible for the farming as well as the grazing of sheep and livestock. Women are also centrally involved in Hopi arts and crafts. By tradition the women's products are specialized and determined by their residence. Women make ceramics on First

Mesa, coiled basketry on Second Mesa, and wicker basketry on Third Mesa. Hopi men do the weaving.

COURTSHIP AND WEDDINGS

Many marriage customs are still observed, but others have fallen into disuse. Fifty years ago, for example, courtship was an elaborate procedure involving a rabbit hunt, corn grinding, and family approval of the marriage. The bride was married in traditional white robes woven for the occasion by her uncles. The couple lived with the bride's mother for the first year. Today the courtship is much less formal. The couple often marry in a church or town and then return to the reservation. Since not all men know how to weave anymore, Page and Page pointed out that it may take years for the uncles to produce the traditional robes. They also described several marriage customs still in practice, however. These include a four-day stay by the bride with her intended in-laws. During this time she grinds corn all day and prepares all the family's meals to demonstrate her culinary competence. Prior to the wedding, the aunts of both the bride and groom engage in a sort of good-natured free-for-all that involves throwing mud and trading insults, each side suggesting the other's relative is no good. The groom's parents wash the couple's hair with a shampoo of yucca in a ritual that occurs in other ceremonies as well. A huge feast follows at the bride's mother's house. Once married, the bride wears her hair loose or in braids.

Clan membership plays a role in partner selection. The rule against marrying another member of the same clan has prevented interbreeding, keeping genetic lines strong. Although marriage into an associated clan was forbidden as well, Page and Page suggest that this tradition is breaking down. Marriage to non–tribal members is extremely rare, a fact that has helped preserve Hopi culture. The clan system is matrilineal, meaning that clan membership is passed down through the mother. One cannot be Hopi without a clan of birth, so if the mother is not Hopi, neither will her children be. Adoption into the tribe is also extremely rare.

FUNERALS

Old age among the Hopis is considered desirable, because it indicates that the journey of life is almost complete. The Hopis have a strong respect for the rituals of death, however, and it is customary to bury the dead as quickly as possible because the religion holds that the soul's journey to the land of the dead begins on the fourth day after death. Any delay in burial can thus interfere with the soul's ability to reach the underworld. The ritual called for the hair of the deceased to be washed with the yucca shampoo by a paternal aunt. Leitch added that the hair was then decorated with prayer feathers and the face covered with a mask of raw cotton, symbolizing clouds. The body was then wrapped—a man in a deerskin robe, a woman in her wedding robe—and buried by the oldest son, preferably on the day or night of death. Leitch wrote that "the body was buried in a sitting position along with food and water. Cornmeal and prayersticks were later placed in the grave." A stick is inserted into the soil of a grave as an exit for the soul. If rain follows, it signifies the soul's successful journey.

INTERACTIONS WITH OTHER TRIBES

The Hopis have maintained historical relations with the Zuñi as well as the Hano and Tewa groups in the Rio Grande River valley to the east. During the Pueblo Revolt of 1680, Pueblo groups united to drive Spanish influence out of the region. Moreover, extensive trading networks existed among the groups prior to the revolt. The complex land issues with the Navajo have led to complex relations. The Hopi elective government have fought for defense of their original reservation, while traditionalists support the Navajo families' efforts to remain on the disputed lands.

NAMING CEREMONY

Page and Page explained the special rituals observed when naming a new baby. A newborn is kept from direct view of the sun for its first 19 days. A few days prior to the naming, the traditional Hopi stew is prepared at the home of the maternal grandmother, who figures prominently in the custom. The baby belongs to her of his mother's clan but is named for the father's. In the naming ritual, the grandmother kneels and washes the mother's hair, then bathes the baby. The baby is wrapped snugly in a blanket, with only its head visible. With the baby's Corn Mother, the grandmother rubs a mixture of water and cornmeal on the baby's hair, applying it four times. Each of the baby's paternal aunts then repeats this application, and each gives a gift and suggests a name. The grandmother chooses one of these names and then introduces the baby to the sun god just as the sun comes up. A feast follows.

RELIGION

The Hopi religion is a complex, highly developed belief system incorporating many gods and spirits, such as Earth Mother, Sky Father, the Sun, the

Moon, and the many kachinas, or invisible spirits of life. Waters described this religion as "a mytho-religious system of year-long ceremonies, rituals, dances, songs, recitations, and prayers as complex, abstract, and esoteric as any in the world." The Hopi identity centers on this belief system. Waters explained their devotion, writing, "The Hopi . . . have never faltered in the belief that their secular pattern of existence must be predicated upon the religious, the universal plan of Creation. They are still faithful to their own premise." The Pages stated in 1982 that 95 percent of the Hopi people continue to adhere to these beliefs.

According to oral tradition, the Hopis originated in the First of four worlds, not as people but as fractious, insect-like creatures. Displeased with these creatures' grasp of the meaning of life, the Creator, the Sun spirit Tawa, sent Spider Woman, another spirit, to guide them on an evolutionary migration. By the time they reached the Third

"She knew it was the duty of the youngest member of a Hopi family to feed the family gods and she was the youngest present, but she was in a hurry to be off and would have neglected the duty had not her grandmother reminded her."

Polingaysi Qoyawayma, *No Turning Back: A True Account of a Hopi Girl's Struggle,* (University of New Mexico Press, Albuquerque, 1964).

World, they had become people. They reached the Fourth, or Upper, World by climbing up from the underworld through a hollow reed. Upon reaching this world, they were given four stone tablets by Masaw, the world's guardian spirit. Masaw described the migrations they were to take to the ends of the land in each of the four directions and how they would identify the place where they were intended to finally settle. And so the migrations began, some of the clans starting out in each direction. Their routes would eventually form a cross, the center of which was the Center of the Universe, their intended permanent home. This story of the Hopi Creation holds that their completed journeys finally led them to the plateau that lies between the Colorado and Rio Grande Rivers, in the Four Corners region. As Waters explained, "the Hopi . . . know that they were led here so that they would have to depend upon the scanty rainfall which they must evoke with their power and prayer," preserving their faith in the Creator who brought them to this place. The Hopis are thus connected to their land with its agricultural cycles and the constant quest for rainfall in a deeply religious way.

EMPLOYMENT AND ECONOMIC TRADITIONS

For more than 3,000 years the Hopis have been farmers in an arid desert climate, dry farming in washes as well as constructing irrigated terraces on the mesas, and supplementing their subsistence economy with small game hunting. Farm and garden plots have traditionally belonged to the women of each clan.

The federal government attempted to subdivide the Hopi reservation in 1910, assigning small parcels to individual Hopi. But the effort failed, and the reservation remained intact. Congress passed the Navajo-Hopi Long Range Rehabilitation Act in 1951, allocating approximately $90 million to improve reservation roads, schools, utilities, and health facilities. In 1966 the Hopi tribal council signed a lease with Peabody Coal Company to strip mine a 25,000 acre area in the Navajo-Hopi Joint Use Area. Traditionalists attempted to block the mining through the federal courts but failed; the case went all the way to the U.S. Supreme Court. In 1998, the Hopis won a $6 million judgment that ordered the Navajo to share with the Hopi taxes collected from the Peabody coal mining operation in the Joint Use Area. That same year the Hopis signed an agreement with the federal government for almost $3 million of water and wastewater construction for the villages of First Mesa.

By the 1970s, farming income was declining and wage labor was gaining importance in the Hopi economy. An undergarment factory was established in Winslow, Arizona, in partnership with the Hopis in 1971 but failed in only a few years. By the late twentieth century, the Hopis had a diverse economy of small-scale farming and livestock grazing, various small businesses, mineral development royalty payments, government subsidies for community improvements, and wage-labor incomes. Many traditional Hopi objects were transformed from utilitarian and sacred items to works of art. Commercial art includes the making of kachina dolls, silver jewelry, woven baskets, and pottery. Cooperative marketing organizations and various enterprises for Hopi craftspeople, including Hopicrafts and Artist Hopid, are available on-reservation and off. In addition to arts and crafts shops, small businesses on-reservation include two motels, a museum, and several dining facilities and gas stations.

POLITICS AND GOVERNMENT

The Hopis have always been organized according to a matrilineal clan system, which in the late 1990s

This Hopi dancer
is performing
at El Tovar,
Grand Canyon.

was made up of some 30 clans. An elected Tribal Council has existed since 1934 to interact with the federal government, but its function is representative; it does not govern the tribe. The individual villages are each governed independently by a *kikmongwi*, or village chief. Susanne and Jake Page, in their book, *Hopi*, described this system as "a loose confederation of politically independent villages, rather like the city-states of ancient Greece, knit together by basically similar views of their history, [and] by similar religious beliefs and ceremonial practices." They noted also that the clan system is "one of the main forms of social glue that has historically held the separate Hopi villages together." Clan membership provides the singular Hopi identity.

The Hopis, protecting their sovereignty, never signed a treaty with the U.S. government. The Hopi Tribal Council and government was established in 1935 with a written constitution but disbanded in 1943. The government was reestablished in 1950, and the nation received federal recognition again in 1955, making available a range of social services and funding opportunities. With coal, natural gas, oil and uranium minerals resources, the Hopis are members of the Council of Energy Resource Tribes. Founded in 1975, the council speaks with a unified Native American voice to the federal government on mineral exploration and development policies and provides technical information to the member tribes.

INDIVIDUAL AND GROUP CONTRIBUTIONS

ACADEMIA

Don C. Talayesva (b.1890) was born on the Hopi reservation in Oraibi and was raised in the traditional Hopi Way for the early part of his life. After attending the Sherman School for Indians in Riverside, California, Talayesva returned to the reservation to resume the traditional Hopi way of life. He became the subject of study by anthropologist Leo Simmons in 1938, which led to the noted 1942 publication *Sun Chief: The Autobiography of a Hopi Indian*, which has remained a popular account of Hopi life.

Elizabeth Q. White (c.1892–1990), also known as Polingaysi Qoyawayma, was born at the traditional village of Old Oraibi. She graduated from Bethel College in Newton, Kansas, after studying to become a Mennonite missionary at the Hopi reservation. She became a teacher in the Indian Service on the reservation, where she became a noted educator, eventually earning the U.S. Department of Interior's Distinguished Service Award. White wrote several books on Hopi traditional life and founded the Hopi Student Scholarship Fund at Northern Arizona University.

ART

Traditional Hopi anonymity changed in the twentieth century as many individuals began to be recognized for their work. Nampeyo (1859–1942), born in Hano on First Mesa, helped revive Hopi arts by reintroducing ancient forms and designs she had noted in archaeological remains into her pottery. Her work became uniquely artistic. Nampeyo was used in promotional photographs by the Santa Fe Railway and others, and her pots were added to the collection of the National Museum in Washington, D.C. Nampeyo's daughters and granddaughter, Hooee Daisy Nampeyo (b.1910) carried on her artistry in ceramics. Her granddaughter Hooee also grew up in Hano, learning ceramics from her grandmother. She furthered Hopi and Zuni art in the Southwest, working in ceramics and silver.

Born at the traditional village of Shongopavi at Second Mesa, Fred Kabotie (1900-1986) attended the Santa Fe Indian School as a teenager, where his talent for painting was recognized. Kabotie became noted especially for his depictions of kachinas, which vividly portrayed supernatural powers. In 1922, Kabotie won the first annual Rose Dugan art prize of the Museum of New Mexico, and by 1930 his paintings were on permanent exhibit in the museum. Kabotie went on to become internationally recognized and his work was exhibited at such major museums as the Museum of Modern Art in New York, the Peabody Museum of Harvard University, and the Corcoran Gallery in Washington, D.C. His work toured internationally in Europe and Asia. He received a Guggenheim Foundation fellowship in 1945, and he was elected to the French Academy of Arts in 1954. In the 1940s, Kabotie founded the Hopi Silvercraft Cooperative Guild, teaching unemployed World War II veterans the art of silverworking. Charles Loloma was a noted student. From 1937 to 1959, he taught art back home in Oraibi, Arizona furthering a tribal artistic tradition. In 1958, Kabotie was awarded the U.S. Indian Arts and Crafts Board's Certificate of Merit. His son, Michael, co-founded Artist Hopid to promote Hopi artists.

Charles Loloma's (1921–1991) jewelry is among the most distinctive in the world. The originality of his designs stems from the combination of nontraditional materials, such as gold and diamonds, with typical Indian materials such as turquoise. He also received great recognition as a potter, silversmith, and designer. Loloma was born in Hotevilla on the Hopi reservation and attended the Hopi High School in Oraibi and the Phoenix Indian High School in Phoenix, Arizona. In 1939 Loloma painted the murals for the Federal Building on Treasure Island in San Francisco Bay, as part of the Golden Gate International Exposition. The following year, the Indian Arts and Crafts Board commissioned him to paint the murals for the Museum of Modern Art in New York. In 1940, Loloma was drafted into the army, where he spent four years working as a camouflage expert in the Aleutian Islands off the Alaskan coast. After his discharge, he attended the School for American Craftsmen at Alfred University in New York, a well-known center for ceramic arts. This choice was unprecedented on Loloma's part, since ceramics was traditionally a woman's art among the Hopis. After receiving a 1949 Whitney Foundation Fellowship to study the clays of the Hopi area, he and his wife, Otellie, worked out of the newly opened Kiva Craft Center in Scottsdale, Arizona. From 1954 to 1958 he taught at Arizona State University, and in 1962 he became head of the Plastic Arts and Sales Departments at the newly established Institute of American Indian Arts in Santa Fe, New Mexico. In 1963 Loloma's work was exhibited in Paris. After 1965, Loloma spent the rest of his years on the Hopi reservation, where he continued working and teaching his art to several apprentices. By the mid-1970s, his jewelry had been exhibited throughout the country and in Europe, and his pieces had won numerous first prizes in arts competitions. Loloma was one of the first prominent Indian craftsmen who had a widely recognized unique personal style.

Otellie Loloma (1922–1992), born at Shipaulovi on Second Mesa, received a three-year scholarship to the School of the American Craftsmen at Alfred University in New York, where she specialized in ceramics. At Alfred she met and later married Charles Loloma, an internationally famous Hopi artist. Otellie herself received world acclaim for her ceramics and was considered the most influential Indian woman in ceramics. Loloma taught at Arizona State University, at the Southwest Indian Art Project at the University of Arizona, and at the Institute of American Indian Arts (IAIA). She also performed traditional dance, performing at the 1968 Olympics in Mexico and at a White House special program. Her work has been internationally shown and is exhibited at a number of museums, including the Museum of the American Indian, Heye Foundation, the Heard Museum, and Blair House in Washington, D.C. One of her last awards was an Outstanding Achievement in the Visual Arts award from the 1991 National Women's Caucus for Art.

EDUCATION

Eugene Sekaquaptewa (1925–) was born on the Hopi reservation at Hotevilla. He earned an M.A. from Arizona State University before joining the U.S. Marines in 1941. He survived the U.S. invasion of Iwo Jima and other intense battles. Sekaquaptewa returned to Arizona State University to teach education courses and participate in the university's Indian Community Action Project, in addition to teaching at the Indian boarding school in Riverside, California, the Sherman Institute. He has published a number of professional papers on Hopi education.

FILM, TELEVISION, AND THEATER

Actor Anthony Nukema was of Hopi and California Karok ancestry, and appeared in *Pony Soldier* (1952) and *Westward Ho the Wagons!* (1957). As independent filmmakers documenting experiences of the native peoples of the Southwest, Maggi Banner produced *Coyote Goes Underground* (1989) and *Tiwa Tales* (1991). The prolific Victor Masayesva Jr. produced *Hopiit* (1982), *Itam Hakim Hopiit* (1984), *Siskyavi: A Place of Chasms* (1991), and *Imagining Indians* (1992) among others.

JOURNALISM

An influential periodical publisher and editor, Rose Robinson (1932–) was born in Winslow, Arizona and earned degrees from the Haskell Institute and the American University in Washington, D.C. in journalism studies. Robinson was a founding board member of the American Indian Press Association (later renamed Native American Journalist Association) before becoming its executive director. She also served as a member of the U.S. Department of the Interior's Indian Arts and Crafts Board, as information officer for the Bureau of Indian Affairs' Office of Public Instruction, as vice president and director of the Phelps-Stokes Fund's American Indian Program, and in various leadership roles with the North American Indian Women's Association. Robinson guides publication of periodicals for the Native American–Philanthropic News Service, including *The Exchange* and *The Roundup*. In 1980 she received the Indian Media Woman of the Year award.

LITERATURE

Poet Wendy Rose (1948–) was born Bronwen Elizabeth Edwards in Oakland, California and grew up in the San Francisco area. She studied at Contra Costa College and earned an M.A. in anthropology at the University of California at Berkeley. Some early work was published under the name Chiron Khanshendel. Her work, which focuses on modern urban Indian issues, has been included in numerous anthologies, in feminist collections such as *In Her Own Image* (1980) and more general collections, including *Women Poets of the World* (1983), in addition to her own published collections, *Hopi Roadrunner Dancing* (1973), *Lost Copper* (1980), *What Happened When the Hopi Hit New York* (1982), *The Halfbreed Chronicles and Other Poems* (1985), *Now Poof She Is Gone* (1994), and *Bone Dance: New and Selected Poems, 1965–1993* (1994). Rose has also served as editor for the scholarly journal *American Indian Quarterly* and has taught at Fresno City College, where she was director of the American Indian Studies Program.

SCIENCE AND TECHNOLOGY

Al Qoyawayma (c.1938–) became a prominent Hopi engineer as well as a noted ceramic artist. Born in Los Angeles, he earned an M.S. in mechanical engineering from the University of California at Berkeley in 1966. Working for Litton Systems, Inc., Qoyawayma developed high-tech airborne guidance systems. He moved to Arizona, becoming manager for environmental services for the Salt River Project. As an understudy of his aunt, Polingaysi Qoyawayma (Elizabeth White), he has also become an accomplished ceramicist, with his works displayed at the Smithsonian Institute and the Kennedy Art Center in Washington, D.C.

A geneticist and the first Hopi to receive a doctorate in sciences, Frank C. Dukapoo (1943–) founded the National Native American Honor Society in 1982. Duckapoo, born on the Mohave Indian reservation in Arizona, has specialized in investigating factors contributing to birth defects in Indians, among other research topics. He is also an accomplished saxophone player. Duckapoo earned his Ph.D. from Arizona State University and has taught at Arizona State, San Diego State University, Palomar Junior College, and Northern State University. Besides holding an executive position with the National Science Foundation from 1976 to 1979, he was also director of Indian Education at Northern Arizona University in Flagstaff, Arizona, and executive secretary for the National Cancer Institute.

SPORTS

Louis Tewanima (1879–1969) was not only the teammate of the famous American Indian athlete Jim Thorpe, but a world-class athlete in his own right. Born at Shongopovi, Second Mesa, on the Hopi Indian reservation, Tewanima chased jackrabbits as a boy. He was on the track team of the famous Carlisle Indian School in Pennsylvania under legendary coach Glenn "Pop" Warner. Tewanima established world records in long-distance running. At one track meet, Tewanima, Jim Thorpe, and Frank Mount Pleasant of Carlisle beat 20 athletes from Lafayette College. The U.S. Olympic Team selected Tewanima and Thorpe without requiring them to undergo trials—a rare honor. In 1912 they sailed to Stockholm, where they became U.S. heroes. Thorpe was proclaimed "the greatest athlete in the world" by the king of Sweden, and Tewanima won a silver medal in the 10,000 meter race. His performance set a U.S. record that lasted more than 50 years, until Billy Mills, a Sioux distance runner, surpassed it in the 1964 Tokyo Olympics. Tewanima returned home to Second Mesa, where he tended sheep and raised crops. Just for fun, to watch the trains go by, he would run to Winslow, Arizona, 80 miles away. In 1954, he was named to the All-Time United States Olympic Track and Field Team and in 1957 was the first person inducted, to a standing ovation, into the Arizona Sports Hall of Fame at a dinner given in his honor. The Tewanima Foot Race is run every September at Kykotsmovi. The tribe established a 2002 Winter Olympic Committee to mark a return of the Hopis to the Olympics and showcase Hopi arts and crafts.

VISUAL ARTS

Weaver Ramona Sakiestewa (1949–) was born in Albuquerque, New Mexico, to a Hopi father. She attended New York's School of Visual Arts and specialized in the treadle loom. Sakiestewa combines ancient design elements with contemporary weaving techniques, establishing a unique tradition in Native American arts. She co-founded ATLATL, a national Native American arts organization. Her tapestries have been shown at various shows and galleries including the Heard Museum of Phoenix and the Wheelwright Museum of American Indian in Santa Fe.

Award-winning artist and teacher Linda Lomahaftewa (1947–) was born in Phoenix, Arizona. She attended the Institute of American Indian Arts in Santa Fe and earned an M.A. in fine arts in 1971 from the San Francisco Art Institute. Lomahaftewa's drawings and paintings reflecting Hopi spirituality and storytelling have been exhibited through-

out the United States. She has received numerous awards and has taught at various colleges and universities, including University of California at Berkeley and back at the Institute.

MEDIA

The surrounding Navajo reservation established Navajo Communications, which provides various telecommunications services. However, the Hopis have no comparable utility and remained unconnected to the Navajo system.

Tutu-Veh-Ni.

A biweekly newsletter published by the Hopi Office of Public Relations.

Address: P.O. Box 123, Kykotsmovi, Arizona 86039.
Telephone: (602) 734-2441.

ORGANIZATIONS AND ASSOCIATIONS

Hopi Cultural Center.

Opened in 1970, the on-reservation facility houses various collections of Hopi arts and crafts and the Hononi Crafts shop.

Address: P.O. Box 67, Second Mesa, Arizona 86043.
Telephone: (602) 734-2401.

The Hopi Foundation.

The nongovernmental Foundation is based on Third Mesa, promoting cultural preservation led by Hopi professionals and laypersons.

Address: P.O. Box 705, Hotevilla, Arizona 86030.

Silvercraft Cooperative Guild.

Supports and sponsors Hopi artists.

Address: Box 37, Second Mesa, Arizona 86043.
Telephone: (602) 734-2463.

MUSEUMS AND RESEARCH CENTERS

Hopi Cultural Preservation Office.

Established in 1989 to implement a 1987 tribal historic preservation plan protecting important Hopi sacred and cultural sites, including traditional subsistence gathering areas.

Contact: Leigh Kuwanwisiwma.
Address: 123 Kykotsmovi, Arizona 86039.
Telephone: (520) 734-2244.

Hopi Tribal Museum.
Address: P.O. Box 7, Second Mesa, Arizona 86035.
Telephone: (602) 234-6650.

Museum of Northern Arizona.
Hosts the Hopi and Navajo Arts and Crafts Show annually in June and July.

Address: Route 4, Box 720, Flagstaff, Arizona 86001.
Telephone: (602) 774-5211.

SOURCES FOR ADDITIONAL STUDY

Benedek, Emily. *The Wind Won't Know Me: A History of the Navajo-Hopi Land Dispute.* New York: Knopf, 1992.

Leitch, Barbara A. *A Concise Dictionary of Indian Tribes of North America.* Algonac, MI: Reference Publications, 1979.

Loftin, John D. *Religion and Hopi Life in the Twentieth Century.* Bloomington: Indiana University Press, 1991.

Page, Susanne and Jake. *Hopi.* New York: Harry Abrams, 1994.

Parsons, Elsie Clews. *Hopi and Zuñi Ceremonialism.* New York: Harper and Bros., 1950. Reprint. Millwood, NY: Kraus Reprint, 1976.

Waters, Frank. *Book of the Hopi.* New York: Viking Press, 1963.

By the 1920s, most immigrants had resolved to stay permanently in the United States. They established families, had American-born children, and became intimately involved in the social lives of their churches, fraternal societies, and cultural institutions that in the past served as their extended families.

HUNGARIAN AMERICANS

by
**Steven Béla Várdy and
Thomas Szendrey**

OVERVIEW

Hungary is a small landlocked country in the Carpathian Basin of Central Europe. It is about the size of Indiana (35,919 square miles, or 93,030 square kilometers) with twice the latter's population. It is bounded by Slovakia in the north, Ukraine in the northeast, Romania in the east, the former Yugoslavia (Serbia, Croatia, Slovenia) in the south, and Austria in the west.

Hungary is inhabited almost exclusively by Hungarians (Magyars), who constitute 96.1 percent of its population. The remaining 3.9 percent is made up of Germans, Slovaks, South Slavs, Gypsies, and Romanians. Since the dismemberment of Greater Hungary after World War II—complemented by several waves of overseas emigration—about one-third of all Hungarians live abroad. The majority of them live in parts of former Greater Hungary in such newly created or enlarged neighboring states as Romania (more than two million), Slovakia (700,000), the former Yugoslavia (500,000), Ukraine (200,000), and Austria (50,000). Another two million reside in Western Europe, the Americas, and Australia—the majority of them in the United States.

According to statistics compiled in 1992, 67.8 percent of Hungarians are Catholic, 20.9 percent Calvinist (Reformed), and 4.2 percent Lutheran (Evangelical). The three religious groups together make up 92.9 percent of the population. Of the remaining portion, 2.3 percent belong to several minor denominations (Greek or Byzantine Catholic, Orthodox Christian, Baptist, Adventist), while 4.8 percent claim no religious affiliation. Jews, who in 1941 constituted 4.3 percent of Hungary's population, do not show up in these statistics. This is in part because the Holocaust or subsequent emigration to Israel decimated their ranks and in part because of the reluctance of some to identify themselves as Jews. Learned estimates, however, put their numbers close to 100,000 (about one percent of the country's population), which still makes them the largest Jewish community in East Central Europe. As the result of half a century of communist rule, relatively few people practice their religion in Hungary. The religious revival following the collapse of communism, however—which includes the return of organized religious education—is in the process of changing this lack of attention to religion.

HISTORY

Medieval Hungarian traditions count even the fifth-century Huns among the Magyars' ancestors, but their immediate forebears arrived in the Carpathian Basin as late as the seventh century. Known as the "late Avars," they established the center of their empire in the region that is part of modern Hungary. The last of several Magyar migratory waves took place in the late ninth century, when under the leadership of Prince Árpád, they conquered this region, gradually extending their rule over the entire Carpathian Basin.

In A.D. 1000, one of Árpád's successors, Stephen I (king of Hungary 997-1038; canonized 1083) Christianized his people and made Hungary part of the Western Christian world. During the next four centuries, the Hungarians continued to expand beyond the Carpathian Basin, especially into the northern Balkans. At the end of the eleventh century they conquered and annexed Croatia as an autonomous kingdom, while in the twelfth and thirteenth centuries they extended their influence over Bosnia, Dalmatia, and northern Serbia—largely at the expense of the declining Byzantine Empire. Moreover, in the fourteenth century, under the Angevin rulers Charles Robert (who ruled from 1308 until 1342) and Louis the Great (who ruled from 1342 to 1382), they expanded their control over the newly formed Vlach (Romanian) principalities of Wallachia and Moldavia and for a brief period (1370-1382) even over Poland. With the expansion of the Ottoman Turkish Empire into the Balkans in the late fourteenth and fifteenth centuries, Hungarian influence over

the northern Balkans declined and was replaced by that of the Turks. Even so, Hungary still experienced moments of greatness, particularly under Regent John Hunyadi (who ruled from 1444 to 1456) and his son King Matthias Corvinus (who ruled from 1458 to 1490). Matthias even conquered Moravia and eastern Austria (including Vienna) and also established a brilliant Renaissance royal court at Buda (now part of Budapest).

Medieval Hungary's greatness ended with its defeat at the hands of the Ottoman Turks at the Battle of Mohács in 1526. Turkish conquest was followed by the country's trisection, which lasted for nearly two centuries. Western and northwestern Hungary ("Royal Hungary") became part of the Habsburg Empire ruled from Vienna; central Hungary was integrated into the Ottoman Turkish Empire; and eastern Hungary evolved into the autonomous principality of Transylvania, whose semi-independence under Turkish suzerainty ended with the country's reconquest and reunification by the Habsburgs of Vienna in the late seventeenth and early eighteenth centuries.

Although dominated by Vienna throughout the eighteenth and nineteenth centuries, Hungary retained considerable autonomy within the Habsburg Empire. In the mid-nineteenth century the Habsburgs and the Hungarians clashed in the Hungarian Revolution and War of Independence (1848-1849), and two decades later they united in the Austro-Hungarian Compromise of 1867. This compromise—engineered by Francis Deák (1803-1876) and Emperor Franz Joseph (who ruled from 1848 to 1916)—resulted in the dual state of Austria-Hungary, which played a significant role in European power-politics until nationality problems and involvement in World War I on the German side resulted in its dissolution in 1918-1919.

The demise of Austria-Hungary was accompanied by the dismemberment of historic Hungary, codified in the Peace Treaty of Trianon in 1920. This treaty turned Hungary into a small truncated country, with only 28.5 percent of its former territory (35,900 square miles versus 125,600 square miles) and 36.5 percent of its former population (7.6 million versus 20.9 million). Trianon Hungary became "a kingdom without a king" under the regency of Admiral Nicholas Horthy (who ruled from 1920 to 1944), who devoted most of the country's energies to the effort to regain at least some of Hungary's territorial losses. These efforts did result in temporary territorial gains in 1938-1941, but as these gains were achieved with German and Italian help, they landed Hungary in the unfortunate German alliance during World War II.

After the war Hungary again was reduced in size and became one of the communist-dominated Soviet satellite states under the leadership of the Stalinist dictator, Mátyás Rákosi (who ruled from 1945 to 1956). Communist excesses and the relaxation that followed Stalin's death in 1953 led to the Hungarian Revolution of 1956, the most significant anti-Soviet uprising of the postwar period. Put down by Soviet military intervention, it was followed by a brief period of retribution and then by a new communist regime under János Kádár (who ruled from 1956 to 1988), who initiated a policy of political liberalization (1962) and economic reform (known as the New Economic Mechanism of 1968). By the 1970s these reforms—supported by generous Western loans—made Hungary and its system of "goulash communism" the envy of the

"**W**hen we were getting off of Ellis Island, we had all sorts of tags on us. Now that I think of it, we must have looked like marked-down merchandise in Gimbel's basement store or something."

Anna Vida in 1921, cited in *Ellis Island: An Illustrated History of the Immigrant Experience,* edited by Ivan Chermayeff et al. (New York: Macmillan, 1991).

communist world. In the 1980s, however, the system began to flounder, and economic problems resurfaced. These problems, together with Mikhail Gorbachev's reforms in the Soviet Union, undermined the Kádár regime. Kádár was ousted in 1988, and in 1989 Hungary came under the control of reform communists, who, unable to control the situation, relinquished power in 1990. They were replaced by a new multiparty government under the leadership of the Hungarian Democratic Forum (HDF), headed by József Antall (who ruled from 1990 to 1993). The HDF regime immediately began to transform Hungary from a communist to a democratic state, but the economic and social problems it encountered—rapid social polarization, the collapse of the protective social welfare system, and pauperization of a large segment of the society—proved to be too much. The HDF government was also plagued by amateurism in leadership. Voted out of office in May 1994, it was replaced in July of the same year by a coalition of the Hungarian Socialist Party and the Federation of Free Democrats. The new prime minister is the ex-Communist Gyula Horn (1932–), who had served as Hungary's foreign minister during the peaceful transition from communism to democracy in 1989-1990.

THE FIRST HUNGARIANS IN AMERICA

According to Hungarian tradition, the first Hungarian to reach the shores of America was a certain Tyrker who had arrived with the Viking chief Eric the Red around A.D. 1000. This is alleged to have happened concurrently with Stephen I's transformation of Hungary into a Christian kingdom. If the Tyrker story is discounted, the first documented Hungarian to land in America was the learned scholar Stephen Parmenius of Buda (c. 1555-1583), who participated in Sir Humphrey Gilbert's expedition in 1583 and later drowned off the coast of Newfoundland.

The next two and one-half centuries belonged to the explorers, missionaries, and adventurers who came to North America in increasing numbers during the colonial and early national periods. The most noted among the latter was Colonel Michael de Kováts (1724-1779), a member of the Pulaski Legion during the Revolutionary War, who is generally credited with being one of the founders of the American cavalry. The late eighteenth and early nineteenth century also saw the arrival of the first sporadic settlers, most of whom came from the middle and upper classes, were motivated by personal reasons to immigrate, and usually settled in such coastal cities as Boston, New York, Philadelphia, Charleston, and New Orleans. In the 1830s and 1840s came a number of learned travelers, including Sándor Bölöni-Farkas (1795-1842) and Ágoston Haraszthy (1812-1869), both of whom wrote influential books about their experiences in the New World under the identical title *Journey to North America* (published in 1834 and 1844, respectively). In 1844 Haraszthy returned permanently with his family and became the founder of California viticulture. The two decades prior to the Hungarian Revolution of 1848 also saw the initial scholarly contacts between the Hungarian Academy of Science and the American Philosophical Society.

The long period of individual migration was replaced in 1849-1850 by the first Hungarian group immigration to America. These were the so-called "Forty-niners," who emigrated to escape retribution by Austrian authorities after the defeat of the Hungarian Revolution of 1848. Several thousand strong, the numbers included only educated men, many of them from the gentry class (middle nobility), who found it difficult to adjust to America's frontier society. A large number of them joined the Union armies during the Civil War, and a few of them returned to Hungary during the 1860s and 1870s, but most of them became a part of American society. Many of the latter rose to important positions, usually in fields other than their original calling.

The next wave was the turn-of-the-century "Great Economic Immigration" that landed about 1.7 million Hungarian citizens, among them 650,000-700,000 real Hungarians (Magyars), on American shores. These immigrants came almost solely for economic reasons, and they represented the lowest and poorest segment of the population.

The outbreak of World War I in 1914 halted mass migration, while the exclusionary U.S. immigration laws of 1921 and 1924 pushed the Hungarian quota down to under 1,000 per year. This situation did not change until the new Immigration Law, the Hart-Celler Act of 1965, ended the quota system. Yet, during the intervening four decades, there were a number of nonquota admissions, which brought completely different types of Hungarian immigrants to American shores. These included the refugee intellectuals (2,000 to 3,000) of the 1930s, who were fleeing the spread of Nazism; the post-World War II political immigrants or the so-called displaced persons or DPs (17,000), who came under the Displaced Persons Acts of 1948 and 1950; and the "Fifty-sixers" or Freedom Fighters (38,000), who left Hungary after the failed Revolution of 1956. Although the com-bined numbers of these last three groups (60,000) were less than 10 percent of that of the turn-of-the-century economic immigrants, their impact on American society was much more significant.

SETTLEMENT PATTERNS

Although the turn-of-the-century economic immigrants were from rural areas, almost all of them settled in the industrial cities and mining regions of the northeastern United States. According to one set of statistics, of all the Hungarians (Magyars) in the United States in 1920, fewer than 0.2 percent were engaged in agriculture. Virtually all of them worked in mining and industry—most of them in the unskilled or semiskilled category. This was primarily because the majority of them came to America not as immigrants but as migrant workers who intended to repatriate to Hungary. Their goal was to return with enough accumulated capital to be able to buy land and thus become prosperous farmers. To do this, however, they had to work in industry, where work was readily available, because during the Gilded Age the rapidly expanding American industrial establishment was in grave need of cheap immigrant labor.

Most of the immigrants were never able to fulfill their original goal of repatriation, although perhaps as many as 25 percent did return permanently. Factors contributing to this included their inability to accumulate the capital to buy enough land; the difficulties they encountered in readjusting to Hungary's class-conscious society; the influence of their American-born children who viewed Hungary as an alien land; and most important, Hungary's post-World War I dismemberment, which transferred the immediate homelands of most of the immigrants to such newly created states as Czechoslovakia or Yugoslavia or to the much-enlarged Romania. They did not wish to join the ranks of Hungarians who had been forcibly transferred to these states, two of which had gone out of existence twice since their creation (Czechoslovakia and Yugoslavia) and one of which had become the home base of postwar Europe's most oppressive and chauvinistic communist regime (Romania).

According to the 1920 U.S. Census, 945,801 persons in the United States either had been born in Hungary or had Hungarian-born parents, slightly over half of whom (495,845 or 52.9 percent) were Magyars. In 1922 the Hungarian-born Magyars numbered 474,000, of whom 427,500 (90 percent) were concentrated in 10 northeastern states: New York (95,400), Ohio (88,000), Pennsylvania (86,000), New Jersey (47,300), Illinois (40,000), Michigan (26,200), Connecticut (14,800), Wisconsin (11,600), Indiana (10,900), and West Virginia (7,300). They congregated in this region because of the coal mines of Pennsylvania, northern West Virginia, and southeastern Ohio, as well as because of the steel mills, textile mills, and machine factories of Pittsburgh, Cleveland, Youngstown, Chicago, Philadelphia, and the Greater New York area.

This settlement pattern remained unchanged until the 1960s when—partially because of the coming of the more mobile political immigrants, and partially because of the general population shift in previous decades—many Hungarians began to move to the West and to the South. The younger and more daring souls flooded to California and Texas, while the retirees favored Florida. Thus, by 1980 the Hungarian population of these states rose, respectively, to 165,000, 28,000, and 90,000.

INTERACTIONS WITH ANGLO-AMERICAN SOCIETY

The relationship of the Hungarians to Anglo-American society varied with the diverse waves of immigrants. The Forty-niners, also known as the "Kossuth immigrants" (after the leader of the revolution, Lajos Kossuth), had been received with awe and respect. Because of their gentry-based background and education, they established the image of the Hungarians as a "nation of nobles." This image was undermined by the turn-of-the-century economic immigrants, the majority of whom were poor and uneducated. They were the ones who unwittingly created the negative "Hunky" image of Hungarians, which then was transferred to all of the East and Southeast European immigrants. This image survived well into the post-World War II period, even though by that time the intellectual immigrants of the 1930s and the political immigrants of the 1950s began to diversify the immigrants' social composition. Although far fewer in number, these newer immigrants were the ones who gave birth to the revised Hungarian image that Laura Fermi, the author of the highly praised study *Illustrious Immigrants* (1968), defined as the "mystery of the Hungarian talent." This was a natural by-product of the fact that many of these intellectual and political immigrants made impressive achievements that had a measurable impact on American society.

KEY ISSUES

Cultural survival and relationship to Hungary are prominent issues for some Hungarian Americans. The third-, fourth-, and fifth-generation descendants of the economic immigrants have already melted into American society. Most of them have lost their ability to speak Hungarian and no longer have a true identity of themselves as Hungarians. Most have only a minimal acquaintance with modern Hungary and know very little about Hungarian traditions. This is somewhat true of the post-World War II immigrants as well, even though a sizable percentage of their American-born offspring does speak Hungarian and has some knowledge of Hungarian culture. Moreover, in light of the collapse of communism in 1989-1990, a significant number of them have found their way back to the land of their ancestors. This was and is being done largely in the form of employment with some of the major American or Western European corporations that have established branches in Hungary. This temporary return does create a set of new ties, but because of the radical transformation of Hungarian society during the four decades of communist rule, the experience is not always positive.

Despite renewed contacts with the homeland, Hungarian Americans are losing their struggle to survive as a separate ethnic group in America. This is evident both in their declining numbers, as well as in the decreasing number of their ethnic institutions, churches, cultural organizations, and fraternal organizations. This phenomenon is best seen when comparing the census statistics of 1980 with those of 1990. The number of those who claimed to be fully or primarily Hungarian during those two census years has declined by nearly 11 percent (from 1,776,902 to 1,582,302), while the number of those who speak primarily Hungarian in their families has dropped by almost 18 percent (from 180,000 to 147,902). During the same period Greater Pittsburgh alone lost about half a dozen Hungarian churches; the remaining ones are struggling for survival. The same fate befell Hungarian cultural and social organizations of western Pennsylvania, few of which are active today. This trend appears to be equally true for the entire Northeast, embracing the above-mentioned 10 states. It should be noted here, however, that this decline is not as evident in California and Florida, which experienced a rapid growth of Hungarians from the 1960s through the 1990s. More recently, however, even California experienced a 3.5 percent decline in its Hungarian population (from 164,903 to 159,121), and Florida gained 11.4 percent only because of its extreme popularity with retirees (from 89,587 to 99,822).

ACCULTURATION AND ASSIMILATION

Notwithstanding earlier immigrations, the Hungarian presence in the United States was established by the large mass of rural immigrants in the three decades before World War I. These immigrants fostered their Hungarian identity and a sense of community because of their social, cultural, and psychological needs and also because of Anglo-American society's unwillingness to accept them. The same cannot be said of their American-born children, who tended to assimilate at a rapid pace. They were driven by the socioeconomic drawing power of American society, as well as by their own conscious desire to separate themselves from the world of their simple immigrant parents. Most of them managed to move up a notch or two in social status, but perhaps for this very reason many of them also left the ethnic communities founded by their parents. Their efforts to assimilate, however, were not fully successful, for although native born, they were still viewed as outsiders by the Anglo-American majority.

The situation changed significantly with the second native-born generation, whose rise to adulthood coincided with the birth of the "ethnic revolution" of the 1960s. Their embracing of this revolution led to the rediscovery of their ethnic roots. It was impeded, however, by their inability to speak Hungarian and by the gradual disintegration of viable Hungarian ethnic communities, a disintegration that began precisely at the start of this ethnic revolution. At present, most self-contained Hungarian American communities are in the process of final dissolution. A few of their cultural and religious institutions still exist, but they serve only the needs of the older generation, and very briefly those of some of the new arrivals. This dying-out process is best demonstrated in the institutional life of the oldest and largest Hungarian Catholic church and parish in the United States, St. Elizabeth of Cleveland (founded in 1892), where the ratio of burials to baptisms is nearly 20 to one.

The early twentieth century immigrants and their descendants provided the foundations of Hungarian American life, but their role and influence were much more limited than those of the later waves, who brought with them a high level of learning and a strong sense of historical and national consciousness. The latter were less prone to buckle under assimilative social pressures. Moreover, if they assimilated, they did so consciously. Most of them, however, retained a large degree of dual identity, which they also passed on to their second- and third-generation descendants. The latter usually moved rapidly into American professional and business circles and—with the exception of those in the vicinity of greater New York, Cleveland, Chicago, and Los Angeles—were forced to live outside the influence of their ethnic communities. Thus, they experienced their Hungarian identity in isolation. This sense of isolation has permeated the lives of most upward-moving professionals, especially since the 1960s. Consequently, their success or lack thereof in passing their traditions on to their offspring depended and still largely depends on their dedication to the idea of dual identity. But because relatively few had the time to deal with this issue, the next generation is rapidly losing its facility to speak Hungarian and along with it its true Hungarian identity.

American-born offspring of the various immigrant waves still practice some of their folk traditions, partially during social events held at their churches and social clubs, but mostly during major folk festivals and "Hungarian Days" that are still celebrated in such large centers of Hungarian life as New Brunswick, New Jersey; Pittsburgh; and Cleveland. Although declining in numbers, the quality of these major performances has actually improved in recent years because of closer contact with Hungary and Hungarian professionals.

Misconceptions about Hungary and the Hungarians abound in the United States, although this is much less true today than in the early part of the century when they were often misidentified as Mongols or Gypsies. This was due in part to American society's minimum knowledge about Central and Eastern Europe and in part to conscious distortions by politically motivated propagandists. Today, the situation has improved significantly because of the impact of the Hungarian Revolution of 1956 and because of the enhanced number and quality of publications about Hungary, produced mostly by the American-educated offspring of the political immigrants. This improvement, however, is more noticeable among the educated classes than among the general public.

HOLIDAYS

Hungarian Americans generally celebrate three major national holidays: March 15 (Revolution of 1848), August 20 (Saint Stephen's Day), and October 23 (Revolution of 1956). These celebrations may combine patriotic and religious elements. There is no such thing as a specifically Hungarian American holiday, perhaps because the attention of most unassimilated Hungarian Americans is focused on the mother country.

HEALTH ISSUES

Hungary has the highest suicide rate in the world (45-48 per 100,000). The factors connected with this suicide rate, however, appear to be limited to Hungarian society, and Hungarian Americans are no more prone to mental health problems than are other ethnic groups in the United States.

The Hungarian medical profession is of high quality, even though it does not have access to much of the modern equipment available in the United States. This does not prevent Hungarian physicians from being among the best educated, as is demonstrated by, among other things, the virtually nonexistent failure rate of Hungarian medical students on American medical examinations. This holds true both for Hungarians who have emigrated after their medical training in Hungary and Hungarian Americans who attend Hungarian medical schools and then return to take their examinations in the United States.

LANGUAGE

Hungarian is classified as a Finno-Ugric language and is part of the larger Ural-Altaic linguistic family. The most distinctive characteristic of these lan-

guages is that they are agglutinative—that is, words are extended into complex expressions through the use of prefixes and suffixes. One example will conveniently serve to illustrate. The meaning of a single word, *szent* (saint), can be changed by adding numerous prefixes and suffixes as follows (hyphens indicate the additions): *szent-ség* (sanctity), *szent-ség-ed* (your sanctity), *szent-ség-ed-del* (with your sanctity), *szent-ség-eid-del* (with your sanctities), *meg-szent-ségel-és-ed* (your sanctification), *meg-szent-ség-telenít-hetetlen-ség-ed-del* (with your ability to withstand desanctification).

The closest linguistic relatives of the Hungarians are the Finns and the Estonians, but the Hungarians are also distantly related to the Turkic peoples. This is due both to their common roots and to the renewal of contacts through the mixing of Finno-Ugric and Turkic tribes during the first nine centuries of the Christian Era.

Before the conquest of Hungary, the Hungarians had their own runic script. After their conversion to Christianity, they borrowed the Latin liturgical language and alphabet and adapted this alphabet to the phonetic properties of the Hungarian language. This was done by doubling up letters to represent a single sound: "cs" ("ch"), "gy" ("dy"), "ly" ("y"), "ny" (soft "n"), "sz" ("s"), "ty" (soft "t"), "zs" ("zh"), "dzs" ("dzh"); or by adding diacritical marks ("á," "é," "í," "ö," "ő," "ü," "ű"). In many instances the accent marks not only signify the pronunciation but also alter the meaning of the word—for example: *sor* (row), *sör* (beer); *bor* (wine), *bőr* (skin); *sas* (eagle), *sás* (sedge); *szar* (excrement), *szár* (stem). The meaning of a single word can be changed several times simply by adding or subtracting a diacritical mark—for example: *kerek* (round), *kerék* (wheel), *kérek* (I am requesting), *kérék* (I have requested).

The English language has had an impact on how Hungarian Americans speak Hungarian. This was particularly true for the less educated immigrants, who readily mixed their simple Hungarian with working-class English. Thus, they rapidly developed a language of their own known as "Hunglish" (Hungarian English), which introduced English words into the Hungarian, but transformed them to fit Hungarian pronunciation and orthography: *trén* (train), *plész* (place), *szalon* (saloon), *bedróm* (bedroom), *atrec* (address), *tájm* (time), *szendsztón* (sandstone), *gud báj* (good-bye), *foriner* (foreigner), *fandri* (foundry), *fanesz* (furnace), *bakszi* (box), *burdos* (boarder), *burdosház* (boarding house), *görl* (girl), *groszeri* (grocery).

There was also a reverse version of Hunglish that may be called "Engarian" (English Hungarian), which adjusted the primitive English to the ears of

the immigrants. The result was two hodgepodge languages that were barely comprehensible to Hungarians or Americans who did not speak both languages—for example: *Szé, miszter, gimi order, maj hen trók brók!* (Say, Mister, give me the order. My hand truck broke.). Such usage is no longer common, largely because the Americanized offspring of the turn-of-the-century immigrants have switched to English but also because the more educated post-World War II immigrants never really acquired it.

GREETINGS AND POPULAR EXPRESSIONS

Common greetings are as follows (all words are pronounced with the accent on the first syllable): *Jó reggelt* ("yo reggelt")—Good morning; *Jó napot* ("yo nahpote")—Good day; *Jó estét* ("yo eshtayt")—Good evening; *Jó éjszakát* ("yo aysahkaht")—Good night; *Kezitcsókolom* ("kezeet choakholohm")—I kiss your hand; *Szervusz* or *Szerbusz* ("servoos, serboos")—Hello, Hi; *Szia* ("seeyah")—Hi, Hello; *Viszontlátásra* ("veesoant-lahtahshrah")—Good-bye, See you again; *Isten áldjon meg* ("eeshten ahldyoan meg")—God bless you. Other popular expressions include: *Boldog újévet* ("bohldogh ooy-ayveth")—Happy New Year; *Kellemes húsvétot* ("kellehmesh hooshvaytoth")—Happy Easter; *Kellemes karácsonyi ünnepeket* ("kellehmesh karahchoanyi ünnepeketh") —Merry Christmas; *Boldog ünnepeket* ("bohldogh ünnepeketh")—Happy Holidays; *Egészségedre* ("eggayshaygedreh")—To your health (spoken when toasting).

FAMILY AND COMMUNITY DYNAMICS

After the early and predominantly male phases of economic immigration abated, Hungarian American immigrant communities assumed a traditional and stable family structure. By the 1920s, most immigrants had resolved to stay permanently in the United States. They established families, had American-born children, and became intimately involved in the social lives of their churches, fraternal societies, and cultural institutions that in the past served as their extended families. The structure survived almost intact into the 1960s, although with only limited participation by the political immigrants of the interwar and postwar periods. Unable to agree on a common platform with the earlier economic immigrants, the latter usually founded their own organizations and pursued their familial and social activities within these more politically oriented groups.

With the exception of the relatively few immigrants who came during the 1960s through the 1980s—many of them from the Hungarian-inhabited regions surrounding Hungary—very few Hungarians have ever received public assistance. Traditionally, accepting handouts has been perceived in Hungarian society as an admission of failure. This view was much less prevalent among the more recent immigrants, who had become accustomed to state assistance under the communist social system.

Immigrant life and ethnic experience in America transformed basic traditional patterns of family life, resulting in a hybrid set of customs. In terms of everyday existence, Hungarian family life conforms to American patterns, but with a greater emphasis on education. The role of women has been enhanced compared with the still male-dominated Hungarian model. Adjustment to American custom is also evident in the area of dating, marriage, and divorce. Until a generation ago, dating practices were very strict and circumscribed. More recently, they have loosened, as has the commitment to a lasting marriage. Thus, whereas a generation ago divorce among Hungarian immigrants was rare, today it is almost as common as it is for American society as a whole.

Philanthropic activities among Hungarian Americans tend to be aimed at specific groups of Hungarians. During the past three decades, these were oriented almost exclusively toward the Hungarian minorities in the areas surrounding Hungary. There are, of course, exceptions to the rule, but these exceptions are usually connected with the philanthropic activities of the few super-rich, the best-known of whom is the billionaire investor George Soros.

RELIGION

Hungary has been a Roman Catholic country since its conversion to Christianity in the late tenth and early eleventh centuries. This religious uniformity was shattered only in the sixteenth century, when Protestantism entered the country and spread, especially in its Calvinist form. After a century of intense struggle, Catholicism remained strong in the country's western and central regions, while Calvinism came to dominate its eastern regions. This Catholic-Calvinist rivalry was complicated somewhat by the presence of a significant minority of Lutherans (Evangelicals), Jews, Greek/Byzantine Catholics, and Unitarians, as well as by a few other small Christian sects. Yet, in spite of its losses to rival faiths, Roman Catholicism retained its dominant position as Hungary's only official "state religion" until the communist takeover in 1948.

The religious divisions in Hungary also came to be reflected in Hungarian American society. The Calvinists were the first to establish their pioneer congregations in 1891 in Cleveland and in Pittsburgh, to be followed in 1892 by the Roman Catholics (St. Elizabeth of Hungary Church, Cleveland) and in 1907 by the Lutherans (Cleveland). These early congregations soon sprouted scores of other Hungarian churches throughout the Northeast. As a result, by the 1930s Hungarian Americans had nearly 140 Calvinist, more than 60 Roman Catholic, and about ten Lutheran churches, as well as perhaps two dozen other prayer houses. Although the Calvinists had the greatest number of churches, their congregations were small, and as such they represented only one-third as many faithful as did the Roman Catholics.

Roman Catholics, Calvinists, and Lutherans together constituted slightly over 90 percent of all religious affiliations of Hungarian Americans. The other eight to ten percent was made up of smaller denominations including the Byzantine Catholics, Jews, Baptists, and Adventists. Because of their small numbers, however, none of the latter had more than a limited and passing influence on Hungarian American life.

The religious practices of Hungarian Roman Catholics and Protestants in the United States are basically identical to those of their coreligionists in Hungary and are also similar to the practices of their American counterparts. Although religious practices did not change after emigration, the social significance of the congregations and the position and the role of the parish priests and pastors underwent significant changes. In Hungary the religious congregations and their priests or ministers were supported by their respective mother churches through an obligatory religious tax. As a result these congregations were centrally controlled, with little or no input from the members of the congregations. This was particularly true of the Roman Catholic Church, which had retained its monarchical structure from the Middle Ages. Although Calvinist and Lutheran congregations did elect their pastors even in Hungary, the powers of the presbytery (church council) were much more limited than in the United States. This was true not only because of the somewhat authoritarian nature of traditional Hungarian society but also because the pastors did not depend on the financial support of their parishioners. In Hungary, therefore, it was the priests and the ministers who controlled the congregation, and not vice versa.

After emigration, this relationship changed significantly. Much of the control over church affairs slipped into the hands of the members of the church council. This change in the power relationship was due both to the lack of state support for religion and to the fact that now the members of the congregations were paying for the upkeep of their churches and their pastors.

Just as the role of the church leaders had changed, the function of the church had also changed. Traditionally, American churches have always combined religious and social functions—a phenomenon that was largely unknown in Europe. This American tradition was accepted by the immigrant churches, which consequently ceased to function solely as houses of prayer. They now also assumed the role of social clubs, where members of the congregation combined their search for spiritual salvation with an ongoing attempt to fulfill their earthly social needs. As such, immigrant churches lost some of the sanctity of their Old World counterparts.

The climax of Hungarian religious life in America was reached in the period between the 1920s and 1960s. By the 1970s, however, a process of slow decay had set in, which during the 1980s had accelerated to the point where several Hungarian ethnic churches were closing their doors every year.

During the past 100 years of Hungarian religious life in the United States, all denominations have been plagued by dissension, but none more so that the Hungarian Calvinist (Reformed) Church. Within the first quarter century after having taken root in America, this dissension has led to the establishment of several competing Calvinist denominations—a process that resulted in a new subdenomination as late as 1982. While some of these conflicts and fragmentations were of an ideological and administrative nature (e.g., their relationship to the mother church in Hungary), most of them were really the result of personal animosity among the clergy. American social practices make it easy for anyone to establish a new church, while personality conflicts and group squabbles often result in institutional divorces. At the moment Hungarian Calvinists are still divided into a half dozen rival and competing churches that are held together only by the awareness of their common

roots and by their membership in the Hungarian Reformed Federation (HRF). Founded in 1898 as a fraternal association, the HRF also serves as a force of unity among Hungarian Calvinists.

EMPLOYMENT AND ECONOMIC TRADITIONS

Hungarian immigrants have been involved in all facets of American economic life, with the level of their employment depending for the most part on their social background. Those who came before the mid-nineteenth century were individual adventurers who were well prepared for all eventualities in the New World. Although few in numbers, most of those who stayed proved to be successful. Some of them became well-known merchants in Philadelphia, Baltimore, and New Orleans, while others became well-respected professors at American universities. Whatever they did, they did it well, for they could rely on a good education and on the self-assurance common to well-born individuals.

To a large degree this was also true for the 3,000 to 4,000 Forty-niners who immigrated after the defeat of the Hungarian Revolution of 1848. Belonging mostly to the gentry, they had no intention of becoming dirt farmers or laborers in America. They spread Hungary's image as the land of a valiant "noble nation," but only a minority were able to adjust to America's pioneer society. This was true even though a few of them also became involved in the establishment of Hungarian colonies in the West, such as László Újházy (1795-1870), a high-ranking official of the revolutionary government, who founded New Buda in Iowa in 1852. After trying their hands at many things, a thousand of the Forty-niners joined the Union armies in the Civil War, after which a good number of them went into diplomatic service or into various major business ventures in the West.

The next wave of immigrants came during the late nineteenth and early twentieth centuries with the intention of repatriating after four or five years with enough capital to make themselves into prosperous farmers. Few of them achieved this goal, and virtually all of them became unskilled or semiskilled workers in America's bustling industries. They were the peons of America's Gilded Age, who contributed their brawn to American coal mines and steel smelters, and who produced the mythical Hungarian American hero, Joe Magarac, who could bend steel bars with his bare hands.

Each of the next four immigration waves contributed to the abatement of this stereotype. These waves comprised the interwar "intellectual immigrants"; the post-World War II "political immigrants"; the Fifty-sixers; and finally the political-economic immigrants of the past four decades. Given their achievements in Europe, the intellectual immigrants moved immediately into the highest American intellectual and scientific circles and almost overnight created the myth of the uniqueness of Hungarian talent.

The political immigrants, or DPs, represented the military-legal-administrative leadership of interwar Hungary and had few transferable skills; thus, many of them were forced to engage in physical labor. Yet, their learning, cultural background, and personal bearing immediately revealed to their fellow American workers that they were of a different caliber. Many of them eventually did manage to transfer to white-collar work, although it was largely their American-educated children who moved up rapidly into the professions.

The Fifty-sixers differed from the DPs in their relative youth, orientation toward transferable technical and practical skills, and diminished cultural background—the product of a decade of communist restructuring of Hungarian society. Yet they and the American-educated children of the DPs produced a class of professionals that penetrated all aspects of American scientific, scholarly, artistic, literary, and business life.

The final immigration wave began during the 1960s and is still going on today. It is characterized by a slow but gradual influx of professionals and professionally oriented individuals. During the 1960s through the 1980s, political persecution was the ostensible motive for their immigration. Since the collapse of communism, they have come as needed professionals.

According to a recent survey by the *New York Times*, Hungarians are not among the most highly regarded ethnic groups in America, but they are certainly among the most successful. They have also managed to eradicate the Hunky stereotype that was unwittingly transmitted by their less fortunate predecessors.

POLITICS AND GOVERNMENT

The political activism of the Hungarians in America reaches back to the mid-nineteenth century, when Lajos Kossuth (1802-1894) visited the United States (1851-1852) and in a highly celebrated tour of the country urged Americans to intervene on behalf of defeated Hungary by supporting Hungary's struggle against Austria. Although the Hungarian statesman's presence created a veritable "Kossuth craze" in America, the results were disappointing. Despite its outward expression of sympathy, the U.S. government was unwilling to budge from its policy of isolationism. Although unsuccessful in its political aims, Kossuth's presence did create a positive image of Hungary, as well as stir up pro-Hungarian sentiment among the American public. The image and sentiment survived until the turn of the century. The final blow to the Kossuth-inspired image came during World War I, when Austria-Hungary sided with imperial Germany.

Although the Austro-Hungarian Empire disappeared and historic Hungary was dismembered after the war, anti-Hungarian sentiment resurfaced after Hungary's forced alliance with Italy and Germany during World War II. Following the war, Hungary came to be regarded as a Soviet satellite. The daring anti-Soviet uprising of 1956 once again stirred pro-Hungarian sentiment. The American image of Hungary has been improving ever since, both because Hungary was among the first of the Soviet-dominated nations to liberalize economically and politically during the 1960s and because of the increasingly sophisticated political activism of Hungarian American lobby groups.

Hungarians established several mutual aid societies in the second half of the nineteenth century, but not until 1906 did they create the first successful political organization, the American-Hungarian Federation (AHF), which is still in existence. The twin goals of the AHF were to protect the interests of the Hungarian immigrants and to promote the cause of Hungary in the United States. During the first decade of its existence, the AHF worked toward these goals in close cooperation with Hungary. During World War I, particularly after the United States entered the war on the opposite side, this task became impossible. Following the war the AHF proved unsuccessful in its efforts to influence American foreign policy on postwar treaties. Yet, during the interwar period—in conjunction with the largest Hungarian fraternal organizations (i.e., Verhovay, Rákóczi, Bridgeport, the Reformed Federation)—it conducted a steady propaganda campaign to revise the unfair terms of the Treaty of Trianon (1920). This task became increasingly difficult during the late 1930s, when Hungary began to regain some of its former territory with the help of Germany and Italy.

The darkest and most difficult period in Hungarian political activism came during World War II, when the AHF and the major fraternal organizations were forced to defend Hungary's territorial gains while maintaining their support for the

American war effort. To prove their loyalty to the United States, more than 50,000 Hungarians served in the U.S. armed forces, and all Hungarian American organizations bought U.S. defense bonds and made repeated declarations of allegiance. Toward the end of the war, they organized the American-Hungarian Relief Committee, whose members undertook a major effort to send aid to their devastated homeland, as well as to hundreds of thousands of Hungarians who had been trapped in German and Austrian refugee camps. Moreover, in 1948 and 1950, the AHF and the major Hungarian fraternal societies supported the passage of the two Displaced Persons Acts that brought almost 18,000 Hungarian political refugees to the United States.

The appearance of the post-World War II political immigrants—the DPs during the early 1950s and the Fifty-sixers after the Revolution of 1956—created a completely new situation. Much better educated and more involved politically than most of their predecessors, the newcomers created their own organizations. Some of the most vocal and active of these associations included the American branch of the Fraternal Association of Hungarian Veterans (1947), the Cleveland-based Committee for Liberation (1951), and the Hungarian National Committee (1948)—the last of which was viewed by the U.S. government as a virtual government in exile.

The appearance of the Fifty-sixers added a new color to this political spectrum. Although a number of them joined existing DP organizations, many of them also founded their own associations. The most important of these was the Hungarian Freedom Fighter's Federation (1957), although very soon it was joined by others with nearly identical names. During the 1970s several minority-oriented organizations were created specifically to help the cause of the increasingly oppressed Hungarian minorities in the neighboring states. These included the Committee for Human Rights in Romania, the Transylvania World Federation, the Transylvanian Committee, and the Hungarian Human Rights Committee, all of which were especially concerned with the plight of the Hungarian minorities under the oppressive rule of the communist Ceauºescu regime in Romania.

From the late 1950s through the early 1980s, most of the nonminority-oriented organizations were concerned primarily with the liberation of Hungary and then with soliciting U.S. government help to undermine the communist regime. Throughout this period the politically active new immigrants had little concern for American domestic politics; their attention was turned to Hungary. Thus, after becoming citizens, they usually voted with the Republican Party, which they perceived to be tougher on communism. As opposed to them, the turn-of-the-century economic immigrants and their American-born descendants paid only lip service to Hungary. They were much more concerned with domestic politics, and with bread-and-butter issues, than with the problems of communism. Thus, they voted mostly Democratic.

The rise of a new generation among the political immigrants during the 1970s and 1980s also produced some changes. On the one hand, the American-born or American-educated members of the younger generations became involved in U.S. domestic politics in both political parties. On the other hand, they began to assume a much more realistic approach toward Hungary and its "goulash communism." Some of them assumed the leadership of the AHF and carried their pragmatism into its politics. While understandable, this act split the AHF and brought about the foundation of the National Federation of Hungarian Americans (NFHA) in 1984, and subsequently several rival organizations, including the very active and influential Hungarian American Coalition (HAC) in 1992.

The collapse of communism and the rise of a nationalist government under the Hungarian Democratic Forum (1989-90) produced a general euphoria among Hungarian Americans, and also an upsurge in their desire to help their homeland. The euphoria coincided with Hungary's unheard of popularity in the world for its role in undermining communism. This euphoria and popularity, however, did not last. The country's social and economic problems produced a general disillusionment that was also felt by Hungarian Americans, many of whose hopes also remained unrealized.

At present, most Hungarian Americans have become American citizens and are heavily involved in the political life of both U.S. political parties. At the same time they still display considerable interest in Hungary. Even though somewhat disillusioned with the way things are going in Hungary, they continue to pursue pro-Hungarian lobbying efforts through several umbrella organizations (AHF, NFHA, HAC), as well as through their presence in the U.S. Congress. The most visible and active among the Hungarian congressional representatives is the Fifty-sixer Tom Lantos (1928–) from California (1980–), who in recent years has become increasingly involved in Hungarian-related political activities.

MILITARY

Relative to their size as an ethnic group, more Hungarian Americans served in the Civil War than any other nationality. Of the approximately 4,000 Hungarians in the United States (including women and children) at the outbreak of the war in 1861, more than 800—at least three-fourths of the adult male population—served in the Union armies. Among them were two major generals, five brigadier generals, 15 colonels and lieutenant colonels, 13 majors, 12 captains, about four dozen first and second lieutenants, and scores of noncommissioned officers.

The most prominent of the officers was Major General Julius H. Stahel (1825-1912)—known in Hungary before his emigration as Gyula Számvald. General Stahel became a close confidant of President Lincoln and the first Hungarian recipient of the Congressional Medal of Honor. Among the nearly 1,000 Hungarians in the Union army was the young Joseph Pulitzer (1817-1911), who subsequently became the king of American journalism and the founder of the famous literary prize that bears his name.

INDIVIDUAL AND GROUP CONTRIBUTIONS

Following Hungary's dismemberment after World War I, many educated Hungarians—engineers, physicians, sociologists, educators, and lawyers—came to the United States to pursue their livelihood. In the 1930s their numbers were increased by those fleeing the spread of fascism in Central Europe. In this category were numerous internationally known scientists, social scientists, musicologists, artists, filmmakers, and other persons of unusual talent.

ECONOMICS

From the late nineteenth century, Hungarians have made important contributions to U.S. industry and finance. Two of the earliest entrepreneurs were the Black (Schwartz) and Kundtz families. The Black family founded a series of garment factories and department stores, while Tivador Kundtz (1852-1937) established the White Machine factory. These two families employed and aided thousands of fellow immigrant Hungarians.

Modern entrepreneurs include the billionaire financier George Soros (1930–), who has played a significant role in the transformation of the former Soviet world through philanthropic efforts such as the establishment of the Budapest- and Prague-based Central European University; and Andrew Grove (born András Gróf; 1936–), who as the founder and president of Intel Corporation created the world's largest manufacturer of computer chips.

FILM AND ENTERTAINMENT

Two Hungarians were influential in the development of the Hollywood film industry: Adolph Zukor (1873-1976), the founder of Paramount Pictures; and William Fox (1879-1952), the founder of Twentieth Century-Fox. Zukor and Fox transformed the stylish Biedermeier culture of the Austro-Hungarian Empire into the glamorous society portrayed in Hollywood film.

Other pioneers in the film industry included directors/producers Michael Curtiz (born Kertész; 1888-1962), Sir Alexander Korda (1893-1956), George Cukor (1899-1983), and Joseph Pasternak (1901–), as well as film stars Leslie Howard (born Árpád Steiner; 1893-1943), Bela Lugosi (1883-1956) of Dracula fame, Tony Curtis (born Bernard Schwartz; 1925–), and the Gabor sisters, Zsa-Zsa, Eva, and Magda. In this category also belong the magician Harry Houdini (born Erich Weisz; 1874-1926) and comedian/television actor Freddie Prinze (born Freddie Preutzel; 1954-1977).

MUSIC

By the time the internationally known composers Béla Bartók (1881-1945) and Ernõ Dohnányi (1877-1960) emigrated in the 1940s, the American cultural scene was already peopled by such Hungarian composers as Fritz Reiner (1888-1963), George Szell (1897-1970), Eugene Ormandy (1899-1985), Antal Dorati (1906-1988), and Sir Georg Solti (1912–). Hungarians were also present on Broadway in popular American musicals. The best-loved of them was Sigmund Romberg (1887-1951), who was perhaps the most successful transplanter of the Viennese and the Budapest operetta. Also significant was the contribution of Miklós Rózsa (1907–), who worked with Sir Alexander Korda and wrote the music to some of the great American films.

SCIENCE AND MATHEMATICS

Three Hungarians assisted Enrico Fermi with the breakthroughs in atomic fission that resulted in the development of the atomic bomb: Leo Szilard (1898-1964), Eugene Wigner (1902-1995), and Edward Teller (1908–). Other major contributors are Theodore von Kármán (1881-1963), father of the heat and quantum theory; mathematician and father of the computer Johann von Neumann (1903-1957); and Zoltán Bay (1900-1992), the pioneer in radar astronomy.

George Pólya (1887-1985) and Gábor Szegő (1895-1985) were responsible for making Stanford University one of the world's premier centers of mathematics. A much younger exponent of finite mathematics and its application, John George Kemény (1926–) later became the president of Dartmouth College.

Other leading Hungarian scientists included the Nobel laureates Georg Karl Hevesy (1855-1966), Albert Szent-Györgyi (1893-1986), Georg von Békésy (1899-1972), and Dennis Gabor (1900-1979). The list also includes several members of the Polányi family: the social philosopher Karl Polányi (1886-1964), the physicist-philosopher Michael Polányi (1891-1976), as well as the latter's son, John Charles Polányi (1926–), who won the Nobel Prize for chemistry in 1986.

MEDIA

PRINT

Amerikai-Kanadai Magyar Élet (American-Canadian Hungarian Life).
Founded in 1959 as *Amerikai Magyar Élet*, this weekly has been under the control of Bishop Tibor Dömötör of the Free Hungarian Reformed Church since 1986.

Contact: Elizabeth Schmidt, Managing Editor.
Address: 2637 Copley Road, Akron, Ohio 44321.
Telephone: (216) 666-2637.
Fax: (216) 666-4746.

Amerikai Magyar Szó (American Hungarian Word).
Founded in 1952 as a successor to several earlier socialist newspapers, this is a leftist Hungarian weekly.

Contact: N. Petervary, Editor
Address: 130 East 16th Street, New York, New York 10003.
Telephone: (212) 254-0397.
Fax: (212) 254-1584

Californiai Magyarság (California Hungarians).
Founded in 1924 as a middle-of-the-road regional newspaper, it is now a national paper that has retained its moderate stance.

Contact: Mária Fényes, Editor and Publisher.

Address: 207 South Western Avenue, Suite 201, Los Angeles, California 90004.
Telephone: (213) 463-3473.
Fax: (213) 384-7642.

Hungarian Insights.
A quarterly publication that provides news and information on Hungarian culture, history, and business.

Contact: Lel Somogyi, Editor.
Address: 6020 Pearl Road, Cleveland, Ohio 44130.
Telephone: (216) 842-4651.

Hungarian Studies Newsletter.
Quarterly publication of the American Hungarian Foundation; publishes news of the Foundation as well as information for English-speaking scholars concerned with Hungarian studies.

Contact: August J. Molnar, Editor.
Address: American Hungarian Foundation, P.O. Box 1084, New Brunswick, New Jersey 08903.
Telephone: (201) 846-5777.

Magyar Elet (Hungarian Life).
An independent weekly newspaper published in Hungarian and circulated throughout Canada and the United States.

Contact: Laszlo Schnee, Editor.
Address: 21 Vaughan Road, Suite 201, Toronto, Ontario, Canada M6G 2N2.
Telephone: (416) 652-6370.
Fax: (416) 652-6370.

Magyarok Vasárnapja (Hungarians' Sunday).
Founded in Cleveland in 1894, for its first hundred years this paper was called *Katolikus Magyarok Vasárnapja (Catholic Hungarians' Sunday)*. Since the change in ownership in 1993, it has lost its religious character and has become the voice of populist nationalism.

Contact: Loránt Szász, Editor and Publisher.
Address: P.O. Box 4442, Thousand Oaks, California 91359.
Telephone: (818) 707-1548.
Fax: (818) 597-9867.

Szabadság (Liberty).
Published for the East Coast readership under the title *Amerikai Magyar Népszava (American Hungarian People's Voice)*, the two papers, which were founded in 1891 and 1899 respectively, were once rivals, but after the owner-editor of *Szabadság*

bought its rival in 1949, they were gradually merged into a single paper under two different titles.

Contact: Eva Nadai, Editor; or, Judith Fliegler, English Editor.

Address: 8140 Mayfield Road, Cleveland, Ohio 44026-2441.

Telephone: (216) 729-7200.

Fax: (216) 729-7250.

Új Világ (New World).

Founded in 1971, this paper was a neutral middle-of-the-road weekly until the early 1990s, when it became the voice of the right wing.

Contact: Viktor K. Molnár, Editor and Publisher.

Address: 15005 South Vermont Avenue, Gardena, California 90247.

Telephone: (310) 719-1078.

Fax: (310) 719-8918.

William Penn Life.

Founded in 1965 to replace an earlier Hungarian-language version, *Vehovayak Lapj* (*Verhovay News*), it is a small English-language monthly geared toward the William Penn Association, the largest Hungarian fraternal organization in America. Its influence is limited to its membership, which is made up largely of third- and fourth-generation descendants of the turn-of-the-century economic immigrants.

Contact: Elmer E. Vargo, Editor.

Address: William Penn Association, 709 Brighton Road, Pittsburgh, Pennsylvania 15233-1821.

Telephone: (412) 231-2979.

Fax: (412) 231-8535.

TELEVISION

The Nationality Broadcasting Network

Located in Cleveland, this network broadcasts Hungarian programs everyday via satellite throughout North America.

Contact: Miklós Kossányi, President.

Address: 11906 Madison Avenue, Cleveland, Ohio.

Telephone: (216) 221-0330.

Fax: (216) 221-3638.

ORGANIZATIONS AND ASSOCIATIONS

American Hungarian Federation (AHF) (Amerikai Magyar Szövetség [AMSZ]).

Founded in Cleveland in 1906, the AHF is the oldest umbrella organization of Hungarian Americans.

After being based in Washington, D.C. from the 1940s to the 1970s, in the early 1980s it transferred its office to Akron. Following an internal controversy that resulted in the formation of the rival National Federation of American Hungarians in 1984, the AHF is now the second-largest Hungarian American umbrella organization, with about 55 member organizations. Like its rival organizations, it conducts lobbying activities on behalf of Hungarian causes.

Contact: Rev. Tibor Dömötör, President.

Address: 2631 Copley Road, Akron, Ohio 44321.

Telephone: (330) 666-1313.

Fax: (330) 666-2637.

American Hungarian Folklore Centrum (AHFC).

Supports and promotes Hungarian studies and folk culture within the scholarly and public life of America.

Contact: Kalman Magyar, Director.

Address: P.O. Box 262, Bogota, New Jersey 07603.

Telephone: (201) 836-4869.

Fax: (201) 836-1590.

E-mail: magyar@magyar.org.

Online: http://www.magyar.org.

American Hungarian Reformed Federation (AHRF) (Amerikai Magyar Református Egyesület [AMRE]).

Founded in 1898, the AHRF is the second-largest and only religiously based Hungarian fraternal association in existence. It has about 20,000 members, and although it is now primarily an insurance company, it continues to support Hungarian cultural activities and also engages in some lobbying efforts on behalf of Hungarian causes.

Contact: George Dózsa, President.

Address: 2001 Massachusetts Avenue, N.W., Washington, D.C., 20036-1011.

Telephone: (202) 328-2630.

Fax: (202) 228-7984.

Hungarian American Coalition (HAC) (Magyar-Amerikai Koalíció [MAK]).

Founded in 1992, the HAC is the most recent of the Hungarian umbrella organizations. Politically, it has a moderate-centrist, pragmatic orientation. It attempts to carry out an effective lobbying effort on behalf of Hungarian causes in Washington, D.C.

Contact: Edith Lauer, President.

Address: Suite 850, 818 Connecticut Avenue, N.W., Washington, D.C., 20006.

Hungarian Association of Cleveland (Clevelandi Magyar Társaság).

Founded in 1958 in Austria and transferred to Cleveland in 1952, the Hungarian Association has been the most influential organization of the post-World War II immigrants, or DPs. Since 1961 it has organized annual congresses (the proceedings of which are published in its yearbook *Krónika*). In 1965 it sponsored the foundation of the Árpád Academy (*Árpád Akadémia*) to recognize the scholarly, scientific, and artistic achievements of Hungarians throughout the world. In 1990 it was responsible for the establishment of one of the rival umbrella organizations of the American Hungarian Federation, the National Federation of Hungarian Americans (NFHA) (Magyar Amerikaiak Országos Szövetsége [MAOSZ]). The Hungarian Association of Cleveland and its member organizations are ideologically conservative, representing essentially the views of interwar Hungary. The HAC functions and publishes primarily in Hungarian.

Contact: Gyula Nádas, President.
Address: 1450 Grace Avenue, Cleveland, Ohio 44107.
Telephone: (216) 226-4089.

Hungarian Cultural Foundation (HCF).

Interested in preserving Hungarian cultural heritage in the United States and elsewhere in the English-speaking world.

Contact: Joseph Ertavy-Barath, President.
Address: P.O. Box 364, Stone Mountain, Georgia 30086.
Telephone: (404) 377-2600.

Hungarian Scout Association in Exile (HSAE) (Külföldi Magyar Cserkészszövetség).

Founded in 1947 in Germany and transferred to the United States in 1951, the HSAE is a worldwide organization, with well over a hundred scout troops, whose goal is to uphold the traditions of Hungarian scouting in the Hungarian language.

Contact: Gábor Bodnár, President.
Address: Post Office Box 68, Garfield, New Jersey 07026.
Telephone: (973) 772-8810.
Fax: (973) 772-5145.

National Federation of Hungarian Americans (NFAH) (Amerikai Magyarok Országos Szövetség).

Founded in 1984, as a splinter group of the much older American-Hungarian Federation, the NFAH has since grown into the largest umbrella organization of Hungarian Americans, with more than one hundred institutional members. Its primary function is to serve as a lobby group for Hungarian and Hungarian American causes in Washington, D.C., and to aid Hungary's transformation toward democracy.

Contact: László Pásztor, National President.
Address: 717 Second Street, N.E., Washington, D.C., 20002.
Telephone: (202) 546-3003.
Fax: (202) 543-8425; or, (202) 547-0392.

William Penn Association (WPA).

Founded in 1886, as the Verhovay Aid Association, the WPA is the largest Hungarian fraternal association in North America. It assumed its present name in 1955, when it absorbed its largest rival, the Rákóczi Federation of Bridgeport, Connecticut. Although primarily an insurance company, the WPA still sponsors certain Hungarian cultural functions. Recently, the WPA has transferred much of its archives and library to the Hungarian Heritage Center of New Brunswick, New Jersey.

Contact: Elmer E. Vargo, National President.
Address: 709 Brighton Road, Pittsburgh, Pennsylvania 15233-1821.
Telephone: (412) 231-2979.
Fax: (412) 231-8538.

MUSEUMS AND RESEARCH CENTERS

American-Hungarian Foundation (AHF), Hungarian Heritage Center.

Founded in 1955, the AHF has grown into a major Hungarian cultural foundation that operates the Hungarian Heritage Center in New Brunswick, New Jersey. In addition to its museum and visitors' center, the Hungarian Heritage Center possesses one of the largest collections of archival materials relating to Hungarian Americans, as well as one of the largest Hungarica libraries in the United States (40,000 volumes). The library is by far the best source of material on the Hungarian American past.

Contact: August J. Molnar, President.
Address: 300 Somerset Street, New Brunswick, New Jersey 08903-1084.
Telephone: (908) 846-5777.
Fax: (908) 249-7033.

Hungarian Chair, Department of Uralic and Altaic Studies, Indiana University.

Founded in 1979 within the confines of an internationally known Department of Uralic and Altaic Studies that developed during the 1950s, the Hungarian Chair is in charge of the only Ph.D.-oriented Hungarian Studies program in North America. It draws heavily on the expertise of the other members of the department, as well as on Indiana University's multidisciplinary Russian and East European Institute and its strong library collection in Hungarian (25,000 volumes) and Russian and East European (200,000 volumes) material. It is in charge of organizing several conferences every year, as well as publishing books and periodicals in the field of Hungarian studies. The only other Hungarian chair in North America is at the University of Toronto and publishes the *Hungarian Studies Review*.

Contact: Hungarian Chair Professor.
Address: Department of Uralic and Altaic Studies, Indiana University, Bloomington, Indiana 47405-2401.
Telephone: (812) 855-2223.
Fax: (812) 855-7500.

Hungarian Institute, Rutgers University.
Founded in 1992 with the financial support of the Hungarian government, the Hungarian Institute is in an early stage of development and at the moment is involved only in undergraduate education. It draws heavily on the intellectual and library resources of Rutgers University (Hungarica, 2,000 volumes), as well as on the library of the nearby American-Hungarian Foundation (Hungarica, 40,000 volumes).

Address: Rutgers University, New Brunswick, New Jersey 08903-5049.
Telephone: (908) 932-1367.
Fax: (908) 932-6723.

Institute of Hungarian Studies.
Integral unit of Indiana University Bloomington. Hungarian society and civilization, including contemporary economic and cultural affairs.

Address: Goodbody 233, Bloomington, Indiana 47405.
Contact: Gustav Bayerle, Director.
Telephone: (812) 855-2233.
Online: http://www.indiana.edu/~rugs/ctrdir/ihs.html.

Hungarian Reformed Federation Library and Archives, Bethlen Home.
The Bethlen Home is the center of American Hungarian Calvinism. Located about 50 miles east of Pittsburgh, it houses an Old Age Home and the Archives of the Hungarian Reformed Church, including the papers of all dissolved congregations. The Bethlen Home also has a significant library of Hungarian American materials. The annual meetings of the Hungarian Reformed Federation (founded in 1898 and based in Washington, D.C.) also take place there, with the representatives of all Reformed congregations, irrespective of their current affiliations, in attendance.

Contact: The Reverend Paul Kovács, Director.
Address: P.O. Box 657, Ligonier, Pennsylvania 15658.
Telephone: (412) 238-6711.
Fax: (412) 238-3175.

Several North American libraries have strong Hungarica collections, the most noteworthy of which are: the Library of Congress (60,000 volumes); Columbia University (50,000 volumes); Indiana University (25,000 volumes); University of Chicago (25,000 volumes, including the newly acquired Szathmáry Library and Archives); Harvard University (20,000 volumes); Stanford University and the Hoover Institution (20,000 volumes); New York Public Library (20,000 volumes); University of Illinois (15,000 volumes); University of Toronto (10,000 volumes); Yale University (10,000 volumes); and at least another half dozen libraries with collections of between 5,000 and 10,000 volumes (Berkeley, Cornell, Duke, Notre Dame, UCLA, University of Washington).

SOURCES FOR ADDITIONAL STUDY

Lengyel, Emil. *Americans from Hungary*. Philadelphia and New York: J. B. Lippincott, 1948; reprinted, Westport, Connecticut: Greenwood, 1974.

McGuire, James Patrick. *The Hungarian Texans*. San Antonio: University of Texas, Institute of Texan Culture, 1993.

Papp, Susan M. *Hungarian Americans and Their Communities in Cleveland*. Cleveland: Cleveland Ethnic Heritage Studies, Cleveland State University, 1981.

Puskás, Julianna. *From Hungary to the United States, 1880-1914*. Budapest: Akadémiai Kiadó, 1982.

Tezla, Albert. *The Hazardous Quest: Hungarian Immigrants in the United States, 1895-1920*. Budapest: Corvina, 1993.

Várdy, Steven Béla. *Clio's Art in Hungary and in Hungarian-America.* New York: Columbia University Press, 1985.

———. *The Hungarian-Americans.* Boston: Twayne, 1985.

———. *The Hungarian Americans: The Hungarian Experience in North America.* New York and Philadelphia: Chelsea House, 1990.

Várdy, Steven Béla, and Agnes Huszár Várdy. *The Austro-Hungarian Mind: At Home and Abroad.* New York: Columbia University Press, 1989.

Iceland's language, customs, and historical background link it ethnically to Scandinavia, although Icelanders have always perceived themselves as having a distinct culture.

ICELANDIC AMERICANS

by
Lolly Ockerstrom

OVERVIEW

Iceland is the most westerly nation of Europe, the least populated, and was the last to be settled. A volcanic island, it touches the Arctic circle with its northernmost edge. Located between Greenland and Norway, the Gulf Stream brings mild temperatures to Iceland's otherwise inhospitable climate. Of its 103,000 square kilometers, only 1,000 are cultivated, with glaciers and lava taking up 23,000 square kilometers. It is often referred to as "the Land of Fire and Ice" because of its glaciers and volcanoes. In 1993, 264,000 persons lived in Iceland, residing mainly in towns located on its 5,000 kilometer coastline. The capitol city is Reykjavik, where almost half of the total population lives.

Iceland's fishing industry provides more than 70 percent of Icelandic exports. Aluminum accounts for about 11 percent. Ninety-three percent of Icelanders belong to the Lutheran Church of Iceland. The national language is Icelandic, a northern Germanic language with some resemblance to Middle English. It has changed very little since it was brought to Iceland by the first Icelandic settlers in the twelfth century. Iceland's *Althingi*, or parliament, was established in the year 930 A.D. It is believed to be the oldest national assembly in the world. Iceland has one of the highest standards of living in Europe, with an especially high quality of housing. Education, including university, is provided free for all of its citizens, as are health care and retirement pensions. Its rich literary heritage dates to the thirteenth century Icelandic Sagas of Snorri Sturluson, which are among the world's classics. Iceland's monetary unit is the Icelandic crown, or *kroner* (ISK).

HISTORY

The earliest account of settlers on Iceland was written in the year 825 A.D. by the Irish monk Dicuil. He recorded first-hand accounts of Irish people who lived on the island of Thule, which became known as Iceland. Sometime between 850 and 875, a Swede named Gardar Svavarsson is thought to have arrived on the island, and his arrival was followed by an influx of pagan Norse during the period of 874-930. The first man to settle in Iceland was Ingolfur Arnarson. According to the *Landnamabok*, or Book of Settlements, written in the twelfth century, Arnarson was a chieftain from Norway. Bringing his family and dependents to Iceland, he built a farm in what eventually became the capitol city of Reykjavik. Like many of the first settlers to Iceland, Arnarson had fled Norway to avoid oppression under the tyrannical ruler, Harald the Fairheaded. Harald was attempting to unify the country by conquering all other lords and kings of Norway. Many of the early settlers of this period were seafarers, including Erik the Red (Eirikur Rauthi), who discovered Greenland. In the year 1000 A.D., his son, Leif Eriksson became the first person to travel to North America, predating Columbus by 500 years.

In the year 930 A.D., Iceland's central parliament, the *Althingi* was established, along with a constitutional law code. It is considered to be the oldest parliament in the world. In the tenth century, small numbers of Irish and Scots settled on Iceland, bringing Christianity with them. Christianity was adopted by the parliament in the year 1,000, about 100 years after it made its way to mainland Scandinavia. Bishoprics, or dioceses, were quickly established in the towns of Skalholt in 1056 and Holar in 1106. Both places became centers of learning, typical of medieval universities throughout Europe which were established for training clerics.

Feuds and civil war came to Iceland between 1262 and 1264, and by 1397, Iceland was under the dominion of Denmark. Danish kings took control over the church, forcing Icelanders to abandon Catholicism for Danish Lutheranism. The Danes also established a trade monopoly, devastating the Icelandic economy. By 1662, Denmark had taken total control of Iceland. In 1800 the *Althingi* was dissolved completely.

Famines, natural disasters, and disease decimated the population during the eighteenth century. The first census in 1703 revealed a population of 50,000. It plunged to a low of 35,000 following a smallpox epidemic between 1707 and 1709. Iceland was further plagued with a series of famines and natural disasters until the end of the century, keeping the population below 40,000. By 1800, the population measured half of what it had been in the year 1100.

MODERN ERA

Iceland began to move toward a national identity during the nineteenth century. The National Library of Iceland was established in 1818, followed by the Icelandic National Museum in 1863 and the National Archives in 1882. In 1843, the *Althingi* was reestablished as a consultative assembly. Statesman and Scholar Jon Sigurdsson began to lead the political struggle for national independence, which continued after his death in 1879. By 1904, Iceland acquired home rule, and Hannes Hafstein was appointed as the first Icelandic government minister. In 1918, Iceland gained complete control of almost all its domestic affairs, although the Danish king remained the head of state. In 1940, Iceland was occupied by British forces, and a year later, the United States took over the defense of the North Atlantic island. On June 17, 1944, following a national referendum, the modern Republic of Iceland was established with a 97 per cent voter approval.

Following its independence, the newly formed republic quickly joined four important international organizations, beginning with the United Nations in 1946. In 1947, it became a founding member of what became known as the Organization for Economic Cooperation and Development, or the OECD. It also became a founding member of the North Atlantic Treaty Organization (NATO), in 1949. In 1950, it joined the Council of Europe. In the same year, Iceland turned its attentions homeward and established a National Theatre and Symphony Orchestra.

Iceland's strategic location in the North Atlantic made the country attractive to western allies. In 1951 a defense agreement was established between Iceland and the United States. This was the beginning of the Iceland Defense Force, based at Keflavik. Throughout the second half of the twentieth century, Iceland continued to strengthen its position in Europe, joining the Nordic Council in 1952.

In 1973, the Heimaey volcano erupted on the only inhabited island in the Westmann Islands. A year after this disaster, Iceland marked the 1,100th

anniversary of the settlement of Iceland at Thingvellir. In 1986, Reykjavik celebrated its bicentennial and hosted the Reagan-Gorbachev Summit.

During the 1950s, Iceland concentrated on strengthening its fishing industry. Fishery limits were extended to four miles in 1952, and expanded in 1954 to 12 miles. Fishing limits were extended further in 1972 to 50 miles, reaching 200 miles by 1974. Denmark returned ancient Icelandic manuscripts to Iceland in 1971, a final gesture of restoration to Icelandic culture. In 1994 Icelanders celebrated the fiftieth anniversary of the modern Icelandic Republic.

THE FIRST IN AMERICA

The first Icelandic settlers in North America arrived in Utah in 1855 seeking religious freedom to follow Mormonism. Eleven Mormon converts left Iceland for North America between 1854 and 1857. A few years later nine Icelanders settled in the town of Spanish Fork, Utah, along with other Scandinavians. For the next 20 years, small groups of Icelanders joined the settlement from time to time. Thorarinn Haflidason Thorason and Gudmund Gudmundsson, Icelandic apprentices who had converted to Mormonism in Denmark and travelled to America in the 1850s, were typical of Icelandic emigrants coming to Utah. Skilled artisans, tradespersons, or farmers, the Icelandic emigrants brought with them useful skills for the frontier, although it was some time before they could use those skills in gainful employment.

The United States suffered an economic depression in the mid-1870s, and jobs were scarce. For newly arrived Icelanders who knew little, if any English, jobs were even more scarce. The secondary education most Icelanders had received in their homeland did little to help them find jobs in their new country. Many Icelandic men took laboring jobs as unskilled factory workers and woodcutters, or as dockworkers in Milwaukee when they first arrived. Working to build capital and to learn farming techniques suitable for their new land so that they could start farms of their own, early Icelandic immigrant communities were largely agricultural. Drawing from their backgrounds in farming, the new immigrants maintained their ties to their Icelandic heritage.

SIGNIFICANT IMMIGRATION WAVES

The last three decades of the nineteenth century saw the largest wave of Icelandic immigration. Between 1870 and 1900, about 15,000 of Iceland's population of 75,000 resettled in North America. The majority of these emigrants settled in Winnipeg, Manitoba, Canada, in a colony called New Iceland. Those coming to the United States settled primarily in the upper Midwest, especially Wisconsin, Minnesota, and the Dakota Territories. A sizable Icelandic immigrant community was established in Utah. William Wickmann, a Danish emigrant who had worked for a time in Eyrarbakki on the southern coast of Iceland before coming to Milwaukee in 1856, wrote letters to Iceland describing his new home. His descriptions of the plentiful life in Wisconsin were circulated among his Icelandic friends.

In particular, Wickmann's accounts of the abundance of coffee, of which Icelanders were especially fond, proved irresistible to his friends. In 1870 four Icelanders left for Milwaukee, eventually settling on Washington Island in Lake Michigan, just off the Green Bay peninsula. Others settled in Minnesota.

In 1874 a group of Icelandic immigrants proposed a settlement in Alaska, which they felt would provide a climate and terrain similar to that of Iceland. They managed to interest the United States government enough to assist them in visiting the proposed Alaskan site. Although the Icelanders wanted to follow through with the plan, the United States apparently lost interest in the project, and plans for a new colony were abandoned.

By 1878, over a hundred Icelanders from the Canadian colony, New Iceland, were forced to relocate because of severe weather conditions, outbreaks of smallpox, and religious disputes. Moving south to the United States, they joined more recent Icelandic immigrants in the northeastern section of the Dakota Territory. With the help of more established Norwegian and German immigrant groups, they formed what later became the largest Icelandic community in America. Mostly farmers and laborers, second and third generation Icelanders were drawn into journalism. Many entered politics.

By 1900, new immigration from Iceland had almost completely ceased. It is estimated that about 5,000 Icelanders had taken up residency in the United States by 1910. The exact number is difficult to determine, since until 1930, the United States census, unlike the Canadian census, did not differentiate between Icelanders and Danes. In 1910, however, the census reported that 5,105 U.S. residents had grown up in a home where Icelandic was spoken. Not until after the end of the World War II did Icelanders again immigrate the United States in any substantial numbers. This post-World War II immigration wave was made up almost entirely of war brides of American servicemen stationed in Iceland.

By the late twentieth century, Americans of Icelandic descent showed great interest in tracing their ancestors. Early Icelandic settlements in Winnipeg, Canada, and Utah attracted the greatest amount of interest among amateur genealogists of Icelandic heritage. In the late twentieth century several web sites appeared offering help with tracing Icelandic ancestors.

SETTLEMENT PATTERNS

Settlement patterns during the second half of the nineteenth century placed Icelanders mainly in the upper Midwestern states of Minnesota and Wisconsin, and in the Dakota Territory. However, by the end of the twentieth century, settlement patterns had shifted from rural to urban communities. Early twentieth century industrialization transformed the United States from an agrarian culture into an urban one, affecting traditionally agrarian-based Icelandic communities. By 1970 over half of the second and third generations of Icelandic immigrants had taken up residence in urban areas.

The 1990 Census of the U.S. Department of Commerce revealed a total count of Icelandic-Americans and Icelandic nationals living in the United States as 40,529. Two-thirds of those lived in the West and the Midwest, with 19,891 in the West and 10,904 in the Midwest. Almost 6,000 lived in the South, while 4,140 resided in the Northeast. California, Washington state, and Minnesota were the most heavily populated with Icelanders and Icelandic-Americans. North Dakota was home to the fourth-largest number of persons with Icelandic backgrounds.

ACCULTURATION AND ASSIMILATION

Iceland's language, customs, and historical background link it ethnically to Scandinavia, although Icelanders have always perceived themselves as having a distinct culture. These distinctions have seldom been clear to non-Icelanders, who have collapsed Icelandic culture into Danish, Swedish, or Norwegian cultures. Icelanders were not even accounted for as a separate category by the U.S. census until 1930. Few studies in English have concentrated on Icelanders, and many reference books have omitted them altogether from general accounts of ethnic distinctions such as holidays, customs, and dress. Nonetheless, strong in their self-identity, Icelanders have from the beginning eagerly adopted new customs in the United States, learning English, holding public office, and integrating into the general culture. At the same time, they have retained a strong sense of ethnic pride, as evidenced in the large number of Icelandic-American organizations in existence throughout the United States since the founding of the Icelandic National League in 1919. Toward the end of the twentieth century, widespread attention to multiculturalism kindled interest in understanding ethnic differences, spurring many Icelanders to reclaim their heritage.

TRADITIONS, CUSTOMS, AND BELIEFS

Icelandic Americans continued to celebrate Icelandic holidays well after they and their families settled into Americanized routines. Early immigrants celebrated August 2, 1874, a date significant on two counts: it marked the millennium of Iceland's first settlement, and the date on which the Danish king granted autonomy to Iceland. By the middle part of the twentieth century, Icelandic Independence Day, June 17, 1944, became the major holiday celebrated by immigrant Icelanders.

As with other Scandinavian countries, Icelanders take great delight in stories of trolls, elves, and fairies. Fairies and elves are thought to exist everywhere, beneath rocks and mushrooms. Although most Icelanders never report actually seeing the fairies and trolls, the presence of such creatures is not denied. Often good luck is attributed to the work of elves. In contrast, prior to the twentieth century, trolls were always associated with danger.. For centuries, the myth of Gryla, a troll who was thought to live in the mountains and to appear in

"[A]round here we're all Icelanders or Norwegians. It's like a little Scandinavian town. I didn't even have to talk English the first few years I was here. Not till I started working in the lumber camps.

Gunner Johanson, cited in *American Mosaic: The Immigrant Experience in the Words of Those Who Lived It,* Joan Morrison and Charlotte Fox Zabusky (E.P. Dutton, New York, 1980).

the lowlands at Christmas, was a staple of holiday lore. Icelandic immigrants handed down the story to younger generations, and the myth continued to play an important role in Christmas festivities in their new land. Although the actual character of the main troll, Gryla, changed over the centuries since her first appearance in Icelandic literature in the ninth century, she lives on in Icelandic folklore. Hjorleifur Rafn Jonsson argues in an article in *Nord Nytt* that the myth changed from period to period according to social and economic developments in Icelandic culture. Like the immigrants themselves, who brought the myth with them to North America, the character of Gryla changed through the generations but remained rooted in Icelandic culture.

PROVERBS

Proverbs are common among Icelanders; they are fond of saying that "sometimes we speak only in proverbs." One typical Icelandic saying is "Even though you are small, you can be clever," which speaks to the Icelandic sense of the value of the individual. Another saying,"It is difficult to teach a dog

to sit," is a typical response to a request to change, similar to the English saying, "You can't teach an old dog new tricks." Used in promoting an Icelandic festival in North Dakota was the slogan, "What is as joyful as a gathering of friends?" written in Icelandic as "Hvad er svo glatt sem godra vina fundur?"

CUISINE

Typical Icelandic fare includes fish, lamb, and dark breads. The many variations of basic recipes suggest regional, as well as individual, differences. Each family treasures its own recipes, and each claims that its mother and grandmother produced the finest version. Women, rather than men, traditionally have done the cooking. Icelandic Americans bring many of these traditional foods to summer festivals and Christmas feasts. Among these foods are *vinarterta,* a layered cake made with cardamom, cinnamon and ground, boiled prunes and served with whipped cream. Icelandic brown bread, made with molasses and wheat germ differs from Icelandic black bread, which contains rye. Both are staples in the Icelandic diet. Iceland pancakes, or *ponnukokur,* are similar to the flat, crepe-like Swedish pancakes. They are unsweetened and served with meat fillings. A *flatbroud,* or rye pancake, is another traditional food.

Dried fish, or *hardfiskur;* blood pudding, or *slatur;* and smoked lamb, or *hangikjot* , are all traditional foods associated with the autumn slaughtering season and the limited methods for preserving meat in earlier times. Pastries include *kleinur,* or Icelandic donuts, made of sour cream, buttermilk, vanilla and nutmeg. *Astarbollur,* or raisin donut balls, are rolled in granulated sugar and cinnamon. Icelandic fruit cake is served at Christmas, and eating it is perceived as a special holiday ritual.

Popular in Iceland during the latter part of the twentieth century were *pylsa,* Icelandic hot dogs. Similar to American hot dogs, although longer and skinnier, they are eaten in Iceland with ketchup, onions, and mustard. In addition, Icelanders insist on a topping called *remoladi. Brennivin* is the Icelandic national drink. It is a schnapps, without flavor, with the consistency of syrup. Often drunk with herring or shark, it is consumed in small quantities in much the same way as the Danish drink, *Aqvavit.*

MUSIC

Choral singing is among the most popular arts of Iceland. It was cultivated on the American frontier in all areas of life—religious, social, and domestic. Particularly at Christmas, Icelanders participated in choirs and bands. Iceland's most prominent musical

genre is the *rimur*, an epic song form. The form dates from the thirteenth century. Because the Icelandic language has changed little since that time, some of the oldest songs are still performed and enjoyed by Icelanders in their original form. Iceland's National Hymn, written by Matthias Jochumsson (1835-1920), is sung at the opening of state and national events.

TRADITIONAL COSTUMES

Traditional Icelandic women's costumes include several distinct garments, usually of fine material which has been embroidered. A sweater suit, or *peysufot*, was used for everyday wear well into the twentieth century, particularly in the countryside. More formal wear included a headdress, or *faldbuningur*, which was used from the late eighteenth century until about 1860. The name comes from the Icelandic word for headdress, *faldur*. The *faldur* is a white scarf-like head piece which covered the hair. It was fastened with a scarf or scarves wrapped around the head. Other elements of the headdress included a *skotthufa*, or tail cap. The tail was made

of numerous small strands of material. Just below the top of the tail was a sleeve, richly ornamented in gold or silver threads.

An ornamental vest was worn on special days. Called the *upphlutur*, or upper part, the vest was abundantly embroidered with gold thread. It was worn with a skirt and apron, both of which were sewn of very good material. While some dresses were worn only for certain festivities, other costumes were worn on Sundays and for travelling.

Special dresses and headgear were worn for confirmation in the Lutheran Church. Children were confirmed at the age of 14. The headdress worn by young girls was called *skautbuningur*, a small white cap with a veil trailing down the back. A golden coronet was positioned at the forehead. Like the cap, the dress of the young girl to be confirmed was also white. Its traditional style was called *Kyrtill*. Older women wore a black skirt with a bodice embroidered in silver thread. The skirt was appliqued with velvet. Both younger and older women wore a special belt. The belt for the older woman was embroidered with a buckle of filigree; the belt of the young girl was completely handmade of filigree. Confirmation marked one's transition into adulthood, which included wearing adult attire. In writing of her confirmation day, Holmforidur Arnadottir exclaimed in her autobiography, "How grand, that from that day I should be dressed as the grown-up women!"

DANCES AND SONGS

Icelanders are fond of music and poetry. Iceland's National Hymn, written by Matthias Jochumsson, expresses a national sentiment of submission to God. The song celebrates "Our Country's God" and "Iceland's thousand years." The final lines defer to a deity that can offer guidance: "O, prosper our people, diminish our tears/And guide, in Thy wisdom, through life!" Jochumsson, a clergyman, was also a journalist, dramatist, and Iceland's national poet. Included among his other work are translations into Icelandic of Shakespearean tragedies.

Christmas and New Year's holidays are marked by much singing and dancing around bonfires. Some celebrants dress up as elves. As Holmfridur Arnadottir described Twelfth Night dances in her autobiography, *When I Was a Girl in Iceland,* white and black fairies "with all kinds of head-dresses" come down from high cliffs carrying torches. A procession of celebrants parades to a bonfire, where the fairies sing and dance in a circle and also recite poetry. When the bonfire has burned out, all move to a dance hall, where they continue dancing.

HOLIDAYS

Iceland's holidays are typical of those celebrated in other western, Christian nations, though with a whimsical twist. The Christmas season lasts several days and is traditionally celebrated with bonfires, dancing, and stories of elves and trolls. On New Year's Eve, it was the custom to invite the elves into one's home. Lights, or candles, would be lit throughout the house in order to drive out the shadows. The mistress of the house would walk around the outside of the house three times, chanting an invitation to the elves to come, stay, or go. At least one light would remain burning throughout the night.

Also on New Year's Eve, the pantry window would be left open to receive the hoarfrost, the frozen dew that forms a white coating on surfaces. It does not accumulate, and it fades quickly. A pot would be placed on the pantry floor in an attempt to capture it, and the house mistress would remain in the pantry all night. In the morning a cross-tree would be placed over the pot to keep the hoarfrost in. Known as the "pantry drift," capturing it in this way was thought to bring prosperity to the household.

Twelfth Night, celebrated 12 days after Christmas on January 5, is often called the "Great Night of Dreams" in Iceland. This refers to the night when the Kings of the Orient are thought to have dreamed of the birth of Jesus. In some parts of Iceland, Twelfth Night was referred to as "The Old Christmas," or "The Old Christmas Eve." Twelfth Day is celebrated on January 6 with bonfires and dancing.

Lent is traditionally the six-week period before Easter Sunday in the Christian calendar, and it is observed in Iceland with festive games during the first three days of the holiday. Lenten, or Shrove, Monday is known in Icelandic as *Bolludagur,* or *Flengingardagur,* and means, respectively, the day of muffins or the day of whipping. It is also known as "Bun Day." This holiday is believed to have been transported to Iceland by Danish and Norwegian bakers who immigrated to Iceland in the late nineteenth century. The day begins with early risers "beating" those who are still in bed with small whips or wands made of colored paper by the children of the household. Those who are whipped provide the children with a bun or muffin. The whipping is done mainly by the children, and is done good naturedly. *Bolludagur* is usually a school holiday that allows for visiting friends and neighbors, and it is a day when muffins are served with coffee wherever one goes.

In earlier times, Tuesday was a day of meat-eating, a custom handed down from Iceland's Catholic days. A game called *ad sitja i fastunni,* or to sit in the fast, was played. It consisted of word play in which common terms for meat, drippings, or gravy were substituted with other words. Not all Icelanders played this game; sometimes only household servants did. Children tried to see if they could get through the entire day without being tricked into using the usual language for meats, even as they were trying to get others to slip into using the forbidden words.

Ash Wednesday, or *Oskudagur,* was celebrated by playing a game of ash bag teasing. It was directly related to the tradition of repentance. On the days prior to Ash Wednesday, women and girls made small bags into which ashes or small stones or pebbles were placed. Constructed with drawstrings, the bags were fastened to someone's back with pins. Bags containing ashes were intended for men and boys; bags with stones were intended for women and girls. It is thought that stones were selected because of the old punishment of tying bags of stones around the necks of adulterous women in order to drown them. The person was made to carry a bag on his or her back a certain distance, sometimes three steps or across three thresholds. In Reykjavik, children began to attach ash bags to the backs of adults, who often did not appreciate the joke. At times, as many as thirty bags might be attached to back of a person's clothing. A more recent variation of this game was to sew some symbol of love on the bag and leave it empty. The recipient then had to guess who had sent it. This was particularly popular around the early part of the twentieth century.

As in other Nordic countries, Icelanders view the First Day of Summer as the most significant holiday of the year with the exception of Christmas. As early as 1545, gifts were exchanged among family members on this holiday, and food played a prominent role in the festivities. Although food was scarce after the long winter, Icelanders saved all they could so they could serve their best food and drink during First Day of Summer festivals. Often the amount of food saved indicated the degree of wealth one had. In the western fjords, many Icelanders stored food in a special barrel during the autumn; this was not to be opened until the following summer.

Special summer-day cakes made of rye were served to each person. The large cakes measured one foot in diameter and were three-quarters of an inch thick. Each cake was topped with one day's portion of food, which included *hangiket*, or butter; *lundabaggar*, or flanks; hard fish, halibut fins, and the like. First Day of Summer celebrations included a domestic service in which special hymns were sung and a sermon was given. Later, children played such games as blindman's bluff. After a hard winter, Icelanders kept themselves out of doors for most of the day celebrating the coming of long days filled with sunlight. Prior to 1900, the First Day of Summer was a day to socialize among family and friends, eat, and mark the end of winter. Public performances gradually became more integrated into the holiday. Young people in particular began to give speeches and poetry readings. Sports, singing, and dancing became important activities, as well as plays and theatrical productions.

Two holidays are unique to Iceland: *Krossmessa*, or *Crossmas*; and St. Thorlak's Day. Although celebrated more in the nineteenth and early twentieth centuries than in the late twentieth century, *Krossmessa* was observed on May 14. It was the day when domestic servants moved. Servants were usually hired for a one-year period; many stayed with their employers for several years before moving on. St. Thorlak's Day is celebrated on December 23 to honor Thorlak Thorhalli, who became the Bishop of Skalholt in 1177. On this day, the Christmas *hangiket*, or smoked mutton is cooked, clothes are washed, and the house is cleaned. Throughout the western fjords, a hash of skate is cooked. With a smell similar to ammonia, the skate hash symbolized that the house had been cleaned and Christmas had arrived.

The 1960s brought the revival of another holiday specific to Iceland, an ancient pagan festival called the *Thorrablot*. It was originally observed in mid-winter, when sacrifices to the Norse god, Thorri, were made. The holiday predated Christian Iceland but died out when Christianity was adopted. It first regained popularity when revived in 1873 by some Icelandic students in Copenhagen, and again in 1881 by a group of archaeologists in Reykjavik, who toasted each other using Viking horns.

HEALTH ISSUES

The average life expectancy in Iceland is 80.9 years for women and 75.7 years for men. Icelanders are known to be in generally good physical health. There do not appear to be medical conditions specific to Icelandic Americans.

LANGUAGE

Icelandic is the national language of Iceland, although both English and Danish are understood and spoken by many Icelanders as well. There are no indigenous linguistic minorities in Iceland. Icelandic is a Germanic language and it is a member of the Scandinavian language family. It is thought to have changed very little in the 1,000 years since the first Nordic settlers arrived on Iceland. Many songs and epic poetry dating from the twelfth century are still read and appreciated in their original forms today by Icelandic speakers. The relative purity of the language is largely the result of Iceland's isolation as an island nation. Two letters of the Icelandic alphabet resemble Old English, the "þ," pronounced like the "th" in "thing," and "ð," pronounced like the "th" in "them." Icelandic pride in its language has resulted in legislation regulating the adoption of foreign names for public establishments. In 1959, a bill was passed in the *Althingi* barring the adoption of names not Icelandic in origin. Only one vote was cast in opposition to the bill.

GREETINGS AND POPULAR EXPRESSIONS

Typical Icelandic greetings and expressions, and their approximate pronunciations are *Góðan dag* (gothan dag)—good day; *gott kvöld* (goht kwvold)—good evening; *Komið pér saelie* (komith pearr sauleuh)—How do you do; *Hallo, hvaðer um að vera?* (Hallo, kwath aer uem ath verra)-Hi, what's going on?; *Hvað heitir þú?* (kwath hayterr peu)—What is your name?; *Ég heiti* (ag haete)—My name is...; *Sjáumst* (syoymst)-bye; *góða nótt* (gotha noht)—good night; *Gleður mig að kynnast þér* (glathur may ad kednast pear)—glad to meet you; *Já eða nei?* (Yaah aytha nay)—Yes or no?; *Ég skil ekki* (Ag skeel ahhki)—I don't understand; *Gleðileg jól* (glathelay yawl)—Merry Christmas; and *Gleðileg nýár* (glathelay nyarr)—Happy New Year.

FAMILY AND COMMUNITY DYNAMICS

The 1992 Icelandic census showed that families in Iceland generally consisted of three persons per family, presumably two parents and a child. This trend toward smaller family units mirrors those in other western nations. The sizes of Icelandic American families, like families of many other immigrant groups, reflect national and even international trends. Icelanders show strong familial and ethnic identification. Although perceived by non-Icelanders as serious and quiet, the people of Iceland and Icelandic Americans often show a sense of humor that includes joking at their own expense. They are the first to laugh at themselves.

EDUCATION

Education in Iceland was provided for all its citizens, and literacy among Icelanders has been universal since the end of the eighteenth century. Immigrant Icelanders in the Dakota Territory set up their first school district in 1881, and more districts soon followed. The value Icelanders placed on education on the American frontier had been instilled in them in their native land. School attendance in Iceland was made obligatory in 1907 for all children between the ages of ten and 14 years. Children younger than ten years of age were usually taught at home. In 1946, the age for compulsory attendance was extended, and by the 1990s, the age of compulsory attendance covered all children between the ages of 7 and 17 years.

A theological seminary, the first institution of higher learning in Iceland, was founded in 1847. A medical school followed in 1876 and a school of law in 1908. In 1911, all three merged and became the University of Iceland. Later a fourth division was added, the Faculty of Philosophy, which offered study in philology, history, and literature.

Among the household goods brought with them to America, Icelandic emigrants brought books. Many had books sent to them from Iceland once they were settled in their new homes. With an unbroken literary history dating from the thirteenth century, the new immigrants continued to cherish literary activity. New immigrant communities organized reading circles, and newspapers were quickly established in Icelandic communities. Until the middle part of the twentieth century Icelandic books continued to be published in the new land. Three presses publishing books in the Icelandic language were located in Winnipeg, Manitoba, in Canada, and one in Minnesota.

THE ROLE OF WOMEN

Iceland is largely egalitarian, with an economy more evenly distributed by gender when compared to many countries. Nonetheless, as in other industrialized countries, women earn significantly less money than their male counterparts, even when performing similar tasks. Well represented in the labor force, women are underrepresented on the faculty of the University of Iceland, and in leadership and management positions. Women often occupy the less prestigious and lower-paid positions in such industries as fish processing plants. Women in Iceland tend to remain employed outside the home following marriage.

The institution of marriage does not carry the same importance for Icelanders as it does for inhabitants of other cultures. One result is that motherhood outside of marriage has never carried a stigma for Icelandic women. Women in Iceland, moreover, do not change their names after marriage. The rate of births by unmarried mothers has varied from 13 percent in the nineteenth century to 36 percent in 1977. One result of single parenthood is that many women work fewer hours outside of the home than men. Coupled with the already lower pay scales for women, the fewer number of hours worked further limits single mothers' income levels.

During the 1980s, a national political party known as the Women's List succeeded in winning some parliamentary elections. In 1987, the Women's Party claimed six seats in the *Althingi*, or Parliament, and 10.1 percent of the total vote. In 1991, the Women's Party won five parliamentary seats with 8.3 percent of the vote.

BAPTISMS

Babies are christened according to the principles set down by the Lutheran Church of Iceland. The parents of the child choose godparents, and the baby is brought to the christening font, usually at the age of two or three months. A celebration follows. Christening gowns are treasured items, often handed down to other generations. Icelandic-Americans who remain in the Lutheran Church continue the practice as a form of a spiritual, as well as a community, expression of welcome to the new baby.

WEDDINGS

Icelandic weddings generally follow the forms set down by the Icelandic Lutheran Church, although Icelandic tradition of handing down family names is unique. Icelandic family names generally follow the ancient patriarchal tradition of taking the last name from the first name of the father. In other words, if a man's name is Leifur Eirikur, his last name, Eiriksson, indicates that he is the son of Eirik. The last name of Leifur's son would be Leifursson, or son of Leifur. Maria, the daughter of Hermann Jakobsson, would be called Maria Hermannsdottir. Following her marriage to Haraldur Jonsson, her name would not change, although her daughter Margret would be known as Margret Haraldursdottir. Family members living in the same household, therefore, do not share a common family name. Directories in Iceland are organized alphabetically by first names.

Legislation dating to 1925 regulates Icelandic names and preserves the Icelandic naming tradition. Members of the clergy are vested with veto power over names of infants. The Faculty of Arts at the University of Iceland serves as the court of appeal. A 1958 case brought before the Faculty by a German immigrant upheld the Icelandic tradition. When he became a citizen of Iceland, the man changed his name from the German Lorenz to the Icelandic Larus. When his son was born, he wanted his son to be known as Lorenz. When the pastor of his church refused to conduct the christening, the case went to the Faculty of Arts, which supported the minister.

INTERACTIONS WITH OTHER ETHNIC GROUPS

Because of the relatively small numbers of Icelanders in America, Icelandic immigrants interacted with those of other ethnic backgrounds. As a matter of survival, early immigrants were eager to learn from the experiences of other immigrants, particularly the Norwegians, with whom they felt a kinship. In areas inhabited by few other persons of Icelandic descent, Icelanders gladly worked with Norwegians, Swedes, Danes, and Finns to develop their communities. Although many Icelandic-American societies exist throughout the United States and Canada, many Icelanders join Scandinavian Clubs, which are broader in scope and include those with heritage from all the Scandinavian countries.

RELIGION

According to the Icelandic 1992 census report, 92.2 percent of Icelanders belonged to the Church of Iceland, the Evangelical Lutheran Church. Early Icelandic immigrants did not remain dogmatically Lutheran when they came to North America. They were happy to be relieved of the heavy tax burden imposed by the Icelandic Lutheran Church. However, churches continued to fill important social, spiritual, and community functions for Icelanders as they established settlements in their new land. Two early immigrants, Pall Thorlaksson and Jon Bjarnason, were leaders among Icelandic Lutherans in North America. Both trained in the ministry, but they represented different philosophies, and this led to a temporary split in the Icelandic-American Lutheran Church. In the 1880s, the Unitarian movement drew a number of Icelanders, but the competition only strengthened Lutheran commitment. The Icelandic Lutheran Synod was established in 1885. Some of the early Icelandic immigrants settling in Utah rejected Lutheranism altogether, instead seeking freedom to follow Mormonism.

EMPLOYMENT AND ECONOMIC TRADITIONS

Icelandic immigrants to North America brought with them skills and trades learned in Iceland, including agriculture and building. They were also skilled artisans. Fishing has always played a major role in sustaining the Icelandic economy. As an island economy with a short growing season, Iceland has always depended heavily on trade. Livestock production was among the most important industries, particularly during the period of Danish colonial rule of the late eighteenth and early nineteenth centuries. Fishing and hunting provided major additional support. Icelanders practiced cod-fishing for centuries, and it is believed that cod has been traded commercially since medieval times. Toward the end of the nineteenth century, as Danish rule weakened, fishing communities developed along the coasts as local economies based on foreign trade grew into place.

The economic base of modern Iceland lies in the fishing industry. Fish and fish products account for more than 70 percent of Iceland's exports. Icelandic fishing techniques, using the most up-to-date computer and other technologies, are among most innovative and advanced in the world. The waters around Iceland are rich fishing grounds. The Gulf Stream and cold nutrient currents of the Arctic meet at the continental shelf that surrounds Iceland. These conditions are favorable for many kinds of marine life. While Iceland exports fish and fish products, it imports almost all of its consumer items. Sheep and dairy cattle are the main livestock in Iceland; agricultural land is used mostly for growing grass to feed the livestock. Other exports include aluminum, which accounts for about 11 percent of the country's exports. Given Iceland's heritage in fishing, farming, and engineering, it is not surprising that many Icelandic Americans have often continued in such pursuits.

POLITICS AND GOVERNMENT

Iceland is an independent, democratic republic. It has a multi-party system with an elected president. The parliament, or *Althingi*, is a legislative body with 63 members who are elected by popular vote. They serve for terms of four years, as does the president. There is no term limit. Any eligible voter can run for a seat in the *Althingi*, except the President and the judges of the Supreme Court. The President chooses a cabinet following the election of a new parliament. Leaders of the political parties are called for discussions, and a cabinet is formed. Cabinet ministers remain in power until the next general election. All cabinet members are members of parliament.

The three largest political parties are the Independence Party, the Progressive Party, and the Social Democrats. Together, these parties represented 73 percent of the vote in the 1991 elections. The remaining 27 per cent of the vote was taken by the People's Alliance and the Women's Party, as well as the Citizens/Liberal Party and others.

As developed in the twentieth century, Iceland's political structure resembles the governments of western Europe, Great Britain, and the United States. Icelandic Americans adapted easily to the system of democracy as it is practiced in the United States. A number of Icelandic Americans have entered local and state politics. In North Dakota alone, three state attorneys general have been of Icelandic heritage, as well as three state supreme court judges and 12 state legislators.

MILITARY

Iceland entered into a defense agreement with the United States in 1951, and it does not maintain its own army or navy. The Icelandic Defense Force, located at the Keflavik base, is maintained by members from all branches of the U.S. Armed Forces, as well as military personnel from the

Netherlands, Norway, and Denmark. Icelandic civilians also work at the base. By the late 1990s, twenty-five different commands of various sizes were attached to the Icelandic Defense Force. The base published an online newsletter in the late 1990s called *The White Falconline* and also maintained a webpage.

RELATIONS WITH FORMER COUNTRY

Icelandic Americans take pride in their heritage, as Kate Bearnson Carter illustrated when she sponsored the building of a lighthouse monument in honor of the first Icelandic settlers in Spanish Fork, Utah. As the daughter of Icelanders, Carter wanted to commemorate her ethnic heritage and honor her parents. A three-day festival in Spanish Fork was observed in 1955 to to mark the centennial of Icelandic immigration. The two original Icelandic newspapers in North America, the *Logberg* and the *Heimskingla* merged in 1959 to become the *Logberg-Heimskringla*. The paper continues to be published in Winnipeg, Manitoba, Canada, more than 100 years after the founding of its parent publications. News from Iceland and Icelandic communities across North America are carried in the paper. Each issue of the weekly publication includes articles in both Icelandic and English.

Several important scholarly collections of Icelandic work attest to an active pride in Icelandic culture. The Willard Fiske collection is located at Cornell University in New York and is the largest. Important collections are also found at Brigham Young University in Utah, the University of Wisconsin, and the University of North Dakota.

In the 1990s, the New Iceland Heritage Museum was founded in Gimli, Manitoba, Canada with the mandate "to foster the preservation, understanding and appreciation of the Icelandic culture in North America." It was scheduled to open in the summer of the year 2000, to coincide with the 125th anniversary of the arrival of Icelandic immigrants in Manitoba.

INDIVIDUAL AND GROUP CONTRIBUTIONS

Although comprising far less than ten per cent of the population, Icelanders continue to contribute individually and collectively to American culture. There are a number of important Icelandic American artists, journalists, and literary figures. The Icelandic culture has also contributed to scientific and social service sectors in America.

ART

The abstract painter Nina Tryggvadottir came to New York from Iceland in 1942 to study with the premier painters of the period, Hans Hoffman and Fernand Leger. She had two major shows in New York, one in 1945 and one in 1948. Her work was reviewed favorably by critic Elaine de Kooning in the influential publication *Art News*. Tryggvadottir also designed scenery and costumes for a production of Stravinsky's *Soldier's Tale*, conducted in New York by Dmitri Mitropolous. Again her work received very favorable reviews. She developed friendships with two major artists of the time, Wilhelm de Kooning and Alexander Calder, and with critic Meyer Schapiro. By 1949, her painting style had matured and her future looked very promising. Her work had broad appeal to both Icelandic and American critics.

Tryggvadottir married the American art critic A.L. Copley, who also moved in New York art circles, and had intended to remain in the United States. However, she became blacklisted during the McCarthy era and was accused of being a Communist sympathizer. She was not allowed to return to the United States following a 1949 visit to her family in Iceland. It was not until December 1959 that she finally returned to New York. By then, the New York art world had lost touch with her work, which she had continued to develop while living in Paris and London. Despite her considerable artistic accomplishments, she never reclaimed her position as an abstractionist in the New York art world. Only one of her paintings, donated in 1961, is in the collection of the Museum of Modern Art in New York. She nonetheless made a name for herself as an Icelandic artist in America. She is best known for the nature abstractions she produced between 1957 and 1967.

Another successful Icelandic-American in the art world was Harvard Arnason, an art historian associated with the Guggenheim Museum during the 1940s. Charles Thorson also worked with Disney and Warner Brothers animation.

JOURNALISM

Jon Olafsson served as founding editor of the first Icelandic newspaper in North America, *Heimskringla*. The name comes from the work of medieval Icelandic writer, Snorri Sturleson. The word *heimer* in Icelandic means the world, and *kringla* means a globe. Started in September 1886 in Winnepeg, the paper was published completely in Icelandic except for some advertisements written wholly or partially in English. Other Icelandic-Americans known for their work in journalism include Stephan G. Stephanson, Kristjan Niels Julius, and Richard Beck.

LITERATURE

The ancient sagas of Snorri Sturluson are well-known among medieval literary scholars. Less well known is work written by immigrant Icelandic women. A Canadian scholar at the Department of Icelandic Studies at the University of Manitoba, Kirsten Wolf, was among the first to edit and translate writing by immigrant Icelanders. Referring to Icelandic communities of North America as "Western Iceland," Wolf edited a collection entitled *Writings by Western Icelandic Women* in 1997. The anthology revived long-forgotten pieces of writing by early Icelandic immigrant women, including Undina, a poet, and Laura Goodman Salverson, winner of the Governor General Award. The book covers 75 years of writing, from the first significant wave of Icelandic immigration in the 1870s to the 1950s. The collection includes short stories and poems, many of which were translated for the first time from the original Icelandic. Offering insight into the experiences of pioneer Icelandic writers, the text brings forth women's voices of the Icelandic immigrant experience, about which very little is known. Other literary figures of Icelandic descent are the Canadian poets Stephan Geir Stephansson and Guttormur Guttormsson.

SCIENCE AND TECHNOLOGY

Icelandic immigrants Vilhjalmur Stefansson, 1979-1962, became known for his Arctic explorations. Chester Hjortur Thordarson, 1867-1945, made a name as an inventor and entrepeneur in the electrical field.

SOCIAL ISSUES

Although little known, Icelandic immigrant Emily Long was one of the first qualified nurses on the Canadian prairies. She helped to found several Saskatchewan hospitals. Having trained as nurse in Iceland, she immigrated to Canada prior to 1910 to join relatives when her family in Iceland died of tuberculosis. In Neepawa, Manitoba, Long repeated her nurses' training. When World War I began in 1914, she went to England for the Canadian Red Cross. Before departing from England in 1919, she received honors for her wartime service from Queen Alexandra, the Queen Mother. Back in Canada, Long took a series of nursing positions before retiring to Gimli, Manitoba, in 1953. Before her death, she received honors from the Crown and the Canadian Legion for her service in the Red Cross during the First World War. Tireless and spirited, according to a brief memoir by Darrell Gudmundson, Emily

Long represents one of the many ways in which early Icelandic immigrants contributed to social welfare in her new land.

MEDIA

Islandica.
Annual publication begun in 1908. Irregular. Furnishes bibliographical information.

Address: Cornell University, Kroch Library, Willard J. Fiske Islandic Collection, Ithaca, New York 14853.
Telephone: (607) 255-3530.

ORGANIZATIONS AND ASSOCIATIONS

Embassy of the Republic of Iceland.
Contact: Jon Baldvin Hannibalsson, Ambassador.
Address: 1156 15th Street, N.W., Suite 1200, Washington, D.C. 20005.
Telephone: (202) 265-6653.
Fax: (202) 265-6656.

Icelandic American Chamber of Commerce (IALL).
Founded in 1986, the Icelandic American Chamber of Commerce has eighty members. The Board of Directors meets three or four times a year at a triennial conference. Individual dues are $60.00 a year; corporate annual dues are $200.00. It is a multinational organization and publishes a monthly newsletter.

Contact: Magnus Bjarnason, Executive Director.
Address: c/o Consulate General of Iceland 800 Third Avenue, 36th Floor, New York, New York 10022-7604.
Telephone: (212) 593-2700.
Fax: (212) 593-6269.

Icelandic-American Veterans.
Founded 1950.

Contact: Dave Zinkoff.
Address: 2101 Walnut Street, Philadelphia, Pennsylvania 19103.
Telephone: (215) 568-1234.

Icelandic National League of the United States, Inc.
Formed in 1919 for the purposes of promoting Icelandic culture, customs, and traditions.

Contact: Mr. Jon Sig. Gudmundsson, Sr.
Address: P.O. Box 265, LaGrange, KY 40031.
Telephone: (502) 222-1441.
Fax: (502) 222-1445.

MUSEUMS AND RESEARCH CENTERS

Fiske Icelandic Collection.
A division of the Rare Manuscript Collections in the Kroch Library at Cornell University. Holdings include books, journals, and other serial literature on Islandica with emphasis on Icelandic language, literature, and history.

Contact: Patrick Stevens.
Address: Ithaca, New York 14853.
Telephone: (607) 255-3530.

SOURCES FOR ADDITIONAL STUDY

Arnason, David, and Michael Olito. *The Icelanders.* Winnipeg, Manitoba: Turnstone Press, 1981.

Bjornson, Valdimar. "Icelanders in the United States." *Scandinavian Review* 64 (1976): 39-41.

Bjornsson, Arni. *Icelandic Feasts and Holidays: Celebrations, Past and Present.* Translated by May and Hallberg Hallmundson. Reykjavik: Iceland Review History Series, 1980.

Embassy of Iceland. Basic Statistics. Web site: http://www.iceland.org.

Gudjonsson, Elsa E. *The National Costume of Women in Iceland.* 3rd edition. Reykjavik, 1978.

Houser, George J. *Pioneer Icelandic Pastor: The Life of The Reverend Paul Thorlaksson,* edited by Paul A. Sigurdson. Winnipeg, Manitoba, CA: Manitoba Historical Society, 1990.

Jonsson, Hjorleifur Rafn. "Trolls, Chiefs and Children: Changing Perspectives on an Icelandic Christmas Myth." *Nord Nytt: Nordisk Tidsskrift for Folkelivsforskning.* 41 (1990): 55-63.

Walters, Thorstina Jackson. *Modern Sagas: The Story of Icelanders in North America.* Fargo, ND: Institute for Regional Studies, 1953.

INDONESIAN AMERICANS

by
Eveline Yang

An ethnic group noted for their diverse cultural and religious backgrounds and geographical origins, Indonesians who live in the United States split their affection and loyalty between their new-found country and whatever part of their homeland they or their ancestors once inhabited.

OVERVIEW

The Republic of Indonesia is located in Southeast Asia, on an archipelago of more than 17,508 islands near the equator. The total land area is 782,665 square miles, and the sea area covers 1,222,466 square miles; altogether, the nation is approximately the size of Mexico. The name Indonesia is coined from Greek: *indos,* India and *nesos,* islands.

Indonesia consists of an array of island stepping-stones scattered in the sea between the Malay Peninsula and Australia, astride the equator and spanning about an eighth of the world's circumference. By comparison, the continental United States stretches across about a sixth of the world's circumference. The islands and island groups consist of a Pacific set and an Indian Ocean set. The Indian Ocean islands are Sumatra, Java, Bali, and the Lesser Sundas, or, in Indonesian, *Sumatera, Djawa, Bali,* and *Nusa Tenggara.* The Pacific Ocean Islands are Borneo, Celebes, and the Moluccas, or *Kalimantan, Sulawesi,* and *Malukus.*

Indonesia's climate may be described as tropical, though land temperatures and rainfall vary considerably according to altitude and relative exposure to winds sweeping in from the ocean. On the whole, temperatures vary little at any one place, and rainfall is generally heavy.

HISTORY

By the fifteenth century, when the Renaissance was just pulling Europe from the Middle Ages, the islands of Java and Sumatra already had a thousand-year heritage of advanced civilization, spanning two major empires. From the seventh to the fourteenth century, the Buddhist kingdom of Srivijaya flourished on Sumatra. At its peak, the Srivijaya Empire reached as far as west Java and the Malay Peninsula. By the fourteenth century, the Hindu kingdom of Majapahit had risen in eastern Java. Gadjah Mada, the chief minister who ruled the empire from 1331 to 1364, succeeded in gaining allegiance from most of what is now known as modern Indonesia and much of the Malay archipelago as well.

Islam arrived in Indonesia in the twelfth century and had almost wholly supplanted Hinduism as the dominant religion in Java and Sumatra by the end of the sixteenth century. The island of Bali, however, has retained its Hindu heritage to this day. In the eastern archipelago, both Christian and Islamic proselytizing took place in the sixteenth and seventeenth centuries; currently, there are large communities of both religions on these islands.

Beginning in the early seventeenth century, Indonesia's many kingdoms had become fragmented and the Dutch gradually established themselves on almost all of the islands of present-day Indonesia, controlling the islands' social, political, and economic institutions. The eastern half of the island of Timor was likewise occupied by the Portuguese until 1975. During the 300-year Dutch rule, the region then known as Netherlands East Indies became one of the world's richest colonial territories.

MODERN ERA

Much of Indonesia's history in the modern era revolves around Sukarno (born Kusnasosro; 1901-1979). The Indonesian independence movement began during the first decade of the twentieth century and continued throughout both World Wars. The Japanese occupied Indonesia for three years during World War II. On August 17, 1945, after Japan had agreed to surrender to the Allied Powers, Sukarno and other nationalists declared national independence and established the Republic of Indonesia. Despite several attempts, the Dutch failed to recapture the territory lost to Japan. The victory over the Dutch strengthened Indonesia's sense of national identity and its citizens' belief in nationalism. In 1950 Indonesia became a member of the United Nations.

During the following decade, Sukarno revised the 1945 Constitution and became the President for Life. The Sukarno government badly mismanaged Indonesia's economy; the government seized foreign-owned plantations but did not train people to operate them, and consequently, economic conditions worsened.

The Communist Party began to grow during the early 1960s, with Sukarno's encouragement. In 1965 a group of Indonesian army officers seized power by killing six generals and other officers. This event precipitated more bloodshed as the Indonesian army and civilian mobs later killed between 200,000 and 300,000 people throughout Indonesia. Some of those killed were not Communists, but foreigners who had once controlled a great portion of the Indonesian economy. Shortly thereafter, Lieutenant General Suharto rose to power, outlawed the Communist Party, and reorganized the government. In 1968 Suharto was elected president and has been the head of the state ever since.

The population of the Republic of Indonesia, according to the 1990 census, is 180 million, which makes it the fourth most populous country in the world. The national motto is *Bhinneka Tunggal Ika*, which means "Unity in Diversity," a phrase that captures the people's strong national allegiance despite the variety of ethnicities and cultures.

The physical, cultural, and linguistic diversity of the Indonesian people reflects their country's past history and prehistory. At first, groups of people from the Asian mainland moved southeastward to the islands. Later groups, culturally more advanced than their predecessors, arrived to absorb the earlier immigrants or displace them, pushing them to remoter islands or less favorable habitats. By the early 1990s, Indonesia's society was divided into more than 300 ethnic groups, the largest of which was the Javanese, at 45 percent of the total population. Other groups include the Sundanese (14 percent), followed by the Madurese (7.5 percent), and the coastal Malays (7.5 percent).

Most of those who choose to leave their country for other countries, including the United States, are from larger urban cities on Java. An ethnic group noted for their diverse cultural and religious backgrounds and geographical origins, Indonesians who live in the United States split their affection and loyalty between their newfound country and whatever part of their homeland they or their ancestors once inhabited.

IMMIGRATION TO THE UNITED STATES

Few Indonesians immigrated to the United States prior to the 1950s. In the mid-1950s many Indonesian students came to the United States to study at

American universities and colleges. In 1953 the ICA (now USAID) started providing scholarships for medical faculty members of the University of Indonesia to study at the University of California at Berkeley. In 1956 the ICA likewise provided scholarships for the teaching staff of the Bandung Institute of Technology to study at the University of Kentucky.

In the 1960s, when a number of political and ethnic skirmishes arose in Indonesia, several thousand Indonesians, the majority of whom were Chinese Indonesian, came to the United States. This

immigration wave was short lived, however, due to the rapid reestablishment of peace in Indonesia and the limitations imposed by U.S. immigration quotas. More recent Indonesian immigrants have come to the United States for economic and educational reasons.

Overall, the number of Indonesians entering the United States is relatively low when compared to Chinese, Japanese, and Filipino immigration figures. According to the 1990 census, of the 6,876,394 Asians residing in the United States, only 30,085 (0.4 percent) are Indonesian Americans or Indonesians residing in the United States. The majority of Indonesian Americans reside in such large cities as Los Angeles, San Francisco, Houston, New York, and Chicago. This is partly due to the improved employment opportunities of these areas and to the fact that these cities have established Asian American communities.

ACCULTURATION AND ASSIMILATION

Unlike other immigrant groups, there are no established Indonesian American ethnic enclaves. This may be attributed to the fact that Indonesia has one of the most ethnically diverse populations in the world; their diversity in social classes, language, religion, ethnic and cultural backgrounds, and geographic location has lessened the possibility of forming a community of common traditions. However, there are numerous organizations, clubs, and religious groups in cities where there is a relatively large concentration of Indonesians, including Dharma Wanita, Ikatan Keluarga Indonesia di AS, and Washington Court Gamelan Ensemble Association.

TRADITIONS, CUSTOMS, AND BELIEFS

Assimilation for Indonesian American immigrants has been difficult, often causing them to become more attached to the traditions of their homeland. The Indonesians' sense of art is closely related to their mystic sense of identity with nature and with God. Humanity, nature, and art constitute an unbroken continuity. Artistic expression in Indonesian art is particularly evident in their dress. Much of their traditional dress consists of *batik* cloth. *Batik* is a design and art form that can be achieved by two techniques. The older method is called *tjanting* because a crucible of that name is used to draw the design directly on the cotton, by means of hot wax. When cooled, the wax resists the dye into which the cloth is immersed, so that all of the cloth except the area bearing the design accepts the dye. The wax is then removed, and the dyeing process is repeated. The second technique is regarded by some as inferior because the batik it produces is perceived to be machine-made. Actually, the design is made by a *tjap*, a printing stamp that is applied by hand to the cloth.

Other distinctive arts of the Indonesian people are the dance dramas of Bali and the Mataram court tradition. Both are essentially religious in character, though some Balinese dance is frivolous, flirtatious, or playful. Puppet dramas, or *wajang,* have been popular for a long time. The most popular puppets are flat and made of leather, but wooden puppets are also used. The puppeteer sits in back of a white screen and moves the puppets to act out stories. A palm-oil lamp throws the shadows of the puppets onto the screen. The plots usually involve a virtuous hero who triumphs over evil by means of supernatural powers and his own self-conquest.

Many Indonesians practice Western arts, from oil painting to metal sculpture, the subjects of which are often inspired by Indonesian life and traditions. The literary arts are also popular. Early Indonesian literature consisted largely of local folk tales and traditional religious stories. The works of classical Indonesian authors, such as Prapantja, are still read today, though modern literature in the Indonesian language began in the 1920s.

CUISINE

Rice is a central ingredient to the Indonesian diet. Indonesians boil or fry rice in various ways and serve it with a great variety of other foods. Foods are usually cooked in coconut milk and oil and sometimes wrapped in banana or coconut leaves. Fish, chicken, and beef are cooked with spices and served with rice. Indonesians eat little pork, since most of them are Muslims. Tea and coffee are favorite beverages.

At ceremonial occasions, including modern weddings, funerals, or state functions, foods such as *sate* (small pieces of meat roasted on a skewer), *krupuk* (fried shrimp or fish-flavored chips made with rice flour), and highly spiced curries of chicken and goat are commonly served. These foods are often served buffet style and at room temperature. Food is eaten with fingertips or with a spoon and fork. Water is served after the meal. These dietary customs are usually observed by Indonesian Americans during holidays and special events in the United States. For everyday meals, some Indonesians adapt readily to American food, while others prefer Indonesian or Chinese cuisine.

CULTURAL EVENTS AND HOLIDAYS

Despite their ethnic diversity, there are three major holidays that virtually all Indonesian Americans observe. *Idul Fitri* (in Arabic), which is also known as *Hari Raja* or *Lebaran* (in Indonesian), marks the end to the Muslims' obligatory fast during the 30-day fast of Ramadan. Many Indonesians celebrate with a traditional Muslim feast. The date of this holiday is determined by the lunar calendar; therefore, the date varies from year to year. Christmas and Easter are also national holidays in Indonesia. Independence Day is August 17. On this day, according to officials in the Indonesian Embassy and Consulate Generals, Indonesians in the United States are invited to celebrate along with Indonesian officials in a flag-raising ceremony and reception.

TRADITIONAL COSTUMES

Both Indonesian American men and women wear sarongs, traditional Indonesian garments with *batik* designs. Indonesian men generally wear sarongs only in the home or during informal occasions. Women wear sarongs on formal occasions, along with the *kebaya,* a tight, low-cut, long-sleeved blouse. Women often tie their hair into a bun or attach a hairpiece. Men may also don *batik* shirts that are worn outside their trousers and a black felt cap, called a *peci,* an item once associated with Muslims or Malays that has acquired a more secular, national meaning in the post-independence period.

DANCES AND SONGS

The most popular forms of dance in Indonesia are the Balinese dance and the *wajang kulit.* Though the origins of *wajang kulit* are lost in antiquity, many scholars believe that it is indigenous to Indonesia and that other shadow-drama arts around the world derive from it. This shadow drama is so popular that those who grew up in Indonesia can recognize all the stylized puppets and the episodes of the dramatized epics.

INDONESIAN STUDENTS IN THE UNITED STATES

In recent years, many Indonesians have immigrated to the United States to attend American colleges or graduate schools. Afterward, many choose to apply for permanent residency or for citizenship. Presently, about 26 percent of the Indonesians residing in the United States are between the ages of 25 and 34. The same percentage of Indonesians have bachelor's degrees.

The attitudes of Indonesian graduate students at selected universities in the United States were reported in Dr. Rustam Amir Effendi's doctoral dissertation of 1983. Students attending the University of Illinois at Urbana-Champaign, the University of Michigan, Michigan State University, the University of Minnesota, Ohio University, the Ohio State University, and the University of Wisconsin were polled about their success with academic adjustment and their overall satisfaction with American education. The study disclosed that approximately 80 percent of Indonesian students were male and that 50 percent of them were between the ages of 31 and 35. Slightly more than 50 percent of them had worked as professionals for several years after they acquired their undergraduate degrees in Indonesia and before they came to America. Most of them became university faculty or government officials. Most studied engineering and the social sciences.

The number of Indonesian students in the United States has grown steadily since 1983. The successful personal adjustments and academic achievements of these students are decided by mainly two factors: language efficiency and the ability to adjust to American society. While some of them return to Indonesia, many choose to remain in the United States to continue their professional pursuits.

LANGUAGE

With over 300 regional languages and dialects, there is a considerable diversity in the languages used in Indonesia. The major family of Indonesian language is the Austronesian. Bahasa Indonesian, a modified form of Malay, was named by Indonesian nationalists in 1928 as the official language. The majority of educated Indonesians in urban areas speak at least two languages.

Spoken Indonesian varies depending on the rank or status of the speaking partner. Respected elders are usually addressed in a kinship term— bapak (father or elder) or ibu (mother). Indirect references are usually preferred in conversation.

Most Indonesian names have two parts, although some Indonesians, including President Suharto, use only one name. In most cases it is appropriate to use the last part of the name before the indicator as a second reference. If no such filial indicator appears, the last part of the name is used as a second reference. Names including "Abu" or "Abdul" should use that word plus the word immediately following as a second reference. Some Muslim names include a place name. The part of the name preceding the place name should be used on second reference, for example, Abdullah Udjong Buloh, or Mr. Abdullah.

FAMILY AND COMMUNITY DYNAMICS

Intermarriage is not uncommon between Indonesians and Americans, especially for the younger generation, though the elder-generation Indonesians prefer that their offspring marry others of Indonesian heritage. According to the 1990 *Census of Population: Asians and Pacific Islanders in the United States*, more than 50 percent of adult Indonesians are members of families with two parents.

RELIGION

The religions in Indonesia are as numerous as the languages. Nearly 90 percent of Indonesians observe Islam, with significantly smaller populations observing Protestantism (six percent), Catholicism (three percent), Hinduism (two percent), and Buddhism (one percent). Many Chinese Indonesians follow Buddhist teachings. All five play significant roles in Indonesian communities in and outside the United States

The high percentage of Muslims makes Indonesia the largest Islamic country in the world. Introduced to Indonesia by traders from India between the twelfth and fifteenth centuries, Islam, or *sharia* (in Indonesian), is a strictly monotheistic religion in which God, Allah, is a pervasive, if somewhat distant, figure. The prophet Muhammad is not deified but is regarded as a human who was selected by God to spread the word to others through the Koran, Islam's holiest book. There are significant variations in the practice and interpretation of Islam in various parts of Indonesia. Overall, a less strict interpretation of Islam is practiced than in the Middle East. There has been constant interaction between the Muslims and the Hindu-Buddhist population in Java Island ever since the initial introduction of Islam, and over time they have blended to form a loosely organized belief system called Javanism, or *agama Jawa,* which was officially recognized in the 1945 constitution.

The most rapidly growing religions in Indonesia are the Christian faith:, Roman Catholicism and Protestantism. The number of Christians in Indonesia is very small compared with the number of Muslims, but Christianity has a long history in Indonesia. It was introduced by Portuguese Jesuits and Dominicans in the sixteenth century. When the Dutch defeated Portugal in 1605, the Calvinist Dutch Reformed Church expelled Catholic missionaries and became the only Christian influence in the islands for 300 years. Because Calvinism was a strict, austere, and intellectually uncompromising variety of Christianity that demanded a thorough understanding of scripture, Christianity gained few converts in Indonesia until the nineteenth century, when German Lutherans introduced evangelical freedom and Jesuits established successful missions, schools, and hospitals on some of the islands, including Timor and Flores.

Membership in Christian churches surged after the 1965 coup attempt, when all nonreligious persons were labeled atheists and were suspected to be Communists. By the 1990s, the majority of Christians in Indonesia were Protestants of one affiliation or another. Catholic congregations grew less rapidly, due to the Church's heavy reliance on Europeans in positions of leadership.

Hinduism is perceived to enforce a rigid caste structure, dividing people into classes: priests, ruler-warriors, and commoners-servants. However, the caste system has never been rigidly applied in Indonesia. The majority of the Hindus are in Bali, and they express their beliefs through art and ritual instead of scripture and law. Ceremonies at puberty, marriage, and, most notably, death are closely associated with the Balinese version of Hinduism.

Chinese Indonesians brought Buddhism to Indonesia, along with Taoism and Confucianism. This unique version of Buddhism was introduced by the founder of Perbuddhi, Bhikku Ashin Jinarakkhita. He claimed that there is a single supreme deity, Sang Hyand Adi Buddha. In the wake of the failed coup in 1965, many Indonesians registered as Buddhists—some simply to avoid being suspected as Communist sympathizers and others sincere enough to construct monasteries.

Although there are various schools of thoughts and practices among Indonesian Buddhists, they each acknowledge the Four Noble Truths and the Eightfold Path. The Four Noble Truths concern the suffering of all living beings, resulting from the craving for worldly belongings. The Eightfold Path leads to enlightenment, teaching purified views, speech, conduct, and mind. In Indonesia, Buddhism is highly individualistic, with each person held accountable for his or her own self. Anyone can meditate alone, anywhere. Temples and pagodas exist only to inspire the proper frame of mind for believers' devotion and self-awareness.

In Dr. Fredy Lowell Macarewa's doctoral dissertation (1988), the author chronicled the efforts by the Seventh-Day Adventists, who practice an evangelical Christian faith, to reach Indonesian Americans. These efforts have not been entirely successful, however, because of the failure to comprehend the belief system unique to Indonesians, which grew out of the long transition from Dutch Indonesian rule to Indonesian independence. Macarewa also recognized that evangelizing Muslims is a difficult task, because of prejudice and antagonism between the followers of Christianity and Islamic Indonesia during the past 14 centuries.

Besides Seventh-Day Adventism, there are other religious establishments for the Indonesian residing in the United States, as there are for Korean Americans and other Asian Americans. These churches or religious groups serve not only as sites for worship but also as centers for social and cultural activities.

EMPLOYMENT AND ECONOMIC TRADITIONS

According to the 1990 census, one-third of employed Indonesian adults in the United States are managers;

one-third are professionals; and one-third are in technical, sales, and administrative-support occupations. There is a growing number of Indonesians who make their living in the importing and exporting business. Trade between Indonesia and United States has been robust. In the early 1990s, U.S. imports from Indonesia, consisting mostly of oil, rubber, coffee, tin, spices, tea, plywood, and textiles, amounted to nearly $4 billion. Exports to Indonesia totaled $2.5 billion and included agricultural products, resins, aircraft and parts, and earth-moving equipment. To facilitate trade there are commercial trade organizations such as the American-ASEAN (Association of Southeast Asian Nations) Trade Council, the American Indonesian Chamber of Commerce, the Central Indonesian Trading Company, the Indonesian Investment Promotion Office, and the Indonesian Trade Promotion Center, all located in New York City. However, recently there have been organization branches established in other cities, including Los Angeles and Houston.

POLITICS AND GOVERNMENT

The immigration bill passed by the Indonesian parliament on March 4, 1993 is greatly impacting the influx of Indonesians to the United States or other countries. The bill bars certain individuals from leaving or re-entering Indonesia if doing so could disrupt development, cause disunity among the Indonesian population, or threaten the individual's life or that of his or her family. Furthermore, a time limit of between six months and two-and-a-half years was set on travel in and out of Indonesia, for those affected. There are no public records showing how many Indonesians are barred from leaving the country.

In November 1994, U.S. President Bill Clinton attended the Asian Pacific Economic Summit meeting in Jakarta. Trade relations between the two countries improved after the meeting. However, Indonesia was embroiled in political chaos in 1998-1999 during its election cycle which has made the nations political future and emigration patterns uncertain.

MEDIA

PRINT

Indonesian Journal.

Indonesian communities in the United States are linked by this publication—the first such commercial magazine in the United States. Published since 1988, it is a monthly journal distributed, free of charge, to the larger Indonesian communities in the country: New York, Chicago, Houston, San Francisco, and Los Angeles. Free copies are also distributed at Indonesian restaurants, churches, and other social organizations throughout the United States. Advertising revenues are its sole means of support. With the exception of some of the advertisements, the text of the publication is in Bahasa Indonesian. With reports on cultural, social, and even political events in the United States as well as in Indonesia, this publication serves as an important vehicle of communication for Indonesians who reside in the United States.

Contact: Mr. Mailangkay, Editor and Publisher.

Address: Desktop Designs, P.O. Box 4009, West Covina, California, 91791.

The Indonesia Letter.

This monthly publication enjoys the largest distribution among its kind. It provides commentary and analysis on the subject of Indonesia and news of its economic, political, and social development.

Address: Asia Letter, Ltd., Los Angeles, California.

ORGANIZATIONS AND ASSOCIATIONS

American-ASEAN Trade Council.

The Council membership consists of members of the American Indonesian Chamber of Commerce, the Philippine American Chamber of Commerce, and other ASEAN (Association of Southeast Asian Nations).

Address: 40 East 49th Street, New York, New York 10017.

American Indonesian Chamber of Commerce (AICC).

This unofficial and nonpolitical organization was incorporated in the United States in 1949, before Indonesia received full independence, a fact that signified the willingness of U.S. firms to trade directly with emerging Republic of Indonesia. Since then, its mission has been to foster and promote trade and investment between the United States and Indonesia. Currently, the American Indonesian Chamber of Commerce has over 150 members, including banks; energy companies; shipping lines; engineering firms; exporters; manufacturers; legal, public relations, and financial-service firms; and consulting and trading companies. The Chamber works closely with both Indonesians and Americans who are interested in doing export and import business from the United States or from Indonesia.

Contact: Wayne Forrest, Executive Director.
Address: 711 Third Avenue, 17th floor, New
York, New York 10017.
Telephone: (212) 687-4505.
Fax: (212) 867-9882.

Asian American Arts Centre (AAAC).

Supports exhibition of traditional and contemporary Asian American, Chinese, Japanese, Indonesian, Indian, Korean, and Filipino arts, including dance, music, performance art, and poetry.

Contact: Robert Lee, Director.
Address: 26 Bowery Street, New York,
New York 10013.
Telephone: (212) 233-2154.

East Timor Project.

This organization seeks to draw public attention to the situations of political prisoners in Indonesia, and to conditions in East Timor. It was formerly named the Emergency Committee for Human Rights in Indonesia and Self-Determination on East Timor.

Contact: Arnold S. Kohen, Coordinator.
Address: P.O. Box 2197, Washington, D.C. 20013.

Indonesian American Society.

Address: c/o Major Hal Maynard, 8725 Piccadilly,
Springfield, Virginia 22151.
Telephone: (703) 425-5080.

Indonesian Community Association.

This association serves as the central point of networking among Indonesians residing in the United States. The Chair serves as leader and coordinator for Indonesian American community. Considered the official representation of Indonesia in the United States, the association was formed to support such activities as family-oriented events, lectures, sports, and religious holidays. The association publication, *Warta IKI*, is published quarterly and distributed among Indonesian organizations in the United States.

Contact: Mr. Muchamad Sukarna, Chair.
Address: c/o Embassy of Indonesia, 2020
Massachusetts Avenue, N.W.,
Washington, D.C. 20036.
Telephone: (202) 775-5200.

Indonesian Students Association.

Founded to serve the needs of Indonesian students at colleges and universities in the United States. Branches of the organization are also in San Francisco, Los Angeles and other major cities.

Address: c/o Embassy of Indonesia, 2121
Massachusetts Avenue, N.W.,
Washington, D.C. 20036.
Telephone: (202) 293-1745.

MUSEUMS AND RESEARCH CENTERS

Cornell Modern Indonesia Project.

The Center for International Studies at Cornell University conducts research activities in the United States on Indonesia's social and political development. The research efforts have resulted in the publication of monographs, bibliographies, and biographies of Indonesian historical figures. The research scope also includes cultural, military, and foreign affairs of Indonesia.

Contact: Professor Benedict Anderson, Director.
Address: Cornell University, 640 Stewart Avenue,
Ithaca, New York 14853.
Telephone: (607) 255-4359.
Fax: (607) 277-1904.
E-mail: seap-pubs@cornell.edu.
Online: http://www.einaudi.cornell.edu/
SoutheastAsia/Seapubs.html.

SOURCES FOR ADDITIONAL STUDY

Aznam, Suhaini. "Passport Control: New Immigration Law Can Render Citizens Stateless," *Far Eastern Economic Review*, March 26, 1992, pp. 18-19.

Cordasco, Francesco. *Dictionary of American Immigration History*. Scarecrow, 1990.

Indonesia: A Country Study, fifth edition, edited by William H. Frederick and Robert L. Worden. Washington, D.C.: Federal Research Division, Library of Congress, 1992.

Slowly the Inuit of northern Alaska are trying to reclaim their heritage in the modern world.

INUIT

by

J. Sydney Jones

OVERVIEW

Once known as Eskimos, the Inuit inhabit the Arctic region, one of the most forbidding territories on earth. Occupying lands that stretch 12,000 miles from parts of Siberia, along the Alaskan coast, across Canada, and on to Greenland, the Inuit are one of the most widely dispersed people in the world, but number only about 60,000 in population. Between 25,000 and 35,000 reside in Alaska, with other smaller groups in Canada, Greenland, and Siberia. The name *Eskimo* was given to these people by neighboring Abnaki Indians and means "eaters of raw flesh." The name they call themselves is *Inuit,* or "the people." Culturally and linguistically distinct from Native Americans of the lower 48 states, as well as from the Athabaskan people of Alaska, the Inuit are closely related to the Mongoloid peoples of eastern Asia. It is estimated that the Inuit arrived some 4,000 years ago on the North American continent, thus coming much later than other indigenous peoples. The major language family for Arctic peoples is Eskaleut. While Aleut is considered a separate language, Eskimo branches into Inuit and Yup'ik. Yup'ik includes several languages, while Inuit is a separate tongue with several local dialects, including Inupiaq (Alaska), Inuktitut (Eastern Canada), and Kalaallisut (Greenland). Throughout their long history and vast migrations, the Inuit have not been greatly influenced by other Indian cultures. Their use and array of tools, their spoken language, and their physical type have changed little over large periods of time and space.

Alaskan Inuit inhabit the west, southwest, and the far north and northwest of Alaska, comprising the Alutiiq, Yup'ik (or Yupiat), and Inupiat tribes. As the first two tribes are dealt with separately, this essay will focus on that group regionally known as Inupiat, and formerly known as Bering Strait or Kotzebue Sound Eskimos, and even sometimes West Alaskan and North Alaskan Eskimos. Residing in some three dozen villages and towns—including Kotzebue, Point Hope, Wainwright, Barrow, and Prudhoe Bay—between the Bering Strait and the McKenzie Delta to the east, and occupying some 40,000 square miles above the Arctic Circle, this group has been divided differently by various anthropologists. Some classify the Inuit into two main groups, the inland people or Nuunamiut, and the coastal people, the Tagiugmiut. Ernest S. Burch, Jr., however, in his book *The Inupiaq Eskimo Nations of Northwestern Alaska*, divides the heartland, or original southerly Inupiat, who settled around Kotzebue Sound and the Chukchi Sea, into 12 distinct tribes or nations. This early "homeland" of the Inupiat, around Kotzebue Sound, was extended as the tribes eventually moved farther north. Over 40 percent of Alaskan Inuit now reside in urban areas, with Anchorage having the highest population, and Nome on the south of the Seward Peninsula also having a large group of Inupiat as well as Yup'ik. Within Inupiat territory, the main population centers are Barrow and Kotzebue.

HISTORY

Among the last Native groups to come into North America, the Inuit crossed the Bering land bridge sometime between 6000 B.C. and 2000 B.C., according to various sources. Anthropologists have discerned several different cultural epochs that began around the Bering Sea. The *Denbigh*, also known as the Small Tool culture, began some 5000 years ago, and over the course of the next millennia it spread westward though Arctic Alaska and Canada. Oriented to the sea and to living with snow, the Denbigh most likely originated the snow house. Characterized by the use of flint blades, skin-covered boats, and bows and arrows, the Denbigh was transformed further east into the *Dorset Tradition* by about 1000 B.C.

Signs of both the Denbigh and Dorset cultures have been unearthed at the well-known *Ipiutak* site, located near the Inuit settlement of Point Hope, approximately 125 miles north of the Arctic Circle.

Point Hope, still a small Inuit village at the mouth of the Kukpuk River, appears to have been continuously inhabited for 2,000 years, making it the oldest known Inuit settlement. The population of the historical Ipiutak was probably larger than that of the modern village of Point Hope, with a population of about 2,000 people. Houses at Ipiutak were small, about 12 by 15 feet square, with sod-covered walls and roof. Benches against the walls were used for sleeping, while the fire was kept in a small central depression of the main room. Artifacts from the site indicate that the Ipiutak hunted sea and land mammals, as do modern Inuit. Seals, walruses, and caribou provided the basis of their diet. Though the tools of whale hunting, including harpoons, floats, and sleds, were missing from this site, bone and ivory carvings of a rare delicacy—reminiscent of some ancient Siberian art—were found.

Other Inuit settled in part-time villages during the same epoch. The continuous development of these peoples is demonstrated by the similarities in both ancient and modern Inuit cultures. Called by some the *Old Bering Sea Cultures*, these early inhabitants traveled by kayak and *umiak* skin boats in the warmer months, and by sled in the winter. Living near the coast, they hunted sea and land mammals, lived in tiny semi-subterranean dwellings, and developed a degree of artistic skill.

The Dorset culture was later superseded by the *Norton* culture, which was in turn followed by the *Thule*. The Thule already had characteristics of culture common to Inuit culture: the use of dogs, sleds, kayaks, and whale hunting with harpoons. They spread westward through Canada and ultimately on to Greenland. However, it appears that some of the Thule backtracked, returning to set up permanent villages in both Alaska and Siberia.

Anthropologically classified as central-based wanderers, the Inuit spent part of the year on the move, searching for food, and then part of the year at a central, more permanent camp. Anywhere from a dozen to fifty people traveled in a hunting group. The year was divided into three hunting seasons, revolving around one animal. The hunting seasons were seal, caribou, and whale. The yearly cycle began with the spring seal hunting, continued with caribou hunting in the summer, and fishing in the autumn. A caribou hunt was also mounted in the fall. In the far north, whales were hunted in the early spring. It was a relentless cycle, broken up with occasional feasts after the seal and caribou hunts, and with summer trade fairs to which groups from miles around attended.

Though most Arctic peoples were not organized into tribes, those of present-day Alaska are to

a certain extent. One reason for such organization is the whaling occupation of the northwestern Alaska natives. These people settled north of the Brooks Range and along the coast from Kotzebue in the southwest, up to Point Hope and north and east to Barrow, the mouth of the Colville River, and on to the present-day Canadian border at Demarcation Point. These areas provided rich feeding grounds for bowhead whale. Strong leaders were needed for whaling expeditions; thus, older men with experience who knew how to handle an umiak, the large wooden-framed boat, used to hunt whales.

For thousands of years the Inuit lived lives unrecorded by history. This changed with their first contact with Europeans. The Vikings under Eric the Red encountered Inuit in Greenland in 984. Almost six hundred years later, the British explorer Martin Frobisher made contact with the Central Inuit of northern Canada. In 1741, the Russian explorer, Vitus Bering, met the Inuit of Alaska. It is estimated that there were about 40,000 Inuit living in Alaska at the time, with half of them living in the north, both in the interior and in the far northwest. The Inuit, Aleut, and Native Americans living below the Arctic Circle were the most heavily affected by this early contact, occasioned by Russian fur traders. However, northern Inuit were not greatly affected until the second round of European incursions in the area, brought on by an expanded whale trade.

Russian expeditions in the south led to the near destruction of Aleutian culture. This was the result of both the spread of disease by whites as well as out-

right murder. The first white explorers to reach Arctic Alaska were the Englishmen Sir John Franklin and Captain F. W. Beechey. Both noted the extensive trade carried on between Inuit and Indian groups. Other early explorers, including Alexander Kasherov, noted this intricate trading system as well, in which goods were moved from Siberia to Barrow and back again through a network of regularly held trade fairs. All of this changed, however, with the arrival of European whalers by the mid-nineteenth century. Formerly hunters of Pacific sperm whale, these whaling fleets came to Arctic regions following the bowhead whale migration to the Beaufort Sea for summer feeding. Unlike the Inuit, who used all parts of the whale for their subsistence, the whaling fleets from New England and California were interested primarily in *baleen*, the long and flexible strips of keratin that served as a filtering system for the bowhead whale. This material was used for the manufacture of both buttons and corset hooks, and fetched high prices. One bowhead could yield many pounds and was valued at $8000, a substantial amount of money for that time.

In 1867, the United States purchased Alaska, and whaling operations increased. The advent of steam-powered vessels further increased the number of ships in the region. Soon, whaling ships from the south were a regular feature in Arctic waters. Their immediate effect was the destruction of the intricate trading network built up over centuries. With the whalers to pick up and deliver goods, Inuit traders were no longer needed. A second effect, due to contact between the whalers and the Inuit, was the introduction of new diseases and alcohol. This, in conjunction with an obvious consequence of the whaling industry, the reduction of the whale population, made life difficult for the Inuit. Dependence on wage drew the Inuit out of their millennia-long hunting and trading existence as they signed on as deckhands or guides. Village life became demoralized because of the trade in whiskey. Small settlements disappeared entirely; others were greatly impacted by diseases brought by the whalers. Point Hope lost 12 percent of its population in one year. In 1900, 200 Inuit died in Point Barrow from a flu epidemic brought by a whaler, and in 1902, 100 more were lost to measles.

Although relatively unaffected by the whaling operations, the Inuit of the inland areas, known as *Nuunamiut*, also saw a sharp decline in their population from the mid-nineteenth century. Their independence had not protected them from the declining caribou herds nor from increasing epidemics. As a result, these people almost totally disappeared from their inland settlements, moving instead to coastal areas.

MODERN ERA

A number of actions were undertaken in attempts to improve the conditions of the Inuit at the end of the nineteen century and the early years of the twentieth century. The U.S. government intervened, obstensibly, to ameliorate the situation with improved education. However, the motivations behind this strategy by the U.S. government are the subject of much debate by many Natives and scholars of Inuit culture and history. Schools were established at Barrow and Point Hope in the 1890s, and new communities were only recognized once they established schools. The government also tried to make up for depleted resources, as the whaling trade had died out in the early years of the twentieth century, due to depleted resources as well as the discovery of substitutes for baleen. The U.S. Bureau of Education, the office given responsibility for the Inuit at the time, imported reindeer from Siberia. They planned to turn the Inuit, traditionally semi-sedentary hunters, into nomadic herders. However, after an early peak in the reindeer population in 1932, their numbers dwindled, and the reindeer experiment ultimately proved a failure. Game was no longer plentiful, and the Inuit themselves changed, seeking more than a subsistence way of life. For a time, beginning in the 1920s, fox fur trading served as a supplement to subsistence. Yet, trapping led to an increased breakdown of traditional cooperative ways of life. Fox fur trading lasted only a decade, and by the 1930s, the U.S. government was pouring more money into the area, setting up post offices, and aid relief agencies. Christian missions were also establishing school in the region. Concurrent with these problems was an increase in mortality rates from tuberculosis.

The search for petroleum also greatly affected the region. Since the end of World War II, with the discovery of North Slope oil in 1968, the culture as well as the ecology of the region changed in ways never imagined by nineteenth-century Inuit. Other wage-economies developed in the region. The Cold War brought jobs to the far north, and native art work became an increasing form of income, especially for carvers. In the 1950s, the construction of a chain of radar sites such as the Distant Early Warning system (DEW) employed Inuit laborers, and many more were later employed to maintain the facilities. In 1959, Alaska became the forty-ninth state, thus extending U.S. citizenship rights and privileges to all of state's population. At the end of the twentieth century, a number of issues face the Inuit: the use of technology, urban flight by the young, and thus, the viability of their traditional culture. Caught between two worlds, the Inuit now use snowmobiles and the Internet in place of the umiak and the sled. Nonetheless, they have designed legislative and traditional ways to maintain and protect their subsistence lifestyle. Since 1978, this lifestyle has been given priority, and it is legally protected.

ACCULTURATION AND ASSIMILATION

As with the rest of Native Americans, the Inuit acculturation and assimilation patterns were more the result of coercion than choice. A main tool of assimilation was education. Schools, set up by the state or by missions, discouraged the learning of native languages; English became the primary language for students who were often transported hundreds of miles from their homes. Students who spoke their native Inupiaq language were punished and made to stand with their faces to the corner or by having their mouths washed out with soap. Returning to their home villages after being sent away for four years to the Bureau of Indian Affairs high schools, these Inuit no longer had a connection to their language or culture. They were ill-equipped to pass traditions on to their own children.

By the 1970s, however, this trend was reversed, as the Inuit began organizing, demanding, and winning more local autonomy. More local schools opened that honored the ancient ways of the Inuit. For many this was too little, too late. Though old dances and festivals have returned, and the language is studied by the young, it is yet to be seen if the old cultural heritage can be re-instituted after a century and more of assimilation.

TRADITIONS, CUSTOMS, AND BELIEFS

Inuit social organization was largely based on bilateral kinship relations. There was little formal tribal control, which led to blood feuds between clans. However, hunting or trading provided opportunities for cooperative endeavors, in which different kinship groups teamed up for mutual benefit.

Wintertime was a period for the village to come together; men gathered in the common houses called *kashims* or *karigi*, also used for dancing. Games, song contests, wrestling, and storytelling brought the people of small villages together after hunts and during the long, dark winter months. Much of Inuit life was adapted to the extremes of summer and winter night lengths. Inupiats formerly lived in semi-excavated winter dwellings, made of driftwood and sod built into a dome. Moss functioned as insulation in these crude shelters. A separate kitchen had a smoke hole, and there were storage areas and a meat cellar. These dwellings could house 8 to 12 people. Temporary snow houses were also used, though the legendary igloo was a structure used more by Canadian Inuit.

CUISINE

Subsistence food for the Inuit of Alaska included whale meat, caribou, moose, walrus, seal, fish, fowl, mountain sheep, bear, hares, squirrels, and foxes. Plant food included wild herbs and roots, as well as berries. Meat is dried or kept frozen in ice cellars dug into the tundra.

TRADITIONAL CLOTHING

Traditionally, Inuit women tanned seal and caribou skins to make clothing, much of it with fur trim. Two suits of such fur clothing were worn in the colder months, the inner one with the fur turned inward. Waterproof jackets were also made from the intestines of various sea mammals, while shoes were constructed from seal and caribou hide that had been toughened by chewing. Such clothing, however, has been replaced by manufactured clothing. Down parkas have replaced the caribou-skins, and rubber, insulated boots have replaced chewed seal skin. However, such clothing has become a major source of income for some individuals and groups. Traditional clothing, from mukluks to fur parkas, has become valued as art and artifact outside the Inuit.

DANCES AND SONGS

An oral culture, Inuit danced at traditional feast times in ritual dance houses called *karigi*. These dances were accompanied by drums and the recitation of verse stories. Some of these dances represented the caribou hunt; others might portray a flight of birds or a battle with the weather. Both poetry and dance were important to the Inuit; storytelling was vital for peoples who spent the long winter months indoors and in darkness. The word for poetry in Inupiaq is the same as the word to breathe, and both derive from *anerca*, the soul. Such poems were sung and often accompanied by dancers who moved in imitation of the forces of nature. Many of the traditional singers were also shamans and had the power to cast spells with their words. Thus, dance took on both a secular and religious significance to the Inuit. The Inuit created songs for dancing, for hunting, for entertaining children, for weather, for healing, for sarcasm, and for derision. Some dance and song festivals would last for days with the entire community participating, their voices accompanied by huge hoop drums. These dance traditions have been resurrected among Inuit communities. For example, the Northern Lights Dancers have pioneered this venture.

HOLIDAYS

Major feasts for the Inupiat took place in the winter and in spring. In December came the Messenger Feast held inside the community building. This *potlatch* feast demonstrated social status and wealth. A messenger would be sent to a neighboring community to invite it to be guests at a feast. Invitations were usually the result of a wish for continued or improved trading relations with the community in question. Gifts were exchanged at such feasts. Some southern groups also held Messenger Feasts in the fall.

The spring whaling festival, or *nalukataq*, was held after the whale hunt as a thanksgiving for success and to ask for continued good fortune with next year's hunt. It was held also to appease the spirit of the killed whales. Similar to other Bladder Dances or Festivals of non-Alaskan Inuit groups, these ceremonies intended to set free the spirits of sea mammals killed during the year. At the nalukataq, a blanket toss would take place, in which members of the community were bounced high from a walrus-skin "trampoline." Another spring festival marked the coming of the sun. Dressed in costumes that were a mixture of male and female symbols to denote creation, the Inuit danced to welcome the sun's return.

Trading fairs took place throughout the year. The summer *Kotzebue* fair was one of the largest. In 1991, it was revived, held just after the Fourth of July. For the first time in a century, Russian Inuit came to celebrate the fair with their Alaskan relatives. The Messenger Feast has also been re-instituted, held in January in Barrow.

HEALTH ISSUES

In traditional Inuit society the healing of the sick was the responsibility of the shaman or *angakok,* who contacted spirits by singing, dancing, and drum beating. He would take on the evil spirit of the sick. Shamans, however, proved helpless against the diseases brought by the Europeans and Americans. Tuberculosis was an early scourge of the Inuit, wiping out entire villages. Alcohol proved equally as lethal, and though it was outlawed, traders were able to bring it in as contraband to trade for furs. Alcohol dependency continues to be a major problem among Inuit villages and has resulted in a high occurrence of fetal alcohol syndrome. Thus, ten villages in the Northwest Arctic Borough have banned the importation and sale of alcohol, while Kotzebue has made the sale of liquor illegal but allows the importation of it for individual consumption. Nonetheless, alcohol continues to be a source of major problems despite the implementation of "dry" towns and burroughs. Rates of accident, homicide and suicide among the Inuit are far higher than among the general Alaskan population. Moreover, there is a high rate of infant mortality and sudden infant death syndrome (SIDS) and infant spinal disorders.

Another health issue, particularly for the Inuit of the Cape Thompson region, is cancer, brought on by the dumping of 15,000 pounds of nuclear waste by the Atomic Energy Commission. Also, radiation experiments on flora and fauna of the region as well as Russian nuclear waste dumping offshore have contaminated many areas of northwestern Alaska, putting the native population at risk.

LANGUAGE

The Inuit communities of northern Alaska speak Inupiaq, part of the Eskaleut family of languages. All Inuit bands speak very closely related dialects of this language family. Its roots are in the Ural-Altaic languages of Finland, Hungary, and Turkey. Alaskan Eskaleut languages include Aleut, Yup'ik and Inupiaq.

Many Inuit words have become common in English and other languages of the world. Words such as kayak, husky, igloo, and parka all have come from the Inuit. The worldview of the Inuit is summed up in a popular and fatalistic expression, *Ajurnamat,* "it cannot be helped."

The future of Inuit-speaking Alaska is optimistic. Language instruction in school, as noted, was for many years solely in English, with native languages discouraged. Literacy projects have been started at Barrow schools to encourage the preservation of the language. However, English is the primary language of the region.

FAMILY AND COMMUNITY DYNAMICS

Local groups were formed by nuclear and small extended families led by an *umialik,* or family head, usually an older man. The umialik might lead hunting expeditions, and he and his wife would be responsible for the distribution of food. Beyond that, however, there was little control exerted on proper behavior in traditional Inuit society. Villages throughout northern Alaska have replaced hunting bands, thus preserving to some extent the fluid network of their traditional society.

EDUCATION

Education for the Inuit is still problematic. Each village has its own school, funded by the state with extra funds from the federal government. Yet the dropout rate is still high among their youth. There was a 30 percent dropout rate in grade school in 1965, a rate that climbed to 50 to 80 percent in high school. And for those few who reached college at that same time, some 97 percent dropped out. Ten years later, in 1975, the rates had gone down considerably, in part due to a revival of teaching in Inupiaq, as opposed to English-only instruction. Most Inuit under 15 are minimally literate in English. However, in older generations the same is not true.

BIRTH AND BIRTHDAYS

Birth and pregnancy were traditionally surrounded by many taboos. For example, it was thought that if a pregnant woman walked out of a house backwards, she would have a breech delivery, or if a pregnant mother slept at irregular times during the day this would result in a lazy baby. Also, there were special birthing houses or *aanigutyaks,* where the woman went through labor in a kneeling (or squatting) position. These postures have been recognized by Western culture as often preferable to the hospital bed.

Most children are baptized within a month of birth and given an English name along with an Inuit one. Chosen by their parents, these names are normally of a recently departed relative or of some respected person. Siblings help care for children after the first few months, and the baby soon becomes accustomed to being carried about in packs or under parkas. There is no preference shown for either male or female babies; both are seen as a gift from nature. While moss and soft caribou skin have been replaced with cotton and disposable diapers, the Inuit's attitude toward their young has not changed. They are loved and given much latitude by both parents, and fathers participate actively in raising their children.

THE ROLE OF WOMEN

There is still a recognized division of labor by gender, but it is a fluid one. In traditional societies, the men hunted, while the women tanned skins and made clothing and generally took care of domestic activities, and this occurred under the aegis of the extended family. In the modern era much of this has changed, but in general, outside employment is still the obligation of the male as well as any ancillary hunting activities necessary to help make ends meet. Women are, for the most part, confined to household tasks.

COURTSHIP AND MARRIAGE

In the past, marriages were often arranged by parents; however, today dating openly occurs between teens. Group activities take precedence over individual dating. In traditional times, the most successful hunter could take more than one wife, though this was uncommon. Also in the past, temporary marriages served to bond non-kin allegiances formed for hunting and or warfare. Married couples traditionally set up their home with the man's parents for a time. Plumpness in a wife was a virtue, a sign of health and wealth. While divorce was, and is practiced in both traditional and modern Inuit societies, its incidence is not as high as in mainstream American society.

RELIGION

A central tenet of Inupiat religion was that the forces of nature were essentially malevolent. Inhabiting a ruthless climatological zone, the Inupiat believed that the spirits of the weather and of the animals must be placated to avoid harm. As a result, there was strict observance of various taboos as well as dances and ceremonies in honor of such spirits. These spirit entities found in nature included game animals in particular. Inupiat hunters would, for example, always open the skull of a freshly killed animal to release its spirit. Personal spirit songs were essential among whale hunters. Much of this religious tradition was directed and passed on by shamans, both male and female. These shamans could call upon a *tuunsaq*, or helping spirit, in times of trouble or crisis. This spirit often took the shape of a land animal, into whose shape the shaman would change him or herself. Traditional Native religious practices, as well as the power of the shamans, decreased with the Inuit's increased contact with Europeans.

EMPLOYMENT AND ECONOMIC TRADITIONS

Traditionally, the Inuit economy revolved around the changing seasons and the animals that could be successfully hunted during these periods. The Inuit world was so closely linked to its subsistence economy that many of the calendar months were named after game prey. For example, March was the moon for hanging up seal and caribou skins to bleach them; April was the moon for the onset of whaling; and October was the moon of rutting caribou. Whaling season began in the spring with the first break up of the ice. At this time bowhead whales, some weighing as much as 60 tons, passed by northern Alaska to feeding grounds offshore, which were rich in plankton. Harpooners would strike deep into the huge mammal, and heavy sealskin floats would help keep the animal immobilized as lances were sunk into it. Hauling the whale ashore, a section of blubber would be immediately cut off and boiled as a thanksgiving. Meat, blubber, bone, and baleen were all taken from the animal by parties of hunters under the head of an umialik, or boss. Such meat would help support families for months.

Caribou, another highly prized food source, was hunted in the summer and fall. In addition to the meat, the Inuit used the caribou's skin and antlers. Even the sinew was saved and used for thread. Baleen nets were also used for fishing at the mouths of rivers and streams. Walrus and seal were other staples of the traditional Inuit subsistence economy.

These practices changed with the arrival of the Europeans. As noted earlier, many attempts were made to replace diminished natural resources, including the importation of reindeer and the trapping of foxes for fur. These were unsuccessful, and modern Inuit blend a wage economy with hunting and fishing. A major employer is the state and federal government. The Red Dog Mine, as well as the oil industry on the North Slope, also provide employment opportunities. Smaller urban centers such as Barrow and Kotzebue offer a wider variety of employment opportunities, as does the Chukchi Sea Trading Company, a Point Hope arts and crafts cooperative that sells native arts online. Others must rely on assistance programs, and for most there continues to be a dependence on both wage and subsistence economies. In order to facilitate subsistence economy, fishing and hunting rights were restored to the Inuit in 1980.

In general, living costs are greater in the rural areas of the north than in the rest of Alaska. For example, as David Maas pointed out in *Native North American Almanac*, a family living in Kotzebue could pay 62 percent more per week for food than a family in Anchorage, and 165 percent more for electricity. The incidence of poverty is also higher among Alaskan Natives than for others in the state, with some 3,000 families receiving food stamps and 18,000 families relying on low-income energy subsidies. Over 25 percent of the Native population of the state live below the poverty line, while in some areas of Alaska, Native unemployment rates top 50 percent.

POLITICS AND GOVERNMENT

Traditional Inuit maintained a large degree of individual freedom, surprising in a society that depended greatly on cooperative behavior for survival. Partnerships and non-kin alliances became crucial during hunting seasons and during wars and feuds, but it was mostly based on the nuclear or extended family unit. When bands came together, they were more geographical than political in nature, and while leaders or umialik were important in hunting, their power was not absolute. The social fabric of Inuit society changed forever in the twentieth century, though the people have avoided the reservation system. Natives themselves, such as the Inupiat of Barrow and Shungnak voted against establishing the reservations that formed all over America in the 1930s.

During the mid-twentieth century, there was a great deal of competition for once-native lands, both from the private and public sector. In 1932 a petroleum reserve in the north was set aside, and then developed by the Navy and later by private

companies. The Atomic Energy Commission (AEC) also wanted Inuit land. In 1958, the AEC requested some 1600 square miles of land near Point Hope to create a deep-water port using an atomic explosion many times more powerful than that at Hiroshima. Some of the first political action taken by the Inuit was in opposition to this experiment. As a result, the plan, Project Chariot, was called off.

After their success against Project Chariot, Natives began to organize in a concerted way to protect their lands. In 1961, various village leaders formed the Inupiat Paitot (The People's Heritage Movement) to protect Inupiat lands. In 1963 the Northwest Alaska Native Association was formed under the leadership of Willie Hensley, later a state senator. The Arctic Slope Association was formed in 1966. Both associations mirrored the activities of the statewide Alaska Federation of Natives (AFN) which lobbied for Native rights and claims. Local villages and organizations throughout the state were filing claims for land not yet ceded to the government. In 1968, with Congress beginning to review the situation, oil was dis-

covered on the North Slope. Oil companies wanted to pipe the oil out via the port of Valdez, and negotiations were soon underway to settle Inuit and other Native claims.

The result was the 1971 Alaska Native Claims Settlement Act (ANCSA), which created 12 regional for-profit corporations throughout the state. These corporations had title to surface and mineral rights of some 44 million acres. Additionally, Natives would receive $962.5 million in compensation for the 335 million acres of the state which they no longer claimed. Thus, the way was paved for the construction of the Alaska pipeline.

As a result of ANCSA, all Alaskans with at least one-quarter Native blood would receive settlement money that would be managed by regional and village corporations. Alaskan Inuit villages then organized into several corporations in hopes of taking advantage of the opportunities of this legislation. Amendments in 1980 to the Alaska National Interests Lands Conservation Act restoring Native rights to subsistence hunting and fishing, and in 1988, ensuring Native control of corporations, helped equalize ANCSA legislation. As of the 1990s, however, few of these corporations have managed to reach financial stability, and at least four have reported losses since 1971.

Inuit groups organized in the 1970s to see that high schools were built in their villages. In the Barrow region, local schools broke away from the Bureau of Indian Affairs administration and formed local boards of education more amenable to the teaching of Inupiaq language, history, and customs. The North Slope Borough, formed in 1972, took over school administration in 1975, and the Northwest Arctic Borough, formed in 1986, did the same. These regional political structures are further sub-divided into villages with elected mayors and city councils. Slowly the Inuit of northern Alaska are trying to reclaim their heritage in the modern world.

INDIVIDUAL AND GROUP CONTRIBUTIONS

Academia and Education

Martha Aiken (1926-) is an educator born in Barrow, Alaska, of Inupiat descent. Aiken has authored 17 bilingual books for the North Slope Borough School District, has translated 80 hymns for the Presbyterian Church, and has been a major contributor to an Inupiaq dictionary. She has also served on the board of the Arctic Slope Regional Corporation. Sadie Brower Neakok (1916-) is an educator, community activist and magistrate, from Barrow. A full-time teacher for the BIA, Neakok was appointed by the State of Alaska to be a magistrate, and was instrumental in introducing the American legal system to the Inupiat.

ART

Melvin Olanna (1941-) is an Inupiat sculptor and jewelry designer. Educated in Oregon and at the University of Alaska, Fairbanks, Olanna has had numerous individual and group exhibitions of his work, and has also won a number of Alaskan awards for the arts. A practitioner of the ancient carving traditions of the Inuit, Olanna brings this older design form together with modern forms. He learned carving techniques from masters such as George Ahgupuk and Wilber Walluk, and by age 14 he was already supporting himself with his carving. Olanna's work typically shows broad planes, simple surfaces, and flowing curves similar to the work of Henry Moore. He works in wood, ivory, whalebone, and bronze, and after a year in Europe he brought several tons of Cararra marble home with him to

Suquamish. He and his wife helped found the Melvin Olanna Carving Center, dedicated to training young Inuit in their ancient traditions. Joseph Senungetuk (1940-) is a printmaker and carver of Inupiat descent. An activist as artist, writer, and teacher, Senungetuk has devoted his life to Native issues and the revitalization of Alaskan arts. He grew up in Nome where an uncle first taught him to carve, then attended the University of Alaska in Fairbanks. Senungetuk also wrote an autobiographical and historical book, *Give or Take a Century: An Eskimo Chronicle,* the first book published by his publishing house. He spent many years in San Francisco where he concentrated on printmaking. Returning to Alaska he wrote a regular column for an Anchorage newspaper and also worked on sculpting. Susie Bevins (1941-) is an Inupiat carver and mask maker. Born in remote Prudhoe Bay to an English trader and his Norwegian-Eskimo wife, Bevins moved to Barrow as an infant after her father died. At age 11 her family once again moved, this time to Anchorage. She studied art in Atlanta, Georgia, and Italy, and she is one of the best known Inuit artists of the day. Her masks often speak of the split personality of Natives growing up in two cultures. Larry Ahvakana (1946-) is an Inupiat sculptor and mixed media artist who trained at the Institute of American Indian Art in Santa Fe and at the Cooper Union School of Arts in New York. Ahvakana uses modern sculptural techniques blended with his Native heritage to create lasting pieces in stone and wood. His interpretations of Alaskan myth often appear in his art.

JOURNALISM

Howard Rock (1911-1976) was born in Point Hope, where in the 1960s he joined Inupiat Paitot to stop the government from using the locale as a nuclear test site. Rock became the editor of a newsletter formed to educate other Inuit about the dangers. In 1962 this newsletter became the Tundra Times, with Rock serving as its editor until his death in 1976. In 1965, he helped organize the first Alaska Federated Natives meeting in Anchorage. Rock, who began life as a jewelry maker, was nominated for a Pulitzer Prize the year before he died.

POLITICS

William L. Hensley (1941-), also known as Iggiagruk or "Big Hill," is an Inuit leader, co-founder of the Alaskan Federation of Natives, and state senator. Born in Kotzebue to a family of hunters and fishermen, Hensley left home for his education, attending a boarding school in Tennessee. He earned a bachelor's degree from George Washington University in Washington, D.C., where he first became politicized about the conditions of his people in Alaska. Returning to Alaska, he studied constitutional law at the University of Alaska. In 1966, Hensley became one of the founders of the AFN, which was instrumental in lobbying Washington for Native claims. Since that time he has played an active role in Alaskan politics and has been an untiring spokesperson for the rights of the Inuit. He founded the Northwest Alaska Native Association and was instrumental in the development of the Red Dog Lead and Zinc Mine in northwest Alaska, the second largest zinc mine in the world. Both a state senator and a representative, Hensley was honored with the National Public Service Award from the Rockefeller Foundation in 1980, the Governor's Award for Alaskan of the Year, 1981, and an Honorary Doctorate of Laws from the University of Alaska in Anchorage, 1981.

MEDIA

PRINT

The Arctic Sounder.
Community newspaper serving Kotzebue, Barrow, and Nome.

Contact: John Woodbury, Editor,.
Address: 336 East Fifth Avenue, Anchorage, Alaska 99501.
Telephone: (800) 770-9830.
E-mail: mail@organsociety.org.

Tundra Times.
Bi-weekly newspaper, founded in 1962, devoted to the issues of Native Alaskans.

Contact: Jeff Richardson, Editor.
Address: P.O. Box 92247, Anchorage, Alaska 99509-2247.
Telephone: (800) 764-2512.
E-mail: tundratimes@tribalnet.org.

RADIO

KBRW-AM (680) and KBRW-FM (91.9).
Contact: Steve Hamlin, Program Director.
Address: 1695 Okpik Street, P.O. Box 109, Barrow, Alaska 99723.
Telephone: (907) 852-6811.
E-mail: kbrw@barrow.com.

KOTZ-AM (720).
Contact: Pierre Lonewolf, Program Director.
Address: P.O. Box 78, Kotzebue, Alaska, 99752.

Telephone: (907) 442-3434.
E-mail: kotzam@eagle.ptialaska.net.

ORGANIZATIONS AND ASSOCIATIONS

Alaska Federation of Natives (AFN).
Serves as an advocate for Alaskan Inuit, Native Americans, and Aleut at the state and federal level. Founded in 1966. Publishes the AFN Newsletter.

Address: 411 West Fourth Avenue, Suite 301, Anchorage, Alaska 99501.
Telephone: (907) 274-3611.

Mauneluk Association.
Contact: Marie Green, President.
Address: P.O. Box 256, Kotzebue, Alaska 99752.
Telephone: (907) 442-3311.

MUSEUMS AND RESEARCH CENTERS

Alaska State Museum.
Address: 395 Whittier Street, Juneau, Alaska 99801-1718.
Telephone: (907) 465-2976.
Fax: (907) 465-2976.

Anchorage Museum of History and Art.
Address: 121 West Seventh Avenue, Anchorage, Alaska 99501.
Telephone: (907) 343-4326.

Institute of Alaska Native Art, Inc.
Address: P.O. Box 70769, Fairbanks, Alaska 99707.
Telephone: (907) 456-7406.
Fax: (907) 451-7268.

Kotzebue Museum, Inc.
Collection contains Inuit artifacts, arts and crafts.

Address: P.O. Box 46, Kotzebue, Alaska 99752.
Telephone: (907) 442-3401.
Fax: (907) 442-3742.

Simon Paneak Memorial Museum.
Contains a collection of Nuunamiut Inuit history and traditions.

Address: P.O. Box 21085, Anaktuvuk Pass, Alaska 99721.
Telephone: (907) 661-3413.
Fax: (907) 661-3429.

SOURCES FOR ADDITIONAL STUDY

Burch, Ernest S., Jr. *The Inupiaq Eskimo Nations of Northwest Alaska.* Fairbanks: University of Alaska Press, 1998.

Chance, Norman A. *The Eskimo of North Alaska.* New York: Holt, Rinehart and Winston, 1966.

————. *The Inupiat and Arctic Alaska.* Forth Worth, TX: Harcourt Brace, 1990.

Craig, Rachel. "Inupiat." *Native American in the Twentieth Century: An Encyclopedia*, edited Mary B. Davis. New York: Garland Publishing, 1994.

Handbook of North American Indians, Vol. 5, edited by David Damas. Washington, D.C.: Smithsonian Institution, 1984.

Langdon, Steve. *The Native People of Alaska.* 3rd ed., revised. Anchorage: Greenland Graphics, 1993.

Maas, David. "Alaska Natives," in *Native North American Almanac*, edited by Duane Champagne. Detroit: Gale Research, 1994. pp. 293-301.

Vanstone, James W. *Point Hope: An Eskimo Village in Transition.* Seattle: University of Washington Press, 1962.

The relationship
between the Iranian
American population
and the surrounding
population since the
1979 revolution
appears to be one
characterized by
fear and prejudice
on the one side, and
by anger and sadness
on the other.

IRANIAN
by
Mary Gillis
AMERICANS

OVERVIEW

The Islamic Republic of Iran occupies 635,932 square miles (1,648,000 square kilometers) on the Asian continent. The country is bounded on the north by the Transcaucasian and Turkistan territories of the former Soviet Union (along with the Caspian Sea), on the east by Afghanistan and Pakistan, on the west by Iraq and Turkey, and on the south by the Persian Gulf and the Indian Ocean. Most of Iran is a geographic plateau located about 4,000 feet above sea level; the plateau is spotted with mountains where the annual snowfall provides much of the water needed for irrigation during the hot spring and summer months.

Although most of the country is arid and desert-like, the majority of the population is located in the area around the Caspian Sea, which has a hot and humid climate. As of the early 1980s, approximately one third of the population was occupied in agriculture, one third in the service sector, and another third in manufacturing, mining, construction, and utilities. Unemployment grew throughout the 1980s, however, reaching an estimated 28.5 percent in 1986 due to the nation's faltering economy in the face of the ongoing border war with neighboring Iraq and the drop in worldwide oil prices.

Iran is the nineteenth most populous nation in the world, approaching 50 million people in the late 1980s. Nearly half the Iranian population is ethnically non-Arab, being considered direct descendants of Aryan invaders of the second century B.C. Other significant ethnic groups descend from ancient Arabic and Turkish conquerors; there are also smaller populations of nomadic tribes, including Kurds, Lurs, Bakhtiari, Qashqa'i, Mamasani, Khamseh, Shahsevans, Baluchi, and Turkomans.

The majority of Iran's population converted to the Islamic religion in the seventh century A.D. after invasion by Arab tribes, and the Shi'i sect of Islam has predominated since the sixteenth century. Most of the population (98 percent) is Muslim, and fully 93 percent are members of the Shi'i sect. The remaining Muslims are members of the Sunni sect of Islam. There are minority Christian (about 300,000), and Jewish (about 25,000 in 1984) populations, as well as Zoroastrians (about 30,000) and Baha'i (about 350,000). The latter two religions originated in Iran, but practitioners of both have been subjected to persecution by officials of the regime that came to power with the revolution in 1979. In 1987, there were 270,000 Bahais in Iran and 7,000 in the United States, of which 1,000 were identified as Iranian immigrants.

In discussing possible reasons for the paucity of material available on the Iranian immigrant community in the United States, Diane M. Hoffman summarized its basic characteristics: "The relative recency of the large-scale influx of Iranians (many of whom arrived in the late 1970s and early 1980s), their relatively affluent socioeconomic background, their great religious, political, and ethnic heterogeneity, and their lack of well-defined geographic communities and internal cohesiveness are characteristics that make their status as a minority community somewhat problematic."

This attitude parallels the traditional self-image of the Shi'ism as a minority that must fight off a hostile majority, a paradigm taken from the martyrdom of Husain, commemorated annually during the month of Muharram. Among Shi'i leadership, this attitude evolved into "a quietist stance," according to David Pinault, which entailed "silent opposition to worldly powers, coupled with spiritual authority among a persecuted and excluded minority." Pinault noted that when the Shi'i leadership took political power in 1979, it was able to tap into the traditional Shi'i stance by "portraying the Iranian nation as a righteous minority menaced by powerful external enemies who seek to deprive it of its proper place in the world." A similarity may be found in Hoffman's description of the attitude of the Iranian high school students in Los Angeles in particular.

HISTORY

Iran's strategic location, bridging the Middle East and India, has determined its history as one of invasion by foreign armies. Aryan invaders of the second century B.C. established Zoroastrianism as the dominant religion in the area, lending the people their distinctive ethnic heritage as well as their name. Alexander the Great swept through the area in the fourth century on his way to India, followed by Arab invaders in the seventh, who spread the teachings of Muhammad. By the eleventh century, the religion of Islam dominated the plateau and the advanced Persian sciences, literature, and learning had seduced the leaders of more than one invading army, including Genghis Khan in the thirteenth century and Tamerlane in the fourteenth. Various native rulers controlled the region over the next centuries. The Safavids ruled from the early sixteenth century until 1736. Their founder and first ruler, Shah Ismail, tried to unify the conglomeration of loosely united tribes scattered through the land by their conversion to Shi'ism as the state religion. During this era theologians laid the basis of Shi'ite theology as it is currently practiced in Iran; also, since then, Shi'ism has been a badge of Persian identity in the Islamic world. By the end of the eighteenth century, a Turkish tribe called the Qajars ruled the area now known as Iran.

MODERN ERA

The Qajars governed Iran until the 1920s when Reza Shah (1878-1944) took over the government and established the Pahlavi monarchy. Reza Shah, whose sympathies leaned toward the Nazis at the start of World War II, was forced to abdicate to his son, Mohammed Reza Pahlavi (1919-1980), in 1941 by Britain and the Soviet Union, which had established a presence in the country in order to block Nazi influence in the region. Some see the first episode of the Cold War in the Soviets' refusal to remove their troops from Iran until forced to do so by the United States and the newly formed United Nations in 1946. Iran became an even more significant player on the political scene worldwide as oil began to dominate the postwar world market—Iran possesses as much as ten percent of the world's oil reserves. It was through its oil contacts that Iran gradually became Westernized, a process consciously accelerated during the "white revolution" of 1962-1963, when various reforms were enacted (including giving women the right to vote and to hold public office) and opposition—increasingly centered in the religious community—was suppressed.

Prior to 1979, Iran was ruled by a constitutional monarchy; however, it was in name only, not in practice. Shah Mohammed Reza Pahlavi changed the country's name from Persia to Iran in 1935 under a directive of Iran's representative abroad who believed that the province under which Persia was named (Pars) was only a single part of the entire country, while the birthplace of the *Aryan* race was Iran. After 1962, Iran became less a constitutional monarchy and more a one-man dictatorship. After the revolution, which toppled the Western-backed government of the Shah, who had led the country for nearly four decades, Iran officially became an Islamic republic governed by the laws of the Koran and the traditions of the Shi'i religion as interpreted by the Ayatollah Ruhollah Khomeini (1900-1989). Khomeini was the nation's official spiritual guide (*faqhi*) until his death a decade after the revolution; he was replaced by Ayatollah Ali Khamenei in 1989. Iran has experienced severe economic, social, and cultural turmoil throughout the twentieth century, particularly in the years leading up to the 1979 revolution. Since that time, the country has struggled to work out the details of its dedication to the teachings of the prophet Muhammad in everyday life and in specific government policies while fighting an expensive border war with Iraq and seeing several million of its wealthiest and most highly educated citizenry emigrate to the West.

IMMIGRATION TO THE UNITED STATES

It is difficult to trace immigration to the United States from the region designated by the modern world as the Middle East because of the way in which immigration officials on both sides have kept records. Prior to 1900, the destination of all those leaving the Ottoman Empire was officially Egypt, as the West was considered off-limits; upon arrival in the United States, these immigrants were indiscriminately labeled "Arabs." After 1900, when the popular term became "Syrians," and as late as 1930, all Middle Eastern immigrants were both officially and unofficially designated as Syrians. It appears that more than half of those who immigrated to the United States before 1950 were Lebanese, and 90 percent of the total were Christian, despite the overwhelming predominance of Islam in the Middle East.

The first wave of immigration from Iran to the United States, corresponding to the period 1950-1977, was relatively insignificant in terms of numbers of immigrants. Annually, about 1,500 Iranians entered the United States as immigrants during this period, along with about 17,000 non-immigrants, including students and visitors. The vast majority of Iran's emigrants left their homeland just prior to or as a result of the 1979 revolution, and are often considered de facto political refugees, though they lack that official designation. For the period 1978-1980, the average number of Iranians entering the United States as non-immigrants annually increased to more than 100,000; it is believed that the difference between the figures for the two waves of immigration is explained by the presence of exiles and refugees from the Islamic fundamentalist regime that overthrew the Shah.

Although non-Muslims form a tiny minority of the Iranian population in Iran, non-Muslim religious minorities appear to be overrepresented among Iranians in Los Angeles, where the largest Iranian population outside Iran is concentrated. The reason for the large number of religious minorities among Iranian immigrants compared to their proportion in the feeder population appears to be fear of or actual religious persecution under the fundamentalist Islamic government. For example, at its height, the Iranian Jewish population numbered 90,000 and enjoyed greater freedom and power than in any other Muslim country. But despite Ayatollah Khomeini's assurances of their safety under his government, several Jewish leaders were killed during the regime's early years, and 2,000 Jews leaving temple after Friday night services in 1983 were rounded up and imprisoned. By 1987, an estimated 55,000 Iranian Jews had received permission to emigrate. In 1992, 35,000 of those potential immigrants had settled in Los Angeles, New York City, and in Europe; however, the stream of Iranian Jewish immigrants had slowed considerably by the early 1990s and a few had even returned to Iran to reclaim their former lives and property as living conditions there eased.

Several sources have noted than an estimated two to three million Iranians have fled their homeland since the 1979 revolution; of the more than one million Iranians scattered across the United States, approximately 600,000—as of 1998—are located in southern California. According to U.S. Immigration and Naturalization Services figures through 1991, estimates on Iranian immigrants are much lower, totaling 200,000 Iranian immigrants entering the United States since 1978. The difference in these figures may be the result of counting only those who entered the country as immigrants, leaving out the large numbers of those entering officially as non-immigrants, including students and visitors. This group is often characterized as the former "elite" of Iran, highly educated and skilled professionals of various religions and ethnic backgrounds, many of whom have been financially successful in the United States.

There is some evidence to support the statement, however, that most Iranians who came to the United States did not intend to stay permanently. Only ten percent of those born in Iran and residing in Los Angeles at the time of the 1980 census had become naturalized citizens, and only 18 percent of those admitted into the country that year were relatives of resident aliens. In 1992, more than 100,000 Iranians had returned to their homeland since 1989, due as much to the economic recession in the United States as a state-sponsored campaign that urged reconciliation with the "secular experts." One Iranian questioned pointed to the reversal in the government's attitude toward secular experts as a recognition that the Iranian economy will never recover under the direction of religious experts alone.

INTERACTIONS WITH SETTLED AMERICANS

The relationship between the Iranian American population and the surrounding population since the 1979 revolution appears to be one characterized by fear and prejudice on the one side, and by anger and sadness on the other. Those belonging to the Muslim religion in particular are often subjected to a kind of nationwide backlash that identifies all members of their religion as violent fanatics or terrorists. In 1985 a proposed religious and cultural center for Muslims to be built in central Oklahoma was abandoned due to the protests of local citizens who feared the project would establish a site for a terrorist network in their midst. In addition, the U.S. government has often reinforced the stereotype that all Iranians are potential terrorists. According to an article in *Maclean's* magazine in 1984, some in the American State Department feared any attempt by the United States to protect its interests in the Persian Gulf during the Iran-Iraq war of the 1980s would inspire "'sleeping' terrorist cells in the ranks of Iranian exiles and students" living in the United States ("Iran's 'Sleeping' Threat," *Maclean's* [June 4, 1984]). And in 1987, the *Nation* reported that Iranian visa and green-card holders constituted one of the groups targeted by the American Immigration and Naturalization Service (INS) for a proposed "contingency plan" intended to identify "potential alien terrorists and undesirables" and remove them from the country ("The Untouchables," *Nation* [March 21, 1987], p. 348).

In response, many Iranian Americans feel a "deep sense of helplessness and alienation" in a culture that appears to understand them little and care less for their fate, according to Homayoon Moossavi. "We are, for the most part, only the subject of ridicule by political cartoonists and second-rate comics. We are treated as a faceless mob. This dri-ves us mad, makes us angry and bitter," Moossavi concluded. Prior to the 1979 revolution, many Iranians would try to conceal their identity by identifying themselves as Persians or by speaking in English. Although some believe that this was to avoid American discrimination, the primary reason was a fear of Iran's State Organization for Intelligence and Security (SAVAK). This organization operated freely abroad, especially in the United States, to punish so-called dissidents or anti-Shah groups.

ACCULTURATION AND ASSIMILATION

Although there is little data pertaining specifically to Iranian Americans and their struggle with assimilation into the surrounding culture, most Iranians in the United States are Muslims. Azim A. Nanji has identified several areas of conflict between the traditional Muslim and the secular American cultures. The most significant difference between living in a predominantly Islamic society and living in the United States is the lack of social support for the shariah, the Muslim code of conduct which has evolved over the centuries and which governs every aspect of one's life, from the most private to the most public.

In addition, the place of the extended family network at the center of Muslim life, which traditionally provides one's social identity as well as the all-important comforts of the private domain, is often not possible for immigrants, who may have left most or all of their family behind. Furthermore, Nanji noted, women may experience the greatest changes in the new environment due to the more frequent necessity of working outside the home. "This has meant that the essentially separate worlds of Muslim men and women in the public spheres have now become fused," Nanji remarked, adding that Muslim women in America tend to participate more actively in the mosque, though traditionally women pray primarily in the home.

Finally, Nanji identified Muslim youth in the United States as an area for deep concern among Muslim families. Peer pressure to experiment with drinking, dating, and other aspects of the lives of secular American adolescents which are forbidden by Islam, as well as pressure from the school system to practice individualistic values such as self-reliance and independent thinking—values that contradict the family-centered Muslim tradition—are sources of anxiety to Muslim parents. In response to these concerns, Nanji noted, some Muslims have attempted to recreate a totally Islamic

atmosphere in the North American context by building schools, mosques, and communes.

Hoffman suggested that unlike other immigrant groups, degree of language acquisition and length of residence in the United States indicate only the most superficial identification with the surrounding culture for Iranian Americans. Indeed, most Iranian immigrants speak English with some degree of fluency upon arrival in the United States. The prestige accorded those fluent in a second language—especially French or English—in Iran meant that conversations held in public or on social occasions were rarely conducted in Farsi; this attitude was carried over to the American context, reflecting the longstanding Iranian fascination with Western culture prior to the 1979 revolution. Indeed, despite a statistical downturn in education level of Iranian immigrants pre- and post-revolution, Iranian immigrants as a group display an extremely high incidence of English proficiency, particularly compared to other recent immigrant groups, according to Georges Sabagh and Mehdi Bozorgmehr in their study of the demographic, social, and economic characteristics of the Iranian immigrant community in Los Angeles.

Hoffman noted that since the 1979 revolution, however, and thus for the majority of Iranian immigrants in the United States, the attitude toward use of Farsi has reversed itself. This has resulted in a resurgence of interest among immigrants in traditional Persian culture and literature, and a new insistence on using Farsi in public and in private unless compelled to use English by an authority fig-

ure (for example, a teacher), or by the exigencies of the situation itself (for example, if one or more people present do not speak Farsi).

Hoffman argued that the resistance to speaking English among Iranians living in the United States indicates a renewed pride in their own cultural heritage as "a response to the twin threat to cultural identity posed by the revolutionary changes in Iran itself and the stresses of living in the United States." Just as the native population was able to maintain its distinctive culture despite centuries of invading armies, so in the United States, Iranians seem to cling to their ethnic heritage in the face of pressures to assimilate. Hoffman found that Iranian immigrants were often less interested in acquiring knowledge about American culture than they were in learning more about their own cultural heritage. Among Iranian American high school students in Los Angeles, Hoffman found both an acknowledgement of the necessity to acquire proficiency in English in order to achieve scholastically and a resistance of the typical association of language acquisition with value acquisition. Among the Los Angeles students and businessmen studied by Hoffman, "American work culture, and perhaps the notion of work as applied to self, such as in the philosophy of self-help or self-development, were the only domains in which Iranians enthusiastically espoused American values."

MISCONCEPTIONS AND STEREOTYPES

Due to the oil shortage experienced in the United States in the 1970s the romantic or exotic image of the Middle East, based on such fairy tales as "Aladdin and His Magic Lamp" and "Ali Babba and the Forty Thieves," became a negative stereotype of "greedy Arab oilmen" and of terrorists crazed by Islamic fundamentalism, as noted in "Media Blitz" (*Scholastic Update*, October 22, 1993). Iranian Americans in particular have been subjected to the latter stereotype because of the political radicals who held 52 Americans hostage for more than a year in 1979 in the American Embassy in Teheran, Iran's capital city. And when four Muslim immigrants were arrested for the bombing of the World Trade Center in New York City in 1993, one Middle Eastern immigrant remarked in "Media Blitz" that "this trial is not about the guilt or innocence of a few men. All Islam is on trial."

Some Muslims blame the American media and popular culture for propagating negative stereotypes about their culture and religion. For example, Disney's popular film *Aladdin* features a Middle Eastern character who sings about cutting off ears as legal punishment and calls his home "barbaric." Middle Eastern critics of American popular culture point to the recent predominance of Arabs or Muslims in the role of villain in movies and television shows. Furthermore, these critics contend in "Media Blitz" that through the media's reliance on such terms as "Islamic terrorists" and "Islamic fundamentalists," Americans are encouraged to confuse the few Islamic radicals who espouse violence with the majority of the adherents of the Islamic religion who reject violence.

HOLIDAYS

The most significant Iranian holiday is Muharram, which focuses on the seventh-century martyrdom of Husain, the grandson of the prophet Muhammad, who is considered the rightful heir to the caliphate (leadership of the religion) by Shi'i Muslims. Muharram is a period of mourning and penitence as all Shi'ites grieve the murder of Husain, his family, and followers at Karbala. The first eight days represent the period they were besieged in the desert; the eighth and ninth days of Muharram are thus the most intense days of this holiday. The tenth day, *Ashura*, is the height of Muharram festival.

Muharram festivities include processions during which banners or commemorative tombs are displayed, narrative readings are performed, and most important, *ta'ziyeh khani* (mourning songs)—traditional plays in honor of the martyrs of Karbala—are enacted in every village. Despite the essentially religious subject matter of the *ta'ziyeh* plays—which traditionally depict the death of Husain and his family or related events, such as the awful fate that awaits their assassins in the afterworld—"they are political as well as religious ceremonies during which a community reaffirms its commitment to the shared set of social values inherent in communally-held religious beliefs," according to Milla C. Riggio. Food is often shared throughout the performance of the play, reinforcing the communal feeling among the audience, and the audience interacts with the players onstage by singing along, crying, and beating their breasts in sorrow or penitence.

In her study of a *ta'ziyeh* performed in the United States, Riggio emphasized the ways in which Mohammed Ghaffari, the play's Iranian American director, altered the original play because of the differences in the American versus the Iranian audience. Because his American audience could not—or would not, given the constraints of Western theatergoing—verbally respond to the spectacle onstage, the play's traditional "call for vengeance against the cultural as well as religious enemies of Shi'ism" was not available to Ghaffari. Instead, the community-affirming message of the play was transformed into a personal expression of the director's feelings about his own exile. This was achieved in part by altering the traditional costuming, action, and theme of the play, "which abstracted and universalized the idea of cruelty rather than localizing it in Shi'i martyrdom," argued Riggio. "Replacing the call to martyrdom with a mystical dance which affirms the beauty of his life while recognizing human cruelty, Ghaffari displaced the communal values of the *ta'ziyeh* tradition in favor of the existential experience of the isolated individual," Riggio concluded.

TRADITIONAL CLOTHING

Hejab, modest garb appropriate for women, is a controversial aspect of Islamic culture, and public conformity to its dictates is often considered a signal of fluctuations in the political atmosphere. During the reign of the Westernized Pahlevi monarchy, women were discouraged from wearing the *chador*, the enveloping robe that ensures women's hair and skin are hidden from view, and among the upper and middle classes the garment came to be associated with oppression. After the revolution, although the *chador* itself was not mandated, it was required that all women appearing in public obey the dictates of modesty in covering themselves completely except for the skin of the hands and face. Although no data was found on the degree of conformity to *hejab* among Iranian women in the United States, given what is known about the high socioeconomic status of most Iranian Americans before immigration, it is unlikely that wearing the *chador* would be widespread among this group.

LANGUAGE

The official language of Iran is Farsi, known in the West as Persian, which combines the ancient Persian language with many Arabic words and is written with Arabic characters and script. Turkish and Turkic dialects are also spoken in several areas in the country. The nomadic tribes that migrate vertically every spring and fall from the Zagros mountain range to the surrounding lowland plains speak a variety of other languages and dialects. Iranian immigrants to the United States are more highly educated than most immigrant groups; this fact, along with the prestige associated with the use of such foreign languages as French or English in Iran, has meant that the majority of Iranian Americans report a high level of proficiency in English. Sabagh and Bozorgmehr concluded that "Iranian migrants as a whole probably have a better command of English ... than most other immigrants in Los Angeles."

GREETINGS AND OTHER POPULAR EXPRESSIONS

Common Farsi greetings and other expressions include: *Salam!*—Greetings!; or, more informally, *Cheh khabar?*—What's new?; and *Cheh khabareh?*—What's happening?; *Khoda Hafez*—Good-bye; *Loftan*—Please; *Mamnoon am*—Thank you; *Khabeli nadereh*—You're welcome. *Inshallah*—If God be willing; *Maashallah*—May God preserve, is often used with expressions of admiration, or by itself to express admiration of someone. Other expressions of admiration include *Cheghadr ghashangeh!*—How beautiful!; *Kheili jaleheh*—Very interesting; and *Aliyeh!*—Great!

FAMILY AND COMMUNITY DYNAMICS

Although half the Iranian population claims a non-Arab ethnicity, all Muslim Iranians—the vast majority of the population—share a common tradition with other Muslims of the Middle East, Arab or non-Arab. Muslim society in general, according to Nanji, is centered on extended family networks headed by the father. Traditionally, business and political life as well as social life has been determined by the family network. According to *Iran: A Country Study*, "Historically, an influential family was one that had its members strategically distributed throughout the most vital sectors of society,

each prepared to support the others in order to ensure family prestige and family status." Thus the family is at the center of the individual's economic and political as well as social and emotional life. The extended family is enlarged through marriage with other Muslims and continues through a strong tradition of family inheritance. "On the whole, this heritage of social grouping and family values characterized the value system of immigrant Muslims." The family has undergone change, however, as Iranian Americans, especially the women, become assimilated in the United States.

COURTSHIP AND WEDDINGS

The father, as head of the family, is considered responsible for the family's social, material, and spiritual welfare, and in return expects respect and obedience. Marriage, often within the extended family network, is encouraged at a young age both officially and unofficially, and though multiple marriages (as many as four) are allowed for men by Islamic law, it has often been discouraged both by the government and by the family. In addition, the Shi'i religion, the predominant sect of Islam in Iran, allows the practice of temporary marriage, or *muta*. Muslim women are forbidden to marry non-Muslims, as it is feared the woman and her children will most certainly be lost to Islam, but Muslim men may marry non-Muslims if they are Jewish or Christian. These religions are traditionally considered kin to the Muslims, but intermarriage is nevertheless allowed on the assumption that the woman will convert to Islam and raise the children according to Islamic law.

Changes in the characteristic Middle Eastern family structure in the North American context have resulted in part from the loss of power that had been accorded to elders as purveyors of important cultural knowledge and to the father as head of the family. The knowledge elders possess may not be considered relevant in the context of immigration. Power relations are sometimes reversed when the second generation finds it necessary to instruct the first on various aspects of the new culture or to represent the family to the outside world due to its greater knowledge of English. Furthermore, influenced by the culture around them, members of the second generation often desire greater freedom to determine their own lives while their elders struggle to maintain control over the family. One area that has not changed is adherence to the Islamic law to take care of the elderly when they cannot take care of themselves. Other changes among immigrant families include a decrease in the likelihood that marriages will be arranged.

THE ROLE OF WOMEN

Women of the middle and upper classes—many of whom had adopted secular, Westernized values—were among those most affected when the conservative Islamic government came to power with the revolution in 1979. Strict enforcement of the traditional dress code might extend to flogging for violations such as wearing make-up or nail polish, even if covered by sunglasses and gloves. Throughout the 1980s, the official attitude toward women as indicated by police enforcement of the dress code through patrols and roadblocks varied somewhat by region (women are more severely restricted in rural areas than in Teheran, the capital city) and with fluctuations in the political realm. Still, a woman may be censured or fined for wearing perfume, letting some hair escape from her *chador*, or for speaking to a man in public in an animated fashion. Although Iranian women believe they are allowed more independence than women in Saudi Arabia, this is still far less than was accorded them before the revolution, and the inconsistency with which the laws have been applied is nerve-wracking.

Nevertheless, the sphere of women's power primarily remains the home, extending only to the initiation of social activities there and in the mosque. Nanji refuted the "stereotype of Muslim women as either concubines or oppressed baby-making machines," stressing that despite the interpretation given the laws of the Koran governing women by the most conservative adherents of Islam, "in the overall context of Muslim history and society, the status and role of women accorded with the larger view of the integrity and vitality of the family as the cornerstone of all social relationships." That is, though the home has traditionally been the seat of women's power in Islamic cultures, and is frequently perceived to be the only sphere where it is appropriate for women to assert themselves, the role that home life plays in Islamic cultures is central to all other aspects of the social structure.

It has been suggested that, among Iranians in Los Angeles at least, the authority of women within the family actually decreases after immigration. Parvin Abyaneh noted that 66 Iranian families in Los Angeles were surveyed on the following four points: amount of time women spent doing housework; amount of help women received while performing household chores; degree of control women had over family income; and, amount of control women had over major family decisions ("Immigrants and Patriarchy," *Women's Studies* 17, 1989). Survey results showed that Iranian American women spend more time doing household chores, receive less help with these chores from their husbands (or others), and have less ability to control the way family income is spent in the United States than when they resided in Iran. Although Iranian women exert little influence outside the home before immigration, that sphere of influence appears to deteriorate after migration to the United States.

Not all Iranian American women led such circumscribed lives. About 48 percent of Iranian American women living in Los Angeles worked outside the home in 1990. By 1997, many women led more western-style lives: they had pursued college educations and jobs. Iranian American women worked as professors, in business, and in hospitals as doctors or other specialists. Sometimes these women were shunned by traditionalists. Still, Iranian American girls, especially of the second generation, saw the possibilities of life in the United States and wanted to take advantage of them. Some protested family rules that decreed more freedom for their brothers. For example, many Iranian American families prevented their daughters from attending college outside of their home city or state. The family pressure had the potential of being psychologically damaging. Yet some families embraced western ways for their daughters, arguing that her potential lifetime earnings could take the place of a dowry.

Groups have sprung up to help first generation Iranian American women with the transition to American life, especially those in a problematic marriage. Organizations such as the Coalition of Women from Asia and the Middle East helped by providing shelters, counseling, and legal assistance to victims of domestic violence and others. Few Iranian American women expressed a desire to return to Iran.

RELIGION

Although Shi'ism predominates, there are several minority religious groups in Iran. Less than ten percent of the Iranian population practices the Sunni version of Islam, a sect that differs from Shi'ism in its attitude toward the imamate, the spiritual descendants of Muhammad. Bahaiism is the second largest religious minority in Iran. Formed in the nineteenth century as an offshoot of Shi'ism, the Baha'i religion believes in pacifism and equality of the sexes, and maintains that all people are brothers. Shi'i leadership officially regards the Baha'i as heretics and, except during the reign of the Pahlavi dynasty, Bahais have been persecuted in Iran. The country's Christian population includes Catholics, Anglicans, and Protestants of mainly Armenian and Assyrian descent. Although this primarily urban population has not suffered official persecution by the government of the Islamic Republic, it has been subjected to many Islamic-oriented laws and to government oversight in its schools, both of which often impinge on the traditional practice of the Christian religion. The small population of Iranian Jews has an ancient history, and was officially recognized in the constitution set down by the revolution of 1979. Nevertheless, the Iranian government's unfriendly relations with Israel have influenced the treatment of its native Jewish population, and many have emigrated to the United States and Israel. The small population of remaining Zoroastrians are also officially recognized by the Iranian constitution and have not been officially persecuted by the government.

The Islamic Republic of Iran tolerates some religious variation, as long as it does not act against the government or the sanctity of Islamic values. The vast majority of Iranians practice the Islamic faith, which originated with Muhammad (572-632 A.D.), who came to believe he was the prophet of Allah, the one true God. Islam, which means "submission to God," requires the belief in God and His Prophet, the recitation of prescribed prayers, the giving of alms, the observance of the feast of Ramadan, and the making of a pilgrimage to Mecca.

The Muslim religion is divided into two main sects, the Sunni, which predominates worldwide, and the Shi'i, which is the minority sect except in Iran, Iraq, and in parts of India. The Shi'i sect of Islam was established in the first years after Muhammad's death when a dispute arose over leadership of the religion. The Sunnis restrict accession to the caliphate to members of the tribe of Muhammad; the Shi'ites restrict right of accession to members of Muhammad's family. The origin of the name Shi'i is thus *Shi'at Ali* (supporters of Ali), Muhammad's cousin and son-in-law.

EMPLOYMENT AND ECONOMIC TRADITIONS

Of Iranian immigrants residing in Los Angeles, nearly 30 percent identified themselves as students in the 1980 census. According to Sabagh and Bozorgmehr, because students are younger than the average Iranian immigrant, generally have greater facility with the English language, tend to work fewer hours than non-students, are less likely to be self-employed, and have a lower occupational profile and consequent lower level of income, their inclusion in a statistical profile of Iranians residing in the United States is believed to distort the group profile. Significantly, this study revealed a higher incidence of self-employment among Iranian immigrants than among Korean

Americans, an immigrant group reputed to have one of the highest rates of entrepreneurship in Los Angeles. Fully one-third of the Iranian immigrants in Los Angeles, regardless of when they entered the country, reported that they were self-employed. Furthermore, later immigrants—those who fled Iran due to the revolution—tended to bring a great deal of money into the United States with them, and reported a significant income from interest and rental properties. Fluctuations in the American economy have affected this group to the extent that the downswing in the economy in the late 1980s, along with the relaxation of conditions in Iran, had encouraged as many as 100,000 Iranians to return to their homeland. Iranian American women living in Los Angeles in 1990 had an employment rate of 48 percent, compared with a 27 percent rate in 1980.

POLITICS AND GOVERNMENT

Shi'ism has traditionally shown a disdain for both secular authority and direct involvement in political life. Iranian leaders of Twelver Shi'ism (*Ithna 'Ashariyah*), the dominant form of Shi'ism, have followed the ancient tradition of remaining separate from the world's political concerns, avoiding the ministering of justice, and seeking a spiritual victory in defeat. There is also a tradition of revolt against injustice within Shi'ism, however, and an inability to suffer the corruption of political figures except when to protest would put one's life in danger. This stance is known as *taqiyah* ("necessary dissimulation") and is traced back to Ali, Muhammad's son-in-law, who quietly accepted the promotion of three others to the caliphate before him in order to avoid civil war. Pinault identified *taqiyah* as a "guiding principle for any Shiite living under a tyrannous government too powerful to be safely resisted; one may given an external show of acquiescence while preserving resistance in one's interior, in one's heart."

The U.S. government was concerned with the political sympathies of Iranians residing in the United States throughout the 1980s but no material was found implicating Iranians in terrorist acts in this country.

INDIVIDUAL AND GROUP CONTRIBUTIONS

ACADEMIA

Vartan Gregorian (1935–) is a former university professor and president of the New York Public Library who has been president of Brown University since 1989.

FASHION

Bijan (1940–) is a fashion designer of exclusive men's apparel and perfumes.

LITERATURE

Sadeq-i Chubak (1916–), considered one of the foremost modern Iranian writers, is the author of short stories, novels, and dramatic works.

THEATER

Lotfi Mansouri (1929–) is a Canadian theatrical director who directed the Canadian Opera Company from 1976 to 1988, and has directed the San Francisco Opera since 1988.

MEDIA

PRINT

Asre Emrooz Daily Newspaper.
Address: 16661 Ventura Blvd., #212,
    Encino, California 91436.
Telephone: (818) 783-0000.
Fax: (818) 783-3679.

Iran Nameh: A Persian Journal of Iranian Studies.
A quarterly academic publication published by the Foundation for Iranian Studies.

Contact: Hormoz Hekmat, Managing Editor.
Address: 4343 Montgomery Avenue, Suite 200,
    Bethesda, Maryland 20814.
Telephone: (301) 657-1990.
Fax: (301) 657-4381.
Email: gafkhami@ fisiran.org.
Online: http://www.fisiran.org/iraname.htm.

Iran Times International.
A weekly newspaper in English and Farsi.

Contact: Javad Khakbaz, Editor.
Address: 2727 Wisconsin Avenue, N.W.,
    Washington, D.C. 20007.
Telephone: (202) 659-9868.
Fax: (202) 337-7449.

Iranian.
Magazine focusing on art, science, philosophy, history, and cultural issues.

Contact: Korosh Bozorg, Editor-in-Chief.

Address: 2220 Avenue of Stars #2301,
    Los Angeles, California 90067 .
Telephone: (310) 553-8150.

Iranian Studies.
Contact: R. D. McChesney, Editor.
Address: New York University, Department of
    Middle Eastern Studies, 50 Washington
    Square South, New York, New York 10003.
Telephone: (212) 998-8902.
Fax: (212) 995-4689.
E-mail: iranian.studies@nyu.edu.
Online: http://www.iranianstudies.org/isfr.html.

Par Monthly Journal.
A monthly publication of the Par Cultural Society.

Address: P.O. Box 703, Falls Church,
    Virginia 22040.
Telephone: (703) 533-1727.

Persian Heritage.
Quarterly magazine published by Persian Heritage, Inc. with a circulation of 15,000.

Contact: Shahrokh Ahkami, Editor in-Chief.
Address: 1110 Passaic Avenue, Passaic,
    New Jersey 07055.
Telephone: (973) 471-4283.

RADIO

KPFT-FM.
Contact: Mary Helen Merzbacher, General
    Manager.
Address: 419 Lovett Boulevard, Houston,
    Texas 77006.
Telephone: (713) 526-4000.

ORGANIZATIONS AND ASSOCIATIONS

American Institute of Iranian Studies.
This organization of educational institutions seeks to improve Iranian studies programs and facilitate the research efforts of Iranian and North American scholars of Iranian studies.

Contact: Dr. Marilyn R. Waldman, President.
Address: c/o Ohio State University, History
    Department, 106 Dulles Hall, 230 West 17th
    Avenue, Columbus, Ohio 43210-1311.
Telephone: (614) 292-1265.
Fax: (614) 292-2282.

Iran Freedom Foundation.

This organization opposes the Islamic Republic of Iran, and attempts to protect human and civil rights in Iran and help establish a secular, constitutional government there by disseminating information to the media, universities, and political institutions, and at demonstrations and gatherings.

Contact: M. R. Tabatabai, President.

Address: P.O. Box 422, Bethesda, Maryland 20817.

Telephone: (301) 608-3333.

Fax: (301) 608-3333.

Iranian B'Nei Torah Movement.

This is an organization for rabbinical students seeking to aid Iranian Jews in the United States and Israel in their religious, charitable, and educational requirements.

Contact: David Zargart, President.

Address: P.O. Box 351476, Los Angeles, California 90035.

Telephone: (310) 652-2115.

Fax: (310) 652-6979.

National Council of Resistance of Iran.

This is a coalition of organizations opposed to the rule of Ayatollah Ruhollah Khomeini and his successors in Iran and favoring their replacement with a democratic government. Organizes opposition worldwide through diplomatic efforts and demonstrations and strikes in Iran.

Contact: Dr. Masoud Banisadr.

Address: c/o Representative Office in the U.S., 3421 M Street, N.W., Suite 1032, Washington, D.C. 20007.

Telephone: (202) 783-5200.

Society for Iranian Studies.

This is an organization of students and scholars of Iranian studies intended to promote scholarship in the field.

Contact: Hamid Dabashi, Executive Secretary.

Address: c/o Middle East Institute, Columbia University, SIA Building, Room 1113, 420 West 118th Street, New York, New York 10027.

Telephone: (212) 854-5284.

SOURCES FOR ADDITIONAL STUDY

Bill, James A. *The Eagle and the Lion: The Tragedy of American-Iranian Relations*. New Haven, Connecticut: Yale University Press, 1988.

Hoffman, Diane M. "Language and Culture Acquisition among Iranians in the United States," *Anthropology and Education Quarterly*, 1989.

Iran: A Country Study, edited by Helen Chapin Metz. Washington, D.C.: U.S. Government, 1989.

Irangeles: Iranians in Los Angeles, edited by Ron Kelley. Berkeley: University of California Press, 1993.

Kordi, Gohar. *An Iranian Odyssey*. Serpent's Tail Press, 1993.

Milani, Farzaneh. *Veils and Words: The Emerging Voices of Iranian Women Writers*. Syracuse, New York: Syracuse University Press, 1992.

Moossavi, Homayoon. "Teheran Calling," *Progressive*, August 1988.

Nanji, Azim A. "The Muslim Family in North America," in *Family Ethnicity*. Newberry Park, California: SAGE Publications, 1993.

Pinault, David. *The Shiites: Ritual and Popular Piety in a Muslim Community*. New York: St. Martin's Press, 1992.

Riggio, Milla C. "Ta'ziyeh in Exile," *Comparative Drama*, spring 1994.

Sabah, Georges, and Mehdi Bozorgmehr. "Are the Characteristics of Exiles Different from Immigrants?" *Sociology and Social Research*, January 1987.

Wright, Robin. *In the Name of God: The Khomeini Decade*. New York: Simon and Schuster, 1989.

IRAQI AMERICANS

by

Paul S. Kobel

For Iraqi, as well as Iraqi-American, women the burden of reproducing Muslim values is placed on their shoulders. Unlike other ethnic minorities that migrate to the United States, the Arab female generally benefits less from the liberal environment of American society.

OVERVIEW

Iraq lies the furthest east of all the Arab nations. It has a total area of 167,975 square miles (435,055 square kilometers), which is comparable to the size of California. It is bordered by Iran to the east, Syria and Jordan to the west, Turkey to the north, and Saudi Arabia and Kuwait to the south. A small portion of Iraq's coast in the north meets the Persian Gulf. The capital of Iraq is Baghdad. Iraq is a level region in a dry climate fed by the Tigris and Euphrates Rivers. Rain is sufficient for agriculture only in the northeast.

The population of Iraq is roughly 16,476,000. The Iraqi population is fairly evenly divided between the Shiite and Sunnite Muslim sects (53 percent and 42 percent respectively). The Kurds are the largest minority group in Iraq, making up about 15 percent of the population. Oil production, which began in 1928, is the engine behind Iraq's economy. Less than half of the Iraqi workforce is employed in agriculture. Iraq's national flag has three horizontal stripes colored red, white, and black from top to bottom, with three green stars in the middle of the white stripe.

HISTORY

The word *iraq* is a geographic term used in early Arabic writings to refer to the southern portion of the contemporary parameters of Iraq. Originally, the area now called Iraq was known as Mesopotamia and was one of the first culturally developed areas of the world. The Semites were the first to inhabit the region in 3500 B.C. The Semites that settled in the north were called Assyrians, and those that settled in the south were called Babylonians. The northern portion of Iraq was originally known as Al-Jazirah, which means "the island," because the Tigris and Euphrates Rivers surrounded it. In 600 A.D. Iraq was ruled by the Persian Sesanian Empire, which employed the Tigris and Euphrates Rivers for irrigation. Southern Iraq was inhabited by Arabian tribesmen, some of whom recognized the Sesanian monarchy. From early on, Iraq enjoyed a rich cultural diversity. Some of the ethnic minorities that migrated to the region included Persians, Aramaic-speaking peasants, Bedouin tribal groups, Kurds, and Greeks.

In 627 A.D. the Byzantines invaded Iraq, although efforts to seize control of the region failed. A period of civil strife followed, which left the region open to Muslim raiders. Iraq subsequently became a province of the Muslim *caliphate* (A caliphate is the highest office within the structure of Islamic religion). Early caliphs were the successors of Mohammed, the founder of Islam. In 632 the Muslims of Medina elected Abu Bakr as the first caliph. The Omayyad dynasty of caliphs ruled from Damascus until 750, when Shiite Muslims, who descended from the caliph Ali, massacred the Omayyad family. The Shiite Muslims subsequently established the Abbasid as the caliph. The revolution that brought the Abbasid family to power prompted a period of medieval prosperity for Iraq, whose center was Baghdad (known as the "city of peace"). The peak of prosperity came with the reign of Harum ar-Rashid (786–809), during which time Iraq was the pillar of the Muslim world. Shortly after the ninth century, however, the caliphate began to disintegrate.

Mongols led by Hulegu, the grandson of Genghis Khan, captured Baghdad in 1258. This resulted in a long period of decline. Baghdad was crushed during the invasion, and nearly one million people perished. After a period of internal chaos, Iraq was drawn into the Ottoman Empire. Although rule under the Turks was despotic, Iraq profited from Ottoman rule, as economic conditions as well as overall quality of life improved for most inhabitants. Ottoman rule resulted in Muslim Sunnite dominance in the north, although the Shiites in the south were generally free to practice Islam as they chose. The weakening of the Ottoman Empire led to local control of Iraqi provinces, which was often tyrannical. Centralized control was restored to the region with the rise of the Mamluk regime in the eighteenth century. The Mamluks were Christian slaves who converted to Islam. Throughout the first half of the eighteenth century, Iraq was dominated by the Georgian Mamluk regime, which succeeded in restoring political and economic order to the region and included the rule of Suleiman II (1780-1803). In 1831, the reign of Daud, the last Mamluk leader, ended. Iraq once again fell under Ottoman rule, during which time the governorship of Midhat Pasha exerted its modernizing influence. Midhat restructured the city of Baghdad by tearing down a large section of the city. Midhat then established a transportation system, new schools and hospitals, textile mills, banks, and paved streets. Also at this time, the first bridge across the Tigris River was constructed.

After World War I Great Britain occupied Iraq and helped the nation achieve gradual independence through a mandate issued by the League of Nations. However, Great Britain's influence in the region was undermined by a growing sense of nationalism in Iraq. In 1921 a monarchy was established, and shortly thereafter Iraq entered a treaty alliance with Great Britain and drafted a constitution. Complete independence would not be achieved until 1932. The new monarchy under the rule of King Faisal had difficulty controlling minority unrest. Assyrians rebelled in 1933 and were brutally put down. In 1936 another coup toppled the monarchy. Despite the political instability that characterized the new government until World War II, Iraq made significant improvements in its infrastructure.

During World War II economic progress stagnated, and communism was growing in popularity. In 1945 the Kurds, an ethnic minority group, attempted to establish an autonomous republic but failed in 1945. Iraq was occupied by Western forces and used as a conduit for supplying Russia during the war. After the war foreign troops left the region, and Iraq enjoyed a period of peace and prosperity under the monarchy of Nuri al-Said. Iraq helped establish the League of Arab States in 1948. Prosperity continued under King Faisal II, during which time new irrigation, communication, and oil production facilities were put in place.

In large part because the monarchy neglected the masses, a military coup took place in 1958 in which the king and his family were murdered. General Abdul Karim Kassem formed a military dictatorship and abolished the frail democratic institutions that had been in place. Kassem was assassinated in another coup, and a revolution in 1968 brought the Ba'th party to power under General Ahmad Hassan al-Bakr.

MODERN ERA

By 1973 the Iraqi Communist Party had full control of governmental affairs. In 1974 the Ba'th Party placated the Kurds, who made another push for independence, by offering them an autonomous region. Bakr resigned from office in 1979 and was succeeded by Saddam Hussein, who was next in command. One of his first acts as head of state was the invasion of Iran in 1980 when Iran failed to honor a 1975 treaty, according to which land bordering the two countries was to be returned to Iraq. Although the campaign was initially successful, it ultimately plunged the country into an eight-year battle with Iran from which neither side profited in the end. Iraq lost more than one million of its men during the war. Throughout the war Iraq was supported by several Western nations, including the United States, which furnished Iraq with military information about Iran's strategic movements in the Persian Gulf and attacked Iranian ships and oil platforms.

After the war with Iran, Saddam Hussein made efforts to implement democratic reforms, including the drafting of a new constitution that would introduce a multiparty system and provide for freedom of the press. Before the plans could be implemented, however, Iraq invaded Kuwait in August of 1990. One of the reasons behind the invasion was that Iraq had accumulated more than $80 billion in war debt during the war with Iran, a substantial portion of which was owed to Kuwait. When Hussein's effort to seize control of border territories diplomatically (claiming a historical right to them) failed, he resorted to force. On the same day as the invasion the United Nations passed Resolutions 660 and 661, which ordered Iraq's withdrawal from Kuwait and imposed economic sanctions, respectively. Hussein ignored the resolutions and declared Kuwait a province of Iraq in late August of 1990. A UN effort that included the support of several Arab nations issued air strikes and sent ground troops into the region in early 1991. The United States participated heavily in the conflict, in large part to protect Saudi Arabia, as well as to maintain the balance of power in the Middle East. By April of 1991 Iraq capitulated and withdrew from Kuwait.

The Persian Gulf War nearly destroyed Iraq's military forces and devastated the infrastructure of its major cities. In addition, damage to oil refineries and economic sanctions left Iraq in economic disarray. Internal political conflict followed the war as Kurds and Shiites rebelled. Hussein crushed the insurrections, however, driving thousands of Kurds to Turkey seeking refuge. Iraq later entered into negotiations with the Kurds in an effort to establish autonomy for the ethnic minority and legalized opposition parties to the central government.

SIGNIFICANT IMMIGRATION WAVES

Although there are roughly two million Arabic-speaking immigrants in the United States, a very small portion of that group (approximately 26,000) came from Iraq. There were two general immigration waves that ushered Middle Eastern groups to the United States: the World War II wave, and the post–World War II wave. Immigration to the United States from the Arab community between 1924 and 1965 was extremely limited. During this period a quota of no more than 100 Arabs were admitted, in accordance with the Johnson-Reed Act of 1924. Early immigration reports suggest that immigrants from the Arab community did not come to the United States in response to persecution or political repression. Most Muslims came seeking economic wealth that they ultimately planned to transport back to their native countries.

SETTLEMENT PATTERNS

A large portion of current Iraqi refugees migrated to the United States after the Gulf War. Roughly 10,000 Iraqi refugees were admitted to the U.S. after the 1991 war. The two main groups admitted were the Kurds, a minority group in Iraq who were the target of Iraqi persecution, and Muslim Shi'a, from southern Iraq, who demonstrated animosity toward Saddam Hussein in 1991 by orchestrating an uprising against the regime.

The Muslim immigrants that came to the United States from Iraq in the 1990s were unlike previous groups from the Middle East. Other Muslim immigrants, such as the well-educated Lebanese and Iranians who came to the United States in the 1950s and 1960s, had sufficient exposure to Western culture to adapt easily to American society. The Muslims from Iraq, however, were much more conservative, believing in such traditional customs as arranged marriages and raising children with a firmness that could easily be construed as child abuse in the United States. Belief in traditional Muslim values made for a difficult transition for some Iraqi families. In one instance an Iraqi family that migrated to Lincoln, Nebraska, was the subject of national attention. The father of the household arranged marriages for his 13- and 14-year-old daughters to two Iraqi American men ages 28 and 34, when he suspected they intended to engage in premarital sex. Although the legal marrying age in Iraq is 18, fathers customarily marry their daughters at an earlier age in order to preclude the temptation to have sexual contact before marriage. The incident brought to light the distance between Muslim custom and law and American custom and law.

Some observers believe that not enough is being done to acculturate Middle Eastern refugees. Although Christian organizations such as Catholic Social Services (which contracts with the federal government to assimilate various refugee groups) make a concerted effort to orient Muslims and other incoming refugees to American laws and customs, it sometimes is not enough to bridge the gap between cultures. The arranged marriage in Nebraska to the two minor girls, although clearly a transgression of American law, is somewhat common among Iraqi immigrants in the United States. In fact there are often public advertisements put out by Iraqi fathers seeking single Iraqi men to wed their daughters.

Historically, immigrant groups profit from the experience of their predecessors. In the case of Iraqi immigrants, however, many of who are first-generation refugees, assimilation is something accomplished in large part on their own. Some scholars have noted that in the past, a sort of "assimilation contract" existed, by which immigrants would be able to retain their cultural diversity in the United States in exchange for committing to learning and accepting American law and custom. However, the "contract" is now being undermined by court decisions that have begun to recognize cultural and legal ignorance as a valid defense against violations of American law.

ACCULTURATION AND ASSIMILATION

As one might expect, life for Iraqi Americans has not been as harmonious as other immigrant groups, given the history of relations between the United States and Iraq. Many Iraqis living in the United States are torn between their loyalty to their former country and their allegiance to their new home. However, the majority, if not all, of the Iraqi people living in the United States agree that Saddam Hussein is at the root of the domestic unrest in their homeland. Moreover, most believe that Iraq will not reach a point of domestic tranquility and earn the respect of the international community unless and until Saddam Hussein's regime falls. Nonetheless, out of concern for their friends and family at home, Iraqi Americans tend not to endorse trade sanctions and air strikes against Iraq.

CUISINE

One of the main Arab dishes is called *hummus*, which is ground chickpeas and garlic with spices served with flat pita bread. Some of the staples of the Muslim diet include rice, garlic, lemon, and olive oil. Pork is forbidden for religious reasons. Most dishes are eaten with one's hands. Traditionally, the right hand is used because it is considered the cleaner of the two. A common expression extended to the chef out of appreciation is *tislam eedaek*, which means "bless your hand."

Other common Arab dishes include shish kebab and *falafel*, which are deep fried balls of chickpeas served with *tahini* (sesame sauce). Some of the less common dishes include *bistilla*, meat and rice served inside a pastry shell, and *musakhem*, roasted chicken with onions and olive oil. The traditional Arab dessert is *baklava*, which is an exquisite pastry with layers of *phyllo* dough covered with nuts and honey.

HEALTH ISSUES

Health care is free in Iraq, and the vast majority of medical facilities have been nationalized. In rural areas there is a shortage of adequate health care facilities and personnel. Despite the advances Iraq has made in health care since the 1970s, outbreaks of infectious diseases such as malaria and typhoid are somewhat common in Iraq. In recent years, genetic defects and children born with permanent disabilities have been on the rise in Iraq because of the chemicals used during warfare over the past two decades. These problems translate into poor health statistics among Iraqi immigrants in the United States, since many come here seeking the health care that was unavailable or require an extensive waiting period in their native country.

LANGUAGE

The official language of Iraq is Arabic, though there are many different dialects spoken throughout the nation. The largest minority group is the Kurds, who speak Kurdish. Roughly 80 percent of the population speak some derivation of Arabic.

Although there are nearly as many different Arabic dialects spoken in Iraq as there are towns and villages, the variation between the towns and villages are not as pronounced as they are in other Arabic-speaking nations such as Syria and Lebanon. Arabic derives from the ancient Semitic languages. There are 28 letters in the Arabic language, none of which are vowels, which makes it extraordinarily complex. Vowels are expressed by positioning points or by inserting the consonants *alif*, *waw*, or, *ya* in places where they are not usually used. Arabic is written from right to left. Modern-day Arabic is slightly different from the classical literary Arabic that was used to write the Koran, though it follows the same stylistic format. Devout Muslims see the Koran as God's word in both style and substance and view any colloquial deviation from pure Arabic as an assault on the integrity of the language. However, the majority of Muslims have adapted the language to meet their needs. In Iraq as well as most Arabic-speaking nations, the majority of the educated population are essentially bilingual, having a command of both classical literary Arabic and their local variation. In public forums, schools, media, and in parliament pure classical Arabic is used.

FAMILY AND COMMUNITY DYNAMICS

EDUCATION

Since the revolution of 1958 there has been an increased emphasis on education within the Ministry of Education and the Ministry of Higher Education and Scientific Research in Iraq. Iraq leads the Arab world in the numbers of qualified scientists, administrators, and technicians it produces. Education is free and is compulsory to the age of 12, and there is easy access to education to the age of 18. The government guarantees jobs to students affiliated with the Ba'th party after they graduate. Many Iraqi students come to the United States for their postgraduate education. Although women have generally suffered limited access to education, their enrollment has been consistently rising. In higher education institutions in Iraq, female enrollment is around 50 percent. The number of Iraqi American women attending institutions of higher learning has increased as well, with some women immigrating to the United States, alone or with their families, solely for this opportunity.

THE ROLE OF WOMEN

Iraq, like many Arab nations, is a patriarchal society. Women historically have had less access to education beyond primary school and have been discouraged from entering the workforce. This trend, however, has been changing in the 1990s, as more and more women have been attending Iraqi universities and contributing to the workforce, in large part out of economic necessity. In general, female refugees tend to come to the United States with their families, as wives and daughters, which facilitates the transfer of traditional patriarchal values to their host country.

Iraqi women, as well as Iraqi American women, bear the burden of reproducing Muslim values. Unlike other ethnic minorities that migrate to the United States, the Arab female generally benefits less from the liberal environment of American society. Because women are expected to propagate cultural values, their role is often limited to family affairs, which leaves little opportunity to expand their existence beyond child rearing. In addition, there is some pressure among individual Arab immigrant groups to convince other groups to conform to traditional Islamic values, one of which is the belief that women should be submissive and subservient to men. Though this is not the experience of all Arab females that migrate to the United States, it seems to be common for many.

WEDDINGS

Traditional Iraqi American weddings are elaborate affairs. The bride and groom sit in miniature thrones while guests join hands and dance in a circle before them. For those who can afford it, a ballroom is rented, an orchestra is hired, and elaborate feasts are prepared. It is customary for the groom to demonstrate financial security before he is accepted as an adequate husband by the bride's parents. The divorce rate in Iraq, which has historically been low in Arab nations, has been on the rise because of the hardships brought on by a lack of economic opportunity. This has not been the case with the divorce rate among Iraqi Americans, which remains quite low.

RELIGION

Islam came to Iraq in roughly 632 A.D. and has been the dominant religion ever since. Islam has been divided into two major sects: the Sunni and Shiite. The Sunnite sect is the more prevalent of the two throughout the Arab world, but in Iraq the division is nearly equal. For the most part religious tensions between the two denominations has given way to economic and political tensions. Islam is the state religion of Iraq, though minorities of Christians, Jews, Yezidis, and Mandaens are tolerated.

Islam, which means "submission," dominates cultural and political life in most Arab nations, and Iraq is no exception. Mecca is the holy city of Islam because it is where the prophet Mohammed first preached his teachings from God. The beginning of the Muslim calendar corresponds with Mohammed's pilgrimage. The Kaaba, in Mecca, is the holy shrine of Islam.

The teachings of Mohammed, which are considered by Muslims to be the word of God, were transcribed to the holy book of Islam called the Koran. Mohammed illustrated a code of conduct for life. Islamic tradition holds that religion, law, commerce, and social life are one entity. The central law of Islamic religion is called the *shahada*, or testimony, which holds that: "There is no God but Allah and Mohammed is his Prophet." One need only recite the *shahada* with unquestioning conviction in order to convert to Islam, and devout Muslims must declare the *shahada* aloud and with full conviction once in their life. Other tenets of Islam include the belief in resurrection, the final judgment of man, and the predetermination of man's every act. Islam holds that God sends a prophet to earth to lead mankind back to God's path. There have been thousands of prophets sent by God, including Adam, Noah, Abraham, Moses, Jesus, and Mohammed.

There are five central teachings of Islam, which are called the Five Pillars: declare the oneness of God; pray often; fast; give alms; and make a pilgrimage to the holy city. The Five Pillars play a central role in the lives of Muslims, who are required to pray five times each day, first standing and then kneeling. Practitioners of Islam are expected to fast from sunrise to sunset during Ramadan, which is the ninth month of the Muslim calendar. During fasting periods Muslims, with the exception of the sick and wounded, must refrain from food, drink, and all other worldly pleasures. Muslims are instructed by the Koran to give to the poor in money or in kind on a regular basis. Lastly, Muslims are required to make a pilgrimage to Mecca once in their lifetime. The pilgrimage, called the *hajj*, is considered the culmination of Islamic practice.

Another component of Islamic teaching is the *jihad*, which literally means "exertion." Muslims are asked to spread the word of God to all the peoples of the world. Many Westerners mistakenly refer to *jihad* as "holy war," or an endorsement by the Koran to wage war on those who do not follow the Islamic faith. In fact, the Koran emphasizes that conversions are not to be executed by force. Some Arab nations have employed the term, however, to mobilize and inspire their forces during times of war.

POLITICS AND GOVERNMENT

RELATIONS WITH IRAQ

Many Iraqi Americans have mixed emotions about their former homeland. On the one hand, they love their country and want to see it flourish, but on the other they despise Saddam Hussein and the international disrepute and social and economic devastation he has brought to the country. Some Iraqi Americans have the same ambivalence about UN and U.S. air strikes against Iraq. Although they support deposing the tyrannical Iraqi leader, they fear for the lives of their friends and family back home.

Some Iraqi Americans who participated in an uprising against Iraqi president Saddam Hussein after the war are critical of U.S. attacks designed to punish the Iraqi leader for failing to comply with UN resolutions. Although they stand in decisive opposition to Saddam Hussein, they are critical of U.S. attacks (recently carried out in December of 1998) because, they contend, they have not accomplished their stated objective of removing Saddam Hussein from power. For instance, one Iraqi refugee, Muhammad Eshaiker, a California resident, summed up his feelings in a news article by Vik Jolly in the *Orange County Register*: "I am torn apart between my love for America and my love for Iraq. I reconcile that with the hope that one day Saddam [will be gone] and the relations between the U.S. and Iraq will improve."

Iraq was declared a republic under a provisional constitution adopted in 1970. In theory, an elected body heads the legislative branch, a president and a council of ministers leads the executive branch, and the judiciary is independent. In practice, however, the constitution has little bearing on political affairs. Opposition to the central government has been consistently repressed throughout Iraq's history. All of the influential governing duties are carried out by the Revolutionary Command Council (RCC), a veritable extension of the ruling Arab Socialist Ba'th party, which came to power in 1968 and has remained the ruling party.

MEDIA

The Arab News Network (ANN).
The ANN has a website that provides access to a variety of newspapers published in Arabic.

Contact: Eyhab Al-Masri.
E-mail: ealmas01@fiu.edu.
Online: http://www.fiu.edu/~ealmas01/ann-online.html.

Iraq Opposition Daily News.
Affiliated with ABC News; provides up-to-date information on Iraqi-United States political affairs.

Online: http://www.abcnews.go.com/sections/world/dailynews/iraq0220_opposition.html.

RADIO

Free Iraq Service.

Provides weekly broadcasts in Arabic on current political and social developments in Iraq. The Free Iraq Service also publishes a weekly magazine (*Free Iraq*) that updates political events associated with post–Gulf War developments in Iraq.

Online: http://www.rferl.org/bd/iq/magazine/index.html.

ORGANIZATIONS AND ASSOCIATIONS

The Iraq Foundation.

The Iraq Foundation is a nonprofit nongovernmental organization striving for political democracy in Iraq and the protection of human rights for Iraqi citizens. Their website provides news and updates on political and social events related to Iraq.

Address: The Iraq Foundation, 1919 Pennsylvania Avenue, NW Suite 850 Washington, D.C. 20006.
Telephone: (202) 778-2124 or (202) 778-2126.
Fax: (202) 466-2198.
E-mail: Iraq@iraqfoundation.org.
Online: http://www.iraqfoundation.org.

Iraqi National Congress (INC).

The INC was founded in Vienna in June of 1992 and has a National Assembly of decision makers consisting of 234 members. The objective of the INC is to establish an operating base in Iraq from which to provide humanitarian relief to victims of Saddam Hussein's repressive regime. The INC is also soliciting the support of the international community to enforce UN Security Council resolutions.

Address: Iraqi National Congress 9 Pall Mall Deposit 124-128 Barlby Road, London W10 6BL.
Telephone: (0181) 964-8993.
Fax: (0181) 960-4001.
Online: http://www.inc.org.uk/.

SOURCES FOR ADDITIONAL STUDY

Harris, George, et al. *Iraq: Its People, Its Society, Its Culture*. New Haven, CT: HRAF Press, 1958.

Longrigg, Stephen H. and Frank Stoakes. *Iraq*. New York: F. A. Praeger, 1958.

McCarus, Ernest, ed. *The Development of Arab-American Identity*. Ann Arbor: University of Michigan Press, 1994.

al-Rasheed, Madawi. "The Meaning of Marriage and Status in Exile: The Experience of Iraqi Women." *The Journal of Refugee Studies*, Vol. 6 no. 2, 1993.

IRISH AMERICANS

by
Brendan A. Rapple

OVERVIEW

The island of Ireland lies west of Great Britain across the Irish Sea and St. George's Channel. It is divided into two separate political entities: the independent Republic of Ireland, and Northern Ireland, a constituent of the United Kingdom. Dublin is the capital of the former, Belfast of the latter. The country is divided into four provinces: Leinster, Munster, Connaught, and Ulster. All of the first three and part of the fourth are situated within the Republic of Ireland. Ulster is made up of nine counties; the northeastern six constitute Northern Ireland. The area of the Republic of Ireland is 27,137 square miles, that of Northern Ireland is 5,458 square miles. The entire island, with a total area of 32,595 square miles, is a little larger than the state of Maine. The population of the Republic of Ireland in 1991 was approximately 3,523,401, that of Northern Ireland 1,569,971. About 95 percent of the Republic's population is Roman Catholic; most of the rest are Protestant. Over 25 percent of Northern Ireland's population is Roman Catholic; about 23 percent is Presbyterian; about 18 percent belong to the Church of Ireland; the rest are members of other churches or of no stated denomination.

HISTORY

Ireland was occupied by Celtic peoples, who came to be known as Gaels, sometime between 600 and

400 B.C. The Romans never invaded Ireland so the Gaels remained isolated and were able to develop a distinct culture. In the fifth century A.D. St. Patrick came to Ireland and introduced the Gaels to Christianity. Thus began a great religious and cultural period for the country. While the rest of Europe was swiftly declining into the Dark Ages, Irish monasteries—preserving the Greek and Latin of the ancient world—not only became great centers of learning, but also sent many famous missionaries to the Continent. Toward the end of the eighth century Vikings invaded Ireland and for over two centuries battled with the Irish. Finally in 1014 the Irish under King Brian Boru soundly defeated the Viking forces at the Battle of Clontarf. An important legacy of the Viking invasion was the establishment of such cities as Dublin, Cork, Waterford, Limerick, and Wexford. In the second half of the twelfth century King Henry II began the English Lordship of Ireland and the challenge of the Anglo-Norman Conquest commenced. By the close of the medieval period many of the Anglo-Norman invaders had been absorbed into the Gaelic population.

English kings traveled to Ireland on several occasions to effect order and increase allegiance to the Crown. The English were generally too occupied with the Hundred Years War (1337-1453) and with the War of the Roses (1455-1485) to deal adequately with the Irish, however. By the sixteenth century English control over Ireland was limited to a small area of land surrounding Dublin. Consequently, Henry VIII and his successors endeavored to force the Irish to submit through military incursions and by "planting" large areas of Ireland with settlers loyal to England. A forceful resistance to the English reconquest of Ireland was led by the Northern chieftain Hugh O'Neill at the end of the sixteenth century. Following O'Neill's defeat in 1603 and his subsequent flight to the Continent, the Crown commenced the large-scale plantation of Ulster with English; Scottish Presbyterians soon followed. During the seventeenth century Ireland, continuing its steady decline, came increasingly under England's rule. In 1641 the Irish allied themselves to the Stuart cause; however, after the defeat and execution of King Charles I in 1649 Cromwell and his Puritans devastated much of Ireland, massacred thousands, and parceled out vast tracts of land to their soldiers and followers. Hoping to regain some of their property, the Catholic Irish sided with the Catholic James II of England but their fortunes further declined when James was defeated by William of Orange at the Battle of the Boyne in 1690. To keep the Irish subservient and powerless the English enacted a series of brutal penal laws, which succeeded so well that eighteenth century Catholic Ireland was economically and socially wasted.

In 1800, two years after the defeat of the rebellion of Protestant and Catholic United Irishmen led by Wolfe Tone, the Act of Union was passed, combining Great Britain and Ireland into one United Kingdom. The Catholic Emancipation Act followed in 1829 chiefly due to the activities of the Irish politician Daniel O'Connell. During the 1830s and 1840s a new nationalist movement, Young Ireland, arose. A rebellion that it launched in 1848, however, was easily defeated. The second half of the 1840s was one of the grimmest periods in Irish history. Due to the great famine caused by the crop failure of Ireland's staple food—the potato—millions died or emigrated. The second half of the nineteenth century saw increased nationalistic demands for self-government and land reform, most notably in the activities of the Home Rule Movement under the leadership of Charles Stewart Parnell. Though home rule was finally passed in 1914, it was deferred because of the onset of World War I. On Easter Monday in 1916 a small force of Irish nationalists rebelled in Dublin against British rule. The rising was a military failure and had little support among the public. However, the harsh response of the British government and particularly its execution of the rising's leaders won many over to the cause. After the Anglo-Irish Treaty was signed in 1921, the Irish Free State, whose constitutional status was tied to the British Commonwealth and required allegiance to the Crown, was established. The Free State was composed of 26 of Ireland's 32 counties; the other six remained part of Britain. In 1949 the 26 counties became the Republic of Ireland, an independent nation. Although the Republic has consistently maintained its claim over the six counties of the U.K.'s Northern Ireland and declared its wish to reunite the whole island into a sovereign nation, in recent decades it has placed more emphasis on economic and social rather than nationalistic issues. Nevertheless, the status of the six counties of Northern Ireland remains a highly critical concern for politicians in Dublin, Belfast, and London.

IRISH EMIGRATION

The Irish like to boast that St. Brendan sailed to America almost a millennium before Christopher Columbus; but even if St. Brendan did not make it to the New World, Galway-born William Ayers was one of Columbus's crew in 1492. During the seventeenth century the majority of the Irish immigrants to America were Catholics. Most were poor, many coming as indentured servants, others under agree-

ments to reimburse their fare sometime after arrival, a minority somehow managing to pay their own way. A small number were more prosperous and came seeking adventure. Still others were among the thousands who were exiled to the West Indies by Cromwell during the 1640s and later made their way to America. There was an increase in Irish immigration during the eighteenth century, though the numbers were still relatively small. Most of the century's arrivals were Presbyterians from the northern province of Ulster who had originally been sent there from Scotland as colonists by the British crown. Many of these, dissenters from the established Protestant church, came to America fleeing religious discrimination. In later years, especially in the second half of the nineteenth century, it was common to assign the term Scotch-Irish to these Ulster Protestant immigrants, although they thought of themselves as strictly Irish. There were also numerous Irish Quaker immigrants, as well as some Protestants from the south. A significant minority of eighteenth century immigrants were southern Catholics. Most of these were escaping the appalling social and economic conditions as well as

the draconian penal laws enacted by the British to annihilate the Celtic heritage and the religion of the Catholic majority. Some of these Catholic arrivals in America in time converted to Protestantism after encountering severe anti-papist discrimination as well as an absence of Catholic churches and priests. The preferred destinations of most of the eighteenth century Irish immigrants were New England, Maryland, Pennsylvania, the Carolinas, and Virginia.

IMMIGRATION UNTIL THE FAMINE YEARS

In the early years of the nineteenth century Protestants, many of whom were skilled tradesmen, continued to account for the majority of Irish immigrants. There were also numerous political refugees especially after the abortive United Irishmen uprising of 1798. However, by the 1820s and 1830s the overwhelming majority of those fleeing the country were unskilled, Catholic, peasant laborers. By this time Ireland was becoming Europe's most densely populated country, the population having increased from about three million in 1725 to over eight million by 1841. The land could not support such a number. One of the main problems was the absence of the practice of primogeniture among the Irish. Family farms or plots were divided again and again until individual allotments were often so small—perhaps only one or two acres in size—that they were of little use in raising a family. Conditions worsened when, in the wake of a post-Napoleonic Wars agricultural depression, many Irish were evicted from the land they had leased as tenants because the landlords wanted it used for grazing. The concurrent great rise in population left thousands of discontented, landless Irish eager to seek new horizons. Moreover, the increase in industrialization had all but ended the modest amount of domestic weaving and spinning that had helped to supplement the income of some families. In addition, famine was never distant—a number of severe potato failures occurred during the 1820s and 1830s before the major famine of the 1840s.

As the passage from Britain to the Canadian Maritimes was substantially cheaper than that to the United States, many Irish immigrants came first to Canada, landing at Quebec, Montreal, or Halifax, and then sailed or even walked down into America. After about 1840, however, most immigrants sailed from Ireland to an American port. Whereas most of the Irish Catholic immigrants during the eighteenth century became engaged in some sort of farming occupation, those in the subsequent century tended to remain in such urban centers as Boston, New York, and Philadelphia or in the textile towns where their unskilled labor could be readily utilized. The immigrants were impoverished but usually not as destitute as those who came during the famine. Many readily found jobs building roads or canals such as the Erie. Still, times were tough for most of them, especially the Catholics who frequently found themselves a minority and targets of discrimination in an overwhelmingly Protestant nation.

FROM FAMINE YEARS TO THE PRESENT

It was the cataclysmic Potato Famine of 1845-1851, one of the most severe disasters in Irish history, that initiated the greatest departure of Irish immigrants to the United States. The potato constituted the main dietary staple for most Irish and when the blight struck a number of successive harvests social and economic disintegration ensued. As many as 1.5 million individuals perished of starvation and the diverse epidemics that accompanied the famine. A great number of the survivors emigrated, many of them to the United States. From the beginning of the famine in the mid-1840s until 1860 about 1.7 million Irish immigrated to the United States, main-

ly from the provinces of Connaught and Munster. In the latter part of the century, though the numbers fell from the highs of the famine years, the influx from Ireland continued to be large. While families predominated during the Famine exodus, single people now accounted for a far higher proportion of the immigrants. By 1880 more single women than single men were immigrants. It has been estimated that from 1820 to 1900 about four million Irish immigrated to the United States.

Though the majority of Irish immigrants continued to inhabit urban centers, principally in the northeast but also in such cities as Chicago, New Orleans, and San Francisco, a significant minority went further afield. Only a small number went west to engage in farming, however. Most Irish immigrants were indeed peasants, but few had the money to purchase land or had sufficient skill and experi-

"The first time I saw the Statue of Liberty all the people were rushing to the side of the boat. 'Look at her, look at her,' and in all kinds of tongues. 'There she is, there she is,' like it was somebody who was greeting them."

Elizabeth Phillips in 1920, cited in *Ellis Island: An Illustrated History of the Immigrant Experience,* edited by Ivan Chermayeff et al. (New York: Macmillan, 1991).

ence to make a success of large-scale agriculture. Still, despite the great exploitation, oppression, and hardships suffered by many nineteenth-century Irish immigrants, the majority endured and their occupational mobility began to improve slowly. Their prowess and patriotic fervor in the Civil War helped to diminish anti-Irish bigotry and discrimination. As the years went by, the occupational caliber of Irish immigrants gradually improved in line with the slow amelioration of conditions in Ireland. By the end of the century a high proportion were skilled or semi-skilled laborers or had trades. Moreover, these immigrants were greatly aided by the Irish American infrastructure that awaited them. While life was still harsh for most immigrants, the parochial schools, charitable societies, workers' organizations, and social clubs aided their entry into a society that still frequently discriminated against Irish Catholics. Furthermore, the influx of even poorer southern and eastern European immigrants helped the Irish attain increased status.

In the twentieth century immigration from Ireland has ebbed and flowed. After World War I Irish immigration to the United States was high. After Congress passed legislation limiting immigration during the 1920s, however, the numbers declined. Numbers for the 1930s were particularly low. After World War II numbers again increased; but the 1960s saw emigration from Ireland falling dramatically as a result of new quota laws restricting northern Europeans. Accordingly, the number of Irish-born legal residents now in the United States is far lower than it was in the mid-twentieth century. From the 1980s onward, however, there has been an unprecedented influx of undocumented Irish immigrants, especially to such traditionally Irish centers as New York, Boston, Chicago, and San Francisco. These have been mainly young, well-educated individuals who have left an economically troubled country with one of the highest rates of unemployment in the European Community (EC). They prefer to work illegally in the United States, frequently in Irish-owned businesses, as bartenders, construction workers, nannies, and food servers, exposed to the dangers of exploitation and apprehension by the law, rather than remain on the dole at home. Their number is unknown, though the figure is estimated to be between 100,000 and 150,000.

ACCULTURATION AND ASSIMILATION

The Irish have been present in the United States for hundreds of years and, accordingly, have had more opportunity than many other ethnic groups to assimilate into the wider society. Each successive generation has become more integrated with the dominant culture. In the eighteenth century the Protestant Irish relatively easily became acculturated and socially accepted. However, it was far more difficult for the vast numbers of Catholic Irish who flooded into the United States in the post-famine decades to coalesce with the mainstream. Negative stereotypes imported from England characterizing the Irish as pugnacious, drunken, semi-savages were common and endured for at least the rest of the nineteenth century. Multitudes of cartoons depicting the Irish as small, ugly, simian creatures armed with liquor and a shillelagh pervaded the press; and such terms as "paddy-wagons," "shenanigans," and "shanty Irish" gained popularity. Despite the effects of these offensive images, compounded by poverty and ignorance, the Irish Catholic immigrants possessed important advantages. They arrived in great numbers, most were able to speak English, and their Western European culture was similar to American culture. These factors clearly allowed the Irish Catholics to blend in far more easily than some

other ethnic groups. Even their Catholicism, once disdained by so many, came to be accepted in time. Though some prejudices still linger, Catholicism is now an important part of American culture.

Today it is no longer easy to define precisely what is meant by an Irish American ethnic identity. This is especially so for later generations. Intermarriage has played a major role in this blurring of ethnic lines. The process of assimilating has also been facilitated by the great migration in recent decades of the Irish from their ethnic enclaves in the cities to the suburbs and rural regions. Greater participation in the multicultural public school system with a corresponding decline in parochial school attendance has played a significant role as well; another major factor has been the great decrease of immigrants from Ireland due to immigration laws disfavoring Europeans. Today, with 38,760,000 Americans claiming Irish ancestry (according to the 1990 census), American society as a whole associates few connotations—positive or negative—with this group. Among these immigrants and their ancestors, however, there is still great pride and a certain prestige in being Irish.

Still, there exists in some circles the belief that the Irish are less cultured, less advanced intellectually, and more politically reactionary and even bigoted than some other ethnic groups. The results of numerous polls show, however, that Catholic Irish Americans are among the best educated and most liberal in the United States. Moreover, they are well represented in law, medicine, academia, and other prestigious professions, and they continue to be upwardly socially mobile. Traditionally prominent in the Democratic ranks of city and local politics, many, especially since the Kennedy presidency, have now attained high positions in the federal government. Countless more have become top civil servants. Irish acceptability has also grown in line with the greater respect afforded by many Americans to the advances made by the Republic of Ireland in the twentieth century.

DANCES AND SONGS

Ireland's cultural heritage, with its diverse customs, traditions, folklore, mythology, music, and dance, is one of the richest and most distinctive in Europe. Rapid modernization and the extensive homogenization of western societies, however, has rendered much of this heritage obsolete or, at best, only vaguely perceived in contemporary Ireland. With their extensive assimilation into American culture there has been a decline in continuity and appreciation of the domestic cultural heritage among Irish Ameri-

cans as well. Nevertheless, there exist many elements in the Irish American culture that are truly unique and lend this group a distinct cultural character.

Irish music and song brought to America by generations of immigrants have played a seminal role in the development of America's folk and country music. Elements of traditional Irish ballads introduced during the seventeenth and eighteenth centuries are easily discernible in many American folk songs. Irish fiddle music of this period is an important root of American country music. This earlier music became part of a rural tradition. Much of what was carried to America by the great waves of Irish immigration during the nineteenth century, on the other hand, became an important facet of America's urban folk scene. With the folk music revival of the 1960s came a heightened appreciation of Irish music in both its American and indigenous forms. Today Irish music is extremely popular not only among Irish Americans but among many Americans in general. Many learn to play such Irish instruments as the pipes, tin whistle, flute, fiddle, concertina, harp, and the *bodhrán*. Many also attend Irish *céilithe* and dance traditional reels and jigs to hornpipes.

ST. PATRICK'S DAY

March 17 is the feast of St. Patrick, the most important holiday of the year for Irish Americans. St. Patrick, about whose life and chronology little definite is known, is the patron saint of Ireland. A Romano-Briton missionary, perhaps from Wales, St. Patrick is honored for spreading Christianity throughout Ireland in the fifth century. Though Irish Americans of all creeds are particularly prominent on St. Patrick's Day, the holiday is now so ubiquitous that individuals of many other ethnic groups participate in the festivities. Many cities and towns hold St. Patrick's Day celebrations, parties, and, above all, parades. One of the oldest observances in the United States took place in Boston in 1737 under the auspices of the Charitable Irish Society. It was organized by Protestant Irish. Boston, especially in the districts of South Boston, still holds great celebrations each year, though the holiday is now more closely identified with Catholic Irish. The largest and most famous parade is held in New York City, with the first parade in that city dating back to 1762. In the early years this parade was organized by the Friendly Sons of St. Patrick; in 1838 the Ancient Order of Hibernians became sponsor and still holds the sponsorship today. New York's main cathedral is dedicated to St. Patrick. Most people celebrating St. Patrick's Day strive to wear something green, Ireland's national color. Green dye is often put in food and drink. The mayor of Chicago regularly has the Chicago River dyed green for the day. If people cannot find a shamrock to wear they carry representations of that plant. According to legend the shamrock, with its three leaves on the single stalk, was used by St. Patrick to explain the mystery of the Christian Trinity to the pagan Irish. In Ireland St. Patrick's Day, though still celebrated with enthusiasm, tends to be somewhat more subdued than in the United States due to a greater appreciation of the religious significance of the feast.

TRADITIONAL COSTUMES

Hardly any true folk costume is still worn in Ireland. The *brat,* a black hooded woolen cloak, is sometimes seen on old women in County Cork. During the nineteenth century the shawl was found by many women to be a cheaper substitute for the cloak and even today older rural women might be shawled. The heavy white *báinín* pullovers, traditionally worn in the west and northwest of Ireland by fishermen whose sweaters each bore a unique and identifiable cable pattern, is now frequently seen throughout the nation. Traditional homespun tweed trousers are still sometimes worn by Aran Islander men. In America the Irish rarely wear any traditional costume. The main exception is the kilt which is sometimes worn by members of *céilí* bands and traditional Irish dancers. This plaid skirt is actually Scottish, however, and was adopted in the early twentieth century during the Gaelic Revival.

CUISINE

For the most part Irish Americans eat generic American food as well as the cuisine of other ethnic groups. Many Irish Americans do cook some of the dishes that make up the distinctive Irish cuisine, which is frequently served in Irish restaurants and pubs throughout America. There is a good market for the many shops in America that sell such Irish favorites as rashers (bacon), bangers (sausages), black and white pudding, and soda bread. Potatoes have traditionally constituted the staple of the Irish diet. The Irish also consume such dairy products as butter, milk, and cheese in large quantities. Many eat oatmeal stirabout or porridge for breakfast. Irish stew is a favorite dish. Smoked Irish salmon, imported from Ireland, is a popular delicacy. Other traditional foods include: soda bread, made with flour, soda, buttermilk, and salt (sometimes with raisins); coddle, a dish originating in Dublin that is prepared with bacon, sausages, onions, and potatoes; and *drisheens,* made from sheep's blood, milk, bread crumbs, and chopped mutton suet. Corned beef and cabbage, sometimes served with juniper berries, was a traditional meal in many parts of Ireland on Easter Sunday and is still consumed by many Irish Americans on this and other days. Boxty bread, a potato bread marked with a cross, is still eaten by some on Halloween or the eve of All Saint's Day. Also on the table at Halloween are colcannon, a mixture of cabbage or kale and mashed potatoes with a lucky coin placed inside, and barmbrack, an unleavened cake made with raisins, sultanas, and currants. A ring is always placed inside the barmbrack. It is said that whoever receives the slice containing the ring will be married within the year. Tea, served at all times of the day or night, is probably the most popular Irish beverage. Irish coffee, made from whiskey and coffee, is truly an Irish American invention and is not drunk much in Ireland. Though Scotch and whiskey are synonymous to many in other countries, the Irish believe that their whiskey, *uisce beatha* (the water of life), is a finer drink. Irish stout, particularly the Guinness variety, is well-known throughout the world.

PROVERBS

Sceitheann fíon fírinne (Wine reveals the truth); *Níl aon tinteán mar do thinteán féin* (There's no fireside like your own fireside); *Más maith leat tú a cháineadh, pós* (Marry, if you wish to be criticized); *Mol an óige agus tiocfaidh sí* (Give praise to the young and they will flourish); *An té a bhíos fial roinneann Dia leis* (God shares with the generous); *Is maith an scáthán súil charad* (The eye of a friend is a good mirror); *Is fada an bóthar nach mbíonn casadh ann* (It's a long road that has no turn); *Giorraíonn beirt bóthar* (Two people shorten the road).

HEALTH ISSUES

The health of Irish Americans is influenced by the same factors affecting other ethnic groups in the western world: old age, pollution, stress, excessive use of tobacco and alcohol, overly rich diet, employment and other economic problems, discord in marriage and personal relationships, and so on. The chief cause of death is heart-related diseases, exacerbated by the Irish fondness for a rich diet traditionally high in fat and caloric content. Alcohol plays a strong role in Irish American social life, and alcohol-related illnesses are common—the rate of alcoholism is high. Irish Americans also have an above-average rate of mental health diseases, with organic psychosis and schizophrenia being particularly prevalent.

In the earlier days of emigration the Irish, like numerous other groups, brought their folk medical remedies to America. Most of these, especially those associated with herbs, are unknown to the majority of contemporary Irish Americans; however, a number of traditional medical beliefs survive. In order to maintain good health and prevent illness many Irish recommend wearing holy medals and scapulars, blessing the throat, never going to bed with wet hair, never sitting in a draft, taking laxatives regularly, wearing camphor about the neck in influenza season, taking tonics and extra vitamins, enjoying bountiful exercise and fresh air, and avoiding physicians except when quite ill. Some traditional treatments are still used, such as painting a sore throat with iodine or soothing it with lemon and honey, putting a poultice of sugar and bread or soap on a boil, drinking hot whiskeys with cloves and honey for coughs or colds, and rubbing Vicks on the chest or breathing in hot Balsam vapors, also for coughs and colds.

Just as other groups in America, the Irish worry about the ever rising cost of medical care. Many would like improved medical insurance plans, whether national or private. The thousands of undocumented Irish throughout the United States who are not medically insured are particularly apprehensive of the frequently high expense of medical treatment.

LANGUAGE

Irish is a Celtic language of Indo-European origin, related to the ancient language of the Gauls. Linguistic scholars usually consider at least four distinct stages in the development of Irish: Old Irish (c. 600-900); Middle Irish (c. 900-1400); Early Modern Irish (c.1400-1600); and Modern Irish (c.1600-present). There are three fairly distinct dialects, those of Ulster, Munster, and Connaught. Beginning in the nineteenth century, Irish—until then widely spoken throughout Ireland—began a rapid decline mainly due to the Anglicization policies of the British government. Since the founding of the Irish Free State in 1921, however, the authorities have made great efforts to promote the widespread usage of Irish. Under the Constitution of the Republic of Ireland, Irish is decreed as the official language, though special recognition is given to English. Irish is still extensively taught in most schools. The result is that competence in Irish—as well as general interest in the language—is higher today than at any time in the Republic's history. Nevertheless, despite all efforts to render Irish a living national language, it is clear that it remains the daily language of communication for only about four percent of the population, most of whom live in small *Gaeltacht* (southwest, west, and northwest) areas. Only a tiny number of Northern Ireland's population speak Irish.

The decline in the usage of Irish and the triumph of English as the first language for most Irish throughout the nineteenth century, though undoubtedly a great loss for nationalistic and cultural reasons, proved to be a boon to Irish immigrants to the United States. Almost alone among new immigrants, apart from those from the British Isles, most spoke the language of their adopted country. Today, there is a resurgence of interest in the Irish language among many Irish Americans. In cities such as New York, Chicago, Boston, and San Francisco, classes in learning Irish are extremely popular. A growing number of American colleges and universities now offer courses in Irish language.

GREETINGS AND OTHER COMMON EXPRESSIONS

Dia dhuit ("dee-ah guit")—Hello; *Conas atá tú?* ("kunus ah-thaw thoo")—How are you; *Fáilte romhat!* ("fawilteh rowth")—Welcome; *Cad as duit?* ("kawd oss dit")—Where are you from; *Gabh mo leithscéal* ("gauw muh leshgale")—Excuse me; *Le do thoil* ("leh duh hull")—Please; *Tá dhá thaobh ar an scéa* ("thaw gaw hayv air un shgale")—There's something to be said on both sides; *Más toil le Dia* ("maws tule leh dee-ah")—God willing; *Tá sé ceart to leor* ("thaw shay k-yarth guh lore") It's all right; *Beidh lá eile ag an bPaorach!* ("beg law eleh egg un fairoch")—Better luck next time; *Buíochas le Dia* ("bu-ee-kus leh dee-ah")—Thank God; *Is fusa a rá ná a dhéanamh* ("iss fusa ah raw naw ah yea-anav")—Easier said than done; *Go raibh míle maith agat* ("guh row meela moh ugut")—Thank you very much; *Slán agat go fóill* ("slawn ugut guh fowil")—Good-bye for the present.

FAMILY AND COMMUNITY DYNAMICS

It is difficult to discuss the Irish American family in isolation from the broader society. Irish assimilation into the American culture has been occurring for a long time and has been quite comprehensive.

MARRIAGE

Traditionally the average age of marriage for the Irish was older than for numerous other groups. Many delayed getting married, wishing first to attain a sufficient economic level. Large numbers did not marry at all, deciding to remain celibate, some for religious reasons, others, it has been suggested, due to a certain embarrassment about sex. Today delayed marriages are less common and there is probably less sexual dysfunction both within and outside marriage. Furthermore, those Irish whose families have long been established in America tend to have a more accepting attitude towards divorce than do the more recently arrived Irish. Many young Irish Americans are more inclined than their elders to look favorably on divorce. The negative attitude of the Catholic church toward divorce still affects perceptions, however. Many Irish Americans, even those who obtain a civil divorce, seek to procure a church annulment of their marriages so that they may remarry within Catholicism. Though Irish Americans frequently intermarry with other groups there remains a strong leaning toward marrying within one's own religion.

WAKES

In remote times in Ireland the Irish generally treated death in a boisterous and playful manner. It is possible that the storytelling, music playing, singing, dancing, feasting, and playing of wake diversions during the two or three days the dead person was laid out prior to burial owed something to pre-Christian funeral games. Such activity may also have stemmed in part from a welcoming of death by an exploited and destitute people. Today, however, wakes among Irish Americans are much more sedate and respectable and generally last only one night. The main purpose of a wake is for relatives, neighbors, and friends to visit in order to pay their respects to the dead person and to offer condolences to the family. Though food and drink are still invariably offered to visitors, the traditional over-indulgence of eating and drinking rarely occurs. In years past the dead body was laid out on a bed in the person's own house. Today the wake often takes place in a funeral home with the body lying in a casket. Catholic dead often have rosary beads entwined in their crossed hands, and some are dressed in the brown habit or shroud of the Franciscan Third Order. Flowers and candles are usually placed about the casket. The laid-out corpse always has somebody standing beside it. This is mainly out of respect for the dead person. Many years ago, however, there was a practical reason for watching the body, namely to guard it from the predations of body-snatchers who would sell it to medical schools. The *caoine* or keening of women over the corpse is no longer heard in America. This custom has also, except for rare occasions, died out in Ireland. It is common for visitors to a wake to say a short silent prayer for the soul of the dead person.

THE ROLE OF WOMEN

The traditional Irish American mother remained at home to take care of the household. Female dominance of domestic life was common and the mother generally played a disproportionate role in raising the children. Not all Irish women were tied to the house, however. Many were also active in community oriented projects, such as charity activities, parochial work, and caring for the old and sick. In addition, many others displayed great independence and resolve last century when, fleeing the famine and terrible conditions in Ireland, they emigrated alone to the United States, a bold act for women of the period. This will and determination remains one of the most dominant character traits of contemporary Irish American females. Modern Irish American women are as likely, if not more so, to be as successful as their peers from other groups. Few today are content to devote their lives to traditional housework, with the great majority working in either part-time or full-time jobs. Great numbers have thrived in such professional spheres as academia, law, business, politics, and a variety of other occupations.

CHILDREN

Irish American families have traditionally been large. Today many families still tend to produce an above-average number of children. This may be due in part to the continued adherence of many Irish to the teachings of the Catholic church on contraception. How Irish Americans rear their children depends to a great extent on the socio-economic background of the family. Generally, however, children are treated firmly but kindly. They are taught to be polite, obey their parents, and defer to authority. The mother often plays the dominant role in raising children and imparting values; the father is frequently a distant figure. In many families negative reinforcement, such as shaming, belittling, ridiculing, and embarrassing children, is as common as positive reinforcement. There has always been a tendency to imbue children with a strong sense of public respectability. It even has been argued that this desire to be thought respectable has deterred many Irish from taking chances and has impeded their success. Overt affection displayed by parents toward their children is not as prevalent as in some other ethnic groups.

EDUCATION

In earlier generations, often more attention was paid to the education of sons than to that of daughters. It was generally thought that girls would become homemakers and that even if some did have a job such work would be considered secondary to their household duties. Today, however, though some Irish parents, particularly mothers, still "spoil" or indulge their sons, the education of daughters is a major concern.

Irish American families encourage achievement in school. In this they follow the traditional respect of the Irish for education. This dates back to when Irish monks helped preserve Latin and Greek learning in Europe, as well as the English language itself, by copying manuscripts during the fifth through eighth centuries when Ireland attained the name of "Island of Saints and Scholars." In addition, Irish Americans well understand that academic success facilitates achievement in wider social and economic spheres. The result is that Irish Catholics are among the top groups in the United States for educational attainment. They are more likely than any other white gentile ethnic group to go to college and are also more likely than most other ethnic groups to pursue graduate academic and professional degrees. While many Irish attend public schools, colleges, and universities, numerous others go to Catholic educational institutions. During the nineteenth century, however, many Irish parochial schools placed a greater emphasis on preventing Irish children from seduction by what many felt to be the Protestant ethos of the public schools. There is strong evidence that attendance at today's Catholic educational institutions, many of which have high standards, facilitates high levels of educational achievement and upward social mobility. Contrary to some beliefs, they are not deterrents to either academic or economic success. Among the most renowned Catholic universities attended by Irish Americans are Boston College and the University of Notre Dame.

RELIGION

Some early Catholic Irish immigrants converted to the pervasive Protestantism in America. However, the vast majority of subsequent Catholic immigrants, many holding their religion to be an intrinsic part of their Irish heritage as well as a safeguard against America's Anglo establishment, held steadfastly to their faith and, in so doing, helped Roman Catholicism grow into one of America's most powerful institutions. Since the late eighteenth century many aspects of American Catholicism have possessed a distinctly Irish character. A disproportionate number of Irish names may be found among America's past and present Catholic clergy. Scores of Irish laymen have been at the forefront of American Catholic affairs. The Irish have been particularly energetic supporters of the more concrete manifestations of their church and have established throughout America great numbers of Catholic schools, colleges, universities, hospitals, community centers, and orphanages, as well as churches, cathedrals, convents, and seminaries.

Until the mid-twentieth century, the life of Catholic Irish Americans revolved around their parish. Many children went to parochial schools, and the clergy organized such activities as sports, dances, and community services. There was little local politics without the participation of the priests. The clergy knew all the families in the community and there was great pressure to conform to the norms of the tightly knit parish. The parish priest, generally the best-educated individual of the congregation, was usually the dominant community leader. At a time when there were far fewer social workers, guidance counselors, and psychologists, parishioners flocked to their priest in times of trouble. Today the typical parish is less closed mainly due to the falling off in religious practice over the last decades of the twentieth century and the increased mainstreaming of parishioners. Nevertheless, there still remains a strong identification of many Catholic Irish with their parish.

The American Catholic church has undergone great changes since the 1960s, due largely to the innovations introduced by the Second Vatican Council. Some Catholic Irish Americans, wishing to preserve their inherited church practices, have been dismayed by the transformation. Some, alienated by the modernization of the liturgy, have been offended by what they consider a diminution of the mystery and venerability of church ritual with respect to the introduction of the vernacular, new hymns, and guitar playing at services. Some have attempted to preserve the traditional liturgy by joining conservative breakaway sects, and others have adopted different branches of Christianity.

Most Irish Americans have embraced the recent developments, however. The traditional Irish obedience to ecclesiastical authority is no longer certain as Rome asserts an uncompromising stance on many issues. Many Irish Catholics are now far more inclined to question doctrines and take issue with teachings on such subjects as abortion, contraception, divorce, priestly celibacy, and female priests. Certain members of the clergy have shown discontent; priests, nuns, and brothers have been leaving their orders in large numbers and there has been a concurrent decline in Irish vocations to the religious life. The numbers of Irish receiving the sacraments and attending mass and other church services have substantially declined; and many have abandoned puritan attitudes toward lifestyle issues, especially sex. Nevertheless, most Irish American Catholics are still faithful to many teachings of their church, and continue to identify as Catholics despite some disagreements with Vatican teachings.

EMPLOYMENT AND ECONOMIC TRADITIONS

The great majority of Catholic Irish immigrants in the eighteenth and the first half of the nineteenth century languished at the bottom of America's economic ladder as unskilled laborers. Though some were farm workers, many more worked in such areas as mining, quarrying, bridge and canal building, and railway construction. So many Irish were killed working on the railroad that it was commonly speculated that "there was an Irishman buried under every tie." Others were dockworkers, ironworkers, factory-hands, bartenders, carters, street cleaners, hod-carriers, and waiters. Irish women generally worked in menial occupations. Multitudes were employed as domestic servants in Anglo-Protestant households, while others worked as unskilled laborers in New England textile mills. Some Irish became quite successful but their numbers were few. The handful who attained white-collar status were frequently shopkeepers and small businessmen. There was an exceedingly meager number of Irish professionals. Those Irish who made the long trip to the western states tended to have somewhat more prestigious jobs than their compatriots in the East and North. This is due in part to the large numbers of Chinese in the West who did much of the manual laboring work. Many Irish participated in the California Gold Rush.

In the years after the Civil War the occupational lot of the Irish began to improve as more entered skilled trades. Many moved into managerial positions in the railroad, iron, construction, and other industries. Some went into business for themselves, especially in the building and contracting sectors. Numerous others became police officers, firefighters, streetcar conductors, clerks, and post-office workers. The Irish held many leadership positions in the trade union movement. Entertainment and athletics were other fields in which they began to attain greater recognition. It was more difficult for Irish women to move into higher prestige jobs, as there were far fewer opportunities for women in general at this time. Still, many attained upward occupational mobility by becoming teachers, nurses, and secretaries. Many Irish American nuns held positions of responsibility in hospitals, schools, and other Catholic social institutions.

By the beginning of the twentieth century Catholic Irish Americans were clearly ascending the occupational ladder. Though most remained members of the working class, large numbers moved into the ranks of the lower middle classes. Throughout the century this improvement in socioeconomic status has continued. Today the Irish are well represented in academia, medicine, law, government service, politics, finance, banking, insurance, journalism, the entertainment industry, the Catholic clergy, and most other professions.

POLITICS AND GOVERNMENT

The vast majority of Irish Catholic immigrants to the United States during the eighteenth and nineteenth centuries arrived as Democrats, a political stance imbued by years of oppression at the hands of the British. Not surprisingly, most favored the democratic policies of Thomas Jefferson and their vote greatly assisted his election to the presidency in 1801. Their political inclinations were again manifest in 1829 in their support for the populist politics of Democrat Andrew Jackson, America's seventh president and the nation's first of Irish (Protestant) background. Understanding that they were clearly unable to match the Anglo-Protestant establishment in the world of business and economics, Irish Catholics, many of whom entered the United States with fundamental political experience gained through mass agitation movements at home, realized that politics would provide them with a potent vehicle for attaining influence and power. In the years after the Civil War the Irish metier for political activity became increasingly evident. To many today the Irish control of New York's Tammany Hall, the center of the city's Democratic Party, is a resolute symbol of their powerful and sometimes dubious involvement in American urban politics. Though graft, cronyism, and corruption were once an integral part of many of their political "machines" in New York and other cities, Irish politicians were frequently more successful than their Anglo-Protestant counterparts in reaching the people, feeding the poor, helping the more unfortunate obtain jobs, and organizing other practical social welfare activities. The Irish political "machine" generally had a strong democratic, reformist, and pragmatic agenda, which frequently extended to Jews, Italians, Germans, Poles, and other nationalities.

The phenomenon of Irish domination of the political life of numerous cities continued well into the twentieth century. Two extremely influential and powerful figures of the old "machine" style were James Michael Curley (1874-1958), mayor of Boston for four terms, and Richard J. Daley, mayor of Chicago from 1954 to 1976. Irish involvement in both state and national politics also gained prominence in the twentieth century. Alfred Emanuel Smith (1873-1944), the grandson of Irish immigrants, was the first Irish Catholic to receive the nomination of a major party (Democratic) in a presidential election; he was defeated by Herbert Hoover. An Irish Catholic reached the White House in 1960 with the election of the Democrat John Fitzgerald Kennedy, who was assassinated in 1963. His brother, Senator Robert F. Kennedy, another prominent Democratic politician who served as attorney general in the Kennedy administration, was assassinated in 1968. A third brother, Edward, has been one of the most liberal and effective champions of social reform in the history of the Senate. Two other twentieth century Presidents, Richard M. Nixon and Ronald Reagan (both Republicans) were of Irish Protestant background. Numerous other Irish American politicians have gained state and national attention in recent decades. Both Mike Mansfield and George J. Mitchell were Senate majority leaders. Thomas O'Neill and Thomas S. Foley both served as Speaker of the House of Representatives. Another influential politician and 1976 presidential candidate was Eugene J. McCarthy of Minnesota.

Despite the notable presence this century of such influential reactionaries as the demagogue Father Charles Coughlin and the communist-baiter Senator Joseph McCarthy, Catholic Irish Americans are among the most likely to advocate the right of free speech. They also tend to be more supportive of liberal issues than many other white ethnic groups. For example, they have traditionally promoted such causes as racial equality, welfare programs, environmental issues, and gun control. Irish Americans have been and still are among the most stalwart supporters of the Democratic Party. Beginning in the late twentieth century, however, there has been a movement by some toward the Republican Party.

ARMED FORCES

The Irish, either as regulars or as volunteers, have served in all of America's wars. They fought with distinction in the Revolutionary War, most siding with Washington. It is estimated that as many as 38 percent of Washington's army was composed of Irish Americans, even though they made up only 10 percent of the population. Of the generals, 26 were Irish, 15 of whom were born in Ireland. In the Civil War most Irish sided with the Union and great numbers fought in the Yankee armies. "The Fighting 69th" was probably the most famous Irish regimental unit, though 38 other Union regiments had "Irish" in their names. The contribution of the Irish to the Confederate cause was also significant. As many as 40,000 Confederate soldiers were born in

Ireland and numerous others were of Irish ancestry. Irish Americans continued to fight in America's armies in subsequent wars and were particularly prominent, with many gaining decorations, in the two World Wars, the Korean War, and the Vietnam War. Their ready and distinguished participation in America's military conflicts has helped the Irish to gain respectability in the eyes of generations of other Americans and to assimilate into mainstream American life.

LABOR MOVEMENT

The Irish have contributed greatly to the labor movement in America. Their struggle for American workers' rights began as an outgrowth of their fight against oppression in Ireland. American capitalist injustice in industry was not too different in principle from persecution by English landlords at home. Even in the antebellum years the Irish were active in workers' organizations, many of which were clandestine, but it was during the second half of the nineteenth century that their involvement in labor activities became especially prominent. Particularly well known are the activities of the Molly Maguires, anthracite coal miners of Pennsylvania who in the 1860s and 1870s violently resisted the mostly English, Scottish, and Welsh mine bosses. Found guilty of nine murders, ten Mollies were hanged in 1876. This did not deter Irish involvement in American labor activities, however. Terrence V. Powderly (1849-1924), the son of an Irish immigrant, was for years leader of the Knights of Labor, the first national labor organization, which was founded in 1869. He later became commissioner general of immigration. Peter James McGuire (1852-1906), a carpenter, was another leading union activist. A founder of the American Federation of Labor, he was its secretary and first vice-president. He is perhaps best known today as the "Father of Labor Day." Irish women have also been prominent in America's labor movement. The Cork-born Mary Harris ("Mother") Jones (1830-1930), after losing all her possessions in the Chicago fire of 1871 began a 50-year involvement in organizing labor unions and in striving to improve workers' conditions and wages throughout the United States. Today, a nationally circulated magazine devoted to liberal issues bears her name. Another famous Irish female in the labor movement was Elizabeth Gurley Flynn (1890-1964) who co-founded the American Civil Liberties Union in 1920 and later became head of the United States Communist party. Kerry-born Michael Joseph Quill (1905-1966) founded the Transport Workers Union of America in 1934 and was its first president. In 1937 Joe Curran became the National

Maritime Union's first president. George Meany (1894-1979), grandson of an Irish immigrant, was president of the combined American Federation of Labor and Congress of Industrial Organizations (AFL-CIO) from 1955 to 1979. Irish American participation in America's unions and labor movement has been and continues to be of vital importance and benefit to the well-being of American society.

NORTHERN IRELAND

The attention of many Irish Americans of different generations has been sharply focused on the political affairs of Ireland ever since the Catholic civil rights movement began in Northern Ireland in the late 1960s. This movement was a response to decades of institutionalized and private discrimination against Catholics in this region since the creation of Northern Ireland as part of the United Kingdom in 1921. This discrimination by the Protestant majority was pervasive in such spheres as voting, housing, and employment. For the past three decades Northern Ireland has been convulsed by political upheaval, the frequently controversial tactics of an occupying force of British soldiers, Protestant and Catholic paramilitary activity, riots, killings, bombings, hunger strikes, internment without trial, and patent violations of human rights. The reactions of numerous Irish Americans have been forceful. In 1970 the Northern Ireland Aid Committee (NORAID) was formed to provide material help to Catholics in Northern Ireland. The Irish National Caucus, a Washington-based lobbying group, has been vociferous in its call for a British withdrawal from Northern Ireland and for a reunification of the whole nation. Many Irish American politicians have campaigned intensely to find a settlement to Northern Ireland's problems. Among the most prominent have been Senator Edward Kennedy of Massachusetts, Senator Daniel P. Moynihan of New York, former Speaker of the House of Representatives Tip O'Neill, and former Governor of New York Hugh Carey. These and other Irish American politicians and lobbying groups have consistently exerted pressure on successive administrations to use their influence with London, Belfast, and Dublin to help amend human rights abuses in Northern Ireland and to aid in the provision of social and economic justice in that region. After the Anglo-Irish Agreement was reached in England in November 1985 Congress, responding in part to pressure from Irish Americans, passed a multi-billion-dollar aid bill for Northern Ireland. The future of this region is by no means clear, despite the recent cease-fire by the Irish Republican Army (IRA), but it is expected that

Irish Americans will continue influence the policy of the major players in this conflict.

INDIVIDUAL AND GROUP CONTRIBUTIONS

It would constitute a thoroughly invidious task to provide a comprehensive record of the vast number of Irish Americans who have attained prominence over the past few centuries. The following list is necessarily selective, and countless other individuals might also have been named.

ART

There have been numerous Irish Americans who have achieved prominence in the arts. In the fine arts, for example, the following three achieved particular fame: Mathew Brady (1823-1896), Civil War photographer; James E. Kelly (1855-1933), sculptor; Georgia O'Keeffe (1887-1986), painter. Others include: Mathew Carey (1760-1839), author, book publisher, and political economist; Edgar Allan Poe (1809-1849), one of the greatest figures in American literature; Ring Lardner (1885-1933), short story writer and sports journalist; Mary O'Hara Alsop (1885-1980), popular novelist who focused on animal life; Eugene O'Neill (1888-1953), one of America's most eminent playwrights; F. Scott Fitzgerald (1896-1940), popular novelist and short story writer; James T. Farrell (1904-1979), author whose work, notably his Studs Lonigan trilogy, centered on working-class Irish American families on Chicago's South Side; John O'Hara (1905-1970), novelist and short story writer; Mary McCarthy (1912-1989), novelist and critic; Mary Flannery O'Connor (1925-1964), novelist and short story writer of the American South; and William F. Buckley (1925-), editor, critic, commentator, novelist.

BUSINESS AND FINANCE

Numerous Irish Americans have made their mark in the world of business and finance: William Russell (1812-1872), founder of the Pony Express; William Russell Grace (1832-1904), entrepreneur and first Roman Catholic mayor of New York; John Philip Holland (1840-1914), Clare-born father of the modern submarine; Anthony Nicholas Brady (1843-1913), wealthy industrialist whose interests extended from railroads to electric companies; Andrew Mellon (1855-1937), banker, art collector, and philanthropist; Samuel S. McClure (1857-1949), leading journalist and newspaper publisher; Henry Ford (1863-1947), auto manufacturer; James A. Farrell (1863-1943), head of United States Steel Corporation; and Howard Hughes (1905-1976), wealthy and eccentric industrialist, aerospace manufacturer, and movie maker.

EDUCATION

John R. Gregg (1867-1948), inventor of the Gregg system of shorthand; and William Heard Kilpatrick (1871-1965), philosopher and leader in the Progressive Education movement, are among prominent Irish American educators.

ENTERTAINMENT

A great number of Irish Americans have attained distinction in the entertainment industry: Victor Herbert (1859-1924), Dublin-born conductor and popular composer of operettas; Will Rogers (1879-1935), humorist and actor; John McCormack (1884-1945), popular Westmeath-born tenor; Buster Keaton (1895-1966), famous silent film comedian; Emmett Kelly (1898-1979), well-known circus clown; James Cagney (1899-1986), movie actor; film director John Ford (born Sean Aloysius O'Feeny; 1895-1973); Spencer Tracy (1900-1967), movie actor; Ed Sullivan (1901-1974), newspaper columnist and television personality; Bing Crosby (1901-1977), singer and movie and radio actor; Pat O'Brien (1900-1983), movie, radio, and television actor; John Huston (1906-1987), film director; John Wayne (1907-1979), movie actor; Errol Flynn (1909-1959), movie actor; Maureen O'Sullivan (1911-), movie actor; Gene Kelly (1912-), dancer, actor, singer; Tyrone Power (1913-1958), movie actor; Mickey Rooney (1920-), movie actor; Maureen O'Hara (1920-), movie actor; Carroll O'Connor (1924-), television actor; Grace Kelly (1929-1982), movie actor and later Princess of Monaco; Jack Nicholson (1937-), movie actor; and Mia Farrow (1945-), movie actor.

LABOR

Activists in the labor movement not mentioned already include: Leonora Barry (1849-1923), feminist and activist for women's suffrage; Mary Kenney O'Sullivan (1864-1943), active labor organizer; and Daniel Tobin (1875-1955), president of the Teamsters Union and a leader of the American Federation of Labor.

MILITARY

Several Irish Americans who have won renown in the military field have been mentioned. Others include: Lydia Barrington Darragh (1729-1789), Dublin-born heroine of the Revolutionary War and spy for George Washington; John Barry (1745-1803), Wexford-born "Father of the American Navy"; Margaret Corbin (1751-1800), heroine of the Revolutionary War; General Douglas MacArthur (1880-1964), leader of the Allied forces in the Pacific during World War II; William J. Donovan (1883-1959), World War I hero and later founder of the Office of Strategic Services; and Audie Murphy (1924-1971), the United States's most decorated soldier of World War II who later became a movie actor.

POLITICS AND LAW

The fields of politics and law have had more than their share of eminent Irish Americans; the following few may be added to those named earlier: Sir Thomas Dongan (1634-1715), Irish-born governor of New York in 1682; Sir William Johnson (1715-1774), army officer and superintendent of Indian Affairs; Pierce Butler (1744-1822), Carlow-born American political leader who signed the U.S. Constitution; Nellie Tayloe Ross (1876-1977), first female governor (of Wyoming 1925-1927) and first female director of the Mint (1933-1953); Sandra Day O'Connor (1930–), the first female Supreme Court Justice; William G. Brennan (1906–), Supreme Court Justice.

RELIGION

Famous Irish American religious leaders include: Archbishop John Joseph Hughes (1797-1864), first Roman Catholic archbishop of New York; John McCloskey (1810-1885), first American cardinal of the Roman Catholic church; James Gibbons (1834-1921), Francis Joseph Spellman (1889-1967), Richard J. Cushing (1895-1970), and Terence Cooke (1921-1983), all Roman Catholic cardinals; Archbishop Fulton John Sheen (1895-1979), charismatic Roman Catholic church leader; Father Andrew Greeley (1928–), priest, sociologist, and novelist. Two famous humanitarians are Father Edward Joseph Flanagan (1886-1948), Roman Catholic priest who worked with homeless boys and who founded Boys Town in Nebraska; and Thomas A. Dooley (1927-1961), medical doctor who performed great humanitarian work in southeast Asia.

SPORTS

Irish Americans have been eminent in sports as well, including: John L. Sullivan (1858-1918), James John "Gentleman Jim" Corbett (1866-1933), Jack Dempsey (1895-1983), and Gene Tunney (1898-1978), all heavyweight boxing champions; Babe Ruth (1895-1948), baseball player; Ben Hogan (1912–), golfer; Maureen "Little Mo" Connolly (1934-1969), tennis star who won the U.S. women's singles championship three times; and Jimmy Connors (1952–), another famous tennis player.

MEDIA

PRINT

Gryfons Publishers and Distributors.
Publisher specializing in new and reprinted works on Irish history and culture, particularly focusing on Gaelic royalism and heritage.

Contact: David Wooten.
Address: P.O. Box 1899, Little Rock, Arkansas 72203-1899.
Telephone: (501) 834-4038.
Fax: (501) 834-4038.
E-mail: ballywoodn@aol.com.
Online: http://gryfons.hypermart.net.

Irish America Magazine.
Established in 1984, the magazine publishes information about Ireland and Irish Americans, including book, play, and film reviews.

Address: Irish America, Inc., 432 Park Avenue South, No. 1000, New York, New York 10016-8013.

Irish Echo.
Established in 1928, this publication contains articles of interest to the Irish community.

Contact: Jane M. Duffin, Editor.
Address: 803 East Willow Grove Avenue, Wyndmoor, Pennsylvania 19038.
Telephone: (215) 836-4900.
Fax: (215) 836-1929.

Irish Herald.
Established in 1962, this newspaper covers Irish American interests.

Contact: John Whooley, Editor.
Address: Irish Enterprises, 2123 Market Street, San Francisco, California 94114.

Stars and Harp.

Carries profiles of Irish Americans and their contributions to the formation of the United States.

Contact: Joseph F. O'Connor, Editor.
Address: American Irish Bicentennial Committee, 3917 Moss Drive, Annandale, Virginia 22003.
Telephone: (703) 354-4721.

The World of Hibernia.

Upscale lifestyle magazine devoted to Irish American culture and notable Irish Americans.

Contact: Thomas P. Farley, Editor.
Address: 217 First St., Ho-Ho-Kus, New Jersey 07423.
E-mail: hibernia@interport.net.
Online: http://www.twoh.com.

RADIO

WFUV-FM (90.7).

"Míle Fáilte" presented by Séamus Blake, Saturdays 8:00 a.m. to 9:00 a.m.; "A Thousand Welcomes" presented by Kathleen Biggins, Saturdays 9:00 a.m. to 12:00 p.m.; "Ceol na nGael" presented by Eileen Fitzsimons and Marianna McGillicuddy, Sundays 12:00 p.m. to 4:00 p.m.

Contact: Chuck Singleton, Program Director.
Address: Fordham University, Bronx, New York 10458.
Telephone: (718) 817-4550.
Fax: (718) 365-9815.

WGBH-FM (89.7).

Celtic program presented by Brian O'Donovan, Sundays 12:00 to 2:00 p.m.

Contact: Martin Miller, Programming Director.
Address: 125 Western Avenue, Boston, Massachusetts 02134.
Telephone: (617) 492-2777.
Fax: (617) 787-0714.

WNTN-AM (1550).

"The Sound of Erin," Saturdays 10:30 a.m. to 7:00 p.m.

Contact: John Curran or Bernie McCarthy.
Address: P.O. Box 12, Belmont, Massachusetts 02178.
Telephone: (617) 484-2275 (John Curran); (617) 326-4159 (Bernie McCarthy).

WPNA-AM (1490).

Irish programming each Saturday 8:00 a.m. to 1:00 p.m., 6:30 p.m. to 9:00 p.m.

Contact: Bud Sullivan, the Hagerty Family, Mike O'Connor, Mike Shevlin, or Joe Brett.
Address: Alliance Communications, Inc., Radio Station WPNA, 408 South Oak Park Avenue, Oak Park, Illinois 60302.
Telephone: (708) 974-0108 (Bud Sullivan); (708) 834-8110 (the Hagerty Family); (708) 771-2228 (Mike O'Connor); (708) 282-7035 (Mike Shevlin); (312) 746-4561 (Joe Brett).

ORGANIZATIONS AND ASSOCIATIONS

American Irish Historical Society (AIHS).
The goal of the AIHS is to promote awareness among Americans of Irish descent of their history, culture, and heritage. To attain that end the AIHS presents lectures, readings, musical events, and art exhibitions. Each year the Society awards its gold medal to an individual who best reflects the Society's ideals. The Society's journal, *The Recorder*, is published semi-annually in the winter and summer, and contains articles on a wide range of Irish American and Irish topics with a primary focus on the contribution of the Irish in American history.

Contact: Thomas Michael Horan, Executive Director.
Address: 991 5th Ave., New York, New York 10028.
Telephone: (212) 288-2263.
Fax: (212) 628-7927.
E-mail: amerirish@earthlink.net.
Online: http://www.aihs.org.

Ancient Order of Hibernians in America (AOH).
Founded in Ireland in the early sixteenth century the AOH established its first American branch in New York City in 1836. Today the AOH, its membership almost 200,000, is the largest Irish American organization with divisions throughout the country. Originally founded to protect the Catholic faith of its members, the AOH still has this as one of its chief aims. It also seeks to promote an awareness throughout America of all aspects of Irish life and culture. The AOH publishes a bimonthly newspaper, *The National Hibernian Digest*.

Contact: Thomas D. McNabb, Secretary.
Address: 31 Logan Street, Auburn, New York 13021.
Telephone: (315) 252-3895.

Irish American Cultural Association (IACA).
Promotes the study and appreciation of Irish culture.

Contact: Thomas R. McCarthy, President.
Address: 10415 South Western, Chicago,
 Illinois 60643.
Telephone: (773) 238-7150.

Irish American Cultural Institute (IACI).

Founded in 1962 this non-profit foundation, whose purposes are non-political and non-religious, fosters the exploration of the Irish experience in Ireland and America. Among its programs are: Irish Perceptions, which facilitates tours and presentations in America of leading Irish actors, lecturers, musicians, and artists; Irish Way, which takes American high school students on a summer educational tour of Ireland; Art and Literary Awards, which provides grants aimed at stimulating the arts in Ireland; and the Irish Research Fund, which supports scholarly work by citizens of any country that illuminates the Irish American experience. IACI also awards a visiting fellowship in Irish Studies at University College, Galway, and scholarships for American undergraduate students to the University of Limerick. IACI publishes *Éire-Ireland*, a quarterly scholarly journal of Irish studies, and *Dúcas*, a bimonthly newsletter. The Institute has 15 chapters throughout the United States.

Contact: James S. Rogers, Director of Operations.
Address: University of St. Thomas, 2115 Summit
 Avenue, Mail No. 5026, St. Paul, Minnesota
 55105-1096.
Telephone: (612) 962-6040.
Fax: (612) 962-6043.

Irish American Partnership.

Individuals and organizations promoting stronger cultural ties between the United States and the Republic of Ireland. Encourages participation in the unique cultural practices and appreciation of the histories of both countries.

Contact: Joe Leary, President.
Address: 33 Broad Street, 9th Floor, Boston,
 Massachusetts 02109.
Telephone: (617) 723-2707.
Fax: (617) 723-5478.
E-mail: iap@irishap.org.

Irish Genealogical Society (IGS).

Promotes and encourages the study of Irish genealogy and other types of Irish studies.

Contact: Joseph M. Glynn, Jr., Director.
Address: 21 Hanson Avenue, Somerville,
 Massachusetts 02143.
Telephone: (617) 666-0877.

Irish Heritage Foundation (IHF).

Promotes Irish heritage and cultural awareness in the United States.

Contact: John Whooley, President.
Address: 2123 Market Street, San Francisco,
 California 94114.
Telephone: (415) 621-2200.

Irish National Caucus.

Founded in 1974, the Irish National Caucus, with a membership of about 200,000 Irish Americans, is a powerful lobbying group that seeks to publicize the violations of human rights in Ireland. Though it does not support any specific solution to the Irish problem, its ultimate objective is to achieve, by political, legal, and non-violent means, a peaceful Ireland free of British rule.

Contact: Fr. Sean McManus, President.
Address: 413 East Capitol Street, S.E.,
 Washington, D.C. 20003.
Telephone: (202) 544-0568.
Fax: (202) 543-2491.

Irish Institute (II).

Founded in 1950. Formerly known as Irish Feis Institute. Provides financial support for cultural projects in Ireland and the United States for U.S. citizens of Irish birth or extraction.

Contact: Kevin Morrissey, President.
Address: c/o Kevin Morrissey, P.O. Box 173,
 Woodside, New York 11377.
Telephone: (718) 721-3363.
Fax: (718) 721-3805.

MUSEUMS AND
RESEARCH CENTERS

American Conference for Irish Studies.
Founded in 1962.

Contact: Dr. Lucy McDiarmid, President.
Address: 1931 Panama Street, Philadelphia,
 Pennsylvania 19103.
Telephone: (215) 545-3015.
Fax: (215) 545-3015.
E-mail: mcdiarmid@acis.vill.edu.

American Irish Historical Society.

The library of the AIHS contains more than 30,000 volumes together with major manuscript and archival collections. It is probably the premier repository of library materials on the Irish in America. The library is open to the public by appointment.

Contact: Alec Ormsby.
Address: 991 Fifth Avenue, New York, New York 10028.
Telephone: (212) 288-2263.
Fax: (212) 628-7927.
E-mail: amerirish@earthlink.net.
Online: http://www.aihs.org.

An Claidheamh Soluis—The Irish Arts Center.
Aims to develop an understanding of Irish culture and arts among the Irish, Americans, and others. It offers a variety of courses in such subjects as Irish language, history, literature, dance, and traditional music. It has an excellent resident theater company. It also sponsors Irish dances, poetry-readings, lectures, and concerts. In addition, the Center publishes the monthly newsletter *Irish Arts—Ealaíona Éireannacha.*

Contact: Nye Heron, Executive Director.
Address: 553 West 51st Street, New York, New York 10019.
Telephone: (212) 757-3318.
Fax: (212) 247-0930.

Boston Public Library.
With more than 6,000,000 volumes, this library is one of the nation's major research libraries. It has particularly strong holdings, including numerous important manuscript and archival collections, relating to many aspects of the national and local history of the Irish in America. Irish American literature and music are also well represented.

Contact: Gunars Rutkovskis, Assistant Director, Resources and Research Library Services.
Address: Boylston Street, Boston, Massachusetts 02117-0286.
Telephone: (617) 536-5400.

Georgetown University, Joseph Mark Lauinger Library, Special Collections.
Contact: George M. Barringer, Head of Special Collections Division; or Nicholas B. Scheetz, Manuscript Librarian.
Address: 3700 O Street N.W., D.C. 20057-1006.
Telephone: (202) 687-7444.
Fax: (202) 687-7501.

Irish American Heritage Museum.
The exhibits, artifacts, and archives of this museum's collection cover many aspects of the Irish American experience from the earliest immigrants up to the present. There are plans to move the museum's research library of Irish American material from its present location at The College of St. Rose in Albany, New York, to the museum itself.

Contact: Monique Desormeau.
Address: Route 145, East Durham, New York 12423.
Telephone: (518) 634-7494.

John J. Burns Library, Boston College, Special Collections and Archives.
The Irish collection at Boston College's Burns Library is widely regarded as one of the most comprehensive collections of its kind outside of Ireland. Burns is also recognized for its extensive and important holdings in materials relating to Irish America. Included in the collection are papers of former Speaker of the House Tip O'Neill, the archives of the Charitable Irish Society (1889-present), the Eire Society of Boston (founded 1937), and the George D. Cahill (some 600 letters and ephemera, 1857-1900) and Patrick A. Collins (some 100 letters, 1880-1882) collections. Numerous other books and periodicals and several more manuscript collections relate to the history of the Irish, particularly in Boston.

Contact: Robert K. O'Neill, Burns Librarian.
Address: Chestnut Hill, Massachusetts 02167.
Telephone: (617) 552-3282.
Fax: (617) 552-2465.

St. John's University, Special Collections.
Contact: Szilvia E. Szmuk, Special Collections Librarian.
Address: Grand Central and Utopia Pkwys, Jamaica, New York 11439.
Telephone: (718) 990-6737.
Fax: (718) 380-0353.

SOURCES FOR ADDITIONAL STUDY

Blessing, Patrick J. *The Irish in America: A Guide to the Literature and the Manuscript Collections.* Washington, D.C.: Catholic University of America, 1992.

Bradley, Ann Kathleen. *History of the Irish in America.* Secaucus, New Jersey: Chartwell, 1986.

Eleuterio-Comer, Susan K. *Irish American Material Culture: A Directory of Collections, Sites, and Festivals in the United States and Canada.* Westport, Connecticut: Greenwood, 1988.

Feagin, Joe R., and Clairece Booher Feagin. "Irish Americans," in their *Racial and Ethnic Relations*, fourth edition. Englewood Cliffs, New Jersey: Prentice Hall, 1993; pp. 85-114.

Greeley, Andrew M. *That Most Distressful Nation: The Taming of the American Irish*. Chicago: Quadrangle, 1972.

Griffin, William D. *The Book of Irish Americans*. New York: Times Books, 1990.

Horgan, Ellen Somers. "The American Catholic Irish Family," in *Ethnic Families in America: Patterns and Variations*, third edition, edited by Charles H. Mindel, Robert W. Habenstein, and Roosevelt Wright, Jr. New York: Elsevier, 1988; pp. 45-75.

The Irish in America: Emigration, Assimilation and Impact, Volume 4 of *Irish Studies*, edited by P. J. Drudy. Cambridge: Cambridge University Press, 1985.

McCaffrey, Lawrence J. *Textures of Irish America*. Syracuse, New York: Syracuse University Press, 1992.

Shannon, William V. *The American Irish*. New York: Macmillan, 1963.

IROQUOIS
CONFEDERACY

by
Loretta Hall

The Iroquois have been willing to adapt to a changing world, but they have resisted efforts to substitute a European culture for their own heritage.

OVERVIEW

The Iroquois Confederacy, an association of six linguistically related tribes in the northeastern woodlands, was a sophisticated society of some 5,500 people when the first white explorers encountered it at the beginning of the seventeenth century. The 1990 Census counted 49,038 Iroquois living in the United States, making them the country's eighth most populous Native American group. Although Iroquoian tribes own seven reservations in New York state and one in Wisconsin, the majority of the people live off the reservations. An additional 5,000 Iroquois reside in Canada, where there are two Iroquoian reservations. The people are not averse to adopting new technology when it is beneficial, but they want to maintain their own traditional identity.

HISTORY

The "Five Tribes" that first joined to form the Iroquois Confederacy, or League, were the Mohawk, Oneida, Onondaga, Cayuga, and Seneca (listed in order from east to west according to where they lived in an area that roughly corresponds to central New York state). They called themselves Haudenosaunee (pronounced "hoo-dee-noh-SHAW-nee"), or people of the longhouse, referring to the construction of their homes, in which extended families of up to 50 people lived together in bark-covered, wooden-framed houses that were 50 to 150 feet long. They also envisioned their extended community as occupying a symbolic longhouse some 300 miles long, with the Mohawk guarding the eastern door and the Seneca the western.

The origin of the name Iroquois is uncertain, although it seems to have involved French adaptations of Indian words. Among the possibilities that have been suggested are a blending of *hiro* (an Iroquois word used to conclude a speech) and *koué* (an exclamation); *ierokwa* ("they who smoke"); *iakwai* ("bear"); or the Algonquian words *irin* ("real") and *ako* ("snake") with the French *-ois* termination. One likely interpretation of the origin of the name is the theory that it comes from the Algonquian word "Irinakhoiw," which the French spelled with the -ois suffix. The French spelling roughly translates into "real adders" and would be consistent with the tendency of European cultures to take and use derogatory terms from enemy nations to identify various Native groups.

The Mohawk called themselves Ganiengehaka, or "people of the flint country." Their warriors, armed with flint arrows, were known to be overpowering; their enemies called them *Mowak*, meaning "man eaters." The name Oneida means "people of the standing stone," referring to a large rock that, according to legend, appeared wherever the people moved, to give them directions. The Onondaga ("people of the hills"), the Cayuga ("where they land the boats"), and the Seneca ("the people of the big hill") named themselves by describing their homelands.

Because the Algonquian people living on both sides of the Iroquois corridor are of a different culture and linguistic stock, it appears likely that the Iroquois migrated into this area at some time. No evidence has been found to indicate where they came from, however. The Cherokee people, whose historic homeland was in the southeastern United States, belong to the same linguistic group and share some other links with the Iroquois. Where and when they may have lived near each other is unknown.

Despite their common culture and language, relations among the Five Tribes deteriorated to a state of near-constant warfare in ancient times. The infighting, in turn, made them vulnerable to attacks from the surrounding Algonquian tribes. This period, known in the Iroquois oral tradition as the "darktimes," reached a nadir during the reign of a psychotic Onondaga chief named Todadaho. Legend has it that he was a cannibal who ate from bowls made from the skulls of his victims, that he knew and saw everything, that his hair contained a tangle of snakes, and that he could kill with only a Medusa-like look.

Into this terrible era, however, entered two heroic figures. Deganawidah came from his Huron homeland in the north, travelling unchallenged among the hostile Iroquois. Finally, he encountered a violent, cannibalistic Onondagan. According to legend, Deganawidah watched through a hole in the roof while the man prepared to cook his latest victim. Seeing the stranger's face reflected in the cooking pot, the barbarian assumed it to be his own image. He was struck by the thought that the beauty of the face was incompatible with the horrendous practice of cannibalism and immediately forsook the practice. He went outside to dispose of the corpse, and when he returned to his lodge he met Deganawidah. The foreigner's words of peace and righteousness were so powerful that the man became a loyal disciple and helped spread the message.

Deganawidah named his disciple Hiawatha, meaning "he who combs," and sent him to confront Todadaho and remove the snakes from the chief's hair. After enduring terrible hardships at his adversary's hands, and after convincing the other Iroquoian chiefs to accept the Good Message, Hiawatha finally convinced Todadaho as well. On the banks of Onondaga Lake, sometime between 1350 and 1600, Deganawidah established the Iroquois Confederacy, a league of nations that shared a positive code of values and lived in mutual harmony. Out of respect, the Iroquois refer to him as the Peacemaker.

When the first white explorers arrived in the early seventeenth century, they found the settled, agricultural society of the Iroquois a contrast to the nomadic culture of the neighboring Algonquians.

RELATIONS WITH NON-NATIVE AMERICANS

The French had established a presence in Canada for over 50 years before they met the Iroquois. During that period, the Iroquois began to acquire European trade goods through raids on other Indian tribes. They found the metal axes, knives, hoes, and kettles far superior to their implements of stone, bone, shell, and wood. Woven cloth began to replace the animal skins usually used for clothing materials.

The recurring raids prompted the French to help their Indian allies attack the Iroquois in 1609, opening a new technological era for the people of the Confederacy. French body armor was made of metal, whereas that of the Iroquois was made of slatted wood. Furthermore, the French fought with firearms, while traditional Iroquois weapons were bows and arrows, stone tomahawks, and wooden warclubs.

In response to European influence, the Iroquois gradually changed their military tactics to incorporate stealth, surprise, and ambush. Their motives for fighting also changed. In the past, they had fought for prestige or revenge, or to obtain goods or captives; now they fought for economic advantage, seeking control over bountiful beaver hunting grounds or perhaps a stash of beaver skins to trade for European goods.

Although it provided the Indians with better tools, European incursion into the territory was disastrous for the indigenous people. In the 1690s alone, the Iroquois lost between 1,600 and 2,000 people in fighting with other Indian tribes. In addition, European diseases such as smallpox, measles, influenza, lung infections, and even the common cold took a heavy toll on them since they had developed no immunity and knew no cures.

These seventeenth century population devastations prompted the Iroquois people to turn increasingly to their traditional practice of adopting outsiders into their tribes to replace members who had died from violence or illness. While some captives were tortured unmercifully to death, others were adopted into Iroquois families (the leading clanswomen decided prisoners' fates, sometimes basing their decision on the manner in which a relative of theirs had been killed). The adopted person, who was sometimes the opposite gender or of a significantly different age than the deceased Indian he replaced, was treated with the same affection, given the same rights, and expected to fulfill the same duties as his predecessor.

Most, if not all, of the Indians who were educated by the English returned to their native cultures at the first opportunity. Many colonists, on the other hand, chose to become Indians, either by joining Indian society voluntarily, by not trying to escape from captivity, or by staying with their Indian captors in the wake of peace treaties that gave them the freedom to return home.

Early in the eighteenth century the Tuscarora, another Iroquoian-speaking tribe living in North Carolina, moved into the territory occupied by the Confederacy. They had rebelled against the encroachment of colonial settlers, against continual fraudulent treatment by traders, and against repeated raids that took their people for the slave trade. They suffered a terrible defeat, with hundreds of their people killed and hundreds more enslaved. Those who escaped such fates made their way north and became the sixth nation of the Iroquois League.

The first half of the eighteenth century was a period of rebuilding. The Iroquois made peace with the French and established themselves in a neutral position between the French and the English. This strategy lasted until the French and Indian War erupted in 1754; though the Confederacy was officially neutral, the Mohawk sided with the English, and the Seneca with the French.

Before long, another conflict arose among the European colonists, and the Iroquois were faced with the American Revolutionary War. Again, the various tribes failed to agree on which side to support. Without unanimous agreement on a common position, each nation in the Confederacy was free to pursue its own course. The Oneida fought on the side of the colonists, eventually earning official commendation from George Washington for their assistance. A major faction of the Mohawk sided with the British and recruited other Iroquois warriors to their cause. The League as a political entity was severely damaged by the conflict, and the war itself brought death and devastation to the member tribes. After the war, American retaliatory raids destroyed Iroquois towns and crops, and drove the people from their homelands.

The Six Nations remained fragmented in political, social, and religious ways throughout the nineteenth century. The development of the New Religion, beginning in 1799, helped revitalize the traditional culture and facilitated the transition to reservation life. Finally, beginning in the 1950s, the Mohawk, Seneca, and Tuscarora became involved in major land disputes over power-production and flood-control projects proposed by the New York State Power Authority and the United States Army Corps of Engineers. Paired with the social climate favoring ethnic assertion in the mid-twentieth century, these land disputes helped foster a resurgence in Iroquois solidarity.

KEY ISSUES

The Iroquois see themselves as a sovereign nation, not as merely another ethnic group within the United States population, and gaining further recognition of that status is a major objective. They have asserted their position in interesting ways. For example, when the United States declared war on Germany in 1917, the Iroquois Confederacy issued its own independent declaration and claimed status as an allied nation in the war effort. In 1949 a Haudenosaunee delegation attended groundbreaking ceremonies for the United Nations building in New York City. Iroquois statesmen and athletes use Haudenosaunee passports as they travel around the world.

Protecting the land is another priority. Since the 1940s, the Haudenosaunee have been involved in land issues involving projects as varied as the Kenzua Dam project, the St. Lawrence Seaway, and the Niagara Power Plant. After New York state attempted to condemn a portion of the Seneca's land for use in building a highway, a federal court ruled in the 1970s

that the state would have to negotiate with the Iroquois as equal sovereigns. In another land issue, the St. Regis (Akwesasne) Mohawk reservation has been affected by off-reservation pollution sources, including a neighboring toxic-waste dump and nearby air-fouling industrial plants. In the 1990s, struggles over land rights and protection of the land have also included the extension of leases on property and towns in western New York, as well as ongoing conflicts over pollution and the environment.

Resolving the question of gambling on the reservations is also an important issue. In 1990 the controversy erupted into a gun battle that left two Mohawk dead. The Onondaga Council of Chiefs issued a "Memorandum on Tribal Sovereignty" that said: "These businesses have corrupted our people and we are appalled at the Longhouse people who have become part of these activities. They have thrown aside the values of our ancient confederacy for personal gain" (*The Onondaga Council of Chiefs Memorandum on Tribal Sovereignty*). On the other hand, the Oneida tribe saw a dramatic decrease in unemployment after building a bingo hall in 1985; first year profits of over $5 million were used by the tribe to acquire additional land adjacent to the reservation.

ACCULTURATION AND ASSIMILATION

TRADITIONAL CULTURE

Even before the Europeans came to America, the Iroquois were an agricultural society. The men set out on hunting expeditions in dugout or bark canoes to provide meat and hides, while the women tended to the farming. They were a relaxed society with a minimum of rules.

The longhouses in which they lived were constructed with a vestibule at each end that was available for use by all residents. Within the body of the house, a central corridor eight feet wide separated two banks of compartments. Each compartment, measuring about 13 feet by six feet, was occupied by a nuclear family. A wooden platform about a foot above the ground served as a bed by night and chair by day; some compartments included small bunks for children. An overhead shelf held personal belongings. Every 20 feet along the central corridor, a fire pit served the two families living on its opposite sides. Bark or hide doors at the ends of the buildings were attached at the top; these openings and the smoke holes in the roof 15 to 20 feet above each hearth provided the only ventilation.

Villages of 300 to 600 people were protected by a triple-walled stockade of wooden stakes 15 to 20 feet tall. About every 15 years the nearby supplies of wild game and firewood would become depleted, and the farmed soil would become exhausted. During a period of two years or so, the men would find and clear an alternate site for the village, which would then be completely rebuilt.

The primary crops, revered as gifts from the Creator, were called the "Three Sisters": Corn provided stalks for climbing bean vines, while squash plants controlled weeds by covering the soil. The complimentary nutrient needs and soil-replenishing characteristics of the three crops extended the useful life of each set of fields. In addition to providing food, the corn plants were used to make a variety of other goods. From the stalks were made medicine-storing tubes, corn syrup, toy warclubs and spears, and straws for teaching children to count. Corn husks were fashioned into lamps, kindling, mattresses, clotheslines, baskets, shoes, and dolls. Animal skins were smoked over corn cob fires.

Although bows and arrows tipped with flint or bone were the primary hunting weapons, blow guns were used for smaller prey. Made from the hollowed stem of swamp alder, blow guns were about six feet long and one inch thick, with a half-inch bore; the arrows were two and a half feet long.

Elm bark was put to many useful purposes, including constructing houses, building canoes, and fashioning containers. Baskets were woven of various materials, including black ash splints. Pottery vessels were decorated with angular combinations of parallel lines.

Wampum (cylindrical beads about one-fourth inch long and one-eighth inch in diameter) was very important in the Iroquois culture. The beads were made of quahog, or large, hardshell clam shells and could only be obtained through trading or as tribute payments from coastal tribes. White and purple beads were made from the different sections of the shells. Although the beads were used as ornamentation on clothing, wampum had several more important uses. Strings of the beads were used in mourning rituals or to identify a messenger as an official representative of his nation. Wampum belts served as symbols of authority or of contract. Patterns or figures woven into wampum belts recorded the terms of treaties; duplicate belts were given to each of the contracting parties. Because of its important uses, wampum became a valuable commodity and was sometimes used as a form of currency in trading.

Traditional Iroquois games ranged from lively field contests like lacrosse to more sedentary activities involving the bouncing of dried fruit-pit "dice" from a wooden bowl. The games were played both as entertainment and as elements of periodic ceremonies. A favorite winter game called "snow-snake" involved throwing a long wooden rod and seeing how far it would slide down an icy track smoothed out on a snowy field.

The Iroquois had no stringed musical instruments. The only wind instrument, the wooden "courting flute," had six finger stops and was blown from the end. Single-tone rhythm instruments provided the only musical accompaniment for ceremonial dancing and singing. Rattles were made by placing dried corn kernels inside various materials including turtle shells, gourds, bison horns, or folded, dried bark. The traditional drum was about six inches in diameter, made like a wooden pail, and covered with stretched animal skin; just the right amount of water was sealed inside to produce the desired tone when the drum was tapped with a stick.

TRANSFORMATION OF CULTURE

The Iroquois have been willing to adapt to a changing world, but they have resisted efforts to substitute a European culture for their own heritage. For example, in 1745 the Reverend David Brainerd proposed to live among them for two years to help them build a Christian church and become accustomed to the weekly worship cycle. They were direct in declining his offer: "We are Indians and don't wish to be transformed into white men. The English are our Brethren, but we never promised to become what they are" (James Axtell, *The European and the Indian: Essays in the Ethnohistory of Colonial North America*. [New York: Oxford University Press, 1981] p. 78).

Yet changes were inevitable. In 1798 a Quaker delegation worked among the Seneca, teaching them to read and write. They also instructed them in modern farming methods and encouraged men to work on the farms, which represented a major cultural shift. A respected Seneca warrior named Gaiantwaka, known as The Cornplanter, helped bring about this change, as did his half brother, Ganiodayo (Handsome Lake).

More Iroquois began to accept the concept of private ownership of land; historically, tribal lands were held in common, although individuals might have the right to farm certain parcels during their lifetime. During the nineteenth century, the Iroquois sold large amounts of land in exchange for useful trade goods. Leading chiefs were sometimes induced to support such sales by the offer of lifetime pensions. Shrinking land holdings made hunting increasingly difficult and left the men with little to do, which contributed to the Quakers' success in turning them to agricultural work. Families were encouraged to leave the longhouses and live separately on small farms so the men could work in their fields without being embarrassed by being seen doing women's work. Today, longhouses are used only for religious and ceremonial purposes.

In the mid-1800s a rather abrupt change occurred in the style of artwork used to decorate clothing with beads, quills, and embroidery. Rather than the traditional patterns of curving lines and scrolls, designs became representational images of plants and flowers, influenced by the floral style prominent among the seventeenth- and eighteenth-century French.

Eventually, the Onondaga discovered that non-Indians would be willing to pay to see their ceremonial dances, and they experimented with public performances. In 1893 the annual Green Corn Festival was delayed several weeks for the convenience of the audience, and the council house was filled three times with spectators who paid 15 cents admission. The contemporary historian William M. Beauchamp wrote, "Of course, this deprived the feast of all religious force, and made it a mere show; nor did it quite satisfy those who saw it" ("Notes on Onondaga Dances," *An Iroquois Source Book, Volume 2*, edited by Elisabeth Tooker. [New York: Garland Publishing, 1985] p. 183).

As was the case with other Native Americans, much of the friction between the Iroquois and non-Indians has involved different attitudes toward land. During the 1950s and 1960s the long-standing disparity was brought into sharp focus during the planning and construction of the Kinzua Dam, which flooded over 9,000 acres of Seneca Land. The Indians fought the dam, claiming it violated the treaty between the Six Nations and the United States. The government reimbursed the tribe financially, but the reservation was disrupted. The grave of the revered Cornplanter had to be moved to accommodate the dam; his descendant Harriett Pierce commented, "The White man views land for its money value. We Indians have a spiritual tie with the earth, a reverence for it that Whites don't share and can hardly understand" (Alvin M. Josephy, Jr., *Now That the Buffalo's Gone: A Study of Today's American Indians* [New York: Alfred A. Knoph, 1982] p. 129).

Traditional values are sustained on the various Iroquois reservations. The ancient languages are spoken and taught, traditional ceremonies are observed, and baskets are woven. Material wealth is not characteristic of reservation Indians, but Tonawanda Seneca Chief Corbett Sundown, keeper of the Iroquois "spiritual fire," disputes the assessment that the people are poor. He told a *National Geographic* writer: "We're rich people without any money, that's all. You say we ought to set up industries and factories. Well, we just don't want them. How're you going to grow potatoes and sweet corn on concrete? You call that progress? To me "progress" is a dirty word" (Arden Harvey, "The Fire that Never Dies," *National Geographic* [September 1987] p. 398).

MISCONCEPTIONS AND STEREOTYPES

"Hiawatha" is one of the most widely recognized Indian names among non-Indian Americans, thanks to Henry Wadsworth Longfellow. Unfortunately, his character is a classic case of mistaken identity. The real subject of the poem, an Ojibwe hero named Nanabozho, was confused with the Iroquoian Hiawatha in a mid-nineteenth century work by Henry Rowe Schoolcraft that inspired Longfellow.

The Longfellow poem, at least, presented a sympathetic image of an Iroquois-named character. In his eloquent history of the Tuscarora Indians, Chief Elias Johnson wrote in 1881: "Almost any portrait that we see of an Indian, he is represented with tomahawk and scalping knife in hand, as if they possess no other but a barbarous nature. Christian nations might with equal justice be always represented with cannon and balls, swords and pistols, as the emblems of their employment and their prevailing tastes" (Elias Johnson, *Legends, Traditions and Laws of the Iroquois, or Six Nations, and History of the Tuscarora Indians* [New York: AMS Press, 1978 (reprint of 1881 edition)] p. 13).

CUISINE

Corn is the traditional staple of the Haudenosaunee diet. It was baked or boiled and eaten on or off the cob; the kernels were mashed and either fried, baked in a kettle, or spread on corn leaves that were folded and boiled as tamales. Some varieties of corn were processed into hominy by boiling the kernels in a weak lye solution of hardwood ashes and water. Bread, pudding, dumplings, and cooked cereal were made from cornmeal. Parched corn coffee was brewed by mixing roasted corn with boiling water.

Besides corn, and the beans and squash they raised with it, the Iroquois people ate a wide variety of other plant foods. Wild fruits, nuts, and roots were gathered to supplement the cultivated crops. Berries were dried for year-round use. Maple sap was used for sweetening, but salt was not commonly used.

The traditional diet featured over 30 types of meat, including deer, bear, beaver, rabbit, and squirrel. Fresh meat was enjoyed during the hunting season, and some was smoked or dried and used to embellish corn dishes during the rest of the year. The Iroquois used the region's waterways extensively for transportation, but fish was relatively unimportant as food.

TRADITIONAL CLOTHING

The fundamental item of men's clothing was a breechcloth made of a strip of deerskin or fabric.

Passing between the legs, it was secured by a waist belt, and decorated flaps of the breechcloth hung in the front and back. The belt, or sash, was a favorite article; sometimes worn only around the waist, and sometimes also over the left shoulder, it was woven on a loom or on the fingers, and might be decorated with beadwork.

The basic item of women's clothing was a short petticoat. Other items that were worn by both sexes included a fringed, sleeveless tunic, separate sleeves (connected to each other by thongs, but not connected to the tunic), leggings, moccasins, and a robe or blanket. Clothing was adorned with moose-hair embroidery featuring curved line figures with coiled ends. Decorated pouches for carrying personal items completed the costumes. Women used burden straps, worn across the forehead, to support litters carried on their backs.

By the end of the eighteenth century, trade cloth replaced deerskin as the basic clothing material. Imported glass beads replaced porcupine quills as decorative elements.

FESTIVALS

The annual cycle consists of six regular festivals, which are still observed among the Iroquois. In addition, ceremonies are held as needed for wakes, memorial feasts, burials, adoptions, or sealing of friendships.

The new year began with the Mid-Winter Festival, which was held in late January or early February when the men returned from the fall hunt. It lasted five days, followed by another two or three days of game playing. This was a time of spiritual cleansing and renewal, and included a ritual cleaning of homes. Public confessions were made, and penitents touched a wampum belt as a pledge of reform. Playing a traditional dice game commemorated the struggle between the Creator and his evil twin brother for control over the earth. Thanks were offered to the Creator for protection during the past year. Dreams were always considered to be supernatural messages, and everyone was obliged to help the dreamer by fulfilling the needs or desires expressed in the dream; particular attention was devoted to dream guessing during the Mid-Winter Festival. On a pre-festival day, names were conferred on babies, young adults, and adoptees so they could participate in the upcoming ceremonies.

In the spring, when the sap rose, it was time for the Thanks-to-the-Maple Festival. This one-day celebration included social dances and the ceremonial burning of tobacco at the base of a maple tree.

In May or June, corn seeds saved from the previous year were blessed at the Corn Planting Ceremony. This was a half-day observance in which the Creator was thanked and spirit forces were implored for sufficient rain and moderate sun.

Ripening strawberries in June signaled time for the Strawberry Festival. Dancers mimicked the motions of berry pickers. This one-day celebration was a time for giving thanks.

In August or early September, the corn was ready to eat. This event was marked by the Green Corn Festival, which involved ceremonies on four successive mornings. The first day included general thanksgiving, a Feather Dance honoring those who worked to put on the festival, and the naming of children. The second day saw more dances and the bestowing of names on young adults and adoptees. The third day was dedicated to personal commitment and sacrifice, and included a communal burning of tobacco. Speeches and dancing were followed by a feast. On the fourth day the ceremonial dice game was played as it was at the Mid-Winter Festival. Finally, the women who worked the fields sang thanksgiving for the crops.

When all the crops had been harvested and stored away, and before the men left for the fall hunt, the Harvest Festival was held. This one-day celebration took place in October.

The use of masks, or "false faces," is a major component of Iroquois rituals. They symbolized spirit forces that were represented by the person wearing the mask at festivals or healing ceremonies. One group of spirits was depicted by masks carved from living trees, while another group was represented by masks made from braided corn husks. Miniature corn husk masks, three inches across or less, were kept as personal charms; in ancient times the miniatures were also made of clay or stone.

DEATH AND BURIAL

When a person died, everyone who had similar names gave them up until a period of mourning was completed. Later, if another person was adopted into the clan, he was often given the name of the deceased person whose place he took.

A wake was held the night following a death. After a midnight meal, the best orators of the village spoke about the deceased, and about life and death in general. The body was placed on a scaffold for several days on the chance that the person only appeared dead and might revive, which happened occasionally. After decomposition began, the remains might be buried, or the cleaned bones

might be housed in or near the family lodge. When the village relocated, all of the unburied skeletons were interred in a common grave. By the end of the nineteenth century, burials were conducted according to European customs.

Upon death both the soul and the ghost left the body. Using food and tools offered by the survivors, the soul journeyed to the land of the dead. The ghost, on the other hand, became a spiritual inhabitant of the village. At a yearly Feast of the Dead, tobacco and songs were offered to the resident ghosts.

HEALTH ISSUES

Traditional Iroquois rituals addressed both physical and mental health issues. Medicine men (or women) used herbs and natural ointments to treat maladies including fevers, coughs, and snake bites. Wounds were cleaned, broken bones were set, and medicinal emetics were administered.

Another type of healer, known as a conjurer, sang incantations to combat maladies caused through witchcraft. They might remove an afflic-

tion from the patient's body by blowing or sucking. Twice a year groups of False Faces visited each house in the village, waving pine boughs and dispelling illness. Shamans were empowered to combat disorders caused by evil spirits.

In the realm of mental health, modern psychologists see the value in the Iroquois practice of dream guessing. Everyone in the community had a responsibility to resolve conflicts and unmet needs made evident through any person's dreams.

LANGUAGE

The six Iroquoian dialects are similar enough to allow easy conversation. The Mohawk and Oneida are quite similar, as are the Cayuga and Seneca; the Onondaga and Tuscarora are each different from the five others. One common characteristic is the lack of labial sounds formed by bringing the lips together.

The language is rich in words for tangible things, but lacking in abstract expressions. A 1901 treatise noted, "for the varieties, sexes, and ages of a single animal they would have a multitude of terms, but no general word for animal. Or they would have words for good man, good woman, good dog, but no word for goodness" (Lewis H. Morgan, *League of the Ho-de-no-sau-nee or Iroquois* [New Haven: Human Relations Area Files, 1954] p. 243).

Historically, the Iroquois language was oral. In the mid-1800s a Congregational missionary named Asher Wright devised a written version using the English alphabet and edited a Seneca newspaper. During the latter half of the 1900s, written dictionaries and grammar texts have been developed for teaching the languages on the reservations. However, Barbara Graymont noted at the 1965 Conference on Iroquois Research that no written material existed in Tuscarora, other than an "unreadable" nineteenth century hymnal (Barbara Graymont, "Problems of Tuscarora Language Survival," *Iroquois Culture, History, and Prehistory* [Albany: The University of the State of New York, 1967] pp. 27-8).

GREETINGS AND OTHER POPULAR EXPRESSIONS

Some of the basic Mohawk expressions are: *shé:kon* ("SHAY kohn") or *kwé kwé* ("KWAY KWAY")—hello; *hén* ("hun")—yes; *iáh* ("yah")—no; *niá:wen* ("nee AH wun")—thank you.

FAMILY AND COMMUNITY DYNAMICS

CLAN AND FAMILY STRUCTURE

The Iroquois tribes were organized into eight clans, which were grouped in two moieties: Wolf, Bear, Beaver, and Turtle; and Deer, Snipe, Heron, and Hawk. In ancient times, intermarriage was not allowed within each four-clan group, but eventually intermarriage was only forbidden within each clan. Tribal affiliation did not affect clan membership; for example, all Wolf clan members were considered to be blood relatives, regardless of whether they were members of the Mohawk, Seneca, or other Iroquois tribes. At birth, each person became a member of the clan of his or her mother.

Within a tribe, each clan was led by the clan mother, who was usually the oldest woman in the group. In consultation with the other women, the clan mother chose one or more men to serve as clan chiefs. Each chief was appointed for life but the clan mother and her advisors could remove him from office for poor behavior or dereliction of duty.

MARRIAGE

Traditionally, a man and woman wishing to marry would tell their parents, who would arrange a joint meeting of relatives to discuss the suitability of the two people for marriage to each other. If no objections arose during the discussion, a day was chosen for the marriage feast. On the appointed day the woman's relatives would bring her to the groom's home for the festivities. Following the meal, elders from the groom's family spoke to the bride about wifely duties, and elders from the bride's family told the groom about husbandly responsibilities. Then the two began their new life together.

In ancient times adultery was rare. When it was discovered, the woman was punished by whipping, but the man was not punished. If a couple decided to separate, both of their families would be called to a council. The parties would state their reasons for wanting a divorce, and the elders would try to work out a reconciliation. If those efforts failed, the marriage ended. In ancient times, fathers kept their sons and mothers kept their daughters when a divorce occurred; by the early eighteenth century, however, mothers typically kept all of the children.

CHILDREARING

Children were valued among the Iroquois; because of the matrilineal society, daughters were somewhat more prized than sons. The birth of a couple's first child was welcomed with a feast at the mother's family home. The couple stayed there a few days, and then returned to their own home to prepare another feast.

Birthing took place in a hut located outside the village. As her time drew near, the mother and a few other women withdrew to the hut and remained there until a few days after the birth. Until he was able to walk, an Iroquois baby spent his days secured to a cradleboard, which his mother would hang from a tree branch while she worked in the fields.

Babies were named at birth; when the child reached puberty, an adult name was given. Names referred to natural phenomena (such as the moon or thunder), landscape features, occupations, and social or ceremonial roles; animal names were very rare. Some examples of the meanings of names are: In the Center of the Sky, Hanging Flower, He Carries News, and Mighty Speaker. A person was never addressed by his name during conversation; when speaking about a person, especially to a relative, the name was only used if he could not otherwise be clearly identified by terms of relation or the context of the discussion.

Mothers had primary responsibility for raising their children and teaching them good behavior. In keeping with the easy-going nature of Haudenosaunee society, children learned informally from their family and clan elders. Children were not spanked, but they might be punished by splashing water in their faces. Difficult children might be frightened into better behavior by a visit from someone wearing the mask of Longnose, the cannibal clown.

Puberty marked the time of acceptance into adult membership in the society. On the occasion of her first menses, a girl would retire to an isolated hut for the duration of her period. She was required to perform difficult tasks, such as chopping hardwood with a dull axe, and was prohibited from eating certain foods. The period of initiation for a young man was more lengthy; when his voice began to change, he went to live in a secluded cabin in the forest for up to a year. An old man or woman took responsibility for overseeing his well-being. He ate sparsely, and his time was spent in physically demanding activities such as running, swimming, bathing in icy water, and scraping his shins with a stone. His quest was completed when he was visited by his spirit, which would remain with him during his adult life.

EDUCATION

A speaker at the 1963 American Anthropological Association convention described the Iroquois as "virtually 100% literate today" (Cara E. Richards, "Women Use the Law, Men Suffer From It: Differential Acculturation Among the Onondaga Indians in the 1950's & 60's," *Iroquois Women: An Anthology* [Ohsweken, Ontario: Iroqrafts Ltd, 1990] p. 167). The 1980 Census found that 60 percent of the Iroquois over the age of 25 were high school graduates, and nine percent were college graduates.

Iroquois children attending reservation schools learn not only the subjects typically taught at non-Indian schools, but also study their tribal culture and history. The stated goals of the Akwesasne Freedom School, for example, are "to facilitate learning so that the students will have a good self-concept as Indians, promote self-reliance, promote respect for the skills of living in harmony with others and the environment and master the academic and/or vocational skills necessary in a dualistic society" (*The Native North American Almanac*, edited by David Champagne [Detroit: Gale Research, 1994] p. 886).

RELIGION

From ancient times the Haudenosaunee believed that a powerful spirit called Orenda permeated the universe. He created everything that is good and useful. The Evil Spirit made things that are poisonous, but the Great Spirit gained control of the world.

During the seventeenth century, French Jesuit missionaries converted many of the Iroquois to Catholicism. Kateri Tekakwitha, who was baptized in 1635, became the first Native American nun. She was extraordinarily devout; since her death many visions and miraculous cures have been attributed to her intervention. She was beatified by the Catholic Church in 1980 and is a candidate for canonization to sainthood. The "Blessed Kateri" is revered at the feasts and celebrations of many Native American nations, particularly those who have incorporated Catholicism into their spiritual belief systems.

In 1710 three Mohawk chiefs, along with another from the Mahicans, visited Queen Anne in England to ask for military assistance against the French and for Anglican missionaries to teach their people. As the years passed, Quakers, Baptists, Methodists, and an interdenominational Protestant group called the New York Missionary Society joined the effort of proselytizing the Iroquois. An intense rivalry developed between the pagan and Christian factions. In fact, in 1823 a group of Oneidas led by Eleazar Williams, a Mohawk from Canada who had become an Episcopalian minister, left their New York homeland and moved to Wisconsin, where they established a reservation.

In 1799, amidst the Christian missionary efforts, a revival of the ancient Longhouse religion developed. A Seneca known as Handsome Lake had spent much of his life in dissolute living and fell gravely ill when he was about 65 years old. He expected to die, but instead, he experienced a profound vision and recovered. Inspired, he began to spread the Good Word among his fellow Iroquois. The New Religion was essentially a revitalization of the ancient pagan beliefs, although some Quaker influence can be detected.

Major tenets of the New Religion included shunning of alcoholic beverages, abandonment of beliefs in witchcraft and love potions, and denunciation of abortion. The fact that Handsome Lake's message had come in a dream gave it a profound impact among the Haudenosaunee. The religion was instrumental in showing many Iroquois how to retain their own culture while adapting to a world dominated by non-Indians.

The Longhouse religion continues to be a major spiritual focus among the Iroquois people. Some adhere solely to its practice, while others maintain a parallel membership in a Christian church.

EMPLOYMENT AND ECONOMIC TRADITIONS

Although the Haudenosaunee's bond to the land remains, most no longer live as farmers. Census data from 1980 show that two-thirds of the Iroquois people lived in urban areas. About half of those living outside urban settings actually lived on reservations. Ties to the homeland and the tribal culture are strong, however, and those who live off the reservation return from time to time to visit relatives and to spiritually renew themselves.

In a modern rendition of their ancient sojourns away from the village to hunt, Iroquois men today may support their families by living and working in a city but returning home periodically. In particular, there is a cohesive group of Indians, including many Mohawk, living in Brooklyn during the week but returning to their families on weekends.

Iroquois men, especially Mohawk, are famous as ironworkers in construction. They walk steel girders high in the air unhampered by any fear of heights. Consequently, they are in demand around the country for skyscraper and bridge building projects, which have included such landmarks as the World Trade Center and the Golden Gate Bridge. Fathers pass their ironworking tools on to their sons (or sometimes daughters) in an atmosphere reminiscent of ancient rituals.

The 1980 census indicated that about nine percent of the employed Iroquois were engaged in construction, although over half of the men of the St. Regis Mohawk Reservation are members of the ironworker union. Factory work was actually the largest occupation, accounting for one-fourth of the jobs held by Iroquois people. Nineteen percent of the employed Iroquois worked in "professional and related services," including health and education. Another 13 percent were engaged in retail trade.

Cara E. Richards of Cornell University conducted an acculturation study focusing on the Onondaga tribe during the 1950s and early 1960s (Richards, pp. 164-67). At that time 70 percent of the tribal women who held jobs worked as domestics in off-reservation homes. This put them in the position of interacting with upper- and middle-class families in home environments that exposed them to radio and television programs, non-Indian lifestyles, modern home appliances, and even different types of foods. Onondaga men, on the other hand, worked primarily in factories or on construction sites. Although they interacted with non-Indian men, there was little exchange of cultural information. Differential patterns of acculturation resulted, in which the women were more comfortable and successful in relating to non-Indian agencies, including law enforcement.

Economic activity varies markedly among the various Iroquois reservations. For example, the Onondaga reservation does not offer services for tourists, but the Mohawk welcome tourists to their museum and marinas.

POLITICS AND GOVERNMENT

The Great Peace forged by Deganawidah and Hiawatha produced an unwritten but clearly defined framework for the Iroquois Confederacy (a written constitution was developed about 1850). Three principles, each with dual meanings, formed the foundation of the League government. The Good Word signified righteousness in action as well as in thought and speech; it also required justice through the balancing of rights and obligations. The principle of Health referred to maintaining a sound mind in a sound body; it also involved peace among individuals and between groups. Thirdly, Power meant physical, military, or civil authority; it also denoted spiritual power. The founders envisioned the resulting peace spreading beyond the original League members, so that eventually all people would live in cooperation. Law and order remained the internal concern of each tribe, but the League legally prohibited cannibalism.

Under the structure of the Confederacy, the 50 clan chiefs (called sachems) from all the tribes came together to confer about questions of common concern. The successor of the Onondaga chief Todadaho served as a chairman who oversaw the discussion, which continued until a unanimous decision was reached. If no consensus could be achieved, each tribe was free to follow an independent course on that matter.

The League functioned well for generations, fostering peace among the Six Nations. Even when the tribes failed to agree regarding an external dispute, such as one between the French and the Dutch, they would find a way to fight their respective enemies without confronting another League tribe. However, they were unable to do this during the American Revolution. The Confederacy nearly collapsed in the wake of that war, and traditionalists are still trying to rebuild it. During the latter half of the twentieth century, it has strengthened significantly.

In 1802 the Mohawk living within the United States officially discarded their traditional clan-based structure and established an elective tribal government. In 1848 a faction of Seneca instituted a similar change, establishing the Seneca Nation. Voting rights were denied to Seneca women, who had historically chosen the tribal leaders; women's suffrage was not reinstated until 1964. Other tribes eventually followed suit, either abandoning their ancestral governments or modifying them to incorporate elections. Traditionalists clung to the ancient structure, however, and today two competing sets of governments exist on several reservations. Violence occasionally erupts between the opposing factions.

The United States government has tried in various ways to relocate, assimilate, or disband Indian tribes. A core group of the Iroquois people has steadfastly resisted these efforts. In 1831 some Seneca and Cayuga moved to Indian Territory (now Oklahoma) as part of the federal removal effort; other Iroquois factions held their ground until the policy was overturned in 1842 and ownership of some of the Seneca land was restored. In 1924 Congress passed legislation conferring U.S. citizenship to all American Indians; the Haudenosaunee rejected such status.

The Iroquois have actively worked to reclaim sacred artifacts and ancestral remains from museums. In 1972 a moratorium was enacted prohibiting archaeologists from excavating native burial sites in New York state; tribal members would be notified to arrange proper reburials for remains unearthed accidentally. Wampum belts held by the New York State Museum in Albany were removed from public display in deference to the Indians' belief that they should not be treated as curiosities, and were finally returned to the Onondagas (as Keeper of the Central Fire for the Iroquois League) in 1989. Years of effort were rewarded in the early 1990s when the Smithsonian Institution and its National Museum of the American Indian committed to returning human remains, burial artifacts, sacred objects, and other articles of cultural patrimony to Indian tribes.

INDIVIDUAL AND GROUP CONTRIBUTIONS

Although disputed by some, there is significant evidence that the Iroquois Confederacy served as a model or inspiration for the U.S. Constitution. Benjamin Franklin and Thomas Paine were well acquainted with the League. John Rutledge, chairman of the committee that wrote the first draft of the Constitution, began the process by quoting some passages from the Haudenosaunee Great Law. The Iroquois form of government was based on democracy and personal freedom, and included elements equivalent to the modern political tools of initiative, referendum, and recall. In 1987 Senator Daniel Inouye sponsored a resolution that would commemorate the Iroquois' contributions to the formation of the federal government.

Many Iroquois people have made notable contributions to society and culture that transcend political boundaries. A dramatic example is Oren Lyons (1930–), an Onondaga chief who has led political delegations to numerous countries in support of the rights of indigenous people. Twice named an All-American lacrosse goal-keeper, he led his 1957 team at Syracuse University to an undefeated season and was eventually enrolled in the sport's Hall of Fame. He was a successful amateur boxer in both the U.S. Army and in the Golden Gloves competition. He worked as a commercial artist for several years before returning to the reservation to assume his position as faithkeeper. An author and illustrator, he has served as Chairman of American Studies at the State University of New York (SUNY) at Buffalo and as publisher of *Daybreak*, a national quarterly newspaper of Native American views. In 1992 he became the first indigenous leader to have addressed the United Nations General Assembly.

ACADEMIA AND SCHOLARSHIP

Arthur C. Parker (Seneca, 1881-1955) was a leading authority on Iroquois culture as well as museum administration. He joined the New York State Museum at Albany as an archeologist in 1906 and became director of the Rochester Museum of Arts and Sciences in 1925. He wrote 14 major books and hundreds of articles.

Dr. John Mohawk (Seneca) teaches Native American law and history at SUNY in Buffalo. He has written extensively on the Iroquois philosophy and approach to government. He founded *Akwesasne Notes*, a quarterly activist magazine, and the Indigenous Press Network, a computerized news service focusing on Indian affairs.

The poetry of Roberta Hill Whiteman (Oneida) has been published in anthologies and magazines including *American Poetry Review*. She has been involved with Poets-in-the-Schools programs in at least seven states and has taught at the University of Wisconsin-Eau Claire.

GOVERNMENT

Robert L. Bennett (Oneida) and Louis R. Bruce Jr. (Mohawk) served in the 1960s and early 1970s as commissioners of the United States Bureau of Indian Affairs. Ely Parker (Seneca, 1828-1895), the first Native American to hold that post, had been appointed by Ulysses S. Grant in 1869.

Katsi Cook (Mohawk), a midwife and lecturer on women's health, is active is the Akwesasne Environment Project. Her health-related writings have appeared in national magazines as well as in medical books.

Amber Coverdale Sumrall (Mohawk), a writer and poet, has been active in the Sanctuary Movement. She also lectures and teaches workshops on the topic of disabilities.

Tahnahga (Mohawk) has a degree in Rehabilitation Counseling; she incorporates traditional Native American healing methods into her work with chemical dependency. She also uses her talent as a poet and storyteller to show Indian youth how to use visions and dreaming to enhance their lives.

VISUAL ARTS AND LITERATURE

Richard Hill (1950–) followed in his father's footsteps and became an ironworker in construction before enrolling in the Art Institute of Chicago. His watercolor paintings include a series on Iroquois culture, and he has also documented the culture through photography. Since the early 1970s, he has curated numerous art shows, prepared museum exhibits for such clients as the Smithsonian Institution, and written many articles about history and art. A past Director of the North American Indian Museums Association, he has also taught at the State University of New York at Buffalo.

Maurice Kenny (Mohawk), a poet nominated for the Pulitzer prize, received the American Book Award in 1984 for *The Mama Poems*. His work has been widely anthologized, and he has been Writer-in-Residence at North County Community College in Saranac Lake, New York. He is described as having "a distinctive voice, one shaped by the rhythms of Mohawk life and speech, yet one which defines and moves beyond cultural boundaries" (Joseph Bruchac, *New Voices from the Longhouse: An Anthology of Contemporary Iroquois Writing* [Greenfield Center, NY: Greenfield Review Press, 1989] p. 161). He has also received the National Public Radio Award for Broadcasting.

Daniel Thompson (Mohawk, 1953–) has been a photographer, graphic artist, and editor of several publications including the *Northeast Indian Quarter-ly* published by Cornell University. He writes poetry in both English and Mohawk and is working to devise an improved written form for the Mohawk language. He has also served as news director for the Mohawk radio station.

Using the knowledge she acquired when earning bachelor's and master's degrees in zoology, Carol Snow (Seneca) has written and illustrated a dozen reports on endangered and rare species for the Bureau of Land Management. As an artist, in 1980 she created a technique incorporating ink and acrylic paint, which she employed in her renderings of Native American and wildlife themes.

Tuscarora sculptor Duffy Wilson works in both wood and stone. Tom Huff, another stone sculptor, is also a writer and poet; he served as editor of the Institute of American Indian Arts' literary journal in 1979. Alex Jacobs (Mohawk), whose sculptures, paintings, and prints can be found in New York galleries, has had his written works included in several Native American poetry and literature anthologies.

FILM TELEVISION, AND THEATER

Jay Silverheels (Mohawk,1918-1980) was born on the Six Nations Indian Reservation in Ontario. Siverheels was an actor perhaps best known for his portrayal of Tonto, the loyal Indian sidekick to the Lone Ranger series, which ran from 1949 to 1957. His noted performances include his depiction of the Apache Indian chief, Geronimo, in *Broken Arrow* (1950), a film acclaimed by many as the first picture to portray Native Americans in a sympathetic light, as well as three "Lone Ranger" films. Silverheels was the first Native American to be given a star on Hollywood's Walk of Fame.

Gary Dale Farmer (Cayuga, 1953-), born on the Six Nations Indian Reservation, is an actor, film producer and activist. Farmer appeared in the movies *Friday the Thirteenth* and *Police Academy*. He also appeared on the television series *Miami Vice* and *China Beach*. After 1989, Farmer began lecturing on Native American culture and issues on many campuses in the United States and Canada, focusing on media, environmental, and social topics relevant to Native communities. In 1998, Farmer had a role in the well-received film *Smoke Signals*.

Graham Greene (Oneida, 1952-) is a film actor who has found success in both Canada and the United States. Greene is one of the most visible Native American actors working on the stage and in film today. He is best known for his roles in *Dances with Wolves* (1990), for which he was nominated for an Academy Award for Best Supporting Actor, and *Thunderheart* (1992). Greene also appeared in the films *Maverick* (1994) and *Die Hard: With a Vengeance*, as well as on the television series *Northern Exposure*.

MEDIA

PRINT

Akwesasne Notes.

This quarterly magazine is published by the Mohawk tribe.

Contact: Mark Narsisian, Editor.
Address: P.O. Box 196, Rooseveltown, New York 13683-0196.
Telephone: (518) 358-9535.

Ka Ri Wen Ha Wi.

This monthly newsletter contains reservation news and items about the Akwesasne Library/Cultural Center.

Contact: Janice Brown, Editor.
Address: Akwesasne Library, Rural Route 1, Box 14 C, Hogansburg, New York 13655.
Telephone: (518) 358-2240.
Fax: (518) 358-2649.

The Seneca Nation of Indians Official Newsletter.

Quarterly publication that prints news and special interest pieces about the Seneca Nation.

Contact: Debbie Hoag, Editor.
Address: G.R. Plummer Building, P.O. Box 321, Salamanca, New York 14779-0321.
Telephone: (716) 945-1790.

RADIO

CKON-FM (97.3).

Radio station owned and operated by the Mohawk tribe on the St. Regis Reservation in New York. It broadcasts music 24 hours a day, including country, adult contemporary, rock, and blues segments. In addition, it airs hourly local news summaries, community announcements (sometimes in Mohawk or French) three times a day, and live coverage of local lacrosse games.

Contact: Kallen Martin, General Manager.
Address: P.O. Box 140, Rooseveltown, New York 13683-0140.
Telephone: (518) 358-3426.

ORGANIZATIONS AND ASSOCIATIONS

The Onondaga Nation.
Contact: Chief Irving Powless, Jr.
Address: Box 319B, Onondaga Reservation, Nedrow, New York 13120.
Telephone: (315) 492-4210.
Fax: (315) 469-1725.

St. Regis Mohawk Tribe.
Contact: Edward Smoke, CEO.
Address: St. Regis Reservation, Rural Route #1, Box 8A, Hogansburg, New York 13655.
Telephone: (518) 358-2272.
Fax: (518) 358-3203.

The Seneca Nation, Allegany Reservation.
Contact: Dennis Bowen Sr., President.
Address: G.R. Plummer Building, P.O. Box 321, Salamanca, New York 14779-0321.
Telephone: (716) 945-1790.
E-mail: sni@localnet.com.
Online: http://www.sni.org/.

The Seneca Nation of Indians, Cattaraugus Reservation.
Contact: Adrian Stevens, Treasurer.
Address: William Seneca Building, 1490 Route 438, Irving, New York 14081.
Telephone: (716) 532-4900.
E-mail: sni@localnet.com.
Online: http://www.sni.org/.

Tonawanda Band of Senecas.
Contact: Chief Emerson Webster.
Address: 7027 Meadville Road, Basom, New York 14013.
Telephone: (716) 542-4244.
Fax: (716) 542-4244.

MUSEUMS AND RESEARCH CENTERS

Akwesasne Cultural Center/Akwesasne Museum.
Displays traditional Mohawk artifacts and basketry, contemporary Iroquois artifacts, and ethnological exhibitions.

Contact: Carol White, Director.
Address: Rural Route 1, Box 14 C, Hogansburg, New York 13655.

Telephone: (518) 358-2240; or 358-2461.
Fax: (518) 358-2649.

The Iroquois Indian Museum.
Features the history of the Iroquois and displays contemporary arts and crafts. A library is available for research.

Contact: James Schafer, Director.
Address: P.O. Box 7, Caverns Road, Howes Cave, New York 12092.
Telephone: (518) 296-8949.
Fax: (518) 296-8955.
E-mail: info@iroquoismuseum.org.
Online: http://www.iroquoismuseum.org/.

The National Shrine of the Blessed Kateri Tekakwitha and Native American Exhibit.
Displays artifacts and maintains the only completely excavated and staked-out Iroquois village in the United States.

Contact: Fr. Jim Plavcan.
Address: P.O. Box 627, Fonda, New York 12068.
Telephone: (518) 853-3646.

The Oneida Nation Museum.
Preserves the culture of the Wisconsin tribe and serves as a point of contact for the Oneida Reservation.

Contact: Denise Vigue, Director.
Address: P.O. Box 365, Oneida, Wisconsin 54155-0365.
Telephone: (414) 869-2768.

The Rochester Museum and Science Center.
Offers changing exhibits as well as a permanent display, "At the Western Door," that focuses on relations between the Seneca Indians and European colonists. Also on display are a furnished 1790s Seneca cabin, six life-size figure tableaus, and over 2,000 artifacts.

Contact: Richard C. Shultz, Director.
Address: 657 East Avenue, P.O. Box 1480, Rochester, New York 14603-1480.
Telephone: (716) 271-1880.
Online: http://www.rmsc.org/.

The Seneca-Iroquois National Museum.
Located on the Allegany Reservation, this museum houses 300,000 articles portraying the life and culture of the Seneca and other Iroquois Indians, including wampum belts, costumes, games, and modern art.

Contact: Midge Deanstock, Director.
Address: 794 Broad Street, Salamanca, New York 14779.
Telephone: (716) 945-1738.

SOURCES FOR ADDITIONAL STUDY

Arden, Harvey. "The Fire That Never Dies," *National Geographic*, September 1987.

Axtell, James. *The European and the Indian: Essays in the Ethnohistory of Colonial North America.* New York: Oxford University Press, 1981.

A Basic Call to Consciousness. Rooseveltown, NY: Akwesasne Notes, 1978.

Bruchac, Joseph. *New Voices from the Longhouse: An Anthology of Contemporary Iroquois Writing.* Greenfield Center, NY: Greenfield Review Press, 1989.

Fenton, Willam N. *The Great Law and the Longhouse: A Political History of the Iroquois Confederacy.* Norman: University of Oklahoma Press, 1998.

Graymont, Barbara. *The Iroquois.* Norman: University of Oklahoma Press, 1991.

"Indian Roots of American Democracy," *Northeast Indian Quarterly*, edited by Jose Barreiro. Winter/Spring, 1987/1988.

An Iroquois Source Book, Volumes 1 and 2, edited by Elisabeth Tooker. New York: Garland Publishing, Inc., 1985.

Iroquois Women: An Anthology, edited by W. G. Spittal. Ohsweken, Ontario: Iroqrafts Ltd, 1990.

Johnson, Elias. *Legends, Traditions and Laws of the Iroquois, or Six Nations, and History of the Tuscarora Indians.* New York: AMS Press, 1978 (reprint of 1881 edition).

Josephy, Alvin M., Jr. *Now That the Buffalo's Gone: A Study of Today's American Indians.* New York: Alfred A. Knopf, 1982.

Snow, Dean R. *The Iroquois.* Cambridge, MA: Blackwell, 1996.

Tooker, Elisabeth. *Lewis H. Morgan on Iroquois Material Culture.* Tucson: University of Arizona Press, 1994.

As the Jewish
persecution in
Europe continued
unabated, the idea
of an all-Jewish state
was offered as a
potential solution.
The idea was given
further credence
in 1896 when
Theodore Herzl
published *The
Jewish State,* a
book which called
for the establishment
of a Jewish state
in Palestine.

ISRAELI
by
Laura C. Rudolph

AMERICANS

OVERVIEW

Located in the Middle East and slightly larger than the state of Massachusetts, Israel measures 7,992 miles (20,700 square kilometers). It is bordered to the north by Lebanon, Syria and Jordan to the east, Egypt to the southwest, and the Mediterranean Sea to the west. The capital is Jerusalem, the largest city in Israel.

Israel has a population of slightly over five million people from various ethnic backgrounds. Approximately 80 percent are Jews who have emigrated from nearly every corner of the world. The rest are largely Arabs, the majority of whom are Muslim (14 percent), with smaller numbers of Christians, Druze, Circassians, and Samaritans. Israel's official languages are Hebrew and Arabic. The national flag displays the Star of David between two horizontal bands of blue.

HISTORY

The complex history of Israel can be traced as far back as 2000 B.C., to the events described in the first five books of the Old Testament that comprise the Hebrew Bible, or Torah. At that time, a Biblical figure, Abraham, was commanded by God to lead a group of nomads from Mesopotamia into Canaan, the "Promised Land." Known as Hebrews, they called themselves the "chosen people of God" because of their faith in the covenant made between Abraham and God. The covenant included God's promise that the Hebrews would prosper and multiply in Canaan so long as they were faithful to Him. Abraham's grandson, Jacob, fathered 12 sons who established the twelve tribes of Canaan (Israel). After a series of famines, Abraham's descendants traveled to Egypt, where they initially prospered. Eventually, however, the Hebrews were enslaved by Ramses II, and suffered under appalling conditions. In approximately 1250 B.C. Moses, at God's command, delivered the Hebrews from Egypt to lead them back to the Promised Land. The liberated Hebrews passed through the Sinai Desert, where they spent 40 years before reaching Canaan.

A series of judges presided over the Canaanites before the kingship of Saul (c.1023-1004 B.C.). Saul's adopted son, David (1000-965 B.C.), is credited with capturing Jerusalem and establishing the capital of Canaan and the Ark of the Covenant containing the Ten Commandments. After the rule of King Solomon (968-928 B.C.), political factions forced the dissolution of the twelve tribes of Israel. Ten of the tribes formed the northern kingdom of Israel, while the other two tribes became the southern kingdom of Judah. An uneasy peace existed between Israel and Judah until about 700 B.C., when the Assyrians conquered both kingdoms. The ten tribes of Israel were destroyed and exiled, and were henceforth known as the "Ten Lost Tribes." Judah was allowed to exist until 586 B.C., when the Assyrians themselves were defeated by the Babylonians. Under the command of King Nebuchadnezzar, the Babylonians conquered Israel and Judah, destroying Jerusalem and the temple containing the Ark of the Covenant. Those who remained fled to Babylon in exile until they returned in 538 B.C., after the Persians defeated the Babylonians. Jerusalem was rebuilt and a Second Temple erected. Israel was then ruled by a series of kings under whom the Hebrews were allowed to remain.

Co-existence proved impossible under the Roman occupation, which began about 63 B.C. In 66 A.D., the Hebrews revolted against their oppressors, but were unsuccessful. The Second Temple was destroyed and the Hebrews were either exiled or annihilated. A second revolt in 132 A.D. proved equally unsuccessful. The Romans renamed Jerusalem "Palestine" and decreed the city permanently off-limits to Hebrews. In what is known as the *Diaspora*, exiled Jews dispersed widely throughout other lands such as Rome and Egypt; eventually many settled in Eastern Europe. Jews continued to keep the covenant, practicing their faith and remaining steadfast in their commitment to the Promised Land.

During this period, the spread of other religions fueled new claims to Palestine. In 326 A.D., Empress Helena (mother of the Christian emperor, Constantine of Byzantium), established the Church of the Nativity in Bethlehem. Other Christian churches were also founded. Following the defeat of the Byzantines by Caliph Omar, the Muslims ruled Palestine. In 638 A.D., Jerusalem became an Islamic holy city, in accordance with the belief that the prophet Mohammed had ascended to heaven from within the city. Islamic claims to Jerusalem generated centuries of conflict with the Christians. Around 1100 A.D., the Christians began a series of crusades to wrest the Holy Land from the Muslims. The Crusades proved disastrous for Christians, Muslims, and Jews alike, and ended with Palestine in the hands of the Egyptian Mameluks. By the sixteenth century, Palestine was part of the Ottoman Empire. The Jews, many of whom were suffering at the hands of Christians, quietly began returning to Palestine.

Jewish settlements in Palestine grew slowly during the next three centuries. However, during the 1870s and 1880s, Jews fleeing *pogroms* (a term for the massacre of helpless people) in Eastern Europe began flooding into Palestine in what is known as the First Aliyah, the mass waves of Jews "ascending to the land." As the persecution of the Jews in Europe continued, Theodore Herzl in *The Jewish State* (1896) proposed the idea of an all-Jewish state in Palestine. Herzl's book led to the formation of a movement termed Zionism. Proponents of Zionism lobbied for an independent Jewish nation, a nation free from religious persecution. In 1897, the first Zionist Congress introduced the formation of the World Zionist Organization (WZO). The WZO established the Jewish National Fund in 1901, and Jews all over the world were urged to contribute to the Zionist cause. Jews, particularly American Jews, responded favorably and donated large amounts of money to the cause. The WZO soon began purchasing land in Palestine.

In 1904, Jews fleeing pogroms in Russia arrived in Palestine, thus creating the Second Aliyah. The city of Tel Aviv was founded in 1909. That same year the Kibbutz Degania, a collective-living experiment, was founded near the Sea of Galilee. As more Jewish immigrants arrived, tensions increased between Jews and Palestinian Arabs. At this time, Palestine was a protectorate of Great Britain. In 1917 the British issued the Balfour Declaration, which advocated the establishment of a Jewish state in Palestine. The Nazi persecution of the Jews during World War II resulted in a flood of immigrants from Europe to Palestine.

Following the end of World War II, Palestine was handed over to the United Nations. In November of 1947, the United Nations voted to partition Palestine into separate Jewish and Arab states, and Jerusalem was proclaimed an international territory. On May 14, 1948, David Ben-Gurion, the first prime minister, declared the state of Israel an independent nation.

MODERN ERA

The declaration of Israel's independence precipitated immediate internal and external crises for the new nation. Although some countries (including the United States and the Soviet Union) were quick to recognize Israel, neighboring Arab states refused to do so. In 1948, Israel was invaded by Iraq, Jordan, Egypt, Syria, and Lebanon. The Israelis were able to repel the invaders and, in the process, actually expanded its boundaries. Although the United Nations arranged a cease-fire agreement between the five neighboring Arab countries and Israel, more obstacles loomed ahead. In particular, tensions dramatically increased between the Jews and the Palestinian Arabs, many of whom had been displaced from their land.

In 1950, Israel enacted the Law of Return, which guaranteed citizenship to all Jews. The number of immigrants continued to grow, and Israel's economy and military slowly gained strength. In 1967, the armies of Egypt, Jordan, and Syria again invaded Israel. The Israelis routed the invaders and captured large amounts of territory from their Arab neighbors. By the end of war, Israel had gained control of the Golan Heights, the West Bank, the Gaza Strip, and the Sinai Peninsula. They also annexed Jerusalem. Dismayed by the growth of Israeli power in the region, the Palestinian Arabs formed the Palestinian Liberation Organization (PLO). The PLO often used terrorism as a means of retaliating against Israel. In 1973, the Egyptians and Syrians launched an attack against Israel during the Jewish holy season of Yom Kippur. The Israelis were initially caught off guard and were nearly defeated. They recovered quickly, however, and were able to successfully defend their land. Eventually, the United Nations negotiated a peace deal that ended the fighting. In 1979, Egypt and Israel signed the Camp David peace accords. Egypt officially recognized Israel as an independent nation while Israel returned control of the Sinai Peninsula, which had been captured in the 1967 war, to Egypt.

Although a peace agreement had been reached between Egypt and Israel, the Palestinians continued to resent Israeli occupation of the Gaza Strip and West Bank. During the late 1980s, the Palestinians and Israelis mutually agreed to seek peace.

Several attempts to broker a peace agreement between the two peoples were unsuccessful. In 1993, after a series of intense negotiations, the Palestinians and Israelis signed the Oslo peace accords. The Palestinians were given control of the Gaza Strip and parts of the West Bank and offered the opportunity to hold democratic elections in those areas under their control. In return, the Palestinians agreed to halt terrorist attacks against Israel. Many Palestinians and Israelis were critical of the agreement, however, and tension between the two peoples remains high.

SIGNIFICANT IMMIGRATION WAVES

Israelis began immigrating to the United States soon after Israel's independence in 1948. During the 1950s and early 1960s, over 300,000 Israelis immigrated to the United States. Another wave of immigration began in the mid-1970s and has continued ever since. Although estimates vary greatly, anywhere from 100,000 to 500,000 immigrants arrived in America during this period. The actual number of Israeli immigrants to the United States has been a subject of intense debate since the 1980s. Many Israeli citizens are emigrants from other countries, and when these Israelis immigrated to the United States, their native-born country was often listed on census records. This may explain in part the low number of Israeli immigrants (90,000) recorded on the 1990 U.S. Census, a figure incongruent with the significant number of Israeli communities in larger cities.

Several key factors contributed to increased Israeli immigration into the United States during the last two decades of the twentieth century. Many Israeli immigrants cited the political unrest in the Middle East and the relative insecurity of the region as their primary reason for emigrating. Shortly after the Yom Kippur War in 1973, an event that left many Israelis shaken and disillusioned, the number of immigrants rose dramatically. It is important to note that many Israelis are exposed to American culture by virtue of the close relationship between Israel and the United States. American fashions, fads, and forms of entertainment are commonplace in Israel. In many cases, the "Americanization" of Israel added to the immigrants' desire to take advantage of the economic and educational opportunities in the United States. During the 1980s and 1990s, Israel produced more qualified and educated workers than there were skilled positions, a situation that resulted in fierce competition within the Israeli job market. Heavy taxation and a lack of available housing also dismayed many Israelis. Israelis looked to the United States as a place to fulfill financial and educational goals in a manner not possible in Israel. As one Israeli immigrant stated in the book *Migrants from the Promised Land*, "It is not for nothing that they [the United States] are referred to as the land of endless opportunities. There are opportunities in every area of life, everywhere. I don't say that here things are blocked, they're not blocked . . . just smaller, more compact."

However, financial or educational fulfillment was not the only incentives for Israeli immigrants. During the 1990s, many Israelis immigrated as a result of their ideological dissatisfaction with Israel. For some, the ideal of an egalitarian community free from religious persecution had paradoxically resulted in an excessive amount of intervention from a highly stratified government that favored Ashkenazic Jews (Jews of European origin). Sephardic Jews (those of North African and Middle Eastern ancestry) have long been the victims of ethnic discrimination by Ashkenazic Jews, who represent the overwhelming majority of Israelis. The socioeconomic discrepancies that arose from discrimination in Israel led many Sephardic Jews to seek economic opportunities elsewhere.

SETTLEMENT PATTERNS

The main areas of Israeli settlement in the United States include New York, California, Michigan, Florida, and Illinois. However, pockets of Israeli settlement can be found throughout the country. Israeli immigrants are fairly mobile and tend to migrate to several locations in the United States before permanently settling down. Chain migrations are often a determining factor in the immigrants' choice of residence. The heaviest concentrations of Israeli Americans are located in New York and Los Angeles, which contain nearly half of those living in the United States. Not surprisingly, Israeli Jews gravitate toward other Jews and a sizable number live in older, established Jewish neighborhoods such as Queens and Brooklyn in New York City, and West Hollywood and the San Fernando Valley in Los Angeles. Similarly, Israeli Arabs tended to settle near other Arabs, particularly in the industrial cities of the Midwest, such as Chicago and Detroit.

ACCULTURATION AND ASSIMILATION

On average, Israeli Americans have enjoyed a smoother transition to American life than other groups of immigrants. A good number of Israeli immigrants are well-educated and possess specialized job skills that have allowed them to bypass the often frustrating experiences of less trained immigrants. In addition, a number of Israeli immigrants have relatives living in the United States, which further eases the adjustment. Within a short period of time, many Israeli Americans attain a relative degree of financial security. However, even though Israelis are attracted by the vast economic opportunities available in the United States, many often feel at odds with many of American society's materialistic values. Many Israeli Americans are accustomed to the closely-knit community and shared ideological experience of Israel. In order to compensate for this loss, Israeli Americans have formed extensive and vibrant communities within the larger American culture, particularly in the Los Angeles and New York areas. This network of organizations ensures that many Israeli Americans remain connected to Israeli culture and the Hebrew language. The extensive Israeli network includes Hebrew newspapers and radio and television broadcasts, as well as organizations such as the Israeli Flying Clubs, the Israeli Musicians Organization, and the Israeli Organization in Los Angeles (ILA).

The Israeli American network has provided a valuable service to immigrants, many of whom initially intended to remain in the United States only long enough to finish their educational or financial goals before returning to Israel. An overwhelming majority of Israeli immigrants believe they will eventually return to Israel and are thus reluctant to fully assimilate into American culture. Also, their status as "temporary sojourners" serves as a buffer against the open hostility they have suffered from both the Israeli government and American Jews. Although American Jews have traditionally welcomed Jewish immigrants, the Israeli immigrants represent a failure of the Zionist cause that Americans Jews have generously supported. Israeli Americans are given the derogatory label of *yordim*, which signifies that they have descended from Israel to the diaspora, as opposed to *olim*, those who have ascended from the diaspora to Israel. The negative connotations and sense of betrayal associated with immigration prevent many Israelis from openly declaring themselves permanent citizens of the United States.

A sizable number of Israeli immigrants eventually become permanent citizens, particularly through marriage. It is estimated that over a third of Israelis marry U.S. citizens. Likewise, a number of Israeli immigrants have established businesses in the United States, which further strengthens their ties to America. However, even those immigrants who eventually become naturalized continue to remain active in Israeli organizations long after the initial

settling process. A strong identification with Israel, coupled with the stigma attached to immigration, helps explain why the majority of immigrants continue to refer to themselves as "Israelis" as opposed to "Americans" or even "Israeli Americans."

TRADITIONS, CUSTOMS, AND BELIEFS

Israelis have a variety of traditions, the majority of which are connected to the Jewish faith. The Torah outlines the strict observance of certain rules called the 613 Holy Obligations, as well as certain holidays and the weekly Sabbath. Other traditions associated with these celebrations have evolved over the centuries. Special foods, objects, and songs are all equally important to Jewish celebrations and the observance of the Sabbath, although they are not explicitly referred to in the Torah. During Rosh Hashanah, it is customary to send cards to friends and family bearing the words "L'shana tovah," which means "to a good and healthy year." Other traditions reflect geographical differences. For example, the Eastern European Jews began the tradition of eating gefilte fish to break the Yom Kippur fast. The custom of eating *cholent*, a stew prepared the night before the Sabbath, also emerged because cooking on the Sabbath is strictly forbidden.

Other customs are only loosely based on the Jewish religion and originate from earlier superstitions, such as the belief in the "evil eye." For example, it is customary to hold a baby shower after the baby is born. A baby's name is revealed only at the naming ceremony, and a red ribbon is tied to the baby's crib. These folk customs originated as precautions designed to fend off the evil forces accompanying the good fortune of a baby's birth. Although the traditions related to the practice of Judaism are still diligently observed, many of the superstitions have gradually been forgotten.

CUISINE

Israeli cuisine is savory and flavorful, and reflects the influence of its diverse cultural inheritance as well as the strict dietary laws practiced by Jews. Israeli Jews observe the *kashrut*, which is a set of food restrictions outlined in the book of Leviticus. The acceptable foods to eat (termed *kosher*) include meat from animals with cloven hoofs, breads, fish with scales and fins, fruits and vegetables, poultry, and kosher dairy products. Foods that are not acceptable (termed *trefa*) include pork, fish that do not have scales and fins (like lobster or shrimp), and meals that combine meat and dairy products. In addition, meat is butchered in a special manner in order to observe the rule that forbids the drinking of blood. Both the Oriental and the Eastern European Jews have contributed to Israel's unique cuisine: the former introduced *shashlik* (cubed meat such as lamb or chicken) and *kebabs* (minced meats), and the latter contributed *schnitzels*, *goulashes*, and *blintzes*.

There is a strong Middle Eastern influence in Israeli cooking. Some favorite dishes include *hummus* (chickpeas, onions, and spices); *falafel* (fried hummus); *fuul* (fava beans); and *mashi* (stuffed pita breads). Israelis enjoy sweet desserts including *baklava* (a dessert of wheat, honey, and nuts) and

katayeef (cheese, wheat, sugar, and honey). Although kosher food is readily available in the United States, many Israeli Americans have opened restaurants that serve the Middle Eastern dishes prominent in Israeli cuisine.

DANCES AND SONGS

Israeli folk dancing is admired around the world and there are thousands of different dances that are performed. Traditional dances include circle, line, or partner dances and they are intricately choreographed. Some of the more popular dances include: "Al Kanfe Hakesef;" "Lechu Neranena;" "Ahavat Itamar;" "Al Tiruni;" "Bakramim;" and "Bat Teiman." Since Israeli folk dancing has long been admired by American Jews, several Jewish organizations have established community folk dancing classes. Klezmer music, the traditional music of the Eastern European Jews, is also popular in Israel and became increasingly popular in the United States during the late 1990s. Traditional klezmer songs include: "Az Der Rebbe Elimeylekh," "A Heymisher Bulgar," and "A Nakht in Gan Edent."

HOLIDAYS

Israeli Americans celebrate Jewish holidays, which are public holidays in Israel. The holidays are based on the Hebrew lunar calendar, which contains twelve 28-day cycles, for a total of 336 days a year, with an extra month added periodically. The holidays do not, therefore, fall on the same day every year, although they remain seasonal. The Jewish New Year begins in the fall with the celebration of *Rosh Hashanah*, which means "The Head of the Year" and is celebrated in September or October. As the sun sets on the first day of the first month, Jewish families gather together to say a blessing over wine and bread and to reflect on the significance of the holiday and renewal of the world. It is customary to bake *challah* bread in the form of a circle as a symbol of the cyclical year. *Yom Kippur*, the holiest day of the Jewish calendar, occurs on the tenth day of the New Year. The ten days between Rosh Hashanah and Yom Kippur are known as the "days of awe" and are meant to provide a quiet, reflective time in which Jews can cleanse their souls and focus on their relationship with God. There is a strict fast on the night before

Yom Kippur and the day and nighttime are usually spent in the synagogue. Special prayers are recited, including the *Kol Nidre, Musaf, Minchah, Neilah,* and ending with the symbolic intonation of "*L'shana ha-ba-ah b'Yerysgakatun,*" which means "next year in Jerusalem."

The *sukkot,* or "festival of the booths," is celebrated immediately after the end of Yom Kippur and commemorates the exodus of the Jews from Egypt. At this time, it is customary to construct huts in order to observe the rule that Jews "live in nature" during the duration of the festival. *Hannukah,* the "festival of the light," lasts for eight days in November or December. Hannukah celebrates the victory of the Maccabees over the Syrians in 165 B.C. After the defeat, the oil for the Temple miraculously lasted for eight days until it could be renewed. During Hannukah, candles in a *menorrah* are lit for each one of the eight days. Traditional foods associated with this holiday include those cooked in oil and dairy foods. *Purim,* "the feast of lots," is a joyous celebration that takes place in late winter and celebrates the victory of the Jewish community in Persia by Queen Esther. It is customary to fast the day before Purim, called the "Fast of Esther." *Passover,* "the festival of freedom," takes place in March or April, and celebrates the time when the Jews put a sign on their doors that enabled God to "pass over" his chosen people when he delivered ten plagues upon their Egyptian captors. The Passover Seder celebrates not only the end of winter, but also the release of oppressed Jews throughout the world. *Shavuot,* the "festival of weeks," occurs seven weeks after Passover and commemorates the anniversary of the receiving of the Ten Commandments by Moses on Mount Sinai. Shavuot is also considered an agricultural celebration, as it celebrates the festival of the first fruits when wheat is harvested. A custom practiced during Shavuot is the ritual of staying up all night and reading the Torah.

Other festivals or holidays are the *Yom Haaho'ah,* which takes place in the spring and commemorates those who died in the Holocaust. *Yom Hazikaron* is the Israeli Memorial Day and is a day of remembrance for those who died in battle for Israel. *Yom Ha-Atzma'ut* takes place in May the day after Yom Hazikaron and celebrates the day Israel declared its independence.

Israeli Americans often express disappointment concerning the way that Jewish holidays are celebrated in the United States. Although American Jews celebrate Jewish holidays, Israeli Americans are accustomed to a national celebration, and find it difficult to adjust to the fact that Jewish holidays are ordinary days to the majority of Americans. Israeli Americans usually prefer to celebrate Israeli holidays with each other, particularly those that American Jews are not comfortable observing.

HEALTH ISSUES

Israeli Americans have not been prone to any specific medical conditions and tend to be in generally good health. Most Israelis have health insurance that is covered by their employers and those that are self-employed provide coverage for themselves and their employees. There are several nationwide organizations of Israeli health professionals.

LANGUAGE

The official languages of Israel are Hebrew and Arabic, but the vast majority of Israelis speak Hebrew, which dates back to 2,000 B.C. and serves as an important bond for Jews throughout the world. Israeli Americans generally learn the English language faster than other immigrant groups, and only five percent of Israeli immigrants are not proficient in English. However, immigrants continue to place an importance on Hebrew as a link to both their Jewish faith and their Israeli background. Eighty percent of first-generation Israeli Americans speak Hebrew at home, although the percentages decrease as the immigrants become more entrenched in American culture. In addition, the Ashkenazic Jews speak *Yiddish,* which is a peculiarly Eastern European mixture of German and Hebrew, while the Sephardic Jews speak *Ladino.* Both languages are increasingly less heard, although Yiddish-speaking Israeli Americans are more likely to be found among those who have settled in New York.

GREETINGS AND OTHER POPULAR EXPRESSIONS

Common Hebrew greetings and other expressions include: *shalom*—hello; *shalom*—goodbye; *bokertov*—good morning; *erev tov*—good evening; *todah*—thank you; *bevakasha*—please; *ken*—yes; *loh*—no; *sleekha*—excuse me; *mazel tov*—good luck; *hag same'ah*—a happy holiday; *shanah tovah*—a good year.

Common Arabic greetings and other expressions include: *a-halan*—hello; *salaam aleicham*—goodbye; *sabah-l-kheir*—good morning; *min fadlach*—please; *shoo-khran*—thank you; *afwan*—you are welcome; *ay-wah*—yes; *la*—no.

FAMILY AND COMMUNITY DYNAMICS

The constant pressure of living in an insecure and dangerous environment has fostered the importance of the family and community among Israelis. Moreover, Judaism encourages strong family relationships, and many observances of the faith, such as the weekly Sabbath, serve to draw the family together. Most immigrants are married and place a strong emphasis on raising children. Because Israeli American parents are accustomed to relying on a national community of resources that aid in the socialization of their children, they often express disappointment with the lack of support systems available in the United States.

One of the greatest concerns of Israeli Americans is the preservation of their identity and their values within the alien culture of the United States. Israeli Americans are opposed to American values, such as competitiveness, materialism, and low motivation, which they perceive as antithetical to their own. However, they are often unable to foster an Israeli identity in their more "Americanized" children. One Israeli American mother described the dilemma in the article "Israeli Immigrants in the United States," "There is a big gap between Israelis and their kids that were born here. This is a special problem for the Israelis because we are raising a generation that are Americans, beautiful American children. Highly educated, high achievers, but still, American children. You cannot raise Israeli children in [the] United States, for heaven's sake."

In order to expose their children to Israeli culture, Israeli Americans and the Israeli government have created various programs and workshops to help strengthen bonds with Israel. Toward the end of the twentieth century, the American Jewish community began to establish similar programs through such groups as the New York Board of Jewish Education, which sponsors folk-dance groups, parent workshops, summer camps, and religious training. *Tzabar*, the American branch of Tzofim (Israeli Scouts), enrolls groups of children between the ages of ten and nineteen. Each summer, over 200 Israeli Americans spend a summer in Israel as part of *Hetz Vakeshet*, a program similar to Outward Bound.

EDUCATION

Israeli Americans value education highly and often immigrate in order to take advantage of the excellent university programs available throughout the United States. According to the 1990 U.S. census, 56% of Israeli American men and 52% of women in New York, and 56% of Israeli American men and 62% of women in Los Angeles had attended college, and only 20% did not finish high school. On the whole, over one-third of all Israeli American immigrants have college degrees.

Although Israeli immigrants appreciate the large number of educational institutions available in the United States, they are cautious about placing their children in public schools. Some Israeli Americans are fearful that negative values such as low achievement, a lack of respect toward parents, and American individuality are being taught to their children. Similarly, Israeli American parents are disturbed by the availability of drugs and sexual permissiveness in some American schools. Israeli immigrants generally prefer to place their children in private schools that emphasize values that are more similar to those taught in the Israeli educational system. Israeli Americans have also relied on a number of instructional courses and after-school programs for their children such as the AMI, which is an Israeli Hebrew course.

THE ROLE OF WOMEN

The Jewish faith is inherently patriarchal and, over the centuries, women have played a nominal role in Jewish communities worldwide. Traditionally, wives and daughters were restricted to running the household and caring for children. Education was not considered necessary for women and, in many instances, was forbidden. During the last few generations, however, Jewish women across the world have made tremendous strides in gaining access to educational and career opportunities. Female Israeli American immigrants tend to be as educated as their male counterparts and are often able to secure high-status jobs within the United States. However, nearly one-half of all married Israeli American women choose to stay at home in order to raise their children.

WEDDINGS, BAPTISMS, AND FUNERALS

Israeli Americans observe weddings, baptisms, and funerals in the tradition of their Jewish faith. The circumcision ceremony (*berit milah*) occurs on the eighth day after the birth of a baby boy. The Covenant of Circumcision celebrates the covenant between God and Abraham and is traditionally performed by a *mohel*, a person who is specially trained in circumcision. The celebration is an important family ritual and the duties of those who take part in the ceremony are strictly designated: those who carry the baby are the baby's chosen godfather (*kvatter*) and godmother (*kvatterin*). Although there is generally not a special naming ceremony for Jewish girls, a special prayer is said at synagogue, at which time the daughter receives her Hebrew name.

Jewish weddings are lavish and festive occasions that are filled with many traditions. The ceremony takes place under a *chupah* (marriage canopy, which symbolizes the bridal chamber and the home that the couple is creating together). The wedding begins with a procession in which the groom (*chatan*) and the bride (*kalah*) are led to the chupah by their parents, where seven blessings (*sheva berachot*) are chanted before the bride and groom drink a glass of wine as a symbol of the sharing of their lives. After the couple exchange rings, they sign the marriage contract, or *ketubah*. The couple is then pronounced man and wife, and the groom steps on a glass as everyone shouts *mazel tov*. Following the ceremony, a large reception takes place, at which there is much singing and dancing.

Following a death in a Jewish family, the funeral is usually held within 24 hours after death. During this time, a *shomer* (person who stays in the same room) guards the body, which is never to be left alone before the burial. In accordance with custom, the casket remains closed and there is no embalming or cosmetology performed. The casket is made of wood so that nature may follow its course quickly. All mirrors in the house are covered, so that vanity may not be allowed to interfere with the mourning and grief owed to the dead. At the graveside service, there is a ceremonial tearing of the mourner's skirt, ribbon, or shirt, which is called *keriah*. The mourners recite a prayer (*kaddish*) over the dead. During the next seven days, the family of the deceased sits *shivah*, and friends and family come to mourn and pay their respects. After a period of eleven months, the grieving process is considered over.

RELIGION

Judaism represents the foundation of the state of Israel. Israeli Judaism is both national and secular, and does not necessarily include the observance of the faith. Expression of a person's Jewish heritage is not restricted simply to the synagogue or to certain days of the year, but encompasses all daily activities, whether in the workplace, government, or during recreation. The observance of the Jewish holidays, the Hebrew language, and Jewish traditions are all performed on a national level. This has led to a greater secularization of Judaism within Israel. Israelis do not regard the practice of their faith as the defining factor of Judaism.

Israeli immigrants to the United States are often unprepared for the highly organized religion practiced by American Jews, who comprise over one-third of the world's Jewish population. American Jews have maintained their faith through a well-established system of synagogues, organizations, and branches of Judaism. Differing attitudes toward Judaism have created tension and conflict between Israeli Americans and American Jews. Unaccustomed to being in the minority, the Israelis are critical of what they perceive as an excessive amount of religious practice by American Jews. Furthermore, Israeli immigrants often accuse American Jews of succumbing to materialistic American values. American Jews, in turn, are often appalled with the cavalier attitude that some Israeli Americans have toward Judaism, and by their indifference to the sacrifices made by American Jews for the Zionist cause.

Israeli Americans are ultimately forced to choose between American Judaism and the more secular Judaism that is practiced in Israel. Immigrants, particularly those with children, often feel torn between the two choices. Even if they are not entirely comfortable with American Judaism, Israeli Americans are fearful that their children will lose their Jewish identity altogether and embrace only American values. The majority of Israeli Americans reluctantly choose to place their children in American Jewish schools and day care centers. However, these children then become accustomed to American Jewish practices and demand the same excessive religiosity in their home. This generates conflict and tension between Israeli American parents and their children.

Toward the end of the twentieth century, American Jews sought to improve relations with Israeli Americans. During the 1980s, the American Jewish community began to encourage Israeli Americans to become more involved in Jewish community centers, organizations, and federations. Israeli Americans responded to these overtures favorably and began to forge bonds with American Jews. Not surprisingly, many Israeli Americans discovered that their practice of the Jewish religion increased considerably after they immigrated to the United States. As they did in Israel, Israeli Americans continued to worship with those of similar ethnic background. The traditional discrimination between the Sephardic and Ashkenazic Jews remains strong in the United States. Generally, the Sephardic Jews tend to have a higher rate of synagogue membership and observance of kosher food laws.

Employment and Economic Traditions

The importance that Israeli Americans place on education has allowed them to find well-paying, highly skilled jobs within the American workforce. Even during the initial adjustment period to life in the United States, Israeli Americans are much less likely to use welfare than other immigrant groups, and tend to have a high employment rate overall. Almost half of all male Israeli Americans in New York and Los Angeles are managers, administrators, professionals, or technical specialists, and another quarter are employed in sales. Israeli American professionals include doctors, architects, entertainers, small businessmen, and teachers. A fairly large number of Israeli American women teach Hebrew.

As is typical of other Jewish immigrants, Israeli Americans are extremely entrepreneurial and have the second highest rate of self-employment among all immigrant groups in the United States. The 1990 census found that one-third of Israeli men in both New York and Los Angeles were self-employed, particularly in the garment and retail industries. Other immigrants opened businesses such as restaurants, nightclubs, and retail shops within the Israeli communities to serve the growing needs of Israeli immigrants. Many newly arrived immigrants view their work in Israeli American businesses as a type of apprenticeship before opening their own business. Although Israeli employers feel a sense of obligation toward other Israelis, they are aware that the employees will eventually become competitors, a situation that sometimes creates conflicts.

The average income for Israeli immigrants is high compared to the rest of the country. The 1990 census reported that Israeli American men in New York and Los Angeles earned an annual income of $35,000 and $49,000, respectively. Israeli American women in New York and Los Angeles made $25,000 and $22,000, respectively.

Politics and Government

Many Israeli Americans expect to return to Israel and are more inclined to follow Israeli, rather than American, politics. Sometimes referred to as "transnationals," over 85 percent of Israeli Americans read Israeli newspapers and 58 percent listen to Hebrew broadcasts. Many Israeli Americans retain ownership of their homes in Israel and make frequent trips between Israel and the United States. Those Israeli Americans who do become naturalized citizens of the United States continue to follow events in Israel and tend to vote for American political candidates that support Israeli interests. For instance, 54 percent of Israeli Americans voted for President Richard Nixon in the 1972 presidential election because of his strong commitment to Israel.

American Jews generously support the state of Israel, and have enough political clout to ensure that Israel remains a focal point of American interests. There has been so much financial, military, and cultural exchange between the two countries that some Israelis refer to Israel as the "51st" state of the United States. Historically, the Israeli government has discouraged immigration to the United States. However, during the late 1990s, the Israeli government began to encourage the formation of services and organizations specifically designed to assist Israeli American immigrants.

Individual and Group Contributions

ACADEMIA

Nadav Safran has received national recognition for his expertise on the Middle East. During his tenure at Harvard University, he published the following books, all of which were well-received: *Egypt in Search of Political Community; An Analysis of the Intellectual and Political Evolution of Egypt, 1804-1952* (1961); *From War to War: The Arab-Israeli Confrontation, 1948-1967* (1969); *Israel, the Embattled Ally* (1978); and *Saudi Arabia: The Ceaseless Quest for Security* (1985). Amos Twersky is considered one of the leading authorities on mathematical models in psychology and has been a Professor of Psychology at Stanford University. He co-authored the following publications: *Mathematical Psychology: An Elementary Introduction* (1970); and *Decision Making: Descriptive, Normative, and Prescriptive Interaction* (1988).

BUSINESS

The Nakash brothers (Joe, Ralph, and Aviv), established Jordache Enterprises, Inc. in 1969. Their trademark Jordache jeans enjoyed immediate success and were soon distributed worldwide. By the late 1990s, they had amassed a fortune of over $600 million.

MUSIC

Yitzhak Perlman (1945-), a world-renowned violinist, has appeared with the New York Philharmonic, the Cleveland Orchestra, the Philadelphia Orchestra, and other orchestras throughout the United States. He received the Leventritt Prize in 1964, 15 Grammy awards between the years 1977-1987 and the Medal of Liberty in 1986. Pinchas Zuckerman (1948-), is also a world-renowned violinist and the recipient of the Leventritt Prize. He was selected as the music director of the St. Paul Chamber Orchestra in Minnesota, where he served from 1980-1987. From 1990 to 1992, he was the guest conductor of the Dallas Symphony Orchestra. Since 1993, Zuckerman has taught at the Manhattan School of Music in New York.

POLITICS

Amitai Etzioni (1929-) served as an advisor to President Carter from 1979-1980. In addition, he has served on the faculty of Columbia University (1958-1980) and George Washington University (1980-). He has also held positions at the Center for Policy Research (1968-), the Brookings Institution (1978-1979), and the Institute for War and Peace Studies (1967-1978).

FILM AND THEATER

Theodore Bikel (1924-) is an award-winning actor and singer. He has appeared in staged productions of *The Sound of Music* (1959-1961) and *Fiddler on the Roof* (1968-1996). He has also appeared in *The African Queen* (1951); *The Defiant Ones* (1958), for which he received an Academy award nomination; *My Fair Lady* (1964); *Sands of the Kalahari* (1965) and *Crime and Punishment* (1993). He also hosted a weekly radio program entitled "At Home with Theodore Bikel" (1958-1963), and recorded various folk songs. He has been the recipient of the Emmy Award (1988) and the Lifetime Achievement Award for the National Foundation for Jewish Culture (1997).

MEDIA

PRINT

Ha'aretz.
An Israeli, Hebrew-language daily, which is distributed across the country

Contact: Bejamin Landau, Los Angeles correspondent.
Address: 356 South LaPeer Drive, Beverly Hills, CA 90211.
Telephone: (310) 854-3797.

Hadoar (The Post).
A Hebrew-language biweekly publication that deals with broad issues of concern to the Jewish person.

Address: 426 W. 58th St., New York, NY 10019-1102.
Telephone: (212) 929-1678.

Young Israel Viewpoint.
Established in 1920, the quarterly publication contains news of interest to the Israeli-Jewish communities.

Address: 3 W. 16th St., New York, NY 10011.
Telephone: (212) 929-1525.

RADIO

WELW-FM.
Address: P.O. Box 1330, Willoughby, OH 44096.
Telephone: (440) 946-1330.

WRSU-FM.
Address: 126 College Avenue, New Brunswick, NJ 08901.
Telephone: (732) 932-7800.

WUNR-FM.
Address: 160 N. Washington St., Boston, MA 02114.
Telephone: (617) 738-1870.

TELEVISION

Israel Broadcasting Authority.
Address: 1101 30th Street, Washington, DC 20007.
Telephone: (202) 338-6091.

Israel Broadcasting Authority Radio and Television.
Address: 10 Rockefeller Plaza, New York, NY 10020.
Telephone: (212) 265-6330.

ORGANIZATIONS AND ASSOCIATIONS

America-Israel Cultural Foundation.
Encourages, promotes, and sustains cultural excellence in Israel. Provides scholarships in music, the visual and design arts, filmmaking, dance, and theater to gifted students; advanced-study fellowships

to teachers and young professionals; and grants to institutions and special projects in Israel. Allocates approximately $2.3 million for underwriting over 600 scholarships, projects, and institutions. Sponsors Israel Philharmonic Orchestra, Tel Aviv Museum of Art, Jerusalem Film and Television School, Batsheva Dance Company, and the Beit Zvi School of Drama.

Contact: Kathleen Mellon, Executive Director.
Address: 51 East 42nd Street, Suite 400,
New York, New York 10017.
Telephone: (212)557-1600.
Fax: (212)557-1611.
Online: http://www.aicf.webnet.org.

America Israel Friendship League.
Seeks to maintain and strengthen the mutually supportive relationship between people of the United States and Israel. Seeks to promote the friendship between the two democracics.

Contact: Ms. Ilana Artman, Executive
Vice President.
Address: 134 East 39th Street, New York,
New York 10016.
Telephone: (212) 213-8630.
Fax: (212) 683-3475.
Online: http://www.usa50israel.org.

Chabad West Coast Headquarters.
Nationwide organization that addresses Jewish issues; lends aid and sponsors events for Jewish immigrants, including newly-arrived Israelis.

Contact: Shlomo Cunih.
Address: 741 Gayley Avenue, Los Angeles,
CA 90024.
Telephone: (310) 208-7511.

Israeli Students' Organization in the U.S.A. and Canada.
Israeli citizens who are in the United States or Canada for study and/or training purposes. Gives aid and advice to members in solving their problems during their study or training and upon their return to Israel; sponsors cultural, social, and informative activities in the Israeli spirit and tradition; represents the Israeli student body before Israeli, American, and Canadian authorities and maintains contact with these author-

ities. Promotes friendship between Israeli students, American Jewish students, other foreign students, American Jewry, and the American public. Maintains a loan fund; provides medical insurance program and discount airfare to Israel.

Contact: Menahem Rosenberg, Executive Officer.
Address: 17 East 45th Street, Suite 907, New
York, New York 10017
Telephone: (212) 681-9810.
Fax: (212) 681-9815.
E-mail: mailbox@isoa.org.
Online: http://www.isoa.org.

SOURCES FOR ADDITIONAL STUDY

Blumberg, Arnold. *The History of Israel.* Westport, CT: Greenwood Press, 1998.

Cohen, Yinon. "Socioeconomic Dualism: The Case of Israeli-born Immigrants in the United States." *International Migration Review* 23: 267-88.

Gold, Steven J. "Israeli Immigrants in the United States: The Question of Community." *Qualitative Sociology.* 17: 325-345.

Gold, Steven J., and Bruce A. Phillips. "Israelis in the U.S." *American Jewish Yearbook, 1996.* New York: The American Jewish Committee, 1996: 51-104.

Mittelberg, David, and Mary C. Waters. "The Process of Ethnogenesis among Haitian and Israeli Immigrants in the United States." *Ethnic and Racial Studies* 15: 412-435.

Ritterbrand, Paul. "Israelis in New York." *Contemporary Jewry* 7: 113-26.

Rosenthal, Mirra, and Charles Auerbach. "Cultural and Social Assimilation of Israeli Immigrants in the United States." *International Migration Review*, pp. 982-991.

Sobel, Zvi. *Migrants From the Promised Land.* New Brunswick: Transaction Books, 1986.

The family (*la famiglia*) rested at the heart of Italian society. Family solidarity was the major bulwark from which the rural population confronted a harsh society, and the family unit (including blood relatives and relatives by marriage) became the center of allegiances.

ITALIAN
by
George Pozzetta

AMERICANS

OVERVIEW

Moored by Alpine mountains in the north, the boot-shaped Italian peninsula juts into the central Mediterranean Sea. Along its European frontier, Italy shares borders with France, Switzerland, Austria, and Slovenia. The nation's land mass, which includes the two major islands of Sicily and Sardinia and numerous smaller ones, measures 116,324 square miles (301,200 square kilometers)—almost exactly double the size of the state of Florida. Italy's population in 1991 stood at 57.6 million. With the exception of the broad north Italian Plain at the foot of the Alps, the peninsula is crosscut through much of its length by the Apennine mountain chain. The obstacles created by the highlands, valleys, and gorges found in the mountain regions fostered strong cultural and linguistic differences.

HISTORY

Italy's modern state traces its mythological roots to the founding of the city of Rome in 753 B.C. More historically verified is the fact that the Romans engaged in territorial expansion and conquest of neighboring lands, devising effective colonization policies that ultimately sustained a widespread realm. By 172 B.C., Rome controlled all of the Italian peninsula and began moving outward into the Mediterranean basin. At its peak, the Roman empire extended from the British Isles to the

Euphrates River. The *Pax Romana* began to crumble, however, by the end of the first century A.D. The sack of Rome by the Visigoths in 410 A.D. presaged the more complete disintegration of the empire in the later fifth and sixth centuries. With its political integration shattered, the country remained fragmented until the late nineteenth century. Italy was, in the view of many Europeans, a "mere geographic expression."

Italy is a relatively young nation state, achieving full unification only during the *Risorgimento* of 1860-1870. Prior to this, the peninsula consisted of often mutually antagonistic kingdoms, duchies, city-states, and principalities. Some of these regions had a history of autonomous rule, while others came under the periodic control of foreign powers as a result of recurrent wars and shifting political alliances. Over the centuries, therefore, powerful regional loyalties emerged, and persisted well after unification. Although local cultural variations remained notable, the most significant internal distinctions have been those stemming from the contrast between a relatively prosperous, cosmopolitan, urban North and a socially backward, economically depressed, agricultural South.

Southern Italy (*Mezzogiorno*), the source of more than 75 percent of immigration to the United States, was an impoverished region possessing a highly stratified, virtually feudal society. The bulk of the population consisted of artisans (*artigiani*), petty landowners or sharecroppers (*contadini*), and farm laborers (*giornalieri*), all of whom eked out meager existences. For reasons of security and health, residents typically clustered in hill towns situated away from farm land. Each day required long walks to family plots, adding to the toil that framed daily lives. Families typically worked as collective units to ensure survival. Angelo Pellegrini, who became a successful immigrant, remembered his sharecropping family: "The central, dominating fact of our existence was continuous, inadequately rewarded labor.... Education beyond the third grade was out of the question.... At eight or nine years of age, if not sooner, the peasant child is old enough to bend his neck to the yoke and fix his eyes upon the soil in which he must grub for bread. I did not know it then, but I know it now, that is a cruel, man-made destiny from which there is yet no immediate hope of escape." (Angelo Pellegrini, *Immigrant's Return*. New York: Macmillan, 1952; pp. 11, 21.)

The impact of unification on the South was disastrous. The new constitution heavily favored the North, especially in its tax policies, industrial subsidies, and land programs. The hard-pressed peasantry shouldered an increased share of national expenses, while attempting to compete in markets dominated more and more by outside capitalist intrusions. These burdens only exacerbated existing problems of poor soil, absentee landlords, inadequate investment, disease, and high rates of illiteracy. With cruel irony, as livelihoods became increasingly precarious, population totals soared. Italy jumped from 25 million residents in 1861 to 33 million in 1901 to more than 35 million in 1911, despite the massive migration already underway.

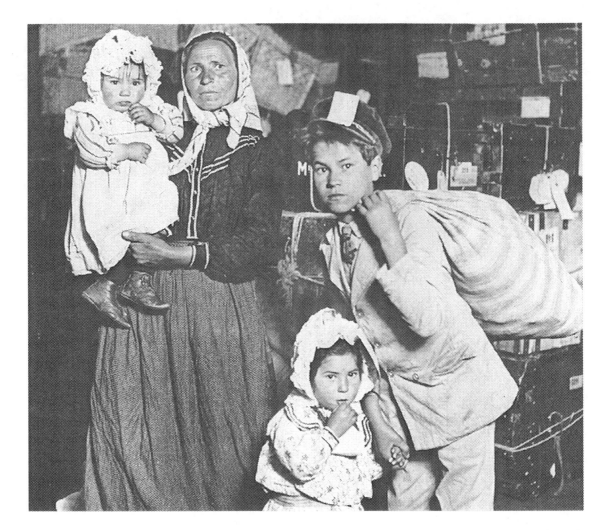

EARLY IMMIGRATION

An exodus of southerners from the peninsula began in the 1880s. Commencing in the regions of Calabria, Campania, Apulia, and Basilicata, and spreading after 1900 to Sicily, Italian emigration became a torrent of humanity. From 1876-1924, more than 4.5 million Italians arrived in the United States, and over two million came in the years 1901-1910 alone. Despite these massive numbers, it should be noted that roughly two-thirds of Italian migration went elsewhere, especially to Europe and South America. Immigration to the United States before and after this period accounted for approximately one million additional arrivals—a considerable movement in its own right—but the era of mass migration remains central to the Italian immigrant experience.

Yet, there were important precursors. Italian explorers and sailors venturing outward in the employ of other nations touched America in its earliest beginnings. The most famous was, of course, Christopher Columbus, a Genoese mariner sailing for Spain. Other seafarers such as John Cabot (Giovanni Caboto), Giovanni da Verrazzano, and

Amerigo Vespucci, and important missionaries such as Eusebio Chino and Fra Marco da Nizza, also played roles in early exploration and settlement.

After the American Revolution, a small flow of largely northern-Italian skilled artisans, painters, sculptors, musicians, and dancers came to the new nation, filling economic niches. With the failure of the early nineteenth-century liberal revolutions, these immigrants were joined by a trickle of political refugees, the most famous of whom was Giuseppe Garibaldi. By the second half of the century, American cities also typically included Italian street entertainers, tradesmen, statuette makers, and stone workers, who often established the first beachheads of settlement for the migrations to come. Many of these pioneers were merely extending generations-old migratory patterns that had earlier brought them through Europe. An old Italian proverb instructed: *Chi esce riesce* (He who leaves succeeds).

This initial Italian movement dispersed widely throughout America, but its numbers were too small to constitute a significant presence. By 1850, the heaviest concentration was in Louisiana (only 915 people), the result of Sicilian migration to New

Orleans and its environs. Within a decade, California contained the highest total of any state—a mere 2,805—and New York, soon to become home to millions of Italian immigrants, counted 1,862.

Everything changed with mass migration, the first phase of which consisted primarily of temporary migrants—"sojourners"—who desired immediate employment, maximum savings, and quick repatriation. The movement was predominately composed of young, single men of prime working age (15-35) who clustered in America's urban centers. Multiple trips were commonplace and ties to American society, such as learning English, securing citizenship, and acquiring property, were minimal. With eyes focused on the old-world *paese* (village), a total of at least half of the sojourners returned to Italy, although in some years rates were much higher. Such mobility earned Italians the sobriquet "birds of passage," a label that persisted until women and families began to migrate and settlement became increasingly permanent in the years following 1910.

Migrants brought with them their family-centered peasant cultures and their fiercely local identifications, or *campanilismo*. They typically viewed themselves as residents of particular villages or regions, not as "Italians." The organizational and residential life of early communities reflected these facts, as people limited their associations largely to kin and *paesani* fellow villagers. The proliferation of narrowly based mutual aid societies and *festas* (*feste*, or feast days) honoring local patron saints were manifestations of these tendencies. Gradually, as immigrants acclimated to the American milieu, in which others regarded them simply as Italians, and as they increasingly interacted with fellow immigrants, *campanilismo* gave way to a more national identity. Group-wide organization and identity, nonetheless, have always been difficult to achieve.

THE EMERGENCE OF "LITTLE ITALIES"

In terms of settlement, immigrants were (and are) highly concentrated. Using kin and village-based chain migration networks to form "Little Italies," they clustered heavily in cities in the Northeast region (the Mid-Atlantic and New England states) and the Midwest, with outposts in California and Louisiana. More than 90 percent settled in only 11 states—New York, New Jersey, Pennsylvania, Massachusetts, California, Connecticut, Illinois, Ohio, Michigan, Missouri, and Louisiana—and approximately 90 percent congregated in urban areas. These patterns largely hold true today, although immigrants have branched out to locations such as Arizona and Florida. In every settlement area, there

has been, over time, a slow but steady shift from central cities to suburbs.

Immigrants often sought out Little Italies as a result of the hostility they encountered in American society. As a despised minority rooted in the working class and seemingly resistant to assimilation, Italians suffered widespread discrimination in housing and employment. American responses to the immigrants occasionally took uglier forms as Italians became the victims of intimidation and violence, the most notorious incident being the 1890 lynching of 11 Italians in New Orleans. Italian mass migration coincided with the growth of a nativism that identified southern and eastern Europeans as undesirable elements. Inspired by the pseudo-scientific findings of eugenics and social Darwinism, turn-of-the-century nativists often branded southern Italians as especially inferior. Powerful stereotypes centering on poverty, clannishness, illiteracy, high disease rates, and an alleged proclivity toward criminal activities underscored the view that southern Italians were a degenerate "race" that should be denied entry to America. Criticism of Italians became integral to the successful legislative drives to enact the nativist Literacy Test in 1917 and National Origins Acts in 1921 and 1924.

Within Little Italies, immigrants created New World societies. A network of Italian language institutions—newspapers, theaters, churches, mutual aid societies, recreational clubs, and debating societies—helped fuel an emerging Italian-American ethnic culture. Aspects of the folk, popular, and high culture intermixed in this milieu yielding an array of entertainment options. Saloons or club buildings in larger urban centers often featured traditional puppet and marionette shows while immigrant men sipped wines and played card games of *mora*, *briscola*, and *tresette*. By the early 1900s, a lively Italian language theater brought entertainment to thousands and sustained the careers of professional acting troupes and noted performers such as the comedic genius Eduardo Migliacco, known as "Farfariello." On a more informal level, Italian coffee houses often presented light comedies, heroic tragedies, and dialect plays sponsored by drama clubs. Italian opera was a staple in most American urban centers, and working-class Italian music halls attracted customers by offering renditions of Neapolitan or Sicilian songs and dances. Band performances and choral recitals were regularly staged on the streets of Italian settlements. Although illiteracy rates among immigrants often ran well above 50 percent, newcomers in larger cities had access to Italian language bookstores stocked with poetry, short stories, novels, and nonfiction. In 1906 one New York bookseller published a catalogue of 176 pages to advertise his merchandise.

The cultural patterns of Little Italies were constantly evolving, providing for a dynamic interplay between older forms brought from Italy and new inventions forged in the United States. Many immigrants attempted to recreate old-world celebrations and rituals upon arrival in the United States, but those that directly competed with American forms soon fell away. The celebration of Epiphany (January 6), for example, was the principal Christmas time festivity in Italy, featuring the visit of *La Befana*, a kindly old witch who brought presents for children. In the United States the more popular Christmas Eve and Santa Claus displaced this tradition.

Even those cultural forms more sheltered from American society were contested. Immigrant settlements were not homogenous entities. Various members of the community fought for the right to define the group, and the ongoing struggle for dominance invariably employed cultural symbols and events.

"My first impression when I got there, I tell you the God's truth, you're in a dream. It's like in heaven. You don't know what it is. You're so happy there in America."

Felice Taldone in 1924, cited in *Ellis Island: An Illustrated History of the Immigrant Experience,* edited by Ivan Chermayeff et al. (New York: Macmillan, 1991).

The commercial and political elites (*prominenti*)—usually aided by the Italian Catholic clergy—sought to promote Italian nationalism as a means of self-advancement. These forces invested great energy in celebrations of Italian national holidays (such as *venti di settembre*, which commemorated Italian unification), and in the erection of statues of such Italian heroes as Columbus, the poet Dante, and military leader Giuseppe Garibaldi.

These activities were challenged by a variety of leftist radicals (*sovversivi*), who sought very different cultural and political goals. Anarchists, socialists, and syndicalists such as Carlo Tresca and Arturo Giovannitti considered Italian Americans as part of the world proletariat and celebrated holidays (*Primo Maggio*—May Day) and heroes (Gaetano Bresci, the assassin of Italian King Umberto) reflecting this image. These symbols also played roles in mass strikes and worker demonstrations led by the radicals. Meanwhile, the majority of Italian Americans continued to draw much of their identity from the peasant cultures of the old-world *paese*. Columbus Day, the preeminent Italian American ethnic cele-

bration, typically blended elements of all these components, with multiple parades and competing banquets, balls, and public presentations.

World War I proved an ambiguous interlude for Italian immigrants. Italy's alliance with the United States and the service of many immigrants in the U.S. military precipitated some level of American acceptance. The war also produced, however, countervailing pressures that generated more intense nationalism among Italians and powerful drives toward assimilation—"100 percent Americanism"—in the wider society. Immigration restrictions after 1924 halted Italian immigration, although the foreign-born presence remained strong (the 1930 census recorded 1,623,000 Italian-born residents—the group's historic high). As new arrivals slowed and the second generation matured during the 1920s and 1930s, the group changed.

Several critical developments shaped the character of Italian America during the interwar years. National prohibition provided lucrative illegal markets, which some Italian Americans successfully exploited through bootlegging operations. During the 1920s, the "gangster" image of Italians (exemplified by Al Capone) was perpetuated through films and popular literature. The celebrated case of Nicola Sacco and Bartolomeo Vanzetti further molded the group's national image, underwriting the conception of Italians as dangerous radicals.

The Great Depression overshadowed earlier economic gains, often forcing Italian Americans back into their family-centered ethnic communities. Here, the emerging second generation found itself in frequent conflict with the first. Heavily influenced by the traditional *contadino* culture passed on from their parents, the second generation uneasily straddled two worlds. Traditional notions of proper behavior, stressing collective responsibilities toward the family, strict chastity and domestic roles for females, rigid chaperonage and courting codes, and male dominance, clashed with the more individualist, consumer-driven American values children learned in schools, stores, and on the streets. Problems of marginality, lack of self-esteem, rebellion, and delinquency were the outcomes.

Partly because of these dynamics, the community structures of Little Italies began to change. The more Americanized second generation began to turn away from older, Italian-language institutions founded by immigrants, many of which collapsed during the depression. Italian theaters and music halls, for example, largely gave way to vaudeville, nickelodeons, organized sports, and radio programming. During the 1920s and 1930s, these transformations were also influenced by Benito Mussolini's fascist regime, which sponsored propaganda campaigns designed to attract the support of Italian Americans. The *prominenti* generally supported these initiatives, often inserting fascist symbols (the black shirt), songs ("Giovinezza"—the fascist anthem), and holidays (the anniversary of the March on Rome) into the ichnography and pageantry of America's Little Italies. A small, but vocal, anti-fascist element existed in opposition, and it substituted counter values and emblems. Memorials to Giacomo Matteotti, a socialist deputy murdered by fascists, and renditions of *Bandiera Rossa* and *Inno di Garibaldi* became fixtures of anti-fascist festivities. Thus, the cultural world of Italian America remained divided.

Any questions concerning loyalties to the United States were firmly answered when Italy declared war on the United States in 1941, and Italian Americans rushed to aid the American struggle against the Axis powers. More than 500,000 Italian Americans joined the U.S. military, serving in all theaters, including the Italian campaign. The war effort and ensuing anti-communist crusade stressed conformity, loyalty, and patriotism, and in the 1940s and 1950s it appeared that Italian Americans had comfortably settled into the melting pot. The second generation especially benefited from its war service and the postwar economic expansion as it yielded new levels of acceptance and integration. In the 1950s, they experienced substantial social mobility and embraced mass consumerism and middle-class values.

Since the end of World War II, more than 600,000 Italian immigrants have arrived in the United States. A large percentage came shortly after passage of the Immigration Act of 1965, at which time yearly totals of Italian immigrants averaged about 23,000. Beginning in 1974, the numbers steadily declined as a result of improved economic conditions in Italy and changing policies in other immigrant-receiving nations. In 1990 only 3,300 Italian immigrants were admitted to the United States, but 831,922 Italian-born residents remained in the country, guaranteeing that Italian language and culture are still part of the American cultural mosaic.

ACCULTURATION AND ASSIMILATION

Assimilation takes place at many different levels, but for the individual, it is likely that few captured the essence of the experience better than Rosa Cavalleri. Cavalleri came from the Italian town of Cuggiono in 1884 as a frightened young woman, joining her husband in a mining camp in remote Missouri. After undergoing numerous tribulations, Cavalleri settled in Chicago, where she cleaned floors and bathrooms, while remarrying and successfully raising a family. As Cavalleri neared death in 1943, she mused: "Only one wish more I have: I'd love to go in *Italia* again before I die. Now I speak English good like an American I could go anywhere—where millionaires go and high people. I would look the high people in the face and ask them questions I'd like to know. I wouldn't be afraid now—not of anybody. I'd be proud I come from America and speak English. I would go to Bugiarno [Cuggiono] and see the people and talk to the bosses in the silk factory.... I could talk to the *Superiora* now. I'd tell her, `Why you were so mean—you threw me out that poor girl whose heart was so kind toward you? You think you'll go to heaven like that?' I'd scold them like that now. I wouldn't be afraid. They wouldn't hurt me now I come from America. Me, that's why I love America. That's what I learned in America: not to be afraid." (Marie Hall Ets, *Rosa: The Life of an Italian Immigrant.* Minneapolis: University of Minnesota Press, 1970; p. 254.)

The integration of Italians like Cavalleri into American life was a result of changes in both the group and the larger society. Italians were beginning to make a commitment to permanent settlement. This process was substantially underway by 1910, cresting in the 1920s when new immigration fell off. After this, perpetuation of the old-world public culture became increasingly difficult, although the family-based value structure was more resilient. During the 1920s and 1930s, the second generation continued to display many of its hallmarks: children of immigrants still held largely blue-collar occupations and were underrepresented in schools, tied to Little Italy residences, and attracted to in-group marriages—choices that demonstrated the continuing power of parental mores.

Changing contexts, however, diminished the "social distance" separating Italians from other Americans. In the 1930s, second-generation Italian Americans joined forces with others in labor unions and lobbied for benefits. They also began to make political gains as part of the Democratic Party's New Deal coalition. Also for the first time, the national popular culture began to include Italian Americans among its heroes. In music, sports, politics, and cinema the careers of Frank Sinatra, Joe DiMaggio, Fiorello LaGuardia, Frank Capra, and Don Ameche suggested that national attitudes toward Italians were in transition.

World War II was a critical benchmark in the acceptance of Italian Americans. Their wholehearted support of America's cause and their disproportionately high ratio of service in the military legitimized them in American eyes. The war also transformed many Little Italies, as men and women left for military service or to work in war industries. Upon their return, many newly affluent Italian Americans left for suburban locations and fresh opportunities, further eroding the institutions and *contadino* culture that once thrived in ethnic settlements.

The Cold War pushed the group further into the mainstream as Italian Americans joined in the anti-communist fervor gripping the nation. Simultaneously, structural changes in the economy vastly expanded the availability of white collar, managerial positions, and Italian Americans jumped to take advantage. Beginning in the 1950s, they pursued higher education in greater numbers than ever before, many receiving aid as a result of the G.I. Bill. Such developments put them into more immediate and positive contact with other Americans, who exhibited greater acceptance in the postwar years.

Ironically, a resurgent Italian American ethnicity emerged at the same time, as the group experienced increasing integration into the larger society. Italian Americans were active participants in the ethnic revival of the 1960s and 1970s. As American core values came under assault in the midst of Vietnam, Watergate, and the rising counterculture, and the nation's urban centers became torn by riots and civil protest, Italian Americans felt especially vulnerable and besieged. Unlike other ethnic groups, they had remained in urban enclaves, manifesting high rates of home ownership, where they now found themselves in contact and conflict with African Americans. Many interpreted the ensuing clashes in cultural terms, seeing themselves as an embattled minority defending traditional values in the face of new compensatory government programs. In response, ethnic traditions surrounding family, neighborhood, and homes gained heightened visibility and strength. New Italian American organizations and publications fostering ethnic identity came into being, and many old rituals experienced a resurgence, most notably the celebration of the *feste*.

Intermarriage rates increased after the 1950s, especially among the third and fourth generations who were now coming of age. By 1991, the group's overall in-marriage rate was just under 33 percent, above the average of 26 percent for other ethnic groups. But among those born after 1940—by now a majority—the rate was only 20 percent, and these marriages crossed both ethnic and religious lines. Once a marginalized, despised minority, Italian Americans are now among the most highly accepted groups according to national surveys measuring "social distance" indicators (Italians ranked fourteenth in 1926, but fifth in 1977). All of the statistical data point to a high level of structural assimilation in American society, although Italian American ethnicity has not disappeared.

That Italian American identity has lost much of its former negative weight is suggested further by recent census figures for ancestry group claiming. The 1980 census recorded 12.1 million individuals who claimed Italian ancestry (5.4 percent of national population). By 1990 this figure had risen to 14.7 million (5.9 percent), indicating that ethnicity remains an important and acceptable component of self-identification for substantial numbers of Italian Americans.

Despite strong evidence of integration, Italian Americans retain distinguishing characteristics. They are still geographically concentrated in the old settlement areas, and they display a pronounced attachment to the values of domesticity and family loyalty. Italian Americans still rely heavily on personal and kin networks in residential choices, visiting patterns, and general social interaction. Perhaps most distinctive, the group continues to suffer from stereotypes associating it with criminal behavior, especially in the form of organized crime and the mafia. These images have persisted despite research documenting that Italian Americans possess crime rates no higher than other segments of American society and that organized crime is a multi-ethnic enterprise. Television and film images of Italian Americans continue to emphasize criminals, "lovable or laughable dimwits" who engage in dead-end jobs, and heavy-accented, obese "Mamas" with their pasta pots.

These representations have influenced the movement of Italian Americans into the highest levels of corporate and political life. The innuendos of criminal ties advanced during Geraldine Ferraro's candidacy for vice-president in 1984 and during Mario Cuomo's aborted presidential bids illustrate the political repercussions of these stereotypes, and many Italian Americans believe that bias has kept them underrepresented in the top echelons of the business world. Since the 1970s, such organizations as the Americans of Italian Descent, the Sons of Italy in America, and the National Italian American Foundation have mounted broad-based anti-defamation campaigns protesting such negative imagery.

HOLIDAYS

The major national holidays of Italy—*Festa della Republica* (June 5), *Festa dell'Unità Nazionale* (November 6), and *Festa del Lavoro* (May 1)—are no longer occasions of public celebration among Italian Americans. Some religious holidays, such as *Epifania di Gesù* (January 6), receive only passing notice. Most Italian Americans celebrate Christmas Day, New Year's Day, and Easter Day, but usually without any particular ethnic character. The principal occasions of public celebration typically revolve around Columbus Day, the quintessential Italian American national holiday, and the *feste* honoring patron saints. In both cases, these events have, in general, become multi-day celebrations virtually devoid of any religious or Italian national connotation, involving numerous non-Italians.

In New Orleans, Louisiana, St. Joseph's Day (March 19) is celebrated by some members of the Italian-American community. The tradition began in Sicily, the origin of much of New Orleans' Italian-American population. The day was commemorated by the building of temporary three-tiered alters, loaded with food offerings for the saint. The alters were found in private homes, churches, some restaurants, and public places associated with Italians, with the general public invited. Visitors to the alters are often given *lagniappe* (a sack of cookies and fava beans, a good luck charm) to take home.

Preparations for St. Joseph's Day began several weeks in advance with baking of cookies, breads and cakes. Cookies, such as twice-baked biscotti and sesame-seed varieties, could be shaped into forms with religious significance. Bread, cannoli, seafood and vegetable dishes are also found on the alter. Such dishes include *forschias* and pasta Milanese covered with *mudriga*. Mudriga was also called St. Joseph's sawdust, made of bread crumbs and sugar. No meat was found because the holiday almost always falls during Lent. In addition to food, the alter often had an image of St. Joseph, home grown flowers, candles and palm branches.

Italian immigrants utilized traditional costumes, folk songs, folklore, and dances for special events, but like many aspects of Italian life, they were so regionally specific that they defy easy characterization. Perhaps the most commonly recognized folk dance, the *tarantella*, for example, is Neapolitan, with little diffusion elsewhere in the peninsula.

CUISINE

The difficult conditions of daily life in Italy dictated frugal eating habits. Most peasants consumed simple meals based on whatever vegetables or grains (lentils, peas, fava beans, corn, tomatoes, onions, and wild greens) were prevalent in each region. A staple for most common folk was coarse black bread.

Pasta was a luxury, and peasants typically ate meat only two or three times a year on special holidays. Italian cuisine was—and still is—regionally distinctive, and even festive meals varied widely. The traditional Christmas dish in Piedmont was *agnolotti* (ravioli), while *anguille* (eels) were served in Campania, *sopa friulana* (celery soup) in Friuli, and *bovoloni* (fat snails) in Vicenza.

In the United States, many immigrants planted small backyard garden plots to supplement the table and continued to raise cows, chickens, and goats whenever possible. Outdoor brick ovens were commonplace, serving as clear ethnic markers of Italian residences. With improved economic conditions, pastas, meats, sugar, and coffee were consumed more frequently. One New York City immigrant remembered asking, "Who could afford to eat spaghetti more than once a week [in Italy]? In America no one starved, though a family earned no more than five or six dollars a week.... Don't you remember how our *paesani* here in America ate to their hearts delight till they were belching like pigs, and how they dumped mountains of uneaten food out the window? We were not poor in America; we just had a little less than others." (Leonard Covello, *The Social Background of the Italo-American School Child*. Totowa, New Jersey: Rowman and Littlefield, 1972; p. 295.)

"Italian cooking" in the United States has come to mean southern-Italian, especially Neapolitan, cuisine, which is rich in tomato sauces, heavily spiced, and pasta-based. Spaghetti and meatballs (not generally known in Italy) and pizza are perhaps the quintessential Italian dishes in the United States. More recently, northern Italian cooking—characterized by rice (*risotto*) and corn (*polenta*) dishes and butter-based recipes—has become increasingly common in homes and restaurants. Garlic (*aglio*), olive oil (*olio d'oliva*), mushrooms (*funghi*), and nuts (*nochi*) of various types are common ingredients found in Italian cooking. Wine (*vino*), consumed in moderate amounts, is a staple. Overall, Italian dishes have become so popular that they have been accepted into the nation's dietary repertoire, but not in strictly old-world forms. Americanized dishes are generally milder in their spicing and more standardized than old-world fare.

HEALTH ISSUES

A number of Italian American organizations have supported the Cooley's Anemia Foundation to fund research into Thalassemia, once thought to be a sickle cell anemia confined to persons of Mediterranean ancestry. Recent research has demonstrated the fallacy of this belief, however, and contributions have largely ceased.

LANGUAGE

Italian is a Romance language derived directly from Latin; it utilizes the Latin alphabet, but the letters "j," "k," "w," "x," and "y" are found only in words of foreign origin. "Standard" Italian—based on the Tuscan dialect—is a relatively recent invention, and was not used universally until well into the twentieth century. Numerous dialects were the dominant linguistic feature during the years of mass immigration.

Italian dialects did not simply possess different tonalities or inflections. Some were languages in their own right, with separate vocabularies and, for a few, fully developed literatures (e.g., Venetian, Piedmontese, and Sicilian). Italy's mountainous terrain produced conditions in which proximate areas often possessed mutually unintelligible languages. For example, the word for "today" in standard Italian is *oggi*, but *ancheuj* in Piedmontese, *uncuó* in Venetian, *ste iorne* in Sicilian, and *oji* in Calabrian. Similarly, "children" in Italian is *bambini*, but it becomes *cit* in Piedomontese, *fruz* in Friulian, *guagliuni* in Neapolitan, *zitedi* in Calabrian, and *picciriddi* in Sicilian. Thus, language facilitated *campanilismo*, further fragmenting the emerging Italian American world.

Very soon after the Italians' arrival, all dialects became infused with Americanisms, quickly creating a new form of communication often intelligible only to immigrants. The new patois was neither Italian nor English, and it included such words as *giobba* for job, *grossiera* for grocery, *bosso* for boss, *marachetta* for market, *baccausa* for outhouse, *ticchetto* for ticket, *bisiniss* for business, *trocco* for truck, *sciabola* for shovel, *loffare* for the verb to loaf, and *carpetto* for carpet. Angelo Massari, who immigrated to Tampa, Florida, in 1902, described preparations in his Sicilian village prior to leaving it: "I used to interview people who had returned from America. I asked them thousands of questions, how America was, what they did in Tampa, what kind of work was to be had.... One of them told me the language was English, and I asked him how to say one word or another in that language. I got these wonderful samples of a Sicilian-American English from him: *tu sei un boia, gud morni, olraiti, giachese, misti, sciusi, bred, iessi, bud* [you are a boy, good morning, alright, jacket, mister, excuse me, bread, yes, but]. He told me also that in order to ask for work, one had to say, `Se misti gari giobbi fo mi?' [Say, mister got a job for me?]." (Angelo Massari, *The Wonderful Life of Angelo Massari*, translated by Arthur Massolo. New York: Exposition Press, 1965; pp. 46-47.)

Italian proverbs tend to reflect the conditions of peasant and immigrant lives: Work hard, work always, and you will never know hunger; He who leaves the old way for the new knows what he loses but knows not what he will find; Buy oxen and marry women from your village only; The wolf changes his skin but not his vice; The village is all the world; Do not miss the Saint's day, he helps you and provides at all times; Tell me who your friends are and I will tell you what you are; He who respects others will be respected.

FAMILY AND COMMUNITY DYNAMICS

The family (*la famiglia*) rested at the heart of Italian society. Family solidarity was the major bulwark from which the rural population confronted a harsh society, and the family unit (including blood relatives and relatives by marriage) became the center of allegiances. Economically and socially, the family functioned as a collective enterprise, an "all-inclusive social world" in which the individual was subordinated to the larger entity. Parents expected children to assist them at an early age by providing gainful labor, and family values stressed respect for the elderly, obedience to parents, hard work, and deference to authority.

The traditional Italian family was "father-headed, but mother-centered." In public, the father was the uncontested authority figure and wives were expected to defer to their husbands. At home, however, females exercised considerable authority as wives and mothers, and played central roles in sustaining familial networks. Still, male children occupied a favored position of superiority over females, and strong family mores governed female behavior. Women's activities were largely confined to the home, and strict rules limited their public behavior, including access to education and outside employment. Formal rituals of courting, chaperonage, and arranged marriages strictly governed relations between the sexes. Above all, protection of female chastity was critical to maintaining family honor.

Family and kin networks also guided migration patterns, directing precise village flows to specific destinations. During sojourner migrations, the work of women in home villages sustained the family well-being in Italy and allowed male workers to actively compete in the world labor market. In America, the extended family became an important network for relatives to seek and receive assistance. Thus, migration and settlement operated within a context of family considerations.

Attempts to transfer traditional family customs to America engendered considerable tension between generations. More educated and Americanized children ventured to bridge two worlds in which the individualist notions of American society often clashed with their parents' family-centered ethos. Still, strong patterns of in-marriage characterized the second generation, and many of their parents' cultural values were successfully inculcated. These carryovers resulted in a strong attachment to neighborhoods and families, consistent deference to authority, and blue-collar work choices. The second generation, however, began to adopt American practices in terms of family life (seen, for example, in smaller family size and English language usage), and the collective nature of the unit began to break down as the generations advanced.

EDUCATION

The peasant culture placed little value on formal instruction, seeking instead to have children contribute as soon as possible to family earnings. From the peasant perspective, education consisted primarily of passing along moral and social values through parental instruction (the term *buon educato* means "well-raised or behaved"). In southern Italy, formal education was seldom a means of upward mobility since public schools were not institutions of the people. They were poorly organized and supported, administered by a distrusted northern bureaucracy, and perceived as alien to the goals of family solidarity. Proverbs such as "Do not let your children become better than you" spoke to these perceptions, and high rates of illiteracy testified to their power.

These attitudes remained strong among immigrants in America, many of whom planned a quick repatriation and saw little reason to lose children's wages. Parents also worried about the individualist values taught in American public schools. The saying "America took from us our children" was a common lament. Thus, truancy rates among Italians were high, especially among girls, for whom education had always been regarded as unnecessary since tradition dictated a path of marriage, motherhood, and homemaking.

Antagonism toward schools was derived not only from culture, but also from economic need and realistic judgments about mobility possibilities. Given the constricted employment options open to immigrants (largely confined to manual, unskilled labor), and the need for family members to contribute economically, extended schooling offered few rewards. From the parental viewpoint, anything

threatening the family's collective strength was dangerous. Generations frequently clashed over demands to terminate formal education and find work, turn over earnings, and otherwise assist the family financially in other ways. Prior to World War I, less than one percent of Italian children were enrolled in high school.

As the second generation came of age in the 1920s and 1930s and America moved toward a service economy, however, education received greater acceptance. Although the children of immigrants generally remained entrenched in the working class (though frequently as skilled workers), they extended their education, often attending vocational schools, and could be found among the nation's clerks, bookkeepers, managers, and sales personnel. The economic downturn occasioned by the depression resulted in increased educational opportunities for some immigrants since job prospects were limited.

Italian Americans were well situated in post-World War II America to take advantage of the national expansion of secondary and higher education. They hastened to enroll in G.I. Bill programs and in the 1950s and 1960s began to send sons and daughters to colleges. By the 1970s, Italian Americans averaged about 12 years of formal education; in 1991 the group slightly surpassed the national mean of 12.7 years.

RELIGION

Although Italian immigrants were overwhelmingly Roman Catholic, their faith was a personal, folk religion of feast days and peasant traditions that often had little to do with formal dogma or rituals. As such, its practices differed greatly from those encountered in America's Irish-dominated Catholic Church. Unlike Irish Americans, most Italians possessed no great reverence for priests (who had sometimes been among the oppressors in Italy) or the institutions of the official Church, and they disliked what they regarded as the impersonal, puritanical, and overly doctrinal Irish approach to religion. As in Italy, men continued to manifest anticlerical traditions and to attend church only on selected occasions, such as weddings and funerals.

For their part, the Irish clergy generally regarded Italians as indifferent Catholics—even pagans—and often relegated them to basement services. The Irish American hierarchy agonized over the "Italian Problem," and suspicion and mistrust initially characterized relations between the groups, leading to defections among the immigrant generation and demands for separate parishes. A disproportionately

low presence of Italian Americans in the church leadership today is at least partially a legacy of this strained relationship. Protestant missionaries were not unaware of these developments. Many attempted to win converts, but met with very little success. With the establishment of "national parishes," however, the Catholic Church hit firmer ground, and Italian parishes proliferated after 1900. In many settlements, parish churches became focal points providing a sense of ethnic identity, a range of social services, and a source of community adhesion.

Italian immigrant Catholicism centered on the local patron saints and the beliefs, superstitions, and practices associated with the *feste*. The *feste* not only assisted in perpetuating local identities, but they also served as a means for public expression of immigrant faith. In the early years, feast days replicated those of the homeland. Festivals were occasions for great celebration, complete with music, parades, dancing, eating, and fireworks displays. At the high point, statues of local saints such as San Rocco, San Giuseppe, or San Gennaro, were carried through the streets of Little Italies in a procession. New Yorker Richard Gambino, in *Blood of My Blood*, recalled the feast days of his youth: "Not long ago there were many such street *feste*. Their aromas of food, the sight of burly men swaying from side to side and lurching forward under the weight of enormous statues of exotic Madonnas and saints laden with money and gifts, the music of Italian bands in uniforms with dark-peaked caps, white shirts, and black ties and the bright arches of colored lights spanning the city streets.... True to the spirit of *campanilismo*, each group of *paesani* in New York had its *festa*. Three *feste* were larger than the

others. Sicilians, especially from the region of Agrigento, went all out for the huge September festival of San Gandolfo. In July, thousands turned out to honor the Madonna del Carmine. And in the fall, Neapolitans paid their respect to the patron of their mother city, San Gennaro."

Worshippers lined the streets as processions moved toward the parish church, and they vied to pin money on the statue, place gifts on platforms, or make various penances (walking barefoot, crawling, licking the church floor [*lingua strascinuni*], reciting certain prayers). Irish prelates frequently attempted to ban such events, viewing them as pagan rituals and public spectacles. A cluster of beliefs focusing on the folk world of magic, witches, ghosts, and demons further estranged Italians from the church hierarchy. Many immigrants were convinced, for example, of the existence of the evil eye (*malocchio* or *jettatura*), and believed that wearing certain symbols, the most potent of which were associated with horns (*corni*) or garlic amulets, provided protection from its power.

As the second and subsequent generations grew to maturity, most strictly old-world forms of religious observance and belief were discarded, leading to what some have called the "hibernization" of Italian American Catholicism. Many feast day celebrations remain, although, in some cases, they have been transformed into mass cultural events which draw thousands of non-Italians. The San Gennaro *feste* in Manhattan's Little Italy is a case in point: once celebrated only by Neapolitans, it now attracts heterogeneous crowds from hundreds of miles away.

EMPLOYMENT AND ECONOMIC TRADITIONS

Throughout the years of mass migration, Italians clustered heavily in the ranks of unskilled, manual labor. In part, this seems to have resulted from cultural preference—men favored outdoor jobs dovetailing old-world skills—and immigrant strategies that sought readily available employment in order to return quickly to Italy with nest eggs. But American employers also imposed the choice of positions since many regarded Italians as unsuited for indoor work or heavy industry. Immigrants thus frequently engaged in seasonal work on construction sites and railroads and in mines and public works projects. Male employment often operated under the "boss system" in which countrymen (*padroni*) served as middlemen between gangs of immigrant workers and American employers. Married women generally worked at home, either concentrating on family tasks or other home-based jobs such as keeping boarders, attending to industrial homework, or assisting in family-run stores. In larger urban centers, unmarried women worked outside the home in garment, artificial flower, and costume jewelry factories, and in sweatshops and canneries, often laboring together in all-Italian groups.

Some Little Italies were large enough to support a full economic structure of their own. In these locations, small import stores, shops, restaurants, fish merchants, and flower traders proliferated, offering opportunities for upward mobility within the ethnic enclave. In many cities, Italians dominated certain urban trades such as fruit and vegetable peddling, confectioniering, rag picking, shoe-shining, ice-cream vending, and stevedoring. A portion of the immigrants were skilled artisans who typically replicated their old-world crafts of shoemaking and repairing, tailoring, carpentry, and barbering.

The dense concentration of Italian Americans in blue-collar occupations persisted into the second generation, deriving from deliberate career choices, attitudes toward formal education, and the economic dynamics of the nation. Italians had begun to make advances out of the unskilled ranks during the prosperous 1920s, but many gains were overshadowed during the Great Depression. Partially in response to these conditions, Italians—both men and women—moved heavily into organized labor during the 1930s, finding the CIO industrial unions especially attractive. Union memberships among Italian Americans rose significantly; by 1937, the AFL International Ladies Garment Workers Union (with vice president Luigi Antonini) counted nearly 100,000 Italian members in the New York City area alone. At the same time, women were becoming a presence in service and clerical positions.

The occupational choices of Italian Americans shifted radically after World War II, when structural changes in the American economy facilitated openings in more white collar occupations. Italian Americans were strategically situated to take advantage of these economic shifts, being clustered in the urban areas where economic expansion took place and ready to move into higher education. Since the 1960s, Italian Americans have become solidly grounded in the middle-class, managerial, and professional ranks. As a group, by 1991 they had equalled or surpassed national averages in income and occupational prestige.

POLITICS AND GOVERNMENT

Italians were slow to take part in the American political process. Due to the temporary nature of early migration, few took the time to achieve naturalization in order to vote. Anti-government attitudes, exemplified in the *ladro governo* ("the government as thief") outlook, also limited participation. Hence, Italian voters did not initially translate into political clout. Early political activity took place at the urban machine level, where immigrants typically encountered Irish Democratic bosses offering favors in return for support, but often blocking out aspiring Italian politicians. In such cities, those Italians seeking office frequently drifted to the Republican Party.

Naturalization rates increased during the 1920s, but the next decade was marked by a political watershed. During the 1930s, Italian Americans joined the Democratic New Deal coalition, many becoming politically active for the first time in doing so. The careers of independent/sometime-Republican Fiorello LaGuardia and leftist Vito Marcantonio benefited from this expansion. As a concentrated urban group with strong union ties, Italians constituted an important component of President Franklin Roosevelt's national support. The Democratic hold on Italians was somewhat shaken by Roosevelt's "dagger in the back" speech condemning Italy's attack on France in 1940, but, overall, the group maintained its strong commitment to the Party. In the early 1970s, only 17 percent of Italian Americans were registered Republicans (45 percent were registered Democrats), although many began to vote Republican in recent presidential elections. Both President Ronald Reagan and President George Bush were supported by strong Italian-American majorities. Overall, the group has moved from the left toward the political center. By 1991, Italian American voter registrations were 35 percent Republican and 32 percent Democratic.

The political ascent of Italian Americans came after World War II with the maturation of the second and third generations, the acquisition of increased education and greater wealth, and a higher level of acceptance by the wider society. Italian Americans were well-represented in city and state offices and had begun to penetrate the middle ranks of the federal government, especially the judicial system. By the 1970s and 1980s, there were Italian American cabinet members, governors, federal judges, and state legislators. Only four Italian Americans sat in Congress during the 1930s, but more than 30 served in the 1980s; in 1987 there were three U.S. Senators. The candidacy of Geraldine Ferraro for the Democratic vice presidency in 1984, the high profile of New York governor Mario Cuomo in American political discourse, and the appointment of Antonin Scalia to the Supreme Court are indicative of the group's political importance.

Since World War II, most Italian Americans have remained largely uninvolved in—even ignorant of—the political affairs of Italy, no doubt a legacy of World War II and the earlier brush with fascism. They have been very responsive, however, to appeals for relief assistance during periodic natural disasters such as floods and earthquakes.

INDIVIDUAL AND GROUP CONTRIBUTIONS

Italians constitute such a large and diverse group that notable individuals have appeared in virtually every aspect of American life.

ACADEMIA

Lorenzo Da Ponte (1747-1838), taught courses on Italian literature at Columbia University and sponsored the first Italian opera house in Manhattan in the 1830s. Prior to becoming president of Yale University in 1977, A. Bartlett Giamatti (1938-1989) was a distinguished scholar of English and comparative literature. He resigned his presidency to become the commissioner of the National Baseball League. Peter Sammartino (1904-1992) taught at the City College of New York and Columbia University before founding Fairleigh Dickinson University. He published 14 books on various aspects of education.

BUSINESS

Amadeo P. Giannini (1870-1949) began a storefront bank in the Italian North Beach section of San Francisco in 1904. Immediately after the 1906 earthquake he began granting loans to residents to rebuild. Later, Giannini pioneered in branch banking and in financing the early film industry. Giannini's Bank of America eventually became the largest bank in the United States. Lido Anthony "Lee" Iacocca (1924–) became president of Ford Motor Company in 1970. Iacocca left Ford after eight years to take over the ailing Chrysler Corporation, which was near bankruptcy. He rescued the company, in part through his personal television ads which made his face instantly recognizable. Iacocca also spent four years as chairman of the Statue of Liberty/Ellis Island Foundation, which supported the refurbishment of these national monuments.

FILM, TELEVISION, AND THEATER

Frank Capra (1897-1991) directed more than 20 feature films and won three Academy Awards for Best Director. His films, stamped with an upbeat optimism, became known as "Capra-corn." Capra won his Oscars for *It Happened One Night* (1934), *Mr. Deeds Goes to Town* (1936), and *You Can't Take It With You* (1938), but he is also well known for *Lost Horizon* (1937), *Mr. Smith Goes to Washington* (1939), and *It's a Wonderful Life* (1947). In addition to directing, Capra served four terms as president of the Academy of Motion Picture Arts and Sciences and three terms as president of the Screen Directors Guild. Francis Ford Coppola (1939–) earned international fame as director of *The Godfather* (1972), an adaptation of Mario Puzo's best selling novel. The film won several Academy Awards, including Best Picture. Among numerous other films, Coppola has made two sequels to *The Godfather*; the second film of this trilogy, released in 1974, also won multiple awards, including an Academy Award for Best Picture.

Martin Scorcese (1942–), film director and screenwriter, directed *Mean Streets* (1973), *Taxi Driver* (1976), *Raging Bull* (1980), and *Good Fellas* (1990), among others, all of which draw from the urban, ethnic milieu of his youth. Sylvester Stallone (1946–), actor, screenwriter, and director, has gained fame in each of these categories. He is perhaps best known as the title character in both *Rocky* (1976), which won an Academy Award for Best Picture (and spawned four sequels), and the *Rambo* series. Don Ameche (1908-1993), whose career spanned several decades, performed in vaudeville, appeared on radio serials ("The Chase and Sanborn Hour"), and starred in feature films. Ameche first achieved national acclaim in *The Story of Alexander Graham Bell* (1941) and appeared in many films, earning an Academy Award for Best Supporting Actor for his performance in *Cocoon* (1986). Ernest Borgnine (born Ermes Effron Borgnino, 1915–) spent his early acting career portraying villains, such as the brutal prison guard in *From Here to Eternity*, but captured the hearts of Americans with his sensitive portrayal of a Bronx butcher in *Marty* (1956), for which he won an Academy Award. Borgnine also appeared on network television as Lieutenant Commander Quintin McHale on "McHale's Navy," a comedy series that ran on ABC from 1962 to 1965. Liza Minnelli (1946–), stage, television, and motion picture actress and vocalist, won an Academy Award for *Cabaret* (1972), an Emmy for *Liza with a Z* (1972), and a Tony Award for *The Act* (1977).

LITERATURE

Pietro DiDonato (1911-1992) published the classic Italian immigrant novel, *Christ in Concrete*, in 1939 to critical acclaim. He also captured the immigrant experience in later works, including *Three Circles of Light* (1960) and *Life of Mother Cabrini* (1960). Novelist Jerre Mangione (1909–) wrote *Mount Allegro* (1943), an autobiographical work describing his upbringing among Sicilian Americans in Rochester, New York. Mangione is also noted for his *Reunion in Sicily* (1950), *An Ethnic at Large* (1978), and *La Storia: Five Centuries of the Italian American Experience* (1992), with Ben Morreale. Gay Talese (1932–), began his career as a reporter for the *New York Times*, but later earned fame for his national bestsellers, including *The Kingdom and the Power* (1969), *Honor Thy Father* (1971), and *Thy Neighbor's Wife* (1980). Talese's *Unto the Sons* (1992) dealt with his own family's immigrant experience. The poetry of Lawrence Ferlinghetti (1919–) captured the essence of the Beat Generation during the 1950s and 1960s. His San Francisco bookstore, City Lights Books, became a gathering place for literary activists. John Ciardi (1916-1986), poet, translator, and literary critic, published over 40 books of poetry and criticism and profoundly impacted the literary world as the long-time poetry editor of the *Saturday Review*. Ciardi's translation of Dante's *Divine Comedy* is regarded as definitive. Novelist Mario Puzo (1920–) published two critical successes, *Dark Arena* (1955) and *The Fortunate Pilgrim* (1965), prior to *The Godfather* in 1969, which sold over ten million copies and reached vast audiences in its film adaptations. Helen Barolini (1925–), poet, essayist, and novelist, explored the experiences of Italian-American women in her *Umbertina* (1979) and *The Dream Book* (1985).

MUSIC AND ENTERTAINMENT

Francis Albert "Frank" Sinatra (1915-1998), began singing with the Harry James Band in the late 1930s, moved to the Tommy Dorsey Band, and then became America's first teenage idol in the early 1940s, rising to stardom as a "crooner." Moving into film, Sinatra established a new career in acting that was launched in 1946. He won an Academy Award for his performance in *From Here to Eternity* in 1953. Since 1954, Sinatra has made 31 films, released at least 800 records, and participated in numerous charity affairs.

Mario Lanza (1921-1959) was a famous tenor who appeared on radio, in concert, on recordings, and in motion pictures. Vocalist and television star Perry Como (born Pierino Roland Como, 1913–) hosted one of America's most popular television shows in the 1950s. Frank Zappa (1940-1993), musician, vocalist, and composer, founded the influential rock group Mothers of Invention in the 1960s. Noted for his social satire and musical inventiveness, Zappa was named Pop Musician of the Year for three years in a row in 1970-1972.

POLITICS

Fiorello LaGuardia (1882-1947) gained national fame as an energetic mayor of New York City, in which capacity he served for three terms (1934-1945). Earlier, LaGuardia sat for six terms as a Republican representative in the U.S. Congress. Known as "The Little Flower," LaGuardia earned a reputation as an incorruptible, hard working, and humane administrator. John O. Pastore (1912–) was the first Italian American to be elected a state governor (Rhode Island, 1945). In 1950, he represented that state in the U.S. Senate. Geraldine Ferraro (1935–) was the first American woman nominated for vice president by a major political party in 1984 when she ran with Democratic presidential candidate Walter Mondale. Her earlier career included service as assistant district attorney in New York and two terms in the U.S. Congress. Mario Cuomo (1932–) was elected governor of New York in 1982 and has been reelected twice since then. Prior to his election as governor, Cuomo served as lieutenant governor and New York's secretary of state.

John J. Sirica (1904-1992), chief federal judge, U.S. District Court for the District of Columbia, presided over the Watergate trials. He was named *Time* magazine's Man of the Year in 1973. Antonin Scalia (1936–) became the first Italian American to sit on the U.S. Supreme Court when he was appointed Associate Justice in 1986. Rudolph W. Giuliani (1944–), served for many years as U.S. Attorney for the southern district of New York and waged war against organized crime and public corruption. In 1993, he was elected mayor of New York City.

RELIGION

Father Eusebio Chino (Kino) (1645-1711) was a Jesuit priest who worked among the native people of Mexico and Arizona for three decades, establishing more than 20 mission churches, exploring wide areas, and introducing new methods of agriculture and animal-raising. Francesca Xavier Cabrini (1850-1917), the first American to be sainted by the Roman Catholic Church, worked with poor Italian immigrants throughout North and South America, opening schools, orphanages, hospitals, clinics, and novitiates for her Missionary Sisters of the Sacred Heart.

SCIENCE AND TECHNOLOGY

Enrico Fermi (1901-1954), a refugee from Benito Mussolini's fascist regime, is regarded as the "father of atomic energy." Fermi was awarded the 1938 Nobel Prize in physics for his identification of new radioactive elements produced by neutron bombardment. He worked with the Manhattan Project during World War II to produce the first atomic bomb, achieving the world's first self-sustaining chain reaction on December 2, 1942. Salvador Luria (1912-1991) was a pioneer of molecular biology and genetic engineering. In 1969, while he was a faculty member at the Massachusetts Institute of Technology, Luria was awarded the Nobel Prize for his work on viruses. Rita Levi-Montalcini (1909–) was awarded a Nobel Prize in 1986 for her work in cell biology and cancer research. Emilio Segre (1905-1989), a student of Fermi, received the 1959 Nobel Prize in physics for his discovery of the antiproton.

SPORTS

Joseph "Joe" DiMaggio (1914-1999), the "Yankee Clipper," was voted the Greatest Living Player in baseball. DiMaggio set his 56 consecutive game hitting streak in 1941. (The record still stands.) In a career spanning 1936 to 1951, DiMaggio led the New York Yankees to ten world championships and retired with a .325 lifetime batting average. At the time of his death, Vincent Lombardi (1913-1970) was the winningest coach in professional football, and the personification of tenacity and commitment in American sports. As head coach of the Green Bay Packers, Lombardi led the team to numerous conference, league, and world titles during the 1960s, including two Super Bowls in 1967 and 1968. Rocky Marciano (born Rocco Francis Marchegiano, 1924-1969) was the only undefeated heavyweight boxing champion, winning all his fights. Known as the "Brockton Bomber," Marciano won the heavyweight championship over Jersey Joe Walcott in 1952 and held it until his voluntary retirement in 1956. Rocky Graziano (born Rocco Barbella, 1922–), middleweight boxing champion, is best known for his classic bouts with Tony Zale. Lawrence "Yogi" Berra (1925–), a Baseball Hall of Fame member who played for the New York Yankees as catcher for 17 years, enjoyed a career that lasted from 1946 to 1963. He also coached and managed several professional baseball teams, including the New York Mets and the Houston Astros. Joseph Garagiola (1926–) played with the St. Louis Cardinals (1946-1951) and several other Major League clubs.

VISUAL ARTS

Frank Stella (1936–) pioneered the development of "minimal art," involving three-dimensional, "shaped" paintings and sculpture. His work has been exhibited in museums around the world. Constantino Brumidi (1805-1880), a political exile from the liberal revolutions of the 1840s, became known as "the Michelangelo of the United States Capitol." Brumidi painted the interior of the dome of the Capitol in Washington, D.C., from 1865 to 1866, as well as numerous other areas of the building. Ralph Fasanella (1914–), a self-taught primitive painter whose work has been compared to that of Grandma Moses, is grounded in his immigrant backgrounds.

MEDIA

PRINT

Since the mid-1800s, more than 2,000 Italian American newspapers have been established, representing a full range of ideological, religious, professional, and commercial interests. As of 1980, about 50 newspapers were still in print.

America Oggi (America Today).
Currently the only Italian-language daily newspaper in the United States.

Contact: Andrea Mantineo, Editor.
Address: 41 Bergentine Avenue, Westwood, New Jersey 07675.
Telephone: (212) 268-0250.
Fax: (212) 268-0379.
E-mail: americoggi@aol.com.

Fra Noi (Among Us).
A monthly publication in a bilingual format by the Catholic Scalabrini order; features articles on issues primarily of interest to Chicago's Italian community.

Contact: Paul Basile, Editor.
Address: 263 North York Road, Elmhurst, Illinois 60126.
Telephone: (708) 782-4440.

Italian Americana: Cultural and Historical Review.
An international journal published semi-annually by the University of Rhode Island's College of Continuing Education.

Contact: Carol Bonomo Albright, Editor.
Address: 199 Promenade Street, Providence, Rhode Island 02908.

Italian Tribune News.

Publishes a heavily illustrated journal that features articles weekly in English on Italian culture and Italian American contributions.

Contact: Joan Alagna, Editor.
Address: 427 Bloomfield Avenue, Newark, New Jersey 07107.
Telephone: (201) 485-6000.
Fax: (201) 485-8967.
E-mail: italtribnews@viconet.com.

The Italian Voice (La Voce Italiana).

Provides regional, national, and local news coverage; published weekly in English.

Contact: Cesarina A. Earl, Editor.
Address: P.O. Box 9, Totowa, New Jersey 07511.
Telephone: (201) 942-5028.

Sons of Italy Times.

Publishes news bi-weekly concerning the activities of Sons of Italy lodges and the civic, professional, and charitable interests of the membership.

Contact: John B. Acchione III, Editor.
Address: 414 Walnut Street, Philadelphia, Pennsylvania 19106-3323.
Telephone: (215) 592-1713.
Fax: (215) 592-9152.
E-mail: info@sonsofitalypa.org.

VIA: Voices in Italian Americana.

A literary journal published by Purdue University.

Contact: Fred L. Gardophe, Editor.
Address: Department of Foreign Languages and Literatures, 1359 Stanley Coulter Hall, Purdue University, West Lafayette, Indiana 47907-1359.
Telephone: (765) 494-3839.
Fax: (765) 496-1700.

RADIO

WHLD-AM (1270).

Broadcasts eight hours of Italian-language programming a week.

Contact: Paul A. Butler.
Address: 2692 Staley Road, Grand Island, New York 14072.
Telephone: (716) 773-1270.
Fax: (716) 773-1498.
Online: http://www.wnybiz.com/whld.

WSBC-AM (1240).

Presents seven hours of Italian-language programming each week.

Contact: Roy Bellavia, General Manager.
Address: 4900 West Belmont Avenue, Chicago, Illinois 60641.
Telephone: (773) 282-9722.

WSRF-AM (1580).

Features 12 hours of Italian-language programming weekly.

Contact: Tony Bourne, Program Director.
Address: 3000 S.W. 60th Avenue, Ft. Lauderdale, Florida 33314.
Telephone: (305) 581-1580.
Fax: (305) 581-1301.

WUNR-AM (1600).

Features 12 hours of programs of ethnic interest.

Contact: Jane A. Clarke.
Address: 160 North Washington Street, Boston, Massachusetts 02114-2142.
Telephone: (617) 367-9003.
Fax: (617) 367-2265.

ORGANIZATIONS AND ASSOCIATIONS

America-Italy Society (AIS).

Fosters friendship between Italy and the United States based upon mutual appreciation of their respective contributions to science, art, music, literature, law, and government.

Contact: Gianfranco Monacelli, President.
Address: 3 East 48th Street, New York, New York 10017.
Telephone: (212) 838-1560.

American Committee on Italian Migration.

A non-profit social service organization advocating equitable immigration legislation and aiding newly arrived Italian immigrants. It sponsors conferences, publishes a newsletter, and disseminates information beneficial to new Italian Americans.

Contact: Rev. Peter P. Polo, National Executive Secretary.
Address: 373 Fifth Avenue, New York, New York 10016.
Telephone: (212) 679-4650.
E-mail: acimny@aol.com.

American Italian Historical Association.
Founded in 1966 by a group of academics as a professional organization interested in promoting basic research into the Italian American experience; encourages the collection and preservation of primary source materials, and supports the teaching of Italian American history.

Contact: Fred L. Gardaphe, President.
Address: 209 Flagg Place, Staten Island, New York 11304.
E-mail: fgardaphe@notes.cc.sunysb.edu.

Italian Cultural Exchange in the United States (ICE).
Promotes knowledge and appreciation of Italian culture among Americans.

Contact: Professor Salvatore R. Tocci, Executive Director.
Address: 27 Barrow Street, New York, New York 10014.
Telephone: (212) 255-0528.

Italian Historical Society of America.
Perpetuates Italian heritage in America and gathers historical data on Americans of Italian descent.

Contact: Dr. John J. LaCorte, Director.
Address: 111 Columbia Heights, Brooklyn, New York 11201.
Telephone: (718) 852-2929.
Fax: (718) 855-3925.

The National Italian American Foundation.
A nonprofit organization designed to promote the history, heritage, and accomplishments of Italian Americans and to foster programs advancing the interests of the Italian American community.

Contact: Dr. Fred Rotandaro, Executive Director.
Address: 666 Eleventh Street, N.W., Suite 800, Washington, D.C. 20001-4596.
Telephone: (202) 638-0220.
E-mail: info@niaf.org.
Online: http://www.niaf.org.

Order Sons of Italy in America (OSIA).
Established in 1905, the organization is composed of lodges located throughout the United States. It seeks to preserve and disseminate information on Italian culture and encourages the involvement of its members in all civic, charitable, patriotic, and youth activities. OSIA is committed to supporting Italian-American cultural events and fighting discrimination.

Contact: Philip R. Piccigallo, Executive Director.
Address: 219 E Street, N.E., Washington, D.C., 20002.
Telephone: (202) 547-2900.
Fax: (202) 546-8168.

MUSEUMS AND RESEARCH CENTERS

American Italian Renaissance Foundation.
Focuses on the contributions of Italian Americans in Louisiana. Its research library also includes the wide-ranging Giovanni Schiavo collection.

Contact: Joseph Maselli, Director.
Address: 537 South Peters Street, New Orleans, Louisiana 70130.
Telephone: (504) 891-1904.

The Balch Institute for Ethnic Studies.
Contains many documents addressing the Italian American experience in Pennsylvania and elsewhere, most notably the Leonard Covello collection. A published guide to the holdings is available.

Contact: Pamela Nelson, Associate Curator/Registrar.
Address: 18 South Seventh Street, Philadelphia, Pennsylvania 19106.
Telephone: (215) 925-8090.
Fax: (215) 9258195.
E-mail: balchlib@hslc.org.
Online: http://libertynet.org/~balch.

The Center for Migration Studies.
Houses a vast collection of materials depicting Italian American activities. It features extensive records of Italian American Catholic parishes staffed by the Scalabrini order. The center also provides published guides to its collections.

Contact: Dr. Lydio F. Tomasi, Director.
Address: 209 Flagg Place, Staten Island, New York, 10304.
Telephone: (718) 351-8800.
Fax: (718) 667-4598.
E-mail: cmslft@aol.com.
Online: http://www.cmsny.org.

Immigration History Research Center (IHRC), University of Minnesota.
IHRC is the nation's most important repository for research materials dealing with the Italian American experience. The center holds major documentary collections representing a wide cross-section of Ital-

ian American life, numerous newspapers, and many published works. A published guide is available.

Contact: Dr. Rudolph J. Vecoli, Director.
Address: 826 Berry Street, St. Paul,
   Minnesota 55114.
Telephone: (612) 627-4208.
Fax: (612) 627-4190.
Email: ihrc@tc.umn.edu.
Online: http://www.umn.edu/ihrc.

The New York Public Library, Manuscripts Division.
Holds many collections relevant to the Italian American experience, most notably the papers of Fiorello LaGuardia, Vito Marcantonio, Gino C. Speranza, and Carlo Tresca.

Address: 42nd Street and Fifth Avenue,
   New York, New York 10018-2788.
Telephone: (212) 930-0801.

SOURCES FOR ADDITIONAL STUDY

Alba, Richard. *Italian Americans: Into the Twilight of Ethnicity.* Englewood Cliffs, New Jersey: Prentice-Hall, 1985.

Battistella, Graziano. *Italian Americans in the '80s: A Sociodemographic Profile.* New York: Center for Migration Studies, 1989.

DeConde, Alexander. *Half Bitter, Half Sweet: An Excursion into Italian American History.* New York: Charles Scribner's Sons, 1971.

Gabaccia, Donna. "Italian American Women: A Review Essay," *Italian Americana*, Volume 12, No. 1 (Fall/Winter 1993); pp. 38-61.

Gambino, Richard. *Blood of My Blood.* New York: Anchor, 1975.

Mangione, Jerre, and Ben Morriale. *La Storia: Five Centuries of the Italian American Experience.* New York: HarperCollins, 1992.

Orsi, Robert A. *The Madonna of 115th Street: Faith and Community in Italian Harlem, 1880-1950.* New Haven: Yale University Press, 1988.

Pozzetta, George E., "From Immigrants to Ethnics: The Italian American Experience," *Journal of American Ethnic History*, Volume 9, No. 1 (Fall 1989); pp. 67-95.

Vecoli, Rudolph J. "The Search for Italian American Identity: Continuity and Change," in *Italian Americans: New Perspectives in Italian Immigration and Ethnicity*, edited by Lydio Tomasi. Staten Island: Center for Migration Studies, 1985; pp. 88-112.

First generation
Jamaican Americans
cherish traditional
family values, such
as practicing
religion, respecting
elders and marital
vows, being with
one's family in times
of need, supporting
one's family, and
correcting and
punishing one's
disobedient children.

JAMAICAN AMERICANS

by
N. Samuel Murrell

OVERVIEW

One of the four large islands of the Caribbean archipelago, Jamaica measures 4,441 square miles, slightly smaller than the size of Connecticut. Its mountainous terrain, which exceeds 7,400 feet at its Blue Mountain peak, makes traveling from one end of the island to another more interesting than one would expect. Jamaica's northern shores are lined by many miles of lovely white sand beaches that attract thousands of American, Canadian, and a growing number of European tourists annually. Kingston, the capital and largest English-speaking city south of Miami, is Jamaica's chief commercial and administrative center. The island is well known for its rich-tasting Blue Mountain coffee and its bauxite mining and aluminum processing industries.

Jamaica's motto, "Out of Many, One People," is a national ideal for its diverse population of 2,506,000 in 1990. As many as 90 percent of all Jamaicans can lay claim to African ancestry. About 26 percent of the population is mixed and approximately nine percent is composed of people of Chinese, European, and East Indian descent. Intermarriage among races over centuries accounts for the diverse physical features of Jamaicans. In addition to English, many Jamaicans speak *Patois* (pronounced patwa)—or what Jamaican intellectuals call Jamaican Talk—a mixture of English and African dialects. Jamaica was once called a "Christian country" because approximately 80 percent of its citizens have some form of association with Christianity. Protestants have traditionally outnumbered Catholics by a wide margin and Rastafarianism, a twentieth-century religious movement, claims a following of approximately eight percent of the population. A number of small Afro-Caribbean, Asian, and Middle-eastern religious groups also exist in Jamaica.

HISTORY

As early as 600 A.D., Jamaica was settled by Arawaks who called the island Xaymaca. In 1494 Columbus claimed the island for Spain and in 1509, Juan de Esquivel began transporting Jamaican Arawaks to Hispaniola as slaves. Within a few decades, the original population, which was made extinct by European disease, kidnapping, enslavement, and genocidal methods of war, was later replaced by Africans. From 1509 until the early 1660s Jamaica served as a sparsely populated Spanish-held way station for galleons en route to Cuba and the Spanish Main. It became the headquarters for pirate ships. Whoever controlled the island controlled much of the Southern Atlantic Ocean and the Caribbean Sea. After a failed expedition to the larger Spanish Caribbean, British Admiral Penn and General Vernables captured the island in 1655 and driving off the Spaniards. Later Spain officially ceded Jamaica to Britain at the Treaty of Madrid, and the British then left the island to the pirates until 1670. During this time, some of the Spaniards' black slaves fled to the hills. Known as *Maroons,* they were an organized band of fierce-fighting fugitive slaves who hampered British rule until a peace treaty was executed with them in 1738.

Britain turned the island into a vast sugar plantation based on slave labor. Since the British one-crop sugar economy in Barbados was in sharp decline by 1650, many planters in Barbados relocated to Jamaica with their slaves. They were followed by hundreds of British colonizers and hundreds of thousands of enslaved Africans. By 1730 Jamaica's 75,000 slaves produced 15,500 tons of sugar and the island replaced Barbados as Britain's most prized colony. In 1808 the slave population exceeded 324,000 and produced 78,000 tons of sugar. Oliver Cromwell's government attempted to balance the white to black population ratio by shipping criminals, prisoners of war, prostitutes, and other undesirable persons to Jamaica as a form of punishment and as indentured servants. However, when the slave trade was abolished in 1807, blacks outnumbered whites by as many as ten to one.

Prior to 1834, when slavery was abolished, blacks in Jamaica fought a bitter and often futile battle to free themselves from the savage institution of slavery. The *Maroons* were well known as Jamaica's only successful black resistance movement. For centuries, they menaced British troops, looted plantations, and carried off slave recruits to the precipitous mountains in retaliation against abuses. Their successful guerrilla warfare abated in 1739 and 1795 when *Maroon* chiefs signed peace treaties with the British government.

As the anti-slavery campaign in Britain heated up in 1830 the slave population gathered in large numbers in Afro-Christian Baptist circles—the most vocal anti-slavery organization in Jamaica—in anticipation of freedom. A different kind of revolt called the Baptist War occurred in Jamaica in 1831. Sam Sharpe, a black Baptist lay preacher, perceived that "free paper" had come but the government was concealing it from the slaves. He led a large revolt in western Jamaica, which resulted in massive destruction of property and a bloody and brutal repression by the government. It is believed that this violent slave resistance, the unprofitability of slavery, and mounting pressure from abolitionists, forced Britain to abolish the institution in 1834.

MODERN ERA

Blacks in post-emancipation Jamaica lived in freedom but had no rights or access to property. They were exploited by the white ruling class and treated with contempt by British governors, whose fiscal policies were designed only to benefit whites. In 1865, the unheeded plea of the peasant masses for farm land erupted into a second major revolt, the Morant Bay Rebellion. This was led by Paul Bogle and supported by George William Gordon, Baptist leaders who became two of Jamaica's national heroes. The suppression of the rebellion by the ruling class was ruthless. A blood thirsty Governor Eyre court-marshaled and executed almost 400 suspects, including dozens of innocent Baptist peasants. In the aftermath, the British government appointed a Royal Commission of Inquiry, which found Eyre's penalty "excessive, barbarous, reckless, and criminal." On December 1, 1865, the secretaries of state for the colonies tore up the Jamaican Constitution and recommended a Crown Colony government for the island. The new political system limited the powers of the governor and the Assembly and allowed Britain to retain direct control over the legislative and executive decisions of the colony. Adversely, however, the Crown Colony government inhibited national leadership and allowed the colonials to dominate and exploit the black masses.

As late as the 1930s the political system continued to be closed to most Jamaicans. In the post World War I period, blacks voiced their discontent by supporting trade unions and other organizations led by young political activists such as Dr. Love (a Jamaican physician and anti-colonialist), Marcus Moziah Garvey, Brian Alves, A.G.S. Coombs, and Alexander Bustamante. The lingering unameliorated political inequity and economic hardship led to the 1938 rebellion in which the working class staged a national strike when the West Indian Sugar Company (WISCO) failed to keep its promises of new jobs, higher wages, and better working conditions in its new massive, centralized factory in Westmoreland. Garvey, Bustamante, William Grant, and Norman Manley played key roles in this organized political agitation, which resulted in better workers' compensation. The strike also put new political leaders in the spotlight and renewed interest in political change. The Peoples' National Party (PNP) and the Jamaica Labour Party (JLP) were born in the throes of these upheavals under the Westminster form of government. It was not until 1944 that the country was granted limited self-government and adult suffrage. The Westminster system created the two-party parliamentary democracy that led Jamaica into independence in 1962; it is in effect today under a prime minister, elected by the people, and a governor general (a Jamaican) who represents the Queen.

THE FIRST JAMAICANS IN AMERICA

The documented history of black emigration from Jamaica and other Caribbean islands into the United States dates back to 1619 when 20 voluntary indentured workers arrived in Jamestown, Virginia, on a Dutch frigate. They lived and worked as "free persons" even when a Portuguese vessel arrived with the first shipload of blacks enslaved in 1629. Since Jamaica was a major way station and clearing house for slaves en route to North America, the history of Jamaican immigration in the United States is inseparably tied to slavery and post-emancipation migration.

After 1838, European and American colonies in the Caribbean with expanding sugar industries imported large numbers of immigrants to meet their acute labor shortage. Large numbers of Jamaicans were recruited to work in Panama and Costa Rica in the 1850s. After slavery was abolished in the United States in 1865, American planters imported temporary workers, called "swallow migrants," to harvest crops on an annual basis. These workers, many of them Jamaicans, returned to their countries after harvest. Between 1881 and the beginning of World War I, the United States recruited over 250,000 workers from the Caribbean, 90,000 of whom were Jamaicans, to work on the Panama Canal. During both world wars, the United States again recruited Jamaican men for service on various American bases in the region.

SIGNIFICANT IMMIGRATION WAVES

Since the turn of the twentieth century, three distinct waves of Caribbean immigration into the United States have occurred—most of these immigrants came from Jamaica. The first wave took place between 1900 and the 1920s, bringing a modest number of Caribbean immigrants. Official black immigration increased from 412 in 1899 to 12,245 in 1924, although the actual number of black aliens entering the United States yearly was twice as high. By 1930, 178,000 documented first-generation blacks and their children lived in the United States. About 100,000 were from the British Caribbean, including Jamaica. The second and weakest immigration wave occurred between the 1930s and the new immigration policy of the mid-1960s. The McCarran-Walter Act reaffirmed and upheld the quota bill, which discriminated against black immigrants and allowed only 100 Jamaicans into the United States annually. During this period, larger numbers of Jamaicans migrated to Britain rather than to the United States due to the immigration restrictions.

The final and largest wave of immigration began in 1965 and continues to the present. This wave began after Britain restricted immigration in its former black Commonwealth colonies. The 1965 Hart-Celler Immigration Reform Act changed the U.S. immigration policy and, inadvertently, opened the way for a surge in immigration from the Caribbean. In 1976, Jamaicans again relocated to the United States in large numbers after Congress increased immigration from the Western Hemisphere to a maximum of 20,000 persons per country. Although about 10,000 Jamaicans migrated to the United States legally from 1960 to 1965, the number skyrocketed in succeeding years—62,700 (1966-1970), 61,500 (1971-1975), 80,600 (1976-1980) and 81,700 (1981-1984)—to an aggregate of about 300,000 documented immigrants in just under a quarter of a century.

At present, Jamaicans are the largest group of American immigrants from the English-speaking Caribbean. However, it is difficult to verify the exact number of Jamaican Americans in this country. The 1990 census placed the total number of documented Jamaican Americans at 435,025, but the high Jamaican illegal alien phenomenon and the Jamaican attitude toward census response may increase that number to 800,000 to 1,000,000 Jamaicans living in the United States. Government statistics report that 186,430 Jamaicans live in New York, but the number is closer to 600,000.

Jamaican migration became so large that it caused a national crisis in Jamaica. The exodus has resulted in a serious "brain drain" and an acute shortage of professionals, such as skilled workers, technicians, doctors, lawyers, and managers, in essential services in Jamaica. For example, the mail often takes one to three months to reach its final destination because of a shortage of postal service supervisors. During the 1970s and early 1980s about 15 percent of the population left the country. In the early 1990s the government began offering incentives to persons with technical, business, and managerial skills to return to Jamaica for short periods of time to aid in management and technical skills training.

REASONS FOR MIGRATING

Jamaicans migrate to the United States for many socio-economic reasons. Migration is encouraged by economic hardship caused by a failing economy based upon plantation agriculture, lack of economic diversity, and scarcity of professional and skilled jobs. Since the nineteenth century Jamaica has had a very poor land distribution track record. The uneven allotment of arable crown lands and old plantations left farmers without a sufficient plot for subsistence or cash crop farming, which contributed to high unemployment statistics and economic hardship. During the 1970s the standard of living declined due to economic inflation and low salaries. When companies and corporations lost confidence in Michael Manley's Democratic Socialist government and his anti-American rhetoric and close business ties to Cuba, the flight of capital from Jamaica and the shift in U.S. capital investments worsened the situation. Jamaica's huge foreign debt and the International Monetary Fund's (IMF) restructuring of the economy further exacerbated the island's economic woes in the 1980s and 1990s. An increase in crime, fueled by unemployment and aggravated by the exporting of criminals from the United States back to Jamaica, forced thousands of Jamaicans to flee the island for safety. Today, unemployment and under-employment continue to rise above 50 percent, wages continue to fall, the dollar weakens, and the cost of goods and services continues to increase.

The Jamaican mentality that one must "go ah foreign" and "return to him country" to "show off" evidence of success has become a rite of passage for thousands of Jamaicans. This began when the Unit-ed States imported Jamaicans to work on various projects in the 1800s and early twentieth century. Before long, Jamaicans saw migration as an attractive solution to the harsh social and economic conditions on the island. Since 1930 an important part of Rastafarian theology is the idea of repatriation to Africa in order to escape oppression in "Babylon." However, many Rastas conveniently "followed the star" of the Yankee dollar instead of the "Star of David" (Emperor Haile Selassie of Ethiopia). After 1966, Ethiopia as a haven for Rastafari faded in the bright lights of U.S. metropolitan centers. In addition, many Jamaican students and trainees study at American institutions. Not all return to Jamaica upon completion of their studies. Many stay because of the lack of job opportunities at home and an entrenched British-colonial bias among Jamaica's elite against American education.

SETTLEMENT

Of the Jamaicans documented in the 1990 census 410,933 reported at least one specific ancestry. Of this number 94.5 percent are persons of first ancestry, and the remaining 5.5 percent are of second ancestry. The regional composition is as follows: 59 percent live in the Northeast; 4.8 percent in the Midwest; 30.6 percent in the South; and 5.6 percent in the West. The Northeast and the South have the largest number of immigrants and are home to most illegal Jamaicans in the United States. Jamaicans refer to Miami and Brooklyn colloquially as "Kingston 22" and "Little Jamaica" respectively. Accessibility, family connections, the help of friends or church, jobs, group psychology (including gangs), access to college and university education, and weather conditions explain the heavy concentration of Jamaican immigrants along the eastern coast.

Jamaicans have a saying, "Anywhere you go in the world you meet a Jamaican." According to the 1990 census, there are Jamaicans in every state in the Union. The census shows that regionally, there are 30,327 in New England, 223,310 in the middle Atlantic, 18,163 in east north central, 2,698 in the west north central, 121,260 in the south Atlantic, 2,882 in the east south central, 9,117 in the west south central, 2,696 in the mountain region, and 21,571 in the Pacific region.

ACCULTURATION AND ASSIMILATION

Jamaican immigrants generally have four options once they arrive in the United States. The first option is to remain a "bird of passage" by viewing oneself as a temporary alien accumulating some Yankee dollars to return home. The second option is to immerse oneself within the culture and work for the improvement of the African American community. The third option is to settle in white suburbs, secure a good-paying job at a white institution or company, and live a life of being the conspicuous black family in town who enhances the diversity of the community. The fourth option is to engage in academic and professional training while intending to return to Jamaica upon completion. Most early Jamaican immigrants chose the first option because they did not intend to become part of the American mainstream. However, since the 1970s more Jamaicans have sought permanent residence in the United States because of social and economic problems back home.

In addition to adjusting to severe weather variations, especially in northern states, Jamaican immigrants must make many other adjustments to American society. First, they must adjust to their new citizenship or residency. Those who are naturalized American citizens often wrestle with the issue of a split national allegiance to Jamaica and to the United States. Immigrants who are resident aliens enjoy the same privileges as all legal residents and are generally more settled than illegal aliens, who exist in a state of vulnerability—a voice-with-no-vote status in the United States. Thousands of Jamaican American professionals, academics, and skilled workers fall in this category.

A second adjustment must be made to the cultural traditions and social roles of racial or ethnic groups with which the immigrants must identify. Today, Jamaicans enter a more prosperous society than that left behind. However, the first and second waves of immigrants suffered much of the racial prejudices of Jim Crow laws and the economy of pre-civil rights United States. Recent immigrants may not encounter the older blatant forms of segregation, but they suffer from the effects of subtle discrimination and stereotypical perceptions based upon color and ethnicity. Although Jamaica is not immune to color distinctions, immigrants to the United States become much more conscious of their blackness (often as a disadvantage) than they did back home in Jamaica, where blacks are the majority and many are highly respected leaders. In the United States, they must adjust to living in communities where blacks are treated as a numerical, political, social, and economic minority.

Third, Jamaicans also must learn to adjust to life in some of America's toughest neighborhoods. They become street-wise very early and learn where to walk and work, and which apartment buildings and neighborhoods to live in. Occasionally, they become victims of inner-city crimes, but many Jamaican youths have penetrated the gangs and drug culture in New York City, Miami, Los Angeles, Washington, D.C., and Boston. Some are named in organized- crime raids by the FBI and other law-enforcement bodies. Finally, because of their large numbers in many U.S. neighborhoods, uninformed Americans often classify any foreign black with a different accent as Jamaican. When Africans, Haitians, Barbadians, and other groups commit felonies, Jamaicans are often de facto implicated in the act by the media.

CULTURE

Jamaica's ethnic distinctions are not as large as those of Trinidad, Guyana, or the United States, but Jamaicans are rich in cultural traditions and ethnic diversity. Although the population is predominantly black, small enclaves of East Indians, Chinese, Lebanese, Europeans, Jews, and other ethnic groups enhance the rich cultural heritage of the country. The motto "Out of Many One People" brings Jamaicans together to celebrate a wide range of local, national, and international cultural events throughout the year.

FESTIVALS

The Accompong Maroon festival is kicked off in Accompong, St. Elizabeth, in January. The annual Jamaica Carnival takes place in April and May in Kingston and Negril, respectively; and the Labor Day celebration is observed on May 23. In June, there is a Jamaica Festival National Heroes Tribute at National Heroes Park, in anticipation of National Heroes Day, celebrated on October 17. The Jamaica Festival Performing Arts Final also takes place in June, and the Jamaica Festival Amateur Culinary Arts, as well as the Jamaica Festival Popular Song Contest, are staged at the National Arena in July. Independence Day observed in August is the most celebrated cultural event in Jamaica. The Portland Jamboree follows Independence Day, providing ten days of colorful street parades, parties, street dancing, cultural and sporting events, fashion and cabaret shows.

HOLIDAYS

Jamaicans celebrate religious holidays like Christmas, Good Friday, New Year's Day, Ash Wednesday, and Easter Monday. Additional holidays include

Bob Marley's Birthday (in February) and Boxing Day. The National Heroes Day celebration occurs on October 17, during which local communities come alive with music, folk dance, and colorful dress. Politicians or other prominent citizens give speeches and pay tribute to fallen heroes at National Heroes Park. The Independence Day celebration is Jamaica's grandest holiday. Between March and August, the Jamaica Cultural Development Commission offers an interesting array of colorful events that exhibit local talents, featuring visual arts, performing arts, and entertainment. On the first Monday in August, a profusion of color and excitement fills the air as community cultural groups showcase their abilities, and preachers and politicians thunder patriotic sermons and speeches. This culminates with the spectacular Grand Gala in Kingston. Jamaican Americans usually observe these holidays by staging their own local activities, such as traveling to Jamaica for the Big Splash. On Labor Day, Jamaican Americans join other Caribbean people during the Carnival celebration in New York.

MUSIC

Many Jamaican festivals celebrate Jamaica's rich musical tradition. In the 1960s, Count Ossie merged native Jamaican, Afro-Caribbean, and Afro-American musical rhythms with rock and other influences to create a distinctively black music called "reggae." This music, which the Rastafarians and Bob Marley popularized, is a plea for liberation and a journey into black consciousness and African pride. Like calypso, reggae began as a working-class medium of expression and social commentary. Reggae is the first distinctly Caribbean music to become global in scope. Each August, Jamaica stages its internationally acclaimed music festival at the Jamworld Center in Kingston. Over the five-day period, the premier music festival of the Caribbean attracts over 200,000 visitors. Each year it features top reggae stars like Ziggy Marley, Jimmy Cliff, Third World, and Stevie Wonder. This is followed immediately by the Reggae Sunfest at the Bob Marley Performing Center in Montego Bay. In the post Lenten period, the streets of Kingston come alive to the pulsating sounds of calypso and soca music. For nine emotionally charged days, local and international artists treat revelers to the best of reggae, soca and calypso "under the tents." During this time, thousands of glittering costumed celebrants revel and dance through the streets in a festive mood. The National Mento Yard is kicked off in Manchester in October with a potpourri of traditional and cultural folk forms which have contributed to Jamaica's rich cultural heritage. Many of these cultural events are

These Jamaican American women are entertaining people with their talent for playing steel drums.

observed by Jamaican Americans in local public celebrations or in the privacy of their homes.

DANCES AND SONGS

Jamaica is known worldwide for its African folk dances, Jan Canoe and Accompong. Jamaica's carnival Jump-up is now very popular in Kingston and Ocho Rios. The National Dance Theater (NDTC), established temporarily in 1962, is a world-renowned troupe that celebrates the unique traditional dance and rich musical heritage of Jamaica and the other Caribbean islands. Under the distinguished leadership of Professor Rex Nettleford, NDTC has made many tours to the United States, Britain, Canada and other countries.

Jamaica also has many other musical forms. Calypso and soca music sway the body of festive dancers to a mixture of Afro-Caribbean rhythms with witty lyrics and heavy metal or finely tuned steel drums. There is also "dub poetry" or chanted verses, "dance hall" music (with rap rhythms, reggae beat, and rude or suggestive lyrics), and Ska, with its emotionally charged, celebrative beat. Jamaican Americans listen to a great variety of music: jazz, reggae, calypso, soca, ska, rap, classical music, gospel, and "high-church" choirs.

CUISINE

The national dish in Jamaica is *ackee and saltfish* (codfish), but curried goat and rice, and fried fish and *bammy* (a flat, baked cassava bread) are just as popular and delicious. A large variety of dishes are known for their spicy nature. Patties, which are hot and spicy, turtle soup, and pepper pot may contain meats such as pork and beef, as well as greens such as okra and kale. Spices such as pimento or allspice, ginger, and peppers are used commonly in a number of dishes. Other Jamaican American foods are: plantain, rice and peas, cow-foot, goat head, jerk chicken, pork, oxtail soup, stew peas and rice, rundown, liver and green bananas, *calaloo* and dumplings, *mannish water* from goat's intestine, and hard dough bread and pastries.

Dessert is usually fruit or a dish containing fruit. An example is *matrimony*, which is a mixture of orange sections, star apples, or guavas in coconut cream with guava cheese melted over it. Other desserts are cornmeal pudding, sweet potato pudding, totoes, plantain tarts, and many other "sweet-tooth" favorites. Coffee and tea are popular nonalcoholic beverages, as are carrot juice, roots, and Irish or sea moss, while rum, Red Stripe Beer, Dragon and Guinness stouts are the national alcoholic beverages. In Miami and New York City, especially Flatbush, Nostrand, Utica, and Church Avenues, one sees groceries filled with a variety of other Caribbean foods, including sugar cane, jelly coconut, and yarns, and black American foods that Jamaicans use for supplementary dishes.

TRADITIONAL COSTUMES

Jamaica's traditional folk costume for women is a bandana skirt worn with a white blouse with a ruffled neck and sleeves, adorned with embroidery depicting various Jamaican images. A head tie made of the same bandana material is also worn. Men wear a shirt that is also made of the same fabric. The colors of the national flag are black, green, and gold. However, because of the popularity of the clothes and colors of Rastafari, many people mistake Rastas' colors (red, green, and gold) as Jamaica's national colors. Jamaicans wear their costumes on Independence Day, National Heroes Day, and other national celebrations. In New York, Jamaican Americans participate in the Caribbean Carnival Jamboree and dress in lavish and colorful costumes during the festive celebration.

SPORTS

Jamaica's primary sports are cricket and soccer. Cricket is more than a sport in Jamaica; it is like a religion, a rallying point for the spirit of patriotism, Caribbean unity and pride, and an occasion for national and individual heroism. Other national sports include horse racing, tennis, basketball, netball, track and field, and triathlon. Some local sports specifically designed for tourists are golf, boating, diving, fishing, and polo.

HEALTH ISSUES

There are no documented medical problems that are unique to Jamaicans. In the 1950s and 1960s, polio appeared in some communities but was later contained by medical treatment. Since the 1980s, drug abuse, alcoholism, and AIDS have also plagued Jamaicans. Crime and economic hardship have taken a heavy toll on the health and life expectancy in Jamaica during the last two decades.

In 1994, the government of Jamaica admitted that most violent crimes committed in the country are drug related. Many of the Caribbean drug kingpins in New York City and Jamaica were trained in the slums of Kingston. The distribution and use of marijuana and crack cocaine accompany Jamaican gang members to New York, New Jersey, Pennsylvania, Florida, Massachusetts, California, and West Virginia, thus perpetuating drug abuse problems.

LANGUAGE

English, Jamaica's official language, is spoken with many variations ranging from British English to Jamaican *Patois*, which is now a language of its own. Jamaicans adapt their speech to the social context of the moment. They speak English in formal discourse or political discussions and shift to Patois in informal conversation and gossip. A large number of people from rural Jamaica, however, experience great difficulty in switching to standard English in formal conversation. In addition, thousands of Jamaicans who live in Brooklyn, speak mainly *Patois*. In recent years, the Rastafarians have developed their own non-Western vocabulary and Afro-Jamaican way of speaking.

PROVERBS AND SAYINGS

Before the 1960s, working-class Jamaicans used numerous *Patois* sayings and verbal expressions, which were usually scorned by the upperclass, and not easily understood by foreigners. In more recent years, the language and its proverbial expressions have been used by most Jamaicans. The use of animal characters is quite frequent in Jamaican proverbs: "When Jon Crow wan go a lowered, im sey a cool breeze tek im;" "When tiger wan' nyam, him seh him favor puss;" "Cow seh siddung nuh mean ress;" "Every dawg have im day;" "Yu see yu neighbor beard on fire, yu tek water an wet yu own;" "When man can't dance, him say music no good;" "One time nuh fool, but two times fool, him a damn fool;" "Mi t'row mi corn but mi nuh call nuh fowl;" "One one cocoa full basket."

There are many Anglicized African proverbs that are popular in Jamaica: When the mouse laughs at the cat there is a hole nearby; No matter how long the night, the day is sure to come; No one tests the depth of a river with both feet; He who is bitten by a snake fears a lizard; If you are greedy in conversation you lose the wisdom of your friend; When a fowl is eating your neighbor's corn, drive it away or someday it will eat yours. Often, the purpose of these sayings is to give caution, play with social and political conventions, make uncomplimentary remarks, crack smutty jokes, or give a new twist to a conversation. They are also used to teach morality, values, and modes of conduct.

GREETINGS AND OTHER COMMON EXPRESSIONS

Some casual colloquial Jamaican greetings are: "Cool man;" "Wah the man ah seh?" "How di dahta doin'?" "Me soon come man" (See you soon); "Likle more" (See you later); "How you doin' man?" "Wah 'appen man?" "Mawning Sah!" "How yu deh do?" Some Rastafari greetings are: "Hail the man," "I an I," "Selassi I," "Jah, Ras Tafari," and "Hey me bredren" (hello brother).

FAMILY AND COMMUNITY DYNAMICS

First generation Jamaican Americans cherish traditional family values, such as practicing religion, respecting elders and marital vows, being with one's family in times of need, supporting one's family, and correcting and punishing one's disobedient children. The emotional bond between parents and children is very strong, often stronger than between spouses. Parents with legal status often are active in civic and political affairs and take an interest in their children's education by joining the PTA, attending open school board meetings, and participating in programs designed to address racism, crime, and poor SATs. Jamaica was once proud of its high literacy rate but the constant migration of teachers and other professionals has taken a heavy toll on the school system and educational achievement since the 1970s.

Unfortunately, the modern Jamaican immigrant family is plagued by many problems. Immigration restrictions and financial limitations make it difficult for an entire family to migrate to the United States simultaneously and to keep their family values intact. One parent often precedes the other family members by many years. Jamaican women are more likely than men to migrate to the United States first. The filing of papers for family members becomes a top priority five to ten years after one becomes a permanent citizen. In some cases, during such long periods of separation, parents, especially men, sever ties with their Jamaican family and begin new ones in the United States. Before they migrate, mothers are forced to leave their children with relatives, grandparents, or friends. These children are often left unsupervised in Jamaica and are introduced to drugs and crime at a young age. They rarely remain in school and others who do become very disruptive because they believe they are in the process of migrating and see no need to complete their studies. When they join their parents in inner-city communities in the United States, Jamaican American children are often left on their own for many hours a day while their single parent, who lacks the family support that they had back home, works more than one job to make ends meet. The net result is that a significant number of Jamaican American families suffer a fair amount of dysfunction as part of the migration phenomenon. The situation is rather acute among blue-collar immigrants who migrate to the United States. Quite often, their children find it difficult to adjust to the new social setting and the resentment which they encounter from students and teachers in the American school environment.

WEDDINGS

Most Jamaican American weddings follow Christian tradition. an engagement period lasts a few months or years. Traditionally, in Jamaica the bride's parents were responsible for supplying the bridal gown and the reception; the groom and his parents provided the ring and the new home. In the United States, substantial variation in this practice exists due to changes in family structure and values. In many cases, the parties are already cohabiting and the wedding ceremony, often performed by a judge or Justice of the Peace, only legalizes the relationship. However, lovers who are practicing Christians do not live together before marriage and the wedding ceremony is performed in a chapel or church. Traditionally, the bride wears white as a sign of chastity, and large numbers of people are invited to observe the ceremony. In rural Jamaica, weddings are community events—the community feels that they are a part of the couple's life and they

view a public invitation to observe the ceremony also as an invitation to attend the reception, which includes lots of food and a large supply of rum and other beverages. In the United States, however, the ceremony and reception are kept within a small circle of close friends and relatives.

The wedding menu usually includes traditional Jamaican cuisine. It starts off with *mannish water*—a soup made from goat tripe (intestine). Guests are often given a choice of curry goat and white rice, rice and peas or kidney beans with fried chicken, or stewed chicken or beef for the main course. A light salad is served with the meal along with sorrel or rum punch. After the meal, the wedding cake is cut and served to the guests. It is usually a black cake with dried fruits presoaked in rum or wine and decorated with icing. Among the poorer people, port wine is used for toasting the couple. Some weddings include dancing by the bride and groom as well as guests and revelry, which can go into the wee hours of the morning.

BAPTISMS

Jamaicans practice two types of baptisms: infant baptism and adult baptism. Among Catholics, Anglicans, Lutherans, Presbyterians, Disciples of Christ, and Methodists, an infant is baptized into the body of believers and of Christ by sprinkling water on its head. When the child reaches the age of accountability, a confirmation ceremony is performed. In other Protestant-Christian and Afro-Caribbean Christian traditions, the infant is blessed at "dedication" but baptized only after faith is confessed voluntarily in Christ. In this baptism by immersion, the "initiate" is submerged bodily under the water by a minister of religion or elder of the faith, in a river, the sea, or a baptismal font located near the sanctuary.

FUNERALS

Jamaican funeral rituals and beliefs are influenced by African, Caribbean, and European-Christian traditions. The basic West African-Jamaican and Christian beliefs concerning death are as follows: the individual has three components—body, soul, and spirit; death marks the end of mortal life and the passage into immortality; at death, the spirit returns to the Supreme God where it joins other spirits; and the deceased's shadow or *duppy* wanders for several days, after which it is laid to rest through special rites. Consequently, Jamaican Christians and Afro-centric religions (Myalism, Pocomania, Shango) bury their dead after performing special rites or a formal church service. A Catholic priest gives the last rites to the dying and may offer a mass for a soul that departed to purgatory before making peace with God. In Jamaica, the high-church Protestants have stately funerals for their communicants who are prominent citizens. Around election time, these funerals are usually attended by high-ranking government officials and distinguished persons in the community. On the night before the funeral, there is a wake for the dead in which friends and family come to offer condolences, sing dirges, and "drink up."

A highlight of the funeral in Afro-centric religions is the "Nine Night" service, conducted to ensure that the shadow of the deceased does not return on the ninth evening after death to visit with family members. In most funerals, it is a custom for men to carry the corpse in a coffin on their shoulders. During the funeral, a phase of ritual mourning and howling in a sorrowful manner occurs. An offering of libation and sacrifices accompanies communication with the deceased at the gravesite. A phase of ritual joy mixed with mourning precedes and follows the interment, which is concluded with a second ceremony at the gravesite. Funeral rites involve dancing, singing, music, and grand incantations. There are often elaborate superstitious grave decorations to fend off evil spirits or bad omens from the deceased who lived a wicked life.

INTERACTION WITH OTHERS

Working-class Jamaican Americans have certain characteristics that set them apart from other groups. They dress differently (especially the Rastas), speak with a different accent, favor certain types of foods, and in some parts of New York City and Miami live as a self-contained group with distinct social and economic habits. They use special verbal expressions and linguistic codes to communicate (mostly in *Patois*). They are a hard-working and confident people, proud of their Jamaican heritage and the international reputation Jamaica receives from reggae and sports. Although often described as very assertive and not easily dominated, Jamaican immigrants generally establish good relations with other groups in their community. Jamaicans own or operate most of the successful Caribbean businesses in communities where they live. They are able to maintain strong friendly social, religious, economic, and political ties with both black and white American institutions and communities simultaneously. Many of the Caribbean nurses and nurses aides are Jamaican; and Jamaican American scholars and professionals establish collegial relations at American universities, colleges, and other institutions of learning.

On the other hand, Jamaican immigrants and native-born African Americans often misunderstand each other as a result of stereotypes and misconceptions, which often leads to intraracial conflict. For example, some Jamaicans believe that their attitudes of hard work, community building, and family values are superior to that of African Americans. Jamaicans see themselves as more ambitious and greater achievers than African Americans. Caribbean people also believe that they have healthier relations with whites than that of their counterparts because they do not carry anti-white rhetoric into all social, political, and economic discussions. Some American blacks see Jamaicans as interlopers who are making it more difficult for African Americans to find jobs and live peacefully in their neighborhoods. The fact that Jamaican Americans have dual national allegiance and, as a result, often pursue a different social and political agenda from other African Americans, adds to the misunderstanding.

Evidence shows that with time, many of the differences between African Americans and Jamaican Americans will become less distinct. Marriage patterns, for example, demonstrate that first-generation Jamaicans marry and have relations with other Jamaicans, while second and third generations tend to marry African Americans as well. This is due to their contact in school, interaction in their living environments, and that the second and third generation Jamaican Americans have lived in the United States all their lives and share very similar life experiences with African Americans. The combined efforts of Jamaicans and African Americans to deal with racial incidences and injustice in their neighborhoods also helps to improve relations.

RELIGION

The majority of Jamaica's population is Christian with small Hindu, Muslim, Jewish, and Bahai communities. The older, established Christian denominations are Baptist, Methodist, Anglican, Roman Catholic, Moravian, and the United Church (Presbyterian and Congregationalist). Jamaica's most vibrant religious experience comes from the less formal or liturgical Protestant religious confessions: the Pentecostals, Church of God, Associated Gospel Assembly, Open Bible Standard Churches, Seventh Day Adventist, Jehovah Witnesses, the Missionary church, and a number of independent churches all of which are called "Evangelical."

A number of African Caribbean revivalist religious groups also exist in Jamaica, which survived under slavery. Among these are Myalism, Bedwardism (founded by Alexander Bedward in 1920), Pocomania Kurnina, Nativism or the Native Baptist church, and Rastafarianism. Myalism is a religion with African origins. It is one of the oldest religions from Africa and involves the practice of magic and spirit possession. It is community-centered and refuses to accept negatives in life such as sickness, failure, and oppression. Kumina, which is related to Mayalism, began around 1730. Membership into Kumina "bands" is inherited at birth rather than by conversion or voluntary membership. The Native Baptist church began as an indigenous church among black American slaves who were taken to Jamaica by their owners when they migrated to the island as Baptist loyalists. One of the distinguishing characteristics of the Native Baptist church is immersion baptism.

Rastafari is Jamaica's most famous Afro-Caribbean religion. It was founded in 1930 by wandering Jamaican preachers who were inspired by the teachings of Marcus Garvey, a political activist. Rastas established their beliefs on messianic interpretations of Christian scripture and the idea that Haile Selassie, the former Emperor of Ethiopia, is divine. Distinguishing features of Rastafari are the wearing of dreadlocks and loose-fitting clothes. The movement has made its presence felt on every continent. There are about 800,000 Rastas and Rasta supporters in the United States, about 80,000 of whom live in Brooklyn.

EMPLOYMENT AND ECONOMIC TRADITIONS

Jamaican American employment is quite diverse. A large number of older Jamaican women work for low wages taking care of predominantly white senior citizens in American metropolitan cities. However, many Jamaican Americans bring technical and professional skills with them to the United States, which often allow them to secure better paying jobs than other blacks. Before 1970, white-owned institutions and corporations tended to hire skilled and highly educated Jamaicans in preference to black Americans. This gave American blacks the distinct impression that Jamaicans were specially favored in the job market.

Both Caribbean and American blacks suffer job discrimination in the United States. Jamaican immigrants who are illegal aliens or who are in a transitional stage of residency are particularly vulnerable to injustice and exploitation. Often, unskilled immigrants work for long hours in two or three part-time low-paying jobs in order to survive. However, a significant number of Jamaican Americans are successful in entrepreneurial enterprises. In New York City, many have benefited from affirmative action policies in housing and jobs in Flatbush, Crown Heights, Bedford Stuyvesant, and elsewhere. Some Jamaicans have used the open enrollment at the City University of New York to improve their skills in order to obtain higher paying jobs and upward mobility.

After the late 1970s, Jamaican businesses in New York City proliferated, including grocery stores, parlors, and shops, restaurants, travel agencies, realtor brokerages, bakeries, bars, beauty salons, music and record shops, and disco and dance clubs. A number of Jamaicans are subcontractors in building construction, masonry, carpentry, woodwork and cabinet making, electrical wiring, plumbing, heating and central air installations, printing, typing and stenographic services. Jamaican professional businesses include computer consulting and training in word processing, law firms, private medical practices, immigration agents or counselors.

Crime has become such a way of life in Jamaica that in the post independence period, both of the ruling parties, the JLP and the PNP, recruited gangsters to "eliminate" opponents in electoral districts, stuff ballot boxes to control election results, hand pick the tenants for scarce housing, launder money, and funnel government jobs to supporters. Since the late 1970s, the gangs have had almost unlimited power in Jamaica and are now bodyguards for government officials. They prey on the defenseless and vulnerable and compete with rivals for turf, both in Jamaica and the United States. In recent years, the U.S. government has adopted a policy of deporting violent Jamaican criminals who are now a serious menace to national security.

POLITICS AND GOVERNMENT

Jamaicans have been involved in issues of political significance in the United States since the early 1800s. In 1827, Jamaican-born John B. Russwurm co-founded and co-edited the first black press in America, *Freedom's Journal*. Russwurm's vocal political views and anti-slavery criticism forced him to leave the paper under pressure from contributors and his own colleagues. After slavery was abolished in the British West Indies in 1834, a number of Jamaicans supported the Back to Africa movement and worked for the abolition of American slavery in collaboration with their black counterparts in the United States.

This political activity led to the founding of the Pan-African Movement, which Marcus Garvey and W.E.B. Dubois championed. Garvey attracted the largest single political gathering in American history prior to the Civil Rights March on Washington. He spurred blacks in Harlem into political action with self-confidence and black pride. He established the Universal Negro Improvement Association (UNIA), which helped to cement the bonds of racial consciousness between American and Caribbean blacks. The majority of Garvey's

UNIA in the United States comprised West Indians, especially from Jamaica. Garvey's movement intimidated the National Association for the Advancement of Colored People (NAACP), which envied the power and support that Garvey enjoyed before he was arrested on charges of alleged embezzlement and later incarcerated in Atlanta, Georgia. After Garvey was deported in the late 1920s, he established the Peoples' Political Party (PPP), which called for many reforms, including minimum wages, guaranteed employment, social security benefits, workers' compensation, the expropriation of private lands for public use, land reform, and the creation of a Jamaican university. While working in the American political context, W. A. Domingo, a Jamaican-born Harlem Renaissance figure and writer, supported black rights and advocated Jamaican independence in the Caribbean. Domingo did not want to emphasize the differences between African Americans and West Indian Americans, because both are black and experience some of the same effects of racial oppression and discrimination.

The influences of Jamaican politics and culture on places like New York City, East Orange, Miami, and elsewhere extend beyond the mere establishment of cultural enclaves. Jamaicans were very vocal and assertive during the early twentieth century black struggle, often paving the way for new black professional opportunities not previously open to blacks. Jamaican Americans who experience racial discrimination in the work-place, in their neighborhoods, and in their communities, combine political efforts to address the concerns of the entire black population. In the 1930s, Jamaican-U.S. political activity reached a new level as Jamaican, Trinidadians, Guyanese, and other Caribbean immigrants began playing an important role in the Democratic Party in New York City. Years later, Una Clarke, a Jamaican-born educator who won one of New York's predominantly Caribbean districts, rose to be one of the prominent Jamaican American politicians in New York.

POLITICAL RELATIONS WITH JAMAICA

Jamaica and the United States have never engaged in a major military confrontation. U.S. involvement in Jamaica includes little intervention. There has never been a need for a "Bay of Pigs" invasion, as in Cuba, a "vertical insertion," as in Grenada, or a military occupation as in Haiti and the Dominican Republic. The United States did not contemplate annexing Jamaica as it did with Puerto Rico and Cuba in the Spanish Cuban American War of 1898. The United States also did not have military bases in Jamaica as it did in Trinidad. The relationship between Kingston and Washington has been very cordial, except for a period under Michael Manley's administration. Today, American tourists frequently visit the island in large numbers, adding substantially to the economy. A busy flow of air traffic exists between Jamaica and United States as Jamaicans make frequent business trips to the United States. Immigrants make regular remittances to family and relatives in Jamaica and visit their "land of origin" regularly. Many of them maintain dual residence and vote in local elections.

In recent decades, the U.S. government has used economic and diplomatic clout to influence political and fiscal direction in Jamaica. In the late 1970s and 1980s, the U.S. government used clandestine activities to destabilize Manley's democratic socialist government. Consequently, Washington came under heavy criticism from Jamaican political analysts and politicians for supporting political violence in Jamaica during elections.

MILITARY

Jamaican membership in the U.S. Armed Forces began during World War I and continued during World War II. Jamaicans both in America and on the island were recruited for service in Europe and some of them were stationed at U.S. bases in the region. Since then, Jamaican Americans have worked in many different wings of the Armed Forces. During the Gulf War, the Head of the Joint Chiefs of Staff, General Colin Powell (born in New York City in 1937) was recognized as the America's most eminent second-generation Jamaican American. He served his country in the Armed Forces with academic and political distinction. He became a household name under the Bush administration and earned the admiration and respect of the nation; Random House paid the retired four-star general $6.5 million to publish his memoirs.

INDIVIDUAL AND GROUP CONTRIBUTIONS

Jamaican immigrants contribute substantially to American political, cultural, religious, and educational life. Jamaican-born writers, athletes, teachers, musicians, poets, journalists, artists, professors, sports writers, actors, and other professionals who have lived in the United States have greatly enriched the American culture in many ways.

ACADEMIA

Jamaican-born John B. Russwurm was one of the first blacks to enter an American academy; he graduated with a B.A. from Baldwin College in 1826; Russwurm distinguished himself as the co-founder of *Freedom's Journal*, black America's first newspaper. Jamaican-born Leonard Barrett lived most of his adult life in the United States and taught at Temple University and other institutions for more than 30 years. Jamaican-born Orlando Patterson, professor of sociology at Harvard University, and economist George Beckford are recognized as leading social scientists in America.

FILM, TELEVISION, THEATER, AND OTHER VISUAL ARTS

Jamaicans have made contributions to the film and television industry in the United States. Louise Bennett-Coverly, better known as "Miss Lou," Jamaica's premier and world-renowned folklorist, has lived and performed in the United States for many years. She was born in Kingston, Jamaica, in 1919 and became a performer of stories, songs, and rhymes. At the age of 14, she began to write and dramatize poems using *patois* rather than standard English. In 1996, she marked her sixtieth anniversary as a performer of poetry, story, and song. For her 50 years of contribution to Caribbean culture, she was named Jamaica's national poet and poet laureate in 1986. Her dramatic style, physical presence, and debonair theatrical equity have made her a legend in Jamaican and Jamaican American theater and has brought distinction to Jamaican *patois* on stage.

Other Jamaican American folklorists like Ranny Williams and Leonie Forbes have made a substantial contribution to the performing arts. Choreographer, scholar, literature laureate, and performer, Rex Nettleford, now vice chancellor of the University of the West Indies, has taken the Caribbean's premier National Dance Theater Company (NDTC) around the world and performed with distinction. The NDTC has won several awards and made several tours of the United States. The Sister Theater Group has also made several U.S. tours. The comedian Oliver Samuels has starred in *Oliver At Large* and *Doctors in Paradise*.

JOURNALISM

Modern Jamaican American journalists who have lived and studied in the United States are John Maxwell, John Heame, Barbara Gloudon (former editor of the *Jamaica Gleaner* and the *Star*), Ronnie Thwaites, Adrian Robinson, Dennis Hall, and Morris Cargill (columnist). Carl Williams, editor and founder of *Black Culture* (1989), lives and works in the United States. Winston Smith, who lives in Brooklyn, works with *The Paper*.

LITERATURE

A number of contemporary Jamaican American scholars are well known in the field of literature. Claude McKay migrated from Jamaica to the United States in 1912 and became an important voice in the Harlem Renaissance; he wrote many novels, among them *Banana Bottom* and *This Island*. Many Jamaican poets have distinguished themselves in the field of literature: Adriza Mandiela wrote *Life of the Caribbean Immigrant, Living in America*. Louise Bennett-Coverly, poet laureate, has written dozens of poems and books on Caribbean life. Two literature laureates and scholars, Rex Nettleford and Sir Arthur Lewis, are well known in the United States. Afoa Cooper, Lillian Allen, Oliver Senior, Mutabaruka, Linton Kwasii Johnson, Gene Binta, Breeze, Opaimer Adisa, D'Janette Sears, Michael Smith, and a-dziao Simba, who wrote *25.40 P.M. Past Morning*, are only a few of the dozens of outstanding Jamaican American poets of modern times. Sheila Winter taught literature at Princeton University and Sir John Mordecai was a visiting professor at the same institution.

MUSIC

Well-known Rasta artists are: The Wailers, Big Youth, We the People, Ras Michael and the Sons of Negus, Peter Tosh, The I Threes, Light of Saba, and United Africa. Reggae rhythms are so popular and powerful that jazz musicians in Jamaica and the United States—Herbie Mann, Sonny Rollins, Roberta Flack, Johnny Nash, Eric Clapton, and Lennie Hibbert—are exploiting the potential of Rasta music with huge financial success. Other well-known Jamaican music stars are: Marjorie Wiley, a Jamaican folklorist, musician, and dancer; Marcia Griffiths, Tiger, Shine Head, and Freddie McGregor.

SPORTS

A number of Jamaicans and Jamaican Americans have excelled in international competition and carried home many trophies. Sir Herbert McDonald was an Olympian; Donald Quarrie won the 200 and the 4 x 100 meters Olympic Gold Medal; Marlene Ottey won the 200 and the 4 x 100 meters. Some of the world's most outstanding cricketers were Jamaicans; they include: O. J. Collier Smith, Alfred Valentine,

Roy Gilcrist, Michael Holding, Easton McMorris, Franze Alexander, and George Headley, who was born in Panama in 1909, transported to Cuba, grew up in Jamaica and lived in the United States.

MEDIA

PRINT

Caribbean Newsletter.

First published October 1, 1980, as "Friends for Jamaica," this quarterly acts as the voice of Friends for Jamaica, "a small collective of New York City residents" which supports the struggles of Jamaican workers and peasants. Also concerned with "the struggles of people in other countries in the English-speaking Caribbean." Contains articles on political, economic, social, and agricultural issues.

Address: Friends for Jamaica, Box 20392, Cathedral Finance Station, New York, New York 10025.

There are many other newspapers and tabloids in the United States that cater to the Jamaican population in America. The journal *Cimmarron*, published by the City University of New York, discusses a variety of Caribbean issues, as does the Afro-centric magazine, *Black Culture*. *Everybody's Magazine* has a very wide readership, as does *New York Carib News*, founded in 1981 by Karl Rodney, the former president of the Jamaican Progressive Party. Additional publications include *Viewpoint* and *The Paper*. These publications provide news about different aspects of Jamaican life such as politics, current events, sports, and other issues of importance to the Caribbean. Newspapers also cover issues and concerns facing Caribbean Americans in the United States. The *Jamaican Gleaner* and *The Star* are favorite daily papers in Miami and New York City.

RADIO AND TELEVISION

Jamaicans in the United States and Jamaica also receive up-to-the-minute news on CNN, C-Span, and other television stations in the international network. At the same time, the Jamaica Broadcasting Corporation (JBC) and Jamaican radio stations (like RJR) supply Jamaican Americans with current news of the island.

ORGANIZATIONS AND ASSOCIATIONS

Various organizations and funds exist to help Jamaican Americans. These include the St. Vincent Benefit and Education Fund, Jamaican Nurses Association and the Jamaican Policemen's School Alumni Association of New York. The Brooklyn Council on the Arts, Caribbean Festival, The Jamaican Association of Greater Cleveland, The Cleveland Cricket Club, The New York Cricket Club (of Brooklyn), and The Third World Foundation located in Chicago are additional Jamaican organizations. Several Jamaican American clubs and organizations comprise alumni of several high schools in Jamaica, including MICA Old Student Association (MOSA), Cornwall College Association (CCA), St. Hughes High School Alumni Association (SHHAA), and the Montego Bay Boys Alumni Association (MBBAA).

SOURCES FOR ADDITIONAL STUDY

Alleyne, Mervyn C. *Roots of Jamaican Culture.* London: Pluto Press, 1988.

Barrett, Leonard E. *The Rastafarians.* Boston: Beacon Press, 1997.

Campbell, Marvis C. *The Maroons of Jamaica 1655-1796: A History of Resistance, Collaboration and Betrayal.* Massachusetts: Bergin & Publishers Inc., 1988.

Carty, Hilary S. *Folk Dances of Jamaica: An Insight.* London: Dance Books, 1988.

Kessner, Thomas, and Betty Boyd Caroli. *Today's Immigrants: Their Stories; A New Look at the Newest Americans.* New York: Oxford University Press, 1982.

Luntta, Karl. *Jamaica Handbook.* California: Moon Publications, 1991.

The economic
position and
socioeconomic
mobility of Japanese
Americans is much
higher now than
at any time in
American history.

JAPANESE AMERICANS

by
Stanley E. Easton and
Lucien Ellington

OVERVIEW

A country slightly larger than the United Kingdom (about the size of California), Japan lies off the eastern coast of the Asian continent. An archipelago, Japan consists of four main islands—Honshū, Hokkaidō, Kyūshū, and Shikoku—as well as 3,900 smaller islands. Japan has a total land area of 145,825 square miles (377,688 square kilometers). Much of Japan is extremely mountainous and almost the entire population lives on only one-sixth of the total land area. Of all the world's major nations, the Japanese have the highest population density per square mile of habitable land. Japan has virtually no natural resources except those found in the sea. To Japan's north, the nearest foreign soil is the Russian-controlled island of Sakhalin while the People's Republic of China and South Korea lie to the west of Japan.

The word, "Japan," is actually a Portuguese misunderstanding of the Chinese pronunciation of the Chinese term for the country. The actual name for the country is Nippon or Nihon ("source of the sun"). Japan has a population of approximately 124 million people. By the standards of other nations, the Japanese are one of the most homogeneous people on earth. Under two million foreigners (less than one percent of the total Japanese population) live in Japan. Koreans constitute well over one-half of resident minorities. There are also two indigenous minority groups in Japan, the Ainu and the

Burakumin. The Ainu, a Caucasian people, number around 24,381 and live mainly in special reservations in central Hokkaidō. Ethnically, the approximately two million Burakumin are no different than other Japanese, but have traditionally engaged in low-status occupations; and although they have the same legal status as their fellow citizens, they are often discriminated against. Shinto, an indigenous religion, is the most popular spiritual practice in Japan, followed by Buddhism, a Korean and Chinese import. Followers of other religions constitute less than one percent of the Japanese population. Culturally, the Japanese are children of China but have their own rich native culture and have also borrowed extensively from Western countries. Tokyō is Japan's capital and largest city. The national flag of Japan is a crimson disc, symbolizing the rising sun, in the center of a white field.

HISTORY

The oldest identified human remains found in Japan date from upper Paleolithic times of the last glacial period, about 30,000 B.C. While there is some dispute, most historians believe that political unity in Japan occurred at the end of the third century or the beginning of the fourth century A.D. The Yamato chiefs who unified the country developed an imperial line, which is the oldest in the world. However, early in Japanese history, emperors lost political authority. Compared to China, ancient and medieval Japan was undeveloped culturally. From early in Japanese history many Chinese imports, including architecture, agricultural methods, Confucianism, and Buddhism, profoundly influenced the Japanese. The Japanese established a pattern that still exists of selectively importing foreign customs and adapting them to the archipelago.

Medieval and early modern Japan was marked by long periods of incessant warfare as rival families struggled for power. While power struggles were still occurring, the Japanese had their first contact with Europe when Portuguese traders landed off southern Kyūshū in 1543. In 1603, through military conquest, Tokugawa Ieyasu established himself as ruler of the entire country. Early in the Tokugawa era, foreigners were expelled from Japan and the country was largely isolated from the rest of the world until Commodore Matthew C. Perry of the U.S. Navy forced Japan to open its doors in 1853.

MODERN ERA

Japan's modern history began in 1868 when a number of citizens led by Satsuma and Chosū domains

The Japanese samurai is a very respectable warrior. Those who immigrated to the United States no longer had a need for the traditional costume, but they were worn occasionally for celebrations or ceremonies.

overthrew the Tokugawas. In the decades that followed Japan feverishly modernized in an attempt to end Western efforts at dominance. By the early twentieth century, Japan possessed a rapidly industrializing economy and a strong military. At first the rest of Asia was excited by Japan's rise. However, the militarization of Japan in the 1930s, and Japan's attempt to dominate the rest of Asia, resulted in the Pacific War that pitted much of Asia and a number of Western countries (including the United States) against Japan. In August 1945, a devastated Japan accepted the surrender terms of the Allied powers. The subsequent American occupation resulted in major political and economic change as Japan became a democracy, renounced militarism, and resumed its impressive economic growth. Today, Japan is a stable democracy among the world's economic superpowers.

MIGRATION TO HAWAII AND AMERICA

In 1835, American settlers established the sugar plantation system in Hawaii, which was then an independent monarchy. The sugar plantations required large numbers of workers to cultivate and harvest the cane fields and to operate the sugar refineries. Beginning in 1852, the plantation owners imported Chinese laborers. In many ways, this "coolie" trade resembled the African slave trade.

By 1865, many of the Chinese were leaving the plantations for other jobs. Hawaii's foreign minister, a sugar planter, wrote to an American businessman in Japan seeking Japanese agricultural workers. On

May 17, 1868, the *Scioto* sailed from Yokohama for Honolulu with 148 Japanese—141 men, six women, and two children—aboard. These laborers included samurai, cooks, *sake* brewers, potters, printers, tailors, wood workers, and one hairdresser. Plantation labor was harsh; the monthly wage was $4, of which the planters withheld 50 percent. The ten-hour work days were hard on the soft hands of potters, printers, and tailors. Forty of these first Japanese farm laborers returned to Japan before completion of their three-year contracts. Once back home, 39 of them signed a public statement charging the planters with cruelty and breach of contract.

On May 27, 1869, the Pacific Mail Company's *China* brought a party of samurai, farmers, tradesmen, and four women to San Francisco. These Japanese had been displaced from their homes by the ending of the Tokugawa shogunate and the restoration of the Meiji emperor. Followers of lord Matsudaira Katamori established the 600-acre Wakamatsu Tea and Silk Farm Colony on the Sacramento River at Placerville. The colony failed in less than two years because the mulberry trees and tea seedlings perished in the dry California soil. A few of the settlers returned to Japan while the rest drifted away from the colony seeking new beginnings. Such were the origins of the first-generation Japanese (*Issei*) on Hawaiian and American shores.

EFFORTS TO BAN JAPANESE IMMIGRATION

The U. S. Congress passed the Chinese Exclusion Act in 1882, prohibiting further Chinese immigration. In 1886, Hawaii and Japan signed a labor convention that led to large numbers of Japanese contract workers in Hawaii and student laborers in California. The increase of Japanese in California gave rise to an anti-Japanese movement and a 1906 San Francisco school board order segregating Japanese American students. Ninety-three students of Japanese ancestry and a number of Korean students were ordered to attend the school for Chinese. The Japanese government was insulted. President Theodore Roosevelt, wishing to maintain harmonious relations with Japan, condemned anti-Japanese agitation and the school segregation order. He advocated naturalization of the Issei, but never sponsored introduction of a bill to accomplish it. Political reaction against Roosevelt in California was fierce. Several anti-Japanese bills were introduced in the California legislature in 1907. President Roosevelt called San Francisco school officials and California legislative leaders to Washington. After a week of negotiations, the Californians agreed to allow most Japanese children (excluding overage students and those with limited English) to attend regular public schools.

Roosevelt promised to limit Japanese labor immigration. In late 1907 and early 1908 Japan and the United States corresponded on the matter. Japan agreed to stop issuing passports to laborers in the United States. The United States allowed Japanese who had already been to America to return and agreed to accept immediate family members of Japanese workers already in the country. This was the so-called "Gentlemen's Agreement."

Under the Gentlemen's Agreement some Japanese migration to the United States continued. Between 1908 and 1924, many of the immigrants were women brought by husbands who had returned to Japan to marry. Between 1909 and 1920, the number of married Japanese women doubled in Hawaii and quadrupled on the mainland. Most of the Japanese women who migrated to Hawaii and the U. S. during that period were "picture brides." Marriages were arranged by parents. Go-betweens brokered agreements between families. Couples were married while the bride was in Japan and the groom was in the United States. Husband and wife met for the first time upon their arrival at the pier in Honolulu, San Francisco, or Seattle, using photographs to identify one another. This wave of immigration changed the nature of the Japanese American community from a male migrant laborer community to a family-oriented people seeking permanent settlement.

By 1924, many Americans favored restricting immigration through a quota system aimed primarily at restricting European immigration without discriminating against any country. Such a bill passed the U.S. House of Representatives in April 1924. U.S. Senator Hiram Johnson of California, however, wanted a ban on all immigration from Japan. Hoping to avoid offending the Japanese government further, Secretary of State Charles Evans Hughes asked the Japanese ambassador to write a letter summarizing the Gentlemen's Agreement of 1907-1908 since its provisions were not widely known. Ambassador Masanao Hanihara wrote the letter and included an appeal to the senators to reject any bill halting Japanese immigration. He referred to "the grave consequences" that exclusion would have upon relations between his country and the United States. Senator Henry Cabot Lodge of Massachusetts, who chaired the Foreign Relations Committee, called Hanihara's letter a "veiled threat" and led the Senate to incorporate Japanese exclusion into the immigration bill. President Coolidge signed the Immigration Act of 1924, including the ban on further Japanese immigration, into law on May 24. Japanese immigration was curtailed until 1952, except for post World War II Japanese brides of U.S. servicemen.

POST WORLD WAR II IMMIGRATION

In 1952 the McCarran-Walter Act allowed immigration from South and East Asia. The new law ended Japanese exclusion, but was still racially discriminatory. Asian countries were allowed 100 immigrants each, while immigration from European countries was determined by the national origins quotas of the Immigration Act of 1924. The McCarran-Walter Act also repealed the racial clauses in the naturalization law of 1790 that forbade non-white immigrants from obtaining American citizenship. Over 46,000 Japanese immigrants, including many elderly Issei, became naturalized citizens by 1965.

The Immigration Act of 1965 abolished the national origin quotas and annually permitted the admission of 170,000 immigrants from the Eastern Hemisphere and 120,000 from the Western Hemisphere. Twenty thousand immigrants per year per Asian country were allowed to enter the United States. This law opened the way for the second wave of Asian immigration and resulted in a new composition of the Asian American population. In 1960, 52 percent of the Asian American population were Japanese American. In 1985 only 15 percent of Asian Americans were Japanese. Between 1965 and 1985, there were nearly four times as many Asian immigrants as there had been between 1849 and 1965.

MODERN ERA

According to the 1990 census figures, there were 847,562 Japanese Americans in the United States. About 723,000 of the Japanese Americans lived in the West, 312,989 of those in California. Today there are Japanese Americans located in each of the 50 states.

Recent decades have brought not only legal and institutional changes but positive attitudinal change on the part of many white Americans toward Japanese Americans. The combination of legal and attitudinal change, along with the higher levels of education that Japanese Americans tend to attain, compared to whites, have resulted in a reversal of the dismal situation of overeducated and underemployed Japanese Americans that existed in the 1930s. Although a substantial number of Japanese Americans are employed by corporations and are members of professions that require college educations, Japanese Americans still experience problems that are a direct result of racially-based misconceptions that some members of the majority population hold.

Many white Americans, particularly well-educated white Americans, think of Japanese Americans as a "model minority" because of their reputation for hard work and their high educational attainment. Despite this reputation, many Japanese—as well as other Asian Americans—complain that they are stereotyped as good technicians but not aggressive enough to occupy top managerial and leadership positions. Anti-Asian graffiti can sometimes be found at top universities where at least some white students voice jealousy and resentment toward perceived Asian American academic success.

Recent economic competition between the United States and Japan has resulted in a rise in anti-Japanese sentiment on the part of many Americans. The 1982 murder of Vincent Chin, a young Chinese man in Detroit, by two auto workers who mistook him to be Japanese is one grisly example of these sentiments. Third- and fourth-generation Japanese Americans often cite incidents of fellow Americans making anti-Japanese statements in their presence or mistaking them for Japanese nationals.

The issue of cultural revitalization is not related to racial attitudes but is still serious to many Japanese Americans. Because of the amazing success of Japan's economy since World War II, the number of Japanese immigrating annually has been far below the 20,000 quota allotted to Japan. In recent years, Japanese immigrants have constituted less than two percent of all Asian immigrants. As a result, the Japanese towns of large American cities are not being culturally renewed and many second- and third-generation Japanese have moved to the suburbs. Many third- and fourth-generation Japanese Americans are not literate in the Japanese language. Unlike the lingering prejudices toward Japanese Americans, the over-assimilation problem may very well have no ultimate solution.

ACCULTURATION AND ASSIMILATION

In the United States, Japanese Americans built Buddhist temples and Christian churches. They built halls to serve as language schools and as places for dramas, films, judō lessons, poetry readings, potlucks, and parties. They constructed sumō rings, baseball fields, and bath houses. They also established hotels, restaurants, bars, and billiard parlors. Japanese Americans opened shops to provide Japanese food and herbal medicines.

The Issei faced many restrictions. They were excluded from some occupations, could not own land, and could not become U.S. citizens. They faced discrimination and prejudice. The Issei's pleasure was in seeing the success of their children. Despite their poverty, the Issei developed large,

close-knit families. They encouraged their children (Nisei) to become educated and obtain white collar jobs rather than stay in farming communities. This drove the Nisei into close associations and friendships with Caucasians. The Nisei were educated in American schools and learned white middle-class American values. Hierarchical thinking, characteristic of Japanese culture, led to pressure to achieve academically and to compete successfully in the larger Caucasian-dominated society.

Between 1915 and 1967 the proportion of Japanese Americans living in predominantly Japanese American neighborhoods fell from 30 percent to four percent. With the end of World War II, prejudice and discrimination against Japanese Americans declined. The majority of Nisei now live in largely Caucasian neighborhoods. Their children (Sansei) have been schooled there and have mostly Caucasian associations. A majority of Sansei are unfamiliar with the Japanese American world characterized by intimate primary, communal association, and close social control. They rarely see members of their clan. Their world has been that of Little League and fraternities and sororities. Whereas only ten percent of Nisei married outside their ethnic group, about 50 percent of the Sansei did.

Many Sansei long to know more about their cultural roots, although the ways of their grandparents are alien to them. They are concerned over the demise of Japanese values. They seek to preserve their Japanese culture through service to the Japanese community at centers for the elderly, participation in community festivals, involvement with

Asian political and legal organizations, and patronizing Japanese arts.

In *Japanese Americans*, sociologist Harry Kitano observed that Japanese Americans developed a congruent Japanese culture within the framework of American society. This was due to necessity rather than choice, since there was little opportunity for the first Japanese immigrants to enter into the social structure of the larger community. Now most Japanese Americans can enter into that social structure. Nisei and Sansei continue to identify themselves as Japanese Americans, but that identity is of little importance to them as members and partakers of a larger society that is not hostile toward them as it was to the Issei. The degree to which Japanese Americans have been assimilated into the predominant culture is unusual for a nonwhite group. Coexistence between Japanese and American cultures has been successful due to the willingness of both cultures to accommodate to one another.

Japanese American history brings us to some critical questions. What the future holds for fourth-generation Japanese Americans (the Yonsei) is unclear. The Japanese American ethnic community may disappear in that generation, or complete assimilation may bring about the demise of the values that pushed Japanese Americans to socioeconomic success. It is uncertain whether the Yonsei will retain their Japanese characteristics and inculcate them in the next generation.

TRANSPLANTED TRADITIONS

In Japanese American communities many Japanese still celebrate New Year's Day very much in the manner the Issei did, following the customs of Meiji-era Japan. New Year is a time for debts to be paid and quarrels to be settled. It is an occasion when houses are cleaned, baths are taken, and new clothes are worn. On New Year's Eve, many Japanese Americans go to temples and shrines. Shinto shrines are especially popular. Just inside the red tori gate, worshippers wash their hands and rinse their mouths with water from the special basin. Then a priest cleanses them by sprinkling water from a leafy branch on them and blesses them by waving a wand of white prayer papers. The people sip sake, receive amulets (charms), and give money.

In Japanese American homes where the traditions are observed, New Year's offerings are set in various places of honor around the house. The offering consists of two *mochi* (rice cakes), a strip of *konbu* (seaweed), and a citrus arranged on a "happiness paper" depicting one or all of the seven gods of good luck. The offerings symbolize harmony and happiness from generation to generation.

At breakfast on New Year's Day many Japanese Americans eat *ozoni*, a toasted *mochi*, in a broth with other ingredients such as vegetables and fish. *Mochi* is eaten for strength and family cohesiveness. Sometimes children compete with each other to see if they can eat *mochi* equal to the number of their years.

Friends, neighbors, and family members visit one another on New Year's Day. Special foods served include *kuromame* (black beans), *kazunoko* (herring eggs), *konbumaki* (seaweed roll), *kinton* (mashed sweet potato and chestnut), and *kamaboko* (fish cakes). Also, *sushi* (rice rolled in seaweed), *nishime* (vegetables cooked in stock), *sashimi* (raw fish), and cooked red snapper are commonly provided for New Year's guests. At many celebrations the Japanese cheer of "*Banzai! Banzai! Banzai!*" rings out. That salute, which originated around 200 B.C., means 10,000 years.

HEALTH ISSUES

Generally, Japanese Americans are healthier than other Americans. Japanese Americans have the lowest infant death rate of any ethnic group in the United States. In 1986, 86 percent of babies born to Japanese American mothers were born to women who had received early prenatal care, compared to 79 percent for Caucasians and 76 percent for all races. Relatively few Japanese American infants have low birth weight and only eight percent of Japanese American births were preterm, compared to ten percent for all races in 1987. Asian Americans have fewer birth defects than Native Americans, Caucasians, or African Americans, but more than Hispanic Americans. Asian and Pacific Islanders were two percent of the U.S. population in 1981-1988, but accounted for only one percent of all U.S. AIDS cases during that period. In October of 1987 less than one percent of drug abuse clients in the United States were Asian Americans.

A study comparing the health status of Japanese and Caucasians over the age of 60 in Hawaii revealed that better health could be predicted from younger age, higher family income, maintenance of work role, and Japanese ethnicity (Marvelu R. Peterson and others, "A Cross-Cultural Health Study of Japanese and Caucasian Elders in Hawaii," *International Journal of Aging and Human Development*, Volume 21, 1985, pp. 267-279). The better health of Japanese Americans in Hawaii may be due to cultural values such as the priority of family interests over those of the individual, reverence for elders, and obligation to care for elders.

Many Japanese Americans consider the use of mental health services as shameful. They tend to use them only as a last resort in severe disorders, such as schizophrenia. Japanese Americans underuse mental health services in comparison to other ethnic groups. They believe the causes of mental illness to be associated with organic factors, a lack of will power, and morbid thinking. They tend to seek help from family members or close friends, rather than from mental health professionals. Further, since Japanese Americans tend to somaticize psychological problems, they may seek help from traditional medical practitioners instead of mental health professionals. There are, however, a number of Japanese American psychiatrists in practice today, indicating greater acceptance of the need for professional mental health care.

LANGUAGE

The Japanese language is unique and has no close relationship to any other language, such as English does to German, or French does to Spanish. It is a popular misconception that Japanese and Chinese are similar. Although many kanji, or ideograms, were borrowed from classical Chinese, the two spoken languages do not have a single basic feature in common. The origins of Japanese are obscure, and only Korean can be considered to belong to the same linguistic family. Spoken Japanese was in existence long before kanji reached Japan. While there is some variation in dialect throughout Japan, variance in pronunciation and vocabulary is, in general, quite small.

Japanese is easy to pronounce and bears some similarity to the Romance languages. The five short vowels in Japanese order are "a," "e," "i," "o," and "u." They are pronounced clearly and crisply. The same vowels in the long form are pronounced by doubling the single vowel and making a continuous sound equal to two identical short vowels. Japanese consonants approximately resemble English.

Some useful daily expressions include: *Ohayōgozaimasu*—good morning; *Konnichiwa*—hello; *Kombanwa*—good evening; *Sayōnara*—goodbye; *Oyasumi nasai*—good night; *Okaeri nasai*—welcome home; *O-genki desu ka*—how are you; *Dōmo arigatō gozaimasu*—thank you very much; *Chotto matte kudasai*—wait just a moment please.

Many linguists believe that Japanese is the world's most difficult written language. Written Japanese consists of three types of characters: kanji, hiragana, and katakana. Kanji, which means "Chinese characters," are ideograms, or pictorial representations of ideas. Kanji were imported into Japan sometime during the fifth century A.D. from China via Korea. Although there are said to be some 48,000 kanji in existence, roughly 4,000 characters are commonly used. The Ministry of Education identified 1,850 kanji (called tōyō kanji) in 1946 as essential for official and general public use. In 1981 this list was superseded by a similar but larger one (called jōyō kanji) containing 1,945 characters. These are taught to all students in elementary and secondary school. Kanji are used in writing the main parts of a sentence such as verbs and nouns, as well as names. Kanji are the most difficult written Japanese characters, requiring as many as 23 separate strokes.

Since spoken Japanese existed before kanji reached Japan, the Japanese adopted the Chinese ideograms to represent spoken Japanese words of the same or related meanings. Since the sounds of Japanese words signifying the ideas were not the same as the sounds of the Chinese words, it became important to develop a writing system to represent the Japanese sound. Therefore, the Japanese developed two sets of characters, hiragana and katakana, from original Chinese characters. Each kana, as these two systems are called, is a separate phonetic syllabary and each hiragana character has a corresponding katakana character. Hiragana and katakana characters are similar to English letters in that each character represents a separate phonetic sound. Hiragana are used in writing verb endings, adverbs, conjunctions, and various sentence particles and are written in a cursive, smooth style. Katakana, which are used mainly in writing foreign words, are written in a more angular, stiff style. Both hiragana and katakana are easy to write compared with kanji. In modern written Japanese, kanji, hiragana, and katakana are combined. Traditionally, Japanese is written vertically and read from top to bottom and right to left. Now, most business writing is done horizontally because it is easier to include numerals and English words. Even though the written language is illogical, in many ways, it has aesthetic appeal and contributes to a feeling on the part of many Japanese that they are unique among the world's peoples. For a variety of reasons, including negative pressures by the majority population and a lack of new Japanese immigrants in the United States, many third- and fourth-generation Japanese Americans do not know the language of their ancestors.

FAMILY AND COMMUNITY DYNAMICS

Communalism did not develop in overseas Japanese communities as it did among the overseas Chinese.

In the fifteenth and sixteenth centuries Japan's land-based lineage community gave way to downsized extended families. Only the eldest son and his family remained in the parental household. Other sons established separate "branch" households when they married. In Japan, a national consciousness arose while in China, the primary allegiance remained to the clan-based village or community. Thus, Japanese immigrants were prepared to form families and rear children in a manner similar to that of white Americans. The "picture bride" system brought several thousand Japanese women to the United States to establish nuclear branch families.

The "picture bride" system was fraught with misrepresentation. Often old photographs were used to hide the age of a prospective bride and the men sometimes were photographed in borrowed suits. The system led to a degree of disillusionment and incompatibility in marriages. The women were trapped, unable to return to Japan. Nevertheless, these women persevered for themselves and their families and transmitted Japanese culture through child rearing. The Issei women were also workers. They worked for wages or shared labor on family farms. Two-income families found it easier to rent or purchase land.

By 1930, second-generation Japanese Americans constituted 52 percent of the continental U.S. population of their ethnic group. In the years preceding World War II, most Nisei were children and young people, attempting to adapt to their adopted country in spite of the troubled lives of their parents. For many young people the adaptation problem was made even more ambiguous because their parents, concerned that their children would not have a future in the U.S., registered their offspring as citizens of Japan. By 1940, over half of the Nisei held Japanese as well as American citizenship. Most of the Nisei did not want to remain on family farms or in the roadside vegetable business and with the strong encouragement of their parents obtained high school, and in many cases, university educations. Discrimination against Japanese Americans, coupled with the shortage of jobs during the Great Depression, thwarted many Nisei dreams.

The dual-career family seems to be the norm for Sansei households. Recently, spousal abuse has surfaced as an issue. If it was a problem in previous generations, it was not public knowledge. In San Francisco an Asian women's shelter has been established, largely by third-generation Asian women.

In Japanese tradition, a crane represents 1,000 years. On special birthdays 1,000 hand-folded red *origami* cranes are displayed to convey wishes for a long life. Certain birthdays are of greater impor-

tance because they are thought to be auspicious or calamitous years in a person's life. For men, the forty-second birthday is considered the most calamitous. For women it is the thirty-third year. Especially festive celebrations are held on these birthdays to ward off misfortune. The sixty-first birthday is the beginning of the auspicious years and the beginning of a person's second childhood. Traditionally, a person in his or her second childhood wears a crimson cap. The seventy-seventh birthday is marked by the wearing of a loose red coat (*chanchan ko*) over one's clothes. The most auspicious birthday is the eighty-eighth, when the honoree wears both the crimson cap and the *chanchan ko*.

At a wedding dinner, a whole red snapper is displayed at the head table. The fish represents happiness and must be served whole because cutting it would mean eliminating some happiness. Silver and golden wedding anniversaries are also occasions for festive celebrations.

RELIGION

While virtually all Issei came to the United States as Buddhists, Christian missionaries worked at converting the immigrants from the very beginning. The Methodists were particularly successful in this effort and records of the Pacific Japanese Provisional Conference of the Methodist Church indicate that three immigrants from Japan were converted in 1877, 11 years before Japan legally allowed citizens to emigrate. In the beginning the Japanese, even though they understood no Chinese, were segregat-

ed into Chinese churches. By the latter part of the nineteenth century and the early years of the twentieth century, separate Japanese Christian churches and missions were established in various California cities as well as in Tacoma, Washington, and Denver, Colorado. These early Japanese Christian organizations usually offered night English classes and social activities as well. While Methodism remained, other denominations such as Presbyterians, Baptists, Congregationalists, Episcopalians, and Catholics also claimed converts.

Organized Buddhism was somewhat slow in attempting to minister to the spiritual needs of Japanese Americans. The first record of Japanese Buddhist priests in the United States was in 1893 when four of them attended the World Parliament of Religions in Chicago. The priests had limited contact, however, with Japanese Americans. The success of one San Francisco Methodist minister, Yasuzo Shimizu, in winning converts stimulated a Japanese American to return to his native land and pressure priests of the Nishi Honganji sect of the Jodo Shinshu denomination to begin establishing Buddhist churches in the United States. The arrival in San Francisco of two Nishi Honganji priests, Shuyei Sonoda and Kukuryo Nishijima, on September 2, 1899, is regarded as the founding date for the Buddhist Churches of America. By the early years of the twentieth century, a number of Buddhist churches were founded on the West Coast. In the 1990s, Jodo Shinshu, organized as the Buddhist Churches of America with headquarters in San Francisco, is the dominant Buddhist denomination in the United States. However, Zen, Nichiren, and

Shingon sects of Buddhism are represented in various cities throughout the United States. While only a minuscule number of Japanese Americans practice Zen Buddhism, this particular sect has exercised a profound influence on many artists, musicians, philosophers, and writers who are members of the majority American population.

Because of cultural assimilation it is difficult to obtain statistics on the religious practices of Japanese Americans. However, followers of Christianity are probably more numerous than Buddhists.

EMPLOYMENT AND ECONOMIC TRADITIONS

The Issei, who came to the United States in the late 1800s and early twentieth century, worked on the West Coast as contract seasonal agricultural workers, on the railroad, and in canneries. For the most part, working conditions were abysmal; and because of racism and pressure by organized labor, Issei were barred from factory and office work. As a result many Japanese Americans created small businesses such as hotels and restaurants to serve their own ethnic group or became small vegetable farmers. The term "ethnic economy" is often used to describe the activities of pre-World War II Japanese Americans. While Japanese produce interests sold to the majority population from the beginning, the grower, wholesaler, and retailer networks were Issei. Issei were remarkably successful in both of these endeavors for several different reasons. Small businessmen, farmers, their families, and work associates toiled an incredible number of hours and saved much of what was earned. Also, the Issei community was well organized, and small businesses and farms could rely upon their tightly knit ethnic group for capital, labor, and business opportunities. Ethnic solidarity paid off economically for Japanese Americans. By the eve of World War II, 75 percent of Seattle's Japanese residents were involved in small business, and Japanese farmers were responsible for the production of the majority of vegetables in Los Angeles County.

Japanese economic success caused a substantial white backlash spearheaded by elements of the majority population who felt their livelihoods threatened. Unions were consistently anti-Japanese for a variety of reasons and California agricultural groups assumed leadership roles in the land limitation laws. The laws resulted, between 1920 and 1925, in the number of acres owned by Issei declining from 74,769 to 41,898 and the acreage leased plummeting from 192,150 to 76,797.

POST WORLD WAR II ECONOMIC CHANGES

No event in history has resulted in more economic change for Japanese Americans than World War II. Before the war Japanese Americans constituted mostly a self-contained ethnic economy. The internment of Japanese Americans and societal changes in attitudes toward Japanese destroyed much of the pre-war economic status quo. Since the war a minority of Japanese Americans have been employed in Japanese American-owned businesses. Many Japanese American farmers, because of the internment, either sold their land or never were able to lease their pre-war holdings again. As a result of the internment, Japanese Americans also sold or closed many family businesses. A comparison of pre-war and post-war economic statistics in Los Angeles and Seattle illustrates these major changes. Before World War II, Japanese Americans in Seattle operated 206 hotels, 140 grocery stores, 94 cleaning establishments, 64 market stands and 57 wholesale produce houses. After World War II, only a handful of these businesses remained. In Los Angeles, 72 percent of Japanese Americans were employed in family enterprises before World War II. By the late 1940s, only 17.5 percent of Japanese Americans earned their livelihood through family businesses.

While these economic changes were largely forced upon Japanese Americans because of the events surrounding the internment, other societal factors also contributed to the end of the Japanese American ethnic economy. The pre-war racial prejudice against Japanese Americans declined substantially in the late 1940s and 1950s. Japan no longer constituted a geo-political threat; many Americans were becoming more sympathetic about the issue of minority rights; and Japanese American West Coast agricultural interests no longer were seen as threatening by other Americans. As a result of these events, the large majority of Japanese Americans in the post-war years have experienced assimilation into the larger economy.

THE CONTEMPORARY ECONOMIC POSITION OF JAPANESE AMERICANS

Today, because of the changes in the post-war years, Japanese Americans are well-represented in both the professions and corporate economy. The pre-war discrimination against university-educated Japanese Americans is largely ended. Japanese Americans today have higher levels of education on average than the majority population and comparable to slightly higher incomes. Studies documenting the absence of Asian Americans from top corporate management and public sector administrative positions provide some evidence that there is some sort of "glass-ceiling" for Japanese Americans still present in the larger economy. Still, the economic position and socioeconomic mobility of Japanese Americans is much higher now than any time in American history.

POLITICS AND GOVERNMENT

LABOR MOVEMENTS

In February 1903, 500 Japanese and 200 Mexican farm workers in Oxnard, California, formed the Japanese Mexican Labor Association, the first farm workers union in California history. Led by Kozaburo Baba, the union called a strike for better wages and working conditions. By March 1903, membership had grown to 1,200 members, about 90 percent of the work force. On March 23 a Mexican striker was shot and killed and two Mexicans and two Japanese were wounded in a confrontation with the Western Agricultural Contracting Company, the major labor contractor. Negotiations led to a settlement by the end of March. Despite such effective organization and leadership, however, the American Federation of Labor denied the Japanese Mexican Labor Association a charter, due to its opposition to Asians.

In Hawaii there were 20 strikes by Japanese plantation workers in 1900 alone. In 1908 the Higher Wage Association asked for an increase from $18 to $22.50 per month. In May 1909, 7,000 Japanese workers struck all major plantations on Oahu. The strike lasted four months. The planters branded the strike as the work of agitators and evicted the strikers from plantation-owned homes. By June, over 5,000 displaced Japanese were living in makeshift shelters in downtown Honolulu. The leaders of the Higher Wage Association were arrested, jailed, and tried on conspiracy charges. The Association called off the strike about two weeks before their leadership was convicted.

In 1920 the Japanese Federation of Labor struck the Hawaiian plantations for higher wages, better working conditions, and an end to discriminatory wages based on race and ethnic background. The strike lasted six months and cost the plantation owners an estimated $11.5 million. The union saw their cause as part of the American way. Hawaii's ruling class—the plantation owners and their allies—called the strike anti-American and painted it as a movement to take control of the sugar industry. The planters evicted over 12,000 workers from their homes. Many deaths resulted from unsanitary conditions in the tent cities that arose.

WARTIME INTERNMENT OF JAPANESE AMERICANS

The great plantation strike of 1920 generated fears within the U.S. government that the labor movement in Hawaii was part of a Japanese plot to take over the territory. Japanese Americans accounted for about 40 percent of the Hawaiian population in the 1920s and 1930s. Beginning in the 1920s, the U.S. Army viewed the presence of Japanese in the Hawaiian Islands as a military threat. The army formulated plans for the declaration of martial law, registration of enemy aliens, internment of Japanese who were considered security risks, and controls over labor. On the afternoon of December 7, 1941, the United States declared martial law, suspension of *habeas corpus*, and restrictions on civil liberties, following the attack by the Japanese navy on U.S. naval and army bases at Pearl Harbor.

Immediately after the bombing of Pearl Harbor American officials in Hawaii began rounding up Japanese Americans. A concentration camp was established on Sand Island, a flat, barren, coral island at the mouth of Pearl Harbor. Terror and punishment were applied to the internees. Terror techniques included strip searches, frequent roll calls, threats to shoot, and excessive display of firepower by the guards who were armed with machine guns and pistols. The prisoners were often forced to eat in the rain, use dirty utensils, and sleep in tents. Ultimately, the army held 1,466 Japanese Americans in Hawaii and sent 1,875 to mainland camps such as Fort Lincoln (North Dakota), Fort Missoula (Montana), Santa Fe (New Mexico), and Crystal City (Texas).

General Delos Emmons, military governor of Hawaii, recognized that Japanese American labor was essential to the territory's economic survival. Therefore, he resisted pressure from Washington to intern more Japanese Americans. Those Japanese Americans in Hawaii who were not interned were required to carry alien registration cards at all times. They were to observe a curfew that applied only to them and were forbidden to write or publish attacks or threats against the U.S. government.

On the U. S. mainland, Japanese Americans were not considered essential to the economy or the war effort. On February 19, 1942, President Franklin D. Roosevelt signed Executive Order 9066 authorizing the army to designate military areas from which "any or all persons may be excluded" and to provide transportation, food, and shelter for persons so excluded. Lt. General John L. DeWitt, commander of the Western Defense Command, issued proclamations dividing Washington, Oregon, California, and Arizona into military areas from which enemy aliens and all Japanese Americans would be excluded.

These proclamations also laid down a curfew between 8:00 p.m. and 6:00 a.m. for enemy aliens and all Japanese, aliens and citizens alike.

RESPONSES TO THE INTERNMENT

While some in the majority population objected to the oppressive treatment of loyal American residents and citizens, most Americans either approved or were neutral about the actions of our government. Wartime American propaganda about the Japanese reflected long-held racist attitudes of many Americans. While cartoonists depicted Germans as buffoons, Japanese were typically caricatured as apes or monkeys.

On December 7, 1941, there were about 1,500 Nisei recruits in U.S. Army units in Hawaii. On December 10 the army disarmed them and confined them to quarters under armed guard. Two days later they were re-armed and placed on beach patrol. On June 5, 1942, after rounding them up and disarming them again, the army organized 1,432 Japanese American soldiers into the Hawaiian Provisional Battalion and shipped them to Camp McCoy, Wisconsin. There, they trained for seven months, initially with wooden guns. The Nisei from Hawaii were joined by other Japanese American soldiers, mostly volunteers and draftees from mainland concentration camps, to form the segregated 100th Infantry Battalion and the 442nd Regimental Combat Team. Many Nisei argued that serving the United States in war against Japan and her Axis allies would prove their loyalty and worth as citizens and overcome the discrimination from which they suffered. In all, about 33,000 Japanese Americans served the United States's cause in World War II.

Other patriotic Japanese Americans saw the situation differently. In 1943, about 200 Nisei at the Heart Mountain concentration camp in Wyoming formed the Fair Play Committee (FPC) to resist conscription into the armed services. The FPC published a manifesto that read in part, "We, the Nisei, have been complacent and too inarticulate to the unconstitutional acts that we were subjected to. If ever there was a time or cause for decisive action, IT IS NOW!" The Fair Play Committee protested denial of their rights as citizens without due process, without any charges being filed against them, and without any evidence of wrongdoing on their part. In June 1944, at the end of the largest draft resistance trial in U.S. history, 63 Nisei resisters were sentenced to three years in prison. On Christmas Eve 1947, President Harry S Truman pardoned them.

From the beginning, Japanese Americans sought to right the wrong of interning up to 120,000 innocent civilians. Mitsuye Endo agreed to serve as the test case against the internment program in 1942. On December 18, 1944, the U.S. Supreme Court unanimously declared the detention of Japanese Americans unconstitutional and ordered Endo's immediate release. One day before the ruling, and in anticipation of it, the Western Defense Command of the U.S. Army announced the termination of its exclusion of loyal Japanese Americans from the West Coast, effective January 2, 1945.

After the war, many Japanese Americans returned home from the camps or the armed services and went to work to secure their rights and redress the wrongs committed against them. In Hawaii, Daniel K. Inouye, a decorated veteran, entered politics. He served in the U.S. House of Representatives from 1959 to 1962. He was elected to the U.S. Senate in 1962. Along with three other Japanese American legislators (Senator Spark M. Matsunaga of Hawaii and Representatives Norman Y. Mineta and Robert T. Matsui of California), Inouye sponsored a bill to apologize for the wartime internment and offer cash payments of $20,000 (tax-free) to each of the 60,000 victims still living. Congress enacted the bill in 1988, but because Congress failed to appropriate the necessary funds, a second bill had to be passed in 1989 to assure the payments.

INDIVIDUAL AND GROUP CONTRIBUTIONS

ACADEMIA

Harry H. L. Kitano (1926–), a native of San Francisco, is a professor of sociology at UCLA, where he holds an endowed chair in Japanese American studies.

ARCHITECTURE

Minoru Yamasaki (1912-1986) designed the World Trade Center in New York City. Its twin towers, erected in 1970-1977, rise 110 stories high.

ART

Perhaps the most famous Japanese American sculptor was Isamu Noguchi. His work extended beyond sculptures to include important architectural projects and stage designs, including designs for the Martha Graham Dance Company.

Ruth Asawa (1926–) is a Nisei artist known for her wire mesh sculptures and bronzed "baker's clay" sculptures. She is co-founder of the School of the Arts Foundation in San Francisco.

Isami Doi (1903-1965) exhibited his art works widely. Born and reared in Hawaii, he studied art at the University of Hawaii, Columbia University, and in Paris.

Toyo Miyatake (1895-1979) was a noted photographic artist and a leader in the Los Angeles Little Tokyo Community. During World War II, he and his family were interned at Manzanar, California, where he was allowed to take photographs documenting life in the camp. After the war he reopened his studio.

FILM, MUSIC, AND ENTERTAINMENT

Philip Kan Gotanda (1949–), a playwright, musician, and director, is best known for musicals and plays about the Japanese American experience and family life. His plays include *The Avocado Kid, The Wash, A Song for a Nisei Fisherman, Bullet Headed Birds, The Dream of Kitamura, Yohen, Yankee Dawg You Die,* and *American Tatoo.*

Sessue Hayakawa (1890-1973) was a leading figure in silent films. After an absence of many years, he returned to Hollywood filmmaking in the 1950s and won an Academy Award for his portrayal of Colonel Saito in *The Bridge on the River Kwai.*

Hiroshima is a Sansei pop music group which blends traditional Japanese instruments into jazz.

Makoto (Mako) Iwamatsu (1933–) was the founding artistic director of the East West Players, an Asian American theater company in Los Angeles. He was nominated for an Academy Award for his supporting role as a Chinese coolie in *The Sand Pebbles.*

Nobu McCarthy (1938–) was a Hollywood star in the 1950s and is currently artistic director of the East West Players in Los Angeles. Her early film roles were mostly stereotypical (geisha girls and "lotus blossoms"). In the 1970s and 1980s, she appeared in more rounded roles in *Farewell to Manzanar, The Karate Kid, Part II,* and *The Wash.*

Midori (1971–) is a celebrated violinist who has performed with many of the world's great orchestras.

Noriyuki "Pat" Morita (1932–) became a major television and film actor in the 1980s. In 1984 he starred as Miyagi, a kind-hearted karate instructor, in *The Karate Kid,* and was nominated for an Academy Award for best supporting actor.

Sono Osato (1919-) is an important dancer who worked with Diaghilev, the Ballet Russe, Balanchine, Tutor, Fokine, Massine, the American Ballet Theatre, and performed in the original production of the Jerome Robbins/Leonard Bernstein *On The Town.*

Seiji Ozawa (1935–), conductor, became music director of the San Francisco Symphony Orchestra in 1970 and the Boston Symphony Orchestra in 1973.

Pat Suzuki (c. 1930–), singer and actress, was the first Nisei to star in a Broadway musical, Rodgers and Hammerstein's *Flower Drum Song,* in 1958.

Miyoshi Umeki (1929–) received an Academy Award as best supporting actress in 1957 for her role in *Sayonara*.

GOVERNMENT

John Fujio Aiso (1909-1987) was director of the Military Intelligence Service Language School which trained about 6,000 persons in Japanese for intelligence work during World War II. In 1953 he became the first Japanese American judge.

George Ryoichi Ariyoshi (1926–) served as governor of Hawaii from 1973 to 1986. He was the first Japanese American lieutenant governor and governor in U.S. history.

S. I. Hayakawa (1906-1992), a professor of English, gained national attention for his strong stand against dissident students during his tenure as president of San Francisco State College (1968-1973). He served as a Republican U.S. Senator from California from 1977 to 1983.

Daniel K. Inouye (1924–) of Hawaii was the first Nisei elected to the U.S. Congress. A Democrat, he served in the House of Representatives from 1959 to 1962. He was elected to the U.S. Senate in 1962. He was a decorated veteran of the 442nd Regimental Combat Team during World War II.

Clarence Takeya Arai (1901-1964), a Seattle lawyer, was a key figure in the founding of the Japanese American Citizens League. He was active in Republican politics in the state of Washington in the 1930s. He and his family were sent to the relocation camp at Minidoka, Idaho, during World War II.

JOURNALISM

James Hattori is a television correspondent for CBS News.

Harvey Saburo Hayashi (1866-1943) was both a physician and newspaper editor for the rural Japanese American community of Holualoa in Kona, Hawaii. He founded the *Kona Hankyo* in 1897. The newspaper was published for the next 40 years and reached a circulation of 500 at its peak.

William K. "Bill" Hosokawa (1915–) has served as a writer and editor for the *Denver Post*. He is the principal historian for the Japanese American Citizens League. During his wartime internment at Heart Mountain, Wyoming, he edited the *Heart Mountain Sentinel*.

Ken Kashiwahara (1940–) is a television correspondent for ABC News and one of the first Asian American journalists to work in network television.

James Yoshinori Sakamoto (1903-1955) began the first Nisei newspaper, the *American Courier*, in 1928. He was a strong supporter of the Japanese American Citizens League from its beginning and served as its national president from 1936 to 1938.

LAW

Lance A. Ito (1950–), Los Angeles County superior court judge, is a highly respected jurist who gained national prominence as the judge in the O. J. Simpson murder trial.

LITERATURE

Velina Hasu Houston (1957–) is known for her plays and poetry reflecting on the experiences of Japanese American women and her own experience as a multiracial Asian woman. Her plays include *Asa Ga Kimashita*, *American Dreams*, *Tea*, and *Thirst*.

Jun Atushi Iwamatsu (1908–) is best known as author and illustrator of children's books. He has been runner-up for the Caldecott Medal for *Crow Boy* (1956), *Umbrella* (1959), and *Seashore Story* (1968). He has held several one-man exhibitions of his paintings.

Tooru J. Kanagawa (1906–), a journalist and decorated veteran of the 442nd Regimental Combat Team, published his first novel at the age of 83. His novel, *Sushi and Sourdough*, is based on his youth in Juneau, Alaska.

Toshio Mori (1910-1980) chronicled the lives of Japanese Americans in numerous short stories and six novels. Most of his writings, however, remain unpublished.

SCIENCE

Leo Esaki (1925–) is a Nobel Prize-winning physicist who invented the tunnel diode while working for the Sony Corporation in Japan. In 1960, Esaki immigrated to the United States to work at IBM's Watson Research Center in Yorktown Heights, New York.

Makio Murayama (1912–), a biochemist, received the 1969 Association for Sickle Cell Anemia award and the 1972 Martin Luther King, Jr. medical achievement award for his research in sickle cell anemia.

Hideyo Noguchi (1876-1928), a microbiologist, devoted his life to fighting diseases such as bubonic plague, syphilis, Rocky Mountain spotted fever, and yellow fever.

Jokichi Takamine (1854-1922) was a chemist who developed a starch-digesting enzyme (*Takadiastase*), which was useful in medicines. In 1901 he isolated adrenaline from the supradrenal gland and was the first scientist to discover gland hormones in pure form.

SPORTS

Masao Kida (1968–), a major league baseball player for the Detroit Tigers, Kida is a pitcher and was born in Tokyo.

Hideo Nomo (1968–), a major league baseball player for the Milwaukee Brewers, Nomo was born in Kobe, Japan.

Kristi Yamaguchi (1971–), a figure skater, won the women's gold medal in figure skating at the 1993 Winter Olympics in Albertville, France.

MEDIA

PRINT

Chicago Shimpo.
Bi-lingual newspaper. The only Japanese publication in the Midwest.

Contact: Akiko Sugano, Editors.
Address: 4670 North Manor Avenue, Chicago, Illinois 60625.
Telephone: (773) 478-6170.
Fax: (773) 478-9360.

The Hawaii Hoichi.
A bilingual publication intended to keep non-English fluent Japanese Americans informed about the United States.

Contact: Mr. Mamoru Tanji.
Address: 917 Kokea Street, Honolulu, Hawaii 96817-4528.
Telephone: (808) 845-2255.
Fax: (808) 847-7215.

Hokubei Mainichi.
A bilingual publication. Covers Japanese politics as well as national news. Receives strong support from local Japanese American organizations.

Contact: Ms. Atsuko Saito.
Address: 1746 Post Street, San Francisco, California 94115.
Telephone: (415) 567-7323.
Fax: (415) 567-1110.

Nichi Bei Times.
A bilingual publication geared toward both visitors from Japan and Japanese Americans. Covers world, national, local, and lifestyle news.

Contact: Ms. Keiko Asano.
Address: 2211 Bush Street, San Francisco, California 94115.
Telephone: (415) 921-6820.
Fax: (415)-921-0770.

Rafu Shimpo.
A bilingual publication. Main source of Japanese American news in Southern California.

Contact: Ted Ubukata.
Address: 259 South Los Angeles Street, Los Angeles, California 90012.
Telephone: (213) 629-2231.
Fax: (213) 687-0737.

RADIO

KALI-FM (106.3).
Japanese language news broadcast weekdays from 7 to 9 AM. Affiliated with *Bridge, U.S.A.* magazine.

Contact: Mr. Ono.
Address: 20300 South Vermont Avenue, Suite 200, Torrance, California 90502.
Telephone: (310) 532-5921.
Fax: (310) 532-1184.

KJPN.
Japanese language news broadcast daily.

Contact: Ms. Ikuko Tomita.
Address: 711 Kapiolani Boulevard, Honolulu, Hawaii 96813.
Telephone: (808) 593-1950.
Fax: (808) 593-8040.

KZOO-AM (1210).
Largest exclusively Japanese broadcast in the United States.

Contact: David Furuya.
Address: 250 Ward Avenue, Suite 209, Honolulu, Hawaii 96814.
Telephone: (808) 593-2880.
Fax: (808) 596-0083.

TELEVISION

The following television stations offer programming in Japanese language: KDOC-TV, Anaheim, California; KTSF (Channel 26), Brisbane, California;

KHNL, Hilo, Hawaii; KSCI (Channel 18), Pasadena, California; WMBC (Channel 63), New York City, New York; and WNYE (Channel 25), New York City, New York.

ORGANIZATIONS AND ASSOCIATIONS

Japan-America Society of Washington (JASW).
Contact: Patricia R. Kearns, Executive Director.
Address: 1800 Ninth Avenue, Suite 1550, Seattle, Washington 98101-1322.
Telephone: (206) 623-7900.
Fax: (206) 343-7930.
E-Mail: admin@us-japan.org.
Online: http://www.us-japan.org.

Japanese American Citizens League (JACL).
Educational, civil, and human rights organization founded in 1929 with 115 chapters and 25,000 members.
Contact: Herbert Yamanishi, National Director.
Address: 1765 Sutter Street, San Francisco, California 94115.
Telephone: (415) 921-5225.
Fax: (415) 931-4671.
E-mail: jacl@jacl.org.

Japan Hour Broadcasting.
Founded in 1974, it produces radio and television programs in Japanese for Japanese residents in the United States, and English language programs on Japan to promote American understanding of Japan and U.S.-Japanese relations.
Contact: Raymond Otami, Executive Director.
Address: 151-23 34th Avenue, Flushing, New York 11354.

Japan Society (JS).
Organization for individuals, institutions, and corporations representing the business, professional, and academic worlds in Japan and the United States; promotes exchange of ideas to enhance mutual understanding.
Contact: William Clark, Jr., President.
Address: 333 East 47th Street, New York, New York 10017.
Telephone: (212) 832-1155.
Fax: (212) 755-6752.
E-mail: gen@jpnsoc.com.
Online: http://www.jpnsoc.com.

Nippon Club.
Organization for persons who take special interest in Japanese affairs.
Contact: Tsutomu Karino, Executive Director.
Address: 145 West 57th Street, New York, New York 10019.
Telephone: (212) 581-2223.
Fax: (212) 581-3332.

MUSEUMS AND RESEARCH CENTERS

Japanese American Cultural and Community Center.
A performing and visual arts center founded in 1980.
Address: 244 South San Pedro, Suite 505, Los Angeles, California 90012.
Telephone: (213) 628-2725.
Fax: (213) 617-8576.
E-mail: jaccc@ltsc.org.
Online: http://www.jaccc.org/.

Japanese American Curriculum Project.
Address: 234 Main Street, P.O. Box 1587, San Mateo, California 94401.
Telephone: (800) 874-2242.

Japanese American National Museum.
The first national museum dedicated to preserving and sharing the history of Japanese Americans.
Address: 369 East First Street, Los Angeles, California 90012.
Telephone: (800) 461-5266; or (213) 625-0414.
Fax: (213) 625-1770.
Online: http://www.lausd.k12.ca.us/janm/main.htm.

Japanese American Society for Legal Studies.
Contact: Professor Daniel H. Foote.
Address: University of Washington Law School, 1100 Northeast Campus Parkway, Seattle, Washington 98105.
Telephone: (206) 685-1897.
Fax: (206) 685-4469.
E-mail: wjackson@u.washington.edu.

U.S.-Japan Culture Center (USJCC).
Seeks to promote mutual understanding between the United States and Japan; to help the public, scholars, government officials, and businesspersons

of both countries increase their knowledge of U.S.-Japan relations.

Contact: Mikio Kanda, Executive Director.
Address: 2600 Virginia Avenue, N.W., Suite 512, Washington, D.C. 20037.
Telephone: (202) 342-5800.
Fax: (202) 342-5803.
E-mail: info@usjpcc.com.
Online: http://www.usjpcc.com/.

SOURCES FOR ADDITIONAL STUDY

Ellington, Lucien. *Japan: Tradition and Change*. White Plains, New York: Longman, 1990.

Hosokawa, Bill. *Nisei: The Quiet Americans*. New York: William Morrow, Inc., 1969.

Japan: An Illustrated Encyclopedia. Tokyo, Japan: Kodansha, 1993.

Japanese American History: An A to Z Reference from 1868 to the Present. New York: Facts on File, 1993.

Kitano, Henry E. *Japanese Americans: The Evolution of a Subculture*. Englewood Cliffs, New Jersey: Prentice-Hall, 1969.

———. *Generations and Identity: The Japanese American*. Needham Heights, MA: Ginn Press, 1993.

Lyman, Stanford M. *Chinatown and Little Tokyo: Power, Conflict, and Community Among Chinese and Japanese Immigrants in America*. Millwood, New York: Associated Faculty Press, 1986.

Montero, Darrel. *Japanese Americans: Changing Patterns of Ethnic Affiliation Over Three Generations*. Boulder, Colorado: Westview Press, 1980.

Nakano, Mei T. *Japanese American Women: Three Generations 1890-1990*. Berkeley, California: Mina Press, 1990.

Takahashi, Jere. *Nisei/Sansei: Shifting Japanese American Identities and Politics*. Philadelphia: Temple University Press, 1997.

Takaki, Ronald. *Strangers from a Different Shore: A History of Asian Americans*. Boston: Little, Brown and Company, 1989.

JEWISH AMERICANS

by
Jim Kamp

OVERVIEW

Jews represent a group of people rather than a distinct race or ethnicity. Although Jews originally came from the Middle East, many races and peoples have mixed together in Jewish communities over the centuries, especially after the Jews were forced out of Palestine in the second century C.E. What binds the group together is a common Jewish heritage as passed down from generation to generation. For many Jews, the binding force is Judaism, a term usually referring to the Jewish religion but sometimes used to refer to all Jews. There are, however, Jewish atheists and agnostics, and one does not have to be religious to be Jewish. In general, one is Jewish if born of a Jewish mother or if he or she converts to Judaism.

Most Jews consider the State of Israel the Jewish homeland. Located in the Middle East with a land mass of 7,992 square miles, Israel is only slighter larger than New Jersey. It is bounded by Lebanon in the north, by Syria and Jordan in the east, by Egypt in the southwest, and by the Mediterranean Sea in the west. With a population of approximately 4.2 million Jews, Israel is home to about one-third of the world Jewry, estimated at 12.9 million at the end of 1992. However, not all Jews consider Israel home. Some feel the United States, with 5.8 million Jews, is the de facto home of Jews, evidenced in part by the fact that Israel is sometimes called "Little America" because of its similarities to the United States. Accounting for more than three-fourths of the world Jewry, Israel and the United States represent the two major Jewish population regions.

Although Jews comprise less than three percent of the American population, Jews have generally had a disproportionately larger representation in American government, business, academia, and entertainment. American Jews have suffered their share of setbacks and have had to combat anti-Semitism during the early twentieth century. On the whole, however, Jews have enjoyed greater acceptance in America than in any other country and have figured prominently in American culture and politics.

HISTORY

Jewish history dates back 4,000 years to the time of Abraham, the biblical figure credited for introducing the belief in a single God. Abraham's monotheism not only marked the beginning of Judaism, but of Christianity and Islam as well. Following God's instructions, Abraham led his family out of Mesopotamia to Canaan, later renamed Palestine, then Israel. Abraham and his descendants were called Hebrews. ("Hebrew" is derived from "Eber," which means "from the other side." This is a reference to the fact that Abraham came from the "other side" of the Euphrates River.) According to the Bible, God made a covenant with Abraham promising that if the Hebrews followed God's commandments, they would become a great nation in the land of Canaan. Subsequently, Hebrews referred to themselves as "God's chosen people."

After Abraham, the Hebrews were led by Abraham's son Isaac, then by Isaac's son Jacob. Jacob, also known as "Israel" ("Champion of God"), was the father of 12 sons, who became leaders of the 12 tribes of Israel. For hundreds of years these tribes lived in Canaan and comprised all of Hebrew civilization. By about 1700 B.C.E., food shortages compelled the Hebrews to leave Canaan for Egypt, where they were social outcasts and were eventually forced into slavery by pharaoh Ramses II around 1280 B.C.E. From these bleak conditions emerged perhaps the greatest leader of the Jews, Moses. In about 1225 B.C.E., Moses led the Hebrews out of Egypt (the Exodus) into the Sinai Desert, where Moses is said to have received the Ten Commandments from God on Mount Sinai. For 40 years the Israelites lived in the desert, obeying God's commandments.

After Moses, Joshua led the Israelites back into Canaan, now called Palestine, representing the "Promised Land." There the people were ruled by benevolent Judges and later by Kings until social tensions after the death of King Solomon caused the Israelites to break apart. Ten tribes organized into the northern kingdom of Israel, while the other two tribes formed the southern kingdom of Judah. The people of Israel, however, lost much of their Hebrew identity after the Assyrians invaded the northern kingdom in 721 B.C.E. By contrast, when the people of Judah, or Jews, were captured by Babylonians in 586 B.C.E., these Jews remained faithful to their traditions and to the Ten Commandments. Fifty years later Jews returned to Palestine after the Persians defeated the Babylonians.

For centuries Jewish culture thrived in Palestine until the Roman occupation beginning in 63 B.C.E. For more than 100 years Jews endured life with the oppressive, violent Romans. By 70 C.E., when the Romans destroyed the Jewish Temple in Jerusalem, Jews had begun migrating to the outer regions of the Roman Empire, including the Near East, North Africa, and southwestern, central, and eastern Europe. In 135 C.E. the Romans officially banned Judaism, which marked the beginning of the diaspora, or the dispersal of Jews. Forced out of Palestine, Jews in exile concentrated less on establishing a unified homeland and more on maintaining Judaism through biblical scholarship and community life.

EUROPEAN LIFE

European Jews are divided mainly between the Jews of Spain and Portugal, the Sephardim, and the Jews from German-speaking countries in central and eastern Europe, the Ashkenazim. The distinction between the Sephardim and Ashkenazim—Hebrew terms for Spanish and German Jews—continues to be the major classification of Jews, with 75 percent of today's world Jewry being Ashkenazic. In medieval Europe, Sephardic Jews enjoyed the most freedom and cultural acceptance. Between the ninth and fifteenth centuries Sephardic Jews made significant cultural and literary contributions to Spain while it was under Islamic rule. By contrast, Ashkenazic Jews in the north lived uneasily among Christians, who saw Jews as "Christ killers" and who resented Jews for thinking of themselves as a chosen people. Christians subjected Jews to violence and destroyed Jewish communities beginning with the First Crusade in 1096. Jewish populations were driven from England and France in the thirteenth and fourteenth centuries. By the beginning of the Spanish Inquisition in 1492, Jews from Spain faced similar oppression, violence, and expulsion from Spanish Christians. As a result, Sephardic Jews spread out to Mediterranean countries, while the majority of Ashkenazic Jews moved east to Poland, which became the center of European Jewry.

In Poland, Jews were permitted to create a series of councils and courts that together represented a minority self-government within the country. In individual Jewish communities, the *kehillah* was the governing structure comprised of elected leaders who oversaw volunteer organizations involved in all aspects of social and religious life in the community. The disintegration of the Polish state in the eighteenth century, however, disrupted community life and caused many to emigrate. By the nineteenth century, Jews in eastern Europe were primarily split between Prussia, Austria, and Russia. The governments in these countries, however, oppressed Jews through military conscription, taxation, and expulsion. Though relatively impoverished, the four million Jews in the Pale of Settlement (a region encompassing eastern Poland and western Russia) maintained their Jewish traditions through close community life.

By contrast, Jews in Western Europe fared much better economically and socially as they gained acceptance in England, France, and Austria-Hungary after the Protestant Reformation. Northern European cities with large Protestant populations such as London, Hamburg, and Amsterdam increasingly opened their doors to Jews. In order to fully assimilate and become citizens, these Jews sometimes had to renounce Jewish laws, self-government, and the quest for nationhood. Still, many Jews were eager to comply, some even becoming Christians. As a result, many western European Jews attained significant wealth and status, generally through banking and trade. In addition to material prosperity, German Jews also enjoyed a period of heightened cultural activity during the Jewish Enlightenment of the eighteenth and early nineteenth centuries, a period marked by free inquiry and increased political activism. Political turmoil by the mid-nineteenth century, however, brought upheaval to Jewish communities, prompting many to emigrate.

IMMIGRATION WAVES

The first Jewish immigrants to settle in the United States were 23 Sephardic Jews who arrived in New Amsterdam (later known as New York) in 1654. Although this group of men, women, and children from Dutch Brazil initially faced resistance from Governor Peter Stuyvesant, they were allowed to settle after Jews in Amsterdam applied pressure on the Dutch West India Company, Stuyvesant's employer. In addition to Spain, Sephardic Jews came from various Mediterranean countries as well as from England, Holland, and the Balkans. The number of Jews in Colonial America grew slowly but steadily so that by 1776 there were approximately 2,500 Jews in America.

The wave of German Jewish immigrants during the mid-nineteenth century represented the first major Jewish population explosion in America. While there were just 6,000 Jews in the United States in 1826, the number of American Jews climbed above 50,000 by 1850 and rose to 150,000 only a decade later. The German Jews actually came from Germany and various other central European countries, including Bavaria, Bohemia, Moravia, and western Poland. Challenges to the monarchies of central Europe in the 1840s caused considerable social unrest, particularly in rural villages. While wealthy Jews could afford to escape the turbulence by moving to cities such as Vienna or Berlin, poorer Jews could not. Consequently, many chose to immigrate to America.

The largest wave of Jewish immigrants were eastern European Jews who came to America between 1881 and 1924. During these years one third of the Jewish population in eastern Europe emigrated because of changing political and economic conditions. The assassination of Russian Tsar Alexander II in 1881 ushered in a new era of violence and anti-Jewish sentiment. Pogroms, or massacres, by the Slavs against the Jews had occurred since the mid-seventeenth century, but the pogroms of 1881 and 1882 were particularly numerous and intense, wiping out entire villages and killing hundreds of Jews. Also, industrialization made it difficult for Jewish peddlers, merchants, and artisans to sustain themselves economically. As a result, a mass exodus of Jews from eastern Europe occurred, with approximately 90 percent bound for America. During the late nineteenth and early twentieth centuries, tens and sometimes hundreds of thousands of Jews arrived in America annually. The immigration of some 2.4 million eastern European Jews boosted the American Jewish population from roughly a quarter million in 1881 to 4.5 million by 1924.

The Immigration Restriction Act of 1924 decreased the annual Jewish immigration from more than 100,000 to about 10,000. Subsequently, U.S. immigration policy remained strict, even during World War II when the need to emigrate was a matter of life and death for German Jews. The 150,000 Jews who managed to immigrate to America between 1935 and 1941 were primarily middle-class, middle-aged professionals and businessmen. These refugees from Nazi Germany represented a different type of immigrant from the young, working-class Jews who emigrated from eastern Europe at the turn of the century. After a period of increased immigration during and immediately following World War II (within the quotas set by Congress), Jewish immigration leveled off for several decades. The most recent immigration wave occurred during the 1980s, when political and economic changes in the Soviet Union prompted hundreds of thousands of Soviet Jews to come to Israel and America. The American quotas by this time had risen to 40,000 Jews per year. This immigration wave of Soviet Jews has been the largest since the immigration of Russian Jews at the beginning of the twentieth century.

Jewish population in relation to the general U.S. population peaked in 1937 at 3.7 percent. Limits on immigration and a Jewish birthrate of less than two children per family—lower than the national average—have lowered the Jewish proportion of the American population to under three percent. This proportion has remained relatively stable, even as the American Jewish population approached six million in the 1990s.

SETTLEMENT PATTERNS

The Sephardic Jews who settled in the American colonies established themselves in cities along the eastern seaboard. From the mid-seventeenth to the mid-eighteenth centuries, the largest Jewish population centers were in New York, Newport, Savannah, Philadelphia, and Charleston, the only cities with synagogues during the period. Jewish businessmen from these cities were supported by influential businessmen from Sephardic communities in London and Amsterdam.

The influx of German Jews in the nineteenth century contributed to the westward expansion of the Jewish population in the United States. By the mid-nineteenth century, there were approximately 160 Jewish communities from New York to California, with Jewish population centers in the major hubs along the trade routes from east to west. Cities such as Cleveland, Chicago, Cincinnati, and St. Louis all became centers of Jewish business, cultural, and religious life. Jewish peddlers and retailers also followed the economic growth of the cotton industry in the South and the discovery of gold in the West. Most of the Jewish immigrants from this period were young, single Germans hoping to escape unfavorable economic conditions and repressive legislation that restricted marriage. Individuals from the same community would typically immigrate together and continue their congregation in the New World.

The wave of eastern European Jews at the turn of the century gravitated toward big cities in the East and Midwest. The result was that by 1920 Jews had their greatest population centers in New York, Newark, Cleveland, Philadelphia, Boston, Baltimore, Pittsburgh, Chicago, St. Louis, and Detroit. Within these cities, eastern European Jews established their own communities and maintained their cultural heritage and identity much more so than nineteenth-century German Jews, who were eager to assimilate into American culture.

Jewish settlement trends in the twentieth century have shown population decreases in the midwest and increases in cities such as Los Angeles and Miami. During the 1930s and 1940s, refugees from Nazi Germany predominantly settled in Manhattan's West Side and Washington Heights as well as in Chicago and San Francisco. After World War II the population of American Jews decreased in midwestern cities such as Chicago, Detroit, and Cleveland and increased in Los Angeles, Miami, and Washington, D.C. For each major city with a significant Jewish population, there has been a steady postwar trend of outward movement toward the suburbs. The young and middle-aged professionals have led this movement, while working-class, Orthodox, and older Jews continue to inhabit the old neighborhoods closer to the city.

By the end of 1992, the largest Jewish population centers were in New York City (1.45 million), Los Angeles (490,000), Chicago (261,000), Philadelphia (250,000), Boston (228,000), San Francisco Bay Area (210,000), Miami (189,000), and Washington, D.C. (165,000).

ACCULTURATION AND ASSIMILATION

Until the late nineteenth century, Jewish settlers desired and found it relatively easy to assimilate into American society. Jews had left Europe because of poor social and economic conditions and were eager to establish themselves in an open, expanding society. Occasionally, Jews would have to combat anti-Semitism and negative stereotypes of "dirty Jews," but for the most part Americans appreciated the goods and services provided by Jewish merchants. The religious freedom guaranteed by the U.S. Constitution coupled with the increasing prosperity of nineteenth-century German Jews enabled Jews to enjoy considerable acceptance in American society.

The basic division between Jews during the nineteenth century was between Polish and German congregations. However, in large population centers such as New York, subgroups emerged to accommodate the local traditions of various Dutch,

U. S. Senator
Alfonse D'Amato
(left center),
comedian Jackie
Mason (center),
and others
celebrate the
annual Salute to
Israel Parade in
New York City.

Bavarian, English, or Bohemian Jews. The desire to assimilate to American culture was felt in the larger synagogues, where decorations were added and sermons were changed from German to English or abandoned altogether.

Beginning in 1881, the immigration of eastern European Jews marked the first significant resistance to acculturation. These immigrants tended to be poor, and they settled in tight-knit communities where they retained the traditions and customs from the old world. They consciously avoided assimilation into American culture and continued to speak Yiddish, a mixture of Hebrew and medieval German that further separated them from other Americans. Some American institutions applied pressure to assimilate into mainstream culture by banning the use of Yiddish in public programs. But the ban was removed by the beginning of the twentieth century as efforts to limit Americanization became more popular. Increasingly, rapid assimilation into American culture was viewed as unnecessary and harmful to Jewish identity. Still, a conflict remained between younger and older generation Jews over how much Americanization was desirable.

STEREOTYPES, ANTI-SEMITISM, AND DISCRIMINATION

The arrival of eastern European immigrants prompted the first significant tide of anti-Semitism in America. During the 1880s, clubs and resorts that once welcomed Jews began to exclude them. European anti-Semitism influenced a growing number of Americans to adopt various negative stereotypes of Jews as clannish, greedy, parasitic, vulgar, and physically inferior. To mitigate these sentiments, Americanized Jews developed aid societies to provide jobs and relief funds to help eastern European Jews fit into American society. In addition, American-born German Jews fought against restrictive legislation and formed philanthropic societies that funded schools, hospitals, and libraries for eastern European Jews. The hope was that if the hundreds of thousands of newly arriving Russian Jews had access to homes, jobs, and health care, the decreased burden on American public institutions would ease ethnic tensions.

Despite efforts by Americanized Jews to reduce ethnic hatred and stereotyping, discrimination against Jews continued into the twentieth century.

Housing restrictions and covenants against Jews became more common just prior to World War I. During the 1920s and 1930s, Jews faced significant difficulty obtaining employment in large corporations or in fields such as journalism. Jews were also increasingly subjected to restrictive quotas in higher education. In particular, Jewish enrollment dropped by as much as 50 percent at Ivy League schools such as Harvard and Yale during the 1920s. By the 1930s most private institutions had Jewish quota policies in place. In politics, one of the motivating forces behind the Immigration Restriction Act of 1924 was the negative image that some held of immigrant Russian Jews, who were thought to live a lowly, animal-like existence. This "dirty Jew" stereotype was based on a perception of ghetto Jews, who were forced to endure squalid living conditions out of economic necessity. Another stereotype was of the Jew as Communist sympathizer and revolutionary, a characterization stemming from the belief that Jews were responsible for the Russian Revolution. All of these negative stereotypes were reinforced in American literature of the 1920s and 1930s. Authors such as Thomas Wolf, F. Scott Fitzgerald, and Ernest Hemingway all depicted Jewish caricatures in their novels, while poets such as T.S. Eliot and Ezra Pound freely expressed their anti-Semitism.

Fueled by a Worldwide Depression and the rise of German Nazism, Jewish discrimination and anti-Semitism reached a peak during the 1930s. One of the more influential American voices of anti-Semitism was Roman Catholic priest Charles E. Coughlin, who argued that the Nazi attack on Jews was justified because of the communist tendencies of Jews. Coughlin blamed New York Jews for the hard economic times, a message intended to appeal to Coughlin's Detroit audience of industrial workers hurt by the Depression.

At the end of World War II, when the atrocities of the Nazi Holocaust became widely known, anti-Semitism in America diminished considerably. Though some Jews in academia lost appointments as a result of Communist fears instigated by Senator Joseph McCarthy, Jews generally enjoyed improved social conditions after 1945. Returning war veterans on the G.I. Bill created a demand for college professors that Jews helped fulfill, and entrance quotas restricting admission of Jewish students at universities were gradually abandoned. As discrimination waned, Jews enjoyed substantial representation in academia, business, entertainment, and such professions as finance, law, and medicine. In short, Jews during the postwar years resumed their positions as contributing and often leading members of American society.

TRADITIONS, CUSTOMS, AND BELIEFS

Immigrant Jews passed on Jewish traditions in the home, but subsequent generations have relied on religious schools to teach the traditions. These schools have helped Jewish parents accommodate their goal of having their children become familiar with Jewish tradition without interfering with their children's integration into American culture. Today, many Jewish children attend congregation school a few days a week for three to five years. During this time, they learn Hebrew and discover the essential traditions and customs of Jewish culture.

Jewish traditions and customs primarily derive from the practice of Judaism. The most important Jewish traditions stem from the *mitzvot*, which are the 613 holy obligations found in the Torah and Talmud. Consisting of 248 positive commandments (Thou shall's) and 365 negative commandments (Thou shall not's), these commandments fall into three categories: *Edot*, or "testimonies," are rules that help Jews bear witness to their faith (e.g., rules on what garments to wear); *Mishpatim* (judgments) are rules of behavior found in most religions (e.g., the rule against stealing); and *Hukim* (statutes) are divine rules that humans cannot fully understand (e.g., dietary rules). No one person can possibly fulfill all 613 *mitzvot* since they include laws for different people in different situations. Even the most Orthodox Jew in modern times is expected to observe less than half of the obligations.

The basic beliefs common to all Jews, except atheists and agnostics, were articulated by Moses Maimonides (1135-1204). Known as the Thirteen Principles of the Faith, they are: (1) God alone is the creator; (2) God is One; (3) God is without physical form; (4) God is eternal; (5) humans pray only to God; (6) the words of the prophets are true; (7) the greatest prophet was Moses; (8) today's Torah is the one God gave to Moses; (9) the Torah will not be replaced; (10) God knows people's thoughts; (11) the good are rewarded and the evil are punished; (12) the Messiah will come; and, (13) the dead will be revived. Although most of the Jewish faithful share these broad beliefs, there is no specific requirement to commit all 13 to memory.

CUISINE

There is no specific Jewish cuisine, only lists of permissible and impermissible foods for Orthodox Jews and others who observe *kashrut*. Delineated in the Book of Leviticus and dating back to 1200 B.C.E., *kashrut* is a system of food laws for eating *kosher* foods and avoiding *trefa* foods. *Kosher* foods are simply ones that are, by law, fit for Jews; they include

fruits, vegetables, grains, meat from cud-chewing mammals with split hooves (e.g., sheep, cows, goats), fish with scales and fins (e.g., salmon, herring, perch), domesticated birds (e.g., chicken, turkey, duck), and milk and eggs from kosher mammals and birds. *Trefa* foods are forbidden by Jewish law, simply because of biblical decree, not because such foods are unfit for human consumption; they include meat from unkosher mammals (e.g., pork, rabbit, horse), birds of prey (e.g., owls, eagles), and water animals that do not have both scales and fins (e.g., lobster, crab, squid). *Kashrut* also prescribes that the slaughter of animals shall be painless. Thus, a Jewish butcher (*shohet*) studies the anatomy of animals to learn the precise spot where killing may occur instantaneously. After the animal is killed, the blood must be completely drained and any diseased portions removed. Finally, kashrut involves keeping meat and milk separate. Because of the biblical commandment not to "stew a kid in its mother's milk," Jewish law has interpreted this to mean that meat and dairy products cannot be prepared or consumed together.

HOLIDAYS

Because there is a separate Jewish calendar based on the lunar cycle, Jewish holidays occur on different secular days every year. The first holiday of the Jewish year is the celebration of the new year, *Rosh Hashanah,* which occurs sometime in September or October. It is a ten-day period in which Jews reflect on their lives during the previous year. Three basic themes are associated with this holiday: the anniversary of the creation of the world; the day of judgment; and the renewal of the covenant between God and Israel. On the night before the beginning of *Rosh Hashanah,* one popular custom is to eat honey-dipped apples so that the new year will be a sweet one. *Yom Kippur,* the "Day of Atonement," occurs at the end of *Rosh Hashanah.* For 25 hours observant Jews fast while seeking forgiveness from God and from those against whom they have sinned. There are five services at the synagogue throughout the day, most centering on the themes of forgiveness and renewal.

In the winter, usually in December, Jews celebrate the festival of *Hanukkah.* This is a joyous eight-day period that marks the time when in 164 B.C.E. the Jews, led by Judah the Maccabee, successfully reclaimed the Temple in Jerusalem from the Syrians. When the Maccabbees prepared to light the perpetual flame in the Temple, they only found one jar of oil, enough for only one day. Miraculously, the oil lasted eight days until a new supply of oil arrived. Thus, the celebration of Hanukkah, also known as the Festival of Lights, involves lighting a candle for each night of the festival, one on the first night, two on the second, and so forth. Over time, Hanukkah has become a time of family celebration with games and presents for children.

Other holidays and festivals round out the Jewish year. In late winter Jews celebrate *Purim*, a period of great drinking and eating to commemorate the biblical time when God helped Esther save the Jews from the evil, tyrannical Haman, who wanted to destroy the Jews. In late March or early April, Jews participate in the week-long festival of Passover, which marks the Jewish Exodus from Egypt. The Passover Supper, or *Seder*, is the central feature of this celebration and is a gathering of family and friends (with room for the "unexpected guest") who eat a traditional meal of unleavened bread, parsley, apples, nuts, cinnamon, raisins, and wine. Seven weeks after Passover, *Shavout* is celebrated, marking the giving of the Torah by God and the season of wheat harvest. In autumn Jews celebrate *Sukkot*, an eight-day festival honoring the time when the Israelites spent 40 years in the desert after the Exodus and before returning to Palestine. Because the Israelites spent 40 years living in the wilderness, this holiday season is celebrated by living for eight days in a temporary home called a *sukkah*. Though a *sukkah* is small and typically does not protect well against the increasingly harsh fall weather, Jews are expected to be joyous and grateful for all that God has provided.

HEALTH ISSUES

Before coming to America, Jews living in small communities in Europe occasionally suffered from amaurotic idiocy, an inherited pathology attributed to inbreeding. During the early twentieth century, when the largest waves of Jewish immigrants arrived in America, Russian Jewish immigrants were afflicted with nervous disorders, suicides, and tuberculosis more often than other immigrants. Despite these afflictions, Jews had a lower death rate than other immigrants at the time. Recently, the National Foundation for Jewish Genetic Diseases published a list of the seven most common genetic diseases suffered by Jews:

Bloom Syndrome: a disease causing shortness in height (usually less than five feet), redness of skin, and susceptibility to respiratory tract and ear infections. Affected men often experience infertility and both sexes have an increased risk of cancer. Just over 100 cases have been reported since the disease was discovered in 1954, but one in 120 Jews are carriers and children from two carriers have a 25 percent chance of contracting the disease.

Familial Dysautonomia: a congenital disease of the nervous system resulting in stunted growth, increased tolerance of pain, and lack of tears. One in 50 Ashkenazi Jews in America carries the gene, and the risk of recurrence in affected families is 25 percent.

Gaucher Disease: a disease that in its mildest form—the form common to Jews—is characterized by easy bruising, orthopedic problems, anemia, and a variety of other symptoms. The more advanced forms of the disease are fatal but rare and not concentrated in any one ethnic group. One out of 25 Ashkenazi Jews carries the recessive gene, and one in 2,500 Jewish babies is afflicted.

Mucolipidosis IV: a recently discovered disease (1974) involving the deterioration of the central nervous system in babies who later develop mild or more severe retardation. Thus far only handful of cases have been reported, all by Ashkenazi Jews. The disease only occurs when both parents are carriers, with 25 percent of babies from such parents being affected.

Niemann-Pick Disease: a usually fatal disease characterized by a buildup of fatty materials causing enlargement of the spleen, emaciation, and degradation of the central nervous system. Afflicted babies typically die before the age of three, but survival into young adulthood is possible in milder cases. The disease affects about 25 Ashkenazi Jews each year in the United States.

Tay-Sachs Disease: a biochemical disorder causing retardation in babies as early as the fourth month and leading to a deterioration of the central nervous system that ends in death, usually between the ages of five and eight. Approximately one in 25 Jews is a carrier, with the risk that 25 percent of babies from two carriers will have Tay-Sachs. Screening techniques have enabled carriers to bring only normal babies to term.

Torsion Dystonia: a disease involving an increasing loss of motor control coupled with normal to superior intelligence affecting children between the ages of four and 16. One in 70 Ashkenazi Jews in America is a carrier, with one out of every 20,000 Jewish babies developing the disease.

LANGUAGE

One of the strongest unifying links between Jews throughout the world is the Hebrew language. From the time of Abraham in 2000 B.C.E. until the Babylonians captured Judah in 586 B.C.E., Hebrew was the everyday language of Jews. Since then, Jews have generally adopted the vernacular of the societies in which they have resided, including Arabic, German, Russian, and English. Hebrew continued to be spoken and read, but primarily in sacred contexts. Most of the Torah is written in Hebrew, and religious services are mostly in Hebrew, though Progressive synagogues will make greater use of the language of the community. The use of Hebrew in religious worship enables Jews from all parts of the world to enjoy a common bond. In the twentieth century, Hebrew regained its status as an everyday language in Israel, where it is the official language.

During the diaspora, as Jews left Palestine to settle in various parts of Europe, two distinctly Jewish languages emerged. The Sephardic Jews of Spain and Portugal developed Ladino, a mixture of Spanish and Hebrew, while Ashkenazic Jews in central and eastern Europe spoke Yiddish, a combination of medieval German and Hebrew. These two languages were spoken by immigrants when they came to America, but were not typically passed on to the next generation. The exception to this occurred during the turn of the century when Russian Jews helped Yiddish gain a strong foothold in America through Yiddish newspapers and theater. At its high point in 1920, Yiddish was spoken by half of the Jewish population in America. By 1940, however, the proportion of American Jews who spoke Yiddish had dropped to one-third, and its presence as a world language was severely threatened by the Holocaust, which killed most of the Yiddish-speaking Jews. Today, a small but growing minority of Jews are attempting to revitalize Yiddish as a language uniquely capable of transmitting Jewish cultural heritage.

GREETINGS AND OTHER POPULAR EXPRESSIONS

Commonly heard expressions are: *Shalom*—Peace (a general greeting); *Shalom lekha*—Hello/Goodbye (an everyday greeting); *Barukh ha-ha*—Blessed be the one who comes (a general welcome to guests often used at weddings or circumcisions); *Mazel tov*—Good luck (a wish for luck commonly used at births, *bar mitzvahs*, and weddings); *Le-hayyim*—To life/Cheers (a traditional toast wishing someone good health); *Ad me'ah ve-esrim shana*—May you live until 120 (an expression meaning good wishes for a long life); *Tizkeh le-shanim*—Long life to you (an expression wishing someone happy birthday or happy anniversary); *Hag same'ah*—A happy holiday (a general holiday greeting used for all Jewish festivals); *L'shana tova*—Good year (a shortened version of "may you be inscribed in the Book of Life for a good year," which is wished during Rosh Hashanah).

FAMILY AND COMMUNITY DYNAMICS

As Jews have spread to Europe and America after being forced out of Palestine, their cultural heritage has depended on strong family and community relations. One of the chief ways in which Jews, particularly Orthodox Jews, have maintained family and community values has been through the keeping of *Shabat*, the Sabbath. Observing *Shabat*, or "the day of delight," is one of the Ten Commandments and is essentially a matter of taking a break from work to devote one day of the week to rest, contemplation, and family and community togetherness. Just prior to Sabbath, which lasts from sunset on Friday to late Saturday night, the family must complete all the preparations for the day because no work should be done once the Sabbath begins. Traditionally, the mother starts the Sabbath by lighting candles and saying a special prayer. Afterward, the family attends a short service in the synagogue, then returns home for a meal and lighthearted conversation, perhaps even singing. The following morning the community gathers in the synagogue for the most important religious service of the week. On Saturday afternoon observant Jews will continue to refrain from work and either make social visits or spend time in quiet reflection. A ceremony called *havdalah* (distinction) takes place Saturday night, marking the end of Sabbath and the beginning of the new week.

The relative importance of *Shabat* and the synagogue for American Jews has declined over the years. In fact, the history of Jews in America reflects an ongoing secularization of Jewish values. Beginning in the nineteenth century, the Jewish community center developed as an important nonsectarian counterpart to the synagogue. Modeled after the Young Men's Hebrew Association, Jewish community centers became dominated by the 1920s by professionals who wanted to establish a central place for younger Jews to acquire such American values as humanism and self-development. While such community centers continue to play a role in Jewish population areas, many of today's American Jews no longer associate with a synagogue or community center, but may live in a Jewish neighborhood as the only outward sign of their Jewish identity.

COURTSHIP AND MARRIAGE

According to Judaism, marriage is the fulfillment of one of God's purposes for human beings. Consequently, all Jews are intended to experience both the joy and hardship of matrimony, including rabbis. To facilitate the finding of a mate, the matchmaker plays a role in Jewish society of bringing together suitable but perhaps reluctant individuals. The matchmaker only helps the process along; the final choice must be made freely by both partners according to Jewish law.

Traditionally, intermarriage between Jews and Gentiles has been forbidden. A Jew who married a Christian faced ostracism from family and community. Jews who immigrated to America during the Colonial period and after, however, intermarried with non-Jews with relative impunity. This tolerance of religious freedom lasted until the 1880s when the arrival of Russian Jews ushered in a conservative era with a more traditional view of marriage. For the first half of the twentieth century, intermarriage among Jews remained low, with only about five percent choosing to marry non-Jews. By the 1960s and 1970s, however, intermarriage became more common, with as many as 20 to 30 percent of Jews choosing non-Jewish mates, and by 1999 had risen to 52 percent. Increased assimilation and intermarriage has sparked concern over the continued existence of American Jewry. A recent survey of American rabbis found opinion divided on performance of mixed marriages by rabbis, with disagreement on whether performing such marriage ceremonies encourages those marrying non-Jews to maintain their connection with Judaism and perhaps encourages the non-Jewish partners to convert.

The question of "who's a Jew" in Israel also has American Jews concerned. Recent legislation makes conversions to Judaism legal only when performed by Orthodox rabbis. This has political implications, given the close relationship of religious affiliation and political power in Israel; for example, 150 religious councils distribute more than $70 million in government funds annually. More important for American Jews is that along with the authority over conversions comes the authority to determine eligibility for automatic Israeli citizenship under the Law of Return. Eighty-five percent of American Jews are Reform, Conservative, or unaffiliated and thus feel that such legislation is shutting them out, in effect telling them that they are not really Jews. In 1997 many withheld charitable contributions or redirected them to more secular organizations in response.

BIRTHS, WEDDINGS, AND FUNERALS

Jewish babies usually receive two names, an everyday name and a Hebrew name used in the synagogue and on religious documents. The naming of the baby occurs after birth at a baby-naming service or, for many male babies, when they are circumcised. Since the emergence of Judaism some 4,000 years ago, Jews have observed the tradition of *brit milah* (covenant of circumcision). Although the practice of cutting the foreskin of male babies probably served a hygienic purpose originally, circumcision has come to represent the beginning of life in the Jewish community. To be sure, many non-Jews are circumcised, and being born of a Jewish mother is sufficient to make a baby Jewish. Nonetheless, circumcision is traditionally associated with the keeping of the covenant between Abraham and God as well as with physical and ethical purity. The *brit milah* must occur eight days after birth, unless the baby is sick. The ceremony takes place in the home and is usually performed by a *mohel*, an observant Jew who may be a rabbi, doctor, or simply one skilled in the technique. After the circumcision, which occurs very quickly and without much pain, a celebration of food, prayers, and blessings follows.

Bar mitzvah, which varies according to local traditions (Ashkenazic, Sephardic, or Oriental) is the ceremony that initiates the young Jewish male into the religious community. By reading in the synagogue, he becomes an adult. According to Talmudic tradition, this ususally occurs at the age of 13. Following the reading in the synagogue, there is a celebration (*seudat mitzavah*). In the twentieth century, the *bas* or *bat mitzvah* has been introduced for young girls; however, this occurs more frequently in the Reform and Conservative groups than the Orthodox ones.

Jewish weddings are marked by several distinct traditions. The ceremony occurs under a *huppah*, a canopy open on all four sides, symbolizing the openness of the bride and groom's new home. The huppah can be placed in a home or outdoors but is most often used in a synagogue. Under the *huppah*, the bride circles the groom a set number of times, the couple is blessed, and they both drink from the same cup of wine, a sharing which demonstrates that from this point forward they will share a life together. The heart of the ceremony, the only part required to make the marriage legally binding, occurs next. The groom places a ring on the right-hand index finger of the bride, proclaiming, "Behold you are consecrated to me by this ring according to the law of Moses and Israel." If at least two witnesses observe her accept the ring, the marriage is complete. The ceremony is rounded out by the signing of the marriage contract (the *ketubah*), the singing of seven blessings (the *Sheva brahot*), and the traditional smashing of the glass by the husband. Breaking a glass symbolizes the destruction of the Temple in Jerusalem and the fact that the couple will have to face hard times together. When the glass is broken, guests exclaim, "*Mazel tov*" (good luck), and a wedding feast ensues.

Jewish funerals and mourning are characterized by a sense of frankness toward the reality of death. Funerals occur soon after a person dies, usually within a day or two unless family travel plans or the observance of Sabbath delays the service for an extra day. Arrangements for the deceased are handled by the *hevra kadisha* (holy society), which is a volunteer organization within the synagogue responsible for preparing the body. Such preparation does not involve make-up or embalming but instead consists of dressing the person in white, perhaps wrapping the deceased with his or her prayer cloth, or *tallit*. In modern times, the *hevra kadisha* are sometimes assisted by professionals, but not for profit. The ceremony is usually short and is followed by burial at the cemetery, where family members will recite the *Kaddish*, a traditional prayer celebrating God and life.

For Orthodox survivors, four stages of mourning have evolved over the years which encourage expression of grief so that the healing process may occur without delay. From the time a person dies until the funeral, mourners cease working, gather together, and do not generally receive visitors, primarily because any comfort at this point is premature and only causes unnecessary strain. The second stage occurs during the first week after the funeral, when the family observes *shiva*. At this time, mourners do not generally work but open their homes to visitors who offer their sympathy. The next stage is *shaloshim*, which lasts for three weeks after shiva and is marked by a resumption of work and other obligations, but entertainment is avoided. Finally, there is a last phase of light mourning for spouses or immediate family members that ends 11 months after the funeral. By the anniversary of a person's death, mourning is complete.

THE ROLE OF WOMEN

Jewish culture over the years has been male-dominated. Women's roles were limited to household activity, including raising children and performing minor religious functions, such as lighting the Sabbath candles. Although women are subject to the same negative biblical commandments as men, they are not expected to observe the same positive commandments. For example, men are expected to pray three times a day at fixed times, while women only pray once at a time of their choosing. This difference has been variously attributed to the demanding nature of women's household duties and to men's higher proclivity to sin. For centuries, women could not study the Torah and could not receive a formal education. While Orthodox Jews have eased their stance against education for women, they have nevertheless maintained that women should serve a secondary role to their husbands. Other Jews have taken a more liberal view, holding that women are equals who can fully participate in religious ceremonies. In Reform and Conservative Judaism, women are permitted to become rabbis. Many Jewish women rabbis played a role in the American feminist movement of the 1960s and 1970s. The movement liberated women from having to serve traditional roles, and Jewish women such as Congresswoman Bella Abzug and authors Gloria Steinem and Betty Friedan paved the way for women to enter a variety of fields once dominated by men.

EDUCATION

For years Jews have placed strong emphasis on the importance of education. In the nineteenth century, the ability to read gave German Jewish immigrants a competitive edge over other German immigrants. Later, American-born Jews pursued education as a means of entering such professions as law and medicine. Although Jews currently represent less than three percent of the American population, the proportion of Jews in academia has been significantly higher since World War II, with Jews comprising ten percent of the teaching faculty at American universities. By 1973, nearly 60 percent of all Jewish graduate students were enrolled in the nation's top ten institutions of higher learning. Approximately 20 to 30 percent of the leading scholars who taught at such universities were Jewish.

Religious education was once taught in a *heder*, an eastern European elementary school for boys. While girls generally did not have access to formal education, boys would attend the *heder* all day long, studying the Hebrew prayerbook and the Torah. In America, the *heder* played a secondary role to public schools. As priorities changed with acculturation, the *heder* diminished in significance. However, the Talmud Torah school, a charitable school first established in Europe, began to usurp the role of the *heder* as a place for Judaic instruction. Today, a number of Jewish children attend some type of religious school a few hours each week for three to five years in order to learn Jewish history, traditions, and customs as well as the Hebrew language.

PHILANTHROPIC TRADITIONS

The Jewish philanthropic tradition reaches back to biblical times when Israeli Jews practiced *tzedakah*, or charity, as one of their primary duties in life. One common form of *tzedakah* was to allocate a portion of the harvest for the poor, who were free to take crops from certain parts of a farm. During the Middle Ages, Jewish self-governing communities called *kehillahs* would ensure that the community's poor would have the basic necessities of life. The spirit of the *kehillah* survived into the twentieth century in the form of *landsmanshaft*, separate societies existing within congregations in cities such as New York. The *landsmanshaft* were comprised of townspeople from congregations who pooled resources to provide such benefits as insurance, cemetery rights, free loans, and sick pay.

While the tradition of lending assistance began in the synagogue, over the years philanthropic organizations became increasingly independent. Organizations such as the Order of B'nai B'rith and the Young Men's Hebrew Association became major sponsors of charitable projects. These and other benevolent societies were responsible for the establishment of Jewish orphanages, hospitals, and retirement homes in major cities across the United States throughout the nineteenth century.

Jewish philanthropy increased tremendously during the twentieth century. Scientific philanthropy—a method of providing aid through modern methods and without assistance from religious institutions—gained favor at the beginning of the twentieth century in response to the problem of helping settle the large waves of Russian immigrant Jews. One outgrowth of this movement was the establishment of the National Conference of Jewish Charities, which formed national agencies to deal with immigrant issues. During World War I, Jewish philanthropic efforts were consolidated through the establishment of the American Jewish Joint Distribution Committee, an organization formed to provide relief to eastern European Jews suffering from famine and pogroms. By raising more than $66 million by 1922, the Committee was able to expand its relief efforts to include health care and economic reconstruction programs that reached some 700,000 Jews in need of assistance. Several organizations supplied economic relief to European Jews during and after World War II. One such organization, the United Jewish Appeal, was initially established to help Holocaust survivors and to promote Israel as a homeland for Jews. During the postwar decades, however, it has blossomed into the largest private charity in America, providing financial aid to Israel and Jews worldwide. In recent decades, the Jewish philanthropic tradition has extended beyond the Jewish community. Mazon, for example, was founded in the 1980s as a national hunger relief organization that is funded by Jews who voluntarily donate three percent of the costs of such celebrations as weddings and *bar mitzvahs*.

RELIGION

The basic message of Judaism is that there is one all-powerful God. Originally established as a response to polytheism and idol worship, Judaism has been quite successful in perpetuating its belief in monotheism in that it is the parent religion of both Christianity and Islam. The basic difference between these three religions centers on the Messiah, or savior of the world. While Christians believe the Messiah was Jesus Christ and Muslims believe in several divinely inspired prophets, the greatest being Mohammed, Jews believe the Messiah has not yet appeared.

"Everybody had something to give me for help. It wasn't a question of money, it was a question of being a human being to a human being. And in those days people were apparently that way. There were so many nice people that were trying to help us when we came to this country."

Clara Larsen in 1908, cited in *Ellis Island: An Illustrated History of the Immigrant Experience,* edited by Ivan Chermayeff et al. (New York: Macmillan, 1991).

The centerpiece of Judaism is the Torah. Strictly speaking, the Torah refers to the first five books of the Bible (Five Books of Moses), but it can also mean the entire Bible or all of Jewish law, including the Talmud and the Midrash. The Talmud is oral law handed down through the generations that interprets the written law, or Torah. The Talmud consists of the Mishnah, which is the text version of the oral law as compiled by Rabbi Judah the Patriarch in 200 C.E., and the Gemara, which is the collected commentary on the Mishnah. The Midrash refers to the collection of stories or sermons, or *midrashim*, which interpret biblical passages. Taken as a whole, Jewish law is known as *halahah*, which guides all aspects of Jewish life.

Two other vital components of Judaism are the rabbi and the synagogue. Since the Middle Ages, rabbis served as spiritual leaders of communities. Though equal with the rest of humanity in the eyes of God, the rabbi was chosen by the community as an authority on Jewish law. Rabbis were paid to teach,

This boy reads
from the Torah
during his Bar
Mitzvah.

preach, and judge religious and civic matters. While the role of the rabbi was well established in Europe, American synagogues were reluctant to preserve the social and economic position of rabbis. Congregation members no longer felt the need for such an authoritative figure. Consequently, some congregations hired ministers rather than rabbis in order to restrict the influence of their religious leaders. Today, many congregations continue to be led by rabbis who perform traditional duties as well as a variety of other functions, including visiting the sick and attending to wedding and funeral services. The synagogue is the place for Jewish worship, study, and social meetings. Although synagogues have generally played a secondary role to Jewish secular organizations in America, the postwar years saw a revival in the importance of the synagogue in Jewish life. The synagogue expanded to become the center of community life and the organization through which Jewish children developed a Jewish identity. Membership in synagogues rose dramatically, though attendance at services did not increase proportionately.

Though not known as such, Jews were all basically Orthodox until the French Revolution. Orthodoxy as a separate branch of Judaism developed in eastern and central Europe during the eighteenth and nineteenth centuries when the Jewish Enlightenment and Emancipation ushered in a new era of freedom of thought and living. Rejecting such changes, Orthodox Jews sought to maintain Jewish traditions through strict observance of Jewish law as expressed in the Torah. While most Jewish immigrants were Orthodox when they arrived in the United States, economic pressure and differences in social

climate between Europe and America caused many to abandon Orthodoxy. As a result, Orthodox Judaism has only been practiced by a small minority of American Jews. (Roughly ten percent of American Jews are Orthodox, 30 percent are Reform, and 40 percent are Conservative.) The survival of Orthodox Judaism is due in part to its tolerance of American ways and modern educational practices, which have appealed to middle-class Jews. Other factors include the founding of Yeshiva College in 1928 and the development of an Orthodox parochial school system, which grew from just 17 schools in the 1930s to more than 400 schools by the 1970s.

For many years, the dominant branch of American Judaism has been Reform. Though some Jews maintain that Judaism has always been Reform, Reform Judaism as a distinct segment of Judaism can be traced to eighteenth-century German Jewish Enlightenment. Some Reform synagogues began to appear in Germany in the early nineteenth century, but Reform Judaism gained its largest following among German Jews who immigrated to America during the mid-nineteenth century. Unlike Orthodox Jews, members of Reform Judaism view Jewish laws as adaptable to the changing needs of cultures over time. As a result, Reform Jews look to the Bible for basic moral principles. They do not believe in a literal reading of the Bible and have felt free to ignore outdated passages, such as those that make reference to animal sacrifice. In general, Reform Judaism represents the most liberal strain of Judaism: Reform was the first to let women become rabbis (1972); it is accepting of intermarriage and converts; and it does not stress such traditional teachings as the coming of the Messiah or the need for separate nationhood (Israel). These liberal views reflect Reform's emphasis on reason over tradition, a shift that represents a transformation of the traditional Jewish identity into a Jewish American identity.

As assimilation has proceeded and intermarriage greatly increased, many Reform Jews seeking to reinforce their Jewish identity have rediscovered traditional practices such as keeping kosher households and the wearing of yarmulkes as well as the study of Hebrew, the use of which has increased in religious services. In May of 1999 the Central Conference of American Rabbis, meeting in Pittsburgh Pennsylvania, adopted a new platform, known as the Pittsburgh Principles. The document, while not requiring such observances, strongly recommended the study and practice of mitzvot, many of which are obligatory in more conservative Jewish sects.

With a theological perspective that falls somewhere between Orthodoxy and Reform, Conservative Judaism has become the largest branch of

American Judaism. Conservative Judaism first developed in nineteenth-century Germany and later gained an American following by the early 1900s. The American roots of this branch of Judaism can be traced to the 1887 founding in New York City of the Jewish Theological Seminary, which has since become the center of Conservative Judaism and home to the world's largest repository of books on Judaism and Jewish life. With its blend of tradition and openness to change within the confines of Jewish law, Conservative Judaism steadily attracted new members until World War II, when membership sharply increased and ultimately attained its current status as the largest branch of Judaism in America. Theologically, Conservatives look to the Talmud and its interpretations of the Torah as an example of their own views on the evolving nature of Jewish law. As long as change does not violate the basic tenets outlined in the Torah, change is welcomed by Conservatives. Thus, religious ceremonies do not have to be in Hebrew, and women can serve as rabbis. Because Conservatives have not formally articulated their ideology, individual congregations are able to style themselves around the needs of the community.

Another segment of American Judaism is Reconstructionist Judaism, which is sometimes lumped together with Reform and Conservative Judaism as Progressive Judaism. Developed in the 1920s and 1930s by Mordecai M. Kaplan and influenced by the thinking of American pragmatist philosopher John Dewey, Reconstructionism emphasizes Democratic culture and humanistic values. Reconstructionists value Jewish traditions not merely for their religious significance, but because such traditions reflect Jewish culture. Thus, Judaism is more a way of life than a religion. Reconstructionists may learn Hebrew, observe Jewish holidays, and eat kosher foods, but not out of a sense of obligation but as a way of preserving Jewish culture. Of the four major branches of Judaism, Reconstructionism has the smallest following.

Although most American-born Jews do not practice traditional Judaism or attend religious services, nearly three-fourths of American Jews align themselves with either Reform or Conservative Judaism.

EMPLOYMENT AND ECONOMIC TRADITIONS

Over the years, Jews have attained a high level of economic prosperity through keen business sense and dedication to hard work. Such prosperity has been achieved over the course of several generations, dating back to medieval Europe when Jews first became associated with the world of finance and trade. Because they were not allowed to hire Gentiles and were excluded from craft guilds, Jews took on the jobs that Christians found repugnant, such as money-lending and tax-collecting. In time Jews became involved in trade and the clothing business as well. By the time the Sephardic Jews began settling in America in the seventeenth and eighteenth centuries, most earned their livings as independent retailers; they were bakers, tailors, merchants, and small business owners.

Jews in the mid-nineteenth century were predominantly tailors or peddlers. Many of those who worked in the city were tailors or were otherwise affiliated with the garment business. Those who sought their fortune outside of the city were usually peddlers, who played a key role in bringing merchandise from the city to the country. The successful peddler could eventually earn enough to set up his own retail store on the outskirts of town or in rural areas. Credit was at the heart of the emerging network of these retail businesses. German Jews were the chief creditors at the time, and they would minimize their credit risks by dealing with relatives whenever possible. The close connection between creditor and businessman led to the emergence of a Jewish business elite between 1860 and 1880 that had established profitable ventures in such fields as investment banking, the garment industry, shoe manufacturing, and meat processing. By the end of the century, American Jews were no longer primarily tailors or peddlers (those trades represented just three percent and one percent, respectively, of American Jews in the 1890 census). Instead, Jews had attained a substantial measure of wealth by becoming retailers, bankers, brokers, wholesalers, accountants, bookkeepers, and clerks; together, these occupations represented 67 percent of all American Jews in the 1890 census.

The immigration of Russian Jews in the early twentieth century brought vast numbers of workers into the clothing industry in large cities. Newly arriving immigrants would work in the factories for long hours, often 70 or more hours a week, honing their skills and developing their own specialties. As with the German Jews before them, the Russian Jews worked their way into more affluent positions over the years, becoming business owners and professionals. While German Jews comprised the majority of the 1,000 clothing manufacturers in the late nineteenth century, by the eve of the World War I Russian Jews owned more than 16,000 garment factories and employed more than 200,000 Russian Jews. The slowing of immigration during and immediately after World War I coupled with increasing wages in the garment industry enabled Russian Jews to raise their standard of living and attain the same socio-economic status as German Jews by the 1920s.

The educated professional has long been a highly valued member of Jewish culture. The entrepreneurial success of first-generation Jews enabled subsequent generations to move into the professional ranks of society. In large eastern and midwestern cities such as New York and Cleveland, the disproportionate share of Jewish doctors, lawyers, and dentists represented two to three times the proportion of the Jewish population in those cities. For example, Jews in the 1930s comprised 25 percent of the population of New York City, yet accounted for 65 percent of all lawyers and judges in the city.

As with the general population, Jews enjoyed considerable economic prosperity during the Postwar years. After World War II, the institutional discrimination against Jews that had developed during the first part of the twentieth century disappeared. With unprecedented access to education and advancement in American society, younger Jews entered colleges and embarked upon successful professional careers at about twice the rate of the preceding generation. Rather than gravitating toward the clothing industry, as many of their parents and grandparents had done, postwar Jews turned to a range of fields, including management, communications, real estate, entertainment, and academia.

POLITICS AND GOVERNMENT

Since the first Jews arrived in Colonial America, Jews have enjoyed a high degree of political freedom and have taken an active role in politics and government. Although early Jewish settlers in America faced some political and social discrimination, laws restricting Jewish religious and business activities were generally not enforced. By 1740, Parliament granted Jewish aliens the right to citizenship without having to take a Christian oath. After America gained its independence, the Mikveh Israel Congregation urged the Constitutional Convention to make a provision guaranteeing the freedom of religious expression, which became a reality with the passage of the First Amendment in 1789. Since then, Jews have been involved in all levels of American civic and political life, with the presidency being the only office a Jew has not held. By 1992, Jews held 33 seats in the U.S. House of Representatives and a full ten percent of the Senate. The

Republican congressional victories in 1994 reduced the number of Jews in the House to 24, while the retirement of Democrat Howard Metzenbaum brought the number of Jewish senators to nine.

Over the years Jews have developed a rich political tradition of fighting for social justice as liberals and radicals primarily affiliated with the Democratic party. Jews have been staunch supporters of Democratic political leaders. When in 1944 President Roosevelt's New Deal policies caused the president to lose popularity, 90 percent of Jews continued to support him. The tendency to side with an unpopular liberal candidate continued through 1972, when Democratic presidential candidate George McGovern won only 38 percent of the popular vote, but garnered more than 60 percent of the Jewish vote. The majority of Jews have continued their allegiance to the Democratic party, even during the 1980s when Republicans Ronald Reagan and George Bush won the presidency in landslide victories. Beginning in the 1970s, however, a growing number of Jews abandoned liberal politics in favor of pragmatism and conservatism. Leading this movement were Nathan Glazer, Irving Kristol, Sidney Hook, and Milton Friedman.

UNIONS AND SOCIALISM

The more radical Jewish political activists have been involved in unions and socialism. During the first part of the twentieth century, Jewish union leaders had strong ties to the Socialist party and the Jewish Socialist Federation. This support reflected a socialist leaning on the part of several Russian Jews who had participated in the failed Russian Revolution of 1905. The Socialist party enjoyed its greatest success in New York City between 1914 and 1917 when Socialist Meyer London was elected to represent the Lower East Side in the U.S. Congress and more than a dozen Socialists won seats in city government.

Influenced by eastern European socialist thought and American free enterprise, Jews found themselves on both sides of the labor disputes of the early twentieth century. The clothing industry provided the battleground. For a time Russian Jewish manufacturers refused to recognize unions, many of which contained a significant proportion of Jewish members. Tensions came to a head during two major strikes: The "uprising of twenty thousand," which involved Jewish and Italian young women striking against shirtwaist manufacturers in 1909, and "the great revolt," a massive strike in 1911 involving thousands of cloak makers. Both strikes pitted thugs and police against union workers. The workers received community support from various Jewish benefactors, ranging from wealthy women who posted bail for the arrested workers to lawyers and community leaders who helped mediate settlements. As a result of the strikes, the work week was lowered to 50 hours and permanent mediation procedures were established. Two key unions at the time were the International Ladies Garment Workers Union and the Amalgamated Clothing Workers Union, both of which included a significant proportion of Jewish members. Another union with significant Jewish membership was Arbeter Ring, or Workmen's Circle. With approximately 80,000 Jewish families on board by the mid-1920s, this union provided health care and cemetery services and involved itself in Yiddish culture by sponsoring Yiddish newspapers, schools, and theaters.

MILITARY PARTICIPATION

Throughout American history, Jews have served with distinction in the U.S. military. Of the approximately 2,500 Jews in America during the Revolutionary War, hundreds fought against the British while others supported the struggle for independence by refusing to recognize British authority. Just as the Civil War divided North against South, so too did it divide the American Jews. While most Jewish soldiers served in the Union army, many Jews in the South remained loyal to the Confederate cause. Several prominent Jews supported the South, notably Judah P. Benjamin, the Confederate Secretary of War and Secretary of State. Jews also figured prominently in the two world wars, with 250,000 Jews participating in World War I and 550,000 in World War II.

The participation of Jews in America's major wars demonstrates that while they are generally known as a peaceful people, Jews are prepared to fight for just causes. For some Jewish Americans, this principle extends beyond national concerns. The Jewish Defense League (JDL), for example, is a militant organization established in New York in 1968 by radical Rabbi Meir Kahane. The JDL's guiding principle is "Never Again," a reference to the Nazi Holocaust. The group's method of combatting worldwide anti-Semitism with violence has made the JDL controversial among Jews and non-Jews alike.

ISRAEL

For centuries Jews have sustained a commitment to establishing a homeland for Jews at some point. The longing to return to Zion, the hill on which Jerusalem was built, remained a vague dream until 1896, when Theodor Herzl wrote *The Jewish State*, which called for modern Palestine to be the home for Hebrew culture. The following year the first Zionist Congress convened in Basle, which along with Herzl's book marked the beginning of Zionism as an official movement. By 1914, some 12,000 American Jews had become Zionists. The movement was bolstered by the 1934 publication of Conservative Mordecai M. Kaplan's influential *Judaism as a Civilization*, which argued that Judaism as a religion reflected the totality of the Jewish people's consciousness. As such, Kaplan asserted that Jewish culture deserved its own central location, Palestine. After World War II, the effort to establish a Jewish state was helped considerably when the British gave the United Nations control of Palestine. In November of 1947 the United Nations approved a resolution to partition Palestine into Arab and Jewish regions. When Israel declared itself a nation on May 14, 1948, President Harry Truman decided to officially recognize Israel, despite a longstanding warning from the U.S. State Department that such recognition could anger oil-producing Arab countries.

Since the late 1930s American Jews have contributed billions of dollars in aid to help Israel deal with its immigration burdens and tenuous relations with Arab neighbors. While the periods of military strife in 1948, 1967, and 1973 brought forth the greatest contributions from the American Jewish community, financial support for various philanthropic projects has been steady over the years.

INDIVIDUAL AND GROUP CONTRIBUTIONS

Countless Jews have made significant contributions to American culture over the years. Only a partial listing of notable names is possible.

ACADEMIA

Jews have been particularly influential in academia, with ten percent of faculty at American universities comprised of Jews, the number rising to 30 percent at America's top ten universities. Notable Jewish scholars include historians Daniel J. Boorstin (1914–), Henry L. Feingold (1931–), Oscar Handlin (1915–), Jacob Rader Marcus (1896-1995), Abram Sachar (1899–), and Barbara Tuchman (1912–), linguist Noam Chomsky (1928–), Russian literature and Slavic language experts Maurice Friedman (1929–) and Roman Jakobson (1896-1982), Zionist scholar and activist Ben Halpern (1912–), and philosophers Ernest Nagel (1901-

1985), a logical positivist influential in the philosophy of science, and Norman Lamm (1927–), Yeshiva University president and founder of the orthodox periodical *Tradition*.

FILM, TELEVISION, AND THEATER

Jews have had an enormous influence in Hollywood. By the 1930s Jews dominated the film industry as almost all of the major production companies were owned and operated by eastern European Jews. These companies include Columbia (Jack and Harry Cohn), Goldwyn (Samuel Goldwyn—born Samuel Goldfish, 1882), Metro-Goldwyn-Mayer (Louis B. Mayer and Marcus Loew), Paramount (Jesse Lasky, Adolph Zukor, and Barney Balaban), Twentieth Century-Fox (Sol Brill and William Fox), United Artists (Al Lichtman), Universal (Carl Laemmle), and Warner Brothers (Sam, Jack, Albert, and Harry Warner).

Actors/performers: The Marx Brothers—Chico (Leonard; 1887-1961), Harpo (Adolph; 1888-1964), Groucho (Julius; 1890-1977), Gummo (Milton; 1894-1977), and Zeppo (Herbert; 1901-1979); Jack Benny (Benjamin Kubelsky; 1894-1974); George Burns (Nathan Birnbaum; 1896–); Milton Berle (Milton Berlinger; 1908–); Danny Kaye (Daniel David Kominski; 1913-1987); Kirk Douglas (Issur Danielovitch; 1918–); Walter Matthau (1920–); Shelly Winters (Shirley Schrift; 1923–); Lauren Bacall (Betty Joan Perske; 1924–); Sammy Davis, Jr. (1925-1990); Gene Wilder (Jerome Silberman; 1935–); and Dustin Hoffman (1937–).

Directors: Carl Reiner (1922–); Mel Brooks (Melvyn Kaminsky; 1926–); Stanley Kubrick (1928–); Woody Allen (Allen Konigsberg; 1935–); and Steven Spielberg (1947–).

GOVERNMENT

Mordecai M. Noah (1785-1851) was the most widely known Jewish political figure of the first half of the nineteenth century. A controversial figure, Noah was U.S. consul in Tunis from 1813 to 1815, when he was recalled for apparently mismanaging funds. He went on to serve as an editor, sheriff, and judge. In 1825 he created a refuge for Jews when he purchased Grand Island in Niagara River. The refuge city, of which Noah proclaimed himself governor, was to be a step toward the establishment of a permanent state for Jews.

In 1916 the first Jew joined the U.S. Supreme Court, noted legal scholar Louis Brandeis (1856-1941), whose liberalism and Jewish heritage sparked a heated five-month Congressional battle over his nomination. After his confirmation, Brandeis used his power to help Zionism gain acceptance among Jews and non-Jews alike. Other prominent Jewish Supreme Court jurists include Benjamin Cardozo (1870-1938), a legal realist whose opinions foreshadowed the liberalism of the Warren court, and Felix Frankfurter (1882-1965), who prior to his Supreme Court appointment had been influential in promoting New Deal policies as a key advisor to President Franklin D. Roosevelt.

After the 1994 elections, nine Jews were members of the U.S. Senate: Barbara Boxer (California), Russell Feingold (Wisconsin), Diane Feinstein (California), Herbert Kohl (Wisconsin), Frank Lautenberg (New Jersey), Carl Levin (Michigan), Joseph Lieberman (Connecticut), Arlen Specter (Pennsylvania), and Paul Wellstone (Minnesota). With the exception of Specter, all are Democrats.

JOURNALISM

During the late nineteenth century Joseph Pulitzer operated a chain of newspapers, many of which often featured stories of public corruption. After his death in 1911, he left funds for the Columbia University School of Journalism and for the coveted annual prizes in his name. Since then, many Jewish journalists have won the Pulitzer Prize, including ABC news commentator Carl Bernstein (1944–), *Washington Post* columnist David Broder (1929–), syndicated columnist and satirist Art Buchwald (1925–), syndicated columnist Ellen Goodman (1927–), former *New York Times* reporter and author David Halberstam (1934–), journalist Seymour Hersh (1937–), *New York Times* columnist Anthony Lewis (1927–), former *New York Times* reporter and Harvard journalism professor Anthony J. Lukas (1933–), *New York Times* executive editor and author A. M. Rosenthal (1922–), stylist, humorist, and former presidential speech writer William Safire (1929–), *New York Times* reporter Sydney Schanberg (1934–), and journalist and political historian Theodore H. White (1915–). Other notable Jewish journalists include sportscaster Howard Cosell (William Howard Cohen; 1920-1995), *Village Voice* columnist Nat Hentoff (1925–), NBC television journalist Marvin Kalb (1930–), financial columnist Sylvia Porter (Sylvia Feldman; 1913–), investigative journalist I. F. Stone (Isador Feinstein; 1907–), "60 Minutes" television journalist Mike Wallace (Myron Leon Wallace; 1918–), and television journalist Barbara Walters (1931–).

LITERATURE

Novelists: Saul Bellow (Solomon Bellows; 1915–)—*The Adventures of Augie March* and *Mr. Sammler's Planet*; E. L. Doctorow (1931–)—*Ragtime* and *Billy Bathgate*; Stanley Elkin (1930–); Joseph Heller (1923–)—*Catch 22*; Erica Jong (Erica Mann; 1942–)—*Fear of Flying*; Jerzy Kosinski (1933-1991)—*Being There*; Ira Levin (1929–)—*Rosemary's Baby* and *Boys from Brazil*; Norman Mailer (1923–)—*The Naked and the Dead* and *Tough Guys Don't Dance*; Bernard Malamud (1914-1986)—*The Natural* and *The Fixer*; Cynthia Ozick (1928–)—*The Pagan Rabbi*; Philip Roth (1933–)—*Portnoy's Complaint*; Isaac Bashevis Singer (1904-1991)—*In My Father's House*; Leon Uris (1924–)—*Exodus*; Nathaniel West (Nathan Weinstein; 1903-1940)—*Miss Lonelyhearts* and *The Day of the Locust*; and Herman Wouk (1915–)—*The Caine Mutiny* and *War and Remembrance*.

Playwrights: Lillian Hellman (1907-1984)—*Children's Hour* and *The Little Foxes*; David Mamet (1947–)—*American Buffalo* and *Glengarry Glen Ross*; and Arthur Miller (1915–)—*Death of a Salesman* and *The Crucible*.

Poets: Allen Ginsberg (1926–)—"Howl" and "Kaddish;" Stanley Kunitz (1905–)—"Green Ways;" and Howard Nemerov (1920-1991).

Essayists/critics: Irving Howe (1920–)—*World of Our Fathers* and *How We Lived*; Alfred Kazin (1915–)—*New York Jew*; Susan Sontag (1933–)—*Against Interpretation*; and Elie Wiesel (1928–)—*Night*.

MUSIC

Broadway and popular composers: Irving Berlin (1888-1989)—"Blue Skies," "God Bless America," and "White Christmas;" George Gershwin (1898-1937)—*Of Thee I Sing* and *Porgy and Bess* (musicals) and "Rhapsody in Blue;" Richard Rodgers (1902-1979)—*Oklahoma!*, *Carousel*, *South Pacific*, *The King and I*, and *The Sound of Music* (musicals; with Oscar Hammerstein II); Benny Goodman (1909-1986)—"Let's Dance" and "Tiger Rag" (swing band music); pianist, composer, and conductor Leonard Bernstein (1918-1990)—*West Side Story* and *Candide* (musicals) and *On the Waterfront* (film score); Burt Bacharach (1929–); Herb Alpert (1935–); and Marvin Hamlisch (1944–).

Classical performers/composers: pianist Arthur Rubinstein (1887-1982); violinist Jascha Heifetz (1901-1987); pianist Vladimir Horowitz (1904-1989); violinist Nathan Milstein (1904-1992); violinist Itzhak Perlman (1945–); operatic soprano Beverly Sills (Belle Silverman; 1929–); and composer Aaron Copeland (1900-1990).

Popular songwriters/performers: Bob Dylan (Robert Zimmerman; 1941–)—"Like a Rolling Stone" and "Blowing in the Wind;" Neil Diamond (1941–)—"Solitary Man" and "I'm a Believer;" Carole King (Carole Klein; 1941–)—"You've Got a Friend" and "Been to Canaan;" Paul Simon (1941–); Art Garfunkel (1941–); and Barbra Streisand (1942–).

SCIENCE AND TECHNOLOGY

Perhaps the best known thinker of the twentieth-century is Albert Einstein (1879-1955), the German Jewish physicist who had completed his most important scientific work before coming to America in 1934. Though best known for his theory of relativity, for which he won the Nobel Prize in 1922, Einstein played a critical role in American history as part of team of scientists who researched atomic power during World War II. At that time, Jewish emigres joined native-born Jews in the famous Los Alamos nuclear project that led to the explosion of the first atomic bomb in 1945. Robert Oppenheimer (1904-1967), Lewis Strauss, and I.I. Rabi (born 1898), all American-born Jews, teamed up with such Jewish immigrant scientists as Einstein, Enrico Fermi (1901-1954), Leo Szilard, Theodor von Karman, and John von Neumann. Einstein was part of "brain drain" of Jews from Nazi Germany that also included psychoanalysts Erich Fromm (1900-1980), Bruno Bettelheim (1903-1990), and Erik Erikson (1902–), as well as social scientists Hannah Arendt (1906-1975) and Leo Strauss (1899-1973).

Other American Jews made notable contributions to science as well. Albert Michelson, who measured the speed of light, was the first American to win the Nobel Peace Prize. Jonas Salk (1914-1995) and Albert Sabin (1906-1993) discovered polio vaccines during the 1950s, and Robert Hofstadter (1916-1970) won the Nobel Prize for creating a device for measuring the size and shape of neutrons and protons. Medical science pioneer Joseph Goldberger (1874-1929) laid the foundation for modern nutritional science with his study of the dietary habits of poor whites and blacks in the South. Finally, chemist Isaac Asimov (1920-1992) popularized science with his 500 fiction and nonfiction books on science.

SPORTS

Children of Jewish immigrants at the beginning of the twentieth century gravitated toward sports to break up the routine of daily life. Boxing was especially popular, with Jewish boxing champions Abe Attell (Albert Knoehr; 1884-1969), Barney Ross

(Barnet Rasofsky; 1909-1967), and Benny Leonard (Benjamin Leiner; 1896-1947), all hailing from New York's Lower East Side. Other world champions from various weight classes for two years or more include Benny Bass (1904-1975), Robert Cohen (1930–), Jackie Fields (Jacob Finkelstein; 1908–), Alphonse Halimi (1932–), Louis "Kid" Kaplan (1902-1970), Battling Levinsky (Barney Lebrowitz; 1891-1949), Ted Lewis (Gershon Mendeloff; 1894-1970), Al McCoy (Al Rudolph; born 1894), Charley Phil Rosenberg (Charles Green; 1901–), "Slapsie" Maxie Rosenbloom (1904-1976), and Corporal Izzy Schwartz (1902–).

Beyond boxing, Jews have made their mark in many other sports as well. The Jewish Sports Hall of Fame in Israel includes the following Americans: Red Auerbach (basketball), Isaac Berger (weightlifting), Hank Greenberg (baseball), George Gulak (gymnastics), Irving Jaffe (ice skating), Sandy Koufax (baseball), Sid Luckman (football), Walter Miller (horse racing), Dick Savitt (tennis), Mark Spitz (swimming), and Sylvia Wene Martin (bowling).

MEDIA

PRINT

Commentary.
An organ of the American Jewish Committee and published monthly, this influential Jewish magazine addresses religious, political, social, and cultural topics.

Contact: Neil Kozodoy, Editor.
Address: 165 East 56th Street, New York, New York 10022.
Telephone: (800) 551-3252; or (212) 751-4000.
Fax: (212) 751-4017.
E-mail: info@ajc.org.

Jewish Forward.
Published in English and Yiddish by the Forward Association. With a circulation of 25,000, the daily paper covers local, national, and international news, with special emphasis on Jewish life.

Contact: Mordecai Shtrigler, Editor.
Address: 45 East 33rd Street, New York, New York 10016.
Telephone: (800) 266-0773; or (212) 889-8200.
Fax: (212) 684-3949.

Jewish Press.
A national weekly newspaper covering issues and events related to Jewish life. Established in 1949, it has a circulation of 174,000.

Contact: Sholom Klass, Editor.
Address: 338 Third Avenue, Brooklyn, New York 11215.
Telephone: (800) 992-1600; or (718) 330-1100.
Fax: (718) 935-1215.
E-mail: jpeditor@aol.com.

Nashreeye B'nei Torah.
A bimonthly journal published by the Iranian B'Nei Torah Movement that carries articles on Jewish history, tradition, and culture for Iranian Jews.

Contact: Rabbi Joseph Zargari.
Address: P.O. Box 351476, Los Angeles, California 90035.
Telephone: (310) 652-2115.
Fax: (310) 652-6979.

Reform Judaism.
An organ of Union of American Hebrew Congregations, this quarterly concentrates on religious, political, and cultural issues of concern to Reform Jews.

Contact: Aron Hirt-Manheimer, Editor.
Address: 838 Fifth Avenue, New York, New York 10021.
Telephone: (212) 650-4240.
Online: http://shamash.org/reform/uahc/rjmag/ .

The Sentinel.
An English-language weekly paper established in 1911 with a circulation of 46,000. It publishes local, national, and international news stories and commentary as well as listings of events of interest to the Jewish community.

Contact: Jack I. Fishbein, Editor and Publisher.
Address: 6 North Michigan, Suite 905, Chicago, Illinois 60602.

RADIO
More than a dozen Jewish radio programs are broadcast weekly in cities across the United States. Typically lasting one to two hours, the programs are found on such stations as the following:

KCSN-FM (88.5).
Address: 18111 Nordhoff Street, Northridge, California 91330.
Telephone: (818) 677-3089.
E-mail: kcsn.request@csn.edu.
Online: http://www.kcsn.org.

WCLV-FM (95.5).
Address: 26501 Renaissance Parkway, Cleveland, Ohio 44128.

Telephone: (216) 464-0900.
Fax: (216) 464-2206.
E-mail: wclv@wclv.com.
Online: http://www.wclv.com.

WMUA-FM (91.1).
Address: 105 Campus Center, University
 of Massachusetts, Amherst,
 Massachusetts 01003.
Telephone: (413) 545-2876.
Fax: (413) 545-0682.
E-mail: wmua@stuaf.umas.edu.

TELEVISION

There are several Jewish television broadcasting stations, including:

Israel Broadcasting Authority.
Address: 1101 30th Street, Washington, D.C.
 20007.
Telephone: (202) 338-6091.

Israel Broadcasting Authority Radio and Television.
Address: 10 Rockefeller Plaza, New York, New
 York 10020.
Telephone: (212) 265-6330.

Jewish Television Network.
Address: 617 South Olive Street, Suite 515, Los
 Angeles, California 90014.
Telephone: (213) 614-0972.

Jewish Video Cleveland.
Address: Jewish Community Federation, 1750
 Euclid Avenue, Cleveland, Ohio 44115.
Telephone: (216) 566-9200.

Tele-Israel.
Cable channels 23, 24, 25, and M in New York City.
Telephone: (212) 620-7041.

ORGANIZATIONS AND ASSOCIATIONS

American Jewish Committee (AJC).
Founded in 1906, the AJC is an influential organization dedicated to the protection of religious and civil rights. Representing more than 600 Jewish American communities, the AJC sponsors educational programs, maintains its own library, and publishes the noted journal, *Commentary*.

Contact: David Harris, Executive Director.
Address: c/o Institute of Human Relations, 165
 East 56th Street, New York, New York 10022.
Telephone: (212) 751-4000.
Fax: (212) 838-2120.
E-Mail: info@ajc.org.
Online: http://www.ajc.org.

American Jewish Joint Distribution Committee (JDC).
Founded 1914, the JDC is a charitable organization created by the American Jewish Relief Committee, the Central Committee for Relief of Jews of the Union of Orthodox Congregations, and the People's Relief Committee. In addition to providing economic assistance to needy Jews in 25 countries, the organization fosters community development through an assortment of educational, religious, cultural, and medical programs with an annual budget of $90 million.

Contact: Michael Schneider, Executive Vice
 President.
Address: 711 Third Avenue, New York, New York
 10017-4014.
Telephone: (212) 687-6200.
Fax: (212) 682-7262.
E-mail: info@jdcny.org.

Anti-Defamation League of B'nai B'rith (ADL).
Founded in 1913, the ADL was created by B'nai B'rith, an international organization founded in 1843 to foster Jewish unity and protect human rights. The ADL was established to counter the rising tide of anti-Semitism during the early twentieth century, but it has since expanded its focus to protect against defamation of any group of people. Though the ADL has broadened its mission and sought to improve interfaith relations, one of the group's primary goals is to further American understanding of Israel. The ADL sponsors a number of bulletins, including its *Anti-Defamation League Bulletin*, as well as articles, monographs, and educational materials.

Contact: Abraham H. Foxman, Director.
Address: 823 United Nations Plaza, New York,
 New York 10017.
Telephone: (212) 490-2525.
Fax: (212) 867-0779.

92nd Street Young Men's and Young Women's Hebrew Association (YM-YWHA).
Founded in 1874, the YM-YWHA resulted from the merger between the Young Men's Hebrew Associa-

tion, the Young Women's Hebrew Association, and the Clara de Hirsch Residence. It provides Jewish cultural, social, educational, and recreational programs for 300,000 Jews in New York City. The association serves a variety of functions by maintaining several facilities in New York, including residence facilities for Jewish men and women between 18 and 27, men's and women's health clubs, swimming pools, gymnasiums, and a library containing more than 30,000 volumes on Jewish life and thought. Scholarships are also offered to Jewish undergraduate and graduate students.

Contact: Sol Adler, Executive Director.
Address: 1395 Lexington Avenue, New York, New York 10128.
Telephone: (212) 996-1100.
Fax: (212) 828-3077.
Online: http://www.92ndsty.org.

World Jewish Congress, American Section (WJC).

Founded 1936, the WJC is an international organization representing three million Jews in 68 countries. The American Section of the WJC represents 23 Jewish organizations. Guided by its mission to protect human rights worldwide, the WJC serves a consultative capacity with various international governing bodies, including the United Nations, UNESCO, UNICEF, International Labour Organization, and Council of Europe. The WJC is responsible for such periodicals as *World Jewry*, *Journal of Jewish Sociology* and *Patterns of Prejudice*.

Contact: Elan Steinberg, Executive Director.
Address: 501 Madison Avenue, 17th Floor, New York, New York 10022.
Telephone: (800) 755-5883; or (212) 755-5770.
Fax: (212) 755-5883.

MUSEUMS AND RESEARCH CENTERS

American Jewish Historical Society.

Founded in 1892 in an effort to gather, organize, and disseminate information and memorabilia related to the history of American Jews. The society has a library with more than ten million books, documents, manuscripts, pictures, and miniatures.

Contact: Justin L. Wyner, President.
Address: 2 Thornton Road, Waltham, Massachusetts 02154.
Telephone: (617) 891-8110.
Fax: (617) 899-9208.
E-mail: ajhs@tiac.net.

U.S. Holocaust Memorial Museum.

Sponsored by the President's Commission on the Holocaust and the U.S. Holocaust Memorial Council, it presents a moving tribute to the millions of Jews who perished in Nazi concentration camps during World War II. Opened in 1994, the museum features photographs, documents, and video.

Contact: Sam Eskenazi, Public Information Director.
Address: 100 Raoul Wallenberg Place, S.W., Washington, D.C. 20024-2150.
Telephone: (212) 488-0400.
E-mail: archives@ushmm.org.
Online: http://www.ushmm.org/.

The Jewish Museum.

Boasts the largest collection in the Western Hemisphere of materials related to Jewish life. Covering 40 centuries, the collection features paintings, drawings, prints, sculpture, ceremonial objects, coins, broadcast material, and historical documents.

Contact: Anne Scher, Director of Public Relations.
Address: 1109 Fifth Avenue, New York, New York 10128.
Telephone: (212) 423-3200.
Online: http://www.jewishmuseum.org/.

Leo Baeck Institute.

A research center dedicated to the preservation and study of materials related to the culture and socioeconomic history of German-speaking Jews of the nineteenth and twentieth centuries. The institute maintains a library with more than 500 unpublished memoirs and 60,000 volumes on the German Jewish experience from the Jewish Enlightenment to the emergence of National Socialism. There is also an art collection featuring more than 3,000 works by German-Jewish artists.

Contact: Carol Kahn Stauss, Executive Director.
Address: 129 East 73rd Street, New York, New York 10021.
Telephone: (212) 744-6400.
Fax: (212) 988-1305.
E-mail: lbi1@lbi.com.
Online: http://www.users.interporl.net/~lbi1.

YIVO Institute for Jewish Research.

A secular research institute dedicated to scholarship on all aspects of the American Jewish experience, with particular emphasis on Yiddish language and literature. Established in 1925, the institute has gathered a massive collection of some 22 million documents, photographs, manuscripts, audiovisuals, and other items related to Jewish life.

Contact: Dr. Tom L. Freudenheim, Executive Director.
Address: 555 West 57th Street, Suite 1100, New York, New York 10019.
Telephone: (212) 246-6080.
Fax: (212) 292-1892.
E-mail: tom@fruedenheim.com.
Online: http://www.baruch.cuny.edu/yivo/.

SOURCES FOR ADDITIONAL STUDY

American Jewish History: The Colonial and Early National Periods, 1654-1840, edited by Jeffrey S. Gurock. New York: Routledge, 1997.

Dimont, Max I. *The Jews in America: The Roots, History, and Destiny of American Jews.* New York: Simon & Schuster, 1978.

Glazer, Nathan. *American Judaism.* Chicago: University of Chicago Press, 1972.

Golden, Harry. *The Greatest Jewish City in the World.* Garden City, New York: Doubleday, 1972.

Hertzberg, Arthur. *The Jews in America: Four Centuries of an Uneasy Encounter.* New York: Simon & Schuster, 1989.

Howe, Irving. *World of Our Fathers.* New York: Harcourt Brace Jovanovich, 1976.

Kushner, Harold. *To Life! A Celebration of Jewish Being and Thinking.* Boston: Little, Brown, 1993.

Sachar, Howard M. *A History of the Jews in America.* New York: Knopf, 1992.

Silberman, Charles E. *A Certain People: American Jews and Their Lives Today.* New York: Summit Books, 1985.

Sklare, Marshall. *America's Jews.* New York: Random House, 1971.

Sorin, Gerald. *Tradition Transformed: The Jewish Experience in America.* Baltimore: Johns Hopkins University Press, 1997.

Waskow, Arthur I. *Seasons of Our Joy: A Handbook of Jewish Festivals.* New York: Summit Books, 1986.

JORDANIAN AMERICANS

by
Norman Prady
and Olivia Miller

OVERVIEW

Jordan is a kingdom near the Mediterranean Sea in the Southwest Asia area known as the Middle East or Near East. Its neighbors are Israel to the west, with which it shares the Dead Sea; Syria to the north; Iraq to the northeast; and Saudi Arabia to the east and south. Amman, the largest city, is the capital. Jordan is the site of the city of Petra, an archeological treasure that was the religious center for the nomadic Arab people called the Nabateans. Jordan's land area is about 35,000 square miles (almost 92,000 square kilometers).

Accurate demographic figures have been difficult to compile because of the substantial number of Jordanians living and working abroad and the continuous flow of West Bank Palestinians using Jordanian passports to travel back and forth between the East and West Banks of the Jordan River. Jordan's 1994 census estimated its population to be almost 4.3 million. Arabs represented 98 percent of the population, Circassians one percent, and Armenians one percent. Within the category of Arabs, a significant distinction exists between Palestinians—estimated at 55 to 60 percent of the population—and Transjordanians. A Palestinian is defined narrowly as a citizen of the British-mandated territory of Palestine, which existed from 1922 to 1948, and more broadly as a Muslim or Christian native or descendant of a native of the region between the Egyptian Sinai and Lebanon and west of the Jordan River-Dead Sea-Gulf of Aqaba line. A Transjordanian is a Muslim or Christian native of the region east of the Jordan River-Dead Sea-Gulf of Aqaba line and within the approximate boundaries of the contemporary state of Jordan. In addition to Circassians and Armenians, the small numbers of non-Arabs originating elsewhere include Shishans—also known as Chechens—and Kurds.

More than 90 percent of Jordanians are Sunni Muslims, and most of the rest are Christians of various denominations. There are a few Shia Muslims and even fewer adherents of other faiths. Arabic is the official language, and English is widely understood among the upper and middle classes. Almost all Jordanians speak a dialect of Arabic; increasing numbers speak or understand Modern Standard Arabic. Most people who have another native language, such as Circassians and Armenians, also speak Arabic.

The flag has three equal horizontal bands of black, white, and green with a red isosceles triangle based on the hoist side bearing a small white seven-pointed star. The seven points on the star represent the seven fundamental laws of the Koran. The King's website explains the flag's symbols as follows: "The flag symbolizes the Kingdom's roots in the Great Arab Revolt of 1916, as it is adapted from the revolt banner. The black, white and green bands represent the Arab Abbasid, Umayyad and Fatimid dynasties respectively, while the crimson triangle joining the bands represents the Hashemite dynasty. The seven-pointed Islamic star set in the center of the crimson triangle represents the unity of Arab peoples in Jordan."

HISTORY

As an independent nation, Jordan is relatively young. The land it occupies, however, has been inhabited for thousands of years. The archaeological record indicates that people who survived by hunting and gathering lived in the area during the Paleolithic and Mesolithic eras. They developed agriculture in the region in the Neolithic period, which began about 10,000 B.C. By 8000 B.C. these peoples were largely sedentary, settling in the region. The cities of Bayda and Jericho grew up during this time. After the Bronze Age, Amorites, Western Semites, Hyksos and Hittites successively invaded the area.

Since biblical times, the area came under the control of various political and military powers-Assyrians, Babylonians, Persians, Jews, Greeks, Nabateans, and Romans, to name a few—until 1516, when the Ottoman Turks incorporated the region into their empire. Shortly after the fall of the Ottoman Empire during World War I, the Allied Powers—the countries that won the war—made the area part of the British mandate of Palestine. Britain then established the Emirate of Transjordan in the portion of Palestine east of the Jordan River. In 1946 the country became independent of Britain. Three years later King Abdullah renamed it the Hashemite Kingdom of Jordan. Hashemite is the name of the dynasty, or hereditary line, through which the country's rulers descend.

Jordan captured and occupied territory on the west bank of the Jordan River in the Arab-Israeli war of 1948. It formally annexed the occupied area in 1950. It lost this land, however, in 1967, when Israel took control of East Jerusalem and the west bank following another war with Arab nations.

MODERN ERA

Jordan is a constitutional monarchy, meaning that its government consists of a hereditary king, plus a constitution guaranteeing citizens' rights. King Hussein took the throne in 1952 following the abdication of his ailing father. At that time Hussein was a teenager ruling a country where fewer than a third of the people were literate. Hussein made education a priority, and by the 1980s the literacy rate had doubled. Jordanians' standard of living also improved during this period, as the country received much aid from other Arab nations during the oil boom of the late 1970s and early 1980s.

In 1970 and 1971, Hussein successfully fought a civil war against Palestinian rebels. In 1974, under pressure from other Arab leaders, he recognized the Palestine Liberation Organization as the legitimate representative of the Palestinian peoples. Hussein worked hard to prevent Palestinian activity against his government. He brought many Palestinians into the government and into positions of power in the private sector. Jordan's policy toward other Arab nations generally has been moderate and flexible, with Arab unity as a priority. Jordan was, however, the most outspoken of the Arab states supporting Iraq during the Iran-Iraq war of 1980, partly out of a fear of the spread of Islamic fundamentalism from Iran. In 1988 Jordan abandoned its attempts to regain the West Bank from Israel.

Foreign aid declined in the 1980s, and Jordan's debts grew. In mid-1989 the Jordanian government began debt-rescheduling negotiations. The Persian Gulf crisis that began in August 1990 aggravated Jordan's already serious economic problems. The economy rebounded in 1992, largely due to the influx of capital repatriated by workers returning from the Gulf, but the recovery was uneven. In 1994 Hussein signed a peace treaty with Israel, the neighbor with which Jordan had fought three wars in 50 years. Still, debt, poverty, and unemployment remained ongoing challenges. Water shortages and disputes with Israel over water use became serious problems in the late 1990s. Hussein died February 7, 1999, following a seven-month battle with cancer. His oldest son, Abdullah, a 37-year-old career Army officer who was educated in the United States, succeeded him.

THE FIRST JORDANIANS IN AMERICA

It appears that the relatively small Jordanian immigration began shortly after World War II. Other Arab-Americans, notably those from Syria and Lebanon, have been coming to the United States since about 1850. West Bank Palestinians, as well as East Bank Jordanians, might travel to the United States with Jordanian passports, creating the indefinite category "Palestinian/Jordanian."

SIGNIFICANT IMMIGRATION WAVES

In the 1950s, 5,762 Jordanians immigrated to the Unites States. This number almost doubled in the 1960s, when 11,727 Jordanians immigrated. Then in the 1970s, 27,535 Jordanians arrived, reflecting an era of civil strife in Jordan. In the 1980s, immigration averaged around 2,500 a year. The total number of Jordanian immigrants from 1820 to 1984 was 56,720.

SETTLEMENT PATTERNS

From World War II until the 1980s, the typical Jordanian immigrant was a married male between the ages of 20 and 39. His education level was higher than that of the average person on the East Bank. More than 30 percent of those working in the United States were university graduates, and 40 percent were in professional positions. Many immigrants stayed four and a half to eight years, then returned to Jordan. American salaries were higher than those in Jordan, and attracted immigrants. More than other Middle Eastern immigrants, Jordanians tended to take their families with them when working in the United States. Since the 1980s, many Jordanians have remained in the United States and have formed cohesive communities. The Jordanian American community in Washington, D.C., held a candlelight vigil after the death of King Hussein.

ACCULTURATION AND ASSIMILATION

As comparative newcomers to the United States, few Jordanian Americans are at or beyond the third generation. As a result, they are much less Americanized, if at all, than groups with longer histories here. Guided by family and friends, these new Americans understandably find comfort in neighborhoods established by others from their home country. In such surroundings they continue their familiar practices in social activities, shopping, and religion. Continued use of their native language and dialect sustains homeland ties and delays acculturation. Language is a key factor in the acculturation process. Those who are fluent in English have greater communication and interaction with the larger community. Other factors that can accelerate acculturation include educational levels and how much contact with the larger community occurs on the job. Also, people from urban areas of Jordan adjust more quickly to America's cities than do some from rural areas. Children often adapt more easily to new surroundings and, as with other immigrant groups, tend to assimilate faster than their parents.

TRADITIONS, CUSTOMS, AND BELIEFS

While Jordan is modern and Western-oriented, Islamic ideals and beliefs provide the conservative foundation of the country's customs, laws and practices. The workweek for Jordanian government offices and most businesses is Saturday through Thursday. Along with religion, hospitality is an important value of Jordanians. A small gift is acceptable in return for hospitality.

Many elements of Jordanian American life provide cultural continuity. Among these are events offering music and dancing, which are typically provided by a larger Arab group. The events range from live stage presentations to shows on radio or cable television in many major metropolitan areas of the United States. Additionally, some cable networks show Arabic movies. This ongoing exposure to traditional entertainment is especially comforting to new immigrants and reassuring even to longer-term residents.

PROVERBS

Like many other Arab peoples, Jordanians use proverbs in place of slang. Here are some common proverbs: When elephants begin to dance, smaller creatures should stay away; Do not cut down the tree that gives you shade; The dogs may bark but the caravan moves on; Eat whatever you like, but dress as others do; The hand of God is with the group; He that plants thorns must never expect to gather roses; I am a prince and you are a prince, who will lead the donkeys; If begging should unfortunately be thy lot, knock at the large gates only; If you do what you've always done, you'll get what you've always gotten; Judge a man by the reputation of his enemies; A kind word can attract even the snake from his nest; Knowledge acquired as a child is more lasting than an engraving on stone; The man who can't dance says the band can't play; Older than you by a day, wiser than you by a year; Silence is the door of consent; Trust in God, but tie your camel; The wound of words is worse than the wound of swords; All sunshine makes the desert; The ass went seeking for horns and lost his ears; Beware of one who flatters unduly for he will also censure unjustly; Dawn does not come twice to awaken a man; Death is a black camel that lies down at every door; Sooner or later you must ride the camel.

CUISINE

Jordanian food is popular in the United States, and many cities boast Jordanian restaurants such as the Petra House in Portland, Oregon. Jordanian food is based on traditional Bedouin cooking. A good example is *mensef*, feast for special occasions that has altered little over the years. Usually, a whole sheep is roasted. Large chunks of the roasted meat are served with rice on a huge platter. A yogurt-based sauce, chopped parsley, and fried nuts are the dish's toppings. One generally eats *mensef* with the hand. The guests of honor at the feast are presented with the softly cooked eyes of the sheep, which is a delicacy.

In Jordanian meals, the main course usually starts with several varieties of *mazza*, or hors d'oeuvres, such as *humus*, *fuul*, *kube*, and *tabouleh*. *Felafel* consists of deep-fried chickpea balls. *Shwarma* is spit-cooked sliced lamb. *Fuul* is a paste of fava beans, garlic, and lemon. Lentils, *adas* in Arabic, are a common ingredient in Jordanian dishes, and there are many recipes for *Shorabat 'adas*, lentil soup. *Magloube* is a meat, fish, or vegetable stew served with rice. For example, one *Magloube* recipe calls for alternating layers of chicken, fried aubergines, and rice. *Magloube* is often served with a lettuce and tomato salad and some plain yogurt. Salads are an important side dish. Jordanian foods are seasoned with spices typical of the Mediterranean, including cumin, garlic, lemons, coriander, and especially saffron. Arabic unleavened bread, or *khobz*, is eaten with almost everything. A meal finishes with dessert or fresh fruits, and Arabic coffee without which no meeting, whether formal or informal, is

complete. Arabic coffee will normally be served continuously during social occasions. To signal that no more is wanted, one slightly tilts the cup when handing it back; otherwise it will be refilled.

There are several other typical Jordanian recipes. *Musakhan* is a chicken dish, cooked with onions, olive oil, and pine seeds and baked in the oven on a thick loaf of Arabic bread. *Mahshi Waraq 'inab* is made of grape leaves stuffed with rice, minced meat, and spices. Also popular is the famous Middle Eastern shish kebab, consisting of chunks of lamb or marinated chicken speared on a wooden stick and cooked over a charcoal fire with tomatoes and onions. The local drink is known as *arak*, an anise-flavored beverage that is served mixed with ice and water. Traditionally, lunch is Jordanians' main meal. They usually have a light breakfast and supper. Most Jordanians do not eat pork, which is forbidden to Muslims.

TRADITIONAL COSTUMES

As late as the 1980s, the style of any Middle Eastern costume conveyed the wearer's ethnic and regional identity as well as the identity of its maker. Men traditionally wore an ankle-length, cool, loose-fitting garment with a high neck and long sleeves called the *kandoura* or *dishdash*. The headdress was a *taqia* or *qahfa*, a skullcap covered by a long cloth, usually white, called a*gutra*, and was secured by a wool rope, known as *al iqal* or *al ghizam*. The headdress was wound around the crown, to protect the head and neck from the blistering sun. The *bisht*, a sleeveless flowing black or beige cloak trimmed with gold, whose material depended on the social status of the wearer, was the outfit for ceremonial occasions. Many people throughout the Arabian peninsula still wear traditional dress, with minor variations, because it is suitable for the desert climate.

Bedouin men typically carried weaponry of some kind. The *khanjar*, a curving double-edged blade, six to eight inches long, with hilt of local horn overlaid with sliver, was once necessary for defense and has since become a status symbol. The *khanjar*'s curving wooden scabbard has more extensive decoration, the upper part usually with engraved silver, the lower section consisting of strips of leather overlaid with silver and decorated with silver rings and wire, often in a geometric pattern, and capped with a silver tip. Scabbards also were decorated with gold. A single-edged tapering blade dagger with straight carved wood scabbard, silver overlaid at both ends, was another popular weapon, as was the *yirz*, an axe combining a three-foot shaft with a four-inch steel head. The *saif*, a double-edged sword, and the scimitar-like *qattara* are usually only seen in museums or in ceremonial dances. Silver and copper were used to decorate containers for gunpowder and long-barreled pistols. Bedouin men also carried less deadly items such as beautifully decorated silver purses, pipes, toothpicks, ear-cleaning spoons, and tweezers, all hanging from silver chains. Modern rifles and cartridge belts slung around the waist were eventually added to the customary dress of the Bedouin.

Women dressed in accordance to their lifestyle and to Islamic ordinances. As with men, traditional dress among women is still very popular. Bedouin women, for practical and monetary reasons, have chosen wool and cotton for their garments, whereas urban women favor silks, brocades, satins and chiffons. Women's clothing often bears intricate decoration. The *burqa*, a veil of coarse, black silk with a central stiffened rib resting on the nose leaving only the eyes clearly visible, is still worn in the street, particularly by older women. An all-enveloping black *abaya* is made from lightweight cloth embroidered with tapestried threads. The *kandoura*, a loose, full-sleeved dress reaching to midcalf, exquisitely embellished on cuffs and collar, is usually of colorful material, with its quality and design varying with the economic status of the wearer. Older Bedu, or Bedouin women of the village, and sometimes the younger ones too, still make and wear the traditional dress, a long black *thobe*, with hems, yokes and sleeves decorated with tiny embroidered stitches that form intricate and colorful patterns. Women make the most of their eyes and hands, as these are often the only visible parts of their bodies. They accentuate their eyes with kohl, while they apply henna to make detailed designs on palms of their hands and sometimes the soles of their feet.

Many tribal women still carry their savings around their necks, wrists, or ankles in their jewelry. These pieces have at various times included intricately designed necklaces formed from beads and coins; elaborate forehead decorations of coins and chains; earrings of ornate loops or dangling shapes, including inverted pyramids with embossed geometric designs; heavy bossed bracelets covering much of the lower arm; elaborate hinged anklets; rings for fingers, toes, and noses, sometimes inset with bone or horn and studded with stone, glass, or coral. Many fine examples of silver Bedouin jewelry can still be found in markets and museums.

DANCES AND SONGS

Bedouin musical traditions are important in Jordan. Jordanian music encompasses both vocal and instrumental performances. Groups of men sing trance-like chants to accompany belly dances. Arabian flute music is also popular. "Lamma Bada Yatathanna" is a classical Arabic song played on the *oud* (Arabic lute).

HOLIDAYS

Jordanian Americans celebrate Jordanian Independence Day on May 25, Labor Day on May 1, Army Day on June 10, the accession of the king, and the king's birthday.

HEALTH ISSUES

Jordanian-Americans' attitudes about health care show the influence of the culture's profound sense of family bonds. An elderly parent, for example, who is not able to live on his or her own, in a nearby private home, would become part of another family member's household. A retirement center or nursing home would not be an option. This attitude that family members should take care of one another extends to all relatives as well as the larger kinship group, which might include persons not directly related but considered family.

In February of 1999, the Cyprus Institute of Neurology and Genetics, in collaboration with two Jordanian hospitals, identified a new form of nerve and muscle-wasting hereditary disease that strikes a particular tribal population of Jordanians. The researchers also isolated the gene on chromosome nine that causes the crippling motor neuropathy, which is unique to people of the ancient Roman-Greek Jordanian city of Jerash and is transmitted by intermarriage among them. It is a recessive disorder, meaning both parents can carry the gene and not pass it to their children, although the risk is greater in this case than if only one parent is a carrier. The disease's victims are strictly Arab Jordanians, all from the Jerash area, and include no Palestinians. The disease causes selective weakness and wasting of the nerves controlling the muscles of the hands and feet, while not necessarily affecting the arms and legs.

LANGUAGE

Arabic is the official language of Jordan, but the number of languages listed for Jordan is eight, including Adyghe, Armenian, Chechen, Arabic, and four Arabic dialects. Levantine Bedawi Arabic dialect was the language of Jordan before the arrival of Palestinian refugees in the wake of the wars with Israel. It remains the language of the army and many TV programs for Bedouin people or to promote Bedouin culture. Most Jordanians speak an Arabic dialect common to Syria, Lebanon, Jordan, and parts of Iraq. Arabic is a Semitic language related to Aramaic, Hebrew, various Ethiopic languages, and others. The language exists in three forms: the classical Arabic of the Koran, the literary language developed from the classical and known as Modern Standard Arabic, and the local form of the spoken language. Standard Arabic is used for education, official purposes, and communication among Arabic-speaking countries. Arabic is rich in synonyms, rhythmic, highly expressive and poetic, and can have a strong emotional effect on its speakers and listeners. As the language of the Koran, believed by Muslims to be the literal word of God, it has been the vehicle for recounting of the historic glories of Islamic civilization. Arabic speakers are more emotionally attached to their language than are most peoples to their native tongues. Poetic eloquence has been one of the most admired cultural attainments and signs of cultivation in the Arab world.

Many Jordanians speak English, so Jordan's radio and television stations offer some English programming. There is a daily English newspaper in Amman as well a weekly newspaper that offers a French section. Additionally, some Jordanians who have business or cultural connections with France and Germany speak French and German; Jordan television offers some daily programming in French. Jordanian Americans have access to national newspapers published in Arabic. There is sometimes a local Arabic newspaper in a community with a large Arab population, such as metropolitan Detroit.

GREETINGS AND POPULAR EXPRESSIONS

In Arabic the Hashemite Kingdom of Jordan is called *Urdoun*. *Ahlan Wa Sahlan* means "welcome,"and *Marhab* means "hello." *Mat el malak, ash el malak* means "The king is dead; long live the king." This expression was heard frequently after the death of Hussein and the swearing in of King Abdullah, to signify both grief and optimism. The expression *inshallah*, "God willing," often accompanies statements of intention, and the term *bismallah*, "in the name of God," accompanies the performance of most important actions.

FAMILY AND COMMUNITY DYNAMICS

Jordanians' upbringing emphasizes generosity, warmth, openness and friendliness. The ideals of tribal unity and respect for the family form the core of Jordanian society. The father is the head of the Jordanian family and has authority over all members. These statements are equally true of Jordanian American families.

EDUCATION

As of 1998 Jordan had the second-highest literacy rate, 85 percent, in the Arab world. Nearly 68 percent of the adult population is literate, and nearly 100 percent of 10-to-15 age group is literate. The first nine years of education are compulsory and free; the next three are also free. In 1987 more than 900,000 students were enrolled in 3,366 schools with approximately 39,600 teachers. Also in 1987, about 69,000 students were enrolled in higher education. Nearly half of these were women.

Jordanian American families place a premium on education. Parents are very active in their children's schools, regardless of their own levels of education. They value education because it improves children's future prospects and brings honor to the family. Jordanian Americans have a higher rate of college graduation than other Arab groups, partly because so many Jordanians come to the United States specifically for education and then stay here.

THE ROLE OF WOMEN

In Jordan, as in many other Arab nations, there is an ongoing campaign for women's equal rights. Since the 1960s, increasing numbers of women have entered the work force. As women's education levels rose, they generally delay marriage. They also tend to have fewer children, partly because of the economic strain of supporting a large family. Still, marriage and childbearing confer status on women.

In a 1988 study of women and work in Jordan, journalist Nadia Hijab argued that cultural attitudes were not the major constraint on women's employment; rather, need and opportunity were more significant factors. Most employed women were single. In the mid-1980s, when unemployment surged, Jordan's leaders pressured women to return to their homes. Publicly and privately, Jordanians hotly debated the issue. Letters to the editors of daily newspapers argued for and against women's working. Hijab observed that by 1985 there was "almost an official policy" to encourage married women to stay at home. That year Prime Minister Zaid ar Rifai bluntly suggested in 1985 that working women who paid half or more of their salary to foreign maids who sent the currency abroad should stop working.

In the 1990s women organized to influence Jordanian society. The Jordan National Committee for Women was established as a policy forum in March of 1992. The committee worked to increase Jordanian women's awareness of the National Strategy, ratified in 1993, that aims to improve women's status, involve them in national development and economic activities, promote their legal status, and increase their participation in decision-making. In the late 1990s, the United Nations Development Fund for Women collaborated with the Jordan National Committee for Women in a meeting in Amman to discuss how to eliminate violence against women in Muslim society. Jordanian women led women's movements in Arab countries, and in 1998 Jordanian women gathered outside the U.S. embassy protesting against U.S. missile strikes against Sudan and Afghanistan. Princess Basma attended workshops on prioritizing women's research. In 1999 Queen Noor spoke out against "crimes of honor," specifically the murder of a woman by her husband whom she had allegedly dishonored by immodest or otherwise unacceptable behavior. Legal reform for women's rights appeared to be imminent in Jordan in 1999.

COURTSHIP AND WEDDINGS

Jordanian Americans want their children to marry within the culture or, at least, within the larger Arab-American community. Sometimes a Jordanian American man will travel to Jordan to find a woman he considers a suitable wife. On the other hand, marriage to a non-Jordanian is tolerable, and husband and wife are welcomed into each other's families.

According to Jordanian tradition, brought to the United States, the bride, groom, and both families plan weddings, and the groom and his family pay for them. Marriage is for life in the Jordanian American culture. If a couple has marital problems, parents and relatives from both families will intervene. Their focus will be on preserving the marriage. If there are children, the culture dictates that the couple resolve past their own problems for the children's sake. Divorce is uncommon.

In Jordan, arranged marriage was once the norm, but this changed toward the end of the twentieth century. Social interaction between single men and women, once rare, has increased. Jordanian society has become more accustomed to the idea of romantic love.

FUNERALS

Jordanian Americans have modified their homeland custom of quick burial to conform to fairly common U.S. practices. They generally use the facilities and services of a funeral director instead of having a home-based rite. Jordanian American Christians might display the body for several days while family and friends visit and offer their sympathies. Jordanian American Muslims, however, do not display the body. Well-wishers usually send food to the home of the deceased person's immediate family each day before the burial. Following the burial, family and friends will gather for a meal and to share memories. Visiting might continue for some days after.

INTERACTIONS WITH OTHER ETHNIC GROUPS

Jordanian Americans tend to be identified with and identify themselves with the larger Arab community. Along with language, they share culture and Middle Eastern history. Jordanian Americans sometimes conflict politically with Israeli organizations in the United States as well as with the pro-Israel policies of the U. S. government.

RELIGION

The religious affiliations of Jordanian Americans contrast sharply with those of homeland Jordanians. Jordan's government states that the country is 96 percent Muslim and four percent Christian. The Jordanian American community is almost the opposite, with the majority Christian and eight percent Muslim. The largest group of Jordanian American Christians belongs to the Eastern Orthodox Church, the next largest to the Roman Catholic Church, and the remainder to Protestant and evangelical churches. Jordanian American Christians and Muslims often share their church buildings and mosques with compatible congregations from other Arab groups, with the institutions bolstering identity and cultural continuity.

Jordan's constitution guarantees freedom of religion, but the official religion is Sunni Islam, and the government supports Sunni institutions. Sunni is the larger branch of Islam, with Shia being the smaller. The 1952 constitution stipulates that the king and his successors must be Muslims and sons of Muslim parents.

Muslims and Christians in Jordan have not had major conflicts. Even the interest of some Jordanians in Islamic fundamentalism during the late 1970s and the 1980s did not produce significant tensions. The largest of the Christian sects in Jordan, as among Jordanian Americans, is Eastern Orthodox.

EMPLOYMENT AND ECONOMIC TRADITIONS

Jordanian Americans have careers in education, business, engineering, and science. Women formed a little over 12 percent of the labor force in Jordan in the late twentieth century; the male-female breakdown in the Jordanian American work force is similar. Many Jordanians come to the United States to pursue advanced degrees in medicine and engineering. Most of the Jordanian students in Western Europe and the United States receive financing from their families, but some obtain assistance from the government of Jordan. Students from Western European and American schools tend to gain the more desirable and prestigious positions on their return home. The perceived higher quality of education in the West helps make these graduates more competitive in the job market.

POLITICS AND GOVERNMENT

Jordanians began arriving in the United States at a time—the latter half of the twentieth century—when their new country was rethinking its own structure. Civil rights laws have helped immigrants feel they do not have to totally submerge their ethnic identity to fully participate in American society. As a result, Jordanian Americans and members of other groups have felt increasingly secure in taking part in local and national political activity, both inside and outside their own groups' interests. They have welcomed interactions with their mother country as well. Jordan's deputy prime minister opened a Detroit trade show in 1997 and urged the United States to take a more active role in the peace process in the Middle East.

RELATIONS WITH JORDAN

Jordan established diplomatic ties to the United States in 1949. The United States began providing limited military aid to Jordan in 1950, then became its principal source of assistance in 1957, after the British discontinued financing. The United States supported Hussein against the Palestinian insurgents in the 1970-71 civil war but did not intervene directly. There were some conflicts between Jordan and the United States over Jordan's weapons requests during the 1980s. The two countries remained on largely cordial terms, however, with the United States providing specialized training for Jordan's military, and senior officers from each country visiting the other in exchange programs. The United States considered Hussein one of the most moderate Middle Eastern leaders and often relied on him to assist in peace negotiations in the region. Shortly before his death, he was instrumental in developing a peace agreement between Israel and the Palestinians.

In 1997 Jordan had a $400 million trade deficit with the United States and was eager to attract American tourists. About 80,000 Americans visited Jordan in 1998, according to the *St. Petersburg Times*. In May of 1999, the U.S. State Department announced it would grant two scholarships yearly to Jordanian students pursuing studies in fields relevant to the Middle East peace process. The department's U.S. Information Agency will award two highly qualified Jordanian students money for advanced studies from the King Hussein Memorial Fulbright Scholarship Program.

INDIVIDUAL AND GROUP CONTRIBUTIONS

LITERATURE

Diana Abu-Jaber, a second-generation Jordanian-American, received her doctorate in English literature from the State University of New York. She has taught literature and creative writing at the University of Michigan, the University of Oregon, and the University of California, Los Angeles. Her first novel, *Arabian Jazz*, won the Oregon Book Award and was a finalist for the national PEN/Hemingway award. For her second novel, *Memories of Birth*, she won a National Endowment for the Arts grant for the manuscript. In 1998 she returned from Amman, where she was on a Fulbright research grant award, conducting interviews with Jordanian and Palestinian women about their lives to develop background for her next novel. In 1999 Abu-Jaber was writer in residence at Portland State University.

SOCIAL ISSUES

Lily Bandak is a renowned photographer who founded an organization to help disabled workers in Arab nations. Born in Amman, Jordan, Bandak went to grade school in Bethlehem on the West Bank. She has lived in the United States since 1960, residing in Newark, Delaware. She studied at the Académie De La Grande Chaumiér in Paris, the Philadelphia College of Art, the University of Delaware, and the Antonelli College of Photography.

Her work with major public figures in the Middle East has included assignments as the personal photographer of Mrs. Anwar Sadat and King Hussein and Queen Noor. She also has photographed Yasser Arafat. In 1978 the government of Egypt invited her to document the people and monuments of that country. These photographs were exhibited in Egypt, in Washington, D.C., and across the United States, and were later compiled into a book, *Images of Egypt*. She has also exhibited at the World Trade Center in New York City. She was the first photographer to have work accepted into the permanent collection of the White House during the Carter administration.

In 1984 Bandak was diagnosed with multiple sclerosis. She designed a camera mount to be attached to her wheelchair that makes it possible for her to return to work. In 1994 she set up the Bandak Foundation, which encourages people with disabilities to enter the work force and participate fully in society.

MEDIA

There are no publications in the United States for Jordanian Americans. *The Jordan Times* is an English-language independent political newspaper, published daily except Friday in Jordan by the Jordan Press Foundation. *Jordan Today* is a monthly English-language magazine on tourism, culture, and entertainment, published by InfoMedia International in Amman. An online weekly newspaper in English can be found at http://star.arabia.com.

ORGANIZATIONS AND ASSOCIATIONS

American Arab Anti Discrimination Committee.
Nonsectarian, nonpartisan organization committed to defending the rights of people of Arab descent and promoting their rich cultural heritage. The largest Arab-American grassroots organization in the United States, founded in 1980 by former Senator James Abourezk, with chapters nationwide.

Address: 4201 Connecticut Avenue, N.W., Suite 300, Washington, D.C. 20008.
Telephone: (202) 244-2990.

Bandak Arab African Foundation.
Nonprofit organization that urges Middle Eastern governments, particularly Jordan, to help people with disabilities in the work force.

Address: 345 New London Road, Newark, Delaware 19711.
Telephone: (302) 737-4055.

Embassy of the Hashemite Kingdom of Jordan.
Address: 3504 International Drive, N.W., Washington, D.C. 20008.
Telephone: (202) 966-2664.

Palestine Children's Relief Fund.
Nonprofit, nonpolitical relief fund to provide humanitarian assistance to children suffering from crisis in the Middle East.

Contact: Steve Sosebee, Director.
Address: P.O. Box 1926 Kent, Ohio 44240.
Telephone: (330) 678-2645.

Palestinian Heritage Foundation.
A nonprofit cultural and educational organization aimed at promoting awareness and understanding of Arab and specifically Palestinian culture and traditions.

Address: P.O. Box 1018, West Caldwell, New Jersey 07006.
E-mail: palherf@aol.com.

Sisterhood Is Global Institute.
Established in 1984, the Sisterhood is Global Institute seeks to deepen the understanding of women's human rights at the local, national, regional and global levels, and to strengthen the capacity of women to exercise their rights. With members in 70 countries, it currently maintains a network of over 1,300 individuals and organizations. It has a regional office in Jordan that was inaugurated by Princess Basma Bint Talal.

Address: 4343 Montgomery Avenue, Suite 201, Bethesda, Maryland 20814.
Telephone: (301) 657-4355.
E-mail: sigi@igc.apc.org.

United Palestinian Appeal.
Nonprofit, nonpolitical, tax-exempt American charity based in Washington, D.C., established in 1978, dedicated to alleviating the suffering of Palestinians, particularly those living in the Occupied Territories.

Address: 2100 M Street N.W., #409, Washington, D.C. 20037.
Telephone: (202) 659-5007.

SOURCES FOR ADDITIONAL STUDY

Hijab, Nadia. *Womanpower: The Arab Debate on Women at Work*. Cambridge Middle East Library Series. Cambridge: Cambridge University Press, 1988.

Hitti, Philip K. *History of the Arabs from the Earliest Time to the Present*. New York: St. Martin's Press, 1956.

Jureidini, Paul A., and R. D. McLaurin. *Jordan: The Impact of Social Changes on the Role of the Tribes*. The Washington Papers, No. 108, Center for Strategic and International Studies, Georgetown University. New York: Praeger, 1984.

Matusky, Gregory, and John Hayes. *King Hussein*. New York: Chelsea House, 1987.

Metz, Helen Chapin. *Jordan, A Country Study*. Washington, DC: Federal Research Division, Library of Congress, 1991.

Satloff, Robert B. *Troubles on the East Bank: Challenges to the Domestic Stability of Jordan*. Center for Strategic and International Studies, Georgetown University. New York: Praeger, 1986.

Kenyan immigrants enjoy a linguistic advantage over other immigrants because English is widely spoken in Kenya. Within a short amount of time, many Kenyan Americans achieve a relative degree of financial security.

KENYAN AMERICANS

by
Laura C. Rudolph

Overview

Located in East Africa near the equator, the Republic of Kenya measures 224,960 square miles (582,650 square kilometers). It is bordered to the north by Ethiopia and Sudan, the Indian Ocean to the east, Somalia to the northeast, Tanzania to the south, and Uganda to the west. The capital is Nairobi is Kenya's largest city, with close to 2 million people.

Kenya has a total population of just under 29 million people and represents a mixture of over 40 indigenous ethnic groups. The groups fall into one of four categories that comprise over 98 percent of the entire population: the Bantu, Nilotic, Nilo-Hamitic, and Hamitic peoples. The Bantu peoples are comprised of the Kikuyu (22 percent), Luhya (14 percent), and Kisii (6 percent); the Nilotics include the Luo (13 percent) and the Kalenjin (12 percent); the Nilo-Hamitics include the Masai, Samburu, Kipsigis, and Nandi; and the Hamitics include the Tugen and Elgeyo. Asians, Arabs, and Europeans compose the remaining 2 percent of the population.

The majority of Kenyans are Christians, including Protestants (38 percent) and Roman Catholics (28 percent), while others practice indigenous beliefs (26 percent). Other religious denominations include Muslim (6 percent), and smaller numbers of Hindus, Sikhs, and Bahais. The country's official languages are Kiswahili and English. Kenya's national flag consists of three horizontal bands of black, green, and red, and contains a shield with crossed spears in the center.

HISTORY

The history of Kenya may be that of humankind. Toward the end of the twentieth century, excavated bones and artifacts convinced many archaeologists and scientists that human evolution began in Kenya. Throughout the first few centuries A.D., Kenya was the destination of numerous migrating tribes, such as the Luo and the Bantu peoples. The tribes spread across the country and established themselves in various areas. The Kalenjin settled around the western part of what became Kenya, while the Kikuyu covered the fertile ground of the Highlands and the Rift Valley. Each group was a self-contained community with its own language, customs, and beliefs.

During years of drought or other natural disasters, tensions increased between tribes as they vied for fertile ground. The Bantus, particularly the Kikuyu, established a stronghold in Kenya's interior around Mount Kenya, largely as a result of their sophisticated tools and weapons. The Kikuyu prospered and established a rich agricultural economy, developing a sound economic and political infrastructure. However, in the nineteenth century, the Masai peoples, famous for their hunting and fighting skills, challenged the Bantu domination and eventually exerted a great influence on customs and styles before severe droughts and disease ended their reign.

Arabs settled on the Kenyan coast as early as the tenth century, and the Portuguese contested for the coast during the fifteenth and sixteenth centuries. The Arabs regained control during the eighteenth century, and by the early-to-mid nineteenth centuries, Sayyid Said of Oman loosely controlled the coast. By this time, Africa's largely untapped wealth attracted scores of Europeans, and in 1885 Africa was partitioned into several sectors controlled by various European nations.

Great Britain received control of Kenya and Uganda, and the British Empire lost little time in issuing a commercial license in 1888 to The Imperial British East Africa Company (IBEA). The IBEA, headed by Sir William MacKinnon, attempted to establish trading centers and a unified control across the regions. However, the British government was not altogether satisfied with their efforts and formally established Kenya as a British protectorate in 1895 and a crown colony in 1920.

British rule was not kind to native Kenyans. Although they quickly built a railroad that promot-ed economic development by linking the regions together, the rights of Africans were restricted, while white settlement was encouraged. The Africans were overtaxed, undereducated, and lacked political representation. In addition, they were not allowed to grow certain exportable crops, and could not settle in the Highlands and the Rift Valley, regarded as the richest farmland in the country. In many instances, tribal peoples were forced to relocate to designated areas in Kenya.

During World War I, a large number of Kenyan soldiers were recruited to fight for the British. Following the war, many Africans, particularly the Kikuyus, who had lost much of their land, began organizing to lobby for reform. One such group, the East African Association (EAA), encouraged protests and demonstrations. Although the EAA dissolved shortly thereafter, the Kikuyu Central Association (KCA) quickly took its place and continued the fight against white supremacy. The KCA lobbied for political representation, lower taxes, and the right to inhabit restricted lands. Although the organization enjoyed some success, it was unable to achieve its goals before it was banned in 1940, shortly after World War II began. However, the KCA helped pave the way for future organizations, which would ultimately achieve independence for Kenya.

MODERN ERA

World War II provided the impetus Kenya needed to achieve independence. Many Kenyans fought in the war and they learned both organizational and military skills. In 1944, the Kenyan African Union (largely comprised of Kikuyus) was formed to continue the fight against white supremacy. In 1947, Jomo Kenyatta was elected the president of the KAU. Although most members were Kikuyus, they encouraged all ethnic groups to join together to achieve independence.

Other Africans, frustrated with the slow response to their demands, turned to more violent means. The *Mau Mau* uprising of 1952-56 was characterized with numerous acts of violence and terrorism against the colonial government and settlers. Brutally suppressed, the uprising left thousands of Africans dead, while only a handful of British were killed.

However, the uprising was not wholly unsuccessful. In response to changes occurring throughout European-dominated countries across Africa, the colonial government was ready to capitulate in Kenya. Africans were allowed representation in the government, and they continued to lobby to gain autonomy. In 1960 they formed the Kenya African

National Union (KANU). However, political infighting between the dominant Kikuyus and other groups led to the formation of a rival party, the Kenya African Democratic Union (KADU).

In 1962, the two parties laid aside their differences and united to form a coalition government. Jomo Kenyatta was elected the first prime minister. Kenya was officially declared independent on December 12, 1963, and became a republic in 1964. Shortly thereafter the KADU dissolved, and Kenya was ruled chiefly by the KANU until 1966 when the Kenya People's Union (KPU) was formed.

From the start, the KPU was at odds with the KANU and did not gain much support beyond the Luo peoples. The group was ordered to disband after an important member of government personnel was assassinated, a crime that was attributed to the KPU. The Kenyan government, largely under Kikuyu control, turned its attention to ongoing social and economic problems. In an effort to boost their flagging economy, they welcomed foreign investors, and Kenya rapidly became the most prosperous country in East Africa.

Although Kenya was fearful that its political stability would be shaken by the death of Jomo Kenyatta in 1978, Daniel arap Moi succeeded without challenge. In 1982 the Royal Air Force staged a coup attempt, but Moi remained in office. In 1991, largely at the urging of foreign investors, Moi pledged to further address social and economic problems and encouraged the formation of a multiparty system, which prevailed through the end of the twentieth century.

SIGNIFICANT IMMIGRATION WAVES

Kenyans have a recorded presence on American soil for over 300 years. The earliest Kenyans were not voluntary immigrants, but were victims of the American slave trade that was not outlawed until 1808. Partly as a result, voluntary migration remained negligible until the last decades of the twentieth century. Between 1980 and 1990, Kenyan immigration more than doubled.

Several factors contributed to increased Kenyan immigration to the United States. Many Kenyans were already exposed to different facets of American culture because of the close relationship between Kenya and the United States. American cuisine and entertainment had become commonplace in Kenya. Exposure to American culture encouraged Kenyans to take advantage of numerous economic and educational opportunities available in the United States.

Kenya's depressed economy and high unemployment rate (over 35 percent), coupled with the importance the country places on education, resulted in more qualified and educated workers than available skilled positions. Toward the end of the twentieth century, Kenyan immigrants were particularly attracted to technology-oriented careers in the United States, an occupation virtually impossible to pursue in Kenya where over 75 percent of the jobs are agricultural-based.

The main areas of Kenyan settlement in the United States include Washington, D.C., where 50 percent of Kenyan Americans can be found, Texas, California, and parts of the Midwest. A number of Kenyans also settled in Georgia and North Carolina, two states with important technological centers.

ACCULTURATION AND ASSIMILATION

For the most part, Kenyan Americans have enjoyed a fairly smooth assimilation process. Many Kenyan immigrants are well educated and possess specialized job skills. They have little trouble finding employment in the technological and health care professions, where they are most numerous. In addition, Kenyan immigrants enjoy a linguistic advantage over other immigrants because English is widely spoken in Kenya. Within a short amount of time, many Kenyan Americans achieve a relative degree of financial security.

Although Kenyans enjoy a smooth transition, their assimilation has not been completely free of difficulties. Unfortunately, Kenyan Americans are sometimes subject to the same prejudice that other African Americans often face. Although blatant discrimination is socially frowned upon, a covert bias is frequently directed toward those of African heritage. Kenyan immigrants often expressed disappointment in this aspect of their assimilation into the larger American society.

The vast majority of Kenyans do become naturalized citizens; less than two percent return to Kenya. The strict immigration quota creates obstacles for many of the immigrants desiring to become citizens and the process can be long and difficult. A small number of Kenyans become U.S. citizens through marriage to Americans. Although many Kenyan Americans would eventually like to return to Kenya after they have completed their education or achieved financial goals, the instability of Kenya's economy deters them. They do maintain contact with their Kenyan relatives and make frequent trips to Kenya.

TRADITIONS, CUSTOMS, AND BELIEFS

Kenyans have a variety of traditions, most of which are connected to indigenous religious beliefs and thus vary from group to group. Many customs and beliefs originate from an agricultural lifestyle and contain special prayers, dances, and rituals to encourage different natural events. During droughts, for instance, the Masai strip the bark off of tree, bury a skin around the root of the tree, and pour water over it while placing charms and praying for rain.

Other traditions stem from hunting and warring practices, where prayers and rituals would be performed before and after the hunt or raid. The Masai sacrifice a sheep before a raid. Reverence of various animals plays a role in other customs. The Suk revere snakes and if a snake were to enter a hut, the animal could not be killed but was to be fed milk. Traditions also centered around life events, particularly the initiation of a child into adulthood or the birth of a baby.

Toward the end of the twentieth century, traditional Kenyan customs and beliefs were gradually fading despite attempts to preserve them. Many agricultural and hunting traditions were not easily transferable to the United States and disappeared as Kenyans immigrated. Although Kenyan Americans maintain a close connection to their cultural heritage, they have abandoned many of the older customs that are no longer relevant to their life in the United States.

PROVERBS

Many proverbs from Kenyan culture have survived through the generations. They include: Even when the shield covering wears out the frame survives; When a drum has a drumhead, one does not beat the wooden sides; When a scorpion stings without mercy, you kill it without mercy; A man does not rub backs with porcupines; Rooster, do not be so proud. Others are: Your mother was only an eggshell; The canoe must be paddled on both sides.

CUISINE

Traditional Kenyan cuisine reflects the agricultural products of the region. Kenyan recipes are generally inexpensive and nourishing, relying heavily on potatoes, rice, and maize. Maize is found in a variety of recipes, especially a porridge called *ugali*, which is cooked with meat (chicken, goat, or beef) or greens and is eaten nearly every day. Other dishes include: *karanga*, a stew cooked with goatmeat, carrots, onions and potatoes; *pillau*, a spiced rice dish that sometimes includes meat; *sukima wiki*, a fried dish with chopped spinach, onions, tomatoes or other vegetables; *kienyeji*, a dish with mashed corn, beans, potatoes, and greens; and *michicha*, which contains spinach, onions, and tomatoes.

Fruits are an important part of the Kenyan diet. People commonly eat bananas, mangos, pineapples, and avocados. Snacks include roasted maize; *samosa* (fried mincemeat and vegetables); *kitumbuo* (fried rice bread); and *mandaazi* (fried dough cakes). Like most regions of the world, Kenyans also eat at international and fast food restaurants.

DANCES AND SONGS

Ngoma, the traditional form of Kenyan music, is generally used to describe both music and dance centered around the drum. Many Kenyan dances and songs serve specific purposes and have a variety of themes such as agricultural (for example, harvest, rain, or fire), mourning, jubilation, fertility, war, and peace. Most of the dances include stamps, hops, squats, slides, and hip swivels, reflecting the occasion for which it is intended. For instance, the battle dance of the Samburu contains fierce jumping motions, which simulate actions of a raid. There are numerous traditional Kenyan instruments, including the drum; bow harp; lute; lyre; instruments made from animals' horns; wood trumpet; flute; rattle; bell; gong; and the pit xylophone. Some songs are sung in unison, while others are call-and-response, in which one person shouts a line and the others respond.

TRADITIONAL COSTUMES

The traditional clothing of Kenyans varies from region to region. Although the clothing of each ethnic group can appear similar, they are actually unique representations. For example, the traditional clothing of the Masai men, who were known for their fierce warrior status, includes headdresses of lion's mane and ostrich feathers. In addition, their faces are painted with white and red paint.

The Suk men wear elaborate shoulder-length chignons, jewelry from animals' horns, capes made of skins, lip plugs, and pierced nose discs. Turkana women shave their hair at the sides and twist the top into strands, and wear oval-shaped plate earrings. Their shoulders are covered with disc-shaped ornamentation chipped from ostrich eggs. Married Turkana women also wear an apron decorated with beads, which is held with a beaded belt.

During special events, particularly those related to the life cycle, clothing serves a special purpose. When girls and boys undergo initiation via

circumcision or clitoridectomies, they wear certain clothing that reveals their status. Njemps boys undergoing circumcision wear a dyed black skin held in place by a belt of cowry shells and two ostrich feathers in their ears. Njemps girls don metal beads around their neck or faces as a symbol of their on-going clitoridectomy process. Other life cycle events require particular costumes as well. Women who have just given birth to a baby often paint the area around their eyes. The majority of Kenyans—including Kenyan Americans—wear more modern clothing and no longer don traditional garments except on special occasions.

HOLIDAYS

Kenyan Americans celebrate Good Friday, Easter Monday, and Christmas Day along with American holidays such as New Year's Day, Labor Day, and other secular holidays. Specific Kenyan holidays include the anniversary of the country's independence (December 12) and Kenyatta Day (October 20), which honors Kenya's first prime minister, Jomo Kenyatta. The small number of Kenyan immigrants in the United States prohibits lavish celebrations in honor of these events, but Kenyan-American organizations sometimes hold a special event in honor of these holidays.

HEALTH ISSUES

Despite recent efforts to address health issues, Kenyans have a fairly low life expectancy (47 years for males and 48 years for females) and a high percentage of infant deaths (59.38 per 1,000 births). Poor living conditions increase the risk of disease and several diseases are particularly troublesome to Kenyans: poliomyelitis, schistosomiasis, intestinal parasites, malaria, respiratory ailments, and, increasingly, HIV infection. Most Kenyan Americans conform to the rules established for immigrants and are in good health when they enter the United States. Like most Americans, Kenyan Americans are able to take advantage of the medical insurance offered as a benefit of employment.

LANGUAGE

Most Kenyans are multilingual and speak at least three languages. Kiswahili and English are the official languages of Kenya. Each indigenous group has a fully developed language of their own. Kiswahili, a Bantu language that gradually incorporated Arabic words over the centuries, serves as a common language for the various regions in Kenya. Although everyday activities are conducted in Kiswahili, government and court business continue to use the English language. Other ethnic languages include Luo, Kikuyu, Kamba, Luyia, Gusii, and Kalenjin, which are usually spoken at home. In addition, English words have become incorporated into Kiswahili, which has led to a hybrid language composed of Kiswahili and English called *Sheng*. Since most Kenyans speak English, Kenyan immigrants generally do not face linguistic obstacles, and are comfortable switching to English as their principal language.

GREETINGS AND OTHER POPULAR EXPRESSIONS

Common Swahili greetings and other expressions include: *Jambo*—hello; *si jambo*—no problems; *habari*—how are you doing?; *nzuri*—fine; *karibu*—welcome; *kwaheri*—goodbye; *asante*—thank you; *tutaonana*—see you; *ndiyo*—yes; *hapana*—no; *jina langu*—my name is; *zuri*—good; *baya*—bad; *si mbaya*—not bad; *sawa*—ok; *kabisa*—perfect; *samahani*—sorry; *hebu*—excuse me; *inshallah*—if God wills it; and *tafadhali*—please.

FAMILY AND COMMUNITY DYNAMICS

Kenyans place a high value on family relationships and the importance of kinship. Close attention is paid to the maintenance of ancestry and lineage, particularly along the paternal lines. The individual is considered less important than his or her community, which centers around the extended family. Households normally contain at least one extended family member. Often several generations are present. Children sometimes refer to their cousins as "brother" or "sister," and call their aunts and uncles "mother" and "father." Grandparents and great-grandparents are revered for their wisdom.

Because of the emphasis placed on the survival of lineage, marriage is a sacred duty. Men are often allowed to marry more than one woman in order to ensure the continuance of the patriarchal line. Women are expected to raise large families. Women who do not have many children often face public derision. Large families are rewarded in many instances, both financially and through the elevation of their status. Kenyan homes are traditionally conservative and strictly patriarchal. Husbands work outside the home while the women are expected to stay within the boundaries of the household.

As a result of strict immigration laws, many Kenyans initially immigrate alone and are separated from their families for a long period of time. Kenyans often have a difficult time adjusting to American values, which they perceive as antithetical to their own, especially individualism, competitiveness, and materialism. Most Kenyan immigrants are accustomed to a closely-knit community surrounded by many family members, and they sometimes feel isolated when they first arrive.

One of the greatest concerns of Kenyan immigrants is their inability to foster a sense of Kenyan identity in their children, who are born and raised in the United States. The gap between immigrants and their children often fosters tensions as the chil-dren have a more difficult time understanding the importance of ancestry and lineage. While Kenyans usually marry within their own ethnic group, the children of Kenyan immigrants are much more likely to marry outside of it. Many Kenyan American parents are involved in Kenyan American organizations that sponsor events to help expose their children to Kenyan culture.

THE ROLE OF WOMEN

Through the end of the twentieth century, Kenyan households maintained rigid rules concerning women's roles within the patriarchal household. Wives and daughters were expected to stay strictly within the domestic sphere, except for designated agricultural tasks. The importance of these responsibilities is attested by the custom of paying bride-price, which compensated the parents for the loss of their daughters.

From the moment they were considered ready for betrothal, women were under an enormous amount of societal pressure to marry. Married women were under the protection of their husbands and forced to obtain permission from them to open a bank account or acquire a driver's license.

Families were always traced from the father's line and all children from a marriage "belonged" to the father. The frequent pregnancies of Kenyan women further reduced their opportunities to break out of traditional domestic-related roles. Contraception remained difficult to obtain and was regarded with suspicion by communities. During the last two decades of the twentieth century, the emerging women's movement began lobbying for changes in educational, health, and other matters.

Kenyan American women are appreciative of the opportunities they find in the United States. Unlike their native-born country, immigrants are able to obtain contraception, driver's licenses, and bank accounts without permission from their husbands. Since Kenyan women are usually well educated, they do not have difficulties finding employment and enjoy the freedom of pursuing a career outside the home.

WEDDINGS

Since much emphasis is placed on family relationships, Kenyan marriages are taken very seriously and must be met with approval by both families. After it has been granted, there is an engagement period, before the marriage ceremony takes place. The vast majority of Kenyans are Christians and their weddings usually conform to the dictates of their religion.

There are also traditional indigenous customs that vary from group to group. For instance, the Kikuyu men choose their wives after carefully examining their personalities, integrity, and sociability. However, it is not customary for women to accept a marriage offer immediately, but to hesitate and refer the question to her father.

After she does accept, the bridegroom presents his bride with gifts, which are termed bridewealth. In addition to more practical items such as cattle or livestock, the gifts sometimes include a *mukwar* (leather strap), *neguo ya maribe* (woman's dress made out of skins and beads, presented to the mother of the bride), a *ruhiu* (sword), and an *itimu ria nduthu* (a man's coat made out of skins, presented to the father of the bride). Other indigenous groups practice similar marriage customs, which are sometimes performed in addition to the Christian ceremonies.

CIRCUMCISIONS

An important life cycle event that takes place in Kenyan culture concerns the initiation of boys and girls into adulthood. This event is traditionally marked with male circumcision and female clitoridectomy rituals. Although male circumcision is regularly practiced fairly among many different groups, the practice of female circumcision (clitoridectomy) is less common. These initiations are an important event for those involved as well as the entire community. Although the customs vary from tribe to tribe, circumcision usually occurs between the twelfth and sixteenth birthday of a boy or girl.

Before undergoing the ceremony, the initiates spend up to a year in preparation, undergoing a series of rituals. For instance, Nandi boys are circumcised around their thirteenth birthday. Their preparation includes learning their groups' folklore, shaving their heads, passing courage tests, and wearing certain garments. After the event, they are placed in seclusion and not allowed to eat with their hands for the first week. After undergoing another series of rituals, they take an oath of secrecy about what they have learned. They are then considered part of Nandi manhood and wear certain clothing to indicate their new status.

Nandi girls undergo a similar process. During their preparation, time they wear certain garments and enter into seclusion. They are generally not allowed to see men during this time. At the end of the initiation period, following the clitoridectomy, the girls can wear different clothing to display their new status. They are then eligible for marriage. Both girls and boys are expected to undergo the experience without complaining.

Toward the end of the twentieth century, these customs were gradually abandoned. Clitoridectomies, in particular, were heavily criticized, in part due to the unhygienic conditions under which they were performed. Kenyan immigrants generally do not observe the practice of male or female circumcision in the United States.

FUNERALS

The majority of Kenyans practice Christian burials and funeral services. Their reverence of ancestry dictates proper respect for the dead and funerals are carefully performed. There are also many indigenous beliefs regarding the afterlife and the spirit world, which are reflected in older customs of burial and funeral services.

The Suk traditionally buried their dead so that their stomachs were tilted toward the Seker, the sacred mountain of the Suk. The Maragoli give a widow her husband's spear and shield. During the funeral she would carry them before handing them to his eldest brother immediately afterwards. The Taveta bury their dead in a sitting position. Men were buried with their left arm positioned on the knee to support the head while the women were buried near the door of their hut in a sitting position with their right arm positioned on their knee. Kenyan American funerals usually do not vary greatly from the funerals of other Americans of their same religion.

RELIGION

Over 60 percent of the Kenyans are Protestant or Roman Catholic, while six percent are Muslim. There are also numerous tribal religions. For example, the Suk believe in a god called the sky (*terorut*) whose his son is the rain (*ilat*). This traditional religion demands regular rituals and sacrifices that demonstrate their loyalty to their god.

The Maragoli believe in a god named *Nyasaye* who is aided by spirits. The Maragolis make offerings to these spirits in a shrine made out of a pole surrounded by eight stones. Once a year, followers drink a brew of water and millet and spit the mixture on the heads and feet of women and children. Blood from a dead chicken is smeared on the heads and feet of women and children as well as the eight stones. The beak is cut off from the dead chicken and put around the neck of the youngest child. The rest of the chicken is roasted and mixed with the millet, cooked to a paste, and then arranged on the stones. If the necessity arises, for example illness taking hold of the group, the Maragoli repeat the ritual.

Most indigenous groups also believe in witchcraft and spirit matter. Witch doctors are commonly called upon during times of distress from illness, drought or other natural disasters, and other disruptive events. The last part of the twentieth century saw a decline in the practice of older customs.

The vast majority of Kenyans that immigrate to the United States are Protestant or Catholic. They generally maintain the practice of these beliefs. Kenyan immigrants look for churches in which they feel comfortable with both the congregation and the manner in which their faith is practiced. The immigrants often find that their church helps ease the adjustment process to their new country, particularly if other Kenyan immigrants belong to the same church.

EMPLOYMENT AND ECONOMIC TRADITIONS

The high value that Kenyan Americans place on education has allowed them to find skilled positions. Even during the initial adjustment period, Kenyan Americans are less likely to need assistance than other immigrants, and they tend to have an overall high employment rate. Because most Kenyans are already fluent in English, they have an even greater advantage over other immigrant groups. Over 50 percent of Kenyans gravitate toward technology fields. There is also a large number of Kenyan Americans in the health care professions, especially nursing. Smaller numbers of Kenyan Americans work as doctors, lawyers, college professors, and business owners and managers.

RELATIONS WITH KENYA

Kenya and the United States have maintained good relations since Kenya declared its independence in 1963. The United States has provided both political and financial support to Kenya. Kenyans and Americans alike were shocked when the U.S. Embassy was bombed in Nairobi in 1998, and during which both Americans and Kenyans lost their lives.

Not surprisingly, relations with Kenya are important to the Kenyan American immigrants. Most Kenyan Americans have left family and friends behind and they are sensitive to the situation that Kenya's floundering economy has produced. Kenyan Americans actively lobby to increase aid to Kenya. There are a number of organizations designed to provide such support. One such organization is the Kenyan-American Chamber of Commerce (KACC, Inc.), which was formed in 1999 from the existing

Kenyan American Association. KACC, Inc. is an influential private investment company that strives to increase development of Kenyan communities through investments in technology, educational, and other sectors, and to promote trade and culture between Kenya and the United States.

A similar organization is the American-Kenyan Educational Corporation. The corporation raises money to purchase textbooks and other items for primary school children and to help secondary school students pay their tuition. The corporation has also set up a sponsor program in which individuals or businesses provide for the needs of an entire classroom.

ORGANIZATIONS AND ASSOCIATIONS

Kenyan-American Chamber of Commerce (KACC).
Established in 1999, the KACC is devoted to the development of communities in Kenya through educational, technical, and other sectors. In addition to providing assistance to Kenyan immigrants, the KACC provides links to cultural, linguistic, academic programs, and news of interest to Kenyan immigrants.

Contact: John Gakuha.
Address: 13829 South Darnell #307, Olathe, Kansas 66062.
Telephone: (913) 491-7388.

SOURCES FOR ADDITIONAL STUDY

Adamson, Joy. *The Peoples of Kenya*. New York: Harcourt, Brace & World, 1967.

Azevedo, Mario. *Kenya: The Land, The People, and the Nation*. Durham: Carolina Academic Press, 1993.

Ochieng, William R, ed.. *Themes in Kenyan History*. Athens: Ohio University Press, 1990.

Whiteley, W. H., ed. *Language in Kenya*. London: Oxford University Press, 1974.

KOREAN AMERICANS

by
Amy Nash

Coming from a traditional society greatly influenced by the Confucian principle of placing elders, family, and community before the individual, Korean immigrants struggle to make sense of the American concept of individual freedom.

OVERVIEW

Known to its people as *Choson* (Land of Morning Calm), Korea occupies a mountainous peninsula in eastern Asia. Stretching southward from Manchuria and Siberia for close to 600 miles (966 kilometers), it extends down to the Korea Strait. China lies to Korea's west, separated from the peninsula by the Yellow Sea. Japan lies to its east on the other side of the Sea of Japan.

Western societies have traditionally viewed the Korean peninsula as a remote region of the world. They have often referred to it as "The Hermit Kingdom" because it remained isolated from the western world until the nineteenth century. Yet it actually holds a central position on the globe, neighboring three major world powers—the former Soviet Union, China, and Japan.

At the end of World War II in 1945, the United States and the Soviet Union divided the peninsula along the 38th Parallel into two zones of occupation—a Soviet controlled region in the north and an American controlled one in the south. In 1948, North Korea (the Democratic People's Republic of Korea) and South Korea (the Republic of Korea) were officially established. North Korea is run by a Communist government, with Pyongyang as its capital city. South Korea's government is an emergent democracy, and Seoul—Korea's largest city—is its capital.

An estimated 67 million people live on the Korean peninsula, with a population of approximately 43.9 million in South Korea and another 23.1 million residing in North Korea. Together they are racially and linguistically homogeneous. They are the ethnic descendants of a Tungusic branch of the Ural-Altaic family. Their spoken language, Korean, is a Uralic language with similarities to Japanese, Mongolian, Hungarian, and Finnish.

EARLY HISTORY

In its 5,000-year history, Korea has suffered over 900 invasions from outside peoples. Accordingly, the Korean people have found it necessary to defend fiercely their identity as a separate culture. Tungusic tribes from the Altai mountain region in central Asia made the peninsula their home during the Neolithic period around 4000 B.C. These tribes brought with them primitive religious and cultural practices, such as the east Asian religion of shamanism. By the fourth century B.C. several wall-town states throughout the peninsula were large enough to be recognized by China. The most advanced of these, Old Choson, was located in the basin of the Liao and Taedong rivers, where Pyongyang is situated today. China invaded Choson in the third century B.C. and maintained a strong cultural influence over the peninsula for the next 400 years.

Historians commonly refer to the first period of recorded Korean history (53 B.C.-668 A.D.) as the Period of the Three Kingdoms. These kingdoms were Koguryo, Paekche, and Silla. Toward the end of the seventh century A.D. Silla conquered Koguryo and Paekche and united the peninsula under the Silla dynasty. This period saw many advancements in literature, art, and science. Buddhism, which had reached Korea by way of China, was practiced by virtually all of Silla society. By the mid-eighth century the Silla people began using woodblock printing to reproduce sutras and Confucian writings.

In 900, the three kingdoms divided again. Within 36 years the Koguryo kingdom took control and its leader, General Wang Kon, established the Koryo dynasty. The word Korea comes from this dynastic name. During Koryo's 400-year reign, artistic, scientific, and literary achievements advanced further. Improving upon earlier Chinese printing methods, Korea became the first country in the world to use movable cast metal type in 1234. Medical knowledge also developed during the thirteenth century. Evolving out of local Korean folk remedies and Chinese practices, Korean medical science was recorded in books such as *Emergency Remedies of Folk Medicine* and *Folk Remedies of Samhwaja*.

Mongolian forces invaded Koryo in 1231 and occupied the kingdom until 1368. The Chinese Ming dynasty forced the Mongols back to the far north. This struggle eventually led to the fall of Koryo in 1392, when General Yi Song-Gye revolted against the king and founded the Yi dynasty. In control until the early twentieth century, it proved to be Korea's longest reigning dynasty and one of the most enduring regimes in history. The increasingly militant Buddhist state of the former Koryo dynasty yielded to the thinking of the new Choson kingdom, which was ruled by civilians who devotedly followed Confucian principles. Confucianism is not a religion but a philosophy of life and ethics that stresses an individual's sense of duty to family members and society as a whole. The Yi regime emphasized hierarchical relationships, with highest respect given to family elders, the monarch, and China as the older, more established country.

The Yi dynasty remained peaceful until 1592, when Japan invaded the peninsula. Chinese soldiers helped Korea seize control over its land from the Japanese armies. Japan attacked again in 1597, but Korea was able to force its withdrawal by the end of the year. Still, the country was left in tatters from the war. Korea suffered more attacks in 1627 and 1636, this time at the hands of the Manchus, who later conquered China. Western scientific, technological, and religious influences began to make their way to Korea during this period, by way of China. France, Great Britain, and the United States had already begun to dominate areas within China and other Asian countries. Calling Korea "The Hermit Kingdom" because of its closed-door policy toward non-Chinese foreigners, Western countries became interested in the peninsula in the nineteenth century.

In 1832 an English merchant ship landed off the coast of Chungchong province, and in 1846 three French warships landed in the same area. Eight years later two armed Russian ships sailed along the Hamgyong coast and killed a few Korean civilians before leaving the region. In 1866 the U.S.S. *General Sherman* sailed up the Taedong River to Pyongyang. The crew's goal of drawing up a trade agreement was thwarted by an enraged mob of Koreans who set fire to the ship, killing everyone aboard. Five U.S. warships appeared near the Korean island of Kanghwa the following year and also were fought off. Korean animosity toward Western countries stemmed largely from their awareness of China's troubles with these same nations, particularly Great Britain, which had devastated China during the First Opium War of 1839-1842. Despite Korean resistance, Japan forced the country to open to trade in 1876. In 1882 Korea reluctantly agreed to trade with the United States.

For two centuries China and Japan fought for control over Asia. China's defeat in the Sino-Japanese War (1894-1895) greatly weakened Chinese dominance. After this victory Japan invaded the Korean peninsula. Korean students from American-founded schools resented this invasion. These schools had become a place to learn about democracy and national liberation. The Japanese army despised the American missionaries who had established these schools but knew better than to confront citizens of the powerful U.S. government. Instead, they took advantage of Korean citizens and outlawed Korean customs. Korea turned to Russia for financial support and protection. What followed was a ten-year struggle between Russia and Japan for control over the Korean peninsula. The Russo-Japanese War of 1904-1905 ended in another Japanese victory. U.S. president Theodore Roosevelt mediated the treaty agreement and won a Nobel Peace Prize for his role in creating the Treaty of Portsmouth. Korea became a protectorate of Japan, and Japan officially annexed the country in 1910.

MODERN ERA

During its 35 years as a Japanese colony, Korea experienced major economic and social developments, such as soil improvement, updated methods of farming, and industrialization in the north. Japan modernized the country along Western lines, but Korea did not reap the benefits. Japan used half of the Korean rice crop for its own industry. Most Korean farmers were forced off their land. All Korean schools and temples were controlled by the Japanese. By the 1930s Koreans were forced to worship at Shinto shrines, speak Japanese in schools, and adopt Japanese names. Japan also prevented them from publishing Korean newspapers and organizing their own intellectual and political groups.

Thousands of Koreans participated in demonstrations against the Japanese government. These marches were mostly peaceful, but some led to violence. On March 1, 1919, a group of 33 prominent Koreans in Seoul issued a proclamation of independence. Close to 500,000 Koreans, including students, teachers, and members of religious groups, organized demonstrations in the streets, protesting against Japanese rule. This mass demonstration, which became known as the March First Movement, lasted two months until the Japanese government suppressed it and expanded the size of its police force in Korea by 10,000. According to conservative estimates from Japanese reports, the Japanese police killed 7,509 Koreans, wounded 15,961, and imprisoned another 46,948 in the process of quelling the movement.

Japan sided with Nazi Germany during World War II. The Japanese government put Koreans to work in munitions plants, airplane factories, and coal mines in Japan. Before the war, Korean nationalists living outside of the country (in Siberia, Manchuria, China, and the United States) organized independence efforts, often using guerrilla tactics against the Japanese. One of these nationalists residing in the United States, Syngman Rhee, went on to become the first president of South Korea. Another Korean who was making a name for himself as a rebel was Kim Song-Je. Born in 1912 near Pyongyang, Kim spent most of his childhood in Manchuria and took the pseudonym Kim Il Sung in 1930. He organized one of the first anti-Japanese guerrilla units in Antu, Manchuria, on April 25, 1932, and became North Korea's first president. North Koreans still celebrate April 25 as the founding date of the Korean People's Army.

When Japan attacked Pearl Harbor, Hawaii, on December 7, 1941, bringing the United States into World War II, the Korean provisional government created by such nationalists as Syngman Rhee finally had an opportunity to take a stand against Japan. On December 8, this provisional government declared war on Japan and formed the Restoration Army to fight alongside the Allies in the Pacific theater.

When Japan surrendered to the Allies on August 15, 1945, ending the Japanese occupation of Korea, Koreans took to the streets in celebration of the end of 36 years under oppressive rule. But the freedom they expected did not follow. The Soviet Union immediately occupied Pyongyang, Hamhung, and other major northern cities. The United States followed by stationing troops in southern Korea. This division, which was supposed to have been a temporary measure, remained a source of turbulence and tragedy for Koreans at the dawn of the twenty-first century.

In the months that followed the end of World War II, postwar international decisions were made without the consent of the Korean people. The Soviet Union set up a provisional Communist government in northern Korea, and the United States created a provisional republican government in the South. In 1948 the Republic of Korea was founded south of the 38th Parallel, followed by the establishment of the Democratic People's Republic of Korea in the north. Both governments claimed authority over the entire peninsula and tempted fate by crossing the border at various points along the 38th Parallel.

On June 25, 1950, North Korea launched a surprise attack on South Korea, beginning a costly, bloody, three-year struggle known as the Korean

War. It was perhaps the most tragic period in modern history for the Korean people. In the end, neither side achieved victory. On July 27, 1953, in the town of Panmunjom, the two sides signed an armistice designating a cease-fire line along the 38th Parallel and establishing a surrounding 2.5-mile-wide (four-kilometer-wide) demilitarized zone, which remains the boundary between the two Koreas. The war left the peninsula a wasteland. An estimated four million soldiers were killed or wounded, and approximately 1 million civilians died.

Both Koreas moved swiftly to rebuild after the war and have emerged into modern, industrialized nations. North Korea, which was more industrialized than South Korea before the war, restored the production of goods to prewar levels within three years. North Korea's economy and industry suffered, however, as a result of the break-up of the Soviet Union, one of its major trading partners. South Korea has evolved from a rural to post-industrial society since the 1960s. It has become an important exporter of products such as Hyundai cars, GoldStar televisions, and Samsung VCRs. In the late 1980s the United States was the second largest exporter to South Korea, after Japan. In 1989, South Korea was the seventh largest exporter country to the United States.

Kim Il Sung ruled as a Communist dictator in North Korea for more than four decades, until his death in July 1994. South Korea, on the other hand, has undergone several political upheavals since the Korean War. South Koreans have become increasingly dissatisfied with the U.S.-South Korea alliance and with the presence of U.S. troops in the country. Corruption in the government and the lack of free elections have caused many student uprisings. President Kim Young-Sam, who took office in February 1993, has instituted economic reforms and an aggressive anti-corruption campaign. As of 1995, it was too soon to tell if his programs would bring the country closer to a true democracy.

All measures introduced to reunify the Korean peninsula have ended in a stalemate. U.S. concern over North Korea's nuclear weapons program during the 1990s has threatened to increase tensions between the two Koreas. North Korea's refusal to allow full international inspection of its nuclear facilities brought the United States close to proposing a resolution for a United Nations economic embargo against North Korea in June 1994. Before sanctions were implemented, former U.S. President Jimmy Carter met with the North Korean government and reported back that the country would be willing to freeze all activity that produces fuel for nuclear weapons if Washington would initiate high-level talks. In the past, planned meetings between the two Korean governments have broken down. Officials were cautiously hopeful that this time would be different, until Kim Il Sung's death once again put negotiations between the two countries on hold. Reunification remains the most pressing issue on the minds of virtually all Koreans.

THE FIRST KOREANS IN AMERICA

The first recorded emigration of Koreans from their homeland occurred in the eighth century, when thousands moved to Japan. Korean communities also existed in China as early as the ninth century. By the middle of the nineteenth century, the Yenpien section of Manchuria and the Maritime provinces of Russia became home to many Koreans escaping famine on the peninsula. Emigration was illegal in Korea, but by the end of the century, 23,000 Koreans were living in the Maritime provinces. Natural disasters, poverty, high taxes, and government oppression were given as their reasons for leaving. As Japanese control over the peninsula began to spread, so did Korean discontent. The United States became a refuge for a small number of Koreans at the end of the nineteenth century. Three Korean political refugees moved to America in 1885. Five more arrived in 1899 but were mistaken for Chinese. Between 1890-1905, 64 Koreans had traveled to Hawaii to attend Christian mission schools. Most of these students returned to Korea after completing their studies.

SIGNIFICANT IMMIGRATION WAVES

The first major wave of Korean immigrants to the United States began in 1903, when Hawaiian sugar plantation owners offered Koreans the opportunity to work on their plantations. By 1835 sugar had become the main crop produced on the Hawaiian Islands, largely due to the prolific yield of the Koloa Plantation on the island of Kauai. Initially the sugar planters hired native Hawaiians to work as contract laborers on the plantations. By 1850 the native population had declined, the laborers became increasingly dissatisfied with the hard work, and the demand for sugar continued to grow. The resulting labor shortage forced the planters to form the Royal Hawaiian Agricultural Society to recruit outside sources of labor. Hawaii was not yet a part of the United States, and contract labor was therefore still legal. In 1852, the first immigrant laborers arrived in Hawaii from China. By the time the United States annexed Hawaii in 1898, 50,000 Chinese immigrants lived in Hawaii. Low wages, long work days, and poor treatment caused many Chinese laborers to leave the plantations in order to find work in the cities. The sugar planters then began to recruit Japanese immigrants to supplement the work force on the plantations.

In 1900 Hawaii became an official U.S. territory, making it legal for the Chinese and Japanese workers to go on strike. Many of them did. America's Chinese Exclusion Act of 1882 prohibited immigration of Chinese people to the United States. When Hawaii became a U.S. territory, Chinese workers were not allowed to immigrate to Hawaii. To offset another labor shortage and weaken the unions, Hawaiian sugar planters turned to Korea. In 1902 growers sent a representative to San Francisco to meet with Horace Allen, the American ambassador to Korea. Allen began recruiting Koreans to work on the plantations with the help of David William Deshler, an American businessman living in Korea. Deshler owned a steamship service that operated between Korea and Japan. The Hawaiian Sugar Planters Association paid Deshler 55 dollars for each Korean recruited. The Deshler Bank, set up in the Korean seaside town of Inchon, provided loans of 100 dollars to each immigrant for transportation.

With conditions worsening in their homeland, the offer appealed to a great number of Koreans. They would be paid a monthly wage of 16 dollars; receive free housing, health care, and English lessons; and would enjoy a warmer climate. Newspaper advertisements and posters promoted Hawaii as paradise and America as a land of gold and dreams. Recruiters used the slogan *Kaeguk chinch wi* ("the country is open, go forward") to encourage potential recruits. American missionaries also helped persuade Koreans with stories of how life in the West would make them better Christians. Reverend George Heber Jones of the Methodist Episcopal Church in Inchon was one of the more well-known American preachers who encouraged Koreans to go to Hawaii.

In December 1902, 121 Koreans left their homeland aboard the U.S.S. *Gaelic,* and all but 19 of the recruits (who failed their medical examinations in Japan) arrived in Honolulu on January 13, 1903. This original group included 56 men, 21 women, and 25 children. Over 7,000 Korean immigrants joined them on the Hawaiian sugar plantations within two years. Most of these immigrants were bachelors or had left their families behind. They hoped to save their wages and return to Korea to share the wealth with their families. With the higher cost of living in Hawaii, only about 2,000 Koreans were able to return to Korea. By 1905 the Japanese government banned emigration from the peninsula because so many Koreans were leaving to avoid Japanese oppression.

The next wave of Korean immigration to the United States occurred when Japan issued the Gentlemen's Agreement of 1907. This pact forbade further immigration of Japanese and Korean workers but included a clause that allowed wives to rejoin their husbands already in the United States. This law initiated the "picture bride" system, enabling immigrant men to have wives and families in America. Of the 7,296 Korean immigrants in Hawaii, only 613 of them were women. To improve the male/female ratio, Korean village matchmakers and the groom's family selected the women to contact. The men exchanged photographs with the prospective brides, and when a match was agreed upon, the groom's family would write the bride's name into the family register to legalize the union. The bride would then travel to the United States by boat and meet her new husband. Marriage ceremonies were often performed on the boat, so that the women could touch American soil as legal wives of the immigrants. Between 1910 and 1924, over 1,000 Korean picture brides came to the United States, mostly to Hawaii. These women were motivated to become picture brides by the opportunities for education and wealth they heard existed in America. Traditional Korean society placed many restrictions on women. Education, travel, and careers were not open to them at home.

The picture brides, however, did not find America paved with gold. Many discovered that their husbands were much older than they looked in the pictures. In fact, an alarming number of these women became widows at a very young age. They faced hard work and long hours, leaving little free time to learn English. In her introduction to *Making Waves: An Anthology of Writings By and About Asian American Women* (Boston: Beacon Press, 1989; p. 9), Sucheta Mazumdar recounts Anna Choi's description of her life in Hawaii as a picture bride: "I arose at four o'clock in the morning, and we took a truck to the sugar cane fields, eating breakfast on the way. Work in the sugar plantations was back breaking. It involved cutting canes, watering, and pulling out weeds.... The sugar cane fields were endless and twice the height of myself. Now that I look back, I *thank goodness* for the height for if I had seen how far the fields stretched I probably would have fainted from knowing how much work was ahead."

In the years between 1907 and World War II, a few Korean political refugees and students also came to the United States. Some were members of a secret Korean patriotic society called *Sinmin-hoe* (New People's Society). To escape persecution by the Japanese government, they crossed the Yalu River and took trains to Shanghai. From there, they made their way to America. By 1924, 541 Koreans living in America claimed to be political refugees. Among the political activists residing in the United States at this time were Ahn Chang Ho, Pak Yong-Man, and Syngman Rhee, the future first president of South Korea. Rhee immigrated to the United States as a student and earned a doctorate from Princeton University in 1910. He returned to Korea to organize a protest against the Japanese. He then came back to the United States to avoid arrest and remained there until the end of World War II. During his years in America, he founded one of the major Korean independence movements.

Korean emigration was discouraged by the South Korean government after World War II, and North Korea forbade any kind of emigration. Most of the Koreans who did immigrate to the United States after the war were women. The quota system created by the United States Office of Immigration in the 1940s allowed between 105 and 150 immigrants from each of the Asian nations into the country. This law favored immigrants with post-secondary education, technical training, and specialized skills. Most of the Koreans allowed to immigrate were women with nursing training. The War Brides Act of 1945 also helped women and children obtain papers to immigrate.

More women who had married American soldiers were allowed into the United States after the Korean War. By this time, Koreans and all Asians in America were able to acquire citizenship through naturalization as a result of the McCarran-Walter Act of 1952. Foreign adoption of Korean babies also began at the end of the Korean War. The war had left thousands of children orphaned in Korea. Over 100,000 South Korean children have been adopted abroad since the war, and roughly two-thirds of these children have been adopted by American families. An estimated 10,000 Korean children have been adopted by Minnesota families alone. Criticized by other countries for running a "baby mill," the South Korean government began to phase out the practice in the 1990s. Although adopting children is traditionally frowned upon in Korean society, social workers are attempting to encourage domestic adoption.

RECENT IMMIGRATION

In 1965 the U.S. Congress passed the Immigration and Naturalization Act. The quota system was replaced with a preference system that gave priority to immigration applications from relatives of U.S. citizens and from professionals with skills needed by the United States. Thousands of South Korean doctors and nurses took advantage of the new law. They moved to America and took jobs in understaffed, inner-city hospitals. Koreans with science and technological backgrounds also were encouraged to immigrate. These new immigrants came from middle-class and upper-class families, unlike the earlier immigrants. The portion of the law informally known as the "Brothers and Sisters Act" has also been a factor in the dramatic increase in the Korean American population. In 1960, 10,000 Koreans were living in the United States. By 1985 the number had increased to 500,000. According to the U.S. Department of Commerce's 1990 Census of Population, 836,987 Korean Americans had settled in the United States. The 1991 Statistical Yearbook of the Immigration and Naturalization Service states that 26,518 Koreans were admitted to the United States in 1991, making up 1.5 percent of the total immigrants arriving in America that year.

SETTLEMENT PATTERNS

Virtually all of the first Koreans who immigrated to the United States settled in Hawaii and the West Coast. As Korean immigrants working on the Hawaiian sugar plantations became increasingly frustrated by the harsh conditions, they moved to cities and opened restaurants, vegetable stands, and small stores, or worked as carpenters and tailors. Some returned to Korea if they could save the money for transportation. Approximately 1,000 Korean plantation workers remigrated to the U.S. mainland by 1907. They settled in San Francisco or moved farther inland to Utah to work in the copper mines, to Colorado and Wyoming to work in the coal mines, and to Arizona to work on the railroads. Some Koreans moved as far north as Alaska and found jobs in the salmon fisheries. The majority of those who remigrated, however, settled in California.

Recent Korean immigrants have settled in concentrated areas around the country. In 1970 the highest percentage of Korean Americans lived in California, followed by Hawaii, New York, Illinois, Pennsylvania, and Washington. In 1990 the U.S. Census reported 260,822 Korean Americans in California, 93,145 Korean immigrants in New York, 42,167 in Illinois, 38,087 in New Jersey, 35,281 in Texas, 32,918 in Washington, and 32,362 in Virginia. Maryland, Hawaii, and Pennsylvania each have over 25,000 Korean American residents. Every state has at least a small population of Korean Americans. Most Koreans who settle in the United States reside in large cities where jobs are available and Korean communities have been established. Koreatowns have developed in areas such as the Olympic Boulevard neighborhood west of downtown Los Angeles, where over 150,000 Korean

Americans live. The Flushing, Woodside, and Jackson Heights neighborhoods within the New York City borough of Queens also have substantial Korean American populations. Unlike the early immigrants, later immigrants generally traveled to America to take up permanent residence. Korean American professionals who can afford it have begun moving to the suburbs.

ACCULTURATION AND ASSIMILATION

Like all immigrants arriving in the United States, Koreans have had to make major adjustments to live in a country that is vastly different from their homeland. Coming from a traditional society greatly influenced by the Confucian principle of placing elders, family, and community before the individual, Korean immigrants struggle to make sense of the American concept of individual freedom. Since the first immigrants arrived in Hawaii, Korean Americans have preserved their identity by creating organizations, such as Korean Christian churches and Korean schools. The Korean word *han*, used to describe an anguished feeling of being far from what you want, accurately conveys the longing that accompanies most Koreans to America. Korean American organizations provide a sense of community for new immigrants and a way to alleviate this longing.

TRADITIONS, CUSTOMS, AND BELIEFS

Korean immigrants bring with them a culture that incorporates aspects of Chinese, Indian, Japanese, and Western cultures. These influences have filtered into Korean society throughout its long history. Yet Koreans have also maintained native elements of their literature, art, music, and way of life. The result is a wonderful collage of elements, both foreign and indigenous to the peninsula. Korean Americans tend to maintain aspects of their culture, while also adopting elements of mainstream America.

LITERATURE, ART, AND MUSIC

Korean literature draws from Chinese and Japanese roots but has its own distinctive features. Poems, romances, and short stories represent only a portion of the breadth of the Korean literary tradition. This tradition includes both folk and highly advanced literary writings and works written in Chinese, as well as Korean. Korean poems, called *hyangga*, dating back to the sixth century, were written in Chinese characters. Hyangga were sung by Buddhist

monks for religious purposes. Korean myths and legends were first recorded in Chinese in the thirteenth century. The first literary work written in the Korean alphabet, *hangul*, was the *Songs of Flying Dragons*, a multi-volume account written between 1445 and 1447 by King Sejong's father during the Yi dynasty. Novels began to appear in the seventeenth century. Among the best known are Ho Kyun's *Life of Hong Kiltong* and *Spring Fragrance*, written anonymously in the eighteenth century.

Chinese, Japanese, and Korean art forms have many similarities, but Korea has also preserved its own creative elements in this field. Korean art is characterized by simple forms, subdued colors, humor, and natural images. Korea is known for its ceramics, especially the celadon. This highly sophisticated form of pottery was first introduced during the Koryo dynasty.

Korean music incorporates Confucian rituals, court music, Buddhist chants, and folk music. Ancient instruments used for court music include zithers, flutes, reed instruments, and percussion. Folk music, which usually includes dancing, is played with a *chango* (a drum shaped like an hourglass) and a loud trumpet-like oboe. *P'ansori*, stories first sung by wandering bards in the late Choson dynasty, are an early form of Korean folk music. Modern Korean composers often draw from Western classical music. Korean American musicians, like Jin Hi Kim, use traditional Korean elements in their compositions. Kim is a *komungo* harpist who came to the United States in her twenties. She incorporates traditional Korean musical styles with other non-Western styles. Kim is one of the leaders in the No World Improvisations movement, which promotes the performance and composition of new improvisational music.

SPORTS

Several sports native to Korea have become popular around the world. For instance, *tae kwon do*, a method of self-defense that originated in Korea more than 2,000 years ago, has now become a commonly taught form of karate in the United States. It involves more sharp, quick kicking than the Japanese style of karate. It was a demonstration sport in the 1988 Summer Olympics in Seoul.

SPECIAL EVENTS

The importance placed on family in Korean society is apparent from the way special events in family members' lives are celebrated. Traditionally parents—with the help of a marriage broker or go-between—chose their children's marriage partners. The parents also planned and prepared the wedding ceremony. Female relatives spent days preparing special dishes for the wedding feast and making the wedding clothes. The picture bride system used to increase the population of Korean American females in Hawaii is one example of how this traditional system was maintained in America. While still common in rural areas of Korea, these customs are no longer standard practice in cities. Similarly, Korean Americans, who generally come from urban areas, usually allow their children to choose their own spouses. As members of Christian churches, most modern Korean Americans have Western-style wedding ceremonies and wear Western-style bridal gowns and formal suits. Another event that Koreans traditionally celebrate with great flourish is a baby's first birthday. The child is dressed in a traditional costume and seated amidst rice cakes, cookies, and fruits. Friends and relatives offer the child objects, each one symbolizing a different career. A pen represents a writing career, and a coin signifies a career in finance. The first object the child picks up is said to indicate his or her future profession.

PRESERVING TRADITION

Korean culture is maintained within Korean American communities through church organizations, Korean schools, and Korean-culture camps. Since the beginning of this century, Korean Protestant churches have offered classes in Korean culture and language. In 1990 an estimated 490 Korean-lan-guage schools operated in the United States. Approximately 31,000 students attend these schools, which are run by 3,700 teachers. Classes are held during the week and sometimes on the weekends. The April/May 1994 issue of *The U.S.-Korea Review* lists 19 summer Korean-culture camps across the country. Located predominantly in California, Minnesota, New Jersey, and New York, these camps offer Korean American children, usually adoptees, an opportunity to learn about their heritage with other Korean American children.

CUISINE

Korean cooking is similar to other Asian cuisines. Like the Chinese and Japanese, Koreans eat with chopsticks. Common ingredients in Korean food, such as tofu, soy sauce, rice, and a wide variety of vegetables, are also staples in other far eastern cuisines. But Korean food is also distinct in many ways. It is often highly seasoned, including combinations of garlic, ginger, red or black pepper, scallions, soy sauce, sesame seeds, and sesame oil. Blander grain dishes such as rice, barley, or noodles offset the heat of the spices. Red meat is scarce in both North and South Korea and typically is reserved for special occasions. Koreans do not usually designate certain foods as breakfast, lunch, or dinner dishes. A standard meal consists of rice, soup, *kimchi* (a spicy Korean pickle), vegetables, and broiled or grilled meat or fish. Fresh fruit is usually served at the end of a meal. *Kimchi* is considered the national dish and is served at virtually every meal. Made from cabbage, turnips, radishes, or cucumber, *kimchi* can be prepared many ways, from mild to very spicy. Korean cuisine includes many different kinds of *namul* (salads). A common type of *namul* is *sukju namul*, or bean sprout salad. Made with bean sprouts, soy sauce, vinegar, sesame oil, black pepper, and other ingredients, it is easy to make and serve. A common soup served at breakfast is *kamja guk* (potato soup). It is often spiced with chopped onion and chunks of tofu. Koreans serve *mandu* (Korean dumplings) at winter celebrations. They are deep-fried wonton skins, usually filled with beef, cabbage, bean sprouts, onions, and other ingredients. Another common Korean dish is *chap ch'ae* (mixed vegetables with noodles). This popular stir-fry dish features cellophane noodles, which are made from mung beans and prepared with vegetables in a wok.

TRADITIONAL CLOTHING

Traditional Korean clothing is rarely worn in either the United States or in Korea on a daily basis. Modern Western-style clothes are standard attire in most of South Korea, with the exception of some rural areas. During holidays, however, Koreans in both the United States and Korea often wear traditional costumes. Women may wear a *chi-ma* (a long skirt, usually pleated and full) and *cho-gori* (a short jacket top worn over a skirt) during New Year's celebrations. Traditional attire for men includes long white overcoats and horsehair hats or colorful silk baggy trousers known as *paji*.

HOLIDAYS

Koreans in both the United States and Korea celebrate several important days throughout the year. Following Buddhist and Confucian traditions, Koreans begin the new year with an elaborate three-day celebration called *Sol*. Family members dress in traditional clothing and pay homage to the oldest members of the family. The festivities include several feasts, kite-flying, board games, and various rituals intended to ward off evil spirits.

The first full moon is also an ancient day of worship. Torches are kept burning all night, and often people set off firecrackers to scare away evil spirits. *Yadu Nal* (Shampoo Day) is celebrated on June 15. Families bathe in streams or waterfalls to protect them from fevers. *Chusok* (Thanksgiving Harvest) is celebrated in autumn to give thanks for the harvest. *Kimchi* is also prepared for the winter at this time. Other traditional holidays observed in many Korean American households include Buddha's birthday on April 8, Korean Memorial Day on June 6, Father's Day on June 15, Constitution Day in South Korea on July 17, and Korean National Foundation Day on October 3. Korean American Christians also observe major religious holidays such as Easter and Christmas.

PREJUDICE AND STEREOTYPES

Anti-Asian prejudice first erupted in the United States when Chinese and Japanese immigrants began arriving in the nineteenth century. Early Korean immigrants suffered discrimination but were not specifically targeted until they became a significant percentage of the population. Americans generally knew nothing about Korea when Koreans first came to the United States. What little information they could find was written by non-Asians and claimed Western superiority over Asian cultures. William Griffis' *Corea: The Hermit Kingdom*, Alexis Krausse's *The Far East*, and Isabella Bird Bishop's *Korea and Her Neighbors* are examples of books that perpetuated the myth of Western superiority. American writer Jack London was also responsible for giving Ameri-

cans an unfavorable view of Korea. As a war correspondent covering the Russo-Japanese conflict in 1904, London voiced his opinions in dispatches that appeared on the front pages of newspapers across the country. In an article entitled "The Yellow Peril" (*San Francisco Examiner*, September 25, 1904; p. 44), London wrote that "the Korean is the perfect type of inefficiency—of utter worthlessness."

Anti-Asian sentiments grew during the early twentieth century when San Francisco workers accused Koreans, along with Japanese and Chinese immigrants, of stealing jobs because the immigrants would work for lower wages. Restaurants refused to serve Asian customers, and Asians were often forced to sit in segregated corners of movie theaters. Violent white gangs harassed Korean Americans in California, and the government did nothing to help the victims. In fact, California laws in the first few decades of the twentieth century supported anti-Asian attitudes. Asian students were banned from attending public schools in white districts in 1906. The 1913 Webb-Heney Land Law prohibited Asians from owning property, and the Oriental Exclusion Act of 1924 banned all Asian immigration to the United States for close to 30 years.

Korean Americans continue to be discriminated against in the job market, often receiving lower pay and having fewer opportunities for promotion than non-Asian co-workers. The view of Korean Americans as "super immigrants" has also caused discord. Korean American success stories in business and education have led to resentment from outside groups. These stories are often exaggerated. Rumors that the

U.S. government gives Korean immigrants money when they arrive are untrue. Only refugees receive aid from the U.S. government, and very few Korean immigrants qualify as refugees. Also, statistics that show the mean income of Korean American families to be higher than that of the general public are misleading because most Korean Americans live in large cities where the cost of living is much higher. These stereotypes have led to boycotts of Korean greengrocers in Brooklyn, Chicago, and elsewhere. In the April 1992 Los Angeles uprising that followed the verdict in the trial of African American assault victim Rodney King's attackers, black rioters targeted Korean grocers, destroying countless Korean American businesses. Korean immigrants refer to this tragic episode as the *Sa-i-kup'ok-dong* (April 28 riots). Korean Americans have come to represent wealth, greed, materialism, and arrogance because they have started businesses in inner-city neighborhoods that have been abandoned by corporations. The people still living in these neighborhoods often use the Korean small businessperson as a scapegoat for their anger against corporate America. Organizations such as the Korea Society in New York and the Korean Youth and Community Center in Los Angeles have begun to address these issues.

HEALTH ISSUES

Korean Americans hold a prominent position in the field of medical science. The proportionally large number of Korean American doctors and nurses attest to this fact. Data on the status of the health of Korean Americans is limited. Asian Americans in general have a longer life expectancy than Americans as a whole. Job-related stress and other factors have contributed to mental health problems within the Korean American community. Most Korean Americans receive health insurance through their employers. New immigrants and the elderly, however, often do not have access to medical care because of language barriers. Organizations such as the Korean Health Education Information and Referral in Los Angeles address this problem.

LANGUAGE

Virtually every citizen in North and South Korea is an ethnic Korean and speaks Korean. Spoken for over 5,000 years, the Korean language was first written in the mid-fifteenth century when King Sejong invented the phonetically-based alphabet known as *hangul* ("the great writing"). The King created the alphabet so that all Korean people, not just the aristocracy who knew Chinese characters,

could learn to read and write. As a result both North and South Korea have among the highest literacy rates in the world.

While most second- and third-generation Korean immigrants speak English exclusively, new immigrants often know little or no English. As time goes by, they begin to learn necessary English phrases. The earliest Korean immigrants in Hawaii learned a form of English known as pidgin English, which incorporated phrases in English, Chinese, Japanese, Korean, Filipino, and Portuguese—all languages spoken by the different ethnic groups working on the plantations. Learning English is crucial for new immigrants who hope to become successful members of the larger American community. Yet most Korean American parents also hope to preserve their heritage by sending their American-born children to Korean-language schools.

Several American universities offer undergraduate, graduate, and doctoral programs in Korean language and Korean studies. These universities include Brigham Young University, Columbia University, Cornell University, Harvard University, the University of Hawaii, Manoa, and the University of Washington, Seattle.

GREETINGS AND OTHER COMMON EXPRESSIONS

The following greetings are translated phonetically from the *hangul* alphabet according to the McCune-Reischauer System of Romanization: *Annyonghasipnigga*—Hello (formal greeting); *Yoboseyo*—Hello (informal greeting); *Annyonghi kasipsio*—Good-bye (staying); *Annyonghi kyeshipsio*—Good-bye (leaving); *Put'akhamnida*—Please; *Komapsumnida*—Thank you; *Ch'onmaneyo*—You're welcome; *Sillyehamnida*—Excuse me; *Ye*—Yes; *Aniyo*—No; *Sehae e pok mani padu sipsiyo!*—Happy New Year!; *Man sei!*—Hurrah! Long live our country! Ten thousand years!; *Kuh reh!*—That is so! True!

FAMILY AND COMMUNITY DYNAMICS

Historically, the family-kinship system was an extremely integral part of Korean society. The male head of a household played a dominant role, as did the oldest members of the family. Parents practiced control over their children's lives, arranging their marriages and choosing their careers. The eldest son was responsible for taking care of parents in their old age. Inheritances also went to the son. These systems have changed in modern Korea, particularly in cities, but the family remains very important to Koreans in

The basic Korean alphabet consists of 10 vowels and 14 consonants.

Basic Vowels: ㅏ ㅑ ㅓ ㅕ ㅗ ㅛ ㅜ ㅠ ㅡ ㅣ

a ya o` yo` o yo u yu u` i

Basic Consonants:

		Name	Sound			Name	Sound
ㄱ	기역	kiyo`k	k,g	ㅇ	이웅	iu`ng	(ng)
ㄴ	니은	niu`n	n	ㅈ	지옷	chiu`t'	ch,j(t)
ㄷ	디귿	tiku`t	t,d	ㅊ	치옷	ch'iu`t'	ch'(t)
ㄹ	리율	riu`l	r,l	ㅋ	키옥	k'iu`k'	k'
ㅁ	미음	miu`m	m	ㅌ	티옷	t'iu`t'	t'
ㅂ	비옵	piu`p	p,b	ㅍ	피옵	p'iu`p'	p'
ㅅ	시옷	siot'	s(t)	ㅎ	히옷	hiu`t	h(t)

( ) sound of final consonants

There are also 11 compound vowels and 5 compound consonants in the Korean alphabet.

Compound Vowels: ㅐ ㅒ ㅔ ㅖ ㅘ ㅙ

ae yae e ye wa wae

ㅚ ㅝ ㅞ ㅟ ㅢ

oe wo` we wi ui

Compound Consonants: ㄲ ㄸ ㅃ ㅆ ㅉ

kk tt pp ss tch

their homeland and in America. Parents still pressure their children to marry someone who has a good relationship with the family. Children—both male and female—usually are responsible for the care of elderly parents, although the government has begun to carry some of the financial burden. Tight family bonds continue to exist among Korean Americans. The current U.S. immigration laws encourage these bonds by favoring family reunions. Korean Americans who invite relatives to come to the United States have a responsibility to help the new immigrants adjust to their new home. Korean American families often include extended family members. The average Korean American household consists of more members than the average American family. The 1980 U.S. Census Bureau reported an average of 4.3 members in the Korean American household, compared to an average of 2.7 persons in the American household at large. The family ties also extend to strong networks of support within Korean American communities.

PUBLIC ASSISTANCE

Because of the well-defined familial structure in Korean society, Koreans traditionally rely less on public assistance. Receiving welfare is often considered to be disgraceful. Family support, however, began to break down in the 1980s and 1990s. Larger numbers of recent Korean immigrants, particularly the elderly, are in need of assistance. Organizations within the Korean community have begun to address this problem. The Korean Youth and Community Center in Los Angeles offers numerous programs and activities for children and their families who have recently immigrated or are economically disadvantaged. Services include employment assistance and placement, family and youth counseling, and education and tutorial programs.

MARRIAGE

In Korean American communities, the marriage bond has in some ways become stronger than filial piety. While honoring one's parents remains important, physical distance and cultural barriers between Korean Americans and their parents have shifted priorities. Korean Americans are less likely to have arranged marriages than their ancestors, because marrying outside of the Korean community has also become increasingly common. Recent surveys show that Korean American women in college are expressing a preference for mates from other ethnic groups.

Traditionally Koreans have frowned upon divorce. Even with the marriages arranged through the picture bride system in Hawaii, few ended in divorce. Recent statistics suggest that the stigma against divorce no longer exists. The divorce rate among Korean Americans has reached and is possibly surpassing the national average. Exhaustion due to working extremely long hours in order to survive contributes to failed marriages. Women in particular suffer from stress. They often work long hours in garment factories or managing small businesses and are also responsible for running their households. Again, Korean American community organizations attempt to address these problems in order to make life in America more fulfilling.

EDUCATION

Koreans have always valued education, and Korean Americans place a strong emphasis on academic achievement. Employment in the civil service, which required passing extremely difficult qualifying examinations, was considered to be the most successful career path to take. Koreans take great pride in their educational achievements. Recent immigrants are strongly motivated to perform well in school and come to the United States better educated than the general population in Korea. Korean American parents pressure their children to perform well. In 1980, 78.1 percent of Korean Americans over the age of 25 had at least a high school education, compared with 66.5 percent of Americans overall. While 33.7 percent of Korean Americans had four or more years of college education, only 16.2 percent of the general U.S. population did.

Korean society gives priority to the education of males. Many of the Korean women who chose to come to the United States as picture brides hoped to find more educational opportunities than they were offered in their home country. In the United States, the bias in favor of educating males persists. Of all Korean American males over 25, 90 percent were high school graduates in 1980. Only 70.6 percent of Korean American women had high school educations. In 1980, 52.4 percent of Korean American males had attended four or more years of college, compared with 22 percent of Korean American females. It is a common stereotype that Korean Americans excel in math and science. Although this is often true, they tend to perform well in all subjects.

THE ROLE OF WOMEN

Korean husbands traditionally work outside the home, while their wives take full-time responsibility for the children and household. Living in a modern industrialized nation, South Korean women do have full-time jobs today, especially in urban areas. Still, the majority of full-time female employees in South Korea are unmarried. In the United States, economic needs often require both parents to work. Running the household, however, usually remains solely the responsibility of the woman. Second-, third-, and fourth-generation Korean American women face conflicts between traditional familial values and mainstream American culture. These women have more opportunities than their mothers and grandmothers. Some of them have careers as lawyers, doctors, teachers, and businesswomen, but most have behind-the-scenes positions or are clerks, typists, and cashiers. Korean American women, like American women in general, are still discriminated against in the job market. Korean immigrant women often come to the United States with professional skills but are forced to work in garment factories or as store clerks because of the language barrier.

The view that Korean American women are passive also persists. Contrary to popular perceptions, Korean American women have a long history of political activism. Unfortunately their work has gone largely unrecorded. Korean female immigrants played a significant role in organizing protests against Japanese occupation both in Korea and America. They established organizations like the Korean Women's Patriotic League, wrote for Korean newspapers, and raised $200,000 for the cause by working on plantations, doing needlework, and selling candies. They also participated in labor strikes on the Hawaiian plantations. Korean American women of the 1990s joined other Asian American women in fighting unfair work practices in the hotel, garment, and food-packaging industries. Korean American women also participate fully in efforts to reunify Korea.

RELIGION

Throughout Korea's long history, religion has played a prominent role in the lives of the its citizens. A variety of faiths have been practiced on the peninsula, the most common being shamanism, Buddhism, and Christianity.

Shamanism, the country's oldest religion, involves the worship of nature; the sun, mountains, rocks, and trees each hold sacred positions. Based on a belief in good and evil spirits that can only be appeased by priests or medicine men called shamans, early shamanism incorporated pottery making and dances such as the *muchon,* which was performed as part of a ceremony to worship the heavens.

China brought Buddhism to Korea sometime between the fourth and seventh centuries A.D. This religion, based on the teachings of the ancient Indian philosopher Siddhartha Gautama (Buddha), has as its premise that suffering in life is inherent and that one can be freed from it by mental and moral self-purification.

Christianity first reached Korea in the seventeenth century, again by way of China where Portuguese missionaries came to promote Catholicism. American Protestant missionaries arrived in Korea in the nineteenth century. The Korean government persecuted these missionaries because the laws of Christianity went against Confucian social order. By the mid-1990s, the majority of South Koreans were still Buddhists, but an estimated 30 percent of the population practiced some type of Christianity.

CHRISTIANITY

Of the original 7,000 Korean immigrants in the United States, only 400 were Christian. Those 400 immediately formed congregations in Hawaii, and by 1918 close to 40 percent of the Korean immigrants had converted to Christianity. Koreans immigrants relied heavily on their churches as community centers. After Sunday service, immigrants spoke Korean, socialized, discussed problems of immigrant life, and organized political rallies for Korean independence. The churches also served as educational centers, providing classes in writing and reading Korean. They remain an integral part of the Korean immigrant community. In 1990 there were an estimated 2,000 Korean Protestant churches in the United States. Most Korean Protestants are evangelical Christians, who study the Bible extensively and follow the word of the gospel closely. In large cities like Los Angeles, New York, and Chicago, Korean Protestants have their own buildings and hold several services a week. The Oriental Mission Church and Youngnak Presbyterian Church in Los Angeles are two of the largest Korean Protestant churches in America with 5,000 members each. Most Koreans in the United States today practice Protestantism.

Over two million Catholics live in South Korea. The Korean American Catholic Community was established by Korean immigrants in the 1960s. The first Korean Catholic center opened in Orange County, California, in 1977. As of 1995, an estimated 35,000 Korean Americans practiced Catholicism. Most Korean American Catholic parishes are part of larger American Catholic parishes.

There are about 100 Korean American Catholic communities in the United States, most of which are headed by priests from Korea, who usually serve four-year periods. Many speak little English and are perceived as being ignorant of contemporary American life, insensitive to the problems of Korean Americans, and more loyal to the their dioceses in Korea than to their Korean American congregations. Some have been accused of having affairs with married women and of financial misdealing. To address these problems by providing a forum for open discussion of them, Korean immigrant Kye Song Lee founded the newspaper *Catholic 21* in 1996. He felt that the two official Catholic newspapers for Koreans—both published in Korea—did not adequately address the problems. *Catholic 21* has been controversial since its inception, with some welcoming its perspective and others labeling it divise, offensive, and even anti-Catholic.

BUDDHISM

Although Buddhism has undergone many upheavals on the Korean peninsula, nearly 14 million South Koreans practice Buddhism today. A Buddhist monk named Soh Kyongbo founded Korean Buddhism in the United States in 1964. Most Korean American Buddhists belong to the Chogye sect. Prominent Buddhist organizations in the United States include the Zen Lotus Society in Ann Arbor, Michigan, the Korean Buddhist Temple Association, the Young Buddhist Union in Los Angeles, the Buddhists Concerned with Social Justice and World Peace, the Western Buddhist Monk's Association, the Southern California Buddhist Temples Association, and several Son and Dharma centers across the country. According to the Korean Buddhist Temple Association's reports, there were 60 temples in the United States and Canada in 1990. The Young Buddhist Union holds an annual arts festival where Buddhist monks dance, sing, read Son poetry, and perform comedy sketches, plays, and piano recitals. Still, Buddhism has not become widespread in the United States and is often viewed as a cult.

EMPLOYMENT AND ECONOMIC TRADITIONS

Early Korean immigrants living on the West Coast were restricted from many types of employment. Discriminatory laws prohibited Asian immigrants from applying for citizenship, which meant that they were ineligible for positions in most professional fields. They took jobs with low pay and little advancement potential, working as busboys, waiters, gardeners, janitors, and domestic help in cities. Outside the cities, they worked on farms and in railroad "gangs." Many Korean immigrants opened restaurants, laundries, barbershops, grocery stores, tobacco shops, bakeries, and other retail shops. With the changes in immigration laws after World War II, Korean immigrants have been able to move into more professional fields such as medicine, dentistry, architecture, and science. Recent immigrants, those who have come to America since 1965, are mostly college-educated, with professional skills. The language barrier, however, often prevents new immigrants from finding jobs within their fields. Korean doctors often work as orderlies and nurses' assistants. In 1978, only 35 percent of Korean teachers, administrators, and other professionals were working in their respective fields in Los Angeles.

According to the U.S. Census Bureau's *Asian and Pacific Islander Population in the United States: 1980 Report*, the average Korean American household income was $22,500, which was higher than the average household income for Americans overall ($20,300). However, Korean Americans have, on the average, more persons living in each household and, as noted earlier, tend to live in urban areas where the cost of living is higher. The same report indicates that 13.1 percent of Korean American families had incomes below the poverty level, which is higher than the 9.6 percent reported for the total U.S. population. Asian American adults have lower unemployment rates than the U.S. adult population overall. In 1980 the U.S. Census Bureau also reported that 24 percent of Korean Americans age 16 or older held managerial or professional positions; 26 percent had technical, sales, or administrative jobs; 16 percent worked in service fields; nine percent held precision production, crafts, or repair jobs; 19 percent were laborers or operators; and six percent were unemployed.

SMALL BUSINESSES

Out of economic need, large numbers of recent Korean immigrants start their own businesses. Most of these immigrants did not run small businesses in Korea. In 1977, 33 percent of Korean American families owned small businesses, such as vegetable stands, grocery stores, service stations, and liquor stores. As a whole, they have a high success rate. In the 1980s an estimated 95 percent of all dry-cleaning stores in Chicago were owned by Korean immigrants. By 1990, 15,500 Korean-owned stores were in operation in New York City alone. Since then, a recession and internal competition has slowed the growth. New Korean immigrants are opening businesses in cities other than New York, Los Angeles, and Chicago, where the competition is less fierce.

ECONOMIC ORGANIZATIONS

Support within Korean communities has contributed to the success of small businesses. Recent immigrants still use the ancient Korean loan system, based on the *kye*, a sum of money shared by a group of business owners. A new grocer, for instance, will be allowed to use the money for one year and keep the profits. The *kye* is then passed to the next person who needs it. Organizations like the Korean Produce Association in New York and the Koryo Village Center in Oakland, California, are another source of support for new immigrants hoping to set up their own businesses.

POLITICS AND GOVERNMENT

Koreans have a general distrust of central governments. Historically, individual citizens have had little power in Korea and have suffered through scores of tragic episodes at the hands of other governments controlling the peninsula. As a result, most Korean immigrants come to America unaccustomed to participation in the democratic process. Discriminatory laws against Asian Americans on the West Coast have contributed to this distrust. Korean American communities have traditionally isolated themselves, relying on their family and neighborhood networks. Korean American participation in these grass-roots organizations and in U.S. government politics in general is growing and evolving slowly.

GRASS-ROOTS ORGANIZATIONS

From the church meetings on Hawaiian plantations in the early 1900s to the efforts of the Black-Korean Alliance in the 1990s, Korean immigrants have created settings to voice their opinions. Racial tensions within Korean American communities have led to the establishment of several grass-roots organizations. The Black-Korean Alliance in Los Angeles and the Korea Society in New York have set up programs to educate the two ethnic groups about each other's cultures. In 1993, the Korea Society launched its Kids to Korea program. Designed to improve the strained relationship between the Korean and African American communities, the program enabled 16 African American high school students from New York

City and Los Angeles to travel to South Korea in order to learn about its people, culture, and history. This successful program has been expanded to include students from other cities. The Korea Society also sponsors a program called Project Bridge in Washington, D.C., which offers classes in both Korean and African American cultures.

UNION ACTIVITY

While research experts have studied extensively the economic development and work patterns of Korean American professionals and entrepreneurs, the general American public knows little about Korean immigrant laborers. Yet since the beginning of the twentieth century, American industries have employed Koreans. By the 1990s, Korean Americans had begun to join forces with other Asian Americans to educate themselves about labor unions and their rights. Founded in 1983, the Asian Immigrant Women Advocates (AIWA) organizes Chinese and Vietnamese garment workers and Korean hotel maids and electronics assemblers in the Oakland, California area. They have staged demonstrations and rallies to draw attention to the unfair labor practices within the garment, hotel management, and electronics industries. The Korean Immigrant Worker Advocates (KIWA) in Los Angeles is another group that is bringing labor issues to the forefront. The KIWA is unique among Asian American organizations in Los Angeles because most of the members of its board of directors are workers themselves.

VOTING PATTERNS

Studies have shown that voter participation among Korean Americans is low. Historically, Korean immigrants have rarely been active in election campaigns and have seldom made financial contributions to individual candidates. Groups such as the Coalition for Korean American Voters (CKAV) in New York are working hard to address this problem. In just three years CKAV has registered 3,000 voters and sponsored programs that educate Korean immigrants about local and national government. The Coalition's efforts include airing public service announcements on Korean American television channels, establishing a college internship program to foster community service and leadership skills in students, and joining forces with other Asian American organizations to increase Asian American involvement in government.

MILITARY PARTICIPATION

In his book *Strangers from a Different Shore: A History of Asian Americans*, Ronald Takaki describes the plight of a Korean immigrant named Easurk Emsen Charr. He was drafted and served in the U.S. Army during World War I. Afterward he argued in court that as a U.S. military veteran, he should be entitled to citizenship and the opportunity to own land in California. The court ruled that the military should not have drafted him because he was Asian and therefore ineligible for American citizenship. Despite such discriminatory treatment, Korean Americans were eager to volunteer for military service during World War II. Doing so gave them a chance to support the American effort to curtail Japanese imperialism. Some Korean Americans served as language teachers and translators, and 100 Korean immigrants joined the California Home Guard in Los Angeles. They also participated in Red Cross relief operations. The American government, however, was somewhat suspicious of Korean-immigrant support because Koreans were technically still part of the Japanese empire. In Hawaii, Korean immigrants were referred to as "enemy aliens" and banned from working on military bases. Today, many Korean American men and women hold positions in the military.

INVOLVEMENT IN POLITICS OF KOREAN PENINSULA

Since Koreans first began immigrating to the United States, they have remained active in the politics of their homeland. Studies have shown that Korean Americans are generally more actively involved in the politics of Korea than in that of their new home. The lives of early Korean immigrants revolved around the Korean independence movement. In the 1960s Korean Americans staged mass demonstrations and relief efforts in response to the massacre of civilians by the South Korean dictatorship in Kwangju, the capital of South Cholla province. Today virtually every Korean American organization supports reunification of the peninsula. Groups such as the Korea Church Coalition for Peace, Justice, and Reunification were formed specifically for this purpose. Other American-based organizations, including the Council for Democracy in Korea, seek to educate the public about the political affairs of Korea.

INDIVIDUAL AND GROUP CONTRIBUTIONS

EDUCATION

Margaret K. Pai (1916–) taught English at Kailua, Roosevelt, and Farrington high schools on the

Hawaiian island of Oahu for many years. Her father, Do In Kwon, immigrated to Hawaii to work on the sugar plantations in the early 1900s. Her mother, Hee Kyung Lee, was a picture bride and met and married her husband in Hawaii at age 18. Since retiring, Margaret Pai has been writing short Hawaiian legends, poems, and personal reminiscences, including *The Dreams of Two Yi-Men* (1989), a vivid account of her parents' experiences as early Korean immigrants in America.

Elaine H. Kim (1943–) is a professor of Asian American studies and faculty assistant for the status of women at the University of California-Berkeley. Kim is also president of the Association for Asian American Studies and founder of the Asian Immigrant Women Advocates and Asian Women United of California. She is the author of *Asian American Literature: An Introduction to the Writings and their Social Context*.

FILM, VIDEO, TELEVISION, THEATER, AND MUSIC

Peter Hyun (1906–) worked in the American theater for many years. He was a stage manager for Eva LeGallienne's Civic Repertory Theatre in New York, director of the Children's Theatre of the New York Federal Theater, and organizer and director of the Studio Players in Cambridge, Massachusetts. During World War II, he served as a language specialist in the U.S. Army. After settling in Oxnard, California, he taught English to immigrant students from Asia. He is the author of *Man Sei!: The Making of a Korean American* (1986), a personal account of growing up as the son of a leader in the Korean independence movement.

Nam June Paik (1932–) has built a worldwide reputation as a composer of electronic music and producer of avant-garde "action concerts." He grew up in Seoul and earned a degree in aesthetics at the University of Tokyo before meeting American composer John Cage in Germany. His interest in American electronic music brought him to the United States. His work has been exhibited at the Museum of Modern Art, the Whitney Museum, and the Kitchen Museum, all in New York City, the Metropolitan Museum in Tokyo, and the Museum of Contemporary Art in Chicago. Among his video credits are *TV Buddha* (1974) and *Video Fish* (1975). He also produced a program called *Good Morning, Mr. Orwell*, which was broadcast live simultaneously in San Francisco, New York, and Paris on New Year's Day 1984 as a tribute to George Orwell's novel *1984*.

Myung-Whun Chung (1953–) was born in Seoul into a family of talented musicians. He made his piano debut at age seven with the Seoul Phil-

harmonic Orchestra and then moved with his family to the United States five years later. He studied piano at the Mannes School of Music and conducting at the Juilliard School of Music in New York City. He has served as assistant conductor of the Los Angeles Philharmonic Orchestra, music director and principal conductor for the Radio Symphony Orchestra in Saarbrucken, Germany, and principal guest conductor of the Teatro Comunale in Florence, Italy. He is now music director and conductor for the Opera de la Bastille, located in the legendary French prison.

Margaret Cho (1968–) is a second-generation comedian who has broken barriers and stereotypes with her numerous television and film appearances. In 1994 Cho became the first Asian American to star in her own television show, the ABC-sitcom *All-American Family*, which centered on a Korean American family.

GOVERNMENT AND COMMUNITY ACTIVISM

Herbert Y. C. Choy (1916–) became the first Asian American to be appointed to the federal bench in 1971. Educated at the University of Hawaii and Harvard University, he practiced law in Honolulu for 25 years. He served as attorney general of the Territory of Hawaii in 1957 and 1958 and continued his law practice until President Richard Nixon appointed him to the U.S. Court of Appeals.

Grace Lyu-Volckhausen comes from a family of female activists. Her mother and grandmother were members of organizations supporting women's needs in Korea. Moving to New York in the late 1950s to study international and human relations at New York University, Lyu-Volckhausen established an outreach center for women at a YWCA in Queens in the 1960s. The program now offers sewing classes, after-school recreation for children, counseling for battered women, and discussion groups. She has served on the New York City Commission on the Status of Women, on the Mayor's Ethnic Council, and on Governor Mario Cuomo's Garment Advisory Council. Still chairperson of her YWCA youth committee in the mid-1990s, she also worked with the New York mortgage agency to provide affordable housing for minorities.

INDUSTRY

Kim Hyung-Soon (1884-1968) immigrated to the United States in 1914 and started a small produce and nursery wholesale business in California with his friend Kim Ho. The Kim Brothers Company developed into a huge orchard, nursery, and fruit-packing shed business. Kim is credited with having developed new varieties of peaches known as "fuzzless peaches," or "Le Grand" and "Sun Grand." He also crossed the peach with the plum and developed the nectarine. Kim helped establish the Korean Community Center in Los Angeles and the Korean Foundation, a fund that offers scholarships to students of Korean ancestry.

LITERATURE

Younghill Kang (1903-1972) was one of the first Korean writers to offer Americans a firsthand, English-language account of growing up in occupied Korea. He wrote his first novel, *The Grass Roof* (1931), after spending many years struggling to survive as an immigrant living in San Francisco and New York. He later taught comparative literature at New York University and devoted the rest of his life to fighting racism in the United States and political oppression in his homeland.

Kim Young Ik (1920–) is the author of several novels and stories for children and adults. His books have won numerous awards and have been translated into many languages. They include *The Happy Days* (1960), *The Divine Gourd* (1962), *Love in Winter* (1962), *Blue in the Seed* (1964), and *The Wedding Shoes* (1984).

Marie G. Lee (1964–) is at the forefront of the current boom in children's literature being written by and about Korean Americans. Raised in Hibbing, Minnesota, she graduated from Brown University and lives in New York City. She is the author of the young adult novel *Finding My Voice* (1992), which won the 1993 Friends of American Writers Award. Her other young adult novels include *If It Hadn't Been for Yoon Jun* (1993) and *Saying Goodbye* (1994). Her work has appeared in many publications, including *The New York Times* and the *Asian/Pacific American Journal*, as well as several anthologies. She is president of the Board of Directors of the Asian American Writers' Workshop and a member of PEN and the Asian American Arts Alliance.

SPORTS AND MEDICINE

Dr. Sammy Lee (1920–) has made a name for himself in both sports and medicine. He won the gold medal for ten-meter platform diving in the 1948 Olympic Games in London and again in the 1952 Games in Helsinki, along with a bronze medal in three-meter springboard diving. He received his M.D. in 1947 and practiced medicine in Korea as part of the U.S. Army Medical Corps. Lee was named outstanding American athlete in 1953 by the Amateur Athletic Union and inducted into the International Swimming Hall of Fame in 1968. He served on the President's Council on Physical Fitness and Sports from 1971 to 1980 and coached the U.S. diving team for the 1960 and 1964 Olympics. He has also been named Outstanding American of Korean Ancestry twice—by the American Korean Society in 1967 and the League of Korean Americans in 1986. After retiring from sports, he ran a private practice in Orange, California, for many years.

MEDIA

PRINT

Korean Culture.
Published quarterly by the Korean Cultural Center of the Korean Consulate General in Los Angeles.

Contact: Robert E. Buswell, Jr., Editor in Chief.
Address: 5505 Wilshire Boulevard, Los Angeles, California 90036.
Telephone: (323) 936-7141.
Fax: (323) 936-5712.
E-mail: kcc@pdc.net.

Korean Studies.
Journal addressing a broad range of topics through interdisciplinary and multicultural articles, book reviews and scholarly essays.

Contact: Edward J. Shultz, Editor.
Address: Journals Department, Hawaii 96822.
Telephone: (808) 956-8833.
Fax: (808) 988-6052.
E-mail: uhpjourn@hawaii.edu.

The New Korea.
A bilingual magazine published weekly for the Korean American community.

Contact: Woon-Ha Kim, Editor and Publisher.
Address: 141 South New Hampshire Avenue, California 90004-5805.
Telephone: (213) 382-9345.
Fax: (213) 382-1678.

The U.S.-Korea Review.
The bimonthly newsletter of the Korea Society, it is designed to improve the depth and breadth of information, news, and analysis in U.S.-Korea relations. It features chronologies of current affairs and trends in trade and business. It also includes literary excerpts and reviews.

Contact: David L. Kim, Editor.

Address: 412 First Street, S.E., Washington, D.C. 20003.
Telephone: (202) 863-2963.
Fax: (202) 863-2965.

RADIO

FM-Seoul.
News programs broadcast in both Korean and English. Affiliated with *Korean Times* and KTAN-TV.

Address: 129 North Vermont Avenue, Los Angeles, California 90004.
Telephone: (213) 389-1000.
Fax: (213) 487-8206.

KBC-Radio.
Contact: Jung Hyun Chai.
Address: 42-22 27th Street, Long Island City, New York 11101.
Telephone: (718) 482-1111.
Fax: (718) 643-0479.

KBLA-AM (1580).
Korean broadcasts around the clock, seven days a week.

Contact: Ron Thompson.
Address: 1700 North Alvarado Street, Los Angeles, California 90026.
Telephone: (213) 665-1580.
Fax: (213) 660-1507.

Korean-American Radio (AM 1400).
Contact: Mr. Chin P. Kim.
Address: 475 El Camino Real, Suite 202, Millbrae, California 94030.
Telephone: (415) 259-1400.
Fax: (415) 259-1401.

Radio Korea NY (AM 1480).
Contact: Byung Woo Kim.
Address: 44 East 32nd Street, New York, New York 10016.
Telephone: (212) 685-1480.
Fax: (212) 685-6947.

Radio Seoul (106.9 FM).
Contact: Ms. Rae Park.
Address: 1255 Post Street, Suite 315, San Francisco, California 94109.
Telephone: (415) 567-3585.
Fax: (415) 567-0909.

TELEVISION

KBC-TV (Channel 28).
Contact: Dave Kang.
Address: 5225 N. Kedzie Ave., #200, Chicago, Illinois 60625.
Telephone: (800) 236-0510; or (773) 588-0070.
Fax: (773) 588-8750.

Korean Broadcasting Corporation (Channel 53).
First East Coast television company owned and operated by Koreans.

Contact: Priscilla Ahn.
Address: 42-22 27th Street, Long Island City, New York 11101.
Telephone: (718) 426-5665.
Fax: (718) 937-0162.

Korean Cultural Television.
Contact: Seung Ho Ha.
Address: 111 West 30th Street, New York, New York 10001.
Telephone: (212) 971-0212.
Fax: (212) 629-0982.

KTAN-TV (Channel 62).
Diverse programming in Korean.

Contact: Ms. Kyung Chung.
Address: 4525 Wilshire Boulevard, Los Angeles, California 90010.
Telephone: (213) 964-0101.
Fax: (213) 964-0102.

KTE-TV.
Exclusive distributor for Korean Broadcasting System's programming.

Contact: Mr. Cha Kon Kim.
Address: 625 South Kingsley Drive, Los Angeles, California 90005.
Telephone: (213) 382-6700.
Fax: (213) 382-4265.

ORGANIZATIONS AND ASSOCIATIONS

M. Y. Han at Duke University has an extensive list of links to Korean and Korean American interest websites (http://www.duke.edu/~myhan/C_KAWWW .html), including organizations and media.

Coalition for Korean American Voters, Inc.
Founded in 1991, this nonprofit, nonpartisan, volunteer organization promotes voter registration and

education of Korean Americans in the New York City metropolitan area.

Contact: Johnny Im, Coordinator.
Address: 38 West 32nd Street, Suite 904,
    New York, New York 10002.
Telephone: (212) 967-8428.
Fax: (212) 967-8652.

The Korean American Coalition.
Founded in 1983, this organization seeks to bring together Korean communities within the United States through fundraising and educational programs. It also sponsors programs designed to educate non-Koreans about Korean culture. The Coalition publishes a monthly newsletter called the *KAC Newsletter*.

Contact: Charles J. Kim, Executive Director.
Address: 610 South Harvard Street, Suite 111,
    Los Angeles, California 90005.
Telephone: (213) 380-6175.
Fax: (213) 380-7990.
E-mail: kaclal983@aol.com.

Korean National Association (KNA).
Contact: Woon-Ha Kim, President.
Address: 141 South New Hampshire Avenue,
    Los Angeles, California 90004-5805.
Telephone: (213) 382-9345.
Fax: (213) 382-1678.

The Korea Society (U.S.-Korea Society).
The Korea Society is the result of the 1993 merger of the work and programs of the New York-based Korea Society and the U.S.-Korea Foundation based in Washington, D.C. This nonprofit organization is dedicated to strengthening the bonds of awareness, understanding, and cooperation between the United States and Korea, and among Koreans, Korean Americans, and all other Americans. The Society's efforts extend to education, public policy, business, the arts, and the media. Its Washington branch publishes *The U.S.-Korea Review*.

Contact: Ambassador Donald P. Gregg, President.
Address: 950 Third Avenue, Eighth Floor,
    New York, New York 10022.
Telephone: (888) 355-7066; or (212) 759-7525.
Fax: (212) 759-7530.
E-mail: korea.ny@koreasociety.org.
Online: http://www.koreasociety.org.

National Association of Korean Americans (NAKA).
Individuals of Korean descent living in the United States. Seeks to safeguard the human and civil rights of Korean Americans; promotes friendly relations between Korean Americans and other racial and ethnic groups. Conducts educational programs.

Contact: John H. Kim, General Secretary.
Address: 276 Fifth Avenue, #806, New York, New
    York 10001.
Telephone: (212) 679-3482.
Fax: (212) 481-9569.
E-mail: nakausa@naka.org.

MUSEUMS AND RESEARCH CENTERS

Many major universities have a "Centers for Korean Studies," including: Columbia University, State University of New York at Stony Brook, University of California at Berkeley, and University of Hawaii at Manoa.

Association for Korean Studies.
University professors and other scholars interested in the promotion of research in Korean studies. Sponsors six to eight seminars a year which are open to the public, featuring distinguished speakers. Presently inactive.

Contact: John Song, President.
Address: 30104 Avenue, Tranquila, Rancho Palos
    Verdes, California 90275.

Korean Cultural Center.
Founded in 1980, this cultural center offers programs that introduce Korean culture, society, history, and arts to the American public. It organizes exhibitions, lectures, symposiums, and multicultural festivals. The Center houses a 10,000-volume library and an art museum and gallery. *Korean Culture Magazine* is published by the Center.

Contact: Joon Ho Lee, Director.
Address: 5505 Wilshire Boulevard, Los Angeles,
    California 90036.
Telephone: (213) 936-7141.
Fax: (213) 936-5172.
E-mail: KCCLA@PDC.NET.
Online: http://www.kccla.org/.

The Korea Economic Institute of America.
Founded in 1982, this educational group includes politicians, academics, trade organizations, banks, and other Americans concerned with the Korean economy. The Institute publishes a quarterly update on economic issues in Korea.

Contact: W. Robert Warne, President.
Address: 1101 Vermont Avenue, N.W., Suite 401,
   Washington, D.C. 20005.
Telephone: (202) 371-0690.
Fax: (202) 371-0692.
E-mail: rbw@keia.com.
Online: http://www.keia.com/.

Korean Institute of Minnesota.
Founded in 1973, this nonprofit organization is dedicated to preserving Korean language and culture. It brings together Korean American and adoptive families with a variety of classes and social opportunities for all ages.

Contact: Yoonju Park, Director.
Address: 1794 Walnut Street, St. Paul,
   Minnesota 55113.
Telephone: (612) 644-3251.
E-mail: lschulte@wavefront.com.

SOURCES FOR ADDITIONAL STUDY

The Korean American Community: Present and Future, edited by Tae-Hwan Kwak and Seong Hyong Lee. Seoul: Kyungnam University Press, 1991.

Lehrer, Brian. *The Korean Americans*. New York: Chelsea House Publishers, 1988.

Mangiafico, Luciano. *Contemporary American Immigrants: Patterns of Filipino, Korean, and Chinese Settlement in the United States*. New York: Praeger Publishers, 1988.

Patterson, Wayne. *The Korean Frontier in America: Immigration to Hawaii, 1896-1910*. Honolulu: University of Hawaii Press, 1988.

Patterson, Wayne, and Hyung-Chan Kim. *Koreans in America*. Minneapolis: Lerner Publications, 1992.

The State of Asian America: Activism and Resistance in the 1990s, edited by Karin Aguilar-San Juan. Boston: South End Press, 1994.

Takaki, Ronald. *From the Land of Morning Calm: The Koreans in America*. Adapted by Rebecca Stefoff. New York: Chelsey House Publishers, 1994.

———. *Strangers from a Different Shore: A History of Asian Americans*. Boston: Little, Brown, 1989.

Won Moo Hurh. *The Korean Americans*. Westport, CT: Greenwood Press, 1998.

LAOTIAN AMERICANS

by
Carl L. Bankston III

Many Laotian Americans have retained the values they brought with them from their homeland. Most significant among these values is the practice of Buddhism, which pervades every aspect of Laotian American life.

OVERVIEW

Located in Southeast Asia, Laos measures approximately 91,400 square miles (236,800 square kilometers), making it slightly larger than the state of Utah. The country shares its borders with Thailand in the southwest, Cambodia in the south, Burma in the west, China in the north, and Vietnam in the east. Laos has a tropical climate, with a rainy season that lasts from May to November and a dry season that lasts from December to April.

Laos has about 4,400,000 residents and an estimated population growth rate of 2.2 percent each year. Minority groups in this small, mountainous country include the Mon-Khmer, the Yao, and the Hmong. Approximately 85 to 90 percent of employed persons in Laos work in subsistence agriculture. Rice is the country's principal crop; other significant agricultural products include corn, tobacco, and tea. The majority of Laotians practice Theravada Buddhism, a form of Buddhism popular in Cambodia, Thailand, Burma, and Sri Lanka. In Laos, however, Buddhism is heavily influenced by the cult of *phi* (spirits) and Hinduism.

The Laotian flag has three horizontal bands, with red stripes at the top and bottom and a blue stripe in the middle. A large white disk is centered in the blue band. Many Laotian Americans identify more with the pre-1975 flag of the Kingdom of Laos than with the present-day flag of the country. This flag was red, with a three-headed white elephant situated on a five-step pedestal, under a white parasol. The elephant was symbolic of the ancient kingdom of Laos, known as "The Kingdom of a Million Elephants." The parasol represented the monarchy and the five steps of the pedestal symbolized the five main precepts of Buddhism.

HISTORY

Laotians trace their ancestry to the T'ai people, an ethnolinguistic group that migrated south from China beginning in the sixth century. Originally part of the Khmer (Cambodian) Empire, Laos achieved independence in 1353 when Fa Ngum, a prince from the city of Luang Prabang, claimed a large territory from the declining empire and declared himself king, calling the newly established state Lan Xang, or "The Kingdom of a Million Elephants." Luang Prabang was the nation's capital for 200 years until, in 1563, a later king, Setthalhiralh, moved the capital to Vientiane, which serves as the capital of Laos today.

The Lao kingdom reached its height in the late 1600s, under King Souligna Vongsa. After his death in 1694, three claimants to the throne broke the kingdom into three distinct principalities, the kingdoms of Vientiane, Luang Prabang, and Champassak. Each kingdom struggled for power, causing the weakened Lao states to become vulnerable to the more powerful nations of Siam (Thailand) and Vietnam. While the Siamese took Vientiane, the Vietnamese took other parts of Laos. By the mid 1800s, almost all of northern Laos was controlled by Vietnam, and almost all the southern and central parts of the country were controlled by Thailand. Only the area around Luang Prabang remained independent.

MODERN ERA

Vietnam suffered from its own internal problems in the late 1700s and early 1800s, and in 1859 French Admiral Rigault de Genouilly attacked and seized Saigon. By 1862, the emperor of Vietnam was forced to recognize French possession of the southern provinces, and Vietnam became a French colony 21 years later.

In 1893 the French entered Thailand's Chao Phya River and forced the king to relinquish Thailand's suzerainty over Laos. Four years later, King Oun-Kham of Luang Prabang was forced to seek the help of France against invaders from China and, consequently, Luang Prabang also fell to France's growing Indochinese empire. Laos then became a protectorate, or colony, of France. By 1899, Vien-

tiane had become the administrative capital of French Laos with French commissioners holding administrative power in all the provinces.

Although there were some local rebellions against French rule—mainly by the tribes of the hills and mountains—widespread Laotian resistance to the French did not begin until after World War II, when Japan, which had assumed control over Indochina during the war years, was defeated. In 1945 the Laotian prime minister, Prince Phetsarath, declared Laos an independent kingdom and formed a group known as the Lao Issara, or "Free Lao." Some Laotians supported a return to French colonization, feeling that their country was not ready for immediate independence. The Lao Issara, however, were strongly opposed to French rule in Laos. The prime minister's half-brother, Prince Souphanuvong, called for armed resistance and sought support from the anti-French movement in neighboring Vietnam, the Viet Minh, led by Ho Chi Minh. This Laotian political group became known as the Pathet Lao ("Lao Nation").

The Viet Minh defeated French troops at Dien Bien Phu in 1954. Afterward, an international conference held in Geneva separated Vietnam at the 17th parallel to prevent Ho Chi Minh's communist government from assuming control over the entire nation. Many Laotians supported the Viet Minh and, when North Vietnam invaded South Vietnam in 1959, Laos was drawn into the war.

The United States also became involved in the war to deter the spread of Communism in Southeast Asia. In Laos, American forces provided tactical and economic support to the royal government but were unsuccessful in their efforts. U.S. troops withdrew from the area in 1973 and South Vietnam fell to its northern enemy in April 1975. Later that same year, Pathet Lao forces overthrew the Laotian government, renaming the country the Lao People's Democratic Republic. Thousands of Laotians fled to Thailand where they were placed in refugee camps.

SIGNIFICANT IMMIGRATION WAVES

While there was some migration from Laos to the United States prior to 1975, the immigrants were so few that there is no official record of them. Available records do suggest, however, that they were highly professional and technically proficient. After 1975, thousands of Laotian people fled their homeland for the United States; the passage of the Indochina Migration and Refugee Assistance Act of 1975 by Congress aided them in this effort. Early Laotian immigrants included former government administrators, soldiers from the royal army, and shopkeepers. More recent immigrants from Laos included farmers and villagers who were not as educated as their predecessors.

While large numbers of Vietnamese and Cambodians began to settle in the United States almost immediately after socialist governments came to power in the spring of 1975, Laotian refugees did not begin to arrive in America in great numbers until the following year. In contrast to the 126,000 Vietnamese and 4,600 Cambodians who arrived in 1975, only 800 refugees from Laos were admitted into the United States. This is partially due to the fact that the new Laotian government obtained power in a relatively peaceful manner, despite fighting between the Hmong and the Pathet Lao. Moreover, the U.S. government was reluctant to accept refugees who had fled Laos for bordering Thailand, many of whom U.S. officials viewed as economic migrants rather than refugees from political oppression.

In 1976, 10,200 refugees from Laos, who had fled across the border into Thailand, were admitted to the United States. The number of Laotian refugees dipped to only 400 in 1977 and then climbed to 8,000 in 1978. In the years between 1979 and 1981, the number of Laotians entering the United States increased dramatically, due to international attention given to the plight of Indochinese refugees in the late 1970s and to the family unification program, which allowed refugees already in the United States to sponsor their relatives. During these three years, about 105,000 people from Laos resettled in America: 30,200 in 1979, 55,500 in 1980, and 19,300 in 1981. Although migration from Laos to America never again achieved the stature of this period, the resettlement of Laotians in the United States continued throughout the late 1980s and early 1990s.

SETTLEMENT PATTERNS

According to the U.S. Census, in 1990 there were about 150,000 Laotian Americans living in the United States. (This figure does not include the Hmong and other minority groups from Laos.) The majority of Laotian Americans (58,058) lived in California, primarily in Fresno (7,750), San Diego (6,261), Sacramento (4,885), and Stockton (4,045). Texas held the second largest number of Laotian Americans (9,332), with the majority living in Amarillo (1,188) and Denton (1,512). Minnesota and Washington State had the third and fourth largest Laotian American populations, with 6,831 and 6,191 residents, respectively. Thirty-four percent (2,325) of Minnesota's Laotian American population lived in Minneapolis and 46 percent

(2,819) of Washington's Laotian American community lived in Seattle.

ACCULTURATION AND ASSIMILATION

While few Laotian residents live in cities, Laotian Americans are an overwhelmingly urban people, with most living in large metropolitan centers. Of the 171,577 people in America born in Laos (this figure includes both ethnic Laotians and Hmong and excludes members of both groups born in America), 164,892 people (96 percent) lived in urban areas in 1990. The remaining four percent lived in rural communities. This is largely due to the fact that the vast majority of Laotians who immigrated to the United States were unaccustomed to an industrial society and spoke either very little or no English; they migrated to urban areas where they could find work that did not require many skills or language proficiency.

As a group, Laotian Americans are substantially younger than the national average. In 1990, the median age for Laotian Americans was 20.4 years while the median age for other Americans was 34.1 years. Moreover, Laotian Americans have larger families than other Americans. In 1990, the average number of people in each Laotian American family was 5.01 members, compared to an average of 3.06 members in white American families and 3.48 members in African American families. These figures demonstrate that Laotian Americans are a dynamic, rapidly growing community.

Because Laotian Americans are relatively new members of American society, it is difficult to predict to what extent they will assimilate. According to interviews given by Laotian Americans, however, it is apparent that many individuals have had to alter their viewpoints considerably to better adapt to American society. For example, such common "American" acts as touching, kissing, slapping someone on the back, waving, pointing one's feet at another person, and looking directly into someone's eyes are considered rude in Laotian culture. As Saelle Sio Lai has explained in John Tenhula's *Voices from Southeast Asia*, "Some of the Laotian customs I can use in my own way and some I must forget."

The majority of Laotian Americans have maintained a low profile in the United States. Consequently, few Americans have much knowledge of Laotian culture and people and, as a result, there are few stereotypes—positive or negative—regarding Laotian Americans.

"My children will surely be influenced by their scholastic environment and be Americanized very fast. I can't and don't intend to stop this natural process. I just want them not to forget their own culture. The ideal is the combination of the positive traits of the two cultures."

A Laotian refugee, cited in *Voices from Southeast Asia: The Refugee Experience in the United States*, edited by John Tenhula (New York: Holmes & Meier, 1991).

VALUES

Many Laotian Americans have retained the values they brought with them from their homeland. Most significant among these values is the practice of Buddhism, which pervades every aspect of Laotian American life. While individual Laotian Americans may not follow all Buddhist teachings, its philosophy serves as a behavorial guide.

The family is also highly important to Laotian Americans. In Laos, where the majority of people work in agriculture, families often work together to produce the goods necessary for their livelihood. In the United States, this practice has been altered somewhat since the majority of Laotian Americans work outside the home in urban communities. Nonetheless, Laotian Americans often live in close proximity to their extended family and such family values as respect for one's parents have remained constant. Laotian American children are expected to respect and care for their parents throughout their adult life.

Education has also become extremely important among Laotian Americans. Often, the family's future is dependent upon their children's success in school. "My husband and I always remind [our children] to study first, study hard, not play, not go out without permission from us," explained one Laotian American woman in *Voices from Southeast Asia*, "We tell them that we want to go to school, too, but we have to work to feed them. We sacrifice for them, and the only thing they can pay back is to study well."

PROVERBS

Laotian proverbs often express an earthy and practical sort of folk wisdom that is rooted in the experiences of generations of hard-working farmers. The Lao have brought countless proverbs to America with them, including the following examples: If you're shy with your teacher, you'll have no knowledge; if you're shy with your lover, you'll have no bedmate; Don't teach a crocodile how to swim; Keep your ears to the fields and your eyes on the farm; If you have money, you can talk; if you have wood, you can build your house; Water a stump and you get nothing; Speech is silver, silence is gold; Follow the old people to avoid the bite of a dog; It's easy to find friends who'll eat with you, but hard to find one who'll die with you; It's easy to bend a young twig, but hard to bend an old tree.

FESTIVALS

Most Laotian holidays and festivals have religious origins. The Lao word for "festival," *boon*, literally means "merit" or "good deed." Scheduled according to the lunar calendar, festivals usually take place at Buddhist temples, making it difficult for Laotian Americans to participate due to the limited availability of monks and temples in the United States. Two of the most important festivals are the *Pha Vet*, which commemorates the life of the Buddha in the fourth lunar month, and the *Boon Bang Fay*, or "rocket festival." Held in the sixth month to celebrate the Buddha, it is marked by fireworks displays.

CUISINE

Laotian cuisine is spicy. Most meals contain either rice (*khao*) or rice noodles (*khao poon*). The rice may be glutinous (*khao nyao*) or nonglutinous (*khao chao*), but glutinous, or "sticky," rice is the food most often associated with Laotian cuisine. The rice is accompanied by meat, fish, and vegetables. Meats are often chopped, pounded, and spiced to make a dish known as *lap*, and fish is usually eaten with a special sauce called *nam ba*. The sticky rice is usually taken in the thumb and first three fingers and used to scoop up other foods. A papaya salad spiced with hot peppers,

Laotian
tribeswomen
gather near the
Vietnam Veterans
Memorial in
Washington, D.C.

which is known as *tam mak hoong* to Laotians and *som tam* to Thais, is a popular snack food.

Many Laotian Americans still eat Lao-style foods at home. These dishes are also available at most Thai restaurants, since the cooking of northeastern Thailand is almost identical to that of Laos. Sticky rice and other ingredients for Lao foods are likewise available at most stores that specialize in Asian foods. In areas that have large Laotian American communities, there are also a number of Lao markets where these ingredients may be purchased.

TRADITIONAL DRESS

On special occasions marked by the *sookhwan* ceremony, some Laotian American women wear traditional costumes. The staple of their attire is the *sinh*, a skirt made from a piece of silk brocade about two yards long that is wrapped around the waist. It is often held in place by a belt made of silver buckles or rings. Accompanying the *sinh* is a shawl, or a strip of material, which is draped over the left shoulder and under the right arm. Some Laotian American men wear ethnic costumes at weddings, especially during the *sookhwan* ritual, and on stage during a *maw lam* performance, when actors sometimes don the *sampot*, or baggy trousers worn in Laos before French occupation.

HEALTH ISSUES

Traditional Laotian medicine involves massages and herbal cures. Practitioners of traditional medicine may be laypeople or monks. Since sickness is often seen as a problem of spiritual essence, the *khwan*, chants, and healing rituals are often used to cure illnesses. Although some traditional Lao medicine may be found in the United States, particularly in places that have large Laotian American communities, the practice of mainstream western medicine in America appears to be much more common.

Laotian Americans are more likely to visit a community clinic than any other type of medical establishment. As new arrivals, their mental health generally follows a pattern common to refugees. The first year in the United States tends to be a period of euphoria at having reached their destination. The second year tends to be a time of psychological shock, producing feelings of helplessness as the strangeness of the new environment becomes apparent. New Laotian Americans usually begin to adjust during the third or fourth year in the United States.

LANGUAGE

Lao is a tonal language; therefore, the meaning of a word is determined by the tone or pitch at which it is spoken. Although the tones vary somewhat from one part of the country to another, the dialect of the capital, Vientiane, is considered standard Lao. In Vientiane there are six tones: low, mid, high, rising, high falling, and low falling. Changing the tone of a word makes it a different word. The sound "kow," pronounced much like the English "cow," spoken with a high tone means "an occasion, a time." "Kow" spoken with a rising tone means "white."

Spoken with a mid tone, this word means "news." These tones give the Lao language a musical quality, so that its speakers often sound like they are singing or reciting melodic poetry.

The Lao alphabet is phonetic, meaning that each Lao letter stands for a sound. Lao writing has 27 consonant symbols that are used for 21 consonant sounds. There are more symbols than sounds because different consonants are used to begin words of different tones. The Lao alphabet also has 38 vowel symbols, representing 24 vowel sounds. These 24 sounds are made up of nine simple vowels and three diphthongs (vowels made up of two vowel sounds), each of which has a short form and a long form. The sounds are written with more than 24 symbols because some of them are written differently at the end of a word and in the middle of a word. All Lao words end in a vowel or in a consonant sound similar to the English "k," "p," "t," "m," "n," or "ng." Some English diphthongs (including "th" and "oh") do not exist in the Lao phonetic system. This is why some Laotian Americans who learned English as a second language may occasionally pronounce "fish" as "fit" or "stiff" as "stip."

The graceful, curving letters of the Laotian alphabet are based on the Khmer (Cambodian) alphabet, which, in turn, was developed from an ancient writing system in India. Although the Lao writing system is not the same as the Thai writing system, the two are very similar, and anyone who can read one language can read the other with only a little instruction.

GREETINGS AND OTHER COMMON EXPRESSIONS

Common Laotian American greetings and expressions include: *Sabai dee baw*—How are you? (literally, are you well?); *Koy sabai dee*—I'm well; *Jao day*—And how are you? (used when responding to *Sabai dee*); *Pai sai*—Where are you going? (used as a greeting); *Kawp jai*—Thank you; *Kaw toht*—Excuse me; *Baw pen nyang*—You're welcome, never mind (literally, it's nothing); *Ma gin khao*—Come eat! (literally, come eat rice); *Sab baw*—Is the food good?; *Sab eelee*—It's delicious.

LITERATURE

Most Laotian literature consists of oral tales and religious texts. Laotian oral literature often takes the form of poetry and is sung or chanted to the accompaniment of a hand-held bamboo pipe organ called the *khene* (pronounced like the word "can" in American English). Such poetry is most often used in theater, or opera, known as *maw lam*. The *maw*

lam leuang, or "story *maw lam*," is similar to European opera; a cast of actors in costume sing and act out a story, often drawn from historical or religious legend. *Maw lam khoo*, or "*maw lam* of couples," involves a young man and a young woman. The man flirts with the woman through inventive methods and she refuses him with witty verse responses. *Maw lam chote*, or "*maw lam* competition," is a competition in verse sung between two people of the same gender, in which each challenges the other by asking questions or beginning a story that the other must finish. In *maw lam dio*, or "*maw lam* alone," a single narrator sings about almost any topic.

Among the many legends and folktales told by Laotians and Laotian Americans, the stories about the character Xieng Mieng are among the most popular. Xieng Mieng is a trickster figure who plays pranks on people of various social classes. Other popular tales involve legends taken from Buddhist writings, especially the *Sip Sat*, stories about the last ten lives of the Buddha before he was reborn and achieved enlightenment. All Laotian religious literature is made up of the same Buddhist texts used by other Theravada Buddhists. These include the *Jataka*, the five *Vinaya*, the *Dighanikaya*, and the *Abhidamma*, all of which are scriptures written in Pali, an ancient language from India still used for religious purposes in countries practicing Theravada Buddhism. Verses in Pali known as the *parittam* are also important to Laotian Buddhists and are chanted by monks to protect people from a variety of dangers.

In the United States, Laotian monks have successfully retained Laotian religious literature. In addition, secular legends and stories, told through the medium of *maw lam*, may be heard at gatherings in cities with large Laotian American communities.

FAMILY AND COMMUNITY DYNAMICS

In Laos, men represent their family in village affairs, while women are responsible for running the household and controlling the financial affairs of the family. Among Laotian Americans, however, female employment is an important source of family income, and it is common for Laotian American women to work outside the home. Fifty percent of Laotian American women and 58 percent of Laotian American men participate in the American labor force. Because of the relative equality between men and women in Laotian American society, many Laotian American men share responsibility for completing household tasks. While Laotian American men almost always hold the official positions of leadership in community organizations, women are also quite active in their communities and are often important (though usually unacknowledged) decision makers.

The most common family arrangement in Laos is that of a nuclear family that lives in close proximity to their extended family. In the United States, extended families have, in many cases, become even more important to Laotian Americans for social and financial support. This interdependence may account for the low divorce rate among Laotian Americans. In 1990, only about four percent of Laotian Americans over the age of 15 who had been married were divorced, while nearly 12 percent of the American population over 15 years of age who had been married were divorced.

The practice of dating is also new to Laotian American immigrants, as it simply was not done in their homeland. In Laos couples usually come to know one another in the course of village life. In the United States, however, many young people date, although this custom is not always embraced by their parents.

EDUCATION

Since Laotian Americans are such a young group, their prospects for continuing adaptation are good, especially considering the scholastic successes of Laotian American children. In *The Boat People and Achievement in America*, an influential book on the academic achievement of young Indochinese Americans, Nathan Caplan, John K. Whitmore, and Marcella H. Choy asserted that refugee children, including Laotians, "spoke almost no English when they came, and they attend predominantly inner-city schools whose reputations for good education are poor. Yet by 1982, we find that the Indochinese had already begun to move ahead of other minorities on a national basis, and, two years later, their children are already doing very well on national tests."

Despite these accomplishments, few Laotian American young people attend college; this may be attributed to the economic disadvantages of their families. Only 26.3 percent of Laotian Americans (not counting the Hmong) between the ages of 18 and 24 attended college in 1990 (compared to 39.5 percent of white Americans and 28.1 percent of African Americans). Laotian American young people also had relatively high dropout rates; 12.2 percent of Laotian Americans between the ages of 16 and 19 were neither high school graduates nor enrolled in school in 1990 (compared to 9.8 percent of white Americans and 13.7 percent of African Americans).

IMPORTANT RITUALS

Many Laotian Americans retain the ritual practices of their culture. The most common of all Laotian rituals is the *baci* (pronounced "bah-see") or *sookhwan*, which is performed at important occasions. The word *sookhwan* may be interpreted as "the invitation of the *khwan*" or "the calling of the *khwan*." The *khwan* are 32 spirits that are believed to watch over the 32 organs of the human body. Together, the *khwan* are thought to constitute the spiritual essence of a person. The *baci* is a ritual binding of the spirits to their possessor. Even Laotians who do not believe in the existence of the *khwan* will usually participate in the *baci* as a means of expressing goodwill and good luck to others.

In the *baci* ceremony, a respected person, usually an older man who has been a monk, invokes the *khwan* in a loud, song-like voice. He calls on the spirits of all present to cease wandering and to return to the bodies of those present. He then asks the *khwan* to bring well-being and happiness with them and to share in the feast that will follow. After the invocation to the *khwan* is finished, the celebrants take pieces of cotton thread from silver platters covered with food, and tie them around each other's wrists to bind the *khwan* in place. While tying the thread, they will wish one another health and prosperity. Often an egg is placed in the palm of someone whose wrist is being bound, as a symbol of fertility. Some of the threads must be left on for three days, and when they are removed they must be broken or untied, not cut. Non-Laotians are not only welcomed to this ceremony, they are frequently treated as guests of honor.

WEDDINGS

The *khwan* is also significant to traditional Laotian wedding ceremonies. When a couple adheres to Laotian traditions strictly, the groom goes to the bride's house the day before the wedding feast, where monks await with bowls of water. The bride's and groom's wrists are tied together with a long cotton thread, which is looped around the bowls of water and then tied to the wrists of the monks. The next morning, friends and relatives of the couple sprinkle them with the water and then hold a *baci* ceremony. Afterward, the couple is seated together in front of all the guests and the monks chant prayers to bless the marriage.

RELIGION

In Laos almost all lowland Laotians are Buddhists, and the temple, or *wat*, is the center of village life. Most Laotian Americans are Buddhists as well, although many have converted to Protestant Christianity, especially in areas where there are no large Laotian concentrations to sustain traditional religious practices. Laotian American Buddhist temples are frequently established in converted garages, private homes, and other makeshift religious centers.

Buddhism is divided into two schools of thought. The "Northern School," known as Mahayana Buddhism, is a school of Buddhism most often found in China, Japan, Tibet, Korea, and Vietnam. The "Southern School," or Theravada Buddhism, is predominant in Laos, Thailand, Cambodia, Burma, and Sri Lanka. Theravada Buddhists stress the importance of becoming a monk and achieving *Nirvana,* an ideal state in which an individual transcends suffering. Mahayana Buddhists rely more on *Bodhisattvas,* enlightened beings who delay achieving *Nirvana* in order to help others become enlightened.

Essential to the Buddhist faith is the belief that all worldly things are impermanent. Those who are not aware of this concept become attached to worldly things, and this leads to suffering. Their suffering continues as the soul goes through a cycle of rebirths, and they are continually drawn back to worldly desires. An individual may break this cycle by overcoming desire through meditation and a moral, disciplined life. The soul that successfully overcomes all worldly desires reaches *Nirvana.*

Also significant to Buddhism is *karma,* which is form of spiritual accounting: good deeds performed in this life enable the soul to be reborn in better circumstances; bad deeds cause the soul to be reborn in worse circumstances. Accordingly, performing good deeds, or "making merit," is important to all Laotians and Laotian Americans. One can make merit through acts of kindness; however, becoming a monk or supporting monks or a temple are considered the best methods for making merit. All Laotian men are expected to become monks, usually in early manhood, before marriage. It is also common for older men, especially widowers, to become monks. Laotian women may become nuns, although nuns are not as respected as monks. In Laos, some men are not able to fulfill their religious duty of entering the temple for a time. This is even more difficult for Laotian American men because of demands in the workplace and the scarcity of temples in the United States. Laotian American monks sometimes share temples with Thai American or Cambodian American monks, since the latter also adhere to Theravada Buddhism.

A belief in spirits, or *phi* (pronounced like the English word "pea"), dates back to the time before the Lao were introduced to Buddhism. Since then, the spirit cult has become a part of popular Buddhist practices in Laos. Some of these spirits are "ghosts," the spirits of human beings following death. Other *phi* are benevolent guardians of people and places or malevolent beings who cause harm and suffering.

EMPLOYMENT AND ECONOMIC TRADITIONS

Although Laotian Americans have earned a reputation as hardworking people, many find themselves among the most disadvantaged in their new country. In 1990, while one out of every ten Americans lived below the poverty line, about one out of every three Laotian Americans lived below the poverty line. The median household income of Laotian Americans in that year was only $23,019, compared to $30,056 for other Americans. Unemployment among Laotian Americans is high (9.3 percent in 1990) and those with jobs tend to be concentrated in manual labor. Fully 44 percent of employed Laotian Americans held jobs classified as "operators, fabricators, and laborers" in 1990.

Many of the economic hardships of people in this ethnic group stem from to their newness in America and from the difficulties in making the change from life in a predominantly agricultural country to a highly industrialized country. Nearly 34 percent of Laotian Americans over the age of 25 had not completed fifth grade in 1990, compared to 2.7 percent of other Americans. While 75.2 percent of all adult Americans had completed high school, only 40 percent of adult Laotian Americans had finished high school. With regard to higher education, over 20 percent of Americans over 25 had finished college, while only about five percent of adult Laotian Americans were college graduates.

Learning English has hindered the economic adjustment of Laotian Americans. Over two-thirds (68 percent) of Laotians over five years of age reported that they did not speak English very well in 1990. While adult education programs and classes in English as a second language in community colleges and other institutions have helped, the transition has not been easy.

Despite their economic difficulties, Laotian Americans generally have positive views of life in the United States, probably because they tend to contrast life in America with their experiences in war-ravaged Laos.

POLITICS AND GOVERNMENT

As a group, Laotian Americans are very concerned about occurrences in their homeland and many would like to return but are unable to because of Laos's communist government. Laotian Americans have not yet become very active in American politics. At present, their first priority appears to be achieving economic independence. In general, they tend to have a positive view of American society and government, as might be expected of recent political refugees.

INDIVIDUAL AND GROUP CONTRIBUTIONS

Although Laotian Americans are relatively new to the United States, many professional individuals have made significant contributions to the Laotian American community and American society in general, specifically in professions requiring strong communication skills. Many Laotian American professionals are multilingual and serve as interpreters, negotiators, counselors, organization executives, and educators. For example, Banlang Phommasouvanh (1946–), a respected Laotian American educator, is the founder and executive director of the Lao Parent and Teacher Association. As such, she assists in promoting Lao culture, language, and arts through classes and support services. In 1990, Phommasouvanh received the Minnesota Governor's Commendation, Assisting the Pacific Minnesotans, State Council of Asia. In 1988, Lee Pao Xiong (1966-) served as an intern in the U.S. Senate. That same year he was one of 25 people chosen in a nationwide competition to attend the International Peace and Justice Seminar. From 1991 to 1993, Xiong was executive director of the Hmong Youth Association of Minnesota. Currently, he is executive director of the Hmong American Partnership in St. Paul, Minnesota. William Joua Xiong (1963–), who is proficient in Lao, Hmong, Thai, English, and French, served as an interpreter and translator at the U.S. Embassy in Bangkok in 1979. Presently a guidance counselor, he is also co-author of the *English-Hmong Dictionary* (1983).

MEDIA

PRINT

Because Laotian Americans are still establishing themselves in the United States, there are very few Laotian publications. Worthy of mention is the monthly, multilingual publication *New Life*, which has attained a wide readership among Laotian Americans. Published by the federal government, it provides international news and articles covering American culture and institutions. *New Life* circu-

lates 35,000 copies in Vietnamese, 10,000 in Lao, and 5,000 in Cambodian.

Khosana.

The semi-annual newsletter of the Thai / Lao / Cambodian Studies Group. News about scholarly activities and endeavors.

Circulation contact information.

Contact: Arlene Neher.
Address: Association for Asian Studies, Thailand-Laos-Cambodia Studies Group, Department of Anthropology, Northern Illinois University, Dekalb, Illinois 60115.
Telephone: (815) 753-8577.

Editorial contact information.

Contact: Michael R. Rhum, Editor.
Address: Khosana, 5100 South Kimbark Avenue, Chicago, Illinois 60615.
E-mail: mrrhum@worldnet.att.net.

ORGANIZATIONS AND ASSOCIATIONS

Most Laotian organizations in the United States were established to help Laotian Americans adapt to life in a new country. Therefore, these organizations concentrate heavily on providing English language tutoring, job counseling, psychological counseling, and other social services.

Coalition of Lao Mutual Assistance.

Located in Washington State, this organization coordinates the activities of ten Laotian organizations (including Hmong organizations and organizations of other minority groups from Laos). The Coalition also provides social services, including transitional counseling, transportation, and tutoring. This is probably the best source for information on the Laotian American community of Washington.

Contact: Udong Sayasana, President.
Address: 4714 Rainier Avenue, Seattle, Washington 98118.
Telephone: (206) 723-8440.

Lao-American Association of Oklahoma.

Address: 2433 Northwest 44th Street, Oklahoma City, Oklahoma 73112-8301.

Lao American Community Service.

Address: 4750 North Sheridan Road #369, Chicago, Illinois 60640-5042.

Lao Assistance Center of Minneapolis.
Provides social services to the Laotian American community in Minneapolis.

Contact: Manivah Foun, Executive Director.
Address: 1015 Olson Memorial Highway,
    Minneapolis, Minnesota 55405.
Telephone: (612) 374-4967.

Lao Family Community of Stockton.
Provides training in English as a second language, vocational education, a variety of youth programs, and a gang prevention program for people from Laos and other countries in Southeast Asia.

Contact: Pheng Lo.
Address: 807 North Joaquin, Suite 211, Stockton,
    California 95202-1716.
Telephone: (209) 466-0721.

Migration and Refugee Services.
Public policy and social action office of the U.S. Catholic Conference, on matters of migration, refugee, and immigration. Provides program support ad regional coordination for a network of 110 diocesan refugee resettlement offices. Office for the Pastoral Care of Migrants and Refugees provides the pastoral foundation for all MRS programs and assists the Bishops in encouraging the integration of immigrants, migrants, and refugees into the life and mission of the local Church. The Catholic Legal Immigration Network (CLINIC), a related organization, ensures that all newcomers have access to affordable immigration related services.

Contact: Mark Franken.
Address: 3211 Fourth Street NE, Washington, DC
    20017-1194.
Telephone: (202) 541-3352.
Fax: (202) 722-8755.
E-Mail: mrs@nccbuscc.org.
Online: http://www.nccbuscc.org/mrs.

National Association for the Education and Advancement of Cambodian, Laotian, and Vietnamese Americans (NAFEA).
Seeks to provide equal educational opportunities for and advance the rights of Indochinese Americans; acknowledge and publicize contributions of Indochinese in American schools, culture, and society; and encourage appreciation of Indochinese cultures, peoples, education, and language.

Contact: Ms. Ngoc Diep Nguyen, President.

Address: Illinois Research Center, 1855 Mt.
    Prospect Road, Des Plaines, Illinois 60018.
Telephone: (708) 803-3112.

MUSEUMS AND RESEARCH CENTERS

Laotian Cultural and Research Center (LCRC).
Individuals interested in preserving Laotian culture by collecting documents that illustrate the history of Laos. Maintains library of more than 500 items.

Contact: Seng Chidhalay, President.
Address: 1413 Meriday Lane, Santa Ana,
    California 92706.
Telephone: (714) 541-4533.
Fax: (714) 953-7693.

SOURCES FOR ADDITIONAL STUDY

Caplan, Nathan, John K. Whitmore, and Marcella H. Choy. *The Boat People and Achievement in America: A Study of Family Life and Cultural Values.* Ann Arbor: University of Michigan Press, 1989.

Mansfield, Stephen. *Culture shock! A Guide to Customs and Etiquette: Laos.* Portland, OR: Graphic Arts Center Pub. Co., 1997.

Proudfoot, Robert. *Even the Birds Don't Sound the Same Here: The Laotian Refugees' Search for Heart in American Culture.* New York: Peter Lang Publishing, 1990.

Stuart-Fox, Martin. *Laos: Politics, Economics, and Society.* Boulder, Colorado: Lynne Rienner Publishers, 1986.

————. *A History of Laos.* New York: Cambridge University Press, 1997.

Tenhula, John. *Voices from Southeast Asia: The Refugee Experience in the United States.* New York: Holmes & Meier, 1991.

LATVIAN AMERICANS

by
Andris Straumanis

The majority of
Latvians who came
to the United States
after World War II
had received at
least some higher
education in their
homeland. Many
were already
academic or cultural
leaders, and they
placed high value
on education for
their children.

OVERVIEW

Latvia is situated in Eastern Europe on the Baltic Sea, bordered by Estonia to the north, Russia to the east, Belarus to the southeast, and Lithuania to the south. With a population in 1993 of about 2.6 million and a surface area of 24,903 square miles (64,600 square kilometers), Latvia—one of the three Baltic nations—is larger than Estonia but smaller than Lithuania. Nearly 69 percent of Latvia's population lives in cities, especially the capital, Rîga, which is home to about a third of the nation's people.

Although Latvia has always had a diverse population, the country's ethnic composition has become a growing issue among Latvians concerned with preservation of their culture. In 1993, according to Latvian government statistics, 53.5 percent of inhabitants were ethnic Latvians, while 33.5 percent were Russians. In some regions, particularly in southeastern Latvia as well as in the capital city of Rîga, ethnic Russians outnumber ethnic Latvians. Other ethnic groups often found in Latvia include Belarussians, Estonians, Germans, Gypsies, Jews, Lithuanians, Poles, and Ukrainians. The leading religions in Latvia include Lutheran, Russian Orthodox, and Roman Catholic. The official language of the country is Latvian, and the national flag consists of three horizontal stripes (maroon on top and bottom, white in the middle).

HISTORY

Latvia's experience as an independent nation has been limited. Inhabited as early as 9000 B.C., the region now called Latvia only began taking on a national identity in the mid-nineteenth century. The Latvians' ancestors—early tribes of Couronians, Latgallians, Livs, Selonians, and Semgallians—were established in the area by about 1500 B.C. Through the centuries, these pagan tribes gradually developed their society and culture, but beginning in the late twelfth and early thirteenth centuries they came under subjugation from German invasions. In particular, the Teutonic Knights of the Holy Roman Empire forcibly Christianized the tribes and built an economic and political system that continued in power until the twentieth century. The Germans were responsible for the growth of Rîga, established in 1201, as an important Baltic Sea port that continues today to serve as a transportation link between western Europe and Russia.

As the Russian Empire expanded in the 1600s, German military control of the Baltic region weakened. Beginning in the 1620s and into the 1700s, the northern part of Latvia was under Swedish rule, while the south and the east came under Polish-Lithuanian domination. Only the Duchy of Courland, in western Latvia by the Baltic Sea, maintained some independence. The Duchy of Courland even managed to briefly extend its influence beyond its home, establishing colonies in Gambia in Africa (1651) and on the Caribbean Sea island of Tobago (1654).

With the signing of the Treaty of Nystad in 1721, settling the Great Northern War between Russia and Sweden, the region that would later become Latvia came under the political and military rule of the Russian czar. Its economy, however, continued to be controlled by German barons who lived off the labor of Latvian peasants. Latvians began to gain some economic power after 1819, when serfs in the Baltic provinces were emancipated by the Russians.

Industrialization and the emergence of the so-called "National Awakening" in the late nineteenth century created discontent among Latvians over their social and political relationships with the Russians and the Germans. That discontent led to the 1905 Revolution in Latvia. Although the revolution failed, it served to bring together the Latvian working class and intelligentsia and to heighten hopes for independence. A year after the 1917 Russian Revolution, Latvia declared its independence and was a sovereign nation until its occupation by Soviet troops in 1940. In June of 1941, during the final three days of the Russian occupation of Rîga

before its fall to the Germans, an estimated 30,000 Latvians were shepherded onto boxcars and deported to Siberia. Thousands died in what is now known among Latvians as the *Baigais gads* ("The Year of Terror"). "Liberated" by German troops in 1941, Latvia again fell under Soviet rule by the end of World War II. Forcefully incorporated into the Soviet Union, Latvia only regained independence in 1991 with the collapse of the Soviet Union.

THE FIRST LATVIANS IN AMERICA

Some historical evidence suggests that the first Latvians in North America may have settled with Swedish and Finnish migrants in the area of Delaware and Pennsylvania around 1640. In the late 1600s, a group from the island of Tobago migrated to Massachusetts. Latvians were also among the thousands of fortune seekers who headed to California during the 1849 Gold Rush. Two histories of Latvians in America claim that Mārtiņš Buciņš, believed to be a Latvian sailor, was among the first to die during the American Civil War.

SIGNIFICANT IMMIGRATION WAVES

Latvian American immigrants consist of two distinct groups: those immigrants—often called *veclatvieši*, or Old Latvians—who settled in the United States before World War II, and those who arrived after the war. Immigration before World War II is generally divided into three phases. The first phase began in 1888 with the arrival of several young men in Boston. (Among them was Jēkabs Zîbergs [1863-1963], who became one of the most important Latvian American community leaders in the pre-World War II era.) Like other Latvian immigrants who followed in the early years of the twentieth century, these men journeyed to America in search of their fortunes—or to escape being drafted into the Russian czar's army. Politically, the early immigrants were further divided into two groups: one devoted to the creation of an independent Latvia; the other, influenced by socialism, concerned with freeing Latvian workers from the oppression of imperial Russia. This division was mirrored in Latvian American society.

The early immigrants were usually young, single men, although some single women and families also came to the States at the end of the nineteenth century. They settled primarily in East Coast and Midwest cities, such as Boston, New York, Philadelphia, Cleveland, and Chicago, as well as in some cities on the West Coast, including Seattle, Portland, and San Francisco. Scattered immigrants also settled in rural areas, although usually not in great enough numbers to form long-lasting communities. In most cities, in fact, Latvians were so few in number that they failed to create the sort of ethnic neighborhoods for which other groups, such as the Italians or Poles, are known. Only in the Roxbury district of Boston did an urban Latvian neighborhood develop. Latvians also attempted to create a rural colony in Lincoln County in north central Wisconsin, but political differences and hard economic conditions sapped the community of its members, which at one point is said to have numbered about 2,000. The first Lutheran church built by Latvians in America was erected in Lincoln County in 1906.

Among the early wave of immigrants were several hundred Latvian Baptists who also settled in various East Coast locations. Perhaps the best-known Latvian Baptist settlement was in Bucks County, Pennsylvania, not far from Philadelphia, where beginning in 1906 a community was formed that eventually grew to about 100 individuals.

The next wave of immigration of Old Latvians began around 1906, following the failed 1905 Revolution in the Latvian province of the Russian empire. Many Latvian political leaders, as well as rank-and-file revolutionaries, faced certain death if caught by Russian soldiers, so they chose instead to emigrate and to continue the revolutionary movement from abroad. Most of the revolutionaries who arrived in the United States had more radical political views than the earlier Latvian immigrants, and this resulted in splits not only between conservative and leftist Latvians but also among the leftists themselves.

With the beginning of World War I, Latvia became a battleground between German and Russian forces. Latvian migration came to a halt until the aftermath of the 1917 Russian Revolution, when many revolutionary Latvians returned to their homeland to work for the creation of a Bolshevik government (a forerunner to the Communist party) in Latvia as well as in Moscow. Among those returning was Fricis Roziņš (1870-1919), a radical Marxist philosopher who had immigrated to America in 1913. He returned in 1917 to head a short-lived Latvian Soviet government. A few nationalist Latvian Americans returned to Latvia after the country declared independence in 1918.

The next wave of immigration was more of a trickle. U.S. immigration quotas put in place in 1924 limited the number of Latvians who could settle in America, while the creation of a free Latvia and the promise of better economic times in the homeland—coupled with the Great Depression in the United States—generally discouraged immigration.

The number of Latvians who journeyed to America before World War II is difficult to determine. Figures compiled by Francis J. Brown and Joseph Slabey Roucek, published in *Our Racial and National Minorities* in 1937, show that 4,309 Latvians came to the United States before 1900; 8,544 from 1901-1910; 2,776 from 1911-1914; 730 from 1915-1919; 3,399 from 1921-1930; and 519 from 1930-1936. Until the 1930 census, the U.S. government lumped Latvians in with Lithuanians and Russians. Ten years later, the census counted 34,656 people of Latvian origin, about 54 percent of them foreign-born.

World War II's ravages of Latvia turned many Latvians into refugees. Fearing the Soviet communists, they headed to western Europe. By the end of the war, an estimated 240,000 Latvians—more than a tenth of the country's population—were camped in Displaced Persons (DP) facilities in Germany, Austria, and other countries. About half were eventually repatriated to Latvia, but the rest resettled in Germany, England, Sweden, Australia, Canada, and the United States, as well as in other countries. As documented by Andris Skreija in his unpublished thesis on Latvian refugees, an estimated 40,000 Latvians immigrated to the United States from 1949 to 1951 with the help of the U.S. government and various social service and religious organizations. Many of these Latvians had been members of the professional class in their homeland, but in America they often had to take jobs as farmhands, custodians, or builders until they managed to find better paying positions.

Most Latvian DPs settled in larger cities, such as New York, Boston, Philadelphia, and Chicago. As with the Old Latvians, the DPs failed to create neighborhoods and had to rely on social events, the telephone, the mail, and the press to create a sense of community. In a few eastern cities, the newer immigrants found that some Old Latvian colonies remained active. (Some organizations and congregations begun by the Old Latvians, such as the Philadelphia Society of Free Letts, founded in 1892, continue to operate today.) In most cases, however, the Latvian DPs had to start from scratch and within a few years had managed to create a rather complete social and cultural world that included schools, credit unions, choirs, dance groups, theater troupes, publishers and book sellers, churches, veterans' groups, and political organizations.

Unlike the Old Latvians, many of whom considered themselves immigrants, the Latvian DPs saw themselves as living in *trimda*, or exile, and dreamed of the day they could return to a free Latvia. Since the reestablishment of an independent Latvia in 1991, however, few have returned,

although about 9,000 have declared dual citizenship as a way to offer political support to the reemerging nation. Many frequently travel to their homeland and provide financial and material support for relatives and various organizations. A number of Latvian Americans have been elected to the *Saeima*, or Parliament, in Latvia. According to the 1990 report of the U.S. Bureau of the Census, a total of 75,747 persons claimed Latvian ancestry, 27,540 of whom were born abroad. From 1980 to 1990, the census reports, 1,006 Latvians arrived in the United States.

ACCULTURATION AND ASSIMILATION

The Latvians of the pre-World War II immigration are generally thought to have assimilated quickly into the American mainstream, while the exiles of the post-World War II period have maintained their ethnic distinctiveness but now are facing deepening concerns about their future.

In a 1919 article in *Literary Digest*, the attitude of Latvians (or Letts, as they were known then)

toward acculturation was described thus: "Their first aim, except among the radical element, is to secure admission to American citizenship. Their children all are educated in our public schools, and the second generation of Letts are thorough Americans in the majority" ("Letts in the United States," *Literary Digest*, 21 June 1919; p. 37). While it may be true that many of the Old Latvians were eager to seek American citizenship, many also continued to keep up their interest in Latvia, especially between 1918 and 1920, when Latvia declared and fought for independence. At the same time, as the *Literary Digest* article noted, some Latvians who held leftist political views may have resisted becoming part of the American system. In 1919, for example, about 1,000 Latvians were among those immigrants who helped found the Communist Party of America.

Except for the political radicals among them, pre-World War II Latvian immigrants tended to assimilate easily. According to Brown and Roucek, 60.9 percent of the 20,673 foreign-born Latvians in the United States had been naturalized by 1930, while another 10.5 percent had declared their intention to be naturalized. Most Latvians, like other immigrants, started out in low-paying, unskilled jobs, but over the years gained experience and higher socioeconomic status. A report of the Committee on Racial Groups of the Massachusetts Bay Tercentenary Inc., written about 1930, had this to say about the Latvians in Massachusetts: "The Lettish people cannot be classified among the rich, but neither are they poor. Many of them own their own homes. Partly due to the fact that the Letts are scattered, there are no Lettish banks, corporations, or big businesses that are worth mentioning. The same is true of the professional workers. Mostly, they are skilled workers, such as carpenters, machinists, painters, wood finishers, tool makers, railroad workers, garage mechanics. Some of them, however, have taken up farming as their chosen profession and are successful farmers" (Committee on Racial Groups of the Massachusetts Bay Tercentenary Inc., *Historical Review*, 1930).

Latvians did not experience much of the stereotyping that plagued southern, central, and eastern European immigrants during the early twentieth century. This is most likely due to the fact that the Latvians were a little-known group. In one incident in Boston in 1908, however, Latvians as a group briefly made the front pages of local newspapers after three Latvians robbed a saloon at gunpoint. The newspaper coverage, the Boston-based magazine *Arena* complained, made the Latvians look like "a bloodthirsty, murderous people, lawless, criminal and altogether undesirable citizens" (Andris Straumanis, "'This Sudden Spasm of Newspaper Hostility': Stereotyping of Latvian Immigrants in Boston Newspapers, 1908," *Ethnic Forum*, Volume 13, No. 2, and Volume 14, No. 1, 1993-1994).

The arrival of the Latvian DPs after World War II sparked an era of heightened ethnic maintenance. Fiercely anticommunist, they saw the Soviet occupation of their homeland not only as an infringement on their right to autonomy but also as an effort to eradicate Latvians altogether. Migration of Russians and other non-Latvian groups into Latvia, part of a Soviet effort at "Russification," became a threat to Latvian culture. Latvian DPs in the United States reacted by launching a number of political and cultural movements to fight assimilation and help make Americans aware of Latvia's plight. Weekend Latvian schools were organized in several cities, while summer camps offered children and adults cultural immersion. *Runāsim latviski* ("Let's speak Latvian") was as much a political statement as an expression of cultural preservation. Marriage outside of the Latvian group often was discouraged, because it might mean that children of mixed couples would not learn the language.

As with the Old Latvians, few cultural misconceptions exist about post-World War II Latvians. Indeed the biggest difficulties Latvians have faced are their small numbers and the erasure, before 1991, of Latvia from many world maps. As a result, few Americans know anything about Latvians—and often confuse Europe's Balkan states with the Baltic countries, of which Latvia is a part.

TRADITIONS, CUSTOMS, AND BELIEFS

Like many other ethnic groups, the Latvians in the United States have adopted some American ways, but they also maintain a cultural heritage from the homeland. Until the late nineteenth century, when industrialization created demand for workers in several Latvian cities, Latvians remained rural. As a result, many of the traditions, customs, and beliefs still acknowledged by Latvian Americans are based on agricultural life. Others are drawn from more ancient Latvian culture. For example, in the Latvian tradition, a bride-to-be proved her worthiness by knitting many intricately designed wool mittens, as well as linen handkerchiefs and wool socks. The more she had in her dowry, the more worthy she might appear to her suitor. In the States, wool mittens and socks are sometimes used as adornments in wedding ceremonies.

Among the Latvian people's strongest traditions are their songs, called *dainas*, and their interest in folk culture. The *dainas*—simple verses that tell old stories and reveal the wisdom of centuries of Latvian culture—were handed down orally over generations. Beginning in the nineteenth century, as interest in Latvian nationalism grew, folklorists transcribed about 900,000 of these songs, culminating in a multi-volume collection compiled by Krisjānis Barons (1835-1923). Even at the end of the twentieth century, dozens of Latvian ensembles maintained the musical tradition in the United States, often performing at community events and in ethnic festivals. On a grander scale, Latvians in America and in Latvia have organized song festivals that feature performances of traditional folk songs and dances, choral music, and even musicals and plays. These song festivals serve as a ritual, reminding Latvians of their common ideals. The first such festival was held in Latvia in 1873; the tradition has since been carried on in the States, beginning in Chicago in 1953.

CUISINE

Traditional Latvian foods include *pīrāgi*, pastry stuffed with bacon or ham; *Jāņu siers*, a cheese usually made for the Midsummer Eve's holiday; various soups; sauerkraut; potato salad; smoked fish and eel; and beer. At major celebrations, such as holidays and birthdays, a popular sweetbread—the *klingeris*, flavored with raisins and cardamom and shaped like a large pretzel—is served. Because of the work involved in preparing many of these dishes, as well as the difficulty in obtaining some ingredients, many of these foods are now prepared only for special occasions. The foods tend to be rich, although Latvian Americans have been known to modify recipes by using lower-fat ingredients and less salt.

TRADITIONAL COSTUMES

Folk costumes are worn by Latvian Americans primarily when performing in song groups or dance troupes. Men's costumes are characterized by monotone (white, gray, or black) wool trousers and coats, white shirts, and black boots. Women's costumes usually include an embroidered white linen blouse and a colorful ankle-length wool skirt. Both men and women wear wide, bright belts and silver jewelry. Unmarried women wear a *vainags* (crown) on their heads, while married women wear a cap or kerchief. The designs of costumes are characteristic of specific locales in Latvia.

HOLIDAYS

Latvian Christians observe Easter and Christmas, attending church services and getting together with relatives and friends. At Easter, eggs are colored using onion skins rather than paint. The skins are wrapped around uncooked eggs, which are then boiled. One Easter dinner custom is to play a game to determine whose egg is strongest: two people each hold an egg, the ends of the eggs are knocked together, and the person whose egg does not break goes on to challenge someone else. At Christmas, an evergreen tree is brought into the home and decorated. Before Christmas gifts are opened, a line of poetry or words from a song are recited. At New Year's, some Latvians still observe a custom of "pouring one's fortune." The person who wishes to know what his or her fortune will be in the New Year pours a ladle filled with molten lead into a bucket of cold water. The shape of the hardened lead is then examined to determine the future.

Perhaps the favorite Latvian holiday, however, comes in June, during the summer solstice—the longest day of the year. Called *Jāņi* (also known as St. John's Eve or Midsummer's Eve) in Latvia the day was a traditional celebration of nature's fertility. An elaborate feast was prepared—including the symbolic *Jāņu siers*, a rich cheese—and the home was decorated with oak leaves and flowers. The celebration, featuring bonfires and sing-alongs, lasted through the night and well into the following morning. In the United States, many of these customs survive; in modern Latvia, *Jāņi* is an official holiday.

HEALTH ISSUES

Latvians in the United States have largely accepted modern medical treatments, although some folk cures are still used by some families. A number of Latvians have entered the medical profession. In addition to health insurance offered through their place of employment or through government programs, many Latvians also have joined the Latvian Relief Fund of America (*Amerikas latviešu palīdzības fonds*), founded in 1952. No illnesses specific to Latvian Americans are known.

LANGUAGE

Latvian, along with Lithuanian, is considered part of the small Baltic language group of the Indo-European family. It is one of the oldest languages still spoken in Europe. Latvian uses the Latin alphabet, although the letters "q," "w," "x," and "y" are not part of the alphabet. In addition, Latvian uses diacritical marks on some letters ("ā," "č," "ē," "ģ," "ī," "ķ," "ļ," "ņ," "ŗ," "š," and "ž") to differentiate long or soft sounds from short or hard sounds. Latvian words are stressed on the first syllable, and written Latvian is largely phonetic.

Due to Latvia's location and its history, the country's language has been influenced by German, Russian, and Swedish. During the 50-year occupation of Latvia by the former Soviet Union, the influence of Russian became particularly strong. A few dialects in addition to standard Latvian can still be heard in Latvia, most notably Latgallian, spoken in the heavily Catholic southeastern province of Latgale. In the United States, Latvian cultural leaders and schools have battled against the encroachment of English into their mother tongue; since Latvia regained independence in 1991 and declared Latvian rather than Russian the official language, more and more English words are creeping into Latvian.

Latvian continues to be used in the United States most widely among the first generation of post-World War II immigrants. According to the 1990 U.S. Census Bureau report, about 13 percent of those persons who claim Latvian ancestry—most of them aged 65 and older—said they do not speak

English very well. Among second and third generation Latvian Americans, usage has dropped significantly, in some cases because of intermarriage. Latvian is still used in church services in many congregations, although some churches have begun to use English as a way to attract and serve non-Latvian speakers. In the United States, only one Latvian-language newspaper is published (the semi-weekly *Laiks* of Brooklyn, New York), but there are several small Latvian-language magazines and numerous church newsletters.

GREETINGS AND OTHER POPULAR EXPRESSIONS

Perhaps the most widespread salutation in Latvian is *Sveiks!* ("svayks")—Greetings! It is commonly used when greeting friends but is also seen on bumper stickers on cars driven by Latvian Americans. Other terms include: *Apsveicu* ("ap-svay-tsu")—Congratulations; *Atā* ("a-tah")—Goodbye; *Daudz laimes dzimšanas dienā* ("daudz laimes dzim-shan-as dien-ah")—Happy birthday; *Labdien* ("labdien")—Good day; *Labrīt* ("labreet")—Good morning; *Labvakar* ("labvakar")—Good evening; *Lūdzu* ("loodz-u")—Please; *Paldies* ("pal-dies")—Thank you; *Priecīgus svētkus* ("prie-tsee-gus sveht-kus")—Happy holidays, used at Christmastime; *Uz redzēšanos* ("uz redz-eh-shan-os")—Until we meet again.

FAMILY AND COMMUNITY DYNAMICS

Latvians in the United States tend to have small nuclear families, usually not exceeding two adults and two children. According to the 1990 census, a total of 37,574 households of Latvian ancestry were reported. Of those, 12,341 had only one family member (32.8 percent); 14,211 (37.8 percent) had two; 5,010 (13.3 percent) had three; and 3,985 (10.6 percent) had four. A total of 86.9 percent of children under the age of 18 were living with two parents. Most families are middle-class; the median household income in 1989 was $38,586. Four percent of Latvian families received public assistance in 1989.

Within the post-World War II Latvian emigre population, young men and women have been encouraged to seek each other out in the hope that new Latvian families would result. For some youth, however, the close-knit nature of Latvian community life made it difficult to transform longtime acquaintances into romantic involvement. Others, perhaps realizing that their involvement in the Latvian community would make a relationship outside

the ethnic group difficult, seem to have deliberately sought out Latvian mates. But because the rate of marriage to non-Latvians has continued to increase over the years, older Latvians have become concerned that Latvian culture in the United States might be threatened. At one point in the early 1970s, it was even suggested that Latvian newspapers should not carry announcements of marriages involving non-Latvians. Among Latvian men, according to the 1990 census, 62.3 percent were married, one percent were separated, and 6.4 percent were divorced. Among women, 50.9 percent were married, one percent were separated, and 8.8 percent were divorced.

THE ROLE OF WOMEN

Latvia extended broad democracy to its inhabitants and guaranteed equal rights to women. In the States, women have often been placed in such traditional roles as homemaker and cook. Despite their accomplishments in the professions, women for many years were not seen at the helm of the most influential local and national Latvian institutions. In recent years, however, that has been changing. For example, the Latvian newspaper *Laiks*, published since 1949, is now edited by a woman, Baiba Bičole.

EDUCATION

The Old Latvians, while recognizing the value of education, did not appear to want or to be able to afford college degrees. By 1911—more than 20 years after the first Latvian immigrants had arrived in the United States—only two individuals had obtained American university degrees, the first one being a woman, Anna Enke, who studied at the University of Chicago.

The majority of Latvians who came to the United States after World War II had received at least some higher education in their homeland. Many were already academic or cultural leaders, and they placed high value on education for their children. The 1990 census indicates that about 34 percent of people claiming Latvian ancestry had earned bachelor's degrees or higher. Between 1940 and 1982, according to a 1984 study, 28 percent of Latvian men outside the Soviet Union who had earned bachelor's degrees studied in the engineering sciences, while another 15.6 percent studied in the humanities. Among women, 22.5 percent studied humanities and 16.9 percent studied medicine.

RELIGION

In 1935, 55.1 percent of religious Latvians followed the Lutheran faith, 24.4 percent were Roman Catholic, and 8.9 percent were Greek Orthodox (*Cross Road Country—Latvia*, edited by Edgars Dunsdorfs [Waverly, Iowa: Latvju Grāmata, 1953]; p. 360). Although it is difficult to obtain accurate figures, the majority of Latvians in the United States follow the Lutheran faith, but there also are adherents of the Catholic and Baptist faiths, as well as a small group of *dievturi*, followers of a folk religion.

The first Latvian Lutheran church service in the United States was organized by the Boston Latvian Society in 1891. The earliest known congregation, St. John's Latvian Evangelical Lutheran Church, was formed in 1893 in Philadelphia and continued to operate more than a century later. The Rev. Hans Rebane (1862-1911) became the first Latvian Lutheran minister ordained in America. Rebane, of Estonian and Latvian heritage, also served Estonian and German congregations. Together with Jēkabs Zībergs, he began *Amerikas Vēstnesis* (*America's Herald*, 1896-1920), a nationalist and religiously oriented newspaper based in Boston; Zībergs also published an almanac and other religious materials. In a few short years, additional Latvian congregations were established in New York, Philadelphia, Baltimore, Cleveland, Chicago, northern Wisconsin, San Francisco, and other locations. Radical Latvians in the United States criticized these early churchgoers; to them, the church in Latvia—largely controlled by German-appointed pastors—contributed to the oppression of Latvian peasants. By World War II, only a few congregations remained, but the arrival of Latvian DPs beginning in 1949 gave them new life.

Latvian Lutheran DPs saw theirs as a church in exile. Although a Lutheran church still existed back in Latvia, its activities were suppressed by the Soviet regime. The Latvian Lutheran church in the United States remains conservative but in many cities has become a focus of community activity. Many congregations have organized Saturday or Sunday schools offering language and cultural heritage lessons in addition to religious instruction. In cities where Latvians acquired their own church buildings, the facilities often double as cultural centers where concerts or other programs might be presented.

A key issue for Lutheran clergy has been whether they can continue to preach Christianity at the expense of Latvian ethnic maintenance. Attempts by some pastors to introduce English into religious instruction have in the past been met by resistance. Like other Latvian social and cultural institutions in the United States, the Lutheran church is concerned about decreasing membership, which erodes both the vitality of congregations as well as their financial base. According to Latvian statistics published in 1993, the number of church members totaled 26,265 in 1978, but dropped steadily to 18,557 over the next 15 years.

Latvian Baptists were also active in the States by the late 1880s. The first Latvian Baptist congregation was founded in Philadelphia in 1900; by 1908 congregations were also meeting in Boston, Chicago, and New York, as well as in Bucks County, Pennsylvania. Latvian Baptists published a number of magazines and newsletters before World War II, including the monthly *Amerikas Latvietis* (*America's Latvian*, 1902-1905) and *Jaunā Tēvija* (*The New Fatherland*, 1913-1917).

Latvian American Catholic groups also sprang up after World War II, but they were not large enough in any city to have their own church. Latvian Catholics are represented by the American Latvian Catholic Association (*Amerikas latviešu katoļu apvienība*), formed in 1954.

Also active in the United States are the *dievturi*, followers of a folk religion registered as the Latvian Church Dievturi Inc., which developed in the 1920s in Latvia. The *dievturi* look to ancient Latvian culture, particularly folk songs, for their beliefs and are credited for their efforts in maintaining old folkways.

EMPLOYMENT AND ECONOMIC TRADITIONS

Many of the Old Latvians who left their homeland were either farmers or factory workers. Upon arriving in the United States, they at first took jobs as unskilled laborers; later, however, some moved into management and professional positions. Unlike the Old Latvians, many of the DPs had held professional positions in Latvia before migrating to America. Most, however, were unable to immediately resume their professional careers—at least until they had mastered English and proven their qualifications.

According to the 1990 census, 38,132 persons of Latvian ancestry were counted in the nation's civilian labor force, of which 1,653 (4.2 percent) were unemployed. About 48 percent of Latvians in the labor force had positions in management and the professions; 30 percent had jobs in technical, sales, and administrative support occupations. Almost three-fourths of the Latvians in the labor force worked in the private sector, about 16 percent had jobs in government and education, and about 10 percent were self-employed.

Like other Americans, Latvians were among those affected by the economic recession of the late 1980s and early 1990s. When a family was forced to relocate to other parts of the mainland States in search of employment, the move sometimes had a dramatic effect on Latvian social and cultural life. In Minneapolis, for example, when two young but large families had to move in the mid-1980s, their departure resulted in enrollment in the small Latvian Saturday school being trimmed by about a third.

POLITICS AND GOVERNMENT

Latvian Americans have always been politically active. Before Latvia declared its independence, radical Old Latvians were particularly active in working for the creation of a socialist government in their homeland as well as in the United States. The first Latvian socialist organization, the Lettish Workingmen's Society, was started in Boston in 1893. By World War I, almost every city where Latvians could be found also had at least one socialist club. With the arrival of revolutionary Latvians after the failed 1905 Revolution, Latvian radicalism moved further to the left. Latvians were among those immigrants who helped form the American communist movement in 1919. Radicals produced a number of newspapers and other publications, but the most important was the Boston-based weekly *Strādnieks* (*The Worker*, 1906-1919). The failure to

establish a permanent socialist government in Latvia following the 1917 Russian Revolution—compounded by U.S. government repression of radical activities during the "Red Scare" of the 1920s—largely put an end to Latvian radical activity in America.

The radicals were opposed by nationalist Latvians who sought independence for their homeland. Under the leadership of Jēkabs Zībergs, Christopher Roos (1887-1963), and others, the nationalists organized in 1917 to support the American World War I military effort by selling Liberty Bonds. The American National Latvian League (*Amerikas latviešu tautiskā savienība* [ALTS]) was formed the next year in Boston to represent Latvian interests in the United States. When their homeland declared independence later in 1918, ALTS representatives urged America to recognize the new nation of Latvia; *de jure* recognition came in 1922.

Soviet occupation of Latvia during World War II was criticized by nationalist Latvians in the States, who sought to inform the American public about atrocities committed by the Russians. The arrival of Latvian DPs after the war heightened political activity among Latvian Americans. A number of Latvian civic and political organizations were founded, including the American Latvian Association in 1951 and the American Latvian Republican National Federation in 1961. Latvians also joined with Estonians and Lithuanians to form groups such as the Baltic Appeal to the United Nations (BATUN), to press world governments to oppose Soviet power in their homelands.

Officially, the U.S. government never recognized the incorporation of the Baltic countries into the Soviet Union. Attempts by U.S. diplomats to ease tensions with the Soviets usually drew swift criticism from the Baltic groups. At election time, the Republican party tended to evoke more support from Latvians than the Democrats—particularly among the first generation of Latvian immigrants, who felt the Republicans had a stronger anticommunist foreign policy platform. Within the Latvian community, efforts during the 1970s and 1980s by some Latvian Americans to establish cultural exchanges with Soviet Latvia were viewed with suspicion and criticism.

Reestablishment of Latvian independence in 1991 opened the door to direct political involvement in the homeland. Latvian immigrants and their descendants were allowed to reclaim their pre-World War II citizenship and voting rights; by May of 1993 more than 8,700 Latvian Americans held dual U.S. and Latvian citizenship, according to American Latvian Association statistics. In June of

1993, during the first free democratic elections after the end of Soviet rule, a number of Latvian Americans were elected to Parliament. Among them were twin brothers Oļǵerts Pavlovskis (1934–) and Valdis Pavlovskis (1934–), both of whom returned to Latvia to take government posts.

INDIVIDUAL AND GROUP CONTRIBUTIONS

Latvians have made a number of contributions to American culture and society. The following sections list some of their achievements.

ART

Florida's famed Coral Castle, a sculpture garden carved from coral, was created over a 30-year period by Edward Leedskalnin (1887-1951), a Latvian immigrant. Leedskalnin, jilted by the girl he wanted to marry, journeyed to the United States and decided to build the sculpture garden as a testament to his love for her. The garden (located in Homestead, Florida) was completed in 1940 and was placed on the National Register of Historical Places in 1984.

EDUCATION

Edgars Andersons (1920-1989) was a prolific historian who taught at San Jose State University in California. A specialist in European and early American history, he received a Distinguished Academic Achievement Award in 1978. Oswald Tippo (born 1911), a botanist by training, held several top academic posts during his career, including chancellor of the University of Massachusetts at Amherst.

FILM, TELEVISION, AND THEATER

Actress Rutanya Alda (1942–) has appeared in numerous film, stage, and television productions, including *The Long Goodbye* (1973), *Pat Garrett and Billy the Kid* (1973), *The Deer Hunter* (1978), and *Prancer* (1989). Actor Buddy Ebsen (born 1908), best known for his television roles as Jed Clampett in *The Beverly Hillbillies* and as the title character in *Barnaby Jones*, is of Latvian and Danish parentage. Chicagoan Mārīte Ozere (1944–) was crowned Miss U.S.A. in 1965. Actress Laila Robins (1959–) has appeared in several feature films, including *Planes, Trains & Automobiles* (1987), *A Walk on the Moon* (1987), *An Innocent Man* (1989), and *Welcome Home, Roxy Carmichael* (1990). Anita Stewart (1895-1961) appeared in the silent movies *Hollywood* (1923) and *Never the Twain Shall Meet* (1925).

INDUSTRY

Augusts Krastiņš (1859-1942) began building gasoline-powered automobiles in 1896, several years before Henry Ford. The Cleveland, Ohio-based Krastin Automobile Company operated until 1904. Leon "Jake" Swirbul was a cofounder of the Grumman Aircraft Company and helped lead the company's production of fighter planes for the U.S. Navy during World War II. In 1946 Swirbul became president of the company, which is now part of Northrop Grumman Corporation.

LITERATURE AND JOURNALISM

Anšlevs Eglītis (1906-1993), a novelist and movie critic, wrote many popular Latvian books and was a frequent contributor to the Latvian American newspaper *Laiks*. Jānis Freivalds (1944–) has worked as a journalist, consultant, and entrepreneur. In 1978 he published a novel, *The Famine Plot*. Peter Kihss (1912-1984) spent nearly 50 years working as a journalist, including 30 years for the *New York Times*.

MUSIC

Several Latvian Americans have made significant contributions to symphonic music and opera, such as concert pianist Artūrs Ozoliņš (1946–), who has recorded with the Toronto Symphony Orchestra, and composer Gundaris Pone (1932-1993), whose work received international recognition but whose radical politics did not endear him to Latvian Americans. Alternative pop singer-songwriter Ingrid Karklins (1957–) of Austin, Texas, has released two albums, *A Darker Passion* (1992) and *Anima Mundi* (1994), some of which draws inspiration from traditional Latvian instruments and songs. The Quags, a Latvian rock group in Philadelphia, have made some recordings.

SCIENCE

John Akerman (1897-1972), a professor of aeronautics, had a long career teaching and researching at the University of Minnesota. Akerman Hall on the Minneapolis campus is named in his honor. Lectures about the Star of Bethlehem by retired astronomy professor Kārlis Kaufmanis (1910–) have become a popular Christmas attraction in Minnesota. Mārtiņš Straumanis (1898-1973) was a professor of metallurgy at the University of Missouri at Rolla.

SPORTS

Latvians in America and in Latvia have become ardent fans of the San Jose Sharks team of the

National Hockey League. Two Latvians, goalie Arturs Irbe (1967–) and defenseman Sandis Ozolinsh (1972–), were acquired by the team in 1991. Gundars Vetra (c. 1967–) was the first Latvian to play for a National Basketball Association team. He was recruited by the Minnesota Timberwolves after playing for the Russian-led Unified Team in the 1992 Olympics.

MEDIA

PRINT

Laiks (Time).

A semi-weekly Latvian-language newspaper published in Brooklyn, New York.

Contact: Ilavars Spilners, Editor.
Address: 7307 Third Avenue, Brooklyn,
New York 11209-2466.
Telephone: (718) 836-6382.
Fax: (718) 748-1426.

Latvian Dimensions.

Published by the American Latvian Association, it offers a national perspective on issues of interest to Latvians.

Contact: Elisa Freimanis, Editor.
Address: American Latvian Association, P.O. Box
4578, 400 Hurley Avenue, Rockville,
Maryland 20850-3131.
Telephone: (301) 340-1914.
Fax: (301) 340-8732.

RADIO

WVVX-FM (103.1).

Chicago Association of Latvian Organizations (Čikāgas latviešu organizāciju apvienība) sponsors a program.

Contact: Juris Valainis.
Address: 210 Skokie Valley Road, Highland Park,
Illinois 60035.
Telephone: (847) 831-5250.
Fax: (847) 831-5296.

ORGANIZATIONS AND ASSOCIATIONS

American Latvian Association in the U.S. (Amerikas latviešu apvienība, ALA).

Founded in 1951, the ALA is largest Latvian association in the United States; it has about 9,000 members and represents approximately 160 organizations. In the past, it served as an umbrella organization that coordinated the political, cultural, and educational activities of Latvian communities and lobbied the U.S. government for legislation and policies supporting independence for Latvia. Since independence was achieved, the ALA has given increased attention to welfare and education efforts in Latvia.

Contact: Anita Terauds, Secretart General.
Address: 400 Hurley Avenue, Rockville, Maryland
20850-3121.
Telephone: (301) 340-1914.
Fax: (301) 340-8732.
E-mail: alainfo@alausa.org.
Online: http://www.alausa.org/.

American Latvian Catholic Association (Amerikas latviešu katoļu apvienība, ALKA).

Founded in 1954, the ALKA represents the interests of Latvians of the Roman Catholic faith, many of whom trace their heritage to the Latgale province in southeastern Latvia.

Address: 2235 Ontonagon Street, S.E.,
Grand Rapids, Michigan 49506.

American Latvian Youth Association (Amerikas latviešu jaunatnes apvienība, ALJA).

Founded in 1952 and incorporated in 1964, the ALJA is a national organization for Latvian youth, generally those under age 30. It has served as a voice for its members in the exile community. During the 1970s and 1980s, it was especially active on the political front, organizing demonstrations at the Soviet embassy in Washington, D.C., and in other locations. Some former officers of the association have gone on to other leadership posts in the Latvian American community as well as in newly independent Latvia.

Contact: Pçteris Burìelis, Information Director.
Address: 10 Lois Lane, Katonah, New York 10536.
Telephone: (914) 232-2192.
E-mail: burgelis@pitnet.net.
Online: http://www.alja.org/.

Latvian Evangelical Lutheran Church in America (Latvieš evaņģeliski luteriskā baznīca Amerikā, LELBA).

Founded in 1975, the LELBA carries on the work of a Latvian American church association formed in 1957. Before 1975, local Latvian Lutheran congregations belonged to one of the U.S. churches, such as the American Lutheran Church. Since then, many have dropped their ties to U.S. churches and now are only members of LELBA. As of 1994, LELBA included 53 congregations in the United States; not all congregations, however, have their own churches or ministers.

Contact: Rev. Uldis Cepure, Chairman of the Board.
Address: 2140 Orkla Drive, Golden Valley, Minnesota 55427.
Telephone: (612) 546-3712.

Latvian Welfare Association (*Daugavas Vanagi*).

Founded in 1945 in Belgium, this is a global organization of war veterans—primarily those who fought in the two Latvian divisions organized during the German occupation of Latvia in World War II. Aside from offering support for disabled Latvian veterans, *Daugavas Vanagi* also supports cultural and educational efforts and works to preserve the history of the Latvian military. The organization has national and local chapters in several countries.

Address: 3220 Rankin Road, Minneapolis, Minnesota 55418.
Telephone: (612) 781-7132.
Fax: (612) 789-2602.

MUSEUMS AND RESEARCH CENTERS

Association for the Advancement of Baltic Studies, Inc.

Independent, nonprofit research association. Focuses on Baltic area, including the people of Estonia, Latvia, and Lithuania and Baltic literature, history, and economics.

Contact: Kalle Merilo.
Address: 3465 East Burnside Street, Portland, Oregon 97214-2050.
Telephone: (908) 852-5258.
Fax: (908) 852-3233.
E-mail: aabs@teleport.com.
Online: http://www.lanet.lv/members/aabs/ aabs.html.

Balch Institute for Ethnic Studies.

Houses Latvian material in its archives, including some records of St. John's Latvian Evangelical Lutheran Church.

Contact: John Tenhula, President.
Address: 18 South Seventh Street, Philadelphia, Pennsylvania 19106.
Telephone: (215) 925-8090.

Fax: (215) 925-8195.
E-mail: balchlib@hslc.org.
Online: http://libertynet.org/~balch.

Immigration History Research Center.

Devoted to collecting archival materials concerning eastern, central, and southern European immigrants, as well as immigrants from the Middle East, the IHRC continues to expand its Latvian collection of books, newspapers, serials, and manuscripts. In 1993 the center embarked on a two-year project to organize materials pertaining to Displaced Persons from Latvia and Ukraine.

Contact: Joel Wurl, Curator.
Address: University of Minnesota, 826 Berry Street, St. Paul, Minnesota 55114.
Telephone: (612) 627-4208.
Fax: (612) 627-4190.
E-mail: ihrc@tc.umn.edu.
Online: http://www.umn.edu/ihrc.

Latvian Museum.

Housed in the Latvian Lutheran Church in Rockville, Maryland, the museum opened in 1980 and provides an overview of Latvian life in the homeland and in exile.

Address: 400 Hurley Avenue, Rockville, Maryland 20850.

Latvian Studies Center.

Serves as a focus for students of Latvian heritage. It includes a growing library and archives of Latvian materials that have been donated to the center by Latvians from throughout the country.

Contact: Maira Bundža.
Address: Western Michigan University, 1702 Fraternity Village Drive, Kalamazoo, Michigan 49006.
Telephone: (616) 343-1922.
Fax: (616) 343-0704.

SOURCES FOR ADDITIONAL STUDY

Andersons, Edgars, and M. G. Slavenas. "The Latvian and Lithuanian Press," *The Ethnic Press in the United States: A Historical Analysis and Handbook*, edited by Sally M. Miller. Westport, Connecticut: Greenwood Press, 1987; pp. 229-245.

The Baltic States: A Reference Book. Tallinn, Estonia: Tallinn Book Printers, 1991.

Dreifelds, Juris. *Latvia in Transition*. New York: Cambridge University Press, 1996.

Kārklis, Maruta, Līga Streips, and Laimonis Streips. *The Latvians in America, 1640-1973: A Chronology and Fact Book*. Dobbs Ferry, New York: Oceana Publications, 1974.

Latvia, prepared by Geography Department. Minneapolis: Lerner Publications, 1992.

Lieven, Anatoly. *The Baltic Revolution: Estonia, Latvia, Lithuania and the Path to Independence*. New Haven, Connecticut: Yale University Press, 1993.

Misiunas, Romuald J., and Rein Taagepera. *The Baltic States: Years of Dependence, 1940-1980*. Berkeley: University of California Press, 1983.

Plakans, Andrejs. *The Latvians: A Short History*. Stanford: Hoover Institution Press, Stanford University, 1995.

Šīmanis, Vito Vitauts. *Latvia*. St. Charles, Illinois: Book Latvia, 1984.

Straumanis, Alfreds. "Latvian American Theatre," *Ethnic Theatre in the United States*, edited by Maxine Schwartz Seller. Westport, Connecticut: Greenwood Press, 1983; pp. 277-318.

Veidemanis, Juris. *Social Change: Major Value Systems of Latvians at Home, as Refugees, and as Immigrants*. Greeley: Museum of Anthropology, University of Northern Colorado, 1982.

Though Lebanese in
America today are
both Christian and
Muslim, Christians
remain the majority.
There are also many
Jews from the
earliest migration,
"as well as a smaller
number of Druze
from both
immigration waves.

LEBANESE AMERICANS

by
**Paula Hajar and
J. Sydney Jones**

OVERVIEW

The earliest immigrants from the Eastern Mediterranean were generally lumped together under the common rubric of Syrian-Lebanese, and it is consequently difficult to separate the number of ethnic Lebanese immigrants from ethnic Syrian immigrants. Neither of these countries came into being as nation-states until the mid-twentieth century; thus records and statistics for both groups are generally combined for early immigration patterns. Such difficulties with early immigration records are further exacerbated because of religious affiliation, both Muslim as well as myriad Christian denominations, which cut across national and ethnic lines in the region.

Early Lebanese settlers in America came mostly from Beirut, Mount Hermon, and surrounding regions of present-day Lebanon, a nation located at the extreme eastern end of the Mediterranean Sea. Syria forms Lebanon's northern and eastern borders. Israel lies directly south of Lebanon, with the Mediterranean Sea to the west. Lebanon's land mass is 4,015 square miles (10,400 square kilometers), and its population is estimated at between 3 and 3.5 million. The capital, Beirut, was often referred to as the "Paris of the Middle East." Beirut was also considered the commercial center of the Middle East before the Lebanese civil war of the 1970s. Lebanon is named for the major mountain range that runs north to south through the middle of the country. The Cedars of Lebanon, famous since Biblical times, are now protected in a few mountain groves. Arabic is the official language of the country, and is even spoken by the minority population of Lebanese Jews. The Armenian population speaks mostly Armenian or Turkish, while Assyrians speak Syriac. French and English are also widely spoken. A land of varied terrain, Lebanon encompasses coastline, mountain, and fertile growing regions such as the Bekáa Valley, which is a primary cereal-producing region. The population of the country is made up of ethnic groups from every Middle Eastern country, which is reflective of Lebanon's long history.

In Lebanon, there is no religious majority. Both Muslims and Christians have many sectarian subdivisions, 17 in all. Among the Muslim population, the Shi'a are the most numerous with about 35 percent, the Sunni number around 23 percent, and the Druze comprise 6 percent. Christians, who account for under two-fifths of the total Lebanese population, include the Maronites (the most numerous and the most powerful) at 22 percent, the Eastern Orthodox at 10 percent; Melkites (Greek Catholics) and Armenians, each at 6 percent, and Protestants at 2.5 percent. Through Lebanon's unwritten National Pact of 1943, political power was apportioned between Christians and Muslims. Originally, the ratio was six to five, Christian to Muslim. Since 1992, power has been shared equally by both groups. Various government offices are still reserved for specific sects: the prime minister is always a Sunni Muslim; the president is always a Maronite, and the speaker of the house is always a Shiite. Throughout its history, there have been movements within Lebanon to "deconfessionalize"—to create a one-person, one-vote system instead of apportioning representation and political offices by religious affiliation. These efforts are ongoing at the end of the twentieth century.

HISTORY

From 1516 until 1916, when the Ottoman Empire was dismembered by the victors of World War I, the area that is now Lebanon was part of the Ottoman province of Greater Syria. At the time of the first immigration wave to the West, Lebanon was not yet a sovereign nation; Because the Ottomans administered their subject peoples according to their religious affiliation, early immigrants from Greater Syria identified with their religious sect rather than any nationality. A sense of national identity did not begin to form among the Greater Syrians until the 1920s, when Lebanon became a separate French protectorate. This identity strengthened in the 1940s, when Lebanon gained independence.

As a witness to the rise and fall of the Mesopotamian, Hittite, Egyptian, Assyrian, Babylonian, Persian, and Greek empires, Lebanon has a distinct history. In the second and early first millennium B.C., the Canaanites, who became known as Phoenicians, were the first inhabitants of Lebanon. Famous as sailors and traders, the Phoenicians lived along the Lebanese coast in the port cities of Tyre, Sidon, and Biblos. They also founded colonies in North Africa, Europe, and the Mediterranean. A succession of peoples, including Persians, Greeks, and Romans, challenged Phoenician power. With the rise of Islam in the East, the population adopted Arabic culture but also maintained its multi-religious character as the mountains of Lebanon became a haven for various religious sects. After the Ottoman Empire gained general control of the area in 1516, Lebanon continued to maintain a feudal system of rule by local chieftains. After 1860, the year many Christians were massacred by the Druze in Lebanon and Damascus, the French, who had economic and strategic interests in Lebanon since the Crusades, created a protectorate. During the next 50 years, the people of Lebanon became increasingly interested in Western culture, independence from the Ottomans, and a revival of the Arabic language.

MODERN ERA

With the fall of the Ottoman Empire during World War I, England and France divided the area into English and French protectorates. England assumed control of what became Palestine and Jordan, and France took over what became Syria and Lebanon. At this time, France divided Mount Lebanon from Syria and, adding the coastal area, created an entity called "The State of Greater Lebanon." In 1926 the Republics of Lebanon and Syria were created, but it was not until 1941 that each gained full independence, and the last French troops did not depart until 1946.

After gaining independence from the French in 1943, Lebanon became known as the "Switzerland of the Middle East." However, its delicate political and demographic equilibrium was shattered in 1975 when civil war erupted. The political inequities that had existed within Lebanon for decades were exacerbated by severe economic divisions, the resistance of those in power to addressing the needs of the poor, and the weakness of the public sector. For 16 years, Lebanon was torn apart by fighting between Christians and Muslims.

Although a tentative peace agreement in 1991 ended the war, many problems remain. Several thousand Syrian troops, who entered Lebanon during the civil war, remain in the country. Relations with Israel have long been contentious and border skirmishes are fought periodically between the two nations. Israel also occupies areas of southern Lebanon. Meanwhile, Lebanon is striving to reconstruct itself physically, economically, and politically.

THE FIRST LEBANESE IN AMERICA

Immigrants from the region of the former Greater Syria account for close to two-thirds of the estimated 2.5 million people in the United States who are of Arabic descent. Christian Lebanese were the first Arabic-speaking people to come to the Americas in large numbers. Their earliest immigration to the United States began in the late 1870s, peaked in 1914 at 9,023, dropped to a few hundred a year during World War I, and rose again during the early

"**W**herever they went, Lebanese carried with them their derbakke, as small drum held under the arm and played with the finger tips. To the beat of the derbakke and the music from their voices, they danced traditional circle and handkerchief dances."

Saud Joseph, *Where the Twain Shall Meet-Lebanese in Cortland County,* (New York Folklore Quarterly, v. XX, no. 3, September, 1964).

1920s, fluctuating between 1,600 and 5,000. Later, with the passage of the Immigration Quota Act (1929–1965), it dropped to a few hundred a year. When the second wave of Arab immigration to the United States began in the late 1960s, the descendants of the early Lebanese immigrants were in their third generation and had almost completely assimilated into mainstream America. In the 1970s and 1980s, the Arabic-speaking population of the United States began to grow again, and Lebanese Americans assumed a higher ethnic profile.

Many factors spurred large-scale Lebanese immigration to America in the late nineteenth century. For instance, many emigrants were inspired by tales of American freedom and equality that were told by American missionaries (doctors and teachers). Also, the world fairs that took place in Philadelphia (1876), Chicago (1893), and St. Louis (1904) exposed participating Greater Syrians to Americans and American society. For the majority of Lebanese emigrants, the determining factors were economic ambition and family competition. For

many Lebanese families, having a son or daughter in America became a visible mark of status. Young men were the first to emigrate, followed by young women and later wives and entire families. Some villages lost their most talented young people. Between the late 1870s and World War I (1914-1918), Lebanon lost over one quarter of its population to emigration. During World War I, it lost about another fifth to famine. Immigrants abroad played a major role in the country's postwar reconstruction and subsequent independence.

The 1975-1991 civil war sparked a new wave of emigration from Lebanon. Many Lebanese went to Europe. Those who came to the United States reinvigorated Lebanese American ethnic life. Most of the new immigrants were better educated and were more conscious of their Arab identity than their predecessors. Many Lebanese Americans who are Muslims devoutly maintain their Islamic traditions and are cautious about assimilating fully into American culture.

SETTLEMENT PATTERNS

Lebanese Americans have settled all over the United States. Peddlers who traveled to New England and upstate New York communities, as well as those in the Midwest and the West, often stayed on and opened general stores. Lebanese developed important communities in Utica, New York; Boston, Lawrence, Lowell, and Springfield, Massachusetts; Fall River, Rhode Island; and Danbury, Connecticut. They also settled in New Orleans, Louisiana; Jacksonville, Florida; Detroit and Dearborn, Michigan; and Toledo, Ohio. Some of the largest concentrations of Lebanese Americans are found in the Northeast and Midwest. Detroit has one of the largest Lebanese American communities in the country, and there are new communities in Los Angeles and Houston.

ACCULTURATION AND ASSIMILATION

The first Lebanese who came to America were considered exotic—their baggy pants (*shirwal*) and fezzes made them stand out even among other immigrants. Later, when enclave living and the ubiquitous peddler made immigrants from Greater Syria a visible presence, attitudes toward them darkened. During a Senate debate on immigration quotas in 1929, Senator David Reed of Pennsylvania referred to Syrian-Lebanese as the "trash of the Mediterranean." Working as peddlers allowed

Lebanese immigrants to meet regularly with other Americans, and helped them to quickly absorb the English language and American culture. Service in the American armed forces during World Wars I and II also hastened the assimilation of Lebanese Americans. Many Lebanese American women worked in war-related industries during World War II, which hastened their assimilation into American culture. By the end of World War II, it was not uncommon for Lebanese American women to work outside the home or family business. Lebanese Americans worked hard to assimilate rapidly into mainstream American society. Many Anglicized their names, joined Western churches, and focused their energies on becoming financially successful.

In the late 1990s, Lebanese Americans faced many of the same problems as other Arab Americans. They have often been the victims of negative stereotyping, especially in films, theater, books, and cartoons. Lebanese Americans have also experienced anti-Arab sentiments in American politics. Because the United States has strong ties with Israel, Arab Americans have often felt that American politicians have little interest in understanding Arab hostility toward Israel. During the 1980s, some political candidates rejected financial support from Arab Americans in order not to appear unsympathetic toward Israel.

TRADITIONS, CUSTOMS, AND BELIEFS

Lebanese Americans are a deeply religious people. In Lebanese culture, age is greatly respected, and respect for parents is extremely valued. Family is at the core of Lebanese social identity and loyalty to family has traditionally superseded all other allegiances. Each person is expected to protect the family's honor. In Lebanese culture, roles are often defined by gender, and this social definition anchors both men and women in their respective roles. Women are to be protected by other family members. Men are the undisputed heads of families, and take the concerns of other members into consideration. In Lebanese American families, the welfare of the group is considered more important than the needs of the individual. Lebanese Americans are known for their elaborate and warm hospitality, and it is considered rude not to offer food and drink to a guest.

Americanization, with its emphasis on youth, personal achievement, individualism, and independence, has eroded some of these traditional beliefs and practices. The Arab respect for age, though still stronger in comparison to the larger society, has decreased. Though the family is highly valued among Lebanese Americans, the belief in family honor has lessened, in part because families are not longer living together in close circles. Family roles are less gender-defined in the United States. Hospitality has also changed: doors are locked, schedules are tight, and people are preoccupied with their own personal concerns. New immigrants who come expecting the kind of help from settled relatives that they themselves would have offered back in the village are often sorely disappointed; they soon discover that they are expected, like everyone else in America, to make it on their own.

CUISINE

Some common Lebanese dishes are described in this section, and it should be noted that the seasoning used in Lebanese cuisine is always subtle. *Kibbee* is ground lamb meat mixed with bulgur wheat and eaten either baked or raw. Yellow and green squash, called *koosa*, are hollowed out, stuffed with rice and ground lamb meat, and cooked in a tomato sauce. The insides of the squash are often fried in olive oil as a separate dish. The ground lamb and rice stuffing mixture (*mahshee*) is sometimes wrapped in grape leaves (*wara' 'anab*) and served with yogurt, or in cabbage leaves (*malfoof*) and served with lemon juice. *Sfeeha* are small, open square pies of ground lamb meat and pine nuts, sometimes made with a thin tomato sauce.

Lebanese food is widely available in gourmet food shops and health food restaurants. Pita bread, hummus (chickpea dip), *baba ghanouj* (eggplant dip), and *tabbouleh* (a salad of parsley and bulgur or cracked wheat), have become mainstays on health food menus. Lebanese Americans also eat fresh fruits and vegetables, cheese, yogurt and yogurt cheese (*labnee*), pickles, hot peppers, olives, and pistachio nuts. One of the most popular Lebanese desserts is *baqlawa*, which is filo dough laced with sugar syrup and wrapped around finely chopped walnuts. The national alcoholic beverage of Lebanon is *'arak*, which is a liqueur flavored with aniseed.

TRADITIONAL CLOTHING

Western dress is the norm in Lebanon and among most Lebanese Americans. Religiously observant Muslim women wear the *hijab*, a long-sleeved coat or dress, and a scarf (often white) that completely covers the hair. Young girls and married women can decide whether or not to wear the *hijab*.

Traditional Lebanese clothing is worn only by performers at ethnic dance festivals. Men wear the *shirwal* (baggy black pants that fit at the shin), high black boots, white blousy shirts, dark vests, and a fez. Women wear long dresses with embroidered bodices and side panels, and tall hats with long white veils.

HOLIDAYS

Different sects within Lebanon celebrate different religious holidays. Christians celebrate the feast days of saints, as well as Easter and Christmas. Easter is celebrated on the Sunday after the first full moon following the vernal equinox. The Orthodox Easter must also come after Passover, and thus Western Easter often falls on a different Sunday than Orthodox Easter. Muslims celebrate three major holidays: Ramadan (the 30-day period of daytime fasting); 'Eid al Fitr, a five-day holiday that marks the end of Ramadan; and 'Eid al-Adha, the "Feast of the Sacrifice," which commemorates Abraham's agreement with God that he would sacrifice his son Ishmael. Lebanon's National Independence Day, which is celebrated on November 22, receives little attention from Lebanese Americans.

HEALTH ISSUES

Except for higher-than-average incidences of anemia and lactose intolerance, Lebanese have no incidence of medical disease specific to them as a group. As a rule, they support the conventional medical establishment.

LANGUAGE

Most Lebanese speak Arabic. Arabic is a poetic language, and poets are prized in Arab culture. In its first 50 years in America, the Lebanese American community enjoyed a golden age of letters, with the literature of such New York experimental poets as Khalil Gibran, Ameen Rihany, and Elia Abu-Madey casting their influence on literary circles of the Middle East. However, in their desire to embrace American culture, many Lebanese Americans did little to teach their American-born children to read Arabic. Immigration quota restrictions accelerated the problem. Without a continuous influx of new readership, once-flourishing Arab American newspapers and journals experienced a steep decline. Christian churches streamlined their Arabic services, and changed many of them to English. Newly arrived Lebanese immigrants to the United States, however, have reinvigorated Arabic language usage within the community. Many Arabic churches now have bilingual announcements, bulletins, and sermons, and the business signs in Arab commercial neighborhoods are often painted prominently in Arabic. In particular, Lebanese Muslim immigrants have contributed to the increase in Arabic usage and have developed Arabic-language classes for children.

GREETINGS AND OTHER COMMON EXPRESSIONS

Greetings in Arabic are elaborate, and there is usually a response and counter-response to every one. *Ahlein*—"Welcome"; or the longer *Ahlan wa Sahlan*—"You are with your people and in a level place"(a greeting appropriate at the door or when being introduced to someone for the first time); the more casual *Marhaba*—"Hello," responded to with *Marhabteen*—"Two hellos"; to which the response is *Maraahib*—"A bunch of hellos." Similarly, the response to the morning greeting, *Sabaah al-kheir*—"The morning is good," is *Sabaah an-noor*—"The morning is light." The evening greeting and response are *Masa al-kheir* and *Masa n-noor*. Leave-takings are extremely elaborate: the person leaving says *Bkhatrak* to a woman, *Khatrik* and to a group, *Khatirkum*, which translates as "By your leave." The response is *Ma'a salaame*—"With safety," or "Go in peace"; to which the counter-response is *Allay salmak*, or *Allay salmik* to a female, and *Allay salimkum* to a group—"May God keep you safe." The holiday greeting is *'Eid Mubarak*—"Holiday blessings"; and *Kull sane w'inte saalim*—"Every year and you are safe." *Sahteen* is the Arabic toast—"May your good health be twofold." Arabic is filled with references to God. For example, the most common response to *Keif haalak?*—"How are you?" is *Nushkar Allah*—"(We) Thank God." Often heard after a statement of intention are the words *In sha Allah*—"If God wills it." Such phrases imply the belief in human impotence to control the affairs of the world.

FAMILY AND COMMUNITY DYNAMICS

Traditionally, Lebanese families and extended families operate as a unit, relying on each other implicitly in social, financial, and business affairs. The father is the decision maker, and the mother his close advisor. Her domain is the daily life of the children and all that happens within the home; The man's domain is strictly outside the home. The firstborn son plays a special role in the family, for he brings his bride to live with his parents, raises his family in his parents' household, and cares for them in their old age.

As Lebanese American families have adopted the American pattern of nuclear families, the dividing line between gender roles has blurred. Fathers spend more time with their small children, and mothers frequently represent the families in public, for example, at school meetings. Independent households are now the norm, and daughters no longer become part of their marital families. Consequently, sisters share responsibility with their brothers for aging parents.

MARRIAGE AND CHILDREARING

Because marriage was traditionally an opportunity for a family to strengthen its prestige and economic situation, marriages in Lebanon were often arranged. This custom is still practiced among some conservative Lebanese Americans. To arrange a marriage, parents and other relatives seek out mates for their children. They set up a chaperoned meeting, which allows the prospective couple to get acquainted. Courtship is conducted under the watchful eye of family members and always carries with it a sense of responsibility and purpose. Casual dating is frowned upon by more conservative Lebanese Americans because it can jeopardize the reputations of the couple and families involved. Among assimilated Lebanese Americans, however, dating is the usual form of courtship.

The majority of early Lebanese American immigrants married within their ethnic and religious groups. Many men returned to Lebanon to find a bride, particularly in the years when single men outnumbered single women in the immigrant community. Most of the first American-born generation of Lebanese Americans also married within the community.

Divorce among Lebanese Americans is less common in arranged marriages than in marriages based on love. The basis of the arranged marriage is a contract of shared responsibility and self-sacrifice. There is no expectation that the needs of the individual will be satisfied in the marriage. The purpose of such marriages is to build a family. In fact, divorce on the grounds of personal unhappiness is frowned upon. Since divorce has traditionally been viewed as a source of family shame, families often become involved in solving marital problems.

Lebanese American families often indulge babies and younger children. Boys are coddled, but are expected to be strong and independent. Girls are restrained, taught to work within existing social schemes, and trained to be dependable as well as interdependent. As they mature, girls assume many household responsibilities. They often take charge of the younger siblings or, if the mother is absent, the entire household.

EDUCATION

By the time they began immigrating to the United States, the immigrants from Greater Syria had attended British, French, Russian, and American schools in their homeland for half a century or longer. These foreign schools had also stimulated the establishment of local government schools, and many of these schools encouraged the education of girls. When they arrived in the United States, the Lebanese adapted to the American school system and culture. Their attitudes paralleled the evolution of the attitudes of other Americans toward education. By the third generation, the education of girls was considered equal in importance to that of boys. The generation of Lebanese Americans born after World War II attended college at the same rate as the rest of the nation's youth, studying business, medicine, law, pharmacy, computer science, and engineering. Because the vast majority of third-generation Lebanese Americans are middle class, they enjoy a higher educational level than Americans on average.

Many Catholic Lebanese children receive their education at Catholic schools. Muslim Lebanese immigrants to the United States occasionally send their children to Catholic schools, where there is more discipline and emphasis on respect for authority. Many Muslim immigrants have set up Islamic schools, some as supplements to their children's education, and a few as full-day parochial schools that teach Arabic language, history, and culture in addition to basic subjects.

THE ROLE OF WOMEN

Women have always been the heart of the Lebanese family. Although men have the final say in family decisions, the opinions of women are also valued. Husbands depend on their wives to maintain the household and raise the children. Many Lebanese American women also work outside the home. They often play key roles in running family businesses, and often take over if their husband dies or becomes incapacitated. As Lebanese American men have become more active in public life, women have begun to follow suit. Donna Shalala, a Lebanese American woman, was the chancellor of the University of Wisconsin and president of Hunter College in New York City, before becoming President Clinton's secretary of health, education and welfare.

PHILANTHROPY

Just as each family must take care of its own, each religious community traditionally takes care of its members. Lebanese Muslims are required to give 2.5 percent of their income, a tithe called *zakkat* to the needy within the community. Philanthropic efforts within the Lebanese American community also cut across religious lines. One is Save Lebanon, an organization formed in 1982 to bring Lebanese children injured during Israel's 1982 invasion of Lebanon, to the United States for medical treatment. More prominent is the Saint Jude Children's Research Hospital in Memphis, Tennessee. Established in 1962, it is funded by an organization called Aiding Leukemia-Stricken American Children, American

Lebanese Syrian Associated Charities, and individual donations. Founded by entertainer Danny Thomas (1914–1991), a Lebanese American, ALSAC and St. Jude's have assumed the leading position in the field of research and treatment of childhood leukemia.

RELIGION

For centuries, religious affiliation in Greater Syria was tantamount to membership in a small nation, or at least a political party. The millet system, which the Ottomans used to divide people into political entities according to religion, gave religion social and political meaning. The millet system also served to create a sense of boundaries among differing sects that went beyond doctrinal disputes. Because brides often converted to the faith of their husbands, all of the major religions within Lebanon competed for converts to their faith. Interfaith marriage was considered taboo.

Although Lebanese Americans include Christians and Muslims, Christians are in the majority. Many Lebanese Jews and a smaller number of Druze are also a part of the Lebanese American community. The vast majority of Lebanese Christians in America belong to one of three Eastern-rite Christian churches: the Maronite, the Eastern Orthodox, and the Melkite/Greek Catholic. Orthodox and Melkite liturgies are in Arabic and Greek; Maronite liturgy is in Arabic and Aramaic. In the United States, all three are sung partly in English.

The differences among these churches are jurisdictional rather than dogmatic. In particular, they differ on the question of the infallibility of the pope in matters of faith. Since its beginnings in the fourth century, the Maronite Church has been steadfast in its allegiance to Rome and the West, and resistant to the Arabic identity embraced by the Eastern Orthodox and Melkite/Greek Catholic churches.

All three churches administer confirmation at Baptism, and use bread soaked in wine for the Eucharist. The marriage ceremony in each rite contains similar components: the blessing of the rings, the crowning of the bride and groom as queen and king, and the sharing of bread and wine—the couple's first meal together. In the Orthodox and Melkite churches, the bride and groom walk around the altar as a symbol of their first journey together as a couple.

Orthodox priests can marry, but those who do cannot climb the clerical hierarchy. While Melkite and Maronite Catholic priests in the Middle East are encouraged by their own Eastern canon law to

marry, they are forbidden to by Western canon. Unlike the Roman Catholic church, Eastern-rite churches have icons rather than statuary.

Most Lebanese American Muslims arrived after 1965. Generally, Muslims pray five times a day and attend Friday prayers. When no mosque is available, they rent rooms in commercial and business districts where they can go for midday prayers. These small prayer places are called *masjids*. Muslims are supposed to fast during the daylight hours for the month of Ramadan. Many, including young schoolchildren, do keep the fast.

EMPLOYMENT AND ECONOMIC TRADITIONS

Upon their arrival in the United States, many Lebanese engaged in peddling. These peddlers carved out routes from New England through the West. Many developed a regular clientele, and eventually opened their own general stores. Some of those who stayed in the city developed their small dry goods businesses into import/export empires. By

1910, there were a handful of Lebanese American millionaires. Other early immigrants were factory workers, particularly those that settled in Detroit and Dearborn, Michigan, where many Lebanese worked in the auto industry.

The occupational profile of Lebanese Americans is very broad, although they are still disproportionately concentrated in retail occupations. Lebanese Americans tend to be self-employed and enter managerial and professional positions at a higher rate than Americans as a whole. Lebanese Americans are well represented in medicine, law, banking, engineering, and computer science.

POLITICS AND GOVERNMENT

Lebanese American political involvement has revolved around American policies in the Middle East, particularly those relating to Israel. Through the Eastern Federation of Syrian-Lebanese Organizations, which was established in 1932, Lebanese Americans quietly protested the 1948 partitioning of Palestine. Following the 1967 war between Israel and its Arab neighbors, Lebanese Americans began to work with other Arabs to form organizations that promoted their common interests.

Members of the Association of Arab American University Graduates, which was established in 1967, focused on educating the American public about the Arab–Israeli conflict. Five years later, the National Association of Arab Americans was created to lobby the American Congress and White House administrations on Middle Eastern issues. In 1980, former senator James Abourezk established the American Arab Anti-Discrimination Committee to combat defamation of Arab Americans in the media. As conditions in the Middle East continued to worsen during the 1980s Lebanese Americans, along with other Arab Americans, became the targets of government surveillance and civil rights infringements. When the United States bombed Libya in 1986, for example, it was revealed that the Immigration and Naturalization Services (INS) had a list of thousands of Arab (including Lebanese) and Iranian students, permanent residents, and even U.S. citizens, for possible detention in internment camps in the United States.

From 1985 to 1987 it was illegal for Americans to visit Lebanon. The travel ban was allowed to expire in 1997 with assurances from the Lebanese government of cooperation on anti-terrorism measures and security. Among the Arab American organizations who lobbied was the American Task Force for Lebanon. This group of prominent Lebanese Americans meets regularly with congressmen and administration officials to advise them on American support for the reconstruction of Lebanon, and the normalization of diplomatic relations between Lebanon and the United States.

Lebanese Americans have traditionally supported the Republican party due, in part, to its support of business interests. Lebanese Americans have also been influenced by the Arab American Institute (AAI). The AAI, which was founded in 1985, is designed to foster Arab American participation in American politics, support candidates who champion Arab American causes, and encourage Arab Americans to run for public office. During the 1988 presidential election, the AAI had gathered more than 300 Arab Americans to serve as delegates to the national Democratic convention. At the 1988 Democratic Convention, Lebanese Americans successfully introduced platforms that supported Palestinian statehood and the restoration of Lebanon as a sovereign state. This convention also marked the first time that an Arab American, served as co-chairperson of the Democratic National Committee.

INDIVIDUAL AND GROUP CONTRIBUTIONS

ENTERTAINMENT

Casey Kasem, (1933–) is America's most famous disc jockey and originator of radio show *American Top 40,* the host of *American Top 10,* and the principal voice-over for NBC-TV.

FASHION

Norma Kamali (1945–) and Joseph Abboud (1950–) are prominent New York fashion designers. J. M. Haggar (1892–1987) founded a major manufacturer of men's slacks; and Mansour Farah (1895–1937) established Farah Brothers, a large competitive pants manufacturer.

FILM AND TELEVISION

Jamie Farr (1934–) played Corporal Klinger for 11 years on the popular television series *M*A*S*H;* actor-singer-comedian Danny Thomas (1914–1991) starred in the popular 1950s television situation comedy *Make Room For Daddy;* his daughter Marlo Thomas (1943–) is an Emmy Award–winning actress who starred in the 1960s television situation comedy *That Girl;* his son Tony Thomas (1948–) is a television and film producer who has won many Emmys for his work on *Golden Girls* and other television series; Tony Shalhoub starred in the television show *Wings;* Vic Tayback (1930–1990) played Mel in *Alice;* Kristy McNichol (1962–) was one of the co-stars of *Empty Nest;* Kathy Najimy (1957–) was a co-star of the film *Sister Act* with Whoopi Goldberg; guitarist and musician Frank Zappa (1940–1993) was a legend in the rock world; and Callie Khoury (1957–) was the first woman to receive an Oscar for Best Original Screenplay, for *Thelma and Louise.*

GOVERNMENT SERVICE AND DIPLOMACY

Career diplomat Philip Habib (1920–1992) helped negotiate an end to the Vietnam War and the Israeli war in Lebanon in 1982; Senator James Abourezk (1931–) from South Dakota was the first Lebanese American to serve in the U.S. Senate (1974–1980), and he founded the American Arab Anti-Discrimination Committee; Nick Rahal (1949–) has served as a U.S. congressman from West Virginia since 1976; Donna Shalala (1941–) was the president of New York City's Hunter College and serves as the Secretary of Health, Education, and Welfare in the Clinton administration; George Mitchell (1933–), was a Senator from Maine who served as the Senate Majority Leader from 1989 to 1995.

LITERATURE AND JOURNALISM

William Blatty (1928–) is the author of the book and screenplay *The Exorcist.* Vance Bourjaily (1922–) is the author of *Confessions of a Spent Youth,* and *The Man Who Knew Kennedy.* Khalil Gibran (1883–1931), poet and artist, is the author of *The Prophet,* perhaps the best- selling volume, after the Bible, of all time; Gibran's exhortation "Ask not what your country can do for you; ask what you can do for your country" in his "Letter to Syrian Youth" was quoted in John F. Kennedy's inaugural address and remains the most-quoted sentence of any inaugural address in American history. American-born poets who are descendants of the Greater Syrian diaspora include D. H. Milhelm (1926–), Sam Hazo (1928–), Joseph Awad (1929–), Sam Hamod (1936–), Lawrence Joseph (1948–), Gregory Orfalea (1949–), and Elmaz Abinader (1954–). Journalist Helen Thomas (1920–) has been the UPI White House correspondent for half a century and opens and closes every White House press conference.

MUSIC AND DANCE

Paul Anka (1941–) wrote and recorded popular hit songs beginning in the 1950s, including "Diana," "She's a Lady,"and "My Way." Rosalind Elias (1931–) is a soprano with the New York City Metropolitan Opera; Elie Chaib (1950–) is a 20-year veteran dancer with the Paul Taylor Company.

PIONEERS

Ralph Nader (1934–) is one of America's most prominent consumer advocates. He is the author of *Unsafe at Any Speed* and founder and head of Public Citizen, an organization that has spawned a number of other citizen action groups such as Congress Watch and the Tax Reform Research Group. Najeeb Halaby (1915–) is the former head of the Federal Aviation Agency and was head of Pan-American Airlines. Candy Lightner (1946–) is the founder of MADD (Mothers Against Drunk Driving). Christa McAuliffe (1948–1986) was the teacher aboard the ill-fated space shuttle *Challenger.* Paul Orfalea (1946–) founded Kinko's, the world's largest international chain of copying and business service stores.

SCIENCE AND MEDICINE

Heart surgeon Michael DeBakey (1908–) invented the heart pump and pioneered the bypass operation in the United States. Harvard University professor Elias J. Corey, (1928–) won the Nobel Prize in chemistry in 1990. The St. Jude Research Hospital in Memphis, Tennessee, founded by Danny Thomas, is the leader in the field of research and treatment of childhood leukemia.

SPORTS

Race-car driver Bobby Rahall won the Indianapolis 500 in 1986; the late Joe Robbie (1916–1990) was owner of the Miami Dolphins.

MEDIA

PRINT

Jusoor (Bridges).
An Arabic/English quarterly periodical that publishes poetry and essays on politics and the arts.

Address: P.O. Box 34163, Bethesda, MD 20817.
Telephone: (301) 869-5853.

Lebanon Report.
A monthly magazine that describes political events in Lebanon in great detail.

Contact: Michael Bacos Young, Editor.
Address: Lebanese Center for Policy Studies, Box 1377, Highland Park, New Jersey 08904.
Telephone: (908) 220-0885.

News Circle.
A socially oriented magazine published in English that reports on the activities of West Coast Arabs.

Contact: Joseph Haiek, Publisher.
Address: P.O. Box 3684, Glendale, CA 91201-0684.

RADIO

Arab Network of America.
Every city with any concentration of Arabic-speaking people, including Lebanese, has at least one or two hours of radio programming a week. The Arab Network is a national Arabic-language radio network whose programs are broadcast in Washington, D.C., Detroit, Chicago, Pittsburgh, Los Angeles, and San Francisco.

Contact: Bruce Finland, CEO.

Address: 150 South Gordon Street,
    Alexandria, VA 22304.
Telephone: (703) 823-8364.

TELEVISION

Arab Network of America (ANA).
Contact: Bruce Finland, CEO.
Address: 150 South Gordon Street, Alexandria,
    Virginia 22304.
Telephone: (703) 823-8364.

TAC—Arabic Channel.
Contact: Jamil Tawfiq, Director.
Address: P.O. Box 936, New York, NY, 10005.
Telephone: (212) 425-8822.

ORGANIZATIONS AND ASSOCIATIONS

American Arab Anti-Discrimination Committee (ADC).
The largest grassroots Arab American organization;
combats stereotyping and defamation in the media
and in other venues of public life, including politics.

Address: 4201 Connecticut Avenue, Washington,
    DC 20008.
Telephone: (202) 244-2990.

American Task Force for Lebanon (ATFL).
Lobbies Congress and various administrations on
issues related to Lebanon and its reconstruction.

Contact: George Cody, Executive Director.
Address: 2213 M Street, N.W., Third Floor,
    Washington, DC 20037.
Telephone: (202) 223-1399.

Arab American Institute (AAI).
Fosters participation of Arab Americans in the
political process at all levels.

Contact: James Zogby, Executive Director.
Address: 918 16th Street, N.W., Suite 601,
    Washington, DC 20006.
Telephone: (202) 429-9210.

Association of Arab American University Graduates (AAUG).
Publishes monographs and books on Arab interests;
holds symposia and conferences on current Middle
East issues.

Contact: Ziad Asali, President.
Address: P.O. Box 408, Normal, IL, 61761-0408.
Telephone: (309) 452-6588.

National Association of Arab Americans.
Lobbies Congress and current administrations on
Arab interests.

Contact: Khalil Jahshan, Executive Director.
Address: 1212 New York Avenue, N.W.,
    Suite 300, Washington, DC 20005.
Telephone: (202) 842-1840.

MUSEUMS AND RESEARCH CENTERS

Communities and churches have begun to archive
some of the memorabilia of the Arab American
experience. The following two centers are of
national importance.

Faris and Yamna Naff Family Arab American Collection Archives Center, National Museum of History, Smithsonian Institution, Washington, DC
Contains artifacts, books, personal documents, pho-
tographs, oral histories, and doctoral dissertations pertaining to the Arab American immigrant experience,
beginning with the earliest wave of immigrants.

Contact: Alixa Naff.
Telephone: (202) 357-3270.

Near Eastern American Collection, Immigration History Research Center, University of Minnesota.
Contains the Philip Hitti archives.

Contact: Rudoph Vecoli.
Address: 826 Berry Street, St. Paul, MN 55114.
Telephone: (612) 627-4208.

SOURCES FOR ADDITIONAL STUDY

Arab Americans: Continuity and Change, edited by
Baha Abu-Laban and Michael Suleiman. Normal,
IL: Association of Arab American University Grad-
uates, Inc. 1989.

Helou, Anissa. *Lebanese Cuisine*. New York: St. Martin's Press, 1995.

Hoogland, Eric. *Crossing the Water*. Washington,
DC: Smithsonian Institution Press, 1987.

Kayal, Philip, and Joseph Kayal. *The Syrian Lebanese in America: A Study in Religion and Assimilation.* Boston: Twayne, 1975.

The Lebanese in the World: A Century of Immigration, edited by Nadim Shehadi and Albert Hourani. London: Centre for Lebanese Studies in association with I. B. Taurus, 1992.

Naff, Alixa. *Becoming American: The Early Arab Immigrant Experience.* Carbondale and Edwardsville: Southern Illinois University Press, 1985.

Orfalea, Gregory. *Before the Flames.* Austin: University of Texas Press, 1988.

Taking Root, Bearing Fruit, Volume 1, edited by James Zogby; Volume 2, edited by Eric Hooglund. Washington, DC: ADC Research Institute, 1984; 1985.

Wakin, Edward. *The Syrians and the Lebanese in America.* Chicago: Claretian Publishers, 1974.

Walbridge, Linda S. *Without Forgetting the Imam: Lebanese Shi'ism in an American Community.* Detroit: Wayne State University Press, 1997.

Zogby, John. *Arab America Today: A Demographic Profile of Arab Americans.* Washington, DC: Arab American Institute, 1990.

LIBERIAN AMERICANS

by
Ken R. Wells

OVERVIEW

Liberia is a country slightly larger than the state of Tennessee, measuring 44,548 square miles (111,370 square kilometers). Located in Western Africa, it is bordered by Sierra Leone to the northwest, Guinea to the north, Ivory Coast (Cote D'Ivoire) to the east, and the Atlantic Ocean to the south. It has a hot, humid tropical climate. The summers (from May to October) consist of frequent, heavy showers. The slightly drier winters, in turn, are characterized by dust-laden winds (called *harmattan*) blowing in from the Sahara Desert during December. Annual rainfall averages 183 inches (465 centimeters) on the coast and 88 inches (224 centimeters) inland. The country's primary natural resources are iron ore, timber, rubber, diamonds and gold. The principal food crops are rice, coffee, palm oil, cassava, and cocoa. About 3 percent of Liberia's land is used for agriculture.

Liberia has a population of nearly 2.8 million people, with an annual population growth rate of about 5.75 percent. Approximately 95 percent of the population are made up of ethnic tribes, with the largest tribes being Kpelle, Bassa, Gio, Kru, Grebo, and Mano. Descendants of immigrants from former slaves in the United States, called Americo-Liberians, make up 2.5 percent of the population. The life expectancy at birth is just under 60 years. The literacy rate is about 38 percent. About 70 percent of the population practice traditional African religions, 20 percent are Muslim, and ten percent are Christian. English is the official language, although 16 tribal languages, each with numerous dialects, are also spoken. The capital city is Monrovia (population 350,000). The Liberian flag consists of 11 horizontal red and white stripes with a white five-point star on a blue square in the upper left corner. The flag is modeled after the U.S. Stars and Stripes.

HISTORY

The history of Liberia started nearly 5,000 years ago. Anthropologists believe people from northern and western areas of Africa began settling in what is now Liberia around 3000 B.C. Most came because the rich, fertile soil of the coastal areas was conducive to agriculture and the tropical rain forests of the interior held an abundance of game. But over a few centuries, these people dispersed to other areas of Africa. It is believed that present day Liberians are descendants from several African tribes that migrated into the area between the eleventh and seventeenth centuries from the belt of Sudan, which stretches from the North African Atlantic coast to the Red Sea. Scientists speculate these people came to Liberia for two reasons. First, they were seeking new land to farm since the Sahara Desert was slowly expanding into their existing homelands. Second, the invasion of Ghana in 1076 by a Muslim sect called the Almoravids forced thousands to flee south and west. By the eleventh century, more than a dozen ethnic groups had settled in Liberia. Over time, these groups formed tribal territories, each with its own culture and oral language.

The first known outsiders to visit Liberia were a group of Portuguese explorers, led by Pedro de Sintra, in 1461. De Sintra named the region the Malagueta Coast, after a green spicy pepper grown in the area. From this first contact, trade routes developed between Europe and coastal Liberia. The name Liberia is Latin for "place of freedom" and was given to the country, formerly known as Cape Mesurado or Cape Montserrado, by the American Colonization Society, which acquired the land from local tribal chiefs in 1821. Liberia was conceived by American political and religious leaders of the time as a place to relocate Africans who were brought to America as slaves. The first African American settlers, known as Americo-Liberians, landed in 1822. By 1864 approximately 15,000 African Americans had settled there. The colony declared itself an independent nation in 1847. The flow of immigrants dwindled to nearly zero following the end of the U.S. Civil War and the emancipation of slaves in America. Despite making up only about one percent of the population, Americo-Liberians became the intellectual and ruling class, modeling the government after that of the United States. Rising economic problems, including a large foreign department, led to the overthrow of the government in 1871. Instability, fueled by a sour economy, continued into the early twentieth century. The first major economic development came in 1926 when the Firestone Rubber Co. leased large areas of Liberia for rubber production.

MODERN ERA

In 1930, the government of president Charles D. B. King resigned after a League of Nations' (now the United Nations) investigation revealed that the government was involved in the slave trading of Liberia's native peoples. With the election of William V.S. Tubman in 1944, Liberia began a period of sustained economic growth and democracy. Under Tubman, Liberia's native tribes were given a greater voice in the political process. They were able to vote in presidential and legislative elections, a privilege previously reserved only for Americo-Liberians. Liberia remained a close ally of the United States, siding with the Allies during World War II. After a visit to Liberia by U.S. President Franklin D. Roosevelt in 1943, the United States agreed to develop a modern port in Monrovia. Liberia was a founding member of the United Nations (UN) and Liberians helped write the UN Charter. Under Tubman's benevolent rule, Liberia prospered. A road system was developed, a major port built in Monrovia, and investment by foreign corporations was encouraged. A strong economy and expanded rights for all ethnic groups proved popular and Tubman was reelected president six times.

Tubman died from prostate cancer in 1971 and the vice president, W.R. Tolbert, became president. He was formally elected to that position in 1972. Soon after, an organized opposition to Tolbert began to rise, including support from some Liberian college students in the United States. It reached its peak in 1979 when increases in the price of rice, the Liberian staple, led to widespread civil unrest and riots. Tolbert was assassinated in a bloody 1980 military coup led by Army Master Sergeant Samuel K. Doe. Democracy collapsed and a prolonged period of dictatorship, corruption, and human rights abuses followed. Civil war broke out in 1989 and was followed by Doe's assassination by a rebel group led by Prince Yormie Johnson in 1990. Another rebel force opposed to Doe, led by Charles Taylor, took over the government and Taylor proclaimed himself president. After Taylor threatened to take foreign residents hostage in late 1990, the United States sent a naval unit with 2,500 Marines to Liberia to evacuate American and other foreign citizens. The Economic Community of West African States (ECOWAS) brokered a peace between the warring factions, but the peace agreement soon fell apart.

The civil war raged on between Taylor's forces (the National Patriotic Front of Liberia) and rebel factions. According to the United Nations High Commission on Refugees, nearly one-third of the population, 755,000 Liberians, fled into neighboring countries and several hundred thousand were killed. The scope of the problem could be seen in Monrovia, which went from nearly one million residents in 1990 to about 350,000 by 1996. In 1990 a peacekeeping force of 10,000 troops from the 16 ECOWAS nations led by Nigeria entered Liberia and installed an interim government headed by Amos Sawyer. Despite several peace agreements, civil war continued until 1997 when citizens elected a new government, again headed by President Charles Taylor. Opposition parties charged that Taylor rigged the election and that many opposition voters did not turn out at the polls because they feared violence. Despite sporadic fighting throughout 1998, the country began the slow and difficult task of rebuilding its economic, social, and political structures. Thousands of refugees who fled into neighboring countries began returning to Liberia. However, the situation remained unstable and uncertain into 1999. Opposition parties and the U.S. State Department accused the Taylor regime of various human rights violations, including murder, rape, torture, and arbitrary arrest and detention. As of mid-1999, freedom of speech and of the press continued to be restricted by the government. Although some refugees who fled the civil war returned to Liberia to begin rebuilding their lives and their country, hundreds of thousands remained outside Liberia.

THE FIRST LIBERIANS IN AMERICA

Liberia is unique among nations because it was settled by former slaves from the United States. Nearly all immigration between the two countries was from the United States to Liberia. In the first half of the twentieth century, only several hundred Liberians immigrated to the United States, an extremely small number compared to those that came here from Europe, Asia and Latin America. The probable reason is that Liberia had one of the most stable democracies and prosperous economies in Africa up until the military coup in 1980. For example, from 1925 to 1929 only 27 Liberians immigrated to the United States, according to statistics from the U.S. Immigration and Naturalization Service (INS). From 1930 to 1939, the number was 30, and from

1940 to 1949 the total number was 28. In the 1950s, the number increased to 232, then to 569 in the 1960s. The number jumped to 2,081 during the 1970s and then more than doubled in the 1980s. It was not until the last decade of the twentieth century that there has been significant immigration of Liberians to America. This influx can be attributed to the civil war, which sent thousands fleeing to the United States.

SIGNIFICANT IMMIGRATION WAVES

The civil war, which started in 1989 and continued through 1997, sent a wave of immigrants from Liberia to the United States. Until 1989, less than 1,000 Liberians left their homeland for the United States each year. But in 1989, the number jumped to 1,175 and increased to 2,004 in 1990. From 1990 through 1997, the INS reported 13,458 Liberians fled to the United States. This does not include the tens of thousands who sought temporary refuge in the United States. In 1991 alone, the INS granted Temporary Protective Status (TPS) to approximately 9,000 Liberians in the United States, according to the August 1998 issue of *Migration News*, published by the University of California at Davis. The INS revoked the status in 1997 following national elections in Liberia. However, many of these Liberian Americans resisted returning to Liberia. As of mid-1999, the U.S. Congress was considering legislation to give the Liberian refugees permanent status in the United States. While many of the immigrants have set down roots in America, some still vow to return to their homeland once the political and social situation stabilizes. Many of the Liberian refugees granted temporary protection have children born in the United States and Liberian American groups are concerned about these children's fate should their parents be forced to return to Liberia. "Unfortunately, security and general living conditions in Liberia are unlikely to improve in the near future and forcing families to return will subject them to undue hardship and suffering," said Joseph D. Z. Korto, president of the Union of Liberian Associations in the Americas, in a 1999 letter to members.

SETTLEMENT PATTERNS

There are no official figures regarding the number of Liberians in the United States, since the number granted immigration visas by the U.S. government only tells part of the story. Including Liberians in the country on temporary status, and children born here to Liberian families, Liberian American organizations estimate there are between 250,000 and 500,000 Liberians in the United States. Liberian immigrants tend to settle on the East Coast of the United States, with large communities in New York, New Jersey, Minnesota, Rhode Island, Ohio, Georgia, North Carolina and South Carolina. Liberians are attracted to Georgia and the Carolinas because the hot, humid summers resemble weather conditions in Liberia. Minneapolis and Rhode Island also draw them because of the lower cost of living. Cities with the largest Liberian populations are the greater New York City area, with an estimated population of 35,000 to 50,000, followed by the Washington, D.C. metropolitan area, with an estimated 20,000. Other cities with significant numbers of Liberians include Boston, Atlanta, Detroit, and Philadelphia. On the West Coast, Liberians are concentrated in California, with the primary settlement points being Los Angeles, San Francisco, Oakland and Stockton. The Liberian Community Foundation in Vallejo, California estimates that there are about 4,000 Liberians living in Northern California. Another 2,000 live in Southern California, according to the Liberian Community Association of Southern California. The INS reported the most popular states for Liberian immigrants in 1997 were Maryland (320), New York (279), New Jersey (241), Pennsylvania (200), and Minnesota (155).

ACCULTURATION AND ASSIMILATION

Since most Liberians immigrated to the United States in the late twentieth century, fleeing civil war and a social and economic collapse in their homeland, many of the children have little education. Therefore, students often have a difficult time catching up with their American counterparts. Newer immigrants are also unfamiliar with American culture and sometimes have difficulty in adapting to their new environment.

Lanla Labi came to the United States from Liberia in 1977 when she was seven years old. She went to live with her mother, already in this country, in Los Angeles. In a January 1999 article in *Essence* magazine, Labi recalls her difficulty in adjusting to a new culture. "My initial excitement about attending an American school quickly faded. My thick accent and sudden shyness alienated me from my classmates, who taunted me with names like 'Cheetah,' Tarzan's chimpanzee companion. After school, I rode the bus home and entered the solitary world of a latchkey child." Author Stephen Chicoine, in his book, *A Liberian Family*, writes about a Liberian family who fled to the United States in 1990 to escape the civil war. Chicoine

details their new life in Houston, Texas, including problems adjusting to living in a small apartment, low-wage jobs for the adults, and isolation from their culture. Although such experiences still happen, they are less common today because there are more Liberians in the United States, and communities of Liberian expatriates have developed in many major metropolitan areas.

One advantage for Liberian Americans is that many Liberian customs, as well as social and economic traditions, originally came from the United States with the first wave of freed African American slaves in the early and mid-nineteenth century. Social gatherings, such as weddings, birthdays, and funerals, are similar in nature to those of Americans in general and more specifically to African Americans. Liberians also celebrate many of the same holidays as Americans, including Christmas, Easter, New Year's Day, and Thanksgiving. These holidays are generally celebrated according to American custom, although occasionally some Liberian and African traditions are incorporated.

TRADITIONS, CUSTOMS, AND BELIEFS

Nearly any occasion is cause for celebration among Liberians, both in Liberia and America. Ethnic Liberians will sing and dance, sometimes for days, during weddings, funerals, the birth of a child, circumcision ceremonies, and initiation into the traditional ethnic societies (usually around puberty). A group of dancers, singers, and musicians may perform in one location, or move from one neighborhood house to another. It is customary for the neighbors to provide drinks and sometimes money to the musicians and dancers.

A unique custom among Liberians is the "snapshake" greeting. When shaking hands, you grasp the middle finger of the other person's right hand between your thumb and ring (third) finger, and bring it up quickly with a snap. The custom is derived from the days of slavery in the United States when a slave owner often would break the middle finger of a slave's hand to indicate bondage. The "snapshake" greeting began in the nineteenth century as a sign of freedom among former slaves. It is sometimes used by Liberian Americans to greet dinner guests.

The ethnic groups of Liberia are known for their collective rather than individual artwork. Members of the secret Poro men's society make ceremonial masks used in various rituals. The Dan group is noted for their carved wooden masks representing spirits of the forest, and for large spoons carved with the features of humans and animals. Another form of Liberian art is drums and other

musical instruments, usually made from wood, animal skins, raffia, and gourds. Since nearly all of the ethnic languages of Liberia are oral rather than written, there is very little traditional Liberian literature.

PROVERBS

Liberian folklore is filled with proverbs and parables, most of which are specific to particular tribal groups. Animals are a common theme in the sayings. A general proverb is: "He who knows the way must conduct others". Two proverbs from the Kpelle tribe are: "When pointing an evil finger at a man, three fingers are also pointed at yourself" and "The stones that you throw into the well to kill frogs are the same stones that will cause you to suffer when you drink the dirty water." A common saying from the Bassa tribe is "He who steps in (a river) first shows the depth of the current." Proverbs from the Krahn tribe include: "To cure a bad sore, you must use bad medicine" and "The leaf that is very sweet in a goat's mouth sometimes hurts his stomach;." From the Gola tribe, sayings include: "A man cannot be taller than his head" and "Washing with dirty water does not clean a dirty object." Two sayings from the Vai tribe are "Do not look where you fell, but where you slipped" and "A curled snake never gets fat."

CUISINE

Traditionally, Liberians eat a healthy diet consisting mainly of fish, rice, greens, and vegetables. Rice is often served with breakfast, lunch, and dinner. Liberians like their food hot, and cayenne and other peppers are usually added to Liberian dishes. Another staple of Liberian cuisine is *cassava*, a tropical plant with starchy roots from which tapioca is obtained. *Dumboy* is fresh cassava roots, which are boiled, then beaten with a mortar and pestle, and finally cut into small pieces. It is usually served with a soup made of peanuts and okra. *Fufu* is made from granulated cassava that is fermented, then the liquid is boiled until it thickens. It is served with soup.

Cassava leaves are also used in Liberian cooking. They are washed and beaten, mashed, or finely chopped with pepper and onion. They are then boiled with beef or chicken until well done and most of the liquid has evaporated. Palm oil is added and, after simmering a few minutes, the dish is served with rice. Another dish is potato greens, called potato "grains" by Liberians, which are fried with onions and hot peppers. Water is then added to the dish and it is boiled until done. The resulting taste and texture is similar to spinach.

Stews and soups are popular dishes among Liberians, and goat soup is considered the national soup. Other favorites are pigs' feet with bacon and cabbage, fish with sweet potato leaves, shrimp and palm nuts in fish or chicken stock, and a combination of rice and platto leaves or okra called check rice. Sweet desserts, such as sweet potato, coconut, and pumpkin pie, are a favorite of Liberian Americans. Peanuts are commonly used in cookies and other desserts. Another delicacy is a sweet bread made from rice and bananas. The preferred drinks are ginger beer (usually homemade), palm wine, and Liberian coffee.

DANCES AND SONGS

The tapestry of Liberian life, both in the homeland and in America, is woven together by the thread of music. Birth, death, planting, harvesting, and other major events have their own music. Traditional Liberians dance according to the sounds of various musical instruments. The heart of Liberian music is the drum, ranging from large ones three or four feet tall and placed on the ground, to smaller ones that fit between the legs or under the arms. At the center is the "talking drum" player, who tells a proverb or story through musical tones that imitate the native languages. The *tardegai* is the traditional Liberian drum, which is played with a stick shaped like a hammer. Another instrument is the *saa-saa*, usually played by women. It is made from a dried gourd enclosed in a net tied into a knot at the top and decorated with shells. By shaking the gourd, the basic rhythm is established, accompanied by the sound made by pulling on the netting.

Among the Kpelle ethnic group, a popular instrument is a foot-long drum made of hollow wood and shaped like an hourglass. The top and bottom drumming surfaces are made from monkey skin. A set of raffia strings connect the skins on either end. It is held under the arm, and by pressing these strings between the arm and body, the drum's pitch is changed. Another musical instrument of Liberia is the *gowd*, the dried round shell of a gourd that is fitted between a string of beads. When the gourd is moved around between the beads, it creates a rhythmic rattling sound. Liberians also play a trumpet-like instrument made out of logs, animal horns, or elephant tusks. Since each instrument has its own sound quality, several are usually played together, creating a unique melody.

SONGS

Traditionally, Liberians sing as a group, repeating a verse over and over. Sometimes the lead singer interrupts the song with parables on Liberian culture. A common subject of the songs and parables is animals, including the monkey, spider, leopard, dog, chicken and frog. Each ethnic group has its own songs and parables. Probably the only commonly sung song is the Liberian National Anthem, "All Hail, Liberia, Hail." The words are: "All hail, Liberia, hail! All hail, Liberia, hail! This glorious land of liberty, Shall long be ours. Though new her name, Green be her fame, And mighty be her powers, And mighty be her powers. In joy and gladness, With our hearts united, We'll shout the freedom, Of a race benighted, Long live Liberia, happy land! A home of glorious liberty, By God's command! A home of glorious liberty, By God's command! All hail, Liberia, hail! All hail, Liberia, hail! In union strong success is sure, We cannot fail! With God above, Our rights to prove, We will o'er all prevail, We will o'er all prevail! With heart and hand, Our country's cause defending, We'll meet the foe, With valor unpretending. Long live Liberia, happy land! A home of glorious liberty, By God's command! A home of glorious liberty, By God's command."

TRADITIONAL COSTUMES

If one word had to be used to describe traditional Liberian costumes and dress, it would be colorful. Both men and women's clothing is very loose fitting and flowing. Among women, the most traditional garment is the *lappa*, a skirt made from hand woven material, called country cloth, in an assortment of bright colors, sometimes with intricate designs woven in. The women also wear a headband or bandana that often matches the *lappa*. The style and design can vary according to ethnic group. Traditionally, the clothing is woven into cloth from cotton picked and twined into thread on a spool. Gowns for men are made by cutting a hole in the center of a piece of cloth for the head to go through. The entire process usually takes weeks or months to complete. Liberian Americans have generally adopted western styles of dress and traditional clothing is usually reserved for special events, such as holidays, weddings, and Liberian Independence Day celebrations.

HOLIDAYS

Christmas Day is traditionally celebrated with a large feast, but without a Christmas tree or exchanging presents. However, more Liberian Americans are adopting the Western traditions of the holiday. New Year's Day is also celebrated by Liberians much the same way as by Americans. Although Easter is celebrated among some Christian Liberian Americans, a more traditional holiday is Fast and Prayer Day on the second Friday in April. July 26 is National Independence Day and Liberian Americans celebrate it with communal picnics and other outdoor gatherings. As with all Liberian celebrations, there is plenty of music, song, and dance. Thanksgiving is celebrated on the first Thursday in November. The birthdays of Liberia's presidents are also formal holidays, but few Liberians in the United States commemorate the dates. The only exception is former President William V. S. Tubman's birthday on November 29. Much like the birthdays of George Washington and Abraham Lincoln are to Americans, Tubman's birthday is a matter more of remembrance rather than celebration for Liberian Americans.

HEALTH ISSUES

There are no documented medical or mental health problems that are specific to Liberian Americans. In Liberia, the major health issue is infectious diseases, including yellow fever, cholera, typhoid, polio and malaria. These problems are almost non-existent in Liberian Americans because of improved health care, housing, and sanitation conditions. Instead, the major health concerns are the same as those affecting all African Americans, including hypertension (high blood pressure), diabetes mellitus Type 2 (adult onset or non-insulin dependent diabetes), high cholesterol levels, stroke and heart disease. These conditions are not widespread in Liberia, and physicians suggest the increased risk among Liberians in the United States is due to a less healthy diet and less exercise. Specifically, a Liberian American's diet generally has less fiber and more fat and cholesterol than the typical diet in Liberia.

LANGUAGE

English is the official language of Liberia, but it is the primary language of only about 20 percent (69,000) of the population. There are 34 ethnic languages spoken in Liberia and within each are multiple dialects, most of which are oral and cannot be written. Because of this, there is a dearth of recorded historical and other information on Liberians prior to the arrival of European and American missionaries in the mid nineteenth century. The primary tribal languages and the number of people who speak them are: Kpelle (487,400), Bassa (347,600), Mano (185,000), Klao (184,000), Dan (150,800), Loma (141,000), Kisi (115,000), Gola (99,300) and Vai (89,500). Other languages include Bandi, Dewoin, Gbii, Glaro-Twabo, Glio-Oubi, nine forms of Grebo, two forms of Krahn, Krumen, Kuwaa, Maninka, Manya, Mende, Sapo, and Tajuasohn. About half the population (1.5 million) speaks English as a second language, mainly for communication between different ethnic language groups. In the mid-nineteenth century, a member of the Vai invented an alphabet for his tribe. Later that century, European missionaries reduced two other tribal languages, Bassa and Grebo, to writing. The ethnic languages are very tonal in quality and are often spoken with musical characteristics. Ethnic Liberian languages usually contain two or three distinct tones, based on pitch, which indicate semantic or grammatical differences. The Liberian "talking drum" can imitate these sounds. Proverbs, songs, and prose narratives are the primary forms of verbal expression within many Liberian ethnic groups. In many of the ethnic languages, there are

up to 20 classes of nouns, compared to three (masculine, feminine and neutral) in English. For example, one set of nouns designates human beings, another is for animals, and a third is for liquids.

Among Liberians in the United States, English is almost universally spoken. Kru is the most widely spoken ethnic Liberian language in the United States and it is ranked thirty-fifth among the top non-English languages spoken by Americans, according to Census Bureau data from 1990. The number of American who spoke Kru was 65,848 in 1990, compared to 24,506 in 1980, which is a 168.7 percent increase. Another language spoken by some Liberian Americans is Gullah, a Creole language with influences from the Gola ethnic group of Liberia. It is limited mainly to a small group of people in the Carolina Sea Islands and middle Atlantic coast of the United States. Several Gullah words have become common in American English, including *goober* (peanut), *gumbo* (okra), and *voodoo* (witchcraft).

FAMILY AND COMMUNITY DYNAMICS

Extended families are the cornerstone of the Liberian American community. Each member is held in high esteem and treated with deep respect by the others. The elderly in particular command veneration, and younger family members respect their elders' opinions and thoughts. Family elders are considered sources of wisdom and knowledge, and therefore are often asked to make important decisions. It is rare to find an elderly Liberian American in a rest home because families take care of their elders. A household is often composed of a husband and wife, their children and the parents of the couple. The typical Liberian American household is an extended family, which can also include brothers, sisters, nieces, nephews and cousins. Children are very important and their parents endeavor to make sure they receive an education. Financial sacrifices are commonly made by the family to pay for schooling.

EDUCATION

Education is extremely important to Liberian Americans, with adults often taking general education and self-improvement classes. A number of Liberian organizations in the United States fund college scholarships for students. Graduates remain very loyal to their high schools and universities, and often sponsor students from Liberia who want to attend school in the United States. However, school-age children who have recently immigrated to the United States often have difficulty in American schools, mainly because the educational system in Liberia was severely damaged during the seven years of civil war. Many schools were destroyed and teachers were killed or forced to flee the country. Also, when children arrive in the United States, their English may be limited and flavored with a heavy accent. Likewise, many Liberian Americans find the accent, tone, and idioms of American English challenging to understand and learn. With all of these challenges, many Liberian American children initially struggle to keep up with their American counterparts. But since education is so valued in the Liberian community, they are motivated to overcome these difficulties. Many Liberian Americans go on to colleges and universities, receive degrees, and find employment in a wide range of professional fields, such as teaching, medicine, science, engineering, and technology.

BIRTH AND BIRTHDAYS

The birth of a child and subsequent birthday celebrations are steeped more in American, rather than African, traditions. A typical celebration is marked by a birthday cake, festive decorations, and gifts. There is almost always music and dance. A birth is usually preceded by a shower, in which the expectant mother receives gifts for the child.

THE ROLE OF WOMEN

The role of Liberian women in the United States is somewhat different from the traditional role of women among Liberia's ethnic groups. In Liberia the main responsibility for women is child rearing, although women are responsible for some agricultural work. In the United States, Liberian women are still the center of the family but many also have jobs, are more educated than their counterparts in Liberia, and are more involved in community dynamics. One significant difference is the practice of female circumcision, also called female genital mutilation. While at least half of females in Liberia undergo the painful experience, the practice is largely non-existent among Liberian American females born or raised in the United States.

WEDDINGS

A traditional Liberian wedding is a verbal contract between the groom and the bride's family. The prospective groom must give the bride's family a dowry to compensate for the loss of a daughter. The dowry usually consists of any combination of money, animals, and household goods. The wedding itself is a festive affair, with singing, dancing, drumming, and a lavish feast. At the conclusion, the guests lead the bride and groom to the home they will live in together.

A Liberian American wedding is deeply rooted in American customs, slightly influenced by Liberian tradition. A dowry is rarely involved. Since most Liberians in the United States belong to a Christian denomination, the ceremony follows along the lines of what is prescribed by the particular church, whether it is Catholic, Mormon, Lutheran, or Methodist. Marriage vows are exchanged and the ceremony is conducted by a priest or minister. The groom usually wears a long, baggy ceremonial gown, which is usually brightly decorated with traditional African colors: red, yellow, green, and black. The groom also wears a traditional hat that is as colorful as the wedding gown. The bride and other women in the entourage wear dresses that are flowing and brightly colored. They also wear their hair tied up with a piece of cloth. Women wear a lot of jewelry, including multiple necklaces, bracelets and earrings.

A popular saying among the Liberian American community is that a prospective couple need only send out a dozen wedding invitations. This is because the word will get around so quickly that ten times that number will show up for the ceremony. Like traditional American weddings, the Liberian ceremony is followed by a reception with a lot of food, song, and dance. In America, as in their homeland, one or several traditional drummers are usually on hand to provide the underlying beat of the festivities.

FUNERALS

A Liberian funeral is a time for both grief, since the departed will be missed by loved ones, and a time for joy, since it is believed the deceased has gone on to a better life among his or her ancestors. On the night before the funeral, a wake is held in the family home where the extended family and friends of the deceased gather for a feast, replete with drinking, the singing of spiritual songs, and often a Liberian drummer. The purpose is to be jovial, to console the immediate family, and to wipe away the grief.

INTERACTIONS WITH OTHER ETHNIC GROUPS

Although the bulk of Liberians in the United States have only been here since 1989, the community has sought to develop strong ties with other West African immigrants, particularly those from the Ivory Coast and Sierra Leone. They also have close ties with African Americans in general. Several U.S. civil rights groups have embraced the Liberian community, including support for granting permanent residency to tens of thousands of Liberian immigrants who have temporary status in the United States. There are also efforts by groups such as civil rights leader Jesse Jackson's PUSH/Rainbow Coalition and the National Association for the Advancement of Colored People (NAACP) to bring Liberian Americans into the mainstream of African American society and culture.

RELIGION

About 70 percent of Liberians in Liberia practice traditional African religious beliefs, 20 percent are Muslims, and 10 percent Christian. However, few Liberians in the United States carry on African traditions. The majority is Christian, while a much smaller number is Muslim. Christian Liberians are spread among a wide range of denominations, including Lutheran, Episcopal, Methodist, Baptist and Catholic. Liberian Americans have established several churches in the United States, including four in the Washington, D.C. metropolitan area. Two more are the African United Methodist Church in Trenton, New Jersey, and the International Christian Fellowship in Atlanta founded in 1986.

EMPLOYMENT AND ECONOMIC TRADITIONS

Liberian Americans have sought employment in a variety of fields, including health care, law, education, service, and hospitality. A few have started their own businesses. Their professions often depend on where they live. For example, Liberian Americans in the Central Valley of California tend to find agricultural jobs. In Washington, D.C., Maryland, and Virginia, many work for the federal government. In the San Francisco Bay area, Liberian women lean toward the health care professions, such as nursing, nursing assistants, and even a few physicians. Many Bay area males have gravitated to the security profession as guards. This is because a Liberian who emigrated to the United States shortly after the Liberian Civil War started his own security firm, which also served as a training ground for guards to go on to other security companies, according to Roosevelt Tarlesson, founder and chairman of the Liberian Community Foundation serving the Bay area. However, many newer immigrants start with low paying jobs, such as kitchen workers, janitors, or in home health care, because of limited education, a lack of English proficiency, and unfamiliarity with the American work culture.

POLITICS AND GOVERNMENT

Politics plays an important role in the life of Liberian Americans, especially when it involves their homeland. Liberia is divided into 13 local government subdivisions called counties. A fierce identification with these counties has caused dozens of county organizations to spring up in areas of the United States with large numbers of Liberian immigrants. These include the Sinoe County Association of Georgia, the United Nimba (County) Citizens' Council, and the Grand Cape Mount County Association of Georgia.

Liberian Americans have taken an active role in lobbying the federal government to more actively support freedom and democracy efforts in Liberia. They also have organized in support of various issues affecting Liberia, including humanitarian assistance, wildlife and nature preservation, and women's rights.

RELATIONS WITH LIBERIA

Although Liberian Americans still maintain close ties with family, friends, and organizations in Liberia, there is widespread dissatisfaction with the current economic and political situation. Many Liberian Americans are working to help rebuild the political, social, educational, and commerce institutions of their homeland. Yet that does not mean all Liberian Americans speak with a unified voice. The Liberian community in the United States is divided between several political parties in Liberia, including the ruling National Patriotic Party, and the opposition Liberian National Union, National Democratic Party, and the United People's Party, all of which have organizations in the United States. Despite the political differences, the Liberian American community is united in the goal of helping the people of Liberia recover from ten years of civil war. Of particular interest is rebuilding schools and restoring the freedom Liberians enjoyed under the leadership of former president William V. S. Tubman's administration.

INDIVIDUAL AND GROUP CONTRIBUTIONS

Liberian Americans represent between one-eighth and one-tenth of one percent of the total American population, so their contribution to popular American culture is limited. This may change as more and more Liberian families become integrated into American culture. However, the following sections list a few Liberian Americans and their achievements.

ACADEMIA

Benjamin G. Dennis (1929–) was born in Monrovia, Liberia but emigrated to the United States. Educated in the United States, Dennis received his doctorate in 1964 from Michigan State University. He is a sociology and anthropology professor at the University of Michigan, Flint. He wrote *The Gbandes: A People of the Liberian Hinterland* (1973) and is researching another book about the effects of industrialization and urbanization on the people of Lofa County, Liberia. He is also a contributor to the *American Sociological Review*.

MUSIC

Liberians in America continue many of the musical traditions of their homeland. A popular contemporary Liberian singer and songwriter is Gbanjah, who mixes American soul music with traditional Liberian percussion. Another is Kaipai, a drummer, dancer, and storyteller from the Vai ethnic group who migrated from Liberia to the United States. His credits include former director of the National Dance Troupe of Liberia and a member of the Jungle Dance Troupe.

In 1996, Liberian immigrant Jacob M. Daynuah started an independent record production company and label in Minneapolis, Minnesota, called Zoto Records, specializing in Liberian music and artists. *Zoto* means "lizard ears" in the Dan language of Liberia. Daynuah has released three albums under the pseudonym Jake D: *African Lady* in 1990, *Unity* in 1992, and *Banjay* in 1996. His musical style is known as *Korlor*, an infectious and happy sound from Nimba County in northeast Liberia. Two other Zoto artists are Joseph Woyee, a singer and composer from southeast Liberia, and Naser, a drummer from Nimba County, Liberia who now lives in Minneapolis. Her traditional *sokay* sound comes from the harmonica and a conga drum known as a *balah*. Her first album, *Sokay*, was released in 1998.

SPORTS

Soccer (football) is the national sport of Liberia and is enjoyed by Liberian Americans. Many large outdoor gatherings of Liberian Americans will include a soccer match. The most famous Liberian soccer player is George Weah (1966–). He is the only soccer player ever to simultaneously hold the titles of World Player of the Year, European Football Player of the Year, and African Football Player of the Year, all in 1995. He has played for national championship teams in Liberia, Cameroon, France (Paris and Monaco), and Italy (Milan). He lives in New York.

Liberian Americans also represented their homeland in the 1996 Summer Olympics in Atlanta, Georgia. Of particular note are four members of the Liberian national men's track and field 100-meter relay team. They are Sanyon Cooper and Robert H. Dennis III of Maryland, Kouty Mawenh of Indiana, and Eddie Neufville of South Carolina. Liberian American Grace Dinkins competed for the Liberian women's track and field team in the 1996 Olympics.

MEDIA

There are a very limited number of newspapers, magazines, and broadcast sources aimed specifically at Liberian Americans. Many keep up with news of their community through newsletters distributed by Liberian American organizations. The Internet's World Wide Web is probably the top media source of news and information for the Liberian American community. There are several Internet sites associated with Liberian American organizations. Dozens of Liberian Americans have their own Web home pages, often using them to post news of themselves and to seek information on missing or lost friends and family members. The embassy of Liberia also maintains a website. Some Liberian Americans keep up with news from their homeland by listening to Star Radio broadcasts from Monrovia, Liberia, on the Internet.

PRINT

Liberian Studies Journal.

Publishes articles on scholarly research in a wide range of disciplines, including social sciences, arts, humanities, science, and technology.

Contact: William C. Allen, Editor.
Address: University of South Carolina, Division of Fine Arts, Languages and Literature, 800 University Way, Spartanburg, SC 29303.
Telephone: (864) 503-5602.
Fax: (864) 503-5825.

INTERNET

The Liberian Connection.

An on-line magazine of news from Liberia and within the Liberian American community. Contents include news, features, sports, entertainment, an email directory of Liberians in the United States, and several chat rooms. It also has dozens of links to other Liberian Web sites.

Contact: Ciata Victor-Baptiste, Webmaster.
Address: P.O. Box 4292, Brockton, MA 02301-4292.

Telephone: (508) 559-0552.
E-mail: toadoll@gis.net.
Online: http://www.liberian-connection.com/
  liberia.htm.

The Perspective.

An on-line newspaper featuring news, sports, entertainment, opinion and commentary on issues affecting Liberia and the Liberian American community. Also includes some regional news, mainly from North Carolina, South Carolina and Georgia.

Contact: Abraham M. Williams, Editor in Chief.
Address: P.O. Box 2824, Smyrna, GA 30081.
Telephone: (770) 435-4829.
E-mail: perspective@mindspring.com.
Online: http://www.mindspring/~perspective/.

ORGANIZATIONS AND ASSOCIATIONS

Coalition of Progressive Liberians in the Americas (COPLA).

COPLA, based in New York with an office in Georgia, describes itself as "a watchdog of vice and virtue" in the Liberian community.

Contact: Bodioh Siapoe, Founder and Chairman.
Address: 108-109 91st Avenue, Queens,
  NY 11418.
Telephone: (718) 849-8243.

Liberia First, Inc.

Established in 1998, Liberia First is a non-profit organization serving the metropolitan Triangle Area of Raleigh, Durham, and Chapel Hill, North Carolina. It promotes cultural and social values among Liberians in the Triangle Area. It also seeks to help with rebuilding the social, economic and education structures in Liberia.

Contact: Siaka Kromah, President.
Address: P.O. Box 5655, Raleigh,
  NC 27650-5655.
Telephone: (919) 286-5774.
Online: http://www.liberiafirst.com/
  membership.htm.

Liberian Association of Southern California.

The Liberian Association of Southern California is a social and economic support group for the estimated 2,000 Liberians living in the Los Angeles area. Services include helping newly arrived immigrants adjust to life in the United States and providing community outreach, especially to the young and elderly. It was founded in the early 1960s to serve the needs of Liberian American students. It later broadened its scope to include all Liberians in Southern California.

Contact: David Beyan, President.
Address: P.O. Box 77818, Los Angeles,
  CA 90007.
Telephone: (213) 382-8339.

Liberian Community Association of Washington, D.C.

The association has 400 members and serves the social and economic needs of Liberians in Washington D.C., Maryland, and Virginia. It holds quarterly general assembly meetings.

Contact: John G. F. Lloyd, President.
Address: P.O. Box 57189, Washington, D.C.
  20037.
Telephone: (301) 681-6560.
Online: http://www.geocities.com/capitolhill/
  lobby/9152/info.html.

Liberian Community Foundation (LCF).

A non-profit organization founded in 1995, the LCF has an office and warehouse where it dispenses information, food, clothing and small appliances to needy Liberians in the San Francisco Bay area. It also provides relief supplies, including food and medical equipment, to Liberia. It is staffed by unpaid volunteers and is run solely on private contributions.

Contact: Roosevelt Tarlesson.
Address: 406 Georgia St., Vallejo,
  CA 94590-2310.
Telephone: (707) 557-2310.

Liberian Social Justice Foundation (LSJF).

Founded in 1995, the LSJF has 2,000 members in the United States. Its primary focus is to provide humanitarian assistance to Liberians abroad and in the United States, and to promote freedom, justice and, democracy in Liberia. It also has a scholarship program, and promotes cultural awareness.

Contact: Edwin G. K. Zoedua, Executive Director.
Address: P.O. Box 31438, Cincinnati,
  Ohio 45231.
Telephone: (513) 931-1872.
Fax: (513) 931-1873.

Union of Liberian Associations in the Americas.

An umbrella organization for Liberian Community Associations in the United States. Activities including lobbying the federal government for immigration and other rights for Liberians in the United States.

Contact: Joseph D. Z. Korto, President.
Address: P.O. Box 57189, Washington, D.C. 20037.
Telephone: (202) 478-4659.

MUSEUMS AND RESEARCH CENTERS

James E. Lewis Museum of Art.
Located in the Carl Murphy Arts Center, the university art museum has a large collection of art works from Africa, including several dozen from Liberia. The Liberian collection includes Dan masks, drums, wood statues, clay bowls, and carved figurines.

Contact: Gabriel S. Tenabe, Director.
Address: Morgan State University, 1700 East Cold Spring Lane, Baltimore, MD 21239.
Telephone: (443) 885-3030.
Fax: (410) 319-4024.

Liberian Museum of City College.
The collection of Liberian art and handcrafted artifacts includes eating and cooking utensils, musical instruments, and traditional clothing donated by citizens in Monrovia, Liberia, Baltimore's sister city in Africa. The museum is in the library of Baltimore City College, a college preparatory high school in Baltimore.

Contact: Joette Chance, Librarian.

Address: Baltimore City College, 3320 The Alameda, Baltimore, MD 21218.
Telephone: (410) 396-7423.

Liberian Studies Association (LSA).
Founded in 1968 and based in Georgia, the LSA is a scholarly research organization with members from cultural, scientific, and educational institutions throughout the United States. It discusses and presents information and opinions on issues involving Liberia and Liberian Americans.

Contact: Ciyata Dinah Coleman, Coordinator.
Address: Morris Brown College, Department of Business and Economics, 643 Martin Luther King Jr. Drive, NW, Atlanta, GA 30314.
Telephone: (404) 220-0157.

SOURCES FOR ADDITIONAL STUDY

Chicoine, Stephen. *A Liberian Family*. Minneapolis: Lerner Publications Co., 1997.

Henries, A. Doris Banks. *Liberian Folklore*. London, England: Macmillan and Co. Ltd., 1966.

Hope, Constance Morris. *Liberia*. Broomall, Pennsylvania: Chelsea House Publishers, 1987.

Newton, Alex, and David Else. *West Africa*. Oakland, California: Lonely Planet Publications, 1995.

Owen, Harrison. *When the Devil Dances*. Los Angeles: Mara Books. 1970.

LITHUANIAN AMERICANS

by
Mark A. Granquist

OVERVIEW

Located in northeastern Europe on the east coast of the Baltic Sea, Lithuania is the most southern of the Baltic Republics—a trio of countries that were formed in 1918. Lithuania measures 25,174 square miles (64,445 square kilometers) and is bordered by Latvia to the north, Belarus to the east, and Russia and Poland to the south and southwest. Its capital is Vilnius, which has a population of 590,000, making it the largest city in the country.

The 1993 census estimated the population of Lithuania at just over 3.75 million people; approximately 80 percent of the citizens are ethnic Lithuanians, 9 percent are Russians, and the remaining 11 percent are largely of Polish, Latvian, and Ukrainian descent. Roman Catholics constitute the largest religious group in Lithuania (85 percent), with smaller numbers of Lutherans, Orthodox Christians, and Jews. The official language of the country is Lithuanian, and the country's flag consists of three equal horizontal bands—yellow on the top, green in the middle, and red on the bottom.

HISTORY

The Lithuanians are ethnically part of the Baltic group of Indo-European peoples, most closely related to the Prussians (a people with Polish and German roots who populated a former northern European state) and the Latvians. The Lithuanians settled along the Neman River perhaps as early as 1500 B.C., founding small agricultural settlements in the area's thick forests. The eastward expansion of medieval German Christianity—under the guise of the crusading religious-military Teutonic Order—brought a number of important changes to the Lithuanians. This outside pressure forced the Lithuanians to unite and sparked Lithuanian expansion south and eastward, into the Belarus and Kievan territories.

Lithuania soon became one of the largest kingdoms in medieval Europe and remained pagan despite attempts by the Catholics and the Orthodox church to Christianize it. The region forged a close alliance with Poland, and the two crowns united in 1386. Lithuania accepted Roman Catholicism at that time, and the combined forces began to push back German incursions, most notably at the battle of Tannenberg-Grünberg in 1410. By 1569 the union of Lithuania and Poland was complete, and the Polish language and culture began to dominate the Lithuanian upper classes, although the peasantry remained culturally and linguistically Lithuanian.

The rise of Russia, combined with the weakness of the Polish-Lithuanian state, led to increasing Russian domination of Lithuania in the eighteenth century. This movement was completed in 1795, when the Russians executed their third division of Poland, effectively ending Polish sovereignty. Some of the northern regions of the division's Lithuanian-speaking territory came under German control as a part of East Prussia. Russia attempted a program of so-called "Russification" of the Baltic states throughout the next century, including the prohibition of Lithuanian language and literature, the imposition of Russian legal codes, and the forcible integration of Uniate (or Byzantine Rite) Catholicism into the Orthodox church. Lithuanian consciousness was maintained in ethnic regional cultures and through a variety of linguistic groupings, but not with a particular sense of national feeling. Beginning in the 1880s, however, a rising nationalistic movement emerged, challenging both Polish cultural domination and Russian governmental controls. With the Revolution of 1905 and the organization of the *Lietuvių Socialistaų Partija Amerikoje* (Lithuanian Socialist Party of America), a Lithuanian assembly convened and demanded a greater degree of territorial and cultural autonomy.

Russian rule of Lithuania came to an end with the German invasion and occupation of the territory during World War I, and 1918 marked the proclamation of the Lithuanian Republic. Achieving actual independence proved more complicated, with opposing forces of Germany, Poland, and the Soviet Union involved, but within two years the region was exercising self-rule.

The dawn of World War II brought political upheaval to Lithuania. In 1940 the Soviet Union took over control of the country—only to lose it to the Germans from 1941 to 1944. Soviet forces then retook Lithuania, though many thousands of Lithuanian refugees fled westward along with the retreating German army. Soviet authorities ordered the deportation of many Lithuanian people from their homeland and from eastern Europe in general between 1945 and 1949, at which time they also collectivized Lithuanian agriculture. During the late 1980s, growing Lithuanian nationalism forced the communists to grant concessions, and, after two years of contention with Soviet authorities, Lithuania finally declared its independence in 1991.

SIGNIFICANT IMMIGRATION WAVES

A number of Lithuanians immigrated to the New World before the American Revolution. The first may have been a Lithuanian physician, Dr. Aleksandras Kursius, who is believed to have lived in New York as early as 1660. Most of the other Lithuanians who ventured to the Americas during this period were members of the noble class or practitioners of particular trades. The first really significant wave of Lithuanian immigration to the United States began in the late 1860s, after the Civil War. During the late nineteenth and early twentieth centuries, an estimated 300,000 Lithuanians journeyed to America—a flow that was later halted by the combined effects of World War I, the restriction of immigration into the United States, and the achievement in 1918 of Lithuanian independence. This number is hard to document fully because census records did not officially recognize Lithuanians as a separate nationality until the twentieth century, and the country's people may have been reported as Russian, Polish, or Jewish.

Several key factors brought about the first surge of Lithuanian immigration to the United States. These included the abolition of serfdom in 1861, which resulted in a rise in Lithuania's free population; the growth of transportation, especially railroads; and a famine that broke out in the country in the 1860s. Later, other conditions, such as a depressed farm economy and increased Russian repression, prompted even more Lithuanians to leave their home soil. In 1930 the U.S. Census Bureau listed 193,600 Lithuanians in the United States. This figure represents six percent of the total population of Lithuania at the time.

The initial wave of immigrants to the United States can also be viewed as part of a larger move-

ment of the Lithuanian peasantry off the land, in search of a better life. Lithuanian peasants moved into Russia and western Europe as agricultural and industrial workers, often intending to return to their native country when they had earned enough money. Their pattern was cyclical, with the numbers of migrating workers shifting along with the seasons and economic cycles. This wave of intra-European immigration consisted mostly of young males, either single or having left their families behind; approximately 48 percent of them were illiterate.

The second wave of immigration had a greater impact on U.S. census figures. Following World War II, a flood of displaced refugees fled west to escape the Russian reoccupation of Lithuania. Eventually 30,000 *Dipukai* (war refugees or displaced persons) settled in the United States, primarily in cities in the East and the Midwest. These immigrants included many trained and educated leaders and professionals who hoped to return someday to Lithuania. The heightening of tensions between the United States and the Soviet Union—known as the Cold War—dampened these expectations, and many Lithuanians sought to create a semipermanent life in the United States. By 1990 the U.S. Bureau of the Census listed 811,865 Americans claiming "Lithuanian" as a first or second ancestry.

SETTLEMENT PATTERNS

The main areas of Lithuanian settlement in the United States included industrial towns of the Northeast, the larger cities of the Northeast and the Midwest, and the coal fields of Pennsylvania and southern Illinois. According to the 1930 census report, only about 13 percent of Lithuanians lived in rural areas, and even fewer—about two percent—were involved in agriculture.

Many of the first immigrants were very mobile, searching for work all over the United States and returning to Lithuania from time to time. Slowly, however, settlement patterns became apparent, and stable Lithuanian American communities were established in the smaller industrial towns in Massachusetts, Connecticut, New Jersey, and Pennsylvania. But by 1930 almost 50 percent of all Lithuanian Americans lived in just ten metropolitan areas. The large cities of Chicago, Cleveland, Detroit, Pittsburgh, New York, and Boston saw the greatest rise in Lithuanian American population. Nearly 20 percent of all Lithuanian immigrants settled in Chicago alone.

When the World War II refugees started entering the United States after 1945, they set up their own communities in many of the same areas as the previous immigrants. The 1990 census lists the leading areas of Lithuanian American settlement as Illinois (109,400), Pennsylvania (103,200), New York (70,300), Massachusetts (68,400), California (63,800), and New Jersey (49,800).

INTERACTIONS WITH SETTLED AMERICANS

Lithuanian immigrants were seen by settled Anglo-Americans as part of the "immigration problem" of the late nineteenth century: the poverty and illiteracy of many of the new arrivals, their Eastern European language and culture, and their devotion to Roman Catholicism put them at a distinct disadvantage in a country where scores of immigrant groups were competing for jobs, housing, and a better life—the so-called "American Dream." Because Lithuanians often took low-paying, unskilled laboring positions, they were not considered as "desirable" as other immigrants. In addition, their involvement in the U.S. labor movement at the turn of the twentieth century led to even more discrimination and resentment from a frightened and suspicious American public. (Lithuanians played an important role in the growth of the United Mine Workers Union and the United Garment Workers Union and were involved in labor unrest in the meat packing and steel industries.)

Throughout the twentieth century, however, Lithuanian Americans began to climb up the economic ladder and gain an important place in their local communities. This mobility allowed them to enter the American mainstream. Members of the post-1945 immigration surge—with their fierce opposition to Russian communism and their middle-class professionalism—have adjusted smoothly and rapidly to the American way of life.

ACCULTURATION AND ASSIMILATION

In 1930 only about 47 percent of Lithuanian immigrants had become American citizens, despite the formation of Lithuanian citizens clubs to promote naturalization. But with their rise toward economic and social success in the twentieth century, Lithuanian Americans began to adapt more easily to life in the States. The American-born second generation, which by 1930 made up the majority of the immigrant community, assimilated much more quickly than their predecessors.

But along with assimilation came the development of an extensive network of immigrant institutions that sought to preserve and advance the immigrant community's native traditions. Foremost among these institutions were the Lithuanian parishes of the Roman Catholic church, which were joined together by various religious orders and lay and clerical organizations. Each immigrant community also boasted numerous immigrant social and fraternal organizations, newspapers, and workers' societies, all of which helped to buttress an immigrant identity.

Two important developments in Lithuania led to the growth of a strong Lithuanian American ethnic identity: the late nineteenth-century rise of Lithuanian national consciousness and the achievement of Lithuanian independence in 1920. Lithuanian Americans were staunch supporters of their newly independent homeland during the 1920s and 1930s, and some even returned to assist in the restructuring of the country's economy and government.

The post-World War II wave of Lithuanian immigrants—the *Dipukai*—also experienced a surge of Lithuanian consciousness. These later immigrants saw themselves as an exiled community and clung to their memory of two decades of freedom in Lithuania. They developed an extensive network of schools, churches, and cultural institutions for the maintenance of Lithuanian identity in the United States. But among the second and third generations of this community, assimilation and acculturation have taken deep hold; ethnic identity, while still important, is no longer central to the community's existence. Given the mass of those American citizens who claim at least partial Lithuanian heritage, most observers feel that this ethnic identity will not be completely forgotten, but many of the institutions that maintained the earlier generations of immigrants have declined in numbers and vitality.

"**I**t was kind of bad for awhile till we got to know people and speak the language and quit being called greenhorns. People say, you ought to preserve your own heritage or something, but all we could think of was, we didn't want to be different, we wanted to be like the rest of the Americans."

Walter Wallace in 1923, cited in *Ellis Island: An Illustrated History of the Immigrant Experience*, edited by Ivan Chermayeff et al. (New York: Macmillan, 1991).

CUISINE

Lithuanian cuisine is influenced by the foods of the land itself and by the various cuisines of its neighbors. More than the other Baltic nations, Lithuanian cooking looks to the east and the south, having much in common with the cooking of Russia, Belarus, and the Ukraine; this is not surprising, as these were the directions taken by the expansion of the medieval kingdom of Lithuania. Lithuanian recipes rely heavily on pork, potatoes, and dairy products such as eggs, milk, cream, and butter. (One specialty is a white cottage-type cheese called *suris*.) Dark, flavorful mushrooms, herring, eels, sausages, and dark rye breads are also central to the Lithuanian diet. Holiday foods included jellied pigs feet, goose stuffed with prunes, and roasted suckling pig.

TRADITIONAL DRESS

The colorful regional dress of Lithuania was used at times of festivals, market days, and special events in the old country. Some immigrants may have brought these costumes with them when they immigrated, but the wearing of such dress was not common in the United States, except for ethnic festivals. The daily working clothes of the immigrants never really differed from that of other Americans holding the same positions.

HOLIDAYS

Along with the traditional Catholic and American holidays, there are several festival days of special significance to the Lithuanian American community. February 16 is Lithuanian Independence Day, marking the formal declaration of independence in 1918. September 8 is known as Lithuanian Kingdom Day. Roman Catholics celebrate the Feast of St. Casimir on March 4, with special celebrations led by the Knights of Lithuania fraternal organization.

HEALTH ISSUES

With the formation of a solid Lithuanian American community at the end of the nineteenth century, the need for health care among immigrants became a key issue. Immigrant fraternal and benefit societies sought to provide help for sick or injured Lithuanians, as did social and charitable organizations. Roman Catholics organized Holy Cross Hospital in Chicago, as well as homes for the aged and infirm. Many of these activities came under the control of Lithuanian Roman Catholic orders, especially the Sisters of St. Casimir. Few Lithuanian medical professionals set up practice in the United States until after 1945, when a postwar influx of Lithuanian doctors from the European refugee community took place.

LANGUAGE

The Lithuanian language—a part of the Baltic branch of the Indo-European language family—is closely related to Latvian and the now-extinct language known as Old Prussian. Wider relationships, whether to German or the Slavic languages, are difficult to establish. Spoken Lithuanian is a very

ancient language; it maintains many early features of speech and grammar that other Indo-European languages have lost. Although written Lithuanian came into existence in the sixteenth century, strong Polish cultural influences and Russian Imperial domination effectively suppressed the development of Lithuanian as a written, literary language—at least until the rise of Lithuanian nationalism in the late nineteenth century.

Lithuanian is divided into Low and High dialects, with numerous subdialects. The language uses 11 vowels ("a," "ą," "e," "ę," "ė," "i," "į," "y," "o," "u," "ų," "ū") along with six diphthongs ("ai," "au," "ei," "ui," ie," and "uo"). In addition to most of the standard consonants of the English language, Lithuanian makes use of "č," "š," and "ž," however, the consonants "f" and "h" and the combination "ch" are used only in foreign words.

The preservation of the Lithuanian language was a key concern among the initial wave of immigrants to the United States. The cultural domination of the Poles led to considerable dissension among the members of the Lithuanian American community. Especially in the Roman Catholic church, Polish prevailed as the official language used in worship and religious education, a practice that came under bitter attack from Lithuanian Americans. Religious organizations and their priests were divided along this issue; eventually, however, the Polophile party lost, and modern Lithuanian became the language of the community. The later immigrants who came after World War II have worked to keep the Lithuanian language alive within the community by developing a network of schools to encourage the preservation of the language. There are still quite a few Lithuanian American publications issued at least partially in Lithuanian, including some local Lithuanian daily newspapers. Several universities and colleges offer Lithuanian language courses, including Yale University, University of Illinois-Chicago, Indiana University-Bloomington, Tulane University, Cornell University, and Ohio State University. There are also dozens of public libraries with Lithuanian language collections, including the Los Angeles Public Library, Chicago Public Library, Donnell Library Center at the New York Public Library, Ennoch Pratt Free Library, and the Detroit Public Library.

GREETINGS AND OTHER POPULAR EXPRESSIONS

Common Lithuanian greetings and other expressions include: *labą rytą* ("lahba reehta")—good morning; *labą vakara* ("lahba vahkahra")—good evening; *labanaktis* ("lahba-nahktees")—good night; *sudievu* ("sood-yeeh-voo")—goodbye; *kaip tamsta gyvuoji* ("kaip tahmstah geeh-vu-oyee")—how are you; *labai gerai* ("lahbai gar-ai")—quite well; *dėkui* ("deh-kooy")—thanks; *atsiprašau* ("aht-see-prah-show")—excuse me; *sveikas* ("say-kahs")—welcome; *taip* ("taip")—yes; *ne* ("nah")—no; *turiu eiti* ("toor-i-oo ay-tee")—I must go.

FAMILY AND COMMUNITY DYNAMICS

During the first wave of Lithuanian immigration to the United States, a stable immigrant community developed rather slowly. Since many of the first immigrants were young males seeking temporary employment, an immigrant community identity was hard to establish. Long hours, grinding poverty, and isolation increased the pressures that fragmented the immigrants. Slowly, as the immigrants began to settle permanently in the United States, family, religious, and community institutions were formed. A growing sense of nationalism within the community allowed the Lithuanians to see themselves as a people separate from the Poles and the Russians.

The immigrant community of the early twentieth century was beginning to mature, with second and third generations rapidly becoming Americanized. The arrival of Lithuanian refugees after World War II brought a fresh wave of immigrants and an intensified sense of Lithuanian nationalism. The size and strength of the Lithuanian American community has allowed its people to maintain a certain sense of ethnic heritage, even as the immigrant population evolves and its succeeding generations become thoroughly Americanized.

INTERACTION WITH OTHER ETHNIC GROUPS

In the late eighteenth and early nineteenth centuries, the Lithuanian American community was closely tied to the Polish community. Since the borders of these nations were fluid—and since a long history of Polish religious and cultural dominance existed in Lithuania—Polish American and Lithuanian American immigrants tended to settle in many of the same areas of the United States. The early struggle for Lithuanians in America involved a move away from the Polish community and toward the definition of a pure Lithuanian national and ethnic identity. In later years a significant relationship developed between Lithuanian Americans and the other Baltic immigrants, Estonians and Latvians. These groups banded together in the interest of freeing the Baltic Republics from Soviet rule:

their solidarity is especially evident in the creation of groups such as the Joint Baltic-American National Committee (1961) and other joint organizations.

EDUCATION

Like many other immigrant groups, Lithuanians have seen that the road to success in America lies with education. Many of the immigrants, especially before 1920, arrived in the States as illiterate peasants. Despite their limited resources, the community soon established a system of parochial schools among the Lithuanian Roman Catholic parishes in the United States, many of which were run by the Sisters of St. Casimir. A smaller network of Lithuanian American Roman Catholic high schools and academies appeared later, numbering approximately ten by 1940.

Responding to a plea from the immigrant community, the Marian Fathers opened a high school and college in Hinsdale, Illinois, in 1926. Later the college was relocated to Thompson, Connecticut, and renamed Marianapolis College. Another early center of Lithuanian education was Indiana's Valparaiso University. Though not an ethnic institution, this university attracted a number of Lithuanian students early in the twentieth century; between 1902 and 1915 the school graduated 29 Lithuanian doctors, 15 lawyers, and 14 engineers. Lithuanian refugees of World War II—many of whom were highly educated, skilled professionals—exhibited an intense interest in education. Their main educational contribution to the community was the formation of a series of Lithuanian schools to transmit Lithuanian language and culture to succeeding generations of Lithuanian Americans.

THE ROLE OF WOMEN

Coming from an extremely traditional agricultural society, the first wave of Lithuanian immigrants brought with them a very rigid set of beliefs about women's roles in the community. Male domination of the family was a given, and women's roles were strictly defined. This social system was very hard for the immigrants to maintain in the United States, especially in the urban areas where the majority of the immigrants settled. As the immigrants became assimilated into the mainstream of American life, women's roles began to change and grow, though not without stress and conflict. One new independent role for women came through the formation of Lithuanian American religious orders, which afforded Lithuanian women a leading role in the immigrant religious community, and beyond: they headed parochial schools and established institutions of mercy, such as hospitals, orphanages, and nursing homes. Later, lay women's organizations—such as the American Lithuanian Roman Catholic Women's Alliance (founded in 1914) and the Federation of Lithuanian Women's Clubs (founded in 1947)—began to spring up in Lithuanian American communities, further empowering the female population.

RELIGION

The large majority of Lithuanian immigrants to America were Roman Catholics; there were also small numbers of Lutherans, Jews, and Orthodox Christians. The dominance of Roman Catholicism in the Lithuanian American community is even more pronounced because of the influence of Catholicism in the formation of the institutions of Lithuanian identity. However, the Roman Catholic presence was neither monolithic nor universal, and significant tensions existed within the Catholic community.

Lithuania adopted Roman Catholicism along the lines of its western neighbor, Poland, and for many centuries Lithuanian Catholicism was Polish in language and orientation. Lithuanian was considered to be a barbarous language, unworthy of religious use, so Polish was used for all official religious business. This dominance in religious matters extended to the immigrant communities of America as well; early Lithuanian immigrants tended to merge into Polish-language Roman Catholic parishes, and Polish-leaning priests dominated many of the early institutions of the Lithuanian American community.

But the rising tide of Lithuanian nationalism and ethnic identity toward the end of the nineteenth century sparked profound changes in the Lithuanian American religious community. Under the leadership of Aleksandras Burba, a priest from Lithuania, some Lithuanian Americans began to pull away from Polish parishes and Polish-dominated institutions and establish their own Lithuanian parishes. More than 100 Lithuanian parishes were formed by 1920. This movement created considerable tension within the immigrant community but also helped heighten and define a sense of ethnic consciousness among Lithuanian Americans. Not all Lithuanians wanted to distance themselves from Polish Roman Catholicism though, and divisiveness soon clouded the ranks of many Lithuanian American institutions and organizations.

The development of Lithuanian Roman Catholicism took hold early in the twentieth century, cementing a Lithuanian ethnic consciousness in America. Many of these efforts were led by an immigrant priest, Father Antanas Staniukynas, who formed the Lithuanian American Roman Catholic Priest's League in 1909. Staniukynas also contributed to the establishment of religious orders in the immigrant community, including the Sisters of St. Casimir and an American branch of the Lithuanian Marian Fathers. Around the same time, many lay Roman Catholic organizations were also founded; fraternal and social organizations were formed for men, women, workers, students, and other lay groups. But probably the most lasting and impressive achievement was the formation of a large parochial school system in affiliation with the Lithuanian American Roman Catholic parishes, a system run largely by the immigrant religious orders.

Religious life in the United States was not without conflict for the Lithuanian Roman Catholics. The old style of autocratic priestly leadership soon gave way to the realities of a democratic and pluralistic America, and the laity demanded an increased role in parish government. After 1945 the influx of war refugees brought new members to Lithuanian American Roman Catholicism; new religious orders, such as the Sisters of the Immaculate Conception and the Lithuanian Franciscan and Jesuit priestly orders were also established.

In 1914 the Lithuanian National Catholic Church was formed in Scranton, Pennsylvania. This movement, which broke away from the Roman Catholic hierarchy in the United States, stressed the national dimension of Lithuanian Catholicism. Lithuanian National Catholic parishes flourished in areas of heavy Lithuanian settlement early in the twentieth century.

Lithuanian Lutherans hailed mainly from the northern and western areas of Lithuania, areas that had been influenced by German and Latvian Lutheranism. The Lutheran reformation—a sixteenth-century Protestant reform movement—took hold in Lithuania until it was largely eliminated by the counter-reformation, yet over the centuries a small Lutheran minority remained. When these immigrants came to America during the initial surge of Lithuanian immigration, they tended to develop separate Lutheran congregations apart from the mainstream Lithuanian American community. The German-speaking Lutheran Missouri Synod sponsored several pastors who sought to reach out to this community. After 1945 a second wave of Lithuanian Lutherans formed the Lithuanian Evangelical Lutheran Church in Exile, headquartered near Chicago. This church has 19 congregations and 10,000 members worldwide.

Although a sizable Jewish community was established in Lithuania prior to World War II, it was forced to coexist with the Christian ethic of the country's wider Roman Catholic world. Many members of the Lithuanian Jewish community immigrated to America during the latter part of the nineteenth century and formed their own communities in the United States, mainly in the cities of the Northeast and the Midwest. One estimate from about 1940 puts the number of Lithuanian American Jews at around 25,000. During the assimilation process, these communities became affiliated with the larger Jewish communities throughout the United States. At the same time back in Europe, the Nazi-engineered Holocaust of World War II had a devastating effect on the Lithuanian Jewish community, leaving it almost completely destroyed by war's end.

EMPLOYMENT AND ECONOMIC TRADITIONS

The first wave of Lithuanian immigration, which ended around 1920, included mostly unskilled and often illiterate immigrants who settled in the cities and coal fields of the East and the Midwest and provided the raw muscle power of urban American factories; they were especially drawn to the garment trade in the East, the steel mills and forges of the Midwest, and the packing houses of Chicago and Omaha. Other immigrants opened businesses within their communities, supplying the growing needs of Lithuanian Americans.

To assist their people in the economic transition to life in the United States, the immigrants established many institutions, including fraternal and benefit societies and building and loan associations. The fraternal societies assisted needy immigrants and provided inexpensive insurance and death benefit protection. The building and loan associations met the immigrants' banking needs and helped them to purchase their own homes. By 1920 there were at least 30 such associations within the Lithuanian immigrant community.

The war refugees who came to the United States after 1945 were a different class of immigrants, mainly educated and professional. Although they had been the leaders of an independent Lithuania from 1918 to 1940, many of these new immigrants had difficulty finding suitable employment in the United States. The language barrier and professional differences meant that many of them had to take positions that were beneath their level of training and education. These refugees were

Lithuanian Americans protest Soviet policies concerning the Baltic States in this 1990 photograph.

an enterprising group, however, and they began a tradition of economic success in the United States.

POLITICS AND GOVERNMENT

Much of the initial political activity of the Lithuanian Americans was confined to the immigrant community itself, as immigrants sought to define themselves, especially in terms of the rising tide of Lithuanian nationalism that dominated the latter part of the nineteenth century. But slowly the immigrant community began to look outside itself toward the wider American world. The first examples of immigrant political activity came in areas that directly affected the new immigrants—namely labor issues and the condition of American relations with the new Lithuanian state. Lithuanians were active in the formation of some of the American labor unions, especially in coal mining and the garment trade. For some, this activity grew into a wider push for socialism (a political and economic doctrine espousing collective rather than private ownership of property), especially with the formation of the Lithuanian Socialist Party of America in 1905. This prewar socialism collapsed, though, after 1918, as the so-called "Red Scare" put great pressure on all socialist groups. The first major political push among Lithuanian Americans came after 1918, when they tried to influence American foreign policy to recognize and support Lithuanian independence.

Since the Lithuanian immigrant community was mostly urban and working class, many Lithuanians aligned themselves with the Democratic party during the twentieth century. Although they were not a real force in national politics, Lithuanian Americans used their numbers to dominate local politics, electing local officials, state legislators, judges, and occasionally members of the U.S. House of Representatives. In turn they became loyal supporters of the local Democratic political machines in areas such as Chicago, Cleveland, and Detroit. In many communities Lithuanians formed their own Democratic clubs for the support of political and ethnic priorities. A smaller number of Lithuanians were attracted to the Republican party, especially after 1945. Along with some members of the other Baltic groups, these Lithuanians blamed the Democrats for the "betrayal" of Lithuanian independence in the Yalta agreement of 1945, which extended Soviet territories to the West. Post-World War II immigrants, because of their strongly anticommunist feelings, favored mostly the Republicans.

UNION ACTIVITY

Lithuanian immigrants were involved in a number of industries that saw a great deal of union activity at the end of the nineteenth century. The Lithuanian coal miners of Pennsylvania and Illinois became members of the United Mine Workers unions, and local unions of Lithuanian garment workers soon merged with either the Amalgamated Clothing Workers Union or the United Garment Workers Union. In other industries, such as steel or meat packing, union organization was slower, but Lithuanian workers were an omnipresent force in labor agitation. A number of nationalist, Roman Catholic, and socialist immigrant organizations were developed to provide support to laborers. Socialist and radical workers groups, such as the Industrial Workers of the World (IWW), succeeded in recruiting Lithuanian workers in the first part of the twentieth century, but these groups declined rapidly after 1920. The Lithuanian community was generally sympathetic to the union cause and supported their fellow immigrants during labor unrest.

MILITARY

Lithuanians have served in the American armed forces in every war since the Civil War; in that war 373 Lithuanians fought on the Union side, and 44 fought on the side of the Confederacy. Lithuanian Americans were especially interested in both World Wars, since they directly influenced the fate of Lithuanian independence. In 1918 a group of 200 Lithuanian Americans who had served in the American military went to Lithuania to help in the fight for freedom.

RELATIONS WITH LITHUANIA

Relations with Lithuania have always been important to the Lithuanian American community. Tensions ran especially high among Lithuanians in the United States during those periods when the Russian state had control over Lithuania. Immigrant communities in America were fertile ground for nationalistic sentiment, and during the last decades of the nineteenth century many radical Lithuanian nationalists sought refuge in the United States from political oppression in Russia. Most Lithuanian Americans supported the nationalist cause, although a small group of radical communists backed Soviet attempts to forcibly annex Lithuania to the Soviet Union.

When Lithuania was declared a republic in 1918, the immigrant community supported independence with financial, military, and political help. A number of the leaders of independent Lithuania had even lived and studied for a time in the United States. Lithuanian Americans pressured the American government to recognize Lithuanian independence and support Lithuanian border claims in the dispute with Poland. This support of the homeland helped strengthen Lithuanian American group solidarity in the United States during the 1920s and 1930s.

With the Soviet invasion of Lithuania in 1940, the Lithuanian American community had new cause for common action. War refugees from Lithuania flooded the United States after 1945, and many new groups and organizations were formed to rally for an independent Lithuania—and to support this cause with money and publicity. Lithuanian Americans worked to keep the dream of an independent Lithuania alive with publicity, lobbying efforts, and various political and cultural activities. These actions moved Lithuanian Americans into the wider sphere of the Lithuanian exile community worldwide, uniting American organizations with others in Europe and elsewhere. Agitation efforts also brought Lithuanian Americans into closer contact with other Baltic Americans, with whom they shared the dream of independence for the Baltic states.

INDIVIDUAL AND GROUP CONTRIBUTIONS

BUSINESS AND INDUSTRY

Lane Bryant (1879-1951), born Lena Himmelstein, arrived in New York in 1895 and began working in the garment industry. With the help of her second husband, Lithuanian-born Albert Maislin (1879-

1923), Bryant expanded her business, introducing the first maternity wear and later manufacturing larger-sized women's clothing. The family of Nicholas Pritzker, a Lithuanian immigrant born in 1871, started numerous businesses that now comprise the Hyatt Corporation.

FILM

Actor Laurence Harvey (1928-1973) was born Laurynas Skinkis in Lithuania. He had an active career in England and the United States, appearing in such films as *Room at the Top, Butterfield 8,* and *The Manchurian Candidate.* Charles Bronson (1920–), born Casimir Businskis, is a popular movie actor known for his action roles in such movies as *The Great Escape, Once Upon a Time in the West, Death Wish,* and *Hard Times.* Actress Ruta Lee, born Ruta Kilmonis, appeared in the 1950s and 1960s motion pictures *Witness for the Prosecution, Marjorie Morningstar,* and *Operation Eichmann.*

GOVERNMENT

Alexander Bruce Bialaski, an American of Lithuanian descent, was the first director of the Federal Bureau of Investigation (FBI), serving in that capacity from 1912 to 1919. Sydney Hillman (1887-1946), a Lithuanian Jewish immigrant, was the leader of the Amalgamated Clothing Workers Union for over 30 years. He moved into the national political arena in 1941, when he became director of the U.S. Office of Production Management.

PHOTOGRAPHY

Lithuanian photographer and journalist Vitas Valaitis (1931-1965) worked for several major publications, including *Newsweek, Saturday Evening Post,* and *U.S. News and World Report,* and won numerous prizes for his work.

SOCIAL ISSUES

Father Jonas Zilinskas (1870-1932) was instrumental in developing the Lithuanian Alliance of America and served as its president. Emma Goldman (1869-1940) was a radical anarchist and supporter of communism. She immigrated to America in 1886 and quickly became a leader in radical movements in the United States. Her bold lectures promoting atheism, revolution, birth control, and "free love" often led to trouble with the authorities. Goldman was imprisoned in 1917 and deported to Russia in 1919. An early supporter of Soviet ideals, she eventually grew disenchanted with the course of the rev-

olution. When she died in 1940 her body was returned to the United States for burial.

SPORTS

Johnny Unitas (1933–) was one of the greatest quarterbacks in the National Football League (NFL). As a star player for the Baltimore Colts in the 1960s, he set a number of professional records and was repeatedly named to the all-star team. Dick Butkas (1942–), a key player for the Chicago Bears during the 1960s and 1970s, is widely regarded as the best middle-linebacker ever to play professional football. Johnny Podres (1932–) pitched for the Brooklyn Dodgers and other professional baseball teams. Jack Sharkey (born Juozas Žukauskas; 1902–) was a World Heavyweight champion boxer whose career peaked in the 1920s and 1930s. Billie Burke, born Vincas Burkauskas, made her mark as a professional golfer on the women's circuit. Vitas Gerulaitis (1954-1994) was a top-ranked tennis professional whose career flourished in the 1970s and 1980s.

THEATER

Elizabeth Swados (1951–) is an award-winning composer, writer, and director whose works include the Broadway musicals *Doonesbury* and *The Beautiful Lady.* She has also written music for many classical dramatic productions and television specials.

VISUAL ARTS

Victor D. Brenner (1871-1924; surname originally Baranauskas) designed the Lincoln penny in 1909. Many of the first Lincoln pennies, now collector's items, bear his initials, "VDB."

MEDIA

PRINT

Bridges.
A Lithuanian American news journal.

Contact: Rimantas Stirbys, Editor.
Address: 2715 East Allegheny Avenue, Philadelphia, Pennsylvania 19134.
Telephone: (215) 739-9353.
Fax: (215) 739-6587.

Dirva (The Field).
Lithuanian-language newspaper that contains items of interest to the Lithuanian community.

Contact: Vytautas Gedgaudas, Editor.
Address: Viltis, Inc., 19807 Cherokee Avenue, Cleveland, Ohio 44119-1090.
Telephone: (216) 531-8150.
Fax: (216) 531-8428.

Draugas (The Friend).

Newspaper published by the Lithuanian Catholic Press Society.

Contact: Ms. Danute Bindokas, Editor.
Address: 4545 West 63rd Street, Chicago, Illinois 60629-5589.
Telephone: (312) 585-9500.
Fax: (312) 585-8284.
E-mail: draugas@earthlink.com

Garsas (The Echo).

Published by the Lithuanian Alliance of America, this monthly bilingual publication contains general news for and about the Lithuanian American community.

Contact: Florence Eckert, Editor.
Address: 71-73 South Washington Street, Wilkes Barre, Pennsylvania 18701.
Telephone: (717) 823-8876.

I Laisve (Toward Freedom).

Lithuanian-language magazine of politics that contains articles of interest to the Lithuanian community.

Contact: Vacys Rociunas, Editor.
Address: Friends of the Lithuanian Front, 1634 49th Avenue, Cicero, Illinois 60650.

Journal of Baltic Studies.

Published by the Association for the Advancement of Baltic Studies, this quarterly provides a forum for scholarly discussion of topics regarding the Baltic Republics and their peoples.

Contact: William Urban and Roger Noel, Editors.
Address: Executive Offices of the ARABS, 111 Knob Hill Road, Hacketstown, NJ 07840.

Lietuviu Dienos (Lithuanian Days).

A general interest, bilingual monthly publication that covers Lithuania and the Lithuanian American community.

Contact: Ruta Skurius, Editor.
Address: 4364 Sunset Boulevard, Hollywood, California 90029.
Telephone: (213) 664-2919.

Lituanus: Lithuanian Quarterly Journal of Arts and Sciences.

Established in 1954, this quarterly publication features scholarly articles about Lithuania and Lithuanians around the world. Published by the Lituanus Foundation, Inc.

Address: P.O. Box 9318, Chicago, Illinois 60690.

Metmenys.

Lithuanian-language scholarly publication.

Contact: Vytautas Kavolis, Editor.
Address: A M & M Publications, 7338 South Sacramento, Chicago, Illinois 60629.
Telephone: (312) 436-5369.

Sandara (The League).

Monthly fraternal magazine published by the Lithuanian National League of America in English and Lithuanian; first published in 1914.

Contact: G. J. Lazauskas, Editor.
Address: 208 W. Natoma Avenue, Addison, Illinois 60101.
Telephone: (630) 543-8198
Fax: (630) 543-8198

Tevyne.

Weekly Lithuanian interest newspaper published by the Lithuanian Alliance of America.

Address: 307 West 30th Street, New York, New York 10001.
Telephone: (212) 563-2210.

World Lithuanian.

Established in 1953 by the Lithuanian World Community, Inc., this is a monthly publication that seeks to unite Lithuanians around the world for ethnic solidarity.

Address: 6804 Maplewood Avenue, Chicago, Illinois 60629.
Telephone: (312) 776-4028.

RADIO

KTYM-AM (1460).

Contact: Bobby A. Howe.
One-half hour of Lithuanian programming weekly.

Address: 6803 West Boulevard, Inglewood, California 90302-1895.
Telephone: (213) 678-3731.

WCEV-AM (1450).

Seven hours of Lithuanian programming weekly.

Address: 5356 West Belmont Avenue, Cicero,
　　Illinois 60641-4103.
Telephone: (312) 282-6700.
Fax: (773) 282-0123.

WPIT-AM (730).

One hour of Lithuanian programming weekly.

Address: 7 Parkway Center, Suite 625, Pittsburgh,
　　Pennsylvania 15220.
Telephone: (412) 937-1500.
Fax: (412) 937-1576.

ORGANIZATIONS AND ASSOCIATIONS

Institute of Lithuanian Studies (ILS).

Seeks to sponsor and encourage research on
Lithuanian language, literature, folklore, history,
and other fields related to Lithuania and its culture.

Contact: Violeta Kelertas, President.
Address: University of Illinois at Chicago,
　　Department of Slavic and Baltic Studies (m/c
　　306), 601 South Morgan, Chicago, Illinois
　　60607-7116.
Telephone: (312) 996-7856.
Fax: (312) 996-0953.

Lithuanian Alliance of America.

Founded in 1886, the LAA was one of the first
social organizations established by Lithuanians in
America. Though originally a fraternal benefit association, the alliance quickly became the center of
organized Lithuanian life in the United States,
especially in the early part of the twentieth century.

Contact: Genevieve Meiliunas, Secretary.
Address: 307 West 30th Street, New York,
　　New York 10001.
Telephone: (212) 563-2210.

Lithuanian American Community (LAC).

Founded in 1952, this organization focuses on educational and cultural activities, sponsoring regional
cultural festivals, providing grants and scholarships
to support academic and cultural activities, and
calling for freedom in Lithuania.

Contact: Joseph Gaila, President.
Address: 2713 West 71st Street, Chicago,
　　Illinois 60629.
Telephone: (312) 436-0197.

Lithuanian American Council (LAC).

Founded in 1940, the LAC functions as an umbrella organization to coordinate the work of Lithuanian American groups, clubs, and religious and fraternal organizations. Its primary purpose is to unite
the Lithuanian American community and to
advance Lithuanian independence.

Contact: John A. Rackauskas, President.
Address: 6500 South Pulaski, Chicago,
　　Illinois 60629.
Telephone: (312) 735-6677.
E-mail: lrsc@mcs.net.

Lithuanian National Foundation (LNF).

Collects, researches, analyzes, and disseminates
information on Lithuania and the Lithuanian
nation.

Contact: Mr. Vilgalys Jonas, Chairman.
Address: 351 Highland Boulevard, Brooklyn,
　　New York 11207-1910.
Telephone: (718) 277-0682.
Fax: (718) 277-0682.

Lithuanian Roman Catholic Federation of America.

Founded in 1906. Composed of Lithuanian-American Catholic organizations, parishes, religious
orders, and publications; agencies and institutions;
individuals. Seeks to unite Lithuanian-American
Catholics; promotes Catholic action; upholds
Lithuanian culture. Operates a camp and retreat
center in Michigan; collects archival material about
immigration history; is establishing audio- and
videocassette library in Lithuanian and English on
educational and religious topics.

Contact: Saulius V. Kuprys, President.
Address: 71-73 South Washington Street,
　　Wilkes-Barre, Pennsylvania 18703.
Telephone: (717) 823-8876.

Lithuanian World Community (LWC).

Founded in 1949, LWC is the largest ethnic organization for the Lithuanian community in exile. It was
formed by immigrants who fled Lithuania following
the Soviet takeover during World War II. It seeks to
unite the Lithuanian exile community around the
world and helps maintain an extensive Lithuanian
educational presence in the United States.

Contact: V. J. Bieliauskas, President.
Address: 14911 127th Street, Lemont,
　　Illinois 60439.
Telephone: (708) 257-8457.

Lituanus Foundation (LF).

Organizes, sponsors, and publishes research material on the language, history, politics, geography, economics, folklore, literature, and arts of Lithuania and the Baltic States.

Contact: A. Damulis, Administrator.
Address: 6621 South Troy Street, Chicago, Illinois 60629-2913.
Telephone: (312) 434-0706.

National Lithuanian Society of America (NSLA).

Fosters Lithuanian fine arts, handicraft, cultural, and educational activities. Publishes bimonthly newsletter.

Contact: Peter Buckas, President.
Address: 13400 Parker Road, Lemont, Illinois 60439.
Telephone: (708) 301-8183.

MUSEUMS AND RESEARCH CENTERS

Balzekas Museum of Lithuanian Culture.

A museum and research library dedicated to the study of Lithuania and Lithuanian Americans. Displays feature Lithuanian art, collectibles, and memorabilia.

Contact: Stanley Balzekas, Jr., Director.
Address: 6500 South Pulaski Road, Chicago, Illinois 60629.
Telephone: (312) 582-6500.

Immigration History Research Center.

Located at the University of Minnesota, it is a valuable library and archival resource on eastern and southern Europeans, including Lithuanians. In addition to serials and newspapers, the center has a large holding of books and monographs on the immigrant community, along with archival resources and manuscripts.

Contact: Joel Wurl, Curator.
Address: 826 Berry Street, St. Paul, Minnesota 55114.
Telephone: (612) 627-4208.

Lithuanian American Cultural Archives.

Run by the Lithuanian Marian Fathers, it focuses on Lithuanians in America. It has an extensive collection of early materials on the immigrant community, especially on Lithuanians in the Northeast and Middle Atlantic states.

Address: Thurber Road, Putnam, Connecticut 06260.
Telephone: (203) 928-9317.

Lithuanian Museum.

Founded to promote and further an understanding of the Lithuanian American immigrant experience, it sponsors both permanent and traveling exhibits and also houses a library. The Lithuanian Museum is affiliated with the World Lithuanian Archives, a major repository of materials by and about the Lithuanian American community, gathered by the Lithuanian Jesuit Fathers Provincial House in Chicago.

Contact: Nijole Mackevincius, Director.
Address: 5620 South Claremont Avenue, Chicago, Illinois 60636.
Telephone: (773) 434-4545.
Fax: (773) 434-9363.
E-mail: lrsc@mcs.net.

Van Pelt Library, University of Pennsylvania.

The library houses one of the largest collections of materials about Lithuania and Lithuanian Americans in the United States.

Address: 3420 Walnut Street, Philadelphia, Pennsylvania 19104.
Telephone: (215) 898-7088.

SOURCES FOR ADDITIONAL STUDY

Alilunas, Leo J. *Lithuanians in the United States: Selected Studies.* San Francisco: R&E Research Associates, 1978.

Budreckis, Algirdas. *The Lithuanians in America, 1651-1975: A Chronology and Factbook.* Dobbs Ferry, New York: Oceana Publications, Inc., 1975.

Encyclopedia Lithuanica, six volumes, edited by Simas Suziedelius. Boston: Juozas Kapocius, 1970-78.

Fainhauz, David. *Lithuanians in the U.S.A.: Aspects of Ethnic Identity.* Chicago: Lithuanian Library Press, Inc., 1991.

Kantautas, Adam. *A Lithuanian Bibliography.* Edmonton, Alberta, Canada: University of Alberta Press, 1975.

Kučas, Antanas. *Lithuanians in America.* San Francisco: R&E Research Associates, 1975.

Lithuanian Cooking. New York: Darbininkas, 1976.

Wolkovich-Valkavičius, William. *Lithuanian Religious Life in America: a Compendium of 150 Roman Catholic Parishes and Institutions.* Norwood, MA: Corporate Fulfillment Systems, 1991-98.

LUXEMBOURGER AMERICANS

by
Drew Walker

Luxembourgers are fond of sayings that mark important moments in history and the formation of national identity. One such saying is "Et get fir de glaf!" or "Here goes for faith!" a saying that was used in the Kloppelkrieg rebellion against the French during the reign of Napoleon.

OVERVIEW

The small country of Luxembourg, also known as the Grand Duchy of Luxembourg, is contained within some 998 square miles, or 2,586 square kilometers of land in western Europe. Luxembourg is surrounded by Belgium to its north and west, France to its south and Germany to its east. The history and culture of Luxembourg have been significantly affected by this geographical location. Since Luxembourg has fused the traditions of the surrounding countries and is the product of various immigration movements throughout its history, the population of Luxembourg (some 410,000) is ethnically diverse. Because of its location and history, it is referred to as one of Europe's most important crossroads. Along its border with Belgium are the Ardennes Mountains, forming a plateau between 1,300 and 1,600 feet (400 to 490 meters). This area is known as the Oesling. To the south of the Ardennes is an area known as Gutland or Bon Pays (literally "good land"), which contains various contours of fertile farmland.

HISTORY

In early ancient times the land of Luxembourg was inhabited by two Belgic tribes named the Medioatrici and the Teveri. In the fifth century A.D. the Franks began to occupy the area. In the following centuries, the people began to convert to Christianity. Under the domination of the Holy Roman Empire of Charlemagne, the area was first a section of the Kingdom of Austrasia and then the Kingdom of Lotharinga. From an exchange of land in 963 by Siegfried, the Count of Ardennes, the Kingdom of Luxembourg became an independent land. Involved in this exchange was Siegfried's acquisition of a Roman castle on the Alzette River. The present name of Luxembourg was derived from the name of the castle "Lucilinburhuc," or "Little Fortress." After the death of Siegfried, he was succeeded by a long line of his descendants. Near the year 1060 one of these descendants, Conrad, became the first Luxembourger ruler to take the title of the "Count of Luxembourg." In 1354, Luxembourg was made a duchy by Holy Roman emperor Charles IV.

Perhaps the greatest point in the history of Luxembourg in this era came in 1443, when the then Duchess of Luxembourg, Elizabeth of Görlitz, gave up the throne to the duke of Burgundy, Philip the Good (Philip III). When all of Burgundy and its lands passed into the hands of the Hapsburg rulers in 1477, so did the Duchy of Luxembourg. In 1556, through a series of changes brought about by the abdication of Hapsburg emperor Charles V, Luxembourg became a property of Spain and part of what were known as "The Spanish Netherlands." Through the two turbulent centuries that followed, Luxembourg often found itself at the geographic and political center of wars and disputes; when these conflicts ended, Luxembourg, along with Belgium, passed from the Spanish into the hands of the Austrian Hapsburgs.

MODERN ERA

Austrian rule continued until 1795 when the French took over the duchy. Following this occupation by French revolutionary forces, a modern state bureaucracy was installed in Luxembourg resembling the French system at the time. In their zeal to institute these reforms, along with their disempowerment of the clergy and the call for mandatory military service by the Luxembourgers, the French created dissent. This dissent eventually led to a rebellion against French rule in 1798, which in turn was brutally put down.

With the fall of Napoleon in 1814 and the end of French rule came the decision of the Allied Powers in 1815 to cede parts of the duchy to Prussia and to give the rest to William I, King of the Netherlands, and to elevate it to the status of a grand duchy. This resulted in confusion over Luxembourg's identity. While owned by William I of the Netherlands, it was also a member of the German Confederation and had close ties with Prussia. In addition, it was, technically, an independent state as well. What ensued in the decades immediately following the possession of Luxembourg by the Netherlands was a struggle against this rule, which was undertaken in cooperation with the Belgians. In a revolution against Dutch rule, the Belgians also declared Luxembourg to be a part of Belgium against the claim of the Netherlands. The series of international reactions that followed led in 1831 to a decision by the "Great Powers" of France, Prussia, Russia, and Britain. Despite Belgium's claim, Luxembourg was to remain the possession, albeit in altered form, of William I and was also to remain a part of the German Confederation. Dividing Luxembourg once again, the French-speaking part of Luxembourg was given to Belgium while the Netherlands retained the parts that spoke the native Luxembourger language. After a series of disputes on this decision between the Netherlands and Belgium, it eventually came to be accepted, and the Netherlands ruled this area alone from 1839 until 1867.

While William I and his successor William II made several moves on behalf of the Luxembourg-Netherlands union, including making Luxembourg a part of the Customs Union directed by Prussia, dissent against this and other decisions continued to grow among the Luxembourgers. The constitution of 1841 given by the Netherlands was met with hostility, which led to a series of constitutional changes thought to be more just. When the German Confederation was dissolved in 1866, Luxembourg became a sovereign nation. In the years that followed, however, a series of disputes between the Great Powers regarding the status of Luxembougian independence led to the decision in 1867 that Luxembourg be deemed an independent nation with perpetual neutrality. While still a part of the Dutch house of Nassau, which had been ruled by the royal family of the Netherlands for generations, Luxembourg at that time was controlled by William III , who remained ruler until his death in 1890. At that time the grand duchy passed into the hands of Adolf, Duke of Nassau

Following the death of Adolf in 1905, his son William ruled for seven years before dying in 1912. Led by William's daughter, the Grand Duchess Marie Adélaïde, the grand duchy cooperated with the Germans in their unlawful violation of Luxembourg's neutrality during World War I (1914-1918). Disliked by her people and severely criticized by the victorious Allied Powers in 1919, Marie Adélaïde was forced to abdicate in favor of her sister Charlotte. Shortly afterward the people of Luxembourg voted to retain Charlotte as grand duchess and not to turn Luxembourg into a republic.

In the following decades, Luxembourg established and pursued an economic union with Belgium with mixed results. When the German army invaded and occupied Luxembourg again in May 1940, Grand Duchess Charlotte went into exile with her family. When Luxembourg was liberated in the late summer of 1944, Charlotte returned and the country formed an economic union with both Belgium and the Netherlands. In 1948 Luxembourg abandoned its perpetual neutrality by taking part in forming the North Atlantic Treaty Organization (NATO). Upon the death of Grand Duchess Charlotte in 1964, her son Prince Jean assumed the throne as the Grand Duke of Luxembourg.

THE FIRST IN AMERICA

The earliest Luxembourgers to emigrate to America came in 1630 with the Dutch to New York City (then New Amsterdam). The first Luxembourger is thought to be Philip de la Noye (or de Lannoy), who arrived on the ship *Fortune*, the sister-ship of the *Mayflower*. Another notable figure from the early years in of Luxembourgers in North America was Father Raphael de Luxembourg who arrived in Louisiana in 1723. Chosen by the King of France to represent the King's interests in the then French colony of Louisiana, Father Raphael also became a leading figure in the Christianization of Native Americans. Noted for his work to provide just pay for Native Americans and blacks, he founded a seminary for Native Americans and the first primary school in the colony.

The greatest influx of Luxembourgers into the United States, however, was during the mid- and late nineteenth century. Between 1841 and 1891, an estimated 45,000 Luxembourgers emigrated to the United States. In the 1830s and 1840s the Luxembourgers arrived in such areas as Maryland, New York and Louisiana. The greatest attraction of the Midwest, where most of them eventually settled, was the availability of fertile and inexpensive farmland. By the 1880s community networks among the settled Luxembourger Americans made further Luxemburger immigration easier and less costly. During this time many came on board ships of the Red Star Line, which sailed from Antwerp, Belgium.

SIGNIFICANT IMMIGRATION WAVES AND SETTLEMENT PATTERNS

The first significant wave of immigration took place between 1830 and the mid-1840s. These immigrants settled in western New York state, in towns such as Sheldon, in Wyoming County, and New

Oregon, in Erie County. Significant numbers of settlers also settled in Ohio in such places as Alvada, in Seneca County and New Riegel and Kirby, in Wyandot County.

The second important wave between 1846 and 1860 led to a great expansion in the population of Luxembourger Americans. Moving westward, they settled in Illinois. A large number settled in Chicago while smaller, yet significant, numbers settled in Rogers Park, Rosehill, Evanston, Aurora, and what is now Skokie. Further settlements were in eastern Wisconsin's Ozaukee County, including such towns as Port Washington, Belgium, Lake Church, Holy Cross, and Dacada. In the Mississippi Valley there were settlements in Winona County, Minnesota, in the towns of Elba, Rollingstone, and Oak Ridge. There were also settlements in Wabasha County, Minnesota, in such towns as Wabasha and Minnieska. In western Wisconsin settlements were made in La Crosse County in places like St. Joseph and La Crosse. In Eastern Iowa's Jackson County there were settlements in St. Donatus, Springbrook, Bellevue, and St. Catherine, and in Dubuque County settlements were made in Dubuque, Luxemburg, Holy Cross, Cascade, and Worthington.

The third major wave of immigration took place between 1860 and 1900. During the American Civil War (1861-1865) this movement slowed but slowly rose to an all-time high in the 1880s. Following the general trend of earlier settlement patterns, many of these people made their homes in the midwestern states. Those who settled in northern and southeastern Minnesota concentrated in towns like Hastings and Vermillion in Dakota County; Belchester and Luxemburg in Stearns County; and Caledonia in Houston County. Moving into South Dakota, settlers in this wave chose places like Alexandria, Hanson County, and White Lake. In western Iowa the towns of St. Joseph and Algona in Kossuth County were settled, as well as the town of Gilbertville. Moving further south and west, the settlers established the towns of Bellwood, David City, Juniata and Roseland, Nebraska. A smaller influx of Luxembourgers took place between 1937 and 1940, when 200 to 300 Luxembourger Jews fleeing Nazi persecution settled in the United States.

ACCULTURATION AND ASSIMILATION

TRADITIONS, CUSTOMS, AND BELIEFS

Like many long-settled groups in the United States, very few Luxembourger Americans can speak the language of their ancestors. Despite this, however, a considerable number still practice traditions handed down through the generations. Even though they have been interacting for over a century with German Americans, many of these people continue to identify themselves as being Luxembourger.

PROVERBS

Luxembourgers are fond of sayings that mark important moments in their history and the formation of national identity. One such saying is *Et get fir de glaf!* or "Here goes for faith," a saying that was used in the Kloppelkrieg rebellion against the French during the reign of Napoleon. This motto was used by peasants when they rose up and by their captured leaders before they were executed.

CUISINE

Among the indigenous Luxembourger foods found in Luxembourger American settlement areas, two stand out. The first is *traïpen* (*moustraipen*), a sausage consisting of hog's head, pork blood, cabbage, and spices. It is similar to black pudding. Included in a tradition in which a large meal with traïpen would be served after midnight mass on Christmas day, traïpen was a winter food, produced at a time when pigs would be butchered to be made into smoked ham and other foods. A second popular food is known as *stärzelen* (*sterchelen*), buckwheat dumplings with lard greaves.

MUSIC, DANCES, AND SONGS

A number of traditional forms of music and dance were a part of holiday celebrations. In Luxembourg, people would travel to towns such as Echternach, to take part in well-known national festivals. Although there is little information on the exact forms of dance and music carried through the generations of Luxembourger-Americans, bands with horns and tubas were likely included. In places like New York and Chicago, military bands were made up of Luxembourger-Americans whose repertoire included tunes from the homeland. Among the variety of songs brought to the United States by Luxembourgers, perhaps the most well known would have been the national song called the "Wilhelmus." Other well known Luxembourger songs included "*De Feierwon, D' Fëscher an d' Jëer,*" "*De Kueb an de Fuuss,*" "*Den Éim Steffen,*" "*De Schmatt,*" "*D' Pierle vum Da,*" "*Léiwer Härgottsblieschen,*" "*Marsch vun der Iechternacher Sprangprëssessioun,*" "*Ons Hemecht*" (the national hymn), "*Rommelpott,*" "*Schuebermëss,*" "'*Tass Fréijor,*" and "*Wéi meng*

Mamm nach huet gesponnen." For more information on the dance of Echternach one can check the website http://www.restena.lu/primaire/consdorf/luxmidi/luxmidi.html. Songs and audio can be found at http://www.restena.lu/primaire/consdorf/luxmidi/luxmidi.html.

HOLIDAYS

In Luxembourg, around sunset on the first Sunday of Lent, fires are lit in every community. This tradition, called *Burgbrennen,* is one of the four times of the year when such fires are lit. The other times are Easter, the summer solstice, and in the late fall. According to the popular "solar theory" of such festivals found throughout Europe and elsewhere, it is thought that the fires are in some sense a magical imitation of the sun. These fires are lit in the hopes that its imitation might make the sun cooperate in the coming months. Besides the desire for practical results, a strong element of revelry and excess is also displayed at such festivals. A great sacrifice to the spirits of the dead, ancestors, and nature is symbolized in the massive destruction of such bonfires. Often accompanied by feasting and carnivalesque behavior, these bonfires are important elements in communal sentiment and the preservation of tradition.

Burgbrennen began with a form of trick-or-treat. Village youngsters go from house to house begging for wood and kindling for the fire. Carrying these materials up the hill to the site of the fire, the boys hold the stack of wood and kindling while a large pole with a wooden cross is hoisted and planted into the ground. As the cross is secured, the youngsters heap the combustible material around the pole, and it is set ablaze by the man to last marry in the village. Other variations of this ritual involved affixing a large wheel and streamers to the top of the pole, which would in turn be set ablaze and spun.

Burgbrennen has not remained a strong custom among Luxembourger Americans. While many communities in the United States have retained bonfire-like festivals, usually in the late fall, the tradition of fires at Lent seems to have greatly faded. In Vermillion, Minnesota, however, memories remain of its existence earlier in this century. One account was told by a village elder: "*Bjork Sonntag* was the First Sunday of Lent and the last day of drinking alcohol during Lent. They had a very unusual custom in this area during the evening of *Bjork Sonntag.* Many of the farmers would erect a pole on the highest point of the farm, put rags on top of the pole or put a wheel on top of the pole and cover that with old rags, pour oil on the rags and start the rags/wheel and pole on fire. As to the reason for the fire on *Bjork Sonntag*, at this time I cannot find out. The people who remember these fires, just remember that this was a custom from the old county that their grandfathers and fathers took part in."

In late August and early September of every year there is a festival called the *Schueberfouer*, or "Shepherd's Fair." This festival was founded by then ruler John the Blind in 1340. Lasting 18 days (except every fifth year when it lasts 25 days), the *Schueberfouer* began as a livestock fair. In addition to livestock and pottery, cloth and woolen articles were also displayed and sold. Craftsmen and weavers were originally the organizers and directors of the fair, giving way to a broader sponsorship and direction in the late eighteenth century. Traditionally, each Schueberfouer began with the marching of a flock of sheep called the *Hämmelsmarsch*. A shepherd and his sheep were followed by a band playing the Hämmelsmarsch tune. During this procession a door to door collection was made. The origin of the tune for the Hämmelsmarsch is unknown. It is known, however, that the carillon of the cathedral was said to have played it in the eighteenth century. The Schueberfouer was brought to the United States by Luxembourgers in the nineteenth century.

There is a noted observance of the Schueberfouer near the end of the Civil War. An immigrant publication named the *Luxemburger Gazette*, published on September 20, 1917, reported that there had been a northern army military unit founded in 1865 in the Williamsburg area of Brooklyn, New York, which was referred to as the *Lëtzebörger Gard*. When the 80 members of this unit met for a reunion after the war, they decided to organize a yearly gathering on the first Monday of September and to organize this event as a Schueberfouer as they had known it in Luxembourg. This event, like the festival in the old country, included a parade, games, dance, and target shooting.

As a result of this reunion and annual *Schueberfouers*, a united group of Luxembourger-Americans was formed. By 1871 this veterans' group had grown and changed into a new organization called the "Luxembourger Mutual Aid Society." The growth of this organization was not, however, unique among Luxembourger Americans across the country. Several organizations grew out of organized *Schueberfouers*, in this way, including Chicago's "Luxembourger Brotherhood of America," which was founded on the occasion of its annual *Schueberfouer* in 1904. Despite the growth of *Schueberfouers* and similar organizations, the twentieth century has seen a gradual decline in their presence in traditionally Luxembourger communities, including Chicago, Rollingstone, Minnesota, and Remsen, Iowa.

Among Luxembourger-Americans Santa Claus is not a Christmas figure. Rather, a special day was marked early in December to celebrate a "St. Nicholas Day." It is the custom one week before this day for children to put their slippers in front of their bedroom doors so that they might be filled with a small gift by St. Nicholas while they slept. On the eve of December 6 it is also a tradition for children to place plates on dining room or kitchen tables to be filled overnight with sweets and gifts from St. Nicholas.

Many Luxembourger-Americans continue to follow Christmas traditions handed down from the old country. Many celebrate Christmas Eve with family and friends after attending midnight mass. It is not uncommon for local clubs and association to organize nativity plays with children as actors and to arrange concerts to be given later on Christmas day. Many families of Luxembourger descent today also include traditions from the more mainstream Anglo- and German-American cultures.

LANGUAGE

The native language of the majority of Luxembourgers is *Letzebuergesch* or *Luxembourgisch*. This language descends from a Frankish dialect spoken by people who moved into this area between the fourth and sixth centuries A.D. The closest relatives to this language are Flemish, Dutch, and the Plattdeutsch dialects still spoken Germany's Rhineland. Only a few words derive from Celtic tongues exist in Letzebuergesch today. Perhaps the most important retention of Celtic influences are those in the very name of the country and language itself. The presence of French words and phrases is evident in the modern usage of *Letzebuergesch*, yet French has not had the influence on this language that might have been expected over so many years. Since the year 1830 the two legal languages of Luxembourg have been German and French. It was not until 1984 that Letzebuergesch was actually named the official language of the country. Very little Letzebuergesch has ever been taught in schools, as the language has been mainly learned at home. Although German has been a more popular language within the media, a great many Luxembourgers are wholly conversant in French as well.

GREETINGS AND POPULAR EXPRESSIONS

In Luxembourgisch the following are equivalent expressions used in daily life: "Good morning/hello" is *Moien*; "Goodbye" is *Äddi* or *a'voir*; "Thank you (very much)" is *Merci* (*villmols*);

"Sorry" is "Pardon;" "Excuse me" is *Entschëllegt*; and "Please" is *Wannechglift*. The national motto, found everywhere in Luxembourg, is *Mir Wöelle Bleiwe Wat Mir Sin*, or "We want to remain what we are."

FAMILY AND COMMUNITY DYNAMICS

In Luxembourger communities of the Midwest, people interacted with one another in several ways. The first was the sharing of farm work. Luxembourger immigrants who were farmers often came to possess land in America ten times or more in size than that of their forebears in the old country. So much land created a great need to organize labor at crucial times of the planting, growing and harvesting seasons. In these crucial times farmers of an area would band together to share in each others' labor. It was thought of as one's responsibility not only to one's neighbor, but to one's family, to offer aid and participate in such communal work. These times of year would provide opportunities for people to come together and share their lives, often holding feasts, dances and other events when the seasonal work was finished. The second important factor in family and community dynamics was the church. Whether providing a time for meeting or providing religious services, the local parish was the focus of community pride. The third major factor was the everyday socializing that took place in towns and farm communities. Among these activities were card playing and quilt making. In town during the summer, people would also go for walks and visit neighbors, often inspecting each other's gardens and discussing their growth, variety, and arrangements.

EDUCATION

In many settlement towns, Luxembourger American education went hand-in-hand with religion. Many of the schools were Catholic and largely staffed by priests, nuns, and lay persons of the Catholic faith. Thus religious and academic instruction were given together, with moral education having great priority. Lessons related to the Catholic rite of catechism were always a part of the school curricula. In the country far from towns, Luxembourger American immigrants often had a one-room schoolhouse education not affiliated with the Catholic church. Despite their isolation from Catholic school instruction in towns, many children were sent to towns to receive weeks of religious education to prepare them for the rite of confirmation or to receive first communion. In some towns

there also were literary societies that aided in the advancement of education within their communities by raising funds and establishing libraries.

THE ROLE OF WOMEN

The role of women among Luxembourger immigrants was varied. In towns, women worked in shops and other businesses, raised families, and did the great share of domestic chores. They also took part in church activities involving education, community awareness, and minor fundraising for projects. In the country, women were responsible for much of the overall work of the business of the farms, often relying on one another for mutual support in the tasks of child-raising, health care, education, and household economizing.

COURTSHIP AND WEDDINGS

In Luxembourger American communities, there were many opportunities for courtship between persons of all ages. Going to church, dances, and school and community events provided a means for socializing. Most persons were allowed to choose whom they wished to court or be courted by, although issues of class, ethnicity and faith often acted as barriers to courting outside of one's own group as defined by parents or other family members.

Marriages are traditionally performed along with a Catholic mass. After the marriage a great feast is held, sometimes lasting days, during which gifts are given, traditional dishes are served, songs are sung, and games are played.

FUNERALS

The rites of funerals in Luxembourger American communities are detailed and depend upon many circumstances, including family choice. Luxembourger Americans have changed many of the nineteenth-century customs that followed them from the old country. All funerals, however did share and continue to share common symbolic meanings of the Catholic faith. The funeral is a time for the affirmation of one's own faith and a time to pray for the Christian salvation of the deceased.

INTERACTIONS WITH OTHER ETHNIC GROUPS

In Luxembourger-American communities, there has traditionally been a close alliance and kinship of custom with German-Americans. Many Luxembourgers spoke German and shared many customs, songs, cuisine and morals with Germans. Although this helped forge a bond between the two groups, religious differences between many Protestant Germans and Catholic Luxembourgers could still result in friction. Politics from the homeland also came to influence relations between older Luxembourgers and Germans as seen in the many anti-Prussian sentiments expressed by this group around the turn of the twentieth century, in places like Chicago, Milwaukee, and New York City. In time, however, German and Luxembougian-Americans overcame most of their differences in opinion and have since assimilated to a much greater degree. In relation to other groups Luxembourgers living in towns were often taken for Germans and were sometimes embroiled in anti-German sentiments that arose during World War I.

RELIGION

Throughout their history, the vast majority of Luxembourgers and Luxembourger-Americans have been Catholic. The country of Luxembourg is covered by one diocese that contains 13 deaneries and 265 parishes in total. Luxembourg has also traditionally been the home of a great number of convents and religious orders, a number that has dwindled since the last century. A small number of Protestants and Jews have also been active for centuries in Luxembourg.

Among Luxembourger-Americans, Catholic churches have served important roles in preserving their heritage. As is common with many immigrant groups, religious practices maintain certain continuities and ties to the homeland. In the beginning of their settlement in the midwestern states there were very few, if any, established churches or assigned priests to minister to the settlers. The building of a church or the establishment of membership to one nearby was often a top priority. Often many of the community's resources went into the establishment of such local religious institutions. In the year 1877, 92 priests of Luxembourg extraction were ministering to these communities.

A great of number of saints popularly venerated in Luxembourg also serve as patron saints of churches in those areas settled by Luxembourger immigrants. In Jackson County, Iowa, for example, one finds a parish dedicated to St. Donatas, the martyr who is thought to protect against storms and lightning, two threats to farmers. Another example is St. Henry's parish, founded in the Luxembourger settlement area north of Chicago and named after a saint who was closely related to Siegfried, the first count of Luxembourg. Symbols of Luxembourg, including the Luxembourg crest, are often found in such shrines dedicated to Luxembourger saints.

Among the many traditions that center on the church, perhaps the most prominent is the one called the *Kiirmes*. This term, which is a contraction of the words *kirch* (church) and *messe* (mass) signifies the mass that is performed when a church is consecrated This celebration traditionally took place on the Sunday following the feast day of the patron saint of the consecrated church. The more secular aspects of this event and celebration in Luxembourger culture involved the gathering of families during the anniversaries of such church consecration masses. At such times, usually between April and November, and most in late fall, very special meals were prepared, and the celebration would last for days.

In America Kiirmes took a different form. It was not the consecration of their own churches that was celebrated, but rather the day in which Kiirmes had been celebrated in the village in Luxembourg from which they came. Kiirmes was, then, an occasion for reunions of families and old country family friends. As those born in Luxembourg grew older and died, this tradition faded, along with the memories of ancestral villages and parishes from where they came.

POLITICS AND GOVERNMENT

Luxembourger-Americans did not shy away from politics or government in their new home. Many were active proponents of political causes and a several held elected and non-elected positions in public service. Among their group's notable political sentiments was anti-Prussianism, a position that reflected both concerns with the government of the Luxembourg and Luxembourgers' place in relation to German-Americans in many parts of the United States. Another notable moment in Luxembourger-American political history occurred when the United Staes entered the war against Germany in 1914. At this time Luxembourger-Americans came out in numbers strongly for the United States effort and against Germany.

MILITARY

One example of a Luxembourger who found success through the military was Dominik Welter. At the age of 11, Welter came from Luxembourg to settle with his family in Ohio. As a young man Welter struck out and traveled west to seek a fortune in the Gold Rush but eventually returned to his family in

Ohio without having had success. In 1861, at the advent of the Civil War, Welter joined the Fourth Ohio Cavalry and worked his way up the ranks to become a captain. Captured at the battle of Chickamunga, he was detained in a prisoner of war camp until the war's end in 1865. After the war in 1877, still a member of the army he traveled to Chicago were he was given the command of a cavalry unit. After resigning from the army Welter was hired as Secretary of Police for Chicago and given the rank of inspector. In the following years he, along with a fellow Luxembourger named Michael Schaack, were the leaders of a political and social organization named the Luxembourg Independent Club of Chicago.

RELATIONS WITH LUXEMBOURG

Throughout the nineteenth century contacts between the Luxembourgers in the United States and in Luxembourg were maintained in various ways. It was not uncommon for visitors from either land to stay awhile and work, often to return with news from either side of the Atlantic. These visitors, some from one's extended family, were not the only conduits on information, however. The Catholic church itself provided many forms of exchange between the two countries as well. It was not uncommon for Luxembourg bishops to keep contact with their emigrated countrymen. One bishop named Koppes made two trips from Luxembourg to America, one in 1901 and one in 1910. Much later, in 1965, another bishop named Lommel is noted for having made a trip to America to invite Luxembourger-Americans to the bicentennial of the Marial festivities in Luxembourg. Another bishop, Jean Hengen, made a trip to Carey, Ohio, in 1975 to participate in the centennial celebration in honor of the founding of the pilgrimage to that community's Our Lady of Consolation shrine.

The importation and circulation of religious objects and figures have also helped to maintain contacts. For example, a church in St. Donatus, Iowa, received a pieta sculpture of Luxembourg artist Victor Thibeau for its pietal chapel. Another of Thibeau's creations was also donated to a church in Schewebsange, Luxembourg.

In addition to these religious and artistic realms, several organizations are dedicated to issues concerning Luxembourger-Americans, including the Luxembourg Jewish Society, begun in 1958 in New York, the Luxembourg-American Social Club established in Chicago in 1960, and the American Luxembourg Society, founded in 1963.

INDIVIDUAL AND GROUP CONTRIBUTIONS

While Luxembourger Americans have been a relatively small group in population with only some 50,000 total immigrants, they have made a great many contributions to American society.

ACADEMIA

Eduard Conzemius gained acclaim in the earlier part of this century as one of the foremost ethnographers of Central American peoples. Emigrating from Luxembourg to the United States to join his brother, Conzemius moved to Chicago and was first employed by the Sherman House Hotel. In the following years he studied English and Spanish while making money as an accountant in Chicago and New Orleans. In 1916 he decided to pursue his dream to study Central American Indians. Leaving the US, he spent time in Honduras and Nicaragua living with the Miskito, Sumu and Rama Indians. In 1932 the Smithsonian Institution published the results of his work on the native languages of these people in a monograph entitled *Ethnological Survey of the Miskito and Sumu Indians of Honduras and Nicaragua.*

ART

Jean Noerdinger, a prominent modernist artist and proponent of modernism emigrated from Diekirch, Luxembourg to the Chicago area in 1925. While in Luxembourg, Noerdinger had been an outspoken critic of the Luxemburg Artists Union, whose power in support of conservative art he opposed, along with a group of artists he led. While in America he continued to exhibit his art and paint portraits.

FILM, TELEVISION, AND THEATER

Perhaps the greatest star of Luxembourger-American descent was the actress Loretta Young. Born in Salt Lake City, Utah, in January 1913, Young received her first part when she was four through her uncle, who was working as an assistant director in Hollywood. In 1927 she had another small part in the film *Naughty, But Nice.* From this point into the early thirties, Young was acting in six to nine films each year. In the mid-1930s Young joined the Fox studios and by then had become one of Hollywood's most prominent leading ladies. In 1947 she was awarded the Academy Award for best actress in *The Farmer's Daughter*, a film about a girl from a rural area who works her way into the U.S. House of Representatives as a congresswoman. In 1949 she was nominated again for an Academy Award. In 1953 Young began her television career with her series *The Loretta Young Show.* This show gained Young Emmy Awards in 1954, 1956, and 1958. After 1962 Young did not appear before the camera until 1986, when she starred in a made-for-television film called *Lady in the Corner.* In 1996 she was retired and living happily in Palm Springs, California.

JOURNALISM

Nicholas Gonner is chiefly known as the author of an authoritative study of the emigration of Luxembourgers into the New World entitled *Die Luxemburger in der neuen Welt: Beiträge zur Geschichte der Luxemburger* (Luxembourgers in the New World: Contributions to the History of the Luxembourgers). This work was written for and published by the *Luxembourger Gazette,* published in Dubuque, Iowa, in 1889 and was meant to be not only a chronicle of Luxembourger success in the New World, but also to be read in Europe as a testament to the success in "the land of opportunity," as the United States imagined itself.

LITERATURE AND MUSIC

Although Luxembourg itself has been home to a great many writers in French, Luxembourgisch and German, Luxembourger-Americans have yet to make conspicuous inroads into American literature.

SCIENCE AND TECHNOLOGY

Among prominent scientists of Luxembourger descent are Johann and Joseph Druecker, two brothers from Ozaukee County, Wisconsin. In 1884, the Drueckers invented a gas lime-kiln that greatly improved their own business and the lime industry overall. Also notable is biologist Francois Mergen.

SOCIAL ISSUES

The first Luxembourger-American to serve in the United States Congress was Nicholas Muller. Born in Luxembourg on November 15, 1836, he attended common schools in the city of Metz and thereafter attended the Luxembourg Athenaeum. Upon immigrating to the United States, the family settled in New York City. Muller was employed as a railroad ticket agent for over 20 years, during which time he was one of the promoters and directors of the Germania Bank in New York. From 1875 to 1876 Muller served as a member of the State Assembly of New York and was also a member of the State Cen-

tral Committee. In 1876 Muller was elected as a Democrat to the Forty-fifth and then re-elected to the Forty-sixth Congress, serving from March 4, 1877, to March 3, 1881. Losing his seat after an unsuccessful re-election bid in late 1880, Muller regained it in 1882, serving another five years until 1887. In 1888, Muller was appointed president of the New York City Police Board and to one other minor office until he was again elected to the U.S. Congress, where he served until his resignation on December 1, 1902. After holding and attempting to hold other minor offices, Muller died in New York City, December 12, 1917.

Another addition to the history of Luxembourger-Americans was the thirty-second President of the United States, Franklin Delano Roosevelt. Roosevelt is said to be descendant of Philip de la Noye (or de Lannoy), who arrived on the ship *Fortune.* De la Noye is thought to be the first Luxembourger to emigrate to North America. Roosevelt was born on January 30, 1882, in Hyde Park, New York, and served as President from 1933 until his death on April 12, 1945.

SPORTS

Perhaps the most famous athlete of Luxembourger-American descent is tennis star Chris Evert. Born in Fort Lauderdale, Florida, on December 21, 1954, Evert came to dominate the sport of tennis throughout the late 1970s and early 1980s and continued to win many important matches into the late 1980s. In 1970, at the age of 15, Evert made her first mark in an important match, beating top-ranked Margaret Court in a small tournament. Having become a professional on her eighteenth birthday in 1972, by the time of her retirement in the late 1980s she had earned nearly $9,000,000. Evert won the U.S. Open women's singles title from 1975-1978, as well in the years 1980 and 1982. She won the Wimbledon singles title in 1974, 1976, and 1981, the French Open singles title in 1974, 1975, 1979, 1980, 1983, 1985, and 1986, and the Australian Open singles title in 1982 and 1984. Her World Tennis Association singles titles number 157. In 1995 Evert was inducted into the International Tennis Hall of Fame. In 1985, she was named Greatest Woman Athlete of the last 25 years by the Women's Sports Foundation.

VISUAL ARTS

Edward Steichen, one of the most prominent American figures in the art of photography, was born in Luxembourg on March 27, 1879. In 1882 his parents moved from Luxembourg to settle in Hancock,

Michigan. By the age of 21, Steichen had achieved a moderate degree of success as a photographer, having had his pictures shown in Chicago and Philadelphia. His photographs portrayed a distinctive soft and fuzzy quality. In his day these photographs were considered highly innovative. In the following decades, Steichen became one of the most sought after and lauded photographers in the United States, showing his photos in many of the major shows of this era. During his service in the First World War Steichen's artistic philosophy and direction changed profoundly. Returning home after the war, he loudly proclaimed his rejection of impressionism and the other elements of style he had made famous and strongly supported a stark form of realism. Steichen then burned all his paintings in a bonfire and took up commercial photography in a studio that he operated from 1923 to 1938. During this time he photographed literary and artistic personalities as well as members of the elite of New York City, and he became the chief photographer for *Vanity Fair* and *Vogue* magazines. With the outbreak of World War II, Steichen, then 62 years of age, was commissioned by the U.S. Navy to photograph the war at sea. During and after the war Steichen continued to have major shows and became the director of photography at the Museum of Modern Art in 1947, a post that he held until 1962. He worked until his death on March 25, 1973.

MEDIA

PRINT

Luxembourg News of America.

This monthly publication is meant to serve as a medium of communication for Luxembourgers living in the United States and also for their descendants and friends. It contains news of Luxembourg societies and anything of interest in the Grand Duchy of Luxembourg.

Address: 496 North Northwest Highway, Park Ridge, Illinois 60629.
Telephone: (312) 394-8253.

Although there are no other well known papers, or radio or television programs that address Luxembourger-American cultural issues today, the various organizations and associations that concern themselves with Luxembourger-American issues have a wealth of printed and printable, audio and visual materials, accessible by phone, fax or the internet.

INTERNET

Both of the following sites contain many helpful links to more information about Luxembourger American culture and heritage.

Michaelus Luxembourg Links.
Online: http://artmichaelis.com/links/luxlinks.html.

Luxembourg Connections.
Shelby County, Iowa, Genealogy.

Online: http://www.rootsweb.com/~iashelby/lux.htm.

MUSEUMS AND RESEARCH CENTERS

Stearns History Museum.
Address: 235 33rd Avenue South, St. Cloud, Minnesota 56301.
Telephone: (320) 253-8424.
Fax: (320) 253-2172.
E-mail: info@stearns-museum.org.
Online: http://www.stearns-museum.org.

SOURCES FOR ADDITIONAL STUDY

American Luxembourg Society 1882-1982. Luxembourg: Imprimerie Saint-Paul, 1991.

Klein, Frank W., and Suzanne L. Bunkers *Good Earth, Black Soil.* Winona, MN: Saint Mary's College Press, 1981.

Lies, Joseph J. *Luxemburger Immigrants to Aurora.* Aurora, IL: Aurora Historical Society, 1976.

Nilles, Mary E. Dann. *Singen Wir' Victoria! Luxemburger Immigration to America. 1848-1872: A Selective Bibliography.* Brussels: Center for American Studies, 1979.

———. *Rollingstone. A Luxembourgisch Village in Minnesota.* Luxembourg: Editions Guy Binsfeld, 1983.

MACEDONIAN AMERICANS

by
Elizabeth Shostak

Easter is the greatest holiday in the Eastern Orthodox Church, and Macedonians in the United States continue to observe it seriously. Easter is celebrated two weeks after the Roman Catholic Easter, in accordance with the Eastern Orthodox Church's adherence to the Gregorian calendar.

OVERVIEW

The Republic of Macedonia is a country slightly larger than the state of Vermont and measures 25,333 square kilometers. Located on the Balkan Peninsula in southeastern Europe, Macedonia is bordered on the north by Yugoslavia, on the south by Greece, on the west by Bulgaria, and on the east by Albania. It is a landlocked and mountainous country, and only about four percent of its land is suitable for crops. The region experiences a high rate of seismic activity, making it susceptible to earthquake damage. It has few natural resources other than mineral deposits. Macedonians have traditionally made their living from farming, herding, and mining.

Macedonia's population is estimated at approximately 2,194,000 and is comprised of a mix of ethnic groups. Sixty-seven percent are identified as ethnic Macedonians. Albanians make up the largest minority, with 21 percent of the population, and small Turkish and Serbian populations are also represented. The majority of Macedonians, 59 percent, belong to the Eastern Orthodox Church, while 26 percent are Muslims. Small Catholic, Protestant, and Jewish communities are also present. Eight languages are spoken in Macedonia. The official language, Macedonian, is spoken by 70 percent of the population. Twenty-one percent speak Albanian, three percent speak Turkish, and three percent speak Serbo-Croatian. Smaller numbers speak

Adyghe, Romanian, Romani, and Balakan Gagauz Turkish. The capital of Macedonia is Skopje (SKOHP-yeh). The Macedonian flag consists of a 16-point gold sun centered on a red field.

HISTORY

The Republic of Macedonia was created in 1991 when the country obtained independence from Yugoslavia. But Macedonian history is long and complex. The Macedonians are a Slavic people, with close ethnic and linguistic ties to Bulgaria, as well as political and church ties to Greece. The earliest civilizations in the Macedonian region have been traced back to at least 3500 B.C., and by about 1000 B.C., several population groups, including Dacians, Thracians, Illyrians, Celts, and Greeks, coexisted in the area. Macedonia had perhaps its greatest period of political power during the fourth century B.C., when King Philip of Macedon and his son, Alexander the Great, strengthened and expanded the Macedonian empire. By 29 A.D., however, Rome had subdued the region and ruled it for several centuries. The Romans incorporated Macedonia into their Eastern Empire, controlled by Constantinople. Beginning in the third century A.D., tribes of Goths, Huns, and Avars invaded the region. By about the middle of the sixth century, Slavic peoples began to settle in Macedonia. A century later, Bulgars, a Turco-Ugrian people of remote Mongolian origin, invaded and were assimilated by the Slavs. The Bulgars established the First Bulgarian Kingdom, which included much of Macedonia's territory. During the ninth century A.D., future saints Cyril and Methodius brought Christianity to the region. Their disciples devised a Slavic alphabet (the Cyrillic alphabet that is also used in Russian) in order to promote literacy in the vernacular.

In the tenth century, the Bulgarian Kingdom split into two. The western kingdom, with its capital in Ohrid, is considered the first Slavic Macedonian state. It was ruled by Tsar Samuil (997-1014) but was conquered by the Byzantine Empire in 1018. Except for a brief period of Serbian control under Stefan Dusan (1331-55), Macedonia remained under Ottoman rule until 1912. This long period of Turkish control was considered the most stable in Macedonian history, and deeply influenced language and social traditions throughout the Balkan region. At the same time, however, Ottoman rule was harsh and authoritarian, and fueled increasing dissent from the subjected population. In 1876, the Bulgarians staged an armed revolt against the Turks, which was brutally subdued and resulted in an indiscriminate massacre of civilians. From that time, intense anti-Turkish sentiment continued, and the region became increasingly destabilized.

MODERN ERA

The early twentieth century was a period of intense conflict and volatility throughout the Balkans as various states competed for power. When the Ottoman Empire began to dissolve at the end of the nineteenth century, Serbia, Greece, and Bulgaria all sought cultural and territorial claims over Macedonia. In response to these threats, Macedonians organized the Internal Macedonian Revolutionary Organization (IMRO) in 1893. IMRO's aim was to preserve "Macedonia for the Macedonians," and on August 2, 1903, it proclaimed independence from the Turks. Though this rebellion was harshly suppressed, it made the "Macedonian Question" an international concern for several years. In 1912, Serbia, Montenegro, Greece, and Bulgaria successfully united in the First Balkan War to eject the Turks from Europe, after which the competing states sought to strengthen their claims to Macedonia. The Serbian army occupied Skopje and claimed "Vardar Macedonia" as a Serbian colony. The Greek army occupied Salonika, which it deemed part of "Aegean Macedonia," virtually excluding Bulgaria from the region. The occupying forces instituted harsh campaigns to force the population to renounce its Macedonian identity. They encouraged Serbian and Greek colonists to move to these regions, suppressed the Macedonian language, and forced priests to convert to the Greek or Serbian Orthodox religions.

Bulgaria's loss of Macedonia precipitated decades of conflict and violence, which arguably contributed to the ethnic hostilities that resurfaced in the Balkans during the 1990s. After a surprise attack on Serbian forces in Macedonia in 1913, which initiated the Second Balkan War, Bulgaria was again defeated and stripped of its claims to Macedonian territory. Despite alliances with Germany in both the First and Second World Wars, during which Macedonia suffered brutal invasions and "Bulgarization" campaigns, Bulgaria was unable to reestablish its hold on Macedonia. In 1945, the new Federal Socialist Republic of Yugoslavia, controlled by a Communist party actively sympathetic to the Macedonian cause, created a People's Republic of Macedonia. This region, which incorporated the boundaries of the later independent republic, was a semi-autonomous constituent republic within the Yugoslav federation. The Communist party encouraged the renewal of Macedonian cultural life, promoting the Macedonian language and restoring the Macedonian Orthodox Church.

After the Yugoslav federation broke up in 1989, Macedonia declared independence on November 20, 1991. A new constitution went into effect that day, and Kiro Gligorov was elected president. Ethnic and political discord, however, remained. Greece, which has a province called Macedonia in its northern region, objected to the country's use of that name. Bulgaria, which has a significant Macedonian minority population, has also historically objected to the idea of an independent Macedonian nation.

THE FIRST MACEDONIANS IN AMERICA

Although Macedonian immigration to the United States did not truly begin until the early twentieth century, there is evidence to suggest that the first Macedonian to arrive in America, Dragan of Ohrid, sailed with Christopher Columbus. There are different accounts of Dragan. One story claims he was a religious heretic who escaped persecution in Macedonia by fleeing to Spain. He was later discovered, however, and condemned to death. Columbus saved Dragan from burning at the stake by recruiting him for his first trip to America. Another account claims that Dragan was expelled from Ohrid with his family when he was a child, after the city fell to the Turks. The family moved to Spain, where Dragan advanced in the military, became a favorite of the crown, and sailed with Columbus on his second voyage. According to this story, after Dragan returned to Europe he formed his own expedition and sailed with this crew to Venezuela. Seeing that the native people there lived along the water in marshy areas, as in Venice, he bestowed the name "Venezia" on the land. He then went to Panama, allegedly becoming the first white man to set foot in that country.

SIGNIFICANT IMMIGRATION WAVES

Macedonian immigration to the United States began in the early twentieth century, as poverty forced many peasants to seek economic opportunities abroad. Most of these early immigrants considered themselves Bulgarians from Macedonia, and entry records from the period usually listed them as Bulgarian, Turkish, Serbian, Albanian, or Greek nationals. For this reason, it is difficult to determine precise numbers of Macedonian immigrants. It is estimated, however, that between 1903 and 1906, approximately 50,000 Macedonian Bulgarians entered the United States. From 1906 to the outbreak of the Balkan Wars and World War I, a few thousand more arrived. The first Macedonian immigrants came primarily from the western parts of Macedonia, near the towns of Kastoria, Florina, and Bitola. About 80 percent of these immigrants were peasants, with small craftsmen, workers, and intellectuals making up the remainder. The vast majority of early Macedonian immigrants were *gurbetchii* or *pechalbari*, single men driven by poverty to seek their fortunes in America, but who expected to return to their homeland after a few years.

American Protestant churches played a notable role in Macedonian immigration. Congregational and Methodist churches began missionary activities in the Balkans in the 1860s and 1870s, and sent many Bulgarians and Macedonians to the United States to attend college. When these individuals returned, they spoke highly of their experiences in America. In addition, the churches established numerous schools in Balkan cities and towns. These activities created a positive image of America and prompted interest in immigration.

After World War I, many Macedonians in America returned to Europe, with only about 20,000 Macedonians remaining in the United States. Further immigration was seriously affected by passage of the Immigration Act of 1924 (the Johnson-Reed Act), which established quotas for each national group based on their numbers in the American population in 1920. Because Macedonian immigration had begun so late, and because many immigrants had returned to their homeland, the basis for the Macedonian quota was extremely low. Nevertheless, though new immigration was much slower during the period between the world wars, Macedonians continued to enter the United States. Many arrived via Canada, crossing the border into Detroit to evade quota restrictions. During this period, increasing numbers of Macedonians also arrived from Greece. By 1945, the number of Macedonians in the United States had reached an estimated 50,000 to 60,000 people.

When the Yugoslav Federation was created after World War II, however, Macedonian immigration slowed significantly. Yugoslavia's support of Macedonian autonomy, as well as economic improvements in Macedonia, encouraged Macedonians to remain there. From 1945 to 1960, only about 2,000 Macedonians arrived in the United States from Yugoslavia. During the 1960s and 1970s, however, after emigration policies were liberalized, as many as 40,000 Macedonians left Yugoslavia for Canada, Australia, and the United States. Few from Bulgaria, however, were allowed to leave. As many as 70,000 Macedonians living in Greece left that country after World War II, when Slavs were expelled from the area. Many settled in Canada, where the Macedonian community in

Toronto grew to more than 100,000. Smaller numbers moved to Australia and the United States.

During the 1990s, Macedonian immigration again increased. Newcomers followed the same settlement patterns of earlier immigrants, settling in large urban centers in the Midwest. Like earlier generations, most came to take advantage of economic opportunities. Others entered the United States to enroll in colleges and universities. The 1990 U.S. census listed the number of Macedonian Americans as 20,365 but that figure almost certainly under represents the actual population.

SETTLEMENT PATTERNS

Though a small proportion of Macedonians who came to the United States from Yugoslavia in the 1950s and 1960s were political dissidents, the majority of Macedonian immigrants were compelled by economic motives. Early Macedonian immigrants from Bulgaria settled in America's northern and eastern industrial centers, especially in the Midwest, where they were able to find unskilled jobs in heavy industries. A large community sprang up in Detroit, which numbered from as many as 15,000 to 20,000 Macedonian Americans by the 1980s. Macedonians also settled in large numbers in Gary, Indiana, Chicago, Illinois, and the Ohio cities of Columbus, Akron, Lorain, Cincinnati, Canton, and Massilon. Other communities were established in Passaic, New Jersey and in New York City, Lackawanna, Buffalo, Rochester, and Syracuse, New York.

Adjusting to industrial jobs and a competitive economic setting was often difficult for Macedonian immigrants, who had come from relatively poor rural areas dominated by an authoritative political regime. Upon their arrival in the United States, they often took hazardous jobs in mines, steel mills and foundries, and railroad construction. Since most immigrants were single men, residents from the same village or region in their homeland tended to stay together in America for social support. Coffee houses and boarding houses became important places where immigrants could socialize and share job prospects, read newspapers and discuss politics, and participate in their associations. Where Macedonians were few in number, they often associated with other Slavic or Orthodox communities.

Macedonian immigrants established fraternal, mutual aid, and cultural societies in America that offered assistance when members lost their jobs or became ill. These societies were organized according to place of origin, and often sent material aid back to their respective villages in Macedonia. The Orthodox Church also served as an important cohesive presence.

ACCULTURATION AND ASSIMILATION

The first Macedonian immigrants endured poverty and harsh working conditions when they first arrived in the United States. Many received daily wages below $2.50, and lived in crowded and unhealthy conditions in large cities. It was customary for several men from the same village in Macedonia to share a small flat or house, often without running water and electricity. Space was so limited that the men had to sleep in shifts, sharing the same bedding. Most lived extremely frugally, reluctant to spend their hard-earned money on anything except the most basic necessities so that they could more quickly save enough to return to their homeland. Though many did eventually return, a large number eagerly embraced Americanization. Some Anglicized their surnames and severed all ties with Macedonia. Others, however, developed identities tied to both their new American homes and their native traditions.

Much about American life was exciting or even shocking to Macedonian immigrants, who had come from a very isolated and impoverished area. Electricity, telephones, and other modern inventions amazed them. However, the large buildings, crowded conditions, pollution, and frantic pace of industrialized cities often demoralized them. In his memoir, *The Eagle and the Stork: An American Memoir,* Macedonian immigrant Stoyan Christowe described the profound disappointment and alienation his uncle and his father found in the factory work and anonymity of the city: "My uncle was here only with his body. His mind, his heart, his whole being were back in the homeland where life had meaning for him, where life was rooted in decency and dignity. The man he worked for there was his host and not his boss. That was because he was building him a house to live in, or a barrel to keep his wine in, or a wedding chest for his daughter. He could sit down with him for a glass of brandy or a cup of Turkish coffee. This America was boring into his life like a worm into the core of an apple, hollowing out the soundness, the meaning."

For other immigrants, however, American offered opportunities they were eager to exploit. Christowe himself avidly learned English and sought an education, and others were able to establish themselves in better-paying jobs as they increased their job skills and experience. Younger generations of Macedonian Americans have become fully integrated into the mainstream American culture.

TRADITIONS, CUSTOMS, AND BELIEFS

Many Macedonian customs and traditions were associated with religious holidays, pre-Christian beliefs, or were tied to the agricultural cycle. Making and jumping over bonfires, a practice that probably originated in pagan times, was often incorporated into the celebration of Christian holidays. On festive occasions throughout the year, villagers would visit their neighbors to wish them good luck, health, and prosperity. On the Eve of St. John (midsummer's day), it was customary to tell omens. Bulgarian and Macedonian housewives observed several customs to ensure prosperity and to keep their homes free of dangers. For example, they used cakes to rid their homes of evil spirits. On Mice Day, October 27, they would spread mud over the threshold and hearth to "muddle over" the mice's eyes, preventing them from seeing food stored in the house. During Wolf Days in November, women would tie their scissors shut to keep wolves from opening their mouths and would refuse to sew any clothes for their husbands to keep them from turning into werewolves. On November 30, St. Andrew's Day, women cooked wheat, lentils, and beans to keep bears away.

CUISINE

Traditional Macedonian foods reflect both the region's indigenous crops and its ethnically mixed history. Ingredients such as feta cheese, yogurt, peppers, cucumbers, tomatoes, and eggplant are commonly used. Food is often flavored with paprika, lemon juice, garlic, or vinegar. When meat is served, it is usually lamb or mutton. Seasonal fruits such as sour cherries, plums, quinces, and grapes are made into thick jam (*slatko*), which is traditionally served to visitors and eaten from a glass jar with a spoon. Milk is used to make a rich cheese-like appetizer, *kajmak*, or is fermented into yogurt. There are several versions of *pindzhur*, a traditional Macedonian vegetable dish made from tomatoes, green peppers, and eggplant. It is usually either baked or stir-fried, and served with feta cheese and fresh bread. *Tarator* is a cucumber salad seasoned with yogurt, vinegar, and garlic, and sometimes garnished with walnuts. Other traditional dishes include stuffed peppers (*polneti piperki*), stuffed grape leaves (*sarma od lozov list*), and mousaka (*musaka*), a casserole of meat, eggplant, and rice bound with a custard sauce. A popular item at barbecues is *kjebapchinja*, a sea-soned mixture of beef or veal and lamb that is grilled and served with scallions, tomatoes, and hot peppers. Also served is *muchkalica*, seasoned mutton grilled on skewers. Festive occasions call for special baked goods such as *baklava*, a honey- dipped layered pastry often filled with ground walnuts, and *burek*, a yeast pastry filled with feta cheese. Macedonians also enjoy Turkish coffee (*Tursko Kafe*), a legacy from centuries of Turkish rule.

MUSIC

Macedonian folk music combines influences from several ethnic traditions. Centuries of Ottoman rule brought to Macedonian music a distinctly eastern tone and style, which was further enhanced by the significant contributions of Gypsy (Rom) musicians. A notable legacy from the Turks was the introduction in the nineteenth century of brass bands, which Macedonian and Gypsy musicians adapted to their own musical traditions. The popularity of brass bands waned in the late twentieth century, however, as Macedonian nationalism gained momentum.

Macedonian folk songs were to be played or sung by shepherds in their fields, and are distinguished by very slow introductory parts and sections of intricate improvisations known as *trepaza*. These variations are thought to resemble the several courses of a grand feast, in which many flavors are mingled in one meal. Their melodies show an eastern influence which ethnic musicologists have linked to the ancient oboe technique of circular, continuous breathing. Instruments commonly used in Macedonian music include the *zurla*, an ancient folk oboe similar to those used in Turkey, Central Asia, and Northern Africa, and the *kaval*, a vertical flute. One of the region's most characteristic instruments is the *gaida*, or Bulgarian bagpipe, which is often used as a solo instrument but is also sometimes accompanied by the *dumbek*, a hand-held drum. The *tambura*, a pear-shaped stringed instrument, is similar to the Bulgarian *gadulka*, and has been compared in tone to the American banjo. The clarinet and the accordion are also popular instruments.

TRADITIONAL COSTUMES

Costumes worn for ceremonial occasions in Macedonia are often heavily embroidered and very colorful. The Valley Bridal Dress worn in the Prilep region is dominated by red and bright yellow, while the Bitola Valley Dress is mostly yellow and black. According to an article in James Nicoloff's *Macedonia*, the Prilep dress is heavily ornamented with embroidery and metal and bead ornaments. It consists of a smock (*golema*) which is almost completely covered with embroidered circles on the sleeves and with stylized blossom and horseshoe patterns on the front and the border of the skirt. Knitted multicolored cuffs are worn on the lower arms. An embroidered cotton upper garment, the *valanka*, is embellished with tufted fringes and braid along the seams. The *chulter*, an intricately woven apron, is worn below the black wool girdle or belt. In back, the *potkolchelniche*, trimmed with beads and old silver coins, is worn beneath the girdle. Scarves and a necklace, both trimmed with old coins, are also worn. On the head is placed a *fes*, ornamented with rows of silver coins that hang down beside the face. A garland of spruce is placed above the *fes*. A hair decoration, the *kocelj*, is made from twisted woolen yarn and hangs down from the shoulders. Flame-colored stockings and homemade slippers complete the costume.

The corresponding men's dress consists of the *aba*, an undershirt made of hand-woven wool, a long linen smock with embroidered sleeves, front, and skirt, knitted cuffs worn on the arms below the elbow, and white broadcloth breeches. A brightly-colored girdle (*kemer*) is worn beneath a black broadcloth waistcoat, which is embellished with multicolored embroidery, buttons, and flame-colored trimmings. A distinctive black astrakhan and velvet cap is worn on the head, and white stockings, decorated garters, and cowhide slippers with straps complete the costume. Men also wear a knife (*zhrenche*) with a chain and a horn sheath as part of this traditional garb.

DANCES AND SONGS

Many Macedonian folk songs were influenced by Gypsy (Rom) music, which was in turn affected by Macedonian traditions. A humorous song popular among Gypsy musicians but sung in Macedonian is "*Da Me Molat Ne Se Zhenam*" ("I Won't Get Married"). The singer laments that if he married a young girl, she would never stay home but if he married an older one she would quarrel with him. If he married a village girl, she would call him Daddy, and if he took a widow for his wife she would already have children. He decides a divorcee would leave him, and a town girl would drive him away. So he will marry no one at all. "*Pesna I Devojka*" ("The Song and the Girl") is also performed in Macedonian. A haunting Macedonian pastoral melody is "*Aj Zajdi Zajdi Jasno Sonce*," sung to kaval accompaniment. Other traditional Macedonian songs include "*Makedonsko Kevojce*" ("Macedonian Girl"), "*Majko Mila Moja Makedonijo*," and "*Katerino*."

Balkan dances are colorful and festive. As with music and songs, they show some borrowing from Gypsy traditions. Many Macedonian dances are based on the *Horo*, or circle dance.

HOLIDAYS

Easter is the most significant holiday in the Eastern Orthodox Church, and Macedonians in the United States continue to observe it seriously. Easter is celebrated two weeks after the Roman Catholic Easter, in accordance with the Eastern Orthodox Church's adherence to the Gregorian calendar. Macedonian American families dye eggs a deep red, to symbolize the blood of Christ, and enjoy the custom of tapping an egg against another person's to try to crack it without cracking one's own. The egg that remains intact symbolizes good luck. Christmas Day (*Bozhik*) is also important. Though the traditions of Santa Claus and Christmas trees did not exist in Macedonia, they have become a part of holiday celebrations in many Macedonian American families.

LANGUAGE

Macedonian is a South Slavic language closely related to Bulgarian. Like Russian, it is written in the Cyrillic alphabet. Unlike Russian, however, modern Macedonian does not change the endings of nouns according to their grammatical case. Standard Macedonian is based on the country's western dialects, which are the most distinct from Bulgarian and Serbo-Croatian. Northern dialects are similar to Serbian dialects, and eastern dialects are closest to Bulgarian. Macedonian has 31 sounds and a letter for each sound, making it a completely phonetic language that is easy to learn to read and write. A Macedonian-English dictionary of 50,000 words, scheduled for publication around 1999 and the largest edition to that date, reflects a strong interest in the Macedonian language among communities in English-speaking countries.

GREETINGS AND POPULAR EXPRESSIONS

The usual Macedonian greeting is *zdravo* (ZDRA-vuh), or "hi." More formal greetings are *dobro utro* (DOE-bruh OO-troh), "good morning" or *dobar den* (DOE-bar DAIN), "good day." "Good night" is *dobra nok* (DOE-bruh NOK-yih). *Kako cte?* (KAK-uh STAI) means "how are you?" and *dobrodojdovte* (DOE-bruh DOY-duv-tai) means "welcome."

FAMILY AND COMMUNITY DYNAMICS

Macedonian immigrants who chose to remain in the United States in the early 1900s often returned to their native land when it was time to marry, bringing their new brides back with them to America. Those who chose their wives in the United States often favored women of Macedonian or Bulgarian ancestry. Though marriage outside the ethnic group was tolerated, Macedonians practiced a high rate of endogamy (same-group marriage), which strengthened family and community bonds. It was not unusual for several generations of Macedonian American families to remain in the same geographic area and to maintain close personal and professional contacts. Perhaps because the Macedonian American population is relatively small, the community has organized associations and festivities, such as folk dancing, concerts, and picnics, to foster group solidarity.

EDUCATION

Though the earliest Macedonian immigrants arrived in the United States with little or no formal education, they quickly availed themselves of new opportunities to improve their literacy skills. Political organizations such as the American Socialists were an important means of spreading literacy. They published several newspapers and magazines in Macedonian and other Slavic languages, and found an interested readership. Many immigrants eagerly studied English and went to school to learn the skills that would enable them to take full advantage of opportunities in America. Within a few generations, Macedonian Americans were attending college and universities and entering the professions.

BIRTH AND BIRTHDAYS

It is a Macedonian custom to prepare a special type of fritter, called *pituli*, to celebrate the birth of a baby. Babies are ceremonially baptized according to the rites of the Eastern Orthodox Church.

THE ROLE OF WOMEN

When Macedonian women followed their husbands to the United States, they often took jobs outside the home a departure from their customary role in Europe. Women in America often worked with their husbands in family businesses. In addition, they played a central role in maintaining Macedonian culture in America. They preserved culinary traditions in their homes and were active in church groups, Sunday schools, and social organizations.

WEDDINGS

Macedonian Americans have continued to celebrate many wedding traditions from earlier generations. The night before the wedding (*kolak* or *kvas*) is spent feasting and dancing. The next morning, friends and family of the groom gather at his home for the groom-shaving ritual. The godparents, known as *kym* and *kyma*, ceremoniously give the groom his last shave as a single man as the guests sing, dance, and feast. During the wedding ceremony, the bride and groom, sometimes joined by their fathers, participate in the "breaking of the bread" to see who will "wear the pants" in the new household. After the wedding ceremony, the male members of the wedding party often perform the Macedonian Pig Dance at the reception. Holding bottles of wine as well as forks and knives, they dance into the reception area carrying a roasted pig. They dance, shout, and whistle in front of the *kym* and *kyma*, demanding "payment" for the feast, and continue until the pig bearer is satisfied with the amount paid.

> **"O**ne of the first customs to be lost in this country, and indeed, a custom which lost favor some years ago in Macedonia, is the arranged marriage. Match-makers (Macedonia: *posturnitsi*; Bulgarian: *svatovnitsi*), usually older women, were contacted by one of the sets of parents and it was she and she alone who completed the necessary negotiations. The bride and groom-to-be were simply not consulted."
>
> Philip R. Tilney, *Immigrant Macedonian Wedding in Ft. Wayne,* (Indiana Folklore, vol. III, no. 1, 1970).

INTERACTIONS WITH OTHER ETHNIC GROUPS

The first groups of Macedonian Americans tended to congregate in areas where there were other Southern Slavic populations. They lived among their fellow Macedonians and Bulgarians, as well as Croats and other immigrants from the Balkan region. In areas with only small numbers of Macedonians, they tended to be most comfortable with other Orthodox Slavs. Their pan-Slavic attitudes often brought them into contact with Poles, Ukrainians, and Russians, with whom they frequently associated in left-wing political groups.

After the creation of the Republic of Macedonia in 1991, tensions escalated between Slavic and Greek Macedonians in the United States and

Canada. When a Macedonian group organized a pavilion at the Toronto Carvan in 1991, the Greek pavilion boycotted the festival, claiming that the Republic of Macedonia had stolen territory from Greece. Macedonians coined the derogatory term "Gerkoman" to refer to ethnic Macedonians who considered themselves Greek instead of Slavic.

RELIGION

The vast majority of Macedonians who immigrated to the United States were members of the Eastern Orthodox Church, and religious affiliation played a central role in maintaining ethnic identity, language, and native traditions. Early immigrants established parishes under the jurisdiction of the patriarch (head of the church) in Sofia, Bulgaria. The first Bulgarian Orthodox church in America was Sts. Cyril and Methodius, established in Granite City, Illinois in 1909. Others included St. Stephen in Indianapolis, founded in 1915, St. Clement Ohridsky in Detroit, founded in 1929, and St. Trinity in Madison, Illinois, founded in 1929. The Bulgarian Orthodox Mission for the entire United States and Canada, which in 1937 was renamed the Bulgarian Eastern Orthodox Church, Diocese of the United States and Canada, was centered in Indianapolis. In 1962, a group of Macedonian Americans in Gary, Indiana founded a separate Macedonian Orthodox Church, which was recognized by the Holy Synod of the Macedonian Orthodox Church in Skopje. Within 20 years, 11 Macedonian Orthodox parishes had been established. By the late 1990s, 19 parishes were listed in the United States. However, Bishop Kyril, head of the Bulgarian Church in the United States and Canada, refused to recognize the Macedonian Orthodox Church, and this rift continued to cause bitter feelings between Macedonian and Bulgarian immigrant communities.

Macedonian Orthodox churches are organized under the guidance of a metropolitan (a bishop who is head of an ecclesiastical province) for the United States, Canada, and Australia. Parishes offer liturgical services in both Macedonian and English and provide a variety of social and cultural activities such as festivals, dinners, and holiday bazaars. Women's groups contribute a great deal to the church's social functions. Sunday schools, which teach the Macedonian language, are also important cultural institutions.

Like other Eastern Orthodox churches, the Macedonian Orthodox Church follows the Julian calendar, which is 13 days behind the Gregorian calendar. Orthodox sacraments and liturgy closely resemble those of the Roman Catholic Church, but

in the Orthodox church, great reverence is attached to icons of Christ, the Virgin Mary, and the saints. Often, homes as well as churches have icons in a place of honor. Unlike the Roman Catholic Church, the Orthodox church allows married men to become priests. Orthodox churches adhere to the Nicene Creed and follow the liturgy of St. John Chrysostom (c.347-407 AD). They observe seven sacraments: the Eucharist, Baptism, Confirmation, Penance, Matrimony, Holy Orders, and the Anointing of the Sick. The Macedonian Orthodox Church also observes the ritual of *Agiasmos*, or Holy Water, as a means of bestowing grace upon the congregation. There are Greater and Lesser Blessings of Water. The Lesser Blessing can be performer on any day of the year, either in the church or within a home or designated space. The Greater Blessing of Water is performed on the Feast of the Epiphany (in the Julian calendar, January 19). On this day, churchgoers often take a bottle of holy water to their homes, where it is kept until the following year.

EMPLOYMENT AND ECONOMIC TRADITIONS

Macedonian Americans were known as hard workers in their new country. Because they often arrived with little education and limited job skills, they frequently took the most hazardous and poorly paid industrial jobs. According to George Prpic in *South Slavic Immigration in America*, immigrants from the Macedonian region enjoyed railroad work, which, though demanding, at least allowed them to labor under the open sky and escape the crowded conditions that beset them in the cities. For several months at a time, these workers lived together in railroad cars and ate meals prepared by their own cooks. Data from 1909 estimated that as many as 10,000 immigrants from Bulgaria and Macedonia were then working on the railroads in North and South Dakota, Montana, Iowa, and Minnesota. Among the Macedonians who sought railroad work was the future writer Stoyan Christowe, who described his living conditions as very harsh. Railroad work, however, paid a little better than some of the industrial jobs available in the cities.

By 1910, almost 15,000 Bulgarian and Macedonian immigrants worked in the steel mills near Chicago, Illinois. Living and working conditions here were, according to Prpic, extremely primitive and unsanitary. Similar communities of Balkan immigrant workers existed throughout the industrial belt. Though they did not have the skills to move immediately into more prestigious jobs, Macedonian immigrants developed a reputation as hard-working, strong, sober, intelligent, and eager workers. Often a Macedonian immigrant dreamed of saving up enough money to open a store or to buy a small farm. Although many immigrants were illiterate in their native land, they acquired reading and writing skills in America, which in time enabled them to move into more highly paid jobs. By the 1940s, many Macedonian Americans had opened small businesses such as stores or bakeries. In the city of Pittsburgh alone, 33 Bulgarian and Macedonian bakeries were in business during this period.

With access to education, subsequent generations of Macedonian Americans have made careers in medicine, law, academia, broadcasting, and other professions, as well as in business. By the end of the 1900s, new immigrants brought more specialized skills to their adopted country, and individuals trained in the sciences, technology, and business have established themselves in those fields. One of the most prominent business leaders in the United States, Frank Popoff, who is president and CEO of Dow Chemical, is of Bulgarian- Macedonian descent. Another business mogul, Mike Ilitch (originally Iliev), began his career in the United States with a single pizza shop, which he built into the successful Little Caesar's franchise.

POLITICS AND GOVERNMENT

The long struggle of Macedonians to free themselves from Ottoman rule and to maintain autonomy amidst the political turmoil of the Balkan region prepared Macedonian immigrants for active political engagement in the United States. As early as 1908, for example, a group of 600 unemployed and starving immigrants from Bulgaria and Macedonia marched on Chicago's city hall to demand work. Such an action was extremely shocking at the time and the incident had little effect, but it indicated the determination of these immigrants to stand up for their rights. Like other Slavic groups, Macedonians tended to support leftist causes more than the general U.S. population, but few were outright radicals.

A commitment to pan-Slavic solidarity also contributed to Macedonian Americans' interest in Socialism. Macedonians had been traditionally friendly toward Russia, with whom they shared ethnic, linguistic, and church ties, and the American Communist Party was very active in enlisting their support for the Soviet cause. Official Soviet support for Macedonian independence further strengthened the bond between Macedonian Americans and Russia. The Socialist Labor Party of America, too, worked to gain Bulgarian and Macedonian membership, and published many newspapers and periodicals to promote their political education. George Pirinsky (born George Zaikoff), a Bulgarian Communist leader in the United States, was the most active leader in this cause.

During World War II, pro-socialist activity among Macedonian Americans and other Slavic groups intensified. On April 25 and 26, 1942 an All-Slavic Congress was held in Detroit, out of which was created the American Slav Congress. The Macedonian-American People's League was a member organization. Macedonian Americans attended the Michigan Slav Congress held in Detroit in 1943 and were involved in the creation of the United Committee of South Slavic Americans. Macedonian Americans also were attracted to the International Workers Order, a Communist front organization that included special sections for individual South Slavic groups. Throughout the war years, these groups criticized American foreign policy toward the Soviet Union, arousing the suspicion of the conservative political establishment. In 1948, the House Committee on Un-American Activities and the U.S. Attorney General accused the American Slav Congress and its affiliate groups of being Communist organizations under the influence of Moscow. For the next several years, Congressional investigations conducted a witch hunt against left-wing radicals, among them some leaders of the South Slavic groups. During this difficult period, many either chose to leave the country or were deported. Despite the leftist orientation of many Macedonian Americans, the vast majority of them, according to Prpic, were loyal to the U.S. government and found such political hostility troubling. They supported American involvement in World War II, served in the military, and worked on the home front to help the war effort.

MILITARY

Though many Macedonian immigrants were actively opposed to World War I, in which their homeland was occupied by Serbia and Greece, thousands of them served in the U.S. armed forces during World War II. Hundreds were killed or wounded on several fronts.

RELATIONS WITH FORMER COUNTRY

Macedonians in the United States generally maintained great interest in events in their homeland. Political strife in the Balkans and the Macedonian struggle for autonomy were frequent subjects of discussion when Macedonians gathered to socialize. They organized material relief for Macedonian villages, sending parcels of clothing and financial assistance to areas in need. They were also very active politically. During the 1920s and 1930s, increased violence in Serbian and Greek occupied Macedonia caused intense concern among Macedonians in the United States. To support the cause of Ivan Mihajlov's Internal Macedonian Revolutionary Organization, they founded the Macedonian Patriotic Organization (MPO) in October 1922. This organization, which originated in Fort Wayne, Indiana and later moved to Indianapolis, was dedicated to the "liberation and unification of Macedonia." Anastas Stephanoff became president of its Central Committee and Atanas Lebanoff was elected secretary. The MPO began publishing the *Makedonska Tribuna* (*The Macedonian Tribune*) on February 10, 1927. This weekly newspaper is still in publication.

Because of their cultural bonds with Russia and their appreciation of the Soviet Union's support for Macedonian autonomy, Macedonian Americans tended not to adopt the anti-Communist attitudes common throughout much of the American population. They appreciated Yugoslavia's official efforts to promote Macedonian autonomy.

INDIVIDUAL AND GROUP CONTRIBUTIONS

FILM, TELEVISION, AND THEATER

Filmmaker Milcho Manchevski, born in Skopje in 1959, immigrated to the United States in 1982 to study film and photography at the University of Southern Illinois. After directing dozens of commercials and music videos, for which he became well-known, he made his feature film debut in 1994 with *Before the Rain*. A three-part story set in contemporary Macedonia and London, the film explores love and fate within the context of ancient Macedonian traditions and conflicts. The film won the Golden Lion award at the Venice Film Festival.

Nick Vanoff (1929-1991), born in Vevey, near the Greek port of Salonika, enjoyed a highly successful career as a Hollywood television and film producer. Vanoff was associate producer for such programs as *The Perry Como Show* and the *Tonight Show*. He originated several others, including the *Bing Crosby Specials*, the *Perry Como Specials*, the *Phil Silvers Specials*, *Hollywood Palace*, the *Andy Williams Specials*, the *Sonny and Cher Show*, and the *Kennedy Center Honors Show*. Vanoff was the creator of the comedy series *Hee-Haw*, which he later syndicated. He served as co-producer for the acclaimed film *Eleni* (1985), based on the memoir of his close friend Nicholas Gage, who grew up near Vanoff.

Other Macedonian Americans have affected television in the 1990s. Actress Starr Andreeff appeared in several daytime television roles, among them Jessica on *General Hospital*. Michael Stoyanov played the role of Anthony, a recovering substance abuser, in the NBC sitcom *Blossom*, which ran from 1991 to 1995.

JOURNALISM

The first editor of the *Macedonian Tribune* was Boris Zografoff, who came to the United States from Bitola to accept the position. He wrote and edited the paper's first issue, published on February 10, 1927, and served as editor for three years. Zografoff was admired as a talented editor with a sophisticated understanding of the Macedonian independence movement. His most renowned successor, Christo N. Nizamoff, worked for the *Macedonian Tribune* for more than 40 years. In the early 1920s, Nizamoff was a member of the Macedonian Press Bureau in New York City. He was the first foreign-born writer to be invited to join the Indianapolis Literary Club. Nizamoff was a founding member of the Indianapolis Press Club as well as its Man of the Year, and was elected to the Indiana Journalism Hall of Fame.

LITERATURE

The most esteemed Macedonian American writer, Stoyan Christowe, was born in Konomlady, Macedonia, in 1898. He came to the United States as a child, and attended Valparaiso University in Indiana. Christowe published six books, including *This is My Country* (1938), *My American Pilgrimage* (1947), and *The Eagle and the Stork: An American Memoir* (1976). As a young man, Christowe identified himself so wholeheartedly as an American that when he returned to the Balkans to visit, he found it easier to converse with the Bulgarian King in English than in Bulgarian. In his books, Christowe explored both the process of assimilation and the strong ties that he continued to feel for his native land. In the late 1930s, Christowe moved to Vermont, where he served for 12 years in the state legislature.

SCIENCE AND TECHNOLOGY

Dr. Boris P. Stoicheff, a professor of physics at the University of Toronto who worked closely with American Nobel laureate Arthur L. Schawlow, contributed to the development of laser technology. Dr. Stoicheff worked with NASA on the Apollo space project.

Peter T. George, D.D.S., an Olympic weightlifter who became an orthodontist after retiring from athletics, has pioneered treatments for obstructive sleep apnea. He holds a patent for the Nocturnal Airway Patency Appliance (NAPA), a device used to prevent the stoppage of breathing during sleep. The NAPA also prevents snoring.

SPORTS

Macedonian Americans have participated actively in both amateur and professional sports. Businessman Mick Ilitch, who was born in Bitola, Macedonia, owns both the Detroit Red Wings, a professional hockey team, and the Detroit Tigers, a professional baseball team. National Basketball Association (NBA) hall-of-famer Pete Maravich (1947-1988), born in Pennsylvania to parents of Serbian and Macedonian backgrounds, scored more points during his college career than any other player and was named a three-time All American as well as the 1970 College Player of the Year. He went on to a professional career with the Atlanta Hawks, the New Orleans Jazz, the Utah Jazz, and the Boston Celtics.

Peter T. George, born in Akron, Ohio in 1929 to Tony and Para George (Tryan and Paraskeva Taleff) won three Olympic medals for the United States in weightlifting. He won a gold medal in 1952 in Helsinki and silver medals in 1948 in London and 1956 in Melbourne. Beginning his athletic career in his teens, George won five world championships from 1947 to 1952, and was middleweight champion at the Pan-American Games in 1951 and 1955. George was named coach of the 1980 Olympic team, but did not attend the games in Moscow because of the U.S. boycott.

Since the early 1990s, soccer in the United States has been greatly enhanced by the presence of foreign-born players, among them Jovan Kirovski, a U.S. citizen of Macedonian descent. Kirovski scored the winning goal in the British 1992-93 Youth Cup semifinal for Manchester United before joining the U.S. national team.

MEDIA

PRINT

The Macedonian Tribune.
A weekly newspaper published since 1927 by the Macedonian Patriotic Organization. It is printed in Macedonian and English.

Address: 124 West Wayne Street, Fort Wayne, Indiana 46802.
Telephone: (219) 422-5900.
Fax: (219) 422-1348.

ORGANIZATIONS AND ASSOCIATIONS

Bulgarian-Macedonian National Educational and Cultural Center (BMNECC).
BMNECC was formed in 1980 from the Bulgaro-Macedonian Beneficial Association, which had originally been established in 1930. The BMNECC offers exhibits, displays, and educational programs, maintains an archive of folk artifacts, runs a museum and library, and has done research on the contributions of individual Macedonians and Bulgarians in America.

Contact: Patricia Penka French, President.
Address: 449-451 West 8th Avenue,
    West Homestead, Pennsylvania 15122.
Telephone: (412) 461-6188.

Macedonian Patriotic Organization (MPO).
MPO was established in 1922 in Fort Wayne, Indiana. Its purpose was to advocate for the liberation of Macedonia, and it began publishing the *Macedonian Tribune* in 1927. Since 1991, the MPO has focused on increasing awareness of Macedonian history and culture.

Contact: Chris Evanoff, President.
Address: 124 West Wayne Street, Fort Wayne, Indiana 46802.
Telephone: (219) 422-5900.
Fax: (219) 422-1348.

MUSEUMS AND RESEARCH CENTERS

Allen County Public Library.
The Fred J. Reynolds Historical Genealogy Department, the second largest genealogical repository in North America, includes federal and state census and mortality records, state indexes, Soundex, and Michigan state census data for selected years. It also contains passenger lists, naturalization records, city and town histories, military records and regimental histories, cemetery and church records, land and probate records, city directories, etc. It maintains the largest English-language genealogy and local history periodical collection in the world.

Address: 900 Webster Street, Fort Wayne, Indiana 46801; P.O. Box 2270, Fort Wayne, Indiana 46801-2270.
Telephone: (219) 421-1200.
Fax: (219) 422-9688.

Russian and East European Studies Consortium. This organization administers inter-university academic exchange program with the University of Sts. Kiril and Metodij (UKIM) in Skopje, Macedonia.

Address: P.O. Box 872601, Arizona State
   University, Tempe, Arizona 85287-2601.
Telephone: (602) 965-4188.

The University of Minnesota's Less Commonly Taught Languages (LCTL) Project lists seven institutions in the United States that offer courses in Macedonian: Cornell University, Lawrence University (Appleton, WI), Ohio State University, University of Chicago, University of Kansas, University of North Carolina, and University of Virginia.

SOURCES FOR ADDITIONAL STUDY

Kaplan, Robert D. *Balkan Ghosts: A Journey Through History.* New York: St. Martin's Press, 1993.

Nicoloff, James. *Macedonia: A Collection of Articles About the History and Culture of Macedonia.* Toronto: Selyani Macedonian Folklore Group, 1982.

Prpic, George J. *South Slavic Immigration in America.* Boston: Twayne Publishers, 1978.

MALAYSIAN AMERICANS

by
Karl Heil

Since Malaysia is an Islamic country, the traditional clothing of Malaysia reflects Islamic beliefs in modesty—that is, keeping the body covered, especially among women. Nevertheless, Malaysian clothing tends to be colorful with abstract and floral patterns and embroidery.

OVERVIEW

The country of Malaysia is composed of 13 states. It is located in Southeast Asia on the Malay Peninsula, which divides the Indian Ocean and the South China Sea, as well as the northern corner of the island of Borneo. The peninsular portion of the country, which lies between Thailand to the north and Singapore to the south, is referred to as Western Malaysia, and the northern portion of Borneo as Eastern Malaysia. About 400 miles (644 kilometers) of the South China Sea separates East and West Malaysia. Malaysia has a combined area of 127,320 square miles (329,758 square kilometers), slightly larger than the state of New Mexico. The country's capital was Kuala Lumpur since it gained independence beginning in 1957. However, in June of 1999, the country planned to move its capital 20 miles (32 kilometers) south to Putrajaya. Putrajaya was designed as a high-tech capital featuring buildings linked with fiber-optic cable and a "paperless" office environment for banks and government buildings. The capital also is slated to have a floating mosque in the city's lake.

The country's population is composed of ethnic Malays and other aboriginal people, who represent 62 percent of the country's population; ethnic Chinese (26 percent) and ethnic Indians (7 percent) make up the country's largest minorities. Other groups include Arabs, Armenians, and Eurasians. The country's indigenous population includes the *orang asli*, which is commonly divided into the Negritos (a nomadic hunting people), the Senoi (an agrarian people), and the Jakun (an agrarian people). These three groups number around one million people. Overall, Malaysia has a population of more than 20 million people, with most residing in Western Malaysia. In addition, Islam is the religion of more than 50 percent of the population, and the official language is Bahasa Malaysia, which is derived from the indigenous Malay language. The country includes two federal territories, Kuala Lumpur and Lubuan, and 13 states, Johor, Kedah, Kelantan, Melaka, Negeri Sembilan, Pahang, Perak, Perlis, Penang, Selangor, Terengganu, Sabah, and Sarawak.

The Malaysian economy, once based mostly on the extraction of raw materials such as rubber and tin, has shifted to manufacturing, tourism, and technology. About 15 percent of the country's land is devoted to agriculture, and rice is the country's leading crop. Furthermore, Malaysia is the world's leader in palm oil production. Production of natural gas and petroleum also constitute significant industries in Malaysia. Malaysia's currency unit is the ringgit, which is also called the Malaysian dollar. The Malaysian flag contains horizontal red and white stripes as well as a blue square in the upper left corner that includes a crescent moon and the sun.

HISTORY

Because of a scarcity of information on Malaysia's history prior to the fifteenth century, historians have been unable to construct with any certainty a picture of Malaysia for this earlier era. Around 1400, however, a major trading port developed in Melaka on the west coast of the Malay Peninsula, and after its rise the area became known to other countries around the world. Nevertheless, some Chinese, Indian, and Arab documents prior to 1400 contain references to the area that is now Malaysia. These sources suggest that the Chinese, Indians, and Arabs made contact with the Malay people before 1400. In addition, archaeological evidence indicates that the original human inhabitants came to the Malay Peninsula in spurts beginning about 35,000 years ago. The original inhabitants apparently came from South China, migrating southward to Malay, Indonesia, and Australia. Somewhat later, immigrants from India traveled to the Malay Peninsula around the beginning of the common era, bringing with them an alphabet, laws, literature, and the Hindu and Buddhist religions. The Indians set up trade centers along the peninsula and retained influence over them until around the thirteenth century, when China began to expand its trade substantially in the region. China's influence over the Malay Peninsula lasted through the fifteenth century.

In the fifteen century, Islamic sultans arrived in Malay and founded the state or sultanate of Melaka (also spelled Malacca). This port city became a nexus for trade, the spread of Islam, and the dissemination of the Malay language to other parts of the island chain (including what are now Indonesia and Singapore). Paramesvara became the sultanate's first ruler, and he received recognition as such by the Chinese around 1405. During this period, a few significant changes took place that helped form aspects of contemporary Malaysia. First, Islam supplanted Hinduism as the dominant religion. Second, the country's sultanate structure of different states ruled by an Islamic leader developed along with its Islamic aristocracy, which remains today in that Malaysia's Muslims are afforded certain privileges because of their religion. Furthermore, Melaka became one of the greatest powers in the region during this period and eventually included all of Malaya, a federation of nine Malay states (Johor, Kedah, Kelantan, Negeri Sembilan, Pahang, Perak, Perlis, Selangor, and Terengganu). With its good harbor and fleet, Melaka became a major center for international trade and the source of spices in the region. The burgeoning wealth of Melaka during this period because of its spice trade and its key location between China and India piqued the interest of Europeans. The Portuguese first seized the state from the Sultans Mahmud Shah and Ahmad Shah in 1511. Although they defeated the sultans and their followers, the Portuguese faced frequent attacks from the sultans' followers as well as from Siam, China, and Japan. However, the Portuguese retained control of Melaka for until 1641, when the Dutch conquered the state and became the region's dominant European trader.

Under Dutch rule, Maleka's importance and size diminished. The Dutch tried to exploit trade in Malay, especially trade of gold, tin, and pepper. To do so, they exacted high duties from merchant vessels passing through Maleka. Hence, many ships navigated around Dutch controlled territories to avoid paying these duties. However, the Dutch efforts proved successful overall and Malay remained under Dutch rule for over two centuries. Nevertheless, Britain eventually came to control sizable interests in the area, too. In 1786, the British East India Company established a port to the north, on the island of Penang, and competed with the Dutch-held ports. The British took over control of Maleka in 1795 under the Anglo-Dutch Treaty. To facilitate governing Penang, Maleka, and Singapore, Britain combined them to form the Straits Settlements Presidency in 1867. This designation allowed the British to control Malay and neighboring territories without direct rule. Because British interest was exclusively in trade, the British established a policy of non-interference with the occurrences in Malay states. Social upheaval in the region eventually forced Britain to play a greater role in the governing of Malaya and nearby British-controlled states, however. Beginning in 1895, Britain formed a variety of federations of Malay states to help restore peace and stability. These federations involved both Malay and British governors, although the British had the ultimate control. British rule became increasingly centralized in the region, until Japan seized Malaya, Sarawak, and North Borneo during World War II and occupied them until the war ended in 1945. In the postwar period, a complicated independence movement began.

MODERN ERA

The independence movement had to overcome the differences among the various ethnic groups in the peninsula, especially those of the Malays, the Chinese, and the Indians. Around 1950, the Alliance party emerged as a voice for independence representing the country's three major ethnic groups. The party came to power in 1955 after the country's first national elections. Tunku Abdul Rahman became the country's first prime minister. The Federation of Malaysia was formed in 1957, and nine Malay states, along with Penang and Melaka, became a country independent of British rule. Before achieving independence, a Communist guerrilla movement fought for independence from British control. In 1963, the Borneo states Sabah and Sarawak joined the states of the Malay Peninsula as part of the Federation of Malaysia. Singapore entered the federation in 1963, too, but defected in 1965 because of disputes with the Malaysian leadership.

During its infancy, Malaysia faced resistance from Indonesia, which attacked Malaysian states in an effort to break up the fledgling country. Indonesia saw Malaysia as a throwback to the colonial era with its dependence on British military assistance. In addition, Communist guerrilla attacks continued in the Borneo states through the early 1970s. The country also saw growing conflict between its Malay and ethnic Chinese citizens, which prompted the New Economic Policy of 1970. This policy was designed to reduce the economic inequality between the rural Malays and urban Chinese.

The economic changes ultimately proved successful to a large extent and helped rural Malays move into urban areas and reap a greater share of the country's economic benefits. Consequently, the country has enjoyed relative prosperity and stability since the early 1970s, and relations with its neighbors

also have been positive during this period. In addition, the country's economic policies are still based on the New Economic Policy, although it is now called the National Development Policy. Malaysia's economic policies of the late 1990s included the expansion of the country's technology industries, promotion of entrepreneurship, and maintenance of harmony among different ethnic groups.

ACCULTURATION AND ASSIMILATION

CUISINE

The cuisine of Malaysian Americans depends on the particulars of ethnicity, although rice is common across all groups. Traditional Malay food features hot chilies, coconut milk, shallots, garlic, ginger, which go into Malay curries and belacan, a fermented shrimp cake. Since the Malays are Islamic, they do not eat pork; they instead rely on beef and seafood for their dishes. One of the most popular Malay dishes is the *satay*, or barbecue meat and vegetables on wooden skewers. In addition, peanut sauces are a prominent ingredient of many a Malay dish.

Ethnic Chinese Malaysians developed their own brand of Chinese cuisine, which varies from the food of mainland China, after spending centuries on the Malay Peninsula. This cuisine is often regional, and its ingredients and methods depend on the specific areas in which the Chinese Malaysians reside. Consequently, specific dishes come from specific cities. For example, *nasi ayam*, or chicken rice, comes from the city of Ipoh and consists of chicken, rice, and bean sprouts. Chinese Malaysian cuisine includes many of the spices that Malay food does—shallots, ginger, garlic, and even chilies—but it generally lacks the spiciness of Malay or Indian Malaysian cuisine.

Indian Malaysian food varies based on religion: those who are Hindus do not eat beef and those who are Islamic do not eat pork. Nevertheless, the cuisine of all Indian Malaysians tends to reflect the cooking of South India, from where most Indians emigrated. Hence, spicy Indian-style curries are popular; they include meat, seafood, and vegetarian curries served with rice. Although all Indian Malaysian food tends to be spicy, those who are Islamic often prefer even spicier food.

TRADITIONAL COSTUMES

Since Malaysia is an Islamic country, the traditional clothing of Malaysia reflects Islamic beliefs in

This elaborate
Malaysian
American float was
created for the
Tournament of
Roses Parade in
Pasadena.

This elaborate Malaysian American float was created for the Tournament of Roses Parade in Pasadena.

modesty—that is, keeping the body covered, especially among women. Nevertheless, Malaysian clothing tends to be colorful with abstract and floral patterns and embroidery. Indian and Chinese Malaysians sometimes retain their respective attire in Malaysia.

HOLIDAYS

Malaysian Americans may celebrate a variety of standard Malaysian holidays such as Worker's Day or Labor Day on May 1, National Day or Independence Day on August 31, and Christmas on December 25 (celebrated by Christian Malaysian Americans, who also celebrate Easter and other Christian holidays). In addition, Malaysian Americans may observe a number of other holidays, depending on their ethnicity. Since Islamic, Chinese, and Hindu calendars are all lunar calendars, these holidays do not set have dates and change from year to year. Islamic Malaysian Americans, for example, may observe *Hari Raya Puasa* (sometimes shortened to *Hari Raya*), which comes at the end of Ramadan (called Puasa in Mala). This holiday involves special prayers at the mosque and gatherings of families and friends. For the occasion, houses are usually decorated with lights, and people dress formally.

Ethnic Chinese Malaysian Americans, on the other hand, might celebrate China's three important holidays: the Chinese New Year, the Feast of the Hungry Ghosts, and the Moon Cake Festival. The Chinese New Year usually falls in January or February, and its traditional Malaysian celebration involves the closing of businesses for two days, parades, and dances. In addition, the holiday brings families and friends together, usually for dinner and celebration. The Hungry Ghosts Festival usually is held between July and August when it is believed that the spirits of the dead circulate on earth and hence need to be fed. When celebrating this holiday, Malaysian Americans may offer food to the spirits and hold feasts for themselves. Finally, the Moon Cake Festival, which is held in September around the autumn moon, commemorates the defeat of the Mongols in ancient China. The celebration includes the preparation and eating of pastries shaped like the moon.

Hindu Malaysian Americans may celebrate the major Hindu holidays. The most popular of these holidays is Deepavali, the Festival of Lights, which usually takes place in October or November. For the holiday, family and friends gather to celebrate the stories of good overcoming evil. Families usually have open houses for the holiday and decorate their homes with colored lights, lamps, fruit, flowers, and other kinds of decorations. Another important Hindu holiday is Thaipusam, which usually takes place in January or February. The holiday honors Lord Subramaniam, and it is day of giving thanks for answered prayers and courage. Traditionally, the holiday includes more elaborate celebration such as parades and processions.

LANGUAGE

Bahasa Malaysia simply means the "Malaysian language" and is a standardized version of Malay. Not only is it the official language of Malaysia but also of Brunei, Indonesia, and even Singapore. Malay began

as a trade language and adopted words from its trading partners, the Chinese, Indians, Arabs, Portuguese, Dutch, and English. While the traditional Malay alphabet Jawi is based on Arabic, Malay script has been converted to roman characters.

The pronunciation of Malay is similar to English and other European languages. However, there are some important differences. The letter *c* is pronounced "ch" as in "church." Hence, the Malay word *cat* is pronounced "chat" and means "paint." The letter *g* also has the hard consonantal sound as in "grade," and so a word such as *garam* ("salt") will have the hard sound. *H* has a soft sound or is not pronounced at all, and *kh* is always hard, as in "kill." *Ng* has the soft sound, as in "song," whereas *ngg* has the hard sound, as in "mango." *Sy* is pronounced like "sh," and *r* rolled as in Spanish. Malay has five vowels as English does: *a, e, i, o,* and *u.* The vowels *i, o,* and *u* are long, while *a* is short. Finally, *e* can be unstressed, as in *u* in "put" or stressed, as in "bench." The diphthongs *au* and *ai* are pronounced like those in "cow" and "sky," respectively.

GREETINGS AND OTHER POPULAR EXPRESSIONS

Some Malay greetings and salutations include: *selamat datang* ("welcome"), *selamat pagi* ("good morning"), *selamat petang* ("good afternoon"), *selamat malam* ("good evening"), *selamat tidur* ("good night"), *selamat jalan* ("goodbye"). Basic Malay phrases and expression include: *Apa khabar?* ("How are you?"), *Khabar baik* ("I'm fine"), *Siapa nama kamu?* ("What's your name?"), *Nama saya . . .* (My name is . . .") *Dimana . . .?* ("Where is . . ."), *Ma'af* ("Excuse me" or "Sorry"), *bari ini* ("Today"), *besok* ("tomorrow"), *semalam* ("yesterday"), *tidak* ("no," "not"), *ya* ("yes"), *lelaki* ("man"), *perempuan* ("woman"), *orang* ("person"), *Terima kasih* ("Thank you"), *tolong* ("please" in a request for help), *minta* ("please" in a request for something), *makan* ("to eat"), *minum* ("to drink"), *saya mau* ("I would like"), *beli* ("to buy"), *saya tidak mengerti* ("I don't understand").

FAMILY AND COMMUNITY DYNAMICS

WEDDINGS

Malaysian weddings are colorful ceremonies, traditionally held in the home of the bride. The groom and his entourage enter the bride's home in procession, accompanied by musicians and singers and bringing gifts. While customs may vary depending on which region Malaysian Americans come from, the bride and the groom both typically wear profusely decorated garments. The bride's costume is decorated with the Malay colors, gold and silver. The ceremony features a lavish feast for the guests as well as the *bersanding,* in which the bride and groom sit together on ornate chairs while the guests come forth individually to offer their congratulations and blessings. The ceremony also may involve the *tepong tawar,* a ritual performed by guests of honor who anoint the groom's forehead with a gold ring, apply rice flour or sandalwood to it, and dapple the groom's head and hands with flowers or rice grains.

RELIGION

Like other aspects of Malaysian American culture, religion also depends on ethnic background. In Malaysia, most Malays and a smaller percentage of Chinese and Indian Malaysians are Muslims. Consequently, more than 50 percent of the population is Islamic, and Islam is the country's official religion. Nonetheless, the government ensures freedom of religion. Most of the Chinese Malaysians follow Buddhism, Taoism, and Confucianism, and the majority of the Indian Malaysians are Hindus or Sikhs—although some are Muslims. In addition, Malaysia has a small Christian segment located mostly in the states of Sabah and Sarawak.

Islamic Malaysians are Sunni Muslims from the Shafi denomination of Islam. The beliefs and obligations of Malaysian Muslims are epitomized in the Five Pillars of Islam: the belief in the omnipotence of Allah and in the Prophet Muhammad, the divine messenger; participation in ritual prayers and purification; the giving of alms; fasting during Ramadan; and at least one pilgrimage to Mecca during one's lifetime.

Since Malaysian Sunnis believe that the prayers and language of Islam came from Allah through Muhammad, they consider the very words powerful in and of themselves. Hence, their religious practices involve chants and readings of the holy words and prayers of Islam.

The Chinese Malaysians tend to believe or follow part of the three main religions of this ethnic group: Confucianism, Taoism, and Buddhism. Depending on where they came from in China, Chinese Malaysians may emphasize particular aspects of one of these religions. Unlike Islam and other religions, these three are largely philosophical and ethical systems, not organized theologies. Buddhism and Taoism, however, have temples and monasteries. The doctrines of Confucianism call for strong family ties; Taoist beliefs emphasize spiritual and mystical life over materialism; and Buddhism

holds that there is salvation and reincarnation and that people must venerate their ancestors.

Most Malaysian Indians are Hindus, and they worship a pantheon of gods. They also try to live up to a variety of ideals and practice a range of rituals. The beliefs of the Hindus emphasize family welfare, land cultivation, and veneration of the family home. Hindu temples are designed as homes for the gods rather than for communal worship. Hindus go to temples to give offerings and receive blessings. Hindu priests tend to the temples, maintaining shrines, accepting offerings, and serving as intermediaries between humans and gods; however, overall there are not that many Hindu priests in Malaysia.

ORGANIZATIONS AND ASSOCIATIONS

Harvard Club of Malaysia.

This organization serves Malaysian and Malaysian American students and alumni and seeks to build ongoing friendships among its members.

Address: Harvard Club of Malaysia c/o Proven Resources Sdn. Bhd. Suite 15.03, Level 15 Menara IMC No. 8, Jalan Sultan Ismail 50250 Kuala Lumpur.
Fax: (603) 201-9934.

The Malaysian American Society (MAS).

MAS was founded in 1967 to promote cultural exchanges between the Malaysia and the United States. The organization has a registered membership of 200 Malaysians and Malaysian Americans.

Address: 48B, Jalan SS 22/21, Damansara Jaya, 47400 Petaling Jaya, Selangor.
Telephone: (603) 716-4848.
Fax: (603) 716-6048.

Malaysian Students Association at the University of Michigan (U.M.I.M.S.A.).

U.M.I.M.S.A. has some 50 members who are Malaysian Americans or Malaysians studying in the United States and serves to foster friendships and camaraderie among Malaysian students.

Contact: Nasir Sobri.
Address: Malaysian Students Association at the University of Michigan Ann Arbor, MI 48107-7054.

Malaysia Student Association of St. Louis, Missouri (MASA).

Established in the 1980s by Malaysian students,

MASA has about 100 members and serves students from five different universities in the St. Louis area. The objective of the association is to maintain close relationships among the students after their graduation.

Contact: Abdul Shukor Ali.
Address: The New Straits Times Press, (M)
    Berhad Balai Berita, 31 Jalan Riong 59100
    Kuala Lumpur.
Telephone: (603) 282-3131 ext. 847.

University of California-Berkeley Alumni Club of Malaysia.
The UC–Berkeley Alumni Club of Malaysia strives to promote congenial relations among members in Malaysia and throughout Southeast Asia and to foster an ongoing and mutually enriching exchange between UC–Berkeley and Malaysia in the areas of professional discourse and cultural understanding. Founded in 1996, the club has a membership of about 40.

Contact: Mr. Victor Kong, President.
Address: 6, USJ 4/1G, 47600 UEP,
    Subang Jaya, Selangor.
Telephone: (603) 202-8330.

SOURCES FOR ADDITIONAL STUDY

Andaya, Barbara Watson, and Leonard Y. Andaya. *A History of Malaysia.* New York: St. Martin's Press, 1982.

King, Victor. *The Simple Guide to Malaysia: Customs and Etiquette.* Kent, England: Global Books, Ltd., 1998.

The greatest number
of Maltese people
came to the United
States during the first
decades of the
twentieth century.
Their move
coincided with the
discharge of skilled
workers from the
Royal British
Dockyard in 1919
following the end of
the World War I.

MALTESE AMERICANS

by
Diane Andreassi

OVERVIEW

A European country often called "the mouse that roars," Malta is also referred to as "the island of sunshine and history." Malta covers 122 square miles in the center of the Mediterranean Sea and is comprised of three inhabited islands: Malta, Gozo, and Comino. Malta, 17 miles long and about nine miles across, is the largest of the three islands. Gozo, the northern island, is 35 square miles and is known for its grottoes, copper beaches, and the third-largest church dome in the world. Comino, at one square mile, has a small population and is located between Malta and Gozo. The uninhabited islands in the archipelago are Filfla and St. Paul's. The topography of Malta lacks mountains and rivers, but the island is characterized by a series of low hills with terraced fields.

The weather, more than any other feature, has made Malta a key tourist resort in the center of the Mediterranean. It never snows in Malta, and the total average rainfall is 20 inches annually. The summers are warm and breezy and the winters are mild, with an average winter temperature of 54 degrees. About 606,000 tourists from all over the world, including the United States and Europe, arrive annually. Tourists boost the economy significantly by spending approximately $3.6 million each year on the island. The Maltese weather and lifestyle also call for afternoon breaks, when shop owners close and the island people rest. Everything resumes again later in the day, when the sun is not as tiring. The climate, sea, and terrain also provide perfect backdrops for movies; for instance, the movie "Popeye" was filmed on the island in the 1980s.

Malta is located 58 miles south of Sicily and 180 miles north of North Africa. The total population is 350,000, which places it among the most densely populated countries in the world. Ninety-six percent of the population is of Maltese descent, two percent are British, and the remaining people are of various other heritages. The chief languages are Maltese, English, and Italian. Ninety-seven percent of the population is Roman Catholic. A high priority is placed on education, bringing the literacy rate to 96 percent. Education is mandatory for Maltese children from age 5 to 16, and by age four there is already almost 100 percent enrollment. Instruction is available in state as well as private schools, with the private sector catering to about 27 percent of the total population.

HISTORY

The first Maltese were late Stone Age farmers who immigrated to Malta from Sicily before 4000 B.C. Structures believed to be temples were the biggest reward of these early people, and their remains can be seen in the megalithic buildings. At least one underground temple catacomb has been associated with the cult of a Mother Goddess. By the year 2000 B.C. these early arrivers were replaced by bronze-using warrior-farmers of the Alpine race who likely arrived from southern Italy.

Phoenicians were to follow during the Iron Age period around 800 B.C., and they were succeeded by Carthaginians. Due to the Punic Wars, Malta became part of the Roman Empire, and inhabitants were well treated by the conquerors. During this time, the Maltese enjoyed peace and prosperity based on a well-developed agricultural economy. Aghlabite Arabs, by way of Sicily, invaded Malta in 870. Then came Count Roger, a Norman who conquered the Arabs in Sicily and brought Malta back into the Christian and European orbit. For four-and-a-half centuries, beginning in 1090, Malta's history was nearly identical to that of Sicily.

In 1530 Malta was granted as a fief to the Order of St. John of Jerusalem, who as the Knights of Malta defended Christianity against Islam and fortified the island. The Knights of Malta were responsible for building grand churches and palaces, especially in the city of Valletta, Malta's capital. The decline of the order hastened when Napoleon landed with his Republican Army in 1798; however, the insurrection of the Maltese that same year brought the end of the French rule. Malta was granted to Britain in 1814. The British built a first-class dockyard and concentrated her fleet on Malta's magnificent harbors.

Malta's strategic position in the Mediterranean Sea made the islands an important ally during World War II. This key location also made Malta a target for overwhelming bombing by Germany and Italy during the war. Surviving the unrelenting attacks, the Maltese people were awarded the George Cross by English prime minister Winston Churchill for their fortitude and dogged determination. Evidence of the bombings, including buildings reduced to rubble and torn up streets, was still apparent decades after the war. The island became independent after a 164-year British occupancy. In 1974 Malta became a Republic.

MODERN ERA

Malta has limited natural resources, and the land is not suited to agriculture. The small size of the country and its isolation dissuades industrialization. Economic growth was spurred until the eighteenth century by a low rate of population growth, income gained from trade of cotton, and the European estates of the Knights of St. John. This began to unravel, however, following the era of the Napoleonic Wars, when an economic downswing was coupled with a surge in population. Early in the nineteenth century the government tried to obtain an ideal population—220,000 inhabitants by the twentieth century. As part of this plan, the government encouraged immigration to other British colonies in the Mediterranean and to the West Indies. The Maltese preferred northern Africa, and by 1885, 36,0000 Maltese immigrants moved to Algeria, Egypt, Tunis, and Tripoli. The rise in cheap native labor in northern Africa later pushed the Maltese people to find other locations in which to settle.

THE FIRST MALTESE IN AMERICA

The earliest Maltese settlers in the United States came in the mid-eighteenth century, mostly to New Orleans. These settlers were often regarded as Italians, and in fact tombstones sometimes mistakenly noted the deceased as "natives of Malta, Italy." The burial grounds were inscribed with such common Maltese names as Ferruggia (Farrugia), Pace, and Grima. By 1855 there were 116 Maltese living in the United States. In the 1860s, it was estimated that between five and ten Maltese came to the United States every year. The majority of the migrants were agricultural workers, and in New Orleans the majority worked as market gardeners and vegetable dealers.

The greatest number of Maltese people came to the United States during the first decades of the twentieth century. Their move coincided with the discharge of skilled workers from the Royal British Dockyard in 1919 following the end of the World War I. More than 1,300 Maltese immigrated to the United States in the first quarter of 1920, and most found work in automobile manufacturing. The *Detroit Free Press* reported in October 1920 that Detroit had the largest Maltese population in the United States, at 5,000 residents. In 1922, the *Detroit Free Press* reported that the only Maltese colony in the United States was in Detroit. Over the next few years, it is believed that more than 15,000 Maltese people settled in the United States and became citizens. They apparently intended to stay for a short time and return home. However, opportunities in America seemed more plentiful and stable than the uncertainties at home, and many Maltese people remained in the United States. By 1928 New York had an estimated 9,000 Maltese immigrants. San Francisco also had a large Maltese population.

After World War II, the Maltese government launched a program to pay passage costs to Maltese willing to emigrate and remain abroad for at least two years. As a result, a surge of Maltese left their homeland. In 1954, a reported 11,447 Maltese left the islands. This program enticed approximately 8,000 Maltese to come to the United States between 1947 and 1977. For more than a century Malta's government encouraged emigration because of the tiny size of the overpopulated island nation.

SETTLEMENT

Settlement in the United States was concentrated in Detroit, New York City, San Francisco, and Chicago. It has been estimated that more than 70,000 Maltese immigrants and their descendants were living in the United States by the mid-1990s. The largest estimated communities are the more than 44,000 Maltese in the Detroit area and the 20,000 Maltese in New York City, most of them in Astoria, Queens.

ACCULTURATION AND ASSIMILATION

Possibly due to the small size of their nation and the large numbers of countries that once occupied the islands, the Maltese are often ignored or confused with other nationalities when studies are done. However, signs of Malta can be seen in fire stations in most cities, small and large, throughout the United States. Firefighters are identified by a badge that designates their company. The majority of badges worn by firefighters take the shape of the Maltese Cross, which is an eight-sided emblem of protection and badge of honor. The history of the cross goes back to the Knights of St. John, who courageously fought for possession of the Holy Land.

Malta's involvement with the United Nations is substantial. The island country became a full member in December 1964 after gaining independence from Great Britain. Issues Malta has been involved in, or spearheaded, include the Law of the Sea Convention in 1981; the United Nations Conference on the Aged; and an initiative to raise questions about the effects of climate change.

Although the people of the Maltese islands are not particularly well known, there are a number of Maltese influences in United States culture. For instance, many people are familiar with the Maltese, a tiny fluffy white dog. The movie *The Maltese Falcon*, a drama about a detective trying to find a priceless statue, is a classic part of American cinema, although another movie, *The Maltese Bippy*, is less known. Oftentimes people with the surname Maltese are Italian by heritage, not Maltese.

TRADITIONS, CUSTOMS, AND BELIEFS

Maltese have traditions and folklore dating back centuries. They are wide and varied—and mostly forgotten today. One popular belief was that if someone gave you "the evil eye," you would have bad luck. To rid their houses of those bad spirits, some Maltese would undergo an elaborate ritual involving old dried olive branches, which were blessed on Palm Sunday in place of the palm branches commonly used in the United States on the Sunday before Easter. The Maltese would burn the olive branches in a pan and spread the incense through every room of their houses, saying a special prayer and hoping the evil spirit would be chased away.

In other folklore tradition, some Maltese believed women who were menstruating could taint new wine, so they were banned from the cellar while wine was made. The same thinking was applied to making bread.

Others thought bad luck would follow if you dropped a knife. Another sign of bad luck was the sighting of a black moth. Good luck was sure to come when a white moth was seen, however. Some believed, also, that you should never kill a moth.

The tradition of matchmaking involved an elaborate sequence of events. For instance, if a young woman were ready for marriage, her parents would place a flower pot on the front porch. A matchmaker would take note and alert the single men about her availability. Interested suitors would then tell the matchmaker they wanted to marry. Next the matchmaker would approach the father of the prospective bride and obtain his blessing.

In the United States a matchmaker was not involved. However, during the first half of the twentieth century, men interested in marrying a Maltese girl still spoke to the girl's father, and in some cases brothers and other members of her family, for permission to marry. This tradition has faded with time.

Most of these customs and beliefs were gradually forgotten as the Maltese people were assimilated into American society. However, some lingered even if they were only jokingly remembered.

CUISINE

Maltese cuisine involves a tasty mixture with many influences. Garlic is a mainstay. The most popular Maltese dish is *pastitsi*, made of a flaky dough similar to the filo dough used by Greeks. A meat or ricotta cheese mixture is wrapped inside the dough enclave, which is usually about the size of a hand. The ricotta mixture includes ricotta cheese, egg, grated cheese, salt, and pepper. The meat mixture has ground beef, onion, tomato paste, peas, salt, pepper, and curry powder. This cheese or meat mixture also can be cooked in a pie form and served as a meal. Baked macaroni, *imquarrun fil forn*, is another popular dish. The macaroni is cooked in salt water. The sauce includes ground beef, tomato paste, garlic powder, eggs, grated cheese, and a dash of curry powder. This dish can be served without baking, in which case it is called *mostoccoli*.

Rabbit cooked in various ways, including stew, is a Maltese mainstay on the island and in the United States. Pastas with ricotta and tomato sauce are common meals, too. Fish is extremely popular, likely because of the abundance available from the Mediterranean Sea. Fried cod, octopus stew, and tuna are typically on the menu. Stuffed artichoke and eggplant are regular meals as well.

For dessert or treats, date slices, or *imqaret*, are found in most Maltese homes in Malta and the United States. This deliciously deep fried pastry has dates, orange and lemon extract, anisette, chopped nuts, orange rind, and lemon rind. Cream-filled or ricotta-filled cannoli shells are common, too. These Maltese sweets are often served at functions like showers, weddings, and baptisms.

This Maltese American woman is participating in a parade in New York City.

TRADITIONAL COSTUMES

Up until the 1950s some of the women in Maltese villages wore a *ghonella*, or *faldetta*, a black dress with a black cape with a hard board black veil. In the modern era many of the fashions are dictated by Italian styles. In the United States, Maltese Americans wear typically the same fashions as other Americans.

DANCES AND SONGS

The traditional Maltese dance is an interpretive routine called *miltija*, which describes the victory of the Maltese over the Turks in 1565. Old-time singing was called *ghana*. This involves bantering, oftentimes between two people who good-heartedly tease each other. They use rhyme and jokes in a relay of comments about each other. Maltese folk singer Namru Station was best known for this form of singing.

HOLIDAYS

The Maltese love festivals, and between May and October almost every town and village in Malta and Gozo celebrates the feast day of its patron saint. The *festa* is the most important day in each village, where the church is the focal point of the event. The churches are elaborately decorated with flowers. Gold, silver, and crystal chandeliers are placed on display as a backdrop for the statue of the patron saint. After three days of preparation, the statue is carried shoulder-high along the streets of the city or village in a parade like procession, including bands and church bells. Since the Maltese specialize in making elaborate fireworks, colorful displays are part of the party. Cities and villages compete with one another to put on the best show. Maltese in the United States privately commemorate and remember the patron saint of their town, but gone are the big festivals and fireworks.

Since the country is officially Roman Catholic, the Catholic traditions and celebrations dominate in the Maltese culture. Holy days include Christmas, Easter, and an annual observance of February 10, which is the day St. Paul, Malta's patron saint, shipwrecked on the island. Legend has it that when he was shipwrecked with his crew, the people made a bonfire to make them warm. Later, a viper snake came out of the wood and went toward St. Paul. The people were awed that this man had escaped the ravages of the seas, and they were curious to see what would happen with the snake. When he was not bitten, the people thought for sure this man was God. He told them, "I am not a God, but I came to talk to you about God."

Other public holidays in Malta include January 1, New Year's Day; March 19, St. Joseph's feast day; March 29, Good Friday; March 31, Freedom Day; May 1, May Day; June 7, Sette Giugno; June 29, St. Peter and St. Paul feast day; August 15, the Assumption of the Blessed Virgin Mary; September 8, Our Lady of Victories or Victory Day; September 21, Independence Day; December 8, the Immaculate Conception of the Blessed Virgin Mary; December 13, Republic Day; and December 25, Christmas Day.

On patriotic days, the Maltese flag is flown. It has two vertical stripes, white in the hoist and red in the fly. A sign, of the George Cross awarded to Malta by His Majesty King George the Sixth on the April 15, 1942, is carried, edged with red in the canton of the white stripe. According to tradition the national colors were given to the Maltese by Count Roger in 1090. Roger the Norman had landed in Malta to oust the Arabs from the island. Out of regard for their hospitality, Roger gave the Maltese part of the pennant of the Hautevilles to serve as their colors.

PROVERBS

Unless the baby cries, he or she will not be put to the mother's breast; Build your reputation and go to sleep; Who I see you with is who I see you as; Little by little the jar will fill; Essence comes in small bottles; Cut the tail of a donkey and it's still a donkey; If you want it to be it never will be; I'll be there if I'm not dead; A friend in the market is better than your money in the hope chest; God does not pay every Saturday; He who waits will sooner or later be happy; Only God knows when death and rain will happen; Always hold onto the words of the elderly to show respect and to gain from their wisdom.

HEALTH ISSUES

Many Maltese people have been stricken with thalassemia. It is also called Mediterranean anemia, because it usually strikes people from that region. In the United States most cases occur in Americans of Maltese, Italian, Greek, Portuguese, or Levantine background. Thalassemia refers to a group of hereditary disorders of the control of globin synthesis, causing too much or too little synthesis of either the alpha or the beta globin chains. In some cases a wrong kind of chain is produced. In beta-thalassemia deficient amounts of beta chains are produced, and in hemoglobin-Lepore thalassemia the beta chain grows longer than the normal 146 amino acids. When the gene is taken from only one parent, a mild anemia usually results; however, when the gene is from both parents the results are devastating. This blood disease is usually discovered during infancy.

LANGUAGE

Like its people and history, the Maltese language is varied. It is Semitic, chiefly Arabic, written in the Roman alphabet, with words and phrases taken from the Italian, Spanish, English, Greek, and some French. The official languages in Malta are Maltese and English. Many people also speak Italian. When English is spoken it is often heard with a British accent, likely a remnant of the 164-year British occupancy of the country.

GREETINGS AND OTHER POPULAR EXPRESSIONS

Typical Maltese greetings and other expressions include: *bongu* ("bon-ju")—good morning; *bonswa* ("bon-swar")—good night; *grazzi* ("grats-ee")—thank you; *taf titkellem bl-Ingliż?* ("tarf tit-kell-lem bilin-gleez")—do you speak English?; *kemm?* ("kem")—how much? The word *sahha* ("sa-ha") can be used as a greeting, as good-bye, or as a toast—it is the Maltese equivalent of "good health."

FAMILY AND COMMUNITY DYNAMICS

There were many changes in the family structure when the first Maltese immigrants came to the United States. Typically, the patriarchs came to the United States without their families. Sometimes they would bring sons, but the wives and children were often left on the homeland. The plan was that they would bring their entire family after they established themselves in their new country and were more financially stable. Oftentimes years lapsed before the entire family was reunited. In other cases, single men came to the United States and lived with relatives or close family friends who had come to the country earlier. They lived in communities that were heavily populated by other Maltese and often married Maltese women who came to America with their families. These Maltese couples then raised a generation of full-blooded Maltese children who had never lived in the mother country. In downtown Detroit and neighboring Highland Park, the largest Maltese community in the United States, there was a heavily populated Maltese area. However, by the 1970s many, but certainly not all, the Maltese in this area began moving to Detroit suburbs.

Maltese family members were usually very close, and aunts, uncles, and cousins were often regarded as immediate family. Before 1980 most Maltese families were large, with four or more children as the norm. In later years, however, the Maltese, like most other ethnic groups in the United States, were beginning to have smaller families, with two or three children commonly found in each household.

There were a number of gathering places, like clubs, where immigrants and first-generation Maltese could find camaraderie. New immigrants also turned to the Maltese clubs and organizations for information and direction on life in their new country. They were a good place to meet other Maltese, who spoke the language and could help in the assimilation process.

WEDDINGS

A Maltese bridal shower is usually very elaborate, with a multi-course meal and a sweet table. The party often is held in a hall or banquet room to accommodate the large number of family and friends who are invited. In Malta the typical wedding is based on the Roman Catholic mass. The bride would be accompanied by several bridesmaids and the groom had one male, the best man, at his side. In the United States, however, the Maltese wedding is usually dictated by typical traditions followed in the United States.

BAPTISMS

Again the Roman Catholic religion dictates much of what happens at baptisms. A *parrina*, or god-mother, and a *parrinu*, or godfather, are chosen. Usually, these people are close family members, like brothers or sisters of the baby's parents. In Malta a party celebration with tables of cookies, ice creams, and drinks will follow the religious ceremony. However, as the customs changed in their new country, the Maltese Americans adopted new traditions, like having a full meal at the party after the baptism.

FUNERALS

The Maltese in the United States have adopted the wake tradition. In Malta when a person died they were usually buried within 24 hours, and very few people were embalmed. In the villages during the early part of the twentieth century, a local person would visit the home, clean the body, and dress the deceased. This person usually was on the lowest rung of the social ladder. Superstition prevailed, and some people were afraid of the undertaker to the point that when village people saw him walking down the street they would walk on the other side of the road. As time passed, however, these traditions faded in Malta and most certainly were not followed in the United States.

RELIGION

Malta's strong Roman Catholic history has been imprinted on those who came to the United States. The religion dates back to a cadre of important visitors to the island, including the Apostle Paul, who was shipwrecked on the island in 60 A.D. The hospitality shown to him by the locals was well documented in the Acts of the Apostles, Chapters 27 and 28, in the New Testament of the Bible. "The natives showed us extraordinary kindness by lighting a fire and gathering us all around it, for it had begun to rain and was growing cold," a passage reads.

Malta's historical and religious background was also greatly influenced by the Knights of the Order of St. John during the eleventh century. In the Holy Land, the Order's original duties were to care for the sick and wounded Christians. The Knights became soldiers of Christ and maintained huge estates in the Holy Land. With the loss of Acre—their headquarters—to the Moslems in 1291, however, the Knights withdrew to Rhodes. They were shields against the Turks until 1522, when Suleiman the Magnificent ousted the Knights from Rhodes. In 1530 they moved to Malta. They quickly improved trade and commerce on the islands by building new hospitals and erecting strong fortifications. Although heavily outnumbered, the Knights fought off an attack by Suleiman during the Great Siege of

1565. They were assisted by Maltese and Sicilian reinforcements. The Turks retreated and the Knights of St. John protected southern Europe and Christendom. A blossoming era in culture, architecture, and the arts followed, when the fortress city, Valletta, was built. The fall of the Ottoman Empire marked the end of the military life of the Order. To this day, 97 percent of the Maltese are Roman Catholic.

In the United States the Maltese maintain their strong devotion to the Catholic church by attending mass weekly and becoming active in their local parishes. Since attendance among Maltese Americans is high, church is another common place where they meet one another. For instance, in San Francisco, St. Paul of the Shipwreck Church at 1122 Jamestown Avenue is heavily populated by Maltese. And in Detroit, the Maltese have attended St. Paul's Maltese Church since the 1920s.

EMPLOYMENT AND ECONOMIC TRADITIONS

Many of the Maltese who came to the Detroit area worked on the assembly line at one of the three automakers, Ford Motor Company, General Motors, and Chrysler Corporation. Other Maltese immigrants worked at various jobs on ships, in restaurants and hotels, selling real estate, and in religious orders as priests and nuns.

POLITICS AND GOVERNMENT

The Maltese government is a Republic with a president and prime minister. The major political parties are the Malta Labor Party and the Nationalist Party. In Malta, the first American consul was nominated in 1796, which made Malta among the first countries to have a consular office of the United States.

MILITARY

Maltese involvement in supporting the United States during war dates back to at least the American Revolution. Maltese seamen enlisted in the French navy, which was supporting the colonists against Great Britain. About 1,800 Maltese sailors went to Toulon to join the French in this effort.

RELATIONS WITH MALTA

During the first decade of the nineteenth century American ships brought a variety of goods to Malta, including flour, rice, pepper, salted meat, rum, tobacco, and mahogany wood from Boston and Baltimore, as well as dried fruits, cotton, wax, pearls, goat hides, coffee, potatoes, drugs, and sponges from Smyrne and the Greek archipelago. During 1808, 33 American vessels entered Valletta, Malta's capital city. Trade would rise and fall cyclically. Malta's biggest boon of American shipping was during the Crimean War, between 1854 and 1856, when Great Britain and France were fighting Russia. Malta also emerged as a stepping stone in the wool trade between Barbary and the United States because it received wool from different ports in North Africa for shipment to America. Later, American tobacco was shipped to Barbary and Sicily through Malta. About 1,500 Maltese were employed in making cigars, which were exported to Italy, Barbary, Turkey, and the Greek Islands. Malta also imported petroleum, rum, pepper, flour, logwood, pitch, resin, turpentine, coffee, sugar, cloves, codfish, wheat, cheese, butter, and lard. Meanwhile, the island nation exported to America items such as olive oil, lemons, sulphur, ivory, salt, rags, goat skins, stoneware, soap, squills, sponges, and donkeys of the largest and most valuable race in the Mediterranean.

INDIVIDUAL AND GROUP CONTRIBUTIONS

ACADEMIA

Professor Paul Vassallo, formerly of Marsa, Malta, headed a consortium of eight universities in the Washington, D.C. area. The Washington Research Library Consortium is a national model of the U.S. government that demonstrates how university libraries can keep up with the volume of new material. Vassallo, born in 1932, immigrated to the United States when he was 15 years old. His mother and siblings lived in the Detroit area.

FILM, TELEVISION, AND THEATER

Joseph Calleia, a Maltese native and actor, appeared in a number of Hollywood movies, including *Wild Is the Wind* in 1957.

MILITARY

Joseph Borg went to the United States at the time of the American Revolution. He was described as having been a sea captain who fought in many battles for American independence.

Brigadier General Patrick P. Caruana commanded the 50 B-52 bombers flying out of Saudi Arabia, England, Spain, and the Indian Ocean during the Persian Gulf War of 1991. The fleet pounded the Iraqis incessantly and helped break their morale. Caruana, a St. Louis resident, was also a KC-135 tanker pilot in Vietnam and commanded the 17th Air Division and its fleet of bombers refueling tankers and spy planes.

MUSIC

Oreste Kirkop, an opera singer, appeared in *Student Prince*. Legend had it that he was encouraged to change his name to increase his fame, but he refused to take the suggestion and instead returned to Malta.

SCIENCE AND TECHNOLOGY

John Schembri, a Pacific Bell employee, has two patents to his name and a third pending. He holds degrees in electronics, engineering, mathematics, and industrial relations and is a recognized expert in the design and application of optical fiber transmissions systems.

VISUAL ARTS

The Liberty Bell was made in England in 1751 for the Assembly of the Province of Pennsylvania, to be used in the State House of the City of Philadelphia. However, when it was being tested the bell cracked. It was recast in Philadelphia by John Pass, a Maltese immigrant, and John Stow, who added a small amount of copper to make it less brittle. Pass appears in the painting "The Bell's First Note," which hangs in the U.S. National Museum of the Smithsonian Institution in Washington, D.C. Although Pass is not a Maltese surname, there is no doubt about his heritage: the speaker of the Pennsylvania Assembly referred to him as hailing from Malta. It is likely that his name in Malta was Pace, and he either changed it, or it was misspelled in documents.

MEDIA

Malta Messenger.
Contact: Charles Hogan, Editor and Publisher.
Address: 72 West High Street, Ballston Spa, New York 12020-1927.
Telephone: (518) 885-4341.
Fax: (518) 885-4344.

Maltese Center Update.
Formerly *Malta Gazetta.*

Address: 27-20 Hoyt Avenue South, Astoria, New York 11102.

ORGANIZATIONS AND ASSOCIATIONS

American Association, Sovereign Military Order of Malta.
Address: 1011 First Avenue, Room 1500, New York, New York 10022.

Committee for Maltese Unity, Inc.
Address: P.O. Box 456, Mount Vernon,
New York 10551.

Friends of Malta Society, Inc.
Address: 3009 Schoenherr Road, Warren,
Michigan 48093.

Institute of Maltese American Affairs.
Address: Malta Overseas Press News Service,
Allied Newspapers Limited, Malta House, 36
Cooper Avenue, Dumont, New Jersey 07628.

Malta Club of Macomb.
Address: 31024 Jefferson Avenue, St. Clair
Shores, Michigan 48082.

Maltese American Association of L.I., Inc.
Address: 1486 Lydia Avenue, Elmont,
New York 11003.

Maltese American Benevolent Society.
Serves social and patriotic needs of Detroit's Maltese population, estimated to be 66,000 and believed to be the largest in the U.S. Supports children's services. Offers activities for members and their families.

Contact: John Caruana, President.
Address: 1832 Michigan Avenue, Detroit,
Michigan 48216.
Telephone: (313) 961-8393.
Fax: (313) 961-2050.

Maltese American Club.
Address: 5221 Oakman Boulevard, Dearborn,
Michigan 48216.
Telephone: (313) 846-7077.

Maltese American Community Club.
Address: 17929 Eton Avenue, Dearborn Heights,
Michigan 48215.

Maltese American Foundation.
Address: 2074 Ridgewood Road, Medina,
Ohio 44256.

Maltese American Friendship Society, Inc.
Address: 32-57 45th Street, Astoria,
New York 11103.

Maltese American League.
Address: 1977 Le Blanc Street, Lincoln Park,
Michigan 48146.

**Maltese-American Social Club of
San Francisco, Inc.**
Address: 1769 Oakdale Avenue, San Francisco,
California 94134.

Maltese International.
Address: 10 Columbus, Berea, Ohio 44017.

Maltese Social Club.
Address: 27-20 Hoyt Avenue South, Astoria,
New York 11102.

Maltese Union Club.
Address: 246 Eighth Avenue, New York,
New York 10011.

San Pablo Rectory.
Address: 550 122nd Street, Ocean Maraton,
Florida 33050.

Sons of Malta Social Club, Inc.
Address: 233 East 32nd Street, New York,
New York 10016.

MUSEUMS AND
RESEARCH CENTERS

Maltese American Benevolent Society.
Contains a library covering Maltese issues, concerns, and background.

Contact: John Caruana, President.
Address: 1832 Michigan Avenue, Detroit,
Michigan 48216.
Telephone: (313) 961-8393.
Fax: (313) 961-2050.

SOURCES FOR
ADDITIONAL STUDY

Balm, Roger. *Malta.* Blacksburg, VA: McDonald & Woodard Publishing, 1995.

Dobie, Edith. *Malta's Road to Independence.* Norman: University of Oklahoma Press, 1967.

Early Relations Between Malta and U.S.A. Valletta, Malta: Midsea Books, Ltd., 1976.

The Epic of Malta. Odhams Press Limited, 1943.

Luke, Harry. *Malta: An Account and an Appreciation,* second edition. [London], 1968.

The Malta Yearbook. Sliema, Malta: De La Salle Brothers Publications, 1991.

Price, Charles A. *Malta and the Maltese: A Study in Nineteenth Century Migration.* Melbourne, Australia, 1954.

By 1990 over one-
half million Hispanic-
owned businesses
existed in the United
States, the majority
of them in California
and controlled by
Mexican Americans.

MEXICAN AMERICANS

by
Allan Englekirk and
Marguerite Marín

OVERVIEW

Mexico, or Estados Unidos Mexicanos, is bordered by the United States to the north, the Gulf of Mexico to the east, Guatemala, Belize, and the Caribbean Sea to the southeast, and the Pacific to the south and west. The northwest portion of Mexico, called Baja California, is separated from the rest of the nation by the Gulf of California. The Sierra Madre, an extension of the Rocky Mountain chain, divides into the Oriental range to the east and the Occidental range to the west. The central highlands, where the majority of Mexico's 75 million people live, lies in between these two mountain systems. Overall, Mexico occupies 759,530 square miles.

HISTORY

The earliest inhabitants of Mexico are believed to have been hunters who migrated from Asia approximately 18,000 years ago. Over time, these early peoples built highly organized civilizations, such as the Olmec, Teotihuacan, Mayan, Toltec, Zapotec, Mixtec, and Aztec societies, the majority of which were accomplished in art, architecture, mathematics, astronomy, and agriculture. In 1517 Spanish explorer Francisco Fernández de Córdoba discovered the Yucatán, a peninsula located in the southeast of Mexico. By 1521 the Spanish conquistador Hernando Cortéz had managed to conquer the

Aztec empire, the most powerful Indian nation in Mexico at the time. For the next 300 years, Mexico, or New Spain, would remain under colonial rule.

Spain's generally repressive colonial regime stifled the growth of commerce and industry, monitored or censored the dissemination of new and possibly revolutionary ideas, and limited access to meaningful political power to anyone but native-born Spaniards. An unequal distribution of land and wealth developed and, as the nation grew in numbers, the disproportion between the rich and poor continued to increase, as did a sense of social unrest among the most neglected of its populace. Their discontent resulted in a successful revolt against Spain in 1821.

In the latter part of the nineteenth century, under the 30-year authoritarian rule of Porfirio Díaz, noticeable industrialization occurred in Mexico, financed in large part by foreigners. Mining was revitalized and foreign trade increased. Dynamic growth brought relative prosperity to many economic sectors of various regions of the country, complemented by increased levels of employment. As the century ended, however, a vast majority of the nations's inhabitants had realized little if any improvement in their standard of living. Those residing in rural areas struggled to produce enough to survive from their own small parcels of land, or, much more likely, worked under a debt-peonage system, farming lands owned by someone infinitely wealthier than they were. Most residents of urban areas, if they were lucky enough to have full employment, worked long hours under poor conditions for extremely low wages and lived in housing and neighborhoods that fostered diseases. The economic depression of 1907 soured the aspirations of the small but growing middle class and brought financial disaster to the newest members of the upper class (Ramón Ruiz, *Triumphs and Tragedy*, pp. 310-13).

Though he was able to manipulate his reelection in 1910, opposition to the Díaz regime was strong, and when small rebellions began to proliferate in the northern states of the nation, he resigned his post in 1911 and left the country. After Francisco Madero, the newly elected president, failed to define an agenda to satisfy the several disparate groups in Mexico, he likewise agreed to self-exile but was assassinated by supporters of General Victoriano de la Huerta, the man who next assumed national leadership. Violence escalated into a bloody and prolonged civil war known as the Revolution of 1910. The turmoil and bloodshed motivated some people from all levels of society to flee the country, most often northward to the United States.

By the early 1920s, though relative peace had been restored, the social and economic reforms that had become associated with the revolution were still unrealized, chief among them the redistribution of land to a greater percentage of the populace. From the perspective of the government-controlled political party, first designated as the PNR (Partido Nacional Revolucionario/National Revolutionary Party), and finally, in 1946, as the PRI (Partido Revolucionario Institucional/Institutional Revolutionary Party), a nonviolent revolution was to continue until the goals related to social and economic justice were attained (Ruiz, p. 423). National presidents focused on promoting growth in the industrial sector, but the opening of new jobs did not keep pace with the employment needs of a rapidly expanding population.

Since the 1950s, economic conditions in Mexico have improved at a gradual pace. Expanding industrialization has provided additional jobs for greater numbers of workers and increased oil production has brought in needed foreign currencies. The projected benefits from commercial accords such as the North American Free Trade Agreement have yet to materialize, but continued growth of international trade with other Latin American nations may invigorate areas of economic investment and production. Continued single-party rule by the PRI, high levels of unemployment, underemployment, low wages, and the many social problems related to a prolonged period of intense urbanization—coupled with the need for renewed efforts at land redistribution in certain areas of the country—remain as sources of concern for the government and causes of unrest for a significant segment of the population. In increasing proportions since the late 1970s, those people unable to find dependable sources of employment or subsistence wages have moved to the northern borderlands and crossed into the United States, where the economic prospects are more promising. To reverse this movement of manpower out of the country, future administrations in Mexico will have to continue to promote the expansion of economic growth to all regions in the country and the creation of new jobs in the public and private sectors.

THE MEXICAN-AMERICAN WAR AND MEXICAN IMMIGRATION TO THE UNITED STATES

The Mexican government initially promoted American settlement in parts of the territory now known as Texas in the 1820s to bolster the regional economy. As the proportion of North American settlers in these lands multiplied, however, they began to request greater local autonomy, feared the possibility that Mexico might outlaw slavery, and resented the imposition of taxes from the government in Mexico City (Oscar Martínez, *The Handbook of Hispanic Cultures in the United States History*, p. 263). Sporadic insurrections occurred after a new president, General Antonio López de Santa Anna, imposed restrictive controls on commerce between the Anglos living on Mexican land and the United States, and these uprisings precipitated an armed response by the Mexican army. Santa Anna seized the Alamo in San Antonio but was later defeated in the Battle of San Jacinto. Santa Anna later signed the Velasco Agreement in Washington D.C., which formally recognized the independence of present-day Texas. After returning to Mexico, however, he was quick to join other military leaders who rejected the accord.

Relations between the United States and Mexico remained strained, at best, during the late 1830s and early 1840s. The Lone Star Republic was admitted to the Union as the State of Texas in 1845; shortly thereafter the frequency of border skirmishes between the two countries increased. U.S. forces responded to these clashes by moving into New Mexico and California in 1846, as well as southward into Mexico. The capture of Mexico City was the final significant armed conflict.

War between Mexico and the United States ended with the Treaty of Guadalupe Hidalgo in 1848 in which Mexico surrendered 890,000 square miles, close to one-half of its territory. Six years later, in order to finish construction of a transcontinental railway, the United States purchased an additional 30,000 square miles of Mexican land for $10 million. This acquisition was made final through the Gadsden Treaty of 1854 (Carlos Cortés, *Harvard Encyclopedia of American Ethnic Groups*, p. 701).

Approximately 80,000 Mexicans resided in the territory transferred to the United States at the conclusion of the Mexican-American War, the greatest numbers of whom were located in present-day New Mexico and California. Only a small proportion of the total, slightly over 2,000, decided to return to their country of origin after the signing of the treaty. Those who remained north of the border were guaranteed citizenship after two years, along with other privileges and responsibilities related to this status.

SIGNIFICANT IMMIGRATION WAVES

When compared to various periods of the twentieth century, Mexican immigration to the United States between 1850 and 1900 was relatively low. The discovery of gold in the Sierra Nevada of California in 1849 was an initial stimulus for this migration, as was the expansion of copper mining in Arizona beginning in the 1860s. During this same period and on into the twentieth century, ranching and agriculture lured many inhabitants of the northern and central states of Mexico to Texas. By 1900 approximately 500,000 people of Mexican ancestry lived in the United States, principally in the areas originally populated by Spaniards and Mexicans prior to 1848. Roughly 100,000 of these residents were born in Mexico; the remainder were second-generation inhabitants of these regions and their offspring.

A combination of factors contributed to sequential pronounced rises in Mexican migration to the United States during the first three decades of the twentieth century. The Reclamation Act of 1902, which expanded acreage for farming through new irrigation projects, spurred the need for more agricultural laborers. The Mexican Revolution of 1910 and the aftermath of political instability and social violence caused many to flee northward across the border for their safety, and the growth of the U.S. economy in the 1920s attracted additional numbers of immigrants. Though the wages received by most Mexican migrants in these decades were quite low, they were considerably higher than the salaries paid for comparable work in Mexico. Most importantly, the number of jobs for foreign laborers seemed unlimited, especially during World War I and on into the early 1920s.

Only 31,000 Mexicans migrated to the United States in the first decade of the twentieth century, but the next two ten-year periods manifested markedly higher numbers, especially from 1920 to 1929, when almost 500,000 people of Mexican ancestry entered the country. However, since the frontier was virtually open to anyone wishing to cross it until the creation of the Border Patrol in 1924, immigration figures for years prior to this date are of dubious legitimacy. The actual number may be appreciably higher (Cortés, p. 699). Rural areas of California, Arizona, New Mexico, Colorado, and Texas attracted a vast majority of these migrants, but during the years of World War I, mounting numbers of newcomers moved to the upper midwestern states, mainly to the region around Chicago. They were attracted by jobs in industry, railroads, steelmills, and meat-packing.

In these initial periods of heavy immigration, it was most common for Mexican males to cross the border for work and return to Mexico periodically with whatever profits they were able to accumulate over several months. Alternatively, they remained in the United States for a longer duration and sent money southward to family members; between 1917 and 1929, Mexican migrants to the United

States sent over $10 million to relatives in their home country (Carey McWilliams, *North from Mexico*, [New York: Praeger, 1990], p. 171). During these same decades, men might also establish residency in the United States and return for their families, though still quite often with the ultimate objective of returning to Mexico permanently in a not-too-distant future. It is estimated that about one-half of those immigrants who entered the United States from 1900 to 1930 returned to Mexico (Matt Meier and Feliciano Rivera, *Mexican Americans/American Mexicans*, [New York: Hill and Wang, 1993], p. 129).

Mexican immigration to the United States decreased considerably in the 1930s due to the economic depression of this decade. Though approximately 30,000 Mexicans entered the United States during these years, over 500,000 left the country, most of them forced to do so because of the Repatriation Program, which sought to extradite those Mexicans without proper documentation. The Mexican government since the 1870s had attempted to encourage reverse migration to Mexico. In the 1930s jobs and/or land were promised to those who would return, but when this commitment was not fulfilled, many families or individuals moved back to the border towns of the north and often attempted again to return to the United States (Richard Griswold del Castillo, *La familia*, p. 59).

With the exception of the decade of Word War II, legal immigration from Mexico to the United States since 1940 has remained at or above the high levels of 1910 to 1930. Despite federal legislation to limit the numbers of immigrants from most countries to the United States in the 1960s and 1970s, Mexican migrants crossing the border totaled 453,937 and 640,294 for the two decades. It is estimated that approximately one million entered the United States legally between 1981 and 1990. The number of undocumented workers has increased consistently since the 1960s; approximately one million people of this category were deported annually to Mexico in the late 1980s and early 1990s, a proportion of this figure representing individuals deported more than once (Meier and Rivera, pp. 192-95). The availability of jobs in the United States, coupled with high rates of unemployment and periodic slowdowns in the Mexican economy, served to encourage this continued migration northward.

SETTLEMENT PATTERNS

Though in 1900 a vast majority of people of Mexican ancestry lived in rural areas, by 1920, 40 percent of the Mexican American population resided in cities or towns. In 1990 the estimated proportion had risen to 94 percent (Meier and Rivera, p. 250). Los Angeles had among the highest number of Hispanics of major cities of the world and by far the greatest proportion of its population was Mexican in origin.

According to the 1990 U.S. Census Bureau report, approximately 12 million people of Mexican ancestry lived in the United States, a figure which represented 4.7 percent of the total national population and 61.2 percent of the total Hispanic population in the country. Over 66 percent of the people of Mexican ancestry were born in the United States, while 7.5 percent of the total were naturalized citizens. The Pacific states, led by California, held 47.8 percent of the 12 million; 30 percent lived in the West Central states, led by Texas. The states with the highest populations of Mexican Americans are, in descending sequence: California, Texas, Illinois, Arizona, New Mexico, Colorado, Florida, and Washington.

RELATIONS WITH ANGLO AMERICANS

Mexicans who held tracts of land of any appreciable size in Texas, California, and New Mexico prior to 1848 were angered and alienated when they began to lose their properties because of alterations made in the 1848 treaty after its signing or because of other unethical tactics used by Anglo Americans to obtain their land. Luis Falcón and Dan Gilbarg identify the procedures employed to acquire two-thirds of the lands once held by Spanish or Mexican families in New Mexico: "Traditional claims were rejected, and original owners were required to prove their ownership in court. The procedures of these courts were biased against the original owners: the burden of proof fell on them, the courts were conducted in English and in locations less accessible to Mexican landowners, and standards of legal proof were based on U.S. law rather than Mexican law under which the land had originally been acquired" (Luis Falcón and Dan Gilbarg, *The Handbook ... Sociology*, p. 58). Small landholders were particularly vulnerable. Land companies often successfully appropriated the holdings of isolated Mexican villagers who neglected to register their land claims in the appropriate governmental offices or failed to pay sometimes burdensome new taxes demanded on their properties. In some instances, these taxes were increased to excessive levels for Mexicans, then lowered after they were forced to sell their holdings to Anglo American families or land agents (Cortés, p. 707).

The response of many Mexicans in the southwestern United States to the Anglo American presence was retaliatory violence. In New Mexico, Las

Gorras Blancas, a vigilante group, destroyed rail lines and the properties of lumber and cattle interests in an attempt to convince these forces to move elsewhere (Griswold del Castillo, p. 13). In Texas, the decade-long Cortina War started in 1859. After shooting a deputy sheriff for arresting one of his former servants for no apparently just reason, Juan Nepomuceno Cortina and some followers conducted a prolonged series of raids on ranches and small towns around Brownsville, in part to avenge the deputy's act but also because he believed that since shortly after their arrival in the region Anglo Americans had scorned and insulted Mexican locals. In defense of Mexican property rights, Cortina declared: "Our personal enemies shall not possess our lands until they have fattened it with their gore" (McWilliams, pp. 104-05). Most Mexicans perceived Anglo Americans to be "arrogant, overbearing, aggressive, conniving, rude, unreliable and dishonest" because of the unscrupulous actions of some (McWilliams, p. 89).

Disfavor on the part of some Anglo Americans with Mexicans was evident before 1848, but it intensified thereafter. Besides a small minority of well-to-do Mexican families with extensive landholdings, the preponderant number of residents in the territories ceded to the United States in 1848 were of humble origin and negligible financial resources. As greater numbers came north in search of work, the wages of those Mexicans already working in the United States were held down due to the abundant supply of labor, and the standard of living of most of these individuals consequently remained at the same low level for decade upon decade. Though not all Anglo Americans living in the same areas inhabited by Mexicans were appreciably better off, a definite economic disparity existed and was one of the reasons for a division to develop between the two cultures.

Other differences made this division more pronounced, however. Whereas the immigrants from Mexico were predominantly Catholic, most of the people who settled in Texas, California, and the other territories were of Protestant sects. The religious wars on the European continent between these creeds were not too distant in the past to be forgotten. Perhaps most importantly for some, however, the new majority society was decidedly of North European origin and of light skin color. In contrast, most Mexicans living in or moving to these newly acquired lands of the United States were *mestizos* (people of mixed Spanish and Indian ancestry), and a significant percentage of those who immigrated from the northern states of Mexico were primarily of Indian ancestry. The sentiments of a sizable portion of western settlers in the United States in the mid-1800s about the indigenous civilizations whose lands they were slowly appropriating were quite negative. In the words of McWilliams, "Indians were a conquered race despised by Anglo Americans" and "Mexicans were constantly equated with Indians" by the most race-conscious of the early Anglo American westerners (McWilliams, p. 190).

The number of immigrants increased considerably in the first decades of the twentieth century. Though employers in mining, agriculture, and various industries were more than pleased to see ever larger numbers of migrant workers cross the border each year, Anglo American laborers in the same occupations as these immigrants blamed the newcomers for holding their wages down and viewed them as strike busters. Moreover, when urbanization became more pronounced in the 1920s and Mexicans in the Southwest began moving to the major cities, many people in these urban centers perceived these Hispanics as part of the cause of higher crime rates, increased vagrancy, and violence. City chambers of commerce, local welfare agencies, nativist organizations, and various labor unions all began to call for controls on Mexican migration. Bills to place a limit on their immigration were proposed in Congress in the 1920s but never ratified (Cortés, p. 703). Massive unemployment in the 1930s prompted the initiation of the Repatriation Program. Many of the Mexicans who left the country had lived in the United States for over ten years and had started American-born families. Their mandated eviction was a tragic experience that led to a bitter realization: it was clear to those involved that they were only welcome in the United States when the economy needed their labors. This would not be the last time this fact would be dramatized to Mexicans and Mexican Americans in such humiliating fashion.

Approximately 350,000 children born in the United States of Mexican immigrants or Mexican American parents fought in World War II, and a proportionately high number won medals of honor, but relations between Mexican American and Anglo American citizens remained tense in the 1940s. In 1942 in Los Angeles, the purported beating of eleven sailors by a group of Mexican American youths sparked a prolonged retaliation by servicemen and civilians against Hispanics wearing "zoot suits," distinctive clothing interpreted by some Anglo Americans in the city to symbolize a rebellious attitude by the younger Mexican Americans. Many injuries occurred on both sides and the riots in Los Angeles spread to several other metropolitan centers nationwide (Meier and Rivera, p. 164).

After the war, despite the fact that thousands of Mexican Americans lost their lives in battle, many Hispanics remained segregated in neighborhoods out of sight to Anglo American society. They attended segregated schools, ate in segregated restaurants, sat in specially designated areas of theaters, and swam in pools on "colored" days only (Cortés, pp. 707-09). Though in the 1950s several southwestern states attempted to rebuild old sections of certain towns of Spanish heritage to romanticize the local Hispanic traditions, the apparent respect for the Hispanic past in this region of the country contrasted "harshly with the actual behavior of the community toward persons of Mexican descent" (McWilliams, p. 47). Increased tourism, rather than pride in the multicultural heritage of these areas, might have been the primary factor for most reconstruction programs.

Only in the 1960s, when the civil rights of most minorities in the United States were brought under scrutiny, did the negative attitudes of many citizens toward Mexican Americans begin to be called into question. In 1970 the U.S. Commission on Civil Rights proclaimed that Mexican Americans had been denied equal treatment by the legal and judicial systems in the United States (Cortés, p. 714). The press coverage given to the efforts of César Chávez to improve the wages and working conditions of agricultural workers and the vital ideas emerging from the Chicano movement of the 1970s raised the consciousness of non-Hispanic U.S. citizens to the social and economic issues of importance to the Mexican American population of the country. The *Teatro Campesino* of Luis Valdez dramatized visually for audiences the barriers of prejudice faced by most Mexican Americans in the land once possessed by their ancestors.

A significant majority of U.S. citizens in the 1990s recognized that Mexican Americans represent a segment of the population whose contributions to the nation's society have been and will be valuable and praiseworthy. Upward mobility has brought a better life to a minority of Mexican Americans and increased acceptance by some who might previously have repudiated them. Inequalities and discrimination have not disappeared, however, and remain as legitimate and vexing sources of discontent for a significant segment of this Hispanic community. As reasons for misunderstanding or discord diminish, both cultures will realize greater rewards.

ACCULTURATION AND ASSIMILATION

Most immigrant groups in America to a lesser or greater extent have attempted to maintain their dis-

tinctive cultural ways. However, the general pattern has been that with each successive generation the use of the mother tongue and other cultural practices diminishes. Mexican Americans do not fit this pattern for a number of reasons. First of all one must consider their historical experience, particularly their "charter member" status within the United States. Some Mexican Americans can trace their ancestry back ten generations. The ancestors of many Mexican Americans living in rural Colorado and northern New Mexico pre-date the Anglo American presence in that region. Many have not acculturated; some speak English with difficulty and appear to be more traditionally oriented than the newly arrived Mexican immigrant (Joan Moore and Henry Pachón, *Hispanics in the United States*, p. 92). Second, Mexican immigration has been a constant pattern throughout the twentieth century. As a result, each successive wave of Mexican immigration has served to reinforce certain aspects of Mexican culture and maintain and encourage the use of the Spanish language within the United States. In addition, intermarriage between immigrant males and Mexican American women has encouraged the maintenance of Spanish. Immigrants have also encouraged the continuous growth of Spanish language enterprises such as the Spanish-language media, print as well as electronic, and small businesses that cater to the Spanish-speaking community. In fact, McLemore has stated that Mexican Americans "have been the primary contributors to the maintenance of the Spanish language over a comparatively long period of time" (*Ethnic Relations in America*, p. 261).

The size and the distribution of the ethnic group also plays a dominant role in the persistence of traditional cultural patterns. The 1990 census indicates that there are approximately 21,000,000 Hispanic Americans residing in the United States, so about one out of every ten Americans is of Hispanic origin. Mexican Americans form the largest group of Hispanic Americans, at over 12,000,000. Not all speak Spanish, but most have some familiarity with the language, and many who speak English in the larger society will often speak Spanish at home. While most are concentrated in the southwestern United States, there has been a greater integration of Mexican Americans into the larger society, and the vast majority are likely to live in communities with high concentrations of inhabitants of their same ethnic identity. Thus, the potential for interaction with other Mexican Americans is extremely high. Many, on a daily basis, will work, go to school, go to church, and attend various community events with other Mexican Americans. This continuous interaction over the years has served to perpetuate certain elements of Mexican and Mexican American culture.

The Mexican Americans' close proximity to their homeland is yet another factor resulting in their slower rate of assimilation. Since the United States shares a 2,000 mile border with Mexico, Mexican Americans are in a truly unique position. Over the years, the children and grandchildren of Mexican immigrants have been able to maintain close ties with the "old country." Many have the opportunity to visit Mexico on a relatively frequent basis. On extended trips, they may travel to the interior of Mexico, or, if their time is limited, they can visit the border region. These return visits to the old country are not once-in-a-lifetime opportunities as has been the case for most European immigrants who settled in America. Many Mexican Americans are able to maintain strong cultural ties through their contacts with friends and extended family in Mexico (Richard Schaefer, *Racial and Ethnic Groups*, p. 277).

TERMS OF IDENTITY

In the 1990s, two terms were widely used to identify Spanish-speaking people: Hispanic and Latino. The latter term appears to be growing in acceptance, especially by younger people who reject the Hispanic identification. The popular use of "Hispanic" grew out of the federal government's efforts, beginning with the 1980 census, to identify and count all people of Spanish-speaking backgrounds with origins from the western hemisphere. Since the term was employed in most federal government reports, the media soon appropriated it and popularized its use. Some members of the Hispanic community have employed the term to create political alliances among all ethnic groups with ties to the Spanish language. However, according to the Latino National Political Survey, the majority of respondents indicated that they defined their identities in terms of place of origin. Among those of Mexican origin who were born in the United States, 62 percent identified themselves as Mexican; 28 percent as Hispanic or Latino; and ten percent as American (P. Kivisto, *Americans All*, pp. 386-387).

Terms of identity vary greatly from region to region and from generation to generation. Traditionally, residents of northern New Mexico have referred to themselves as Spanish Americans or *Hispanos*, terms which are essentially a reflection of their early ancestors from "New Spain" who settled the region. Persons from Texas, in the recent past, have referred to themselves as Latin Americans, although there is growing use of the term "Tejano" by Texas residents of Mexican ancestry. The identi-

fication of Mexican is more commonly used in the Los Angeles area. More recently, the identification of Mexican American has gained in popularity.

In general, varying group identities are a reflection of the changing self-definitions of an ethnic group. The term "Chicano" is perhaps the best example of this social process. Chicano appeared in the mid-1960s as a political term of choice primarily among the young. The term identified an individual actively promoting social change within the context of the social movements of the 1960s and 1970s. To the older generation and the more affluent, to be identified as a "Chicano" was an insult. In the past the term specifically referred to the unsophisticated immigrant. However, to the generation of political activists, their term of ethnic identity came to signify a sense of pride in one's community and heritage. Thus, as Kivisto states, group identities are social constructs that "human beings are continually renegotiating and articulating" (Kivisto, p. 18).

RESISTANCE TO ASSIMILATION

Following the Mexican-American War, increasing violence perpetrated by Anglo Americans made Mexicans and Mexican Americans intensely aware of their subordinate status within the American Southwest. They did not have equal protection under the law, despite the guarantees of the Treaty of Guadalupe Hidalgo and the U.S. Constitution, and several laws were passed to specifically control their way of life. According to Griswold del Castillo: "A Sunday Law imposed fines ranging from ten to 500 dollars for engaging in `barbarous or noisy amusements' which were listed as bullfights, horse races, cockfights, and other tradition Californio amusements. At the same time, a vagrancy law called `the Greaser Law' was passed.... This law imposed fines and jail sentences on unemployed Mexican-Americans who, at the discretion of local authorities, could be called vagrants" (*The Los Angeles Barrio: A Social History*, p. 115). When Mexican Americans defied Anglo Americans and their newly established laws, lynchings, murders, and kangaroo trials were quite common as Anglo Americans asserted their dominance.

In an attempt to cope with their second-class status, Mexican Americans created a variety of social and political organizations, many of which promoted ethnic solidarity. As sociologist Gordon Allport has noted, one of the results of ethnic persecution is the strengthening of ethnic ties. Within their group, ethnic minorities "can laugh and deride their persecutors, celebrate their own heros and holidays" (*The Nature of Prejudice*, p. 149).

Before the turn of the twentieth century at least 16 Spanish-language newspapers were established in Los Angeles. The Mexican American press took the lead in condemning discrimination against their community. For example, in 1858 the editor of *El Clamor Público* denounced the theft of California lands by Anglo Americans and urged nonconformity to Anglo American culture and domination. The Mexican American press also developed a sense of ethnic solidarity by reporting on such cultural events as Mexican Independence Day and Cinco de Mayo, which celebrates the defeat of the French forces in Mexico in 1862.

The concept of "La Raza" was also promoted by the newspapers of the time. Its use by the Spanish-language press was evidence of a new kind of ethnic identity. The term connoted racial, spiritual, and blood ties to all Latin American people, ties particularly to Mexico. In addition, a number of social and political associations began to reinforce ethnic identity. Griswold del Castillo notes that between 1850 and 1900 at least 15 associations were established in Los Angeles. Their purposes were social and political. However, they overwhelmingly promoted Mexican nationalist sentiments (p. 135).

During the 1960s the Chicano movement specifically challenged assimilationist orientations within the larger society as well as within the Mexican American community itself. The ideology of the Chicano movement, particularly for Mexican American college students, called into question the idea of conformity to "Anglo American" cultural ideals. The beliefs promoted by the movement articulated a sense of personal worth and pride in common history and culture by emphasizing Chicano contributions to American society. The activists also reevaluated former symbols of shame associated with their heritage, culture, and physical appearance. Activists took great care in pronouncing Spanish names and words with the proper accent. Monolingual English-speaking Chicanos took courses to learn Spanish. Cultural relics and artifacts were resurrected. Items such as *sarapes* (serapes, or shawls) and *huaraches* (sandals), as well as other clothing symbolic of Mexican American culture, were displayed and worn with pride. A new perception of self-worth and pride in one's heritage prevailed among the adherents of the Chicano movement. This perspective was not only indicative of a newfound image and self-concept; it was also an assertion of dignity within a society that regarded Chicanos and their cultural symbols as inferior (Marguerite Marín, *Social Protest in an Urban Barrio*, pp. 114-120).

The ethnic movements of the 1960s and 1970s brought to the fore the contemporary debate concerning cultural pluralism. The ethnic movements of this period argued that assimilating into American society entailed the loss of distinctive identities, cultures, and languages. Assimilation was defined as a virtual assault on the way of life of American ethnic minority groups. As a result, a concerted effort is under way to understand, albeit only within certain segments of American society, the internal and external dynamics of the many peoples that make up the American mosaic.

MISCONCEPTIONS AND STEREOTYPES

The first major wave of Mexican immigration during the twentieth century triggered physical as well as verbal attacks by white Americans. Immigrant labor camps were raided by whites espousing white supremacist beliefs. By 1911 certain politicians lobbied against further Mexican immigration. The Dillingham Commission argued that Mexicans were undesirable as future citizens. Nativist scholars and politicians feared "mongrelization" as a by-product of contact with Mexicans, and in 1925 a Princeton economics professor even spoke of the future elimination of Anglo Americans by interbreeding with Mexicans (Feagin and Feagin, p. 265). These themes reemerged in 1928 when a congressional committee attempted to set limits on immigration from the western hemisphere. Congressman John Box called for restrictions on Mexican immigration because the Mexican was a product of mixing by the Spaniard and "low-grade" Indians. This mixture, according to Boxer, was an obstacle to participation in American democracy.

The image of the Mexican American male possessing innate criminal tendencies emerged during the World War II era. For example, in 1943, following the Zoot Suit Riots, the Los Angeles Sheriff's Department issued a report alleging that the Mexican American's desire to spill blood was an inborn characteristic. Further, the report concluded that Mexican Americans were violent because of their Indian blood (Feagin and Feagin, 265). And as late as 1969, a California judge ruling in an incest case reiterated similar racist beliefs. He stated in court: "Mexican people ... think it is perfectly all right to act like an animal. We ought to send you out of this country.... You are lower than animals ... maybe Hitler was right. The animals in our society probably ought to be destroyed" (Feagin and Feagin, p. 266).

One of the most persistent stereotypes is the image of simplemindedness. In 1982 the U.S. Department of Defense issued a report explaining that lower test scores for Hispanics and African Americans as compared to white Americans were due to genetic differences as well as cultural differences. During the same year, the National Educational Testing Service, surprised by the excellent performance of 18 Mexican American students attending Garfield High School (a school situated in one of Los Angeles' poorest Mexican American communities), demanded that all retake the exam. Allegations of cheating by the students was the reasoning of the testing administrators. The students eventually did re-take the exam; once again they received excellent scores.

HEALTH CARE BELIEFS AND PRACTICES

A majority of Mexican immigrants and Mexican Americans relied most frequently on traditional medical beliefs and practices to resolve health problems up through the first decade of the twentieth century. In some situations, a physical ailment might easily be alleviated or eliminated by herbs or other natural medicines or remedies. These cures, prescribed most often by mothers or grandmothers,

"**I** went to the doctor. He made me get undressed and put on a little robe. He examined my hands and knees. Then he told me I had rheumatism. I already knew that! He said he couldn't do anything for me, just give me a shot. He charged me $15; now I go to him only when I feel real sick and need the drugs. Otherwise I go see [a healer]. I don't know why but I have more confidence and faith in him. He gives me herbs, and I feel fine."**

Cited from Robert Trotter, *Curanderismo*, p. 51.

represented the accumulated knowledge gained from personal experience or observation of others passed down from generation to generation. On those occasions in which relief from a specific affliction was not achieved through home remedies, however, individuals or families might solicit the assistance of a *curandero* (folk curer) or other type of folk healer.

In general, all folk healers possessed a certain *don*, or God-given gift or ability, that provided them the power to restore the health of others. They might accomplish this through the use of herbs (*yerberos*, or herbalists), massages or oils, and/or the aid of the spirit of another more powerful healer serving as a medium between this more potent spirit and the afflicted person (Leo R. Chávez and Victor M. Torres, *The Handbook ... Anthropology*, p. 227). Alternatively, some used cards to divine an illness or to prescribe a remedy (Chávez and Torres, pp. 229-30).

Curanderos also have been used to cure ailments more readily recognizable to the medical establishment in the United States. It was not uncommon for some Mexican Americans to seek assistance from both a *curandero* and a physician. Several factors prompted the first generations of Mexican Americans in the late nineteenth and early twentieth centuries to rely more readily on folk healers than on practitioners of the U.S. medical community. The geographic isolation of the rural areas in which they settled or the segregated neighborhoods in which they lived in the cities combined with limited financial resources to restrict the options available to most people or families for several generations. Even those with ready access to medical assistance often were more confident in relying on a local curandero because of the faith their parents and grandparents had placed in these traditional curers or because of the more personal approach they employed. In many cases, the healers were likely to be acquainted with the family and involved relatives in the evaluation or treatment of an illness (Trotter, p. 44). The emotional bond established by the folk healer with the patient was a consistent and compelling element promoting greater trust in these traditional health providers.

As more Mexican Americans emigrated to large cities and greater numbers moved into more integrated settings, a higher percentage of them came to depend on practitioners and services of the U.S. medical community, occasioned either by easier access to these facilities, by the availability of medical insurance through their employers, or because of decreasing contact with families maintaining ties to traditional health practices. By the 1950s, research revealed that the primary source of health care for a dominant percentage of Mexican Americans had become doctors and clinics of the modern medical establishment. Surveys in the 1970s and 1980s in various urban areas of California suggested that as low as five percent of those polled had consulted a folk healer to resolve a health problem. Other studies showed that though close to 50 percent in some mixed urban and rural areas expressed faith in curanderos, over 90 percent of the same sample proclaimed confidence in medical doctors (*Family and Mental Health in the Mexican American Community*, edited by Susan E. Keefe and J. Manuel Casas, pp. 10-11).

Though their importance among Mexican Americans has diminished considerably over the last century, folk healers remain as a viable source for assistance with illness. J. Diego Vigil asserts that "some very acculturated Latinos accept the validity of diagnoses and traditional cures" of these healers

(Chávez and Torres, p. 223). Second-generation families living in rural areas may have easier access to curanderos and therefore use them more frequently, and these curers still may consult with urban dwellers whose family medical doctors, despite the advances in contemporary medicine, are ineffective in treating a given ailment.

HEALTH ISSUES

Though Mexican Americans manifest no congenital diseases that are group-specific, the rates at which they contract certain maladies are considerably above the national average. Some of these diseases are more evident among certain sectors of the Mexican American population, while others are common to the entire community.

The incidence of diabetes is greater among obese persons and studies have shown that one-third of all Mexican Americans fall in this category, the highest rate among Hispanics in the United States. Among those of the 45-74 age group, 23.9 percent had diabetes. Poor eating habits and/or inadequate diets contributed directly to its prevalence (Chávez and Torres, p. 235).

According to recent studies, 14 percent of all AIDS cases in the United States occurred among the Hispanic community and, as a group, they were 2.7 times more likely to contract this disease than Anglo Americans. Evidence of higher rates of AIDS within the migrant farmworking community (a considerable proportion of which is still Mexican or Mexican American) became more pronounced in the 1990s. The mobile nature of existence of this specific populace facilitates its dissemination, as does a lower frequency of condom use (Chávez and Torres, p. 236). Farmworkers are also at higher risk of exposure to tuberculosis. In comparison to the overall population of the United States, they are six times as likely to fall victim to this disease.

Alcoholism afflicts Hispanics at two to three times the national average. Mexican Americans and Puerto Ricans suffer the highest rates. Alcohol abuse is eight percent to 12 percent higher for all age groups among Mexican Americans as compared to "non-Hispanic whites" in these same categories (*The Statistical Record ...*, p. 434). The highest frequencies occur in those families of low economic stability, and many of those afflicted are unaware of, or ineligible for, treatment programs. Cirrhosis of the liver is the most common cause of death for these specific individuals. The frequency level for this disease is 40 percent higher among Mexican Americans than among Anglo Americans.

The underutilization of medical services represents one of the most pressing health issues among a significant proportion of the Mexican American population. For second-generation families whose contacts with Anglo American society have been limited and whose disposable income is low, such fundamental considerations as inadequate language skills, lack of transportation, or inability to pay for services reduce the possibilities for using or even seeking health care facilities. Public health facilities have decreased in number in some urban zones of heavy Hispanic population. In rural areas, medical assistance may be too distant, poorly staffed, or offer medical technologies of limited capacity to detect or cure more complex ailments. Preventative health measures are a privilege too expensive to consider for those whose income is at survival-level.

Research in the 1960s in Texas and California revealed that the proportionate number of Mexicans and Mexican Americans receiving psychiatric assistance in public facilities was significantly lower than their overall population in these areas. The findings in Texas prompted sociologist E. G. Jaco to suggest that Mexican Americans might in fact suffer less from mental illnesses than the Anglo American population, a premise that seemed to contradict generally held assumptions regarding immigrant groups and their families raised in foreign countries—specifically, that individuals of such groups were more likely than people of the dominant culture in a given society to exhibit a higher prevalence of mental disorders due to the psychological stress and tension generated by the immigration experience, discrimination, and the acculturation process in general. Jaco proposed that the existence of strong, supportive family ties among the Mexican and Mexican American population might explain the lower proportion of patients of this ethnic community at these facilities, but other theories have since been put forth. The most often-repeated assertions, some of which have been posited with little or insufficient supporting material to defend their contentions, have suggested that: Mexican and Mexican Americans are more tolerant of psychiatric disorders than Anglo Americans and seek assistance with lower frequency; they suffer from just as many disorders but manifest these conditions more often in criminal behavior, alcoholism and other addictions; they are too proud or sensitive to expose such psychological problems, especially in facilities staffed mainly by Anglo Americans; they utilize priests and family physicians instead of public health specialists or they return to Mexico to seek a cure.

LANGUAGE

Spanish has remained the principal, if not sole, language of almost all Mexicans in the southwestern United States for many decades after the signing of the Treaty of Guadalupe Hidalgo. Since the overwhelming majority of the first generations of Mexican immigrants moved to areas already populated predominantly by people of their heritage and worked side-by-side with these individuals in the same jobs, the need for them to learn more than rudimentary English was of minor importance. Proximity to Mexico and the continued entry of additional immigrants constantly revitalized the culture and native language of those who chose to become permanent residents of the United States.

In the twentieth century, as the proportion of second- and third-generation Mexican American families increased and some of their members moved into a wider range of professions in which more of their co-workers were non-Hispanic, proficiency in English became practical necessary for many. In addition, heightening exposure of the younger generations of Mexican Americans to Anglo American education meant that English became a fundamental part of their curriculum. Moreover, the use of Spanish in and outside the classroom was strongly discouraged and sometimes even prohibited in many school systems until mid-century and beyond. Of equally substantial and enduring impact, English was introduced to ever greater numbers of Hispanic households by means of television. Though few lower income Mexican American families could afford this form of entertainment in the 1950s, it had entered most living rooms by the end of the next decade and brought the language (as well as other aspects) of Anglo American culture nightly to the ears of a growing Mexican American audience.

The persistence of high immigration levels did not allow Spanish to disappear from this community, regardless of the encroachments made by English in their public and private lives, and the Chicano movement of the late 1960s and 1970s renewed the pride of many Mexican Americans in their heritage and in the Spanish language. In the 1980s there were still over 100 Spanish-language newspapers in circulation within the United States, approximately 500 radio stations, and 130 television stations whose programming was partially or completely in Spanish.

MEXICAN SPANISH

Some families in more remote parts of northern New Mexico still speak a Spanish quite similar to the language spoken in Spain at the time of the arrival of the first conquistadors in the Americas. On the other hand, later immigrants, like their immediate ancestors, speak Mexican Spanish. This language differs from Castilian Spanish in the pronunciation of certain consonants and consonant and vowel combinations but is more strikingly distinct in aspects of vocabulary, where the influence of pre-Columbian indigenous languages have added to the language spoken in Mexico. Such words most often apply to agriculture and the natural world. For example, the native word for "grass," *zacate*, replaced the Spanish word *hierba-* and *guajolote* and *tecolote*, of Indian derivation, replaced the Spanish words for "turkey" and "owl."

The Spanish spoken by Mexican Americans is "a spoken and informal dialect" (González-Berry, p. 304). It varies to some extent depending on the rural or urban identity of the speaker, his/her economic standing, length of time in the United States, and level of education. Though some scholars have maintained that Mexican American Spanish may be separated or differentiated by geographic zone in the United States, the intramigration among these areas has made a clear delineation between them difficult. In general terms, it is characterized by and distinguished from Mexican Spanish in differences between the enunciation of certain sounds. For example, whereas the standard Spanish words for "soldier" and the pronoun "you" are respectively *soldado* and *usted*, the corresponding words in Mexican American Spanish for many speakers have altered to *soldau* and *usté* through the elimination of the consonant of the last syllable. Transformations of certain verb conjugations are evident also in Mexican American Spanish, such as the shift from *decía* ("I/she/he/you were saying") to *dijía* (González-Berry, p. 305). Markedly evident also is the incorporation of English words to Spanish, with the appropriate orthographic changes to make the specific terminology more similar in sound to Spanish, for example, *troca* for "truck," *parquear* for "park," or *lonche* for "lunch."

Still prevalent among various urban groups of young Mexican Americans is the use of *caló*, a variation of Mexican Spanish which employs slang from Mexican Spanish, African American English, and Anglo American English to create a new vocabulary. It was used much more extensively in urban settings in the Southwest during the 1940s and 1950s by members of the younger generation who wished to set themselves apart from their parents. As González-Berry illustrates, the combination of languages used in *caló* make it comprehensible only to those who use it, as may be seen by the phrase *gasofla pá la ranfla*—"gas for the car" (p. 306).

Those Mexican Americans who have been exposed extensively to English and Spanish and employ both languages actively in speaking or writing may move from one language to another within a given sentence, a linguistic phenomenon referred to as "code-switching." The alternation may be caused by a momentary memory lapse by the speaker, with use of proper nouns, or when a specific word has no exact equivalent in the other language. The result occasioned by one or more of these factors might be a sentence such as: "*Mucha gente no sabe where Magnolia Street is*" ("Many people don't know where Magnolia Street is") (Lipski, *The Hispanic American Almanac,* p. 224). This linguistic tendency was once perceived in a negative light, and in the case of some speakers is indicative of lexical deficiencies. An expanding percentage of Mexican Americans, however, are now "coordinate bilinguals," able to separate English from Spanish completely and use either language effectively and persuasively depending upon the situation or need (Olivia Arrieta, *The Handbook … Anthropology,* p. 166). Code-switching when employed by these bilinguals by no means signifies confusion or insufficient linguistic aptitude to distinguish between the two languages but an attempt to use the most appropriate phrase to convey a certain word or notion (Lipski, p. 224).

LANGUAGE ISSUES

Despite high levels of Mexican immigration and strong pride in their Hispanic heritage, the primary language of Mexican Americans is English, and with each new generation born in the United States the use of Spanish becomes less frequent in many families. U.S. Census Bureau statistics for 1976 revealed that 68 percent of the Mexican American population possessed good language proficiency in English. According to Meier, polls taken in the 1990s indicate that though 90 percent of those Mexican Americans questioned asserted an ability to speak and comprehend Spanish, only 5.3 percent confirmed that they spoke the language at home (p. 245). Census figures for 1990 calculate that though 65 percent of Mexican Americans "speak a language other than English," 97.8 percent of those persons five years of age and over professed to an "ability to speak English" (*1990 Census of Population—Persons of Hispanic Origin in the United States,* p. 86).

In addition to the factor of progressive acculturation, these figures also in part reflect the effect of bilingual education programs nationwide, programs that began in significant numbers in the late 1960s with passage of the Bilingual Education Act of 1968 but multiplied considerably in the 1970s

due to a decision rendered by the U.S. Supreme Court in the case of *Lau v. Nichols* in 1974. This verdict affirmed that those schools not able or willing to provide language instruction to children of immigrants whose skills in English were deficient were acting in violation of the Civil Rights Act of 1964 and the Fourteenth Amendment to the Constitution. By the close of the 1970s there were still four states in which bilingual instruction was forbidden. Spending for these classes had increased to $107 million (Cortés, p. 715).

The movement to bilingual instruction in the public schools was not received positively by all sectors of society in the United States in this period, however. Towards the end of the 1970s and in the initial years of the 1980s, various individuals and organizations set out to reverse a perceived trend towards bilingualism and/or biculturalism/multiculturalism in the United States, which they saw as a threat to the dominant Anglo American culture. In 1978 Emmy Shafer established the organization English Only and in 1983 United States English was founded, a group whose annual budget is now $5 million with a membership of 400,000. One of the priorities of this second group has been to secure passage of the English Language Amendment, thereby declaring to ratify English as the official language in the United States. Though they had not achieved this goal at the national level as of 1995, 21 states had passed legislation to this effect. Opponents of these proposals assert that the United States has never been monolingual or monocultural and that attempts to establish national or local restrictive language policies are anti-immigrationist and racist.

Though virtually all Mexican Americans endorse the need to learn English and have supported programs in bilingual instruction as a prerequisite to academic and professional advance in the United States, many have found fault with the "language immersion" or "transitional" approaches employed in a large percentage of bilingual programs, which place little or no importance on the retention of the students' native language or culture as they learn English. A method far less commonly employed but defended more positively by many Mexican Americans is "maintenance bilingual instruction," a technique that utilizes the speaker's language of origin to teach English but never abandons the use of the native language nor denies the importance of the student's ethnicity. The goal of this popular alternative is to make the learner totally functional in the two languages in terms of reading, writing, and speaking (Arreta, p. 186). The English Plus proposal endorsed by the League of Latin American Citizens (LULAC), which asserts the necessity of acquiring fluency in English for Hispanics yet also reaffirms the importance of maintaining identity with Hispanic values, has received the support of many Hispanic groups in the United States.

FAMILY AND COMMUNITY DYNAMICS

The average size of the Mexican American family in 1989 was 4.1 persons, as compared to 3.1 for non-Hispanic and 3.8 for all Hispanic families residing in the United States. Though the birth rate among Mexican American women remains high in comparison to the national average and 43 percent of the Mexican American population was 14 years of age or under, the size of the family has declined slowly over the past generations. In 1991, among Mexican-origin families in the United States, 73.5 percent were headed by married couples, and 19.1 percent were female-headed, a figure approximately three percent higher than for non-Hispanic groupings. Among female-headed families, 49 percent were below the poverty line in terms of income. According to the 1990 census, 7.8 percent of Mexican American men over 15 years of age were divorced, as opposed to 6.4 percent of the women in this same category. In 1989 13.5 percent of Mexican American households received public assistance. The mean for this specific income per household was $4,359 (*1990 Census of Population...*).

Intermarriage between Mexicans/Mexican Americans and Anglo Americans was prevalent in the mid-nineteenth century and increased slowly in subsequent generations. After World War II, due in part to a slow movement towards residential integration and greater and more widespread social mobility, the incidence of intermarriage increased at more rapid rates, especially in urban settings. In the mid 1980s in the states of the Southwest of highest Hispanic population, intermarriage rates varied from nine to 27 percent in Texas, 27 to 29 percent in New Mexico, and 51 to 55 percent in California (Rosina Becerra, in Mindel, *Ethnic Families in America: Patterns and Variations,* p. 156). Male exogamy was slightly higher than female exogamy for the same period and occurred most frequently among third-generation Mexican Americans.

TRADITION AND CHANGE IN FAMILY STRUCTURE AND ROLES

In the mid-nineteenth century *la familia,* or the extended family, included aunts and uncles, as well as grandparents and even great grandparents.

Beyond these direct familial ties between generations, *compadres* (co-parents) were most often an integral part of these groupings, as were adopted children and intimate friends, in many instances. As close, personal friends of the mother or father of a child, the *padrinos* (godfathers) or *madrinas* (godmothers) developed a special relationship with their *ahijados* (godchildren), a relationship that started in definitive terms at his/her baptism. From this point forward, in most instances, they provided emotional, financial, or any other form of assistance or advice their *ahijados* might require past that afforded by their actual parents, especially in times of family crisis. They were also essential participants in all events of social or religious importance to the godchild and maintained strong bonds with their *compadres* or *comadres*—lasting friendships based upon mutual admiration and support. As much as any immediate family member, godparents contributed to strong family unity (Griswold del Castillo, p. 42).

A patriarchal hierarchy prescribed a system of male dominance in the traditional family. As the authority figure, the husband was the principal, if not the sole, breadwinner. He made the important social and economic decisions and was the protector of the family's integrity. Wives had general control over household matters but were expected to be obedient and submissive to their husbands (Maxine Baca Zinn, *The Handbook ... Sociology,* p. 164). Though the wife might perform work outside the household, this was usually an acceptable alternative only in cases of extreme economic duress. In such cases, her efforts were limited to a restricted number of options, almost always of a part-time nature, and contributed nothing to improve her subservient status within the house. This division of authority established between man and wife was perpetuated by their offspring. Girls were taught distinct behavior patterns and were encouraged to adopt specifically defined aspirations quite different from their brothers, beginning at an early age. Motherhood was the ideal objective of all young girls and the primary virtue of all those who achieved it (p. 167).

This system of mutual dependence and respect for elders created a close-knit family unit. Family honor and unity were of paramount significance. If problems arose for individual members, the immediate or extended family could be relied upon to resolve the issue. Important decisions were always made with first consideration given to the needs of the group rather than the individual. Traditional social and religious practices passed from one generation to the next virtually unchanged because they were perceived as intrinsic values to the family's cultural heritage.

While extended family households are less common today, the importance of the family as a unit and the ties between these units and their extended members remains strong. Newly arrived immigrants generally continue to seek out relatives in the United States, as did the initial generations after 1848, and may rely upon these individuals and their families for temporary residence as well as assistance in arranging employment, especially in rural regions. Though in a majority of instances each successive generation born in the United States tends to exhibit reduced dependence on extended kin, birthdays, baptisms, marriages, and other family celebrations bring relatives together with a pronounced regularity (Robert R. Alvarez, Jr., *The Hispanic American Almanac*, p. 171).

Modifications also have occurred in the pattern of male dominance and division of work by gender within these families. In the United States in the generations immediately subsequent to 1848, economic necessities provided the initial impulse toward a more egalitarian relationship between husband and wife. The specific forms of employment assumed by the Mexican American husband in the southwestern region during these years frequently made his absence necessary from the household for long periods of time; while drovers, miners, farmworkers, and other laborers often strayed considerable distances from their families in pursuit of work or in performing their labors, the wife was left as the authority figure. Though the male almost always assumed total control upon his return, accommodations or compromise might alter the structure of power within the family somewhat, and it was not uncommon for women to continue to exert a more pronounced role in decision making in those families where this pattern of male absence was prolonged and repetitive (Griswold del Castillo, p. 34).

As a growing proportion of Mexican American women moved into the full-time labor force in the early decades of the twentieth century and thereafter, alterations in role patterns and the division of responsibilities were manifested in greater frequencies. Though in some cases, especially in the early years of the century, the family was less male dominant, equal hours of work outside the house for the wife generally helped to initiate a progressively more egalitarian arrangement with the family structure.

The contemporary Mexican American family exhibits a wide range of decision making patterns, including that of male authoritarianism. Most, but not all, studies in the 1980s and early 1990s have concluded that both parents generally share in the day-to-day management of the family and in determining responses to matters of critical importance to this unit. Among others, Ybarra contends that "egalitarianism is the predominant conjugal role arrangement in Chicano families" (*Journal of Marriage and Family* 1982, p. 177). The mother, as before, is generally seen as the individual most responsible for meeting the domestic needs of husband and children, but in those families in which she has become the disciplinarian, she has frequently found this role is in conflict with her traditional identity as nurturer (Chavira-Prado, p. 258). Alvarez contends that, as in many contemporary cultures, though women most often have taken on new and varied roles, men have altered little with respect to their low participatory level related to household chores (*The Handbook …*, p. 165). Despite the fact that actual family dynamics reveal general egalitarianism, deference to the father as the ultimate authority remains the ideal behavior pattern (Alvarez, *The Hispanic American Almanac*, p. 172).

CHILDREARING AND COURTSHIP

Fairly rigid sex roles were maintained for Mexican American children well into the twentieth century. Beginning in colonial times in Mexico, young girls were taught the tasks and skills of their mother from an early age. The eldest daughter was initially always given the chore of caring for her younger siblings, but, after reaching puberty, the eldest brother replaced her in this responsibility (Becerra, pp. 149-50).

Whereas girls, up through adolescence, were restricted in their activities and spent much time together with their sisters at home, boys of the same age group were given more liberties and were allowed to venture outside the household with peers. There were rules of proper etiquette that prevailed in large cities and small towns for dating. Chaperoning was most common, if not required. Young unwed women were to be perceived by the community as the ideal figures in terms of social behavior. Adolescent boys, on the other hand, were not monitored as closely. The male was seen as "a fledgling (sic) macho who must be allowed to venture out of the home so he may test his wings and establish a masculine identity" (Alfredo Mirandé and Evangelina Enríquez, *La Chicana: The Mexican-American Woman*, 1979, p. 114).

Teen marriages were most prevalent in Mexican American families into the first decades of the twentieth century. The premarital procedures involved in joining a couple in matrimony varied depending on the social background of the families. Up until the 1920s and perhaps later in rural areas, a *portador* (go-between) would deliver a written proposal of marriage to the father of the would-be bride. Fathers decided on the acceptability of the suitor based on the apparent moral respectability of the young man and his family, and though the opinions of his spouse and daughter were important in the final decision as to marriage, the father might often overrule the wishes of either or both of these individuals (Williams, pp. 27-30).

Except among the most traditional Mexican American families, childrearing and dating practices have changed substantially over the past few generations. Among other studies finding similar conclusions, Jesse T. Zapata and Pat T. Jaramillo have found that parents rarely ascribe pronounced roles determined by sex to their children (*Hispanic Journal of Behavioral Sciences* 3, No. 3, p. 286). Family commitments or responsibilities may still curtail the social activities of young girls more than boys, but equal privileges within the family arrangement are the norm rather than the exception. Girls may be monitored more closely in their dating patterns, but few of the restrictions that once prevailed now determine their behavior. Premarital chastity is still expected of young Chicanas, but as Mirandé and Enríquez affirmed, though "premarital virginity prevails ... its enforcement may prove more difficult today than in the past" (p. 114). Parents have far-reduced and sometimes incidental influence with regard to the selection of marriage partners for their offspring, except in the most traditional families, but their sentiments on the issue are most always considered of significance.

EDUCATION

The desire of low-income migrant families from Mexico to provide their children with opportunities for education in the late 1800s and early 1900s was counterbalanced by more fundamental needs: the wages paid these immigrants for their labors in the fields, mines, factories, or railways were most often so low that families needed the additional income provided by their children to meet the basic necessities required for survival. Attendance at the primary level of instruction was relatively high, provided that schools were available in the predominantly rural areas where the first generations of Mexican immigrants resided. But progress past this level and on into secondary schools was less common because of economic factors. The mobile nature of farm and railworker families made it difficult for children to maintain a continuity in their schooling. Finally, the schools and teachers in these rural areas were of inferior quality. It was hard for parents to maintain a positive attitude about the long-range significance of attending classes since it quickly became apparent to

most that, as with other families before them, it would only be a matter of time before economic factors would force them to pull their children out of classes or at least reduce the number of hours or days that they could attend school.

Low-income immigrant families, as well as those with greater financial stability whose children consequently had a better chance of staying in school, were dissuaded from adopting a more positive attitude toward the U.S. educational system because of the tendency of teachers and administrators to deny the existence or importance of Catholic or Hispanic traditions in favor of those held by the majority population. The assimilationist philosophy endorsed by the public school system was designed "to shape desirable behaviors for functioning in America" and encourage uniformity of perspective regardless of differences in the ethnic heritage among the student population (Guadalupe San Miguel, Jr., *The Handbook ... Anthropology*, p. 293). Texts as well as curricula in the public schools well into the twentieth century disregarded or acknowledged only minimally the role and/or contributions of minority peoples to the socioeconomic historic development of the United States.

Religious orders staffed most Catholic schools in the latter decades of the nineteenth century, many of which were located in areas of high Mexican and Mexican American population. Though not founded specifically to educate Hispanics, these schools attracted significant numbers of Mexican Americans because of their religious orientation. As public education facilities began to proliferate at the end of the century, however, an ever-smaller percentage of Chicanos attended parochial schools, either because of easier access to public institutions or because of the cost factor involved with Catholic education (San Miguel, p. 293). By the 1960s, though the Mexican American population of the United States was close to 90 percent Catholic, only 15 percent of Spanish-surname students in Los Angeles attended grades one through six in Catholic institutions, whereas in San Antonio 21 percent attended grades one through eight (Grebler, p. 475). The proportion of Mexican Americans in parochial schools in the 1990s remains at similar or lower levels.

Beginning in the first decades of the twentieth century and continuing thereafter, as greater numbers of Mexican Americans moved to an urban setting, the opportunities for public school education increased measurably. Alternative sources of employment were more plentiful in the cities, and, though a majority of Mexican Americans continued to experience wage discrimination during these decades, the possible advantages of higher levels of education related to salary and employment options made academic preparation more attractive. Segregated educational facilities were the rule, however, until mid-century and beyond. The suits brought by *Menendez v. Westminster School District* in Southern California and *Delgado v. Bastrop Independent School District* represented important steps in the 1940s toward the outlawing of segregation, but some school systems practiced "integration" by joining Mexican American and Afro American students rather than combining these minorities with predominantly Anglo American students (Cortés, p. 718). The separate educational facilities provided to minority students were most often poorly maintained, staffed by undertrained instructors. and provided with inadequate supplies.

As segregated facilities have slowly diminished over time, Mexican Americans who have entered integrated schools have often been classified as "learning disabled" because of linguistic deficiencies or inadequate academic preparation afforded by their previous learning institutions. This factor has caused many of these students to be channeled into "developmentally appropriate" classes or curricular tracks (San Miguel, p. 303). It was only in the late 1960s that the judicial system took steps to mandate the establishment of bilingual programs in education, but continued strong funding for these programs has been challenged by many groups at national and local levels. The pedagogical approach adopted by the vast majority of bilingual programs has stressed rapid conversion to the use of English without regard for the maintenance of skills in the native languages of first- and second-generation immigrants.

Leaders of the Chicano movement focused much of their energies on educational issues. They emphasized the need to lower the high school dropout rate, expand the number of bilingual/bicultural programs, increase the availability of fellowships for Mexican Americans at the college level, support the recruitment of higher percentages of Hispanic instructors and administrators at all levels of the educational system, and diversify class offerings by establishing new courses and programs in Chicano studies (Cortés, p. 718). Several student organizations have evolved to provide forums for the discussion and wider propagation of issues fundamental to improving educational opportunities for Mexican American students. In 1969 a conference at the University of California, Santa Barbara, attempted to unite many of these organizations under MECHA (*Movimiento Estudiantil Chicano de Aztlán*—Chicano Student Movement of Aztlán). A *Plan de Santa Barbara* (Santa Barbara Plan) was for-

mulated related to the procedures necessary for the development of degree programs in Chicano studies (Meier, in McWilliams, p. 287). Strategies emerging from this reunion and other meetings of an academic focus among Mexican Americans have resulted in the creation of a growing number of Chicano studies programs nationwide. These programs feature courses and curricula of more definitive relevance to students at advanced education levels. In 1972 the National Association of Chicano Studies (NACS) was founded, an organization for college students and professors that sponsors annual conferences oriented to social, economic, literary, and other themes pertinent to Mexican Americans. A special session of the annual meeting in 1982 brought under discussion the need to champion recognition and participation by Mexican American women in this organization, a goal that has been accomplished in large part since that time (Teresa Córdova, *The Handbook ... Sociology*, p. 185).

According to U.S. Census Bureau estimates for 1991, 50.5 percent of the "Mexican-origin" population 35 years of age and over had completed four years of high school or more, and 7.4 percent of this same age category had attended four years of college or more. As of 1985, 27.8 percent of women in the United States designated under the identical classification had studied four years or more in high school, whereas 4.6 percent had continued on to four or more years of college. Significant differences existed between first- and second-generation families and their levels of educational attainment in 1988: 34 percent of the first generation received a high school degree while 65 percent of the next generation reached this level (Steven F. Arvizu, *The Handbook ... Anthropology*, p. 288). Though the number of Hispanics with advanced degrees remains low, this number has risen in a consistent, albeit slow, pattern since the 1970s.

THE ROLE OF WOMEN

Beginning in the late 1960s and in increasing proportions thereafter, Mexican American women began to write about themes directly oriented to the socioeconomic and political challenges that had confronted them over many generations: gender/race-based discriminatory practices in almost all areas of the labor market; inequities in educational opportunities and lack of sufficient local or federal support to alter this situation; the specific needs of Chicana women in poor Mexican American neighborhoods (health care, physical abuse, and unemployment, among others); Chicana prisoner abuse and rights; welfare rights and child care issues; lack of equitable political enfranchise-

This elaborate altar is decorated for the celebration of the Mexican Festival *El Dia de los Muertos,* or the Day of the Dead.

This elaborate altar is decorated for the celebration of the Mexican Festival *El Dia de los Muertos,* or the Day of the Dead.

ment; and the virtual nonexistence of gender-specific political representation at local, state, or national levels (Córdova, pp. 177-80).

In the 1970s and early 1980s a significant number of Mexican American women were intrigued, but most often not attracted, by the ideas emerging from the women's movement in the United States. Though, as Maria Gonzalez affirms, it "provided the example and the language with which Hispanic women could challenge traditional attitudes towards women's roles," several basic perspectives identified with the movement were seen in a negative light by most Mexican American women. While they were aware of the need to react to oppression from within and without the Mexican American community, they judged the declarations of Anglo American feminists as somewhat excessive in their demands for independence and self-autonomy and contended that such stances, if adopted by Chicanas, might function to disrupt the unity of the Mexican American family. They also were disenchanted by a perceived racism that was made evident to them from occurrences at various national women's association conferences. As synthesized by

María González: "What has emerged from Hispanic women's experience with feminism is an acknowledgment by Hispanic feminists of pride in their traditional heritage but with a realistic attitude toward its limitations, as well as an acknowledgment of the limitations of feminism" (*The Hispanic-American Almanac,* p. 356).

Since the 1960s, many notable advances for women and women's issues have been made within the Mexican American community. Melba J. T. Vásquez cites two studies (Gándara and Avery) of the 1980s on "high-achieving" Chicanas that suggest a dilemma of a different dimension for these women when set in the context of Mexican American social history in the United States. In both studies, it was revealed that, as opposed to Anglo American professional women, Mexican American women in industry, academia, and politics married at significantly lower rates and, of those who married, only 56 percent of them had children. Avery concluded that for these specific females, "the conflicts involved in maintaining roles within and outside the home may be perceived as too overwhelming and the availability of male partners of comparable educational backgrounds may be limited" (quoted in Vásquez in *Chicano Psychology*, second edition, edited by Joe L. Martínez and Richard H. Mendoza, p. 42).

For the pronounced majority of Chicanas, however, the move to a position of equality in North American society has yet to begin or is only commencing. Insufficient opportunity for an adequate education to allow them to compete in an increasingly challenging job market condemns too many of them to unemployment, underemployment, or work in professions with little promise for upward mobility and jobs with decent salaries. Many Chicanas remain in oppressed situations within their own community, held back by gender-based traditions that deny them a chance to alter their role and define a new identity. The positive advances of the minority of Mexican American women must be viewed by the majority, however, as a promise for a better future.

CUISINE

The basic diet of the inhabitants of Mexico has changed little from the beginning years of recorded human history in the area to the present period. Corn, beans, squash, and tomatoes were staples until the arrival of the Spaniards in the early 1500s. The culinary preferences of these Europeans, plus the addition of some items from trade centered in Manila brought pork, beef, rice, and various spices, among other foods, to the diet of this region.

Pork and beef, in steaks or stews, along with chicken, were the meats eaten in those areas from which migration to the United States was highest in 1848 and subsequent decades. This same cuisine forms the day-to-day food of most contemporary Mexican Americans: prepared with tomato-based sauces flavored by a variety of chiles and/or spices or herbs such as cumin and cilantro, one of these meats is generally served with rice, beans, and corn tortillas.

On festive occasions such as religious holidays or family reunions, one or more of the following traditional meals consumed in Mexico are prepared by most Mexican American families: *tamales* (shredded and spiced pork or beef caked within cornmeal and wrapped in a corn husk before steaming); *enchiladas* (corn tortillas lightly fried in oil then wrapped around sliced chicken, shredded beef, cheese, or ground beef and various spices and coated with a tomato and chile sauce before baking); *mole* (most often chicken, but sometimes pork, combined with a sauce of chiles, chocolate, ground sesame or pumpkin seeds, garlic, and various other spices,

slow-cooked under a low flame on the stove); *chilaquiles* (dried tortilla chips complemented by cheeses, chile, and perhaps *chorizo*—spiced sausage—and/or chicken and a tomato-based sauce of green or red chile stirred into a hash-like dish on the stove); *chiles rellenos* (green chiles stuffed with a white cheese and fried in an egg batter that adheres to the chiles); and *posole* (a soup-like stew which contains hominy as its essential ingredient, as well as stew meat and various spices).

Though some ingredients of the meals described above are at times somewhat difficult to find in major supermarkets in the United States, the proximity of Mexico makes it possible for small markets that specialize in Mexican food to obtain and sell these items at a reasonable price.

TRADITIONAL CLOTHING

The clothing identified as most traditional by Mexicans and Mexican Americans and, according to Olga Nájera-Ramírez, recognized as "official national symbols of Mexico," is now worn most frequently at festivals of historic importance to these people. Men dress as *charros*, or Mexican cowboys, and wear wide-brimmed *sombreros* along with tailored jackets and pants lined with silver or shining metal buttons. Women dress in *China Poblana* outfits, which include a white peasant blouse and a flaring red skirt adorned with sequins of different colors. This apparel is linked most closely in socio-historical terms to people of more humble origin in Mexico.

HOLIDAYS

Two secular holidays of national importance in Mexico are celebrated by a significant number of Mexican Americans. Mexican Independence Day is celebrated on the 16th of September. Commemorating the date that the priest Miguel Hidalgo y Costilla initiated the war for liberation from Spain with the *grito*, or call to battle, "*Viva Mexico y mueran los gachupines*" ("Long live Mexico and death to all *gachupines*"—a derogatory term for Spaniards used during the colonial period and afterwards), part of the festivities may include the pronouncement of the grito and/or a mass with *mariachis*, (Mexican street bands) followed possibly by a speech or parade. In that the central idea related to this date is ethnic solidarity, many of the participants wear the *charro* and *China Poblana* outfits. Along with traditional plates such as *mole*, other condiments and food served on this date traditionally stress the colors of the Mexican flag: white, red, and green. These items may include rice, limes, avocados, chopped tomatoes, peppers, and onions (Eunice Romero Gwynn and Douglas Gwynn, *The Handbook ... Anthropology*, p. 366).

Perhaps the most widely recognized Mexican holiday celebrated by Mexicans and Mexican Americans residing in the United States, as well as by other Hispanics nationwide, commemorates the victory of Mexican troops in the Battle of Puebla over the invading French army on May 5, 1862. The Cinco de Mayo celebration may include parades or other festivities and, as with Independence Day, reinforces for many Mexican Americans a sense of ethnic brotherhood. Many Anglo Americans join in commemorating this date, though its historic importance is known by only a negligible number of revellers.

RELIGION

Approximately 75 percent of the Mexican American population are of the Catholic faith, and in the southwestern United States over two-thirds of the Catholics are Mexican or Mexican American (Julián Samora, *A History of the Mexican-American People*, p. 232). Despite their numerical importance within this church, however, the first Mexican American bishop was not ordained until 1970 and, as of 1992, only 19 of 360 bishops in the country were of Hispanic origin. In recent decades, attempts have been made by church hierarchy to establish a stronger bond between Mexican Americans and the Catholic church in the United States, but various factors and events over time since 1848 created a rift that remains clearly defined between this specific laity and the institutional church with which they are nominally affiliated (Silvia Novo Pena, *The Hispanic-American Almanac*, p. 367).

CATHOLIC CHURCH IN THE UNITED STATES

The presence of the Catholic church on Mexico's northern frontier was weak throughout the first half of the nineteenth century, due in part to the attempts of liberals to reduce its economic and political power nationwide, but also because of the death, departure, or expulsion of Spanish clerics from the region and the failure of the church to replace them (Cortés, p. 710). By 1846 there were only 16 Catholic priests in the lands that were to become the states of California, Arizona, and New Mexico (Alberto L. Pulido, in *Perspectives in Mexican American Studies* IV, p. 106).

Beginning in the colonial period, and increasingly so in the nineteenth century, Mexicans living in the rural areas of this region evolved a "self-reliant," popular religiosity. Though based upon fundamental Catholic tenets, this form of religion manifested practices that deviated in notable ways from those endorsed by the institutional church, especially so after 1848 (Moisés Sandoval, *On the Move: A History of the Hispanic Church in the United States*, p. 21). Home altars and devotional tables became the center of prayer for this isolated laity, and parents or grandparents often instructed the younger members of the family in religious matters. Feasts, festivities, and processions to honor saints or events of historical religious significance became the principal means for local believers to share religion on a community level. Pilgrimages to shrines took on added importance for those hoping for divine intervention in times of despair (Anthony Stevens-Arroyo and Ana María Díaz-Stevens, *The Handbook ... Sociology*, p. 270). A more pronounced devotion to certain saints or the Virgin Mary in one of her various identities frequently dominated a believer's prayers. Religious brotherhoods, such as *Los Hermanos Penitentes* (the Confraternity of Our Father, Jesus of Nazarene) in northern New Mexico and southern Colorado—operating in the absence of priests—directed holy ceremonies for those in the surrounding communities, taught doctrine to the young, and conducted penitential rituals (Sandoval, p. 22).

By the mid-1850s the lands taken over by the United States were included in newly created dioceses placed under the control of bishops and vicars whose origin or heritage, much like the newly ordained clergy of the period, most frequently was European. These leaders were prompt to voice protests over the religious practices of the Mexican laity and priests in their regions and soon proposed several basic reforms. Though they had been prohibited since 1833, the collection of tithes was called for in most dioceses and set fees were established for church marriages, burials, and baptisms. Processions and other public demonstrations of faith not under the direct control of the church were discouraged. Festive religious celebrations often were condemned as immoral and those who selected not to worship or to do so in services not tied officially to the institutional church were chastised. In New Mexico the French apostolic vicar of the Santa Fe diocese, Jean Baptiste Lamy, actively sought to curtail the activities and power of the *Penitentes* and replaced or excommunicated several priests who failed to follow his dictates, among them Father Antonio José Martínez of Taos, who, despite being excommunicated, continued to perform services in a small chapel in his parish (Mirandé, p. 136).

Thus, although they had been guaranteed the right to maintain their religious preferences and practices in 1848, as the nineteenth century ended it was progressively more evident to most Mexican and Mexican American Catholics that they had no institutional voice at any level in the American Catholic church and that the religious traditions they had come to deem important and essential to their convictions were considered inappropriate, if not unacceptable, in the estimation of the Euroamerican Catholic laity and clergy in the United States.

It was not until the mid-1940s that the institutional Catholic church in the United States began to devise strategies and programs to meet the pastoral and social needs of Mexican Americans and other Hispanics. In 1944 meetings and seminars were organized for delegates of western and southwestern dioceses at the request of Robert E. Lucey and Urban J. Vehr, the archbishops of San Antonio and Denver, respectively, to analyze the scope and effectiveness of the church's efforts in these areas (Sandoval, p. 47). In 1945 the Bishop's Committee for the Spanish-speaking was formed, the objectives of which were to construct clinics, improve housing and educational and employment opportunities, and eliminate discrimination.

Hispanic priests increased in numbers slowly during the 1950s and 1960s, and beginning in 1969, some of these pastors organized the PADRES (Priests Associated for Religious, Educational, and Social Rights) to help strengthen the voice of their ethnic community within the national Catholic church (Novo Pena, p. 367). Fifty nuns in 1971 united to form *Las Hermanas* and proclaimed a similar agenda. In response to pressure from these and other associations, a Secretariat of Hispanic Affairs was created within the church to coordinate activities of Hispanic clergy across the country. Three national meetings (*Encuentros*) between Spanish-speaking leaders and higher clerics in the church were held in 1972, 1977, and 1985. Though not all participants involved in these meetings viewed them in positive terms, Sandoval concludes that they provided a means for Hispanics to "come face to face with the top levels of authority in the church to express their frustrations and demands for equality and opportunity in the community of believers. The encuentros have legitimized protest and demonstrated the Church's willingness to listen to the oppressed" (*Fronteras: A History of the Latin American Church in the United States*, p. 431).

One of the most dynamic forces to bring about change between Mexican Americans and the Catholic church and its clergy in the United States was the Chicano movement of the 1960s and early 1970s. In seeking to define their unique identity within North American society by affirming a strong sense of pride in their Spanish and indigenous American heritage, leaders of this movement also condemned U.S. institutions that they believed had fostered or condoned the oppression of Mexican Americans in the past and present. In the early 1970s, the activist group *Católicos por la Raza* dramatized their discontent over lingering evidence of segregation in the church and its failure to bring about reforms to correct inequities in society by organizing a Christmas Eve demonstration. Many of the participants were arrested, but their sentiments were publicized (Meier, p. 227).

By the 1990s, an expanding proportion of Mexican Americans were mainstream Catholics and no longer sensed the same isolation or separation that their parents or grandparents likely experienced. According to Sandoval, however, the basic reality is the same as before: "Hispanics ... remain a people apart. They continue to cling to their culture and maintain at least some of their religious traditions. There is `social distance' between them and the institutional Church. For some it is a vague discomfort of not feeling at home. For others, it is the perception that the clergy are not interested in them. Moreover, Hispanics in the main have no role in ministry: episcopal, clerical, religious or lay. They are the objects of ministry rather than its agents" (p. 131).

RELIGIOUS FESTIVALS AND RITUALS

Various rituals and festivals of Spanish or Mexican Catholic origin continue to represent an important spiritual element in the lives of many contemporary Mexican Americans. In some instances, these public manifestations of faith have remained virtually unchanged since 1848 or before, but the number of those believers who practice them is decreasing with each new generation. The degree to which any single family participates in these activities depends on the nature of their religious convictions and the level of contact they maintain with more tradition-oriented members of churches of the Mexican American Catholic community.

One of the most symbolic celebrations for many Mexican Americans is the Feast of Our Lady of Guadalupe on December 12th. The festivity commemorates the apparitions of the Virgin Mary to a converted Christian Indian, Juan Diego, in Mexico on the hill of Tepeyac (located within the boundaries of present-day Mexico City) on this same date in 1521. Though she had identified herself as the Virgin Mary to Diego, in appearing before him she spoke his language, Nahuatl, related herself to indigenous deities, and, most importantly, was of a skin color similar to his. In the years immediately after her apparition countless thousands of Indians who had previously sought to maintain their native religions converted to the Catholic faith, seeing the coming of the Virgin in a new identity as a symbolic act of supreme consequence.

To commemorate the day of the Virgin's final apparition to Juan Diego on December 12th, some Mexican Americans may rise early and unite at some high point in the area (symbolic of the hill at Tepeyac) and sing "Las Mañanitas," a traditional song which, according to Elizondo, in this festivity represents the Mexican Americans' "proclamation of new life" (*Galilean Journey: The Mexican-American Promise*, p. 44). A special mass is said and roses are an important part of the celebration; most families take these flowers to the service and place them at the altar of the Virgin. Some Mexican Americans, on a given year, may make a pilgrimage to the Basilica of Our Lady of Guadalupe in Mexico City. The importance of the Virgin Mary to Mexican Americans and Hispanics in general cannot be overstated, as affirmed by Silvia Novo Pena: "For the males she is the understanding mother who forgives and intercedes for her errant sons; for the women she sympathizes with the early travails of a mother, sister, or daughter" (p. 381).

Ceremonies and rituals in recognition of events related to the birth and death of Jesus Christ are an essential part of the religious calendar of many Mexican Americans. During the nine days prior to Christmas Day, masses are said at dawn and the festivities of "Las Posadas" honor the arrival of Mary and Joseph to Bethlehem and their search for lodging at an inn (*posada*). Dressing in clothing similar to that likely worn by these personages, a couple visits designated houses of friends or other family members on consecutive nights. It is common for the participants to read dialogues that recreate the probable conversation between the Holy Family and the innkeepers. Though the contemporary Mary and Joseph, like those whom they represent, are denied entry each night, after the dialogues and other ritual acts are completed they may return to the house and unite with friends and family for fellowship. On the ninth night, which is Christmas Eve, Mary and Joseph visit a house that accepts their request for a night's lodging. All those who participated in the events of prior evenings generally attend the *Misa de Gallo* (Midnight Mass), which usually starts with a procession down the main aisle during which two godparents carry a statue of the Christ Child to a manger near the front altar (Samora, p. 227). Festivities include the sharing of food and drink to celebrate the arrival of Mary and Joseph at the inn where the Christ child will be born. During the evening, in most instances, those children present break a *piñata* (a paper maché figure often in the shape of a farm animal filled with candy and hung from a high spot in the house). In all, these joyous events serve to prepare the human spirit for the arrival of the Christ Savior. Christmas Day is spent at home with members of the extended family, and traditional Mexican dishes are principal elements of the menu (Nájera-Ramírez, p. 337).

The final significant event of the Christmas season is *El Día de los Reyes Magos* (Three Kings' Day) on January 6th, when children receive gifts to mark the arrival of the Magi and their offerings for the Christ Child. The night before this special date children leave a note in one of their shoes explaining their behavior during the past year, followed by a list of requests for specific gifts. The shoes often are filled with straw and left under the bed or on a windowsill, along with water, symbolically to provide sustenance to the camels of the kings. In doing so, "they are taught to be mindful of animals and to experience the joy of gratitude" (Samora, p. 227). On the evening of January 6th, families and close friends of this group unite to cut and share a special bread of circular shape with the figure of the infant Jesus in the center.

Activities throughout the Hispanic world also occur to recall the last days of Christ's life on earth. *El Miércoles de Ceniza* (Ash Wednesday), according to Samora, is of particular importance to Mexican Americans "as they reflect on their ties to the earth as a mestizo people" (p. 227). By receiving the imprint of a cross on their foreheads during mass on this day, like Catholics of all countries, they acknowledge the pain and suffering of Christ on the cross and "profess publicly the Christian faith with an awareness of their human sinfulness and limitations." On Good Friday in many parishes, *La Procesión de las Tres Caídas* (The Procession of the Three Falls) in conjunction with religious services brings to the memory of those in attendance the agony associated with Christ's journey to Calvary. Families may visit a statue or altar of Our Lady of Sorrows, a Virgin Mary with tears of anguish for her Son in His last moments on earth. The Mexican American mother, in visiting the statue, demonstrates her pity for the Virgin on this anniversary day. On Easter Sunday, another procession commemorates the reunion of the resurrected Christ and His mother. The burning of an effigy of Judas may also form part of the religious activities (Samora, p. 228).

FUNERALS

Rituals practiced in Spain and colonial Mexico associated with the death of family members are still preserved by some Mexican American families. After passing, the body of the deceased may be dressed in special clothing (*la mortaja*) and remain in the family home overnight, making it possible for relatives and friends to pay respects to the departing soul. Food is generally served at this *velorio* (wake). For years to follow on this same date, those people who attended the *velorio* may reunite to affirm once again their bonds to the deceased person. On the day of burial, the family accompanies the body to the grave, frequently singing songs of a religious theme. Flowers are thrown into the grave and the entire family generally stays at the site until the casket is completely covered. Mexican American families whose deceased members were born in Mexico may sometimes arrange for the body to be transported back to his/her town of origin. It was once customary for the spouse and certain family members to wear black clothing for varying periods and make *promesas* (vows) to honor the dead. This is still the practice with a reduced number of families, but the length of time of mourning differs considerably from group to group. Most significant is the perspective on death held by many Mexican and Mexican American Catholics that, rather than an end, death is seen as "a new beginning" (Stevens-Arroyo and Díaz Stevens, p. 379).

PROTESTANTISM AND OTHER FAITHS

The Anglo American settlers who immigrated in the early nineteenth century to the area of present-day Texas were predominantly of Protestant faith, as were those who in later decades travelled to California and most other regions north of the Rio Grande. Over time, they converted a small number of Mexican Americans to Protestantism. By the 1960s three percent of the Mexican American population were members of Protestant denominations (Cortés, p. 711). Increased efforts in social outreach projects, pronounced support of farmworker protest campaigns, and expanded evangelism, coupled with the continued dissatisfaction of many Mexican Americans with the relative lack of recognition accorded them locally or institutionally, have contributed to a considerable expansion in the proportion of Mexican Americans who have converted to Protestant sects. Pentecostal groups have also attracted growing numbers of Mexican Americans.

EMPLOYMENT AND ECONOMIC TRADITIONS

Mining, agriculture, transportation, and ranching attracted the highest numbers of Mexican immigrants and Mexican Americans in search of work in the United States from shortly after the mid-nineteenth century through the first decades of the twentieth century. As these sectors of the economy grew in importance, their demand for low-wage laborers multiplied, and the completion of local and transcontinental rail lines expanded the markets for ranchers and farmers in this region, prompting further increases in demands for additional workers (Mirandé, p. 29). Laws limiting or excluding Chinese and Japanese immigration made jobs even more abundant for others in certain regions of the western United States. For the Mexican immigrant, repeated downturns in the Mexican economy and the socio-political turbulence related to the Revolution of 1910 made "the North" an attractive location for at least temporary residence.

A reduced percentage of Mexican landowners and merchants crossed into the United States in this early period during the years of the Mexican Revolution. Many were successful in establishing businesses in Mexican American neighborhoods in the Southwest. With more years of formal education in their background than the majority of immigrants in this same period, this minority frequently provided jobs and political leadership within their newly adopted communities (Meier, p. 109).

Though mining, ranching, and transportation employed many new immigrants, the highest percentage of foreign workers were drawn to agriculture, mostly in Texas and California, but also in parts of New Mexico, Arizona, and Colorado. By 1930, 41 percent of the agricultural laborers in the Southwest were Mexicans or Mexican Americans (Cortés, p. 708). Eight-, ten-, or twelve-hour workdays, with few if any days of rest, combined with generally high temperatures to make this work in the fields or orchards extremely demanding and wearing in physical terms. Housing made available to laborers by their employers was of inferior quality. Unsanitary and confining living quarters facilitated the spread of disease. Clean drinking water was not easily accessible and indoor plumbing was uncommon. In areas of colder climate, inadequate heating was the norm. The transitory nature of this work was most difficult on immigrant families, whose children very seldom had the opportunity to attend anything but makeshift schools on a temporary basis and were most often forced, for economic reasons, to begin work in the fields at a young age.

The decade of the 1930s brought severe cutbacks in hiring in agriculture and other industries due to worldwide economic depression. High levels of unemployment nationwide made immigrant labor expendable. Those workers not of U.S. origin were deported in large numbers; over 500,000 were forced to return to Mexico during this ten-year period. Frequently, families were separated: parents of foreign citizenship were returned to their home countries, whereas their children, if born in the United States, and thus, American citizens, sometimes remained in their country of birth with relatives or family friends, hoping for the prompt return of their parents.

Less than ten years after the first of these deportations, however, labor shortages caused by World War II—principally in agriculture—stimulated a renewed need for immigrant labor. To resolve this matter, the governments of the United States and Mexico signed an agreement in 1942 that initiated the *bracero* (someone who works with their arms—*brazos*) program, which allocated temporary work visas to Mexican immigrants seeking farm work in the Southwest. From 1942 to 1948, over 200,000 laborers entered the United States to work in California agribusiness and, in reduced numbers, in the rail industry and other sectors. Though cancelled in 1948, the program was renewed shortly thereafter and continued in force until 1964 when, in part because of socio-political pressures related to the civil rights movement, the U.S. Congress decided against any further extensions of the agreement. Accusations of farmworkers against their employers related to substandard housing and work conditions had been confirmed by studies conducted by the Labor Department in the 1950s; agencies such as the National Council of Churches of Christ in America, the National Catholic Welfare Council, and the National Consumers League had spoken out against these infringements and made many U.S. citizens more fully aware of the abuses repeatedly suffered by these workers.

A major portion of the braceros working in the United States from 1942 to 1964 returned to Mexico, but it is estimated that eight percent of these workers, roughly 750,000, remained in the Southwest to raise families and establish permanent residency or citizenship (Meier, p. 184). To those who participated in this program and to other immigrant Mexican laborers who had come northward for work in this period, it became evident once again, as in the 1930s, that when low-wage workers were needed, they were welcome in the United States. When the demand for laborers diminished, however, their presence was not wanted by significant numbers of the majority community.

Wages for Mexican and Mexican American farmworkers continued at inequitable, low levels and living and work conditions failed to improve to any marked degree in the decades subsequent to the 1960s. Strikes and boycotts organized by César Chávez further publicized the injustices perpetrated by many employers in this rural industry. The formation of the United Farm Workers union gave somewhat greater strength to migrant labor demands, but unfair practices by employers still remain a source of grievance in the fields (Meier, p. 210).

DIVERSIFICATION OF EMPLOYMENT OPPORTUNITIES

Noticeable beginning in the 1920s and increasing measurably in the years after World War II was a shift in the Hispanic labor force in the United States, especially by second- and third-generation Mexican Americans, away from their initial sources of employment into a wider range of occupations. Many of these workers were attracted to other regions of the country. The midwestern states, particularly Illinois, offered jobs in meat-packing and manufacturing to mounting numbers of Mexican Americans seeking alternatives to the transient life of field work. By 1990 only 2.9 percent of the Mexican American working population were employed in agriculture and forestry, with less than one percent in the mining industry. Professional and health and education services employed 20.3 percent of this specific labor force, while 16.4 percent had service occupations and 15.9 percent were in manufacturing. Over 16 percent held managerial and professional specialty positions (*The Statistical Record of Hispanic Americans*, p. 534).

The small Mexican American entrepreneurial sector—evident beginning in the second decade of the 1900s—expanded considerably after World War II. By 1990 over one-half million Hispanic-owned businesses existed in the United States, the majority of them in California and controlled by Mexican Americans. Earnings for these commercial concerns approached $100 billion annually and contributed to the growth of the Mexican American middle class (Meier, p. 253).

Mexican American women entered the labor market as farmworkers, laundresses, and domestics in representative numbers starting in the first decades of the twentieth century. By 1930, 15 percent had employment, and 45 percent of this total worked in domestic and personal service, with smaller percentages in textile and food processing industries, agriculture, or sales (Cortés, pp. 708, 713). The proportion of Mexican American women in the labor force increased substantially in the decades that followed, reaching 21 percent by 1950 and over 50 percent by 1990 (Falcón and Gilbarg, p. 64). In 1991 the sectors of the national economy with highest levels of employment for Mexican American women were technical, sales, and administrative support, including clerical positions at 39 percent, followed by jobs in service occupations at 27 percent. Fourteen percent were in managerial and professional specialty classifications (*The Statistical Record ...*, p. 508). Though Mexican American women are employed at approximately the same percentage as non-Hispanic women, their earnings

are 82 percent of the income of this other group (Meier, p. 262). In general, as asserted by many contemporary sociologists, Mexican American women have had to overcome the triple oppression of class, race, and gender in seeking employment.

Despite the diversification in employment into other sectors of the national economy detailed above, wages have remained low for most members of the Mexican American community. Though well over 50 percent of the families had two wage earners and 15 percent had three workers, as of 1990, the median family income was $23,240, considerably lower than the national average. The median incomes for Mexican American males and females were below those of most other Hispanic groups: while Puerto Rican males and females earned $18,193 and $11,702 respectively, the corresponding wages for Mexican American men and women were $12,894 and $9,286. Unemployment rates for the two genders were 11.7 percent and 9.2 percent (Falcón and Gilbarg, p. 64).

In the early 1990s jobs in manufacturing in the national economy declined, whereas service and information technology hirings increased. Service sector jobs respond more immediately to cyclical trends, and because a large percentage of Mexican Americans are in this line of employment, they are among the first exposed to periodic declines in the contemporary job market. High dropout rates at the high school level and low numbers of Mexican American youth that graduate from two- or four-year colleges allow but a small percentage of Mexican Americans to qualify for positions in the information technology sector. Low educational attainment in general continues to place them consistently at entry-level positions and makes progress to higher rank or pay more difficult. The plant closings of many manufacturing industries in the southwest, and specifically in Southern California in the early 1990s, have forced many thousands of Mexican Americans to look for jobs in other lines of work, but again, low levels of education or technical training limit the alternatives open to these individuals.

POLITICS AND GOVERNMENT

Political participation by Mexican Americans historically has been limited by discrimination. In the early Southwest before 1910, small numbers of Mexican Americans held offices in territorial and state legislatures in California, Colorado, and New Mexico. However, they were usually handpicked by the dominant Anglo Americans of these regions. In other cases, Anglo American businessmen who controlled the railroads, mines, and large ranches dominated the state and local politics of the Southwest. The existing political structure was manipulated to benefit these interests. During the first decades of the twentieth century—to insure Anglo American political control—participation in the voting process for Mexican Americans was maintained at a minimum with the use of various discriminatory devices. Restrictive policies included the poll tax, literacy tests, all-white primaries, and coercion. In this atmosphere it is not surprising that few Mexican Americans voted (Feagin and Feagin, p. 274).

While political participation was limited, Miguel Tirado points out that during the early part of the twentieth century Mexican Americans formed protective organizations—*mutualistas* (mutual aid societies)—which were quite similar to those that developed among European immigrant groups. Members of these organizations found that by pooling their resources they could provide each other with funeral and insurance benefits as well as other forms of assistance. For example, the Lázaro Cardenas Society was formed in Los Angeles soon after World War I to improve municipal facilities available to Mexican Americans (*Aztlán*, 1970, p. 55). By the 1920s it became evident to Mexican Americans that if their interests were to be protected political power was essential.

However, even as Mexican Americans began to adapt to the political and social traditions of the United States they were still viewed as "foreigners" by the larger society. Thus, they set out to demonstrate that they were true Americans. This orientation was reflected in the goals of the emerging organizations of the early twentieth century. The *Orden Hijos de América* (Order of the Sons of America), established in 1921 in San Antonio, Texas, by members of a small emerging middle class, restricted its goals to that of "training members for citizenship." Membership was consequently limited to "citizens of the United States of Mexican or Spanish extraction" (Moore and Cuellar, 1970, p. 41). According to Moore and Cuellar, this orientation strongly suggested that Mexican Americans "were more trustworthy to Anglos than Mexican nationals, and also more deserving of the benefits of American life." Thus, as an organization consisting of upwardly mobile individuals, OSA attempted to demonstrate to the larger community that they were people to be respected. To understand the group's motives, the OSA must be placed within the social climate of the era. Their orientation was a reflection of the social and economic vulnerability of Mexican Americans during the 1920s.

The OSA functioned for approximately ten years. Disagreements about the goals and direction of the group soon lead to schisms. However, the splintering of OSA led to the development of a new organization—the League of Latin American Citizens (LULAC). The theme of unity and the need to provide a united front to the Anglo American community guided the group's decision to call itself LULAC. It also limited its membership to U.S. citizens. LULAC gained power among the Mexican American middle class and it ultimately became their strongest advocate (Moore and Cuellar, p. 41).

THE POLITICIZATION OF MEXICAN AMERICANS

The events of World War II would prove to be a turning point in the Mexican American's bid for expanded political participation. This confrontation profoundly affected Mexican Americans, first by exposing those who served in the armed services to social climates where they were regarded as equals. Secondly, the needs of the industrial wartime economy drew many Mexican Americans into the nation's urban centers seeking employment, thus fostering a greater participation in larger society. In essence, their participation in the war effort at home and abroad served as a solidifying force, setting the stage for political activism (Moore and Pachón, p. 178).

Many political groups organized by returning Mexican American veterans emerged to challenge segregation and other forms of discriminatory practices in American life. The Community Service Organization (CSO) is one example. It was founded in 1947 to promote social change within the Mexican American communities of Los Angeles. The founding members set out to improve social conditions by promoting participation in the political process. CSO was determined to elect individuals responsive to the needs of the Mexican American community. It met with some success. Through the efforts of CSO, the East Los Angeles community elected the first Mexican American to the city council since 1881 (Tirado, pp. 62-66).

The political activism of this period is also exemplified by the actions of the G.I. Forum, the Mexican American Political Association (MAPA), and the Political Association of Spanish-Speaking Organizations (PASSO). Established in 1948, the G.I. Forum emerged to protest the refusal of cemeteries and mortuaries in Three Rivers, Texas, to bury the body of a Mexican American World War II veteran. This incident focused national attention on the discriminatory conditions of Mexican Americans in Texas. The Forum later turned its attention to mainstream politics by organizing voter registration drives and get-out-the-vote campaigns (C. F. García and R. O. de la Garza, *The Chicano Political Experience: Three Perspectives*, p. 29).

Created in 1960, MAPA marks yet another stage of political activism. It was one of the first organizations to clearly articulate ethnic political goals. According to the MAPA Fourth Annual Convention Program, "An organization was needed that would be proudly Mexican American, openly political, and necessarily bipartisan" (Moore and Pachón, p. 179). MAPA met with success. It helped elect several Mexican Americans to office (Garcia and de la Garza, p. 31). PASSO, created a few years earlier in Texas, and MAPA were political groups organized essentially to lobby at the party level for Mexican American interests. Both organizations carried out voter education and registration drives; however, they were primarily oriented toward winning concessions for Mexican Americans at the party level (Moore and Cuellar, p. 45).

In the 1970s, unhappy with both the Democratic and Republican parties, some Mexican Americans opted for an entirely different political strategy. They set out to create an alternative political party—La Raza Unida (LRU). Established in Texas in 1970, the LRU had remarkable successes. Most notable were the party's achievements in Crystal City, Texas, a community of approximately 10,000 where many LRU candidates won control of the city council and the school board. These newly elected officials in turn hired more Mexican American teachers, staff, and administrators. They also instituted bilingual programs and added Mexican American history to the school curriculum. The newly elected officials also made changes throughout the city government, including the police department, to rectify years of neglect by city officials (John Shockley, *Chicano Revolt in a Texas Town*).

The LRU then sent organizers throughout the Southwest in efforts to duplicate their success in South Texas. LRU candidates were placed on many local and statewide ballots, but they were unable to generate the type of support that led to their success in Crystal City. After the mid-1970s, the LRU rapidly declined. Its decline was the result of several factors. Internal ideological splintering and personality conflicts played a part, but harassment and repression of the party was the most significant force (Carlos Muñoz, *Youth, Identity, Power: The Chicano Movement*, 1989).

The LRU is but one of many groups that contributed to the growth of the Chicano Movement during the 1960s and 1970s. Mexican Americans became much more vocal and militant in their demands for social change. Many groups emerged to address such issues as the rights of farmworkers, inferior education, employment opportunities, health care, women's rights, reform within the welfare system and the Catholic church, police brutality, and community self-determination.

National attention during this period focused on the actions of La Alianza Federal de Mercedes (Federal Alliance of Land Grants) and the United Farmworkers of America (UFW). Reies López Tijerina and the members of La Alianza demanded the return of stolen lands to the indigenous peoples of northern New Mexico. In 1966 La Alianza occupied a part of the Kit Carson National Forest in New Mexico. Arrested for trespassing, Tijerina spent the next few years awaiting trial. In 1975 the land dispute was partially resolved when about 1,000 acres of the forest were transferred to 75 Mexican American families (Shaefer, p. 283).

The notable organizing efforts of César Chávez, Dolores Huerta, and the UFW brought the plight of the farmworker to national attention and served as a mobilizing force for many Americans of all walks of life. The UFW's first success was the grape boycott beginning in 1965, which carried the struggle of the farmworkers into the households of many Americans. With the overwhelming refusal to buy table grapes by many American households, the UFW was able to negotiate its first union contract with California growers (the first union contract in the history of California farm labor). During the late 1980s, the UFW altered its labor unionizing strategies by addressing the issue of pestiticide use in agricultural production.

From the Mexican American communities of Denver, Colorado, emerged the Crusade for Justice led by Corky Gonzales. This organization was primarily concerned with civil rights issues of urban Mexican Americans; however, it was also one of the first groups to advocate and promote issues of cultural diversity. During 1969 and 1970, the Crusade for Justice was instrumental in organizing a series of Chicano youth liberation conferences, bringing together hundreds of young Chicanos from throughout the nation and generating a series of discussions concerning the question of ethnic identity (Rodolfo Acuña, *Occupied America*, pp. 241-43).

By the late 1960s high school and college students were calling for social change within the educational system. The high school "blowouts" of East Los Angeles in 1968 galvanized student discontent. Chicano high school students walked out of their classes in mass, demanding quality education and local community control of their schools. In several other communities students staged similar events.

High school students abandoned their classes in Riverside, California; Denver, Colorado; Crystal City and San Antonio, Texas; and several other cities with high concentrations of Mexican Americans. College students also mobilized. In the Los Angeles area, college students came together to support the high school walkouts and the students' demands for a quality education. Throughout the Southwest, college students were instrumental in establishing the first Chicano studies programs and educational opportunities programs on many college campuses (Acuña, p. 243).

In 1968 the Mexican-American Legal Defense and Education Fund (MALDEF) was established by several Mexican American lawyers to protect the constitutional rights of Mexican Americans. Although it does not endorse political candidates, it has made itself felt in the political sphere much like the NAACP has for African Americans. In addition to providing legal advocacy, MALDEF has been involved in litigation involving illegal employment practices, immigrant's rights, biased testing in school settings, educational segregation, inequalities in school financing, and voting rights issues. As of the 1990s, MALDEF has emerged as the primary civil rights group advocating on behalf of Mexican Americans.

VOTING PATTERNS AND ELECTED OFFICIALS

Mexican American voting behavior has traditionally been Democratic, especially at the presidential level. According to the Latino National Political Survey (1992), 59.6 percent of all Mexican Americans identify themselves as Democrats, 16 percent as Republican, and 24.4 as belonging to independent parties. As members of the Democratic Party, they have played a significant role in several elections. In 1960 John F. Kennedy won an estimated 85 percent of the Mexican American vote, which allowed him to win the states of New Mexico and Texas. To insure Kennedy's victory, "Viva Kennedy" clubs were formed throughout the Southwest, promoting voter education and registration drives. In 1964 Lyndon B. Johnson won an estimated 90 percent, and in 1968 Herbert Humphrey won 87 percent of the Mexican American vote (Feagin and Feagin, p. 275).

While Mexican Americans played a significant role in the above elections, there are several factors that have worked against the growth of Mexican American participation in the political process. First, they are a young population, which means that many are below the voting age. Second, a relatively large segment of the population is ineligible

to vote because they are not citizens. Even among those who are eligible to vote, the turnout of 46 percent (for all Hispanics) in the November 1988 elections was 15 percent lower than for non-Hispanics. Third, lower socioeconomic status serves as an obstacle for many Mexican Americans. The educational attainment of Mexican Americans is still far below the general population and the poverty rates are much higher for Mexican Americans than the general population. Thus, many Mexican Americans have not had the opportunity to develop the skills necessary to participate in the voting process. Consequently, Mexican Americans are presented with formidable obstacles that prevent the development of political strength and greatly hinder the election of Mexican American officials (Maurilio Vigil, *The Handbook ... Sociology*, pp. 81-82).

While the percentage of Mexican American elected officials is not representative of their total U.S. population, significant changes have taken place since the mid-1960s. The number of state legislators in 1950 with Spanish surnames totaled 20. By the late 1980s the number had increased to 90. In 1991 the National Roster of Hispanic Elected Officials reported 3,754 elected officials in the five southwestern states, mostly of Mexican American ancestry, and 4,202 Latino elected officials nationwide. The increase in Mexican American officials is due in part to the Twenty-fourth Amendment, which banned the poll tax and eliminated the English-only literacy requirements for voting in some states. Redistricting following the 1980 census, as well as a substantial growth in the Mexican American population, have also contributed to the rise in the number of Mexican American elected officials (Feagin and Feagin, p. 274).

FEDERAL LEGISLATION AND NATIONAL POLICY

With the slow yet steadily increasing number of Mexican American elected officials, significant pieces of federal legislation have been introduced and enacted into law. During the recent past, Mexican American lawmakers have supported the creation of the federal Fair Employment Practices Commission, the Civil Rights Act of 1964, the Voting Rights Act of 1965, and the subsequent series of civil rights and affirmative action legislation. In 1968 the Bilingual Education Act was passed into federal law; in 1974 subsequent amendments were sponsored by New Mexico Congressman Joseph Montoya. That same year, Congress, with the urging of many Hispanic and non-Hispanic elected officials alike, encouraged the adoption of bilingual or multilingual ballots where census data documented a substantial number of non-English-speaking people.

In 1976 the Congressional Hispanic Caucus was created with the election of several Hispanics to the House of Representatives. Since then, the caucus has acted as a viable force within Congress, consistently supporting legislation on behalf of Mexican Americans and other disadvantaged groups (Vigil, pp. 91-92). Two of the most prominent public policies affecting Mexican Americans and Hispanics in general are immigration reform and the "English as Official Language" policy. Although the members of the caucus did not agree with each other on the specific initiatives of the policies, both of these issues were and continue to be a high priority for the caucus.

MILITARY STATUS

According to the 1990 census, there are 59,631 Mexican American men over the age of 16 serving in the armed forces, 7,924 of whom are naturalized citizens, while the remainder are native-born. The number of Mexican American women in the armed services is significantly lower; 5,025 native-born Chicanas are active members of the military.

INDIVIDUAL AND GROUP CONTRIBUTIONS

Mexican Americans have made significant and lasting contributions to virtually every element of American culture and society. The following individuals represent merely a sample of this growing community's achievements.

BUSINESS

Born to undocumented Mexican parents in Miami, Arizona, Romana Acosta Bañuelos (1925–) was deported at the age six during the Repatriation Program of the 1930s. After returning to the United States at age 19, she converted a small tortilla factory into Romana's Mexican Food Products, a multimillion-dollar firm. In 1971 she became the first Mexican American to serve as treasurer of the United States.

EDUCATION

Born in Albuquerque, New Mexico, George I. Sánchez (1906-1972) directed his energies to improving the quality of education available to Mexican Americans as well as defending their civil rights. *Forgotten People: A Study of New Mexico* (1940), one of his many publications, revealed the inadequacies of the educational system for Mexican Americans in his home state. Sánchez served as president of LULAC and, in 1956, founded the American Council of Spanish-Speaking People, a civil rights organization.

FILM, TELEVISION, AND THEATER

Mexican American dancer and choreographer José Arcadia Limón (1908-1972) was a pioneer of modern dance and choreography. Edward James Olmos (1947–), received critical acclaim for his portrayal of the *pachuco* in the stage and film version of Luis Valdez's *Zoot Suit* and for his role as Jaime Escalante in the film *Stand and Deliver*. In addition to his appearances in other movies of merit, Olmos starred in "Miami Vice," a popular television series of the 1980s. Paul Rodríguez, who has worked in a number of television series and movies, is perhaps the most popular and widely recognized comedian of Mexican descent in the United States. The head of his own company, Paul Rodríguez Productions, in 1986 he released his first comedy album entitled "You're in America Now, Speak Spanish." The son of Mexican migrant farmworkers, Luis Valdez (1940–) is the founding director of the Teatro Campesino, an acting troupe that was originally organized to dramatize the oppressive existence of the migrant worker. In addition to directing the stage and film version of *Zoot Suit*, he wrote and directed the film *La Bamba*, about the Mexican American rock star Ritchie Valens.

FOLKLORE

Born in Brownsville, Texas, Americo Paredes (1915–) achieved national and international recognition for his research and scholarship in the area of folklore and Mexican American popular culture and served as president of the American Folklore Society. Among his many noteworthy publications are *Folktales in Mexico* (1970) and *A Texas Mexican Cancionero* (1976).

LABOR

César Chávez (1927-1993) was born in Yuma, Arizona, to a farmworking family. Chávez attended over 30 schools as a youth because of the mobile pattern of existence of migrant agriculture. In 1962, after working as a community organizer in the CSO, he moved to Delano, California, and soon became the head of the United Farm Workers, AFL-CIO. From the mid-1960s to his death, Chavez dedicated his life to improving the living conditions, wages, and bargaining power of Mexican and Mexican American farmworkers by means of organized work stoppages, demonstrations, hunger strikes, and boycotts.

LITERATURE

Lucha Corpi (1945–) is a notable poet and novelist whose works often address the struggles of women in contemporary society. Primarily known as a poet, she is perhaps best known for her series "The Mariana Poems," which appear in her *Palabras de mediodia/Noon Words* (1980). Rolando Hinojosa (1929–) was one of the first Chicano writers to achieve national as well as international fame. His *Estampas del valle y otras obras: Sketches of the Valley and Other Works*, a series of "sketches" that portrayed Mexican American life in a fictional town in Texas, won the Premio Quinto Sol for Chicano literature. Another of his works on the same theme, *Klail City y sus alrededores*, won the prestigious international award, Premio Casa de las Americas, in 1976. Born in Linares, Mexico, in 1907, literary critic Luis Leal is one of the most productive, most respected, and most honored scholars of Latin American and Chicano literature. In addition to teaching at numerous universities, he has written some 16 books and edited dozens of others.

MUSIC

Eduardo Mata (1942–) is among the most respected conductors in the world. The former director and conductor emeritus of the Dallas Symphony Orchestra, he was awarded the White House Hispanic Heritage Award in 1991. Singer and musician Lydia Mendoza (1916–) was the first interpreter of rural popular Tejano and border music to acquire star status through her many recordings. Grammy award-winning Tejano singer and entertainer Selena Quintanilla Perez (1971-1995), best known as Selena, had achieved international fame at the time of her murder in April 1995.

POLITICS

After her election as a state assemblywoman in California in 1982, Gloria Molina (1948–) was voted into the Los Angeles City Council in 1987. In 1991 she was elected to the Los Angeles County Board of Supervisors, thus becoming the first Hispanic in California to be selected by voters to serve at these three levels of government.

RELIGION

The first Mexican American to be named as a bishop of the Catholic church in the United States, Patrick F. Flores (1929–) worked in the diocese of Galveston-Houston and became the director of the Bishop's Committee for the Spanish-Speaking. He has been a strong defender of the civil rights of Hispanics in the United States for over four decades and has won many honors for these efforts, including the Ellis Island Medal of Honor in 1986.

SCIENCE

A renowned physicist and educator, Mexican American Alberto Vinicio Baez (1912–) and his co-researcher, Paul Kirkpatrick, developed the Kirkpatrick-Baez Lamar X-ray telescope, which was later approved for flight on the Freedom Space Station. A pioneer in X-ray radiation, optics, and microscopy, Baez has also made noteworthy achievements in the field of environmental education; he has served as chairman of the Committee on Teaching Sciences of the International Council of Science Unions and as chairman emeritus of Community Education, International Union for the Conservation of Nature and Natural Resources, Glantz, Switzerland. Chemist Mario Molina (1943–) earned national prominence by theorizing, with fellow chemist F. Sherwood Rowland, that chlorofluorocarbons deplete the Earth's ozone layer.

MEDIA

PRINT

El Chicano.
Contact: Gloria Marcias Harrison, Publisher.
Address: P.O. Box 6247, San Bernadino, California 92412-6247.
Telephone: (909) 381-9898.
Fax: (909) 384-0406.
E-mail: iecn@gte.net.

Mexican American Sun.
Contact: Rose Soto, Editor.
Address: 2500 South Atlantic Boulevard, Building B, Los Angeles, California 90040-2004.
Telephone: (213) 263-5743.
Fax: (213) 263-9169.

El Mundo.
Contact: William Fonsea, Editor.
Address: P.O. Box 1350, Oakland, California 94604-1350.

Telephone: (510) 763-1120.
Fax: (510) 763-9670

Saludos Hispanos.
Contact: Maureen Herring, Editor.
Address: 73121 Fred Waring Drive, #100,
    Palm Desert, California 92260.
Telephone: (619) 776-1206.
Fax: (619) 776-1214.
Online: http://www.saludos.com.

El Sol.
Contact: Christine Flores, Editor.
Address: 750 Northwest Grand Avenue,
    Phoenix, Arizona 85007.
Telephone: (602) 257-1746.

RADIO

KQTL-AM (1210).
Covers Southern Arizona and Northern Mexico.

Contact: Bertha Gallego, Director of Operations;
    Raul B. Gamez, General Manager.
Address: P.O. Box 1511, Tucson,
    Arizona 85702-1511.
Telephone: (602) 628-1200.
Fax: (602) 326-4927.

KXKS-AM.
Founded in 1969, went to all-Spanish format in
1982. 10,000 watts, covers 150 miles out from center of Albuquerque.

Contact: Bertha Gallego, Director of Operations;
    Kelly Cunningham, General Manager.
Address: 6320 Zuni S.E., Albuquerque,
    New Mexico 87108.
Telephone: (505) 265-8331.

WIND-AM (560).
Contact: Lucy Diaz.
Address: 625 North Michigan, Suite 300,
    Chicago, Ilinois 60611-3110.
Telephone: (312) 751-5560.
Fax: (312) 664-2472.

TELEVISION

KDB-59 (Telemundo Affiliate).
Contact: Kelly Cunningham-Muson,
    General Manager.
Address: 6320 Zuni S.E., Albuquerque,
    New Mexico 87108.

Telephone: (505) 265-8331.
Fax: (505) 266-3836.

KHRR-40 (Telemundo Affiliate).
Contact: Jay S. Zucker.
Address: 2919 East Broadway, Tucson,
    Arizona 85716.
Telephone: (602) 322-6888.
Fax: (602) 881-7926.

KINT-26 (Univision Affiliate).
Contact: Silvia Martínez, Director of Operations.
Address: 5426 North Mesa, El Paso, Texas 79912.
Telephone: (915) 581-1126.
Fax: (915) 581-1393.

KLUZ-41 (Univision Affiliate).
Contact: Marcela Medina, Director of Operations.
Address: 2725-F Broadbent Parkway, N.E.,
    Albuquerque, New Mexico 87107.
Telephone: (505) 342-4141.
Fax: (505) 344-8714.
E-mail: kluztv41@aol.com.

KMEX-34 (Univision Affiliate).
Contact: Jorge Belón, Director of Operations.
Address: 6701 Center Drive West, 15th Floor,
    Los Angeles, California 90045.
Telephone: (310) 216-3434.
Fax: (310) 348-3597.

KSTS-48 (Telemundo).
Contact: Enrique Pérez, Director of Operations.
Address: 2349 Bering Drive, San Jose,
    California 95131.
Telephone: (408) 285-8848.
Fax: (408) 433-5921.

KTMD-48 (Telemundo).
Contact: Darlene Stephens, Director of
    Operations.
Address: 3903 Stoneybrooke, Houston,
    Texas 77063.
Telephone: (713) 974-4848.
Fax: (713) 974-5875.

KWEX-41 (Univision Affiliate).
Contact: Lillian Almendarez, Director of
    Operations.
Address: 411 East Durango, San Antonio,
    Texas 78204.
Telephone: (210) 227-4141.
Fax: (210) 227-0469.

WGBO-66 (Univision Affiliate).
Contact: Paul Yewowsski, Director of Operations.
Address: 541 North Fairbanks, 11th Floor,
Chicago, Illinois 60611.
Telephone: (312) 670-1000.
Fax: (312) 494-6492.

WSNS-44 (Telemundo Affiliate).
Contact: David Cordoba, Director of Operations.
Address: 431 Grant Place, Chicago,
Illinois 60614.
Telephone: (312) 929-1200.
Fax: (312) 929-8153.

ORGANIZATIONS AND ASSOCIATIONS

**Comisión Femenil Mexicana Nacional, Inc.
(National Mexican Women's Commission)**
Founded in 1970. Current membership: 5,000, in
23 chapters. Supports increased rights and opportunities for Hispanic women in education, politics
and labor. Publication: *La Mujer* ("The Woman")
semiannual.

Contact: Nina Aguayo Sorcin, President.
Address: 379 South Loma Drive, Los Angeles,
California 90017.
Telephone: (213) 484-1515.
Fax: (213) 484-0880.

**Mexican American Legal Defense and
Education Fund.**
Founded in San Antonio in 1968 in response to a
historical pattern of discrimination against Mexican Americans. Protects and promotes the rights of
over 25 million Latinos in the United States in
employment, education, immigration, political
access, and language through litigation and community education.

Contact: Antonia Hernández, President.
Address: 634 South Spring Street, 11th Floor, Los
Angeles, California 90014.
Telephone: (213) 629-2512.
Fax: (213) 629-0266.

**National Association for Chicano and Chicana
Studies, NACCS National Office.**
Founded in 1971. Membership of over 300 consists
of college professors, graduate and undergraduate
students, and diverse others whose professional or
personal interests center on sociological, historical,
political or literary themes or concerns pertaining

to Mexican Americans. Sponsors annual conference and publishes selected proceedings.

Contact: Dr. Carlos Maldonado, Director.
Address: Chicano Education Program, Eastern
Washington University, Monroe Hall 202,
MS 170, Cheney, Washington 99004.
Telephone: (509) 359-2404.
Fax: (509) 359-2310.

National Council of La Raza.
The nation's largest constituency-based Hispanic
organization. Exists to reduce poverty and discrimination and improve life opportunities for all Hispanics nationally. Nearly 200 formal affiliates serve
37 states, Puerto Rico and the District of Columbia.
Programmatic efforts focus on civil rights, education, health, housing and community development,
employment and training, immigration and poverty.

Contact: Raul Yzaguirre, President.
Address: 1111 19th Street N.W., Suite 1000,
Washington, D.C. 20036.
Telephone: (202) 785-1670.

Southwest Voter Registration Education Project.
Founded in 1975. Conducts nonpartisan voter registration drives, compiles research on Hispanic and
native American voting patterns and works to eliminate gerrymandered voting districts. Publication:
National Hispanic Voter Registration Campaign.
Regional planning committees publish newsletters.

Contact: Antonio Gonzalez, President.
Address: 403 East Commerce Street, Suite 220,
San Antonio, Texas 78205.
Telephone: (800) 404-VOTE; or (210) 222-0224.
Fax: (210) 222-8474.

MUSEUMS AND RESEARCH CENTERS

Center for Chicano Studies.
Part of University of California, Santa Barbara.
Supports and conducts research on historical and
contemporary issues related to Mexican-origin population of the United States. Encourages and facilitates academic investigations and training of minority students. Sponsors events that increase public
awareness and appreciation of Mexican and Mexican American culture.

Contact: Dr. Denise Segura, Director.
Address: Room 4518, South Hall, Santa Barbara,
Santa Barbara, California 93106-6040.
Telephone: (805) 893-3895.

Fax: (805) 893-4446.
Online: http://omni.ucsb.edu/ccs/.

Center for Mexican American Studies.
Part of the University of Texas at Austin. Provides financial and technical support for research by faculty and graduate students. Offers courses as part of Ethnic Studies curriculum of College of Liberal Arts. Publication: *Monograph Series.*

Contact: David Montejano, Director.
Address: F 9200, Austin, Texas 78712.
Telephone: (512) 471-4557.
Fax: (512) 471-9639.
E-mail: cmason@uts.cc.utexas.edu.
Online: http://www.utexas.edu/depts/cmas.

Chicano Studies Research Center.
Part of the University of California, Los Angeles. Promotes the study and dissemination of knowledge on the experience of people of Mexican descent and other Latinos in the United States. Publication: *Aztlán: A Journal of Chicano Studies.*

Contact: Dr. Guillermo Hernández, Director.
Address: 180 Haines, Los Angeles,
    California 90095.
Telephone: (310) 825-2363.
Fax: (310) 206-1784.
E-mail: gmo@csrc.ucla.edu.
Online: http://www.sscnet.ucla.edu/csrc.

Guadalupe Cultural Arts Center.
Latino arts and cultural institution. Sponsors instructional programming and presentations.

Contact: Pedro A. Rodríguez, Executive Director.
Address: 1300 Guadalupe Street, San Antonio,
    Texas 78207.
Telephone: (210) 271-3151.

Mexic-Arte Multicultural Works.
Exhibits include work of Mexican artists, pre-Cortez implements, and photographs of the Mexican Revolution.

Contact: Herlinda Zamora, Director.
Address: 419 Congress Avenue, Austin,
    Texas 78701.
Telephone: (512) 480-9373.

Mexican Fine Arts Center Museum.
Collections of Mexican art as well as presentations of current and past Mexican literary works.

Contact: Carlos Tortellero, Director.

Address: 1852 West 19th Street, Chicago,
    Illinois 60608.
Telephone: (312) 738-1503.

Mexican Museum.
Pre-Hispanic, colonial, folk, Mexican, and Mexican American fine arts. Permanent collection as well as temporary exhibits.

Contact: Marie Acosta-Colón, Executive Director.
Address: Fort Mason Building D., Laguna and
    Marina Boulevard, San Francisco,
    California 94123.
Telephone: (415) 441-0404.

Plaza de La Raza.
Offers instruction in theater, dance, music, visual and communication arts. Exhibits include Mexican American folk art of surrounding region.

Contact: Rose Cano, Executive Director.
Address: 3540 North Mission Road, Los Angeles,
    California 90031.
Telephone: (213) 223-2475.

**Southwest Hispanic Research Institute/
Chicano Studies.**
Part of University of New Mexico. Established in 1980. Coordinates and conducts investigations of interdisciplinary scope. Visiting Scholars Program funded by Rockefeller Foundation provides economic support to scholarly research of regional focus. Sponsors colloquium series that allows faculty to present findings of research to academic and local community. Publications: *Working Paper Series.*

Contact: Dr. Felipe Gonzales, Director.
Address: 1829 Sigma Chi, Albuquerque,
    New Mexico 87131.
Telephone: (505) 277-2965.
Fax: (505) 277-3343.
E-mail: gonzales@unm.edu.

SOURCES FOR ADDITIONAL STUDY

Acuña, Rodolfo. *Occupied America: A History of Chicanos*, third edition. New York: Harper & Row, 1988.

Between Two Worlds: Mexican Immigrants in the United States, edited by David G. Gutiérrez. Wilmington, DE: Scholarly Resources, 1996.

del Castillo, Richard Griswold, and Arnoldo de León. *North to Aztlán: A History of Mexican Americans in the United States.* New York: Twayne Publishers, 1996.

Durán, Livie Isauro, and H. Russell Bernard. *Introduction to Chicano Studies,* second edition. New York: Macmillan Publishing Co., 1982.

Grebler, Leo, Joan W. Moore, and Ralph Guzman. *The Mexican-American People: The Nation's Second Largest Minority.* New York: Free Press, 1970.

The Handbook of Hispanic Cultures in the United States, four volumes, edited by Nicolás Kanellos and Claudio Esteva-Fabregat. Houston: Arte Público Press, 1993.

Kanellos, Nicolás. *The Hispanic-American Almanac.* Detroit: Gale Research. 1993.

McWilliams, Carey. *North from Mexico: The Spanish-Speaking People of the United States,* updated by Matt S. Meier. New York: Praeger, 1990.

Meier, Matt S., and Feliciano Rivera. *Mexican Americans/American Mexicans.* New York: Hill and Wang, 1993.

Mirandé, Alfredo. *The Chicano Experience An Alternative Perspective.* South Bend, Indiana: University of Notre Dame Press, 1985.

Samora, Julián, and Patricia Vandel Simon. *A History of the Mexican-American People.* South Bend: University of Notre Dame Press, 1993.

Vento, Arnoldo Carlos. *Mestizo: The History, Culture, and Politics of the Mexican and the Chicano: The Emerging Mestizo-Americans.* Lanham, MD: University Press of America, 1997.

MONGOLIAN AMERICANS

by
Baatar Tsend

The Mongolian American community still retains its Mongolian culture. Most Mongolian American families strive to preserve traditional Mongolian values and transmit these to their children.

OVERVIEW

Mongolia is a large landlocked country, 604,100 sq. miles (1,566,000 sq km.), in area about three times the size of France, over twice the size of the state of Texas, and almost as large as Queensland, Australia. It is located in Northeastern Asia, south of Siberia and north of China and borders with Russia on the north and the People's Republic of China on the south. Mongolia is a land of extremes. It is so far inland that no sea moderates the climate. Only in summer does cloud cover shield the sky. There is very little humidity in Mongolia, but the sunshine is intense. With over 260 sunny days a year, Mongolia is justifiably known as the "Land of Blue Sky." It is also known as the "Land of Chinggis Khan." Until the twentieth century, Mongolia was about twice its present size. A large portion of Siberia was once part of Mongolia but is now securely controlled by Russia, and Inner Mongolia is now firmly a part of China.

Mongols are people with an ancient and glorious history. They constitute one of the principal ethnic divisions of the Asian peoples. In fact, the race of the Asian peoples is known as "mongoloid." Throughout the world there is a birth mark famous as the "Mongolian spot." It is a blue birthmark on the buttock, and it shows up right after a child is born.

Mongolia, the only independent state of Mongolians, has a population of 2.4 million. The great majority (about 85 percent) of Mongolians are

Khalkh Mongols. About 10 percent are members of other Mongol confederations and tribes (Barga, Bayad, Buriad, Dariganga, Darkhad, Khoton, Myangad, Oold, Torguud, Tsaatan, Tuva, Uriankhai, Uzemchin, Zakhchin), and 5 percent are of Kazakh, Russian, Chinese, Korean, or other descent.

More Mongolians live outside of Mongolia than in it—about 3.5 million in China, while in Russia Kalmyk Mongolians number about 175,000 and Buriat Mongolians about 425,000. Many people of Mongolian origin also live in Central Asia, India, some parts of Canada, Europe and in the United States.

The country's capital is Ulaanbaatar; the Mongolian flag is red and blue with a golden soyombo. The Golden Soyombo, the national symbol of Mongolia which dates back at least to the 14th century, signifies freedom and independence. The national language is Mongolian.

HISTORY

Mongolia is one of the world's oldest nomadic civilizations. Archeological digs have uncovered human remains in the Gobi and other regions dating back nearly 500,000 years. Agriculture seems to have preceded nomadic herding of animals, and despite Mongolia's short summers, wheat growing has co-existed with nomadic life for thousands of years. It was only after the Mongols tamed horses, yaks and camels that they took to a nomadic herding lifestyle.

Early Chinese manuscripts refer to 'Turkic-speaking peoples' living in what we now call Mongolia as early as the fourth or fifth century B.C. The name 'Mongol' was first recorded by the Chinese during the Tang dynasty (618-907 A.D.). At that time, Mongolia was dominated by the Uighurs. The Uighurs continued to control most of Mongolia until 840 A.D. The defeat of the Uighurs created a vacuum, which was filled by the Kitans, a Mongol tribe from what is now north-east China. By the tenth century, the Kitans had control of most of Manchuria, eastern Mongolia and much of China north of the Yellow River. The Kitans continued warring with other Mongol tribes, most significantly with the western Xi, during the eleventh and twelfth centuries. The Kitan empire was finally defeated in 1122 A.D.

The Mongols and other nomadic peoples of northern Asia seldom united and had little inclination to do so; they preferred to be nomadic, widely scattered over great areas, frequently on the move with their animals in search of pasture. They wanted to live as separate clans, united only in the face of a common threat.

Until the end of the twelfth century, the Mongols were little more than a loose confederation of rival clans. In 1182, a 20-year-old Mongol named Temujin rose to power to become the leader of the Borjigin Mongol clan, and later managed to unite all the Mongol tribes and founded a united Mongol state. In 1206 he was given the honorary name of Chinggis Khan, meaning 'universal (or oceanic) king'. He would soon conquer adjacent lands and later set up a vast empire that covered most of Asia and Europe. By the time of his death in 1227, the Mongol empire extended from Beijing to the Caspian Sea. Power passed into the hands of Chinggis' favorite son, Ogedei, who continued this program of military conquest. His generals pushed as far west as Hungary and were all set to invade Western Europe when Ogedei died. Mongol custom dictated that all noble defendants of Chinggis had to return to Mongolia to democratically elect a new Khan (king). Chinggis' grandson, Khubilai Khan (circa 1216-1294), completed the subjugation of China, effectively ending the Song dynasty (960-1269). He became the emperor in China, the Mongol Yuan dynasty (1271-1368). Khubilai established his winter capital in Tatu ('great capital', M. Khan Balgasun), today's Beijing. After Kublai Khan died in 1294, the Mongols became increasingly dependent on the people they ruled. The Mongol empire not only strongly influenced the emergence of a united Russian state but it also contributed to reversing the disintegration process in China and laying the foundations of a united China. By the 1350s, Mongol rule began to disintegrate. They were expelled from Beijing by the first emperor of the Ming dynasty (1368-1644). A major civil war occurred from 1400 to 1450 between wto main groups, the Khalkha in the east and the Oirad in the west. A revival of sorts occurred under Altan Khan (1507-83), who united the Khalkha, defeated the Oirad and brought most of Mongolia under his control. After the death of Altan Khan, Mongolia reverted to a collection of tiny tribal domains. Meanwhile, the Manchus, ancient enemies of the Mongols, established the Qing dynasty (1644-1911).

In 1911 China's last dynasty, the Qing, crumbled. Mongolian independence from China was declared on 1 December 1911. On 25 May 1915, the Treaty of Kyakhta, granting Mongolia limited autonomy, was signed by Mongolia, China and Russia. In July 1921, the People's Government of Mongolia was declared. Until 1990, Mongolia was a satellite state of the Soviet Union. It had Soviet style political and economic institutions. In 1990, Mongolia became a free and democratic country with a multi-party parliamentarian system under a president.

THE FIRST MONGOLIANS IN THE UNITED STATES

Few Mongolians came to the United States between 1948 and 1949. Those who did were immigrants from Inner Mongolia. The first Mongolians to come to the United States were Gombojob Hangin and Urgunge Onon. Hangin was a native of Tsakhar, Inner Mongolia and Onon was a native of Daguur, also Inner Mongolia. They came with their families in 1948 to join Owen Lattimore's program in East Asian Affairs at Johns Hopkins University. The Mongolian immigration to the United States continued following the arrests of high-ranking lamas, a purge which began in 1935. At that time some lamas left Mongolia for India. The first Mongolian lama to immigrate to the United States was the living Buddha, Dilowa Gegen Khutukhtu. He was a Khalkha Mongol, who formerly headed a ministry in Mongolia. He came to the United States in 1949 as a political refugee, and also joined Owen Lattimore's the Mongolia Project.

SIGNIFICANT IMMIGRATION WAVES

Mongolians from Europe began to immigrate to the United States in 1951-1952. This large group was the Kalmyk Mongols. The Kalmyks (Western Mongolian), who took up residence on the East Coast of the U.S., had been living in Europe, more precisely, in the Don-Volga region, where they have had state structure since the beginning of the seventeenth century, around 370 years. The Russian Revolution in 1917 brought further changes. During that time, close to 2,000 Kalmyks fled from Russia by way of the Black Sea ports. After debarking in Turkey, they traveled to Yugoslavia and Bulgaria, and some further dispersed into Czechoslovakia and France. In 1945, after the capitulation of Germany, during the years of her political and economical bankruptcy and anarchy, Kalmyk immigrants went through the most difficult times in their lives. After five years of living in the refugee camps, old (since 1920) and new (since 1943-1945) Kalmyk immigrants were in a desperate situation.

In 1950 and 1951, with the help of American friends, the Kalmyk representation was able to found the "Special Committee on the Kalmyk Immigration Affairs." On August 31, 1951, the U.S. Congress passed a law granting Kalmyks the rights to immigrate as Europeans. Between December of 1951 and March of 1952, 571 Kalmyks arrived in the United States. Additional families and individuals arrived later. There are approximately 1000 Kalmyks in the United States, of which 300 are from the Astrakhan area. They are primarily from the Dorvet clan with a few Torgut—and the remainder are Buzava.

The third Mongolian wave to immigrate to this country came in small numbers (between 150-200). In 1965 the United States accorded an equal quota to Asian immigrants via the Immigration and Naturalization Act Amendments. Those from Mongolia and Inner Mongolia as well as western Mongols from Sinkiang and Khukhe-Nuur and those in exile in India and Taiwan came at this time (between 1965 and 1975). For example, among those Mongols immigrating to the United States at this time were the professors, Jagchid Sechen, a Kharcin Mongol and Unen Sechen, a Khorchin Mongol, both of whom had fled to Taiwan. There were also famous lamas who came from India. Jambaldorj, Choijo, Yondonjamps, Gombojab and Jamps, for example. They came from Dharmasala, India, and were nominated by the Dalai Lama.

The most recent Mongol immigrants, those from Mongolia, the Republic of Kalmykia and Buriat, came after the collapse of the Soviet Union in the 1990s. They came to study and for economic reasons. There are no accurate immigration statistics on the most recent wave of immigration. Numbering about 1,500-2000, this group includes both family units and single individuals covering a full range of ages. According to the census, the total population of Mongols in the United States now stands at about 3,500.

SETTLEMENT PATTERNS

The first Mongolian immigrants settled around Baltimore, Maryland, and New York City and then moved to the other cities. Kalmyk Mongol immigrants settled in Lakewood and Freewood Acres, New Jersey in a section of Philadelphia, Pennsylvania. The International Refugee Organization made a special grant to several social service groups, notably the Tolstoy Foundation and the Church World Service, on behalf of the Kalmyk Mongolians, to jointly sponsor efforts to help them find a home. The other group is located in an older section of north central Philadelphia, were successive waves of first-generation immigrants have settled from colonial times until the present day. There are also several families living in New Brunswick and Paterson, New Jersey, and in Valley Forge, Pennsylvania. Since the time they immigrated, the Kalmyk Mongol community has not risen too much. Today there are still only about 1,000 Kalmyks in the United States. Some continue to live in Lakewood and Freewood Acres, New Jersey and in sections of Philadelphia, Pennsylvania. Many of them have moved away. This was started in the 1970s. They are now settled in New York, Washington D.C., West Virginia, Florida, Arizona, Texas, New Mexico and California. Mongol-American communities of recent immigrants are settled in San Francisco, Los Angeles, Chicago, New York, Washington D.C., Philadelphia, and New Jersey.

ACCULTURATION AND ASSIMILATION

The Mongolian American community still retains its heritage. Most Mongolian American families strive to preserve traditional Mongolian values and transmit these to their children. The social interaction that does occur with the host culture is primarily a result of the necessary participation of Mongolians in economic and politico-administrative institutions. In essence, these communities mitigate the shock of transition into a foreign culture, and they also prolong the period of acculturation. The younger generation has been educated in American schools, exposed daily to the media, and interact more frequently than their parents and grandparents with Americans. Young Mongolians are increasingly abandoning many aspects of their ethnic heritage and are adopting more Americanized attitudes and behavior. This can be seen in the greater frequency of interracial dating and marriage, the adoption of Americanized standards of beauty and fashion, and the gradual disintegration of Mongolian families and communities. This, however, is not a simple process of exchanging one heritage for another, nor is it a process which is common to all second and third generation Mongolians. The price exacted from these young people for the transition often entails a high level of disorganization and the complete abandonment of their own cultural heritages.

Mongolian Americans are professionals, others own small businesses, do construction or are employed as semi- or non-skilled workers. Mongolians enjoy relatively high standards of living, attain levels of education, and are well employed. However, most Mongolians are willing to work within a American framework.

TRADITIONS, CUSTOMS, AND BELIEFS

Assimilation for Mongolian American immigrants has been difficult, often causing them to become more attached to the traditions of their homeland. The Mongolian Americans' sense of art is closely related to their mystic sense of identity with nature. Humanity, nature, and art constitute an unbroken continuity. Artistic expression in Mongolian art is particularly evident in their dress. Traditionally,

Mongolian Americans believe in astrology and consider certain days in the year more conducive to the conclusion of business deals or to the purchase of new houses or cars and marriage. They turn to astrology on important days like the beginning of a new job, the commencement of college, or birth of a child. Mongolians use a lunar calendar and have adopted the Chinese zodiac with its 12 animal signs. This is also a very important thing in Mongolian Americans' lives. The beautiful Mongolian landscape abounds with an ecological wonder that is expressed in song and dance, which expresses the varied lives on the Mongolian steppes. Many Mongolians practice Western arts, from oil painting to metal sculpture, the subjects of which are often inspired by Mongolian life and traditions. The literary arts are also popular. Early Mongolian literature consisted largely of local folk tales and traditional religious stories. *The Secret History of the Mongols*, Mongolia's most famous book has no known author. This heroic epic of the Mongols—historic texts of war and feuding, myths of origin, administrative manuals of empire, diplomatic histories of hordes and dynasties and biographies of great Khans—were all first committed to writing over 760 years ago.

The greatest scholar on Mongolian studies, professor Francis W. Cleaves said "*The Secret History of Mongols* is not only the capital monument of thirteenth century Mongolian Literature, but it is one of the great literary monuments of the world."

The Mongols' most famous epic is *Djangar*. This heroic oral-epic literature was found about 560 years ago in Western Mongolia. Also, all Mongolian people, no matter what their tribal affiliation or where they came from, know and admire the writings of the modern Mongolian authors D. Natsagdorg and Ch. Chimid, especially their most famous works, *Minii Nutag* (My Native Land) and *Bi Mongol Khung* (I am Mongolian).

CUISINE

Most of the Mongols' traditional dishes continue to be part of Mongolian Americans' cuisine today although in many instances they are served only on ceremonial occasions. The most popular food continues to be Mongolian tea, which is now made from an infusion of tea, evaporated milk, nutmeg and butter. It is used as a ceremonial drink as well, and it is served at most rites. *Boortsag* or *borts'k*, the small cakes made of flour, water and yeast and fried in oil, are still made, but primarily for use at various ceremonials and rites. *Makhan*, made from lamb in the traditional way—that is boiled in water, cut up into pieces and mixed with fresh cut onions and a little *shulen* (the lamb stock) and rewarmed—is also prepared on festive occasions. *Guriltai shul* or *budan*, a stew of lamb meat or beef, water and flour, and bulmuk, a gravy like dish of broth and flour, are also still prepared. *Tarag* or *chigan*—fermented cow's milk—is at present made and drunk primarily by the older people. It is felt to have great therapeutic value and is believed to insure a long life. Another most popular dish is *Buuz* or *varenk*, made from beef and flour especially steamed mutton dumplings. *Khuushuur*, made from beef and flour and fried in oil, are still made but also primarily for use at various ceremonies and rites. These dietary customs are usually observed by Mongolian Americans during holidays and special events in the United States. For everyday meals, Mongols have readily adapted American food and drink.

HOLIDAYS AND CULTURAL EVENTS

Despite their ethnic diversity, there are several major holidays that virtually all Mongolian Americans observe. Mongolians have been celebrating *Tsagaan Sar* (White Month) for thousands of years, although it may have been held during the summer (possibly in August) when Chinggis Khaan was roaming the steppes. Now held over three days at the start of the lunar new year (in end of January or start of February), Tsagaan Sar celebrates the end of winter and the start of spring. During the Tsagaan Sar, *Zolgokh* is the traditional greeting. Rather like shaking hands in the West, the younger person places his or her forearms under those of the elder person.

The next group-wide ceremony in the annual cycle is the combined celebration of *Urus-Ova*, which is now celebrated for convenience on the first weekend after the commencement of the first month of summer to permit greater lay participation. This ceremony commemorates *Shagja-muni* or the Buddha, and the yearly celebration which took place at the oboo, or shrines, to placate malicious spirits.

The third major ceremony celebrated in much in the same manner as it was traditionally celebrated is the ritual of *Zul* or *Zula* (Lamp), which takes place in the middle of winter on the 25th day of the month of *Ukher* (cow). People still recall that it marks the passing on to the next world of Tsong-Kha-Pa, the great religious reformer.

The Kalmyk Mongolians have proclaimed "Kalmyk Day," a day in which all are invited to come and see on exhibit all types of artifacts, literature, movies and Kalmyk song and dance performances, to see first hand Kalmyk Mongolian culture

and history. Mongolian Americans have to celebrate annual "Chinggis Khan Ceremony." It was the wish of the founders of the Mongol-American Cultural Association to celebrate this ancient ceremony, so that the current and future generations of Mongolian Americans would have the opportunity to observe and participate in this ancient tradition. Also Mongolian Americans were celebrated at the Mongolian Cultural Celebration. Another Mongolian national holiday is Naadam Festival, which is from July 11 to July 13. It is also known as the *eriin gurban naadam*, after the three 'manly' sports of wrestling, archery and horse racing. On this day, along with officials in the Mongolian Embassy and Mongolians in the United States, all people are invited to celebrate along with Mongolian officials in a ceremony and reception.

TRADITIONAL COSTUMES

Mongolian Americans wear western-style clothes, but on some special celebration days they wear traditional Mongolian clothes. The main garment is the *del*, a long, one-piece gown made from wool. The del has a high collar, is often brightly colored, comes with a multipurpose sash. Mongolians, but not untrained westerners, can differentiate ethnic groups by the color, the design and shape of their del. The *gutul* is a high boot made from thin leather. They are easy to fit, as both the left and right boot are the same shape. The Mongolian traditional hat is known as the decorative *toortsog* and *loovuz*. The loovuz is made from fox skins.

MUSIC AND DANCE

Traditional music involves a wide range of instruments and uses the human voice in a way found almost nowhere else. The *khoomi* singing of Mongolia, in which carefully trained male voices produce a whole harmonic from deep in the throat, gives the impression of several notes coming at once from one mouth. It is often sung solo, but when combined with fiddles, lutes, zithers, drums and other python-skin, bamboo, metal, stone and clay instruments, one begins to understand the centrality of music in Mongolian life. The instrument most identified with Mongolia is arguably the horse-head fiddle, known as the *morin khuur*. It has two strings, made from horse hair, with the distinctive and decorative carving of a horse's head on top. Traditionally, the morin khuur often accompanies the unique long songs which regale the beauty of the countryside and relive tales of nomadism.

Some Mongolian music, particularly instrumental music, is intended specifically to accompany dancing. Mongolian dance includes a number of kinds of group folk dance similar to round dancing and square dancing; these might be performed by groups of men, groups of women, or groups of mixed couples. These dances are called *bujig*. The most typical Mongolian dance form, however, is the *bii* or *biyelgee*, "upper-body dance," a dance normally performed by women. Accordingly, leg movements are restricted or entirely absent; some forms of biyelgee are performed in a sitting or kneeling position. The dance consists of intricate, rhythmic movements of the head, shoulders, arms, and upper torso; some dancers display their skill by dancing with bowls of tea or a rag balanced on their wrists, elbows, and heads. Today, the Kalmyk American Dance Ensemble is held in Howell, New Jersey.

MONGOLIAN STUDENTS IN THE UNITED STATES

In recent years Mongolian young people have immigrated to the United States to attend American colleges or graduate schools. Afterward, many choose to apply for permanent residency or for citizenship. Presently, about 80 percent of the Mongolians residing in the United States are between the ages of 18 and 35. The number of Mongolian students in the United States has grown steadily since 1990. Recent numbers show Mongolian students are attending colleges and universities in about 30 states. The successful personal adjustments and academic achievements of these students are decided by mainly two factors: language efficiency and the ability to adjust to American society. While some of them return to Mongolia, many choose to continue their professional pursuits. Mongolian students pursue careers in medicine, business, computer sciences, bio-technology, engineering, administration, law, and social sciences. Young people from Kalmykia, Buriat and Inner Mongolia have also immigrated to the United States to attend American colleges and graduate schools. The American Government, Mongol-American Cultural Association, and family already settled in the United States help Mongolian students get scholarships and to get adjusted to their new country.

HEALTH ISSUES

Most Mongolian Americans accept the role of modern medicine and pay careful attention to health matters. Nevertheless, as noted below in connection with the religious aspects of medical treatment, the services of the Tibetan-trained religious medical practitioners (the *emch*) and of the other clerics are often utilized in concert with western medical science, or sometimes as a last resort. The emch's herbal remedies are still employed by some, primarily the elderly. The dietary advice, blessed water and special prayers of the other clerics is also sought. Diagnosis and treatment is based on the five vital elements of earth, water, fire, wind and wood. Medicines are often made from herbs, plants, mineral water and organs from unfortunate animals, and administered according to the weather, season and individual's metabolism. Acupuncture, massage and blood-letting, as well as prayers, are also important factors. All Mongolian Americans know Cheojey lama from Sunud, Mongolia. He is a famous practitioner of folk medicine. He has approximately 30 people practicing the art of folk medicine in America. He died in 1990, but his students continue to practice.

LANGUAGE

Mongolian is not a single language, but rather a group of closely related languages spoken by the various tribes that make up the Mongolian people. The Mongolian languages are usually considered to belong to four groups: 1) Central Mongolian, including Khalkha (Mongolia), Ordos, Chakhar (Inner Mongolia); 2) Eastern Mongolian, including various Khorchin, Kharchin, Jalaid, Gorlos, Ar Khorchin, Baarin, Naiman, and Onniud. Eastern Mongolian dialects are popular in Inner Mongolian; 3) Northern Mongolian, including various Buriad, Barga, Khamnigan, and Soloon (Mongolian, Russian, Inner Mongolian); 4) Southern Mongolian, including various Mongolian Oirad (Durvet, Bayad, Zakhchin, Torguud, Uriankhai, Uuld), Kirgiz, Xinjiangian Torguud, Khoshuud, Uuld, Uriankhai and Russian Kalmyks (Torguud, Buzava, Durvet), American and France Kalmyk (Buzava, Torguud, Durvet), Chinese Alasha (province), Torguud, Kheisi, Khenanian (province), Khoshuud, Kheisi, Qinkhai (province) Tsoros, Gangsu, Khenianian (province), and Uuld.

The Mongolian languages belong to the Uralic-Altaic language family, named for the Ural Mountains of Russia and the Altai Mountains of western Mongolia. Spread by ancient migrations and the conquests of the Mongol Empire itself, the Uralic-Altaic language family is large and diverse; it includes among others Korean and Japanese, Turkish, Finish, and Hungarian. All of these languages are characterized by a highly inflected grammar, meaning that grammatical structure is indicated by prefixes, suffixes, vowel shifts, and other changes of words within a sentence. In the early thirteenth century the Mongols adopted a script from the Turik Uighurs which is used by many of the Mongolians even today. In 1941 the Government of Mongolia adopted a phonetic alphabet derived from a modified Cyrillic script. Today both scripts can be used. Kalmyk Mongolians are versed in the Zaya Pandita script (Todo Mongol) and Mongolian script.

GREETINGS AND OTHER POPULAR EXPRESSIONS

Some common expressions in the Mongolian language include: *Tiim* ("Yes"); *Ugui* ("No"); *Bayarlaa/Gyalailaa* ("Thanks"); *Uuchlaarai* ("I'm sorry/ Excuse me"); *Yuu genee?* ("Sorry?" or "What did you say?"; *Khun guai!* ("Excuse me, sir/madam!"); *Sain baina uu?* (literally, "How are you?"); *Sain ta sain baina uu?* ("Fine"); *Bayartai* ("Goodbye"); and *Za* ("Okay").

FAMILY AND COMMUNITY DYNAMICS

Mongolian Americans family ties are very strong, and it is considered the responsibility of more prosperous members to look after their less well-to-do relatives. Mongolian parents tend to frown upon the practice of dating, although they are slowly yielding to their offspring's demands to be allowed to do so. The preference is still the selection of a marriage partner from within the origin of the Mongolian community and with the full approval and consent of the parents. Family or community members are often involved in the selection of a suitable mate. The family and educational backgrounds of the potential partner are thoughly examined before introductions are made. Although intermarriage is not uncommon between Mongolians and Americans, many Mongolian Americans believe that their children will be happier if they are married to someone who shares the same history, tradition, religion, and social customs and who will be able to impart these values to their children, thus ensuring the continuity of the community. They believe that such marriages made within the community tend to be more stable and longer lasting than those that cross community borders. The traditional Mongolian American household is a patriarchy in which the head of the household is the eldest male. The principal roles of the wife are to keep house and raise the children. The children have a duty to honor their parents and respect their wishes.

THE ROLE OF WOMEN

Traditionally, Mongolian American women have the responsibility of preserving the memories, customs, and traditions of the Mongolian homeland. A women's first obligation is to be a good wife and raise a family. Girls have not been allowed as much freedom as boys and were not encouraged "to go out." Instead, girls have been kept at home and taught domestic skills. Girls were sent through high school and encouraged to pursue higher education and a career. After graduation and before marriage, women have often helped with the family business. Mongolian women are usually married between the ages of 22 and 26. Today many Mongolian American women feel caught between worlds. They often feel obligated to conform to the standards and mores of their community but, at the same time, are pressured to "Americanize." However, many Mongolian American women have pursued higher education and careers outside the home.

WEDDINGS

Traditionally, before marriage the most important thing is accounts. Accounts of the Mongolians from their earliest period to the recent past contain a great deal of information regarding the marriage institution. Even the small fragments of the ancient Tsaadiin Bichik (Ugin Bichig), which has come down to us from the period of the first Oirad federation in the fifteenth century contains, of its eighth provisions, four provisions relating to the fines to be exacted when adultery was committed with the wife of a prince, with an ordinary man's wife, with a female slave and with the concubine of a priest. Marriage, with its rites and ceremonies, provides a second but non-cyclical focal point for the intensification of social interaction among the Mongolians

in America today. It involves a complex series of formal visits and gift exchanges extending over a period of time and leading up to the marriage rite and beyond. It provides a continuing focus of activity not only for the two families directly involved but also to close and distant relations, and certain events may involve practically the entire Mongolian group. The date which will be presented will show the historical depth and continuity of many of the aspects of this institution as well as its continuing and central importance in Mongolian American life. The account of the rites and ceremonies that are involved in marriage today will also provide examples of the way in which changes and accommodations have been made, particularly in the realm of material objects—new items being equated with and replacing old ones and new content being injected into the traditional patterns which maintain their continuity.

RELIGION

Mongolian Americans have always followed Buddhism of the Tibetan (Lama) variety faithfully.

Shortly after their arrival in the United States, the Kalmyk Mongols began the reconstruction of their religious system. Only 20 priests, a few less than the total number who had emigrated from Russia during the first and second waves of immigration, came to settle in America. All of these priests were over 60 years of age and represented primarily the higher ranks in the traditional ecclesiastical hierarchy. Until his death, the highest ranking cleric was not a Kalmyk but rather a Khalkha Mongol, the Living Buddha, Dilowa Gegen Khutukhtu, who was deferred to in all religious matters and was the final authority in religious decisions. Through he lived in Baltimore, he participated frequently in rituals and ceremonies in Freewood Acres and in Philadelphia and had a residence in one of the religious establishments in Freewood Acres and also in New York. However, several priests have been sent from India by the Dalai Lama to augment the dwindling number of priests. The physical plans of these religious establishments are essentially similar and include a place of worship which is furnished with a multitude of thankas or Tibetan religious pictures, flowers, satin banners, prayer flags and several small tables flanked opposite the door which serve as the altar and on and around it are placed incense and offerings of various types. Along the left side, facing the altar, are the low seats or divans and tables of the clergy, arranged in the order of their hierarchical standing—the highest being closest to the altar. The religious precinct also includes a place of residence for its priests. In effect, the unity is a reconstruction of the traditional monastic establishment. The whole is referred to by the Mongolians in English as the temple and in Mongolian as *Khurul* (Assembly of monks) or *olna gazar* (holy ground). Today American Mongolians have five temples in the United States. Three of them are in Howell, New Jersey, another one is in Philadelphia, and one is in New York. At the various temples in the United States, lamas work to prepare tangkas, forge idols, and build stupas. The most important of these people familiar in the ways of Buddhist practice are Gyamcho and Jambaldorj, a Khalkha Mongol, who was the disciple of the Living Buddha, Dilowa Gegen Khutughtu.

The Mongolian American community in America also includes small numbers, especially young people who are Christian, but their numbers are few.

EMPLOYMENT AND ECONOMIC TRADITIONS

The Mongolians who came to the United States were from rural backgrounds and worked as farmers, while others in most cases have skilled and semi-skilled factory jobs in various soft goods industries and mechanical trades, and lots of people are employed in the house building trades. Most of the working women are employed as seamstresses in the dressmaking industry.

Mongolians have opened their own businesses. The most successful Kalmyk Mongolian businesses are the house building trade and small businesses. Today Mongolian Americans are employed in a variety of professional enterprises. About 45 percent of the Mongolian Americans who live the United States are employed in white-collar work.

POLITICS AND GOVERNMENT

Mongolian Americans have always felt a strong attachment to Mongolia and have supported events that occur in the homeland. During the deportation period of the Kalmyk people to Siberia, the Kalmyk Committee in the USA played an important historical role. One of the leaders of this committee is the well-known Kalmyk human rights activist, Djab

Naminov Burchinov, who also played an important historical role, in returning Russian Kalmyks to their native land. His place in the fight for the national interests and in defense of human rights is not modest but great.

Burchinov sent several memoranda with the request to accept Mongolia into the UN membership. He assisted in solving this problem positively. Burchinov fights not only for the human rights of Kalmyk Mongols but also the rights of the Tibetans and Inner Mongols. During the time of the AIDS epidemic in Kalmykia he obtained donations from the big American companies.

The Mongol-American Association press has played an important role in Mongolian nationalism in the United States. Since 1990, Mongolian Americans have shown an increasing interest in American government policy decisions concerning Mongolia. Well-known professor John Gombojab Hangin was instrumental in the establishment of normal political relations between Mongolia and the United States.

The United States supports Mongolia's reforms and renders it technical and humanitarian assistance. United States Congress has adopted a resolution in support of the reforms in Mongolia. The United States declared in 1995 that independent, democratic, prosperous and secure Mongolia is in their interests. Mongolia's strategic location is important not only geo-politically, but also geo-economically, since it has abundant mineral resources, educated and motivated people and is located between two large, emerging markets with millions of consumers. Despite the long distance, peoples of both countries are interested in developing trade, economic, cultural and people-to-people relations. Bilateral trade in 1997 reached $51 million. Both countries have granted each other most favored nation (MFN) status. Both sides believe that there is enormous potential for developing trade and economic relations.

INDIVIDUAL AND GROUP CONTRIBUTIONS

Djab Nominov Burchinov is a well-known Kalmuk Mongol human right activist, and is the author of *The Struggle for Cvil Rights of the Kalmyk People* (1997). Arash Bormanshinov is the author of *Kalmyk Manual* (1961), which is considered to be the first work in English on Kalmyk Mongol written by an Kalmyk Mongolian. John Gombojab Hangin was Professor of Mongolian studies at Indiana University at the time of his death. He was a principal founder of both the

Mongolia Society and the Mongol-American Cultural Association. He is a author of *A Mongol Reader* (1956), *A Concise English-Mongolian Dictionary* (1970), and *A Modern Mongolian-English Dictionary* (1986). Professor Jagchid Sechin wrote *Essays in Mongolian Studies* (1988), *Mongolian Living Buddha: Biography of the Kanjurwa Khutukhtu* (1983), *Mongolian Cultural and Society* (1979), and *Peace, War, and Trade Along the Great Wall: Nomadic Chinese Interaction Through Two Millenia* (1989). Dr. Sanj Altan is well-known Mongolian American Cultural activist; Lee Urubshurow is well-known Kalmyk Mongolian cultural activist; she was a principal founder both of the Kalmyk-American Cultural Association, and the Kalmyk-American Dance Ensemble.

MEDIA

The Mongol Tolbo Newsletter.

The Mongol-American Cultural Association's newsletter Mongol Tolbo is a quarterly publication enjoys the distribution among its kind. It provides commentary and analysis on the subject of the Mongol culture and news of its economic, political, and social development of Northern and Southern Mongolia, Tuva, Sinjiang, Buryatia and Kalmykia.

Contact: Chinggeltu Borjiged, Editor.
Address: Mongol-American Cultural Association
    Inc., 50 Louis Street, New Brunswick
    New Jersey 08901.
Telephone: (732) 297-1140.
E-Mail: MONGOL@COMPUBELL.COM.

ORGANIZATIONS AND ASSOCIATIONS

Mongol-American Cultural Association, Inc.

The Mongol-American Cultural Association serves as the central point of networking for all Mongolian tribes residing in the United States. Culture, heritage, and customs are shared between all Mongolian Americans no matter what their tribal affiliation or history. The goal of the association is to promote cultural exchange between all of the Mongolian ethnic groups, Khalkha, Buriat, Kalmyk, and Inner Mongolian. They also provide support to Mongolian youth, scholarships to students, aid to the poor, homeless, or handicapped.

Contact: Dr. Sanj Altan, President.
Address: Mongol-American Cultural Association,
    Inc., 50 Louis Street, New Brunswick,
    New Jersey 08901.
Telephone: (732) 297-1140.

Asian American Heritage Council of New Jersey.

The Asian American Heritage Council of New Jersey has been of exemplary service to the Asian American citizens of this state, working diligently to assist and integrate Asian culture.

Contact: Shashi K. Agarwal, President.
Address: 290 Central Ave, Orange,
    New Jersey 07050-3414.
Telephone: (973) 676-1234.
Fax: (973) 676-5858.

Kalmyk-American Cultural Association.

The association has formed classes to teach the Kalmyk Mongolian culture and the language. This organization has not only brought together the young people but has shown them that they have inherited a rich cultural heritage.

Contact: Lee Urubshurow, President.
Address: 55 Schank Road Suite A-1, Freehold,
    New Jersey 07728.
Telephone: (732) 576-5614.

Mongolia Society.

The Mongolia Society has several hundred members and is concerned with presenting information dealing with the history and culture of this area of Inner Asia. Four separate series devoted to Mongolian topics are published. These are Mongolian Studies; Journal of the Mongolia Society: Mongolia Survey; Occasional Papers; and Special Papers. The society is the only importer of Mongolian books in the United States. It also sells Mongolian dictionaries and a wide variety of items that pertain to Mongolia. An annual scholarship is presented to a person of Mongolian heritage.

Contact: Henry Scharz, President.
Address: Indiana University, 321 Goodbody Hall,
    Bloomington, Indiana 47405.
Telephone: (812) 855-4078.
Fax: (812) 855-7500.

U.S.-Mongolia Business Council.

Contact: Steven R. Saunders, Executive Director.
Address: 1015 Duke Street, Alexandria,
    Virginia 22314-3551.
Telephone: (703) 549-8444.
Fax: (703) 549-6526.
E-Mail: Mongolia@erols.com.

US-Mongolia Advisory Group.

Contact: Dr. Alica Campi, President.
Address: 6002 Ticonderoga Court, Burke
    Virginia 22015.
E-Mail: usmagcampi@aol.com.

World Mongolian Association.

The association serves as the central point of networking World Mongolian tribes, culture and heritage.

Contact: Giga Andreyev, President.
Address: 55 Schank Road, Suite A-1,
　　　Freehold, New Jersey 07728.
Telephone: (732) 409-3511.
Fax: (732) 409-6298.

SOURCES FOR ADDITIONAL STUDY

Adelman, Fred. *Kalmyk Cultural Renewal*. PhD dissertation. Ann Arbor: University Microfilms, 1960.

Bormanshinov, Arash. *Kalmyk Manual*. Micro Photo Division Bell & Howell Company Press, 1963.

Burchinov, Djab Nominov. *The Struggle for Civil Rights of the Kalmyk People*. Moscow and Elista Press, 1997.

Major, John S. *The Land and People of Mongolia*. J. B. Lippincott Press, 1990.

Rubel, Paula G. *The Kalmyk Mongols: A Study in Continuity and Change*. Bloomington: Indiana University Press, 1967.

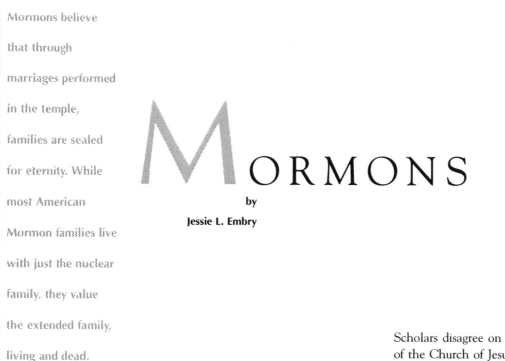

MORMONS

by
Jessie L. Embry

Mormons believe that through marriages performed in the temple, families are sealed for eternity. While most American Mormon families live with just the nuclear family, they value the extended family, living and dead.

OVERVIEW

Scholars disagree on whether Mormons, members of the Church of Jesus Christ of Latter-day Saints (LDS), can rightly be considered an ethnic group. Using survey results, sociologist Armand Mauss shows that Mormons are typical Americans. Canadian anthropologist Keith Parry, however, contends that Mormons have a distinctive lifestyle and language that set them apart from mainstream America. Much of the Mormon identity comes from its history. Members accept the Book of Mormon as a religious history of a people who saw the United States as a land of promise where Christ's church could be restored before His second coming. As historian Dean May explains, "The Mormons have been influenced subsequently by ritual tales of privation, wandering, and delivery under God's hand, precisely as the Jews have been influenced by their stories of the Exodus. A significant consequence of this tradition has been the development of an enduring sense of territoriality that has given a distinctive cast to Mormon group consciousness. It differentiates the Mormons from members of other sects and lends support to the judgment of [Catholic] sociologist Thomas F. O'Dea that the Mormons 'represent the clearest example to be found in our national history of the evolution of a native and indigenously developed ethnic minority'" (*The Harvard Encyclopedia of American Ethnic Groups*, 1980).

The Mormon church has grown to be more than an American religious denomination. Its 8,000,000-person membership in 1991 nearly covered the world and only half (4,336,000) lived in the United States. Of the one million converts in 1988 and 1989, 60 percent of them were from Mexico and Central and South America. Still, Utah is 77 percent Mormon, but only about one-eighth of the church members (1,363,000) live there.

HISTORY

The founder of the Mormon church in the United States, Joseph Smith, Jr., was the third son of a New England farming family. When he was a teenager, he attended a religious revival where his family lived in upstate New York. Confused by the different religions, Smith prayed for direction in 1820 and over the next few years recorded several personal revelations. He organized his first church on April 6, 1830. Members accepted him as a prophet who could speak the will of the Lord. As the church grew and developed, he received additional revelations that the Mormons view as scripture; these teachings are recorded in the *Doctrine and Covenants*.

From his New York base, Smith sent his followers out to seek converts; the majority of growth during this period occurred in Ohio. One of the first groups went to share the *Book of Mormon* with the Native Americans. When there were more Mormons in Ohio than in New York, Smith received a revelation that the church should move west. The first group arrived in Kirtland, Ohio, a few miles east of Cleveland, early in 1831. For the next seven years, Kirtland served as the church headquarters, and the Latter-day Saints built their first temple there.

But Smith made it clear that Kirtland was only a temporary home. In time, he predicted, God would ask Mormons to establish "Zion," a "New Jerusalem" to prepare for the millennium—the return of the Savior who would usher in a 1,000-year reign of peace. During the summer of 1831 Smith declared that this Zion would be established in Jackson County, Missouri. So Mormons started to gather there. However, tension arose between the Mormons, who opposed slavery, and slaveholding immigrants from Tennessee and Kentucky. The Mormons' claims that the territory was their promised land, their voting together as a bloc, and their communal living posed a threat to the Missourians' lifestyle, and the Mormons were eventually forced from the state.

The Mormons moved to Illinois and settled on undeveloped land along the Mississippi River known as Commerce. They renamed the area Nauvoo and started building a city. The Mormons received a liberal charter from the state that allowed them to have their own militia and courts. From here Smith continued to send out missionaries. Those sent to England were very successful, and soon immigrants from there as well as Canada and other areas of the United States arrived and helped establish what became the second largest city in Illinois. The Saints again started to build a temple. Smith continued to receive revelations.

One of Smith's revelations, plural marriage, caused special problems for the Mormons. Historians do not know when Smith received this revelation; there is some evidence that he married his first plural wife, Fanny Alger, in 1831. He did not write down the revelation until 1843, when he attempted to convince his first wife, Emma Hales Smith, of the principle. Although Smith and some of his closest followers practiced polygamy in Nauvoo, the church did not publicly announce the doctrine until 1852, after the Mormons moved to Utah. Some Mormons who knew of the doctrine opposed the practice and in June 1844 published a newspaper expressing their views of Smith as a fallen prophet. Using the powers granted by Nauvoo's charter, Smith destroyed not only the newspaper but also the press. The city courts released him, but the state arrested him for treason. As Smith, his brother Hyrum, and other church leaders were held in jail awaiting trial, a mob broke into the jail and killed Joseph and Hyrum Smith on June 27, 1844.

Following the death of their leader, Brigham Young (1801-1877), the president of the Council of Twelve Apostles, gained the trust of most of Smith's followers. Some Mormons reported that when Young spoke to them he sounded like Smith. These people saw this as a heavenly manifestation that Young was to be the next leader. Eventually, he became church president. Young led the work to complete the temple in Nauvoo and continued to give the members the ordinances he learned from Smith.

Problems between the Mormons and the local residents continued, and by February 1846, the Mormons began to leave Illinois, heading first for Nebraska and then to Salt Lake Valley. Isolated from the rest of the nation, Brigham Young and the Mormons set out to establish "Zion in the tops of the mountains," following Smith's visions. He planned Salt Lake City and other communities using Smith's Plat of Zion, a grid system. He encouraged the Mormons to be self-sufficient and created an independent commonwealth. He sent settlers to southern Utah, where they attempted to raise cotton and manufacture iron so they would not have to

depend on outsiders for these goods. He asked communities to live the "United Order," wherein people shared resources. Communities had varying success for several years, but eventually most communal attempts failed because most Mormons supported the American ideal of free enterprise. Eventually the church adopted free-enterprise policies. The Mormons completed the first temple in the area in St. George, Utah, in 1877. The Salt Lake Temple, which has become a symbol of Mormonism, took 40 years—from ground breaking to dedication—to complete. It was dedicated on April 6, 1893.

Young also announced for the first time publicly that the church endorsed plural marriage. In 1852 Apostle Orson Pratt delivered a discourse on the virtues of plural marriage. While church members now knew the church sanctioned polygamy, most of the Latter-day Saints did not practice it. The practice of polygamy varied by community, apparently based on how strongly local leaders encouraged it. Current research suggests that around 20 percent of the Mormons belonged to plural families.

Because of the Mormons' practice of polygamy and their political and economical isolation, many Americans questioned their loyalty to the nation. In 1857 the U.S. government sent an army to Utah with a federal appointee, Alfred Cumming of Georgia, to replace Brigham Young as governor of the territory. Although the groups resolved the problem peacefully and Cumming took office, the Mormons still contended with the U.S. government. In 1862 Congress passed the Morrill Act, the first legislation against polygamy, and continued to strengthen those laws for the next 25 years. The Edmunds Act (1882) was a series of amendments that strengthened the Morrill Act. It made cohabitation illegal; federal officials only had to prove that husband and wives were living together and not that multiple marriages had been performed for the law to have been broken. Polygamists were disenfranchised and could not hold political office. When the Edmunds Act did not control polygamy, Congress passed the Edmund-Tucker Act (1887), which abolished women's suffrage, required plural wives to testify against their husbands, and allowed the federal government to acquire all church property. The government began plans to confiscate the property, including the temples, in 1890. Church President Wilford Woodruff then issued a "Manifesto" stating that the church would no longer practice polygamy. In 1904 church President Joseph F. Smith presented a second manifesto that disciplined those who continued to practice polygamy or perform plural marriages.

SETTLEMENT

As Mormons arrived in Utah's Great Basin, Brigham Young sent them throughout the West. Although some colonies were short lived, Mormon communities extended from southern Idaho to San Bernardino, California. During the years when the federal government arrested polygamists, Mormons also moved into northern Mexico and southern Alberta, Canada. Young and the presidents who followed him also sent missionaries throughout the United States and northern Europe. The church encouraged the new converts to "gather to Zion." Church-sponsored ships carried emigrants across the Atlantic. Once in the United States, converts traveled by rail as far as possible and then continued by wagon. Some groups who could not afford wagons pulled two-wheeled handcarts. The church established an endowment, the Perpetual Emigrating Fund, to help the new arrivals.

The church encouraged the newcomers to assimilate as quickly as possible. They learned English and the Mormon way of life. Brigham Young proposed an alphabet that spelled English phonetically. Although it was never adopted, the alphabet demonstrated the church's attempt to assimilate newcomers. European immigrants were allowed at first to attend congregations speaking their native languages but were encouraged also to attend the congregation in which they lived, which usually spoke English. In 1903, when a disagreement developed over the celebration of a Swedish holiday, the First Presidency emphasized, "The counsel of the church to all Saints of foreign birth who come here is that they should learn to speak English when possible, adopt the manners and customs of the American people, fit themselves to become good and loyal citizens of this country, and by their good works show that they are true and faithful Latter-day Saints."

Additional factors worked for assimilation in Mormon society; those already in Utah understood the desire of the newcomers to be in Zion and felt a religious obligation to accept and love their brothers and sisters in the gospel. With all groups working together, European immigrants often married out of their cultural groups. So while Salt Lake City's foreign-born population during the 1880s ran as high as 80 percent, there were very few conflicts. Mormon immigrants assimilated into the mainstream of Mormonism's unique culture in one generation.

Throughout the late nineteenth and early twentieth centuries, Mormons remained concentrated in the inter-mountain west. The agricultural and mining depression of the 1920s and the nationwide depression of the 1930s forced some Mormons to leave the area looking for employment. During World War II, Utah's population increased as the government developed military bases and supported wartime industries. In the 1990s, while Mormons can be found throughout the United States, there is still a high concentration in the inter-mountain west.

INTERACTIONS WITH OTHERS

During the nineteenth century, most Americans saw the Mormon church as an eccentric religion that practiced polygamy, voted as a bloc, and lived together. Following the issuing of the Manifesto, though, Mormons not only abandoned polygamy but also gave up many of their unique economic and political practices. In order for Utah to become a state, the federal government required the church to dissolve its political arm, the People's Party. Most Mormons became Republicans and Democrats like the rest of the nation. The church gave up its communal and cooperative efforts and embraced the capitalist economy.

As time passed Mormonism became, as historian Jan Shipps described, "the Reader's Digest church" because members seemed to fit the American ideal. While there are still some misgivings about the church's claims to be the only true church, most Americans now see Mormons as law abiding, peaceful people who embrace all aspects of American life. This image improved in 1978 when the church abandoned its policy that blacks could not hold its lay priesthood.

FUTURE OF THE MORMON CHURCH

One major problem facing the Mormon church is its growing international membership, both worldwide and in American ethnic communities. Church leaders face the dilemma of separating gospel values from the American secular traditions that they have interwoven into Mormon culture. Before the priesthood revelation, there was an informal rule in many missions that they should not recruit blacks. As a result, only a limited number of African Americans joined. After 1978, missionaries actively ministered among blacks, and increasing numbers of African Americans are joining the religion. Hispanic Americans and Asian Americans are also becoming members. Polynesian Americans who joined the church in the islands are immigrating to the United States and bringing extended family members. Not all of them are Mormons, but some join after they have arrived. The church has also continued its efforts, although on a lesser scale, to convert Native Americans.

While the northern European immigrants assimilated in one generation, these new members maintain their language and much of their cultural identity. The Mormon church has tried various approaches to help these members, including establishing separate congregations, integrating them into existing congregations without translation support, and facilitating partial integration—allowing them to "fuse" their culture with the Mormon lifestyle. In the 1960s, for example, church President Spencer W. Kimball (1895-1985) actively organized Indian congregations (generally called Lamanite branches), and congregations of other ethnic groups, including a Chinese branch and a German-speaking ward in Salt Lake City, were formed. In the early 1970s, church leaders again questioned the utility of sponsoring separate branches and urged the integration of ethnic members into the church. However, before the end of the decade, a Basic Unit plan encouraged ethnic branches again. In practice the church's policy has vacillated because neither ethnic branches nor integrated wards have met the needs of all church members. Language and cultural barriers often weaken the ties of religion. Questions about how to resolve these issues still face the Mormon leadership.

In addition, church leaders uphold family values and gender roles that some Americans question. Many see the Mormon church as a conservative voice similar to the South's Bible Belt, and even some Mormons question these conservative stands. In 1993 and 1994 the church excommunicated intellectuals who questioned some basic tenets such as not ordaining women to the priesthood, the historicity of the *Book of Mormon*, and the role of church leaders.

FAMILY AND COMMUNITY DYNAMICS

Mormons believe that through marriages performed in the temple, families are sealed for eternity. While most American Mormon families live with just the nuclear family, they value the extended family, living and dead. They feel that the temple "saving ordinances" such as baptism, a special "endowment" session, and marriages are also essential for family

members who have died. Since these ordinances can only be performed on earth, living Mormons perform them as proxies for deceased relatives. To facilitate this, church leaders encourage Mormons to research their genealogies and collect the names of their deceased relatives.

The LDS church has emphasized family worship, including family scripture reading and weekly family meetings (now called family home evenings) for decades. The practice of family gatherings started in the Granite Stake in the Salt Lake Valley in 1909. Church leaders instructed families to set aside time to learn the gospel, participate in activities, sing songs, read the scriptures together, play games, and enjoy refreshments. Six years later in 1915, the First Presidency of the church announced its official endorsement of the church program. They asked "presidents of stakes and bishops throughout the church [to] set aside one evening each month for a "Home Evening" where "fathers and mothers may gather their boys and girls about them in the home and teach them the word of the Lord." The church formalized the program in 1965 as the "family home evening" program. General church leaders encouraged local leaders to set aside Monday for the weekly meeting, prohibited ward or stake meetings that night, and provided lesson and activity manuals to assist families in their time together.

Mormons also encourage daily family prayer. In a survey of Utah adults by sociologist Stan Albrecht, 42 percent of lifetime Mormons reported having "daily" family prayer, with another 27 percent specifying "often." The comparable figures for converts were 45 percent and 23 percent respectively. While the number of those answering "never" or "only on special occasions" were higher (31 percent for lifetime members and 32 percent for converts), Utah Mormons prayed as families more often than Utah Catholics and Protestants, who collectively reported that 16 percent had daily family prayer, 13 percent less frequently, and 71 percent "never" or "only for special occasions."

Church leaders encourage Mormons to be self-sufficient. Since 1930, the church has operated its own welfare system to help members in need. Leaders ask members to fast once a month and donate the money they would have spent on those meals to help the needy. However, leaders also encourage members to use their own resources and seek their extended families' assistance before coming to the church for aid. To help in times of emergency, leaders ask members to maintain a year's supply of food and other necessities. During the 1930s, the church claimed that it could support its own members, but studies showed that members depended on the federal programs to a greater extent than other Americans. Church members continue to use federal and church programs, but the goal of self-reliance endures.

Church policy discourages teenagers from dating until they are 16 years old. Leaders also encourage no serious dating until after young men serve a two-year full-time mission when they are 19. Leaders stress that young people should marry other Mormons within their own racial group. The 1978 issue of the *Church News* that announced the change in policy toward blacks holding the priesthood included an article restating that the church still discouraged interracial marriages. It pointed out that marriage is always difficult and even more so when the partners come from different backgrounds. While the topic is not discussed as much in the general church, single Mormons from ethnic groups are frequently confused by the church's counsel to marry within the church and to marry someone from their ethnic groups when they do not find potential marriage partners who are Mormons and who belong to their cultural backgrounds.

The church teaches that sexual intercourse outside marriage is a sin. As a result, Mormon women marry at slightly younger ages than other Americans, while men marry at about the same age as the national average. Most Mormons marry rather than cohabit. As divorce has become more acceptable in the United States, more Mormons are separating. Utah has a higher divorce rate than the national average. Some studies show Mormons are more likely to separate in the first five years and less likely to divorce after five years of marriage.

Mormons believe all people existed as spirits before they were born and that to progress they needed to come to this earth to receive a body and to be tested. Many believe that the spirits on the other side need to be provided bodies. For that reason, the church discourages birth control and suggests that Mormons have large families; Latter-day Saints have families larger than the U.S. average. Mormon church leaders also speak against abortion. They view ending a pregnancy as "one of the most ... sinful practices of this day." The only allowable exceptions are where "incest or rape was involved, or where competent medical authorities certify that the life of the mother is in jeopardy, or that a severely defective fetus cannot survive birth."

Mormons value children and provide training for them in the home and in the church. Traditional Mormon gender roles have changed along with overall American values as society has evolved in the twentieth century. But there are still differences in the training of boys and girls. Boys receive the priesthood when they are 12 years old and progress through priesthood offices. Church leaders ask all young men to serve a two-year mission when they are 19 years old. They receive the temple endowment before leaving on their missions. Girls, however, do not have the same advancement. They are allowed but not encouraged to go on missions, and they do not go until they are 21. Young women who serve missions receive the temple ordinances before they leave. Most women attend the temple for the first time just before their marriages. In marriage, a woman is sealed to her husband, and the church teaches that the man, the priesthood holder, is the head of the home; leaders discourage women from working outside the home. While many women work, studies show that women in Utah are more likely to work part time and many Mormon Utah women stay at home.

Despite rather conservative family status for women, however, Utah was the second state (after Wyoming) to give women the right to vote. Although Congress took suffrage away with the Edmunds-Tucker Act, some women continued to campaign for suffrage and were active in the national suffrage movements. The Utah State Constitution gave women back the vote in 1896. Some women, especially those involved in suffrage, became active in political parties. Historically Mormon women have been involved in community health, social welfare, and adoption programs; the best known of these is the Relief Society.

EDUCATION

Mormons place a high value on education. Joseph Smith established a School of the Prophets and stressed the importance of learning, and Mormon scripture encourages members to "seek learning even by study and also by faith." Once the Mormons arrived in Utah, they established and sponsored the first schools on all levels in the state. Formal statehood brought public education, and gradually the church closed or transferred to the state most of its high schools (or academies). Weber State University in Ogden, Utah; Snow College in Ephraim, Utah; and Dixie College in St. George, Utah, are examples of state-sponsored institutions that were first established as Mormon academies. The church did not abandon all of its educational facilities, however. It still sponsors Brigham Young University, a four-year college with a large campus in Provo, Utah, as well as a smaller campus in Laie, Hawaii. It also operates a two-year junior college in Rexburg, Idaho, LDS Business College in Salt Lake City, and high schools and smaller colleges throughout the world in areas with limited public education.

These Mormon
women are tacking
a quilt out in the
yard.

With the closing of its academies, the church feared the loss of religious instruction. To provide the spiritual training other than that provided at Sunday activities, the church established seminaries at high schools and institutes at universities. The first seminary was established at Granite High School in Salt Lake City in 1912; the first institute was created at the University of Idaho in Moscow in 1926.

The Mormons' emphasis on education has led to an educated Mormon populace in the United States. In 1984 sociologists Stan L. Albrecht and Tim B. Heaton found that over half Mormon men (53.5 percent) had some post high school education as compared to 36.7 percent of American men; 44.3 percent of Mormon women had similar training, contrasting with only 27.7 percent of American women overall.

HOLIDAYS

For the most part, American Mormons observe only the national holidays that other Americans celebrate. The exception is July 24, Pioneer Day, in honor of the day that Brigham Young entered the Salt Lake Valley in 1847. This date is a state holiday in Utah, and residents celebrate with parades and fireworks. With the emphasis Mormons place on their history, members throughout the United States celebrate Pioneer Day on a smaller scale.

HEALTH ISSUES

Mormons consider the Word of Wisdom, a revelation received by Joseph Smith, to be a commandment from God. According to Mormon tradition, in 1833 Emma Smith questioned male church leaders using chewing tobacco and spitting in her home. As a result, Joseph Smith asked the Lord for guidance and received Section 89 of the Doctrine and Covenants. It cautioned against "wine and strong drinks," tobacco, and "hot drinks." It also said meat should be "used sparingly" and urged the use of grains, especially "wheat for man," and herbs. When the revelation was first received, the church considered it only advice; violation did not restrict church membership. During the 1890s, though, church leaders started emphasizing the Word of Wisdom more. They led the prohibition fight in Utah and discouraged the use of alcoholic drinks. In 1921 church president Heber J. Grant made obeying the Word of Wisdom a requirement to enter the temple. The church interpreted the revelation to forbid coffee, tea, tobacco, and alcohol, but it does not stress other elements of the teaching, including guidelines about the use of meat and grains.

Strict adherence to the Word of Wisdom has led to greater health among Mormons. Studies have found that Mormons in Utah have fewer cases of diseases, especially cancers, and suggest this may be because they do not use tobacco or alcohol. One study declared that Mormons showed that one-third of the cancers in the United States could be prevented by avoiding these substances. Mormons also helped in cancer research through their high birth rate and the keeping of genealogical records. University of Utah professors have encoded this information and identified high-risk cancer patients. In addition, information provided by the Mormons helped lead to the identification of a gene that frequently occurs in colon cancer patients.

Nineteenth-century Mormon health practices and problems were similar to those of other Americans at the time. Mormons suffered a high rate of infant morality and death from infectious diseases. Their initial mistrust of the medical profession was also common. Some early Mormons believed in herbal treatments. Many practiced faith healing. Leaders encouraged members to depend more on the power of God than on doctors. In the church's early days, men and women gave blessings as a way of healing. Usually women blessed other women at the time of childbirth. Now the church only authorizes men holding the priesthood to give blessings.

Mormon health practices have changed over the years. Some modifications developed in response to changes in American views. After the Mormons moved to Utah, Brigham Young encouraged members to go to doctors for medical treatment. His suggestion slightly preceded the general American shift to greater support of the medical profession. Young asked second-generation Mormons to return to the East to study medicine, and men and women responded. While leaders still stressed faith healing, they also encouraged members to seek the assistance of secular medicine.

Around the turn of the century, Mormons participated in public health programs that were popular throughout the United States. Church leaders encouraged voluntary vaccination programs and supported quarantines. The women's organization, the Relief Society, sponsored maternal and child health programs. It also held milk clinics and organized "Swat the Fly" campaigns. The women worked closely with the state government to implement the services Congress provided through the 1920s Shepherd-Towner Act. Under this law, the stake Relief Society in Cottonwood opened a maternity hospital and other church groups provided layettes and promoted pregnancy and well-baby care.

The Mormon church also sponsored hospitals in Utah to provide assistance to the sick. The Relief Society started the Deseret Hospital in 1882. When that hospital closed 10 years later, members worked to raise money for the W. H. Grover Latter-day Saint Hospital that opened in 1905. The Mormon church owned and operated hospitals in Utah and Idaho until the 1980s, when the leaders turned these hospitals over to a newly created private institution, the Intermountain Health Corporation.

By the end of the twentieth century, Mormons depended as much on doctors as on other members. While blessings at the time of illness continue, leaders recommend that members seek medical advice. Physician and historian Lester Bush concludes, "With regard to most aspects of medical practice, Mormons are indeed no longer a `peculiar people'" (Health and Medicine Among the Mormons: Science, Sense, and Scripture, 1993). There are some minor differences though. Early in the century the Utah state legislature voted against compulsory vaccinations. Later that decision was reversed, but for years Utah had higher cases of smallpox than the rest of the nation because vaccinations were not required. Utah has also resisted water fluoridation. In 1972 the First Presidency asked members to study the issue and make their own decision, but they did not express support. As a result, much of Utah's water is not fluoridated, and children have more cavities.

RELIGION

Though Mormons are found throughout the world, the church is thoroughly American. That is true especially of its leadership. While the church has appointed local leaders that represent its worldwide membership, the most influential, the First Presidency and the Council of Twelve, are all white American males. When a president dies, the senior member of the Council of Twelve replaces him, so future church leaders will come from this group. The two Quorums of Seventies are also General Authorities in the church. The First Quorum is appointed for life and in 1993 included 35 men. Only eight of its members are not from the United States. The Second Quorum is appointed for a five-year term. Of 43 men in 1993, only 14 are not Americans. Since nearly all the General Authorities are Americans, the body tends to represent that perspective.

Mormons attend geographically structured congregations known as wards. In Utah a ward might include only a few blocks; in other areas, wards might encompass an entire middle- sized or metropolitan city. In Utah boundaries frequently split neighborhoods, and there is very little contact outside assigned wards. Wards support religious and social life by sponsoring athletic events, parties, and other activities for all age groups. Five to six wards form a unit known as a stake, which is similar to a diocese.

The importance of "going to church" has changed for Mormons over time. Historian Jan Shipps described the changes in Mormon religious practice: "Hypothetical Saints [travelling to the nineteenth century] ... in a time machine would have been astonished to find so few Saints at sacrament meeting because the twentieth century sacrament meeting is a visible worship sign, whereas in the pioneer era more expressive worship signs were irrigation canals or neatly built or nicely decorated houses or good crops of sugar beets. More significant, living in the nineteenth century was the sign of citizenship in God's elect nation" (*Mormonism: The Story of a New Religious Tradition*, 1985). As the Mormons gave up such distinctive practices as polygamy and the United Orders, the responsibility of "boundary maintenance" shifted from the church to the individual. According to Shipps, "The LDS dietary, behavior, and dress codes" are now important boundary markers, while correspondingly, "worship activity ... seems almost mandatory."

The importance of attending worship services is reflected in contemporary Mormon church statistics. For example, a 1980-1981 study shows that 68 percent of lifetime Mormons in Utah attend church on a weekly basis. Converts are even more devout: 74 percent attend weekly. Sociologist Armand Mauss' study of general U.S. surveys found that 58 percent of Mormons go to church weekly compared to only 29 percent of other Americans. On Sundays Mormons attend a three-hour block of meetings that includes a general worship service—known as the sacrament meeting—for everyone. Adults and teenagers attend Sunday School classes. Men and women then split; women attend Relief Society and men attend priesthood meeting. Teenage girls attend Young Women, and teenage boys attend priesthood classes. Children between the ages of three and twelve go to Primary. A nursery serves those between eighteen months and three years of age. Before 1981, Mormons scattered meetings throughout the week. Partly because of the gasoline

shortage of the late 1970s, these meetings were consolidated into today's Sunday block. The church leaders hoped this would not only cut down travel time, but allow families more time to be together.

Mormons also develop a sense of community by working together in the wards. The only paid full-time clergy in the church are the General Authorities. Ward and stake leaders accept positions to serve as bishop (similar to a pastor or priest), stake president (similar to a bishop in the Catholic church), and staff for other church organizations. Catholic sociologist Thomas F. O'Dea in his extensive study of the Mormons observed that the church's lay ministry means "the church has provided a job for everyone to do and, perhaps more important, has provided a formal context in which it is to be done. The result is a wide distribution of activity, responsibility, and prestige" (*The Mormons*, 1957). O'Dea explained lay structure has historical roots. Mormonism came into being "when lay responsibility in church government was widespread and developed in circumstances that demanded lay participation for the survival of the group and the carrying-out of the program.... If western conditions caused older and established churches to make use of laymen, a new and struggling religious movement had all the more reason to do so, and no inhibiting traditions." Mormonism's already expansive definition of priesthood continued to broaden, becoming universal for men after 1978.

TEMPLES

Early Mormon meeting houses and temples were works of art. The architecture was often similar to Gothic chapels and represented the feeling that the Saints were giving the best to the Lord. The Salt Lake Temple, often seen as the symbol of Mormonism, is a classic example; but the church has had a mixed record of preserving these historic treasures. In the late 1960s local residents along with state citizens fought to prevent the church from tearing down the Heber City, Utah, tabernacle that had served as a meeting place for the Wasatch Stake. Just a few years later similar groups were unable to preserve the Coalville, Utah, tabernacle. In the late 1970s the church preserved the outside of the Logan Temple but gutted the interior. It maintained the original murals in the Salt Lake and Manti temples. In 1994 the church announced plans to convert the tabernacle in Vernal, Utah, into a temple.

Mormon temples provide a special worship atmosphere for members; meeting houses are more practical. They include a chapel for worship, a cultural hall for sports and theater, classrooms, a kitchen, and a library. In the early days the buildings were still decorative; now there is more emphasis on utilitarianism. The church provides standard architectural plans that can be adapted for individual needs. New temples are built to serve functional needs. A good contrast that shows the changes is to compare the Salt Lake Temple with its granite towers and symbolism with the simple concrete design of the Provo, Utah, and Ogden, Utah, temples.

EMPLOYMENT AND ECONOMIC TRADITIONS

Mormons have a variety of occupations. Sociologist Wade Dewey Roof and theologian William McKinney examined religious "streams" in the "circulation of the saints." The "upward movement" from one social and economic class to another is one of these streams. They concluded that the Mormon church moved from the bottom of the lowest scale in the 1940s, based on education, family income, occupational prestige, and perceived social class, to the highest in the middle category by the 1980s.

POLITICS AND GOVERNMENT

Since the breakup of the People's Party, the Mormon church leaders claim to speak out only on political issues that they consider to be of moral concern. In 1968 the church opposed the sale of liquor by the drink, supported Sunday closing laws, and favored right-to-work laws. The Mormon church also took a stand opposing the Equal Rights Amendment (ERA) in the 1970s. While LDS women were split, the church's Relief Society came out against the amendment and in October 1976 a First Presidency statement opposed the ERA. The church's stand influenced the vote in Utah, Florida, Virginia, and Illinois and affected states such as Idaho that attempted to reverse their ratification of the amendment.

Besides opposing the ERA, Mormons attended state activities for the International Women's Year. Mormons tended to vote as a bloc against what they saw as liberal proposals. The Mormon church also made national news when an outspoken supporter of the ERA, Sonia Johnson, was excommunicated from the Mormon church. The Mormon Women's Forum, a group of Mormon feminists seeking to reform the church, looks at what its members see as the suppressive influence of the church on Mormon women and examines such issues as the ordination of women to the priesthood.

The First Presidency also spoke out against the location of the MX missile system in Utah and Nevada in 1981. The church issued a statement declaring, "Our fathers came to this western area to establish a base from which to carry the gospel of peace to the peoples of the earth." It continued, "It is ironic, and a denial of the very essentials of that gospel, that in this same general area there should be a mammoth weapons system potentially capable of destroying much of civilization." The federal government then suggested moving the project to Wyoming and later abandoned the project altogether.

The Mormon church also spoke out on other issues. Leaders came out strongly against abortion. Utah passed one of the most pro-life legislation packages in the United States in 1991. In 1992 the LDS church opposed a pari-mutuel betting proposal in the state of Utah; several general authorities mentioned this subject in the October General Conference just before the election. The measure was defeated.

Other than speaking out on issues and encouraging members to vote and be involved in the political process, Mormon leaders do not officially support any political party. Almost half of the American Mormon population are Republicans. The rest are independents, Democrats, and small political party members. Mormons tend to be conservative no matter which political party they belong to.

MILITARY

One of Joseph Smith's Articles of Faith, a 13-statement creed of belief, says that Mormons believe in being "subject" to governments and "honoring" the laws of the land. Church leaders asked members to participate in the armed forces of their countries, even when that meant that Mormons fought against each other. During World War II and the Korean and Vietnamese conflicts, Mormon leaders restricted the missionary efforts and discouraged draft dodgers and conscientious objectors. Mormons have changed the way that they view wars. In the early church, Latter-day Saints looked for the Second Coming of Jesus Christ. They viewed the Civil War as the beginning of the "wars and rumors of wars" that were prophesied would proceed the millennium. Mormons saw the Spanish American War that came immediately after Utah received statehood as a chance to prove their loyalty to America. Like other Americans, Mormons saw World War I as a "just war" to end all wars. World War II was seen as a necessary battle to save democracy and remove dictators.

INDIVIDUAL AND GROUP CONTRIBUTIONS

ACADEMIA

Laurel Thatcher Ulrich won the Pulitzer Prize for nonfiction for her book *A Midwife's Tale: The Life of Martha Ballard, Based on Her Diary, 1785-1812.* Ulrich is a professor of history at the University of New Hampshire. Mormons also publish scholarly journals that deal with various aspects of LDS life. The first journal addressed to the intellectual community was *Brigham Young University Studies* (1959). In 1966 scholars formed *Dialogue: A Journal of Mormon Thought,* an independent voice, despite disapproval from many in the church's hierarchy. Other autonomous periodicals followed including the *Journal of Mormon History* (1974), *Exponent II* (1974), and *Sunstone* (1975). The Mormon History Association publishes the *Journal of Mormon History.* The rest are published by small groups devoted to the need for an independent organ for Mormon scholars.

ART AND MUSIC

President Spencer W. Kimball (1895-1985) encouraged Mormons to develop an art form of their own. Mormons have attempted to do this throughout the church's history. They formed musical groups, especially bands, during the nineteenth century. They also participated in choral singing on a local and church-wide basis. Several Mormon regional choirs are very successful. The best-known choir is the Mormon Tabernacle Choir that presents a weekly program on CBS Radio and Television. Equally well-known is the Osmond family, which has had many different successful music groups, whether it was the Osmond Brothers, or brother and sister act Donny and Marie. Mormons have also encouraged plays and theatrical productions. In 1861 the church built the Salt Lake Theater that was the center of drama in the Rocky Mountain West for years. Dramas have continued on a local and churchwide basis over the years. The church also sponsors pageants depicting the Mormon past at historic sites throughout the United States. The most noted is the Hill Cumorah Pageant near Palmyra, New York, which enacts the history of the *Book of Mormon* and Joseph Smith's early life.

Mormons have used motion pictures as missionary and teaching tools. One of the first was *Man's Search for Happiness,* produced for the 1967 World's Fair in New York City. Since then, the church has produced television specials and other motion pictures. In 1993, for example, the church started showing *Legacy,* a dramatic presentation of early Mormon history, in the restored Hotel Utah, now known as the Joseph Smith Memorial Building.

Mormon artists have used their talents to express church messages. During the 1880s and 1890s, Mormon painters went as missionaries to Paris to learn the impressionist art. They returned to paint murals for the Salt Lake Temple. Other Mormon painters contributed stained glass windows and other paintings to chapels. As the church has grown worldwide, artists from many countries have adapted their native art forms to portray Mormon themes. The church-owned Museum of Church History and Art sponsors art competitions to help collect and display the art produced from around the world. Brigham Young University has a large collection of painting and sculpture in its Museum of Art.

CHURCH ADMINISTRATION

Amy Brown Lyman (1872-1959) served on the Relief Society general board and as president of that organization from 1940 to 1944. Lyman was active in church and state welfare programs. James O. Mason (1930–) worked in the LDS church welfare services and then in the Utah Department of Health. In 1989 he was appointed head of the U.S. Public Health Service. He retired from the federal government in 1992 and was called to be a member of the Second Quorum of Seventy in the LDS church. Eliza R. Snow (1804-1887) served as secretary of the Relief Society in Nauvoo, Illinois, and president in Utah. Snow wrote poems; some are LDS hymns. She was a plural wife of Joseph Smith, and after Smith's death, she became a plural wife of Brigham Young. Emmaline Blanche Wells (1828-1921) was editor of the *Women's Exponent* for nearly four decades and general president of the Relief Society for over a decade. Active in women's suffrage, she was a friend of Elizabeth Cady Stanton and Susan B. Anthony.

JOURNALISM

Since the early church, Mormons have published newspapers and magazines. Some important U.S. publications include the *Evening and Morning Star* (Independence, Missouri, 1832-1833; Kirtland, Ohio, 1833-1834), the *Times and Seasons* (Nauvoo, Illinois, 1839-1946); and the *Frontier Guardian* (Kanesville, Iowa, 1849-1852). Once in Utah the Mormons started a newspaper, the *Desert News* (1850-) that is ongoing. Women established a quasi-Mormon women's paper, the *Woman's Exponent* (1872-1914). It was replaced by an official magazine, the *Relief Society Magazine* (1914-1970). The church also sponsored a Sunday School magazine, the *Juvenile Instructor*, a young women's magazine, and the *Children's Friend*. The general church magazine was the *Improvement Era* (1897-1970). In 1970 the church started three new magazines, the *Ensign* for adults, the *New Era* for teenagers, and the *Friend* for children.

LITERATURE

Mormons have also written novels, stories, and poems about the LDS experience. Vardis Fisher (1895-1968) wrote from a Mormon background. Others with Latter-day Saint backgrounds who wrote about Mormon themes include Samuel Taylor (1906–), Virginia Sorsensen (1912-1992), and Maurine Whipple (1904-1993). Another contemporary Mormon author is Levi Peterson (1933–), who writes novels (*Backslider*) and short stories (*Canyons of Grace*). Mormon authors formed the Association of Mormon Letters to promote literary study.

SCIENCE AND TECHNOLOGY

Mormons have also been involved in technological inventions, although most of these innovations have had little to do with their Mormon past. One exception is the development of irrigation. The community-minded Mormons worked out a system to share water in the arid west. They developed irrigation companies and ways to share the limited water resources. Later other Mormons improved these methods and shared them throughout the United States and the world. John A. Widstoe (1872-1952) was among the first Mormons who went east in the 1890s to study science at secular universities. Widstoe directed the Utah Agricultural Experiment Station and was a professor of chemistry at the Utah State Agricultural College. He developed dry farming and irrigation methods. Henry Eyring (1901-1981), a chemist, developed the absolute rate theory of chemical reactions and received the National Medal of Science. He served as president of several leading scientific organizations. Harvey Fletcher (1884-1981), a physicist, worked for Bell Labs and helped develop stereophonic reproduction. James Chipman Fletcher (1919-1992) was the director of NASA from 1971 to 1977. He was asked to return to that position after the Challenger disaster and remained from 1986 to 1989.

POLITICS AND GOVERNMENT

Terrell H. Bell (1921–) was the secretary of education in the early 1980s under President Ronald Reagan. Ezra Taft Benson (1899-1994) served as president of the LDS church. Benson also served as secretary of agriculture under President Dwight D. Eisenhower and was active in farm organizations. David M. Kennedy (1925–), a banker, was the secretary of the treasury under president Richard Nixon from 1969-1971, an ambassador-at-large from 1971-1973, and the ambassador to NATO from 1972-1973. He later became an ambassador-at-large for the LDS church. Rex Lee (1935-) was U.S. solicitor general. In 1989 he has became president of Brigham Young University. George Romney (1912–) was president and general manager of American Motors (1954-1962), governor of the state of Michigan (1963-1967), and a candidate for the Republican presidential nomination in 1968. Stewart L. Udall (1920-) served as secretary of the interior in the 1960s under president John F. Kennedy.

SPORTS

Many Mormons have achieved fame in athletics. These include professional baseball players such as Dale Murphy, basketball players such as Danny Ainge, football players such as Steve Young, and golfers such as Johnny Miller. Mormons have also excelled in amateur sports, including athletes Henry Marsh, Doug Padilla, Ed Eyestone, and Jay Silvester in track and field.

MEDIA

PRINT

Affinity.

Monthly publication of the Affirmation/Gay and Lesbian Mormons. Promotes understanding, tolerance, and acceptance of gay men and lesbians as full, equal, and worthy members of the Church of Jesus Christ of Latter-Day Saints and society. Provides a forum for dialogue between members and church leaders and examines the consistency of homosexual behavior and the Gospel. Studies ways of reconciling sexual orientation with traditional Mormon beliefs.

Contact: James Kent, Editor.
Address: P.O. Box 46022, Los Angeles, California 90046.
Telephone: (213) 255-7251.

Church News.
A weekly publication that includes the activities of Mormons worldwide. It is published as an insert in the Mormon-owned *Deseret News*.

Contact: Dell Van Orden, Editor.
Address: 40 E. South Temple, P.O. Box 30178, Salt Lake City, Utah 84130.
Telephone: (800) 453-3876; or (801) 534-1515.
Fax: (801) 578-3338.
Online: http://www.deseretnews.com/cn-home.htm.

Dialogue: A Journal of Mormon Thought.
Quarterly scholarly journal examining the relevance of religion to secular life and expressing Mormon culture.

Contact: Martha Bradley, Co-Editor.
Address: P.O. Box 658, Salt Lake City, Utah 84110-0658.
Telephone: (801) 363-9988.

Ensign.
A monthly magazine published by the Mormon church for its adult English-speaking members. It includes a message from the First Presidency and articles concerning LDS life and members. A section includes "News of the Church."

Contact: Jay M. Todd, Managing Editor.
Address: 50 East North Temple, 23rd Floor, Salt Lake City, Utah 84150.
Telephone: (800) 453-3860; or (801) 240-2950.
Fax: (801) 240-5997.
E-mail: majones@chg.byu.edu.

Exponent II.
Quarterly newspaper for Mormon women.

Contact: Susan L. Paxman, Editor.
Address: P.O. Box 37, Arlington, Massachusetts 02174.
Telephone: (617) 862-1928.
Fax: (617) 868-3464.

Friend.
An LDS church magazine for children. Its stories and articles provide information for youth ages three to 12.

Contact: Vivian Paulsen, Editor.
Address: 50 East North Temple, 23rd Floor, Salt Lake City, Utah 84150.

New Era.
A Mormon publication for teenagers and young adults. Its articles focus on the concerns of young people.

Contact: Richard M. Romney, Editor.
Address: 50 East North Temple, 23rd Floor, Salt Lake City, Utah 84150.

Sunstone: Mormon Experience, Scholarship, Issues, and Art.
Magazine published by Sunstone Foundation, which also sponsors symposiums in the United States. (In 1992 the Mormon church's First Presidency and Council of Twelve issued a statement cautioning against Mormons participating in symposiums, and many felt this referred to Sunstone.)

Contact: Elbert Peck, Editor.
Address: 343 North 300 West, Salt Lake City, Utah, 84103-1215.
Telephone: (801) 355-5926.
Fax: (801) 355-4043.

This People: Exploring LDS Issues and Personalities.
Quarterly magazine for members of the LDS church.

Contact: Jim Bell, Editor.
Address: Utah Alliance Publishing, P.O. Box 50748, Provo, Utah 84605.
Telephone: (801) 375-1700.
Fax: (801) 375-1703.

RADIO

Bonneville LDS Radio Network.
The media corporation owned by the LDS church; provides a 24-hour radio service that is sent by satellite to church members who own satellite receivers. It is also repeated by a few stations across the nation as an FM sideband service.

Contact: Richard Linford.
Address: P.O. Box 1160, Salt Lake City, Utah 84110-1160.
Telephone: (801) 575-7505.

Bonneville International also operates radio stations throughout the United States: KIDR-AM (740) in Phoenix, Arizona; KIRO-AM (710) and KWMX-FM (101) in Seattle, Washington; KOIT-FM (96.5) and KOIT-AM (1260) in San Francisco, California; KZLA-FM (93.9) and KBIG-FM (104.3) in Los Angeles, California; KSL-AM (1160) in Salt Lake City, Utah; KHTC-FM (96.9) and KIDR-AM (740) in Phoenix, Arizona; KMBZ-AM (980) in Westwood, Kansas; KLDE-FM (94.5) in Houston, Texas; KZPS-FM (92.5) and KAAM-AM (1310) in Dallas, Texas; WDBZ-FM (105.1) in New York City; WGMS-AM (103.5) in Washington, D.C.; and WLUP-FM (97.9) and WNND-FM (100.3) in Chicago, Illinois. These are commercial stations. At least one station in each operating area carries the CBS broadcast "Music and the Spoken Word," and some carry one or more sessions of the LDS General Conference.

LDS Public Communications.
Produces a weekly "News of the Church of Jesus Christ of Latter-day Saints" and other public affairs programs that are packaged and sent to radio stations.

Contact: Gerry Pond, Producer.
Address: LDS Church Headquarters, 50 East North Temple, Salt Lake City, Utah 84150.

TELEVISION, BROADCAST, AND CABLE SERVICES

Bonneville International Corporation.
Operates two television stations, KIRO-TV, Channel 7 in Seattle, Washington, and KSL-TV in Salt Lake City, Utah. These operate as commercial stations and do not regularly carry unique Mormon programming. The LDS church Public Communications airs shows on the cable system religious station VISIONS.

Address: LDS Church Headquarters, 50 East North Temple, Salt Lake City, Utah 84150.

ORGANIZATIONS AND ASSOCIATIONS

Affirmation/Gay and Lesbian Mormons.
Members of the Mormon church; friends, relatives, and interested individuals whose purpose is to promote understanding, tolerance, and acceptance of gay men and lesbians as full, equal, and worthy members of the church and society. Studies ways of reconciling sexual orientation with traditional Mormon beliefs.

Contact: Tianna Owens, Executive Director.
Address: P.O. Box 46022, Los Angeles, California 90046.
Telephone: (213) 255-7251.
Online: http://www.affirmation.org/affadmin.

Mormon History Association.
Promotes the study of the Mormon past. It publishes the *Journal of Mormon History*, a biannual scholarly publication.

Contact: Craig and Suzanne Foster, Executive Secretaries.
Address: 2470 North 1000 West, Layton, Utah.
Telephone: (801) 773-4620.
Fax: (801) 779-1348.
E-Mail: suzannefoster@bigplanet.com.

Mormon Social Science Association.
Encourages the study of Mormon life.

Contact: Lynn Payne, Secretary-Treasurer.
Address: Sociology Department, A 800 SWKT, Brigham Young University, Provo, Utah 84602.

Young Women of the Church of Jesus Christ of Latter-Day Saints (YW).
Founded in 1869. Description: Girls between the ages of 12 and 18. Seeks to strengthen the spiritual life of young women through Christian values and experiences. Reinforces the values of faith, divine nature, individual worth, knowledge, choice and accountability, good works, and integrity. Works to develop leadership attributes in young women through service in the community. Bestows Young Womanhood Medallion for special achievement.

Contact: Margaret D. Nadauld, President.
Address: 76 North Main, Salt Lake City, Utah 84150.
Telephone: (801) 240-2141.
Fax: (801) 240-5458.

MUSEUMS AND RESEARCH CENTERS

Charles Redd Center for Western Studies
Integral unit of Brigham Young University. History, anthropology, economic development, literature, folklore, social development, politics, and other activities relating to western development, including studies on Mormon history.

Contact: Dr. Edward A. Geary, Director.
Address: 5042 Harold B. Lee Library, Provo, Utah 84602.
Telephone: (801) 378-4048.
Fax: (801) 378-6708.
E-mail: gearye@jkhbhrc-byu.edu.

Joseph Fielding Smith Institute for Church History.
Integral unit of Brigham Young University. History of Church of Jesus Christ of Latter-day Saints and its followers (Mormons).

Contact: Dr. Ronald K. Esplin, Director.
Address: 127 Knight Mangum Building, Provo, Utah 84602.
Telephone: (801) 378-4023.
Fax: (801) 378-4049.
E-mail: jfsi@byu.edu.

SOURCES FOR ADDITIONAL STUDY

Alexander, Thomas G. *Mormonism in Transition: A History of the Latter-day Saints, 1890-1930.* Urbana: University of Illinois Press, 1986.

Allen, James B., and Glen M. Leonard. *The Story of the Latter-day Saints,* second edition. Salt Lake City: Deseret Books, 1992.

Arrington, Leonard J., and Davis Bitton. *The Mormon Experience.* New York: Alfred A. Knopf, 1979.

Bush, Lester E. *Health and Medicine Among the Mormons: Science, Sense, and Scripture.* New York: Crossroads, 1993.

Cornwall, Marie, Tim B. Heaton, and Lawrence A. Young. *Contemporary Mormonism: Social Science Perspectives.* Urbana: University of Illinois Press, 1994.

Hansen, Klaus J. *Mormonism and the American Experience.* Chicago: University of Chicago Press, 1981.

Hill, Marvin S. *Quest for Refuge: The Mormon Flight from American Pluralism.* Salt Lake City: Signature Books, 1989.

Ludlow, Daniel H. *Encyclopedia of Mormonism.* New York: Macmillan, 1992.

Mauss, Armand L. *The Angel and the Beehive: The Mormon Struggle with Assimilation.* Urbana: University of Illinois Press, 1994.

Shipps, Jan. *Mormonism: The Story of a New Religious Tradition.* Urbana: University of Illinois Press, 1985.

Moroccan Americans

by
Elizabeth Shostak

Evidence indicates that Azemmuri, a Moroccan boat pilot from Azemmour, landed in America before Columbus. It is also possible that a few Sephardic Jews from Morocco made their way to the United States early in the twentieth century by way of South America.

Overview

Morocco, a country slightly larger than the state of California, is situated in northwestern Africa and is the African nation closest in location to Europe. It is bordered on the east by Algeria and to the south by Western Sahara. To its north is the Mediterranean Sea and to its west is the Atlantic Ocean. Morocco's two coasts are separated by the Strait of Gibraltar, a strategic point that guards entry to the Mediterranean from the west. Only 10 miles across the Strait to the north lies Spain. Morocco's total land area is 177,117 square miles (458,730 square kilometers), of which only 21 percent is farmable land. Two northeast-southwest mountain ranges, the Rif and the Atlas Mountains, bisect the country and occupy more than a third of its total area. Morocco's maximum north-south dimension is 825 miles, and its maximum east-west dimension is 475 miles. Its capital city is Rabat, on the Atlantic coast. Its principal economic and cultural center is Casablanca, also on the Atlantic coast.

Morocco's population in 1998 was estimated at 29,114,497. Of this number, the majority of Moroccans—approximately 75 percent—are of Berber ancestry. Arabs make up the second largest group, and smaller numbers of black Africans and French are also represented. Ninety-eight percent of the population is Muslim. Christians comprise only 1.1 percent of the population, and Jews only 0.2 percent. Arabic is the official language of Morocco, although French continues to be used frequently in business and government matters; Spanish is also used. Berber dialects are also spoken, particularly in rural areas. Morocco is a constitutional monarchy; its chief of state is King Mohamed VI (since July 24, 1999). The country is governed by a bicameral Parliament and follows a legal system based on Islamic law and French and Spanish civil law. Morocco's flag consists of a red field with a green five-pointed star—known as Solomon's seal—in its center.

Morocco has relatively high birth and population growth rates, which exacerbate housing shortages and a high level of unemployment. The lack of health care and social services are also significant issues. The country has a mixed economy, but continues to have a relatively low GNP and a surplus of unskilled labor.

HISTORY

Morocco's early history was shaped by pre-Arabic, Arabic, and Jewish influences. The Berbers, a group of non-Arabic tribes scattered throughout North Africa, inhabited Morocco by the end of the second millennium B.C. Many Berbers were settled farmers, though some groups were nomadic. They raised crops and pastured their flocks in Morocco's mountainous inland regions. Phoenician merchants established trading ports along Morocco's Mediterranean coast in the twelfth century B.C. Their presence brought increased commerce to the region and introduced new skills to the Berbers, including weaving, masonry, and iron and metal work. By the fifth century B.C., the Phoenicians had expanded their ports along Morocco's Atlantic coast, as well. After the Roman Empire defeated Carthage, Morocco's Berber King Juba (25 B.C.-24 A.D.) encouraged his country to ally itself with Rome. In 46 A.D. Morocco was annexed as part of the province of Mauretania to the Roman Empire. It is believed that during the period of Roman rule, the province was almost entirely converted to Christianity.

The Jewish presence in Morocco was established before the country became a Roman colony. Small groups of Jews entered the area in the first century A.D. after they had been forced out of their ancestral land. From 1391 through the last decades of the fifteenth century, *Sephardim*, Jews who had settled in Spain and Portugal, fled to Morocco and other North African countries to escape the Inquisition. There they engaged in small crafts or trades, such as silversmithing, and often moved from town to town. By 1438 the Jews in Fez were forced to live in special quarters called *mellahs*. This term derived from the Arabic word for salt, and referred to the

fact that Jews were given the job of salting the heads of executed prisoners to prepare them for public exhibition.

In the late seventh century, the Arab conquest brought Islam to Morocco. Though the Berbers fiercely resisted Arab control, and in 740 staged a successful revolt against Damascus rule, Arab religious, social, and linguistic traditions remained a central part of Moroccan culture. After regaining their independence from the Arabs, various Berber factions vied for control in the area, leading to a series of local wars that spanned almost 300 years. Finally, around the middle of the eleventh century, a confederation of tribes called the Almoravids conquered all of Morocco, as well as much of Spain. Early in the twelfth century the Almohads, another clan, overthrew the Almoravid dynasty and assumed rule. By the thirteenth century, the Almohads were expelled from Spain; in 1269 they were defeated in Morocco by the Marinids. Marinid rule lasted until the mid-fifteenth century, after which the country was partitioned into small independent states. Around 1550, the Sa'dis took control and remained in power for the next century. The North African tribes who conquered Spain were commonly known as Moors.

MODERN ERA

During the 1800s, European interest in North Africa increased, with France and Spain vying for power in the region. France invaded Algeria in 1830, and eventually became the dominant colonial power in the area. The Treaty of Fez, signed in 1912, made Morocco a French protectorate. This new status resulted in improved conditions for Moroccan Jews, who were given equality and religious autonomy. However, when the official French government at Vichy cooperated with Nazi rule during World War II, the situation became more precarious. Although King Muhammed V prevented the deportation of Jews from Morocco during World War II, thereby saving them from almost certain death in Nazi concentration camps, they faced increasingly harsh conditions in Morocco. By 1948 most of the estimated 270,000 Jews in Morocco left its poverty and discrimination for new opportunities in Israel, France, Canada, and the United States. The vast majority of these emigrants settled in Israel.

In the years following World War II, anti-colonial agitation increased throughout Asia and Africa. Morocco pushed for independence from France, which was negotiated in 1956, when Sultan Sidi Muhammad formed a constitutional government. A series of attempted military coups, however, prevented the new parliamentary government from assuming its duties until 1977. Morocco's constitution, signed in 1972 and revised in 1980 and 1992, gives supreme executive power to the hereditary king, who appoints a prime minister. The constitution also created a House of Representatives and an independent judiciary.

Although modern Morocco has instituted land reforms and economic modernization initiatives, and has strenuously developed its tourism industry, by the late 1990s the country was still experiencing problems typical of developing nations: high government spending and inflation, a huge external debt, limited access to health care, poor housing and living conditions, and high unemployment. With an estimated birth rate of 26.37 births per 1,000 people—resulting chiefly from Muslim opposition to family planning measures—Morocco is faced with a relatively high rate of population growth (estimated at 1.89 percent). Moreover, approximately two-fifths of the country's population is younger than 15 years of age. Morocco's high unemployment rate, estimated between 16 and 20 percent, particularly affects this segment of the population. Migration has emerged as a significant means of relieving unemployment, which, according to a 1999 article in *The Economist*, brings about $2 billion a year into Morocco, providing the country with its second-largest source of hard currency.

With average wages in nearby Europe about 20 times higher than that in North Africa, migrants have increasingly attempted to enter Spain, France, and Italy from Morocco to obtain work. But by the end of the 1990s, the European Union began limiting visas for North Africans and barring illegal migrants from entering Europe. The elimination of access to European jobs caused significant problems in Morocco. Some Moroccan workers sought illegal entry to Spain—a practice fraught with dangers: *The Economist* reported in 1999 that, during the preceding five years alone, 3,000 Moroccans had drowned in illegal attempts to cross the Strait of Gibraltar to enter Spain. This situation affected mostly unskilled workers; those Moroccans with higher levels of education and job skills were able to consider emigration to the United States.

THE FIRST MOROCCANS IN AMERICA

Moroccan presence in America was quite rare until the middle of the twentieth century, but it is believed that Moroccans may have been present in the country from the earliest years of European exploration. Evidence indicates that Azemmuri, a Moroccan boat pilot from Azemmour, landed in America before Columbus. It is also possible that a few Sephardic Jews from Morocco made their way to the United States early in the twentieth century by way of South America. In the early 1800s, large numbers of young Moroccan Jewish men, seeking to escape crowded conditions and poverty in their native country, went to the Amazon region in South America. They settled in the cities of Rio de Janiero, Caracas, and Belem, where they established a synagogue in 1824. These young men were instrumental in developing the Amazon's rubber trade, and enjoyed substantial business success. Many returned home after making their fortunes, but others remained in South America. In 1910, however, the South American rubber industry collapsed, and the Moroccan Jews left the area, either returning to North Africa or moving on going to other opportunities in the western hemisphere. Although little documentation exists to trace their various routes, it is possible that some of them entered the United States.

Though the Moroccan American community is relatively new, America's relationship with Morocco dates from the very beginning of U.S. history. Morocco was the first country to grant official recognition to the newly formed United States of America after the country obtained independence from Great Britain.

SIGNIFICANT IMMIGRATION WAVES

Although the vast majority of Sephardic Jews who left Morocco after World War II went to Israel, sporadic waves entered the United States. Motivated by the desire to escape difficult social and economic conditions in North Africa, they tended to settle in areas where earlier Sephardic immigrants from Spain, Turkey, or the Balkans had established communities. Arabized Moroccans, however, did not begin to enter the United States in significant numbers until much later in the century, after American immigration laws lifted national quotas, based on data from the 1920 census, that had favored the entry of immigrants from northern and western Europe. Another factor that inhibited earlier Moroccan migration to the United States was the relative proximity of Europe. Until very late in the 1990s, Spain and France welcomed unskilled migrants from Morocco and other North African countries. It was easy, inexpensive, and quick to go back and forth across the Strait of Gibraltar, making this option attractive for workers who hoped to improve their earnings but then return to their homes and families. Furthermore, Spain's Moorish heritage and France's colonial dominance of the Maghreb had established strong cultural and linguistic connections between these countries and

Morocco. This undoubtedly eased the transition for migrants who sought opportunities there.

While Moroccans who migrated to European countries were typically unskilled workers hoping to escape their country's high unemployment rate, those who came to the United States from approximately the late 1970s through the 1990s tended to have more education and better job skills. They settled in urban areas, especially in New York City, New England, the District of Columbia, California, and Texas, where they often established small businesses or entered professional fields. By the late 1990s, a large proportion of Moroccans in the United States were students or recent university graduates. In general, the number of Moroccan immigrants remains relatively low. The 1990 U.S. census counted only 21,529 foreign-born Moroccans residing in the United States; 15,004 census respondents listed Moroccan as their first ancestry, while 4,074 listed it as their second ancestry.

ACCULTURATION AND ASSIMILATION

Sephardic Jews who immigrated to the United States from Morocco were generally attracted to areas where other Sephardim lived. Within these communities, they shared religious, linguistic, and cultural traditions that both united them with the country's larger Jewish community but also set them apart. The vast majority of American Jews are of *Ashkenazi* descent, meaning that their ancestors had settled in Germany and Eastern Europe. These groups developed cultural traditions that differed from those observed by the Sephardim. Sephardic Jews, for example, spoke Ladino and Arabic rather than Yiddish or German, pronounced Hebrew words differently from the Ashkenazim, used different melodies in religious services, and served North African or Iberian versions of kosher foods during holidays. Some Sephardic Jews in America have felt that their culture is little appreciated, and resent the fact that Ashkenazi traditions have largely determined American conceptions of Jewishness. In addition, some have felt that their relatively dark skin has caused them to be treated with prejudice. Yet their shared Jewish identity still connected Sephardic immigrants with those of Ashkenazi descent and helped them adapt to life in the United States, where the Jewish community has worked hard to combat anti-Semitic attitudes and to achieve social and economic success.

Arabs in the United States have also had to deal with prejudice. Americans have been less exposed to Islam than to Judaism or Christianinty, and have sometimes been suspicious of Muslims. In addition, the country's strong political ties to Israel have also fostered mistrust of Arabic groups—in particular the Palestinian Liberation Organization, which for decades perpetrated terrorist acts against Israel. The activities of other extremist Islamic groups, such as the bombing of the World Trade Center in New York City, have created negative stereotypes of Arabs in the United States. Although Moroccans' history has differed dramatically from that of Middle Eastern Arabs, Americans have tended to view all Arabs as a monolithic group. Because Moroccans typically entered the United States with high levels of education and job skills, however, the Moroccan American community has generally encountered a positive environment.

CUISINE

Situated on the route of the Arabia-North Africa spice trade, Morocco developed traditional foods enhanced by such exotic flavorings as cinnamon, ginger, turmeric, saffron, cumin, cayenne, anise, and sesame seed. Native crops of mint, olives, oranges, lemons, prickly pear, pomegranates, almonds, dates, walnuts, chestnuts, barley, melons, and cherries further increased available ingredients. Fish was plentiful along the Atlantic coast, whereas inland areas produced lamb and poultry as well as honey.

In Morocco, the main meal is eaten at mid-day (except during the holy month of *Ramadan*, in which the Muslim faithful fast until sundown). A typical main meal begins with hot and cold salads. Among the most commonly served are a tomato and green pepper salad, similar to Spanish *gazpacho*. Other popular salads are made with mixed herbs, with eggplant, or with greens and oranges. *Tabbouleh*, a cracked wheat salad flavored with parsley and popular throughout North Africa and the Middle East, is commonly served in Morocco, as are *hummus*, a spicy chick-pea pate, and *falafel*, spicy fried fava bean patties.

Following the salad course, Moroccan cooks typically serve main dishes that include meat and vegetables, followed by *couscous*. One of the most familiar Moroccan foods in American supermarkets, *couscous* is made from grains of very fine semolina (wheat) and is steamed until barely soft. It has a delicate, rather bland taste that sets off the spicier flavors in the dishes that accompany it.

Other dishes include chicken with lemon and olives, a traditional Moroccan favorite. Another popular dish is chicken *tagine*, which includes butter, onions, pepper, saffron, chick peas, almonds, and

lemon. Chicken is also stuffed with raisins, almonds, rice, or eggs. Moroccans often use fish in stews, but also serve it fried or stuffed. A popular recipe that suggests a strong Spanish influence combines fish with tomatoes, green peppers, and potatoes. Lamb, which has been called the "king of the Moroccan table, " is served in a variety of ways. *Mechoui* is a holiday dish in which lamb is seasoned with paprika, cumin, butter and salt and then roasted. Lamb is also roasted on skewers as *shish kebab,* or can be braised, browned, or steamed. *Kefta* is a mixture of spicy lamb or beef that is rolled into a sausage shape and then cooked on a skewer or broiled. It is also rolled into meatballs that are used in tagines.

Other traditional Moroccan dishes include *bisteeya,* a savory pastry with possible Persian or Chinese origins. In this dish, layers of shredded chicken, eggs curdled in lemon-onion sauce, and sweetened almonds are wrapped in a paper-thin pastry called *warka,* then sprinkled with cinnamon and sugar. Moroccans also enjoy both Arab-style bread and pita bread. Though desserts are not frequently served, sweetened green tea flavored with fresh mint traditionally ends the meal on a sweet note.

TRADITIONAL COSTUMES

The *kaftan,* a long, loose-fitting long robe, is still worn throughout much of Morocco in both rural and urban areas. It is a garment well suited to Morocco's climate, protecting wearers from the harsh sun and allowing for ventilation, but also providing warmth for chilly nights. The traditional headgear for Moroccan men is the *fez,* named after the Moroccan city of the same name. It is a close-fitting red felt hat with a flattened top and a tassle worn to the side. The fez became common throughout much of the Islamic world but is thought to have originated in Morocco. In earlier years, Moroccan women, like those in other Islamic countries, wore veils to cover their faces in public. Although this custom has largely disappeared in urban parts of the country, women in rural areas sometimes still wear full or partial veils.

DANCES AND SONGS

An Arabic dance tradition that has become familiar to many Americans is belly dancing. The term refers to the closely-controlled abdominal movements the female dancers make to achieve a rapid rhythmic swaying of the belly and hips. Belly dancers wear a tight garment similar to a brassiere, and wide, flowing trousers gathered at the ankle. They use coordinating long scarves or shawls to accentuate their graceful arm and hand movements, and often ornament their brows with headbands decorated with jewels or old coins. Belly dancing is often offered as entertainment at Moroccan American restaurants. During the 1970s and 1980s, many non-Arabic American women became interested in learning how to do belly dancing. They noted that it requires a surprising degree of athleticism and artistic skill.

Moroccan music reflects the country's hybrid culture, blending Arabic, African, and European influences. *Gnaoua* music, which includes strenuous acrobatic dancing, combines religious Arabic songs with African rhythms. *Andaloussi* music is traced to Abu Hassan Ali Ben Nafi, who fled Baghdad in the ninth century to settle in Cordoba, in the part of Spain then ruled by Morocco. More popular, or folk, music is called *Chaabi*. Many contemporary Moroccan singers record in this style. Instruments used in traditional Moroccan music include the *tbal*, a double-headed drum, and the *querqbat*, or metal castanets. Others are the *tambour* (tambourine); the *oudh*, or lute; the *buzuq*, a larger and deep-toned stringed instrument; the *rebab*, a stringed instrument something like a dulcimer and played with a bow; the *tablah*, a small hand drum; and the *qanun*, similar to a zither. Two reed instruments are also used: the *ney*, a single reed pipe; and the *maqrum*, a double-reed clarinet.

HOLIDAYS

Moroccan Americans who are Muslims celebrate the Islamic holy month of Ramadan. Occurring late in the calendar year, Ramadan is a period of fasting and purification. During the 30 days of Ramadan, nothing—no food, drink, or cigarette smoke—is allowed to pass the lips from daybreak to sunset. This 12-hour fast is then broken each night with the *iftar*, a celebratory family meal. During Ramadan, the faithful donate food and money to the needy, and spend time in prayer. Although non-Muslims might consider Ramadan a period of hardship, for many Muslims it is the favorite time of year. They enjoy the sense of community it brings, and note that it heightens their awareness of the plight of others. They point out that the fast provides physical benefits and helps focus mental attitudes. Ramadan ends with the *Eid el-Fitr*, a special feast during which holiday foods are served and presents are given.

LANGUAGE

Arabic is the official language of Morocco, although French is still widely used in business. Spanish is also frequently spoken, particularly in the northern regions of the country. Standard Arabic, used in newspapers and broadcasts, speeches, and correspondence, is the language of the *Qur'an* (or Koran, the sacred book of Islam), and is understood throughout the contemporary Arab world. There are, however, many different dialects of the language spoken in Arabia, Iraq, Syria, Egypt, and North Africa. Spoken Arabic contains sounds and patterns that differ significantly from those of English or other European languages.

Words in Arabic are composed of the root, usually made up of three consonants which establish the word's basic lexical meaning, and the pattern, which adds the vowels that give the word its grammatical sense. There are three short and three long vowels (a, I, u; a, I, u). The vowel pattern –I-a, for example, makes the root ktb into the word *kitab*, or book; the pattern –a-I creates the word *katib*, meaning "one who writes." Arabic verbs are always regular. There are two tenses: the perfect, which expresses past time by adding suffixes; and the imperfect, which expresses present or future time by adding prefixes.

After the Latin alphabet, the Arabic alphabet is the most widely used writing system in the world. It was created for writing the Arabic language, but has been adapted to such diverse languages as Persian, Turkish, Spanish, Hebrew, Urdu, Berber, Malay, and Swahili. The Arabic alphabet, which was likely derived from Aramaic and Nabataean scripts, probably originated in the fourth century AD. Arabic is written from right to left and contains 28 letters, all of which represent consonants. The letters alif, waw, and ya (representing glottal stop, w, and y) represent the long vowels a, u, and i. The shapes of letters depend on whether they are placed at the beginning, middle, or end of a word. Another form is used for each letter when it is written alone.

GREETINGS AND OTHER COMMON EXPRESSIONS

In Moroccan Arabic, the word for "hello" is *ahlan*. "Goodbye" is *beslama*. "How are you?" is "*Labass alaik*"? "Please" and "thank you" are *affak* and *shoukran*, respectively.

FAMILY AND COMMUNITY DYNAMICS

In Islamic cultures, family dynamics were strictly patriarchal, with the husband accorded power and the wife relegated to a subordinate status. Families tended to be large because of Muslim opposition to birth control. However, Berber attitudes tended to mitigate some of Islam's more misogynistic qualities in Morocco, and as the country modernized, family dynamics also changed. Divorce laws in Morocco, for example, still generally favor husbands but have been used with increasing effectiveness by wives who seek better material conditions or who wish to convince their husbands to agree to divorce. Statistics show that divorce is more common among Moroccan families of lower income than of higher income. Certainly, access to education has changed family relationships throughout much of the country as women have entered the workforce and gained more autonomy. Among Moroccan families in the United States, many women work outside the home and balance careers with family obligations.

The Moroccan American community has adapted relatively easily to America's secular urban society. But their small numbers and their dispersal throughout cities across the country have presented challenges to the maintenance of ethnic unity. Moroccans in the United States, who are scattered across the country in many different urban areas or college towns, have increasingly used the Internet to share information about themselves and keep in touch with others who share their background.

EDUCATION

Schooling in Morocco is compulsory for both girls and boys from ages seven through 15, but the country's literacy rate is only 50 percent. The figure is closer to 60 percent for males, and just above 30 percent for females. Moroccans who have settled in the United States, though, generally had relatively levels of education and skills. Many arrived as students and furthered their education at American colleges and universities. The Moroccan American community values education as an important means of acquiring the knowledge and skills necessary to succeed in a commercial and high-tech economy.

THE ROLE OF WOMEN

Although Moroccan culture was heavily influenced by Arabic traditions, Berber customs generally accorded women more freedoms than they enjoyed in Middle Eastern Arab countries. Moroccan American women, who enjoy a relatively high level of education, are likely to work outside the home. Though women tend to enter traditionally "feminine" professions, such as teaching, increasing numbers are training in more competitive fields, such as computer science or business.

BAPTISMS

Muslim children are not baptized, although male children are circumcised. Among Arab cultures, this custom predated the arrival of Islam, but later became incorporated into Islamic tradition. There are varying opinions among different schools of Islam on the proper importance of ritual circumcision (khitan). Some consider it obligatory, while others consider it recommendable but not required. The age at which it is performed varies from country to country.

WEDDINGS

Weddings in Morocco are festive affairs, and often last for several days. Special garments are painstakingly woven and embroidered for the bride and groom. So important are these costumes that wedding garments from the city of Fez are exhibited on poles during parades on national holidays. Often, the bride orders several garments to be worn during the course of a long wedding. For the ceremony itself, the groom wears a long, loose-fitting garment called a jellaba and the bride wears the traditional long head shawl and kaftan. Special textiles are also used during the bride's henna ceremony, in which intricate patterns are traced on her hands with henna, a red dye. Traditionally, a set of velvet gold-thread embroidered accessories is used for this custom. The mendil, a large rectangular cloth, is placed on the bride's lap while two pillows support her arms. Two special mitts protect her decorated hands. A special domed canopy, also decorated with gold thread, is used to cover the bride and groom while they are carried on trays above their guests.

INTERACTIONS WITH OTHER ETHNIC GROUPS

The experience of Arabized Berbers who came to the United States from Morocco has been similar in some ways to that of Moroccan Jews. Arriving in the country much later than the Sephardim, who made their way here after World War II, Moroccan immigrants found only limited common ground with the existing Arab American community, which, until the influx of Palestinians and other Middle Eastern Arabs after the creation of Israel, had been overwhelmingly Christian. These earliest groups of Arab Americans were the descendants of Syrian Christians, mostly merchants and traders, who had moved to the United States in the late 1800s. The newer Palestinian immigrants, however, were Muslim. Moroccans shared a linguistic tradition with both these groups, and shared a religious affiliation with the Palestinians, but much in

Moroccan history and culture differed from the Middle Eastern Arab experience. Moroccan Americans have not been excluded from the many Arab American associations that emerged to counteract prejudice and advocate for better access to jobs and social services in the United States. However, few Moroccan immigrants have allied themselves with such organizations because their focus is emphatically on the conditions that affect Arab immigrants from the Middle East.

RELIGION

Islam was founded in the seventh century A.D. by the Arabian prophet Muhammed and is the religion of the overwhelming majority of Moroccans. The faith quickly spread throughout the Middle East and North Africa, and was established in Afghanistan, Pakistan, the Balkan Peninsula, Turkey, and Malaysia. By the late twentieth century, Islam was the second largest religion in the world (after Christianity), with approximately 950,726,000 followers worldwide. Those who practice Islam are known as Muslims. The principal sects of Islam include the *Sunni, Shi'ah, Sufi,* and *Ismaili* Muslims. Most Moroccans are Sunni Muslims of the Malakite order.

Islam, which is Arabic for "submission to the will of God," is based on the *Qur'an* (also spelled Koran), the holy book considered God's revelation to humankind. Muslims believe that the Qur'an confirms and replaces earlier books of revelation, such as the Bible, and that the Prophet Muhammed is the last and most perfect of several prophets sent by God, including Adam, Abraham, Moses, and Jesus. Though Muslims consider Jesus a prophet, they reject the Christian belief that he is the Messiah. Muslims believe in one omnipotent God (Allah), angels, revealed books (sacred texts handed down to people from Allah), the prophets, and the Day of Judgment. Muslims also believe strongly in predetermination—sometimes interpreted as fatalism.

Muslims are expected to practice the Five Pillars of Islam: to recite the profession of faith ("There is no God but God, and Muhammed is the prophet of God"); to observe public and collective prayers five times a day; to pay a purification tax (*zakat*) to help support the poor; to abstain from food from sunup to sundown every day during the holy month of Ramadan; and to perform the *hajj,* or pilgrimage to the holy city of Mecca. The most important religious concept of Islam is the *Shari'ah,* or the Law. The Shari'ah was formulated by Muslim theologians during the eighth and ninth centuries,

and encompasses teachings that address the entire way of life as commanded by God. These include such things as dietary restrictions, sexual mores, and other matters of conduct. Though some traditional Islamic countries have adhered to a very strict interpretation of these laws, such as those requiring women to cover and veil themselves in public or punishing adultery by death, more secular Islamic countries tolerate a broader range of behaviors. Morocco has historically allowed women a degree of freedom relatively high in the Islamic world.

EMPLOYMENT AND ECONOMIC TRADITIONS

During the 1980s and 1990s, many Moroccans entered the United States to attend colleges, universities, graduate schools, and medical schools. After completing their education, some remained to begin careers in such professions as banking, engineering, computer science, medicine, architecture, journalism, research, and teaching. Other Moroccan immigrants have set up small businesses such as retail establishments or restaurants. Shops dealing in textiles (especially rugs), pottery, jewelry, and other handcrafts from Morocco have found a receptive clientele in the United States, as have restaurants featuring traditional Moroccan foods and entertainment.

POLITICS AND GOVERNMENT

Moroccan citizens enjoy universal adult suffrage and are familiar with the principles and processes of representative government. The Moroccan American community is still relatively new, however, and has not had sufficient time to develop extensive political networks or to lobby for particular legislation or programs in this country.

RELATIONS WITH MOROCCO

Many Moroccan Americans who have founded retail establishments maintain close business ties with Morocco, from which they obtain many goods for sale in the United States (these include rugs, other textiles, and crafts). Such trade is favorable to Morocco, and organizations in both Morocco and the United States facilitate increased reciprocal business between the two countries. In addition, many Moroccan Americans have close family members in Morocco and maintain frequent contact with them.

INDIVIDUAL AND GROUP CONTRIBUTIONS

Because Moroccan Americans have had such a brief history in the United States, it is not yet possible to provide a comprehensive list of their achievements in various fields. The following limited list represents only the beginning of their contributions to American culture:

LITERATURE

Ruth Knafo Setton, a Sephardic Jew born in Said, Morocco, has established herself as a significant voice in American letters. Her short fiction and essays have appeared in numerous publications. Setton has received a National Endowment for the Arts fellowship and two Pennsylvania Council of Arts fellowships. She is the author of *Suleika*, and teaches at Lafayette College. Ahimsa Timoteo Bodhran, editor of two anthologies of writing by men of color, is of mixed North African Sephardic and Arab descent. His book *Yerbabuena/Mala Yerba (All My Roots Need Rain: Mixed Blood Poetry and Prose)* is forthcoming. Born in New York City, he now lives in Oakland, California.

ORGANIZATIONS AND ASSOCIATIONS

American Moroccan Forum.
The American Moroccan Forum was established to serve the Moroccan American community. The organization maintains a website with useful links to news and other information.

Address: 4200 Cathedral Ave N.W. Suite 408, Washington, DC 20016.
Telephone: (202) 686-1171.
E-mail: Amfor@amfor.com.
Online: http://www.amfor.com.

Association of Moroccans in America.
Contact: Majid Fentas, Acting President.
Address: 1448 Boston Post Road, Larchmont, New York 10538.
Telephone: (914) 833-0329.

Friends of Morocco (FOM).
Established in 1988 with the intention of "promoting educational, cultural, charitable, social, literary and scientific exchange between Morocco and the United States of America." Maintains a "yellow pages" of organizations of interest to Moroccan Americans.

Contact: Tim Resch, President.
Address: P.O. Box 2579, Washington, DC 20013-2579.
Telephone: (703) 660-9292.
Fax: (202) 219-0509.
E-mail: tresch@worldnet.att.net.
Online: http://home.att.net/~morocco/index.htm.

Moroccan American Business Council Ltd. (MABC).
MABC was created to strengthen business ties and friendly relations between Morocco and the United States.

Contact: Ron Leavell, Executive Director.
Address: 1085 Commonwealth Ave., Boston, Massachusetts 02215.
Telephone: (617) 439-5658.
Fax: (617) 923-3725.

Moroccan American National Association (MANA).
Contact: Aziz Abbassi, President.
Address: P.O. Box 2189, Washington, DC 20013.
Telephone: (512) 258-1573.

MUSEUMS AND RESEARCH CENTERS

American Museum of Moroccan Art.
Address: P.O. Box 50472, Tucson, Arizona 85703-0472.
Telephone: (602) 529-0232
Fax: (602) 529-2791.

Moroccan Studies Society.
Contact: c/o Dr. Harvey Munson, Jr.
Address: Anthropology Dept., Stevens Hall South, University of Maine, Orono, ME 04469.

SOURCES FOR ADDITIONAL STUDY

Bibas, David. *Immigrants and the Formation of Community: A Case Study of Moroccan Jewish Immigration to America.* New York: AMS Press, 1998.

Mackie, Louise W. "The Threads of Time in Fez, Morocco." *The Magazine of the Royal Ontario Museum*. Winter 1991, pp. 18-23.

Marks, Copeland. *The Great Book of Couscous: Classic Cuisines of Morocco, Algeria and Tunisia*. New York: Primus, 1997.

Miller, Susan Gilson. "Kippur on the Amazon." *Sephardi and Middle Eastern Jewries: History and Culture*. Jewish Theological Seminary, 1996.

Pratt, Ruth Marcus. *The Sephardim of New Jersey*. Jewish Historical Society of Central New Jersey, 1992.

N AVAJOS

by
D. L. Birchfield

Because they have remained relatively isolated from the centers of European population, because they have been able to hold onto a large part of their ancestral homeland, and because of the great distances and poor roads within the region, Navajos have been more successful than most Native Americans in retaining their culture, language, and customs.

OVERVIEW

The Navajo Nation covers a territory larger than the combined states of Massachusetts, New Hampshire, and Vermont. It is the largest reservation-based Indian nation within the United States, both in land area and population. More than 200,000 Navajos live on the 24,000 square miles of the Navajo Nation. The Navajos' name for themselves is *Diné*, meaning "the people." The Spanish and Mexicans called them "Apaches de Navajo": "Navajo" is a modified Tewa word meaning "planted fields" and "Apache" is the Spanish version of the Zuñi word for "enemies." In 1969 the Navajo Tribal Council officially designated the nation the "Navajo Nation."

HISTORY

In the early nineteenth century, Navajos lived in what is now New Mexico in an area that was under Spanish colonial rule. Navajos lived too far from the colonists, who were concentrated in the upper Rio Grande Valley, to be subjected to the disruption of their lives that the Pueblos suffered at the hands of the Spanish. At times the Navajos were allied with the Spanish against other Indians, principally the Utes; other times the Spanish joined forces with the Utes and fought the Navajos. For the Navajos, the most important by-product of Spanish colonization in New Mexico was the introduction of horses and sheep; the smooth, long-staple, non-oily wool of the Spanish churro sheep would prove ideal for weaving. When the United States claimed that it had acquired an interest in Navajo land by virtue of having won a war with Mexico in 1848, the Navajos were not particularly impressed. But when the U.S. Army arrived in force at the conclusion of the American Civil War, matters took a grim turn for the Navajo. In the army's scorched-earth campaign, led by Colonel Kit Carson, the Navajo homeland was devastated. Half of the Navajos, demoralized and starving, surrendered to the army and were marched 370 miles to the Bosque Redondo concentration camp on the Pecos River, where many of them died—2,000 of them in one year alone from smallpox. After four years of imprisonment they were allowed to return to their homeland in 1868, now reduced to one-tenth its original size by treaty that same year. They began rebuilding their lives and their herds, virtually unnoticed in an area that most Americans considered worthless desert wasteland.

MODERN ERA

Modern Navajos remain in their ancestral homelands in Arizona, New Mexico, and Utah. In both the 1980 and 1990 census, Arizona and New Mexico ranked third and fourth, respectively, for the largest number of Native American residents within each state. The contemporary government of the Navajos is the Navajo Nation in Window Rock, Arizona. The Navajo Nation comprises approximately 16 million acres, mostly in northeastern Arizona, but including portions of northwestern New Mexico and southeastern Utah. It is a land of vast spaces and only a few all-weather roads. Eighty-eight percent of the reservation is without telephone service and many areas do not have electricity.

The local unit of Navajo government is called the Chapter. There are more than one hundred Chapter Houses throughout the nation, which serve as local administrative centers for geographical regions. Before the 1990 tribal elections, the tribal council system of government was reorganized into executive, legislative, and judicial branches. In 1990 Navajos elected a tribal president for the first time, rather than a tribal chairman. The tribal budget exceeds $100 million annually, with much of the revenue coming from mineral leases.

The Navajo reservation, as created by treaty in 1868, encompassed only about ten percent of the ancestral Navajo homeland. The land base soon tripled in size, largely by the addition of large blocks of land by executive orders of presidents of the United States during the late nineteenth century,

when Americans still considered most of the desert Southwest to be undesirable land. Dozens of small increments were also added by various methods until the middle of the twentieth century.

Navajos of the mid-1990s were still adjusting the boundaries of their nation, especially by trading land in an attempt to create contiguous blocks in an area called the Checkerboard, which lies along the eastern boundary of the Navajo Nation. More than 30,000 Navajos live in this 7,000 square-mile area of northwestern New Mexico. They are interspersed with Anglo and New Mexican stock raisers and involved in a nightmare of legal tangles regarding title to the land, where there are 14 different kinds of land ownership. The problems originated in the nineteenth century, when railroad companies were granted rights of way consisting of alternating sections of land. They were complicated by partial allotments of 160-acre parcels of land to some individual Navajos, the reacquisition of some parcels by the federal government as public domain land, and other factors. Crownpoint is the home of the Eastern Navajo Agency, the Navajo administrative headquarters for the Checkerboard. As recently as 1991 the Navajos were still attempting to consolidate the Checkerboard, exchanging 20,000 acres in order to achieve 80,000 acres of consolidation.

There are three isolated portions of the nation in New Mexico—satellite reservations known as the Ramah Navajo, the Cañoncito Navajo, and the Alamo Navajo. Canoncito was first settled around 1818. Ramah and Alamo had their origins in the late 1860s when some Navajos settled in these areas on their way back toward the Navajo homeland from imprisonment at the U.S. Army concentration camp at Bosque Redondo; approximately half the Navajos had been incarcerated there. Ramah is rural and is a bastion of traditional Navajo life. More than 1,500 Navajos live at Ramah, which is between the pueblos of Zuñi and Acoma, near the El Malpais National Monument. More than 1,700 Navajos live at Canoncito, which is to the east of Mt. Taylor near the pueblos of Laguna and Isleta, and more than 2,000 live at Alamo, which is south of the pueblos of Acoma and Laguna.

THE FIRST NAVAJOS IN AMERICA

Navajos and Apaches, as members of the Athapaskan language family, are generally believed to have been among the last peoples to have crossed the land bridge from Siberia to Alaska thousands of years ago during the last Ice Age. The Athapaskan language family is one of the most widely dispersed language families in North America, and most of

its members still reside in the far north in Alaska and Canada.

SETTLEMENT

It is not known, and will probably never be known, exactly when the Navajos and Apaches (Southwestern Athapaskans) began migrating from the far north to the Southwest or what route they took. Linguists who study changes in language and then estimate how long related languages have been separated have offered the year 1000 A.D. as an approximate date for the beginning of the migration. It is clear, however, that the Southwestern Athapaskan did not arrive in the Southwest until at least the end of the fourteenth century. Until that time what is now known as the Navajo homeland was inhabited by one of the most remarkable civilizations of ancient people in North America, the Ancestral Puebloans. Ancestral Puebloan ruins are among the most spectacular ruins in North America—especially their elaborate cliff dwellings, such as the ones at Mesa Verde National Park, and such communities as Chaco Canyon, where multistory stone masonry apartment buildings and large underground kivas can still be seen today.

Scholars originally thought that the arrival of the Southern Athapaskan in the Southwest was a factor in the collapse of the Ancestral Puebloan civilization. It is now known that the Ancestral Puebloans expanded to a point where they had stretched the delicate balance of existence in their fragile, arid environment to where it could not withstand the severe, prolonged droughts that occurred at the end of the fourteenth century. In all likelihood, the Ancestral Puebloans had moved close to the more dependable sources of water along the watershed of the upper Rio Grande River and had reestablished themselves as the Pueblo peoples by the time the Navajos entered the Southwest. The Navajos then claimed this empty land as their own. They first settled in what they call *Dinetah*, which means "homeland of the Diné," in the far northwestern corner of what is now New Mexico. After they acquired sheep and horses from the Spanish—which revolutionized their lives—and acquired cultural and material attributes from the Pueblos—which further enhanced their ability to adjust to the environment of the Southwest—the Navajos then spread out into all of *Diné Bikeyah*, "the Navajo country."

ACCULTURATION AND ASSIMILATION

Because they have remained relatively isolated from the centers of European population, because they have been able to hold onto a large part of their ancestral homeland, and because of the great distances and poor roads within the region, Navajos have been more successful than most Native Americans in retaining their culture, language, and customs. Until early in the twentieth century Navajos were also able to carry out their traditional way of life and support themselves with their livestock, remaining relatively unnoticed by the dominant culture. Boarding schools, the proliferation of automobiles and roads, and federal land management policies—especially regarding traditional Navajo grazing practices—have all made the reservation a different place than what it was in the late nineteenth century. As late as 1950 paved roads ended at the fringes of the reservation at Shiprock, Cameron, and Window Rock. Even wagons were not widely used until the early 1930s. By 1974, however, almost two-thirds of all Navajo households owned an automobile. Navajos are finding ways to use some changes to support traditional culture, such as the adult education program at Navajo Community College, which assists in teaching the skills that new Navajo medicine men must acquire in order to serve their communities. Bilingual education programs and broadcast and publishing programs in the Navajo language are also using the tools of change to preserve and strengthen traditional cultural values and language.

TRADITIONS, CUSTOMS, AND BELIEFS

Navajo traditional life has remained strong. In 1941 an anthropologist interviewed an entire community of several hundred Navajos and could not find even one adult over the age of 35 who had not received traditional medical care from a "singer," a Navajo medicine man called a *Hataali*. Today, when a new health care facility is built on the reservation it includes a room for the traditional practice of medicine by members of the Navajo Medicine Man's Association. Virtually all of the 3,600 Navajos who served in World War II underwent the cleansing of the Enemyway ceremony upon their return from the war. There are 24 chantway ceremonies performed by singers. Some last up to nine days and require the assistance of dozens of helpers, especially dancers.

Twelve hundred different sandpainting designs are available to the medicine men for the chantways.

Large numbers of Navajos also tend to identify themselves as Christians, with most of them mixing elements of both traditional belief and Christianity. In a 1976 survey, between 25 and 50 percent called themselves Christians, the percentage varying widely by region and gender. Twenty-five thousand Navajos belong to the Native American Church, and thousands more attend its peyote ceremonies but do not belong to the church. In the late 1960s the tribal council approved the religious use of peyote, ending 27 years of persecution. The Native American Church had originally gained a stronghold on the Ute Mountain Reservation, which adjoins the Navajo Nation on the northeast. In 1936 the church began to spread to the south into the Navajo Nation, and it grew strong among the Navajos in the 1940s.

HOLIDAYS

The premier annual events open to visitors are the Navajo Fairs. One of the largest is the Northern Navajo Fair, ordinarily held on the first weekend in October, at Shiprock, New Mexico. The dance competition powwow draws dancers from throughout the continent. Another large Navajo Fair is held annually at Window Rock, usually during the first week in July. Other Navajo fairs are also held at other times during the year. All-Indian Rodeos are also popular, as are competition powwows.

NAVAJO DANCES AND SONGS

Except for powwow competition dances and singing, most Navajo traditional dances and songs are a part of healing ceremonies, at which visitors are allowed only with the permission of the family. Photography and video or tape recording of the ceremonies are not permitted without the express authorization of the healers. Charlotte Heth of the Department of Ethnomusicology, University of California, Los Angeles, noted in a chapter of *Native America: Portrait of the Peoples*, that "Apache and Navajo song style are similar: tense, nasal voices; rhythmic pulsation; clear articulation of words in alternating sections with vocables. Both Apache Crown Dancers and Navajo Yeibichei (Night Chant) dancers wear masks and sing partially in falsetto or in voices imitating the supernaturals."

HEALTH ISSUES

The suicide rate among Navajos is 30 percent higher than the national average. Another severe problem is alcoholism. Both of these problems are exacerbated by poverty: more than half of all Navajos live below the poverty line.

Four full-service Indian hospitals are located in northwestern New Mexico. The one at Gallup is the largest in the region. The others are at Crownpoint, Shiprock, and Zuñi. In northern Arizona, full-service Indian hospitals are located at Fort Defiance, Winslow, Tuba City, and Keams Canyon. Indian Health Centers (facilities staffed by health professionals, open at least 40 hours per week, and catering to the general public) are located at Ft. Wingate and Tohatchi in northwestern New Mexico and at Greasewood, Toyei, Dilkon, Shonto, Kayenta, Many Farms, Teec Nos Pos, and Chinle in Arizona. Indian Health Stations (facilities staffed by health professionals and catering to the general public, but open only limited hours, often only one day per week) are located at Toadlena, Naschitti, Navajo, Pinedale, Pueblo Pintado, Ojo Encino, Torreon, Rincon, and Bacca in northwestern New Mexico and at Gray Mountain, Pinon, Dinnebito Dam, Red Lake, Page, Coppermine, Kaibito, Dinnehotso, Rock Point, Rough Rock, and Lukachukai in Arizona. Indian School Health Centers (facilities meeting the same criteria as Indian Health Centers, but catering primarily to school populations) are located at Crownpoint, Sanostee, and Shiprock in northwestern New Mexico and at Leupp, Tuba City, Holbrook, and Chinle in Arizona. Additionally, non-Indian hospitals are located in Flagstaff, Winslow, and Holbrook in Arizona, in Gallup, Rehoboth, Grants, and Farmington in New Mexico, in Durango and Cortez in Colorado, and in Goulding, Utah. In keeping with the recent trend throughout the United States, Navajos are now administering many of their own health care facilities, taking over their operation from the Public Health Service. The Navajo Tribal Health Authority also plans to develop an American Indian medical school at Shiprock, New Mexico.

Traditional Navajo healers are called *Hataali*, or "singers". Traditional Navajo medical practice treats the whole person, not just the illness, and is not conducted in isolation but in a ceremony that includes the patient's relatives. The ceremony can last from three to nine days depending upon the illness being treated and the ceremony to be performed. Illness to the Navajos means that there is disharmony in the universe. Proper order is restored with sand paintings in a cleansing and healing ceremony. There are approximately 1,200 designs that can be used; most can be created within the size of the average hogan floor, about six feet by six feet, though some are as large as 12 feet in diameter and some as small as one foot in diameter. The *Hataali*

may have several helpers in the creation of the intricate patterns. Dancers also assist them. In some ceremonies, such as the nine-day Yei-Bei-Chei, 15 or 16 teams of 11 members each dance throughout the night while the singer and his helpers chant prayers. When the painting is ready the patient sits in the middle of it. The singer then transforms the orderliness of the painting, symbolic of its cleanliness, goodness, and harmony, into the patient and puts the illness from the patient into the painting. The sand painting is then discarded. Many years of apprenticeship are required to learn the designs of the sand paintings and the songs that accompany them, skills that have been passed down through many generations. Most *Hataali* are able to perform only a few of the many ceremonies practiced by the Navajos, because each ceremony takes so long to learn. Sand painting is now also done for commercial purposes at public displays, but the paintings are not the same ones used in the healing rituals.

LANGUAGE

The Athapaskan language family has four branches: Northern Athapaskan; Southwestern Athapaskan; Pacific Coast Athapaskan; and Eyak, a southeast Alaska isolate. The Athapaskan language family is one of three families within the *Na-Dene* language phylum. (The other two, the Tlingit family and the Haida family, are language isolates in the far north, Tlingit in southeast Alaska, and Haida in British Columbia.) *Na-Dene* is one of the most widely distributed language phyla in North America. The Southwestern Athapaskan language, sometimes called Apachean, has seven dialects: Navajo, Western Apache, Chiricahua, Mescalero, Jicarilla, Lipan, and Kiowa-Apache. In 1987 approximately 125,000 Navajos on the reservation still spoke Navajo fluently.

FAMILY AND COMMUNITY DYNAMICS

No tribe in North America has been more vigorously studied by anthropologists than the Navajos. When a man marries, he moves into the household of the wife's extended family. The Navajos joke that a Navajo family consists of a grandmother, her married daughters and their husbands, her daughters' children, and an anthropologist. A Navajo is "born to" the mother's clan and "born for" the father's clan. The importance of clans, the membership of which is dispersed throughout the nation for each clan, has gradually diminished in favor of the increasingly important role of the Chapter House, the significance of which is based on the geographical proximity of its members. Traditional prohibitions against marrying within one's own clan are beginning to break down. The girl's puberty ceremony, her *kinaalda,* is a major event in Navajo family life. Navajos maintain strong ties with relatives, even when they leave the reservation. It is not uncommon for Navajos working in urban centers to send money home to relatives. On the reservation, an extended family may have only one wage-earning worker. Other family members busy themselves with traditional endeavors, from stock tending to weaving.

From the late 1860s until the 1960s, the local trading post was the preeminent financial and commercial institution for most Navajos, serving as a local bank (where silver and turquoise could be pawned), a post office, and a store. One of the most famous, Hubbell's Trading Post, is now a national monument. Traders served the community as interpreters, business managers, funeral directors, grave diggers, and gossip columnists. The automobile and big discount stores in the urban centers at the fringes of the nation have greatly diminished the role of the trading posts.

TRADITIONAL CRAFTS

Navajo jewelry, especially work done in silver and turquoise, is internationally famous. Navajo silversmithing dates from 1853, when a Mexican silversmith arrived at Fort Defiance in what is now Arizona. The Navajo 'Atsidi Sani learned the craft from him and taught it to others. By 1867 several Navajos were working with silver, and by 1880 they had begun to combine turquoise with their designs. At the turn of the century the Fred Harvey Company asked Navajo silversmiths to make lighter pieces for the tourist trade and guaranteed them a sales outlet. Today silversmithing is a widespread craft practiced by many Navajos.

Weaving is also an important economic activity throughout the nation. Navajo weaving has undergone many changes in designs. Navajos are continually creating new ones, and various locations within the nation have become famous for particular types of rugs and patterns. Weaving underwent a revival in the 1920s, when Chinle weavers introduced the multicolored Wide Ruins, Crystal, and Pine Springs patterns. The rug weavers auction at Crownpoint is known worldwide. The Navajo Nation owns the Navajo Nation Arts and Crafts Enterprise at Window Rock, where customers can be assured of purchasing authentic Indian crafts made by Indian people.

EDUCATION

An 1868 treaty provided for schools for Navajo children. The number of schools increased greatly after compulsory school attendance was mandated in 1887. In 1907 a Navajo headman in Utah was imprisoned without trial for a year and a half for speaking out against forced removal of local children to the Shiprock Boarding School. Others were strongly in favor of schools, especially after 19 influential Navajo headmen were exposed to the outside world at the 1893 World's Columbian Exposition in Chicago.

Until 1896 Navajo schools were operated by missionaries, who were frequently more interested in attempting to eradicate the Navajo religion, culture, and language than in educating their charges. The establishment of boarding schools far from Navajo homes, subjected Navajo children to the trauma of being removed from their families and their cultures for extended periods of time. Instruction was conducted only in English. With the secularization of the federally maintained Navajo public school system in 1896 civil servants replaced the missionaries, but lack of understanding and appreciation of Navajo culture—and instruction only in English—continued to be the norm. Some religious-affiliated schools continue to the present day, but they display a greater appreciation for Navajo culture and traditions than their nineteenth-century predecessors. By 1958, 93 percent of Navajo children were in school.

In the 1960s Navajos began to exercise much stronger management of their children's education with the establishment of community-controlled contract schools. The Rough Rock Demonstration School was the first of these schools. It introduced bilingual education for young children, the adult training of Navajo medicine men, and other innovative programs based on the perceived needs of the local community. It should be pointed out that the bilingual education introduced was, and is, to teach Navajo language, not to transition into English. This is not an additional tool of assimilation, but rather a reinforcement of traditional language and culture.

In 1969 the Navajo established Navajo Community College, the first college operated by Indians. At first located at Many Farms High School, it moved to Tsaile, Arizona, with the opening of its new campus in 1974; there is a branch campus in Shiprock, New Mexico. In 1972 the College of Ganado, a junior college in Ganado, Arizona, was incorporated as a successor to the Ganado Mission School. Following the lead of the Navajos, there are now a total of 29 Indian institutions of higher edu-

The Coalition of Navajo Liberation is a strong voice for Navajo affairs. Over 350 Navajo protestors marched on Window Rock, Arkansas to present grievances to tribal officials in 1976.

cation in the United States, all members of an American Indian higher education consortium. Navajo Community College Press is a leading native-owned academic press. A number of state supported baccalaureate institutions are located near the Navajo Nation. These include branch campuses of the University of New Mexico at Gallup and Farmington, Northern Arizona University at Flagstaff, and Ft. Lewis College in Durango, Colorado. In 1987 more than 4,000 Navajos were attending college.

EMPLOYMENT AND ECONOMIC TRADITIONS

Nearly every Navajo extended family has members who engage in silversmithing and weaving as a matter of occasional economic enterprise. Farming and stock raising are still important in the economic life of the nation. But the largest employers of Navajo people are the federal and tribal governments. The Navajos have their own parks and recreation department, fish and wildlife department, police department, educational programs, and health service, as well as many other jobs in tribal government and administration. Many federal agencies have offices either on or near the reservation. Other Navajos are employed at the tribally operated electronics plant at Fort Defiance, Arizona, and at the Navajo Forest Products Industry, an $11 million sawmill also run by the tribe. It is located at Navajo, New Mexico, the only industrial town on the reservation, which was created and planned to serve the needs of its industry.

Until the early twentieth century Navajos were able to continue deriving their livelihood from their traditional practices of stockraising. Since the 1920s fewer and fewer Navajos have been able to maintain themselves in this manner. Chronic high rates of unemployment and dependency on governmental assistance have gradually replaced the traditional way of life. In 1941 Navajos had earned only $150,000 from industry, but World War II was a boom time for the economy, giving the Navajos a taste for money and what it could buy. More than half the Navajos 19 and older had wartime jobs; in 1943 they earned $5 million. After the war in the late 1940s the annual family income averaged $400.

By 1973 a study released by the Navajo Office of Program Development found that only 20,000 people were employed on the reservation, of which 71 percent were Navajos. Nine communities were found to account for 84 percent of the jobs held by Navajo people: Shiprock, 3,616; Chinle, 2,284; Window Rock, 2,100; Ft. Defiance, 1,925; Tuba City, 1,762; Crownpoint, 1,149; Navajo, 697; Kayenta, 571; and Ganado, 311. Public service jobs—health, education, and government—were found to account for nearly three-fourths of all employment on the reservation. In 1975 the Navajo unemployment rate was 67 percent. Median Navajo annual household income declined during the 1970s, standing at $2,520 in 1979. In 1991 the unemployment rate was 36 percent and remained at about that level in 1999.

Since the late 1960s, developing projects have been diversifying employment within the Navajo

Nation. The Navajo Indian Irrigation Project (NIIP) is projected to irrigate 110,000 acres of cropland from water impounded in the upper San Juan River basin, using open canals, pipelines, lift stations, and overhead sprinkler systems. The Navajo Agricultural Products Industry (NAPI), a tribal enterprise, manages the program. It includes agribusiness plant sites, grazing lands and a feedlot for cattle production, and an experimental research station. Instituted by act of Congress in 1962, the first 10,000 acres were brought into irrigation in 1976, producing crops of barley and cabbage. By 1981 the total irrigated acreage had increased to 40,000 acres, and crop diversification had added alfalfa, pinto beans, corn, and milo. In 1982 a cattle feedlot operation began to make use of grain and forage crop production. NAPI showed its first profit in 1986. By 1991 more than half of the projected acreage had been brought under irrigation. A coal-gasification plant near Burnham and Navajo-Exxon uranium leases, along with the irrigation project, are making northwestern New Mexico and the eastern portion of the Navajo reservation the focus of new economic activity. Uranium mining, however, has produced health risks, including alarmingly high rates of cancer. In 1979 a broken tailings dam belonging to United Nuclear Corporation at Church Rock, New Mexico, discharged 100 million gallons of radioactive water into the Puerco River—the largest release of radioactivity in United States history.

Because of their legal status, Navajo businesspeople must deal with state and federal agencies as well as Navajo officials and must pay both state and Navajo taxes. In addition, complicated paperwork requirements for obtaining business licenses and land leases for businesses hamper start-up. IINA (which means "life" in Navajo), an initiative started by Navajo Duane "Chili" Yazzi, is currently underway, and is aimed at reducing red tape by delegating control to local tribal chapters. Another objective is to use part of the nation's assets, some $1.2 billion, as venture capital for Navajo entrepreneurs.

The Navajo people's biggest economic ventures have been coal leases. By 1970 the Navajo Nation had the largest coal mine in the world. The 1964 and 1966 Black Mesa coal leases to Peabody Coal Company have become a source of controversy within the nation, as more and more Navajos decry the scouring of their land, the displacement of families for the sake of mining activity, and the threat to sacred places posed by mining operations.

Little has been done to develop tourism, despite its potential as a source of income. Only four motels exist on the reservation, in contrast with neighboring Gallup, New Mexico, which has more than 35. The Navajo Nation maintains four campgrounds: Monument Valley, Four Corners, Tsaile South Shore south of Lukachukai, and Little Colorado River. Other economic ventures under way include shopping centers and motels. Hunting and fishing provide economic activity and jobs in the portion of the reservation lying in northwestern New Mexico, where 16 lakes offer fishing for trout, channel catfish, bass, northern pike, and bluegill. Hunting permits may be obtained for deer, turkey, bear, and small game.

POLITICS AND GOVERNMENT

The basic unit of local government in the Navajo Nation is the Chapter, each with its own Chapter House. The Chapter system was created in 1922 as a means of addressing agricultural problems at a local level. Before the 1920s, the nation had no centrally organized tribal government. Like many other Indian nations, the tribe was forced to create a central authority by the United States. For the Navajos, the seminal event was the discovery of oil on the reservation in 1921, after which the United States desired some centralized governmental authority for the Navajos for the purpose of executing oil leases, largely for the benefit of non-Navajos. At first the Bureau of Indian Affairs appointed three Navajos to execute mineral leases. In 1923 this arrangement gave way to a plan for each of several Navajo agencies to provide representatives for the Navajo government. After World War II the Navajo Tribal Council became recognized as the Navajo government.

MILITARY

Navajos have served with distinction in the armed forces of the United States in every war in the twentieth century, including World War I, even though they—and other reservation Indians—did not become citizens of the United States until citizenship was extended to them by an act of Congress in 1924. Their most heralded service, however, came during World War II in the U.S. Marine Corps, when they employed the Navajo language for military communication in the field as the Marines stormed Japanese-held islands in the Pacific. They have become known to posterity as the Navajo Code Talkers.

Philip Johnson, born to missionaries and raised on the Navajo reservation, is credited with a leading role in the formation of the Navajo Code Talkers. As a child he learned fluent Navajo, as well as Navajo culture and traditions. At the age of nine he served as interpreter for a Navajo delegation that traveled to Washington, D.C., to present Navajo grievances to President Theodore Roosevelt. After serving in World War I, Johnson was a civil engineer in California. When war broke out with Japan in 1941, Johnson learned that the military hoped to develop a code using American Indians as signalmen. He met with Marine Corps and Army Signal Corps officers and arranged a demonstration of Navajo as a code language. The demonstration took place on February 28, 1942, at Camp Elliott with the cooperation of four Navajos from Los Angeles and one who was in the Navy in San Diego.

Within a year the Marine Corps authorized the program, which at first was classified as top secret. Johnson, though over age, was allowed to enlist in the Corps and was assigned to help supervise the establishment of the program at Camp Pendleton in Oceanside, California. In May 1942 the Marine Corps, with the approval of the Navajo Tribal Council, began recruiting Navajo men at Window Rock, Arizona, for the program. The first group to receive training consisted of 29 Navajos who underwent basic boot camp training at the San Diego Marine Corps Recruit Depot. They were then sent for four weeks to the Field Signal Battalion Training Center at Camp Pendleton, where they received 176 hours of instruction in basic communications procedures and equipment. They were later deployed to Guadalcanal, where their use of the Navajo language for radio communication in the field proved so effective that recruitment for the program was expanded. Eventually, approximately 400 Navajo Code Talkers saw duty in the Pacific in the Marine Corps. By the end of the war they had been assigned to all six Marine divisions in the Pacific and had taken part in every assault—from Guadalcanal in 1943 to Okinawa in 1945. Today the surviving Navajo Code Talkers maintain an active veterans' organization. In 1969, at the Fourth Marine Division Association reunion in Chicago, they were presented with a medallion specially minted in commemoration of their services.

RELATIONS WITH THE UNITED STATES

Much friction has resulted between the Navajos and the United States over the management of Navajo livestock grazing. The original Navajo Reservation in 1868 encompassed only a small portion of the ancestral Navajo rangelands. The size of the reservation tripled between 1868 and the mid-1930s by 14 additions of blocks of land from 1878 to 1934. This would give the appearance of a rapidly expanding amount of rangeland available to the Navajos. In fact, just the opposite was true.

When the Navajos returned to their homeland from the Bosque Redondo in 1869, the government issued them 1,000 goats and 14,000 sheep to begin replacing the herds that the U.S. Army and New Mexico militia had either slaughtered or confiscated. In 1870 the Navajos were issued an additional 10,000 sheep. With practically no Anglo encroachment on their ancestral rangeland, reservation boundaries had little meaning. The Navajos spread out over their old estate and their herds began increasing. The Bureau of Indian Affairs forbade the selling of breeding stock, eager to see the Navajos regain self-sufficiency. The Navajo population increased steadily, from an estimated 10,000 to 12,000 in 1868 to nearly 40,000 by 1930, and their herds increased accordingly, though there were large fluctuations in the numbers year by year due to occasional drought and disease. At the same time the appropriation of the ancestral rangelands outside the reservation boundaries by Anglo cattle operations and other interests had accelerated, forc-

"**O**n the wind-beaten plains once lived my ancestors. / In the days of peaceful moods, / they wandered and hunted.... / Now, from the wind-beaten plains, only their dust rises."

From the poem "Ancestors" by Grey Cohoe, on the rising consciousness of the American Indian.

ing the Navajos onto an ever smaller amount of range. By the 1920s a serious soil erosion problem on the reservation was being blamed on overgrazing. The Navajos tried to alleviate the problem by seeking more land and renewed access to the ancestral rangelands from which they had gradually been forced off. The United States believed that a solution to the problem was to force Navajo livestock reductions by killing the animals it deemed to be unnecessary. Thus began a 20-year conflict between the Navajos and the United States, in which the U.S. government, in attempting to implement its policies, found itself disrupting traditional Navajo economic, social, and political life to a far greater extent than at any time in the past.

The tool of the government in this matter was the creation of land management districts, first established in 1936 and adjusted to their preset boundaries in 1955. In attempting to change Navajo livestock practices, the U.S. government subverted and altered Navajo culture in the process. Today the federal land management districts on the reservation are still important factors in Navajo livestock practices. The grazing committees of the Navajo Chapter Houses must work closely with the districts to set the herd size for each range. The extreme turmoil that the stock reduction crisis caused in traditional Navajo life—and the tactics used by the U.S. government to subvert traditional Navajo culture and government during the height of the crisis in the 1930s and 1940s—are the subject of an extensive, detailed study by Richard White, *The Roots of Dependency: Subsistence, Environment, and Social Change Among the Choctaws, Pawnees, and Navajos.*

Indians in Arizona and New Mexico were not allowed to vote in state and national elections until 1948. In 1957 Utah finally allowed Indians living on reservations to vote—the last remaining state to do so. It required a 1976 U.S. Supreme Court ruling to force Apache County, Arizona, where the population was 70 percent Navajo, to allow Navajos to serve on its board of supervisors. As of 1984 no Native American had ever been elected to public office in Utah. In that year the U.S. Department of Justice ordered San Juan County, Utah, where the population was 50 percent Navajo, to redistrict. The next year a Navajo was elected county commissioner.

The most divisive issue among the Navajos in recent years, and the cause of the greatest strain in relations with the United States, has been the so-called "Navajo-Hopi Land Dispute," in which thousands of Navajos have been forced to relocate from lands that were jointly held by the two tribes since 1882. Many prominent Navajos and some prominent Hopis believe that the relocation of the Navajos and the division of the 1882 Joint Use Area has been undertaken by the U.S. government for the benefit of the American extraction industry, so that valuable mineral deposits within the area can be strip-mined.

INDIVIDUAL AND GROUP CONTRIBUTIONS

ACADEMIA

Among the first Navajos to earn a Ph.D., Ned Hatathli (1923-1972) was the first president of the Navajo Community College—the first college owned and operated by the Navajo people. Annie Dodge Wauneka (1910–) is a public health educator responsible for largely eliminating tuberculosis among the Navajo Indians. Wauneka was later elected to the Navajo Tribal Council and was the first Native American to receive the Presidential Medal of Freedom. Peterson Zah (1937–) is an edu-

cator and leader who has devoted his life to serving the Navajo people and retaining Navajo culture, especially among young people. In 1990 Zah was elected the first president of the Navajo people; he was later awarded the Humanitarian Award from the City of Albuquerque and an honorary doctorate from Santa Fe College.

ART

Harrison Begay (1917–) is one of the most famous of all Navajo painters. Noted for their sinuous delicacy of line, meticulous detail, restrained palette, and elegance of composition, his watercolors and silkscreen prints have won 13 major awards. Carl Nelson Gorman (1907–) is a prominent Navajo artist whose oil paintings and silk screening have won acclaim for their divergence from traditional Indian art forms. His contributions to Navajo and Native American art and culture inspired the dedication of the Carl Gorman Museum at Tecumseh Center at the University of California at Davis. Rudolpf Carl Gorman (1931–) is one of the most prominent contemporary Native American artists of the twentieth century. His art combines the traditional with the nontraditional in style and form.

LITERATURE

Navajo author Vee Browne has achieved national recognition with her retellings of Navajo creation stories. Her books have included *Monster Slayer* and *Monster Birds,* a children's biography of Osage international ballet star Maria Tallchief, and a volume in a new series of Native American animal stories from Scholastic books. Her honors include the prestigious Western Heritage Award from the Cowboy Hall of Fame and Western Heritage Center in 1990. A guidance counselor by training, Browne is active in helping emerging Native American writers hone their skills and find outlets for their work, serving as a mentor in the Wordcraft Circle of Native American Mentor and Apprentice Writers. She has also served on the 1994-1996 National Advisory Caucus for Wordcraft Circle.

Elizabeth Woody (1959–), born on the Navajo Nation but raised mostly in the Pacific Northwest, has been influenced by the Pacific Northwest tribes as well as her Navajo heritage. She returned to the Southwest to study poetry and art at the Institute of American Indian Arts in Santa Fe, New Mexico. Her first volume of poetry, *Hand Into Stone,* published in 1988, won the American Book Award. Her other books include *Luminaries of the Humble* and *Seven Hands, Seven Hearts.* Woody's poetry has been anthologized in *Returning the Gift* and *Durable Breath*; her short fiction, "Home Cooking," has been anthologized in *Talking Leaves*; her nonfiction, "Warm Springs," has been anthologized in *Native America*. Woody now teaches at the Institute of American Indian Arts. Her illustrations can be found in Sherman Alexie's *Old Shirts & New Skins*, and her art has been the subject of a five-week exhibit at the Tula Foundation Gallery in Atlanta, Georgia.

Actress/writer Geraldine Keams has appeared in several films, including *The Outlaw Josey Wales*, and has been published in *Sun Tracks* and *The Remembered Earth*. Jean Natoni has published her work in *The Remembered Earth*, as have Aaron Yava, a Navajo/Hopi, and Genevieve Yazzie. Yava's drawing have appeared in *Border Towns of the Navajo Nation*, *Man to Send Rain Clouds*, and *A Good Journey*. Yazzie's work is also featured in *New America*, and she worked on the Navajo-English dictionary project.

Rex Jim, a highly regarded medicine man, is the first author to have published a volume of poetry in Navajo, with no translation, with a major university press (*Ahi'Ni'Nikisheegiizh*, Princeton University Press). Jim's fiction and nonfiction have also been published by Rock Point Community School in the Navajo Nation and include such works as "Naakaiiahgoo Tazhdiya" and "Living from Livestock."

Laura Tohe's volume of poetry, *Making Friends with Water*, was published by Nosila Press, and her poetry and nonfiction have appeared in such publications as *Nebraska Humanities*, *Blue Mesa Review*, and *Platte Valley Review*. Tohe received her Ph.D. in English literature from the University of Nebraska and teaches at the University of Arizona. Tohe's latest project is a children's play for the Omaha Emmy Gifford Children's theater. Like Vee Browne, Tohe is a mentor in the Wordcraft Circle program and is also a member of its 1994-1996 National Advisory Caucus.

Lucy Tapahonso (1953–) is the author of four books of poetry, including *Saanii Dahataa*. She is an assistant professor at the University of Kansas at Lawrence. Della Frank lives and works on the Navajo Nation. Her poetry has appeared in such publications as *Blue Mesa Review* and *Studies in American Indian Literature* and has been anthologized in *Neon Powwow* and *Returning the Gift*. She is co-author of *Duststorms: Poems From Two Navajo Women*. Rachael Arviso (Navajo and Zuñi) lives and works on the Navajo Reservation; her short fiction has been anthologized in *Neon Powwow*. Esther G. Belini's poetry also appeared in *Neon Powwow*; she received her B.A. degree from the University of California at Berkeley.

Other Navajos whose work has been anthologized in *Neon Powwow* include Dan L. Crank, Nancy Maryboy, Irvin Morris, Patroclus Eugene Savino, Brent Toadlena, Gertrude Walters, and Floyd D. Yazzie. Aaron Carr (Navajo and Laguna Pueblo) has published poetry and short stories in *The Remembered Earth* anthology, in *Sun Tracks*, and in *Planet Quarterly*. Bernadette Chato's work has appeared in *New America* and *The Remembered Earth*. Grey Cohoe's work has appeared in several anthologies, including *Whispering Wind*, *The Remembered Earth*, and *The American Indian Speaks*. Larry Emerson's column "Red Dawn" appeared in a number of Indian newspapers, and his work has been anthologized in *New America* and *The Remembered Earth*. Nia Francisco, who has taught at the Navajo Community College, has been published in *Southwest: A Contemporary Anthology*, *College English*, *The Remembered Earth*, *Cafe Solo*, *New America*, and *Southwest Women's Poetry Exchange*.

SCIENCE

Nuclear physicist and educator Fred Begay (1932–) has served as a member of the technical staff at the Los Alamos National Laboratory since 1971. His research is directed primarily toward the use of laser, electron, and ion beams to demonstrate the application of thermonuclear fusion; this technique will provide future economical and environmentally safe and clean power sources.

MEDIA

PRINT

Bear Track.
Address: 1202 West Thomas Road, Phoenix, Arizona 85013.

Diné Baa-Hani'.
Address: Box 527, Ft. Defiance, Arizona 86504.

Dinehligai News.
Address: P.O. Box 1835, Tuba City, Arizona 86045.

DNA in Action.
Address: DNA Legal Services, Window Rock, Arizona 86515.

Four Directions.
Address: 1812 Las Lomas N.E., Albuquerque, New Mexico 87131.

Indian Arizona.
Address: 4560 North 19th Avenue, Suite 200, Phoenix, Arizona 85015-4113.

Kachina Messenger.
Address: P.O. Box 1210, Gallup, New Mexico 87301.

Navajo.
Covers history, art, culture, events, and people relevant to the Navajo Indians.

Contact: Michael Benson, Editor.
Address: Box 1245, Window Rock, Arizona 86515.
Telephone: (602) 729-2233.

Navajo Assistance.
Address: P.O. Box 96, Gallup, New Mexico 87301.

Navajo-Hopi Observer.
Weekly newspaper in English. Founded in 1981.

Contact: Jay Lape, Publisher; Tanya Lee, Editor.
Address: 2608 North Stevens Boulevard, Flagstaff, Arizona 86004.
Telephone: (520) 526-3115.
E-mail: observer@infomagic.com.
Online: http://www.navajohopiobserver.com.

Navajo Nation Enquiry.
Address: P.O. Box 490, Window Rock, Arizona 86515.

Navajo Times.
Weekly newspaper that contains articles of interest to the American Indian community and the Navajo people.

Contact: Tom Arviso Jr., Editor.
Address: P.O. Box 310, Window Rock, Arizona 86515-0310.
Telephone: (602) 871-6641.
Fax: (602) 871-6409.

Tsa'aszi'.
Address: P.O. Box 12, Pine Hill, New Mexico 87321.

Uts'ittisctaan'i.
Address: Northern Arizona University, Campus Box 5630, Flagstaff, Arizona 86011.

RADIO

The following radio stations are owned by the Navajo Broadcasting Company: KDJI-AM (1270); KZUA-FM (92.1); KTNN-AM (660); KNMI-FM (88.9); KPCL-FM (95.7); KABR-AM (1500); and KTDB-FM (89.7).

TELEVISION

KOBF-TV (Channel 12).
Broadcasts "Voice of the Navajo" on Sunday mornings.

Address: 825 W. Broadway, Box 1620, Farmington, New Mexico 87401.
Telephone: (505) 326-1141.
Fax: (505) 327-5196.
E-mail: shkobf@cyberport.com.

ORGANIZATIONS AND ASSOCIATIONS

Arizona Commission for Indian Affairs.
Contact: Eleanor Descheeny-Joe, Executive Director
Address: 1400 West Washington, Suite 300, Phoenix, Arizona 85007.
Telephone: (602) 542-3123.
Fax: (602) 542-3223.

Diné CARE Citizens Against Ruining our Environment.
Environmental activism group.

Address: 10A Town Plaza, Suite 138, Durango, Colorado 81301.
Telephone: (970) 259-0199.

Navajo Code Talkers Association.
Contact: Dr. Samuel Billison, President.
Address: 1182, Window Rock, Arizona 86515-1182.
Telephone: (520) 871-5468.

Navajo Nation.
Address: P.O. Box 308, Window Rock, Arizona 86515.
Telephone: (602) 871-6352.
Fax: (602) 871-4025.
Online: http://www.navajo.org.

Navajo Tourism Office.
Address: P.O. Box 663, Window Rock, Arizona 86515.

Telephone: (602) 871-6436.
Fax: (602) 871-7381.

Navajo Way, Inc.
United Way for the Navajo Nation.

Address: P.O. Box 309, Window Rock,
Arizona 86515.
Telephone: (520) 871-6661.
Fax: (520) 871-6663.

New Mexico Commission on Indian Affairs.
Address: 330 East Palace Avenue, Santa Fe,
New Mexico 87501.

New Mexico Indian Advisory Commission.
Address: Box 1667, Albuquerque,
New Mexico 87107.

Tseyi Heritage Culture Center.
Contact: Jim Claw Sr., President.
Address: P.O. Box 1952, Chinle, Navajo Nation,
Arizona 86503.
Telephone: (520) 674-5664.
Fax: (520) 674-5944.
Online: http://www.navajoland.com/nn/Tseyi/.

MUSEUMS AND RESEARCH CENTERS

Albuquerque Museum and Maxwell Museum in Albuquerque, New Mexico; American Research Museum, Ethnology Museum, Fine Arts Museum, Hall of the Modern Indian, Institute of American Indian Arts, and Navajo Ceremonial Arts Museum in Santa Fe, New Mexico; Art Center in Roswell, New Mexico; Black Water Draw Museum in Portales, New Mexico; Coronado Monument in Bernalillo, New Mexico; Hubbell Trading Post National Historic Site in Ganado, Arizona; Heard Museum of Anthropology in Phoenix, Arizona; Milicent Rogers Museum in Taos, New Mexico; Navajo National Monument in Tonalea, Arizona; Navajo Tribal Museum in Window Rock, Arizona; Northern Arizona Museum in Flagstaff; and the State Museum of Arizona in Tempe.

SOURCES FOR ADDITIONAL STUDY

Bailey, Garrick, and Roberta Glenn Bailey. *A History of the Navajos: The Reservation Years*. Santa Fe, New Mexico: School of American Research Press, 1986.

Benedek, Emily. *The Wind Won't Know Me: A History of the Navajo-Hopi Land Dispute*. New York: Alfred A. Knopf, 1992.

Correll, J. Lee. *Through White Men's Eyes: A Contribution to Navajo History (A Chronological Record of the Navajo People from Earliest Times to the Treaty of June 1, 1968)*, six volumes. Window Rock, Arizona: Navajo Heritage Center, 1979.

Forbes, Jack D. *Apache, Navaho, and Spaniard*. Norman: University of Oklahoma Press, 1969; with new introduction, 1994.

Goodman, James M. *The Navajo Atlas: Environments, Resources, People, and History of the Dine Bikeyah*, drawings and cartographic assistance by Mary E. Goodman. Norman: University of Oklahoma Press, 1982.

Iverson, Peter. *The Navajos: A Critical Bibliography*. Bloomington: Indiana University Press, 1976.

Navajo History, Vol. 1, edited by Ethelou Yazzie. Many Farms, Arizona: Navajo Community College Press for the Navajo Curriculum Center, Rough Rock Demonstration School, 1971.

Navajo: Walking in Beauty. San Francisco: Chronicle Books, 1994.

Simonelli, Jeanne M. *Crossing Between Worlds: The Navajos of Canyon De Chelly*. Santa Fe, NM: School of American Research Press, 1997.

Thompson, Gerald. *The Army and the Navajo*. Tucson: University of Arizona Press, 1976.

Trimble, Stephen. *The People: Indians of the American Southwest*. Santa Fe, New Mexico: Sar Press, 1993.

Warriors: Navajo Code Talkers, photographs by Kenji Kawano, foreword by Carl Gorman, introduction by Benis M. Frank. Flagstaff, Arizona: Northland Publishing, 1990.

White, Richard. *The Roots of Dependency: Subsistence, Environment, and Social Change Among the Choctaws, Pawnees, and Navajos*. Lincoln: University of Nebraska Press, 1983.

NEPALESE AMERICANS

by
Olivia Miller

OVERVIEW

The Kingdom of Nepal is a landlocked country in southern Asia. It occupies an area of 56,136 square miles and is roughly the size of Tennessee. Located between China and India, Nepal is known for its majestic Himalayas and is the home of Mount Everest and Annapurna. Nepal is also the birthplace of Buddha and is the only official Hindu kingdom in the world. The national capital is Kathmandu.

Nepal has a population of over 23.6 million people. It is one of the poorest and least developed countries in the world, with more than half of its population living below the poverty line. Nepal has 60 ethnic groups, 11 major languages and 70 dialects. Caste and ethnicity are often used interchangeably. The major ethnic groups include Newars, Indians, Tibetans, Gurungs, Magars, Tamangs, Bhotias, Rais, Limbus, and Sherpas. The Rai make up 64 percent of the population; the Singsawa (Bhotias), 18 percent; the Sherpa, eight percent; the Brahmin and the Chhetri, four percent; and other ethnic/caste groups, six percent. Nepali is the official language, but Rai and Tibetan are also spoken. Ninety percent of the population is Hindu, five percent is Buddhist, three percent is Muslim, and two percent are listed as "other." The country's flag is red with a blue border around the unique shape of two overlapping right triangles; the smaller, upper triangle bears a white stylized moon and the larger, lower triangle bears a white 12-

pointed sun. Nepal is governed by a constitutional monarchy, with a judicial system that blends Hindu and Western legal traditions. Nepal was admitted to the United Nations in 1955.

HISTORY

Nepal has been a kingdom for at least 1,500 years and its history has been shaped by Tibetan, Chinese, India, and British influences. In 563 B.C., Siddhartha Gautama, a prince who rejected the world to search for the meaning of existence and became known as the Buddha, or the Enlightened One, was born in Nepal. Since the fourth century, the Nepalese civilization has been based on Buddhism and Hinduism. In the late fifth century, rulers calling themselves *Licchavis* recorded details concerning the politics, society, and economics of Nepal. The Licchavis ruled from the fourth to the eighth century, and the Malla kings ruled from the twelfth to the eighteenth century. In the sixteenth century, there were dozens of kingdoms throughout the Himalayan region. Gorkha, a small kingdom, conquered and united the entire nation in the late eighteenth century. The armies of Nepal conquered territories far to the west and east and challenged the Chinese in Tibet and the British in India. The Anglo-Nepalese War (1814-1816) was disastrous for Nepal. According to the Treaty of Sagauli, which was signed in 1816, Nepal lost its territories west of the Kali River and most of its lands in the Tarai. By the 1850s, a dynasty of prime ministers known as the *Rana* created a dictatorship that lasted 100 years, during which Nepal remained a primitive nation with little interest in modern science or technology.

MODERN ERA

In the mid-nineteenth century, Nepal's prime ministers usurped complete control of the government and reduced the kings to puppets. Following a revolt that overthrew the Ranas in 1950, Nepal struggled to overcome its long legacy of underdevelopment and to incorporate its varied ethnic populations into a single nation. During the rule of the Ranas, only two percent of the adult population was literate, the infant mortality rate was more than 60 percent, and average life expectancy was only 35 years. Less than one percent of the population was engaged in modern industrial occupations, and 85 percent of employment and income came from agriculture. The entire nation had approximately 100 kilometers of railroad tracks and a few kilometers of paved roads. Telephones, electricity, and postal services served only one percent of the population. Government expenditures were focused solely on salaries and benefits for the army, the police, and civil servants. Health and education received less than one percent of the government's expenditures. The nation still contained autonomous principalities (*rajya*), based on deals with former local kings, and landlords acted as small dictators on their own lands.

Between November 1951 and February 1959, a succession of short-lived governments ruled under an interim constitution or under the direct command of the king. In 1959, Nepal held the first national elections in its history. Nepal has two legislative houses: an Upper House (*Maha Sabha*) of 36 members, half elected by the lower house and half nominated by the king; and a Lower House (*Pratinidhi Sabha*) of 109 members, all elected by universal adult suffrage. The leader of the majority party in the Lower House is named prime minister and governs with a cabinet of ministers. The king is allowed to act without consulting the prime minister and has the power to dismiss him. The king also conducts foreign affairs and controls the army. He also has the power to suspend all or part of the constitution and can declare a state of emergency.

In 1960, the Nepalese government established diplomatic relations with the United States, the Soviet Union, China, France, and Pakistan. On December 15, 1960, the king used his emergency powers to dismiss the cabinet and arrest its leaders. This move effectively ended Nepal's experiment with liberal socialism and democracy. Pro-democracy movements in Eastern Europe during the early 1990s led to the formation of the Movement for the Restoration of Democracy in Nepal, and the ban on political parties was lifted. During 1994 and 1995, political turmoil halted democratic reforms. Today, the Nepalese Congress and the United Marxists/Leninists are the two main parties in the government. However, the king reserves the right to name one-fifth of the members of the legislature, and Nepal continues to have a strong monarchy.

THE FIRST NEPALESE IN AMERICA

The first Nepalese to enter the United States were classified as "other Asian." Immigration records show that between 1881 and 1890 1,910 "other Asians" were admitted to the United States. However, it is not likely that many of these were from Nepal. The first time that the Nepalese were classified as a separate group occurred in 1975, when 56 Nepalese immigrated to the United States. The number of immigrants from Nepal remained below 100 per year through 1996.

SIGNIFICANT IMMIGRATION WAVES

Nepalese people make up only a small number of the United States' immigrant population. For example, in 1995 only 55 Nepalese became American citizens and 312 received lawful permanent-resident status. Only 686 Nepalese entered the United States on student visas in 1996. In 1998, 226 Nepalese were winners in the DV-99 diversity lottery. The diversity lottery is conducted under the terms of Section 203(c) of the Immigration and Nationality Act and makes available 50,000 permanent resident visas annually to persons from countries with low rates of immigration to the United States.

"Their culture and Tibetan Buddhist religion have long attracted intense interest in the United States. 'I think Americans have always been interested in the Tibetan peoples – you know, the land of Shangri-La,' said Dawa Tsering, the United States representatives of the Dalai Lama. 'But the 'Everest' film and the recent books, and movies like 'Kundun' and 'Sevens Year in Tibet,' have created a new wave of interest in the culture and traditions.'"

Glenn Collins, *Looking for a Sherpa in Nepal? Try New York,* (New York Times, April 3, 1998).

SETTLEMENT PATTERNS

According to the 1990 U.S. Census, there were 2,616 Americans with Nepalese ancestry. Fewer than 100 Nepalese immigrants become U.S. citizens each year, but the number of Nepalese who become legal residents has grown steadily from 78 in 1987 to 431 in 1996. Significant communities of Nepalese Americans exist in large metropolitan areas such as New York, Boston, Chicago, Denver, Dallas, Portland, Gainesville, and St. Paul. Sizable numbers also live in various cities of California.

ACCULTURATION AND ASSIMILATION

Many Nepalese immigrate to the United States in search of educational and employment opportunities. Because of Nepal's inadequate educational system, wealthy Nepalese send their children to the West for schooling. Many Nepalese students apply for work permits and eventually become citizens of the United States. However, acclimation to life in the United States is often a difficult process. This process was illustrated in *Ista-Mitra* or "Relative-Friends," the first Nepalese feature film produced in the United States. Produced in 1999 by writer and

director Hari Siwakoti, the film chronicles Siwakoti's life from his arrival in America through the assimilation process. Siwakoti described the Nepalese immigrant experience as difficult. "The Nepali culture helps each other," he said. "This is a different culture, a different life."

Second-generation Nepalese Americans continue their family's religious heritage. They often embrace and interpret American culture through the filter of family beliefs and traditions. For example, a recent paper by Mr. Rajan Rajbhandari, a second-generation Nepalese American and a consultant software engineer in Chicago, compared Hindu mythology to that in the movie series *Star Wars*.

TRADITIONS, CUSTOMS, AND BELIEFS

Many Nepalese customs and beliefs are heavily influenced by Buddhist or Hindu values. Many Nepalese American women continue to wear the *Tika*, a red sandalwood dot pasted on the forehead, as an indication of marriage. Although most Nepalese eat with their right hand, Nepalese American diners have adopted silverware. In Nepal, many people believe that metal spoons ruin the flavor of food and make a person thinner. Food may be served in a *thaali*, a metal plate divided into separate compartments.

PROVERBS

Just as there are many different cultures and tribes within the Nepalese population, there are also various proverbs, including the following: The crow does not care for the cow's wound; You don't get smoke without a fire; A person with money has no wisdom and a person with wisdom has no money; The discontented are always unhappy and the contented are always happy; The person who works does not get credit; The country you hear about is always nice, and the country you live in is unhappy; You may talk about everything, but don't talk about your household; No one sees the cat stealing the milk, but everyone sees the cat get beaten; Even a monkey can dance if he is taught; A barking dog never bites; and A dog can't fight with a group of monkeys.

CUISINE

Like Indian food, Nepalese food is full of spice and flavor. The Nepalese use spices such as cumin, chili, turmeric, fennel, fenugreek, mustard seed, coriander, and the mixed-spice masala. *Besaar,* a bright orange spice, gives Nepalese curries their characteristic golden tint. Mustard oil is used for cooking, as well as for oil lamps, temple offerings, and massage. Food is fried in mustard oil and liberally seasoned with garlic, onions, and fresh ginger. Authentic Nepalese food is not overwhelmingly spicy, but it does have a definite flavor of *koorsani,* or chili pepper.

The national dish of Nepal is *daal bhaat,* which consists of boiled rice (*bhaat* with a thin lentil sauce (*daal*), accompanied by curried vegetables (*tarkaari*) and a pungent pickle (*achaar*). Daal bhaat is eaten twice a day in the rice-growing regions of Nepal. The first meal is served around 10:30 a.m. and the second shortly after sunset.

Roasted flour, known as *sattu* or *tsampa* is a staple food made from local grains: maize, wheat, millet, barley, or buckwheat. Sweet, milky tea, beaten or popped rice, flat bread, or curried potatoes are popular snack foods.

Regional foods within Nepal are distinct. The principal food of most hill families is *dhiro,* a cooked mush of maize or millet flour. It can be eaten alone, with fried vegetables, or with a thin soup. The staple food among the highland Bhotia people is Tibetan *tsampa,* which is ground roasted barley flour. In highland mountain regions like the Sherpa homeland of Khumbu, the main dish is boiled potatoes, peeled and eaten with salt and a relish of pounded chilis and garlic. Sherpa women often make *rigi kur,* delicious crispy potato pancakes served with yak butter.

Chiura is made by pounding soaked, uncooked rice. It is served with yogurt, vegetable curry, and fried meat (*chuela*) at Newar ritual feasts. *Bhuja,* or popped rice, resemble puffed rice crisps, and are popped in a pan. Other favorite snacks include curried potatoes (*alu daam*), dried peas in sauce (*kerau*), chewy dried meat (*sukuti*), and deep-fried triangular dumplings (*samosa*). Breads vary from fried rings of rice-flour (*sel roti*), to Gurung corn cakes, to the Indian flat, thin wheat-flour disks (*chapaati*) and the smaller, fried *puri.* Yogurt, called "curd," has a smoky taste from the wood fire it is cooked on. Bhaktapur's thick, creamy *juju dahu,* or "King of Curd," is known as the best. *Chhurpi* is a cheese made from the solids of mahi or yogurt, which is dried in the sun and then cut into squares and strung on cords of yak hair. The chhurpi is very hard when it is first made, but slowly softens when boiled in a soup or stew.

MUSIC

Nepalese music combines whimsical and rhythmical sounds of melodies with a characteristic sharp twang. Traditional folk tunes sung in the remote villages of Nepal celebrate religious and agricultural life. A music group popular with Nepalese Americans is Sur Sudha, a trio of three musicians performing Nepalese music on the flute, sitar and tabla. Performances and recordings by Sur Sudha have received rave reviews around the world. Sur Sudha has performed more than 2000 concerts in Europe, India, Japan, and the United States.

Three of the most popular traditional musical instruments in Nepal are the *bansuri,* the *madal,* and the *sarangi.* The sarangi is the most widely played musical instrument in Nepal. The madal is a double-headed drum made from a hollow tree-trunk and animal skin. Both ends of this drum are played, with each end having its own distinct tone. The madal is traditionally played by hanging the drum over the shoulders or around the neck. The madal drum is an ancient folk instrument that is frequently played during festivals and celebrations in the Kathmandu Valley and surrounding areas. The sarangi is a violin-like, four-stringed wooden instrument, the lower part of which is hollow and wrapped with thin leather. It is played vertically. The bansuri is a flute made of bamboo and is played horizontally. All of these instruments are handmade and they are played in both traditional and modern Nepalese music.

TRADITIONAL COSTUMES

The clothing of Nepal varies according to tribes and regions. Nepal is known internationally for its wool garments, which are made from the fur of the *pashmina,* a mountain goat that scales the snow-capped mountains. Pashmina shawls are usually bright red, green, muted beige, or oatmeal in color. Some pashmina garments are also embellished with embroidery. The intricate stitching on a pashmina can take five years to complete. Wealthy families are expected to include pashiminas in a marriage dowry.

Nepalese women wear *saris,* which consist of unstitched cloth wrapped in a variety of ways. The saris are made of silk and cotton and can be either simple in design or brilliantly adorned. Buddhist monks wear yak-hair boots and beautiful brocade robes in bright colors with wide sleeves. At the annual *Tiji* festival, celebrants wear traditional white silk *khatas* (scarves).

The nomadic Chepang do not have a distinct tribal costume. The men wear loincloths and vest-like clothes called *bhotos,* while the women wear saris and *cholos* (full sleeved blouses). Bangles made of glass and plastic, along with various hair ornaments, are worn by women to show their marital status. In modern Nepal, all Nepalese officials are required to wear black caps, called *topi,* when for-

Gelmu Sherpa rubs a "singing bowl" which resonates with a soft hum in her shop on New York's Upper West Side.

mally dressed. The traditional Nepalese coat, which is often made from maroon velvet, overlaps at the front and is closed with four ties. The *chuba* is a long woolen coat worn by Sherpas.

DANCES AND SONGS

Tharu, the indigenous people of Nepal, perform a stick dance known as the *phejaiti*. The dance has been an important part of Tharu culture and is popular among the Tharu communities in Chitwan, Bardiya, Dang and Nawalparasi. A circle is created by more than a dozen dancers, each with a stick in hand, and in the center is the group leader with a madal. The group leader signals participants to dance, making a circular movement on the ground. As the group leader plays the madal, others dance swinging their sticks in the air, while either standing or sitting. A combination of music and song accompanies the movement of the dancers.

A *jhilli* dance, a version of the stick dance, is also popular in the Tharu society. The jhilli is a musical instrument made of copper that produces an alarming sound. The jhilli dance originated when the cowboys went to the forest to look after their domestic animals and encountered wild animals. To protect themselves and their cows, the herdsmen used the jhilli to scare predators. Twelve to fifteen people participate in the dance and are accompanied by a group of four singers. During the month of September, mask dancing is popular in Kathmandu. Papier-maché masks are used in festivals to frighten evil spirits. Dances are rituals learned at an early age and performed in exact sequences.

HOLIDAYS

Nepalese Americans celebrate Hindu and Buddhist holidays set by an ancient lunar calendar. The one national holiday celebrated by Nepalese Americans is the December 28 birthday of King Birendra Bir Bikram Shah Dev. In Nepal, calendars are printed each spring at the beginning of the Nepalese year showing dates from all three calendars—the lunar, the Nepalese (a solar calendar) and the Gregorian. Major holidays include *Buddha Jayanti*, a celebration of Buddha's birth, in May; *Janai Purnima* (also called *Rakchshya Bandhan*), a celebration of the changing of the protective thread worn by all, in August; *Gai Jatra* (the cow festival), in August; *Krishnaastami*, a Hindu celebration, in September; *Teej*, a festival for women, in September; *Indra Jatra*, a Hindu festival, in September; *Ghatasthapana-Bada Dashain*, a national harvest-type festival, in September and October; *Tihar,* a Hindu animal worship festival, in October and November; and *Maha Shivaratri*, a festival honoring the Hindu god Shiva, in February.

HEALTH ISSUES

There are no known health or medical problems specific to Nepalese Americans. However, in Nepal, goiter, a disease directly associated with iodine deficiency, was endemic in certain villages in the hills and mountains. In most of the villages surveyed, more than half of the population had goiter. In these same villages, the incidence of deafness and mental retardation was much higher than in other villages. Leprosy also was a serious problem. Foreign assistance, specifically through Christian missions, has led to the creation of leprosy treatment centers in different parts of the country. "Wasting," a condition in which a child has very low weight for his or her height, is also evident in hill and mountain regions of Nepal.

LANGUAGE

Nepal's ethnic groups can be roughly divided between the Tibeto-Nepalese, who are related to the Chinese and Mongolians to the north and speak Tibet-Burman languages, and the Indo-Nepalese who are related to the Indians of the south and use Indo-Aryan languages. The Newars, who are thought to be the original inhabitants of the Kathmandu Valley, speak a Tibeto-Burman language known as Newari.

Since the creation of a national educational program in Nepal during the 1950s, the majority of Nepalese, 58.3 percent, speak Nepali. Nepali has twelve vowel sounds and 36 consonants. The vowels are "a," "aa," "i," "ii," "u," "uu," "e," "ai," "o," "au," "an," and "ah."

Even though Nepali is the national language and is the mother tongue of approximately 58 percent of the population, there are several other languages and dialects in Nepal. Other languages include Maithili, Bhojpuri, Tharu, Tamang, Newari, and Abadhi. Non-Nepali languages and dialects are rarely spoken outside their ethnic enclaves.

GREETINGS AND POPULAR EXPRESSIONS

The word *Namaste* is a common expression. It is used for greetings such as "hello," "good morning," and "good night." *Namaskaar* is another form of greeting and is mostly used on formal occasions. The fundamental role of rice in Nepalese culture is evident in the language. Daal bhaat is *khaanaa*, "food," and a common Nepalese greeting is "*Bhaat khaayo?*" meaning literally, "Have you eaten rice?"

FAMILY AND COMMUNITY DYNAMICS

In Nepal, ethnic identity is distinguished primarily by language and dress, and limits the selection of a spouse, friends, and career. This is evident in social organization, occupation, and religious observances. Nepalese Americans are not limited in this way because caste limitations are abandoned for the most part once a Nepalese immigrant becomes an American citizen.

In most areas of Nepal, the basic social unit in a village is the family, or *paribar*. According to the 1990 Nepalese census, the paribar consisted of a patrilineally extended household made up of 5.8 persons. This extended family system does not continue once Nepalese immigrate to the United States. Although Nepalese Americans may offer living assistance for a time to newly arrived relatives, they live mostly in single family units.

One integral part of Nepalese society is the Hindu caste system. The fourfold caste divisions are the *Brahman* (priests and scholars), the *Kshatriya* or *Chhetri* (rulers and warriors), the *Vaisya* (merchants and traders), and the *Sudra* (farmers, artisans, and laborers). The only way to change caste status was to undergo *Sanskritization*. Sanskritization is achieved by migrating to a new area and by changing one's caste status and/or marrying across the caste line. This can lead to the upgrading or downgrading of caste, depending on the spouse's caste. However, given the rigidity of the caste system,

inter-caste marriage carries a social stigma, especially when it takes place between members of castes from opposite ends of the social spectrum.

Social status in Nepal is measured by economic standing. Land ownership is both a measure of status and a source of income. Women occupy a secondary position, particularly in business and the civil service, although the constitution guarantees equality between men and women. Nepalese tribal and communal customs dictate women's lesser role in society, but their status differs from one ethnic group to another and is usually determined by caste. In 1962, a law was passed making it illegal to discriminate against the untouchable castes.

Today, Brahmins have land, work in the fields, and are involved in government service. Some members of the Baisya and Sudra castes are teachers, high officials, and successful politicians. All castes are not equally treated by the law. Historically, Brahmins were not subject to the death penalty and were given the same revered status as cows in the Hindu religion. However, education is free and open to all castes.

EDUCATION

Nepal's literacy rate in 1998 was 27.5 percent. Before the 1950-51 revolution, Nepal had 310 primary and middle schools, eleven high schools, two colleges, one normal school, and one special technical school. In the early 1950s, the average literacy rate was five percent. Literacy among males was ten percent and less than one percent among females. Only one child in 100 attended school. Serious educational system revisions occurred after the revolution in 1951. In 1975, the government took responsibility for providing school facilities, teachers, and educational materials free of charge. Primary schooling was compulsory. It began at age six and lasted for five years. Curriculum was greatly influenced by American models, and it was developed with assistance from the United Nations Educational, Scientific, and Cultural Organization. However, in the early 1980s, approximately 60 percent of the primary school teachers and 35 percent of secondary school teachers were untrained, and there was only one university in Nepal. Foreign educational degrees, especially those obtained from American and West European institutions, carried greater prestige than degrees from Nepal. Higher-caste families sent their children to study abroad.

THE ROLE OF WOMEN

Nepal is a rigidly patriarchal society. In virtually every aspect of life, women were subordinate to men. However, a woman's status varies from one ethnic group to another. The status of women in Tibeto-Nepalese communities was generally better than that of Pahari and Newari women. Women from the low-caste groups also enjoyed relatively more autonomy and freedom than Pahari and Newari women.

The senior female within the family played an important role by controlling resources, making crucial planting and harvesting decisions, and determining the expenses and budget allocations. Nonetheless, women's lives remained centered on their traditional roles of household chores, including childrearing. Statistics from 1985 showed that on average, women had 6.3 children. Moreover, their standing in society depended on their husbands' and parents' social and economic positions.

Women had limited access to markets, reproductive services, education, health care, and local government. In 1981, 35 percent of the male population was literate compared with only 11.5 percent of the female population. Women faced malnutrition and poverty. Female children usually were given less food than male children, especially when the family experienced food shortages. Women generally worked harder and longer than men. By contrast, women from high-class families had maids to take care of most household chores and other menial work and thus worked far less than men or women in lower socioeconomic groups. When women were employed, their wages normally were 25 percent less than those paid to men. In most rural areas, their employment outside the household generally was limited to planting, weeding, and harvesting. In urban areas, they were employed in domestic and traditional jobs, as well as in the government sector, mostly in low-level positions.

Although the Nepalese constitution offers women equal educational opportunities, many social, economic, and cultural factors contribute to lower enrollment and higher dropout rates for girls. Although the female literacy rate improved noticeably by the early 1990s, it was still far short of the level of male literacy. The level of education among female children of wealthy and educated families was much higher than that of female children from poor families. In the early 1990s, a direct correlation existed between the level of education and status. Educated women had access to relatively high-profile positions in the government and private service sectors, and they had a much higher status than their uneducated counterparts. However, within the family, an educated woman did not necessarily hold a higher status than her uneducated counterpart. A woman's status, especially as a daughter-in-law, was more closely tied to her husband's authority and to her parental family's wealth and status than to any other factor.

WEDDINGS

Saipata is the name given to both the official engagement announcement and the wedding day. Among Nepalese Americans, saipata is performed only for symbolic purposes. In this ceremony, the eldest family member from the groom's family, excluding his father and mother, formally requests the bride's hand in marriage while presenting the bride with food, gifts, and clothing. Traditional gifts include fruits, pastries, fish, and sweets. Other presents include clothing, make-up sets, shoes, and jewelry. Saipata is designed to showcase the groom's family wealth. The bride places the red *tika* on her forehead and is given a ceremonial blessing. The *jaanti* is the procession to the bride's home for the *swaymber*, the main wedding ceremony. Traditionally, a marching band performs. In the United States, however, friends of the bride or groom improvise with a few drums and other instruments. The procession arrives at the bride's house. The groom's family circles the bride's car three times, symbolic in Hinduism, to welcome the bride, who wears red, and her family. The bride is welcomed with garlands, and the bride and groom exchange garlands. The families join hands to accept the couple. The bride and groom take turns feeding each other. They exchange rings and wedding vows, which is a Western adaptation of the traditional ceremony, in witness of the eternal *agni*, the ceremonial fire of existence. They circle the *agni* seven times. Then the groom applies a red powder to the bride's head, which is symbolic of marriage. The husband is the first person to apply this powder to the bride. The groom also gives *pothey* (beads) and *toka* and *churi* (bangles), which are accessories worn by a married woman. The couple then receives a blessing from Suyra, the sun god, by standing together in the sun with their arms out in front and their hands cupped to receive the sun.

INTERACTIONS WITH OTHER ETHNIC GROUPS

First-generation Nepalese Americans interacted peaceably with many ethnic groups in Nepal. Nepalese Americans who share Hindu and Buddhist beliefs form a ready bond with other Hindu and Buddhists of other nationalities. There are no major ethnic conflicts traditional to Nepalese that would affect how Nepalese Americans interact with other groups.

RELIGION

Nepal is the only official Hindu country in world. Hindu and Buddhist beliefs intermingle without conflict. About 89.5 percent of the population is Hindu; 5.3 percent is Buddhist; and 2.7 percent embrace other religions, including Christianity. Hinduism generally is regarded as the oldest formal religion in the world. The origins of Hinduism go back to the pastoral Aryan tribes from inner Asia. Unlike other world religions, Hinduism had no single founder and has never been missionary in orientation. It is believed that about 1200 B.C., or even earlier by some accounts, the *Vedas*, a body of hymns originating in northern India were produced. These texts form the theological and philosophical precepts of Hinduism. Hindus believe that the absolute (the totality of existence, including God, man, and the universe) is too vast to be contained within a single set of beliefs. Hinduism embraces six philosophical doctrines (*darshanas*). Individuals select one of these doctrines, or conduct their worship simply on a convenient level of morality and observance. Religious practices differ from group to group. The average Hindu does not need any formal creed in order to practice his or her religion, complying instead with the customs of their family and social groups. Because of this, Hindus can assimilate easily by adding new customs and beliefs according to personal needs.

One basic concept in Hinduism is that of *dharma*, or natural law, and the social and religious obligations it imposes. Dharma holds that individuals should play their proper and determined role in society. The caste system is an integral part of dharma. Each person is born into a particular caste, whose traditional occupation is graded according to the degree of purity and impurity inherent in it. Other fundamental ideas common to all Hindus concern the nature and destiny of the soul and the basic forces of the universe. Hinduism is polytheistic, incorporating many gods and goddesses with different functions and powers. The religion's three major gods are Brahma, Vishnu, and Shiva.

One part of *karma* (universal justice) is the belief that the consequence of every good or bad action must be fully realized. Another basic concept is that of *samsara*, the transmigration of souls. An individual's role throughout life is fixed by his or her good and evil deeds in a previous existence. Veneration for the cow has come to be intimately associated with all orthodox Hindu sects. Because the cow is regarded as the symbol of motherhood and fruitfulness, the killing of a cow, even accidentally, is regarded as one of the most serious of religious transgressions.

EMPLOYMENT AND ECONOMIC TRADITIONS

According to the 1984 U.S. Census, of the 75 Nepalese immigrants admitted to the United States, 33 had professional specialties, and 42 had no occupation. Five were in farming and forestry. In the 1980s, a significant number of college-educated people living in cities within the Kathmandu valley created new firms to meet the needs of foreign donors looking to hire Nepalese consultants. Throughout Kathmandu, a number of consulting firms and associated services emerged. However, in the early 1990s, the Nepalese economy was still 90 percent rural-agricultural.

About 70 percent of the total Nepalese population is of working age, that is, between the ages of 15 and 59 years. More than 65 percent of this segment of the population was considered economically active in 1981. In terms of employment structure, more than 91 percent of the economically active population is engaged in agriculture and allied activities, and the rest in the industrial and service sectors, including government employment.

POLITICS AND GOVERNMENT

Nepalese Americans who participate in lobbying efforts for Nepal are typically in medical and humanitarian assistance projects. Their political activity generally does not involve foreign policy or attempt to influence U.S. relations with Nepal in other arenas.

ORGANIZATIONS AND ASSOCIATIONS

America-Nepal Medical Foundation.
Aims to meet current medical needs in Nepal through programs, studies, research and medical education in Nepal.

Contact: Arjun Karki, M.D.
Address: Division of Pulmonary and Critical Care, Roger Williams Medical Center, 825 Chalkstone Ave., Providence, RI 02908-4735.
Telephone: (401) 456-2000.

America-Nepal Society of California, Inc.
Formed in 1973 to promote harmonious relations between the United States and Nepal and to promote educational opportunity for economically and/or disadvantaged persons.

Address: 22814 S. Berendo Ave., Torrance,
    CA 90502.
E-mail: vbjoshi@aol.com.

Association of Nepalese in Midwest.
Promotes Nepalese culture to second-generation Nepalese Americans and provides community for new immigrants.

Contact: Mrs. Bindu Panth.
Address: 2367 Springdale Road, Cincinnati,
    OH 45231.

Association of Nepalese in Midwest America (ANMA).
Promotes the Nepali culture and language and is concerned about what is being done to keep the Nepali cultural heritage alive in Nepal. Has published a newsletter, *Viewpoint,* since 1982. On May 25-26, 1991, ANMA organized the First National Convention of Nepalese and Friends of Nepal in North America at the University of Maryland. The convention was co-sponsored by six other Nepalese and Nepal-related associations.

Contact: Mr. Dhruba Shrestha.
Address: 3535 Wheeler Road, Bay City, MI 48706.
Telephone: (517) 684-8314.
Online: http://www.anmausa.org/index.html.

Association of Nepalis in the Americas.
An organization of people of Nepali origin in the Americas and international friends of Nepal. ANA was founded on July 1983 in New York and incorporated in Washington, DC, in 1983 as a non-profit, tax-exempt organization.

Address: 11605 Gainsborough Road, Potomac,
    MD 20854.
Telephone: (301) 299-8045.

Empower Nepal Foundation (ENF).
Non-profit organization of individuals of Nepali ethnicity promoting Nepalese culture and relations with Nepal.

Address: 2000 Como Avenue, St. Paul, MN 55108.

Florida-Nepal Association.
Non-profit organization of individuals of Nepali ethnicity promoting Nepalese culture in the Florida area, and relations with Nepal.

Contact: President: Tirtha Mali.
Address: 6320 NW 33rd Terrace, Gainesville,
    FL 32606.

Greater Boston Nepali Community.
Non-profit organization of individuals of Nepali ethnicity promoting Nepalese culture in the Boston area.

Contact: Raju Pradhan.
Address: P.O. Box 893, Watertown, MA 02272. .
Telephone: (617) 924-8852.

International Nepali Literary Society.
Address: 2926 Wetherburn Ct. ,Woodbridge,
    VA 22191.
Telephone: (703) 221-2656.

Nepal Association of Northern California.
Non-profit organization of individuals of Nepali ethnicity promoting Nepalese culture in Northern California.

Contact: President: Gopal Khadgi.
Address: P.O. Box 170253, San Francisco,
    CA 94117.

The Nepal Digest Foundation.
A global non-profit information and resource center committed to promoting issues concerning Nepal, Nepalis, and friends of Nepal.

Address: P.O. Box 8206, White Plains, NY 10601.
E-mail: tnd@nepal.org.

Nepal Human Rights Committee—USA .
A non-profit organization lobbying for humane treatment of all ethnic groups in Nepal. Incorporated in Washington DC.

Address: P.O. Box 53253, Washington, DC 20009.
Telephone: (301) 587-0454.

Nepalese Embassy.
Assists Nepalese citizens living in the United States and maintains diplomatic relations with the United States.

Address: 2131 Leroy Place NW, Washington,
    DC 20008.
Telephone: (202) 667-4550.

Nepali Youth Organization.
Non-profit group for preserving and transferring Nepalese culture to second- and third-generation Nepalese Americans.

Address: P.O. Box 10422, Arlington, VA 22210. .

MUSEUMS AND RESEARCH CENTERS

The Lowe Art Museum at the University of Miami.
A permanent collection of Indian, Nepalese, Tibetan, Chinese, and Japanese sculptures and paintings, "Gods And Goddesses, Myths And Legends In Asian Art," examines the development of myth, legend, and religion in south and east Asia.

Address: P.O. Box 248105, Coral Gables, FL 33124-4020.
Telephone: (305) 284-5500.

Nepal Studies Association
Association of scholars, scientists, development planners, and libraries.

Address: Northern Kentucky University, Department of History & Geography, Nunn Drive, Highland Heights, Kentucky 41099-2205.
Contact: John Metz, President.
Telephone: (606) 572-5461.
Fax: (606) 572-6088.
E-mail: metz@nku.edu.
Online: http://www.macalstr.edu/~guneratn/.

Virginia Museum of Fine Arts.
The Nepalese galleries showcases collections of opaque watercolors on cloth or palm leaf.

Address: 2800 Grove Avenue, Richmond, VA 23221-2466.
Telephone: (804) 367-0844.

SOURCES FOR ADDITIONAL STUDY

Koirala, Niranjan. "Nepal in 1989: A Very Difficult Year," *Asian Survey*, February 1990, pp. 136-43.

Raj, Prakash A. *Kathmandu & the Kingdom of Nepal.* South Yarra, Australia: Lonely Planet Publications, 1985.

Savada, Andrea Matles. *Nepal: A Country Study.* Washington, DC: Library of Congress Federal Research Division, 1993.

Weir, Richard. "Neighborhood Project: Woodside; His Film, Real-Life Misadventures," *New York Times*, February 14, 1999, Sec. 14. page 8.

The Seven Drums
Religion, considered
a direct descendant
of the Prophet
Dance, has long
been a focal point in
the revitalization of
Nez Percé traditional
religious practices.
The religion is a
blend of vision
quests seeking
personal spirit pow-
ers and some Christ-
ian elements in a
Native communal
worship framework.

NEZ PERCÉ

by
Laurie Collier Hillstrom
and Richard C. Hanes

OVERVIEW

The Nez Percé (nez-PURSE or nay-per-SAY) tribe's traditional territory includes the interior Pacific Northwest areas of north-central Idaho, northeastern Oregon, and southeastern Washington. The Nez Percé call themselves Nee-Me-Poo or Nimipu, which means "our people." The name Nez Percé is French for "pierced nose" and was applied to the tribe by early French Canadian fur traders, who apparently observed a few individuals in the region with pendants in their noses. Nose piercing, however, is not a common Nez Percé custom.

Despite maintaining peaceful and friendly relations with non-native peoples for most of their history—such as the celebrated assistance they gave to Lewis and Clark when the famous American explorers were near starvation in 1805—the Nez Percé are perhaps best known for their battles with the U.S. Army during the Nez Percé War of 1877. The 750-member Wallowa band of Nez Percé kept more than 2,000 highly-trained American troops at bay during a four-month, 1,600-mile trek through the rugged high country of Idaho, Wyoming, and Montana. The band was finally forced to surrender only 30 miles short of reaching safety in Canada. At the time, the dramatic "Flight of the Nez Percé" was front-page news in the United States and is still studied by military historians.

The Nez Percé were one of the most numerous and powerful tribes of the Plateau Culture area, living a semi-sedentary existence as fishermen, hunters, and gatherers. They speak a Sahaptian dialect of the Penutian language family, which is common among other Plateau groups in the mid-Columbia River region. According to Michael G. Johnson in *The Native Tribes of North America*, the Nez Percé population was estimated at about 6,000 in 1800. By the beginning of the next century, their numbers had declined to about 1,500 due to newly introduced diseases, the loss of tribal lands, and a reduction of economic resources. Many of the almost 4,000 descendants of the tribe live on the Nez Percé reservation near Lapwai, Idaho, except for the Joseph band, which resides on the Colville reservation of north-central Washington.

HISTORY

Before the Nez Percé acquired horses in the early 1700s, they lived in semi-subterranean pit houses covered with branches and earth. They spent most of their time fishing, hunting, or gathering wild plants for food. The use of horses rapidly changed the lifestyle of the Nez Percé, allowing them to trade with neighboring tribes and make annual trips to the Great Plains to hunt buffalo. The increased contact with tribes of the Great Plains and the Pacific Coast also led to the advent of more decorative Nez Percé clothing styles and new forms of housing, such as hide-covered tepees and pit-tepees. The rich grasslands of the Nez Percé territory enabled the tribe to raise some of the largest horse herds of any Native American group. Skilled horse breeders and trainers, the Nez Percé became particularly well known for breeding the sturdy, spotted horses now called Appaloosas.

Typical of many native groups in the West, the Nez Percé lacked an overall tribal organization, living instead in bands composed of families and extended kinship groups. Each autonomous village or band had a headman who could speak only for his own followers. When a major decision needed to be made, the headmen of the various bands, along with respected shamans, elders, and hunting and war leaders, would meet in a combined council and attempt to reach a consensus.

The first contact between the Nez Percé and non-native people occurred in the fall of 1805, when the Lewis and Clark expedition wandered into western Idaho. The American explorers were cold, tired, and running low on food when they encountered the Nez Percé. The tribe provided assistance that may have prevented members of the expedition from starving. They also helped the explorers build boats and guided them toward the Pacific Coast. Over the next few decades, the Nez Percé similarly established friendly relations with French Canadian and American fur traders, missionaries, and settlers. At the request of the Nez Percé, a Methodist minister named Henry Spalding established a mission near Lapwai in 1836. Three years later, Asa Smith established another mission at Kamiah. The Nez Percé consulted these ministers for the special powers they seemingly held.

As the number of white settlers in the Northwest increased through the mid-1800s, the Nez Percé avoided many of the conflicts that plagued other tribes. At the Walla Walla Council of 1855, the Nez Percé signed a treaty ceding most of their 13 million acre ancestral territory to the government in exchange for money and a guarantee that 7.5 million acres of their lands would remain intact as a reservation. Immediately after the governor of Washington Territory, Isaac Ingalls Stevens, had signed treaties with several Plateau tribes, he wrote a letter to an eastern newspaper proclaiming the Northwest open for settlement. Other area tribes reacted violently to his duplicity by attacking settlers arriving in the territory. This violence led to the Plateau Indian, or Yakima, War of 1855-1858. Although the Nez Percé remained neutral in the conflict, the treaty signing had split the tribe. The Christianized Nez Percé led by Lawyer (Hallalhotsoot), who signed the treaty, supported the agreement, but many of the tribe's traditionalists balked at signing away their lands.

In the early 1860s, gold was discovered on Nez Percé lands. In violation of the 1855 treaty, settlers rushed in and laid claim to the land. They soon began pressuring the U.S. government to open more tribal territory for mining and settlement. In 1863, Governor Stevens again approached the Nez Percé about relinquishing more tribal lands. Although many leaders, including Chief Joseph (Heinmot Tooyalakekt) and White Bird, refused to negotiate, Lawyer and several others signed a new treaty with Stevens. This treaty reduced the Nez Percé reservation to 780,000 acres. In what came to be known among tribal members as the Thief Treaty, the Nez Percé had lost their claim to many important areas, including Joseph's home territory in the Wallowa Valley of northeastern Oregon. Upon hearing this news, Old Chief Joseph (Tu-ke-kas), the peaceful leader of the Wallowa band who had converted to Christianity some years earlier, destroyed his Bible. Despite the anger and resentment caused by this treaty, the Nez Percé remained peaceful in their relations with whites and expressed their discontent through passive noncompliance.

Upon the death of Old Chief Joseph in 1871 his son, Young Chief Joseph, took over leadership of the Wallowa band. In 1873 the government tried to create a Wallowa reservation for Joseph's band, but abandoned the attempt two years later under pressure from the white settlers. Representing his people in a meeting with General Oliver Howard at the Lapwai Council of 1876, Chief Joseph firmly refused to honor the 1863 treaty and give up the tribe's ancestral valley. The following year, however, the government gave the tribe 30 days to vacate Wallowa Valley and move to a reservation near Lapwai, Idaho. When it became clear that war would result if the Wallowa band continued to resist, Chief Joseph agreed to relocate. He stated, "I would give up everything rather than have the blood of my people on my hands."

Before the move could begin, young rebels within the tribe attacked a group of whites in retribution for previous mistreatment of the Nez Percé. Three men were killed and another wounded. Panic spread quickly on both sides, and the U.S. cavalry was mobilized. When the Nez Percé did not leave the Wallowa Valley as ordered, the cavalry attacked Chief Joseph's village. Joseph and the rest of the Wallowa band, which consisted of 250 men and 500 women, children, and elderly, fled into the surrounding mountains. About 2,000 U.S. Army troops under General Howard followed, marking the beginning of the Nez Percé War of 1877. In the *Encyclopedia of Native American Tribes,* this war is described as "one of the most remarkable stories of pursuit and escape in military history." Over the next four months, the Nez Percé traveled 1,600 miles through the rugged wilderness of Idaho, Wyoming, and Montana. During this time, they fought 14 battles against a larger and better-equipped enemy. Until the last battle, Waldman noted, the Nez Percé "consistently outsmarted, outflanked, and outfought the larger white forces."

In one of the more embarrassing moments of the war, the U.S. troops built a barricade across Lolo Pass in the Bitterroot Mountains to prevent the Nez Percé from entering Montana. After the tribe avoided the barricade by leading their horses along the face of a cliff, the ineffective structure came to be known as Fort Fizzle. The final battle between the U.S. cavalry and the Nez Percé took place near Snake Creek in the Bear Paw Mountains of Montana, just 30 miles from the Canadian border. For six days the Nez Percé fought off troops led by Colonel Nelson Miles, who had been dispatched to prevent the Nez Percé from reaching Canada before General Howard's troops could catch up and surround them. After fighting bravely for so long, the Nez Percé finally decided to surrender. An exhaust-ed Chief Joseph delivered his famous surrender speech to his people, in which he stated: "Hear me, my chiefs, I am tired. My heart is sick and sad. From where the sun now stands, I will fight no more forever." Following their surrender, Joseph and other tribal leaders such as White Bird, Lean Elk, and Joseph's brother Ollokot, were not allowed to go to the Nez Percé reservation. Instead, they were taken to Indian Country, first in Kansas, then in Oklahoma. They eventually returned to the Northwest at the Colville reservation in north-central Washington, despite Joseph's repeated attempts to reclaim their home.

For the rest of the Nez Percé, the late nineteenth century was a period of great difficulty. Members of the tribe were forced to attend Christian churches and government schools, which was an attempt to destroy the Nez Percé culture. Under the General Allotment Act of 1887, the U.S. government divided the reservation into relatively small allotments and assigned them to individual tribal members. By 1893, reservation lands not allotted were deemed excess and sold to non-Indians. In all, 90 percent of tribal lands within reservation boundaries were lost. Those retained amounted to 90,000 acres scattered in a checkerboard pattern of ownership. In spite of this, Nez Percé tribal traditions persisted into the twentieth century.

MODERN ERA

In recent times, the Nez Percé have been involved in several fishing rights cases affecting the entire Columbia River Basin. As active sponsors of the Columbia River Inter-Tribal Fish Commission, they have taken a number of steps to revitalize salmon and steelhead runs in the region. In addition, they have been negotiating water rights to the Snake River and trying to reacquire ancestral lands. The Nez Percé of Idaho reached an agreement with the U.S. Army Corps of Engineers, which had built dams on the Columbia and Snake Rivers, that will provide the tribe access to traditional fishing stations. In 1996, the Nez Percé regained 10,000 acres of their homeland in northeastern Oregon from the U.S. Bonneville Power Administration. This land is managed as a wildlife preserve. Additional reacquisitions were also being pursued at the time.

The Nez Percé honor their unique and tragic tribal history. In 1996, descendants of the Wallowa band held their twentieth annual ceremony commemorating the members of the tribe who died in the Bear Paw Mountains during the Nez Percé War of 1877. They gathered to smoke pipes, sing, pray, and conduct an empty saddle ceremony, in which horses are led around without riders in order to appease the spirits of the dead.

SETTLEMENT PATTERNS

Following their surrender to the U.S. cavalry, the Wallowa band of Nez Percé was sent to reservations in Oklahoma and Kansas before finally settling on the Colville reservation near Nespelem, Washington. The remainder of the Joseph band members and other Nez Percé live on the Nez Percé reservation in north-central Idaho. Many also live in various urban areas where better employment opportunities exist. On the Idaho reservation, most of the Nez Percé live in the principal communities of Lapwai, Kamiah, Cottonwood, Nez Percé, Orofino, Culdesac, and Winchester. Some descendants of the Joseph band remained in Oklahoma and others live in Canada.

ACCULTURATION AND ASSIMILATION

TRADITIONS, CUSTOMS, AND BELIEFS

Before acquiring horses, the Nez Percé lived in houses covered with plant material. In the summer, they moved often in search of food, living in lean-tos consisting of a pole framework covered with woven mats of plant fibers. In the winter, they built pole-framed structures over large pits and covered them with layers of cedar bark, sagebrush, packed grass, and earth. Each dwelling usually housed several families, and a village might consist of five or six such pit houses. As horses increased their mobility and contact with other tribes, Nez Percé buildings grew larger and more sophisticated. Their winter pit houses sometimes extended up to 100 feet in length and housed many families. They also adopted the use of hide-covered tepees during summer fishing and hunting trips.

As with many Native American groups in the United States, the Nez Percé began an era of cultural revitalization in the 1960s involving religion, dance, and arts and crafts. In 1978 Phil Lucas produced *Nez Percé—Portrait of a People*, a film documenting the rich history of the Nez Percé. The film uses archival photographs, traditional stories, and scenes of Nez Percé country to tell of their interaction with the Lewis and Clark expedition and the loss of their lands later in the nineteenth century.

CUISINE

In the dry, rugged high country where the Nez Percé lived, gathering food was a time-consuming prospect. They subsisted primarily by fishing, hunting, and gathering vegetables from spring through fall. Surplus food was stored for winter use. During the spring, when large numbers of salmon swam upstream to spawn, the Nez Percé used a variety of methods to catch them, including spears, hand-held and weighted nets, small brush traps, and large enclosures. They also used bows and arrows to hunt elk, deer, and mountain sheep, although hunting was often difficult on the hot, open plateaus of their homeland. The Nez Percé sometimes disguised themselves in animal furs or worked together to surround a herd of animals so that they could be killed more easily.

In the spring, Nez Percé women used sharp digging sticks to turn up cornlike roots called *kouse* on the grassy hillsides. These roots were ground, then boiled to make soup or shaped into cakes and stored for later use. During the summer, the Nez Percé gathered a wide variety of plants, including wild onions and carrots, bitterroots, blackberries, strawberries, huckleberries, and nuts. In late summer, the various Nez Percé bands came together to gather sweet-tasting camas lily bulbs. These were steamed and made into a dough or gruel. Many of these traditional foods are still shared today as key elements of important celebrations.

MUSIC

Music among the Nez Percé was traditionally a dynamic medium of celebration and ritual, marked by improvisation. It involved not only musical instruments and verse, but also improvised vocalizations of sounds, such as sighs, mimicked animal sounds, moans, and yelps. Flutes made from elderberry stems were one of the preferred musical instruments used by the Nez Percé. It usually had six finger holes. For protection in war, men played wing bone whistles to call guardian spirits. The rasp, which involved scraping a serrated stick with a bone, was standard for war dances prior to the nineteenth century. During the nineteenth century, hand drums replaced the rasp. Larger drums associated with Washat ceremonies began to be used in the 1860s. By the 1890s, some drums were large enough to accommodate up to eight drummers. For traditional ceremonies, a shaman used rattles composed of deer hooves on a stick. After the Nez Percé came into contact with white settlers, bells were used instead of hooves. A simple wooden rod beaten rhythmically on a plank was also used as an instrument.

TRADITIONAL COSTUMES

Traditional Nez Percé clothing was made of shredded cedar bark, deerskin, or rabbitskin. Men wore breechcloths and capes in warm weather, adding fur robes and leggings when it turned cold. Nez Percé women were known for the large basket hats they wove out of dried leaves and plant fibers. By the early 1700s, when horses expanded the tribe's hunting range and brought them into contact with tribes of the Pacific Coast and Great Plains, the Nez Percé began wearing tailored skin garments decorated with shells, elk teeth, and beads. As they prepared to make war, Nez Percé men wore only breechcloths and moccasins and applied brightly colored paint to their faces and bodies. Red paint was applied to the part in a warrior's hair and across his forehead, while other colors were applied to his body in special, individual patterns. The warriors also adorned themselves with animal feathers, fur, teeth, and claws representing their connection to their guardian spirits. Elaborate adornments for the horses are characteristic of Nez Percé society, including brightly colored beaded collars and saddlebags, appliquéd with brass tacks and bells added for decorative purposes.

DANCES AND SONGS

Among the Nez Percé, song is considered essentially the same as prayer. Song accompanied most daily activities from morning to night, and most life events. Individuals often had their own personal songs that others might sing to indicate support. Songs and dance still serve to instill community pride and convey tribal heritage, in addition to providing a forum for socialization. Through special songs and dances, the Nez Percé honored the spirit of Hanyawat and Mother Earth in an effort to maintain a balance with nature and express thanks to fish, birds, plants, and animals.

Song and dance focused on guardian spirits, prophet visions, winter ceremonies, and shamanic rituals; seasonal food thanksgivings for first roots, first fruits, first salmon and first game; and for important rites of passage, including birth, naming, puberty, marriage, and death. For instance, each year during the winter traditional Nez Percé hold the Guardian Spirit Dance, or *Wee'kwetset*. In this ceremony, young people who had recently acquired a *wyakin*, a guardian spirit, would dance and sing in prescribed ways in order to become one with their guardian spirits. By watching and participating, other tribal members can often discover the identity of a young people's *wyakin*. The ceremony sometimes involves contests to see who has received the greatest powers from his or her *wyakin*. This Winter Dance was meant to ensure a desirable life, with safety, health, wealth, skill and strength.

The war dance complex consisted of a set of dances focused on various aspects of war-related activities. A five-day Scalp Dance would conclude the sequence upon the return of the warriors. After acquisition of horses in the mid-eighteenth century, the Nez Percé began journeying annually to the northern Plains to hunt buffalo, some staying for years at a time. There they encountered Plains customs and brought some back with them, including certain war dance styles and drumming. New religions also brought new songs and dance. When Smohalla of the Wanapums of central Washington introduced the Washat religion, he also introduced a new dance and song that sought restoration of traditional life and removal of white influence. Later, worship at the Indian Shaker Church consisted of stomp dances with loud vocalizations and bells. In addition, a number of Anglican hymns introduced by the Presbyterian church were translated into Nez Percé language and printed in the later 1830s.

Dance and song continues its importance to Nez Percé life today. Annual festivals consist of powwows and celebrations. Powwows include the Four Nation Pow Wow at Nez Percé County Fair Grounds in Lewiston, Idaho, in the fall; the Chief Joseph and Warriors Memorial Pow Wow at the Nez Percé Reservation in Lapwai, Idaho, in June; the Pendleton Roundup at Pendleton, Oregon; the Nee-Mee-Poo Sapatqayn and Cultural Days at the Nez Percé Reservation in Spalding, Idaho, in late August; and the Chief Looking Glass Pow Wow at the Nez Percé Reservation in Kamiah, Idaho, the third weekend in August. These events commonly include horse parades, cultural demonstrations, speakers, stick games, arts and crafts, and drumming and dancing, including war dances and social and contest dancing. Other celebrations include the Root Festival the first week of May and the Talmaks celebration, which consists of an early summer camp meeting sponsored by the Presbyterian church. Many of the celebrations are an integral part of the process of cultural rejuvenation still occurring. By observing these celebrations, the Nez Percé maintain connections with the earth, their ancestors, and their historic symbols.

HOLIDAYS

The Nez Percé regularly participate at the Celico Wy-Am Salmon Feast at Celilo Village in Oregon each spring. Also in north-central Oregon is the All-Indian Rodeo held in spring at Tygh Valley, sponsored by the Western States Indian Rodeo Association. The event includes Western dances, a fun run, arts and crafts, and baseball tournament. Thanksgiving, Christmas, and New Year are also celebrated.

LANGUAGE

The Nez Percé spoke a Sahaptian dialect of the Penutian language family. According to Alvin M. Josephy Jr. in *The Nez Percé Indians and the Opening of the Northwest*, the Nez Percé belonged to one of the oldest known language stocks in North America. Their language was closely related to that of the Walla Walla, Yakima, and other Plateau tribes. The traditional territory of the Sahaptian speakers extended for almost 400 miles from the Bitterroot Mountains of Idaho westward to the Cascade Mountains of Oregon. However, Deward E. Walker Jr. explains in *Native America in the Twentieth Century* the Nez Percé language was rarely spoken by tribal members under the age of 30 in the late 1990s.

GREETINGS AND POPULAR EXPRESSIONS

Some Washat-related sayings include: *wa·láhsat*—jumping up and *ipnú·cililpt*—turning around while chanting. Other words or expressions are: *tiwe-t*—male medicine doctor; *tiwata a-t*—female medicine doctor; *Aiiiiii*—an amen-like utterance at the end of a series of Washat songs; and *á-šapatwana'aš wíwnu-na*—I mixed huckleberries with salmon flour.

FAMILY AND COMMUNITY DYNAMICS

EDUCATION

Traditionally, the extended family raised the children, with grandparents teaching many of life's basic lessons. The first non-native schools were introduced by the Presbyterian missionaries who settled in Nez Percé country at the tribe's invitation in 1836. Catholic missionaries followed later. By the late nineteenth century, the Bureau of Indian Affairs (BIA) established on-reservation elementary schools operated by Indian agents, designed to "civilize" the Nez Percé. Students were discouraged

Despite the use of modern technology, the Nez Percé family tradition has stayed very much the same over the years.

from practicing long-standing tribal traditions and speaking the Nez Percé language. Reflecting the biases of white society, emphasis was placed on educating the boys. Though many of the basics of U.S. elementary schools were taught, including English, vocational training was emphasised. Older children were sent off-reservation, frequently long distances away from their families, to BIA-operated boarding schools such as Carlisle in Pennsylvania and Haskell in Oklahoma. These forced education policies posed dramatic changes to Nez Percé life.

An increasing number of Nez Percé tribal members earned college degrees in the late twentieth century. A number of Nez Percé attend University of Idaho, Washington State University, and University of Washington, among others. Many returned to the tribe to serve the reservation in various capacities including that of wildlife management and administration.

BIRTH AND BIRTHDAYS

During pregnancy, women were encouraged to exercise vigorously and take a number of medicinal herbs. Nez Percé custom dictated that deformed animals and humans should not be ridiculed for fear of causing similar deformities in the baby. The tying of knots was also avoided because they represented the obstruction of the umbilical cord. Babies were delivered in small separate houses with the help of midwives and female relatives. Shamans were called if major problems arose. The baby's head and feet were shaped immediately upon birth. For good luck the umbilical cord was sown into a small hide pouch and attached to the cradleboard. Feasts and gifts were given to the mother and baby, especially for firstborn children, and at adolescence a formal naming ceremony was held.

THE ROLE OF WOMEN

As in many indigenous societies, Nez Percé women held a prominent role in food acquisition and preparation. Although men were mainly in charge of the fishing, women assisted in gutting, drying, and storing the large volumes of fish that were caught. Women assumed leadership in food and medicinal plant collecting, using digging sticks to collect various types of roots, or tubers. The bulb of the camas lily, which grows primarily in wet meadows, was a principal plant food. With the absence of a pottery tradition, baskets were used for numerous tasks, including food storage and even cooking, which was accomplished by placing heated stones in a basket full of water to boil foods.

Nez Percé women were given more respect within the tribe than women in other American Indian tribes. Nez Percé women were eligible to be shamans, who were believed to have miraculous powers, able to cure the sick by singing sacred songs and prescribing herbal remedies. During tribal council meetings, the women could speak up, although they could not lead the meetings. Women's roles in powwows have changed in the late twentieth century, with increased participation in drumming and war dancing, both prohibited to Nez Percé women several generations earlier.

COURTSHIP AND WEDDINGS

Heads of families often arranged marriages in traditional Nez Percé society, sometimes during childhood. The relative prestige of both families was weighed in making selections. Kin relationships, even distant ones, were avoided; on the other hand, commonly several sons and daughters of two families might marry. In cases where marriage was not arranged, when a male found a female he wanted as a wife, an older female relative of the male initiated negotiations with the female's family. The woman might be observed by the elder relative over a period of time to determine if she was acceptable. The couple might then live together for a while to determine compatibility. Once the couple decided to marry, a ceremony and somewhat competitive gift exchange was held. Relatives of the groom might give horses, equipment for hunting and fishing, and skins. The bride's relatives would give baskets, root bags, digging sticks, and beaded bags. When two prestigious families were involved in an exchange ceremony, many people participated. After a second exchange ceremony, the wedding was considered complete. Since the 1960s, wedding ceremonies are often conducted in traditional longhouses.

FUNERALS

The death of a leader or highly respected elder is a major event in Nez Percé society. Traditional funerals were elaborate and consisted of many components. Close female relatives of the deceased immediately began wailing as criers announced the death in the area. The deceased's face was traditionally painted red, and the body was washed, dressed in new clothes, wrapped in a robe, and buried the following day. A number of the deceased's favorite valuables were placed in the grave. A favorite horse might even be killed and left in the vicinity. The grave was placed on a prominent hill overlooking a valley or in a rocky talus slope. A shaman would perform rituals to prevent the deceased ghost from returning, and individuals who had tended to the body ritually purified themselves. Following burial, a feast was held and the remaining items of the deceased disbursed. For the following year, the surviving spouse cut his or her hair short, wore old clothes, did not smile in public, and was prohibited from remarrying. At the end of the yearlong mourning period, relatives supplied a new set of clothes, and a new spouse if a brother or sister of the deceased spouse was available.

Various religions are still practiced by the Nez Percé and other natives in the region, including Washat, Feather, and Shaker sects. In some instances, a modern-day funeral may include more than 20 Washat songs performed during a night-long wake. Graveside Washat songs may also be performed at the burial.

INTERACTIONS WITH OTHER TRIBES

The Nez Percé maintained friendly relations with most tribes of the Plateau area, including the Walla Walla, Yakima, Palouse, and Cayuse as well as other tribes to their north. The Nez Percé were traditionally part of a large trading network, trading directly with other Columbia River basin tribes to the west, and native groups to the east in western Montana, and even onto the Great Plains. A variety of raw materials and goods passed through this network. The main enemies of the Nez Percé were the Great Basin groups to the south, including the Shoshone, Northern Paiute, and Bannock. Raids motivated by revenge regularly occurred back and forth between the Nez Percé and these groups.

One of the strongest present-day forums for interaction with other tribes is the Columbia River Inter-Tribal Fisheries Commission (CRITFC). The CRITFC was formed to facilitate the restoration of salmon and steelhead runs in the Snake River system, an issue of primary importance in the latter years of the twentieth century. The Nez Percé, the Yakima, Warm Springs, and Umatilla tribes are CRITFC members. The commission developed its own comprehensive restoration plan for the region in the mid-1990s and is a key player with various federal agencies and several states in the major restoration effort.

RELIGION

The Nez Percé felt a deep spiritual connection with the earth and sought to live in harmony with nature. They believed all living things and all features of the natural environment were closely related to each other and to people. Every member of the Nez Percé tribe had a personal link with nature in the form of a guardian spirit, or *wyakin*, that protected him or her from harm and provided assistance during his or her life. For example, a person might pray to his or her *wyakin* for success in war or for help in crossing a dangerous river. A small medicine bundle containing materials that represented one's *wyakin* was often carried.

Around the onset of puberty, a young Nez Percé would leave the village in hopes of acquiring a *wyakin* through a sacred experience. The youth traveled alone to an isolated place, often at a high mountain or along a river, without food or weapons, and sat upon a pile of stones and waited for the *wyakin* to reveal itself. The *wyakin* might appear as something material, such as an elk illuminated in a flash of lightning, or as a hallucination or dream. After returning to the village, the young person did not tell others of the experience but interpreted the power of the *wyakin* privately. From that point on, there were certain rules to follow in order to avoid bad fortune, but one could also appeal to the *wyakin* in times of need.

Until the 1863 treaty, the Nez Percé were generally open to white settlement and Christian missions in the region. However, with the continued loss of tribal lands Christianity became a major issue causing factionalism. The white culture not only introduced new technologies to the Nez Percé in the nineteenth century, but also brought epidemics, guns, whiskey, impacts on traditional food resources, and loss of land. Over time, pronounced despair led to the rise of various prophetic movements focused on restoring traditional ways and ridding the area of whites. These movements arrived in cycles as interest would grow, then wane, only to rise again. The first was the Prophet Dance in the 1820s, followed by the Washat or Seven Drum Religion in the 1850s, an Earth-lodge cult of the late nineteenth century, and the Feather cult of 1905. A series of prophets were among the Nez Percé, including Nez Percé Ellis, Wiskaynatowat-sanmay, and Tawis-waikt. The Prophet Dance, the oldest of the series of prophetic movements, generally involved dancing in a circle with a leader making vision-inspired prophecies in a trance-like state. The messages were deeply religious in tone and emphasized a renewal of life.

The Seven Drums Religion, considered a direct descendant of the Prophet Dance, has long been a focal point in the revitalization of Nez Percé traditional religious practices. The religion is a blend of vision quests seeking personal spirit powers and some Christian elements in a native communal worship framework. It is also known as the Longhouse Religion, as it was performed in traditional longhouses throughout the Columbia Plateau region and led by highly charismatic individuals. The first roots feasts in spring, a first salmon feast slightly later, and a berry feast toward summer's end as well as funerals and memorials are commonly celebrated in the Washat format.

EMPLOYMENT AND ECONOMIC TRADITIONS

The traditional Nez Percé economy was based on fishing, gathering, hunting, and, later, raising large herds of horses. Prior to incursions by white settlers, a number of major villages existed along the lower courses of the Snake, Salmon, and Clearwater Rivers and their tributaries. Having rich fisheries on these watercourses, including seasonal runs of a variety of salmon and steelhead trout, annual fish consumption in the traditional economy was estimated at more than 500 pounds per person. The traditional territory contains a diversity of landscapes with rugged mountains and numerous valleys and high prairies, primarily within the Snake River drainage system. Each area offered something different in terms of resources.

The loss of a viable land base greatly undermined both the traditional Nez Percé economy and the ability to join the burgeoning market economy of the non-Indians. The tribe won several Indian Claims Commission monetary awards in the latter half of the twentieth century in payment for lost lands. They received $3.5 million for lands ceded in the 1855 treaty and more than $5 million for lands lost in the 1863 treaty and 1893 allotments. Along with several other tribes, the Nez Percé also received compensation for the flooding of a key fishery location on the Columbia River in the 1950s by reservoir construction. The Nez Percé share was almost $3 million.

The Nez Percé tribe has occasionally leased approximately 80 percent of its lands to non-Indians. Tribal economy has been largely based on funding from these leases and a timber program. Reacquisition of tribal lands is a key goal of the tribe. In the mid-1990s, as Wallowa Valley encountered difficult economic times with declines in the timber and cattle markets, residents made plans to invite the Nez Percé back to the area. Residents began raising money to build an interpretive center and purchase 160 acres of land for the tribe to use for cultural events. Though valley residents viewed the return of the Nez Percé as an opportunity to promote tourism, most members of the tribe were pleased to recover some of their ancestral territory. "The whites may look at it as an economic plus, but we look at it as a homecoming," tribal member Soy Redthunder informed journalist Timothy Egan. The Nee-Me-Poo National Historic Trail, the Nez Percé National Historical Park, and the burial site of Old Chief Joseph have become major tourist attractions. One tourism-related Nez Percé-owned business enterprise is Old West Enterprises Textiles and Tipis in Lapwai, Idaho.

The Nez Percé received approval in 1992 from the Northwest Power Planning Council for an ambitious $14 million Clearwater River hatchery plan to restore chinook, steelhead and eventually other salmon, trout, and sturgeon to the tribe's fishing sites scattered over two million acres of central Idaho. (Project funding from the Bonneville Power Administration proved more elusive.) Project plans included a central hatchery and rearing facility, an auxiliary hatchery, and a number of satellite monitoring facilities. One goal was to return fish to traditional spawning grounds in the upper reaches of the Clearwater tributaries, strengthening natural fish runs. The long-term goal of the project is to restore salmon to 13 million acres of ceded lands in Oregon and Washington.

The Nez Percé are not reluctant to enter mainstram society. The Nez Percé are receptive to the United States educational system and their members thrive in academics. Nez Percé members are doctors, nurses, engineers, journalists, and teachers. The Nez Percé tribe operates a printing plant and a marina. The unemployment rate of the Nez Percé is lower than that of most other Native American tribes.

POLITICS AND GOVERNMENT

In 1923, the non-traditionalists of the tribe, seeking an elective form of government, formed the Nez Percé Home and Farm Association, with James Stuart as the first president. The Nez Percé rejected the Indian Reorganization Act of 1934 and the Indian New Deal, instead establishing their own tribal constitution in 1948. Under the constitution, Tribal Executive Committee, whose members are elected at large, governs the tribe. The committee oversees the tribe's economic development, including the use of natural resources and the investment of trib-

al income. It is also responsible to the General Council, which consists of all enrolled tribal members. By the 1990s, with an annual budget of $2 million, the tribe employed over 250 people and provided many social services to tribal members.

INDIVIDUAL AND GROUP CONTRIBUTIONS

ACADEMICS

Nez Percé anthropologist and activist Archie Phinney (1903-1949) played a significant role in preserving the traditional language and folklore of the tribe. Phinney was born on the Nez Percé reservation and raised in a traditional manner, including speaking the language. He attended the University of Kansas, where he became the first Native American to receive a degree from that school. Phinney then attended Columbia University and earned a graduate degree. Returning to the Nez Percé reservation, he began a project of preserving the Nez Percé language and folklore. Phinney authored two books and several journal articles. One book, the 1934 Nez Percé Texts, contained traditional stories of the tribe and was published by the prestigious Columbia University Press. Phinney demonstrated that folklore was a legitimate academic field of study. Promoting Native American causes nationwide, Phinney held leadership positions with the Bureau of Indian Affairs, including that of superintendent of the Northern Idaho Agency, and in the National Congress of American Indians. Phinney lobbied the U.S. Congress regarding education issues and land claims. Internationally recognized, Phinney received an honorary degree from the Russian Academy of Science in Leningrad as well as the Indian Council Fire Award in 1946. In 1973 the Nez Percé published its own history, Noon Nee-Me-Poo: We, the Nez Percés co-authored by Nez Percé historian Allen P. Slickpoo Sr.

FILM, TELEVISION, AND THEATER

Hattie Kauffman, winner of four Emmy Awards, has been a national correspondent for CBS This Morning and a former feature reporter for ABC's Good Morning America.

LITERATURE

The works of Phil George (b. 1946), a Wallowa Nez Percé poet, have been published in several anthologies, including The Remembered Earth (1979) and Dancing on the Rim of the World (1990). His poetry has even been read on popular television shows, such as the *Tonight Show* and the *Dick Cavett Show*. Born in Seattle, Washington, George attended Gonzaga University in Spokane, Washington, and the Institute of American Indian Arts in Santa Fe, New Mexico. He is also a champion Traditional Plateau dancer. George wrote, produced, and narrated the program *A Season for Grandmothers* for the Public Broadcasting Service. His work is showcased at the Nez Percé National Historical Park in Spaulding, Idaho.

POLITICAL LEADERS

The Nez Percé have been blessed with a number of influential leaders. These leaders are not only recognized by Native Americans but have also an integral part of American history. Old Chief Joseph (1790?-1871), also known as Tuekakas and Wellaamotkin, was the primary leader of the Wallowa band of Nez Percé in the northeastern Oregon during the period of substantial encroachment of white settlers. Peacefully accepting non-Indians into Nez Percé territory, Joseph was one of the first Nez Percé baptized by the Presbyterian minister Henry Spalding. Joseph reluctantly signed the 1855 treaty with territorial governor Isaac Stevens, since it reserved the Wallowa Valley lands for his band. However, the continued influx of non-Indians into his band's territory led his angry disavowal of Christianity and a stronger alignment with the more militant, anti-treaty Nez Percés. In 1886, nine years after his death, whites opened his grave and displayed his skull in a dental office. In 1926 he was reinterred in his homeland valley.

Lawyer (1796-1876), also known as Aleiya, was the son of Twisted Hair, the Nez Percé leader who welcomed and aided Lewis and Clark in 1805. Following his father's tradition, Lawyer became leader of the band of Nez Percé living along the Clearwater River of north-central Idaho. He also sought friendship with the non-Indians entering the area, serving as guide and interpreter for early explorers and trappers in the region. In addition, Lawyer served as a teacher for Presbyterian missionary Asa Smith at Kamiah. Lawyer was known for his oratorical skills and mastery of English. He became leader of the treaty faction of the Nez Percé, signing both the 1855 and 1863 treaties with territorial governor Isaac Stevens, and even protecting Stevens from attacks by natives. In his latter years, Lawyer traveled to Washington, D.C., to protest the breaking of treaty terms by the United States. He died the year before the Nez Percé War.

Looking Glass (1823?-1877) was born Allalimya Takanin. His father, also known as Looking Glass, was leader of the Asotin band of Nez Percé living in the Clearwater River drainage of north-central Idaho. He was also recognized as leader of the non-treaty Nez Percé in general. Takanin inherited the band leadership and the name. Young Looking Glass was appointed a war leader for the Nez Percé in 1848. Like a number of his contemporary Nez Percé leaders, Looking Glass followed a path of passive resistance to white encroachment into Nez Percé territory. However, as war broke out in northeast Oregon between the Joseph band and the United States, Looking Glass was drawn into the conflict when his own village was attacked by a combined volunteer militia and U.S. Army force. Looking Glass became the initial leader of the fleeing force of Nez Percé attempting to join Sitting Bull's Sioux, already exiled in Canada after the Battle of Little Bighorn the previous year. However, Looking Glass's consistent underestimation of the U.S. determination to track down the Nez Percé lost him his leadership role to others, including Chief Joseph. Looking Glass was killed as the Nez Percé fought their last battle just short of the Canadian border.

Also known as Hin-mut-too-yah-lat-kekht, or Thunder-Traveling-Across-Lake-and-Fading-on-Mountainside, Chief Joseph (c.1840-1904) and other tribal leaders led a large band of Nez Percé in the most successful, sustained resistance to the U.S. cavalry ever achieved by Native American fighters. The Nez Percé War of 1877 broke out after the tribe had suffered years of abuse from white settlers living on their land and unreasonable demands by the federal government for the Indians to confine their living space and accommodate the settlers' demands. Chief Joseph, whose father (also named Joseph) was a prominent leader of the Wallowa band, took charge upon his father's death in 1871. After several years of passive noncompliance with the Treaty of 1863, he prepared to lead his band out of Wallowa Valley in Idaho in 1877 under the threat of war with the United States. When rebels from the band attacked and killed a group of white settlers, however, Chief Joseph and his whole band (men, women, children, the elderly, and their horse herd) began a 1,600-mile trek through Idaho and Montana toward Canada with the army in pursuit. After outsmarting the American troops numerous times and engaging in 14 separate battles, the Nez Percé were finally forced to surrender just 30 miles short of their goal. At that time Chief Joseph uttered the famous words, "I will fight no more forever." He continued to be a respected leader during the early reservation years, as he eloquently pleaded the tribe's case before government representatives. In 1879 he gave a famous interview that was published in the *North American Review* under the title "An

Indian's View of Indian Affairs," which brought national attention to the Nez Percé. He died in 1904 on the Colville reservation in Washington. Other leaders of the period included Timothy, White Bird, Yellow Wolf, and Ollikut.

MEDIA

Indian Art Northwest.
Dedicated to enhancing public awareness and appreciation of Native American arts and culture in the Pacific Northwest. Publishes information related to Native American arts and educational events and products.

Address: 911 Northeast 11th Avenue, Portland, Oregon 97232.
Telephone: (503) 230-7005.

Nez Percé Tribal Newspaper.
Address: Box 305, Lapwai, Idaho 85341.

Wana Chinook Tymoo.
A publication of the Columbia River Inter-Tribal Fish Commission.

Address: 729 Northeast Oregon, Suite 200, Portland, Oregon 97232.
Telephone: (503) 238-0667.

ORGANIZATIONS AND ASSOCIATIONS

Affiliated Tribes of Northwest Indians.
Address: 222 Northwest Davis, Suite 403, Portland, Oregon 97209.
Telephone: (503) 241-0070.

Columbia River Inter-Tribal Fish Commission.
Address: 729 Northeast Oregon, Suite 200, Portland, Oregon 97232.
Telephone: (503) 238-0667.

Nez Percé Arts and Crafts Guild.
A cooperative for Nez Percé craftspersons.

Address: P.O. Box 205, Lapwai, Idaho 83540.

Nez Percé Tribe.
Address: P.O. Box 305, Lapwai, Idaho 83540.
Telephone: (208) 843-2253.

Pi-Nee-Waus Community Center.
Provides information concerning contemporary Nez Percé artists.

Address: P.O. Box 305, Lapwai, Idaho 83540.
Telephone: (208) 843-2253.

White Eagle Trading Post.
Retail sales of Nez Percé arts and crafts, including beaded, feather, and leather pieces.

Address: Highway 1, Orofino, Idaho.
Telephone: (208) 476-7753.

MUSEUMS AND RESEARCH CENTERS

Clearwater Historical Museum.
Holds Nez Percé artifacts, photographic file, and other papers.

Contact: Robert Spencer.
Address: 315 College Avenue, Orofino, Idaho 83544.
Telephone: (208) 476-5033.

Gonzaga University Archives.
Considerable information on traditional Plateau cultures from missionaries' journals and other unpublished archival documents are housed in this independent Catholic college founded in 1887 by Jesuits.

Address: East 502 Boone Avenue, Spokane, Washington 99258.
Telephone: (509) 328-4220.

Idaho State Historical Society Library.
Contains more than 200 volumes of Lapwai Agency records between 1871 and 1883 in addition to photo archives, diaries, and a library of published literature regarding the Nez Percé tribe.

Contact: Arthur A. Hart.
Address: 610 North Julia Davis Drive, Boise, Idaho 83702.
Telephone: (208).

Nez Percé National Historic Park and Museum.
Houses photo archives and exhibits relating to the Nez Percé cultural history.

Contact: Susan J. Buchel.
Address: P.O. Box 93, Spalding, Idaho 83551.
Telephone: (208) 843-2261.

University of Idaho Library Archives and Pacific Northwest Anthropological Archives.

Address: University of Idaho, Moscow, Idaho 83844.

Telephone: (208) 885-6326.

Whitman College Library Archives.

This private college, founded in 1859, houses a collection of unpublished documents on Nez Percé culture.

Address: Whitman College, Walla Walla, Washington 99362.

Telephone: (509) 527-5111.

SOURCES FOR ADDITIONAL STUDY

Brown, Mark. *The Flight of the Nez Percé.* Lincoln: University of Nebraska Press, 1967.

Egan, Timothy. "Expelled in 1877, Indian Tribe Is Now Wanted as a Resource."*New York Times*, July 22, 1996.

Josephy, Alvin M., Jr. *The Nez Percé Indians and the Opening of the Northwest.* New Haven, CT: Yale University Press, 1965.

McWhorter, Lucullus Virgil *Yellow Wolf: His Own Story* Caldwell, Idaho: The Caxton Printers, Ltd. 1948.

Sherrow, Victoria. *The Nez Percé.* Brookfield, Conneticut: The Milbrook Press 1994.

Slickpoo, Allen P., and Deward E. Walker, Jr. *Noon Nee-Me-Poo: We, the Nez Percés.* Lapwai, ID: Nez Percé Tribe of Idaho, 1973.

Trafzer, Clifford E. *The Nez Percé.* New York: Chelsea House, 1992.

Walker, Deward E., Jr. "Nez Percé." *Native America in the Twentieth Century: An Encyclopedia,* edited by Mary B. Davis. New York: Garland Publishing, 1994.

NICARAGUAN AMERICANS

by
Stefan Smagula

For Nicaraguan Americans, the central plazas of Nicaraguan towns may have been replaced by shopping centers and malls, but traditions do not change as easily as one's locale. Having only recently arrived in the United States, most Nicaraguan Americans have maintained their traditions and beliefs.

OVERVIEW

Bordered on the north by Honduras, on the south by Costa Rica, on the east by the Caribbean Sea, and on the west by the Pacific Ocean, Nicaragua is Central America's largest nation. Within its triangular borders there are 57,089 square miles (147,900 square kilometers), making Nicaragua the size of Iowa. Dividing the Caribbean lowlands from the Pacific coast is a range of volcanic mountains whose highest peak, Pico Mogoton, 6,913 feet above sea level, is near the Honduran border. The 3,000-square-mile Lake Nicaragua is the largest lake in Central America, and because it was once part of the Pacific Ocean, it is the only place in the world where freshwater sharks, swordfish, and sea horses live. The Caribbean lowlands, which extend inland from the Mosquito Coast, make up half the national territory, but most of Nicaragua's population has always been concentrated near the fertile Pacific coast.

In 1970 about two million people were living in Nicaragua. In 1995 the population could reach 4.5 million, and by 2025 the population could be over nine million, according to the United Nations Department of International Economic and Social Affairs. The population grows 3.4 percent each year, according to the Inter-American Development Bank. *Mestizos*—people of mixed Spanish-indigenous ancestry—make up about 77 percent of Nicaragua's population. Another ten percent are of European descent, nine percent are of African descent, and four percent are indigenous. However, these numbers oversimplify the complex racial, cultural, and ethnic makeup of a country where, before the Spanish conquest, there lived at least nine distinct indigenous peoples.

In the mid-1990s, the main cultural-racial groups are *mestizos*, *indígenas*, English- and Garífuna-speaking Afro-Karib people, and a small Caucasian elite class. Among the groups living on the Atlantic coast that are commonly defined as indigenous are the Miskito, Sumu, and Rama. The Miskito are not exactly an indigenous group, but a mixture of indigenous peoples and all the travellers who have passed through the Mosquito Coast over the last two centuries. The Sumu and Rama are indigenous people who probably originated in South America. The Garífuna, known historically as the "Black Karibs," are the descendants of escaped African slaves and Karib Indians who intermarried on the island of St. Vincent, where they lived until the British transported them forcibly to the Caribbean coast of Central America in 1796. The Caucasian elite is formed by a small, but typically wealthy, group of people whose ancestors came from Europe—usually Spain, Germany, France, and England. There are minorities of Chinese, Arabs, Cubans, Russians, and others in Nicaragua today.

Indígena, or indigenous, is a cultural and linguistic designation, not merely a racial term. The term "indigenous" refers to people who not only have ancestors who came from Central or South America but who self-consciously identify themselves with a specific indigenous group or tribe, speak the language, and practice the customs of that group. It is possible to be entirely indigenous in the racial sense and to be *mestizo*. *Mestizos* are culturally, linguistically, and often racially mixed people. The word *mestizo* means "mixed race" in Spanish and refers to the race of people that has resulted from hundreds of years of assimilation and intermarriage between Spanish and indigenous people.

About 88 percent of the entire country is nominally Roman Catholic. Many Nicaraguans, especially in rural areas, practice a syncretist form of religion that combines indigenous religious beliefs with Catholicism. A small but growing percentage of the country belongs to evangelical, Pentecostal, and fundamentalist Protestant churches.

HISTORY

Archaeologists working in El Bosque, Estelí, Nicaragua unearthed a pile of Mastodon and Megatherium bones that suggest that prehistoric people used El Bosque as a slaughter site as many as 20,000 to 30,000 years ago. The bones at El Bosque are among the oldest known evidence of a prehistoric human presence in Central America. Archaeologists and others have theorized that the ancestors of the people who lived long ago at El Bosque—and of all indigenous people in the Americas—originally came from Asia across an ice- or land-bridge between Siberia and Alaska. Aside from archeological and geological evidence, there are also some genetic similarities between Asians and indigenous Americans that support the idea of the Asian origin of indigenous American peoples.

INDIGENOUS SOCIETIES

Many thousands of years after the first people arrived in North America between 5000 and 2000 B.C., the Mayan empire first began to develop along the Caribbean coast, and eventually its influence spread through a network of city-states that stretched from present-day southern Mexico into Honduras, just north of Nicaragua. The ancient Maya produced many intellectual and artistic accomplishments. They invented the first system of writing in the New World, developed a sophisticated knowledge of astronomy and mathematics, worshipped at brightly painted temples of stone, lived in large city-like centers, and sustained a rigid and highly structured society. The many Mayan temples and stone-paved roads that remain are testimony to the beauty, ingenuity, and durability of ancient Mayan architecture and engineering. But the Mayan culture that flowered so brilliantly was the same culture that waged the brutal civil wars that may have contributed to the sudden and mysterious downfall of the Mayan empire around 900 A.D. The descendants of the ancient Maya live today in Guatemala and the Yucatán Peninsula in southern Mexico. The influence of the ancient Maya is ubiquitous throughout Central America, and many Mayan-language words are present in the everyday Spanish spoken in modern Nicaragua.

After the fall of the Maya, the Aztecs, a Nahuat-speaking group who originated in northern Mexico, came into full power. They eventually established a series of allegiances that spread from Mexico to El Salvador. The Nicarao and some of the other indigenous groups of Nicaragua may have originally fled south to Nicaragua in order to avoid subjugation by the aggressive Aztecs. These migrating groups of people brought with them the Aztec language and culture, both of which persist in various forms today in Nicaragua.

COLONIAL PERIOD

Before the Spanish conquest in the early 1520s, Nicaragua was inhabited by numerous competing indigenous groups that probably originally came from both the North and the South. Among them were the Niquiranos, the Nicarao (also known as the Nahual or Nagual), the Chorotega, the Chontales (or Mames), the Miskito, the Sumu (or Sumo), the Voto, the Suerre, and the Guetar. The invading Spaniards and the epidemics that followed the conquest all but eradicated the Nicarao, Chorotega, Chontales, Voto, Suerre, Guetar, and numerous other indigenous Nicaraguan peoples. Having been decimated by war and disease, their societies in shambles, the surviving indigenous people were often forced to learn Spanish, to convert to Catholicism, and to work under slavelike conditions for the benefit of the Spanish colonizers and missionary priests. Over the years, many of these indigenous people assimilated and intermarried into Spanish colonial society, forming the racial-cultural group called *mestizo*.

Although a few Nicarao persisted in Nicaragua until the mid-twentieth century, their descendants are now only vaguely aware of their ethnic identity. Unlike the Nicarao, whose culture has been subsumed by mestizo culture, some indigenous groups in Nicaragua have maintained their language, culture, and ethnic identity. Through a combination of fierce resistance to Hispanic control and isolation in the Caribbean lowlands, the Miskito, the Sumu, and the Rama have managed to survive and maintain their ethnic identity into the present.

INDEPENDENCE

From the time of the conquest until 1821, Spain controlled most of Nicaragua. British colonizers controlled some areas along the Caribbean coast. Nicaragua gained independence from Spain first in 1821 as part of the Mexican empire and later as part of the Central American Federation. By 1838 the Federation had collapsed, and rival conservative and liberal factions had begun violent struggles for power in Nicaragua. The rivalry was as much based on political differences as it was on *localismo*—the provincial hatred between Grenada and Leon, the two oldest colonial cities in Nicaragua. In the mid-1800s the United States and Britain aggravated the liberal-conservative feud when the two nations competed for control over a potential transoceanic canal route that would have crossed Nicaragua via the San Juan River and Lake Nicaragua.

In 1855 liberal leader General Francisco de Castellón invited a well-known Tennessee-born adventurer named William Walker to come to Nicaragua as a peaceful "colonist" with the understanding that Walker was to be the defender of the liberals. However, when Walker arrived with a gang of 58 mercenaries named the "American Phalanx of Immortals," he promptly ended the civil war and declared himself president of Nicaragua. The same day he took office, he issued four decrees: the first was an agreement to borrow money from abroad with the Nicaraguan territory as collateral; the second confiscated the property of the conservatives, for sale to U.S. citizens; the third made English the official language of the country; and the fourth reinstated slavery.

Walker next attempted to conquer the other four Central American republics, but a combined effort by the Central American armies eventually forced his retreat in May of 1857. Fortunately for Walker, there was a U.S. ship waiting to take him back to New Orleans, where he was given a hero's welcome. Completely discredited by the Walker incident, the liberals lost control to the conservatives, who established the Nicaraguan capital in Managua. The conservative government was stable but not democratic. In November of 1857, Walker led another failed invasion of Nicaragua and once again was shipped safely back to the United States. Three years later Walker made his third attempt to achieve "manifest destiny," but this time a British ship overcame him and turned him over to the Honduran government; a Honduran firing squad ended Walker's life. It was just the beginning of a long era of U.S. intervention in Nicaraguan politics.

MODERN ERA

In recent years the people of Nicaragua have suffered many disasters, both natural and man-made. Hurricanes, severe earthquakes, dictatorships, revolution, counterrevolution, famines, epidemics, civil war, volcanic eruptions, and foreign machination have all besieged Nicaragua. In 1909 the U.S. government supported a revolution that ousted liberal General Jose Santos Zelaya and instated conservative rule. In 1912 popular revolt against the conservatives led to U.S. Marine intervention, and the Marines essentially did not leave Nicaragua until 1933, after fighting a guerrilla war against General Augusto Cesar Sandino and his followers. At the request of their commander, General Anastasio Somoza, the U.S.-trained Nicaraguan National Guard killed General Sandino.

Somoza seized control of Nicaragua in 1936 and was the country's dictatorial ruler until his assassination by young poet Rigoberto Lopez in

1956. Somoza's sons, Luis Somoza Debayle and Anastasio Somoza Debayle, who both spoke English and were educated in the United States, assumed control of the country. When Luis, better known as Tachito, died a natural death in 1967, Anastasio became leader.

After a severe earthquake leveled Managua in 1972, Anastasio Somoza's detractors claimed that Somoza had embezzled many millions of dollars of earthquake-relief money. Popular dissatisfaction with the perceived widespread corruption and brutality of the Somoza regime, coupled with anger over what many believed was the Somoza-directed murder of opposition leader Pedro Joaquin Chamorro in 1978, prompted nationwide uprisings that led to civil war. The Marxist guerrillas of the Sandinista National Liberation Front (FSLN) led the anti-Somoza fighting. The Sandinistas, who take their name from General Sandino, took power on July 9, 1979 and set up a broad-based coalition government. On July 17, 1979 Somoza, along with many of the top-ranking government officials, fled with their families to Miami, Florida. The coalition government soon broke up when the leadership of the Roman Catholic church, industrialists, and moderate politicians all opposed the FSLN's Marxist elements. Somoza later moved from Miami to Paraguay, where he was assassinated.

POST-REVOLUTION U.S. INVOLVEMENT IN NICARAGUA

President Ronald Reagan imposed an economic embargo against Nicaragua, citing what he saw as the threat of Marxism and Communism in the "backyard" of the United States. Despite a thorough campaign of misinformation by the U.S. Department of State, which denied American support for anti-Sandinistas, the U.S. government secretly aided anti-Sandinista guerrillas, or "Contras." Exiled Nicaraguan Contra leaders who lived in Miami worked together with high-ranking officials in the Marines, the Central Intelligence Agency (CIA), and the National Security Council (NSC) to supply weapons and money to the Contras at a time when Congress had passed a law banning U.S. government support for the Contras. This affair was partially brought to light in 1986 when then-Attorney General Edwin Meese discovered that much of the money for the Contras came from a secret arms-for-hostages deal between the United States and Iran. Marine Lt. Col. Oliver North and other high-ranking officials in the CIA and NSC were later convicted of crimes ranging from perjury to conspiracy to defraud the U.S. government. Presidents Reagan and Bush denied prior knowledge of the Iran-Contra

affair, as the scandal came to be called. In 1992 President Bush pardoned all of the high-ranking officials who were involved with the scandal.

FLEDGLING DEMOCRACY

FSLN leader Daniel Ortega Saavedra was elected president of Nicaragua in 1984, but much of the opposition boycotted the election. As fighting against the U.S.-funded Contras began to grow more and more severe, economic and civil rights conditions continued to deteriorate in Nicaragua, prompting many former Sandinista supporters to flee to the United States and Costa Rica.

Violeta Barrios de Chamorro, wife of slain anti-Somoza leader Pedro Joaquin Chamorro, was elected president in February 1990. She is a conservative who is moderately opposed to the Sandinistas. After Chamorro's election the U.S. trade embargo was lifted, and in November 1993, in response to Chamorro's pledge to place the army under non-Sandinista control, President Bill Clinton approved $40 million in aid for Nicaragua. Chamorro attempted to achieve peace by giving amnesty to both sides for crimes committed during the civil war, but later clashes between the Sandinista-controlled army and "recontras" have revived old anxieties among Nicaraguans.

Sixteen years after the Sandinista revolution, Nicaragua was still in a desperate situation. There were an estimated 1,500 recontras, former right-wing rebels, fighting for land rights. The annual per capita income in 1994 was $540, less than it was in 1960, according to the University of Central America. Some 60 percent of Nicaraguans were unemployed, and 70 percent lived in extreme poverty, according to United Nations estimates. The infant mortality rate was the highest in Central America: 81 deaths per 1,000 live births. Nicaragua had an external debt of about $14 billion and suffered from inflation. In a mid-1990s poll in Nicaragua, 50 percent of the respondents said that Nicaragua was better off under the brutal Somoza regime, and only seven percent said that the country was better off under Chamorro, according to Canadian magazine *Maclean's*. In 1996, a conservative, Arnoldo Aleman, defeated Ortega in the presidential election.

THE FIRST NICARAGUANS IN AMERICA

Little is known about the first Nicaraguans to immigrate to the United States. One early visitor was Padre Augustín Vigil, a priest from Granada, Nicaragua, who served as William Walker's ambassador to the United States. Padre Vigil lived in

Washington, D.C., sometime between 1856 and 1857. The U.S. Census Bureau did not keep separate statistics for individual Central American countries until 1960. Pre-1960 census reports simply lumped Nicaraguans together with all Spanish-surnamed people. Estimates of the number of undocumented early immigrants are not available. Available statistics show a great deal of variation from decade to decade. Documented migration to the United States from Central America rose from 500 individuals entering between 1890 and 1900 to 8,000 individuals between 1900 and 1910. U.S. demand for labor increased during World War I, and 17,000 Central Americans entered the United States legally between 1910 and 1920. Due to 1920s legislation that restricted the flow of immigrants from the Western Hemisphere, the number of Central American immigrants dropped to 6,000 during the 1930s (Nora Hamilton and Norma Stoltz Chinchilla, "Central American Migration: A Framework Analysis," *Latin American Research Review*, Volume 26, No. 1; p. 81). In general, early migration from Nicaragua to the United States was facilitated by Nicaragua's political and economic dependency upon the United States.

Nicaragua's dependence upon the United States has fostered in the Nicaraguans a "perverse esteem" for the United States, according to Judith Thurman in an article written for the *New Yorker*. Esteem for the United States, whether perverse or not, is certainly one of the main factors that has attracted Nicaraguans to move North. Across Central America the United States is thought of as a *país de maravillas* or "country of marvels," where everyone is wealthy, or at least upwardly mobile.

Nearly 7,500 Nicaraguans immigrated legally into the United States between 1967 and 1976. In 1970, 28,620 Nicaraguans were living in the United States, according to the U.S. Census Bureau. Over 90 percent of Nicaraguan immigrants self-reported as "white" on the 1970 census. Most Nicaraguan immigrants during the late 1960s were women: there were only 60 male Nicaraguan immigrants for every 100 female immigrants during this period (Ann Orlov and Reed Veda, "Central and South Americans," *Harvard Encyclopedia of American Ethnic Groups* [Cambridge: Harvard University Press, 1980]; pp. 210-217). This male-to-female ratio may be explained by the large number of Central American women who came to the United States to work as domestic servants so that they could send money home to Nicaragua. Most immigrants during this period settled in urban areas, and many went to live in Los Angeles and San Francisco, California.

DOCUMENTED IMMIGRATION

The 1979 revolution triggered the largest waves of Nicaraguan immigrants. Documented immigration increased two to three times after the revolution, and undocumented immigration rose dramatically. Migration to the United States occurred in three waves. The first wave took place during the time of the revolution, when the wealthy families closely associated with the Somoza regime fled to Miami. Perhaps as many as 20,000 Nicaraguans immigrated to Miami during this period. After the revolution there was a period of repatriation, when people who had left Nicaragua to avoid the conflicts returned home. The second wave occurred during the early 1980s, when the Nicaraguan government was reorganized. Many non-Sandinista members of the coalition as well as industrialists whose companies had been seized by the state left the country—some ending up in the United States. In the mid-1980s, fighting between the Sandinistas and the U.S.-supported Contras became more severe, which caused the country's economic and civil rights conditions to worsen significantly. The real wage paid to workers, for example, declined by over 90 percent from 1981 to 1987, according Sandinista figures, and the opposition newspaper was heavily censored. This economic chaos and social repression prompted the third and largest wave of immigrants to date. Over 62 percent of the total documented immigration from 1979 to 1988 occurred after 1984 (Edward Funkhouser, "Migration from Nicaragua: Some Recent Evidence," *World Development*, Volume 20, No. 8, 1992; p. 1210). The immigrants in the third wave tended to be young men of all classes fleeing the involuntary military draft and poorer families seeking to escape harsh economic conditions and violence.

The three waves together brought the documented population of all Nicaraguans in the United States to 202,658, with a large percentage of that number, 168,659, having been born in Nicaragua, according to the 1990 U.S. Census. However, some sources say that in the late 1980s there were probably about 175,000 documented and undocumented Nicaraguans in Miami alone.

Between 1982 and 1992, approximately ten percent to 12 percent of the population of Nicaragua left their native country. The largest numbers of people went to Costa Rica, but hundreds of thousands went to the United States, Honduras, and Guatemala. Between 1979 and 1988, 45,964 Nicaraguans emigrated to Costa Rica legally, and another 24,000 people were classified as refugees, as reported by the Nicaraguan Instituto Nacional de Estadísticas y Censos. During almost the same period, 21,417 Nicaraguans entered the United States legally, according to the Immigration and Naturalization Service's *Statistical Yearbook*. In 1988 over 44,000 people, or 1.5 percent of the population of 3.6 million, left Nicaragua, according to the Nicaraguan Instituto Nacional de Estadísticas y Censos.

When the Sandinistas tried to relocate the Miskitos away from the war zones, thousands of Miskitos fled to Honduras and Costa Rica to avoid what they felt was mistreatment by the Hispanic Sandinistas. Large numbers of Miskitos also joined the Contras in Honduras. It is not known whether Miskitos traveled in large numbers to the United States, and the same is true of the Garífuna. There is reportedly a Garífuna community living in Houston, Texas, and some of them may be Nicaraguan.

UNDOCUMENTED IMMIGRATION

The majority of Nicaraguans have entered the United States without the knowledge of immigration authorities. Because most Nicaraguan immigrants are undocumented, and therefore deportable, collecting information about them is difficult. When the Immigration Reform and Control Act of 1986 offered amnesty to all undocumented immigrants who could prove that they had entered the United States before 1982, 15,900 Nicaraguans applied for amnesty. This is more than double the number of Nicaraguans who entered the country legally between 1979 and 1982. According to several studies, the number of amnesty applicants suggests that there were about 200,000 Nicaraguans living in the United States during the mid-1980s (Funkhouser, p. 1210). The true number of Nicaraguan immigrants can only be estimated, but by 1995 it was probably over 250,000.

ENTERING THE UNITED STATES ILLEGALLY

Aimed at reducing the numbers of illegal immigrants to the United States, the 1986 Immigration Reform and Control Act had little effect on the numbers of immigrants who entered the United States—it just drove the flow of undocumented immigrants deeper underground and made it more difficult for them to find work once in the United States. Even before the law was passed, large numbers of Nicaraguans were forced to cross the Mexican-United States border illegally with the help of *coyotes*, a Spanish colloquial term for the people who illegally transport immigrants into the United States. After the law was passed, and border control was stepped up, the *coyotes* began to charge more money.

Undocumented Nicaraguans who enter the United States typically cross Honduras, Guatemala, and Mexico before they reach the United States. *Coyotes*, so called because they often prey upon the people they are transporting, rob, rape, enslave, and sometimes even kill the immigrants they carry. The illegal immigrants are known colloquially as *mojados* or wetbacks, illegals, and *pollos*—Spanish for "chickens," the prey of *coyotes*. Sometimes the *coyotes* recruit the *pollos* inside of Nicaragua, even offering to take the immigrant across the border on family credit; otherwise the immigrant gets to the Mexican-United States border on her or his own and then contacts and pays the *coyote*. Whatever the case, the journey is always dangerous and expensive. *Coyotes* charge from between $400 to $1,500 per person—depending upon the distance involved and the current demand—to take the *pollo* into the United States. The entire journey from Nicaragua to Los Angeles, for example, easily could cost $2,000 to $2,500, after paying the *mordidas*, or bribes to Mexican officials at control posts on Mexican highways, the *coyote*'s fee, food, and transportation costs. This is an enormous sum of money for most people in Nicaragua, where the average person makes about $540 dollars a year.

The border towns of Tijuana and El Paso are the crossing points favored by undocumenteds. These towns are notorious for drug cartels and prostitution rings in which many Central American immigrants, Nicaraguans among them, are forced to work. One chapter in *Miami: Secretos de un exilio*, a book written by a Nicaraguan who traveled in the United States, tells the tale of one woman and her four children who narrowly escaped tragedy when they tried to cross at El Paso. The family flew into Mexico City and then traveled to a border town where she claimed the Mexican police robbed her of all the money she had, $970, and even took the clothes of her small children. Penniless, friendless, and homeless, the woman had almost given up hope when a family member living in Miami was able to help her and her children to reach Miami, where she filed a claim for political asylum. The INS allowed her to remain in the United States until her claim could be heard by the court—a process that could take years.

Not every woman who attempts to cross the border illegally has family in the United States and not every woman makes it across the border. Some must struggle to survive waiting on tables at bars or working as prostitutes in the rough bordertowns like Ciudad Juarez, Matamoros, and Nuevo Laredo, hoping to someday save enough to cross into *el norte*, or "the north," as the United States is known. The number of Central American women who are raped in transit to the United States is unknown because most women are too ashamed to tell even family or friends about the crime, but many estimate that rape, along with robbery, is common. On the U.S. side of the border, undocumented immigrants cannot report assault, rape, or exploitation in the cantinas, manual-labor jobs, or the sweatshops that employ them for fear of being deported by the *migra*, as the INS is known in California, Texas, and Florida.

SETTLEMENT PATTERNS

Miami, the capital of the exile, is the center of Nicaraguan American life. The ousted dictator Anastasio Somoza was the first of about 175,000 Nicaraguans who overwhelmed Miami in the 1980s. A small city called Sweetwater, about 16 miles from Miami, has been dubbed "Little Managua" by the locals because of the large number of Nicaraguans who settled there. Nicaraguans have also created communities in other large urban centers where Hispanics live, such as Los Angeles and San Francisco. Smaller numbers of Nicaraguans live in large cities in Texas. All these cities have significant Spanish-speaking populations, and it is possible to work and live in areas where Spanish is spoken. This facilitates networking and the sense of community among the recent immigrants, many of whom speak little English. In 1990, soon after Chamorro was elected, a caravan of cars and buses left Miami headed for Nicaragua, according to several newspaper reports. But only a small portion of the total number of Nicaraguan Americans were repatriated.

REACTION TO NICARAGUAN IMMIGRANTS

Many Americans wished that more Nicaraguans would return to Nicaragua. In 1994, tensions between the haves and have-nots, and between the "legals," and the "illegals," led to the passage of Proposition 187 in California, which would prohibit undocumented immigrants from benefitting from publicly funded services like nonemergency health care and education. Similar legislation banning undocumented immigrant children from public schools was passed in Texas but was eventually overthrown by the U.S. Supreme Court. In 1999 several lawsuits against the enforcement of the law were settled by the state's new governor greatly weakening the law.

The recent animosity toward immigrants in California is in contrast to the welcome that Nicaraguan immigrants received in the early days of the first wave after the revolution. President Reagan painted the Nicaraguan revolution in stark cold-war tones: the Sandinistas were Marxists and Communists who were going to destabilize the Central American isthmus through their close alignment with Communist Cuba and the Soviet Union. According to this cold-war scenario, Nicaraguan immigrants were refugees and exiles who had escaped the Communist regime, and therefore deserved political asylum and assistance. Even though the political affiliation of the parent country is not supposed to enter into questions of asylum Nicaraguan applicants were granted political asylum about 50 percent of the time in 1987. Salvadorans fleeing similar conditions received asylum only three percent of the time in 1987.

During the mid- to late 1980s, in an attempt to make up for what they saw as wrong-headed American immigration laws and foreign policy in Central America, some Americans banded together to support Central Americans and Central American refugees. Over 80 municipal governments created U.S.-Nicaraguan sister city agreements. The U.S. cities sent medical supplies, food, and farming materials to their counterpart cities in Nicaragua. Some churches created what were called "sanctuaries" for undocumented immigrants. The churches offered support and shelter to Central American immigrants. During this period Central American refugee centers appeared in nearly every large urban center in America.

Key issues facing Nicaraguans staying permanently in the United States are questions of identity. They wonder, for example, whether they are considered refugees or immigrants, or whether they are merely living in exile. CARACEN, one of the leading Central American assistance groups, reflected this shift in identity when it recently changed its name from Central American Refugee Center to Central American Resource Center. Another key issue is the return of millions of dollars' worth of property seized by the Sandinistas under a law that gave the government the right to seize property if the owner was absent from Nicaragua for more than 60 days. Many of the former owners of the seized property are now citizens of the United States and are attempting to regain title through U.S. law.

MISCONCEPTIONS AND STEREOTYPES

The most common myth pertaining to Nicaraguan Americans is that they are all former *Somocistas*, as the followers of Somoza are called. This is untrue. Despite significant cultural differences among Hispanics, Nicaraguans are often perceived to be no

These Nicaraguan American girls are participating in a Cinco de Mayo parade.

different from other Hispanics and are thus subject to the same prejudices and stereotypes as other Hispanics. Some common stereotypes are that Hispanics are docile, ignorant, and easily led. On the West Coast and in the Southwest, Mexican Americans and Central Americans have been called "greasers," "beans," "beaners," and "spics" by people of other ethnic groups. According to one stereotype, Hispanics stay within their own group and always protect their own people. A phrase common in the schools and streets of California expresses this stereotype: "If you crush one bean, the whole burrito comes after you."

Undocumented Hispanic immigrants are also portrayed as ignorant workers who enjoy being exploited. In an article about the Southwest's dependence on undocumented workers published by the *Wall Street Journal* in 1985, the author wrote: "But Mexican nationals ... happily dangle in branches and power lines for the minimum wage" (*Wall Street Journal*, May 7, 1985; p. 10). Common among leftist American writers in the 1980s was the stereotype of the happy, friendly Nicaraguan: "But most of all I like the people—their friendliness,

their openness, their courage" (Rita Golden Gelman, *Inside Nicaragua: Young People's Dreams and Fears* [New York: Franklin Watts, 1988], p. 128).

ACCULTURATION AND ASSIMILATION

For Nicaraguan Americans, the central plazas of Nicaraguan towns may have been replaced by shopping centers and malls, but traditions do not change as easily as one's locale. Having only recently arrived in the United States, most Nicaraguan Americans have maintained their traditions and beliefs. Because the Nicaraguan American community in San Francisco, for instance, is relatively diffuse, Nicaraguan Americans there are assimilating into a pan-Latino culture more rapidly than they are assimilating into non-Latino culture.

TRADITIONS, CUSTOMS, AND BELIEFS

Some of the Nicaraguan people's beliefs and traditions date back to pre-Colombian times, and others appeared during colonial times. Most are a mixture of both pre- and post-Colombian culture. *La Llorona* is the name of a legendary woman-spirit who walks along streets and paths on dark nights sighing and sobbing over the children she lost during the time of the Spanish conquest. One version of the legend has it that her children were killed by an earthquake; another says that the children's Spanish father stole them away from her. This may be related to the Mexican legend of La Malinche, the lover and assistant of conquistador Cortés.

There are many folk beliefs in Nicaraguan culture. One belief says that if a person who has walked in the sun for many hours looks at a child with sun-irritated eyes, that child will be "infected with the sun" and will suffer from fever and diarrhea. The treatment is difficult unless the person who has infected the child is known. If the person is known, the treatment is simple: wrap the child in a sweaty shirt that has been worn by the person who originally infected him or her, and hours later the child will be healthy.

LA PURÍSIMA

Until recently, *La Purísima* was a holiday celebrated only in Nicaragua. Now it is also celebrated in Los Angeles, Miami, and other Nicaraguan American communities. The holiday takes place from the last days in November until the night of the seventh of December, which is called the *Noche de Gritería*, or "Night of the Shouting." All through the week women make all sorts of intricate traditional sweets and drinks that are exchanged during the last night. The centerpiece of the holiday is a small statue of the Virgin Mary covered with decorations of flowers, fruits, lights, and candles. Each night the family prays together in front of the statue. Then on the last night, neighbors, friends, and families go traveling from house to house in a secular-religious celebration that takes its name from the shouts raised in honor of the Virgin Mary: "Long live the Conception of Mary!" and "Who causes so much joy? The Conception of Maria!" are heard in the streets. Groups of people also sing traditional religious songs in front of the statue of the Virgin. Typically, the *gritería* culminates at midnight with the explosions of bombs and the reports of thousands of pistols shot into the air.

SEMANA SANTA

In Nicaragua, *Semana Santa*, or Holy Week, a major summer holiday, is a time for relaxing at the beach or vacationing. This holiday may still be celebrated by Nicaraguan Americans. On Easter Sunday villagers all over Nicaragua gather beneath bowers made of palm leaves decorated with fruits, vegetables, and flowers. Accompanied by a brass band, the villagers walk slowly around the town. At the head of the parade are people dressed as symbolic characters: Hebrew elders and Apostles. The Apostles carry a life-size statue of Christ. The procession usually ends up in a public square in front of the town's church, where there is food for sale and carnival-like concessions.

VELORIOS

The observation of a *velorio*, or funeral party, after a person's death is an old tradition with Hispanic origins. During the *velorio* the family and friends of the deceased gather to share their grief. The relatives and close friends sit in the same room as the deceased and maintain a silent prayer vigil throughout the night until morning. Others at the *velorio* talk in small groups to distract themselves from fatigue, tell picaresque stories, drink liquor, eat large amounts of food, and even gamble. Sometimes, after hours of drinking, the *velorio* ends in a raucous, drunken fight. Following the *velorio*, the body is taken to the cemetery in a funeral procession with a brass band. The mourners follow the casket on foot to the cemetery.

The *velorios de los santos*, or *velorios* of the saints are similar affairs in which small candles are lit on altars, festive decorations are hung, and prayers are made, accompanied by music and sometimes drunkenness. The most famous funeral procession of a saint is the procession of Managua's Saint Domingo. In this noisy and colorful parade, a tiny statue of the saint is carried to "sanctuary" in the hills of Managua. Marimbas, dancers, fireworks, and a carnival atmosphere mark the event.

SPORTS

The national sport of Nicaragua is baseball. The first organized baseball game in Nicaragua took place in 1892. For more than two decades in the early part of the twentieth century, U.S. Marines were stationed in Nicaragua. One result of the U.S. Marine occupation is Nicaragua's widespread fascination with baseball. In Nicaragua, the word for baseball is *béisbol* ("bays-bole"). Men and boys in small towns play baseball with whatever equipment they can muster—sometimes they use tough Nicaraguan grapefruits (for which the Nicaraguan word is *grapefruit*), or even an old sock rolled up around a rock, instead of a ball. There is also a professional league. At least five Nicaraguans who may have started by playing with rolled up socks later played for the major leagues in the United States. Cock fighting, a sport in which two trained cocks fight each other, is also popular among Nicaraguans. Men gather around the fighting birds to cheer their favorites and to make bets on the animals, who fight sometimes to their death.

PROVERBS

Seemingly innocuous, the following Nicaraguan proverbs and sayings reveal quite a bit about Nicaragua and Nicaraguans: *Con eme-omo-de-odo, se consigue todo*—With manners, everything can be obtained; *Cada uno tiene su modo de matar pulgas*—Everyone has her or his manner of killing fleas; *De todos modos, moros son todos*—At any rate, *moros* are everyone (A "*moro*" is the color white with

"**T**he Nicaraguan's worst fear is not the fear of losing a job, but the fear of getting sick."

A Nicaraguan American pediatrician in Miami (from Guillermo Corés Domínguez, *Miami: secretos de un exilio*. Managua: El Amanecer, 1986).

dark brown grease stains and may refer in a negative way to *mestizos*.); *El último mono se ahoga*—The last monkey drowns (Figuratively, the last in line will not receive her or his portion of food.); *No creer en santos que orinan*—Don't believe in saints that urinate; *Voltearse la tortilla*—The tortilla is flipped (refers to the way that tortillas are cooked. This is said when one party has fallen and another is ruling.); *Tamal con queso, comida de preso*—Tamale with cheese, food of the prisoner (tamales are made of meat cornmeal wrapped in cornhusks or banana leaves).

CUISINE

The importance of corn to traditional Nicaraguan cuisine, religion, and folklore cannot be overstated. To a large extent, the traditional cuisine of Nicaragua consists of varied and imaginative ways of preparing corn, or *maíz*. Nearly every part of the plant is used—from the fungus that grows on the corn to the husk that covers the cob—and nearly every type of dish and beverage is made of corn. Breakfast cereals, breads, drinks that taste a bit like coffee, puddings, desserts, porridges, and even beer are made from corn. Beans are also important. Unlike most of Central America, which prefers black beans, Nicaraguans tend to eat red beans. While everyday cuisine is based upon abundant corn and beans, the *criollo* ("cree-o-yo"), or Creole, cuisine is based more on meats and sauces that are Nicaraguan adaptations of Spanish and European dishes. The scarcity and high cost of meats in Nicaragua has put meats normally out of reach of everyone but the upper classes. In the United States, where meat is more abundant, Nicaraguans probably eat more meat dishes.

The small, round, unleavened *tortilla* ("tor-tiya"), made of ground and processed corn, is the daily staple of Nicaraguans. The *tortilla* is bread, spoon, and plate for Central Americans. Traditionally made at home by hand, *tortillas* are made by machines in the United States and sold in supermarkets all over California, the Southwest, and in southern Florida.

The *tamal* ("tahmahl") is a bit of corn dough with seasoned meat, sweet chocolate or vegetables, wrapped inside of a corn husk or a banana leaf before it is steamed or boiled. The national *tamal* is called *nacatamal* ("naca-tahmahl") and consists of pork, chicken, or turkey, various vegetables, mint, and hot peppers, all combined with a corn dough made with sour orange juice. A small amount of this mixture is put inside of an individual corn husk or banana leaf and then folded or rolled and sealed before cooking. Restaurants in Miami have signs in their windows that say: "Nacatamales and other Nicaraguan Foods." According to Angélica Vivas, author of *Cocina Nica*, "The silent nacatamal says more about the history of Nicaragua than all the pages of don José Dolores Gámez" (Angélica Vivas, *Cocina Nica* [Managua: Ministerio de Cultura], p. 17). Gámez was a chronicler of Nicaraguan colonial history.

Red bean soup is the most typical soup of Nicaragua. It is made from red beans boiled with garlic, onion, pork, and sweet red pepper. The soup is poured into a bowl, and then an egg is cracked into the hot soup. The heat of the soup partially cooks the egg.

Desserts called *almibares* ("almeebarays") consist of honey- and syrup-coated fruits such as mango, mamey, jocote, papaya, and marañon. *Almibares* are eaten all over the country during *Semana Santa*. Many corn-based desserts also exist. For example, *motlatl atol* ("moetlahtel ahtol") is a yellow pudding-like dessert made from corn, milk, sugar and a fruit, which is also eaten during *Semana Santa*. Chocolate, which is native to Central America, is used not only in sweet drinks and desserts but as a flavoring for meat dishes.

Because so many are undocumented immigrants, and so many work in clandestine jobs for low wages, many poorer Nicaraguan Americans have no health insurance. Those who have health insurance are either professionals who are covered through their employers or are successfully self-employed.

Nicaraguan-educated doctors came to the United States only to find out that without a U.S. medical degree, all those years of study and training were worth almost nothing. Those who had studied in the United States were more fortunate and could more easily transfer their experience to a job in the United States. Frustrated by their situation, some Nicaraguan-educated doctors in Miami founded clandestine clinics to serve the uninsured Nicaraguan American population. These clinics do not appear in telephone books and do not advertise. During the time of the Contra war, some of the medical supplies that were headed for the fighting in Honduras ended up in some of these clandestine clinics, according to a Nicaraguan journalist. Other Nicaraguan-educated doctors found illegal work in clinics that agreed to let them work at wages far below normal.

Nicaraguans, like all people native to the Americas and the Pacific Basin, are genetically prone to develop a small birthmark called a Mongoloid spot. The spot is a small, oval bluish mark found at the base of the spine on babies. Eventually this spot disappears, leaving no trace. In some cases a similar pigmentation, called Nevus of Ota, can appear on the cheeks or on the sclera of the eyes. Nevus of Ota is disfiguring, but usually not debilitating.

According to a study conducted in Los Angeles and published in 1992, post-traumatic stress disorder (PTSD) is common among Nicaraguan immigrant children who have witnessed or experienced violence. Fifteen of the 31 Central American children studied had witnessed violence. Of the children who both witnessed violence and lost contact with a caregiver, 100 percent suffered from some form of PTSD. The combined stress of living in guerrilla war conditions, forced emigration and impoverished living conditions in the United States cause many Nicaraguan refugee children to suffer from the symptoms of PTSD, including nightmares, nervousness, insomnia, loss of appetite, and tearfulness.

The indigenous medicine of Nicaragua is one part magical and one part rational. For every illness there is a specific therapy, usually of vegetal origin. Many potent botanical medicines are part of the traditional medicine—some of them, like the leaves of the coca plant, which are the source of cocaine, have been recognized as potent pharmaceuticals by Western science and medicine. The various leaves, roots, berries, etc. are usually made into a tea that the ill person drinks or a poultice that is applied to the body. Certain foods, like *atol* made from corn, are also believed to have specific curative properties.

La Hechicería, or the belief that some people have supernatural powers, is common among Nicaraguans and stems from indigenous beliefs. Those who practice *hechicería* are known as *brujos* ("brew-hose") or *brujas* ("brew-has"). *Brujos* are believed to have the power to transform themselves into animals, like tigers and dogs, and they are also believed to have the power to heal others.

LANGUAGE

Spanish is the language spoken by most Nicaraguans, but several indigenous groups speak their own languages, sometimes in addition to Spanish or English. The Miskito, Sumu, and Rama on the Atlantic coast all speak related, but distinct, languages. Many Garífuna also speak an Afro-Karib language of their own, sometimes in addition to Spanish and English. It is not known how many Garífuna or indigenous people have immigrated to the United States.

Nicaraguan Spanish has several distinguishing characteristics. The Nicaraguan accent dates back to the sixteenth century in Andalusia, and the relative isolation of Nicaragua meant that the accent did not change in the same ways that the Andalusian accent has. For example Nicaraguans have a tendency to replace the "s" sound with an "h" sound when speaking. Nicaraguans also tend to use grammatical constructions that are now rare in most other Spanish-speaking countries. For example: ¡Y quien sos vos!—And who are you! uses "vos," an antiquated form of "you." Some linguists have noted that onomatopoeic words are common in Nicaragua.

Nicaraguan Spanish also has many indigenous influences. Until the nineteenth century a hybrid form of Nahuat-Spanish was the common language of Nicaragua. Today Nahuat, Mangue, and Maya words and syntax can be found in everyday speech. As the words for two tropical fruits, *mamey* and *papaya*, testify, Nicaraguan Spanish has some Caribbean influences. *Béisbol* and *daime* ("dime") attest to Nicaragua's long association with the United States. However, the greatest number of Nicaraguanisms come from Aztec and Nahuat languages. An example of a Spanish-Aztec hybrid word is *chibola*, the Nicaraguan word for bottled soda. It is formed from two words: *Chi*, meaning small in Aztec, and *bola,* meaning ball in Spanish. Nicaraguan Americans and other Spanish-speaking newcomers in cities like Miami soon learn to speak "Spanglish"—a combination of Spanish and English. For example: "Have a nice day, *Señor.*" This type of language usage is so common that it can be heard on Spanish-language radio shows and television.

The most novel contribution Nicaragua has made to the Spanish language is the word *jodido* ("ho-dee-doe") and its many variants. *Jodido* stems from the most vulgar and indecent of all verbs in Latin American use that describe the act of sexual intercourse. Strangely enough, *jodido* has been used so commonly in Nicaragua by all classes of people that the word has lost much of its original obscenity and now means something like "bothered" or "screwed."

GREETINGS AND OTHER COMMON EXPRESSIONS

Buenos días (Spanish), *Pain lalahurám* (Miskito), and *Buiti binafi* (Garífuna) mean "Good day." *¿Qué tal, amiga?* (Spanish), *Naksá?* (Miskito), and *Numá ¿Ida biñá gia* (Garífuna) are translated as "How's it going, friend?" *Bendiga, mami* (Spanish) and *Busó da* (Miskito) mean "Bless you, mother." *¿Como te llamas?* (Spanish) and *¿Ka gia biri?* (Garífuna) mean "What's your name?" *Adios* (Spanish), *Asabé* (Miskito), and *Ayó* (Garífuna) all mean "Good-bye."

FAMILY AND COMMUNITY DYNAMICS

Partly because of tradition, and partly because of the Catholic prohibition against birth control and abortion, Nicaraguan American families tend to be larger than is typical in the United States. The tradition of larger families may have its origin in Nicaragua's agricultural economy, where more children meant more help to plant and harvest. In the 1960s and early 1970s, few families immigrated together—two-thirds of all Nicaraguan Americans were women. As the reasons for immigration changed over the years, single women gave way to more families and widowed women with children. Sometimes families spanning three generations immigrated together. When immigrants are fleeing from violence and economic problems, as Nicaraguans were in the 1980s, they want to take as many loved ones with them as they can. When the goal is to make money to send home, as it was in the late 1960s, immigrants tend to migrate alone. No records of the number of Nicaraguan American

families who receive public assistance exist, but the number is probably fairly small, because many Nicaraguans are undocumented and are not eligible for any public assistance.

INTERMARRIAGE

In a 1989 San Francisco study of birth records, out of 192 Nicaraguan-born mothers living in San Francisco, 12.5 percent had children with men born in the United States; 56 percent had children with men born in Nicaragua. Nicaraguan-born women were much more likely (28.1 percent) to have children with Mexican- or other Latin American-born men than they were with U.S.-born men. The same study showed that the degree of intermixing between Nicaraguan Americans and other groups is higher than the degree of intermixing between Mexican Americans and other groups. This implies that Nicaraguan Americans, in San Francisco at least, are less likely than Mexican Americans to retain a distinct nationality-based identity (Steven P. Wallace, "The New Urban Latinos, Central Americans in a Mexican Immigrant Environment," *Urban Affairs Quarterly,* Volume 25, No. 2, December 1989; pp. 252-255).

Divisions are deep among Nicaraguan American families and communities. The Sandinista revolution split sister from brother, mother from daughter, and friend from friend. Attitudes for or against the Sandinistas undermined efforts to create cohesive communities in cities like Los Angeles, where Casa Nicaragua, a Nicaraguan American social and political organization, was burned down in 1982, supposedly by Somocistas. However, as Nicaraguan Americans have become more assimilated, the political differences that have divided the community are dissipating. Relatives of the deposed dictator Somoza own a chain of Nicaraguan restaurants in Miami, and these restaurants have become gathering places for a diverse group of Nicaraguans. Speaking of the restaurant, one Nicaraguan American man said: "The Somozas own it and nobody cares. Everybody goes there—Somocistas, Sandinistas, Cubans, Americans. Because in Miami, the war is over. Our children are not even Nicaraguans" (Marc Fisher, "Home, Sweetwater, Home," *Mother Jones,* Volume 13, No. 10, December 1988; p. 40).

EDUCATION

Many Nicaraguan families venture to the United States in order to improve their own or their children's education. It has been common for the wealthier families in Nicaragua to send their children to boarding schools and universities in the United States and Europe. There is no information on typical courses of study among Nicaraguan Americans.

INTERGROUP RELATIONS

Tension exists in Miami between Nicaraguan Americans and African Americans. African American resentment over what they saw as preferential treatment being given to the newly arrived Nicaraguans led, in part, to African American riots in Miami in 1989. African Americans perceived that the Cuban Americans, who have most of the political control in Miami, were looking after Nicaraguan American interests at the cost of African American interests.

RELIGION

Nicaraguan Americans are overwhelmingly Roman Catholic, and Nicaragua's Catholicism is very much centered around the Virgin Mary. There are small numbers of evangelical, Pentecostal, and fundamentalist Protestants. Most, if not all, of Nicaragua's 60 or 70 Jewish families left the country during and after the Sandinista revolution. They cited anti-Semitic harassment by FSLN soldiers as the main reason for leaving. One Managuan synagogue was firebombed, reportedly by people who identified themselves as members of the FSLN. Some of these Nicaraguan Jewish families came to live in the United States. Changes in worshipping practices since Nicaraguans have begun arriving in the United States are not documented.

EMPLOYMENT AND ECONOMIC TRADITIONS

As undocumented immigrants, most Nicaraguan Americans work in clandestine jobs with neither social security nor unemployment benefits. Over the years diverse groups of Nicaraguans have immigrated to the United States—some were doctors or bankers with university educations, and some were 15-year-old boys fleeing the draft. As a group, though, they all have one thing in common: the majority of them are undocumented. Regardless of degrees, experience, and prior social standing, the undocumented Nicaraguan American must take whatever job is available, and usually these jobs are unskilled manual or service-related jobs that, because they are clandestine, sometimes pay below the federally mandated minimum wage.

The Nicaraguans who left Nicaragua between 1979 and 1988 tended to be of working age and were more likely to have been employed in a white-collar occupation before leaving Nicaragua, according to a statistical study published in 1992. They also tended to be from wealthier, larger, better educated families compared to nonmigrating Nicaraguans: 64.2 percent of the immigrants had a secondary education, compared to 43.3 percent of all families surveyed in Managua. About 14 percent of the migrants had a university education, according to the same study (Funkhouser, p. 1211).

Nicaraguan Americans typically find work by word of mouth through family or friends who have established themselves in the community, and they tend to work in specific niches that are related to these unofficial word-of-mouth networks. In San Francisco between 1984 and 1985, for example, it was common for Nicaraguan American men to work as janitors. Nearly nineteen percent of Nicaraguan men worked as building cleaners, according to one San Francisco study that tallied the occupations of Nicaraguan-born men who listed their occupations on their children's birth certificates. Another 21.6 percent of Nicaraguan-born men worked in operations and fabrications, 10.8 percent worked at production and repair, and 1.1 percent worked as farmers, bringing the total percentage of Nicaraguan Americans who worked at blue-collar jobs to 33.5 percent. Nicaraguan Americans were also much less likely to work as food-service laborers than were other Central Americans. Only 6.5 percent of the Nicaraguan Americans worked in food service, compared to 34.5 percent of Guatemalan Americans. Nicaraguan Americans were much more likely to work in white-collar jobs: 36.3 percent held administrative or other white-collar positions, compared to 6.9 percent of the Guatemalan Americans. This discrepancy may be the result of differences in education between Nicaraguans and Guatemalans. Similar information about Nicaraguan American women in the workplace is not available, though many sources say that Central American women commonly work in textiles and housecleaning.

Each year, Nicaraguan Americans send millions of dollars home to their families in Nicaragua. Thirty-six percent of Managuan households with relatives abroad received an average of $79 each month, according to a Sandinista government source. In 1988, Nicaraguan Americans sent somewhere between $50 million and $80 million to Nicaragua, making this nearly the second largest source of foreign exchange in Nicaragua. Coffee exports bring in the most money: $84 million in 1988. The amount of money sent home to Nicaragua has probably increased since 1988.

POLITICS AND GOVERNMENT

Shortly after the revolution, Nicaraguan exiles living in America who were politically opposed to the Sandinistas organized an anti-Sandinista guerrilla army that had its base in Miami and Honduras. Many of the guerrillas and guerrilla leaders were former National Guardsmen or closely associated with the Somoza regime. The Somoza regime's long affiliation with the U.S. government meant that some Nicaraguan exiles already had well-placed U.S. government contacts and friends before they arrived in the United States. U.S.-government support of the Contras grew out of some of these relationships. Secret CIA involvement in the Contras' affairs dates back to at least 1981, according to Edgar Chamorro, former leader of the Contras, in his 1987 book *Packaging the Contras*. In a Senate subcommittee hearing in 1988, Octaviano Cesar, a Contra leader, admitted that the Contras had smuggled drugs into the United States for a profit, but he blamed it on the U.S. Congress, which cut off aid to the Contras in 1984. Notes taken by Marine Lt. Col. Oliver North suggest that North knew about the drug running and that the profits may have been as high as $14 million.

In 1987, about 2,000 Nicaraguan Americans protested publicly against the Immigration Reform and Control Act of 1986, which they said prevented the majority of Nicaraguans from remaining in the United States. About two months later, Attorney General Edwin Meese signed an order that permitted Nicaraguans to stay in the United States "for the present." Two years later, in 1989, the INS changed its regulations in order to streamline its operations. The result was that fewer Nicaraguan refugees received working permits. Nicaraguans who applied for political asylum in the 1980s received preferential treatment. Up to 80 percent of the Nicaraguan asylum applicants were granted asylum in certain years. Only a few nationalities, like Poles and Armenians, received asylum at such a high rate.

INDIVIDUAL AND GROUP CONTRIBUTIONS

What follows is an eclectic listing of individuals who have contributed in various ways to American culture and society.

ACADEMIA

Author of "El mito de paraiso perdido en la literature nicaragüense en los Estados Unidos" ("The Myth of Paradise Lost in Nicaraguan Literature in the United States"), published in *El Pez y la Serpiente* in 1989, Nicasio Urbina is a writer and an assistant professor in the department of Spanish and Portuguese at Tulane University in Louisiana. Born in 1958 in Buenos Aires, Argentina, to parents of Nicaraguan ancestry, Urbina was educated at Florida International University and at Georgetown University. He has been a member of the Modern Language Association since 1984 and has received numerous scholarships and fellowships throughout his academic career.

Eddy O. Rios Olivares was born in Nicaragua in 1942 and educated in Minnesota and Puerto Rico. He has conducted microbiological research in Nicaragua and at the Universidad Central Del Caribe in Puerto Rico, where he is professor and chairman of the department of microbiology. He has received various grants and research awards for his antitumor research.

ARTS

Guillermo Ortega Chamorro (Gil Ortegacham), an actor and musician who lives in Brooklyn, New York, was born in 1909 in San Jorge, Rivas, Nicaragua. Chamorro performed in *The Blood Wedding* on off-off-Broadway in 1987 and 1988. Educated in Nicaragua and at New York University, Chamorro has made many contributions to New York City radio and drama.

HEALTH CARE

Born in Managua in 1940, Norma F. Wilson is an obstetrical/gynecological nurse practitioner who lives in Kansas City. Wilson belongs to many professional associations and organizations relating to public health, family planning, and minority health. The Seward County Republican Women named her one of the women of the year in 1988.

Born in Managua in 1937, Rolando Emilio Lacayo is a physician and surgeon who specializes in gynecology, infertility, and obstetrics. Lacayo was educated in Nicaragua, the United States, and Mexico. From 1970 to 1971 he was an instructor in gynecology and obstetrics at Baylor College in Houston, Texas. He is a member of the American Medical Association, and a junior fellow of the American College of Obstetrics and Gynecology.

LITERATURE

Pancho Aguila was born Roberto Ignacio Zelaya in 1945 in Managua. Aguila immigrated to the United

States in 1947 and wrote and read in coffeehouses in San Francisco during the late 1960s until he was arrested and sentenced to life in prison in 1969. He escaped from prison in 1972 and was reapprehended five months later. While in prison, he has written five books of poetry and has contributed to several periodicals.

Horacio Aguirre is the publisher and editor of *Diario las Américas*, the leading conservative Spanish-language newspaper in Miami. In 1970 he was named man of the year by *Revista Conservadora del Pensamiento Centroamericano*. Horacio's brother, Francisco Aguirre, has been called the godfather of the Contras. Francisco is a former National Guard colonel and has lived in exile in Washington, D.C., since 1947. He is well known in CIA and U.S. Department of State circles.

POLITICS AND BUSINESS

President of the Nicaraguan American Banker's and Businessman's Association, educated at Notre Dame, and a commercial banker in Miami, Roberto Arguello is one of the most visible Nicaraguan Americans. In 1990 Arguello took time off from banking to lobby in Washington on behalf the Nicaraguan government. In the late 1980s, he was a vocal opponent of the U.S. refugee policy for Nicaraguans.

Nadia Pallais is a resident of Miami and in 1988 was the Dade County government's spokeswoman for the Hispanic media. Pallais immigrated to the United States from Nicaragua in 1979. She is the mother of four daughters.

SOCIAL WORK

Born in 1943 in Mexico to a Nicaraguan father and a Mexican mother, Carmela Gloria Lacayo has worked for many years to improve the lives of the poor and elderly. Lacayo established the National Association for Hispanic Elderly and founded Hispanas Organized for Political Equality. She has been appointed to a number of political positions, including vice-chair of the Democratic National Committee, member of the Census Bureau on Minority Populations, and an advisor on Social Security reform.

SPORTS

Nicaraguan American pitcher Dennis Martinez is a native of Grenada, Nicaragua. In 1976 Martinez became the first Nicaraguan ever to play in major league baseball. In 1990 he signed a three-year contract with the Montreal Expos that paid him more

Nicaraguan American baseball palyer Dennis Martinez.

than $3 million per season. In an interview with *Sports Illustrated*, Martinez said that when he broke into the big leagues and told people that he was from Nicaragua, they didn't know where it was. In 1991 he pitched a perfect game against the Los Angeles Dodgers. He has narrowly missed winning the Cy Young award several times. During his off-seasons in Miami, Martinez has put his celebrity among baseball-loving Nicaraguan Americans to good use by participating in drug-prevention programs for young Nicaraguan Americans in Miami. He retired following the 1998 season.

MEDIA

PRINT

Diario las Américas.
Leading conservative Spanish-language paper in Miami; printed in Spanish.

Contact: Horacio Aguirre, Editor.
Address: 2900 Northwest 39th Street, Miami, Florida 33142-5149.
Telephone: (305) 633-3341.
Fax: (305) 635-7668.

La Estrella de Nicaragua.
Newspaper published in Spanish by and for Nicaraguan Americans in Miami, Florida.

Telephone: (305) 386-6491.

Nicaragua Monitor.

Analyzes political and economic situations in Nicaragua, as well as U.S. government policies toward the country. Seeks to inform U.S. activists who support the gains of the Sandinista Revolution. Recurring features include news of research, book reviews, and a column titled "Month In Review."

Contact: Katherine Hoyt, Editor.
Address: Nicaragua Network Education Fund, 1247 E Street SE, Washington, D.C. 20003.
Telephone: (202) 544-9355.
E-mail: nicanet@igc.apc.org.

Nicaraguan Perspectives.

Quarterly political science journal of Nicaragua Information Center.

Address: Box 1004, Berkeley, California 94701-1004.

Voz Summary.

Summary of Nicaraguan news from shortwave radio.

Address: Box 8151, Kansas City, Missouri 64112.
Telephone: (816) 561-0125.

ORGANIZATIONS AND ASSOCIATIONS

American Nicaraguan Foundation.
Provides health care to Nicaraguan people.

Address: 848 Brickell Avenue, Miami, Florida 33131.
Telephone: (305) 375-9248.

Nicaragua Center for Community Action (NICCA).
Publishes quarterly journal with news and analysis about Nicaragua and the Nicaraguan solidarity movement.

Address: 2140 Shattuck Avenue, Box 2063, Berkeley, California 94704.
Telephone: (510) 704-5242.
Fax: (510) 654-8635.
E-mail: nicca@igc.org.

Nicaraguan American Women Civic Association.
Contact: Mauritza Herrera.
Address: 961 Northwest Second Street, Miami, Florida 33128.
Telephone: (305) 326-7700.

Nicaraguan Interfaith Committee for Action (NICA).
NICA is concerned with the problems of Nicaragua and with taking action to alleviate them; the organization also sponsors Nicaraguans in the United States.

Contact: Janine Chayoga, Director.
Address: 833 Market Street, Room 812, San Francisco, California 94103.
Telephone: (415) 495-6057.

Nicaragua Network Education Fund (NN).
Network of organizations and individuals united in opposition to U.S. intervention in the Central American/Caribbean region and in support of the Nicaraguan revolution. Seeks to create a peaceful and friendly relationship between the United States and Nicaragua through public education.

Contact: Chuck Kaufman, Co-coordinator.
Address: 1247 E Street SE, Washington, D.C. 20003.
Telephone: (202) 544-9355.
Fax: (202) 544-9359.

MUSEUMS AND RESEARCH CENTERS

Dallas Museum of Art.
The museum displays an extensive collection of pre-Columbian and eighteenth- to twentieth-century textiles, censers, and other art objects from the Nicaraguan area.

Contact: Karen Zelanka, Associate Registrar, Permanent Collection.
Address: 1717 Harwood, Dallas, Texas 75201.
Telephone: (214) 922-1200.
Fax: (214) 954-0174.
Online: http://www.dm-art.org/.

Documentation Exchange.
Formerly known as the Central America Resource Center, the Documentation Exchange maintains a library of information on human rights and social conditions in many countries, including Nicaragua. Also produces biweekly compilations of current news articles on Central America called NewsPaks.

Contact: Charlotte McCann, Editor.
Address: 2520 Longview Street, #408, Austin, Texas 78768.
Telephone: (512) 476-9841.
Fax: (512) 476-0130.

The Nattie Lee Benson Latin American Collection.

Located at the University of Texas at Austin, this renowned collection consists of Nicaraguan books, books about Nicaragua, and resources relating to Nicaraguan Americans. Excellent electronic information resources.

Contact: Laura Gutiérrez-Witt, Head Librarian.

Address: Sid Richardson Hall 1.109, General Libraries, University of Texas, Austin, Texas 78713-7330.

Telephone: (512) 471-3818.

Nicaraguan Information Center.

Maintains a library of 100 volumes, videotapes, slides, magazines, newspapers and microfilms on Nicaragua.

Contact: Amanda Velazquez, President.

Address: P.O. Box 607, St. Charles, Missouri 63301.

Telephone: (314) 946-8721.

The UT-LANIC Server.

Managed by the Institute of Latin American Studies at the University of Texas at Austin. The UT-LANIC Server is accessible on the Internet. It provides access to academic databases and information services worldwide, as well as information from and about Latin America. To reach UT-LANIC Server via World Wide Web browser: http://lanic.utexas.edu; via Gopher client: lanic.utexas.edu.

Contact: Laura Gutiérrez-Witt, Head Librarian.

Address: Sid Richardson Hall 1.109, General Libraries, University of Texas, Austin, Texas 78713-7330.

Telephone: (512) 495-4520.

SOURCES FOR ADDITIONAL STUDY

Boyer, Edward J. "Nicaraguans in L.A.: A Lively Political Debating Society," *Los Angeles Times*, February 20, 1984; pp. 1, 3.

Chamorro, Edgar. *Packaging the Contras: A Case of CIA Disinformation*. New York: Institute for Media Analysis, 1987.

Chavez, Leo Ralph. "Outside the Imagined Community: Undocumented Settlers and Experiences of Incorporation," *American Ethnologist*, May 1991; pp. 257-278.

Cortés Domínguez, Guillermo. *Miami: secretos de un exilio*. Managua: El Amanecer, 1986.

Crawley, Eduardo. *Nicaragua in Perspective*. New York: St. Martin's Press, 1979.

Fins, Antonio. "For Exiled Nicaraguans, Just Where Is Home?" *Business Week*, March 26, 1990; pp. 28D-28K.

Fisher, Marc. "Home, Sweetwater, Home," *Mother Jones*, 13, No. 10, December 1988; pp. 35-40.

Funkhouser, Edward. "Migration from Nicaragua: Some Recent Evidence," *World Development*, 20, No. 8, 1992; pp. 1209-18.

Gelman, Rita Golden. *Inside Nicaragua, Young People's Dreams and Fears*. New York: Franklin Watts, 1988.

Hamill, Pete. "Any Happy Returns?" *Esquire*, July 1990; pp. 33-34.

Hart, Dianne Walta. *Undocumented in L.A.: An Immigrant's Story*. Wilmington, DE: SR Books, 1997.

Malone, Michael R. *A Nicaraguan Family*. Minneapolis: Lerner Publications Co., 1998.

Misconceptions about U.S. Policy Toward Nicaragua (Department of State Publication 9417, Inter-American Series 117). Washington, D.C.: Department of State, 1985.

Petzinger, Thomas, Jr., Mark Zieman, Bryan Burrough, and Dianna Solis. "Vital Resources: Illegal Immigrants Are Backbone of Economy in States of Southwest," *Wall Street Journal*, May 7, 1985; pp. 1, 10.

Scanlan, David. "Just Like Old Times: The Civil War May Be Only a Memory, But Nicaraguans Are Still Suffering," *Maclean's*, January 17, 1994; p. 32.

Teenage Refugees from Nicaragua Speak Out, edited by K. Melissa Cerar. New York: Rosen Pub. Group, 1995.

Thurman, Judith. "Dry Season," *New Yorker*, March 14, 1988; pp. 44-78.

While in their native country large families are common, Nigerian Americans have fewer children so that they will be able to give them the best education possible. The early immigrants were educated people and they instilled in their children the importance of education as a component of a successful life.

NIGERIAN AMERICANS

by
Kwasi Sarkodie-Mensah

OVERVIEW

With an area of 356,669 square miles (923,768 square kilometers), Nigeria's size approximately equals the combined areas of New Mexico, Arizona and California. A coastal state on the shores of the Gulf of Guinea in West Africa, Nigeria is bounded by Niger to the north, Benin to the west, Cameroon to the east and southeast, and Chad to the northeast.

The November 1991 population census put Nigeria's population at 88,514,501. Nigeria's population is extremely diverse—more than 250 ethnic groups are identified. Ten ethnic groups account for 80 percent of Nigeria's population. English is the official language; however, Yoruba, Ibo, and Hausa represent the principal languages, joined by Kanuri, Fulani, Nupe, Tiv, Edo, Ijaw and Ibibio. Like many other African countries, the distribution of religion can be broken down into three major areas: Christians, Muslims, and animists. In Nigeria, 47 percent of the population practice Islam, while about 36 percent practice Christianity, and 17 percent practice animism or traditional African religion. Nigeria's national flag, believed to have been designed by Taiwo Akinkunmi—a Nigerian student in London, consists of a field of green, white, and green, divided into three equal parts. Green represents the agricultural richness of the nation, while the white stands for unity and peace.

HISTORY

The name Nigeria was coined by Lord Lugard's wife in 1897 in honor of the 2,600-mile-long Niger River. The first Europeans to reach Nigeria were the Portuguese in the fifteenth century. In 1553, the first English ships landed at the Bight of Benin, then known as the "Slave Coast." The present day Nigeria came into existence in 1914, when the Colony of Lagos, the Protectorate of Southern Nigeria, and the protectorate of Northern Nigeria were amalgamated. Even before the arrival of Europeans, the many nationalities or ethnic groups were highly organized and had law and order. There were village groups, clans, emirates, states, kingdoms, and some empires. The Kanem-Bornu empire goes as far back as the tenth century. The Oyo Empire, founded in the late fourteenth century by Oranmiyan, a Prince of Ile-Ife, had a powerful army and maintained diplomatic contact with other kingdoms in the area. The Fulani Empire was established in 1803 by the *jihad*, or holy war against the rulers of the Hausa states by Usman Dan Fodio; it went on to become one of the most powerful kingdoms. Within two decades, parts of the Oyo Empire, Bornu, and Nupe were added by conquest to the Fulani Empire. Though there was no centralized governments, trade and commercial activities existed. Intermarriages flourished among the various groups.

One of the most prosperous trades even before the arrival of the Europeans was the slave trade. It was common practice in many African civilizations to sell war captives, delinquent children, and the handicapped; and Nigeria was no exception. With the arrival of the Europeans, slavery became more lucrative. Intertribal wars were encouraged by the Europeans so that more captured slaves could be sent to the New World. The British Parliament abolished slavery in 1807.

MODERN ERA

When the mouth of the Niger River was discovered in 1830, the British heightened their economic expansion into the interior of the country. Formal administration of any part of Nigeria goes back to 1861 when Lagos, a vital component of the lucrative palm oil trade, was ceded to the British Crown. At the Berlin Conference of 1884-1885, geographical units and artificial borders were created in Africa by European powers without any consideration of cultural or ethnic homogeneity. Britain acquired what is now Nigeria as a result of this scramble for Africa. In 1914 the various protectorates were consolidated into one colony, the Protectorate of Nigeria.

After World War II, nationalism rose in Nigeria. Under the leadership of Nnamdi Azikiwe, Obafemi Awolowo, and Alhaji Sir Abubakar Tafawa Balewa, Nigerians began to ask for self-determination and increased participation in the governmental process on a regional level. On October 1, 1960, Nigeria became an independent country, but this independence brought about a series of political crises. Nigeria enjoyed civilian rule for six years until January 15, 1966 when, in one of the bloodiest coups in Africa, the military took over the government of Tafawa Balewa, assassinated him and replaced him with General J. Aguiyi-Ironsi. Later that month Ironsi was killed in a counter-coup, and replaced by General Yakubu Gowon. In early 1967 the distribution of petroleum revenues between the government and the Eastern Region, where the majority of Ibos come from, sparked a conflict. Gowon proposed to abolish the regions of Nigeria and replace them with 12 states. Colonel Ojukwu, a soldier from the Ibo tribe, announced the secession of the Eastern Region, and declared a Republic of Biafra. Events following this declaration resulted in the Biafra War, one of the most deadly civil wars in Africa, claiming the lives of over two million Nigerians.

Gowon was overthrown in a bloodless military coup on July 29, 1975, when he was attending a summit meeting of the Organization of African Unity. Brigadier General Murtala Ramat Muhammed became the leader of the government. He started a popular purging of the members of the previous government and announced a return of the country to civilian rule. On February 13, 1976 Muhammed was assassinated during a coup attempt. Lieutenant General Olusegun Obasanjo, chief-of-staff of the armed forces in Muhammed's government became the new head of state. In 1978 Nigeria produced a new constitution similar to that of the United States.

The country returned to civilian rule in 1979 when Alhaji Shehu Shagari was sworn in as president on October 1. Shagari's government ended on New Year's Eve 1983 when he was ousted by a group of soldiers, led by Major-General Muhammadu Buhari. Buhari introduced stringent measures to curb corruption. He imprisoned many former government officials found guilty of corruption. Under Buhari's government, the death penalty was reintroduced in Nigeria and freedom of the press was rigorously restricted. Many newspapers were banned and many journalists were imprisoned or tortured.

On August 27, 1985, Major General Ibrahim Babaginda led a bloodless coup d'etat, deposing Buhari as the head of state. Babaginda promised to restore human rights, establish a democratically elected government, and eradicate corruption, which has always been a part of Nigerian politics. Babaginda not only violated his promises, but imprisoned journalists who stood up for the truth. After repeatedly postponing, altering, or scrapping timetables for a return to a democratically elected government, Babaginda annulled the results of the elections held in June 1993, which were won by his opponent Chief Moshood Abiola. Under pressure, Babaginda resigned and left power in the hands of a handpicked and widely opposed interim government headed by Ernest Shonekan, who was prominent in business and supported Babaginda. The military still retains control of the country under the leadership of Abdulsalom Abubakar, who has promised free elections in the future.

THE FIRST NIGERIANS IN AMERICA

Compared with other ethnic groups in America, the presence of Nigerian Americans in the United States does not date back very far. However if the slave trade is considered, then Nigerians have been part of the American society as far back as the eighteenth century. Even though Nigerian Americans of the modern era do not want to be associated with slavery and put in the same category as African Americans, history bears witness to the fact that the coastal regions of modern day Nigeria were referred to as the Slave Coast. Nigeria provided a vast percentage of the Africans who were bitterly separated from their families and forced into slavery by European entrepreneurs.

World War I expanded the horizons of many Africans. Though European colonial masters wanted Africans in their territories to receive an African-based education with emphasis on rural development, Africans wanted to go abroad to study. In the early parts of the twentieth century, it was traditional for Nigerians to travel to European countries such as the United Kingdom and Germany to receive an education and to return to their countries. Two dynamic programs emerged after the war: Marcus Garvey's military platform of Africa for Africans, and W. E. B. Dubois' Pan African movement. The colonial powers in Africa feared that the strong ideas of identity and freedom preached by both Garvey and Dubois would turn the Africans against their colonial masters.

The United States became a center of attraction for Nigerian nationalists who later became the revolutionary leaders. The Nigerians who came to the United States to study saw the white person in the same light as a black individual; white people were subjected to the same grandeur and malaise of human nature and were in no way superior to black people. The most prominent Nigerian symbolizing the spirit of freedom and human respect was the late Chief Dr. Nnamdi Azikiwe, first President of Nigeria and first indigenous governor-general of Nigeria. Arriving in the United States by boat in 1925, Zik, as he was affectionately referred to, entered Storer College and later transferred to Lincoln University and Howard University. While in the United States, Zik experienced racial prejudice and worked as a dishwasher, a coal miner, and a boxer to survive the difficult times in America. However, he later became a professor at several prestigious American institutions. Two other Nigerians from the Eastern Region used their American education in the 1930s to bring change to their people. Professor Eyo Ita and Mbonu Ojike became influential leaders in Nigerian national politics.

SIGNIFICANT IMMIGRATION WAVES

In its 1935 annual report, the New York-based Institute of International Education indicated that in 1926 there were three documented Nigerian students in United States universities. In its subsequent reports, the number of students increased to 22 in 1944. A steady increase in Nigerians continued when the oil boom in the 1970s made Nigeria one of the wealthiest nations in Africa and many came to the United States to study. Most students were sponsored by their parents and relatives both in Nigeria and in the United States, while others obtained financial assistance from universities and colleges in the United States. In the late 1970s and 1980s Nigeria was among the top six countries in the number of students sent to study in the United States. While many returned home, in the 1980s when Nigeria's economy began to decline at a tragic rate, many Nigerians remained in the United States and obtained citizenship. After becoming citizens many Nigerian Americans brought their relatives into the United States. According to 1990 census figures, there were approximately 91,688 people of Nigerian ancestry living in the United States.

SETTLEMENT

Nigerian Americans, like many Africans migrating into the United States, are willing to settle almost anywhere. Family relations, colleges or universities previously attended by relatives and friends, and the weather are three major considerations for settlement by Nigerian Americans. Early Nigerians coming to the United States went to schools in the southern United States. Large metropolitan areas attract modern day Nigerian Americans, many of whom hold prestigious professional jobs. Poor economic conditions have forced many highly educated Nigerian Americans to take up odd jobs. In many metropolitan areas, Nigerian Americans with one or several graduate degrees are taxi drivers or security officers. The heaviest concentrations of Nigerian Americans are found in Texas, California, New York, Maryland, Illinois, New Jersey, and Georgia.

ACCULTURATION AND ASSIMILATION

Mention the name Nigeria, and the average American conjures up the image of the jungle and children living in squalor. This perception is largely due to the erroneous depiction of Africa by Hollywood and the tendency of the American media to publicize only catastrophic events in Nigeria. Nigeria as a country defies easy generalization because the people are as varied as the cultural differences that characterize them as a nation. Nigerian Americans come from a wide variety of rich backgrounds not only in financial terms but in societal values. Despite the negative stereotypes Nigerian Americans have maintained their pride and cultural identity, and contribute immensely to the American society at large.

TRADITIONS, CUSTOMS, AND BELIEFS

Nigerians have a variety of traditions and lore dating back to antiquity. For example, peeking at the eggs on which a hen is sitting was believed to make you blind. Singing while bathing could result in a parent's death. A pregnant woman who ate pork could have a baby with a mouth like that of a pig. Among the Yoruba it was believed that there were spirits hidden in rivers and hills in various cities. Since these spirits were there to protect the people, they were not to be disturbed on certain days of the week. In almost all Nigerian societies, there is a strong belief that most disease and death are caused supernaturally, by witchcraft, curses, or charms. Witches are usually elderly women. For a long time the Ibos believed that twins were an abomination and killed them at birth. Among some of the Hausa people, it was believed that marrying a Yoruba woman could result in mystical dangers such as serious sickness or even death. As the immigrants became acculturated into the American society, these beliefs and superstitions were forgotten.

In many Nigerian cultures elders are supposed to be served first during a meal but leave food in the bowl for the children to eat as leftovers. The proverb, "the elder who consumes all his food will wash his own dishes," attests to this belief. However, in many Nigerian American homes children are served before adults, an indication of the Western influence whereby the needs of the child come first.

PROVERBS

The following are some common Nigerian proverbs: The voyager must necessarily return home; Death does not recognize a king; A foreign land knows no celebrity; An elephant is a hare in another town; The race of life is never tiresome; The nocturnal toad does not run during the day in vain; A child who does not know the mother does not run out to welcome her; If birds do not seek a cause for quarrel, the sky is wide enough for them to fly without interference; It is not a problem to offer a drink of wine to a monkey, but the problem is to take away the cup from him; Many words do not fill a basket; Truth is better than money; If the elephant does not have enough to eat in the forest, it puts the forest to shame.

There is a mine of proverbs in Pidgin English: "Man wey fool na him loss" (It is the fool that loses); "Lion de sick no be say goat fit go salute am for house" (Just because the lion is sick does not mean the goat can go to the lion's house to greet him); "Monkey no fine but im mamma like am so" (The monkey may not look handsome, but his mother likes him as he is); "Cow wey no get tail na God dey drive him fly" (God drives away the flies from the cow without a tail).

CUISINE

Ask anyone who has tasted Nigerian cuisine, and one answer is almost guaranteed—hot. There is no typical Nigerian American dish. Among the Yoruba, a meal may consist of two dishes: a starch form of dough derived from corn or guinea corn, or mashed vegetables that may be served with stew. The stew is prepared in typical Yoruba way using palm oil, meat, chicken, or other game cooked with many spices and vegetables, flavored with onions or bitterleaf leaves. A common Yoruba food is *Garri*, made from the roots of *cassava* (manioc).

Among the Ibo people, *cassava*, *cocoyam* (taro), potato, corn, okra, beans, peanuts, and pumpkins are common foods. In the northern part of Nigeria, grains constitute a good component of the diet. *Tuo* ("tu-wo") is a common dish in the north, and is eaten with different types of soup and sauce made from onions, peppers, tomatoes, okra, meat, or fish.

Akara ("ah-ka-ra"), Nigerian bean cakes, are fried patties made with uncooked, pulverized black-eye peas ground into a batter with onion, tomatoes, eggs, and chili peppers. *Egusi* ("e-goo-she") soup is a hot fiery soup made from *Egusi* seeds—pumpkin seeds can be substituted. Other ingredients required for a typical Egusi soup include okra, hot peppers, onions, any type of meat, poultry, or fish, palm oil, leafy greens, tomato paste, and salt. *Chinchin* ("chin-chin") are fried pastries made from flour mixed with baking powder, salt, nutmeg, butter, sugar, and eggs. *Kulikuli* ("cooley-cooley"), or peanut balls, are made from roasted peanuts (called ground nuts in Nigeria), peanut oil, onions, salt, and cayenne pepper. *Moi-moi* ("moy-moy") is a savory pate made from black-eyed beans, onions, vegetable oil, tomato paste, parsley or fresh vegetables, salt, and pepper. Okra soup is based on meat, smoked fish, seafood and vegetables, and okra. This dish is similar to New Orleans gumbo. Pounded *Yam Fufu* is made from boiled yams pounded in a mortar with a pestle, and served with meat or fish stew and vegetable or okra soup.

TRADITIONAL COSTUMES

Men from various Nigerian groups wear *Sokoto* ("show-kowtow"), a pair of loose-fitting trousers, a *buba* ("boo-bah") or loose-fitting overshirt, and a cap. Yoruba men wear *agbada* ("ah-bah-dah"), which is flowing robe worn to the ankle. It covers an undervest with no sleeves, and a pair of baggy pants. The women wear a wide piece of cloth that goes from below the neck to the ankles. A blouse hanging to the waist is worn over it. A head tie and a thin veil are also worn. Nigerian Americans wear their traditional costumes on special occasions such as National Day, October 1.

DANCES AND SONGS

Nigerian Americans boast of a wealth of traditional and modern music and dances because dancing and music form a focal point in life. At birth and death, on happy and sad occasions, and in worship, dancing and music are present. Traditionally in many Nigerian societies, men and women did not dance together. Western education and influence have changed this tradition, though Nigerian Americans who want to recreate their culture retain this separation.

Drums form an integral part in Nigerian dances and music. Juju music, a very popular form of music from Yorubaland, is a slow, spaced, and very relaxed guitar-based music. Highlife music is popular in all parts of West Africa, including Nigeria. Highlife music usually consists of brass, vocals, percussion, drums, double bass, and electric guitar. Nigerians from the North practicing Islam enjoy music that has origins in North Africa. Such music is varied, but the instruments commonly used include trumpets, flutes, long brass horns, percussion frame drums, cymbals, and kettle drums.

Nigerian Americans returning from visits to Nigeria bring back with them both contemporary and old music in various formats. Nigerian Americans enjoy music from all over the world. In addition to American and British music, reggae, calypso, and Zairian music are popular.

HOLIDAYS

The major public holidays in Nigeria are: New Year's Day; *Id al Fitr*—end of Ramadan; Easter; *Id al-Kabir*—Feast of the Sacrifice; *Mouloud*—birth of the Prophet Mohammed; National or Independence Day—October 1; and Christmas. Nigerian Americans also celebrate the major public holidays in the United States.

National Day is one of the most important holidays for Nigerian Americans celebrating the independence of Nigeria from colonial rule. A whole week of cultural, educational, and political events are scheduled. Activities include lectures on Nigeria, traditional Nigerian dances and music, fashion shows, story telling, myths and legends from various Nigerian communities. Many Nigerian Americans volunteer to talk to neighborhood school children about Nigeria and the African continent at large. When the holiday proper falls on a weekday, parties and other festive celebrations are held on the weekend. The parties and festivities culminating in the celebration of Nigerian's independence are open invitations to Nigerians, people of other African descents, and others associated in one way or the other with Nigerian living in the United States. In New York, for example, the staff of the Nigerian Consulate attend these festivities.

For Moslem Nigerian Americans, *Id al-Fitr* or the end of the Moslem fasting season is the second most important holiday in the Islamic calendar. For the approximately 30 days of Ramadan, Moslems are expected to fast from dawn to sunset. They also abstain from sex, drink, tobacco, and other activities that result in physical pleasure. To celebrate *Id al-Fitr*, Moslems say the special feast prayer in a community format and give special alms to the poor. Nigerian American Moslems also share food and gifts with relatives and friends, and children receive gifts of all kinds.

There are many other holidays and festivities observed by Nigerian Americans to preserve their cultural heritage. Ibos in large metropolitan areas make it a point to celebrate the New Yam Festival every year. Traditionally, the yam has been the symbol of the prowess of the Ibo man. Just before midnight, the *ezejis* or elders offer prayers of thanksgiving and break kola nuts. Drums are played while blessings are offered. Other participants perform libation using Scotch or other similar liquor by pouring from a ram's horn. During the ceremony, prayers are addressed to an almighty being, and to the ancestral gods who control the soil, through whose constant kindness and guidance yams and other foods of the land bear fruit. The ceremony also includes dancing, eating, and exchange of greetings.

HEALTH ISSUES

There are no documented health problems or medical conditions specific to Nigeria Americans. However, like all black people, Nigerian Americans are susceptible to sickle cell anemia, an abnormal hereditary variation in the structure of hemoglobin, a protein found in the red blood cell.

A 1994 deportation victory by a Nigerian immigrant brought the health issue of female circumcision to light. Lydia Oluroro won a deportation case in Portland, Oregon. If she had been sent home, her two children could have had their clitoris and part of their labia minora cut. Nigerian Americans reacted differently to this decision; some praised it, and others expressed concern that Americans might consider female circumcision a common practice in all of Nigeria. This issue is definitely going to be a future health concern among Nigerian Americans.

LANGUAGE

English is the official language in Nigeria, but it is estimated that there are between 250 and 400 distinct dialects. There are three major ethnic languages in Nigeria: Yoruba, Ibo, and Hausa. Yoruba is spoken by over 15 million people, primarily in Southwestern Nigeria. Belonging to the Kwa group of languages, Yoruba is a tonal tongue. Depending on the tone used, the same combination of sounds may convey different meanings. Ibo is also spoken by over 15 million people in Nigeria. Formerly considered as a Kwa language, recent research has placed Ibo in the Benue-Congo family of languages. Hausa is spoken in the Northern part of Nigeria, and is considered to be the most widely spoken language in Africa. It is a member of the Chad group of languages frequently assigned to the Hamitic sub-

family of the Hamito-Semitic family of languages.

Pidgin English has become the unofficial language in many African countries and Nigeria is no exception. It can be loosely defined as a hybrid of exogenous and indigenous languages. It has become the most popular medium of intergroup communication in various heterogenous communities in Nigeria. Nigerian Americans from different tribal entities who may not communicate in English can communicate with each other in Pidgin English.

The first generation of Nigerian Americans speak their native languages at home and when interacting with people from the same tribal groups. English words have found their way into most of the traditional languages spoken by Nigerian Americans. Children born into Nigerian American homes speak English and may learn the native languages if their parents teach them or speak the languages at home. Since English is the official language in Nigeria, and is used for instruction in schools, many Nigerian Americans prefer to have their children learn English as well possible so that upon returning home, the children will be able to communicate with others or do better in schools. The American accent acquired by younger Nigerian Americans is of spectacular interest to people in their home country.

It has been proposed several times that Nigeria needs an African language as its official language. This laudable desire may never become a reality because there are too many languages and dialects to consider. The existence of the diverse tribal and cultural groups makes it hard to single out one native language as the national language.

GREETINGS AND OTHER POPULAR EXPRESSIONS

Common Yoruba expressions include: *Bawo ni?* ("baa wo knee")—Hi, how are things?; *Daadaa ni* ("daadaa knee")—Fine. Common Hausa expressions include: *Sannu* ("sa nu")—Hi; *Lafiya?* ("la fee ya")—Are you well? Common Ibo expressions include: *Ezigbo ututu*—Good morning; *Kedu ka imere?*—How do you do?; *Gini bu aha gi*—What is your name? Popular expressions in Pidgin English are varied: "How now?"—How are you? or How is the going?; "Which thing you want?"— What do you want?' "How body?"—How are you health-wise?

FAMILY AND COMMUNITY DYNAMICS

The first Nigerians came to the United States for educational purposes. Since transportation costs were high, it was common for them to leave their family behind. Painful as this separation was, it also afforded them the opportunity to concentrate on their studies. They saved money and later sent for their wives or children. In some cases, though, Nigerians sponsored by governmental agencies were accompanied by their families. In the modern era, Nigerians who migrated to America were sponsored by their families. Nigerian Americans have always had the reputation of living comfortable lives and maintaining high standards of living. Their industrious nature has made it possible for a great majority of them to purchase cars and houses, or rent nice apartments.

There is no typical Nigeria American household decoration. Depending on which region in Nigeria they come from, Nigerian Americans decorate their houses with various art forms. Many of them bring such artifacts when they travel home to visit. Other Nigerian Americans become so westernized that their households do not have any indication of their heritage.

"Don't misunderstand me. I love America. The freedom, tolerance, and respect of differences that are a part of everyday public life are some of the first things a visitor to America notices. But I also saw a public school system disconnected from society's most important institution—the family. In Nigeria, with all its political and social problems, the family remains strong, and by doing so helps to define the social and economic expectations of the nation."

Jide Nzelibe, a graduate of St. John's College in Annapolis and Woodrow Wilson School of Public and International Affairs at Princeton University (from "A Nigerian Immigrant Is Shocked by His U.S. High School," *Policy Review,* Fall 1993, p. 43).

Africans in general have strong family commitments. It is traditional in Nigeria to have extended families. Unannounced visits are always welcome, and meals are shared even if no prior knowledge of the visit was given. Nigerian Americans continue this tradition. However, as a result of hectic work schedules and economic realities, it is common for Nigerian Americans to make a phone call before paying visits to relatives or friends.

Traditionally, in many Nigerian communities, a man marries as many wives as possible. However, Nigerian Americans marry only one wife. While in their native country large families are common, Nigerian Americans have fewer children so that they will be able to give them the best education possible. The early immigrants were educated people and they instilled in their children the importance of education as a component of a successful life. Over half of Nigerian Americans between the age 18 and 24 go to four-year universities and obtain bachelor degrees. About 33 percent of Nigerian Americans 25 years and over who entered the United States between 1980 and 1990 received masters degree. Close to ten percent received doctoral degrees. About 50 percent of women aged 25 or older received their bachelor degrees. Masters and doctoral degrees for women in the same age group were 32 percent and 52 percent.

Years ago in Nigeria it was traditional for women to stay home and take care of children; however in modern times, both in the United States and at home, educational opportunities are opened equally to men and women. The areas of specialization are not delineated between the sexes.

Children are required by tradition to be obedient to their parents and other adults. For example, a child can never contradict his or her parents; and the left hand cannot be used to accept money from parents, or as a gesture of respectful communication. Nigerian Americans try to maintain these traditional values, but as a result of peer pressure in American society, young Nigerian Americans resist this type of strict discipline from their parents. Even though children are treated equally in Nigerian American families, girls are usually the center of attention for several reasons. With teenage pregnancies on the rise in the United States, many parents seem to keep a closer eye on their female children. As part of sex education, many Nigerian American parents alert their children to the problem of teenage pregnancy and its ensuing responsibilities.

WEDDINGS

Different groups in Nigeria have different types of weddings. Usually, marriages are a combination of the traditional and the modern. Even though the traditional marriage ceremonies seem to be fading, many Nigerian Americans continue to perform it at home and then perform a Western-type wedding in a church or a court of law.

Among the Yoruba for example, on the day of the traditional marriage, there is feasting, dancing, and merriment. At nightfall, the senior wives in the family of the groom go to the house of the bride's family to ask for the bride. At the door, the senior wives in the house of the bride ask for a door opening fee before they are allowed in the house. In addition to this initial fee, there are several others to be paid—the children's fee, the wives' fee, and the load-carrying fee. The family of the bride must be completely satisfied with the amount of monies given before the bride can be taken away. The senior members of the bride's family pray for and bless her, and then release her to the head of the delegation. A senior wife from the groom's family carries the bride on her back to the new husband's home. The feet of the new wife have to be cleaned before she can enter the house. This symbolizes that the new wife is clean and is on the threshold of a new life altogether.

When there are no close relatives of the bride and the groom in the United States, friends take on the roles of the various participants in the traditional wedding. After the traditional wedding, if the couple practices Christianity, the ceremony is performed according to the tradition of the church. Friends, relatives, an well-wishers from the home country and across the United States are invited to the ceremony. Though many guests may stay in hotels, according to the African tradition of hospitality, friends and relatives of the couple living in the immediate surroundings will house and feed the visitors free of charge. The accompanying wedding reception is a stupendous feast of African cuisine, traditional and modern music and dancing, and an ostentatious display of both African and American costumes.

CHILD NAMING CEREMONIES

In many Nigerian American homes the child naming ceremony is even more important than the baptism. Among the Ibos, when a child is born, the parents set a time for this ceremony to take place and friends, relatives, and well wishers are invited to this event. Grandmothers traditionally prepare the dish that will be served, but in modern times all the women in the household take part in the preparation of the food. At the ceremony benches are arranged in a rectangular form with a lamp placed at the center, and guests are ushered in by the new mother. Kola nuts (the greatest symbol of Ibo hospitality) are served followed by palm wine. When the guests have had enough to drink, the new mother asks her mother to serve the food, which is usually a combination of rice, garri, yams, or fufu, and soup and stew made with stock-fish, ordinary fish, meat, and other types of game meat. After the meal, more palm wine is served. The host, usually the most senior man in the household, then repeats one or more proverbs, orders the baby to be brought, and places the baby in the lap. The grandmother gives a name, followed by the child's father, and then the baby's mother. Guests can also suggest names. After more drinking and celebration the guests depart and the household gathers to review the suggested names and to select one, which becomes the name of the child. Possible Ibo names include: *Adachi* (the daughter of God); *Akachukwu* (God's hand); *Nwanyioma* (beautiful lady); and *Ndidikanma* (patience is the best).

The Yoruba naming ceremony takes place on the ninth day after birth for boys, and on the seventh day for girls. Twins are named on the eighth day. By tradition the mother and the child leave the house for the first time on the day the naming ceremony takes place. Relatives, friends and well wishers join together to eat, drink, and make merry. Gifts are lavished on the newborn and the parents. An elder performs the naming ceremony using Kola nuts, a bowl of water, pepper, oil, salt, honey, and liquor. Each of these items stands for a special life symbol: Kola nuts are for good fortune; water symbolizes purity; oil symbolizes power and health; salt symbolizes intelligence and wisdom; honey symbolizes happiness, and liquor stands for wealth and prosperity. The baby tastes each of the above, as do all the people present. The name of the child is chosen before the ceremony. After dipping his hand in a bowl of water, the person officiating at the ceremony touches the forehead of the baby and whispers the name into the baby's ears, and then shouts it aloud for all around to hear. Some Yoruba names are: *Jumoke* (loved by all); *Amonke* (to know her is to pet her); *Modupe* (thanks); *Foluke* (in the hands of God); and *Ajayi* (born face downwards). Nigerian Americans preserve the traditional ceremonies, modifying as needed. For example, an older relative or friend plays the role of the grandmother when the real grandmother of the child is unable to be present.

After the traditional naming ceremony, if the family is Christian, another day is set aside for the child to be baptized in church. Hausa children born to Islamic parents are given personal names of Moslem origin. The Moslem name is often followed by the father's given name. Surnames have been adopted by a few Hausa people, especially those educated abroad. Some given Hausa names are: *Tanko* (a boy born after successive girls); *Labaran* (a boy born in the month of the Ramadan); *Gagare* (unconquerable); and *Afere* (a girl born tiny).

FUNERALS

The African concept of death is considered a transition, not an end. The Ibos, Yoruba, and the Hausa, including those practicing the Christian and Islamic religions, believe in reincarnation. Even though Western education and religion may have changed many traditional African beliefs, many Nigerian Americans hold on to those beliefs. Thus, if a person dies, he is born into another life completely different from the one he had. In addition to our visible world, there is believed to be another world where ancestors dwell and exert influence on the daily activities of the living. In many Nigerian societies, when a person dies, the entire community becomes aware of the death almost immediately. Wailing and crying from family members and unrelated people fill the town or village where the death occurs.

Funeral traditions vary in Nigeria according to group. For example, at the funeral of the Kalabari people of Eastern Nigeria, unless a person dies from what are considered abominable causes such as witchcraft, drowning, or at childbirth, every adult receives an *Ede* funeral, which consists of laying the body in state and dressing the chief mourners. Traditionally the dead were buried the day after death. In the case of an older person, a whole week of ceremonial mourning was set aside. In modern times, the dead are kept in the mortuary up to eight weeks or more so that elaborate preparations can take place and relatives both local and abroad could come to the funeral. The initial wake is usually held on a Friday, and the burial takes places on a Saturday. After elaborate traditional burial ceremonies, those who practice Christianity are taken to the church for the established funeral rites before the corpses are taken to the cemetery. A week after that the final wake is held on a Friday, and the funeral dance and ceremonies on a Saturday. The day of the final funeral is filled with elaborate activities; relatives of the dead person dress up in expensive garments.

Many Nigerian Americans prefer to be buried in Nigeria when they die. For this reason they buy enough life insurance to cover the transportation of their bodies home. Bodies in the United States are usually kept in the funeral homes till the wake is done. When the body is flown home, in addition to the traditional burial ceremonies, Nigerian Americans who practice Christianity will be buried according to established rites. Nigerian American Moslems whose bodies are sent home are buried according to the Islamic tradition.

INTERACTIONS WITH OTHER ETHNIC GROUPS

Nigerian Americans interact with other ethnic minorities and the community as a whole, though most Nigerian Americans will first seek out people from their own tribes. At one time, as a result of the Biafra War, Nigerian Americans from the Yoruba tribe would not interact with others from the Ibo tribe and vice versa; but this situation has improved

in contemporary times. Interaction exists between Nigerian Americans and people from other African countries such as Ghana, Ethiopia, Kenya, and Uganda. Most Africans see themselves as brothers and sisters in the United States since they all left their home countries to come here. There are some Nigerian Americans who prefer not to interact with people of their own heritage. There have been many cases of fraud, crime, and drug smuggling involving Nigerian Americans and some want to avoid any implication in such criminal cases.

RELIGION

As is the case in many African countries, Western religion was imposed on Nigeria. Traditionally, Nigerians believe that there are two types of divinities: the Supreme Being, and the subordinate deities. The Supreme Being can be likened to God and the subordinate deities to the saints and others through whose intercession people can communicate with the Supreme Being. The Ibos, for instance, refer to the Supreme Being in powerful terms, such as *Chukwu*— the Great Providence, and *Chineke*—Creator and Providence. The traditional religion of the Yorubas focuses on different gods, representing aspects of one almighty, all-encompassing God, *Olodumare, Oluwa, Olorun*—owner of heaven and earth, who is too sacred to be directly approached or worshipped.

Through commercial contacts and colonization, Islamic and European religions were introduced in Nigeria. The majority of Nigerian Americans hailing from the northern states in Nigeria are Moslems. Islamic groups in the northern part of Nigeria include the Hausa, Fulani, Kanuris, Kanemis, Bagirimis, and the Wadayans. About 40 percent of the Yoruba population also practice Islam. The majority of Nigerian Americans from the Ibo tribe are Catholics. While many Nigerians worship with the American community in places of worship, members of the Nigerian American community have their own groups in which they can worship together. For example, in Boston, the Igbo community has formed a group that worships in the Catholic tradition, using the native language in both prayers and songs. They inculcate traditional practices such as dancing and drumming into their worship.

A key development in religion in Nigeria was the establishment of *Aladura* or spiritual churches. *Aladura* is a Yoruba word meaning "one who prays." The Aladura movement started among the Yoruba people in Nigeria during the first decades of the twentieth century and spread throughout Africa. Among the many practices of this movement, all participants put on white robes while they worship.

They may worship in a church building, along the beach, on top of hills, or by the mouth of rivers praying, confessing their sins, healing, singing and clapping. The *Aladura* movement can be likened to the charismatic movement in the United States. In many cities in the United States, Nigerian Americans have established their own *Aladura* churches where they gather to worship.

EMPLOYMENT AND ECONOMIC TRADITIONS

Early Nigerian Americans came to the United States to study, acquired terminal degrees, and returned home. This ambitious habit was copied by many Nigerian Americans settling in the United States. Through their status as American citizens or permanent residents Nigerian Americans were able to acquire prestigious jobs in academia and other professions. Other Nigerian Americans without the academic qualifications accept jobs in various sectors of society. Many Nigerian Americans establish their own businesses in the United States. For many, trading in Nigerian and other African costumes has become a profitable business. This requires travelling between Nigeria and the United States to arrange importation of items. In many American cities, it is not uncommon to find Nigerian and other African restaurants owned and operated by Nigerian Americans. Nigerian Americans have established their own small businesses, including travel agencies, parking lots, taxi stands, cultural exchange programs, and health and life insurance agencies. Even though they target the general population for their clientele, Nigerian Americans invest time in acquiring Nigerian and other African clientele.

POLITICS AND GOVERNMENT

Nigerian Americans as a group do not have political clout in the United States. They do work in small groups through established associations or where they reside to raise political consciousness when appropriate issues arise. When the press in the United States reports sensational stories that create stereotypical impressions about Nigeria, Nigerian Americans react in unison to correct such impressions.

RELATIONS WITH NIGERIA

Nigerian Americans maintain a high sense of pride for their country. They remain attached to Nigeria no matter how long they stay away from it. Many go home to visit occasionally while others make a visit to the motherland an annual obligation. Basketball star Hakeem Olajuwon, who recently became a citizen of the United States, expresses the attachment Nigerians have for their country: "There's no place like home. I will always be from Nigeria" ("Hakeem Becomes U.S. Citizen," *The Houston Chronicle*, April 3, 1993).

When Nigerians first came to the United States, they would gather with other African students to promote nationalism and protest against colonial domination in their homeland. In contemporary times, Nigerian Americans have been vociferous in protesting against injustice and despotic rule in Nigeria. In 1989, when Nigeria's military leader Ibrahim Babaginda summarily dissolved several groups that aspired to be registered as political parties to compete in elections, Nigerian Americans throughout the United States held demonstrations to protest against this act of despotism.

In 1993, when Babaginda refused to accept the June elections and proposed a second election in August, Nigerian Americans added their voice to those of freedom-loving people around the world to protest against his disrespect for the choice of Nigerian voters, Chief Moshood Abiola. As the political situation in Nigeria remains in turmoil, Nigerian Americans constantly express themselves and gather to ensure that justice will prevail.

Nigerian Americans forge strong ties with their motherland. By working strongly with both private and governmental groups, Nigerian Americans have succeeded in organizing exchanges between business people in the United States and Nigeria. Individual organizations also pool their resources together to assist their motherland. A good example is the Network of Nigerian Engineers and Scientists whose members sometimes offer free services to the government of Nigeria. As a result of these efforts there has been a boost in trade between the United States and America and a boost of tourism in Nigeria. African American tourists visit Nigeria in huge numbers every year to explore their heritage.

By working closely with universities, other institutions of higher learning, and research centers, Nigerian Americans have ensured that prominent authors, artists, and other researchers visit the United States on a regular basis. Wole Soyinka, the Nobel prize winner from Nigeria, has been a regular visitor to many campuses and art centers in the United States. Chinua Achebe, renowned novelist and scholar comes to the United States to lecture on college campuses and at other literary and cultural events. Top known artists and musicians such as King Sunny Ade, Ebenezer Obey, Sonny Okosun, and Fela Anikulapo Kuti have been invited by Nigerian Americans to perform throughout the United States.

INDIVIDUAL AND GROUP CONTRIBUTIONS

Nigerian Americans vividly portray the philosophy of life evident in all African societies: as long as God has given you the strength and power to live, you have to contribute to society as much as you can. Small in percentage as they are to the American population as a whole, Nigerian Americans distinguish themselves. The following is a sample of notable Nigerian Americans working in various arenas.

ACADEMIA

Known as one of the world's top three scientists in the fields of robotics, Bartholomew Nnaji (1957–), came to the United States on an athletic scholarship in 1977 and is currently a professor at the College of Engineering of the University of Massachusetts, Amherst; author of six books and editor in chief of the International Journal of Design and manufacturing, Nnaji has won many awards including the 1988 Young Manufacturing Engineering Award.

JOURNALISM

Through the popular journal *African World*, Bartholomew Nnaji (1957–), professor of industrial engineering and operations research and past interim federal minister for science and technology in Nigeria, has been working with Okey Ndibe, former editor of *African Commentary* to educate Americans about the distortion of the history of Africans and others of African descent.

MUSIC

Titilayo Rachel Adedokun (1973–) was a finalist in the 1993 Miss America pageant and was the 1993 Miss Ohio. Adedokun graduated from the Cincinnati College Conservatory of Music.

O. J. (Orlando Julius) Ekemode (1942–) born in Ijebu-Ijesha in Nigeria, started playing drums at age eight. His combination of traditional African music with contemporary jazz, religious, reggae, Afro-beat, and soul music in the fashion of James Brown has made him one of the living legends of real African music in the United States.

SCIENCE AND TECHNOLOGY

One of America's top engineers, Olusola Seriki, currently development director for the Rouse Company in Columbia, Maryland, has distinguished himself; born in Ibadan, Oyo, Nigeria, he is a Howard University graduate who has worked on several large-scale international projects; the countless awards he has received include the prestigious African Business Executive of the Year in 1989; an accomplished author and scholar, Seriki is also active in various professional organizations.

SPORTS

According to George Karl, coach of the Seattle Supersonics, Hakeem Olajuwon (1963–) is the second-best player in the world. Akeem, as he is affectionately known, led the University of Houston to three consecutive trips to the Final Four of the NCAA basketball tournament. Olajuwon led the Rockets to NBA titles in 1994 and 1995.

Donald Igwebuike (1961–), kicked five years for the Tampa Bay Buccaneers football team; when he was released in September 1990, he was picked up by the Minnesota Vikings for the 1990 football season; soon after he was arrested and charged with being an accomplice to heroin trafficking, but was later acquitted. Christian Okoye (1961–), known as the "Nigerian Nightmare" is a superior discus thrower and a great football player; his sports career in the United States started when he came on a track scholarship to the Azusa Pacific University in 1982; he is also a former Kansas City Chiefs running back who became the NFL's leading rusher in 1989.

MEDIA

PRINT

Because Nigeria's official language is English, publications regarding Nigerian Americans come out mainly in the English Language. The following are just a few of the available newspapers and similar types of publications on Nigeria.

Nigeria Trade Journal.
Published quarterly, this journal is an important resource for Nigerian Americans and others interested in establishing businesses in Nigeria.

Contact: Nigerian Consulate General.
Address: 828 Second Avenue, New York,
    New York, 10017-4301.
Telephone: (212) 752-1670.

Nigerian Journal.
Quarterly journal published by the Nigerian Consulate in New York. This English language publication provides a vast array of information on Nigeria, and issues of concern to Nigerians at home and those abroad, as well as non-Nigerians interested in Nigeria.

Contact: Nigerian Consulate General.
Address: 828 Second Avenue, 10th Floor, New York, New York, 10017-4301.
Telephone: (212) 850-2200; or (212) 808-0301.

Nigerian Students Union in the Americas Newsletter.

A monthly publication that provides information on Nigeria and the world at large to Nigerians and Nigerian students studying in the Americas.

Contact: Nigerian Consulate General.
Address: 828 Second Avenue, New York, New York, 10017-4301.
Telephone: (212) 752-1670.

Nigerian Times.

Formerly the *African Enquirer.*

Contact: Chika A. Onyeani, Editor.
Address: 368 Broadway, Suite 307, New York, New York 10013.
Telephone: (212) 791-0777.

RADIO

WABE-FM (90.1).

This is a daily evening music broadcast featuring music from all over the world, including Nigeria.

Contact: Lois Reitzes, Program Director.
Address: 740 Bismark Road, N.E., Atlanta, Georgia 30324-4102.
Telephone: (404) 827-8900.
Fax: (404) 827-8956.

WRFG-FM (89.3).

"African Experience" is a two-hour program from 12:00 p.m. to 2:00 p.m. on Saturdays with emphasis on music, opinions, interviews from Africa, including Nigeria.

Contact: B. Kai Aiyetoro.
Address: 1083 Austin Avenue, N.E., Atlanta, Georgia 30307.
Telephone: (404) 523-3471.
E-mail: wrfg@mindspring.com.

ORGANIZATIONS AND ASSOCIATIONS

League of Patriotic Nigerians (LPN).

Founded in 1985, the LPN has a membership of 10,000 Nigerian American professionals, including doctors, lawyers, accountants, and engineers. It promotes professional behavior, and the importance of good citizenship, respect for the law, and community involvement.

Contact: Alex Taire, Vice President.

Nigerian American Alliance (NAA).

Formerly known as the Nigerian American Friendship Fund, the NAA was founded in 1988 and has a membership of 300 business people, government officials, and educators interested in Nigeria and American-Nigerian relations. The NAA promotes improved understanding between the two countries on political, social, and economic issues.

Contact: James E. Obi, Agency Manager.
Address: c/o James E. Obi, 1010 Washington Boulevard, Stamford, Connecticut 06901.

Nigerian American Chamber of Commerce (NACC).

The NACC is a trade group trying to develop closer economic ties between Nigeria and the United States.

Address: 575 Lexington Avenue, New York, New York 10021.
Telephone: (212) 715-7200.

Nigerian Students Union in the Americas (NSUA).

Disseminates information about Nigeria and Africa; cooperates with other African student unions in the Americas and with Nigerian student unions in Nigeria and other parts of the world.

Contact: Granville U. Osuji.
Address: 654 Girard Street, N.W., Apartment 512, Washington, D.C. 20001-2936.

Organization of Nigerian Citizens (ONC).

Founded in 1986, the ONC has a membership of 700 in 21 state groups; it is made up of people of Nigerian ancestry, and works to increase the understanding and awareness of Nigeria and its citizens by promoting educational programs. It also serves as a networking link for people interested in Nigeria. The ONC seeks solutions to problems encountered by Nigerian Americans.

Contact: Chuks Eleonu.
Address: P.O. Box 66220, Baltimore, Maryland 21239.
Telephone: (410) 637-5165.

World Union of Nigerians (WUN).

Promotes democratic principles of government, protection of civil liberties, and economic development within Nigeria.

Contact: Sonnie Braih, Executive Chair.
Address: 2147 University Avenue, W., Suite 101, P.O. Box 14265, St. Paul, Minnesota 55114.
Telephone: (612) 776-4997.

MUSEUMS AND RESEARCH CENTERS

The Afro-American Historical and Cultural Museum.
Maintains a vast collection of African sculpture and artifacts relating to Africa and the slave trade. Nigeria is well represented in the collection.

Contact: Nannette A. Clark, Executive Director.
Address: 701 Arch Street, Philadelphia, Pennsylvania 19106-1557.
Telephone: (215) 574-0380.

Black Heritage Museum.
Holds a vast collection of art and artifacts of black heritage, including many tribal artifacts from Nigeria.

Contact: Priscilla G. Stephens Kruize, President.
Address: Miracle Center Mall, 3301 Coral Way, Miami, Florida 33257.
Telephone: (305) 252-3535.

Museum for African Art.
Has an extensive collection of art from all over Africa, including Nigeria.

Contact: Susan M. Vogel, C.E.O and Executive Director.
Address: 593 Broadway, New York, New York, 10012.
Telephone: (212) 966-1313.

Museum of African American Art.
Has preserved a large collection of Arts of African and African descendant peoples, including Nigeria.

Contact: Belinda Fontenote-Jamerson, President.
Address: 4005 Crenshaw Boulevard, Third Floor, Los Angeles, California 90008.
Telephone: (213) 294-7071.

National Museum of African Art.
Part of the Smithsonian Institution, the museum has over 6,000 objects of African art, wood, metal, ceramic, ivory, and fiber. Its collection on Nigerian art is extensive.

Contact: Roslyn A. Walker, Director.
Address: 950 Independence Avenue, S.W., Washington, D.C., 20560.
Telephone: (202) 357-4600.
Fax: (202) 357-4879.
Online: http://www.si.edu/organiza/museums /africart/start.htm.

SOURCES FOR ADDITIONAL STUDY

Burns, Sir Alan. *History of Nigeria.* London: George Allen and Unwin Ltd., 1929; reprinted, 1976.

Essien, Efiong. *Nigeria Under Structural Adjustment.* Nigeria: Fountain Publications Ltd., 1990.

Footprints of Our Ancestors, edited by Ben Okaba. Port Harcourt, Nigeria: Pan-Unique Publishers, 1998.

Hair, Paul Edward Hedley. *The Early Study of Nigerian Languages: Essays and Bibliographies.* London: Cambridge University Press, 1967.

Nigeria: A Country Study, edited by Helen Chapin Metz. Washington D.C.: Federal Research Division, Library of Congress, 1992.

Offoha, Marcellina Ulunm. *Educated Nigerian Settlers in the United States: The Phenomenon of Brain Drain.* Philadelphia, Temple University, 1989.

Shepard, Robert B. *Nigeria, Africa, and the United States: From Kennedy to Reagan.* Bloomington: Indiana University Press, 1991.

Sofola, Johnson Adeyemi. *American-Processed Nigerians: A Study of the Adjustment and Attitudes of the Nigerian Students in the United States of America.* American University, 1967.

Udofia, Paul E. *Nigerians in the United States: Potentialities and Crises.* Boston, Massachusetts: William Monroe Trotter Institute, 1996.

NORWEGIAN AMERICANS

by
Odd S. Lovoll

The pioneers on the
American frontier
were the new Vikings
of the West; Leif
Ericson became the
quintessential icon of
a glorified Viking
heritage. Norwegians
found a second
identifying quality by
presenting them-
selves as an ethnic
group with whole-
some rural values
and ideals. And, in
fact, Norwegians
were the most rural
of any major
nineteenth-century
immigrant group.

OVERVIEW

Occupying the western part of the Scandinavian peninsula in northwestern Europe, and sharing borders with Sweden, Finland, and Russia, Norway is slightly larger than the state of New Mexico, measuring 125,181 square miles (323,878 square kilometers). The country measures 1,095 miles from south to north, and one-third of its land mass lies north of the Arctic Circle, extending farther north than any other European country.

Norway's population is 4,300,000. Save for an indigenous minority of Samis (estimated at no more than 40,000) confined mainly to the northern half of the country, Norway's population is ethnically and culturally homogeneous. Almost 90 percent of the inhabitants belong to the Evangelical Lutheran state church, five percent are members of other denominations and faiths, and only five percent have no religious affiliation. Norway's form of government is a hereditary constitutional monarchy. The capital city is Oslo. The national flag displays a central blue cross with a white border on a red field. Norwegian is the official language, rendered in two different literary forms, the predominant *bokmål* (Dano-Norwegian) and the rural dialect-based *nynorsk* (New Norse).

HISTORY

Norway (Old Norse: *Norvegr* or *Noregr*) designates the sea-lane—the north way—along the country's extensive coastline as viewed from the south. Maritime connections west and south have, as a consequence of Norway's geography, characterized its history. During the Viking Age (800-1030) expansive forces moved the Norse Vikings onto the historical stage of Europe; their westward expansion extended to Iceland, Greenland, and even to the continent of North America. Some time before 890 Harald Finehair consolidated Norway under the Yngling dynasty. The martyrdom of King Olav II of this royal line on July 29, 1030, at the Battle of Stiklestad, made him Norway's patron saint, secured a national monarchy, and established the Christian church as a dominant institution.

Medieval Norway attained its political height under the reign of Haakon IV Haakonson (1217-1263), with territorial dominance to the western islands (the Orkneys, the Shetlands, the Hebrides, the Isle of Man, and the Faroes), Iceland, and Greenland, and three districts in present-day Sweden. It was then that Norway entered fully into close diplomatic and commercial relations with other European states.

Norwegian national decline manifested itself in dynastic unions with the two other Scandinavian nations, Sweden and Denmark. The Bubonic Plague that ravaged Europe in the middle of the fourteenth century hit Norway, a country with greater poverty and fewer natural resources than the other Nordic lands, especially hard. Norway's population was devastated, resulting in a serious loss of income for the great landowners, the church, and the king. The last king of an independent and sovereign Norway died in 1380 and Norway united with Denmark. In 1397 the three Scandinavian states were joined under one ruler in the Kalmar Union; in the case of Norway the union with Denmark lasted until 1814. The Lutheran Reformation in 1537 resulted in Norway's reduction in administrative arrangements to a province within the Danish state. The idea of Norway as a kingdom, however, remained alive throughout the union period and was evidenced in the term "the twin realms."

MODERN ERA

The big power politics following the Napoleonic Wars yielded a national rebirth. Rejecting the terms of the Treaty of Kiel, which transferred Norway to the King of Sweden, a constituent assembly meeting north of Oslo at Eidsvoll on May 17, 1814, signed a constitution establishing a limited and hereditary monarchy, and declared Norway's independence. Mindful of their pledge to the Swedish throne, but also not wishing to quell Nor-

wegian moves toward independence, the European powers endorsed a compromise that established a union under the Swedish king. The union preserved the Eidsvoll constitution and was based on the will of the Norwegian people rather than the Treaty of Kiel.

The Act of Union signed in 1815 declared, in principle, an equal partnership in the double monarchy of Sweden and Norway. In reality, however, Norway held an inferior position. Politically Norway feared Swedish encroachment and sought full equality in the union. Culturally the new nation struggled against Danish hegemony—a result of the 400-year union—-and engaged in a quest for national identity and cultural independence. There was a surge of nationalism, which was expressed in an idealized and romantic cultivation of the peasantry as the true carriers of the national spirit. Norway's ultimate goal was a separate and respected national status within the Nordic nations. In 1905 the union with Sweden ended after a dispute over foreign affairs, centering on Norway's demand for an independent consular service. The union was unnatural from the start with few, if any, positive elements linking the two countries.

Prince Carl of Denmark was elected King of Norway, taking the name Haakon VII, which linked him to the old Norwegian royal line. The first half-century of full independence witnessed a rapid transformation from mainly an agricultural society to an industrialized and commercial one. The laboring classes gained political influence and from the mid-1930s the Norwegian Labor Party formed the government. German occupation from 1940 to 1945 suspended the Party's political agenda, but in the postwar era it resumed power and transformed Norway into a prosperous social-democratic welfare state. In foreign affairs, the country abandoned its historically neutral stance and joined the western alliance in the North Atlantic Treaty Organization (NATO). In 1994 Norway completed negotiations for membership in the European Union. A pending national referendum will determine whether or not Norway actually becomes a member.

THE PIONEER IMMIGRATION

Norwegian overseas emigration began earlier than in the other Nordic lands, commencing dramatically on July 4, 1825, with the sailing of the tiny sloop *Restauration* from Stavanger on the southwestern coast of Norway. The initial emigration occurred in a district with historical ties to England where the idea of emigration as an alternative to staying at home originated. As early as 1821 the enigmatic wanderer Cleng Peerson, "the pathfinder of Norwegian emigration," traveled to America as an agent for the pioneer emigrants. Many Lutheran pietists and Quakers chose to emigrate as a result of persecution by the Lutheran clergy because of their defiance of ecclesiastical law. Religious oppression did not enter into the subsequent emigration. In 1824 Peerson returned briefly to Norway to advise the emigrants, but was back in the United States to meet "the Sloopers" (as they were called because they sailed on a sloop). The *Restauration* landed in New York on October 9, 1825, with a boatload of 53 immigrants—one of them a baby girl born during an adventurous voyage of 14 weeks.

Annual emigration did not commence until 1836, but a contact had been made with the New World. Individuals had gone to America in the intervening years and even visited Norway to report on life there. The Norwegian exodus rose in the 1840s; by 1865, nearly 80,000 Norwegians had entered the United States. From the southwestern coastal areas the "America fever" had moved along the west coast and inland to the central highland region. Even though no part of Norway was entirely untouched by the overseas exodus, the majority of emigrants in this founding phase of the movement came from the inner fjord districts in west Norway and the mountain valleys of east Norway. It was an emigration of rural folk with a strong family composition. Their move was permanent; they sought a new life in America for themselves and their descendants. As a result, the character of the immigrant community that evolved in America reflected traditions, mores, and religious as well as secular values of the people from their districts in the old country and conveyed a strong familial and communal bond.

SIGNIFICANT IMMIGRATION WAVES

The end of the Civil War brought about a great increase in Atlantic crossings. The number of Norwegian emigrants leaped from 4,000 in 1865 to 15,726 in 1866, heralding the era of mass migration. The migration occurred until 1873 when, in the course of only eight years, some 110,000 Norwegians left their homeland. The second, and also the greatest, period of emigration lasted 14 years from 1880 to 1893, when on the average 18,290 left annually—ten for every 1,000 Norwegians. During this time Norway's emigration intensity was the second greatest in Europe, surpassed only by Ireland. Norway experienced a final mass exodus in the first decade of the twentieth century, although there was considerable emigration in the 1920s as well. Emigration from its beginning in 1825 until the present has affected some 900,000 people. Of the total emigration, 87 percent, or 780,000 Norwegians, left in the period between 1865 and 1930.

In the nineteenth century, Norwegian emigrants headed almost exclusively for the United States. Only since 1900 have other overseas areas, especially Canada, attracted substantial number of Norwegians. Still, the United States remains the most popular destination. A rapid population growth in the last century and a slow industrial expansion left many young Norwegians unable to find gainful employment at home. Surplus labor was syphoned off through emigration. The United States on the other hand had a great need for people to develop its resources. In periods of expanding economy, American society offered seemingly unlimited possibilities. The response in Norway was a rise in emigration. The migration of families gradually changed in the last quarter of the century to an emigration of individuals. It was dominated by a movement of young male laborers who came from the cities as well as the countryside, though the rural exodus was by far the larger. From the 1880s, youths with education and technical training joined the masses who went to America.

Improved transportation facilitated by steam passenger liners, allowed people to move back and forth across the Atlantic, yielding a two-way migration. The Norwegian Bureau of Statistics has estimated that about 25 percent of the immigrants to North America between 1881 and 1930 have resettled in Norway. Still, as of 1990 there were 3,869,395 residents of Norwegian ancestry in the United States, nearly as many as in the home country.

SETTLEMENT

The majority of the pioneer immigrants, the so-called "Sloopers," assisted by the kindly services of American Quakers, went to Orleans County in western New York state and settled in what became Kendall Township. In the mid-1830s the Kendall settlers gave impetus to the westward movement of Norwegians by founding a settlement in the Fox River area of Illinois. A small urban colony of Norwegians had its genesis in Chicago at about the same time.

Immigrant settlements now stood ready to welcome Norwegian newcomers, who, beginning in 1836, arrived annually. From Illinois, Norwegian pioneers followed the general spread of population northwestward into Wisconsin. Wisconsin remained the center of Norwegian American activity up until the Civil War. In the 1850s Norwegian landseekers began moving into both Iowa and Minnesota, and serious migration to the Dakotas was underway by the 1870s. The majority of Norwegian agrarian settlements developed in the northern region of the so-called Homestead Act Triangle between the Mississippi and the Missouri rivers. The upper Midwest became the home for most immigrants. In 1910 almost 80 percent of the one million or more Norwegian Americans—the immigrants and their children—lived in that part of the United States. In 1990, 51.7 percent of the Norwegian American population lived in the Midwest; Minnesota had the largest number. Minneapolis functioned as a Norwegian American "capital" for secular and religious activities.

In the Pacific Northwest, the Puget Sound region, and especially the city of Seattle, became another center of immigrant life. Enclaves of Norwegians emerged as well in greater Brooklyn, New York, in Alaska, and Texas. After Minnesota, Wisconsin had the most Norwegians in 1990, followed by California, Washington, and North Dakota.

In a letter from Chicago dated November 9, 1855, Elling Haaland from Stavanger, Norway, assured his relatives back home that "of all nations Norwegians are those who are most favored by

"**A** newcomer from Norway who arrives here will be surprised indeed to find in the heart of the country, more than a thousand miles from his landing place, a town where language and way of life so unmistakably remind him of his native land."

Svein Nilsson, a Norwegian American journalist (in *Billed-Magazin*, May 14, 1870).

Americans." This sentiment was expressed frequently as the immigrants attempted to seek acceptance and negotiate entrance into the new society. In their segregated farming communities, Norwegians were spared direct prejudice and might indeed have been viewed as a welcome ingredient in a region's development. Still, a sense of inferiority was inherent in their position. The immigrants were occasionally referred to as "guests" in the United States and they were not immune to condescending and disparaging attitudes by old-stock Americans. Economic adaptation required a certain amount of interaction with a larger commercial environment, from working for an American farmer to doing business with the seed dealer, the banker, and the elevator operator. Products had to be grown and sold— all of which pulled Norwegian farmers into social contact with their American neighbors.

In places like Brooklyn, Chicago, Minneapolis, and Seattle, Norwegians interacted with the multicultural environment of the city while constructing a complex ethnic community that met the needs of its members. It might be said that a Scandinavian melting pot existed in the urban setting among Norwegians, Swedes, and Danes, evidenced in residential and occupational patterns, in political mobilization, and in public commemoration. Intermarriage promoted interethnic assimilation. There are no longer any Norwegian enclaves or neighborhoods in America's great cities. Beginning in the 1920s, Norwegians increasingly became suburban, and one might claim, more American.

ACCULTURATION AND ASSIMILATION

Norwegian history in America covers a period of 170 years, beginning with the pioneer immigrants in 1825. Viking ancestors had, however, established colonies in Greenland—outposts of European civilization—as early as 985 A.D. From there they found America, commonly associated with the voyages of the Norse adventurer Leif Ericson, around the year 1000 and formed colonies on Newfoundland. These had no impact on the later European settlement in the New World, but they provided Norwegians, and other Scandinavians, with a claim to a birthright in America and gave them their most expressive identifying ethnic symbols.

The pioneers on the American frontier were the new Vikings of the West; Leif Ericson became the quintessential icon of a glorified Viking heritage. Norwegians found a second identifying quality by presenting themselves as an ethnic group with wholesome rural values and ideals. And, in fact, Norwegians were the most rural of any major nineteenth-century immigrant group. In 1900, for instance, only a little more than a quarter of all Norwegian-born residents in the United States lived in towns with more than 25,000 inhabitants. It was the lowest percentage for any European immigrant population. It has been claimed that the Norwegian farmer in America passed on a special rural bond from one generation to the next. Perhaps the greatest contribution was a dedication to farming as a way of life; in 1900, 54.3 percent of the children of Norwegian immigrants were farmers.

In their farming communities Norwegians exhibited a nationalistic solidarity that had no counterpart among other Scandinavian groups. The homeland's quest for a national identity created a patriotic fervor that was transplanted as immigrant clannishness. Even today, as evidenced by the retention of their institutions, Norwegians appear more focused on culture retention than their Nordic neighbors in America. For example, a Norwegian-language Lutheran congregation survives in Chicago, whereas the Swedes, with a much larger population, have not maintained a Swedish-language church.

PUBLIC CELEBRATIONS

Norwegians' past in the United States was celebrated at the Norse American Centennial in the Twin Cities of Minneapolis and St. Paul in June 1925. A century had passed since the landing of the *Restauration* in New York harbor. President Calvin Coolidge came to honor the Norwegians for being good Americans and validated their claim of sharing nationality with the original discoverer of America as the Norwegian Americans reflected upon a successful 100 years as an immigrant people. The festivities displayed an attachment to traditional rural values and a cultivation of ancient and heroic Norse roots, but featured heroes from their American experience as well. An impressive pageant centered on the life of Colonel Hans Christian Heg, a hero from the Civil War. The hostilities between the North and the South gave Norwegian Americans a sense of a legitimate place in the United States, because Norwegian blood had been spilled in its defense.

The symbols and content of a Norwegian ethnic identity emerged among the more successful of their nationality in such urban centers as Chicago and Minneapolis. They were the ones who most eagerly sought acceptable ethnic credentials and gathered their compatriots around the celebration of such holidays as Norwegian Constitution Day on May 17, which became the most important identifying ethnic symbol. The day is still celebrated with a traditional parade featuring flags, banners, music, and speeches in Norwegian centers across America. The event, observed since the early days of settlement, communicates American patriotism as well as Norwegian memories; ethnic identities are firmly rooted in positive views of the group's place in America and images of the homeland's culture are equally prominent in the celebration.

There are numerous folk festivals in Norwegian centers. *Norsk Høstfest* in Minot, North Dakota (for information, contact [701] 852-2368), and Nordic Fest in Decorah, Iowa (for information, contact [800] 382-3378), annually assemble thousands of Norwegian Americans nationwide around a varied program focusing on a Norwegian American heritage.

At such events Norwegian stereotypes are regularly introduced to the amusement of those assem-

These Leikarring Norwegian Dancers are standing in front of a replica of the Valhalia Viking ship in Petersburg, Alaska.

bled. Invariably there are stories and jokes poking fun at the ignorance and foolishness of Norwegian types, such as the characters of Ole and Lena, who speak in broken English. New tales are constantly being created. A typical one might go as follows: "Ole and Lena invited a well-to-do Uncle for dinner. Little Ole looked him over and finally approached the old Uncle with a request. 'Uncle Knute ... vill you make a noise like a frog for me?' said Little Ole. 'Vy in the world do you vant me to make a noise like a frog?' exclaimed the Uncle. 'Because,' said Little Ole, 'Papa says ve are going to get a lot of money ven you croak!'" (Red Stangeland, *Ole & Lena Jokes*, Book 4 [Sioux Falls, South Dakota: Norse Press, 1989], p. 14).

TRADITIONS, CUSTOMS, AND BELIEFS

In 1879 a Norwegian Unitarian minister and author was amazed after a visit to Wisconsin at "how Norwegians have managed to isolate themselves together in colonies and maintain their Norwegian memories and customs." He had to ask himself if he was really in America. Adjustments were, however, made to American ways in clothing and food, although especially typical Norwegian dishes were retained. These became associated with Christmas celebrations, which in pioneer days were observed for the entire Twelfth-night period, as in Norway. Aaste Wilson of Wisconsin tells how transplanted Norwegians retained such old customs: "They invited one another for Christmas celebration and then they had home-brewed ale, made from malt or molasses or sugar cane.... Nearly everybody slaughtered for

Christmas so that they could have meat and sausages. Then they had potatoes and *flatbrød* (flatbread) and *smultringer* (doughnuts) and sauce made from dried apples. And most of them had *rømmegrøt* (cream porridge). We youngsters liked to stay and listen to the old folks and thought it good fun when they told about old things in Norway." (Wilson, Aaste, "Live blant nybyggjarane." *Telesoga,* September 1917.)

A gradual transition to American life weakened immigrant folkways. Some traditions and customs survived and were cultivated, others were reintroduced and given a heightened importance as a part of an ethnic heritage. Toward the end of the century *lutefisk,* dried Norwegian cod soaked in a lye solution, assumed a role as a characteristic Norwegian American dish. It was served at lodge meetings, festive banquets, and church suppers, most regularly during the Christmas season. The dish is served with *lefse,* a thin buttered pancake made from rolled dough. Madison, Minnesota, has erected a statue of a cod in its city park and advertises itself as the "*Lutefisk* Capital of America" because it reportedly consumes more *lutefisk* per capita than any other American city.

Old-country traditions in food, festive dress, folk arts, and entertainment were given a powerful boost with the establishment of *bygdelag,* or old-home societies, around the turn of the century. These groups were rooted in Norwegian locality and loyalties to the old-country home community. The annual reunions of the 50 or so such societies, each bearing the name of a specific Norwegian home district, became grand celebrations of a regional and rural Norwegian cultural heritage.

Women especially revived the use of the festive rural dress, the *bunad,* wearing specific costumes of their old-country districts. A love for jewelry was demonstrated in the use of heavy silver brooches (*sølje*). The peasant costume of Hardanger on Norway's west coast, a favored region for national romantics, inspired the official dress of the Daughters of Norway organization. These colorful outfits are worn at Norwegian American public events.

There was also renewed interest in the traditional Norwegian Harding fiddle, and old rural dances. Even today, groups meet to practice the old figures and demonstrate their mastery of the country dances. The current popularity of the peasant arts of wood carving and *rosemaling* (rose painting) also grew out of the *bygdelag* tradition. Vesterheim, the Norwegian American Museum in Decorah, Iowa, has promoted the folk arts through instruction and exhibitions.

PROVERBS

Norwegians tend to integrate sayings and proverbs into daily conversations. Some common expressions are: All is not gold that glitters; A burnt child avoids the fire; A dear child has many names; All cats are gray in the dark; As we make our bed, so must we also lie; "Cleanliness is a virtue," said the old woman, she turned her slip inside out every Christmas Eve; Crumbs are also bread; Empty barrels make the most noise; If it rains on the pastor it drips on the sexton; Many small brooks make a big river.

CUISINE

Norwegian cuisine is mainly limited to special occasions—family events like weddings and anniversaries, and such holidays as Christmas, when other customs are revived as well. The *kransekake* a cone-shaped cake of almond macaroon rings, is traditionally served at weddings and anniversaries. It is generally decorated with costumed figures and with flags, snappers, flowers, or medallions. The observance of the Christmas season begins on Christmas Eve, when a big meal is served, followed by the reading of the Christmas gospel and the opening of gifts. Hymns and carols are sung later, accompanied in some families by tradition of holding hands and circling the Christmas tree.

A typical old-country Christmas meal consists of *lutefisk, rømmegrøt,* pork or mutton spare ribs with pork sausages, as well as *fattigmann,* a deep-fried diamond-shaped cookie; *sandkake,* a cookie made of butter, flour, and almonds, baked in small metal molds; *krumkake,* a wafer baked in a special iron and rolled into a cylindrical shape while still warm; *julekake,* a sweet bread containing raisins, citron, and cardamon, and the essential *lefse,* which appears in many regional variations.

The Norwegian *koldt bord,* or cold table, is basically the same as the better known Swedish *smörgåsbord;* with selected hot dishes. Some of the traditional dishes of the Norwegian "cold table" include herring in many forms; sardines; smoked salmon and other fish; sliced cold ham, lamb, and beef; cheeses like Swiss, *geitost* (goat cheese), and *gammelost* (highly pungent sour milk cheese); *sylte* (pickled pork, pressed into loaf shape and sliced); pickles, cranberries, apple sauce, and spiced apples; and various types of bread, including flatbread. The meal is served with *akevitt* (strong distilled alcoholic drink) and beer.

HEALTH ISSUES

In his investigation of Norwegian immigrants in Minnesota, Ørnulv Ødegaard discovered a much

higher incidence of emotional and mental problems than among Norwegians in Norway (Ornulv Ódegaard, *Emigration and Insanity: A Study of Mental Disease among the Norwegian-born Population in Minnesota* [Copenhagen], 1932). The frequency was also much higher than among other ethnic groups in America. At present, no empirical evidence has identified any emotional or cultural causes unique to the Norwegian population.

LANGUAGE

The Norwegian language, along with Danish and Swedish, belongs to the mutually comprehensible northern branch of the Germanic family of languages. During the centuries-long union with Denmark, Norwegians accepted Danish as their written language. Following independence in 1814 efforts to provide a national written standard created conflict between those who worked for a gradual Norwegianization of Danish orthographic forms and those who wished to create a totally new written language. The Norwegian government officially recognizes the existence of the predominant *bokmål* (Dano-Norwegian), which continues the Danish written tradition greatly modified through a series of reforms under the influence of Norwegian speech habits, and *nynorsk* (New Norse), constructed on the basis of modern dialects which most faithfully preserved the forms of Old Norse. Because of the isolated nature of Norwegian rural communities, the local vernacular was distinct with marked dialectal differences from one district to the next.

The cultural baggage of Norwegian immigrants included their specific local dialect and a Danish literary language. The latter played a significant role in the immigrant community, attaining a nearly sacred quality. It was the language of their institutions, secular and religious, and of sacred and profane literature. The immigrants had little appreciation for the linguistic reforms in the homeland; often such changers were viewed as a betrayal to a common cultural heritage. Changes in the official written language in Norway made the older form even more difficult to retain in America. A newspaper such as *Decorah-Posten* in Decorah, Iowa, persisted in using a Dano-Norwegian orthographic tradition from the 1870s well into the 1950s. The situation created confusion among teachers of Norwegian at American high schools, colleges and universities, who felt obligations to the language of the immigrant community. Only just before World War II did they in principle agree to teach the written standard—generally the Dano-Norwegian *bokmål*—which at any one time was recognized as the official one in Norway.

English was another threat to the maintenance of the Norwegian language in America. Rural settlement patterns protected spoken Norwegian so it still can be heard in some Norwegian communities. According to researcher Joshua A. Fishman, about half of second generation Norwegians in the period 1940 to 1960 learned the language; and in 1960 there were as many as 40,000 of the third generation who had learned Norwegian. As of 1990, about 80,000 speakers of Norwegian remained in the United States. In Minnesota, Norwegian, with

16,000 speakers, is the second most common European language after German. Across the country there are still two bilingual newspapers, *Western Viking* in Seattle and *Nordic Times* in Brooklyn. The *bygdelag* promoted the use of rural vernaculars and, indeed, their annual reunions provided an environment where rural speech was honored and encouraged. It was, however, a mixed language with English words and phrases integrated.

GREETINGS AND OTHER POPULAR EXPRESSIONS

Some common Norwegian expressions are: *God dag* ("gooDAAG")—Good Afternoon, How do you do?; *Adjø* ("adyur")—Goodbye; *Hvordan står det til?* ("VOORdahn stawr deh til")—How are you?; *Bare bra, takk* ("BAArer braa tahk")—Just fine, thanks; *Takk* ("tahk")—Thank you; *Mange takk* ("MAHNger tahk")—Thank you very much; *Skål* ("skawl")—Cheers; *God jul!* ("goo yewl")—Merry Christmas; *Godt nyttår* ("got newt awr")—Happy New Year; *Gratulerer!* ("grahtewLAYrerr")—Congratulations.

FAMILY AND COMMUNITY DYNAMICS

Early Norwegian immigration exhibited a pronounced family character. In a typical settlement like Spring Grove Township in Minnesota, for instance, there was in 1870 a near gender balance—107 men for each 100 women—as compared to 128 males to 100 females for all Minnesotans. An extended communal and familial network was encouraged by this circumstance. The regional composition of most rural settlements, so that immigrants from a specific Norwegian home community were preponderant, worked to the same end, recreating a familiar and comforting cultural and social environment.

But opportunities in America, where land was cheap and labor expensive, altered immigrant practices. The family farm, lacking the retinue of servants and landless agricultural workers common in Norway, encouraged greater marital fertility to produce needed labor. The immigrant families were large. The sexual division of labor changed as women moved further into domestic roles. Men took over such farm chores as milking, which had been women's work in Norway.

Norwegian courting patterns were modified in part due to pietistic attitudes rooted in religious awakenings in Norway, but also because they were ridiculed by American neighbors. Greater wealth allowed the immigrants to imitate urban middle-class practices in housing, dress, household amenities (such as pianos), and leisure activities. But the bourgeois lifestyle was colored both by the local Norwegian cultural background and by the dominant position of the immigrant Lutheran church.

The male-dominated youth migration toward the end of the century was also entrenched in kinship and community. Later immigrants traveled increasingly to urban centers to reunite with relatives in America. Carl G. O. Hansen, visiting an aunt in Minneapolis in the 1880s, described the Norwegian environment: "My aunt sent one of her children out to make some purchases. Some things were to be bought at Haugen's, some at Tharaldsen's and some at Olsen & Bakke's. That surely sounded as if it were a Norwegian town." (Carl G. O. Hansen, *My Minneapolis* [Minneapolis, Minnesota: Privately published, 1956], p.52.)

The many single men living as boarders in crowded quarters would foster marriage outside the Norwegian group. Yet, there was a strikingly high percentage of in-marriage only in both the immigrant generation and the American-born second generation. In Chicago in 1910, 77 percent of married first-generation Norwegians had wed another Norwegian, and 46 percent of the married second generation had chosen a mate within their ethnic group. When most Norwegian Americans married outside their nationality, their spouse was Scandinavian, or, if German, at least shared a Lutheran culture.

For most Norwegian families the "American Dream" was the security of a middle-class existence. Only a few Norwegians asserted themselves as financiers and captains of industry. Norwegians typically endorsed the American principle of equality and rejected American materialism. This attitude was reinforced by the Lutheran ethic of renouncing worldly pleasure. According to the census of 1990, 4.3 percent of Norwegian American households received public assistance and 5.1 percent lived under the poverty line.

Current specific data on in-marriage and divorce are not available. With regard to the latter, Norwegian Americans do not seem to deviate much from the average for the American population as a whole. Anecdotal evidence also suggests a continued high degree of in-marriage, attributable to community and church relations, and even to loyalty to an ethnic heritage. A persistent sense of family cohesion and values is evident in the common practice of arranging family reunions and the compilation of family histories. Such activities fortify ties to the past.

EDUCATION

Higher education in America is greatly indebted to religion. In the Norwegian immigrant community the Lutheran church recognized the salutary benefits of education in a Christian spirit. It emulated American denominations in establishing Lutheran church academies and colleges.

Norwegians placed themselves in a singular position among Scandinavian groups in America to question the religionless "common" school. The orthodox Lutheran clergy even dreamed of replacing the public schools with Lutheran parochial schools, but lacked the means to do so. The ability to read and write was common among Norwegian immigrants, and it improved greatly after 1860 when Norway enacted new laws to improve public education. The Norwegian Lutheran church in America did manage to operate congregational schools, some continuing into the 1930s. During the summer months these schools offered lessons on Lutheran faith and rudimentary instruction in the Norwegian language.

The academy movement flourished for a while, with approximately 70 such schools being established. They lasted until about World War I and assisted the immigrants in adjusting to American society. Inevitably they also strengthened a national Norwegian identity. Some academies were transformed into four-year liberal arts colleges. The college movement among Norwegians began in 1861 with the founding of Luther College, now located in Decorah, Iowa. The school was a facet of the church's effort to train Lutheran ministers. As such it was a men's school, with nearly half of the graduates entering the ministry. In the 1930s it began to admit women.

Five other Norwegian colleges have since been established. All were founded before 1900 mainly as academies. Three are in Minnesota: St. Olaf College in Northfield, which admitted female students from its inception; Augsburg College in Minneapolis; and Concordia College in Moorhead. Augustana College is located in Sioux Falls, South Dakota, and Pacific Lutheran University is in Tacoma, Washington.

Norwegian women in America obtained higher education at a time when such studies were closed to women in the homeland. Some of these women were trained as physicians at the Women's Medical School which opened in Chicago in 1870. As feminists and as professionals, they became leaders in the Norwegian community.

According to the 1990 census, of those who declared Norwegian as their primary ancestry, 21 percent of the women and 32 percent of the men 25 years or older had earned bachelor's, master's or doctor's degrees. Most attended public institutions rather than one of the "Norwegian" colleges.

RELIGION

The Norwegian Lutheran church was a focal point and conservative force in rural settlements in the upper Midwest. The congregation became an all-encompassing institution for its members, creating a tight social network that touched all aspects of immigrant life. The force of tradition in religious practice made the church a central institution in the urban environment as well. The severe reality of urban life increased the social role of the church.

In the unbridled freedom of America, Norwegian Lutherans exhibited an extreme denominationalism and established a tradition of disharmony. The Church of Norway largely abandoned the immigrants and provided no guidance. As a consequence, no fewer than 14 Lutheran synods were founded by Norwegian immigrants between 1846 and 1900. In 1917 most of the warring Lutheran factions reconciled doctrinal differences and organized the Norwegian Lutheran Church in America. It was one of the church bodies that in 1960 formed the American Lutheran Church, which in 1988 became a constituent part of the newly created Evangelical Lutheran Church in America.

Even though the terms Norwegian and Lutheran might seem synonymous to many, there were in fact substantial numbers of Methodists among Norwegian immigrants. They were concentrated especially in Chicago; a Norwegian Methodist theological seminary was established in Evanston. Some Norwegians converted to the Baptist faith. There were also groups of Quakers, relating back to "the Sloopers," and Mormons who joined the trek to the "New Jerusalem" in Salt Lake City, Utah.

EMPLOYMENT AND ECONOMIC TRADITIONS

Norwegians succeeded in commercial agriculture in pioneer times—following frontier practice—as wheat farmers but soon diversified into other products as dictated by topography, soil, climate, and market. In Wisconsin such considerations drew some Norwegians to tobacco farming. In Iowa they grew corn or raised cattle and hogs; in parts of Minnesota dairy farming was prominent. In the northwestern part of the state Norwegian farmers engaged heavily in spring wheat cultivation. The hard spring wheat region extended into South and North Dakota where Norwegians adapted to the demands of grassland wheat production on the semiarid northern plains.

In the urban economy, Norwegian men, along with other Scandinavians, found a special niche in construction and the building trades. It was a natural transfer of skills from home, as was their work as lumberjacks in the forests of northern Wisconsin and Minnesota. Norwegian men in Minneapolis earned a livelihood in the large flour mills. In the Pacific Northwest logging and employment in sawmills engaged many. Another significant transplanted skill was shipping. On the Great Lakes, Norwegian sailors and boat owners dominated as long as sailing vessels remained an important means of transportation. In 1870 approximately 65 percent of all sailors on Lake Michigan were Norwegian. Shipping was big on the eastern seaboard and the west coast as well. The coastal areas provided rich opportunity for fishing too. Norwegians on the west coast and Alaska began to develop the halibut industry at the turn of the twentieth century. By 1920 about 95 percent of all halibut fishermen and an even higher percentage of the owners of halibut schooners were of Norwegian birth or descent.

Traditional early employment for Norwegian women involved domestic and personal service. Accessibility to higher education gradually opened up new possibilities—especially for the American-born generations—in commerce, education, and in specialized professions. Looking at the occupational picture in 1950, there is a striking social advance both for women and men. Still Norwegians of both the first and second generation revealed a preference for farming, and men born in Norway were overrepresented in construction work.

The evidence provided in the 1990 census indicates little occupational concentration among Norwegian Americans. Of employed persons 16 years old and over, only 4.5 percent were occupied in farming, forestry, and fishery, and six percent in construction, while 15 percent were employed in manufacturing, and nearly 31 percent in a variety of managerial and specialty occupations. That year 4.4 percent of the civilian labor force was unemployed.

POLITICS AND GOVERNMENT

Norwegians in America have participated in the formation of several aspects of the political culture and are to be found in conservative and liberal camps of both prominent political parties.

Norwegians had a certain passion for the political arena. Familiarity with democratic reform and local self-government in Norway, a dislike of officialdom, and a heightened assertion encouraged them to participate in local government in America. From the community, they made their way to state and even national politics. During the early decades of this century Norwegians in Minnesota and North Dakota were, for instance overrepresented in the state administrations as well as in the legislatures and Congress.

Political affiliation, as expressed in a flourishing Norwegian immigrant press, was strongly influenced by the Free-Soil party. In the late 1850s, this same press abandoned the Democrats for Abraham Lincoln's Republican party, supporting its antislavery stance and for free distribution of frontier land to serious settlers. The Homestead Act of 1862 and the heroic participation of Norwegian Americans in the Civil War assured a strong loyalty to the Republican party and its ideals.

Toward the end of the nineteenth century, however, other issues came to the fore and weakened Republican loyalties. In regions suffering from agricultural depression and exploitation by outside financial interests, independent political thought brought Norwegians into the agricultural protest embodied in the Populist movement. This was especially the case in the wheat-growing regions of North Dakota and western Minnesota.

From around the turn of the century the Progressive movement gained a broad Norwegian following and Norwegians exhibited great faith in the benefits of legislative reform. The Nonpartisan League, organized in North Dakota in 1915, was further evidence of agrarian unrest. Norwegian farmers played a prominent role in its activities and advocacy, which included such socialist goals as public control and operation of grain silos, and the sale of wheat. This radical policy was, however, less a consequence of ethnic predispositions toward social reform than of economic self-interest and the problematic local conditions faced by wheat farmers.

Norwegians were also attracted to the Socialist party, joining local socialist clubs, which again became members of the Scandinavian Socialist Union formed in Chicago in 1910. But they did not do so in great numbers. Due to the high concentration of Norwegians in skilled occupations, especially in the building trades, they did, however, join labor unions in large numbers. The efforts of a Norwegian immigrant, Andrew Furuseth, to improve the working conditions for sailors, resulting in the Seamen's Act of 1915, is one example of the significant contributions made by immigrants to the American union movement.

In the 1920s Norwegians joined a national trend toward the Democratic party. The loyalty to the Republican party was significantly frayed as working class and reform-minded Norwegians took part in third-party movements, increasingly for Democrats, who seemed more committed to labor concerns and social justice than the Republicans. Republicanism remained common among middle- and upper-class Norwegian Americans, however.

Norwegian members of both parties were concerned with prohibition. Under the banner of temperance and local prohibition of the sale of intoxicating beverages, Norwegian politicians gained the support of their compatriots and were elected to public office. North Dakota, influenced by the agitation of the Norwegian American press, adopted a prohibition clause in its state constitution in 1889. National prohibition legislation, passed in 1919 as the Volstead Act, was named for Norwegian American Andrew J. Volstead, Republican congressman from Minnesota. Opposition to prohibition and the corruption and crime it yielded, paradoxically, strengthened the move toward the Democratic party, most especially among urban Norwegians.

MILITARY

Most Norwegians have viewed military service as an affirmation of American patriotism. The first fallen hero was a private in the war with Mexico who had Americanized his name to George Pilson. He had immigrated to Chicago and fell in 1847 in the bloody battle of Buena Vista, with Chicago newspapers claiming that "more patriotic blood does not enrich the field at Buena Vista than that of the Chicago Norwegian volunteer." Norwegian acts of heroism, valor, and sacrifice constituted a watershed experience during the Civil War; Norwegian men have served in great numbers, suffered substantial casualties, and have established themselves in America. Norwegians supported the Spanish-American War and rallied around the American war objectives during World War I. In a patriotic spirit, Norwegian American societies and organizations published lists of "our boys" in the armed forces and memorialized the fallen of their nationality. Occupation of Norway by the Germans during World War II was a calamity that filled Norwegians in America with indignation and sorrow. During the summer of 1942 the U.S. Army established a Norwegian-speaking combat unit, the 99th Infantry Battalion, in case there should be an invasion of Norway. It consisted of immigrants and Norwegians born in America.

RELATIONS WITH NORWAY

Norwegian Americans cultivated bonds with Norway, sending gifts home often and offering aid during natural disasters and other hardships in Norway. Relief in the form of collected funds was forthcoming without delay. Only during conflicts within the Swedish-Norwegian union, however, did Norwegian Americans become involved directly in the political life of Norway. In the 1880s they formed societies to assist Norwegian liberals, collecting money to assist rifle clubs in Norway should the political conflict between liberals and conservatives call for arms. The ongoing tensions between Sweden and Norway and Norway's humiliating retreat in 1895 fueled nationalism and created anguish. Norwegians in America raised money to strengthen Norway's military defenses. The unilateral declaration by Norway on June 7, 1905, to dissolve its union with Sweden yielded a new holiday of patriotic celebration.

INDIVIDUAL AND GROUP CONTRIBUTIONS

As in any large population, certain members of the Norwegian American community have excelled in many disciplines. A sampling of group and individual achievements follows.

ACADEMIA

Thorstein Veblen (1857-1929), a second-generation Norwegian, was a superb social critic. His best known work is *The Theory of the Leisure Class* (1899), a savage attack on the wastefulness of American society. Einar Haugen (1906-) is a prominent linguist and professor emeritus at Harvard University. Marcus Lee Hansen (1892-1938), of Danish and Norwegian descent, was a pioneer immigration historian. Theodore C. Blegen (1891-1969) was also a prominent historian of Norwegians in America, and his book *Norwegian Migration: The American Transition* was published in 1940. Agnes Mathilde Wergeland (1857-1914) was a professor of history at the state university in Laramie, Wyoming, and the first Norwegian woman to earn a doctoral degree.

ARTS

Olive Fremstad (1868-1951) was an internationally renowned Wagnerian opera singer. Ole Bull (1810-1880) was a well-known concert violinist. F. Melius Christiansen (1871-1955) perfected *a capella* singing as director of the St. Olaf College choir. He has been called the "Music Master of the Middle

West." Ole E. Rølvaag (1876-1931), the best-known Norwegian American author, wrote such books as *Giants In the Earth* (1927). Hjalmar Hjorth Boyesen (1848-1895), a realistic novelist, literary critic, and social Darwinist, taught at Cornell and Columbia universities. Kathryn Forbes (1909-1966) authored the best-selling *Mama's Bank Account* (1943), a portrait of a Norwegian family in San Francisco. As *I Remember Mama*, Forbes's work became a hit Broadway play, a motion picture, and a television series. Celeste Holm (1919-), versatile actress of stage and screen, appeared on Broadway and in numerous motion pictures. In 1950 she was an Academy Award nominee for Best Supporting Actress for her role in *All About Eve*.

INDUSTRY AND BUSINESS

Nelson Olson Nelson (1844-1922) founded the N. O. Nelson Manufacturing Company, which became one of the world's largest building and plumbing supply companies. Ole Evinrude (1877-1934), a self-taught mechanical engineer, developed the idea of the outboard motor. He formed the Evinrude Company in 1909. Arthur Andersen (1885-1947) was the founder of the world-famous accounting firm that bears his name. Conrad Hilton (1887-1979), Norwegian on his father's side, established one of the world's largest hotel chains and at the time of his death, owned 260 first-class hotels worldwide.

JOURNALISM

Victor F. Lawson (1850-1925) was editor and publisher of the Chicago *Daily News*, a philanthropist and a community leader. William T. Evjue (1882-1970) gained great influence as the editor of the progressive and reform-minded Madison *Capital Times*. Eric Sevareid (1912-1992), had a distinguished career in journalism and as a radio and television reporter and commentator.

MEDICINE

Ludvig Hektoen (1863-1951) made great progress in cancer research. The Hektoen Institute of Medical Research continues his work. Ingeborg Rasmussen (1854-1938) graduated from the Women's Medical College in Evanston in 1892 and became a prominent physician, feminist, and cultural leader among the Norwegians in Chicago. Helga Ruud (1860-1956) graduated from the Women's Medical College in 1889 and enjoyed a distinguished medical career at the Norwegian American Hospital in Chicago. Ulrikka Feldtman Bruun (1854-1940) was an influential temperance worker among Danes and Norwegians for the Woman's Christian Temperance Union (WCTU).

POLITICS AND GOVERNMENT

Knute Nelson (1843-1923) served as a Republican U.S. senator from Minnesota from 1895 to 1923. Andrew Furuseth (1954-1938) organized American commercial sailors. He was considered their liberator and was referred to as "the Abraham Lincoln of the Sea." Earl Warren (1891-1974) served as Chief Justice of the U.S. Supreme Court from 1953 to 1969. Henry Jackson (1912-1983), Democratic U.S. senator from Washington, served from 1953 to 1983. Hubert Humphrey (1911-1978) served for two terms as U.S. vice president under President Lyndon Johnson and was the Democratic presidential nominee in 1968, losing to Richard Nixon in the national election. Walter Mondale (1928-), served as a U.S. senator from Minnesota (1964-1977); U.S. vice president under President Jimmy Carter (1977-1881); and was the Democratic presidential nominee in 1984. Since 1993, Mondale has been U.S. Ambassador to Japan under the Clinton administration. Warren Christopher (1925-), whose great-grandparents emigrated from Norway in 1853, was named secretary of state in 1993.

SCIENCE

Ernest O. Lawrence (1901-1958), a professor of physics at Yale University, received the Nobel Prize in physics in 1939. Ivar Giaever (1929-), Norwegian-trained engineer and physicist, received the Nobel Prize in physics in 1973. Lars Onsager (1903-1976), received the Nobel Prize in chemistry in 1968. Norman E. Borlaug (1914-), an agricultural scientist, received the 1970 Nobel Peace Prize for his leadership in the "Green Revolution," which helped to dispel the fear of famine in underdeveloped countries. Ole Singstad (1882-1969) was chief engineer for the construction of the Holland Tunnel under the Hudson River.

SPORTS

Norwegian immigrants brought skiing to America in the mid-1800s by introducing cross-country racing and ski jumping, and organizing local clubs, including the National Ski Association. They dominated the sport into the 1930s. Beginning in 1856, John A. "Snowshoe" Thompson (1827-1876) delivered mail on skis across the Sierra Nevada mountains for nearly 20 years during the winter months, ensuring postal connection between Utah Territory and California. Sonja Henie (1912-1969) was an Olympic and World figure skating champion, movie star, and pioneer of ice shows. Torger Tokle (1920-1945), arrived in America in 1939 and was unrivaled by any U.S. ski jumper. Tokle won 42 of 48 competitions and, in so doing, set no fewer than 24 new hill records. He was killed in military action in the mountains of northern Italy while serving in the 86th Mountain Regiment—"The Ski Troops." Knute Rockne (1888-1931), head football coach at the University of Notre Dame from 1918 to 1931, revolutionized American collegiate football; his record consist of 105 wins, 12 losses, and five ties. Mildred "Babe" Didrikson Zaharias (1913-1956), a daughter of Norwegian immigrants, was a champion in basketball, track, and golf. Tommy Moe (1970-) won a gold medal for skiing in the 1994 Olympic Games.

MEDIA

PRINT

News of Norway.
Contact: Marianne Kirkebo, Editor.
Address: Royal Norwegian Embassy, 2720 34th Street, N.W., Washington, D.C. 20008-2714.
Telephone: (202) 333-6000.
Fax: (202) 337-0870.
E-mail: newsnor@interramp.com.
Online: http://www.norway.org.

Norway Times/Nordisk Tidende.
Contact: Tom Røren, Editor.
Address: 123 West 44th Street, Brooklyn, New York 11209.
Telephone: (718) 238-1100.

Western Viking.
Contact: Alf Lunder Knudsen, Editor and Publisher.
Address: P.O. Box 70408, Seattle, Washington 98107.
Telephone: (206) 784-4617.
Fax: (206) 784-4856.

RADIO

KBLE-AM (1050).
"The Scandinavian Hour" every Saturday morning.
Contact: Ron Olsen.

Address: 1114 Lakeside Avenue, Seattle, Washington. 98122.
Telephone: (206) 324-2000.
Fax: (206) 322-4670.
E-mail: operations@kble.com.

WTHE-AM (1520).
"Scandinavian Echoes" every Saturday afternoon.
Contact: Jeanne Widman.
Address: 260 East 2nd Street, Mineola, New York 11501.
Telephone: (516) 742-1520.
Fax: (516) 742-2878.

ORGANIZATIONS AND ASSOCIATIONS

American-Scandinavian Foundation (ASF).
Promotes international understanding by means of educational and cultural exchange with Denmark, Finland, Iceland, Norway, and Sweden. It has an extensive program of fellowships and grants, and publishes the *Scandinavian Review*.
Contact: Lena Bărck Kaplan, President of the Board of Trustees.
Address: 725 Park Avenue, New York, New York 10021.
Telephone: (212) 879-9779.

The Norsemen's Federation (Nordmanns-Forbundet).
An international organization founded in Norway in 1907 to strengthen the ties between men and women of Norwegian heritage in and outside Norway. It functions as a cultural and social organization and has chapters throughout the United States.
Contact: Johan Fr. Heyerdahl, Secretary General.
Address: Rădhusgt. 23 B, 0158 Oslo, Norway.

Norwegian American Historical Association (NAHA).
Founded in 1925, is the main research center for Norwegian American history. It possesses large documentary archives and extensive library holdings. The Association publishes one to two volumes annually; so far more than 80 volumes of high scholarly merit on the Norwegian American experience have been released under its imprint.
Contact: Lloyd Hustvedt, Executive Secretary.
Address: St. Olaf College, 1510 St. Olaf Avenue, Northfield, Minnesota 55057-1097.

Telephone: (507) 646-3221.
Fax: (507) 646-3734.
E-mail: naha@stolaf.edu.

Sons of Norway.

An international order founded as a fraternal society in Minneapolis in 1895 with lodges throughout the United States as well as in Canada and in Norway. It provides insurance benefits for its members and publishes a monthly magazine, *The Viking*.

Contact: Lee A. Rowe, CEO.
Address: 1455 West Lake Street, Minneapolis, Minnesota 55408.
Telephone: (612) 827-3611; or (800) 945-8851.
Fax: (612) 827-0658.
E-mail: fraternal@sofn.com.
Online: http://www.sofn.com.

MUSEUMS AND RESEARCH CENTERS

Little Norway.

Provides guided tours through a Norwegian pioneer homestead settled in 1856, featuring the Norway building patterned after a twelfth century stave church. It was built in Trondheim, Norway, to be exhibited at the Chicago World's Columbian Exposition in 1893.

Contact: Scott Winner, Director.
Address: 3576 Highway JG North, Blue Mounds, Wisconsin 53517.
Telephone: (608) 437-8211.
Fax: (608) 437-7827.
E-mail: info@littlenorway.com.
Online: http://www.littlenorway.com.

Nordic Heritage Museum.

Opened in 1980 in Seattle, Washington. Its purpose is to collect, preserve, and present the Scandinavian heritage in the Pacific Northwest. It has an extensive collection of objects from Scandinavia and the Pacific Northwest.

Contact: Marianne Forssblad, Director.
Address: 3014 Northwest 67th Street, Seattle, Washington 98117.
Telephone: (206) 789-5707.

Norskedalen Heritage and Nature Center.

Features objects specific to Norwegian immigrants who settled in Vernon and LaCrosse counties, Wisconsin, before 1900, and two separate pioneer homesteads. It arranges an annual Midsummer Festival in late June.

Contact: James Nestingen, Director.
Address: P.O. Box 225, Coon Valley, Wisconsin 54623.
Telephone: (608) 452-3424.

Vesterheim, the Norwegian American Museum.

A major ethnic museum, it maintains high professional standards and supports an outdoor museum as well as a large collection of objects dealing with the Norwegian homeland and life in America. It also features a museum store with Norwegian American crafts and books. It conducts workshops in Norwegian folk crafts.

Contact: Darrell D. Henning, Director.
Address: 523 West Water Street, P.O. Box 379, Decorah, Iowa 52101.
Telephone: (319) 382-9681.
Fax: (319) 382-8828.
E-mail: vesterheim@vesterheim.org.
Online: http://www.vesterheim.org/.

SOURCES FOR ADDITIONAL STUDY

Anderson, Wilford Raymond. *Norse America, Tenth Century Onward*. Evanston, IL: Valhalla Press, 1996.

Gjerde, Jon. *From Peasants to Farmers: The Migration from Balestrand, Norway, to the Upper Middle West*. New York: Cambridge University Press, 1985.

Haugen, Einar. *The Norwegian Language in America: A Study in Bilingual Behavior*, two volumes. Bloomington: Indiana University Press, 1969.

Lovoll, Odd S. *A Century of Urban Life: The Norwegians in Chicago before 1930*. Northfield, Minnesota: NAHA, 1988.

———. *The Promise Fulfilled: A Portrait of Norwegian Americans Today*. Minneapolis: University of Minnesota Press, 1998.

———. *The Promise of America: A History of the Norwegian American People*. Revised edition. Minneapolis: University of Minnesota Press, 1999.

Schultz, April R. *Ethnicity on Parade : Inventing the Norwegian American Through Celebration*. Amherst: University of Massachusetts Press, 1994.

OJIBWA

by
Lorene Roy

In traditional Ojibwa culture, an individual lived in a band and was a member of a clan. Most people from the same clan shared a common ancestor on their father's side of the family. Some clans were matrilineal, and children were affiliated with their mother's clan. People of the same clan claim a common totem, the symbol of a living creature.

OVERVIEW

The Ojibwa ("oh-jib-wah") are a woodland people of northeastern North America. In the mid-seventeenth century there were approximately 35,000 Ojibwa on the continent. According to the 1990 census, the Ojibwa were the third-largest Native group (with a population of 104,000), after the Cherokee (308,000) and the Navajo (219,000). Federally recognized Ojibwa reservations are found in Minnesota (Fond du Lac, Grand Portage, Leech Lake, Mille Lacs, Nett Lake [Bois Forte Band], Red Lake, and White Earth), Michigan (Bay Mills Indian Community, Grande Traverse, Keweenaw Bay Indian Community, Saginaw, and Sault Sainte Marie), Wisconsin (Bad River, Lac Courte Oreilles, Lac du Flambeau, Mole Lake or Sokaogan Chippewa Community, Red Cliff, and St. Croix), Montana (Rocky Boy's), and North Dakota (Turtle Mountain). Others have petitioned for federal recognition. While Ojibwa reserves are also found in Ontario and Saskatchewan, this account stresses their history in the United States.

HISTORY

The Ojibwa call themselves the Anishinabeg (also spelled Anishinaabeg, or if singular, Anishinabe) for "first" or "original people." In the eighteenth century the French called Ojibwa living near the eastern shore of Lake Superior Salteaux or Salteurs, "People of the Falls." These terms now used only in Canada. The Anishinabe acquired the names Ojibwa and Chippewa from French traders. The English preferred to use Chippewa or Chippeway, names typically employed on the treaties with the British government and later with the U.S. government. In 1951, Inez Hilger noted that more than 70 different names were used for Ojibwa in written accounts (M. Inez Hilger, *Chippewa Child Life and Its Cultural Background* [originally published, 1951; reprinted, St Paul: Minnesota Historical Society Press, 1992], p. 2).

There are several explanations for the derivation of the word "Ojibwa." Some say it is related to the word "puckered" and that it refers to a distinctive type of moccasin that high cuffs and a puckered seam. Others say that the French used the word *o-jib-i-weg* or "pictograph" because the Anishinabe employed a written language based on pictures or symbols. There is no standard spelling in English, and variations include: Ojibwa, Ojibway, Chippewa and Chippeway. Chippewa is the form used by many tribal organizations recognized by the United States. Ojibwa has become the common English language reference for encyclopedias and entries on this group of peoples. As previously noted, the people call themselves Anishinabe. This name, as with other names chosen by the peoples in question, is the preferred term.

MIGRATION TO THE GREAT LAKES

Early legends indicate that, 500 years ago, the Ojibwa lived near the mouth of the Saint Lawrence River. About 1660 they migrated westward, guided by a vision of a floating seashell referred to as the sacred *miigis*. At the Straits of Mackinac, the channel of water connecting Lake Huron and Lake Michigan, the vision ended, and the Anishinabe divided into three groups. One group, the Potawatomi, moved south and settled in the area between Lake Michigan and Lake Huron. A second group, the Ottawa, moved north of Lake Huron. A third group, the Ojibwa, settled along the eastern shore of Lake Superior. Because of this early association, the Potawatomi, the Ottawa, and the Ojibwa are known collectively as the Three Fires.

FIRST CONTACT WITH EUROPEANS

The Ojibwa met non-Native Americans in the 1600s, possibly hearing about Europeans through the Huron people. The first written European accounts about the Ojibwa appeared in Jesuit diaries, published in collected form as the *Jesuit Relations and Allied Documents*. The Jesuits were followed by French explorers and fur traders, who were succeeded by British fur traders, explorers, and soldiers and later by U.S. government officials and citizens.

Fur trading, especially the exchange of beaver pelts for goods including firearms, flourished until the 1800s. The Ojibwa traded with representatives of fur companies or indirectly through salaried or independent traders called *coureurs des bois*. In addition to furs, the land around the Great Lakes was rich in copper and iron ore, lumber, and waterpower, all natural resources that were coveted by non-Native Americans. Competition in trading led to intertribal conflict. By the 1700s the Ojibwa, aided with guns, had succeeded in pushing the Fox south into Wisconsin. Ojibwa and Sioux fighting extended over a 100-year period until separate reservations were established.

By the mid-nineteenth century the Ojibwa had enlarged their geographic boundaries and had splintered into four main groups. The Southeastern Ojibwa lived southeast and north of Lake Huron, in present-day Michigan and southern Ontario. The Southwestern Ojibwa lived along the south and north shores of Lake Superior. The Northern Ojibwa lived in northern Ontario. The Plains Ojibwa or Bungi lived in the present-day states and provinces of Montana, North Dakota, Manitoba, and Saskatchewan. The Plains Ojibwa adopted a lifestyle that resembled that of other Plains tribes, living in tepees, riding horses, and relying on buffalo for food and clothing.

RELATIONS WITH NON-NATIVE AMERICANS

The history of the contact between non-Native Americans and the Ojibwa dates back more than 350 years. While the Ojibwa did not engage in extended armed conflict with Europeans, the relationship was not always amicable. To the missionaries the Ojibwa were heathens to be converted to Christianity. To the fur traders they were commodities who could be purchased and indentured to company stores through watered-down alcohol and cheaply made goods. To the settlers they were wastrels who did not force the land to release its bounty. To ethnologists the Ojibwa were objects of study. To the government they were impressionable and recalcitrant wards. While there are many people who now value the Ojibwa culture, there are still others who regard the Ojibwa with disinterest or disdain, indicating that long-held stereotypes persist.

KEY ISSUES

Key issues facing the Ojibwa include economic development to reduce unemployment, the defense of the wild rice industry from commercial growers, improved medical treatment to combat illnesses such as diabetes and alcoholism, better management of natural resources, protection of treaty rights and attainment of sovereignty, and increased emphasis on higher education to train specialists and renew cultural ties.

ACCULTURATION AND ASSIMILATION

MISCONCEPTIONS AND STEREOTYPES

The Ojibwa face the same misconceptions and stereotypes applied to other Native peoples. Because they refuse to strip the land of all its bounty, they have been considered lazy and unintelligent. Sports mascots and consumer product labels targeted at the general American public perpetuate Native American stereotypes. Ojibwa have also seen their sacred religious beliefs, such as vision quests, misinterpreted and sold by seekers of New Age thought. Misconceptions about sovereignty are common. Almost all early treaties promised the Ojibwa that they could continue to hunt and fish in ceded land. Yet when the Ojibwa attempt to enforce their treaty rights, conflicts arise with non-Native outdoors enthusiasts and tourists. From 1989 to 1991 anti-treaty organizations such as Stop Treaty Abuse staged protests against spearfishing that led to racial slurs, verbal threats, stoning, and gunfire aimed at Ojibwa. Two widely publicized antitreaty group slogans were, "Save a Deer, Shoot an Indian," and "Save a Fish, Spear a Squaw." The relationship between the Ojibwa and the federal government is often perceived not as a legal entitlement but as a special privilege; many non-Native Americans have been falsely persuaded that the Ojibwa receive extraordinary benefits.

TRADITIONAL CULTURE

Cultural values such as generosity, honesty, strength of character, endurance, and wisdom were instilled through education, religious practice, and by example within the tribe. The Ojibwa counted time by 24-hour intervals (nights), months (moons), and years (winters). Each month had a name, denoting some natural feature or event. For example, the month of September, when tribes harvested wild rice along the lake shores, was called *manoominike-giizis*, or "ricing moon." October was "falling leaves moon." Time was sometimes reckoned by making notches on sticks.

Precontact culture was heavily influenced by the natural terrain as the Ojibwa adapted their lifestyle to survive in a heavily forested land traversed by a network of lakes and rivers. The Ojibwa lived a seminomadic life, moving a number of times each year in order to be close to food sources. Except for the Plains Ojibwa, who rode horses, they traveled on land by foot and wore snowshoes during the winter, transporting goods on dog sleds. The portability of Ojibwa lodging—the wigwam—enabled such moves to be made quickly and easily. Wigwams could be built in a day by bending peeled green ironwood saplings into arches; lashing the arches into a circular or oval shape with basswood fiber; and weaving birch bark strips or rush, cedar bark, or cattail mats around the saplings. The dwelling had two openings, a door and a hole on top to emit smoke from the cooking fire located directly below. When they moved to another camp, the Ojibwa left the frame, taking the lightweight birch bark strips and rush mats. During warm months the Ojibwa slept on cedar bough mattresses, each person wrapped in a bearskin or deerskin robe.

Ojibwa lived in hunting camps in late fall and winter. In winter, men trapped and hunted. Families could become isolated during the winter months, and women occupied their time by tanning hides and sewing, while families engaged in storytelling. Many tales centered on Nanabush, a half-human, half-spirit trickster, who was often entangled in humorous scrapes and brought innovations, such as medicine, to humankind from the spirits (Nanabush went by many other names: Naanabozho, Nanibush, Nenabozho, Manabozho, Minabozho, Waynaboozhoo, Wenabozho, Wenabozhoo, Wenebojo, Winabojo, or Winneboshoo). Gambling was another popular pastime. In the moccasin game, players on different teams guessed the location of a marked bullet or metal ball hidden under a moccasin. Gambling was a social event often accompanied by drumming and singing.

Before the Ojibwa began to trade with Europeans and Americans, they wore clothing made from animal hides, primarily from tanned deerskin. The women wore deerskin dresses, leggings, moccasins, and petticoats made of woven nettle or thistle fibers. The men wore leggings, breechcloths, and moccasins. Girls and women decorated the clothing in geometric designs with bones, feathers, dyed porcupine quills, shells, and stones, using bone or thorn needles and thread made from nettles or animal sinew. Jewelry was made from animal bones, claws, or teeth strung into necklaces. After European contact, the Ojibwa began to wear woven clothing. Europeans introduced the Ojibwa to glass beads inspired by the designs in calico cloth. Both men and women wove and mended fish nets.

Birch bark was a versatile natural product from which the Ojibwa created many items, including canoes, toboggans, and storage containers. The Ojibwa built canoe frames from wood and covered the frame with sewn birch bark strips, sealing the seams with pine or spruce gum. Each canoe weighed from 65 to 125 pounds and was typically 16 feet long, 18 inches deep, and three feet wide across the midpoint. Toboggans also had curved wooden frames covered with birch bark. The Ojibwa decorated birch bark baskets with porcupine quills, sweet grass, birch bark cutouts, or bitten designs that were created by folding thin pieces of birch bark in half and biting them. The dents made dark impressions on the light background. Birch bark torches were fashioned by rolling the bark into tubes and covering the tube with pitch. The Ojibwa also carved wooden objects such as arrows, bowls, boxes, drums, paddles, rattles, spoons, shuttles for weaving fish nets, and war clubs.

TRANSFORMATION OF CULTURE

Traditional life was altered through contact with non-Native Americans. Fur trading resulted in the Ojibwa becoming reliant on traded goods rather than the clothing, utensils, and weapons they had constructed. The establishment of reservations restricted Ojibwa seasonal travel, the formalized educational system removed children from their families, and the government's relocation policies dispersed tribe members. By the late 1880s many Ojibwa lived in one-room log cabins, frame cabins, or tar paper shacks rather than in wigwams. Wigwam construction incorporated new materials: other forms of tree bark were more easily available than long strips of birch bark; blankets covered wigwam doors instead of animal skins; calico, cardboard, and tar paper replaced the rush matting. The rate of acculturation varied by reservation. By the mid-1940s, only the elderly were bilingual, and most Ojibwa had adopted modern clothing. Birch bark canoes were largely replaced by wooden and later aluminum boats. Few Ojibwa practiced their traditional religion.

Ojibwa culture is currently experiencing a renaissance as natives and non-natives are studying Ojibwa botany, crafts, myths, and religion. Wild ricing by canoe is still a valued, even sacred, part of the culture, despite the fact that the once bountiful harvest has been reduced and the Ojibwa must now compete with commercial growers. Making maple sugar is still popular as well, although the sap may be collected in plastic bags rather than in birch bark baskets. Communal festivities such as the "Honor the Earth" powwows held every July at Lac Courte Oreilles have become a focal point of modern day Ojibwa culture and hundreds of dancers of all ages participate.

Many Ojibwa are concerned about the degradation of the environment by industry and mismanagement. Wild rice harvesting has suffered from changing water levels, housing construction, water pollution, boat traffic, and the incursions of alien species of plants and animals. Logging enterprises have destroyed traditional maple sugar camps, and fish caught in freshwater lakes are contaminated with mercury. It is still common for Ojibwa to hunt, trap, and fish. The *Mide* religion has been revived as well, and traditional importance is still afforded to visions and dreams. Ojibwa gatherings often begin with a prayer and a ritual offering of tobacco as an expression of gratitude and respect to the Heavenly Spirit. Powwows, the modern equivalent of multiband gatherings, are now elaborately staged competitions were costumed dancers perform to the accompaniment of vocalists who sing in Ojibwa while beating on bass drums with padded drumsticks. Clan and band affiliation still exists, and many Ojibwa seek to reclaim lands once tribally owned. If they are non-reservation dwellers, they often maintain ties to reservations, especially if they are enrolled or official members. Tribal newsletters are a means for members to stay abreast of local news, issues, and politics.

CUISINE

Native cuisine was closely influenced by the seasons, as the Ojibwa changed camps in seminomadic pattern to locate themselves closer to food sources. For example, because the Ojibwa used maple sugar or maple syrup as a seasoning, during the late spring they lived near maple sugar trees. Each family or group of families returned to a traditional location where they had stored utensils and had marked with an ax cut the trees they would tap. A typical sugar camp or sugar bush encompassed an area of some 900 taps or cuttings, with up to three taps made per tree. The Ojibwa collected maple sap in birch bark containers and poured it into vats made of moose hide, wood, or bark, and later into brass kettles, where it was boiled until it became syrup. The syrup was strained, reheated, thickened, and stirred in shallow troughs until it formed granulated sugar. Birch bark cones were packed with sugar, tied together, and hung from the ceiling of the wigwam or storage building. The Ojibwa also poured the sap into wooden molds or directly into snow to form maple sugar candy. Camps were moved in the summer to be close to gardens and wild berry patches. The Ojibwa cultivated gardens of corn, pumpkins, and squash. Dried berries, vegetables, and seeds were stored in underground pits. They drank teas boiled from plants and herbs and sweetened with maple sugar. The Ojibwa fished throughout the year, using hooks, nets, spears, and traps. Fish and meat were dried and smoked so they could be stored.

In late summer the Ojibwa moved again to be near wild rice fields. Wild rice (in Ojibwa, *mahnomin*, *manomin*, or *manoomin*) is a grain that grows on long grasses in shallow lakes or along streams. As the edible rice seeds began to mature, families marked the area they would harvest by tying the rice stalks together, using knots or dyed rope that would distinguish their claim. The rice harvest was a time of community celebration, starting with the announcement by an annually appointed rice chief or elder that the fields were ready. One team member stood in the canoe pushing a long forked pole to guide the canoe through the grasses. The other team member sat in the canoe, reaching to bend the grass over the canoe and hitting the grass with wooden stocks called beaters in order to shake the wild rice seeds from the grass without permanently injuring the plant. On shore, the rice was dried in the sun, and then parched in a kettle to loosen the hull. A person in clean moccasins then "danced the rice" treading on it to remove the hull and then tossing it into the air to winnow the chaff. A medicine man blessed the first rice harvested, and each ricing pair donated rice to a communal fund to feed the poor. Rice was often boiled and sweetened with maple sugar or flavored with venison or duck broth. Up to one-third of the annual harvest was stored, usually in birch bark baskets. The rice season lasted from ten days to three weeks. Ricers often poled through their sections every few days as the rice seeds matured at differing rates. They were also deliberately inefficient, leaving plenty of rice to seed the beds for the following year.

HEALTH ISSUES

During their first contact with non-Native peoples, the Ojibwa were exposed to a number of diseases and suffered through epidemics of smallpox and other illnesses. The transition from traditional living to permanent settlement in villages led to a reduced lifestyle and to a high incidence of communicable diseases including tuberculosis and trachoma. When the Ojibwa ceded land they often did so in exchange for health care, indicating an early concern for health issues. These rights are still in effect, and Ojibwa living on or maintaining social ties with reservations may have access to federally funded programs including Indian Health Service clinics or hospitals. The Ojibwa, along with other

This woman is dressed in the manner of early Ojibwa mothers.

Native American groups, share concerns over poor health. There are high incidences of chemical dependency, diabetes, fetal alcohol syndrome, obesity, suicide, and accidental death.

Today the Ojibwa use a blend of traditional and modern treatment methods to improve health. Alcohol consumption and chemical dependency is discouraged. Alcohol and drugs are banned from powwow sites, and some powwows are organized to celebrate sobriety. Mash-Ka-Wisen ("Be strong, accept help"), the oldest Native-owned and operated chemical treatment center, on the Fond du Lac Reservation, incorporates elements of Ojibwa culture into its services for its clients. The Minneapolis American Indian Center provides an array of social services, including programs on chemical dependency, developmental disabilities, and rehabilitation.

Traditional herbal cures include sumac fruit made into tea with crushed roots to stop bleeding, blackberry roots boiled and drunk to stop diarrhea or prevent miscarriage, wild onions cooked and sweetened with maple sugar to treat children's colds, yarrow roots mashed into creams for treating blemishes, strawberry roots boiled and eaten to treat stomach aches, and plantain leaves chopped and used as a poultice for bruises, rheumatism, and snake bites.

LANGUAGE

Spoken Ojibwa or Ojibwemowin is an Algonquin language with regional dialectical differences. It is related linguistically to the languages not only of the Ottawa and Potawatomi but also of the Fox, Cree, and Menominee. Since it was a spoken rather than a written language, the spelling of Ojibwa words varies. The Ojibwa language is spoken by between 40,000 to 50,000 people. While once spoken only by elders, there is currently a resurgence of interest in and promotion of the language. Many Ojibwa demonstrate this interest in native identity by preferring to be called Anishinabe. Instruction is available in some public as well as in tribally directed educational settings. Classes and workshops offered at community colleges and state universities are sometimes broadcast to more distant locations. Language texts as well as instructional material in workbooks, bilingual texts, audiotapes, and multimedia formats have also been developed. Tribal newspapers carry regular Ojibwa-language columns.

GREETINGS AND OTHER POPULAR EXPRESSIONS

Common Ojibwa expressions include: *Boozhoo* ("boo shoo")—Hello, greetings; *Miigwech* ("mee gwitch")—Thank you; *Aaniin ezhi-ayaayan?* ("a neen a shay i an")—How are you?; *Nimino-ayaa* ("nay mi no a yah")—I am fine; *Mino-ayaag!* ("minnow a yog")—All of you be well!

FAMILY AND COMMUNITY DYNAMICS

In traditional Ojibwa culture, an individual lived in a band and was a member of a clan. Most people from the same clan shared a common ancestor on their father's side of the family. Some clans were matrilineal, and children were affiliated with their mother's clan. People of the same clan claim a common totem (*dodem, do daim,* or *do dam*), the symbol of a living creature. The seven original clans were the bear, bird, catfish, crane, deer, loon, and marten. Twenty or more clans with additional totems were added later. A totem could denote an attribute such as prowess, leadership, knowledge, healing power, or sustenance. Bands consisted of groups of five to 50 families, up to 400 people, and lived within the same village. Examples are the five large bands of Minnesota: the Superior, Mississippi, Pillager, Red Lake, and Pembina. Bands were formed of people from a number of clans.

SOCIAL ACTIVITIES UNRELATED TO FOOD GATHERING

Traditionally, Ojibwa behavior was controlled by taboos that governed actions during pregnancy, birth, illness, death, and mourning. For example, bereaved relatives were not allowed to participate in food gathering until someone fed them the first wild rice or maple sugar of the season. Within families, Ojibwa humor was expressed through teasing.

Before contact with non-Native Americans, the Ojibwa held annual spring and autumn celebrations at a central location, with singing, dancing, eating, sports competitions, and storytelling. In the early 1700s the celebrations took place in Bowating, near present-day Sault Sainte Marie. In the late 1700s they were held near Lake Superior's Chequamegon Bay and, by the early 1800s, at Fort La Pointe on Madeline Island. These celebrations commemorated significant events in an individual's lifetime: the naming of a child, a boy's first hunt, a girl's first menstrual period, marriage, and death. Music played a central part in these events, as "singers" would perform to the accompaniment of drums, rattles, or, flutes. At the gatherings, men showed off their skill at traditional, fancy, and grass dances, while women joined in the traditional dances and added shawl and jingle dances. Modern costumes for these dancing competitions, which still continue, have incorporated many novel elements; for example, jingle dancers may sew hundreds of snuff can covers onto dresses in place of traditional seashells or bones.

MARRIAGE

Women were allowed to marry soon after puberty, at age 14 or 15. During a woman's first menstrual period she fasted in a small wigwam from five to ten days. During this time the manitou or spirits were considered a strong spiritual presence in her life. Boys were allowed to marry as soon as they could demonstrate that they could support a family through hunting. During courtship the couple's contact was supervised. If both young people were found acceptable to each other and to their families, the man moved in with the wife's family for a year. There was no formal wedding ceremony. If the marriage proved to be disharmonious or if the wife failed to conceive, then the man returned to his parents. A couple that wished to continue living together after the year would build their own separate dwelling. Marital separation was allowed, and after separation people could remarry. Men who could support more than one family might have more than one wife. Intermarriage was acceptable, and by 1900 most Ojibwa were of mixed heritage, typically French and Ojibwa.

This Ojibwa chromolithograph is called "Meda Songs."

CHILDREARING

Parents appointed an elder to give the baby its sacred, or dream, name. The parents would also give the child one or more nicknames. Ojibwa babies were wrapped in swaddling until they were one year old, then kept in cradle boards—rectangular wooden frames with a backrest or curved headboard to protect the baby's head, and a footrest. Dream catchers—willow hoops encircling woven animal-sinew designs that resembled spider webs—and toys of bone, birch bark, shells, or feathers hung from the headboard. Dried moss, cattail down, and rabbit skins served as diapers. Grandparents typically had living with them at least one grandchild, including at least one granddaughter. Childhood was divided into two periods: the time before the child walked, and the time from walking to puberty.

Until girls and boys were around seven years of age, they were tended to and taught by their mothers, aunts, and elders. After that age, boys were taught hunting and fishing skills by the men, while girls continued to learn domestic skills from the women and elders. Moral values were taught by example and through storytelling.

FUNERALS

If a person died inside a wigwam, the body was removed through a hole made in the west-facing side of the dwelling. The body was wrapped in birch bark and buried with items of special significance. During the next four days the individual's spirit or ghost was said to be walking westward to a place where the soul would dwell after death. Food and beverage were left at the grave site for the spirit's consumption during the walk. Grave sites were marked by erecting gabled wood houses over the length of the grave. Placed at the head of the grave was a wooden marker painted with a pictograph illustrating the individual's achievements and clan affiliation; the totem animal was painted upside down, denoting death. Families mourned for periods of up to one year, with some family members expressing grief by blackening their faces, chests, and hands with charcoal and maintaining an unkempt appearance. A Feast of the Dead service, scheduled each fall, was sponsored by families who had lost members over the previous year. Food continued to be left at the grave site at regular intervals over a period of many years.

EDUCATION

Federal policy toward Native education emphasized Native American assimilation into U.S. society. Consequently, instruction in vocational skills was promoted over the teaching of Native traditions. In fact, Native traditions and languages were forbidden in the educational context provided by the government and mission schools. From the 1870s until the 1940s, many Ojibwa children were sent to government day schools, mission schools, or boarding schools (grade schools located as far away as Kansas and Pennsylvania). School attendance for Ojibwa became compulsory in 1893.

A significant step toward Native American education occurred with the passage of the Johnson

O'Malley Act in 1934, authorizing states and territories to contract with the Bureau of Indian Affairs (BIA) for services including education. Public schools were encouraged to incorporate information on Native cultures into their curricula.

Today Ojibwa children living off reservations attend public or private schools. Private schools include those operated by Native American organizations, such as the Red School House in St. Paul and the Heart of the Earth Survival School in Minneapolis. Since 1989 public school curricula in Wisconsin are required by law to incorporate lessons on Native American cultures; by 1994 similar legislation was being considered in Minnesota. Ojibwa living on or near reservations may also be taught in tribally run schools or BIA contract schools. Some academic institutions offer degree programs specializing in Ojibwa culture. In addition, four of the 24 tribal colleges in the United States are located on Ojibwa reservations: Bay Mills Community College (Brimley, Michigan), Fond du Lac Community College (Cloquet, Minnesota), Lac Courte Oreilles Ojibwa Community College (Hayward, Wisconsin), and Turtle Mountain Community College (Belcourt, North Dakota). These institutions offer associate degrees and, in their roles as community centers, serve as focal points of Ojibwa culture.

According to the *Chronicle of Higher Education* (Volume 60, No. 1, August 25, 1993, pp. 13, 15), as of fall 1992, 114,000 (0.8 percent) of 14,359,000 college students in the United States were Native Americans. As with other Native peoples, fewer Ojibwa complete high school and postsecondary education than do other population groups. The composite of Ojibwa students in higher education often differs significantly from that of non-Native American students: they generally are older, drop out or stop out at higher rates, take longer to complete their degrees, and often are married with children. These students face many obstacles including culturally rooted learning differences and homesickness if they relocate. Students requesting financial aid from their tribe may be channeled into certain fields of study such as education, social work, or medicine.

RELIGION

While some aspects of religious observance were communal, traditional Ojibwa religious practice was focused on inward personal experience. There was a belief in spirits, called *manitou* or *manidoo*. The creator was referred to as Gitchie Manitou. Manjimanidoo or evil spirits existed; windigos were especially terrifying spirits who dwelled within lakes and practiced cannibalism. Animate and inanimate

objects possessed spiritual power, and the Ojibwa considered themselves one element of nature, no greater or less significant than any other living being. The cardinal directions were invested with sacred power and were associated with certain colors: white for the north, red or black for the south, yellow for the east, blue for the west. The Ojibwa recognized three additional directions: heaven, earth, and the position where an individual stands. Tobacco was considered sacred and was smoked in pipes or scattered on lakes to bless a crossing, a harvest, or a herd or to seal agreements between peoples of different tribes.

Dreams carried great significance and were sought through fasting or other purgative ceremonies. Dream catchers were used to capture good dreams. The name "dreamer" was reserved for tribal visionaries who would dream of certain powerful objects—such as stones—that they would then seek on waking. Dreamers might also experience prophetic dreams that they would convey to others to forestall danger. At an early age young boys and girls fasted in order to obtain a vision of how to conduct their future. Some visions provided complete messages and songs; others were incomplete and were revealed in their entirety only with the fullness of time. Visions could come during sleep. Since it was difficult to adhere to the advice imparted by visions, men and women went on annual fasts or retreats to renew the vision and reflect on their lives.

Sweat lodges were used to cure illness or to procure dreams. These were wigwams in which steam was created by pouring water over heated rocks and sealing the entrances. Bark and pine boughs might be added to the steam. Fasting was used to cure sickness and, like sweating, was thought to cleanse the body.

The Ojibwa developed a Grand Medicine Society or *Midewiwin* (*Mitewiwin*) religion. Abbreviated *Mide*, *Midewiwin* most likely means "good-hearted" or "resonant," in reference to the belief that the *Mide* priest worked for the betterment of others and employed special sacred drums. The *Mide* culture is a hierarchical priesthood of four to eight degrees, or orders, with each level representing the attainment of certain skills or knowledge. Women as well as men, children as well as adults, could be priests (also referred to as medicine men or women). As many as 20 years of study might be required to progress to the highest degree. After one year of training, an apprentice was initiated as a first-level *Mide* priest and was allowed to perform certain duties. Initiations were held during an annual Grand Medicine Dance in the spring or early fall and lasted from one to five days. Conducted in large wigwams, the ceremonies incorporated the use of a sacred drum and sacred pipe, both of which were guarded by caretakers. Initiates offered gifts such as blankets, cooking utensils, and wild rice. Feasting included wild rice, fresh or dried blueberries, maple sugar, and dog meat. Subsequent training required learning herbology for treating sickness or for acquiring personal power, a skill used much in the way that charms are used. *Mide* priests, therefore, acquired the role of healer. *Mide* members were also reputed to use "bad medicine" to cause sickness or death. *Mide* priests carried personal medicine bundles, cloth squares, or cloth or yarn bags enclosing one or more decorated animal skins called medicine bags. Specific types of skins were associated with each of the *Mide* degrees. At the first level, the *Mide* priest would have a medicine bag made from the skin of an otter, marten, mink, or weasel. Objects found in medicine bags included shells, bear claws decorated with ribbons, glass beads, *kinikinik* (native tobacco), carved figures, dried roots, and herbs. *Mide* songs and instructions were recorded on birch bark scrolls that were placed under the care of an appointed guardian priest.

In the early nineteenth century, many Ojibwa became followers of the Shawnee Prophet and his multitribe Shawano cult whose members advocated a return to traditional living and replacing *Mide* rites with new ceremonies. The Prophet was also known as Lalawethika (Laulewasika) or Tenskwatawa and was the brother of the Shawnee warrior Tecumseh. The Shawano cult lost favor and the *Mide* regained strength after the Prophet's followers failed to defeat the U.S. Army troops in 1811 at the battle of Tippecanoe.

Christianity was adopted slowly, but most modern Ojibwa are Roman Catholics or Protestant Episcopalians. Conflict arose between full-blooded Ojibwa, who tended to follow a more traditional lifestyle focused on *Mide* or Episcopalian values, and the mixed-blood progressive Ojibwa, who typically were Roman Catholic and followed a more acculturated lifestyle. The BIA often settled disagreements between the two factions by siding with the progressives who promoted majority culture values such as agronomy and small business enterprises.

EMPLOYMENT AND ECONOMIC TRADITIONS

Ojibwa culture dictated that excess goods be shared with the less fortunate. With the arrival of the fur trade, the Ojibwa learned to barter for goods that generally could be consumed within a year. They first earned money through the sale of land or timber rights. Since saving money was not a tradition and the amount they received was low, incomes were disposable and might be barely sufficient for a meager living. Often relocated to disadvantaged areas, the Ojibwa faced poverty and bare subsistence through living off the land and/or farming. Reservation life led to reliance on government assistance.

Modern Ojibwa live on reservations and in a variety of nonreservation areas, rural, suburban, and urban. Like other Native peoples, the Ojibwa, particularly those on reservations, have high rates of unemployment. They may support themselves through seasonal work, including forestry, farming, tourism, trapping, and wild ricing. Particularly since the 1970s reservations also support small businesses: bait shops, campgrounds, clothing manufacturing, construction, fish hatcheries, hotels, lumber stores, marinas, restaurants, and service stations.

With the passage of the Indian Gaming Regulatory Act in 1988, reservations were accorded new employment venues related to gaming, including bingo halls, casinos, and spin-off businesses such as gas stations, hotels, and restaurants. While there is some opposition to gaming, profits have contributed to higher employment levels and income. Tribes have invested gaming income in the purchase of ancestral lands, in road and home construction, and in building new social service buildings and/or extending social services. Some reservations have passed employment rights ordinances requiring employers on reservations to give preference to tribal members in hiring, training, and promotion.

Treaty rights allow modern Ojibwa to hunt, fish, and harvest rice on lands once belonging to their ancestors. The Ojibwa right to use the natural resources of reservation lands ceded to the government was reaffirmed by the U.S. Court of Appeals for the Seventh Circuit in the 1983 Voigt Decision. In 1987 federal judge James Doyle found that these rights extended to the use of traditional methods and that the Ojibwa had the right to use their natural resources to the extent that they could support a modest standard of living.

POLITICS AND GOVERNMENT

Federal policy emphasized the assimilation of the Ojibwa into U.S. society. This policy has taken the following forms: treaty making; establishment of reservations and removal; individual allotments; relocation; and self-determination and cultural affirmation.

TREATY MAKING

Until 1871 the Ojibwa tribes were viewed as sovereign nations. As such, the legal relationship between the Ojibwa and national governments and their citizens was largely defined by treaties. Treaties drew boundaries between Ojibwa lands and lands designated for other tribes and/or non-Native Americans, concentrated tribes on reservations, allowed the government to purchase Ojibwa land, or set regulations concerning commerce. A major treaty was signed by Lakota (Sioux) and Ojibwa representatives at Prairie du Chien (in present-day Wisconsin) in 1825 to stop fighting between the two nations and establish boundaries. In 1827 another treaty set the boundary between Ojibwa and Menominee land. The Ojibwa ceded or sold land rights in Michigan, Minnesota, and Wisconsin to the federal government in a number of treaties, including one signed in 1854 that established permanent Ojibwa reservations in three states: Michigan, Minnesota, and Wisconsin. Bands were dispersed geographically, with members spread out in different reservations. In exchange for land or natural resources, the Ojibwa received annuities or annual payments of goods, livestock, food staples, clearance of debt with fur traders or fur company stores, and the services of blacksmiths, physicians, saw millers, and teachers.

ESTABLISHMENT OF RESERVATIONS AND REMOVAL

Federal and state legislation replaced treaty making in 1871. Later some reservations were created by executive order or by public act. Some reservations closely followed traditional Ojibwa boundaries, while others were established in previously unsettled areas. In the 1860s non-Native Americans put forward a plan to move all Minnesotan Ojibwa to a new reservation in the northwest corner of the state. Members of the four bands living in Minnesota were eventually relocated to the White Earth Reservation, beginning in 1868. The history of White Earth is a particularly disruptive one, with much of the land initially designated for the Ojibwa lost through improper taxation and swindling.

INDIVIDUAL ALLOTMENTS

The General Allotment Act of 1887, also known as the Dawes Act, outlined national adherence to allotment, a policy of encouraging assimilation to white culture, primarily through the adoption of agriculture as a means of subsistence, and the allotment or parcelling out of land to individuals rather than to communities, bands, tribes or nations. States also passed their versions of the Dawes Act,

such as Minnesota's Nelson Act of 1889. After Ojibwa families took their allotments, unallotted land on reservations was then sold to the public. The Dawes Act not only severely restricted communal lands and traditional cultural patterns, it opened up huge tracts of native lands to white settlement and exploitation. Arguably, this was as much the reason for the Act as the desired assimilation of native peoples.

Rather than converting the Ojibwa to self-sufficient living, the allotment system resulted in the loss of Native-held land. There were also environmental and cultural reasons the Ojibwa did not succeed as farmers. In some reservation areas the land was sandy, rocky, swampy, or heavily wooded, and the weather limited the varieties of crops that could mature during the short growing season. Farming was also resisted by some Ojibwa who perceived gardening as women's work and disliked the permanency that farming required.

All Native Americans, including the Ojibwa, became U.S. citizens in 1924. Until this time, Ojibwa could attain citizenship through marriage to a non-Native American or by serving in World War I.

In 1934 the passage of the Indian Reorganization Act reversed the allotment system, and tribes held elections to decide whether to reorganize their governments. In 1936 six of the seven Minnesota reservations incorporated as the Minnesota Chippewa Tribe. Red Lake, which elected not to join the Minnesota Chippewa Tribe, is still known for its adherence to traditional culture. The Red Lake Reservation was excluded from the Nelson Act, and, while it did sell some land to the United States, the original tribal areas remained the property of the entire tribe. The six reservations in Wisconsin are governed separately, as are the westernmost Ojibwa in North Dakota and Montana. There are three Ojibwa tribal groups in Michigan. The Sault Sainte Marie band is governed separately as the Bay Mills Indian Community. The Keweenaw Bay Indian Community includes three bands: L'Anse, Lac Vieux Desert, and Ontonagon. The Saginaw Chippewa Tribe comprises the Saginaw, Swan Creek, and Black River bands.

In the 1930s Ojibwa men and women were employed in federal conservation, construction, and manufacturing projects organized under the Civil Works Administration and the Civil Conservation Corps, Indian Division. Ojibwa also received vocational training through Works Progress Administration programs. This brought some economic relief to reservation areas hit hard by the depression.

After World War II federal policy toward Native Americans once again promoted assimilation and integration, a setback for the New Deal philosophy encouraging Native culture and autonomy.

RELOCATION

In the 1950s the BIA instituted the Indian Relocation Services campaign. Like the allotment system, relocation focused on individual Ojibwa rather than tribal group and Native culture. Ojibwa were encouraged to move off reservations to assimilate with non-Native culture in urban areas in order to reduce the need for federal support. Great Lakes Ojibwa moved to urban centers in Minnesota and Wisconsin, most notably Duluth, Milwaukee, and Minneapolis, St. Paul.

SELF-DETERMINATION AND CULTURAL AFFIRMATION

The policy of promoting Native self-sufficiency was termed "self-determination." Under the Johnson administration, the Ojibwa qualified for Office of Economic Opportunity funds to open social programs, such as Head Start, and Native businesses and housing. Federal legislation in the 1970s, most notably the Indian Education Act of 1972, the Indian Self-Determination Act of 1973, and the Education Assistance Act of 1975, provided funding for culturally based education and afforded tribes more direct control of programs once administered by the BIA.

During the late 1960s some urban Ojibwa in Minneapolis formed a Red Power Organization known as the American Indian Movement (AIM). A modern proponent of the Native warrior ethic, AIM supported tribal civil rights through enforced reform rather than legislation. Activism took a different form in the 1980s and the 1990s, with the Ojibwa seeking to enforce treaty rights and working in the legal arena.

Traditional Ojibwa governance followed a multitiered system of elders, civil chiefs, and when necessary war chiefs. Elders—older and respected tribe members—played vital roles in decision making and educating younger members of the band. Civil chiefs could inherit their position or be nominated. Elders met in councils to identify a potential civil chief who would manage day-to-day operations. The nominee, who could be female or male, could accept the invitation to serve as civil chief, though such acceptance was not mandatory. Chiefs had official assistants, including messengers and orators. Civil chiefs could also summon the council of elders to request assistance. Councils of chiefs and elders from a number of bands met to discuss major decisions that would affect more than one band. War chiefs were self-appointed; a war chief was any man who could convince others to join him in battle. Adult men and women were part of the general council, and while votes were not tallied, each individual could join in the discussion at tribal meetings.

Late twentieth-century reservation areas are striving for home rule—the right to set and follow laws of their own making. Ojibwa reservations in Minnesota are each governed by a Reservation Business Council (RBC, also known as a Reservation Tribal Council). There are three districts on each reservation, each of which elects a representative to the RBC. The entire reservation also elects officials: a chairperson and a secretary-treasurer. Members of the RBC serve four-year terms. The RBC discusses approval of loans, petitions requesting enrollment of official membership in the tribe, and issues relating to economic development and sends reports to the U.S. Secretary of the Interior. Two members from each of the six reservations comprising the Minnesota Chippewa Tribe also serve on the statewide Tribal Executive Committee (TEC), which meets every three months. While the RBC governs the reservation, the TEC governs the tribe, as constituted by its six member reservations.

The Red Lake Reservation has a tribal council consisting of three officers (chairperson, secretary, and treasurer) elected from the entire tribal membership and eight council members, two elected from each of four districts. Red Lake also maintains traditional governance through an advisory council of descendants of civil chiefs.

Modern versions of intertribal councils also exist. The Four-State Intertribal Assembly represents the interests of over 30 tribes in Michigan, Minnesota, Iowa, and Wisconsin. Representatives meet at annual conferences.

MILITARY

The Ojibwa culture has traditionally revered the warrior. The Ojibwa often engaged in battles with and against other Native peoples and joined non-Native Americans in their fighting. During the French and Indian Wars (1754-1763), the Ojibwa sided primarily with the French. Ojibwa also participated in Pontiac's Rebellion (1763-1764), most notably in the capture of the British-held Fort Michilimackinac (in present-day Michigan). Their role during the Revolutionary War (1776-1783) was negligible. During the War of 1812, Ojibwa living west of Lake Superior sided with the Americans, while those living in present-day Michigan sided with the British. During World War I, the Ojibwa responded to the war effort by buying war bonds and donating money to the Red Cross. Ojibwa men also served in active duty. Ojibwa men served during World War II (1941-1945), and both men and women moved to urban areas for employment in war industries. The grand entrance march at many powwows begins with an honor guard of Ojibwa war veterans. Ojibwa may still be awarded eagle feathers in recognition of extraordinary achievement.

INDIVIDUAL AND GROUP CONTRIBUTIONS

The Ojibwa have made a number of significant contributions to American life: they discovered maple sugar and wild rice and invented hammocks, snowshoes, canoeing, and lacrosse. The English language contains a number of Ojibwa words (moccasin, moose) and place-names (Mackinaw, Michigan, Mesabi). Many Ojibwa contributions evolved over centuries, before they could be acknowledged by written record. Notable Ojibwa men and women, primarily those living in the late twentieth century, and their achievements are identified below.

ACADEMIA

White Earth enrollee Will Antell (1935–) has served as an educational consultant on Native education for the State of Minnesota. Edward Benton-Banai (1934–) directs the Heart of the Earth Survival School in Minneapolis and has written a series of coloring books to teach Ojibwa culture to young people. Lester Jack Briggs, Jr., (1948–) is director of the Fond du Lac Community College, Cloquet, Minnesota. Duane Champagne (1951–) serves as director of UCLA's American Indian Studies Center where he is also the editor of the *American Indian Culture and Research Journal*. After completing her Ph.D. at the University of Minnesota, Ojibwa educator Rosemary Ackley Christensen (1939–) has continued to publish, lecture, and consult on topics related to Native education. Gwendolyn A. Hill (1952–), of mixed Ojibwa and Cree heritage, is president of the Sisseton-Wahpeton Community College, Sisseton, South Dakota. Modern scholars have increasingly turned to tribal elders, including Maude Kegg (1904–), for instruction in the Anishinabe culture and language.

GOVERNMENT AND POLITICS

Among those credited with organizing AIM are Dennis Banks (1932–) and Clyde Bellecourt

(1939–). Both were instrumental in organizing events such as the 1972 Trail of Broken Treaties caravan to Washington, D.C., resulting in the takeover of the BIA offices. Banks's recent activities include lecturing and acting in the films *The Last of the Mohicans* (1992) and *Thunderheart* (1992). Leonard Peltier (1944–) took part in the 1973 occupation of Wounded Knee, South Dakota. Convicted of killing two FBI agents, he is imprisoned in Marion, Illinois. His controversial conviction is examined in the 1992 film *Incident at Oglala*. A number of foreign countries and organizations regard Peltier as a prisoner of conscience.

LITERATURE

Author and poet Louise Erdrich (1954–) is the best-known modern Ojibwa writer. The characters in Erdrich's fiction follow a rich genealogy of Pillager band Ojibwa and non-Native Americans from the nineteenth century to the modern reservation milieu of gaming and competition dancing. Her novels include: *Love Medicine* (1984), *The Beet Queen* (1986), *Tracks* (1988), and *The Bingo Palace* (1995), *The Antelope Wife* (1998), and *The Crown of Colombus* (1999). Poet, novelist, and journalist, Jim Northrup, Jr., (1943–) writes about modern Anishinabe life on the Fond du Lac Reservation in northeastern Minnesota. A collection of his poems and short stories was published as *Walking the Rez Road* (1993), and his humorous and often biting commentary appears in a column, "Fond du Lac Follies," published in *The Circle* and *News from Indian Country*. Gerald Vizenor (1934–), a member of the Minnesota Chippewa Tribe, is a professor of Native American Studies at the University of California, Berkeley. A poet and novelist, his writing centers on traditional culture and includes such works as *The Everlasting Sky: New Voices From the People Named Chippewa* (1972); *The People Named the Chippewa: Narrative Histories* (1984); *Interior Landscapes: Autobiographical Myths and Metaphors* (1990); *The Heirs of Colombus*(1992); *Fugitive Poses: Native American Indian Scenes of Absence and Presence* (1998); and *Postindian Conversations* (1999).

MEDIA

PRINT

The Circle.

Published by the Minneapolis American Indian Center, this monthly publication provides international, national, and local news relevant to Indian concerns and tracks issues of importance to the Ojibwa.

Contact: Joe Allen, Editor.
Address: 1530 East Franklin Avenue,
    Minneapolis, Minnesota 55404-2136.
Telephone: (612) 871-4749.
Fax: (612) 871-6878.

MASINAIGAN (Talking Paper).

Published by the Great Lakes Indian Fish and Wildlife Commission (GLIFWC). This 40-page quarterly publication reports on GLIFWC activities and on a broader range of issues of importance to the Ojibwa, including antitreaty activity, treaty support, Indian education, Native culture, Native rights, and major federal legislation.

Contact: Susan Erickson, Editor.
Address: P.O. Box 9, Odanah, Wisconsin 54861.
Telephone: (715) 682-6619.
E-mail: pio@win.bright.net.

ORGANIZATIONS AND ASSOCIATIONS

Great Lakes Indian Fish and Wildlife Commission (GLIFWC).

Founded in 1983, the GLWIFC's mission is to assist 13 Ojibwa tribes in Michigan, Minnesota, and Wisconsin to better manage their natural resources in off-reservation areas. The Commission comprises five divisions: Biological Services, Enforcement, Planning and Development, Intergovernmental Affairs, and Public Information. It publishes a free quarterly newsletter, MASINAIGAN (Talking Paper).

Contact: James Schlender, Executive Director.
Address: P.O. Box 9, Odanah, Wisconsin 54861.
Telephone: (715) 682-6619.
Fax: (715) 682-9294.
E-mail: pio@win.bright.net.

Minnetrista Council for Great Lakes Native American Studies (MCGLNAS).

Founded in 1990, it is an organization with representatives from more than 20 tribes. MCGLNAS promotes the study and preservation of woodland tribal culture and sponsors annual powwows, conferences, and workshops.

Contact: Nicholas Clark, Chairman.
Address: P.O. Box 1527, Muncie,
    Indiana 47308-1527.
Telephone: (317) 282-4848.

MUSEUMS AND RESEARCH CENTERS

D'Arcy McNickle Center for the History of the American Indian.

Located within the Newberry Library, it provides access to scholarly material in the E. E. Ayer Collection; the Center sponsors seminars, exhibits, summer institutes, and fellowships, and publishes occasional papers, bibliographies, and monographs.

Address: 60 West Walton Street, Chicago,
    Illinois 60610-3394.
Telephone: (312) 943-9090.

Minnesota History Center.

The headquarters of the Minnesota Historical Society, it includes an extensive research and archival collection on the Native peoples of the state. Among its vast and varied exhibits on the Ojibwa is a detailed exhibit on wild ricing.

Address: 345 Kellogg Boulevard West, St. Paul,
    Minnesota 55102-1906.
Telephone: (651) 296-6126; or (800) 657-3773.

SOURCES FOR ADDITIONAL STUDY

Broker, Ignatia. *Night Flying Women: An Ojibway Narrative*. St. Paul: Minnesota Historical Society Press, 1983.

Densmore, Frances. *How Indians Use Wild Rice Plants for Food, Medicine and Crafts*. New York: Dover, 1974 (originally published as *Uses of Plants by the Chippewa Indians*, 1928).

Hilger, M. Indez. *Chippewa Child Life and Its Cultural Background*. St. Paul: Minnesota Historical Society Press, 1992 (originally published, 1951).

The Jesuit Relations and Allied Documents: Travels and Explorations of the Jesuit Missionaries in New France, 1610-1791, edited by Rubin G. Thwaites. Cleveland: Burrows Brothers Co., 1896-1901.

Johnston, Basil. *Ojibway Ceremonies*. Lincoln: University of Nebraska Press, 1990.

———. *The Ojibway Heritage*. New York: Columbia University Press, 1976.

Summer in the Spring: Anishinabe Lyric Poems and Stories, edited by Gerald Vizenor. Norman: University of Oklahoma Press, 1993.

Tanner, Helen Hornbeck. *The Ojibway.* New York: Chelsea House, 1992.

Vennum, Thomas, Jr. *Wild Rice and the Ojibway People*. St. Paul: Minnesota Historical Press, 1988.

Warren, William Whipple. *History of the Ojibway People*. St. Paul: Minnesota Historical Society Press, 1984 (originally published, 1885).